# PSYCHOMETRIC
# THEORY

# PSYCHOMETRIC THEORY

## THIRD EDITION

## Jum C. Nunnally

Late Professor of Psychology
Vanderbilt University

## Ira H. Bernstein

Professor of Psychology
The University of Texas at Arlington

**McGRAW-HILL, INC.**

New York   St. Louis   San Francisco   Auckland   Bogotá
Caracas   Lisbon   London   Madrid   Mexico City   Milan   Montreal
New Delhi   San Juan   Singapore   Sydney   Tokyo   Toronto

This book was set in Times Roman by The Clarinda Company.
The editors were Jane Vaicunas and James R. Belser;
the production supervisor was Annette Mayeski.
New drawings were done by ECL Art.
R. R. Donnelley & Sons Company was printer and binder.

*Psych
BF
39
.N8
1994*

## PSYCHOMETRIC THEORY

This book is printed on acid-free paper.

3 4 5 6 7 8 9 0   DOC/DOC   9 9 8 7 6 5

ISBN 0-07-047849-X

**Library of Congress Cataloging-in-Publicaton Data**

Nunnally, Jum C.
    Psychometric theory / Jum C. Nunnally, Ira H. Bernstein.—3rd ed.
        p.      cm.
    Includes bibliographical references and index.
    ISBN 0-07-047849-X (alk. paper)
        1. Psychometrics.      I. Bernstein, Ira H.      II. Title.
BF39.N8      1994
150'.28'7—dc20                                        93-22756

# ABOUT
# THE AUTHORS

JUM C. NUNNALLY received a doctorate from the University of Chicago in 1952, working with William Stephenson, Leon Thurstone, and Carl Rogers. Early in his career he was associated with Samuel Beck and Roy Grinker. From 1954 to 1960, he was a faculty member at the University of Illinois. He joined Vanderbilt University in 1960 as professor and became chair in 1961. He published four books besides the previous editions of *Psychometric Theory*. *Popular Conceptions of Mental Health* (Holt) became a basic resource in community mental health. In addition, he published 110 articles. Many involved various issues in measurement, such as $Q$ methodology and confirmatory factor analysis. In fact, he pioneered modern multivariate hypothesis testing. In addition, he also published significant work on language development in deaf children, the acquisition of reward value in previously neutral objects, experimental aesthetics, and the scaling of the evaluative and affective components of language. As an administrator, he was responsible for making the psychology department at Vanderbilt the major force it is today. He served on the editorial board of *Applied Psychological Measurement* and three other journals and was active in many scholarly organizations. He died on August 22, 1982.

IRA H. BERNSTEIN received a doctorate at Vanderbilt University in 1963 under the direction of Prof. Richard L. Blanton, a close friend of and collaborator with the late Prof. Nunnally. He then spent a postdoctoral year at Prof. Nunnally's institution, the University of Illinois, studying perception with Prof. Charles Eriksen. He joined the faculty of the University of Texas at Arlington (then Arlington State College) in 1964. He has remained there ever since, progressing to the rank of professor in 1969. He divides his work equally among basic research (perception/cognition), methodological issues in applied measurement (item-level factoring, categorical modelng), and application (police selection, pain, and other medical topics). He has published approximately 70 articles in such journals as *Educational and Psychological Measurement, Health Education Quarterly, Multivariate Behavioral Research, Perception and Psychophysics, Psychological Bulletin,* and *The Journal of Experimental Psychology: General* and has served on two editorial boards. He is a Fellow of the American Psychological Association and the Society for Personality Assessment and is also the author of *Applied Multivariate Analysis* (Springer-Verlag).

# CONTENTS

# PREFACE

Like the previous edition, the third edition of *Psychometric Theory* is a comprehensive text in measurement designed for researchers and for use in graduate courses in psychology, education, and areas of business such as management and marketing. It is intended to consider the broad measurement problems that arise in these areas once one steps aside from the specific content that often obscures these similarities. This does not mean that all situations are the same. Lee Cronbach (1957) pointed out a major difference between the measurement needs of those who study group differences, as in experimental manipulations, and those who study individual differences. This difference is noted in the pages that follow. I have also attempted to write the book so that the reader needs only a basic background in statistics.

The previous editions of this book were so widely read and accepted that they became a common denominator for more than a generation of scholars. Prof. Nunnally's death a decade ago raised the possibility that this contribution might be forgotten. I cannot, of course, know what he would have written for this edition, however, I hope that I have stood with sufficient solidarity upon his shoulders. My main goal is to express to the readers of this book, the love of solving measurement problems that he inspired in me. It is also with pride that I include some contributions of my own students who have followed this path. They include Victor Bissonnette, Sebiastiano Fisicaro, and Calvin Garbin.

One essential feature that I have tried to maintain is the emphasis upon principles that characterized the previous editions. Now, as then, there are many excellent references that go much further into the details of the various analyses. These are found in the many references, especially the Suggested Additional Readings at the end of each chapter. I have attempted to strike a balance between papers designed for a general audience of psychologists and graduate students, which appear in sources like *Psychological Bulletin* and empirical journals, versus those of a more mathematical orientation, such as *Psychometrika* and *Applied Psychological Measurement*.

I have also maintained the use of several examples that allow hand calculation, since many of the newer procedures do not. Consequently, I have included some procedures that many consider obsolete, specifically centroid factor analysis. Not every reader or instructor will find this useful, but I can speak from my own memories as a student on this point. Most recent developments in measurement have had the unintended effect of taking students further from the data than older methods. To the extent that this reflects the importance of more general, latent variables, it is an important step forward. However, one cannot totally ignore the possibility that the inexperienced data analyst, which we all are at some point, may mistake the spurious for the profound. I have also made use of the general-purpose statistical packages that are now a necessary part of every researcher's repertoire of tools. I currently use SAS, LISREL, and Excel in my own work, but there are no compelling reasons to choose them over their competitors. Moreover, I have also included discussion of other procedures that are considered obsolete because I believe they have a real place in research. The clearest example of this is group centroid confirmatory factor analysis, which Prof. Nunnally stressed in previous editions and in his own work. The appropriate discussions, Chapter 13 in this case, provide detailed rationales.

Without doubt, the major change that has taken place since publication of the previous edition of this book has been the shift away from classical procedures that explain variance to modern inferential procedures. This is also discussed in many areas of the book. This is clearly necessary for those who do fundamental research in measurement, and so there is a corollary need to explore the applicability of these newer methods. However, I strongly feel that Prof. Nunnally would have agreed that modern methods should be viewed as complements and not as replacements. Unfortunately, even some substantive journals have insisted that authors use these inferential methods when the investigator's goals may be more traditional in nature. As of this writing, even basic researchers in measurement are concerned about the many ways that modern methods may provide unnecessarily complicated solutions. These methods are, and should be, used when data-gathering limits are present to cast doubt on the statistical reality of findings. Anyone with serious interest in measurement must therefore be knowledgeable about these methods. However, you should *not* allow their current limitations to lead you astray. Chapter 13 deals with a common situation where both trivial and spurious results may arise. The position I have taken also reflects Prof. Nunnally's stress on the primacy of scientific generalization that was so apparent in the previous editions.

A second major change from the previous edition is that classification has been given explicit status as a form of measurement distinct from scaling. Chapter 1 explicates this necessary distinction. A well chosen categorization can be as fruitful as an improved scaling. I am particularly indebted to Calvin Garbin for discussions on this point, and I hope that Chapter 15 is useful to this end.

The necessity of discussing both classical and modern models and the need to keep the book of manageable length forced the deletion of chapters previously devoted to specific tests. I regret having to do this. There are several excellent texts that deal with specific tests, such as Anastasi (1988) and Cronbach (1990), and also present an excellent discussion of theoretical issues.

Part and chapter overviews and chapter summaries have been added, but the organization is otherwise similar to that of the previous edition. Part One (Chapter 1) considers measurment as a general process. Part Two (Chapters 2–5) deals with statistical foundations of measurment, including a discussion of the crucial concept of validity. Although there has been a noticeable trend toward unifying the major meanings of validity, I have continued to point out Prof. Nunnally's useful distinctions among them. This first part also presents basic concepts in statistics and correlational analysis. My discussion of certain approximations to the ordinary correlation coefficient ($r$), e.g., polyserial and polychoric correlation, somewhat softens Prof. Nunnally's negative views toward them despite our general agreement. I have also expanded the discussion of statistical estimation, as it has become considerably more complex in recent years. Part Three (Chapters 6–10) continues to deal with the internal structure of multi-item measures and the process of aggregating items into scales. The previous edition mentioned generalizability theory in passing; I feel it now needs more detailed discussion. One minor change is that I have moved some material on speed and guessing from the last chapter of the previous edition into Chapter 9 to unify discussion with related material. I have also added material on statistical definitions of test bias and halo effects to this chapter. A full chapter has been added on modern test theory.

Part Four (Chapters 11–13) deals with how measures relate to one another. The previous edition devoted two chapters to factor analysis. Its importance led me to devote three chapters to it. I have provided a detailed contrast between the component and common factor models. In addition, I have provided a detailed discussion of confirmatory factor analysis and the factoring of categorical data (item-level factoring). I have also attempted to maintain the clarity of Prof. Nunnally's discussion of the geometric basis of factor analysis. The first of two chapters forming Part Five, Chapter 14, discusses some alternative models that largely share the geometric assumptions of factor analysis. Finally, the last chapter deals with a variety of emerging topics in measurement: categorical modeling, tests of independence, and alternatives to geometric representation.

I thank several people besides those already mentioned. I am indebted to my recent group of students: Laura Fields, Paul Havig, Matthew Lee, and Meredith O'Brien and apologize for not mentioning by name all of the other fine students who have worked with me. I thank Laurie Liska and Tim Larey for their comments on an earlier draft, and Pauline Gregory, Amy Osborn, and Susan Sterling for clerical assistance. I am particularly indebted to Professor Dennis Duffy at the University of Houston Law School for his suggestions about the legal aspects of test bias. Professor James Tanaka completed his penetrating comments only a short time before the tragic accident that claimed his life. Several colleagues at the University of Texas at Arlington (Jim Bowen, Jim Erickson, Bill Ickes, and Paul Paulus) and elsewhere (Charles Eriksen, Matt Jaremko, Michael Kashner, Judith Keith, Rob Kolodner, Paul McKinney, and Rick Weideman) stimulated my thinking about many issues. The book could not have been written without the help of Professor Nunnally's widow, Kay. Jim Cullum, John Sheridan, the late John B. Gillespie, Ferdinand LaMenthe, Thelonious Monk, and Charles C. Parker played an oblique role but deserve note nonetheless. I especially thank my wife, Linda and daughters, Cari and Dina, for their love and support.

Finally, I extend my appreciation to the following reviewers whose suggestions guided my writing of this text: J. William Asher, Purdue University; Jacob G. Beard, Florida State University; Jeffrey Bjorck, Fuller Theological Seminary; Richard L. Blanton, Professor Emeritus, Vanderbilt University; Donald R. Brown, Purdue University; Joseph M. Fitzgerald, Wayne State University; Calvin Garbin, University of Nebraska; Gene V. Glass, University of Colorado; Richard L. Gorsuch, Fuller Theological Seminary; Frank M. Gresham, Louisiana State University; Larry H. Ludlow, Boston College; Samuel T. Mayo; Michael Pressley, University of Maryland; Louis H. Primavera, St. John's University; John E. Sawyer, Texas A&M University; Roger Schvaneveldt, New Mexico State University; Eugene F. Stone, SUNY, Albany; Michael J. Subkoviak, University of Wisconsin, Madison; J. S. Tanaka, University of Illinois; and David Thissen, University of North Carolina, Chapel Hill.

I conclude this preface with the wisdom of one of my oldest friends, Stan Coren of the University of British Columbia. He told me while I was working on my previous major effort that "You never finish writing a book; they just take it away from you."

*Ira H. Bernstein*

# PSYCHOMETRIC
# THEORY

# INTRODUCTION

The main purpose of Part One (a single chapter in this case) is to define "measurement" in terms of two fairly simple concepts: Measurement consists of rules for assigning symbols to objects so as to (1) represent quantities of attributes numerically (scaling) or (2) define whether the objects fall in the same or different categories with respect to a given attribute (classification). Most of the book is concerned with the first of these meanings. The topics of levels of scaling and the general standards by which measurement rules are evaluated are focal issues.

## CHAPTER 1

# INTRODUCTION

## CHAPTER OVERVIEW

This opening chapter begins with a definition of measurement which we break down into two subtopics: scaling and classification. Some general properties of good measurement are introduced, and the importance of standardization is discussed. The separate roles of measurement and pure mathematics are contrasted. One major, and still controversial, topic in measurement concerns what are known as levels of measurement. According to some, the appropriate level of a measure must be established before employing mathematical and statistical procedures associated with that level. Many look for ostensive (visualizable) properties of measures like the yardsticks and clocks of physics. They view present scales as imperfect correlates of unknown "true" scales. We attempt to show that these strategies easily lead to unreasonable outcomes. One should demonstrate that a measure has the properties ascribed to it, establish scales by convention, but be prepared to change these conventions as better measures become available. The chapter concludes by noting some of the changes brought to the study of measurement that result from the availability of computers.

## MEASUREMENT IN SCIENCE

Although tomes have been written on the nature of measurement, in the end it boils down to two fairly simple concepts: "measurement" consists of rules for assigning symbols to objects so as to (1) represent quantities of attributes numerically (scaling) or (2) define whether the objects fall in the same or different categories with respect to a given attribute (classification). Most of what is historically called measurement involves scaling, and therefore properties of numbers, but classification can be equally important. The objects in psychology are usually people, but they may be lower animals as in some areas of psychology and biology or physical objects as in some market research. The term "rules" indicates that the assignment of numbers must be explicitly stated. Some rules are so obvious that detailed definition is unnecessary, as in measuring height with a tape measure. Unfortunately, these obvious cases are exceptional in science. For instance, assaying a chemical compound usually requires extremely complex procedures. Certainly the rules for measuring most attributes such as intelligence, shyness, or priming are not intuitively obvious.

Rules, in turn, are an important aspect of standardization. A measure is standardized to the extent that (1) its rules are clear, (2) it is practical to apply, (3) it does not demand great skill of administrators beyond that necessary for their initial training, and (4) its results do not depend upon the specific administrator. The basic point about standardization is that users of a given instrument should obtain similar results. The results must therefore be reliable in a sense to be discussed at several points in this book. Thus, measuring the surface temperature of a planet is well standardized if different astronomers obtain very similar estimates. Similarly, an intelligence test is well standardized if different examiners obtain similar scores from testing a particular child at a given time.

The term "attribute" in the definition indicates that measurement always concerns some *particular* feature of objects. One cannot measure objects—one measures their attributes. One does not measure a child per se, but rather his or her intelligence, height, or socialization. The distinction between an object and its attributes may sound like mere hairsplitting, but it is important. First, it demonstrates that measurement requires a process of abstraction. An attribute concerns relations among objects on a particular dimension, e.g., weight or intelligence. A red rock and a white rock may weigh the same, and two white rocks may have different weights. The attributes of weight and color must not be confounded with each other nor with any other attributes. It is quite easy to confuse a particular attribute of objects with other attributes. For example, some people find it difficult to understand that a criminal and a law-abiding citizen can both be equally smart. Failing to abstract a particular attribute from the whole makes the concept of measurement difficult to grasp.

A second reason for emphasizing that one measures attributes and not objects is that it makes us consider the nature of an attribute carefully before attempting measurement. An attribute we believe in may not exist in the form proposed. For example, the many negative results obtained in the efforts to measure an overall attribute of rigidity make it debatable that such an attribute exists. Even highly popular terms used to describe people may not correspond to measurable attributes, e.g., clairvoyance. It is also common for an assumed unitary attribute to confound several more specific attributes. For example, "adjustment" may include satisfaction with one's life, positive mood, skills in coping with stress, and other meanings of the term. Although such conglomerate measures may be partly justifiable on practical grounds, their use can undermine psychological science. As this book will show in detail, a measure should generally concern some one *thing*—some distinct, unitary attribute. To the extent that unitary attributes need be combined in an overall appraisal, e.g., of adjustment, they should usually be rationally combined from different measures rather than being confounded within one measure.

The first part of the definition of measurement stresses the use of numbers to represent quantities in scaling  Technically, quantification concerns how much of an attribute is present in an object, and numbers communicate the amount. Quantification is so intimately intertwined with measurement that the two terms are often used interchangeably. This is unfortunate, as the second part, classification, is at least as important to science.

Although the definition emphasizes that rules are at the heart of measurement, it does not specify the nature of these rules or place any limit on the allowable kinds of rules. This is because a clear distinction must be made between measurement as a process and the standards for validating measures. The measurement process involves such considerations as the levels-of-measurement issue that is discussed later in this chapter. Validation involves issues that are discussed in Chapter 3. Numerous standards can be applied to obtain the usefulness of a measurement method, including the extent to which data obtained from the method (1) fit a mathematical model, (2) measure a single attribute, (3) are repeatable over time if necessary, (4) are valid in various senses, and (5) produce interesting relationships with other scientific measures. Such standards will be discussed throughout this book. Thus, a psychologist might establish rules to measure, say, dogmatism, in a manner that seems quite illogical to other psychologists, but the measure's usefulness cannot be dismissed beforehand.

The rules employed to define a particular measure must be unambiguous. They may be developed from an elaborate deductive model, based on previous experience, flow from common sense, or simply spring from hunches, but the crucial point is how consistently users agree on the measure and ultimately how well the measurement method explains important phenomena. Consequently any set of rules that unambiguously quantifies properties of objects constitutes a legitimate measurement method and has a right to compete with other measures for scientific usefulness. Keep in mind, however, that clarity does not guarantee explanatory power.

## What Is "Meaningful" and "Useful"?

There is both agreement and disagreement among scientists about what is a meaningful and/or useful result. It is fair to say that there is a high degree of agreement on two points. One is that any result should be *repeatable* under similar circumstances. It is quite possible that a finding obtained on April 8, 1991, from a particular group of psychology students at the University of Texas at Arlington was a real effect descriptive of that group of people. However, unless that effect also applied to some other group, e.g., students at the University of Texas at Arlington tested on another day or at some other university on the same day, there is no need for a scientist to be concerned with it.

The second point of agreement that all scientists have learned is that any set of results can be understood after the fact even if it is a chance occurrence or even systematically wrong. Perhaps every investigator has analyzed a set of results and formulated an explanation only to discover that there was a "bug" in the analysis. That bug probably did not hamper a "creative" explanation of the wrong results. In a like manner, some of the more sadistic instructors we have known assign randomly generated results to students for explanation. Students often find the exercise creative until they are let on.

The keys to meaningfulness are to proceed from some position that *anticipates* results. This is where scientists differ. Some are strongly biased toward testing hypotheses derived from highly formalized theories; others are more informal and/or result-oriented in their approach. For a debate on this issue, see Greenwald, Pratkanis, Leippe, and Baumgardner (1986) and a series of commentaries that appeared in the October 1988 issue of *Psychological Review*. As of this writing, the pendulum seems to have swung in a more formal direction, at least in cognitive psychology, but it probably will swing back. Whatever the level of formality preferred, meaningfulness depends upon context. One of the most common phrases one hears about results is "So what?" The answer lies in placing findings in a relevant context.

This is not to rule out unanticipated findings, which are always an exciting part of science. However, before one becomes too enraptured by an interpretation given a set of findings, one should be prepared to replicate them, preferably in some way that broadens their generality.

## ADVANTAGES OF STANDARDIZED MEASURES

Although you may already have a healthy respect for the importance of measurement in science, it is useful to look at some particular advantages that measurement provides. To note these advantages, consider what would be left if no measures were available, e.g., if there were no thermometers or intelligence tests. Measures based upon well-developed rules, usually including some form of norms that describe the scores obtained in populations of interest, are called "standardized." Despite criticisms of standardized psychological tests, the decisions that these are used for would still be made. What would be left would consist of subjective appraisals, personal judgments, etc. Some of the advantages of standardized measures over personal judgments are as follows:

### Objectivity

The major advantage of measurement is in taking the guesswork out of scientific observation. A key principle of science is that any statement of fact made by one scientist should be independently verifiable by other scientists. The principle is violated if scientists can disagree about the measure. For example, since there is no standardized measure of "libidinal energy," two psychologists could disagree widely about a patient's libidinal energy. It is obviously difficult to test theories of libidinal energy until it can be measured.

One could well argue that measurement is *the* major problem in psychology. There are many theories, but a theory can be tested only to the extent that its hypothesized attributes can be adequately measured. This has historically been the problem with Freudian theory: There are no agreed-on procedures for observing and quantifying such attributes as libidinal energy, etc. Major advances in psychology, if not all sciences, are often based upon breakthroughs in measurement. Consider, for example, the flood of research stimulated by the development of intelligence tests and of personality tests like the Minnesota Multiphasic Personality Inventory (MMPI), or, in a very different area, the development of techniques to record from single neurons (Hartline, 1940; Kuffler, 1953). Scientific results inevitably involve functional relations among measured variables, and the science of psychology can progress no faster than the measurement of its key variables.

## Quantification

The numerical results provided by standardized measures have two advantages. First, numerical indices can be reported in finer detail than personal judgments, allowing more subtle effects to be noted. Thus the availability of thermometers makes it possible to report the exact increase in temperature when two chemicals are mixed, rather than for the investigator to intuitively judge only that "the temperature increases." Similarly, teachers may be able to reliably assign children to broad categories of intelligence such as bright, average, and below normal, but intelligence tests provide finer differentiations.

Second, quantification permits the use of more powerful methods of mathematical analysis that are often essential to the elaboration of theories and the analysis of experiments. Although important psychological theories need not be highly quantitative, the trend is and will continue to be clearly in that direction. Mathematically statable theories make precise deductions possible for empirical investigation. Also, other mathematical models and tools, such as factor analysis and the analysis of variance (ANOVA), may be used to analyze various results even when the study does not test any formal theory.

## Communication

Science is a highly public enterprise requiring efficient communication among scientists. Scientists build on the past, and their findings must be compared with results of other scientists working on the same problem. Communication is greatly facilitated when standardized measures are available. Suppose, for example, it is reported that a particular treatment made the subjects "appear anxious" in an experiment concerning the effects of stress on anxiety reaction. This leaves many questions as to what the experimenter meant by "appear anxious," and makes it difficult for other experimenters to investigate the same effect. Much better communication could be achieved if the anxiety measure were standardized, as the means and standard deviations of these scores could be compared across treatment groups. Even very careful subjective evaluations are much more difficult to communicate than statistical analyses of standardized measures.

## Economy

Although standardized measures frequently require a great deal of work to develop, they generally are much more economical of time and money than are subjective evaluations after they have been developed. For example, even the best judges of intelligence need to observe a child for some time. At least as good an appraisal can usually be obtained in less than an hour with any of several inexpensively administered group measures of intelligence. Similarly, one can use a standardized activity measure such as rate of bar pressing in a Skinner box to evaluate the effect of a proposed stimulant on animals.

Besides saving time and money, standardized measures often free professionals for more important work. Progress generally favors measures that either require relatively little effort to employ or allow less highly trained technicians to do the administration and scoring. The time saved allows practitioners and scientists more time for the more scholarly and creative aspects of their work.

It is sometimes difficult to disentangle the measurer from the measurement process, as in individually administered intelligence tests. Although individual intelligence tests are highly standardized, they still require much time to administer and score. Context determines whether there are sufficient advantages to compensate for these disadvantages over even more highly standardized pencil-and-paper tests.

### Scientific Generalization

Scientific generalization is at the very heart of scientific work. Most observations involve particular events—a "falling" star, a baby crying, a feeling of pain from a pin scratch, or a friend remarking about the weather. Science seeks to find underlying order in these particular events by formulating and testing hypotheses of a more general nature. The most widely known examples are the principles of gravitation, heat, and states of gases in physics. Theories, including those in the behavioral sciences, are intended to be general and thereby explain a large number of phenomena with a small, simple set of principles.

Many scientific generalizations, particularly in the behavioral sciences, must be stated in statistical terms. They deal with the probability of an event occurring and cannot be specified with more exactness. The development and use of standardized measurement methods are just as essential to probabilistic relationships as they are for deterministic ones. Figure 1-1 illustrates a simple probabilistic relationship noted by the first author between the complexity of randomly generated geometric forms and the amount of time that subjects looked at the forms. The data are group averages and are much more regular than individual subject data. However, the principle seems clear: People look longer at more complex figures than at simpler figures; but this would have been much less apparent in the data of individual subjects.

## MEASUREMENT AND MATHEMATICS

A clear distinction needs be made between measurement, which is directly concerned with the real world, and mathematics, which, as an abstract enterprise, needs have nothing to do with the real world. Perhaps the two would not be so readily confused if both did not frequently involve numbers. Measurement always concerns numbers relatable to the physical world, and the legitimacy of any measurement is determined by data (facts about the physical world). In particular, scaling, but not classification, always concerns some form of numerical statement of *how much* of an attribute is

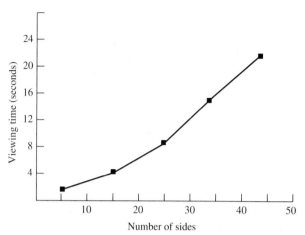

**FIGURE 1-1**    Viewing time as a function of stimulus complexity (number of sides on randomly generated geometric forms).

present, as its purpose is to quantify the attributes of real objects. A measure may be intended to fit a set of measurement axioms (a model), but its fit to the model can be determined only by seeing how well the data fit the model's predictions. Even if there is no formal model, the eventual and crucial test of any measure (scale or classification) is how well it explains relations among variables. As will be discussed in Chapter 3, the various types of validity for psychological measures all require data rather than purely mathematical deductions.

In contrast to measurement, pure mathematics is limited to deductive sets of rules for the manipulation of symbols, of which those used to denote quantities and categories are only one type. Many deductive systems in modern mathematics do not involve numbers, though they may involve classification. Any internally consistent set of rules for manipulating a set of symbols can be a legitimate branch of mathematics. Thus the statement "iggle wug drang flous" could be a legitimate mathematical statement in a set of rules stating that when any iggle is wugged it drang a flous. Mathematical systems could be constructed in which both the objects and the operations are symbolized by nonsense words. This system might not and need not be of practical use, as its legitimacy depends entirely on the internal consistency of its rules.

As a result, scientists *develop* measures by stating rules to quantify attributes of real objects, but *borrow* mathematical systems to examine the structure of the data. Fortunately scientifically useful measurement methods can usually be associated with appropriate mathematical systems.

### Measurement and Statistics

Because the term "statistics" is used broadly, some distinctions among different uses of the term are necessary in order to see their implications for psychometric theory.

There is a basic distinction between descriptive and inferential statistics. "Descriptive statistics" concerns quantitative statements about an attribute of a particular group of observations and does not necessarily imply generalization. Thus, one may compute the arithmetic mean of the scores on a classroom test, the correlation between two presumed measures of anxiety, or the scores of two job applicants without making any broader statements about those not taking the tests. In contrast, "inferential statistics" concerns generalizing from observed sample values (statistics) to their counterparts in a population (parameters), nearly always in the form of probability statements. A common example is to estimate the probability that the observed mean difference between an experimental group and a control group is a chance departure from 0, the expected result if the treatment had no effect.

We will say less in this book about inference than description, as most of the traditional quantitative methods to be presented are primarily designed for description rather than inference. Thus correlational analysis, factor analysis, discriminant analysis, and other procedures can be discussed and employed with minimal use of inference. This is not to say that inferential statistics are unimportant or that they will be totally neglected. We will consider some advances in inferential statistics that have become prominent since the last revision, particularly maximum likelihood estimation. There are three reasons to emphasize description. First, classical psychometric theory and some newer models are large-sample theories that assume that many subjects are studied. Second, even some investigators who have been very concerned with developing these newer inferential measurement models stress the importance of description (Bentler & Bonnett, 1980). Finally, we have enough material to present without going too far into a somewhat ancillary topic. There are excellent books on the relevant inferential statistics for psychometric theory that will be referenced where appropriate.

A second important statistical distinction is that between the sampling of objects (in this context, usually people) and the sampling of content (items). After a measure has been developed, it is often important to make statements about objects as in developing test norms. Before measures are developed, however, measurement is much more closely related to the sampling of content, as in deciding which test items to include. We will later stress how it is useful to think of particular test items as a sample from a hypothetical infinite population or universe of items measuring the same trait. Thus a spelling test for fourth-grade students can be thought of as a sample of all possible appropriate words. Part of measurement theory thus concerns statistical relations between the actual test scores and the hypothetical scores that would be made if all items in the universe had been administered.

There is a two-way problem in all psychology concerned with the sampling of objects to be measured and the sampling of content. The former usually concerns the generality of findings over objects, and the latter concerns the generality of findings over test items. Some item response theory models (Chapters 2 and 10) simultaneously take objects and items into account. However, most analyses take only one of these dimensions into account explicitly and keep the other in mind or, worse, simply ignore it. Thus, a study comparing different approaches to teaching mathematics upon a particular achievement test may explicitly concern gender differences. However, it might have to acknowledge that different results might have been obtained with different achievement measures.

The frequent necessity of considering only one of these two dimensions is not ideal, but it is not necessarily fatal. Subsequent studies can deal with generalizing over the other dimension. The most desirable situation is when one samples so extensively on one dimension that the only sampling error present is on the other dimension. This normally requires an extremely large sample of subjects. At least hundreds, if not thousands, of subjects should be used in the development process. Except as noted, we will assume that all mathematical analyses are based on large numbers of subjects so that issues will be limited to the sampling of content. Studies conducted on relatively small numbers of subjects are usually not sufficient. Thus, even though a few dozen subjects may suffice to establish that the test reliability is greater than zero, a more precise statement of the magnitude is nearly always required.

The idea that sampling content is more important than sampling objects in developing a measure is not easy to grasp. Many students fall into the trap of assuming that a test's reliability increases with the number of objects (subjects) used in the study of reliability, when in fact it is directly related to the number of items on the test and independent of the number of objects.

## MEASUREMENT SCALES

A series of articles by Stevens (1946, 1951, 1958, 1960) evoked considerable discussion and soul searching about the different possible types of measurement scales. Stevens proposed that measurements fall into four major classes (some extensions of these basic types will be noted below): nominal, ordinal, interval, and ratio. The levels allow progressively more sophisticated quantitative procedures to be performed on the measures but in turn demand progressively more of the measurement operations. In addition, the levels restrict the transformations possible upon the data. Table 1-1 provides an illustration of this proposed classification which we will embellish on in the succeeding pages.

Stevens' work evoked a great deal of controversy at the time, some of which continues. One major effect was that it led to a healthy self-consciousness about

TABLE 1-1    STEVENS' LEVELS OF MEASUREMENT, BASIC DEFINING OPERATIONS, PERMISSIBLE TRANSFORMATIONS, EXAMPLES OF PERMISSIBLE STATISTICS, AND EXAMPLES

| Scale | Basic operation | Permissible transformations | Permissible statistics | Examples |
|---|---|---|---|---|
| Nominal | = vs ≠ (equality vs. inequality) | Any one-to-one | Numbers of cases, mode | Telephone numbers |
| Ordinal | > vs. < (greater than vs. less than) | Monotonically increasing | Median, percentiles, order statistics | Hardness of minerals, class rank |
| Interval | Equality of intervals or differences | General linear $x' = bx + a$ | Arithmetic mean, variance, Pearson correlation | Temperature (Celsius), conventional test scores (?) |
| Ratio | Equality of ratios | Multiplicative (similarity) $x' = bx$ | Geometric mean | Temperature (Kelvin) |

*Source:* Adapted from Stevens (1951) by permission of John Wiley, Inc.

psychological measurement, but it also led to some unfortunate conclusions about the legitimacy of employing particular classes of mathematical procedures with measures of psychological attributes. Of these, the issue of whether or not it is meaningful to compute the mean of a series of test scores derived by summing individual items had the greatest implications. We will first present Stevens' position in a simplified, conventional manner, after which we will discuss the nature of psychological measurement in more general terms.

## Nominal scales

Nominal scales contain rules for deciding whether two objects are = (equivalent) or ≠ (not equivalent), i.e., for categorizing. Equivalence means that two objects have a critical property in common, e.g., two people are both females. It does not imply identity or equality with respect to all relevant properties, and it will be discussed in a more formal sense below. The result of a nominal scale is a series of classes which *may* be given a numeric designation. The numbers are frequently used to keep track of things, without implying that they can be subjected to any mathematical analysis. Telephone and social security numbers are common examples of using numbers simply as labels that could just as well be expressed without numbers. These labels have no mathematical properties, and so it makes no sense to average a work and a home telephone number. However, it is important to distinguish between using the category "names" numerically, which is improper, and the category "frequencies," which is quite proper, e.g., to ask whether there are more Democrats, Independents, or Republicans in a political poll.

It is sometimes useful to distinguish between labels and categories even though both can be nominal scales. Labels, numeric or otherwise, are used to identify individual objects. These may be unique, as are the social security numbers given to U.S. citizens and residents, or there may be many duplications, as with given names. In contrast, categories are groupings of objects, in which it is usually desirable to have relatively few categories compared to the number of objects. Common categories are race, ethnicity, and gender.

Although categories and labels need not reflect any specific quantitative relationship, they may lead to the discovery of important correlates. For example, the finding that people of a certain ethnicity are more prone to a particular disease than people of a different ethnicity is vital to geneticists. However, this is an issue of classification, discussed below and in Chapter 15, and not scaling. Labels and categories are nominal scales, but nominal scales have thus far offered little to formal scaling models even though such models exist.

Nominal scales can be transformed in any manner that does not assign the same number to different categories. Thus, males and females could, respectively, be coded 1 and 0, 0 and 1 or even −257.3 and 534.8 without gain or loss of information. These one-to-one transformations are permissible because the names do not have numeric properties. The flexibility with which one can transform nominal scales reflects the limited mathematical operations that can be performed with them. For example, assume that a survey has coded potential voters as 1, 2, or 3 for Democrat, Republican, and Independent and that the frequencies of individuals in these three classes are 35,

25, and 40. One could compute a "mean" as $(35 \cdot 1 + 25 \cdot 2 + 40 \cdot 3)/100$ or 2.05. However, this figure would change capriciously if permissible transformations were made upon the categories. For example, it would change to 2.95 if Independents were coded 0, Democrats were coded 2, and Republicans were coded 9, and there is no logical connection between changes in the scale values and changes in this mean. One important exception to this principle is when there are two categories. This exception underlies much contemporary multiple regression theory, as we will see later in this book. In this case, statistics such as means do change predictably as categories are changed. We will show why this is the case when we consider interval scales.

## Ordinal scales

Ordinal scaling involves rules for deciding whether one object that is $\neq$ to another is $>$ (greater than) or $<$ (less than) with respect to a given attribute (there may also be ties so $\leq$ and $\geq$ are also used). A *ordinal scale* for $N$ persons ($Ss$) allows one to determine that $S_i \geq S_j \geq S_k \geq S_n$ with respect to an attribute (the $=$ part of $\geq$ allows for ties). This implies that (1) a set of objects is ordered from "most" to "least" with respect to an attribute, (2) one does not know how much any of the objects possess of the attribute in an absolute sense, and (3) one does not know how far apart the objects are with respect to the attribute. An ordinal scale is obtained if a group of people are ranked from tallest to shortest. This scale gives no indication of the average height. The mean rank of the height of $N$ jockeys and $N$ professional basketball players will be $(N + 1)/2$. In both cases, the mean of five ranked observations will thus be $(5 + 1)/2$ or 3. Likewise, the variance of the ranks will equal $(N^2 - 1)/12$ regardless of whether the measures are very similar or very dissimilar. If there are five ranked observations, the result will be $(5^2 - 1)/12$ or 2.

Dichotomous (pass-fail) scoring is a special and, indeed, the simplest case of ordering. It is commonly present in true-false or multiple-choice ability tests. A pass is commonly designated 1, and a failure is designated 0. Items using an agree-disagree format in personality or attitude measurement logically also yield pass-fail orderings, since agreeing with the key is a form of passing.

Ordered categories arise when a measure yields relatively precise information, but the investigator lumps scores into a smaller number of successive categories. For example, an economist may categorize family income measures into a small number of levels. This can sacrifice a great deal of information, but it may be needed for data presentation. In contrast, data may be gathered as ranks. Likert scale items are a common example used in personality and attitude measurement in which subjects describe their intensity of feeling toward the item. For example, subjects might be asked whether they "strongly agree," "agree," "are indifferent," "disagree," or "strongly disagree" with the statement "I feel uncomfortable asking professors questions in class." The subject is then assigned a score from 1 to 5, and the total scale score is the sum of individual item scores. This format generates more information than dichotomous scoring, as it may increase the range of scores substantially over dichotomous items scoring, a benefit to the statistical analysis as it more faithfully reflects the individual differences on the attribute.

Rank ordering is basic to higher forms of measurement. Most of the information contained in higher level scales is contained simply in the rank orderings (Coombs, 1964; Parker, Casey, Ziriax, & Silberberg, 1988). Thus, if two sets of measures obtained from higher level scales are correlated and converted to ranks, and the ranked data also correlated (see Spearman's rank order correlation in Chapter 4), the correlation between the original numbers and the correlation between the ranks are usually quite similar in magnitude. In contrast, considerable information is lost if both sets of observations and correlations become much smaller when data are dichotomized. Consequently, methods based upon rank ordering, such as rank order multidimensional scaling considered in Chapter 14, often do justice to the relations contained in higher-level data, but the common practice of dichotomizing variables when the underlying data are of a stronger form should be avoided (Cohen, 1990).

The class of transformations permissible for ordinal scales is more limited than it is for nominal scales. The transformation must preserve the rank-order properties of the data. Thus, category names 1, 2, and 3 may be transformed to 4, 5, and 23 or −1.3, 2.05, and 5.33, but not 3, 1, and 2. These permissible transformations are called "monotonic" and are illustrated in Fig. 1-2. A set of statistical operations has been designed for use with ordinal data. The central tendency may be described in terms of the median or the mode (which is also meaningful with nominal data) rather than the arithmetic mean. The mean and mode will change predictably with permissible transformations, whereas the mean will not. For example, if the median and mode are in the second of four ordinal categories coded from 1 to 4, they will remain so under any permissible transformation, which is not true of the arithmetic mean. A considerably different mean will obtain if the categories are recoded as 2, 4, 17, and 39, for example, but the median and mode simply change to the second category, 4.

## Interval scales

Interval scales reflect operations that define a unit of measurement as well as >, =, and <. They are often referred to as "equal interval scales" for this reason. Consequently (1) the rank ordering of objects on an attribute is known, (2) the distances among objects on the attribute are also known, but (3) the *absolute* magnitudes of the attribute are unknown. Expressing the height of each of a series of children relative to their mean height would yield an interval scale of their height. Thus a child 2 inches taller than average would receive a score of +2, a child 3 inches shorter than average would receive a score of −3, etc. Deviations from any mean can be calculated without actually knowing how far anyone is from a true zero point, e.g., zero height. The absolute magnitudes of the attribute are potentially important but unknown since the tallest child is probably short in a more general sense. However, psychological measures are commonly described as deviations from the mean.

Interval scales do not require an equal number of objects (people) at each point, i.e., a rectangular distribution of scores. The term "equal" describes the intervals on the scale, not the number of people between equally spaced points on the scale. Thus, the difference between intelligence measures of 100 and 105 are assumed equal to the difference between intelligence measures of 120 and 125 even though many more people fall between 100 to 105 than 120 to 125.

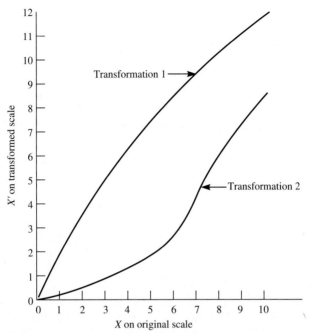

**FIGURE 1-2** Two examples of monotonic transformations permissible on an ordinal scale. The general form of these transformations is difficult to define algebraically.

Interval properties imply that if $a$, $b$, $c$, $\cdots$, $k$ are equally spaced points on the scale, the scale is defined by two statements:

**1** $a > b > c > \cdots > k$

**2** $a - b = b - c = c - d = \cdots = j - k$

An interval scale is defined by algebraic differences between points, and so addition and subtraction of the scale points are permissible operations. Since $a - b = b - c$, the sum of the two intervals equals $(a - b) + (b - c) = a - c$.

The difference between the two intervals equals zero:

$$(a - b) - (b - c) = a - 2b + c$$

The expression equals zero because $a + c = 2b$:

$$a - b = b - c$$
$$a + c = 2b$$

Since points are assumed to be equidistant on an interval scale,

$$\frac{a - b}{b - c} = 1$$

Similarly, the distance from $a$ to $c$ equals twice the distance from $a$ to $b$.

Whereas there is usually little dispute over whether nominal or ordinal properties have been established, there is often great dispute over whether or not a scale possesses a meaningful unit of measurement. Formal scaling methods designed to this end are discussed in Chapters 2, 10, and 15. For now, it suffices to note that many measures are sums of item responses, such as conventionally scored multiple-choice, true-false, and Likert scale items. Data from individual items are clearly ordinal. However, the total score is usually treated as interval, as when the arithmetic mean score, which assumes equality of intervals, is computed. Those who perform such operations thus implicitly use a scaling model to convert data from a lower (ordinal) to a higher (interval) level of measurement when they sum over items to obtain a total score. Some adherents of Stevens' position have argued that these statistical operations are improper and advocate, among other things, that medians, rather than arithmetic means should be used to describe conventional test data. We strongly disagree with this point of view for reasons we will note throughout this book, not the least of which is that the results of summing item responses are usually indistinguishable from using more formal methods. However, some situations clearly do provide only ordinal data, and the results of using statistics that assume an interval can be misleading. One example would be the responses to individual items scored on multi-category (Likert-type) scales.

The only transformation that preserves the properties of an interval scale is called the general linear transformation and is of the form $X' = bX + a$, where $X'$ is the transformed measure, $X$ is the original measure, and $a$ and $b$ are, respectively, additive and multiplicative constants involved in the transformation. Transforming temperatures from Celsius ($C$) to Fahrenheit ($F$), both of which are interval scales, by the relation $F = \frac{9}{5}C + 32$ is a common example. Figure 1-3 illustrates three general linear transformations. Ratios of *individual* values are not meaningful on an interval scale because the zero of an interval scale may be legitimately changed through changes in the additive constant $a$. The ratios, in degrees Fahrenheit of 64 to 32 and of 100 to 50 are both numerically computable in degrees as 2:1. However, these no longer remain equal, and indeed the first of them becomes undefined, if these temperatures are expressed in degrees Celsius. On the other hand, ratios of *differences* in interval scale values are meaningful. For example, assume the summer mean temperature (in degrees Fahrenheit), of a particular city is 90 during the day and 75 at night. These respectively change to 50 and 40 in the winter. The ratio of the difference in summer and winter temperatures is $(90 - 75)/(50 - 40)$ or 1.5. The corresponding ratio in degrees Celsius is $(32.2 - 23.9)/(10 - 4.4)$ or (within rounding error) also 1.5. This is because the effects of changes in $b$ and $a$ cancel in the process of forming ratios of differences.

When there are only two categories, there is only one interval to consider, so that one interval may be considered an "equal" interval. That is why binary (dichotomous) variables may be considered to form interval scales, the point noted above as being so important to modern regression theory and elsewhere in statistics.

## Ratio Scales

A ratio scale is an interval scale with a rational (true) zero rather than an arbitrary zero. A rational zero for children's height in the above example would be physical

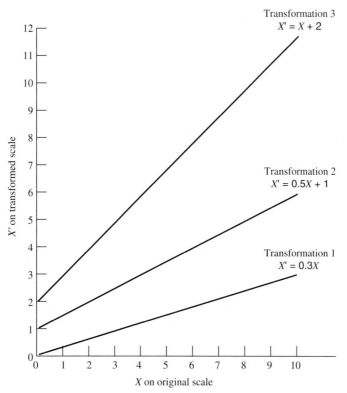

**FIGURE 1-3**  Three examples of general linear transformations permissible on an interval scale: $X' = X + 2$, $X' = 0.5X + 1$, and $X' = 0.3X$. The general form of the transformation is $X' = bX + a$.

zero rather than the mean height. The presence of a meaningful zero makes ratios of any two measures meaningful. Unlike the three lower types of scales, all four fundamental operations of algebra—addition, subtraction, division, and multiplication—may be used with individual values defined on ratio scales.

A rational zero means absence of the attribute and not simply "reasonable," e.g., zero height or weight. It is often reasonable to reference scores to the mean, but the mean clearly does not denote absence of the attribute, and so it is not a rational zero in the present sense. If there is no rational zero, it does not make sense to form ratios since ratios change as the arbitrary zero changes, another way of saying that ratios of individual values on an interval scale are not meaningful. For example, suppose the class average on a test is 30 and two particular students obtain scores of 50 and 40. Relative to a score of zero, the ratios of these two scores is 1.25:1. However, zero correct is not a rational zero because a student obtaining a score of zero might be able to answer some simpler items correctly. Relative to the mean, the ratio becomes (50 − 30)/(40 − 30) or 2:1, but this ratio is just as arbitrary as the 1.25:1 ratio relative to zero.

There are many examples of rational zeros in physics—zero time and absolute zero (Kelvin) temperature being two others. However, it has proven difficult to define absolute zeros for most psychological attributes like intelligence. Zero reaction time is based upon physical time, and so it is a rational zero. This means that it is sensible to form such ratios as the mean reaction time obtained from a more versus a less intense stimulus. The major example of ratio scales comes from the fact that differences between observations on an interval scale form a ratio scale. Thus, if pre- and posttest scores on a measure are obtained, the resulting change score can be assumed to form a ratio scale with 0 representing no change. However, Chapter 5 will discuss why change scores may have other problems—it is difficult to compare two change scores based upon different pretest scores.

Actually, ratio scales are rarely needed to address the most common needs of scaling. Defining an interval is very important, but ordering is the most crucial concept. In contrast, nominal measurement rules suffice for most classification problems. It is not proper to employ the general linear transformation permissible with interval scales, only the more restricted form $X' = bX$ is allowable. This more specific form of linear transformation, depicted in Fig. 1-4, is also called a multiplicative transformation. Employing an additive constant (a) implies that the zero point is not fixed, which it is in a ratio scale, by definition. Changing from feet *(F)* to inches *(I)* by the relation $I = 12F$ is a frequently used multiplicative transformation.

Ratios of height, weight, etc., as measured from their true zero points are meaningful. These ratios do not change with permissible transformations since these permissible transformations do not allow a change in the zero point. This is why the term "ratio scale" is used. Someone who weighs twice as much as another person in pounds will also weigh twice as much in kilograms.

## Other Scales

Those within the tradition exemplified by Stevens have proposed scale types other than these basic four, and it is important not to think that all scales are divided into four levels. Coombs (1964), Coombs, Dawes, and Tversky, (1970) and Stine (1989a) have discussed these in some detail. One additional type is an ordered metric in which (1) the rank order of objects is known, (2) the rank order of intervals between objects is known, but (3) the magnitudes of the intervals are unknown. Such a scale allows one to say that $a$ and $b$ differ more than $c$ and $d$ but does not allow more precise statements about the relative magnitudes of difference. Stevens (1958) proposed a logarithmic interval scale where the ratios of magnitudes corresponding to successive points $a$, $b$, $c$, $d$ are $a/b = b/c = c/d$, etc. Then $\log a - \log b = \log b - \log c = \log c - \log d$, etc. The decibel scale that is familiar to physicists is a logarithmic interval scale (it is not limited to the measurement of sound intensity), since it involves transforming stimulus energies to their logs.

The absolute scale formed from counts is the strongest type of measurement because it has the interesting property of being its own invariant scale of measurement: When one says "There are three people in the room," the meaning of "three" is inherent in the real number system. In contrast, if you were told a room is three units wide, this might refer to yards, meters, or some other unit of measurement. As interesting as some of these other scales are, though, the four basic ones listed above are far and away the most important to psychometric theory and application.

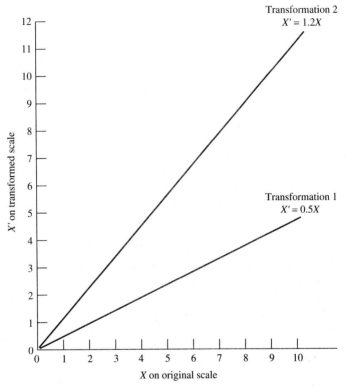

**FIGURE 1-4** Two examples of multiplicative transformations permissible on a ratio scale: $X' = 1.2X$ and $X' = 0.5X$. The general form of the transformation is $X' = bX$.

## Invariance

It is important to consider the circumstances under which a particular type of scale remains invariant, i.e., maintains its properties when the unit of measurement is changed. As we have seen, the more powerful the mathematical operations meaningful with a given scale, the less free one is to change it. Thus, nominal scale labels may be changed in an almost unlimited manner as long as no two categories are given the same label, but at the other extreme absolute scales lose their absolute properties when changed in any way.

Invariance is basic to the generality of scientific statements derived from a scale (Luce, 1959b, 1990). It is easy to imagine the chaos that would result if some physical measures lacked the invariance of ratio scales. Without invariance, a stick that is twice as long as another measured in feet might be three times as long when measured in inches. The range of invariance of a scale determines the extent to which principles remain unaffected by expressing the scale in different units, e.g., feet rather than inches. This does not mean that the results of using the scale will not change. A mean temperature in degrees Fahrenheit will be numerically different than a mean temperature in degrees Celsius even though both are permissible operations. The point is that the means will change in an orderly fashion: Specifically, the same equation will relate the means as the one presented above that relate the individual values. Any permissible transformation of a scale produces an equivalent scale—one that maintains the same general form of relationship. Similar statements apply about operations meaningful on other scales.

## DECISIONS ABOUT MEASUREMENT SCALES

A strong view of measurement is called the representational position (or the "fundamentalist" position in the previous edition of this book) about measurement scales because it states that scale values represent empirical relations among objects (Michell, 1986, also see Stine, 1989b). Its main assertions are that (1) measurement scales have empirical reality in addition to being theoretical constructs, (2) a possible measure of an attribute can be classified into one of a small number of distinct levels, and (3) investigators must document the scale properties of particular measures before analyzing data obtained from the scale because the scale's level limits the permissible mathematical operations. Besides Stevens, the tradition includes Krantz, Luce, Suppes, and Tversky (1971), Luce (1959b), Suppes and Zinnes (1963), and Townsend and Ashby (1984; also see Ashby & Perrin, 1988; Davison & Sharma, 1988, 1990).

Representational theory had great impact in the 1950s. Investigators tended to avoid parametric tests ($t$, the $F$ ratio of the ANOVA, etc.) that required an interval scale (at least according to representational theory) and used nonparametric tests (Siegel & Castellan, 1988) that required only ordinal or nominal assumptions instead. Representational proponents of nonparametric tests argued that these tests were only slightly weaker (less able to detect differences) than their parametric counterparts, a difference that could generally be overcome by gathering slightly more data. However, they largely ignored the greater flexibility of parametric methods in evaluating interactions (combined effects of two or more variables that are not predictable from the individual variables). Starting in the 1960s, investigators returned to the use of parametric tests.

As a simple example of the representational approach, consider this approach to defining the equivalence ("=") of two objects (the presence of a property in common, e.g., being enrolled in the same college course). Equivalence requires transitivity, symmetry, and reflexivity. "Transitivity" means that the relation passes across objects—if John and Richard are enrolled in the course and if Richard and Mary are enrolled in the course, then John and Mary must be enrolled in the course. "Symmetry" means that the relationship extends the same way in both directions—if John is enrolled in the same course as Mary, then Mary must be enrolled in the same course as John. "Reflexivity" states that the relation extends to the object itself—every object is equivalent to itself (if John is enrolled in the course, then John is enrolled in the course but not all examples are that obvious, as we will see in Chapter 15). Parallel considerations yield definitions of the ">" and "<" relationships used to define ordinal scales, the unit used to define interval scales, and the zero point used to define ratio scales. These latter relations are *not* symmetrical, among other things. If Mary is ">", e.g., taller than, Susan, then Susan cannot be ">" Mary. Representationalists have been most concerned with whether a particular measurement achieves interval status so that computing the mean is permissible. We have already stressed the issue of whether scores on a conventionally scored test form an interval scale, and they have often argued that they

do not. We strongly suggest that this position can easily become too narrow and counterproductive. Michell (1986) describes two other traditions that he terms operational
theory (Gaito, 1980; Bridgman, 1928) and classical theory (Rozeboom, 1966). Neither
accepts Stevens' view that one must have achieved a particular level of measurement
to perform a particular statistical operation. Operational theory views a concept as synonymous with the operations that define it. In other words, a score on a test does not
represent (stand for something beyond) a measure. It *is* the measure, but it may contain an error so that it merely estimates the trait; operationalism does not require the
measure to be the trait itself. Finally, classical theory views measurement as the determination of quantity or how much of an attribute is present in an object (as noted
above, we assume that measurement also includes classification).

Gaito (1980; also see Baker, Hardyck, & Petrinovich, 1966) termed his position
"statistical theory" and was highly critical of representational theory (which he called
"measurement theory"). His tone was very clearly pejorative, but his view nonetheless
strikes a sympathic chord with many investigators who have had to defend what they
considered to be obvious aspects of their statistical analyses. Perhaps his major point
is that using presumably impermissible transformations usually makes little, if any,
difference to the results of the most common analyses. For a counterexample, see
Townsend and Ashby (1984).

## Ostensive Characteristics

The physical characteristics of the measurement operations provide one way to judge
the scale characteristics of a particular measure, e.g., length with some form of yardstick. To prove that the attribute in question is measured on a ratio scale requires proof
of both (1) equal intervals and (2) an axiomatically unquestionable zero point. Anyone
can *see* the zero point where the yardstick starts. The beginning of the measuring instrument is the front of the yardstick, and open space is behind that point. Who could
argue for a more meaningful zero point? The equality of intervals is also easy to demonstrate, e.g., saw the yardstick inch by inch and compare the inch long pieces to ensure equality.

To a lesser or greater extent, all other measures employ correlates of the attribute
rather than the attribute itself and are therefore indirect. We can establish equality of
time intervals but, strictly speaking, we observe the effects of time and not time itself—ticks, pendulum swings, and the earth's rotation are only consequences of time.
Nearly all measures of interest to behavioral scientists are indirect. We cannot observe
intelligence per se but only its by-products. Likewise, a subject's perception can only
be inferred from subjects' ability to discriminate and/or report what they experience
(Eriksen, 1960).

Many investigators, who may not even consider themselves representationalists in a
formal sense, tend to evaluate scale properties in terms of ostensive characteristics and
think of actual measures as imperfect correlates of "real" ones even though the scales
may have been developed from a formal scaling model. We suggest that if the data obtained from applying a measurement scale fit the axioms of the particular model under
consideration and the axioms (assumptions) of the model are appropriate, then the
measure has scale properties specified by the model. For example, Chapter 2 contains

a model proposed by Louis Guttman for the construction of ordinal scales. It is based upon assumptions about patterns of responses to test items. Relevant data can be analyzed to determine how well the actual score patterns relate to the patterns predicted by the model. A good fit implies that an appropriate scale exists.

Since, for example, there are no ostensive properties to guarantee the equality of intervals measuring intelligence, some have argued that intelligence tests, for example, provide ordinal scales at best. We hope the above discussion illustrates that few measures in all sciences would be considered more than ordinal scales by these standards; the following sections will show that proper standards for judging the scale properties of a measure do not require observing the ostensive characteristics of an attribute. In particular:

**1** Standards can be based on data rather than ostensive characteristics. One studies the results of applying a measure to real objects when using a scaling model, or one studies the measurement tool directly when using ostensive characteristics. Thus, instead of relying upon the ostensive properties of yardsticks, one could test a model concerning properties of ratio scales and then see if it fits data obtained from yardstick measurements. One could therefore derive the scale properties of the yardstick from the model before seeing a yardstick. People have done this, and the data fit a variety of scaling models beautifully, e.g., produce transitivity. This is what psychological scaling is about: *It is an attempt to work backward from data to test the fit to a model.* In this way, ratio, interval, ordinal, or perhaps nominal scales for psychological attributes which cannot be seen directly may be constructed.

**2** Using scaling models is a healthy trend in the development of measurement methods. Many models are intuitively quite appealing. Because they specify the characteristics that should be found in data, they are subject to refutation (can be falsified, Popper, 1959). Some models have produced scales that have led to interesting scientific findings.

**3** A model is no better and no worse than its assumptions (axioms). There is ample room for disagreement, and there is plenty of it, about the fruitfulness of different models. For example, we have argued that measures like multiple-choice test scores should be viewed as having interval properties. However, if psychologists disagree about the correctness of different scaling models, how are scale characteristics ever determined? If, for example, several interval scaling models are being tried on a particular type of data, a failure of the data to fit one model does not automatically prevent the measure from being considered as an interval scale. Conversely, even if the data fit *all* the models, the measures should not automatically be thought of as constituting an interval scale. A more final decision should be made with respect to standards to be discussed in the following sections.

## Consequences of Assumptions

Even if one believes that there is a real scale for each attribute that is either directly present in a particular measure or mirrored in a monotonic transformation, an important question is What difference does it make if the measure does not have the same zero point or proportionally equal intervals as the real scale? If the scientist assumes, for example, that the scale is an interval scale when it really is not, something will go wrong in the daily work of the scientist. What could go wrong? How could the difficulty be detected? The scientist could misstate the specific form of the relationship between the attribute and other variables. For example, a power function might be found between two measures using an imperfect interval scale, whereas the right scale may produce a linear relationship.

How seriously would such a misstatement affect the progress of the behavioral sciences? At present, the usual answer is "very little." Most results are reported as either correlations or mean differences. We have stressed and will stress that correlations are little affected by monotonic transformations on variables. These correlations are the basis of still more powerful methods like factor analysis. However, we also stress that justifying the rank order is vital. Even if one accepted the representational point of view about measurement scales, what sense does it make to sacrifice powerful methods of correlational analysis just because there is no way of proving the claimed scale properties of the measures?

There is also often major concern about the ratios of variances among different sources of variation in analyzing mean differences among groups, e.g., $F$, the variance among means relative to the variance within groups. This ratio and related statistics are also little affected by monotonic transformations of the dependent measure. If it is granted that the measure used in the experiment is at least monotonically related to the real scale, it usually makes little difference which is used in the analysis. There are some exceptions of import. Two of these are (1) in examining details of functional relationships, such as whether a particular monotonic relation is linear, logarithmic, a power function, or some other form, and (2) for some goodness-of-fit tests used in structural modeling (see Chapters 5, 10, and 15).

A simple rule of thumb is that transformations become more important as the level of sophistication of the research hypotheses increases. Thus, tests simply concerned with looking for group differences and rank orderings of groups typically involve statistical procedures that are little affected by transformations. Numerically, these perhaps account for the vast majority of research. Interval assumptions are therefore not crucial when interest centers on ordinal relations among group means, etc. However, more refined tests of highly quantitative models are very sensitive to the interval properties of the scale, virtually by definition.

After analyzing the results of investigations, as in correlations and/or ratios of variance components, it often is important to make probability statements about the results after applying inferential statistics. Thus, it may be important to set confidence zones for a correlation coefficient or to test the significance of a particular ratio among components of variance. Such statistical methods are completely indifferent to the zero point on a scale and consequently do not require ratio scales. However, they do assume interval properties, but since they are based on ratios of variation and covariation, they are also little affected by monotonic deviations from any true interval scale. Moreover, statistical methods are completely blind to any meaning in the real world of the numbers involved. These methods require only a definable population of numbers that meets the assumptions in the particular statistical method, such as normality of the population error distribution. We suggest that it is perfectly permissible to employ the ANOVA to test hypotheses about the average size of the numbers on the backs of football players on different teams. What use you may make of the result is, of course, a different story, since there is no meaning to a theory of football numbers beyond identifying the position individuals play, rather than how well they play it (see Lord, 1953).

Chapters 14 and 15 will consider some extremely useful consequences of the representational point of view. We merely note that it is easily misused when the usual intent is to compute correlations or infer the ordering among groups means. Moreover, even when the intent is to study specifics of functional relations, one may discover that two perfectly good definitions of attributes are not linearly related to one another so that the "true" relation to other measures depends upon how the attribute is defined.

## Convention

We have thus far considered the representational point of view that scientists normally think in terms of "real" scales and obtain measures as approximations to such "real" scales. Our opinion is that (1) this point of view frequently leads to unanswerable questions and (2) violations of even relatively important assumptions are not harmful in *most* settings. The authors oppose the concept of "real" scales in most settings and deplore the confusion that this conception has wrought to the average investigator. It is much more appropriate to think of measurement scales as conventions or agreements among scientists about a "good" scaling.

In saying that scales are established by convention and not God-given, we do not mean that such conventions should be arbitrary. Before measuring an attribute, all manner of wisdom should be sought as to the nature of the attribute—one cannot measure something unless one has some general conception about what is to be measured. The nature of a "good" scaling of certain measures can be so readily agreed that a convention is easily established, e.g., length, weight, and time. Exasperation about theories of measurement has tempted some to wish that there were no yardsticks and no balances for the measurement of weight so that all scientists could see that measurement always involves convention rather than discovery of the "real" measure.

Sometimes, one person establishes a measurement convention and other scientists often neglect to participate in establishing the particular convention. Consequently, the particular scale becomes accepted as *the* scale. The Fahrenheit thermometer was once taken as *the* scale of temperature. Later, the discovery of absolute zero led to a new and more useful scaling. In psychology, intelligence was once defined as the ratio of mental age to chronological age, i.e., as an intelligence quotient (IQ), but intelligence is now measured relative to performance within a given age distribution. Both these instances illustrate why it is wrong to think that "real" scales had been discovered. It is better to say that conventions changed because better conventions were developed. The key is continued *validation* of measures.

After applying all available wisdom to the problem, it is good to apply some type of formal scaling model when actually constructing measurement scales. Although any set of rules for the assignment of numbers constitutes measurement, silly and/or ad hoc rules probably will not result in a useful measure. It is useful to think of a scaling model as an internally consistent plan for scaling an attribute. When the plan is put to use, the measure may eventually prove unsatisfactory to the scientific community, but having a plan increases the probability that it will be acceptable. Sometimes, useful measures are simply stumbled upon. However, explicit plans based on common sense and past experience improve the probabilities of a useful measurement scale.

A convention establishes the scale properties of a measure. If it is established as a ratio scale, then the zero point can be taken seriously and the intervals may be treated as equal in any form of analysis. If it is established as an interval scale, the intervals may be treated as equal in all forms of analysis. This is not meant to imply that such conventions are, or should be, established quickly or until much evidence is in, but in the end they are conventions, not discoveries of "real" scales.

Certain conventions are not employed because they make no sense or do not lead to useful results. For example, the Celsius scale's use of the freezing point of water to define temperature's zero point has limited scientific utility. Water is an important substance, but it not the only important substance. On the other hand, the absolute zero of the Kelvin scale based upon the absence of molecular activity is useful to a wide range of physical laws. It similarly makes little sense to establish zero points on scales of many, but not all, psychological attributes. Zero intelligence might be defined as the problem-solving ability of a dead person, but the utility of this convention in establishing a ratio scale of intelligence remains to be determined. Psychologists seek to develop interval scales for many attributes because it is reasonable to ask how far apart people are on the scale and not simply their ordering. For example, we frequently need to determine if $a$ is closer to $b$ than to $c$.

Scaling procedures that make sense may still not produce scales that *work well in practice*. These last four words are the key to establishing a measurement convention—a good measure is one that mathematically fits well in a system of lawful relationships. Chapter 3 will emphasize that the usefulness (validity) of a measure is the extent to which it relates to other variables in a domain of interest. The "best" scaling of any particular attribute is that producing the simplest forms of relationship with other variables. An increasing hierarchy of simplicity is (1) a random relationship, (2) a nonrandom pattern fitting no particular line of relationship, (3) an unevenly ascending or descending monotonic relationship, (4) a smooth monotonic relationship, (5) a straight line, and (6) a straight line passing through the origin. The only way to describe a random relationship completely is to describe every point. However, a straight line passing through the origin is completely described by $Y = bX$, and the $b$ (slope) parameter is usually arbitrary. Since the scientist's task is to translate and simplify the complexity of events in the universe through lawful relationships, the simpler these relationships, the better.

One way to make relationships simpler is to change the scaling of one or more of the variables. Thus, an irregular monotonic relationship can be smoothed by stretching some of the intervals, a procedure widely used by Anderson (1981, 1982) under the name "functional measurement." Any monotonic curve can be transformed to a straight line by this device. A straight line can be made to pass through the origin by changing the origin (zero point) on one of the scales. Of course, conventions about a particular attribute should not be altered because of the relationships found with only one or two other measures. One should consider the effects upon several measures. Nonetheless, if many relationships are simplified by a particular transformation, the new scale is logically a better scale. Such transformations are made actually quite frequently. For example, logarithmic transformations are quite common, especially in sensory psychology.

Following this point of view to the extreme, there is no reason why all variables known to science could not be rescaled to simplify all relationships. This would be a wise move if it could be done—a big "if." The new scales are as "real" as the old ones, and there might be every reason to take the zero points and the intervals on the new scales seriously.

There are two major problems with considering scaling merely as a matter of convention. First, it is disquieting to those who think of real scales and futilely wish for infallible tests of the relationships among real scales. Looking at measurement scaling as convention also seems to make the problem "messy." How well a particular scaling of an attribute fits in with other variables is vague. Which variables? How good is a particular fit? To avoid such questions, however, is to blind oneself to the realities of scientific enterprise. To seek shelter in the apparent neatness of conceptions regarding real scales is not to provide answers about the properties of measurement scales but to ask logically unanswerable questions.

A second, and more serious, problem with considering scaling as a matter of convention is that two or more conventions often compete with one another. For example, there has been much dispute about whether Thurstone's law of comparative judgment or Stevens' magnitude-estimation methods better describe the results of measuring sensations (see Chapter 2). As it turns out, Thurstone's procedures are more useful in describing lawful relations involving confusion among stimuli, and Stevens' methods are more useful in predicting how stimuli will appear (the two are also simply related through a logarithmic transformation). More appropriate than asking which is correct would be to ask whether confusion among stimuli or their appearance is at issue in the particular situation.

Having competing conventions regarding the scaling of attributes is not as bad as it sounds for two reasons. First, if the two scalings are monotonically related to each other, as is usually the case, and if one has a monotonic relationship with a third variable, so will the other. Thus the principles established with the two scalings will produce the same general functional relations, even though the specifics may differ. The specific form of relationship is rarely the major issue in contemporary psychology even though it can be. The more common question is the strength of relationship between the two variables. Correlations greater than .60 are the exception rather than the rule, and, as was said previously, such correlations are largely insensitive to monotonic transformations. Consequently if there are two competing, monotonically related conventions for scaling that are equally reliable in the sense to be describe later, both will produce about the same correlation with any other variable. In sum, the specific forms of relationship can be settled only when there are firm conventions for scaling. The specific form of a relationship is relative to the measurement convention. To hope to find the relationship is either to continue to search vainly for real scales or to assume that one measurement convention eventually will win out over others.

## Classification as Measurement

We have devoted nearly all of this chapter to the first part of the definition of measurement, measurement as scaling. This is because measurement as scaling has led to more issues of dispute than has measurement as classification, and because until recently there were few sophisticated techniques to use with categorical (nominal) data, the usual fruits of classification. This has changed, especially since the last edition of this book, and Chapter 15 will focus on some of these new developments.

Classification demands a nominal scale (rules to define "=" and "≠") at a minimum and, conversely, illustrates that a nominal scale, which was considered "lowly" in terms of scaling, can be extremely important. Consider two common statements: (1) "Everyone is unique; no two people are the same" and (2) "People are pretty much alike." Although these two statement appear totally contradictory, both share the characteristic that they lead one away from some useful, if not obvious, results. For example, people who describe themselves as Republicans are quite likely to answer a variety of politically related questions differently from people who describe themselves as Democrats, e.g., "Should prayer be allowed in public schools?" Similarly, the relation between political affiliation and response to the political issue may jointly vary with additional variables such as whether the person lives in a rural, suburban, or urban area. Note that this analysis does not necessarily ignore individuality. Two people who fall within the same "cell" of the analysis (e.g., who are both Democrats, live in a suburban area, and oppose school prayer) may differ in countless ways (e.g., gender, religion, height, or weight). As with scaling, classification assumes *equivalence* and not *identity*.

Although classification is relatively simple conceptually, it can be quite difficult empirically. Useful classification along one dimension implies that the dimension in question will relate to another dimension (which in turn could be at any of the previously mentioned levels). There is no reason to classify people as type alpha versus type beta unless these categories have a useful external correlate. Even such obvious categories as Catholic, Protestant, Jewish, and Muslim may not be widely useful (though religiously orthodox versus religiously nonorthodox, disregarding the specific religion, may be). Moreover, apparent relations between a categorical variable (or any other) and a given criterion may be an artifact of a third variable; religious differences may, for example, be an artifact of differences in education and/or income. Thus, one may obtain apparent differences between Catholics and Protestants on an issue that involves liberal versus conservative attitudes because more affluent individuals also tend to be more conservative and the two groups differ in affluence. Likewise, empirical disputes often arise between "lumpers" (people who favor a small and therefore more parsimonious number of broad categories) and "splitters" (people who favor a larger number of more finely defined categories).

## RECENT TRENDS IN MEASUREMENT

### The Impact of Computers

It is very easy to think that the main role of a computer is to expedite analyses that one would have performed anyway. This is certainly important. Anyone who has used computers for a long time appreciates the increasing flexibility and user-friendliness of major computer packages such as BMDP, SAS, SPSSX, SYSTAT, and UniMult. One likewise appreciates the related factors of greater power, increased reliability, and lower cost in the personal computers that are now beginning to dominate statistical analyses and the availability of supercomputers for massive undertakings. However, one additional point must be stressed—computers now allow fundamentally different kinds of analyses to be performed, i.e., open form analyses that are effectively impossible to do by hand.

### Closed versus Open-Form Solutions

Many of the techniques, concepts, and measurement theories that have recently become popular actually have long histories. However, they were essentially interesting statistical curiosities before computers became generally available. The distinction between closed- and open-form solutions helps make this point more understandable. Consider your first statistics class where you were taught to compute the arithmetic mean of a sample by adding up the scores and dividing by the number of scores and given the associated equation $X = \Sigma X/N$. This is a closed form solution because all you need do is plug the numbers into the formula to obtain the result. You might wish to use a computer if $N$ were very large, but the principle would be the same.

On the other hand, suppose you did not know the formula but for some bizarre reason you remembered that the mean minimizes the sum of squared deviations. This too can be expressed by a kind of formula: $\Sigma(X - C)^2 = $ a minimum when $C = X$, but the formula does not tell you how to obtain $X$. You might use this information to compute $X$ by plugging in different values of $C$, computing the sum of squared deviations for each value, and accepting the one producing the smallest sum. If you performed enough calculations, you could in fact obtain an open-form estimate of $X$.

Many statistical quantities of interest, particularly those of recent prominence, require an open form of estimation because they lack a closed-form solution. This is often true of maximum likelihood estimates discussed at several points in this book. For all intents and purposes, such estimates require a computer and, even then, can be very time-consuming. The process involves repeated calculations or iterations. Numerical analysts often specialize in developing better algorithms to obtain the necessary successive approximations. Iterative proportional fitting and Newton-Raphson algorithms are two such common computational processes. You will not need to know how to use either one yourself, but they are widely employed in programs you may use.

### Computer Simulation

Computers are also invaluable in simulating processes. A particular form of simulation that is widely performed on computers is the Monte Carlo method in which an estimate of a parameter is obtained by random sampling. If you were asked to verify that the probability of obtaining heads on a coin flip is .5, you might actually flip a coin a large number of times and count the actual number of heads, hoping the coin was fair. This would illustrate the Monte Carlo method but would not be a computer simulation. The experiment may be done more efficiently on a computer where the program would conduct a series of trials. On each trial, the program generates a random number from 0 to 1 and adds one to the count of heads if the random number is greater than 0.5. When finished, it prints the proportion of times heads occurred. Computer simulations are often performed when it is difficult to obtain a solution analytically (algebraically) or if no solution is known to exist.

## SUMMARY

Measurement consists of rules for assigning symbols to objects to (1) represent quantities of attributes numerically (scaling) or (2) define whether the objects fall in the same or different categories with respect to a given attribute (classification). Both scaling and classification involve the formulation and evaluation of rules. These rules are used to measure attributes of objects, usually, but not exclusively, people. It is important to remember that we can measure only attributes of objects, not the objects themselves. Among the characteristics of good rules are repeatability (reliability) and, more importantly, validity in senses to be described. Standardization is an important goal of measurement because it facilitates objectivity, quantification, communication, economy, and scientific generalization.

Measurement uses mathematics, but the two serve separate roles. Measurement needs to relate to the physical world, but *pure* mathematics is solely concerned with logical consistency. One traditionally important, but controversial, aspect of scaling that involves mathematics is the concept of levels of measurement: Scales generally fall at one of four levels (others have been suggested): nominal, ordinal, interval, and ratio. These four levels represent progressively better articulated rules. For example, nominal scales simply define whether or not two objects are equivalent to one another with respect to a critical attribute, but ordinal scales determine whether one object that is not equivalent to another is greater than or less than the other. Stronger results are possible from higher levels of measurement. Basic to these levels of measurement is the concept of invariance, which concerns what remains the same as permissible changes are made in the scale (e.g., in its unit of measurement); higher-level scales are more restricted as to how they may be transformed and still preserve key invariances.

Focal to the debate about levels of measurement is what statistical operations are permissible on a given set of measures. The representational position asserts that scale properties must be established before performing relevant operations; e.g., a scale must demonstrably have interval properties before it is proper to compute an arithmetic mean. Alternative positions, classical and operational, do not share this view. Many, who need not be formally aligned with a specific position, look for scales to have ostensive (visualizable) properties like yardsticks or clocks have before accepting a scale as real; they view existing measures as highly imperfect correlates of true scales. We suggest that very few measures in science are ostensive. A much better criterion is the extent to which the results of using the scale fit a scaling model. All measurement use is essentially based upon convention, and progress is made when better conventions are agreed upon. In general, the more well elaborated a hypothesis is stated quantitatively, the more important formal scaling issues are.

The most important single factor in the recent progress in measurement has been the computer. Although computers obviously allow analyses that could be done by hand to be done more easily and accurately, they allow fundamentally different analyses to be performed. Many of these use open-form solutions, so named because the results cannot be defined directly by a formula (closed-form solution). In addition, computers allow simulation of processes that are difficult to study directly.

## SUGGESTED ADDITIONAL READINGS

Cohen, J. (1990). Things I have learned (so far). *American Psychologist, 12,* 1304–1312.

Coombs, C. H. (1964). *A theory of data.* New York: Wiley.

Gaito, J. (1980). Measurement scales and statistics: Resurgence of an old misconception. *Psychological Bulletin, 87,* 564–567.

Michell, J. (1986). Measurement scales and statistics: A clash of paradigms, *Psychological Bulletin, 100,* 398–397.

Stevens, S. S. (1958). Problems and methods of psychophysics. *Psychological Bulletin, 55,* 177–196.

Townsend, J. T., & Ashby, F. G. (1984). Measurement scales and statistics: The misconception misconceived, *Psychological Bulletin, 96,* 394–401.

Note: Sage Publications offers many short monographs on an extremely wide variety of relevant topics aimed at scholars who are not quantitative specialists. Although they should not be used as the sole guide to a given problem because of the innumerable complications that may be present, they are highly recommended as starting points. We will not cite these works individually.

# TWO

---

# STATISTICAL
# FOUNDATIONS

---

Part Two contains four chapters that deal with statistical concepts basic to measurement. First, we look at some models used to construct scales. One central concept is that of the item trace line (item-characteristic curve) which relates the magnitude along a dimension (trait) to the magnitude of response to a particular item. The next chapter deals with the three basic meanings of test validity: content validity, construct validity, and predictive validity. Many have debated whether these are ultimately the same or not. Though they share important similarities, there are also important differences among them. The third chapter considers statistical description and estimation. Much of this involves traditional issues in correlation and regression that you may have been previously exposed to. However, two additional topics may be less familiar: structural relations and alternative forms of statistical estimation. The latter is important because statistical inference plays a much larger role in psychometric theory than it did in the previous edition. The method of maximum likelihood is especially important. Finally, we discuss properties of linear combinations which are central to psychometric theory.

# TRADITIONAL APPROACHES TO SCALING

## CHAPTER OVERVIEW

Scaling was defined in Chapter 1 as the assignment of numbers to objects to represent quantities of attributes. Although any relevant set of rules can be spoken of as measurement, it helps to have some internally consistent plan when developing a new measure. The plan is a "scaling model," and the resulting measure is a "scale" or a "measurement method." The simplest example is a ruler used as a scale of length. The methods for constructing and applying rulers constitute the scaling models. Scaling models are designed to generate one or more dimensions (continua) to locate people or objects. In the following example, persons $P_1$, $P_2$, $P_3$, and $P_4$ fall along one such dimension, which could be social anxiety, spelling ability, attitude toward abortion, etc.

Because this is an interval scale, the distances between people are meaningful. Thus $P_1$ is considerably higher in the attribute than $P_2$, $P_2$ and $P_3$ are close together, and $P_4$ is far below the others.

We begin this chapter with an introduction to the concept of a data matrix, which is central to nearly all measurement data, and some differences between scaling stimuli and scaling people. Next, we present a brief history of "psychophysics," which is the study of the relation between variation in physical dimensions of stimuli and their associated responses—as it forms the foundation for "psychometric" theory. In contrast, "psychometrics" in general may or may not study the effects or variation in a single physical dimension, and so it includes psychophysics as a topic. Then, some distinctions among different types of stimuli and, especially, responses are made. We then consider some general principles underlying the development of ordinal, interval, and ratio scales. Following this, we present what is probably the historically most important scaling model for stimuli, Thurstone scaling. The ensuing section considers some models used to scale people. In particular, we introduce the linear model (also called the summative or centroid model), which simply involves the familiar process of defining a score as the ordinary sum, perhaps weighted, of responses to individual items.

## DATA MATRICES

Most measurement problems begin with a data matrix or two-way array or table (we will describe some other matrices from time to time). Rows typically represent $N$ different objects (usually people), and columns represent $K$ different stimuli (content), e.g., questionnaire items (see Table 2-1). It is convention to denote the entire matrix by an uppercase letter in boldface, e.g., **X.** The data are responses, e.g., 0 = incorrect versus 1 = correct, Likert scales, etc. Individual elements appear in lowercase italics. The first subscript conventionally denotes the row (usually the object being measured, e.g., a person), and the second subscript denotes the column (stimulus, as a questionnaire item number), so that $x_{ij}$ denotes the response of subject i to stimulus j. However, the stimuli and responses can represent anything that the experimenter does to the subjects and anything the subjects do in return. Consequently, we need not limit the discussion to people and test items in the ordinary sense. Subjects might estimate the weights of various objects, for example. It is possible, though rare, that the matrix is a single person's response to a series of stimuli studied over occasions (e.g., Nunnally, 1955), among other variants.

Most classical psychometric models treat scale items as replicates of one another in the sense that differences among the items are ignored in scaling. Thus, a patient's anxiety is typically defined by counting the number of anxiety-related symptoms that are endorsed regardless of which specific items these are. Alternative models, mainly of recent origin, derive scale scores from the pattern of responses. These latter models

**TABLE 2-1**  A BASIC TWO-WAY DATA MATRIX (**X**) CONTAINING RESPONSES OF $N$ PERSONS (ROWS) BY $K$ STIMULI (COLUMNS)

|  |  | Stimuli | | | | | |
|---|---|---|---|---|---|---|---|
|  |  | 1 | 2 | 3 | ... | $j$ | $K$ |
|  | 1 | $x_{11}$ | $x_{12}$ | $x_{13}$ | ... | $x_{1j}$ | $x_{1k}$ |
|  | 2 | $x_{21}$ | $x_{22}$ | $x_{23}$ | ... | $x_{2j}$ | $x_{2k}$ |
| Objects | 3 | $x_{31}$ | $x_{32}$ | $x_{33}$ | ... | $x_{3j}$ | $x_{3k}$ |
| (People, usually) | ... | ... | ... | ... | ... | ... | ... |
|  | $i$ | $x_{i1}$ | $x_{i2}$ | $x_{i3}$ | ... | $x_{ij}$ | $x_{ik}$ |
|  | $n$ | $x_{n1}$ | $x_{n2}$ | $x_{n3}$ | ... | $x_{nj}$ | $x_{nk}$ |

will be introduced here but are discussed in more detail in Chapter 10. Likewise, methods of scaling objects, as in market research studies, often assume that people are replicates of one another. For example, the percentage of persons in a group that prefer one brand of cereal to another is assumed to be the same as the percentage of times a typical (modal) individual would have this preference over occasions. These classical methods, by definition, treat individual differences among items and people as random error. In contrast, newer methods incorporate individual differences in a more systematic manner.

It is only meaningful to obtain a single measure by counting the number of positive responses if the stimuli measure a single attribute. This in turn implies that differences in response to the various stimuli are highly correlated; e.g., if people who admit to one anxiety-related symptom also tend to admit to others, and vice versa for people who deny these symptoms. Various correlational methods are used to evaluate the extent to which people or stimuli can be viewed as replicates. If responses correlate poorly with one another, two or more scales would have to be formed from the items. These involve methods discussed throughout the book, especially in Chapters 11 through 14. This chapter will be limited to models that assume the stimuli measure a single attribute (unidimensional scaling)—situations in which the data under consideration can be summarized satisfactorily with only one "yardstick."

## More Complex Organizations

The two-way organization of Table 2-1 contains the minimal elements of interest to a measurement problem. If there were but a single column (stimulus), there would be no way to evaluate the structure of the stimuli, which is basic to psychometric theory. The only results possible would be descriptive statistics on the single measure (e.g., the mean and standard deviation) for the single group of subjects. These data are rarely of interest to the psychometrician because nothing can be said about the structure. Likewise, data from a single row (subject) in isolation are unlikely to be informative. At a minimum, we need to compare that person's data to normative data.

More complex arrangements of the data are extremely common. First, the two-way matrix may be repeated over occasions, as when a pre- and a posttest are administered. This gives rise to a three-dimensional arrangement in which there are rows and columns, as before, plus "slices" that represent the two or more occasions. Another possibility is that subjects are sampled from two or more groups; e.g., one studies gender differences in response to items measuring depression. A third possibility is that two or more attributes are investigated simultaneously, as when one series of items measures job satisfaction and another series of items reflects job performance. This design involves methods of multidimensional (multivariate) analysis considered later in the book.

Scaling objects often involves a three-dimensional array, as when a market researcher conducts a taste test and has people judge multiple attributes of several brands of cola, e.g., sweetness and intensity of flavor. (As an incidental point, the application of measurement methods to quantify the perceived appearance, including taste, of consumer product preferences is known as "sensory evaluation" to market researchers.) These possibilities may be combined in still higher-order ways, e.g., by obtaining pre- and posttest measures that compare two or more groups.

We have frequently used the phrase "people or objects," but the vast majority of studies examine people's responses to different stimuli. In fact, objects (which may be abstract concepts) play the same role as people in some studies and as stimuli in others.

### "Holes" in the Matrix (Missing Data)

In an ideal situation, there is an outcome at each location in the matrix; e.g., each person is administered each stimulus. Sometimes this is not possible or even meaningful. For example, the number of stimuli may be too large to allow a given person to respond to each one. Similarly, the effects of administering one stimulus may influence subsequent behavior, known as "carryover" effects. Subjects are then often deliberately given a subset of the stimuli chosen according to a predesignated plan usually involving random assignment of stimuli to a given subject. This is part of the experimental design. Perhaps the most comprehensive text dealing with these problems is Winer, Brown, and Michels (1991). Although some statistical power is lost when subjects do not respond to all stimuli, this loss of power can be offset by increasing the sample size. The problem will not be considered further since it poses no additional complications.

Far more serious problems emerge when the resulting holes in the data matrix are nonrandom. For example, the second author once was given neuropsychological test data. The data involved many scales (subtests) that were normally not all administered to each patient. Thus, patients with frontal lobe damage were given one set of subtests, patients with temporal lobe damage were given a different set of subtests, etc. Such limitations on data gathering caused the missing data to be nonrandom. Type of injury was confounded with the particular scales that were administered. The results obtained from analyzing these data might well differ substantially from a study in which all subjects responded to all measures or the pattern of administration was random. Good design dictates minimizing the impact of missing data. If all measures are equally important, randomize the order of administration or administer random subsets if all cannot be administered to each subject. Conversely, if some are relatively unimportant because they are being used for more exploratory purposes, administer these at the end.

### EVALUATION OF MODELS

Often different models can be applied to a given set of data to develop alternative scales. These models and their associated scales sometimes lead to different substantive conclusions. Two different models might produce scales that are not linearly related. One model might suggest that the data do not even possess ordinal properties, whereas another might indicate they clearly form an interval scale. How, then, does one know which model to choose? Chapter 1 noted why this cannot be known in advance. We suggest that the most crucial test is how well the scale provides meaningful, repeatable relations with other variables. Before time and effort are spent on such investigations, however, some additional criteria can be applied.

**1** The intuitive appeal of a scaling model provides one criterion for "reasonable." Although the data of science must be public, a scientist's intuition plays an indisputable role in the gathering and analysis of data. Looked at in one way, a measurement model is nothing more than an explicitly defined hunch that particular operations on data will be useful. In particular, we suggest that psychologists lean toward measurement models that are most analogous to the measurement of simple physical attributes, e.g., length.

**2** Another aspect of "reasonable" is that one should exploit what is already known about similar data. For example, power functions are well known to describe relations between physical and perceived intensity (see below). On the negative side, some models assume that individual test item responses are highly reliable; yet, a wealth of evidence shows that such responses usually are highly *un*reliable.

**3** Preliminary analyses often provide cues about the usefulness of a scale. If the scale values for objects or persons are markedly affected by slight procedural differences, the scale will probably not work well in practice. There are, for example, numerous ways in which subjects can judge weight. If two similar appearing approaches yield very different intervals of judged weight, either or both methods are suspect. Conversely, different models that yield similar results provide converging operations (Garner, Hake, & Eriksen, 1956) that mutually strengthen the confidence one may have about any given method. "Triangulation" is another common term used to describe this.

**4** Another important type of evidence is the magnitude of measurement error in using a particular scale, which we will discuss in detail in Chapters 6 to 10. A scale that yields a great deal of measurement error cannot possibly be useful.

Beyond the standards of good sense, however, the ultimate test of any model is the extent to which it yields useful empirical results.

### Scaling Stimuli versus Scaling People

Although psychometric methods can be used to scale people, stimuli, or both, different methods are often used when the focus is on scaling people than when the focus is on scaling objects. As Cronbach (1957) pointed out in a classical article, clinical, counseling, and school psychologists are more inclined to think in terms of individual differences among people, e.g., in measuring such attributes as intelligence and level of adjustment. These individual differences are a nuisance to experimental psychologists and market researchers who largely ignore individual differences, though both may be interested in group differences. Their problems typically involve scaling stimuli, e.g., measuring which words or advertisements are most readily recalled. Regardless of the focus of the research, the basic data are representable as a two-dimensional array, perhaps extended into other dimensions because of additional considerations.

Unidimensional scaling of people is probably the easiest situation to describe. For example, a spelling test contains words as stimuli and students as subjects. The data are simply 1 = correct and 0 = incorrect. The simplest model for scaling subjects (see the linear model below) collapses the stimulus dimension of words by adding the number of 1s for each person. Although additional analyses are usually conducted to determine the interrelations among responses to different words, these simple sums of correct responses scale students on their spelling ability. Consequently, Dina may obtain a score of 48 and Ralph may obtain a score of 45 out of 50 words. It is quite possible that a simple ranking of the students will suffice so that an ordinal scale may be all that is necessary for such purposes as grading. The major requirement in scaling people is that alternative scalings be monotonically related to one another, i.e., that they rank-order people in the same way. Thus if two different methods for scaling anxiety have a strong monotonic relationship, research results will be much the same regardless of which scale is employed.

The roles of people and stimuli are often reversed to scale objects. Specifically, sums over students for each word describe differences in the difficulty of the words, e.g., if 50 students spell "abacus" correctly but only 35 spell "mnemonic" correctly, "mnemonic" is considered more difficult than "abacus." In fact, these data are usually a standard part of a test analysis, even when interest is directed toward scaling people. However, studies directed toward scaling stimuli are also more likely to be concerned with establishing functional relationships to various attributes, in which case ordinal scales are quite likely to be insufficient. Assume, for example, that the stimuli are tones of different intensity which subjects rate for loudness. Everyone knows that more intense tones will be rated louder; the key to the study is whether the relationship is logarithmic, linear, or of some other form. A unidimensional scale of stimuli should also fit a typical (modal) individual. Such a scale should be typical of a group even if it imperfectly represents the data from any one individual.

Because of the thornier problems in stimulus scaling, most of the issues and more complex scaling models have arisen from scaling stimuli. This difference has influenced the language used to describe psychological research. "Scaling" and "scaling methods" usually denote the scaling of stimuli. Problems of scaling people are more likely to evoke the terms "measurement" and "test construction." Those who are interested in the details of stimulus scaling could well consult the classical works of Guilford (1954), Torgerson (1958), and Woodworth and Schlossberg (1954). Despite their age, all three of these books describe the major models in unique step-by-step detail; more recent books have tended to concentrate on newer models.

Perhaps the main consideration in measurement is what kind of response is to be obtained from the subject, because this has profound effects on what subsequent analyses may be performed—one cannot analyze data that one has not obtained. There are two broad approaches, and both derive from psychophysics. In one, which originated with Gustav Fechner, subjects make only ordinal judgments as to whether a stimulus was seen or not and whether a comparison stimulus is more or less intense than a standard stimulus. The methods require very little of subjects. Indeed, animals can be trained to make requisite responses by means of such devices as bar pressing. In the other approach, most strongly associated with S. S. Stevens (see Chapter 1), subjects are required to use properties of the real-number system to make interval or ratio judgments, as by saying how much more intense a comparison stimulus was than a standard. Such methods normally require adults or older children.

## A BRIEF INTRODUCTION TO PSYCHOPHYSICS

The overview defined psychophysics as the study of the relation between variation in physical dimensions of stimuli, which we will symbolize as $\Phi$ (for physical), and their associated responses, historically called "sensations," which we will symbolize as $\Psi$ (for psychological). The physical dimension need not be intensity, but it will be for all examples in this chapter, and the associated responses will describe apparent intensity. We have already noted the obvious ordinal relation between the physical and apparent intensities of weights, flashes of light, and tones. A 5-pound weight obviously feels heavier than a 1-pound weight. In particular, the probability that a weak event will be detected also increases as the intensity increases. Psychophysics is concerned with making more detailed statements about the relations between $\Phi$ and $\Psi$ which, as was also noted, are usually required by the problem under study. Three particular questions are historically important yet relevant to many contemporary problems:

**1** What is the minimal energy needed for a particular event to be perceived under particular conditions, i.e., the absolute threshold or limen? For reasons to be noted below, this normally involves determining the stimulus event that is perceptible 50 percent of the time.

**2** How different must two stimuli be in order to detect a difference between them or to determine which is of greater intensity? This involves what is variously called the "difference threshold," "difference limen," or "just noticeable difference" (JND) between a standard and a comparison stimulus.

**3** How may the relation between physical intensity and its associated sensation be described in the interval or ratio terms of Chapter 1? This is known as the problem of psychophysical scaling.

The history of these questions is covered in several excellent books on the general history of experimental psychology (Boring, 1950; Robinson, 1981) because early experimental psychology was psychophysics. Simple but useful discussions of current applications may be found in any standard undergraduate textbook on perception such as Coren and Ward (1989). For a more detailed treatment, see Engen (1972a, 1972b) or Woodworth and Schlossberg (1954). Psychophysics is important for its own sake as exemplified by its use in such areas as communications engineering and photography. Audiologists perform psychophysical scaling on individuals in testing for hearing loss when they compare absolute thresholds they obtain with norms. An abnormally high threshold implies hearing loss. Psychophysics is limited to the study of relationships that hold when stimuli vary along a specified physical dimension such as sound intensity. Measuring intelligence, psychopathology, etc., is not psychophysical because no physical dimension underlies these attributes. Nonetheless, concepts like the threshold are applicable to psychometrics in general.

### Psychophysical Methods

Methods used to gather psychophysical data were first developed by Fechner (1860/1966) to study the relation between mind and body. Later, J. M. Cattell, Fullerton (Fullerton & Cattell, 1892), Thurstone (1928), and others expanded upon their use.

Several psychophysical methods developed by Fechner are still widely used. One is called the method of constant stimuli. Assume that a tone whose physical intensity is 185 units is essentially never reported as being heard, but a tone whose physical intensity is 215 units is nearly always reported as being heard. The experimenter might choose to use intensities of 185, 190, 195, …, 215 units. On each trial, one level (magnitude) is chosen at random for presentation. There is no limit upon the number of levels the experimenter may use. The levels need not be equally spaced and they need not occur equally often, but it is typical to use from 5 to 10 equally spaced and equally probable levels. The results are the probabilities of an affirmative response (e.g, saying the tone was heard) for each level.

Two related procedures are the method of adjustment and the method of limits. In the "method of adjustment," a standard is varied until it is barely sensed to determine an absolute threshold, or a comparison is made to barely differ from a standard to provide a difference threshold (JND). The method of limits takes two forms. The "ascending method" as used to determine an absolute threshold starts with a stimulus that is not sensed. The stimulus is progressively increased until it is sensed. The "descending method" starts with a stimulus that is sensed and decreases the intensity. The modification made to determine difference thresholds is straightforward. The comparison stimulus is presented either below (ascending method) or above (descending method) and incremented or decremented.

## Absolute Thresholds

The original idea of an absolute threshold goes very far back in philosophy. It implied a "cut" in $\Phi$—the subject never sensed the stimulus below the cut (threshold) and always detected it above the cut. Imagine that the method of constant stimuli is used to present a series of weights. This predicts a step function relating $\Phi$ to $\Psi$ (in this case, the probability of reporting that the stimulus was sensed or detected), as illustrated in Figure. 2-1a. The general name given to any relation between $\Phi$ and $\Psi$ is a "psychometric" (mind/measuring) function. This particular function describes local psychophysics, because $\Psi$ is defined in terms of sensations in the location of the threshold. However, it is extremely unusual for data to provide a step function, which we will later show is of general importance to psychometric theory. The data will more likely resemble panel (b) of Figure 2-1b, known as an ogive or S-curve.

Figure 2-2a illustrates an ogive and its associated data points as simulated by methods defined below. Although several mathematical functions produce ogives and there are many explicit curve fitting methods (see Chapter 15), curve fitting can often be done by inspection. The point at which the curve crosses the .50 level for $\Psi$ defines the absolute threshold. This is approximately 200 units in the present case.

In order to explain this lack of a step function, the original threshold hypothesis was modified to incorporate sensory noise. "Sensory noise" refers to random error in perceiving an event, causing a fixed stimulus to have variable effects on different trials. The process may be thought of as physiological in origin, but it need not be so viewed. The most popular specific conception of sensory noise is the phi-gamma hypothesis—numerous independent factors contribute to the error, and so it varies

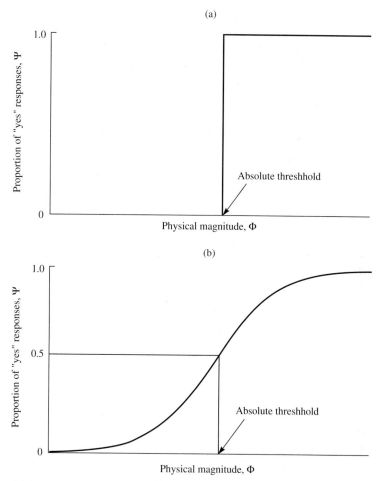

**FIGURE 2-1**    (*a*) A step function representing the initial concept of the threshold and (b) an ogive (*S* curve) representing a more realistic outcome.

normally over trials because of the central limit theorem (see Chapter 5). The specific form of the ogive (psychometric function) is the cumulative normal. An alternative model (Luce, 1959a, 1963) leads to a logistic function, defined below. Cumulative normals and logistic ogives are closely related mathematically and cannot be differentiated by eye. A third, but thus far less fruitful, possibility is neural quantum theory (Stevens, Morgan, & Volkmann, 1941). It leads to a linear function which will not be considered further. The 0.5 point that describes the absolute threshold is therefore arbitrary.

The location of the psychometric function is one of its two basic parameters. If auditory stimuli are used, the function of a subject with more acute hearing and consequently a lower threshold will fall to the left of the function of a subject with less

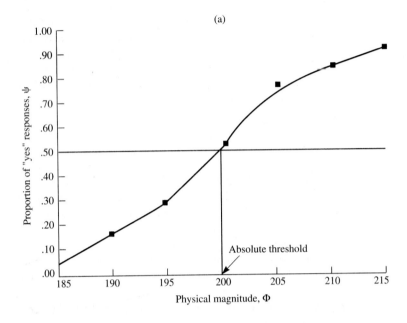

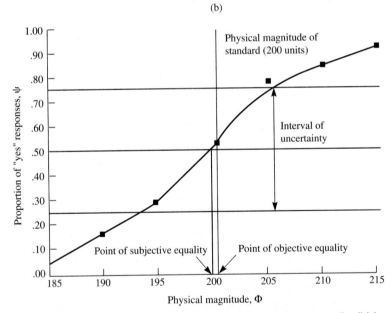

**FIGURE 2-2** Psychometric functions derived from applying the method of constant stimuli (simulated data) to (a) absolute responses (detection) and (b) comparative responses.

acute hearing. Likewise, we hear tones at middle frequencies better than lower- or higher-frequency tones, holding intensity constant, so that middle-frequency tones produce psychometric functions to the left of higher- and lower-frequency tones. Location thus defines task difficulty. The second parameter of importance is the slope of the function or the extent to which it resembles a step function. The steeper the slope, the more discriminating the responses are. Quantities related to these two parameters play a crucial role in psychometric theory, as we will show later in this chapter.

Now consider a question like "Are you unhappy at life" on a depression inventory. The probability that this question will be answered in the affirmative should be quite low for people who are low in the attribute (not depressed) and increase with the level of depression until it reaches 1.0. This implies that there should be a level of depression for which the probability of endorsing the item is .5, and so it is meaningful to think of an absolute threshold associated with the item. Similar considerations hold for items for which there is a correct answer and the underlying dimension is course knowledge or general intelligence. We will exploit the generality of the threshold and psychometric function concepts, especially in this chapter and in Chapter 10. The fact that there are physical dimensions of weight, sound intensity, and light intensity, but none of depression, course knowledge, or general intelligence, might appear to reflect a major difference between psychophysical and other applications. However, as we noted in Chapter 1, such ostensive characteristics are not needed to provide a scale. The scaling models considered in this book allow dimensions that are not defined physically to be inferred.

## Simulating a Threshold

The data in Fig. 2-2 were actually derived from a very simple computer simulation to illustrate the absolute threshold and sensory noise. We defined the absolute threshold as 200 units. Sensory noise was produced by choosing a random number from a normal distribution with a mean of 0 and a standard deviation of 10 in accord with the phi-gamma hypothesis. The mean of any given physical magnitude ($\Phi$) was its physical value (185 to 215 in 5-unit steps), but it varied normally about this mean on any given trial. The sensory effect for a stimulus on any given trial equaled $\Phi$ plus the random number. We ran 100 trials per stimulus.

For example, the two random numbers obtained for the first two trials using the 195-gram stimulus were +20.6, and +2.8. These produce sensory effects of 215.6 and 197.8. If the effect equaled or exceeded the threshold value of 200, the subject said yes (the stimulus was felt); otherwise the subject said no. Consequently, the subject said yes in the first case and no in the second. Note that the sensory effect of any comparison stimulus *can* exceed 200, but the probability of this happening increases as its physical magnitude increases. The resulting proportions of yes responses ($\Psi$) for the seven stimuli were 0.07, 0.17, 0.35, 0.53, 0.66, 0.87, and 0.94, as plotted. The important point to remember is how sensory noise can cause physically unchanging stimuli to vary over trials.

## Difference Thresholds

Defining a difference threshold (JND) is a bit trickier when the subject compares two stimuli in order to determine which is of the greater magnitude. The corresponding point at which the psychometric function is .5 describes the comparison stimulus perceived as equal to a standard half the time, not the threshold. This is called the point of subjective equality. Its value need not match the physical magnitude of the standard (the point of objective equality). For example, suppose the standard and comparison stimuli in Fig. 2-2*b* were weights of different density, e.g., were lead versus wood. A 200-gram lead standard stimulus would obviously be much smaller than a 200-gram wood comparison, and so there might be an illusory difference in weight. The two weights might have to differ in physical magnitude to appear equal.

The "interval of uncertainty" is that range of stimulus differences for which judgments can "go either way" and is usually taken from .25 to .75 on the function, as illustrated in Fig. 2-2*b*. The concept also applies to absolute thresholds, even though that is not depicted here. The difference threshold (not presented in the figure) is usually defined as half this interval of uncertainty, again by convention. The key to both types of threshold is the varied psychological effect of a fixed physical stimulus due to sensory noise.

It is possible to simulate a difference threshold in a manner similar to the absolute threshold. However, sensory noise would affect both the standard and the comparison. Although this might seem to decrease subjects' ability to make judgments, this need not be the case. The covariance (or correlation) between the two noise sources is also important for reasons that will become clear when we consider the logic Thurstone (1928) used to develop his discriminant model.

## The Weber Fraction, Fechner's Law, and Psychophysical Scaling

E. H. Weber noted an important property of the JND which was the main stimulus to Fechner's subsequent ideas—its magnitude is proportional to the standard against which it is derived. Subsequent research indicates that his findings are a good first approximation for a wide variety of sensory dimensions as long as the standard is not extremely weak or strong. Thus, suppose he found that a 1.05-gram weight was just noticeably different from a 1-gram standard weight so that the JND was $0.05(1.05 - 1)$ grams. The Weber fraction is the JND divided by the magnitude of the standard ($\Phi$), or 0.05/1 or 0.05 in this particular case. Weber's results were that a 10.5-gram comparison stimulus was just noticeably heavier than a 10-gram standard, a 105-gram comparison was just noticeably heavier than a 100-gram standard, etc. His results may be generally stated as $\Delta\Phi/\Phi$ equals a constant where $\Delta\Phi$ is the physical magnitude of the JND associated with a given $\Phi$.

Suppose that Weber's law had held exactly, a 1.0-unit standard was also the absolute threshold, and the fraction was 0.05. A 1.05-unit comparison will be 1 JND more intense than this standard. Now, let the resulting 1.05-unit stimulus become a new standard. A 1.10, i.e., $1.05(1 + 0.05)$ unit comparison will be just noticeably more intense. Keep repeating the process of obtaining a stimulus that is 1 JND more intense by multiplying by 1.05 and use it as the next standard. The resulting values will be 1.16, 1.22, 1.28, 1.34, ..., to two decimal places. It does not matter what type of stimulus is being judged.

Fechner made what in essence is a simple yet dramatic (and controversial) proposal: Let each of these steps, separated by a JND, define equal units on an interval scale of sensation. A corollary is that one can speak of two stimuli in terms of how many JNDs separate them—2.3, 0.5, or whatever. Mathematically, this relationship can be expressed as Eq. (2-1), which is called Fechner's law:

$$\Psi = b \log(\Phi) + a \qquad (2\text{-}1)$$

where $\Psi$ = scale value of the sensation (apparent magnitude)
    $\Phi$ = physical magnitude
    $b, a$ = scaling constants

Neither scaling constant is important to our discussion; $a$ is commonly chosen to make $\Psi = 0$ when $\Phi$ is at threshold, but this is usually not viewed as a rational zero in the ratio scale sense. Figure 2-3$a$ depicts Fechner's law. Unlike Figs. 2-1 and 2-2, values of $\Psi$ need not fall near threshold. The relation applies to the entire physical dimension ($\Phi$) and is known as global psychophysics.

Logarithmic functions have several important characteristics. The one particularly important for our purpose is that equal physical ratios yield equal sensory differences. Suppose stimuli $a$, $b$, $c$, and $d$ are, respectively, 10, 20, 100, and 200 grams. Since $a/b = c/d$, $a$ and $b$ are just as many JNDs apart from each other as are $c$ and $d$.

Fechner's methods are called indirect methods because subjects do not define sensory magnitudes directly, and discriminant methods because they concern the subject's ability to discriminate. They are also called confusion methods because scale values require that stimuli generally be confusable with one another in magnitude.

## Direct Psychophysics and the Plateau/Stevens Tradition

Coren and Ward (1989) described a test of Fechner's law made by Plateau in 1872. He had artists mix black and white pigments to make a gray appear midway between the two. Fechner's law predicts that the gray's intensity should be the average of the black's intensity and the white's intensity. Plateau obtained a systematic departure in that the grays fell near the cube roots of the two other intensities. Four important things about Plateau's research and Stevens' (1951, 1956, 1975) subsequent extensions are that (1) unlike Fechner's approach, subjects respond directly through subjective estimates; (2) equal physical ratios provide equal sensory ratios and not differences with these subjective estimates; (3) equal numbers of JNDs between different pairs of stimuli are not equal appearing, the emphasis is upon global and not local psy-

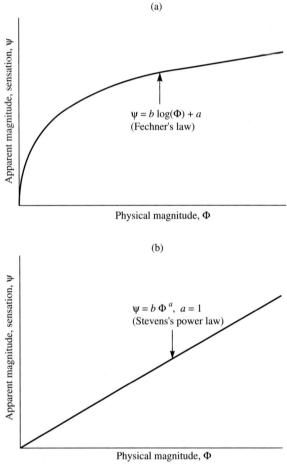

(a)

$\psi = b \log(\Phi) + a$
(Fechner's law)

Apparent magnitude, sensation, $\psi$

Physical magnitude, $\Phi$

(b)

$\psi = b\,\Phi^{a}, \; a = 1$
(Stevens's power law)

Apparent magnitude, sensation, $\psi$

Physical magnitude, $\Phi$

**FIGURE 2-3**   (a) Fechner's logarithmic law for indirect psychophysics, (b) Stevens' power law for direct psychophysics with an exponent $a = 1$.

chophysics. Point 2 may be stated as Eq. 2-2, called Stevens' law, since he examined it so thoroughly, or the power law from its mathematical form:

$$\Psi = b\Phi^{a} \tag{2-2}$$

where $\Psi$ = scale value of the sensation (apparent magnitude)
  $\Phi$ = physical magnitude
  $b$ = scaling constant

The $a$ parameter is more complex. It describes the sensory ratio associated with the physical ratio of two stimuli that differ along the physical dimension in question, $\Phi$. Let the two stimuli be $x$ and $y$, their associated sensory ratio be $\Psi_x/\Psi_y$, and their phys-

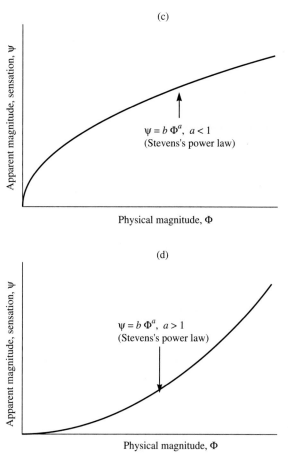

**FIGURE  2-3**   (c) Stevens' law with an exponent $a < 1$, and (d) Stevens' law with an exponent $a > 1$.

ical ratio be $\Phi_x/\Phi_y$. If the two are the same ($\Psi_x/\Psi_y = \Phi_x/\Phi_y$), the relation is linear; $a = 1$. For example, doubling the duration of a noise also makes it appear to last twice as long. However, the sensory ratio is smaller than the associated physical ratio for most dimensions ($\Psi_x/\Psi_y \ \Phi_x/\Phi_y$), and so $a < 1$. The brightness (apparent intensity) of many light sources increases only as the cube root of the change in physical intensity. This means the physical intensity of two lights must be in an 8:1 ratio for the more intense light to appear twice as bright. Finally, a few sensory ratios are larger than their associated physical ratios ($\Psi_x/\Psi_y > \Phi_x/\Phi_y$), and so $a > 1$. If one electric shock is physically twice as powerful as another, it will actually appear more than 10 times as intense. Stevens and his associates devoted many years to a thorough study of different sensory modalities. In particular, Stevens (1961) "cataloged" the exponents of various dimensions. Figure 2-3b through 2-3d depict these three outcomes ($a = 1$, $a < 1$, and $a > 1$). Note that even though the function for $a < 1$ resembles Fechner's law in being concave downward, the two are quite different. Data fitting Fechner's law become linear when the abscissa, but not the ordinate, is logarithmic (semilog graph paper), and data fitting a power law become linear when both axes are logarithmic (log-log graph paper), regardless of the magnitude of the exponent. The slope of the line in the latter case defines the magnitude of the exponent. Although Fechner and Stevens' laws were once regarded as competitors (investigators commonly asked which one was "right"), it is now generally recognized that the $\Psi$ of Fechner's law for discrimination need not be the same as the $\Psi$ of Stevens' law for subjective estimates, and so there need be no incompatibility. Indeed, the two would be completely compatible if Stevens' $\Psi$ were the logarithm of Fechner's (Luce, 1963).

Stevens also developed several methods for inferring the exponents and showing that any given estimate was not an artifact of a single method; i.e., he used converging operations as defined above. The most commonly used of these methods are the following:

**1** *Ratio production.* A subject is shown a standard stimulus and is then asked to adjust a comparison so that it appears in a specified ratio to the standard. The simplest and most common ratio is 2:1, so that the subject is asked to make the second stimulus appear twice as intense. If, for example, the comparison has to be physically four times as intense, the ratio *(a)* will be .5. However, the subject might also be asked to make the second stimulus three times as intense.

**2** *Ratio estimation.* The subject is shown standard and comparison stimuli and asked to define the ratio of their apparent intensities. Thus, they might report that a comparison tone is 1.5 times louder than a standard tone.

**3** *Magnitude estimation.* The subject is shown a single stimulus and simply asked to define its magnitude numerically. Usually, subjects are also shown a different stimulus, called the modulus, which is given an assigned value to fix the units of the scale, making it somewhat similar to ratio estimation.

**4** *Bisection.* As in Plateau's experiment, subjects are shown two stimuli and asked to adjust a third so that it appears midway between the first two. Unlike other subjective estimates, bisection requires interval rather than ratio judgments.

**5** *Cross-modal matching.* The subject is presented a stimulus in one modality and asked to adjust a stimulus in another modality to apparent equality. For example, the task might be to make a tone appear as loud as a light is bright. As bizarre as the task may seem, the exponent relating the two modalities is predictable from the exponents inferred from the other tasks. For example, the sweetness of a sucrose solution and the apparent thickness of wood blocks both have exponents of about 1.3. Suppose a given sucrose solution is matched with a given thickness. Then the concentration of the sucrose is then doubled. According to Stevens' power law, the matching wood block should seem twice as thick, which it does.

In all methods, the procedure is repeated with different stimuli in order to determine the consistency of the exponent.

Although it is not associated as strongly with the Stevens tradition as the above, the method of equal-appearing intervals (category scaling) also tends to fit Stevens' power law (Marks, 1974; Ward, 1974). Subjects simply sort stimuli into categories so that the intervals between category boundaries appear equal. In particular, the sensory difference between the upper and lower boundaries of each category should be the same.

## The Fullerton-Cattell Law

The Fullerton-Cattell (Fullerton & Cattell, 1892) law is a basic link between Fechnerian indirect psychophysics and psychometrics in general. It states, simply and euphoneously, that equally often noticed differences are equal unless always or never noticed. This is certainly true in the psychophysical case since the unit (the JND) is defined by equally often noticed differences. The significance of the Fullerton-Cattell law is that it does not depend upon how the stimuli differ or on the basis of the judgment. In particular, the ">" relationship that meant brighter, heavier, or louder above can also mean "is more preferred," among other things. If you prefer bananas to apples 75 percent of the time and apples to pears 75 percent of the time, the distance between apples and bananas and the distance between apples and pears may be assumed equal; i.e., apples are at the midpoint of a scale defined by these three stimuli. The "always or never" part is simply a caveat that one cannot draw inferences when there is no confusion over trials: If you always prefer bananas to apples and always prefer apples to pears, their relative distances cannot be inferred from these data alone. However, if you sometimes prefer plums over each and sometimes not, a scale can be constructed.

## Signal Detection Theory and Modern Psychophysics

In early studies of the absolute threshold, a stimulus was always presented. Subjects, who were often also the investigators, typically knew this but were trained at analytic introspection to report their sensations and to ignore this knowledge. Sometimes, however, the equipment would malfunction and fail to produce a stimulus, but subjects might say "Yes, I saw (heard, felt, etc.) it," thus committing the stimulus error by responding on the basis of their conceptions of the stimulus rather than the sensation itself. Gradually, "catch" trials were regularly used to "keep subjects on their toes," but no systematic use was made of the data obtained on these trials since the purpose of the experiments was to measure sensations.

Measuring sensations was the exclusive goal of nineteenth-century psychophysical research and is often a valid goal today, but it is not the only goal. Reflecting a variety of factors such as the behavioristic rejection of mental states like sensations, much of psychophysics eventually became concerned with subjects' ability to discriminate the presence of stimulation from its absence. A particular tradition emerged known as the theory of signal detection (TSD) (Egan, 1975; Green & Swets, 1967; Macmillan & Creelman, 1991; Swets, 1986a, 1986b; Swets, Tanner, & Birdsall, 1961; Tanner & Swets, 1954). It bears a close kinship to Thurstone scaling, and we will consider it in more detail in Chapter 15. For the present, it is most important in helping to illustrate the difference between the classical psychophysics of judging sensations and the more modern emphasis upon accuracy of discrimination.

TSD has proven particularly important because of its emphasis upon assessing response bias or differential willingness to use the response alternatives independently of sensitivity or accuracy at discrimination. Threshold measures using psychophysical procedures derived from Fechner are particularly influenced by a subject's willingness to report having sensed the stimulus. A practical example of a response bias involves the diagnostic accuracy of two clinicians who see the same set of patients. Clinician A correctly diagnoses 90 percent of the patients determined to have a given disorder on the basis of some appropriate method, but clinician B diagnoses only 80 percent of the patients correctly. Does this mean that clinician A is the better diagnostician? The data are insufficient since only their hit (true positive) rates in identifying those who have the disease are known. We also need to know the false alarm (false positive) rates of diagnosing normals as having the disease. Perhaps clinician A has a false alarm rate of 90 percent, in which case he or she is just blindly guessing the presence of the disease in 90 percent of the population. If this is true and if clinician B's false alarm rate is less than 80 percent, clinician B could be the better.

## TYPES OF STIMULI AND RESPONSES

Endless distinctions could be made about stimuli and responses that are important to psychometrics, but we will consider only the most important. Most are derived from psychophysics.

### Judgments versus Sentiments

Although no two words perfectly symbolize the distinction, the distinctions between what we call "judgments," where there is a correct response, and "sentiments," which involve preferences, is very basic. There are correct (veridical) versus incorrect answers to "How much is two plus two?" and "Which of the two weights is heavier?" There may also be degrees of correctness, as in line-length judgments of visual illusions. In contrast, sentiments cover personal reactions, preferences, interests, attitudes, values, and likes and dislikes. Some examples of sentiments include (1) rating how much you like boiled cabbage on a seven-category Likert scale, (2) answering the question, "Which would you rather do, organize a club or work on a stamp collection?" and (3) rank-ordering 10 celebrities in terms of preference. Veridicality does not apply to sentiments—a subject is neither correct nor incorrect for preferring chocolate ice cream to vanilla ice cream. This distinction is very close to the difference between making discriminations in TSD and reporting sensations in classical psychophysics. Judgments also tend to be cognitive, involving "knowing," whereas sentiments tend to be affective, involving "feeling."

Ability tests nearly always employ judgments regardless of whether an essay, short-answer, multiple-choice, or true-false format is used. Coversely, tests of interests inherently concern sentiments as the subject identifies liked and disliked activities. Attitudes and personality measures can use either form. Items like "Do you like going to parties?" involve sentiments, but items like "How often do you go to parties?" are essentially judgments. The distinction may be obscured because the perceived frequency may reflect preference as well as actual frequency.

Social desirability may bias sentiments in the signal detection sense so that the popularity of socially endorsed behaviors may be overestimated. This is less likely to be a problem with judgments. However, the internal consistency or extent to which items measure the same thing is important to both. Temporal stability or the extent to which the measure tends to remain the same over time may or may not be important. Chapters 6 through 9 consider how these statistics are obtained. In general, the logic of using judgments is generally clearer than the logic of using sentiments because of advantages inherent in having a correct response. Other terms are frequently employed to describe these two categories. Goldiamond's (1958) distinction between what he called "objective" and "subjective" indicators of perception corresponds in essence to the judgment-sentiment distinction. The word "choice" is frequently used in place of the word "sentiment."

### Absolute versus Comparative Responses

In general, an absolute response concerns a particular stimulus, whereas a comparative response relates two or more stimuli. The distinction applies to both judgments and sentiments. "How many concerts have you been to in the past year?" versus "Have you been to more concerts than movies in the past year?" illustrates this distinction for judgments. Likewise, "Do you like peas?" versus "Do you like peas more than you like corn?" involves sentiments.

One of psychology's truisms is that people are almost invariably better (more consistent and/or accurate) at making comparative responses than absolute responses. This is because there is a frame-of-reference problem present to at least some extent in absolute responses that is avoided in comparative responses. Asking a consumer "Is this cola sweet?" raises the question of how sweet is sweet that is avoided when one is asked to judge which of several colas is the sweetest since the criterion of sweetness can be applied equally to all colas. One possible application of this principle is in ability testing. If there are no "none of the above" or "all of the above" alternatives, multiple-choice tests are comparative judgments of the relative truth of the alternatives. We suggest (and some disagree) that these alternatives be avoided because they compromise the comparative nature of the test by asking whether none or all of the other alternatives are true in an absolute sense. Similarly, true-false tests are absolute judgments of the truth or falsity of a single item, and we suggest the use of multiple-choice questions for this and other reasons to be considered.

People rarely make absolute judgments in daily life, since most choices are inherently comparative. There are thus few instances in which it makes sense to employ absolute judgments. One important exception is when absolute level is important, as in attitudes toward various ethnic groups. A subject could, for example, rank various groups from most to least preferred. However, the subject may dislike all the national groups or like them all, which would not be apparent from the comparative rankings. Absolute responses are especially important when some indicator of neutrality is needed. For example, people who are more neutral with respect to candidates in an election are probably more susceptible to influence and change than those who have a clear preference. By requiring absolute responses from subjects, one is able to approximate a neutral point.

Another case in which it makes sense to phrase items in absolute terms is when the inherent ambiguity of absolute judgments is of interest. For example, the MMPI contains several items like "I often have headaches" and "I frequently have trouble falling asleep." A psychologist is probably not actually interested in the actual frequency of headaches or sleepless nights. If he or she were, more objective tests could be developed through clinical observation. The issue is how the patient interprets words like "often" and frequently." Absolute judgments are perfectly appropriate in that case.

Absolute responses are also useful because they are much easier and faster to obtain than comparative responses. For example, the method of paired comparisons is an extremely powerful way to gather data. A market research example could involve preferences among $K$ brands of cola. The subject is given two brands in succession and asked to state a preference. This is repeated for all possible pairs of brands. Unfortunately, this requires anywhere from $K(K - 1)/2$ pairs (if a given brand is presented in only one of the two possible positions in the pair) to $K^2$ pairs (if all brands appear in all orders and a given brand is paired with itself). The number of comparisons increases rapidly with $K$. For example, if there are 20 brands in the study, from 190 (20)(19/2) to 400 ($20^2$) trials are required per subject. However, it is much quicker to have subjects rate each brand individually. Any of several scaling models can be used to obtain interval estimates of preference from each cola's average rating over subjects. Conversely, paired comparison methods generally give much more reliable results when applicable.

To the extent that a person answering an item phrased absolutely has a criterion to define terms like "frequently," "seldom," or "hardly ever," the judgment becomes partly comparative. Individuals generally have feelings about their absolute liking for an object or activity, but such sentiments are influenced by the range of objects or activities available. An individual who rates how much they like boiled cabbage probably thinks "What else is there to eat?" Differences among subjects and/or time contribute to unreliability. However, temporal instabilities can be of interest in themselves (Spielberger, Gorsuch, Lushene, 1970).

If an absolute format is appropriate, anchoring by specifying the meaning of the response scale is generally important to reducing unwanted error due to differences in implicit bases of comparison. For example, instead of simply asking subjects to rate how often they go to the movies on a five-point scale, indicate that 1 means once a month or less, 2 means at least once a month, etc. (the actual anchors should be developed by pretesting). Similarly, if a pretest reveals that subjects nearly always answer the question "I absolutely adore rutabagas to the point that I must eat them daily" causes everyone to respond in the negative, change the anchor to favor a higher incidence of positive responses, such as "I would eat rutabagas if they were served to me." Not all situations demand anchors, as in the MMPI example where the ambiguity was intentional.

## Preferences versus Similarity Responses

Different methods are required to study responses denoting which stimuli are preferred versus most similar. Preference responses are also known as dominance responses. Examples of these responses (which are nearly always sentiments) include which stimulus is most liked, tastes best, is least filling, would be most likely purchased, etc. Similarity responses denote which stimuli are most like one another. Preferences are clearly asymmetric; preferring A to B means not preferring B to A. In contrast, similarity responses are normally symmetric—saying A is similar to B implies that B is similar to A (Chapter 15 will consider an interesting exception). Thurstone scaling, described below, requires preferential data. However, the most common methods of analysis, (e.g., factor analysis, and multiple and partial correlation) require similarity data because they are based upon the ordinary Pearson correlation coefficient (Chapter 4), a measure of similarity rather than preference.

### Specified versus Unspecified Attributes

By definition, psychophysical responses are obtained with respect to an attribute defined by the experimenter. This may also be the case when the attribute is not a single physical dimension. For example, a marketing study may ask which of several packages differing in height, width, and depth looks largest even though all contain the same volume. Conversely, subjects may be asked to evaluate similarities or preferences among stimuli without being told in what respect. If the stimuli clearly differ in a single, dominant respect, instructions may be unnecessary. However, if the stimuli are multidimensional, the goals of the experiment dictate whether or not some particular attribute should be specified. The study may concern how well subjects ignore a given attribute, so that it is important to tell him or her which attribute is critical. On the other hand, subjects should not be told, implicitly or explicitly, if the goal is to find out which actual attributes subjects actually use.

### METHODS FOR CONVERTING RESPONSES TO STIMULUS SCALES

Fechnerian methods, which provide ordinal data, Stevens' methods, which provide interval or ratio data are applicable outside the confines of psychophysics. Keep in mind that the level at which data are gathered may well differ from the level of the resulting scale, particularly for Fechnerian methods. Scaling models often take data obtained at one level and transform it to a higher level, most specifically to produce an interval scale from ordinal data. Of course, data gathered at a ratio level need not be transformed. One part of successful scaling involves choosing an empirical procedure that is appropriate to the subjects' ability to respond; another part is to use a scaling model appropriate to the resulting data.

### Ordinal Methods

In general, the simplest way to obtain ordinal data is the method of rank order in which subjects rank stimuli from "most" to "least" with respect to the specified attribute.

In the A-B-X method, subjects are presented with stimuli A and B followed by a third stimulus (X) which is either A or B. The subject is asked to say whether X is A or B. The process is repeated, comparing all pairs of stimuli. The probability of confusing any two stimuli is an ordinal measure of their similarity. This method is particularly useful in scaling stimuli that are difficult to describe. For example, suppose Alpha Cola and Beta Cola are fairly similar in taste, but both differ somewhat from Gamma Cola. Subjects' A-B-X judgments may be only 60 percent correct when Alpha and Beta are paired (50 percent is chance), but 80 percent correct when Alpha and Gamma are paired and 85 percent correct when Beta and Gamma are paired.

In contrast, the method of triads uses three different stimuli which may all be highly discriminable from one another and asks which two are most similar. For example, the subject might taste string beans, lima beans, and green peas. It is probable that lima beans and green peas would be found to be the most similar pairing. The data obtained from all possible triads in a larger set (the number of combinations of $K$ things taken three at a time) provide similarity rankings.

In the method of successive categories, the subject sorts the stimuli into distinct piles or categories that are ordered with respect to a specified attribute. For example, subjects could sort the U.S. presidents into five piles ranging from "very effective" to "very ineffective." This information can be obtained most easily by having the subjects mark a printed rating scale. This method has many variants depending on the information sought by the experimenter. If the experimenter is seeking only ordinal information, the subject may be allowed free choice as to the number of stimuli per category and number of categories. In contrast, the categories may be constrained to appear equally spaced in the method of successive categories. Sometimes, subjects are required to place an equal number of stimuli in each category. Perhaps the most important variant is the Q sort where subjects sort the stimuli so that the distribution of stimuli in successive piles forms a normal distribution. These methods necessarily provide numerous tied ranks. Thus if stimuli are placed in a series of categories, those in the first category can be thought of as tied for the top rank. Averaging over subjects eliminates most of these ties.

## Interval Methods

The primary methods used to obtain interval data from subjects are variations upon the method of successive categories and Stevens' methods of bisection. This involves instructing the subject to use the scale as though the distances between successive categories were the same; e.g., the difference between a rating of 2 and 4 is equal to the difference between a rating of 6 and 8. Frequently anchors are also employed. For example, pleasantness could be anchored with adjectives ranging from "extremely pleasant" to "extremely unpleasant." Rating anchors also may be expressed as percentages to further ensure the interval nature of the responses so that subjects can be asked what percent of the general population they feel agrees with each of a series of statements.

The method of bisection may be applied outside psychophysics as follows. Subjects may be given two statements differing in how favorable they are toward the President and asked to select another statement from a list that falls closest to halfway between them. Rather than bisecting the distance between the two stimuli, other ratios may be used, as in psychophysics. For example, subjects may be asked to select a stimulus X such that the interval between one of two fixed stimuli and X appears twice as great as the distance between the two standards. Another approach is to present subjects with two stimuli that are at the extremes of the attribute and have them judge the ratio of intervals formed when a third stimulus is inserted.

In all these methods, the subject evaluates *intervals* of judgment or sentiment. Even though he or she may describe 1:1 ratios in the method of bisection, these ratios are not formed with respect to the absolute magnitudes of the stimuli as in ratio scaling. The experimenter might eventually use a scaling model to obtain these absolute magnitudes, but it is important to maintain the distinction between what the subject is required to do and the experimenter's use of the data in a scaling model.

## Ratio Methods

Ratio methods require subjects to evaluate the absolute magnitudes of stimuli. For example, subjects may be given the name of a food liked moderately well by most people and asked to name a food liked twice as much, half as much, etc. Note that in ratio production, the subject generates the actual stimulus, unlike in other ratio methods. This may be somewhat difficult outside psychophysical applications.

If a zero point can be taken seriously, previously described percentage scales can be employed for ratio estimation. For example, subjects might rate the complexity of 100 geometric forms. The stimulus rated as most complex in pilot research is used as a standard, and the other stimuli are rated in relation to this standard on a percentage scale. If the least complex form is rated at 20 percent, its scale value will be .20, where the standard is 1.0. These ratio scales closely resemble scales obtained from more direct ratio estimation methods (Stevens, 1951, 1958, 1960).

Interval and ratio estimation methods may appear superficially similar. For example, choosing a stimulus that is halfway between two others (bisection) seems similar to choosing a stimulus that is twice as great as another (ratio production). In both cases, the subject forms two equal-appearing intervals. The important difference between these two methods is that the lower interval is bounded by a *phenomenal* zero in ratio production. The subject is essentially required to form an interval between two stimuli that is equal to the interval between the less intense stimulus and zero. Moreover, if subjects are sophisticated enough to provide interval judgments, they can also usually provide ratio judgments, making interval methods somewhat unnecessary.

## MODELS FOR SCALING STIMULI

The next step in scaling is to generate an ordinal, interval, or ratio scale as desired. The models considered in this chapter are considered classical primarily because they have been available for a long time. They may also be considered classical because they provide relatively simple closed-form solutions and therefore do not require a computer (in practice, computers would probably be used). In contrast, modern psychometrics, considered in Chapter 10, usually requires open-form estimation.

Ordinal scales do not require complex models, and the various methods of gathering data and scaling usually produce the same rank ordering. In general, simply average individual subjects' ranks and rank-order the average of these ranks. This final set of ranks is the desired ordinal scaling of a modal subject.

In paired comparison methods, the first step to determine the percentage of subjects that rate each stimulus as being higher on the particular response dimension than each of the other stimuli. Thus, each of 10 stimuli produce 9 percentages comparing that stimulus to the rest. The full data from the group of subjects are summarized by a square matrix containing all possible percentages of paired comparison preferences. These percentages are summed for each stimulus (column of the matrix), and these sums are then ranked from highest to lowest.

Formal scaling models are more important in constructing interval (the more common situation) or ratio scales. The remainder of this section will consider models used for these purposes. They fall into two broad classes of models paralleling the distinction between Fechnerian indirect (discriminant) methods and Stevens' direct (subjective estimate) methods. Stevens' approach will be discussed first because it is simpler.

### Direct (Subjective Estimate) Models

Direct models are usually close to the data because the experimenter takes the subject's interval responses (e.g., bisections or ratio responses, magnitude estimations, ratio estimations, ratio productions) seriously. Often, the experimenter needs only to average responses over repeated measurements of one individual to obtain an individual scale or, more commonly, over subjects in a group to obtain a group scale. The Stevens tradition, like the Fechner tradition, recognizes variability from sensory noise but simply as error rather than as an intrinsic part of scaling.

One example is to use the aforementioned method of equal-appearing intervals. Subjects might sort 100 occupations into 10 successive categories ranging from least to most prestigious. The subjects are instructed to treat the 10 numbered categories as an interval scale. Error is minimized by averaging judgments over subjects or occasions. Thus "psychology professor" may be rated 9, 9, 8, and 8 by four subjects. This yields an average rating, and therefore a scale rating, of 8.5 on the interval scale. Measurements are obtained in a like manner for the 99 remaining occupations. This scale may then be used in any situation requiring an equal-appearing interval scale, e.g., to study the relation between job prestige and job satisfaction. A ratio scale can be formed in a like manner using ratio production. For example, one occupation (e.g., dentistry) can be anchored at 50 and subjects asked to rate others as ratios relative to this norm. See Stevens (1958, 1960) and the Suggested Additional Readings for further details. It is important to test the assumption that the subjects are behaving consistently. One important statistic is the internal consistency reliability (homogeneity) of the data. Chapters 6–8 will illustrate the process.

### Indirect (Discriminant) Models

Although the logic traces back to Fechner, Fullerton, Cattell, and others, L. L. Thurstone's law of comparative judgment (Thurstone, 1928) is the foundation of modern discriminant models. This law takes on numerous forms depending upon more specific assumptions. We will consider only the basic ideas and stress the single most popular model. A more complete discussion may be found in Bock and Jones (1968), Guilford (1954), and Torgerson (1958). The law of comparative judgment led to signal detection theory and general recognition theory (Ashby & Townsend, 1986; Ashby & Perrin, 1988, see Chapter 15).

Although the same computational procedures can be applied to testing one individual repeatedly by pooling individual data, we will illustrate the logic here with the classic example of how one individual's subjective rank orderings can be "brought into the open" as an interval scale. Any stimulus is assumed to yield a discriminal process with respect to a specified attribute. The "discriminal process" is simply a broadly defined reaction which correlates with the intensity of the stimulus on an interval scale for an attribute. Because of what is equivalent to sensory noise, each stimulus has a discriminal distribution (discriminal dispersion) which reflects the variation in response to that stimulus. The model assumes the phi-gamma hypothesis by assuming reactions to a given stimulus are normally distributed, as shown in Fig. 2-4.

These distributions and the attribute continuum on which they fall, most simply called a "strength axis," are entirely hypothetical. Unlike psychophysics, the experimenter cannot locate the stimuli directly on the attribute—any model would be unnecessary if this could happen. Only after the experimenter makes a series of assumpions about what is going on in the subject's head and about the statistical relationship of such covert reactions to the hypothetical dimensions can a suitable model be formulated.

The mean discriminal process (reaction) to each stimulus is the best estimate of the scale value of that stimulus in several senses, such as most likely and least squares (see Chapter 4). If all stimulus means were known, an interval scale would complete the scaling problem, which is unfortunately not directly possible. They must be inferred from the subject's responses. Each of several variants upon the basic model make somewhat different assumptions about the nature of these discriminal processes. The standard deviations depicted in Fig. 2-4 are unequal, and so some stimuli are more variable than others. Because this is a discriminant model, the discriminal processes of at least some stimuli must overlap measurably. If the discriminal distribtion of any stimulus does not overlap with any of the others, its interval location cannot be determined. The major assumptions and deductions of the general model are as follows:

**1** Denote the covert discriminal responses to stimulus j as $r_j$ and the covert discriminal responses to stimulus k as $r_k$.

**FIGURE 2-4**    Discriminal distributions of three stimuli which fall at progressively higher points along the strength axis and are also progressively more variable.

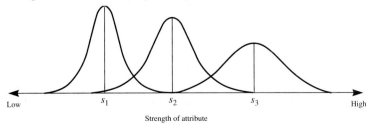

Strength of attribute

**2** The means of these discriminal responses, $\bar{r}_j$ and $\bar{r}_k$, are the best estimates of their respective scale positions. That is, if each stimulus' discriminal processes could be determined directly, its mean (arithmetic average) would be the best estimate of a typical reaction and therefore its location on the interval scale of judgment or sentiment.

**3** The overlap in discriminal distributions causes the difference in response to the two stimuli, $r_d = r_j - r_k$, to be positive on some trials and negative on others, producing the varied response to fixed stimuli that is necessary in discriminant models. In the present case, there is variation in the perception of difference. Understanding distributions of difference scores is absolutely crucial to understanding discriminant models used in comparisons. By analogy, two weight lifters each vary in their skill because of a variety of random factors. The varied amounts of weight they lift at a competition produce distributions analogous to those in Fig. 2-2. Heavier weights quite literally mean greater strength. One lifter may be better than the other on average. However, if their abilities are sufficiently similar, their distributions will overlap; the weaker athlete may sometimes lift a heavier weight than the better athlete. One could subtract the weight of the poorer lifter from the weight of the better lifter in any competition to obtain a difference score. Most of these differences will reflect the fact that the poorer lifter cannot lift as heavy a weight as the better lifter. It is perfectly proper to place these difference scores into a frequency distribution which summarize the overlap of the two separate distributions. In this case, the weights can actually be scaled directly, but this is the exception.

**4** Because the individual discriminal processes $r_j$ and $r_k$ are assumed to be normally distributed, the distribution of their difference, $r_d = r_j - r_k$, will also be normally distributed. This distribution of differences is illustrated in Fig. 2-5. The shaded area is proportional to the percentage of times stimulus j is judged greater than stimulus k, and vice versa for the unshaded area. Note that the mean ($\bar{r}_d$) is positive. This is because the mean discriminal response to stimulus $r_j$ ($\bar{r}_j$) is greater than the mean discriminal response to $r_k$ ($\bar{r}_k$); consequently, the majority of the differences (the shaded portion) are positive rather than negative.

**5** The mean of the differences between responses to the two stimuli on numerous occasions, $\bar{r}_d = \bar{r}_j - \bar{r}_k$, is the best estimate of the interval separating the two. Although this mean cannot be estimated directly because it is entirely hypothetical, Thurstone's

**FIGURE 2-5**   Distribution of discriminal differences for two stimuli, j and k, where j is ordinarily preferred to k.

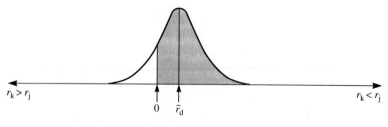

Distribution of difference

law of comparative judgment allows it to be estimated from paired comparisons as follows.

**6** Ask a subject to state whether stimulus j is greater or less than stimulus k with respect to an attribute. Denote the proportion of times j is judged greater as $p_{j>k}$.

**7** Next, assume that discriminal differences are normally distributed with a mean of $\bar{r}_d$ and a standard deviation of 1.0. The zero point will fall to the left or to the right of the mean depending on which stimulus is more frequently judged greater with respect to the attribute. Convert $p_{j>k}$ into a corresponding number of standard deviation units from a table of the normal distribution. If, for example, j is judged greater than k 92 percent of the time ($p_{j>k} = .92$), the corresponding normal deviate ($z_{jk}$) is approximately 1.4. This implies that the zero point is 1.4 standard deviations below the mean. More importantly, $\bar{r}_d = \bar{r}_j - \bar{r}_k$ is 1.4 standard deviations above 0, which moves us close to a solution.

**8** With $\bar{r}_d = \bar{r}_j - \bar{r}_k$ expressed in standard deviations units, all that needs to be done is to express $\bar{r}_d$ in terms of the actual standard deviation of the dispersion of discriminal differences. This is necessary because the standard deviations of discriminal differences might differ for different pairs of stimuli. In the above analogy to weight lifters, this would happen if some lifters are more consistent than others. If that occurs, two pairs of stimuli separated by the same *mean* distance could be separated by different *scale* distances. Thus even if $z_{jl}$ and $z_{jk}$ are the same, the standard deviations of the discriminal differences might require different intervals.

**9** The standard deviation of the dispersion of discriminal differences can be expressed in the same way as the standard deviation of any set of difference scores. The formula is

$$\sigma_d = \sqrt{\sigma_j^2 + \sigma_k^2 + 2r_{jk}\sigma_j\sigma_k} \qquad (2\text{-}3)$$

where $\sigma_d$ = the standard deviation of discriminal differences
$\sigma_j$ and $\sigma_k$ = the respective standard deviations of discriminal distributions for stimuli $j$
       and $k$
    $r_{jk}$ = the correlation between the discriminal distributions of the two stimuli

The standard deviation of the distribution of discriminal differences thus involves the standard deviations of the two discriminal distributions and the correlation between them. A correlation that differs from zero implies that the sensory noise components of the two discriminal processes are correlated over trials. Note that positive correlations reduce the magnitudes of discriminal dispersions. This is in fact the norm. For example, people vary in how highly they rate all the stimuli on the covert continuum. Thus, if people made absolute responses to the stimuli, one person might like all of the stimuli and rate them highly, and a second person might feel the converse. However, the process of comparison eliminates this difference. This is one reason why comparative judgments are more consistent (reliable) than absolute judgments.

**10** The interval separating two stimuli is obtained from the standard deviation of the distribution of discriminal differences using Eqs. 2-4:

$$\bar{r}_d = \bar{r}_j - \bar{r}_k = z_{jk}\sigma_d \tag{2-4a}$$

$$\bar{r}_j - \bar{r}_k = z_{jk} \sqrt{\sigma_j^2 + \sigma_k^2 - 2r_{jk}\sigma_j\sigma_k} \tag{2-4b}$$

Equations (2-4) multiply the normal deviate by the standard deviation of the distribution of discriminal differences between the two stimuli. This allows the proper interval to be found on the underlying measurement scale. These equations define the "complete law of comparative judgments." Their use requires knowledge of (1) the proportion of times each stimulus is judged greater than another with respect to an attribute, (2) the standard deviation of discriminal dispersions for the two stimuli, and (3) the correlation between the two discriminal distributions.

Information is rarely obtained about all three of these statistics; consequently, some simplifying assumptions are usually made. These are discussed in Bock and Jones (1968), Guilford (1954), and Torgerson (1958). The two most common assumptions are (1) the correlations between discriminal dispersions are zero (i.e., responses are independent) and (2) the standard deviations of discriminal dispersions are all equal. Equation 2-4 then reduces to

$$\bar{r}_j - \bar{r}_k = z_{jk} \sqrt{\sigma_j^2 + \sigma_k^2} \tag{2-5a}$$

$$\bar{r}_j - \bar{r}_{jk} = z_{jk} \sigma \sqrt{2} \tag{2-5b}$$

Since all dispersions (standard deviations) of discriminal processes are assumed to be the same, the term under the radical reduces to $\sqrt{2}$ times any of the standard deviations. Since that term is constant for all pairs of stimuli and since the intervals on an interval scale are unaffected when all scale values are multiplied by a constant, the formula reduces to

$$\bar{r}_j - \bar{r}_k = z_{jk} \tag{2-6}$$

Thus, these assumptions allow the normal deviate representing the proportion of times one stimulus is preferred over another to define the interval separating two stimuli. Equation 2-6 is by far the most frequently used form of the law of comparative judgment. Further simplifying assumptions are made when the law of comparative judgment is actually applied. The most general form of the model is based on response distributions of one subject on numerous occasions. This is seldom done for three reasons. First, it is difficult to find subjects who will devote the time to the task. Second, most responses are not independent—subjects tend to remember their previous responses. Third, the usual goal of scaling stimuli is to obtain a scale that applies to a definable group of people. A scale that applies to only one person is usually of limited generality.

The law of comparative judgment can be applied to any form of ordinal data, such as the method of successive categories, but the method of paired comparisons is the most obvious approach. Consequently, each subject is presented with all possible pairs of stimuli in a set, which usually ranges from 10 to 20. The subjects indicate which member of each pair is preferred (greater) with respect to the attribute in question. The

**TABLE 2-2**    PROPORTIONS OF SUBJECTS PREFERRING EACH VEGETABLE (COLUMNS) COMPARED TO EACH OF THE OTHER VEGETABLES (ROWS)

| Vegetable | Vegetable | | | | | | | | |
|---|---|---|---|---|---|---|---|---|---|
| | 1 | 2 | 3 | 4 | 5 | 6 | 7 | 8 | 9 |
| 1. Turnips | .500 | .818 | .770 | .811 | .878 | .892 | .899 | .892 | .926 |
| 2. Cabbage | .182 | .500 | .601 | .723 | .743 | .736 | .811 | .845 | .858 |
| 3. Beets | .230 | .399 | .500 | .561 | .736 | .676 | .845 | .797 | .818 |
| 4. Asparagus | .189 | .277 | .439 | .500 | .561 | .588 | .676 | .601 | .730 |
| 5. Carrots | .122 | .257 | .264 | .439 | .500 | .493 | .574 | .709 | .764 |
| 6. Spinach | .108 | .264 | .324 | .412 | .507 | .500 | .628 | .682 | .628 |
| 7. String beans | .101 | .189 | .155 | .324 | .426 | .372 | .500 | .527 | .642 |
| 8. Peas | .108 | .155 | .203 | .399 | .291 | .318 | .473 | .500 | .628 |
| 9. Corn | .074 | .142 | .182 | .270 | .236 | .372 | .358 | .372 | .500 |

*Source:* Adapted from Guilford (1954) by permission of the author and publisher.

result is a table containing the proportion of persons who prefer one stimulus to another ($p_{j>k}$). Table 2-2 lists typical results from a study of food preferences. Values of .5 are placed in each diagonal position in the table as each stimulus is assumed to be judged greater than itself half of the time. Each value of $p_{j>k}$ is then converted into a normal deviate $z_{jk}$, presented in Table 2-3.

If it is proper to assume Eq. 2-6, each normal deviate in Table 2-3 is an interval between the two stimuli. However, these normal deviates are likely to be affected by sampling error, which can be reduced as follows. The sum of the normal deviates for each column (stimulus) is obtained and then averaged. However, pairs that are widely

**TABLE 2-3**    TRANSFORMATIONS OF THE PROPORTIONS IN TABLE 2-1 TO NORMAL DEVIATES (*z* SCORES)

| Vegetable | Vegetable | | | | | | | | |
|---|---|---|---|---|---|---|---|---|---|
| | 1 | 2 | 3 | 4 | 5 | 6 | 7 | 8 | 9 |
| 1. Turnips | .000 | .908 | .739 | .882 | 1.165 | 1.237 | 1.276 | 1.237 | 1.447 |
| 2. Cabbage | −.908 | .000 | .256 | .592 | .653 | .631 | .882 | 1.015 | 1.071 |
| 3. Beets | −.739 | .256 | .000 | .154 | .631 | .456 | 1.015 | .831 | .908 |
| 4. Asparagus | −.882 | −.592 | −.154 | .000 | .154 | .222 | .456 | .256 | .613 |
| 5. Carrots | −1.165 | −.653 | −.631 | .154 | .000 | −.018 | .187 | .550 | .719 |
| 6. Spinach | −1.237 | −.631 | −.456 | −.222 | .018 | .000 | .327 | .473 | .327 |
| 7. String beans | −1.276 | −.882 | −1.015 | −.456 | −.187 | .327 | .000 | .068 | .364 |
| 8. Peas | −1.237 | −1.015 | −.831 | −.256 | −.550 | −.473 | −.068 | .000 | .327 |
| 9. Corn | −1.447 | −1.071 | −.908 | −.613 | −.719 | −.327 | −.364 | −.327 | .000 |
| Sum | −8.891 | −4.192 | −3.000 | −.073 | 1.165 | 1.401 | 3.711 | 4.103 | 5.776 |
| Average | −.988 | −.465 | −.333 | −.008 | +.129 | +.156 | +.412 | +.456 | +.642 |
| Final scale | .000 | .523 | .655 | .980 | 1.117 | 1.144 | 1.400 | 1.444 | 1.630 |

*Source:* Adapted from Guilford (1954) by permission of the author and publisher.

separated (e.g., $z_{jk} > 2.0$), are eliminated from this averaging process because the assumption that these stimuli overlap is not tenable (the "always or never" part of the Fullerton-Cattell law). The results are normal deviates expressed as deviations from the average stimulus in the set. Finally, the value of the lowest (most negative) stimulus is subtracted from each of the values to eliminate negative values in the final scale. This produces the final interval scale, e.g., of food preferences for the data in Table 2-3. Corn is the most liked vegetable, and turnips are the least liked. The latter is arbitrarily designated as zero on the scale. This zero is arbitrary, by definition, since this is an interval scale.

### Simulating Thurstone Scaling

One can work backward from the scale values presented at the bottom of Table 2-3 to estimate the proportions found in Table 2-2 directly by applying Eqs. 2-3 through 2-6 in reverse order. Consequently, a Monte Carlo approach is unnecessary. However, it is instructive to perform one and compare it to our previous simulation. The first step is to multiply the scale values in the bottom line of Table 2-3 by $\sqrt{2}$ to conform to Eq. 2-5b. This provides values of .000, .740, .926, ..., which are the mean discriminal responses—$r_j$, $r_k$, ....

To compare turnips with cabbage, two numbers were chosen from a normal distribution having a mean of zero and a standard deviation of 1.0. The first number was added to the value associated with turnips (.000), and the second number was added to the value associated with cabbage (.740). These independent, normally distributed random numbers provided discriminal dispersions. When added to the scale values, they yielded the covert discriminal responses, $r_j$ and $r_k$, of assumption 1. They were assumed normally distributed because of assumption 4. The subject preferred turnips over cabbage if $r_j - r_k$ was > 0 but preferred cabbage over turnips if $r_j - r_k$ was < 0. This was repeated 1000 times for each stimulus pair. The resulting probabilities appear in Table 2-4.

**TABLE 2-4    ESTIMATED PROPORTIONS OF SUBJECTS PREFERRING EACH VEGETABLE BASED UPON COMPUTER SIMULATION**

| Vegetable | Vegetable | | | | | | | | |
|---|---|---|---|---|---|---|---|---|---|
| | 1 | 2 | 3 | 4 | 5 | 6 | 7 | 8 | 9 |
| 1. Turnips | .500 | .710 | .745 | .845 | .844 | .870 | .927 | .923 | .956 |
| 2. Cabbage | .290 | .500 | .550 | .684 | .735 | .761 | .813 | .804 | .864 |
| 3. Beets | .255 | .450 | .500 | .614 | .676 | .697 | .748 | .784 | .821 |
| 4. Asparagus | .155 | .316 | .386 | .500 | .525 | .567 | .649 | .668 | .745 |
| 5. Carrots | .156 | .265 | .324 | .475 | .500 | .529 | .601 | .633 | .700 |
| 6. Spinach | .130 | .239 | .303 | .433 | .471 | .500 | .575 | .613 | .675 |
| 7. String beans | .073 | .187 | .252 | .351 | .399 | .425 | .500 | .523 | .585 |
| 8. Peas | .077 | .196 | .216 | .332 | .367 | .387 | .477 | .500 | .548 |
| 9. Corn | .044 | .136 | .179 | .255 | .300 | .325 | .415 | .452 | .500 |

*Source*: Adapted from Guilford (1954) by permission of the author and publisher.

These probabilities are only a first approximation to those in Table 2-2. For example, turnips are preferred to cabbage .810 of the time, but the simulation only predicted a difference of .710. On the other hand, the observed preference for corn over cabbage (.858) is fairly close to the predicted preference (.864). Consider why the fit was not better. One major factor was that the simulation assumed the equal discriminal dispersions of Eqs. 2-5 and 2-6 instead of the more general Eqs. 2-3 and 2-4. Another possibility is that the stimuli vary along more than one axis, i.e., are multidimensional. Should one try a more general model with more parameters to estimate? Perhaps yes; perhaps no. This is a question of the tradeoff of completeness and goodness of fit against parsimony.

## A Comparison of the Two Simulations

Two simulations have been presented in this chapter. The first involved absolute judgments along a single physical dimension, i.e., was psychophysical. The second involved a comparison of two sentiments with stimuli that did not vary along one physical dimension, i.e., was not psychophysical.

The law of comparative judgment has had both historical and continuing importance. The first author had the privilege of sitting in Thurstone's classroom when he indicated that the law of comparative judgment was his proudest achievement. This came from a man for whom the word "genius" is appropriate. Hundreds of journal articles and numerous books have been stimulated by the law of comparative judgment. Although the derivation of the law is not simple, the law itself is held in reverence by some psychometricians, and for good reason.

In the end, the law is very simple. It consists of transforming percentages of "greater than" responses for pairs of stimuli into $z$ scores reflecting their difference. The process uses the inverse of the cumulative normal curve introduced in basic statistics. This inverse function is depicted in Fig. 2-6. The interval between any two stimuli is the $z$ score that corresponds to the percentage of "greater than" responses. Intervals are computed for all pairs of stimuli. Although these $z$ scores themselves can define intervals, they are usually averaged to increase the reliability of the estimates, and the lowest one is set to zero to simplify description.

The point basic to both simulations is that variability due to noise unified the two types of response. The additional factor of a correlation between the separate processes in a comparison is also important in reducing the magnitude of error. The simulations reasonably document what the subjects do.

## The Logistic Distribution and Luce's Choice Theory

Although much statistical theory used in scaling employs the familiar normal distribution, more recent work tends to stress the logistic distribution. The ogival shape of the logistic distribution is visually indistinguishable from the cumulative normal distribution, but it is much more convenient mathematically. This will be especially important in Chapters 10 and 15. Equation 2-7 defines the logistic function:

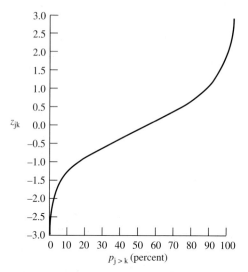

**FIGURE 2-6**   Interval scale values based upon the law of comparative judgment ($z_{jk}$) as a funtion of the percentage of "greater than" responses ($p_{j>k}$).

$$Y = \frac{e^{1.7X}}{1 + e^{1.7X}} \qquad\qquad (2\text{-}7)$$

where $e = 2.718281828+$. The constant 1.7 causes $Y$ to differ from the standard cumulative normal distribution by no more than 0.01 for any value of $X$. Had this distribution been used instead of the cumulative normal, the final scale values would have been indistinguishable.

Just as it is reasonable to use the cumulative normal distribution because the combined effects of independent sources of error tend to form a normal distribution, the logistic distribution may also be justified mathematically through Luce's choice theory (Luce, 1959a, 1963, 1977). Choice theory deals with preferences just as the law of comparative judgment does. Consider choosing one vegetable from menus on which (1) asparagus and beets are the only two choices and (2) there are other options. The probabilities of choosing asparagus and beets are obviously smaller when there are other options since one may prefer corn, cabbage, etc., over either.

The essence of choice theory is the constant ratio rule which predicts that the ratio of choosing asparagus over beets will be the same in both situations. Thus, Table 2-2 indicates that 56.1 percent of subjects chose asparagus over beets when they are the only options. This ratio is $56.1/(100 - 56.1) = 56.1/43.9$ or 1.28. Now suppose that 10 percent of subjects choose beets from a larger menu. According to the model, asparagus should be chosen 12.8 percent of the time. These constant ratios in turn are also the ratios of their scale values. The logistic transformation relates scale values ($X$) to probabilities ($Y$). In contrast, Eqs. 2-3 through 2-6 show that Thurstone's law of comparative judgment is a constant-difference rule.

## Averages as Scale Values

Both Thurstone's law of comparative judgment and choice theory are representational models of interval scaling in the sense of Chapter 1. The reason for choosing either the normal curve transformation that gave rise to Table 2-2 or the logistic transformation follows from the constant-difference and constant-ratio rules (assumptions). Consider what would happen if the scale were simply formed from the preference probabilities in Table 2-2 themselves. One first computes the column sums, which are 1.634, 3.001, 3.438, 4.439, 4.878, 4.947, 5.764, 5.925, and 6.414. Dividing each in turn by 9 to form averages gives 0.181, 0.333, 0.382, 0.493, 0.542, 0.554, 0.640, 0.658, and 0.712. Next, subtracting 0.181 from each average gives values of 0.000, 0.152, 0.201, 0.312, 0.361, 0.373, 0.459, 0.477, and 0.531.

In order to visualize the similarities between these values, based upon simple sums, and either Thurstone's or Luce's formal assumptions, multiply each value by the ratio of the highest scale value in Table 2-3 (1.630) to the highest scale value here (0.531) or 3.07. This makes the first and last values of the two scales the same. Both this and the subtraction of the smallest scale value (0.181) are permissible transformations of an interval scale. The resulting scale values are 0.000, 0.466, 0.615, 0.957, 1.108, 1.145, 1.409, 1.464, and 1.630. The similarities to the proper Thurstone values are apparent and important.

This similarity is one justification for the operationalist position (Gaito, 1980) discussed in Chapter 1. Were the table comprised of outcomes for nine baseball teams, the result would be familiar won-loss percentages. However, the operation and therefore the scale values are meaningless in a representational sense since, unlike the rationale provided by Thurstone and his predecessors, there is none for summing probabilities as opposed to $z$ scores. The operationalist position is that it is difficult to see why one operation is meaningless when it gives results nearly identical to those of another that is meaningful.

## Checks and Balances

So far in this chapter numerous assumptions have been discussed regarding the use of various models for scaling stimuli. How does one know if the assumptions are correct?

**1** We have already noted the importance of internal consistency in developing subjective estimate scales. Similar considerations hold for discriminant models. Basically, an ordinal scale is developed by averaging individual subjects' rankings, and the data are internally consistent to the extent that different subjects give similar rankings. As previously noted, suitable methods for obtaining internal consistency measures are discussed later in Chapters 6 through 8.

**2** As indicated in the simulations, one can work backward from Thurstone scale values to paired comparison probabilities. These estimated probabilities should be similar to the observed probabilities.

**3** One should examine the transitivity of the response probabilities. If stimulus i is preferred to j and j is preferred to k, then i should be preferred to k. Violations of transitivity are an indication that the scale is not unidimensional. Of course, slight violations of transitivity may simply reflect measurement error.

**4** A stronger (interval) criterion for unidimensionality is the additivity of the scale values, an issue we will consider in detail in Chap. 14. Tests of additivity depend upon which form of the model is being used, but the basic idea is simple. Suppose that Eq. 2-6, which assumes that the stimuli have equal variances, is used. Now suppose stimulus i is preferred to stimulus j 65 percent of the time ($p_{i>j} = .65$). A table of the normal curve indicates that stimuli i and j are separated by .39 units. Further, suppose that stimulus j is preferred to stimulus k 70 percent of the time ($p_{j>k} = 0$). This implies that stimuli j and k are separated by .52 $z$-score units. Additivity holds to the extent that the distance between i and k is close to .91 (.39 + .52) $z$-score units. Consequently, $p_{i>k}$ should be .82, the value of $p$ associated with a $z$ score of .91, within measurement error. A failure of additivity could imply that the data are multidimensional, but it could also imply correlated error or unequal variance. Guilford (1954) describes a formal chi-square test of significance.

**5** As in any scientific endeavor, relative scale values should be replicable within the linear transformations permitted by an interval scale. As with any other criterion, the degree of replicability is a function of the sample size: The larger the sample, the more stable the expected results. However, other factors, particularly the care with which the data are gathered, are also important. Thus, the relative sizes of the intervals among the stimuli should remain much the same. If the relative sizes of these intervals change markedly across situations, scalings would be highly context-dependent. These findings would therefore ordinarily not be useful unless the changes occurred in a theoretically interesting way.

## Multi-item Measures

This book stresses the need for multi-item measures, where "item" is broadly used to stand for any stimuli used in measurement. Thus items may be words on a spelling test, comparisons between weights, statements concerning attitudes toward the U.S. Congress, response latencies, etc. There are a number of important reasons for combining several items when measuring a psychological attribute.

**1** Individual items usually correlate poorly with the particular attribute in question.

**2** Each item tends to relate to attributes other than the one to be measured. For example, the ability of children to spell "umpire" correctly may partly depend on their interest in baseball.

**3** Each item has a degree of specificity in the sense of not correlating with any general attribute or factor. The concept of specificity for individual test items will become clearer when factor analysis is discussed in Chapters 11 through 13.

**4** Individual items have considerable random measurement error, i.e., are unreliable. This can be seen when people rerate stimuli. A person who initially rates stimulus A as 3 on one occasion may rerate it as 5. Some of this may reflect changes in the attribute over time, but it may occur even when one has every reason to believe the trait itself is stable. To the extent that some stimuli are rated higher and others are rated lower, measurement error averages out when individual scores are summed to obtain a total score.

**5** An item can categorize people into only a relatively small number of groups. Specifically, a dichotomously scored item (one scored pass versus fail) can distinguish between only two levels of the attribute. Most measurement problems require much finer differentiations.

All of these difficulties are diminished by the use of multi-item measures. The tendency of items to relate to incidental factors usually averages out when they are combined because these different incidental factors apply to the various items. Combining items allows one to make finer distinctions among people. For reasons which will be discussed in Chapters 6 and 7, reliability increases (measurement error decreases) as the number of items increases. Thus, nearly all measures of psychological attributes are multi-item measures. This is true both for measures used to study individual differences and for measures used in experiments. The problem of scaling people with respect to attributes is then one of combining item responses to obtain one score (measurement) for each person.

### Item Trace Lines (Item Characteristics Curves)

Nearly all models for scaling people can be described by different types of curves relating the attribute they measure to the probability of responding one way versus another. Functions of this form are called "item trace lines" or "item characteristic curves" (ICCs). For example, a trace line might denote the probability of recognizing Thurstone as the author of the law of comparative judgment as a function of overall knowledge of psychology. We will define response alpha as passing rather than failing an ability item scored as correct versus incorrect, answering an personality test item in the keyed direction, agreeing rather than disagreeing with an opinion statement, or remembering versus not remembering an item on a list. Response beta is the alternative outcome. More complex models can handle multicategory responses such as Likert scales and the nominal categories of a multiple-choice item. Figure 2-7 depicts four of the possible forms a trace line based upon dichotomously scored items may take: (*a*) a step function, (*b*) an ogive, (*c*) an irregular but monotonic function, and (*d*) a nonmonotonic function.

The point to note about all trace lines is their similarity to local psychometric functions like Figs. 2-1 and 2-2. The difference is that the abscissa of a psychometric function is a physical dimension ($\Phi$) that can usually be described in ostensive terms. The abscissa of a trace line denotes an abstract attribute defined in terms of its strength as in Thurstone scaling and is commonly denoted "$\Theta$". Different models make different assumptions about trace lines. Some are very specific as to form and require trace lines like those in Fig. 2-7*a* and 2-7*b*; others describe only a general form like that in Fig. 2-7*c*. Figure 2-7*d* generally represents what is normally an undesirable outcome. It is most likely to arise when a distractor on a multiple-choice test tends to be chosen by high-ability subjects, perhaps because it is correct in a way that the test constructor did not think of. However, there are some models that use nonmonotone items.

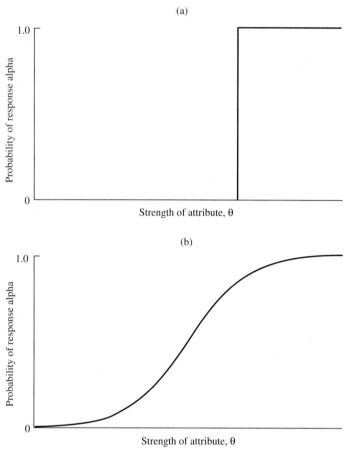

**FIGURE 2-7** Trace lines (item-characteristic curves). (*a*) A step function, (*b*) an ogive.

In general, it is important to distinguish among (1) a single observation (test item), (2) a more general attribute measured by a finite number of items that may be spuriously influenced, an obtained or fallible score, and (3) a hypothetical, perfectly measured attribute or true score perhaps as measured on an infinite number of trials. A critical difference between the classical approach of Chapters 6 and 7 and the modern approaches of Chapter 10 (item response theories) is that classical approaches usually define $\Theta$ in terms of obtained measures (fallible scores), but item response theories always define $\Theta$ in terms of true scores. The ordinate in both cases is the probability or proportion of response alpha, and thus refers to a test item.

Attributes are also commonly called "constructs" or, in the narrower sense of personality theory, "traits." When an attribute is inherently categorical (e.g., political party or religious membership), the attribute is called a "class." Classes may vary complexly, but attributes are otherwise generally assumed to vary in only one way,

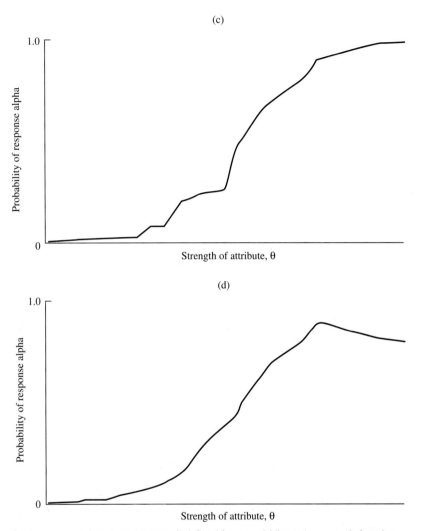

**FIGURE 2-7**    (*c*) A monotonic function with no well-defined form, and (d) a nonmonotonic function.

i.e., be unidimensional. The measurement of constructs is discussed in Chapter 3, and the principles involved in estimating fallible and true scores are considered in Chapters 6 through 10. The response of a subject in recalling a particular word from a list of words presumably relates to a more general attribute of memory. The principles apply to measuring any response, not just pencil-and-paper items.

An attribute is defined somewhat circularly in terms of whatever the items tend to measure in common. Chapter 3 considers the process of validation that is used to "break the circle." Appropriate methods also exist to infer how much the items have in common. Thus a list of spelling words are assumed to measure spelling ability, and the number of words correctly recalled are a (fallible) measure of memory for the particular material. The word "tend" indicates that no attribute is perfectly mirrored in any finite set of items. Perfectly reliable measurement demands that children be administered all words in the English language on a spelling test or subjects in a memory study be given an infinitely long list to recall.

## Difficulty and Discrimination

Two basic properties of a trace line are its difficulty and its discrimination. "Difficulty" refers to how much of the attribute an individual must possess to achieve a given probability of response alpha. Increasing the difficulty of an item is equivalent to "sliding" its trace line to the right, as has been done with the item denoted $a$ in Fig. 2-8. This might occur when a group of primary school children are asked to spell "cattle" instead of "cat." Making the item easier slides the trace line to the left. The classical psychometric index of difficulty is simply the probability of response alpha. However, modern theories use the amount of an attribute ($\Theta$) necessary to achieve a .5 probability of response alpha, i.e., the "threshold." This reflects the analogy to psychophysics.

The "discrimination" of an item describes the extent to which the probability of response alpha correlates with the attribute. An item with a perfectly flat trace line does not discriminate and should be eliminated from the test. Most models are called "monotone" models in that the probability of response alpha is expected to increase with the attribute in the general form of Fig. 2-7$c$. In that case, making an item more discriminating increases its slope, as depicted by the item designated b in Fig. 2-8, which completes the analogy with the psychometric function of psychophysics. The most common classical index of discrimination is the correlation over people between response alpha and total test score, the "item-total" correlation. The concepts of difficulty and discrimination are logically independent, as an item may be difficult or easy regardless of whether it is discriminating or nondiscriminating. However, modern test theorists stress that the probability of response alpha and the item-total correlation are not independent because, as will be noted in Chapter 4, the proportion of alpha responses places limits on the item-total correlation. In fact, item response theories use the slope of the trace line to describe discrimination, just as in psychophysics.

There must be a large number of persons at each point on the trace line. Save for classes, attributes are continuous, so that it is theoretically possible to make infinitely fine discriminations. The trace line thus shows the expected response probability for people at that level of the attribute or class. This expectation either defines the probability of response alpha for dichotomous items or the mean for Likert or other multicategory items. Such expectations inherently contain error. For example, there is a probability of response alpha at each point for dichotomous items, but there is no certainty as to who will respond alpha and who will respond beta. Multicategory items likewise have a band of error (standard error) surrounding the average. Thus, although the expected score on a 5-point Likert scale for a given point on an attribute might be 3.1, scores at that point probably range from 1 to 5.

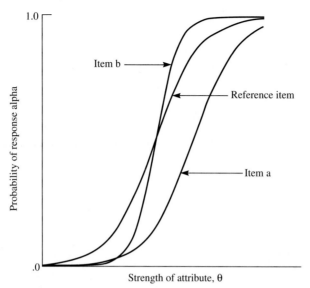

**FIGURE 2-8**    Effects of making an item more difficult (item a) or more discriminating (item b) relative to a reference item.

## DETERMINISTIC MODELS FOR SCALING PEOPLE

Deterministic models are so called because they assume that there is *no error* and so the trace line is a step function as in Fig. 2-7a (or Fig. 2-1a). The most common form assumes that the probability of response alpha to a dichotomous item at each level of the attribute is 0 up to a point (probability of response beta is 1.0), i.e., the threshold. Beyond this point the probability of response alpha is 1.0. Its discrimination is therefore infinite at the threshold. Figure 2-9 contains a family of such items. Each item has a perfect biserial correlation (an estimated correlation between a dichotomous measure and a continuous measure, assuming that both underlying measures are continuous and normally distributed, see Chapter 4) with the attribute. Consequently each item perfectly discriminates at a particular point of the attribute. This is perhaps a very appealing model because it is exactly what one expects to obtain from measurements of length. Thus, one expects to obtain a trace lines like those in Fig. 2-9 for the following items:

|  | Yes | No |
|---|---|---|
| (a) Are you above 6 feet 6 inches in height? | _____ | _____ |
| (b) Are you above 6 feet 3 inches in height? | _____ | _____ |
| (c) Are you above 6 feet in height? | _____ | _____ |
| (d) Are you above 5 feet 9 inches in height? | _____ | _____ |
| (e) Are you above 5 feet 6 inches in height? | _____ | _____ |

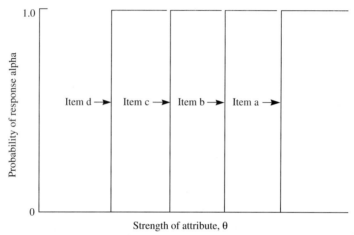

**FIGURE 2-9**   A family of trace lines that discriminate perfectly at different points and thereby form a monotonic deterministic model (Guttman) scale. Items a to d are progressively easier.

Assume "yes" is response alpha. Any person who answered yes to question (a) would answer yes to the others. Any person who answered *no* to (a) but answered yes to (b) would also answer yes to questions (c) through (e). Five people with different patterns of responses would produce a triangular pattern of data like that in Table 2-5. An X symbolizes a yes answer (response alpha).

## The Guttman Scale

Although a trace line usually requires at least some statistical estimation, one can look at data to see if they provide a triangular pattern like that in Table 2-5 (making, however, a subtle logical assumption as discussed below). Some items do produce a pattern of data like that in Table 2-5, perhaps the following:

|  | Yes | No |
|---|---|---|
| (a) The U.S. Congress is the savior of all Americans. | _____ | _____ |
| (b) The U.S. Congress is America's best hope for peace. | _____ | _____ |
| (c) The U.S. Congress is a constructive force in the American political system. | _____ | _____ |
| (d) We should continue our present system of government, including Congress. | _____ | _____ |

Anyone who answers yes to (a) will probably answer yes to the other items; anyone who answers no to (a) but answers yes to (b) will probably answer yes to the other items; etc. Items that produce a pattern of responses like those in Table 2-6 form a

TABLE 2-5    TRIANGULAR PATTERN OF RESPONSES
FITTING A GUTTMAN SCALE

|        | Person |   |   |   |   |
|--------|--------|---|---|---|---|
| Item   | 1 | 2 | 3 | 4 | 5 |
| *a*    | X |   |   |   |   |
| *b*    | X | X |   |   |   |
| *c*    | X | X | X |   |   |
| *d*    | X | X | X | X |   |
| *e*    | X | X | X | X | X |

"Guttman scale." Guttman scales are developed by administering items to a group and then attempting to arrange the responses so that they form the required triangular pattern (see Torgerson, 1958). The data will form a "solid staircase" of alpha responses, and the height of each step will be proportional to the number of people at each level of the attribute. The term "scalogram analysis" describes methods of developing Guttman scales.

Unfortunately, it is very unlikely that the initial set of items will produce a triangular pattern. It is therefore necessary to (1) discard some items and (2) find the best possible ordering among the remaining items. The reproducibility of score patterns is of primary concern regarding the latter issue. If a triangular pattern is obtained, knowing the number of alpha responses allows one to reproduce *all* of an individual's responses. The percentage of people whose patterns are thus reproduced is a basic statistic in scalogram analysis.

Guttman scales could conceivably be developed for any type of dichotomous item such as a spelling test. A triangular pattern of data will be obtained (X denoting a correct spelling) if the items have trace lines like those in Fig. 2-10. If person A has a score of 35 and person B has a score of 34, person A would have to get the same 34 items correct as person B plus the next most difficult item. Knowing how many items an individual passes defines which items are passed.

Figure 2-10 describes a variant upon the Guttman scale which uses nonmonotone items instead of monotone items, i.e., the trace lines go up and then comes down. Our discussion of Guttman scaling in the next paragraph applies to this variant. Subjects falling between two levels of the attribute respond with alpha, and subjects who either fall below the first level or above the second level respond with beta. Each person responds with alpha to only one item. The following four items should fit this model:

|                                                              | Yes | No |
|--------------------------------------------------------------|-----|----|
| (a) Are you between 6 feet 3 inches tall and 6 feet 6 inches? | ___ | ___ |
| (b) Are you between 6 feet tall and 6 feet 3 inches?          | ___ | ___ |
| (c) Are you between 5 feet 9 inches tall and 6 feet?          | ___ | ___ |
| (d) Are you between 5 feet 6 inches tall and 5 feet 9 inches? | ___ | ___ |

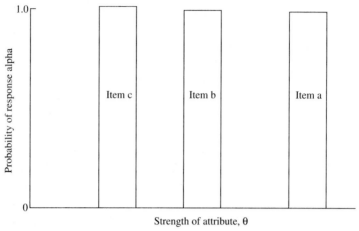

**FIGURE 2-10**    A family of trace lines that meet the requirements of a nonmonotonic, deterministic scaling model. Items a to c are progressively easier.

## Evaluation of the Guttman Scale

The Guttman scale concept has great intuitive appeal, but it is highly unrealistic. First, as rare as step functions are in psychophysics, where there is great control over the stimuli, anything approaching a step function outside that context is even rarer. No item correlates perfectly with any attribute. Although there is no way to obtain the trace line directly, some good approximations are available. Trace lines obtained with virtually all items have a much flatter slope than is consistent with the Guttman model, regardless of whether classical or modern methods are used to estimate them. Individual items rarely correlate higher than .60 with total scores. That is why it is unreasonable to assume a model that assumes perfect biserial correlations between items and an attribute.

Second, having a triangular pattern of data does not guarantee that items have step-function trace lines like those in Fig. 2-11. Items whose thresholds are far enough apart in difficulty will provide a triangular pattern even if their trace lines are fairly flat. This may be illustrated with the following four items:

**a** Solve for $x$: $x^2 + 2x + 9 = 16$.
**b** What does the word "severe" mean?
**c** How much is $10 \times 38$?
**d** When do you use an umbrella? (given orally).

We have not performed the experiment but suspect that the above four items probably would form an excellent Guttman scale if they were administered to subjects ranging in age from 4 to 16. Anyone who got the first item correct probably could get the others correct. Anyone who failed the first item but got the second correct would probably get the other two correct, etc. This would produce the required triangular pattern of data even though they probably measure different attributes ("factors," in the sense of Chapters 11 through 13). They apparently fit the unidimensional scale model because they are administered to an extremely diverse population. Consequently, it does not follow that having a triangular pattern of data is *sufficient* to establish a unidimensional scale. Because triangular data patterns can be obtained any time items vary greatly in difficulty, Guttman scales seldom have more than eight items. To take an extreme case, three items that are, respectively, passed by 10, 50, and 90 percent of the subjects will probably produce a triangular pattern regardless of their content. Scales which have eight or fewer items can make only gross discriminations among people.

A third criticism of the original Guttman scale was that it provided only an ordinal scale. However, recent methods of statistical estimation considered in Chapter 10 allow $\Theta$ to be estimated on an interval scale.

A fourth criticism of the Guttman scale is that it is usually more appropriate to think of items as rubber yardsticks applied by investigators with limited vision rather than as well-defined and well-understood procedures. To complete the analogy, one should think of items as rubber yardsticks that are poor copies of a real yardstick so that some yardsticks may have a zero point at 4 inches. Any single yardstick (item) discriminates poorly. However, the methods discussed in subsequent sections, such as simply adding items evoking response alpha, allow one to combine these various rubber measurements to obtain an approximate linear relationship with "better" yardsticks and thus obtain an interval scale.

In summary, we suggest the deterministic model underlying the Guttman scale is not very applicable to psychological measurement because (1) almost no items fit the model, (2) a triangular pattern is a necessary but not sufficient condition for the fit of the model, (3) the triangular pattern can be (and usually is) an artifact of using a small number of items that vary greatly in difficulty, (4) the model originally provided only an ordinal scale (a problem since overcome), and (5) there are better ways to develop measurement models [Cliff (1983a) presents a well-reasoned defense of Guttman scaling; it is also important to distinguish between Cliff's work in which the Guttman model is applied to a dichotomized composite score and the present discussion, in which individual items are presumed to fit a Guttman scale]. However, impractical models are often very important to the development of more useful models. This is certainly the case with the Guttman scale—the item response theories of Chapter 10 replaced the assumption of a step function with a more realistic ogive of the form presented in Fig. 2-7b. The Guttman scale, while unreasonable in itself, is a basic link to modern test theory.

## PROBABILISTIC MODELS FOR SCALING PEOPLE

Trace lines that are not step functions like Fig. 2-7a describe some probabilistic models. There are numerous types of probabilistic models, depending on what form the trace line is assumed to have.

### Nonmonotone Models

Nonmonotone probabilistic models are analogous to nonmonotone deterministic models as discussed above. Trace lines that change slope from positive to negative, or vice versa, at some point are nonmonotone. The only nonmonotone model that has been used assumes trace lines that are in the shape of normal distributions, as depicted in Fig. 2-11 for three items.

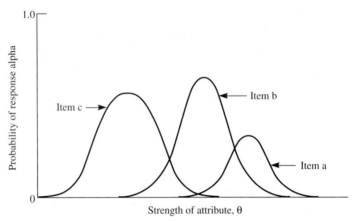

**FIGURE  2-11**    Nonmonotone, normal trace lines for three items that might be used on a Thurstone scale of attitudes.

The trace lines need not be exactly normal, and their standard deviations need not be equal. This model has been used only to develop a few attitude scales. Since Thurstone developed the scaling procedure, it is referred to as a "Thurstone scale of attitudes." However, this model has little to do with and should not be confused with Thurstone's previously discussed law of comparative judgment. Items at three points on a Thurstone scale of attitudes are as follows:

|  | Agree | Disagree |
|---|---|---|
| (a) I believe that the church is the greatest institution in America today. | _____ | _____ |
| (b) I enjoy a fine ritual service with good music when I go to church. | _____ | _____ |
| (c) The paternal and benevolent attitude of the church is quite distasteful to me. | _____ | _____ |

A Thurstone scale of attitudes begins with a large pool of attitudinal statements rated by 100 or more raters. Each statement is rated on an scale consisting of about 11 Likert-type steps, perhaps ranging from "strongly favorable" with respect to the attribute to "strongly unfavorable." Note that the raters do not state how *they* feel about the item; they evaluate the *item* itself, so that both a conservative and a liberal rater might rate a given item as "moderately favorable" with respect to a liberal position. Two standards are used to select a set of 10 to 20 items from the initial pool: (1) The ratings of items should have small standard deviations over raters (i.e., the raters should agree among themselves where the items fall on the scale); and (2) means for different items should vary considerably (i.e., items should reflect a wide range of the attribute). A subject's score is the average score of the items he or she endorses.

For example, if a subject agrees with items that have scale scores of 3.0, 3.1, and 3.2 and disagrees with all of the remaining items, that subject is assigned a score of 3.1. Another approach is to assign the scale score of the *highest* item on the scale with which the person agrees. The consistency of judgments can be inferred from the standard deviation of the endorsed items scale scores.

The Thurstone scale of attitudes model states that each item should evoke response alpha (agreement in this case) in only one limited region of the attribute ($\Theta$). Assuming that the trace line has an approximately normal distribution recognizes that items may be endorsed by people with a range of attitudes and, conversely, that people with a given attitude endorse items near and not necessarily at their preferred position. If only people who fall at 3.1 on the scale were to endorse an item judged to be 3.1, the scale would have to have an infinite number of items to capture the one that epitomizes the subject's attitude.

The major fault of the Thurstone scale of attitudes and, for that matter, any other nonmonotone model, is that good nonmonotone items are very difficult to construct. This is especially true for abilities items and, more generally, judgments. The problem is somewhat less severe with sentiments—a person who likes chocolate ice cream may not want it at every possible occasion. However, the model also has logical difficulties with attitudinal statements and sentiments in general. Items fitting this model tend to be "double-barreled" in saying one good thing and one bad thing. This can be seen in the three attitude statements given earlier. Item (*b*) asks subjects to agree simultaneously with two hidden statements:

($b_1$)    I sometimes go to church.
($b_2$)    I probably would not go to church if it were not for the fine ritual services and good music.

Likewise, item *(c)* is "triple-barreled" because a subject must agree that the church is paternal, benevolent, and distasteful to agree with it. The three modifiers collectively imply a moderately negative attitude toward the church. One constructs such items only by building two or more statements into what is ostensibly one statement. People who are not skilled at constructing questionnaires often unintentionally construct such ambiguous statements. Some subjects respond to one of the hidden statements, some subjects to another. This is ordinarily not useful in defining a relevant trait. One might as well construct statements like the following: The church is a wonderful, horrible institution.

Another important criticism of nonmonotone probability models is that it is very difficult to think of suitable items to define the ends of the scale. This is illustrated with item (*a*) in the previous example. Who could have a very positive attitude toward the church yet disagree with the statement, "I believe the church is the greatest institution in America today"? Such items will be monotone, continuing to increase in probability of endorsement as the level of the attribute increases.

In summary, nonmonotone probability models at best have limited applicability to the measurement of attitudes. One is probably better off restating the items in a monotone form and using an appropriate model for such items. We now turn to such models.

## Monotone Models with Specified Distribution Forms

Some monotone trace line models assume that the trace lines fit a particular statistical function. In particular, those that form the basis of modern psychometrics assume ogives like Fig. 2-7*b*. Another distinguishing characteristic of most of these models is that the pattern of responses defines the scale score rather than simply the number answered in the alpha direction, e.g., correctly. The ideas that are basic to these models have been available for a long time, but computers and recent developments in numerical estimation have spurred their recent growth.

Ogival trace lines are always more discriminating in their steeply ascending middle part than at the extremes. The steeper that section of the trace line, the higher the item-total correlation and other discrimination statistics. If it were a step function, the item would correlate perfectly with the attribute and form part of a Guttman scale. As items correlate less and less with the attribute and therefore become less discriminating, the ogival S shape flattens toward the horizontal.

Ogival models are appealing for two reasons. First, they make good intuitive sense. One can easily think of a critical interval of uncertainty as in psychophysics (see Fig. 2-2*b*) where subjects respond in both directions. This interval of uncertainty is more realistic than the perfect discrimination in a Guttman scale. Moving further away from that zone in either direction markedly reduces the uncertainty. Persons below that zone will choose response beta almost exclusively, and persons above it will choose response alpha almost exclusively. Thus, people of low ability will find a particular item too difficult, and people of high ability will find the same item too easy.

Another reason for the appeal of this model is that it has useful mathematical properties. For example, the sum of a series of ogives is also an ogive of predictable location and slope. The scale score is usually obtained from the probabilities of individual responses. This may require a complex algorithm, but it is a linear function of the attribute under certain assumptions. In contrast, scores derived from item sums typically are not linearly related to the attribute (Lord, 1980, also see Chapter 10), even though this nonlinearity is rarely a major problem. Another useful deduction is that the most discriminating items at any point on the attribute are those whose sum is as steep as possible at that point. This permits some interesting deductions about discriminating at a point, item difficulties, and correlations of items with total scores. It is also possible to deduce the amount of measurement error (unreliability) at different points on the attribute.

Some models make additional assumptions involving correlations among the items or the distribution of the underlying attribute. These assumptions provide a variety of interesting deductions that are useful when the assumptions hold. In particular, one can deduce the score that individuals would make on a test that they have not taken from the score that they made on one that they actually had taken even if the two tests were unequally difficult. These models have been a major, if not the major, focus of psychometric research (see Hulin, Drasgow, & Parsons, 1983; Lord, 1952a; 1974, 1980; Lord & Novick, 1968; Thissen, & Steinberg, 1988; Thissen, Steinberg, & Gerrard, 1986; Wainer & Braun, 1988). At the same time, item response approaches have not supplanted the conventional approach of summing item scores when subjects answer all test items on a test that is administered once.

### Monotone Models with Unspecified Distribution Forms

We finally arrive at the model that underlies most scaling—the linear, summative or centroid model. The model makes three major assumptions:

**1** Each item has a monotonic trace line as in Fig. 2-7c; the form of this monotonic trace line can even vary over items.

**2** The sum of the trace lines for a particular set of items (the trace line for total test scores) is approximately linear. That is, even if items do not all have the same type of monotonic trace line, departures from linearity average out when items are combined.

**3** The items as a whole measure only the attribute in question. This is the same as saying that the items have only one factor in common, a point to be discussed in detail in later chapters. It implies that the total score summarizes all the important information about the attribute being measured.

Figure 2-12 contains a family of such trace lines, and Fig. 2-13 presents the sum of these trace lines, the trace line of expected scores on a four-item test.

The model is called "linear" because the score is derived from a linear combination which is a sum of item responses. Even though the underlying mathematics of the linear model is not as elegant as that of modern psychometric models, it is not devoid of such properties given its use of the algebra of linear combinations. This sum does not require each item to have equal weight. The term "centroid" means average—the total score divided by the number of items gives the centroid or average. This is equivalent to weighting each of the $K$ items used to generate the score by $1/K$. Thus, a person's score on a classroom examination would probably be presented as the equally weighted sum, but performance on a series of reaction time trials might presented as a mean—the choice is a matter of convenience.

**FIGURE 2-12**    A family of four items with monotone trace lines that can be used in a linear model.

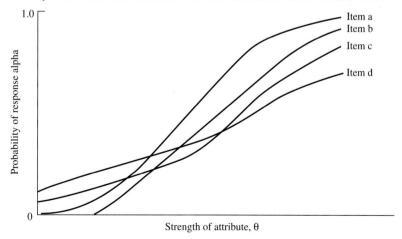

Item a
Item b
Item c
Item d

Probability of response alpha

Strength of attribute, θ

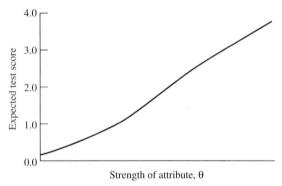

**FIGURE 2-13**   Expected scores on a four-item test—the sum of trace lines in Fig. 2-12.

We will normally assume that each item is given equal weight, called an equally weighted or unweighted model, but occasionally, weighting items differentially is appropriate. The effects of weighting are often trivial, especially when there are many items, and we will later argue against differentially weighting in most scale applications. The major features of the linear model apply to both weighted and unweighted versions. They also apply to multicategory or continuous items as well as to dichotomously scored items. Two slight drawbacks are that there is no formal rationale, in the representational sense, for a unit of measurement, and that the relation between total score and $\Theta$ may be nonlinear. However, as we have stressed, strong relations exist between linear scales and those developed from more complex models, and item sums ordinarily are monotonically related to $\Theta$ despite the nonlinearity.

We have come a long way around in this chapter to the conclusion that the most sensible way to measure psychological attributes of people is to do the obvious—sum item scores. The essence and beautiful point of the model is that it does not take individual items very seriously. It recognizes that any individual item has considerable specificity and measurement error. It does not make stringent assumptions about the form of the trace line. The only assumption made is that each item has some form of monotonic trace line. The model is fairly robust with respect to even that point in the sense that it is not highly sensitive to violations of this assumption. Even a few items with slight nonmonotonicities will not seriously affect the adequacy with which the attribute is measured. Items may have a noticeable *false positive* rate in that they may be answered correctly by subjects of the lowest imaginable ability (e.g., through guessing) and a *false negative* rate of being answered incorrectly by able subjects (e.g., through carelessness).

Much of the remainder of the book is based on the linear model, which makes sense and works well in practice. We will be discussing some newer models. However, there presently is no serious challenge to the linear model for most scaling of people and lower animals with respect to psychological attributes in the vast majority of applications.

## SUMMARY

Constructing a scale begins with a plan, usually leading to a matrix representation of the data with subjects as rows and stimuli as columns. Two important considerations are whether stimuli or subjects (objects) are to be scaled and the types of judgments to be made by the subjects. Scaling models are typically more critical in scaling stimuli. The different kinds of judgments in turn can be traced back to psychophysics, the study of the relation between physically defined dimensions and their associated responses. There are three main questions in psychophysics: (a) How does one obtain the absolute threshold or point at which a stimulus is perceived 50 percent of the time? (b) How does one obtain the difference threshold (difference limen) or just-noticeable difference (*JND*)? (c) What is the overall relation between variation in a physical dimension and associated responses (psychophysical scaling). In particular, although the absolute threshold was thought of as an all-or-nothing effect (an event was either below threshold and not perceived or above threshold and perceived), nearly all data suggest that the function is continuous, usually in the form of an ogive (S curve).

There are two broad traditions in psychophysics. Fechner's indirect (discriminant) approach stresses ordinal judgments, particularly paired-comparison methods, and requires stimuli be confusable; it leads to a logarithmic relationship between physical magnitudes and associated sensations and can be used with a wide variety of subjects. Stevens' direct approach requires subjects to report intervals or ratios of perceived magnitudes as required. Its major methods are ratio production, ratio estimation, magnitude estimation, bisection, and cross-modal matching. It leads to a power function relating physical magnitude and sensation, although there is no necessary incompatibility between the two laws. Both lead to methods generally important in psychometrics. The Fullerton-Cattell *law* states that equally often noted differences are equal unless always or never noted is a basic link between Fechnerian psychophysics and psychometric theory. It led to Thurstone's law of comparative judgment. In turn, Thurstone scaling is closely related to signal detection theory which stresses the separation of bias in responding from accuracy of discrimination.

The concept of an item trace line (item characteristic curve) which relates the probability of a given response (response alpha) to the magnitude of an underlying attribute is extremely important. The Guttman scale was an early formal model for scaling people. It assumes that the item trace line is a step function. However, the similarity of the trace line to the psychometric function was noted, which suggests that the Guttman scale may be unrealistic. There are newer models, considered in Chapter 10, which make more realistic assumptions.

The simplest model for scaling people simply counts the number of responses in the alpha direction, perhaps weighting certain items over others. The only thing it requires of the item trace line is that it be monotonic. The chapter concluded by noting the utility of this linear (summative, centroid) model.

## SUGGESTED ADDITIONAL READINGS

Coombs, C. H. (1964). *A theory of data.* New York: Wiley.

Engen, T. (1972a). Psychophysics I: Discrimination and detection. In J. W. Kling & L. A. Riggs (Eds.). *Woodworth & Schlossberg's Experimental Psychology* (3d ed.), vol. 1. New York: Holt, Rinehart, and Winston, chap. 1.

Engen, T. (1972b). Psychophysics II: Scaling Methods. In J. W. Kling & L. A. Riggs (Eds.). *Woodworth & Schlossberg's Experimental Psychology* (3d. ed.), vol. 1. New York: Holt, Rinehart, and Winston, chap. 2.

Guilford, J. P. (1954). *Psychometric methods.* New York: McGraw-Hill, chaps. 2 and 10.

Hulin, C. L., Drasgow, F., & Parsons, C. K. (1983). *Item response theory.* Homewood, Ill.: Dow Jones-Irwin.

Thissen, D., & Steinberg, L. (1988). Data analysis using item response theory. *Psychological Bulletin, 104,* 385–395.

Thissen, D., Steinberg, L., & Gerrard, M. (1986). Beyond group-mean differences: The concept of item bias. *Psychological Bulletin, 99,* 118–128.

Torgerson, W. S. (1958). *Theory and methods of scaling.* New York: Wiley.

Woodworth, R. S., & Schlossberg, H. (1954). *Experimental Psychology* (rev. ed.). New York: Holt.

## CHAPTER 3

# VALIDITY

## CHAPTER OVERVIEW

The term "validity" denotes the scientific utility of a measuring instrument, broadly statable in terms of how well it measures what it purports to measure. Unfortunately, the term has considerable "surplus meaning"; some take it to mean all things that are good about a measuring instrument rather than to specify how well the instrument has met the standards by which it is judged. We begin with a few of the cardinal considerations in all validation research. We have already stressed the importance of scientific generalization in psychometrics; this will be made explicit throughout the chapter.

Validity has been given three major meanings: (1) *construct* validity—measuring psychological attributes, (2) *predictive* validity—establishing a statistical relationship with a particular criterion, and (3) *content* validity—sampling from a pool of required content. Examples of measures intended to have these three types of validity are a measure of anxiety, a test for admitting students to graduate school, and a test for measuring spelling ability of fifth-grade students.

Since all forms of validity involve scientific generalization and the measurement of attributes is common to all validation, some have argued that there really is only one form of validity, construct validity. Apt as that point is, we will show how these three types of validity also involve somewhat different aspects of scientific generalization and discuss the unique aspects of each below. In particular, we will need to consider how the need for homogeneity of tests varies across situations.

This chapter is relatively brief, but do not confuse its brevity with lack of importance. Indeed, this is *the* most important chapter in this book. No amount of mathematical elegance or related use of sophisticated measurement procedures can substitute for validity in the senses described above.

## GENERAL CONSIDERATIONS

Some instruments are rather easily validated, e.g., the yardstick as a measure of length. It takes very little research to determine that yardstick measurements (1) fit axiomatic concepts of length and (2) relate to alternative definitions of length, e.g., tape measures, and (3) also relate lawfully to other variables, e.g., height and weight are correlated in the general population. If all measures met these standards so perfectly, validation would be simple, but such is not the case. Every area of psychology can provide numerous examples of what turned out to be mismeasurement; apparently good intuitive approaches to measurement have proven invalid by the standards and methods of investigation to be discussed.

Validation always requires empirical investigations, with the nature of the measure and form of validity dictating the needed form of evidence. For example, construct and predictive validity usually stress correlations among various measures, but content validity is largely based upon opinions of various users. To state the principle in reverse: There is no way to prove the validity of an instrument purely by appeal to authority, deduction from a psychological theory, or mathematical proof.

Moreover, validity usually is a matter of degree rather than an all-or-none property, and validation is an unending process. Whereas measures of length and of some other simple physical attributes may have proven their merits so well that no one seriously considers changing to other measures, most psychological measures need to be constantly evaluated and reevaluated to see if they are behaving as they should. New evidence may suggest modifications of an existing measure or the development of an alternative approach.

Strictly speaking, one validates the *use* to which a measuring instrument is put rather than the instrument itself. Tests are often valid for one purpose but not another. For example, a test used to select first-year college students may in fact be highly valid for that purpose but totally invalid for use in graduate school admissions. Although a measure may be valid for several purposes, as intelligence tests often are, the validity of *each* use must be documented empirically (but see the section on validity generalization below). Some measures, unfortunately, have no documentable valid use.

Measures are often validated independently of their development and well after development is complete. There is nothing wrong in doing this. However, we strongly recommend that anyone who develops a measuring instrument think about how its validity could be established at the outset and design at least a preliminary validation study for use in the development stage. Both authors have seen numerous individuals formulate what they consider a clever measure yet have no idea of how to validate it. The "woods are filled" with such measures, and it is difficult to see how they have made any contribution.

## CONSTRUCT VALIDITY

All basic sciences, including psychology, are concerned with establishing functional relations among important variables. Of course, variables must be measured before their interrelations can be studied. For such statements of relationship to have any meaning, each measure must validly measure what it is purports to measure. Some variables that have proven important in various areas of psychology are the perceptibility of briefly flashed words, the time required for various decisions, intelligence, and anxiety. In particular, suppose that an investigator wants to see if a particular approach to psychotherapy reduces patients' anxiety. Ignore, for simplicity, the eventual importance of comparing the patients to an untreated (control) group in order to focus on the problem of defining anxiety—until the measure is defined, one cannot know if it has changed.

An experimenter could simply ask patients to rate their anxiety on a scale. We have already noted in Chapter 1 how a single measure does not provide any structure to evaluate, and in Chapter 2 how the response, a sentiment, may be subject to various distortions. There is a third problem related to both of these. The investigator is not interested in measuring or modifying the rating as a specific behavior. If that were the case, a simple inducement ("I'll give you five dollars to rate yourself calm") or, what is cheaper, a threat, could probably produce the desired results. The investigator is interested in studying the abstract and latent process of anxiety that leads to the rating and hopes that the rating measures that process, which it may not—the subject may act simply to please or displease the investigator.

To the extent that a variable is abstract and latent rather than concrete and observable (such as the rating itself), it is called a "construct." Such a variable is literally something that scientists "construct" (put together from their own imaginations) and which does not exist as an observable dimension of behavior. A construct reflects a hypothesis (often incompletely formed) that a variety of behaviors will correlate with one another in studies of individual differences and/or will be similarly affected by experimental manipulations. Nearly all theories concern statements about constructs rather than about specific, observable variables because constructs are more general than specific behaviors by definition.

Scientists cannot do without constructs. Their theories are populated with them, and they find it all but impossible to discuss their work without using them even in informal conversations. In general, science's two major concerns are (1) developing measures of individual constructs and (2) finding functional relations between measures of different constructs. Corresponding to these two concerns is the notion that any theory has two equally important components—the measurement component that dictates what constructs are to be measured and the structural component that describes the properties of the resulting measures in terms of how constructs interrelate. For example, a proposed new measure of schizophrenic deficit may dictate use of a self-descriptive measure and state that schizophrenics should get higher scores than normals.

Construct validation is an obvious issue in scientific generalization. The goal of studying constructs is to employ one or more measures whose results generalize to a broader class of measures that legitimately employ the same name, e.g., "anxiety." However, these logical issues are complex and need to be considered from complementary points of view. Fortunately, this makes it relatively easy to discuss predictive validity and content validity.

Constructs vary widely in the extent to which the domain of related observable variables is (1) large or small and (2) specifically or loosely defined. When the construct is response latency (speed of response), the domain of related variables is relatively small and any one of the few observable variables in the domain will suffice to measure the construct. There are relatively few alternative methods of measuring reaction time, and their results tend to be closely related. For example, overall reaction time depends in part upon how much warning subjects are given that a trial will start, but differences among conditions tend not to be affected greatly by changes in warning condition. Any form of warning condition can therefore be spoken of as measuring reaction time without doing much injustice to the construct of latency. At a higher level of complexity, anxiety should be reflected in self-reports and clinical observation. Unfortunately, these two types of measures often intercorrelate poorly. This leads to the need for postulating two different types of anxiety. In contrast, self-reports and clinical observations of depression tend to correlate more highly, allowing greater unity.

Domain size and specificity are intimately related; the larger the domain of observables related to a construct, the more difficult it is to specify the variables that belong in the domain. The domain of related observables for many constructs is fuzzy, and scientists are often unsure of the full meanings of their own constructs. Typically, they hold firm beliefs about the more prominent observables related to a construct but can only speculate how far the construct extends. All would agree that a construct of intelligence should include reasoning ability but disagree as to whether perceptual and memory abilities should be considered part of the construct.

Because constructs concern domains of observables, a better measure of any construct is obtained by combining the results from a number of measures than by taking any one of them individually. However, this work is often tedious enough with one measure, let alone a handful. It is sometimes asking too much to expect a scientist to employ more than a few measures in a given investigation. Thus, any particular measure can be thought of as having construct validity to the extent that results obtained from it would remain the same if other measures in the domain were used. Similarly, combining several observables provides greater construct validity and scientific generalizability in the domain as a whole relative to a single measure.

The logical status of psychological constructs used to define individual differences and experimental measures is the same. Thus, even though the construct of intelligence is discussed more frequently within studies of individual differences, and the construct of a threshold is discussed more frequently in experimental studies, the problems of construct validity are essentially the same for both.

If the measurement of constructs is vital to scientific activity, how are such measures developed and validated? This is not a simple question, and there are legitimate disagreements about the correct answer. We will first present the most widely accepted point of view, logically analyze this view, and then conclude that the different points of view are complementary rather than contradictory.

The most prevalent point of view is as follows:  There are three major aspects of construct validation: (1) specifying the domain of observables related to the construct; (2) determining the extent to which observables tend to measure the same thing, several different things, or many different things from empirical research and statistical analyses; and (3) performing subsequent individual differences studies and/or experiments to determine the extent to which supposed measures of the construct are consistent with "best guesses" about the construct.

Aspect 3 consists of determining whether a supposed measure of a construct correlates in expected ways with measures of other constructs and/or is affected in expected ways by appropriate experimental manipulations. Investigators rarely plan these steps completely. There are advantages to undertaking the steps in the order given and, especially, to having some idea in advance about what hypotheses to test. However, psychologists often develop a particular measure of a construct and then leap directly to aspect 3 by relating the presumed measure to measures of other constructs, e.g., correlating a particular measure of anxiety with a particular measure of shyness. Only later is the measure correlated with similar measures. Alternatively, investigators may develop a measure. Skipping aspects 1 and 2, they will move directly to aspect 3 and try to find interesting relations between their measures and measures of other constructs. Still other times, deductions are made from theories that provide new tests of a construct which were not available when the measure was originally developed.

Often, a particular construct becomes popular, and different researchers attempt to devise their own measures. As the number of proposed measures of the construct grows, suspicion grows that they might not all measure the same thing. One or more investigators seek to outline the domain of observables related to the construct (aspect 1). All or part of the outline is subjected to investigation to determine the extent to which these alternative measures are or are not equivalent (aspect 2). The impact of theorizing in aspect 1 and the research results from aspect 2 tend to influence which particular variables are studied (aspect 3).

Most psychologists work as individuals, doing what they please, rather than as a part of some overall plan of attack on a problem. Consequently there is seldom a organized, concentrated effort to develop valid measures of constructs. Instead of tightly defining the initial domain of observables for the construct (aspect 1), the nature of the domain is usually suggested by numerous attempts to develop particular measures of the construct. Subsequently, some investigators attempt an explicit outline of the domain of content. Instead of a planned, frontal attack on the empirical investigations in aspects 2 and 3, evidence usually accrues from diverse studies in which the available evidence accumulates and is evaluated.

Hopefully, this complex process produces a construct that (1) is well defined through a variety of observables, (2) is well represented by alternative measures, and (3) relates strongly to other constructs of interest. We will now consider some of the methods required to reach these goals.

## Domain of Observables

Scientists seldom outline the domain of observables before assuming that any one observable relates to a construct. They typically investigate a single observable and tentatively assume that it relates to the construct. For example, shyness is currently a popular topic, and many investigators use Cheek and Buss' (1981) scale to define shyness.

Scientists should not be criticized for provisionally assuming that particular observables relate to a vaguely understood construct. Each scientist can perform only a relatively small number of major studies in a lifetime. This leaves insufficient time to do all that is required to specify the domain of a construct, develop measures of the construct, and relate these measures to other variables of interest. However, the collective efforts of different scientists interested in a particular construct like shyness make it fruitful to attempt to specify the domain of related variables.

No precise method can be stated to outline the domain of variables for a construct properly. The outline essentially constitutes a theory regarding how variables relate to one another. Although theories themselves should be objectively testable, the theorizing process is necessarily intuitive. Outlining a construct essentially consists of stating what one means by the use of particular words such as "anxiety," "memory," and "intelligence." Early attempts to outline a domain are usually limited to a definition in which the word denoting the construct is related to less abstract words. Binet and Simon's (1905) attempt to define "intelligence" is one example: "The tendency to take and maintain a definite direction; the capacity to make adaptations for the purpose of attaining a desired end, and the power of auto-criticism." Brave as such attempts are, they do little to specify the domain in question when they employ words that are far removed from specific observable variables.

Whether or not a well-specified domain for a construct actually leads to adequate measurement of the construct is an empirical issue. However, there is no way to know how to test the adequacy with which a construct is measured without a well-specified domain. In other words, aspect 1 (outlining the domain) is important in telling you what to do in aspect 2 (investigating relations among different proposed measures of a construct).

## Relations among Observables

The adequacy of a domain's outline is tested by determining how well the measures of observables "go together" (intercorrelate) empirically. The first step in individual differences research is to obtain a sample of scores for individuals on some of the measures. The various measures are then intercorrelated. The resulting intercorrelations describe the extent to which all the measures relate to the same thing. This is essentially the problem of factor analysis, which is discussed briefly later in this chapter and in detail in Chapters 11 through 13.

Investigating construct validity in experiments uses much the same logic as in studies of individual differences. One investigates the extent to which treatment effects are similar for measures that are presumably similar. Figure 3-1 depicts the hypothetical effects of five levels of noise-induced stress (the independent variable) on four presumed measures of fear. Fear measures a and b are affected in much the same way by the experimental treatments, as both are monotonically related to stress. Fear measure c is also monotonically related to stress up to level 4 but falls off sharply at level 5. Consequently, it measures something different from a and b. Fear measure d is, if anything, *inversely* related to stress, so that it cannot measure the same thing as a, b, and c. To determine the extent to which these and other measures of fear go together more fully, it is desirable to study the effects of a different stressor such as electric shock.

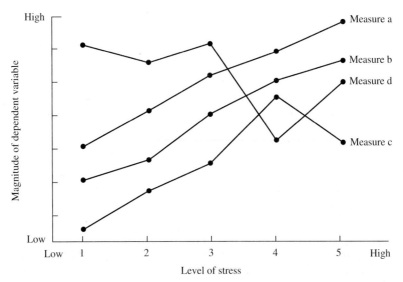

**FIGURE 3-1**  Effects of five levels of stress on four dependent measures.

The test of how well different experimental measures go together is the extent to which their functional relationships are similar when they are affected by different treatment variables. The form of relationship with any particular treatment variable is immaterial as long as these relationships are similar. Thus, two supposed measures of a construct could both increase monotonically with one treatment variable, curvilinearly with a second treatment variable, and not vary at all with a third treatment variable. The key is that both measures are affected in the same way.

If two measures were affected in exactly the same way by all possible experimental treatments, it would be immaterial which one was used in a particular study and one could speak of them as measuring the same thing. This would be the case even if there were slight differences in the exact form of functional relationship, e.g., if one measure varied linearly with a treatment variable and another varied exponentially. An appropriate monotonic transformation could eliminate the disparity in form of function. This transformation usually is not needed when correlational measures are used because it has little effect. In sum, the *degree* to which two measures are affected similarly by a variety of experimental treatments defines their similarity. When a variety of measures behave similarly over a variety of experimental treatments, it becomes meaningful to speak of them as measuring a construct. The measures that most consistently behave as the majority of measures do have the most construct validity.

Methods of investigating construct validity both in individual differences studies and in controlled experiments involve correlations in the broad sense of the term. Actual correlations are computed among measures of individual differences, and a comparison of two curves is a correlational process even if the Pearson correlation coefficient is not used specifically. Regardless of whether correlations are computed over individual differences or over levels of treatment effects, such correlations provide evidence about the structure of a domain of observables relating to a construct.

The results of investigations like those described above lead to one of three conclusions. If all the proposed measures correlate highly with one another, it can be concluded that they all measure much the same thing. If the measures tend to split up into clusters such that the members of a cluster correlate highly with one another and correlate much less with the members of other clusters, they measure a number of *different* things. Spielberger, Gorsuch, and Lushene (1970) noted that responses to self-reports of long-term anxiety (trait anxiety) tend to go together but are at least partially separable from self-reports about present anxiety (state anxiety). Note that the two constructs need not be completely independent to be separable into two meaningful measures. A third possibility is that the correlations among the measures all are near zero, so that they measure different things and there is no meaningful construct. Unfortunately, the evidence is seldom clear-cut regarding the appropriate conclusion, leaving room for dispute.

Evidence of the kind described above should affect both subsequent efforts to specify the domain of observables for a construct and theories relating the construct to other constructs. If all relevant measures of a construct intercorrelate highly, investigators should keep working with the specified domain of observables and encourage continued theory development. If more than one thing is apparently being measured, the old construct should be replaced by two or more new ones, and theories that assume only one construct should be modified to reflect this multiplicity. If none of the variables correlates substantially with any of the others, the scientist has an unhappy state of affairs. Of course, it is possible that one of the measures is highly related to the construct and the others are irrelevant, but it is much more likely that none of them relate well to the construct. The investigator can postulate an entirely new domain of observables for the construct, perhaps by abandoning questionnaire measures for physiological measures. The alternative is to abandon the construct altogether.

## Relations among Constructs

The previous section considered means of studying construct validity in terms of the "internal consistency" of a construct's assumed measures in a domain, i.e., whether they supply the same information by intercorrelating highly over subjects or over experimental treatments. To the extent that the elements of such a domain show this consistency, *some* construct may be employed to account for the interrelationships, but it is by no means certain that the construct name which motivated the research is appropriate. In other words, internal consistency is *necessary* but not *sufficient* for construct validity. A discussion of how one can, if ever, obtain sufficient evidence that a domain of observables relates to a construct requires an analysis of the deepest innards of scientific explanation.

We will begin by assuming that it is possible to find immutable proof that a particular set of variables measures a particular construct and see what forms of evidence are required. That assumption will then be challenged, leading to a different perspective on interpreting evidence about construct validity. If the assumption of immutable "proof" were accepted, sufficient evidence for construct validity would simply be that the supposed measure(s) of the construct *behave as expected*.

Suppose a particular measure is thought to relate to the construct of anxiety. Common sense suggests many expected findings. Higher anxiety scores should be found for (1) patients diagnosed with anxiety reactions versus normals, (2) subjects in an experiment who are threatened with a failure experience versus control subjects, and (3) graduate students undergoing their final oral examination for the Ph.D. versus the same students after passing the examination. Similarly, intelligence measures should correlate at least moderately with measures of academic accomplishment. All constructs have expected correlations with other variables and/or expected experimental effects.

Any immutable proof of the extent to which a measure defines a construct would have to come from determining how well the measure fit lawfully into a network of expected relationships. This pattern of results is often called a "nomological network" (Cronbach & Meehl, 1955). Tests of internal consistency of observables come first and require many studies. The degree of construct validity reflects the extent to which the measures met the theoretical expectations.

One could argue that there is a logical fallacy in claiming evidence such as that discussed previously as proof of construct validity. To determine construct validity, a measure must fit a theory about the construct; but to use this evidence, one must assume the theory is true. The circularity of this logic is illustrated by the following four hypotheses:

**1** Constructs A and B correlate positively.
**2** X is a measure of construct A.
**3** Y is a measure of construct B.
**4** X and Y correlate positively.

To be more specific, assume that A is anxiety, B is stress, X is a questionnaire thought to measure anxiety, and Y is an experimental manipulation thought to induce stress. Even though the four hypotheses are not independent, it should be obvious that one experiment cannot test them all simultaneously. Only hypothesis 4, that X correlates positively with Y can be tested directly; it is necessary to *infer* the truth or falsity of the other hypotheses from this test. Note how many possible outcomes there are. Hypothesis 1 may be correct, but even if hypothesis 4 is correct, it would not prove the truth of either or both hypotheses 2 and 3. Obviously X and Y could correlate positively, not because they relate to constructs A and B, respectively, but rather because they relate to some other construct. As another possibility, hypothesis 2 could be correct, but if hypothesis 3 is incorrect, there would be no necessity for X to correlate with Y.

It is apparent that the above paradigm for determining construct validity is invalid from an inductive standpoint. In the illustrative experiment, the experimenter hoped to obtain some evidence for hypothesis 2 (X is a measure of anxiety). All that can be validly tested by the experiment is whether hypothesis 4 is correct (whether X correlates with Y).

Someone wanting to defend the above paradigm could point out that the situation is not nearly as bleak as it has been painted. What is done in practice is to *assume* that two of the hypotheses 1 through 3 are correct. An empirical test of hypothesis 4 then allows a valid inference about the remaining hypothesis. Thus, one would assume that (1) hypothesis 1 is correct (stress relates to anxiety,) and (2) hypothesis 3 is correct (the threat of painful electric shock is a stressor.) If these assumptions are correct, the actual correlation between X and Y permits a valid inference regarding the truth of hypothesis 2 (X is a measure anxiety).

One could further argue that making such assumptions in the modified paradigm above is not really so dangerous. The danger can be lessened by restricting investigations of construct validity to those situations in which some of the hypotheses are clearly true. The evidence for such truth could be based on either other experiments involving the variables (e.g., prior use of electric shock as a stressor) or on an appeal to common sense. Thus, in construct validation, one relates variables in situations where the assumptions are very safe. Nearly everyone agrees that stress should increase anxiety and that the threat of painful electric shock is a stressor. Such assumptions are made even safer by correlating two supposed measures of constructs where the domain of one has previously been both well defined and highly restricted. Thus, if a proposed measure of anxiety is correlated with reaction time, it is rather safe to assume that the reaction time validly represents the construct of response latency.

In the limiting case, construct validity concerns a hypothesized relationship between a supposed measure of a construct and a particular observable variable. Thus, the specific measures of academic accomplishment that one might hypothesize are correlated with tests of intelligence include grades in school, teachers' ratings of intelligence, and level of professional accomplishment. These academic variables are constructs only in that slight variations are possible in the measurement of each (e.g., which teachers do the rating and how the ratings are conducted), and these variations may have little effect on the resulting correlations with intelligence measures. This reduces the number of hypotheses in the above paradigm from four to three because the hypothesis "Y is related to B" becomes the assumption "Y is B." If the assumption A relates to B (e.g., intelligence relates to progress in school) is very safe, an empirical correlation of X with Y provides a safe basis of inference regarding the construct validity of A as a measure of X. According to this point of view, construct validity studies are safe and should be undertaken only when (1) the domain of the "other" construct is well defined and (2) the assumption of a relationship between the two constructs is inarguable.

## Campbell and Fiske's Contribution to Construct Validation

Campbell and Fiske (1959) published a key article on construct validation. They viewed reliability and validity as points along a continuum rather than as sharply distinguished ideas since each involves degrees of agreement between measures. Their introduction makes four key points:

**1** Validation is typically *convergent* because it is concerned with demonstrating that two independent methods of inferring an attribute lead to similar ends. This often involves correlating a new measure with an existing measure, but it may also involve correlating two existing measures.

**2** In order to justify novel measures of attributes, a measure should have *divergent* validity in the sense of measuring something different from existing methods. Measures of different attributes should therefore not correlate to an extremely high degree.

**3** A measure is jointly defined by a *method* and attribute-related *content*. Two measures may differ in method, content, or both.

**4** At least two attributes, each measured by at least two methods, are required to examine discriminant validity. Table 3-1 contains a matrix of correlations among measures that results from meeting these minimal requirements. In the example, the two attributes (traits) are anxiety and depression, and the two methods are self-report, as on an MMPI scale, and observation, as a clinical rating. These data form a multitrait-multimethod matrix.

Although they did not introduce the concept in their article, divergent validity describes the ability of a measure to produce relevant group differences. For example, people diagnosed as depressed should score higher on a measure of depression than the population at large.

There are four types of correlations in a multitrait-multimethod matrix. "Reliability coefficients" describe the extent to which a measure is internally consistent in the sense that its components all measure the same thing (see Chapter 6) and appear along the diagonal. A "heterotrait-monomethod correlation" denotes the correlation between two measures that share a common method but assess different attributes. These have been shortened to "method correlation" in Table 3-1. Conversely, a "monotrait-heteromethod correlation" ("trait correlation" for short) denotes a correlation between two measures of the same trait using different methods. Finally, a "heterotrait-heteromethod correlation" (neither) is a correlation between different attributes using different methods. One normally expects the reliabilities to have the highest values, although it is mathematically possible for this not to be the case. At the other extreme, heterotrait-heteromethod correlations should be the lowest since they differ both in what is measured and how it is measured. However, these correlations need not to be zero because neither the methods nor the traits need to be independent. There may be shared method variance among alternative approaches. For example, a clinical evaluation of depression by a clinical psychologist shares the method of observation with anxiety ratings made by nonprofessional staff.

**TABLE 3-1**  MULTITRAIT-MULTIMETHOD MATRIX FOR TWO TRAITS (ANXIETY AND DEPRESSION) MEASURED UNDER TWO METHODS (SELF-REPORT AND OBSERVATION)

| | | Self-Report | | Observation | |
|---|---|---|---|---|---|
| Method | Trait | Anxiety | Depression | Anxiety | Depression |
| Self-report | Anxiety | Reliability | Method | Trait | Neither |
| Self-report | Depression | Method | Reliability | Neither | Trait |
| Observation | Anxiety | Trait | Neither | Reliability | Method |
| Observation | Depression | Neither | Trait | Method | Reliability |

Generally, construct validation demands that trait correlations be high to reflect convergent validity, and that method correlations be relatively low to reflect discriminant validity. Neither is particularly easy to achieve. Methods, especially those based upon self-report, are often highly correlated because of method variance. Results are often highly attribute specific. For example, it is not uncommon for self-descriptive, clinical, and physiological evaluations of anxiety to be poorly related. Shared method variance with other traits may make the concept difficult to measure (Martin, 1961; Lang, 1969). On the other hand, magnitudes of depression as inferred by different methods seem more highly related (Rush, 1987).

Recent trends in confirmatory factor analysis, as discussed in Chapter 13 (see Bentler, 1986; Bernstein, 1988; Breckler, 1990; Byrne, 1990; Gorsuch, 1983; Hayduk, 1987; Loehlin, 1987) have attracted a new generation of investigators to multitrait-multimethod matrices. Hammond, Hamm, and Grassia (1986) represent another use of these matrices in studying the coherence or clarity with which raters define their concepts.

## PREDICTIVE VALIDITY

"Predictive validity" concerns using an instrument to estimate some criterion behavior that is external to the measuring instrument itself. Some refer to predictive validity as "criterion-related validity," which defines the processes involved well. However, this use conflicts with other hyphenated terms involving the word "criterion" that are encountered in special problems of testing.

Developing a test for college admission illustrates a predictive validity problem. The test ultimately chosen is useful only insofar as it estimates academic performance, perhaps defined as overall grade-point average. After the criterion is obtained, the validity of prediction is straightforward to determine, as it primarily consists of correlating scores on the predictor with scores on the criterion. The size of the correlation directly indicates the predictive validity.

### The Temporal Relation Between Predictor and Criterion

Used generically, "predictive validity" refers to functional relations between a predictor and criterion events occurring before, during, and after the predictor is applied. Thus a test administered to adults could be used to "predict" childhood events (usually in the form of contemporary reports of what happened then). A test intended to "predict" brain damage is, of course, not intended to forecast who will become brain-damaged in the future but rather to determine who is brain damaged at the time the test is administered. A test used to predict academic success properly involves forecasting. Others have distinguished predictive validity at those three points in time, respectively, as "postdiction," "concurrent validity," and "prediction."

Using different terms, however, implies that the *logic* and *procedures* of validation are different, which is not true. In each case a predictor measure is related to a criterion measure. After the data are available, it does not matter when they were obtained. The nature of the problem dictates when the two sets of measurements are obtained.

Thus to forecast success in college, it is necessary to administer the predictor instrument before students go to college; and to obtain the criterion of success in college, it is necessary to wait.

Although the temporal relation between the predictor and criterion makes no logical or procedural difference, the results may not be interpretable in the same way. For example, consider administering a personality test to a group of veteran salespeople. These individuals typically know how well they have performed compared to their peers since their income often reflects their sales and their sales manager may have told them (especially, if they were performing poorly.) An ineffective salesperson may be painfully aware of his or her low salary. The personality test may reveal depression, anxiety, and other symptoms. However, these need not be the *cause* of the disparity in sales; they may be the *result*. These traits may not have been present when the individual was hired, and the results were of greatest interest to the company. A psychologist has an ethical obligation to reveal this interpretive ambiguity to the company.

Similarly, predictive validity typically decreases as time elapses between the measurements of the predictor and the criterion. Assuming that the predictor is obtained first, anything that happens to influence the criterion after the predictor scores are obtained must reduce the predictive validity, and the longer the interval, the more opportunities there are for such events to occur. Using the same example of predicting how well salespeople will perform, consider a salesperson who performed well and in accord with the predictor for a time but had to cease work because of illness.

In a statistical sense, predictive validity is determined by, and only by, the degree of correspondence between predictor(s) and criterion. If the correlation is high, no other standards are necessary. Thus if it were found that accuracy in horseshoe pitching correlated highly with success in college, horseshoe pitching would be a valid measure for predicting success in college.

Nonetheless, sound theory and common sense are useful in selecting predictor instruments—it is in fact unlikely that horseshoe pitching does predict success in college. Moreover, a rationale for using a particular test for employment and admissions is becoming increasingly important: Courts are increasingly demanding some logical connection between predictor and criterion (i.e., construct validity) because of the often raised issue of cultural bias (see the section titled **The Criterion Problem**). The role of theory in guiding prediction is consistent with the view that all validity is construct validity, but one should not miss the point that predictive validity is tied to a relatively specific criterion, unlike construct validity. No amount of apparently sound theory can substitute for lack of a correlation between predictor and criterion. Similarly, if only one test can be used in selection, the test with the highest correlation with the criterion would be the most valid in that situation.

There clearly are additional considerations that determine the usefulness of an actual test in particular applied situations. There are applications in which a test is useful in forecasting performance even if its correlation with the criterion is modest. Such usefulness depends on the size of the available pool of individuals, the proportion of people selected, the difficulty of the performance situation, and other matters. The overall strategy for employing predictor tests is discussed by Cronbach and Gleser (1965), Ghiselli (1966), Guion (1965), Hills (1971), and Horst (1966).

Early conceptions of validity were phrased exclusively in predictive terms, which is now regarded as a considerable oversimplification. Predictive validity is primarily at issue when tests are employed to make *decisions* about people. If the statistical results (usually correlations) lead to wise decisions, the tests have predictive validity. This is especially true when emphasis is empirical (a high predictor-criterion correlation) rather than theoretical (understanding the processes that underlie the correlation). Although predictive validity has an obvious relation to personnel selection, content validation has been dominant in this area for the past 20 years. Regardless, the importance of thinking in terms of general constructs rather than specific criteria needs be underscored.

Predictive validity is especially important in making academic decisions. Many schools still employ the concept of "readiness," and a test of readiness to enter school is valid only to the extent that it predicts how well children actually perform in the first grade. The same is true for graduate admissions testing—tests have predictive validity only to the extent that they serve prediction functions.

Although there is a clear difference between predictor instruments and the criteria they are meant to predict, the two are often confused. Perhaps the most widely discussed example is the extent to which universities describe the quality of their programs in terms of the entrance scores (SATs, GREs, etc.) obtained by their students rather than what happens to the students once they get there.

## The Criterion Problem

Whereas it is easy to talk about correlating a predictor test with its criterion, obtaining a good criterion may actually be more difficult than obtaining a good predictor. Many times, either no criterion is available or the criteria that are available suffer from various faults. This issue has been considered in detail by Cronbach (1971), Ghiselli (1966), and Hills (1971).

Predictive validation accepts the criterion as a *given*, unlike construct validation. The second author has been involved for many years in the evaluation of applicants to law enforcement and security guard positions. This often involves, by law, screening for emotional stability which, we suggest, can be done, albeit imperfectly, with various measuring instruments in a manner acceptable by construct validity standards. However, employers often ask for more—to pick the "best potential officers." The natural response is, "Fine, but how can I know who is the best officer?" Many psychologists have attempted (for the most part, unsuccessfully) to go beyond maladjustment screening (ensuring adequate intelligence is another relevant consideration), but their failures and the often resulting lost legal battles have turned many against more appropriate uses of psychological tests.

Perhaps the most intriguing comment the second author heard about the problem of identifying good officers was from a government official who said, "Well, *I* know the officers who are and aren't good, but my partner doesn't." Had the partner been asked, it is not unlikely she would have said exactly the same thing; it is more likely that she had a different idea, so that the two sets of ratings generated by their conceptions might even have been negatively correlated. As will be noted at several points in this book, if you haven't heard it before, it is impossible to have predictive validity with a random (totally unreliable) criterion. Obviously, the two individuals had different ideas about what was desired. If their ideas were sufficiently different it would be impossible for a predictive instrument to correlate positively with both.

What is known as the "criterion problem"—deciding what to measure—is a core problem associated with many predictive validity situations and can easily raise a dilemma. A natural way to define who is the best officer is to use supervisory ratings. However, such ratings are often highly contaminated with personal biases (Hunter, Schmidt, & Hunter, 1979). Supervisors often react to incidental aspects of the ratees such as their race or gender. These biases need not be negative. Indeed, "bending over backward to be fair" attenuates validity just as much as a negative bias. Both attenuate correlations between the predictor and the criterion (unless the predictor incorporates the same biases). The second author had a related experience involving a situation in which police officers were evaluated for their performance by their superior officers using personality measures obtained at time of initial hiring. The results apparently indicated that the *more* maladjusted officers received better evaluations from their supervisors. In fact, further research using a variety of other measures indicated that the supervisors were actually rating the officers' subservience. This part of the research fell outside the predictive validity paradigm, although it was clearly relevant to construct validation. Hunter and Schmidt (1976) provide a superb discussion of the problems inherent in the term "bias" which will be considered in Chapters 9 and 10.

Industrial and organizational (I/O) psychologists are not the only people who should be concerned about test bias; ratings are not the only measures subject to bias, and bias is not the only problem one encounters in predictive validity. An example of a different kind of problem may arise when one is teaching a learnable skill, such as a technical vocabulary. At the extreme, the teaching may be so effective that everyone masters the material to a high degree, which was the intent of the instruction. The result is that there is no variance in the criterion to be predicted, and so the predictive validity must be undefined. Fortunately, content validation is appropriate since one can show that the items comprising the test are appropriate to the task demands.

### Other Problems in Prediction

Another reason why a test that has construct (or, as will be discussed, content) validity may not have predictive validity is that something may occur to eliminate or minimize relevant differences on the predictor or criterion, the frequently encountered phenomenon of "range restriction." For example, the SAT is often criticized for relating poorly to college grades (Nairn & Nader, 1980), and the GRE and similar tests are likewise criticized for relating poorly to grades in graduate and professional schools. However, the process of selecting students typically makes them fairly homogeneous in cognitive ability, which is what these tests generally measure. Everyone will be smart at competitive schools which use these as selection devices, so differences in other variables, such as motivation and departmental grading standards will dominate prediction of grades.

Even when a test is not used explicitly for selection, other criteria, such as interviews, which tap general ability may be used, and these surrogates may induce similar range restriction. Moreover, variation in cognitive ability among students at even relatively unselective schools is smaller than in the general population (even when the *average* level of cognitive ability is not especially high because of the limited number of students at the high, as well as the low, end of the scale). Range restriction is not limited to purely academic criteria. Job applicants are often selected by means of a cognitive ability measure and then considered for retention and/or promotion some time after initial (probationary) hiring. The initial test may measure a highly relevant attribute, but test scores may be unrelated to whether or not those initially selected are retained and/or promoted since initial selection may eliminate relevant variance in the attribute. Measures that are appropriate for initial selection may therefore be useless for subsequent decisions about promotion or retention. Decisions about retention and promotion should be made on the basis of what has happened during the training or educational process, not on what was used for initial selection. Presumably, the initial screen ensured sufficient ability; other attributes such as motivation dominated later.

Dawes (1971) noted some interesting consequences of range restriction on one variable when other relevant predictors are not considered. Suppose that cognitive ability and motivation actually contribute equally to success at a task like completing graduate school, but, as is common, selection is based upon cognitive ability alone since motivation is difficult to measure. Those selected will clearly vary more in motivation than in cognitive ability, and achievement will likewise depend more upon motivation than upon ability.

An even more interesting point can be illustrated by assuming that cognitive ability and motivation are uncorrelated in the original group. An institution may not be able to obtain many high ability–high motivation applicants. Eliminating these students leaves a negative correlation between ability and motivation in the remaining students. Even if cognitive ability and motivation are related, their relation will be more strongly negative in this remaining pool than in the general pool. Since the most cognitively able are selected from this pool, those selected will also tend to be relatively unmotivated. The practical consequence is that one should not be too stringent in selecting along one dimension when others are relevant and when one may not be able to get those who are best in the general sense to accept. The cognitive abilities measure may still possess construct validity, but its use at the expense of other considerations can be counterproductive.

Part of the problem in selecting a criterion is that any criterion is influenced to a certain degree by random error and is therefore only partially reliable. Psychometric methods discussed in this book are able to handle this problem fairly well, sometimes leading to improved measurement of the very criteria they were intended to measure. The more serious problem is that the criteria may be systematically influenced by factors that may undercut the decision making process. We have noted how gender and ethnic bias (for, as well as against, as noted above) may play a negative role. In addition, an educational psychologist may wish to predict academic success. An obvious criterion is the grade point average. In some situations, typically professional schools, students take a common curriculum and so their grades are based upon a common set of instructors. Individual instructors have idiosyncrasies and biases, of course, which may pose problems. However, everyone knows that students often take courses because of the grade they expect to earn and that departmental standards vary considerably.

### The "Composite Criterion"

Another variation on the criterion problem is that many times the measure available to you as a criterion is a composite of two separable attributes. For example, assembly line workers can vary in the speed of their work, but they can also vary in the accuracy. Their gross output may or may not be of interest. Some correction for the number of defective items is needed to provide a net output measure. In this case, there may be a simple economic answer if the cost of a defective item and the value of an acceptable item can be measured. Assuming this can be done, a predictor which is sensitive to both attributes, to approximately the same extent that they are reflected in the criterion, will provide superior predictive validity compared to one that is a "pure" measure. Note that predictive validity minimally assumes the purity of the predictor, incorporating concerns about illegal bias, and is concerned only that it work in the appropriate context. This contrasts with the construct validity paradigm which stresses pure measures of attributes.

### Validity Coefficients

All these issues indicate that investigators can rarely have faith in their criterion measures, regardless of the area in which they work. Yet, to use predictive validity in contrast to construct validity is to assume that the criterion is appropriate. In a very real sense, the concept of predictive validity is limited in its applicability; construct validity allows one to evaluate the adequacy of the nominal criterion at the same time the nominal predictor is also evaluated. Consequently, predictive validity represents a very direct, simple, but limited issue in scientific generalization that concerns the extent to which one can generalize from scores on one variable to scores on another variable. The correlation between the predictor test and the criterion variable, commonly termed the "validity coefficient," specifies the degree of validity of that generalization.

The validity of individual predictor instruments and combinations of predictor instruments is determined by bivariate and multivariate correlational methods discussed in several later chapters. The simplest type of validity coefficient arises when an individual predictor test is correlated with an individual criterion in a particular circumstance, e.g., the Scholastic Aptitude Test is correlated with grade point averages of students in school X and year Y.

Correlations based upon a single predictor, save for some settings highly dominated by intelligence (general cognitive ability), rarely exceed .3 to .4 (a figure that is also typical of predicting academic success). People are far too complex to permit a highly accurate estimate of their proficiency in most performance-related situations from any practicable collection of test materials. Equally complex are the perturbations affecting criterion measures, e.g., the immense complexity of all the variables involved in determining the average grades of college students or the total amounts of an insurance agent's sales. These immense complexities make it remarkable that predictor tests correlate as highly as they do. For example, scholastic aptitude tests are no less predictive of college grades than are meteorologists' 10-day advance predictions of the weather.

The proper way to interpret a validity coefficient is in terms of the extent to which it indicates a possible improvement in the average quality of persons that would be obtained by employing the instrument in question. Tests that have only modest correlations with their criteria (e.g., correlations of .30 and .40) can improve the average performance of personnel markedly under optimal circumstances, e.g., many applicants for relatively few positions. Of course, many mistakes will be made in prediction, but on the average persons who score high on the test will perform considerably better than persons who score low on the test.

As a simple example, suppose that a test used to select sales agents correlates .30 with their volume of sales. The scatter plot of this may show that the average sales of the highest scoring applicants is 10 percent greater than the average sales. Given enough applicants, the company could increase gross sales by 10 percent, which might make the difference between going into bankruptcy and becoming very profitable. In a similar way, tests that have only modest correlations with their criteria can often make highly important improvements in the average performance of workers that benefit their clients as well.

## Validity Generalization

Treatments of validity a generation ago properly stressed the importance of treating validation as a continuing process. However, they also tended to view validity in extremely narrow terms. If company X found that a test predicted success in a similar company Y, it would naturally be inclined to adopt that same test. However, perhaps company X was too small to allow its personnel selection methods to be evaluated. Some argued that the evidence gained from company Y is irrelevant; one would have to conduct a separate validity study in company X. A more recent view is that validity evidence *generalizes* across similar situations (Schmidt & Hunter, 1977). Of course, normal considerations of predictive logic apply. Differences between the two companies in such matters as the variance among their applicants, type of clientele served, etc., reduce the degree of generalization.

There is a second component of Schmidt and Hunter's position. Many early I/O psychologists adopted a "lock-and-key" approach to personnel selection and classification—certain patterns of abilities were better suited for some jobs than others. In contrast, Hunter and Schmidt argue that overall cognitive ability is generally (but not totally) a sufficient predictor. We will not review the pros (Hunter & Hunter, 1984; Hunter & Schmidt, 1981; Schmidt, Hunter, & Pearlman, 1981; Schmidt, Pearlman, Hunter, & Hirsh, 1985) and cons (Sackett, Zedeck, & Fogli, 1988; Prediger, 1989) of this issue. However, note that the statistical issue of whether to use differential weights or equal weights is one of the most general questions there is in psychometric theory and statistics. In general, evidence for the advantages of differential weighting tend to be slight unless samples are extremely large.

One major reason why some recent trends have tended to favor at least partial validity generalization is that many early contrary examples turned out to be statistical artifacts of various types. One common problem is range restriction that differentially operates in one situation relative to another. For example, if company X tends to recruit applicants who vary more widely in relevant skills than company Y, validity coefficients will also tend to be higher in company X. Our previous example involving the SAT at schools that vary in selectivity illustrates this point; parallel examples exist in industry among companies that vary in the ratio of applicants to people hired. When apparent differences in validity affect groups defined by gender or ethnicity, the term "differential validity" is used as part of the more general issue of test bias. Chapters 9 and 10 consider these issues which are understandably quite politically sensitive. Chapter 5 will consider a procedure called moderated multiple regression that is apparently less sensitive to differences in variance than comparing correlation magnitudes.

## Meta-analysis

"Meta-analysis" (Hedges & Olkin, 1985; Hunter, Schmidt, & Jackson, 1982) involves aggregating results across studies in order to obtain a more powerful and stable estimate of effect magnitudes. For example, the mean difference associated with a given experimental effect may be too small in each of a series of individual studies to be significant, but it may be significant when the results are pooled, reflecting the increased sample size. Examples of meta-analyses appear in nearly every issue of the *Psychological Bulletin*. Meta-analysis is extremely useful in aggregating well-done studies hampered by small sample size and in averaging out spurious effects that operate in both directions on a difference. Consequently, it can be a useful tool to integrate the literature. However, a significant effect in a meta-analysis may arise because of a spurious influence (confound), just as in a single study. Meta-analysis is no substitute for careful evaluation of individual studies' procedures and results, and it was never intended as a "meat grinder" to average out results of studies that vary in their quality of execution. Careful evaluation of individual studies may suggest why the effect of interest occurred in certain studies and not in others.

## CONTENT VALIDITY

Validity sometimes depends greatly on the adequacy with which a specified domain of content is sampled. A prime example is a final examination in an introductory psychology course. Obviously, predictive validity is not relevant because the test is designed to measure academic performance *directly* and not to predict something else. The test must stand by itself as an adequate measure of what it is supposed to measure. In essence, the test *is* the criterion of performance.

One might argue for a construct validation approach. Even if course examinations were to be validated in terms of some external criterion, what behaviors would be adequate? One might see whether students take another course in that field. However, a student might deserve an A in the course by any standard but never take another course in that area because it was simply an elective. Of course, one would expect the test to correlate with some other variables, and the size of such correlations provides some hints about the test's adequacy.

For example, one would expect to find a substantial correlation between final examination scores in introductory psychology and abnormal psychology among students who took both courses. A correlation of zero would make one suspect that something was wrong with one or both of the examinations or with one or both courses. However, such correlations offer only hints about the validity of the examinations, with verification resting on the adequacy with which content had been sampled. The lack of correlation might well reflect range restriction caused by the inability of students who performed poorly in the introductory course to take the more advanced course—anyone reading this book knows how their desires to take more advanced courses were influenced by earlier course grades. These difficulties suggest an alternative approach to evaluating the examination—content validity reflecting how well the course material was sampled.

Many other measures require content validation. These include course examinations in all types of training programs and at all levels of training. All commercially distributed achievement tests require content validity, as in a comprehensive measure of school progress. Although measures used in personnel selection are not absolutely required to have content validity, their general acceptance is enhanced when they do. For example, both employers and employees react more positively to tests that appear related to job demands.

One should ensure content validity (adequacy of sampling the material on which people are tested) in terms of a well-formulated plan and procedure of test construction *before* the actual test is developed rather than evaluate this *after* construction. One example is to construct a spelling test for fourth-grade students by randomly sampling words occurring in readers used at that level. The plan is to sample randomly from a specified domain of content, and potential users should agree that the procedure ensures a reasonably representative collection of words.

In addition, a sensible procedure is required to transform the words into a test. One possibility is multiple choice—each correctly spelled word is grouped with three misspellings. Alternatively, the teacher may read the word aloud and require the student to write the correct spelling. A variety of factors such as class size would dictate the choice, and there would be a variety of other decisions, such as the specific instructions to be used. The validity of the measure is judged by the character of the plan and the skill with which the plan has been carried out. If most potential users of the test agree that the plan was sound and well carried out, the test has a high degree of content validity. Further information on content validation may be found in Nunnally (1972) and Thorndike (1971).

The spelling test illustrates the two major standards for ensuring content validity: (1) a representative collection of items and (2) "sensible" methods of test construction. Of course, most times these standards are not so easily judged. It is often logically impossible or infeasible to actually sample content. For example, how should one adequately sample items on a geography test, as neither the sampling unit nor the domain is well defined? One could sample sentences from textbooks and turn them into true-false items, but such a test is obviously inadequate. Rather, one must formulate a collection of items that broadly represents the course. To ensure that the items actually represent the course, a syllabus (blueprint) of relevant questions and problems is needed. Judging the quality of the outline in such cases is an important part of the assessment.

A simple random sampling of content is usually unrealistic for a second reason: The selection of content usually involves questions of values. Thus, there may be good reason to stress spelling performance on nouns rather than on adjectives and verbs, or quantitative concepts rather than numerical computations in an arithmetic test. This is true of nearly all measures based on content validity: Values determine the relative stress on different content areas. Of course, where values are important, there will be differences in values among people and therefore about the proper content coverage of particular tests. The values underlying a measure and its construction should be made explicit, e.g., in test manuals (see Krathwohl and Payne, 1971).

Deciding what is a sensible method of test construction further complicates content validation. This is not much of a problem with spelling tests, because it is relatively easy to construct a satisfactory test. Indeed, a domain of content (see Chapter 6 for a more complete discussion of this crucial construct) can be well defined by supplying the list of words to be used in testing. The test itself could then be generated by a random process, although this is not necessary. Other areas often require much more skill. Wesman (1971) discusses the construction of test items. Problems often arise in content validation because it primarily rests on appeals to reason about the adequacy with which important content has been sampled and cast into test items. However, there are ways to analyze test data that provide important circumstantial evidence (see Henryssen, 1971; Cronbach, 1971; Hambleton, 1980; Rovinelli & Hambleton, 1977).

One expects at least a moderate level of internal consistency among the test items; i.e., the items should tend to measure something in common (see Chapter 8). This is not an infallible guide, however, because it is reasonable with some subject matter to include materials that tap somewhat different abilities (just as is appropriate in some predictive situations). For example, skill at numerical computation and ability to quantify are not identical, but a good argument could be made for mixing these two types of content when measuring overall progress in arithmetic.

Another type of circumstantial evidence for content validity is that learning normally causes posttest scores to increase over pretest scores. The improvement on individual items is some evidence for their validity. There are, however, numerous flaws in this reasoning. Any trivial item like spelling the teacher's name may show marked improvement. Conversely, some very important items may improve little on the posttest because of inadequate texts, unskilled teachers, or lazy students.

Another type of evidence for content validity is obtained from correlating scores on different tests purporting to measure much the same thing, e.g., two different commercial tests claiming to measure achievement in reading. It is comforting to find them highly correlated, but this does not guarantee content validity. Both tests may measure the same wrong things.

In spite of efforts to settle every psychological measurement issue by a flight into statistics, content validity is mainly settled in other ways. Although helpful hints are obtained from analyses of statistical findings, content validity primarily rests upon an appeal to the propriety of content and the way that it is presented.

Content validity also relates to a rather direct issue in scientific generalization—the extent to which one can generalize from a particular collection of items to all possible items in a broader domain of items. This type of scientific generalization is obviously at issue in developing an achievement test for spelling. The intention is to obtain a sample of words that is representative of those in the learning environment of students at a particular grade level. Although the item collections are usually formulated rather than statistically sampled in testing spelling ability and other types of achievement (e.g., knowledge of law enforcement practices for a civil service examination for promoting police officers), the intention is still to obtain as representative a collection of item material and relevant content as possible. Similarly, the testing method should produce results very similar to those of alternative approaches. A representative sampling of content and testing method permits the maximum generalizability of results.

## EXPLICATION OF CONSTRUCTS

Our earlier discussion of construct validation is probably well accepted by most theorists, although perhaps some related procedures were specified in more detail than is typically the case. We hope we have provided a workable set of standards for the measurement of psychological constructs. There is, however, a more defensible logic the reader may wish to use in thinking about the measurement of psychological constructs. Rather than refer to this logic as construct *validation,* it is more correct to refer to it as construct *explication*—the process of making an abstract word explicit in terms of observable variables.

A potential problem with our earlier logic in determining construct validity is that it might permit an unwary individual to assume that a construct has objective reality beyond that used to measure the construct. Thus we speak of anxiety as though it were a "real" variable to be discovered empirically. Treating a term as if it denotes a real entity or process is called "reification" and has caused many problems in science.

Evidence is often used to support or refute arguments about whether or not a construct has been measured. One hears psychologists say, "This is not really a measure of anxiety" or "Scale X provides a good measure of anxiety." Inherent in this and other statements used in discussing the measurement of constructs is the implicit assumption that constructs have objective reality, i.e., exist beyond the measures proposed to describe them. It is more defensible to make no claims for the objective reality of a construct name such as "anxiety" and simply use the construct name as a convenient label for a particular set of observable variables. The name is "valid" only to the extent that it accurately describes the kinds of observables being studied to others.

A more airtight set of standards for construct validity starts with the definition of a set of measures concerning observables. Thus set $A$ might consist of measures of observables $X_1$, $X_2$, $X_3$, etc., and set $B$ might consist of observables $Y_1$, $Y_2$, $Y_3$, etc. The $X$'s might be different measures of anxiety and the $Y$'s different measures of retention. Construct validation (the term will be modified later) then consists of forming a network of statements relating the different measures in set $A$, and then in set $B$. The two sets are then related to one another and perhaps to other sets. The resulting conclusions are, of course, probabilistic ("best guesses" given the data).

There are many ways to do this, depending on what types of empirical studies have been and will be undertaken and the types of statements that make the most theoretical sense. The most straightforward example is where individual differences on the different measures within a set are correlated with one another. Thus $X_1$ may correlate .50 with $X_2$ and .45 with $X_3$, and $X_2$ may correlates .55 with $X_3$. One could define confidence intervals for scores on the three measures knowing these correlations. If, for example, a person has a score of 20 on measure $X_1$, one could determine the probability that the person will score between 40 and 60 on $X_2$. Although one seldom needs to derive such confidence intervals explicitly, correlations among the measures determine their properties.

The correlations among the individual observables then make it possible to infer correlations among different combinations of variables using methods described in Chapter 5. Thus, one can deduce the correlation between the sum of one set of three measures in the set and another three measures in the set. More importantly, one can deduce the correlation between any particular measure in the set and the sum of *all* measures in the set.

Additional studies provide more information about how variables in a particular set intercorrelate. The totality of such information forms the internal structure of these elements (observables). As noted above, this structure may indicate that all the variables tend to measure (1) a single construct, which supports retaining the set as originally defined (2) two or more things, which dictates dividing the original set $A$ into several sets $A_1$, $A_2$ ..., or (3) nothing in common (possess no structure), because all correlations are very low. In case 3 it is illogical to speak of the variables as constituting a set, and the investigator should focus on other sets of variables. Factor analysis is invaluable for studying such internal structures.

Statements may also be made about variables in *different* sets. Thus, assume that a particular variable $X_1$ in $A$ is correlated with a particular variable $Y_1$ in set $B$. Depending on the size of the correlation, it might then be possible to infer (probabilistically) unknown correlations involving other variables in the two sets. For example, if $X_1$ and $X_2$ are known to correlate highly and if $Y_1$ and $Y_2$ are known to correlate highly, a high correlation between $X_1$ and $Y_1$ leads one to expect a high correlation between $X_2$ and $Y_2$.

Similarly, if the sum of the variables in $A$ correlates highly with the sum of the variables in $B$, it is possible to estimate the correlation between any particular variable from $A$ and $B$ or the correlation between any two combinations of variables from $A$ and $B$. Thus, in addition to the two internal structures within sets $A$ and $B$ taken separately, there is a cross structure between variables in the two sets. If the internal structure of any set is well defined, a scientist may explore cross structures of that set with other sets. The simplest case is to correlate the average score over the variables in one set with the average score over variables in the other set. Such cross structures provide scientific progress: Theories may be tested and/or interesting discoveries made.

The measurement and validation of constructs ultimately consists of nothing more than determining internal structures and cross structures, usually in the context of some broader theory that suggests variables, constructs, and their relations. However, laypeople and scientists alike are disquieted by looking at things this way. The system requires more meaning. Scientists are not content to say only that particular variables relate to one another; they want to make broader statements. As was mentioned previously, words denoting constructs are essential for the scientist to think about problems, formulate theories, and communicate the results of experiments. This need for names pushes the scientist, and the layperson even more, into assuming that *some* real variable identifying the construct will be discovered some day. For example, some psychologists talk as though some "real" counterpart to the word "anxiety" eventually will be "found." The problem is not one of searching for a needle in a haystack, but of assuming that the needle exists in the first place.

The words that scientists use to denote constructs (e.g., "anxiety" and "intelligence") have no real counterparts in the world of observables; they are only heuristic devices for exploring observables. Whereas, for example, the scientist might find it more comfortable to speak of anxiety than of set *A,* only set *A* and its relations objectively exist, research results relate only set *A,* and, in the final analysis, only relations within members of set *A* and between set *A* and members of other sets can be unquestionably documented.

Although words relating to constructs are undeniably helpful to the scientist, they also can cause real trouble. Such words only designate collections of observables. Thus the word "fear" is a symbol for many possible forms of behavior. The difficulty is that the individual scientist is not sure of all the observables that relate to such a word, and scientists frequently disagree about which observables are related to the set. A word's denotations can be no more exact than the extent to which (1) all possible related observables are specified and (2) all who use the word agree on the specification. Dictionary definitions of words concerning constructs help very little; they serve only to relate one unspecified term to other unspecified terms.

Considering the inexactness of denotations of words defining constructs, it is impossible to *prove* that any collection of observables measures a construct. It is much like an expedition starting out to photograph a rare bird, an "awrk." The scientists may agree that the awrk has red wings, a curved bill, and only two toes, but everything else about the awrk may be either unknown or in dispute. How, then, would the expedition ever know for sure whether it has found an awrk since other birds may have these same three properties? The analogy really is not farfetched; the same inconsistency is apparent in efforts to "find" measures of some constructs such as "rigidity."

Although one can never prove that any set of measurement methods precisely fits a construct name in a strict sense, there are forms of verification that satisfy the major requisite properties. The scientist starts with a word like "anxiety" and hypothesizes a set of related observables from it. The internal structure of those observables can be verified by previously noted methods. If some combination of the members of this set of variables relates strongly to some combination of the members of another set as predicted from the theory, the first set has explanatory power. If it is useful to call these two steps "construct validation," no harm is done, but one should understand what is being tested and how the related evidence is gathered.

It would be good if words denoting constructs were altered as evidence is obtained about relevant sets of observables, but this is unfortunately not done as frequently as it should be. Ideally, one could envision a process whereby gradual refinements of a set of observables are matched by gradual refinements of the words used to denote the set.

Thus, relatively inexact terms like "anxiety" and "intelligence" would be successively replaced by terms that are more denotatively exact for a set of observables, and the set itself would be continually refined as its internal structure and cross structure became better articulated (specific, empirically grounded terms like "state" and "trait anxiety" are a start in this direction). It is doubtful, though, that any terms in common parlance will ever suffice to serve this purpose. Unfortunately, research tends to produce new terms *and* to retain old ones.

Although it may be useful to think of measuring a construct or testing a theory about that construct, these ideas are best viewed as "useful fictions." A construct is only a word, and although the word may suggest explorations of the internal structure of an interesting set of variables, there is no way to prove that any combination of these variables actually "measures" the word. Theories consist of collections of words (statements about natural events), and though such theories may suggest interesting investigations of cross structures among sets of observables, the evidence obtained describes the utility of the theory and not its truth. Call it the measurement and validation of constructs if you like, but science can only provide (1) words denoting constructs, (2) sets of variables presumably related to these constructs, (3) evidence about the internal structures of such sets, (4) words concerning relations among constructs (theories), (5) cross structures among different sets of observables implied by these words, and (6) evidence regarding such cross structures. It can provide nothing more.

### Changing Substantive Theories versus Changing Measurement Theories

The development of any instrument must be guided by a theory even if that theory is relatively informal, and we have stressed that a theory consists of a measurement and a structural component that, respectively, deal with the definitions of constructs and their interrelations. A favorable outcome of any given study effectively supports both aspects of the theory since it is consistent with the premises that the observables defining the construct have been properly chosen and that the relation to other variables is also as it should be. However, even in this situation the support may be illusory: The relations that are observed may arise for a different reason than that postulated. For example, a badly designed study may produce higher scores among schizophrenics than normals because of a failure to motivate schizophrenics; another study properly motivating them may find no difference.

Theories are always incomplete in failing to predict all relevant relations. Virtually every measure that became popular led to new unanticipated theories. This is the "heuristic" value of a theory. Such new discoveries lead to expansions of the original theory to take the new discoveries into account.

The obvious problem is what to do when the results of using measures are inconsistent with the theory. The theory may predict a relationship that is not found, the absence of a relationship when one exists, or a relationship in the wrong direction. The measure, the theory, or both need to be modified if one is to continue this direction of research. There are no guidelines for making an appropriate choice. The investigator may take consolation in the fact that such negative results sometimes are a real contribution. A great many theories grow out of the everyday experience of the researcher and are quite likely to be shared with other investigators. Formalizing a theory is one of the best ways to reveal flawed or overly narrow conceptions.

A final possibility is to abandon the area of research. What to do here has the same uncertainty as the issue of what to revise. Sometimes progress could not be made because of technological limitations that were later overcome. Applications of now-popular techniques based upon complex numerical analysis developed in the days before computers is one important example. Science has numerous recorded instances of individuals who clearly devoted too much of their career to the wrong problem, but it also contains other instances of people who prematurely stopped short.

### A Commonsense Point of View

We have tried to make you properly uneasy if you believed that science could ever establish the "ultimate reality" of a construct. We will now come back down to earth and take a commonsense point of view. Although there is nothing wrong with our previous analysis of constructs, one could rightly argue that our concerns about construct validity really boil down to something rather homespun, namely, the quality of the circumstantial evidence of a new measurement method's utility. New measurement methods and newly defined variables, like most new things, should not be trusted until they have been thoroughly tested. If a measuring instrument produces interesting findings over the course of numerous investigations and fits the construct name applied to it, investigators should be encouraged to continue using the instrument and to use the construct name in referring to it. On the other hand, if the resulting evidence is dismal, as it often is, scientists should be discouraged from wasting their time on the instrument and wonder if it really fits the name of the attribute employed to describe it. If it is not possible to find sets of variables that relate to the construct, the construct itself should be questioned. Essentially this is what construct validity is about from the behavioral scientist's perspective.

## OTHER ISSUES CONCERNING VALIDITY

### Relations among the Three Types of Validity

Whereas the three types of validity were discussed separately in order to emphasize their differences, they actually tend to complement one another in practice (Amastasi, 1986). There are obvious ways in which construct validity supports predictive validity and content validity. It was mentioned that instruments which are essentially intended to measure constructs sometimes are often used as specific predictors, e.g., measures of cognitive ability. Although the measurement functions of an intelligence test often involve construct validity, as in basic research on inheritance, these tests are also useful in predicting academic or occupational success. The extent to which such tests serve prediction functions enhances the overall construct validity of the instrument.

Content validity also supports construct validity: The same procedures required to ensure content validity are intimately related to defining the domain of observables in construct validity.

Whereas content validity mainly depends on a rational appeal to the care with which a domain of content has been sampled, both predictive validity and construct validity provide important auxiliary information of a more empirical nature. Although achievement tests and other instruments that rely mainly on content validity are not specifically constructed to correlate with other variables, they often prove to be excellent predictors of specific criteria, such as success in higher education.

Although predictive validity may be described directly in terms of a correlation between a measure and a relevant criterion, one often must rely heavily on both content validity and construct validity to support the measure's application, particularly in personnel selection or placement. If a predictor test also has content validity in the sense of following from a well-outlined domain of content, sampling that domain well and testing sensibly provide additional circumstantial evidence for the usefulness of the predictor test beyond the sheer correlation with the criterion. However, as noted above, factors such as range restriction may limit the predictive validity of a measure in a specific application.

Construct validity is especially helpful with predictor tests. The fact that a predictor test is known to correlate well with other measures of a construct that is also known to affect the criterion variable is important circumstantial evidence about the predictor's usefulness. Even though a test that is used specifically for a prediction function should be validated as such, there are many cases where the only recourse is to rely on content validity and construct validity. A test must sometimes be selected before there is an opportunity to demonstrate its predictive validity. For example, the criterion measure might not be available for years after it is necessary to use the predictor instrument. In other cases, either there is no sensible criterion available or the available ones may be obviously biased and/or unreliable. Such instances force one to fall back on content and construct validity. In still other cases, the predictive validity study may be ethically dubious. For example, one should not arm individuals with known histories of severe emotional maladjustment as police officers to evaluate the use of an emotional maladjustment screen. Analog experiments, which contribute construct validity, would of course be encouraged.

## Other Names

Other authors have used different names to describe the three types of validity discussed in this chapter. Predictive validity has been referred to as "empirical validity," "statistical validity," and more frequently "criterion-related validity"; content validity has been referred to as "intrinsic validity," "circular validity," "relevance," and "representativeness"; and construct validity has been spoken of as "trait validity" and "factorial validity."

One frequently sees the term "face validity." Although its definition is somewhat vague, it may best be understood as reflecting the extent to which the test taker or someone else (usually someone who is not trained to look for formal evidence of validity) feels the instrument measures what it is intended to measure. For example, consider an item like "Sometimes I feel like people don't fully understand me" on a self-consciousness measure. This item *might* be valid in any of the above senses; e.g., it might correlate with like items and the total test score might correlate with clinical judgments. However, it might also fail to correlate because everyone feels misunderstood at times. The point is that it *looks* like it measures self-consciousness and therefore has face validity in that sense. Face validity has often been criticized as a concept by psychometricians, and properly so, when it is used as a substitute for any of the forms of evidence cited above. However, this is perhaps too simplistic.

It is easy to confuse face validity with content validity. Face validity concerns judgments about items *after* an instrument is constructed. As discussed previously, content validity is more properly ensured by the plan of content and item construction *before* it is constructed. Thus, face validity can be considered as one limited aspect of content validity, concerning an inspection of the final product to make sure that nothing went wrong in transforming plans into a completed instrument.

The predictive validity of an instrument depends almost entirely on how well the instrument correlates with the criterion it is intended to predict. Consequently, face validity has no direct relevance. Many instruments *look* as though they should correlate well with a criterion but do not, and many other instruments bear no obvious relationship to a criterion but do correlate well with the criterion. It is often desirable that the instrument *not* bear an obvious relation to what is being tested in order to avoid distorting the behavior of those tested. Face validity is, however, sometimes important to prediction in suggesting which instruments *might* correlate well with their criteria. Thus, even though the correlations tell the full story, one should not select predictors at random. Before prediction research is done, there must be some hope that a particular instrument will work. Such hope is fostered when the instrument looks as if it should predict the criterion.

Also, tests usually are more predictive of a criterion if their item content is phrased in the language and the terms of the objects actually encountered in the particular type of performance, other considerations being equal. For example, reading comprehension examinations for police officers frequently phrase questions in terms of law enforcement situations. Face validity therefore plays a important indirect role in the construction and use of predictor instruments.

Face validity thus often plays an important public relations role in applied settings. For example, although the MMPI has been found useful in assessing psychogenic involvement in patients suffering from chronic pain, many patients refuse to take the test because of the implication that they may be "crazy." Some recent success at obtaining greater cooperation has been found with tests that focus more specifically on pain-related symptoms, e.g., Melzack (1975). Less logical is the reluctance of some administrators in applied settings like industry to use predictor instruments which lack face validity. Conceivably, a good predictor of a particular criterion might consist of preferences among drawings of differently shaped and differently colored butterflies, but it may be difficult to convince administrators that the test actually selects employees well.

## The Place of Factor Analysis

For those who are not already familiar with factor analysis, it essentially consists of methods for finding clusters of related variables. Each such cluster, or factor, consists of a group of variables whose members correlate more highly among themselves than they do with variables outside the cluster. Each factor is thought of as a unitary attribute which is measured to greater or lesser degree by particular instruments depending on their correlation with the factor. Such correlations are sometimes spoken of as the "factorial validity" of measures, but it is better to speak of such correlations as the "factorial composition" of measures because the word "validity" is somewhat misleading. Methods of factor analysis and their use in the development of measures will be discussed in Chapters 11 through 13 and at other points in the book, but it is helpful to place some related issues in perspective since factor analysis is intimately involved in validation.

The factorial composition of measures plays a part in all three types of validity discussed in this chapter. Factor analysis is important in selecting instruments to be tried as predictors. Instead of constructing a new test for each applied problem as it arises, one should select a predictor instrument from a "storehouse" of available instruments. Factor analysis can construct such storehouses with known factorial composition. It is much easier to formulate hypotheses about the predictive power possible from particular factors than to formulate hypotheses about the predictive power of instruments developed on an ad hoc basis. We argue in Chapter 8 that developing measures ad hoc in applied prediction is not only highly wasteful of energy but also leads to illogical test construction.

Factor analysis provides helpful evidence about measures that are intended to have content validity. For example, suppose a factor analysis is conducted of a battery of achievement tests and that a presumed mathematics test correlates highly with a verbal comprehension factor. This implies that the phrasing of the items was unduly difficult. Rewording the items may eliminate this problem.

Factor analysis is at the heart of the measurement of psychological constructs. As noted previously, explicating constructs mainly consists of determining (1) the internal statistical structure of a set of variables said to measure a construct and (2) the cross structures between the different measures of one construct and those of other constructs. Factor analysis is used directly in addressing both these issues. To take the simplest case, if all the elements of set $A$ correlate highly with one another and all the elements of set $B$ correlate highly with one another, the members of each set then have high correlations with the factor defined by their respective sets. This is evidence that the two sets, corresponding to two supposed constructs, have a "strong" internal structure. The cross structure of the two sets of measures would be supported, in addition, if the two factors correlate substantially. Methods known as confirmatory factor analysis (see Chapter 13) are especially useful when the relations among the measures follow from a reasonably well-defined theory.

Factor analysis plays an important part in all three types of validity, but it plays a somewhat different part in each. Factor analysis mainly is important to predictive validity in suggesting predictors that will work well in practice. Factor analysis is important to content validity in suggesting how to revise instruments. Factor analysis provides some of the tools needed to define internal structures and cross structures for sets of variables in construct validity.

## SUMMARY

Despite its brevity, this chapter is the most central to the book because no measure is useful in the long run without evidence for its validity, which deals with how well it measures what it purports to measure in the context in which it is to be applied. The term "validity" has three major meanings: (1) construct validity deals with the measurement of psychological attributes, as in developing a measure of anxiety; (2) predictive validity deals with establishing a statistical relationship with a particular criterion, as in developing admissions tests; and (3) content validity deals with sampling from a pool of required content as in a spelling test. Because all three have much in common, many stress the unity of the validation process. However, there are some important differences among the three strategies.

Construct validation requires a substantive theory to define the construct to be measured as well as a measurement theory to provide the measure itself. Constructs are inherently abstract and best viewed as explanatory tools invented by scientists rather than realities to be discovered. Three aspects of the process of construct validation are (1) specifying the domain of relevant variables, (2) determining the extent to which observables measure the same or different things, and (3) doing relevant research to determine if the properties of the measure are consistent with the substantive theory. These three aspects are ideally conducted in the indicated order, but a variety of considerations often make this impractical. Measures that presumably define a given construct should all intercorrelate highly, i.e., be convergent (Campbell & Fiske, 1959) in providing similar functional relationships to other relevant variables that are consistent with the substantive theory. A novel measure should also have divergent validity in the sense of measuring something different from existing methods. It is also important to separate the method variance that reflects the *way* constructs are measured from the content variance reflecting the similarity of what is measured as both contribute to observed correlations. Attempts to achieve this separation may involve a multitrait-multimethod matrix.

Predictive validity in one narrow sense can be evaluated simply in terms of how well the measure relates to its designated criterion, but considerations such as test bias that may jointly affect predictor and criterion also need to be considered. The temporal relation between the predictor and the criterion is also important. For example, if the predictor is actually obtained after the criterion has occurred (postdiction), spurious influences may affect the relationship. Similarly, the longer the interval between obtaining the predictor and a subsequent criterion (prediction), the more opportunities there are for spurious influences to affect the outcome. Prediction is often impaired because the criterion is ill-defined or is a composite of multiple attributes. Moreover, range restriction also attenuates correlations with criteria (validity coefficients) in a variety of ways. Another important consideration is that tests with low-validity coefficients may still substantially improve prediction of such variables as work productivity. Validity generalization deals with the extent to which a measure found valid in one setting proves valid in related settings.

Content validation is the least empirical of the three approaches and depends in large measure on the extent to which authorities agree on how well test material was sampled.

The explication of constructs was then considered. The internal structure of a set of measures is defined by their interrelations. This structure may suggest that a set of measures describe a single construct, describe multiple constructs, or have no useful structure. These measures are then related to determine their cross structure with other variables. A difficult issue arises when the internal or cross structures are not as expected—one must decide whether to change the substantive or measurement theory.

Relations among these three forms of validity were then considered. One consideration that is sometimes important is historically termed "face validity" or the extent to which a test appears valid. Face validity differs from content validity because it is assessed (usually informally) after constructing the measuring instrument; content validity follows from a test plan developed before items are generated. Face validity is not evidence for or against the utility of a measure, but it may be valuable in gaining acceptance of the test by users and test takers. Finally, the importance of factor analysis in evaluating the structure of measures was noted.

## SUGGESTED ADDITIONAL READINGS

EEOC et al. (1978). Adoption by four agencies of Uniform Federal Guidelines on Employee Selection Procedures. *Federal Register, 43,* 38290–38315.

EEOC et al. (1979). Adoption of questions and answers. *Federal Register, 44,* 11996–12009.

Hedges, L. V., & Olkin, I. (1985). *Statistical methods for metanalysis.* Orlando, FL: Academic Press.

Hunter, J. E., & Hunter, R. (1984). Validity and utility of alternative predictors of job performance. *Psychological Bulletin, 96,* 72–98.

Linn, R. L. (1989). *Educational measurement.* New York: American Council on Education.

## CHAPTER 4

# ELEMENTS OF STATISTICAL DESCRIPTION AND ESTIMATION

## CHAPTER OVERVIEW

A great many measures, such as tests in the ordinary sense, involve forming scales from items. Scale scores are basically continuous measures, whereas items are inherently categorical (discrete). We therefore begin the chapter with a consideration of the distinction between the two types of data, noting that the standard mathematical definitions of "continuous" and "discrete" are not necessarily the most useful empirically. For our purposes, any measure which can assume 11 or more levels can be regarded as continuous, and any measure which can assume only 10 or fewer levels can be regarded as discrete.

The next main section is primarily devoted to the Pearson product-moment correlation *(r)* and some related concepts such as variance and covariance. Much of this is an extension of concepts taught in basic statistics. The *r* describes the linear relation between two variables, and a universal measure of relationship, eta ($\eta$), that does not assume linearity is introduced.

The Pearson correlation and the next topic, linear regression, are distinct concepts, as *r* describes the joint relation between two measures, whereas regression involves predicting one measure from another. However, *r* plays an important role in regression, as it is the slope of the regression line in predicting one standardized score from another using least-squares estimation. In turn, linear regression is also closely related to structural equations in which observable variables are treated as joint functions of unobservable (latent) variables.

Least squares is a popular method of statistical estimation, but it is only one of many. The chapter concludes with a consideration of some alternatives, in particular, maximum likelihood. If you thoroughly understand the elements of statistical description discussed in this chapter, particularly the variance of measurements and covariance among different measures, you will have little difficulty in understanding the theory of measurement error, measurement of reliability, test construction, and multivariate analysis. Although you may already have been introduced to some of these topics, reminders might prove helpful. Also, we will make an effort in this chapter to relate relevant issues to more complex topics discussed throughout the remainder of the book and to introduce some important recent developments.

## CONTINUOUS VERSUS DISCRETE (CATEGORICAL) VARIABLES

Mathematically, a "continuous" variable or constant is one that may assume a value intermediate between any two other values. The system of real numbers is continuous because at least one number (actually an infinity of numbers) is intermediate between any two other numbers. For example, 1.01121 (or 1.01123) is intermediate between 1.0112 and 1.0113. In contrast, data are discrete or categorical when this is not the case. Integers are discrete (categorical) because there is no integer between 103 and 104, for example.

This definition is not useful in the physical world because the limitations of measurement make any data categorical: The resolution of any measuring instrument, be it the physicist's or the psychologist's, is finite. Improvements in techniques often increase the precision and therefore the number of categories, but the number remains finite and therefore inherently discrete even though the resulting number of categories may be very large.

The fact that all real measurement is discrete limits the utility of this mathematical distinction, but it can be extremely valuable with a slight modification. Much measurement, most obviously ordinary tests scored using the linear model of Chapter 2, consists of aggregating item responses to obtain a total (composite) score. The individual items on this test have two important properties: (1) The data they provide fall into an extremely small number of ordered categories (quite often as few as two, such as right versus wrong) and (2) they are quite "noisy" in the sense described in Chapter 2, i.e., in the sense of being influenced by a large number of factors. In contrast, the total score provides a much larger number of categories and, as will be noted in Chapters 6 through 10, a much more reliable outcome. We concentrate on property 1 in this section.

We will somewhat arbitrarily treat a variable as continuous if it provides 11 or more levels, even though it is not continuous in the mathematical sense. Consequently we will normally think of item responses as discrete and total scores as continuous. The number 11 is not "magical," but experience has indicated that little information is lost relative to a greater number of categories. Moreover, the law of diminishing returns applies, and so using even 7 or 9 categories does little harm if the convenience of reporting data as a single digit is important to the application. In many cases, correlational analysis must be performed with fewer levels of measurement (as low as 2 in some problems), in which case important information is lost.

One factor that determines how much information is lost by restricting the number of categories is how well subjects can discriminate between levels of the stimuli: The easier it is to tell stimuli from one another, the more benefit there is to increasing the number of categories. In the limiting case in which the stimuli are not perceptibly different, even a division into two categories will be meaningless (Garner, 1960).

Many analyses assume that data are continuous. This is implicit in those that assume that error is normally distributed since one cannot have normally distributed error without continuity. Indeed, continuity rather than normality is usually the more important. Most analyses are robust with respect to some underlying assumptions in the sense that even moderately substantial violations can leave the essential results unaffected. This is not the case when one neglects the distinction between discrete and continuous (in the present, nonmathematical sense) and, for example, treats item responses as if they were scale scores. This is especially true for analyses that involve correlations. The reasons for this will be discussed below.

## VARIANCE

One might say that scientific issues are posed only to the extent that objects or people *vary* with respect to particular attributes. The speed of light in a vacuum is a constant, and so there is no room to investigate differences in the speed of light in a vacuum. Likewise, the question "I feel awkward speaking to strangers" would not be useful on a questionnaire if everyone endorsed it. Constants found in nature often prove useful in equations specifying relations among attributes that do vary, but there is otherwise nothing to investigate about a constant per se.

Variation is as necessary to the effects of experimental manipulations as it is to the study of individual differences. For example, if the amount of stress is varied and subjects then respond to an anxiety questionnaire, the results are of interest only to the extent that mean anxiety measures differ among groups. In general, variance among people in an attribute is of interest to studies of individual differences, whereas variance among group means is of interest to experiments. This makes the considerations involved in the two situations somewhat different. Cronbach (1957) offers a cogent discussion of the consequences of this distinction. Scientists look for attributes that vary considerably, develop measures of these attributes, and attempt to "explain" such sources of variation with theories and experimentation.

The purpose of a scientific theory is to explain as much variation of interrelated variables as possible. That is, a theory should have a high level of generalizability in its explanatory power. Variance is explained by studying how measures of different attributes jointly vary (covary). The scientist hopes to find a relatively small number of basic variables that explain the variation in many other variables. The variance of one variable is explained by another to the extent that the variables covary or correlate. Thus, if performance in school correlates highly with measures of intelligence, social background, motivation, and others, performance in school is explained by these other variables. To the extent that familiarity affects ratings of how attractive stimuli are, familiarity explains judgments of attractiveness. At the same time that we focus upon the explanation of variance, we restate the old adage, "Correlation is not causation." It is perhaps easier to lose sight of this point when some of the complex procedures described in this book are used than in the simpler examples you may have been given in earlier books.

Although there are many possible measures of variation, or dispersion, Eq. 4-1 has proven by far the most fruitful:

$$\sigma^2 = \frac{\Sigma x^2}{N} = \frac{\Sigma(X-\overline{X})^2}{N} \qquad (4\text{-}1)$$

where $\sigma^2$ = variance of a measure $X$
$x$ = deviation scores on $X = X - \overline{X}$
$N$ = number of measurements

Each $x$ value is the deviation score for a particular person, obtained by subtracting the mean of a set of scores from each of the raw scores. Since the grand mean of raw scores $(x)$ is usually of little interest, raw scores can usually be converted to deviation scores. The variance is the average squared deviation score. Squared deviations are used because they readily lend themselves to algebraic manipulations. A measure of variation cannot be developed from the deviations themselves because their sum is always zero by definition. It is possible to develop measures of variation from the absolute deviations (disregarding signs), but such absolute deviations are very awkward to work with mathematically. Squared deviations allow use of a very wide variety of least-squares and other statistics that have wide applicability. You may never compute deviation scores or a variance using Eq. 4-1, but both will be referred to extensively in subsequent discussion.

Although the variance is easy to work with mathematically, its square root (the standard deviation, $\sigma$) is more useful in description. The standard deviation is expressed in the same units as the measure involved. Thus, a standard deviation, say of 5, on a 40-item test facilitates visualization of the subjects' variability. It is somewhat more difficult to visualize the variance, 25 in this example. The variance is more useful in statistical theory, but the standard deviation is more useful in "making sense" out of data. Since one is directly convertible to the other, choice is a matter of convenience.

We will symbolize the standard deviation by the Greek letter $\sigma$ rather than the ordinary (Latin) $s$ and likewise use $\sigma^2$ to denote the variance. Greek letters are typically employed to denote the standard deviation of the population as a whole, and ordinary letters are used to denote a sample estimate of $\sigma$. It is also common to employ $N - 1$ (the degrees of freedom) rather than $N$ in the denominator to estimate the sample standard deviation, usually symbolized $s$. However, this makes little difference in large samples, and there is a theoretical justification discussed below for using $N$ when one is interested in a maximum likelihood estimate.

The grand mean of raw scores is usually unimportant, as, in addition, are the *absolute* sizes of deviations about the mean since both typically reflect arbitrary units of scaling. The key data are the *relative* sizes of deviations about the mean. The absolute sizes of deviations are artifacts of measurement, as when heights are expressed in inches or meters. Such artifacts of the unit of measurement are eliminated by dividing each deviation score by the standard deviation to produce a standard score. Thus, if someone has a deviation score of +20 (20 points above the mean) and the standard deviation of scores in the group is 10, that individual has a standard score ($z$) of $2 = 20/10$. Similarly, someone with a deviation score of $-10$ on that measure has a standard score of $-1$, i.e., $-10/10 = 1$.

Standard scores are very easy to interpret—each specifies how many standard deviations an individual is above or below the mean. If a distribution of scores is approximately normal, standard scores can be easily interpreted in terms of the percentage of individuals above and below particular points on the score continuum. Since standard scores have such useful descriptive properties, it is important to think in terms of standard scores in discussing various methods of mathematical analysis. As will be discussed later, the correlation between any two measures is exactly the same whether the analysis started with raw scores, deviation scores, or standard scores. Similarly, the results of a particular analysis of variance are the same whether the analysis employed raw scores, deviation scores about the grand mean, or standard scores about the grand mean. A ratio of variance ($F$) is invariant with respect to any linear transformation, Eq. 4-2

$$X' = bX + a \qquad (4\text{-}2)$$

where $X'$ = set of transformed scores
$\quad b$ = any constant multiplier of $X$
$\quad a$ = any constant added to $bX$

The special case of a dichotomous variable that can have only two values (1 versus 0, pass versus fail, etc.) is important. If $p$ is the proportion of persons who pass the item and $q = 1 - p$ is the proportion of persons who fail the item, the variance is then

$$\sigma^2 = pq \qquad (4\text{-}3a)$$
$$= p(1 - p) \qquad (4\text{-}3b)$$

All dichotomous distributions can be scored as 1 or 0 whether they represent quantitative or qualitative dichotomies. Thus, persons with IQs at or above average or females could be scored 1, and those below average or males could be scored 0. Experimentation with Eq. 4-3a will indicate that $\sigma^2$ reaches a maximum value (.25) when $p$ and $q$ are .5 and decreases as $p$ and $q$ deviate from that point. Since $q = 1 - p$, the variance is entirely determined by the size of either of the two values. Thus, two items have the same variance if 80 percent of the individuals pass one item and 20 percent of the individuals pass the other item.

Some people find it odd to think of a dichotomous distribution as having variance. Not only is it mathematically sound to speak of the variance of a dichotomous item, but a moment's reflection will also show that it makes intuitive sense. Variance is uncertainty. A test with a large variance produces more uncertainty about any person's score than a test with a small variance. Similarly, the nearer $p$ is to .5, the more uncertainty there is about an outcome. The closer $p$ is to 1.0, the more certain you are that any given outcome is positive; and the closer $p$ is to .0, the more certain you are that any outcome is negative.

## Transformations of Distributions

The basic formula for the variance (Eq. 4-1) employs deviation scores $(x)$. Because the variance is computed about the mean, the value of the mean itself is irrelevant to $\sigma^2$ and $\sigma$. Thus $\sigma^2$ is not changed if any arbitrary constant is added to or subtracted from every score in a distribution. That constant changes the mean but has no effect on $\sigma^2$ regardless of the original mean.

If a series of scores $(X)$ are multiplied by a constant $(b)$, $\sigma_x^2$ is multiplied by the square of the constant, and $\sigma_x$ is multiplied by the constant.

$$\sigma_{bx}^2 = \frac{\Sigma(bx)^2}{N}$$

$$= \frac{\Sigma b^2 x^2}{N}$$

$$= \frac{b^2 \Sigma x^2}{N}$$

$$= b^2 \sigma_x^2 \qquad (4\text{-}4)$$

where $\sigma_x^2 =$ variance of the original scores, $x$
$b =$ constant multiplier applied to the scores
$\sigma_{bx}^2 =$ variance of the transformed scores, $bx$.

It is frequently useful to transform a distribution of scores to another having a particular mean and standard deviation. Suppose the mean of a set of obtained scores is 40 and the standard deviation is 5. One might wish to transform the original distribution to one having a mean of 50 and a standard deviation of 10 to compare scores on the test with scores on another test or to make them more interpretable. The principles stated lead to Eq. 4-5:

$$X_t = \frac{\sigma_t}{\sigma_o}(X_o - \overline{X}_o) + X_t \qquad (4\text{-}5)$$

where $X_o =$ original scores
$X_t =$ transformed scores
$\overline{X}_o, \overline{X}_t =$ respective means of $X_o$ and $X_t$
$\sigma_o, \sigma_t =$ respective standard deviations of $X_o$ and $X_t$

In the foregoing example, an original score of 40 becomes a transformed score of 50, and an original score of 25 becomes a transformed score of 20. Because the transformation is linear, the shape of the score distribution does not change.

## CORRELATION AND COVARIANCE AS CONCEPTS

Correlational analysis is so basic to psychometric theory and data analysis in general that a thorough understanding of its basic principles is essential to understanding the more advanced topics in this book. There are different indices of correlation, but they all have one thing in common: They describe the degree of relationship between two variables.

Although it is fine to hope for the day when variables or combinations of variables will correlate perfectly, such a day is a long way off. The temperature of an enclosed gas lawfully relates to the average molecular motion but only in a statistical sense. Similarly, the most that psychologists can hope for is a probabilistic correspondence among variables. Experience has taught that the degree of correspondence will not be high. For example, it is unreasonable to expect a very high relationship between predictors of academic success and college grades even though there is a relationship. Similarly, subjects within groups of an experiment usually show considerable dispersion on the dependent variable, and distributions of different treatment groups usually overlap considerably even though there may be mean differences. Correlational analysis is useful in specifying the form and degree of imperfect relationships among variables and constructs.

The choice of a measure of correlation between two variables depends upon which mathematical operations are assumed permissible on the scores (assumptions about scale properties). It will be recalled from Chapter 1 that numbers may be applied to nominal, ordinal, interval, or ratio scales. Since ratio scales are rarely encountered, we will not deal with that situation. Conversely, we will deal with nominal scales in Chapter 15. This reduces the problem to interval and ordinal scales. We will stress methods of correlational analysis applicable to interval scales but note a measure appropriate to ordinal measures.

## THE PEARSON PRODUCT-MOMENT CORRELATION

The "Pearson product-moment" (PM) correlation of two continuous distributions, commonly symbolized as $r$, specifies the magnitude of linear relationship between two variables. It is sometimes important to identify which variables are correlated, in which case we will use subscripts. For example, if $W$, $X$, and $Y$ are three variables, $r_{WX}$ denotes the correlation between $W$ and $X$, $r_{WY}$ denotes the correlation between $W$ and $Y$, etc. Most cases involve only two variables, and so we will simply use the symbol $r$. It is simplest to assume that these scores have been standardized, which makes the means and standard deviations of the raw scores irrelevant. The scores of nine persons on two tests, $z_X$ and $z_Y$ are shown for illustration:

| Person | $z_X$ | $z_Y$ | $z_X z_Y$ |
|--------|-------|-------|-----------|
| a | 1.55 | 1.18 | 1.83 |
| b | 1.16 | 1.77 | 2.05 |
| c | .77 | .59 | .45 |
| d | .39 | −1.18 | −.46 |
| e | .00 | .59 | .00 |
| f | −.39 | −.59 | .23 |
| g | −.77 | −.59 | .45 |
| h | −1.16 | −.59 | .68 |
| i | −1.55 | −1.18 | 1.83 |
| Sum (Σ) | 0.00 | 0.00 | 7.06 |

The magnitude of $r$ $(r_{XY})$ is simply the *average* of these cross products, which is computed as follows:

$$r = \frac{\Sigma z_X z_Y}{N} \tag{4–6}$$

$$= \frac{7.06}{9}$$

$$= .78$$

Equation 4-6 assumes both variables have been standardized. Numerous formulas for $r$ are much simpler than Eq. 4-6 for those rare occasions when calculation must be done by hand. Virtually every introductory text in statistics presents these formulas, and so we will not. Others reveal useful properties of $r$. One is presented below in our discussion of the covariance. You may find it useful to use Eq. 4-6 on a small data sample and compute $r$ by hand once if you have never done so. A scatter diagram of the above pairs of scores is shown in Fig. 4-1. The concept of line of best fit, as identified in Fig. 4-1a, is discussed below.

## The Meaning of the Pearson Product-Moment Correlation

The Pearson product-moment correlation is used so frequently that the word "correlation" itself implies $r$ unless some other measure is stated explicitly. The reasons for its name are as follows. First, it was developed by Karl Pearson. Second, moments of a distribution play a very important role in statistical theory. The $r$th moment about any constant $(c)$, is defined as

$$\frac{1}{N}\Sigma(X - c)^r \tag{4-7}$$

Thus, take each value $(X)$, subtract it from the constant $(c)$, raise the difference to a power $(r)$, and average the results over the number of observations $(N)$. The mean (strictly speaking, the arithmetic mean) is the first moment about the origin ($r = 1$ and

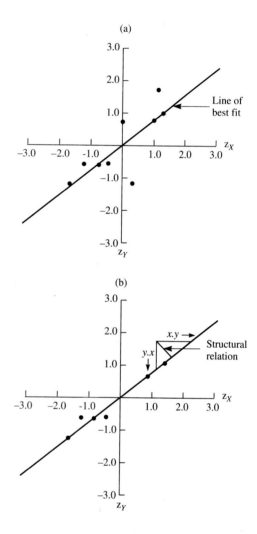

**FIGURE 4-1**    A scatter plot of two sets of standard scores, $z_X$ and $z_Y$. (a) A regression line and (b) how deviations are measured in predicting $Y$ and $X$ ($Y \cdot X$), in predicting $X$ from $Y$ ($X \cdot Y$), and in a structural relation in which it is assumed that $X$ and $Y$ are both funtions of an unobservable (latent) variable and have equal error variance.

$c = 0$); the variance is the second moment about the mean ($r = 2$ and $c = x$ or $\mu$), and various formulas for skewness and kurtosis, used in describing distribution shape, are respectively derived from the third and fourth moments ($r = 3$ and $4$). Not all important statistical concepts are moments, e.g., the median and the mode. Equation 4-6 defined $r$ as the average of the $z_X z_Y$ values, both of which are deviations about a mean raised to the first power and therefore the product-moment. We will return to a consideration of the general concept of moment below.

The $r$ is extremely useful. Its sign and size denote the direction and degree of relationship between two variables. It is easy to show why $r$ cannot be greater than 1.00. If each person had the *same* standard score on $X$ and $Y$, $r$ would equal the variance of a standard score, which is 1.00 as $\Sigma z_X z_Y$ becomes $\Sigma z_X z_X = \Sigma z_x^2$. The maximum negative correlation is when the standard scores of each person are numerically equal but opposite in sign. The average of cross products is $-1.00$.

The advantages of $r$ are that it (1) permits the variance of each of the two measures to be partitioned into meaningful components, (2) may also be used to predict one variable from one other variable (linear regression), (3) is the foundation for predicting one variable from several other variables (multiple regression), and (4) serves as a foundation for many complex methods of correlational analysis, such as multiple correlation, partial correlation, and factor analysis. Points 1 and 2 are considered in this chapter. Point 3 is considered in the next chapter, and point 4 is considered both in the next chapter and in Chapters 11 through 13.

## Computer Applications

Computer packages of any sophistication allow you to compute the correlations among each of a set of variables. They typically also provide univariate statistics (means, standard deviations, etc.). The major complications you are likely to run into are (1) limitations on the number of variables you can intercorrelate in one procedure, (2) problems posed by missing data, and (3) the choice you must make among several options that generate correlations. The first problem can be handled by correlating selected groups of variables. For example, in SAS, you can use the keywords VAR and WITH to delimit the variables you are correlating. Suppose you have 40 variables named X1 to X40. This will pose no problem on a mainframe computer but it might exceed a personal computer's limits. That is, you might run out of memory if you tried to invoke the command PROC CORR;VAR X1-X40; or the equivalent in some other language. In that case, the commands PROC CORR;VAR X1-X20; PROC CORR;VAR X1-X20; WITH X21-X40; and PROC CORR;VAR X21-X40; might achieve the desired end.

Missing data pose more of a conceptual problem. There are three general approaches: pairwise deletion, listwise deletion, and estimation of the missing values from the remaining data. In pairwise deletion, a missing observation for a given variable affects only the specific correlations involving that given variable. In other words, if one subject does not answer question 1 but answers questions 2 and 3, the correlation between variables 1 and 2 and 1 and 3 are based upon one fewer observation than would be the case if the subject had answered question 1, but the correlation between variables 2 and 3 is unaffected. In listwise deletion, the entire case (variables 1, 2, and 3) is eliminated from the analysis.

Pairwise deletion obviously causes fewer data to be lost and may be preferable to listwise deletion when there are but a few, random omissions. However, if there is a pattern to the omissions, say substantially more males than females refuse to answer a given question, correlations between different variables would be more influenced by differences in the subject composition in pairwise deletion. Estimation has become far more common because it can be implemented with relative ease in computer packages. Winer, Brown, and Michels (1991, pp. 479–481) describe unweighted means estimation in the ANOVA. The results obtained from any of these three general approaches should be interpreted with extreme caution when the proportion of missing observations is large, as no method will likely be satisfactory.

### Covariance

*[handwritten margin note: roduct of unstandardized deviation scores]*

The covariance ($\sigma_{XY}$) is defined as the average cross product of two sets of deviation scores:

$$\sigma_{XY} = \frac{\Sigma xy}{N} = \frac{\Sigma(X - \overline{X})(Y - \overline{Y})}{N} \tag{4-8}$$

where $x$ = deviation scores on one measure
$\quad\quad y$ = corresponding deviation scores on another measure
$\quad\quad X, Y$ = raw scores on the two measures
$\quad\quad \overline{X}, \overline{Y}$ = means on the two measures
$\quad\quad N$ = number of pairs (usually persons)
$\quad\quad \sigma_{XY}$ = covariance

Consequently, $\sigma_{xy}$ is the average cross product of *un*standardized deviation scores and therefore also a product of moments. The $\sigma_{xy}$ does not have as many useful properties as $r$. For example, $\sigma_{xy}$ is not restricted to the range of $-1.00$ to $+1.00$. Its magnitude is not directly interpretable unless more is known about the standard deviations of the variables. In other words, the magnitude of $r$ is not affected by the units of measurement, but the magnitude of $\sigma_{xy}$ is. A correlation between weight and height does not depend upon whether weight is expressed in grams, kilograms, or pounds. However, the covariance changes along with the standard deviation (Eq. 4-4) as these units change. The covariance is, however, important to the development of many complex statistics. This is illustrated by the following formula for $r$:

$$r_{XY} = \frac{\sigma_{XY}}{\sigma_X \sigma_Y} \tag{4-9}$$

*[handwritten margin note: r is a standardized covariance ✓]*

The correlation between two measures is therefore the covariance of two measures divided by the product of their respective standard deviations: $r$ is a *standardized* covariance. Phrasing $r$ in this way is very helpful in understanding more complex forms of correlational analysis. Combinations of variables are placed in Eq. 4-9 instead of individual variables at numerous places in the pages ahead.

It is useful to transform Eq. 4-9 as follows:

$$\sigma_{XY} = r_{XY}\sigma_X\sigma_Y \tag{4-10}$$

This shows that the covariance equals $r$ times the product of the two standard deviations.

### Other Measures of Linear Relation

Many other measures of linear correlation have been developed (see Guilford & Fruchter, 1978.) None has achieved the prominence of $r$ because none fits as neatly into the mathematics of general psychometric theory. The closest to an exception is Kendall's (1948) tau, a measure of rank-order correlation, but even this measure has not been used extensively in recent years. Psychometricians argue as to how rigorous the criterion for equality of intervals should be before statistics that assume equal intervals, such as $r$, are used. We again note how experience has generally shown that these criteria need not be extremely rigorous when data are essentially continuous, but the issue should not be ignored in toto.

## Three Special Cases

Many textbooks discuss three special cases of $r$: the phi coefficient ($\Phi$), point-biserial $r$ ($r_{pb}$), and rho ($\rho$). The $\Phi$ coefficient is applicable when both variables are dichotomous. One important application is to correlate pairs of dichotomously scored items. The $r_{pb}$ is used when one variable is dichotomous and the other is continuous. A specific application of importance is to correlate a dichotomous test item with the total score on the test. Finally, $\rho$ is used when the data are in the form of ranks and is therefore applied to ordinal data.

Using $r$ in place of these special formulas makes absolutely no difference to the results: The formulas for all three are simply short cuts useful in hand calculation when the data are in a certain form, e.g., dichotomies. The concepts, however, are useful, as we will consider a different class of correlations in the next section that estimates what the correlations between observed categorical or rank-ordered variables would be if they actually were continuous and normally distributed, e.g., if we knew a subject's true skill instead of pass versus fail. Similarly, if one had access to continuous data which were then dichotomized, the correlation obtained from the original continuous data would be considerably higher than the $\Phi$ or $r_{pb}$ obtained after dichotomization as a result of loss of information even though both correlations would be Pearson PM correlations. The reduction in $r$ is less true with $\rho$ (especially when there are few tied ranks) because the ordinal information in the ranks contains most of the information about the relationship.

There is a very useful relationship between $\Phi$ (and therefore $r$ obtained from two dichotomous variables) and the Pearson chi-square statistic ($\chi^2$):

$$\chi^2 = N\Phi^2 \tag{4-11a}$$
$$\chi^2 = Nr^2 \text{ (for dichotomous variables)} \tag{4-11b}$$

The null hypothesis that $r$ ($\Phi$) is zero can be tested by referring the obtained value of $\chi^2$ to a table of chi-square with 1 degree of freedom ($df$).

## ESTIMATES OF $r$

Although they are not PM coefficients in themselves and therefore not equivalent to $r$ in the sense that $\Phi$, $r_{pb}$, and $\rho$ are, coefficients have been developed to estimate $r$. These assume that the underlying data are continuous and normally distributed instead of categorical. The two most familiar estimates are the "biserial correlation" ($r_{bis}$), where one observable is dichotomous and the other is continuous, and the "tetrachoric correlation" ($r_{tet}$), where both observables are dichotomous. They are special cases of more general measures, polyserial and polychoric correlations, respectively. The $r_{bis}$ and $r_{tet}$ apply only to dichotomous variables; polyserial and polychoric correlations apply to variables divided into any number of categories. We will first describe $r_{bis}$ and $r_{tet}$ and then consider their utility.

## Biserial r ($r_{bis}$)

The formula for $r_{bis}$ is

$$r_{bis} = \frac{X_s - X_u}{\sigma} \cdot \frac{pq}{z} \tag{4-12}$$

where $x_s$ = mean score on a continuous variable for a group that is successful on a dichotomous variable

$x_u$ = mean score on a continuous variable for a group that is unsuccessful on a dichotomous variable

$\sigma$ = overall standard deviation of the continuous variable

$p$ = proportion of individuals in the successful group on dichotomous variable

$q$ = proportion of individuals in the unsuccessful group on dichotomous variable = $1 - p$

$z$ = ordinate of normal curve corresponding to $p$

The $r_{bis}$ is used to estimate the PM correlation that would be obtained from two continuous distributions if the dichotomous variable were normally distributed. For example, one may use $r_{bis}$ with data from individuals scored on a pass-fail basis on a criterion with the intent of later refining the criterion.

If you have already obtained $r_{pb}$ ($r$) and wish to compute $r_{bis}$ from the same data, as with correlations between scores on items and total test scores, the relation is given by

$$r_{bis} = r_{pb} \frac{\sqrt{pq}}{z}$$

$$r_{bis} = r \frac{\sqrt{pq}}{z} \tag{4-13}$$

## Tetrachoric Correlation ($r_{tet}$) and Related Estimates

The tetrachoric correlation coefficient ($r_{tet}$) takes the logic of $r_{bis}$ one step further to estimate the PM correlation between two continuous, normally distributed variables from dichotomies. One use of $r_{tet}$ is with continuous variables that have artificially been "cut" at the median. Another use of $r_{tet}$ is with two variables that are inherently dichotomous at the time of the analysis but which may later be gathered in more continuous form, e.g., to later use actual income rather than rich versus poor.

A polyserial correlation is the generalization of $r_{bis}$ when one of the variables is continuous and the other is categorical, but one wishes to estimate what the correlation would be if both variables were continuous and normally distributed. Whereas $r_{bis}$ applies only to a dichotomy, polyserial correlations may be estimated when the categorical variable is a trichotomy (high, medium, and low), a four-way classification, etc. Likewise, a polychoric correlation is the estimate of what $r$ would be if each of two categorical variables were in fact continuous and normally distributed.

Computing $r_{tet}$, polychoric $r$, and polyserial $r$ is extremely complex, although computer programs are now widely available, e.g., Muthén's (1988) LISCOMP and a Fortran program by Martinson and Hamdan (1975) in the public domain. Be sure to incorporate Beardwood's (1977) modification if you use the latter.

## PEARSON $r$ VERSUS ESTIMATES OF PEARSON $r$

Many circumstances dictate correlating either a categorical variable with a continuous variable or two categorical variables. The following are some considerations relevant to a choice between $r$ ($\Phi$ and $r_{pb}$ for dichotomous variables) and polyserial or polychoric correlation ($r_{bis}$ and $r_{tet}$ for dichotomous variables). The polyserial and/or polychoric estimates will always be somewhat higher than the values of $r$ and, in that sense, properly indicate structure that would be missed using $r$ alone, especially if one were not aware of the effects of categorization (as noted above, there are somewhat fewer problems when data are rank-ordered without ties). At the same time, these estimates may or may not be accurate. In general, we suggest caution about using any estimate of $r$. They are presented here because they have many knowledgeable advocates when used under appropriate circumstances, and they also illustrate the importance of recognizing the problems in dealing with categorical data such as item responses.

**1** *Become familiar with the properties of these estimates.* Take some representative continuous data, categorize it, and obtain $r$ and estimates of $r$ from the original and categorized data, which is simple to do on a computer. You will naturally find that categorization reduces $r$. Equally important is how well the estimates actually regenerate the original correlation. The first author once compared $r$ and $r_{bis}$ using variables that had been dichotomized at the median. The $r$ before dichotomization was .52, but $r_{bis}$ was .71! Misestimation is even more likely when the cut is far from the median and when $r_{tet}$ is used, and it is possible to obtain absolute values in excess of 1.0.

**2** *Consider whether it is reasonable to assume the latent variable is continuous in the first place.* It is often reasonable to view a discrete variable as a reflection of an underlying continuous variable, especially in self-description. For example, answering yes or no to the question "I get very many headaches" may fruitfully be viewed as categorizing the perceived frequency of headaches. On the other hand, people are either alive or dead, registered Democrats or not, Catholics or not. Estimates of the "magnitude of death" do not seem fruitful.

**3** *Use estimates only with very large sample sizes.* Even when their assumptions are met, the sampling error of these estimates is vastly greater than $r$ (Kendall & Stuart, 1967). This is more true of $r_{tet}$ and polychoric estimates than of $r_{bis}$ and polyserial estimates because the former require more numerical estimation. One should be *extremely* cautious in applying them to samples of less than several hundred. Many proponents of these estimates work with huge data bases such as obtained by the Educational Testing Service, and their critics tend to work with smaller data bases. It is not unusual to compound the felonies of insufficient sample size and artificial dichotomization (outside of pilot studies not meant for consumption by others) by using these measures.

**4** *Don't categorize.* Countless studies in personality, educational, and social psychological research, as well as in other areas, have begun with continuous measures which are then categorized. An investigator might therefore compare the frequency of initiating conversations among subjects classified as above or below the median in social anxiety. We cannot stress sufficiently that a great deal of meaningful information is lost since a person who scores one point above the median is treated the same way as the person who obtains the highest score. As Cohen (1983; also see Cohen, 1990; Cohen & Cohen, 1983; Humphreys & Fleishman, 1974) notes, this is approximately the same as randomly discarding a third of the cases; when both variables are dichotomized, it is equivalent to discarding roughly 60 percent of the cases. Relationships that could well be meaningful may well be lost through insufficient power to reject the null hypothesis. Of course, many variables are naturally categorical, and so there is nothing you can do when these are of interest. Sometimes, of course, your data are in that form, and so there may be nothing you can do about the situation.

**5** *Recognize the potentially misleading consequences of both approaches.* There are generally problems present using categorical variables in analyses that assume continuity, a topic we will consider at length in Chapter 13. Our comments criticizing the use of estimates of $r$ need to be balanced by criticisms of those who treat categorical data as if it were continuous. To repeat, $r$ obtained from categorical data systematically underestimates relations that would exist were finer measurement possible. At the same time, point 1 in this section has to be kept in mind. It is easy to reify estimates of $r$ as if they were $r$ itself. Opinions are mixed on the results. Whatever the case, be highly cautious about reporting that $r_{bis}$ is .7 when $r$ for the categorical data is .1 (a hypothetical but not unrealistic example).

Polychoric and polyserial correlations play an important role in developing mathematical models relating to measurement theory. However, their use in determining the correlation between real variables should be quite carefully limited. The previous edition of this book stressed avoiding $r_{bis}$ and $r_{tet}$ in multivariate applications. That conclusion still generally holds despite the availability of better computational algorithms.

### Some Related Issues in Categorization

Categorization provides additional problems if more than one independent variable is categorized. Say that the above investigator decides to add a second independent variable, a measure of social presence, to the social anxiety measure. Four groups might be formed representing subjects below the median on both measures, above the median on social anxiety but below the median on social presence, below the median on social anxiety but above the median on social presence, and above the median on both measures. Quotas are set to produce equal numbers of subjects in the four groups. The experimenter then conducts a two-way ANOVA. Unfortunately, the estimates of the effects are predicated upon the assumption that the variables are uncorrelated in the population and they are not. Consequently, the results will be highly misleading.

Investigators often categorize because they are more familiar with the ANOVA than with multiple regression in general, but artificially categorizing variables costs more than is gained in allowing use of a familiar tool. Experimental psychologists who conduct experiments with multiple independent variables also usually manipulate them independently so that the sample sizes for each combination of treatments is the same. This is legitimate with most experimental manipulations, as opposed to classification variables, and greatly simplifies interpretation compared to nature's more usual case of correlated variables. However, the interpretational problems with correlated predictors are far from insurmountable.

One relatively legitimate use of categorization is to facilitate the presentation of results. For example, suppose an investigator studies ratings of the attractiveness of geometric designs as a joint function of their complexity and the intelligence of the raters. The hypothesis is that there is an optimal level of preferred complexity for any given level of intelligence that is higher for more intelligent people. Assume that appropriate methods exist to measure intelligence, complexity, and perceived attractiveness. Grouping subjects into several intelligence levels and presenting the functions relating complexity to perceived attractiveness within each group may be a good way to present the results. One might find that the lowest-scoring group's ratings decline with complexity, the highest scoring group's ratings increase with complexity, and intermediate groups show nonmonotonic (inverted U-shaped) functions whose peaks increase with intelligence. However, corresponding formal tests are much weaker than methods treating intelligence scores as continuous, e.g., moderated multiple regression, considered in the next chapter. You will therefore still probably find it best to perform your statistical analyses on the continuous data even if you graph the categorical data. Make what you have done clear to the reader, of course.

## ASSUMPTIONS UNDERLYING *r*

Certain assumptions must be met in using *r*:

**1** The relationship between $X$ and $Y$ should be essentially monotonic and, preferably linear. This means in practice that $r$ describes a relationship poorly when the trend line increases and then decreases, or vice versa (is nonmonotonic). Monotonic nonlinearities (curves that do not affect the rank ordering) generally have small effects upon the magnitude of $r$ (Parker, Casey, Ziriax, & Silberberg, 1988), but, as we shall see, these effects cannot be ignored. Methods of handling situations in which the relation is clearly nonmonotonic are considered in the next major section.

**2** The relationship must be homoscedastic so that the spread (errors of estimate) about the best-fitting straight line (discussed below) is approximately the same at all levels of $X$ and $Y$, rather than heteroscedastic, where the spread is much greater at certain levels than others. Heteroscedasticity may arise in correlating an aptitude test with college grades because there may be more spread of grades among those with high aptitude than with low aptitude. Some high scorers do as well as expected, but others do poorly for lack of motivation. In contrast, low scorers may obtain uniformly low grades because they lack the requisite ability, no matter how hard they try; ability is usually *necessary* but not *sufficient* for good grades.

**3** Error affecting each of the variables must be normally distributed (not necessarily the variables themselves) if inferential tests are to be used. Even though this assumption is not necessary to simply describe the relation, extreme skewness can lead to other misleading results even in describing the relationship. As we note at many points, this implies the more important attribute that the data be continuous.

There has been considerable controversy as to whether the these three characteristics should be considered "assumptions" in correlational analysis. They are important to statistical inference (tests of significance), as in deciding whether the population $r$ is zero and to more complex tests. When these three characteristics are present, the relationship is said to be "bivariate normal."

To the extent any of the three assumptions is not met and bivariate normality is not present, probability statements about $r$ will be inexact, but this is usually not a great problem, especially when the probability of obtaining the value of $r$ by chance is clearly greater than .05 or very small. If one or more assumptions are apparently unmet, use a higher level of significance than ordinary, e.g., .001 level. An example of a serious violation is to use $r$ when the relation is clearly nonmonotonic. Computer programs readily output scatter plots like Fig. 4-1 which are useful to inspect. Most relationships are so "noisy" that it is unlikely that you will see a nonmonotonicity, but if you do, use one of the methods designed for use in this case as provided below.

Linearity, homoscedasticity, and normality are also important in *interpreting* the results. Thus, there is nothing to prevent the use of $r$ even if the shapes of the distributions are markedly different, the relationship is far from linear, and/or the spread varies along the line. Unless these assumptions are seriously violated, no real problem in interpretation arises. For example, a moderate departure from linearity (say, the trend tends to "flatten out" at the high end of the independent variable because of a ceiling effect) will usually not affect $r$ greatly. It might be more appropriate to employ a nonlinear measure as discussed later, but the difference between the two is usually not large.

It is wise, nonetheless, to compute the nonlinear measure since the effort required is minimal and extreme violations, such as strong ceiling effects, can have major effects. Also, even though a skewness, nonlinearity, or heteroscedasticity may not affect $r$ greatly, as compared to a nonlinear measure, the existence of any of these may have practical and/or theoretical importance.

## FACTORS INFLUENCING $r$

### Restriction of Range

The $r^2$ may be expressed as the proportion of variance in $Y$ ($\sigma_Y^2$) that is accounted for by its linear relation to $X$ (true variance, $\sigma_t^2$), see Eq. 4-24c below). Likewise, $\sigma_Y^2 = \sigma_t^2 + \sigma_e^2$, where $\sigma_e^2$ = the proportion of $\sigma_Y^2$ that is independent of the relation between $Y$ and $X$ (error variance). Consequently, $r^2$ also equals $1 - \sigma_e^2/\sigma_t^2$. Homoscedasticity causes error variance ($\sigma_e^2$) to be approximately the same in samples that have different total variances ($\sigma_y^2$), and so the difference in $\sigma_Y^2$ tends to be in true variance ($\sigma_t^2$). Thus, as sampling broadens or narrows, error variance tends to remain constant, but true variance and therefore total variance change. The $r$ is a function of these variances; increasing the variance of subjects sampled ($\sigma_Y^2$) increases $r$, and decreasing the variance decreases $r$.

This effect of sampling is the same regardless of whether the $X$ or $Y$ variance is altered. If a change in sampling doubles the variance of $X$, the effect on the correlation would be the same as if a change in sampling doubled the variance of $Y$. The $\sigma_e^2$ and $\sigma_t^2$ will change appropriately in $\sigma_X^2$ rather than $\sigma_Y^2$. On the other hand, $r$ is not affected by artificial changes in the variance due simply to scaling. Scaling changes cause error and total variance change equally (Eq. 4-4), and so $r$ s not altered.

We will frequently document the concern one should have with sampling methods that limit the variance of $X$, $Y$, or both and thereby induce range restriction, as the term was introduced in Chapter 3. That chapter discussed an aptitude test that was being validated for selecting college students. The test was administered to *all* applicants at a particular college, but only a small percentage of the applicants were admitted. Later, aptitude test scores were correlated with grade point averages *on those admitted*. This restricts the range of scores on the aptitude test because its range, and therefore its variance, would have been much larger had every applicant been admitted. The validity of the test in the restricted sample is spuriously low since it is actually to be used with all applicants.

Although the example involves restriction in range and variance, it is no different for an inflation of range. If the measures are obtained from an sample whose range is much larger than the eventual target population, the resulting $r$ will be spuriously high. Any study requires that one consider what variance is appropriate to the investigation, which depends on the intended scientific statements (generalizations) to be made. If the results are to apply to people in general, the appropriate variance is obtained from an unbiased sample of the population in general. If the results are to apply to patients at state psychiatric hospitals, the appropriate variance is found in an unbiased sample of that group.

If the target population's variances are known, they may be compared with the obtained variances. If the two sets of variances differ appreciably, estimates can be made of what the correlation would be if there were no restriction or elevation of range (Guilford & Fruchter, 1978). The formula is

$$r_b = \frac{r_a(\sigma_b/\sigma_a)}{\sqrt{1 - r_a^2 + r_a^2 \, (\sigma_b^2 \sigma_a^2)}} \tag{4-14}$$

where $r_a$ = correlation in the original group (group a)
$r_b$ = correlation in the target group (group b)
$\sigma_a$ = standard deviation in the original group
$\sigma_b$ = standard deviation in the target group

## Distribution Form

Differences in the *shapes* of the two distributions restrict the size of the correlation. The most obvious example is that one cannot obtain a perfect correlation between two variables unless they have exactly the same distribution form (normal or otherwise), as illustrated in Fig. 4-2. Note that the numbers along both axes are frequencies and not scale values, which are arbitrary. These frequencies show that variable *X* is quite negatively skewed and variable *Y* is quite positively skewed even though the relation is positive.

Try to depict a perfect positive correlation by pairing high scores on *X* and *Y* and low scores on *X* and *Y*, leaving the univariate distributions as they are. This is clearly impossible. One cannot place the top eight people on *X* at the highest level of *Y* because only two people are at the highest value of *Y*. Six of the eight highest scorers on *X* would have to fall lower on *Y*. The relationship is also curvilinear, which is not uncommon when the distributions are of different shapes. Note that only the directions and not the amounts of skewness differ, and so one can obtain a perfect negative correlation.

The restriction on the correlation depends on (1) how high the correlation would have been if the distributions had the same shape and (2) how different in shape the distributions are. However, differences in distribution shapes have an effect regardless of the original size of *r*. The extent of the reduction depends on the original size of *r*. Suppose, for example, two variables have the same distribution shape, are linearly related, and *r* is 1.0. If the form of one distribution is artificially altered, *r* might fall to as low as .9 or .8. However, if the original value of *r* were a more likely .35, the reduction might not even be noticeable. Although no formulas are available to forecast the reduction, experience indicates that changes in the shape of one distribution seldom

FIGURE 4-2    A scatter plot of two differently shaped distributions.

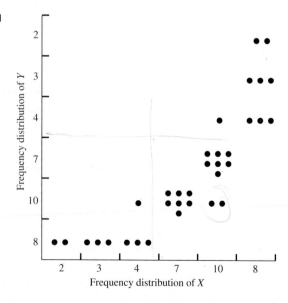

alter a correlation of .50 by more than .05. Thus, differences between two continuous variables in distribution shape usually do not affect $r$ very much. Correlations as high as .70 are rare, and the average of all correlations between two distinct variables reported in the literature probably is less than .40.

The relative insensitivity of differences in distribution shape on moderate-sized correlations assume a relatively large sample, e.g., at least 100. Values of $r$ based upon small numbers of subjects, say, 30 or less, can be affected substantially by any changes in the scores, including transformations of $X$ or $Y$, even though these may have little effect in larger samples. The effect on $r$ can be quite unpredictable because it may capitalize upon sampling error. This is one of the many reasons we have stressed the need for large samples in this book. Even though differences in distribution shapes tend to have slight effects with continuous variables, the effect can be quite large with categorical variables, especially when they are dichotomous. Although it might seem odd to speak of the "shape" of a dichotomous distribution, it is useful. All distributions can be thought of as containing a standard unit area. Imagine pulling and squeezing the area under this unit normal distribution to form differently shaped distributions. The total area available in a dichotomous distribution can be divided into two rectangles proportional to the percentages of scores in each part, and one can talk about the similarity in shape of a dichotomous distribution to another dichotomous distribution or even to a continuous distribution.

The $r$ between two dichotomous variables ($\Phi$) is restricted by the extent to which the percentage of persons who pass one variable differs from the percentage of persons who pass the other variable. Suppose that 70 percent pass and 30 percent fail item a and 50 percent pass and 50 percent fail item b. Table 4-1 illustrates the highest correlation possible in that case. It is quite evident that $r$ cannot be 1.0: All who passed item a would also have had to pass item b, but this is not possible. Because 70 percent passed a and only 50 percent passed b, 20 percent of those who passed a must have failed b even in this "best" case.

A perfect positive correlation cannot be obtained between two dichotomous variables unless they have the same $p$ values, and differences in the respective $p$ values place a ceiling on the maximum value of $r$. The ceiling on negative correlations reflects the extent to which the $p$ value on one item and the $q$ value on the other item are similar. Thus if 30 percent pass one item and 70 percent pass another item, it is possible for $r$ to be $-1.00$ but not $+1.00$. The reverse is true if 70 percent had failed the second item.

**TABLE 4-1**    JOINT FREQUENCIES OF PASSING AND FAILING
TWO ITEMS WITH DIFFERENT $p$ VALUES

| | | | Percentage of persons Item a | | |
|---|---|---|---|---|---|
| | | | Fail | Pass | Total |
| Percentage | | Pass | 0 | 50 | 50 |
| of | Item b | Fail | 30 | 20 | 50 |
| persons | | Total | 30 | 70 | 100 |

Figure 4-3 illustrates the degree to which $r$ is restricted by differences in $p$ values for the two variables. For example, if the $p$ value of one item is .5 and the $p$ value of the other item differs by as much as .3 (being either .2 or .8), $r$ ($\Phi$) cannot exceed .50. This restriction on $\Phi$ reflects the difference in $p$ values for the two variables. A perfect correlation can arise when two variables both have $p$ values of .90, as well as for two variables that both have $p$ values of .50.

The effects of differences in $p$ values on the maximum value of $\Phi$ holds for any two dichotomous variables; responses need not be scored as pass versus fail. For example, one could correlate male versus female gender with yes versus no responses to a question like "Should abortion remain legal?" If the gender distribution differs considerably from the yes versus no distribution, the size of $\Phi$ will be restricted as indicated in Fig. 4-3.

Whereas it is possible for $\Phi$ obtained from two dichotomous variables to equal 1.0, it is not possible for $r$ obtained from a continuous variable and a dichotomous variable ($r_{pb}$) to equal 1.0. A dichotomous variable and a continuous variable cannot have the same distribution shape even though two dichotomous variables can. Figure 4-4 illustrates why there cannot be a perfect relationship between a dichotomous variable and a continuous variable. All scores for the dichotomous variable fall at two points. All scores at these two points must also fall exactly on two points on the other variable for $r$ to equal 1.0, but this is impossible if the other variable is continuous. Consequently, scores for at least one of the two points on the dichotomous variable must span a range of different points on the continuous variable.

**FIGURE 4-3** The maximum possible value of $\Phi$ as a function of the $p$ vaule of one variable when the other has a $p$ of .5.

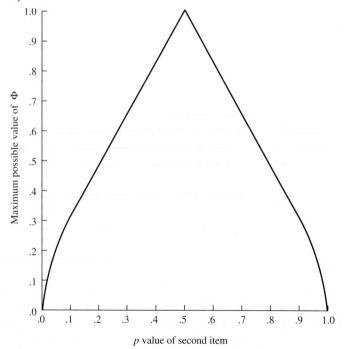

$p$ value of second item

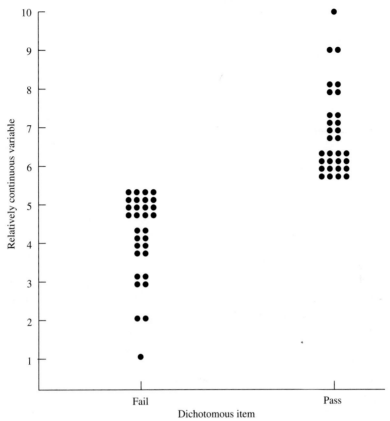

**FIGURE 4-4**   A scatter plot of values on a continuous variable when the other is a dichotomous variable with a *p* value of .5.

The maximum size of $r_{pb}$ between a dichotomous variable and a normally distributed variable is about .80, which occurs when the dichotomous variable has a *p* value of .50. The further *p* deviates from .50 in either direction, the lower the ceiling on $r_{pb}$ because the shape of a dichotomous distribution is most similar to a normal distribution when *p* is .50. The shape of the dichotomous distribution becomes less and less like that of a normally distributed variable as *p* departs from .50. Figure 4-5 describes the maximum value of *r* ($r_{pb}$) between a dichotomous variable and a normally distributed variable as a function of the *p* value of the dichotomous variable. For example, when *p* is as high as .90 or as low as .10, the maximum possible value of *r* is about .58.

## A UNIVERSAL MEASURE OF RELATIONSHIP

We have thus far assumed that relations between variables are linear and used *r* to describe the strength of that relationship. This approach works fairly well in practice for most forms of monotonic relationships, but it is entirely possible that relationships in particular studies will be nonmonotonic and therefore nonlinear. Linear methods are

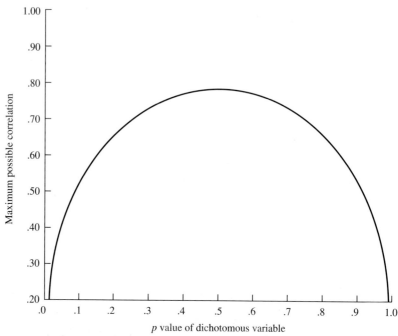

**FIGURE 4-5** The maximum possible point-biserial correlation ($r_{pb}$) between a normally distributed variable and dichotomous variables as a function of the $p$ value of the dichotomous variable.

used wherever possible because they lead to a variety of more complex methods such as factor analysis.

We have previously stated that $r$ may be defined as 1 minus the ratio of error variance ($\sigma_e^2$) in one variable to its total variance ($\sigma_Y^2$, assuming that variable is $Y$), where the error variance is defined in terms of deviations from the linear relation between it and another variable. The same logic provides a universal measure of relationship that can be used regardless of the form of the relationship. The universal measure is called eta ($\eta$) or the correlation ratio (Hays, 1988). The $\eta$ is obtained by computing the variance in $Y$ about *any* curve of relationship. This is error variance ($\sigma_e^2$) as defined above, but the function need not be a straight line. Divide $\sigma_e^2$ by the variance of the dependent variable, $\sigma_Y^2$, and subtract the ratio from 1.0 to obtain $\eta^2$:

$$\eta^2 = 1 - \frac{\sigma_e^2}{\sigma_Y^2} \tag{4-15a}$$

$$\eta^2 = \frac{\sigma_t^2}{\sigma_Y^2} \tag{4-15b}$$

The $\sigma_t^2$ is true variance and equals $\sigma_Y^2 - \sigma_e^2$ as in our previous discussion of $r$. However, it does not assume a linear relation between $X$ and $Y$ (see Eq. 4-24b below). Tak-

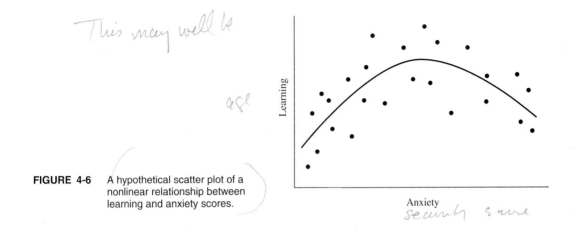

*This may well be*

*age*

**FIGURE 4-6**   A hypothetical scatter plot of a nonlinear relationship between learning and anxiety scores.

*Security score*

ing the square root of Eq. 4-15 produces $\eta$. The $X$ may be used instead of $Y$ and will produce the same value. The definition of $\sigma_e^2$ used in the numerator will change, but $\sigma_X^2$ will be used in place of $\sigma_Y^2$. Figure 4-6 illustrates the principle underlying $\eta$ using a hypothetical relationship between anxiety scores and performance in a learning task. Since the relationship is distinctly nonmonotonic, $r$ summarizes the trend poorly. One computes $\eta$ from the best-fitting smooth curve.

The correlation ratio ($\eta$) is a universal measure of relationship because it (1) applies regardless of the form of the relationship, (2) can be used with either a predicted curve of relationship or a best-fitting curve obtained after the data are obtained, and (3) applies equally well to continuous or categorical independent variables. Point 1 holds because a ratio of error variance to total variance is as meaningful with a complex curve as with a straight line. The predicted relationship may arise from a theory (point 2). For example, an ogive (the cumulative normal or logistic distribution) might be used to predict growth. Curves of appropriate form could be tried on the data, and $\eta$ would indicate how well the curves explained scores on the dependent measure. Issues related to trend analysis, which involves curve fitting, are discussed in Winer et al. (1991). Alternative curves can be used when no particular curve is predicted or if different theories predict different curves. The one with the largest $\eta$ provides the best fit in the sense of the loss function used in fitting, such as least squares. However, Parker et al. (1988) and others show how it may not be easy to make a convincing choice between two models that predict similar functional relationships. For example, a relationship that is logistic in reality will be fit almost as well by a cumulative normal distribution and to only a slightly poorer degree by other monotonic functions including a straight line! For a related critique, see Birnbaum (1974).

Many computer programs are available for curve fitting that provide $\eta$. Polynomials are often used. Thus, one first obtains the best-fitting straight line and associated $\eta$ ($r$ in that case). Next, one obtains the best-fitting quadratic, the best-fitting cubic, etc., for higher-order equations. Both descriptive and inferential criteria can be used to decide at what level to stop, e.g., to see if a linear relationship is sufficient.

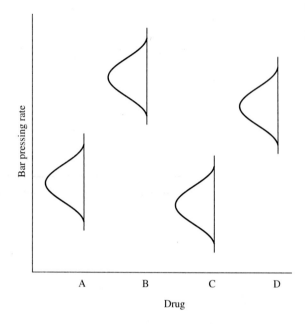

Bar pressing rate

A    B    C    D

Drug

**FIGURE 4-7**  Distribution of effects of four drugs on the rate of bar pressing in a Skinner box.

The $\eta$ can be applied when the independent variable is categorical rather than continuous (point 3). This is illustrated in Fig. 4-7, which shows the effect of four different drugs on bar pressing in a Skinner box. As it is arbitrary which drug is denoted A and which is denoted D, it is not meaningful to talk about the form of the relationship in this case. There is nothing wrong with reordering the drugs on the graph, which changes the visible form of relationship drastically. One may obtain $\eta$ here just as when both variables are continuous. Sums of squares ($\Sigma x^2$) can be calculated about each group mean score on the dependent measure, pooled over groups, and divided by the total number of animals to estimate $\sigma_e^2$. In turn, this can be divided by $\sigma_Y^2$ and subtracted from 1.0 to obtain $\eta$.

The logic of $\eta$ is implicit in the ANOVA. Researchers often focus upon the ANOVA in terms of the $F$ ratio it produces, i.e., the ratio of the variance estimate from a systematic source (the various drugs in this case) to an appropriate error variance such as the pooled variance of scores within groups. Although $F$ is basic to statistical inferences about group mean differences in the population, $\eta$ indicates how *strong* the relationship is, thus describing the independent variable's explanatory power. The statistical significance of $F$ depends on the number of subjects, but $\eta$ is independent of the number of subjects. The $F$ may well be highly significant in a large sample, but a small value of $\eta$ may indicate that the independent variable explains only a small portion of the variance in the dependent measure. As important as inferential statistics like $F$ are, it also is important to determine the strength of relationships using a measure like $\eta$.

The correlation ratio ($\eta$) is a link between the correlational statistics of psychometric theory and the inferential statistics of the ANOVA employed with experimental data. One use of $\eta$ was previously illustrated in the ANOVA of the four drugs depicted in Fig. 4-7. The concept of $\eta$ can be extended to complex correlational problems and ANOVA designs. In ANOVA designs with more than one factor, separate values of $\eta$ can be obtained for each treatment factor. For example, one could vary the dosage of each drug in the experiment depicted in Fig. 4-7. There will be significance tests ($F$) for (1) overall differences among drugs, (2) overall differences among dosage levels, and (3) their interaction. Paralleling these are three correlation ratios.

The squared correlation ratio ($\eta^2$) for any systematic source is obtained by dividing the sum of squares attributable to that source (which may be an interaction) by the total sum of squares. Some complexities arise, especially when one wishes to compare two different effects that are each based upon different numbers of treatment levels. Winer et al. (1991) describe alternative indices. Comparing the complex statistics from correlational analysis employed in psychometric theory with the equally complex ANOVA $F$ ratios derived from psychological experiments reveals that both reflect the same principle—the partitioning of variance.

The $r$ is a special case of $\eta$. When both variables are continuous and the relationship is linear, $\eta$ equals $r$. Magnitudes of $\eta$ and $r$ can be interpreted similarly. "How high is high?" is relative to the context of use for both measures, but if a value of $r$ of .3 can be regarded as "important" in a given situation, so can a value of $\eta = .3$. The one slight difference is that $\eta$ can never be negative since the concept of inverse has no meaning with a nonmonotonic relation. The difference between $\eta^2$ (which will always be the larger) and $r^2$ is used to test for nonlinearity. The logic behind $r$ is very general; likewise, $\eta$ can be used to measure the degree of relationship regardless of whether (1) the investigation concerns individual differences or effects of experimental treatments; (2) the relationship is linear or nonlinear; (3) the form of the relationship is hypothesized ahead of time or derived from the data afterward; (4) the independent variable is measured on a ratio, interval, ordinal, or nominal scale; and (5) there are two or several variables involved in the analysis.

## PREDICTION, REGRESSION, AND STRUCTURAL EQUATIONS

Predicting one variable from another is closely related to describing the correlation between them. Although the two concepts are distinct, we will show how $r$ is a basic link between them. Two basic forms of prediction are (1) linear regression, in which an observable criterion (effect), $Y$, depends upon and is predicted from an observable predictor (cause), $X$, in a linear manner, and (2) structural equations, in which two observables, $X$ and $Y$, both depend upon a third, usually unobservable, variable which we denote $t$ (we will later show that linear regression can also be viewed as a special type of structural equation). In a structural equation, neither $X$ nor $Y$ is a predictor; both are viewed as effects of $t$. Many more complicated forms of prediction are possible, some of which will be considered in the next chapter and Chapter 13. For example, $Y$ may be related to several predictors, $X_1, X_2, ..., X_k$, which is known as multiple regression. In turn, the ANOVA is a special case of multiple regression where the predictors are categorical. In addition, prediction may use relations other than a straight line.

## Regression

The process of using linear regression to relate $X$ to $Y$ can be understood most simply by assuming that $X$ and $Y$ are in standardized ($z$-score) form. A straight line has only two parameters: its slope ($b$) and its intercept with the $z_Y$ axis ($a$), and so the problem is to best estimate scores on $z_Y$ from scores on $z_X$ as follows:

$$z_Y' = bz_X + a \qquad (4\text{-}16)$$

where $z_{Y'}$ is the score on $z_Y$ estimated from $z_X$. The quality of the estimates is gauged by various functions of the differences between the estimated scores for $z_Y$ ($z_Y'$) and the actual scores ($z_Y$). These differences are known as "residuals," symbolized $z_{Y \cdot X}$. The symbol "$Y \cdot X$" denotes that $Y$ is being predicted from $X$ rather than the other way around.

$$z_{Y \cdot X} = z_Y' - z_Y \qquad (4\text{-}17a)$$

This is the same as:

$$z_{Y \cdot X} = z_Y - (bz_X + a) \qquad (4\text{-}17b)$$

The $b$ and $a$ can be obtained in various ways, depending on what specific function of the difference between $z_Y$ and $z_Y'$ is to be minimized. Thus one could try to derive $b$ and $a$ so as to minimize the sum of absolute differences between $z_Y$ and $z_Y'$ (sum of absolute values of $z_{Y \cdot X}$). Alternative functions of this form, known as loss functions, could also be employed (see below). The particular loss function, which has proven most useful traditionally, is ordinary (unweighted) least squares: $b$ and $a$ are determined to minimize the sum of squared differences between actual scores and estimated scores, $\Sigma(z_Y - z_Y')^2$, and thereby to minimize the sum of squared residuals, $\Sigma z_{Y \cdot X}^2$. Thus, least-squares estimation (we will drop the "ordinary" for now) minimizes the following expression given a proper choice of $b$ and $a$:

$$\Sigma z_{Y \cdot X}^2 = \Sigma(z_Y - z_Y')^2 = \Sigma[z_Y - (bz_X + a)]^2 \qquad (4\text{-}18)$$

Summation proceeds over individual observations. Whether or not the foregoing expression has a unique minimum and, if it does, how to determine $b$ and $a$ are simple problems in calculus. The solution indicates that $a = 0$ for standardized scores. Thus, the least-squares regression line always goes through the origin when scores are standardized, as indicated in Fig. 4-1. This simplifies the problem to finding a $b$ that minimizes the expression:

$$\Sigma z_{Y \cdot X}^2 = \Sigma(z_Y - bz_X)^2 \qquad (4\text{-}19)$$

The solution also tells us that $b$ is unique to any set of data; there is only one value of $b$ that minimizes the loss function. This value of $b$ is

$$b = \frac{\Sigma z_X z_Y}{N} \tag{4-20}$$

Eq. 4-20 for $b$ is identical to Eq. 4-6 for $r$: the slope of the line of best fit in predicting one standardized variable from another is their PM correlation ($r$). The problems of correlation (magnitude of relationship) and regression (the slope and intercept of the line producing that relationship) are linked because $r$ describes *both* the magnitude and the slope for standardized data. This is also true if $X$ and $Y$ have the same standard deviation even if they are not standardized. Once $b$ ($r$) is obtained, the line of best fit can be drawn, as in Fig. 4-1. The best estimate of $z_Y$ ($z_Y'$) for any value of $z_X$ is obtained by multiplying $z_X$ by $b$.

Even though $b = r$, an important distinction should be noted between $r$ as a measure of correlation and $b$ ($r$) as a measure of slope in regression. Correlations are symmetric (nondirectional) in that it makes no difference whether one thinks of correlating $z_X$ with $z_Y$ or of correlating $z_Y$ with $z_X$. Regression, on the other hand is asymmetric (directional) in that regressing $z_Y$ upon $z_X$ is conceptually different from its converse. The slope ($b$) in linear regression has same numerical value ($r$) whether one predicts $z_Y$ from $z_X$ or vice versa. However, this is the exception and not the rule. It does not generally hold with nonstandardized variables, for example. Regressing $z_X$ upon $z_Y$ treats $z_X$ as a predictor and $z_Y$ as a criterion. Linear regression assumes that prediction is imperfect ($z_Y \neq z_Y'$) because $z_Y$ contains error; $z_X$ is assumed to be error-free, and the deviations in Fig. 4-1 are measured vertically. The converse is true when one regresses $z_Y$ upon $z_X$. The squared deviations are measured horizontally (see the bottom panel of Fig. 4-1). Thus, two distinct regression lines are obtainable even though only one may be of interest.

## Regression Based upon Raw Scores

We have focussed upon $z$ scores because we could ignore the largely incidental properties of the raw-score units. You may have already been exposed to the raw-score formulas for regression, but we will present them as Eqs. 4-21 since they are both simple to present and are instructive.

$$b_{Y \cdot X} = \frac{\sigma_Y}{\sigma_X} r \tag{4-21a}$$

$$a_{Y \cdot X} = \overline{Y} - b_{Y \cdot X} \overline{X} \tag{4-21b}$$

The $b_{Y \cdot X}$ and $a_{Y \cdot X}$, respectively, denote the slope and $Y$-intercept of the raw-score regression line in predicting $Y$ from $X$. The ratio of the criterion's standard deviation to the predictor's standard deviation in Eq. 4-21a illustrates that one "shrinks" the predictor's variance and "expands" the criterion's variance when the predictor is more variable than the criterion, e.g., when SAT scores (which have a standard deviation of 100 or more, depending on how the scores are used) are used to predict grade-point average (which has a standard deviation of about .2). The reverse is true when the criterion is more variable than the predictor. These differences in variance often simply reflect arbitrary differences in unit of scaling.

Equation 4-21b is also informative. The point that represents the joint mean of the predictor and criterion ($\overline{X}$, $\overline{Y}$, or centroid, a term that will appear later this book) always falls on the line of best fit in least-squares linear regression.

Weights used in regression are generically called "regression weights." Regression weights applied to standardized variables are known as "beta ($\beta$) weights," and regression weights applied to raw or deviation scores are known as "$b$ weights." Had we followed this convention, the $b$ of Eq. 4-20 would have been $\beta$. A more specific notation parallels the distinction between the sample mean ($\overline{X}$) and the population mean ($\mu$) in distinguishing sample estimates from population parameters. The most common convention is to place a circumflex ("hat") over sample estimates, e.g., $\hat{b}$ and $\hat{\beta}$. However, we will not do so in this book for simplicity.

### The Standard Error of Estimate

The $r$ plays a vital role in describing error in prediction (errors in estimating $z_Y$ from $z_X$ through linear regression). The variance of the errors ($\sigma_e^2$) was discussed above, e.g., in Eq. 4-15. It is actually the variance of the residuals ($z_{Y \cdot X}$) and could therefore also be symbolized as $\sigma_{Y \cdot X}^2$. This variance may be derived as follows:

$$\sigma_e^2 = \frac{\Sigma z_{Y \cdot X}^2}{N}$$

$$= \frac{1}{N} \Sigma (z_Y - z_Y')^2$$

$$= \frac{1}{N} \Sigma (z_Y - r z_X)^2$$

$$= \frac{1}{N} \Sigma (z_Y^2 - 2 r z_X z_Y + r^2 z_X^2)$$

$$= \frac{\Sigma z_Y^2}{N} - 2r \frac{\Sigma z_X z_Y}{N} + r^2 \frac{\Sigma z_X^2}{N}$$

$$= 1 - 2r^2 + r^2$$

Thus,

$$\sigma_e^2 = \sigma_{Y \cdot X}^2 = 1 - r^2 \tag{4-22a}$$

and

$$\sigma_e = \sigma_{Y \cdot X} = \sqrt{1 - r^2} \tag{4-22b}$$

estimate when the dependent variable is in $z$-score form. The quantities $r^2$ and $1 - r^2$ are similarly known as the coefficient of determination and the coefficient of nondetermination, respectively, because $r^2$ describes the proportion of variance in one variable that is determined by another. If both variables are expressed as raw scores or deviation scores rather than as standard scores, Eqs. 4-22 become

$$\sigma_e^2 = \sigma_Y^2 (1 - r^2) \qquad (4\text{-}23a)$$

$$\sigma_e = \sigma_Y \sqrt{1 - r^2} \qquad (4\text{-}23b)$$

The $\sigma_Y^2$ is the variance of the criterion. Equation 4-23 is the general form of the standard error of estimate. If the dependent variable is standardized, $\sigma_Y$ "falls out" of the equation, leaving Eqs. 4-22. The variance and standard deviation of errors of estimate depend only on the correlation between the two variables ($r$) and the variance of the dependent variable ($\sigma_Y^2$) in the raw-score form of Eqs. 4-23.

Using linear regression and Eqs. 4-21 through 4-23, you can take a predictor, obtain a least-squares estimate of the criterion, and obtain a confidence interval on this estimate. This is most useful in applied work. Thus, it might be found that the probability is less than .05 that students obtaining grades below a certain score on an admissions test will complete college successfully based upon the correlation between the admissions test and academic performance.

It is important to remember that there is an inverse relationship between the squared correlation ($r^2$) and the variance of the errors of estimate ($\sigma_e^2$). The more points scatter about the best-fit line, the lower $r$ is. In addition, the variance of errors of estimate ($\sigma_e^2$) allows many indices of relationship between variables to be developed. For example, Eq. 4-23a can be rewritten as

$$r^2 = 1 - \frac{\sigma_e^2}{\sigma_Y^2} \qquad (4\text{-}24a)$$

$$r^2 = \frac{\sigma_{Z'}^2}{\sigma_Y^2} \qquad (4\text{-}24b)$$

where $\sigma_{Z'}^2$ = variance in predicted scores and corresponds to $\sigma_t^2$ (true variance) in Eq. 4-15.

Thus, the correlation is inversely related to the ratio of $\sigma_e^2$ to $\sigma_Y^2$, the ratio of error variance to total variance. When $\sigma_e^2$ is as large as $\sigma_Y^2$, the correlation is zero; when $\sigma_e^2$ is very small relative to $\sigma_Y^2$, the correlation is very high. Conversely, we will make frequent use of $r^2$ as the ratio of true variance to total (observed) variance. $\sigma_{Z'}^2/\sigma_Y^2 = \sigma_t^2/\sigma_Y^2$. It often makes sense to reverse the roles of $X$ and $Y$, in which case $\sigma_e^2$ becomes $\sigma_{X \cdot Y}^2$ and $\sigma_Y^2$ becomes $\sigma_X^2$. If $\sigma_Y^2$ and $\sigma_X^2$ are different (e.g., one is obtained from a 20-item test and the other is obtained from a 100-item test), the standard errors will also differ even though $r^2$ is the same. Changes in $\sigma_X$ as produced by different approaches to sampling subjects affect $r$ in the same way that changes in $\sigma_Y$ do.

## Partitioning of Variance

We have noted that one of the important properties of $r$ is that it permits variance to be partitioned into meaningful components. We have already used the terms "coefficient of determination = $r^2$" and "coefficient of nondetermination = $1 - r^2$" to illustrate how the total variance of a standardized variable may be divided into mutually exclusive (nonoverlapping) and inclusive (adding to the total) parts. Again assume that $z_X$ is used to estimate $z_Y$. There are two variables, $z_X$ and $z_Y$, before the correlational analysis is undertaken. The analysis provides two additional variables: $z_Y'$ (estimates of $z_Y$) and $z_{Y \cdot X}$ (residuals or errors in estimation obtained by subtracting $z_Y'$ from $z_Y$). The means and variances of these four variables and the correlations among them are extremely important. Throughout the book, we will demonstrate that many important principles rest on simple properties of these four sets of scores. Because of the importance of this section, we will provide derivations, something we ordinarily do not do because of space.

It should be apparent that the means of all four variables above are zero. The means of $z_X$ and $z_Y$ are zero by definition. Since $z_Y'$ is obtained by multiplying $z_X$ by a constant ($b = r$), the mean remains zero. Since $z_{Y \cdot X}$ is obtained by subtracting estimated ($z_Y'$) from actual ($z_Y$) scores, the mean of $z_{Y \cdot X}$ is also zero because the mean of a difference equals the difference in the means.

The variances of $z_X$ and $z_Y$ are 1 by definition. Since $z_Y' = r z_X$ and multiplying all the scores in a distribution by a constant multiplies the variance by the square of that constant (Eq. 4-4), the variance of the predicted values ($z_Y'$) is $r^2$, and we have already shown how the variance in residuals (error variance = $\sigma_{Y \cdot X}^2 = \sigma_e^2$) is $1 - r^2$.

Multiplying a variable by a constant does not change the correlation of that variable with any other variable. Consequently since $z_Y' = r z_X$ and the correlation of $z_X$ and $z_Y$ is $r$, the correlation of $z_Y'$ and $z_Y$ likewise is $r$. The correlation of $z_{Y \cdot X}$ with $z_X$ is obtained using Eq. 4-9 as follows:

$$r_{z_X z_{Y \cdot X}} = \frac{1}{N} \cdot \frac{\Sigma z_X z_{Y \cdot X}}{\sigma_{Y \cdot X}} \tag{4-25}$$

The numerator is the covariance of $z_X$ and $z_{Y \cdot X}$. The "missing" standard deviation in the denominator is for $z_X$, which does not appear since it is 1.0. One needs only to examine the numerator of the expression to prove that $z_X$ and $z_{Y \cdot X}$ have a correlation of zero since zero divided by any other number is still zero:

$$\frac{1}{N} \Sigma z_X z_{Y \cdot X} = \frac{1}{N} \Sigma z_X (z_Y - r z_X)$$

$$= \frac{1}{N} \Sigma (z_X z_Y - r \Sigma z_X^2)$$

$$= r - r$$

$$= 0 \tag{4-26}$$

Since $z_Y' = rz_X$ correlates 1.0 with $z_X$, the above also proves that predicted scores $(z_Y')$ and residuals $(z_{Y \cdot X})$ are uncorrelated.

The correlation of obtained scores $(z_Y)$ with residuals $(z_{Y \cdot X})$ is obtained as follows:

$$r_{z_X z_{Y \cdot X}} = \frac{(1/N)\, \Sigma z_Y z_{Y \cdot X}}{\sigma_{Y \cdot X}} \tag{4-27}$$

This is another application of Eq. 4-9, but $\sigma_Y$ is missing from the denominator as it is 1.0. The denominator of the equation is the standard deviation of the errors of prediction. Previously the variance of the errors of prediction was shown to be $1 - r^2$; consequently the denominator is the square root of that quantity (the standard deviation). The numerator can be expanded as follows:

$$\frac{1}{N} \Sigma z_X z_{Y \cdot X} = \frac{1}{N} \Sigma z_Y (z_Y - rz_X)$$

$$= \frac{1}{N} \Sigma (z_Y^2 - r\Sigma z_X z_Y)$$

$$= \frac{1}{N} \Sigma z_Y^2 - \frac{1}{N} r\Sigma z_X z_Y$$

$$= 1 - r^2$$

Placing numerator and denominator back in the original equation gives

$$r_{z_X z_{Y \cdot X}} = \frac{1 - r^2}{\sqrt{1 - r^2}}$$

$$= \sqrt{1 - r^2} \tag{4-28}$$

Note that $Y$ is correlated with the residuals, even though $X$ is not. Assuming $r > 0$, people who obtain high scores on $Y$ do so because of (1) high scores on $X$ (talent), and/or (2) the effects of chance upon the criterion (luck) and/or (3) other systematic factors not reflected in the predictor. The residuals encompass (2) and (3). The converse holds for people who obtain low scores on $Y$. Table 4-2 summarizes the above relationships among means, variances, and correlations. You should derive these simple principles on your own, then burn the results into your brain. These simple principles are the foundation of all methods of multivariate analysis. The next chapter contains a numeric illustration.

A number of important points should be understood from the foregoing discussion. The $r$ summarizes the relationship between two variables and also defines a line of best fit between one standardized variable and another. For each score on one variable, there is a corresponding predicted score on the other variable. Unless the correlation is

TABLE 4-2    MEANS, VARIANCES, STANDARD DEVIATIONS, AND CORRELATIONS
AMONG SCORES INVOLVED IN CORRELATION AND LINEAR REGRESSION

| Measure | Score | | | |
|---|---|---|---|---|
| | $z_X$ | $z_Y$ | $z_{\acute{Y}}$ | $z_{Y \cdot X}$ |
| Mean | 0. | 0. | 0. | 0. |
| $\sigma^2$ | 1.0 | 1.0 | $r_{XY}^2$ | $1 - r_{XY}^2$ |
| $\sigma$ | 1.0 | 1.0 | $r_{XY}$ | $\sqrt{1 - r_{XY}^2}$ |
| $r$ with $z_X$ | 1.0 | $r_{XY}$ | 1.0 | 0. |
| $r$ with $z_Y$ | $r_{XY}$ | 1.0 | $r_{XY}$ | $\sqrt{1 - r_{XY}^2}$ |
| $r$ with $z_{\acute{Y}}$ | 1.0 | $r_{XY}$ | 1.0 | 0. |

perfect, predicted scores vary less than scores for the variable being predicted (observed scores). Error scores are uncorrelated with both predictor and predicted scores but are correlated with criterion scores.

Correlational analysis thus partitions the observed variance into two independent (uncorrelated or orthogonal) sources—one source that can be explained by another variable and a second source that cannot be explained by that other variable. The variance of the criterion variable ($z_Y$), is partitioned into two additive components, and the sum of squared correlations with these two components is 1.00. This is why it is meaningful to speak of the squared correlation as equaling a proportion of variance and why it is meaningful to speak of correlational analysis as decomposing the variance of one variable into parts attributable to different sources. This logic is expanded in factor analysis; variables are partitioned into sources of variance that can and cannot be accounted for by combinations of other variables. If you are unclear about any points mentioned thus far, you should reread this material carefully. The complex methods of analysis required in psychometric theory grow from these simple statistical roots.

## Structural Equations

Although linear regression is relatively simple to use and widely applicable, it sometimes makes more sense to think of $z_X$ and $z_Y$ as joint consequences of a third, unobservable variable, construct, attribute, or true score (t) than to think of either $z_X$ or $z_Y$ as a predictor (cause) and the other as a criterion (effect). Consider, for example, two different checklists of depression-related symptoms. These two measures probably correlate highly over subjects, but one does not cause the other; both are outcomes of $t$ (depression in this case). Conversely, lack of perfect correlation is assumed to arise from unique errors ($e_X$ and $e_Y$) that are largely but not exclusively unreliability in the sense of Chapters 6 through 9 and which are also not directly observable. The result may be expressed as structural equations:

$$z_X = t + e_X \tag{4-29a}$$
$$z_Y = t + e_Y \tag{4-29b}$$

We have assumed for simplicity that the two observable quantities, $z_X$ and $z_Y$, are standardized, and so they have means of 0 and variances of 1. The means of the three unobservable terms, $t$, $e_X$, and $e_Y$, may also be defined as zero when there is only one group of subjects, and so the important terms are the relative variances of these unobservables. Note that Eqs. 4-29 contain two known quantities, $z_X$ and $z_Y$, and three unknown quantities, $t$, $e_X$, and $e_Y$. An assumption or constraint is necessary in order to obtain a unique solution. Three possible constraints are the following: (1) The variance of $e_X$ is zero, so $z_X$ is error-free ($z_Y$ can also be assumed error-free); (2) the variances of $e_X$ and $e_Y$ are equal; and (3) the variances of $e_X$ and $e_Y$ are proportional to their reliabilities.

Although we introduced them as separate cases, linear regression becomes a special case of structural modeling when $e_X$ or $e_Y$ is assumed to have zero variance. This is what happens under constraint 1. The subtle distinction is that one thinks of the predictor as an observable in regression and as an unobservable in structural modeling. However, they are perfectly correlated when one variable is assumed error-free, which obscures the distinction. Structural modeling can therefore be used to obtain a least-squares regression line. We have noted that the squared deviations are measured either vertically or horizontally in regression because the predictor is assumed to be error-free. Under different constraints, deviations are measured obliquely. In particular, they are measured perpendicularly to the line of best fit when the variances of $e_X$ and $e_Y$ are assumed equal under constraint 2, as illustrated in Fig. 4-1b. Isaac (1970) provides a useful discussion of this topic.

In more complex situations, several constructs may be modeled, e.g., anxiety and depression; the correlation between their respective true scores may be estimated, and each construct may be defined through multiple indicators. Unfortunately, structural equation modeling requires much more complex computational algorithms than ordinary linear regression or even multiple regression considered in the next chapter. Specialized programs which either "stand alone" or are optional extensions of general-purpose programs are generally necessary to this end. Some of the more commonly used are LISREL (Jöreskog & Sörbom, 1989), EQS and SAS' PROC CALIS (Bentler, 1985), MILS (Schoenberg, 1982), and LISCOMP (Muthén, 1988). LISREL was the first such computer program to achieve widespread use and is perhaps still the most cited. Using any of these programs is quite involved and goes beyond this textbook, but some features will be considered in subsequent chapters, particularly Chapter 13 (confirmatory factor analysis) where we will present a numeric example.

## STATISTICAL ESTIMATION AND STATISTICAL DECISION THEORY

The contemporary conception of statistics is the making of decisions based upon incomplete data and may be traced to Wald (e.g., Wald, 1950). These decisions may have important consequences. One situation that illustrates such varied consequences, testing a null hypothesis, is introduced in basic statistics. Rejecting a null hypothesis based upon sample data can be a correct decision or a type I error, and accepting that hypothesis may also be a correct decision or a type II error. The self-correcting nature of science usually limits the long-range harm of an error, but there may well be short-range negative consequences, such as wasted research effort. A clinical diagnosis clearly can have similar properties. It too involves sample data (an individual's behaviors). A correct decision may suggest a correct plan of therapy, and an incorrect decision may expose the individual to the harm of wrong or no treatment.

In statistics, a great many quantities are estimated (the mean, variance, correlation, regression line slope and intercept, etc.). An "estimator" is a decision rule that results in a particular value or estimate that is a function of the data (sample values—$X_i$ or, generically, $X$). We will use the symbol $\Theta$ to denote any unknown parameter and $\hat{\Theta}$ to denote a corresponding sample estimate. The data in turn are assumed to be functions of $\Theta$ as well as perhaps other quantities such as random error. Estimation involves considering the expected loss given the possible distributions of the data. Good estimation means that $\Theta$ and $\hat{\Theta}$ are numerically close to one another, and the aforementioned concept of a loss function defines how close the two terms are. Unfortunately, there is more than one definition of "close" and associated "loss function." The purpose of this section is to illustrate some alternatives.

Ordinary least squares was defined specifically in the context of linear regression. Equation 4-30 describes its general form:

$$L(\Theta, \Theta) = \frac{1}{N} \Sigma (X_i - \Theta)^2 \tag{4-30}$$

Letting $\Theta$ be the population mean ($\mu$) provides a simple example. Many statistics books prove that the expected value of $\Sigma(X_i - \hat{\Theta})^2/N$ is at a minimum when $\Theta$ = the sample mean ($X$). Consequently, $X$ is the least-squares estimate of the population mean. This least-squares loss function is usable in many situations such as multiple regression.

Ordinary least squares is not the only possible way to estimate, even though it is very popular and usually relatively simple to apply. We will consider five alternatives to ordinary least squares that have reflected areas of recent advance (though the principles they reflect have long been known): (1) generalized (weighted) least squares (Grizzle, Starmer, & Koch, 1969), (2) maximum likelihood, (3) Bayesian methods, (4) the method of moments, and (5) equal weighting. Maximum likelihood is the most important of these and will therefore be considered in the most detail. Once these are discussed, we will then consider some properties of estimators that facilitate comparing them. Most approaches to estimation regard the parameter $\Theta$ as an unknown constant. However, Bayesians are unusual in regarding $\Theta$ as an unknown variable determined by chance from a random variable $\mathbf{\Theta}$ whose distribution will be denoted $h(\Theta)$.

## Generalized Least-Squares Estimation

The generalized least-squares loss function is defined as

$$L(\Theta_i, \hat{\Theta}_i) = \Sigma w_i(X_i - \hat{\Theta}_i)^2 \tag{4-31}$$

where $w_i$ is a weight applied to the $i$th observation. Weighting emphasizes the more important data, e.g., those having the most in common with other data or the most reliable, depending upon the circumstance. In contrast, ordinary least-squares regression weights each observation equally. Draper and Smith (1981, pp. 108–117) describe how generalized least squares may be used to handle some unusual regression problems. Various forms of robust analysis "trim" (eliminate) outlying observations, thereby giving them a weight of 0.

Generalized least squares uses a matrix of variances and covariances of the variables to obtain weights, but the various algorithms are beyond the scope of this text. Some, but not all of these (and maximum likelihood) algorithms are open form (iterative). Certain highly specialized algorithms in factor analysis and categorical modeling currently provide only generalized least-squares estimates. Generalized least squares and maximum likelihood have become attractive because they allow inferential tests that are not possible with ordinary least squares. We will introduce the resulting strategy below but discuss it more fully in Chapters 10, 13, and 15.

## Maximum Likelihood Estimation

The principle of maximum likelihood is fairly simple: Choose the parameter whose value is most probable given the data and assumptions about the distribution(s) of $X$. Symbolically, choose $\Theta$ to maximize $p(\Theta/X)$, meaning "the probability of the parameter given the data." As a simple but highly artificial example, suppose that you are given a coin and told that it is either fair (the probability of a head is .5) or biased (the probability of a head is .6). You flip the coin three times and obtain a head, a head, and a tail. Since the tosses are independent, the joint probability of these three outcomes is the product of the individual probabilities. Were the coin fair, the probability of two heads and one tail in that order = $.5^3 = .125$, since the probability of each head = the probability of the one tail = .5. Were the coin biased, the probability of the joint outcome = $(.6^2)(.4) = .144$, since the probability of the two heads is each .6 and the probability of the one tail = .4. The outcome has a greater probability with the biased coin than with the fair coin, and so $p = .6$ is the maximum likelihood estimate (again assuming that .6 and .5 are the only possible values). The ratio of the two probabilities (.144/.125 = 1.16) is known as the "likelihood ratio." Since this is close to 1.0 (equal probability), the evidence for bias is weak.

Had you been simply asked to estimate the probability of a head, the maximum likelihood estimate would equal the observed probability (2/3 = .67) since $pp(1 - p)$ can be shown to reach its maximum value when $p$ is .67. This value is the same as the least-squares estimator of the sample mean ($X$). However, the maximum likelihood estimator of the population variance involves dividing $\Sigma x^2$ by $N$ instead of $N - 1$, as was noted in the discussion of Eq. 4-1.

## Maximum Likelihood and the Testing of Hierarchical Models

One important use of maximum likelihood estimation is to test a sequence of "hierarchical models," defined as models in which hypotheses about the data become progressively more specific (generalized least squares may be used to the same specific end). For example, assume that a sample of 100 intelligence (IQ) measures has been obtained from a particular group. Three possible models (hypotheses) assume that the data are normally distributed (1) with an unspecific population mean ($\mu$) and unspecified population standard deviation ($\sigma$), (2) with $\sigma = 15$ but an unspecified $\mu$, and (3) with $\mu = 100$ and $\sigma = 15$, the parameters for the general population. Model 3 thus completely specifies the distribution since normal distributions can vary only in location ($\mu$) and variability ($\sigma$).

If model 2 is true, model 1 must also be true. However, model 1 may be true yet model 2 may be false if $\sigma$ is not 15. Model 2 is therefore a special case of model 1, technically called a "nested model." Model 3 is nested relative to model 2 and therefore model 1 for the same reasons. Another possible model, $2'$, states that the data are normally distributed with $\mu = 100$ but makes no statement about $\sigma$. It is also nested within model 1 and model 3 is nested within it, but models 2 and $2'$ are not nested in relation to one another since their respective statements about $\sigma$ and $\mu$ can be true or false independently of each other. It is also useful to consider one more model (0) which makes no statements about the form of the distribution of scores or their parameters. It is the most general possible model. Models 0, 1, 2, and 3 (or 0, 1, $2'$ and 3) thus form a hierarchy of nested models.

One simple and perfectly proper way to test hypotheses about $\mu$ and $\sigma$ is to perform a single-sample $t$ test to see if the sample mean ($X$) differs significantly from 100, and a chi-square test to determine if the sample variance ($s$) differs significantly from $15^2$ or 225. The approach we present is designed to illustrate the testing of hierarchical models and was chosen for simplicity. Future chapters contain more realistic examples. If the data were normally distributed, standardizing them by subtracting $X$ and dividing the result by $s$ would produce scores that are normally distributed with $\overline{X} = 0$ and $s = 1$, regardless of the population parameters. The test treats $\mu$ and $\sigma$ as free parameters to be estimated from the data (we would divide the sample sum of squares by $N$ rather than $N - 1$ to compute $s$ since all tests require maximum likelihood estimates of relevant parameters). A table of the normal distribution indicates that equal proportions (fifths) of the distribution fall above $z = +.84$, between $z = +.26$ and $z = +.84$, between $z = -.26$ and $z = +.26$, between $z = -.84$ and $z = -.26$, and below $z = -.84$. The data should therefore fall in approximately equal proportions using these cutoffs. The observed ($o$) and expected ($e$) frequencies within each of the five categories may be compared by a Pearson chi-square statistic ($\chi^2$), Eq. 4-32, which you may have been introduced to in earlier statistics classes:

$$\chi^2 = \Sigma \left[ \frac{(o - e)^2}{e} \right] \tag{4-32}$$

However, a slightly different statistic, the likelihood ratio chi-square statistic is actually more useful to this same end (Eq. 4-33):

$$G^2 = 2\Sigma o \ln\left( \frac{o}{e} \right) \tag{4-33}$$

Summing proceeds over all cells, and ln denotes the natural logarithm. The chi-square statistic is usually identified as $G^2$ rather than $\chi^2$ to distinguish it from the Pearson statistic. The main advantage of $G^2$ is that it can be applied additively to nested models. However, the same chi-square tables can be used to test the significance of both $G^2$ and $\chi^2$ statistics, and obtained values tend to become numerically equal as sample size increases. The test uses one of the five original degrees of freedom since, as in any chi-square, the sum of the five observed frequencies must equal the sum of the five expected frequencies. In addition, two more degress of freedom estimate $\mu$ and $\sigma$, leaving a total of 2 *df*. A large value of $G^2$ implies the data are not normally distributed.

Next, replace *s* with the proposed $\sigma$ (15) and generate a new distribution of *z* scores. The value assigned $\sigma$ is now fixed rather than free. The observed proportions falling in each of the five categories produce a new value of $G^2$. This value must be at least as large as the first. Both values are sensitive to sampling error and nonnormality, but the second is also sensitive to the possible deviation of $\sigma$ from 15. Since one less parameter ($\sigma$) is estimated, the $G^2$ is based upon three rather than 2 *df*. The difference between the two $G^2$ values is itself a $G^2$ statistic with 1 *df* and specifically tests the hypothesis that $\sigma$ is 15. If it is large, the hypothesis may be rejected. This difference $G^2$ is also relatively robust with respect to violations of assumptions such as normality since nonnormality affects the two $G^2$ values being compared and is thus subtracted out (Agresti & Yang, 1986; Wickens, 1989).

The third step fixes $\mu$ at 100 and $\sigma$ at 15 and recomputes $G^2$ based upon the new distribution of *z* scores. The difference between this $G^2$, which has 4 *df* (there is only one constraint in the five cells—the sum of observed and expected frequencies must be equal), and the value obtained in the previous step tests whether 100 is a plausible estimate of $\mu$, given that 15 is a plausible estimate of $\sigma$. We could also obtain a $G^2$ from fixing $\mu$ at 100 but letting $\sigma$ vary freely (model 2′) and compare it to model 1 or model 3. The difference in $G^2$ between models 1 and 2′ tests the hypothesis that 100 is a plausible value for $\mu$, ignoring $\sigma$.

Models (e.g., model 2) were nested within other models (e.g., model 1) in these examples by fixing parameters rather than letting them vary freely. Constraining parameters to equality with one another that are allowed to vary freely in the more general model is another way to nest. Suppose there are two groups. One model might use separate group means, thus allowing them to vary. Nesting would use the grand mean, and thereby constrain the two group means to equality. The difference $G^2$ tests the null hypothesis that the group means are the same.

We drew 100 observations from a population in which $\mu$ actually was 108 and $\sigma$ was 14. The resulting frequency distributions appear in Table 4-3. The expected values are 20 per category. Because the data were actually sampled from a normal distribution, the $G^2$ for model 1 was quite small and nonsignificant (1.48). Fixing $\sigma$ at 15 (model 2) produced the same numeric value of $G^2$ to two decimal places, and so the difference $G^2$ was 0 and thus nonsignificant. Although it is in fact a type II error to conclude that 15 is an acceptable estimate of $\sigma$, this error illustrates the difficulty of detecting a difference in a small sample. Fixing $\mu$ at 100 and $\sigma$ at 15 (model 3), produced a significant difference $G^2$ of 26.60 because an excess of positive values of *z*. The same value of $G^2$ obtains when $\mu$ is fixed at 100 and $\sigma$ is estimated (model 2′). The large increase in $G^2$ when $\mu$ is fixed at 100 makes it clear that this estimate is not acceptable.

**TABLE 4-3**   FREQUENCY DISTRIBUTION FOR FOUR DIFFERENT MODELS

| Interval | Model 1 $\mu$ = free; $\sigma$ = free | Model 2 $\mu$ = free; $\sigma$ = 15 | Model 3 $\mu$ = 100; $\sigma$ = 15 | Model 4 $\mu$ = 100; $\sigma$ = free |
|---|---|---|---|---|
| $z > .86$ | 17 | 17 | 37 | 37 |
| $.84 \geq z > .26$ | 20 | 20 | 25 | 25 |
| $.26 \geq z > -.26$ | 24 | 24 | 17 | 17 |
| $-.26 \geq z > -.84$ | 18 | 21 | 15 | 1 |
| $-.84 \geq z$ | 21 | 18 | 6 | 6 |

In order to be clear, these examples are much simpler and the analysis is much cruder than the ones used in practice. They do not require open-form estimation since the sample mean and standard deviation can be obtained directly from the data. Real problems often require an iterative solution. Another characteristic of a real problem is that one must consider whether a unique solution is possible, i.e., the issue of identification.

In order to visualize more complex problems, where numerous parameters may be estimated at the same time, simply consider iterative estimation of two parameters, such as the above mean and variance. Any two such values fall somewhere in a two-dimensional plane of outcomes. Start at any arbitrarily chosen point in this plane. Then, move in the direction of greatest parameter change in the plane as determined from the probabilities of the parameters given the data. Each iteration moves closer to the maximum likelihood estimates. The process stops when two successive estimates differ by less than a designated amount.

### Bayesian Estimation

Bayesian estimation treats an unknown parameter $\Theta$ as the outcome of a random variable ($\mathbf{\Theta}$). The prior distribution of $\mathbf{\Theta}$ (its distribution in the absence of data) is denoted $h(\mathbf{\Theta})$. In a great many situations, all values of $\mathbf{\Theta}$ may be viewed as equally probable for lack of an alternative distribution, so that $h(\mathbf{\Theta})$ is uniform. If this is the case and one other condition described below is met, Bayesian estimation reduces to maximum likelihood estimation. However, Bayesian estimation may also reflect knowledge gained about a parameter from previous studies and the differential utility of outcomes by considering the relative cost of estimating too high or too low.

The probability of choosing a given value of $\mathbf{\Theta}$ is the ratio of the product of (1) the prior probability of that value of $\mathbf{\Theta}$, $h(\mathbf{\Theta})$, and (2) the conditional probability of the data (the probability of the data given $\mathbf{\Theta}$), denoted $p(X/\mathbf{\Theta})$, to (3) the unconditional (overall) probability of the data [$p(X)$], where $X$ denotes the data. The latter is obtained by computing the probability of data for each possible value of $\mathbf{\Theta}$ and (in essence) averaging. Equation 4-34 defines the Bayesian estimate of the probability of $\Theta$ given the data,$[p(\Theta/X)]$. Note that this conditional probability of the parameter is the inverse of $[p(\Theta/X)]$—one obtains the probability of the parameter given the data from the probability of the data given the parameter and other information. The maximum likelihood principle for a discrete distribution is as follows (the same ideas hold in a continuous distribution but a more cumbersome notation is needed).

$$p(\Theta/X) = \frac{p(X/\Theta)}{p(X)} \, h(\Theta) \qquad (4\text{-}34)$$

The numerator of this expression, $p(\Theta/X)h(\Theta)$, depends upon $\Theta$, but the denominator, $p(X)$, does not [since $p(X)$ is a constant, it is not really needed in most practical estimations]. Consequently, the ratio describes how choosing a particular value of $\Theta$ increases or decreases the probability of having obtained the data relative to an average outcome. The usual value of $\Theta$ chosen is the value that maximizes $p(\Theta/X)$, the mode of the function. If this is the case and $h(\Theta)$ is uniform, the result is the maximum likelihood estimate. An alternative way to estimate $\Theta$ is to select the expected value of $\Theta$ or average of the function, the a posteriori conditional probability.

## The Method of Moments

We previously obtained the $r$th moment about any constant $c$ by taking deviations of scores about $c$, raising each deviation to the power $r$, and averaging over the number of observations. The mean was therefore describable as the first moment about the origin ($c = 0$ and $r = 1$), and the variance as the second moment about the mean ($c = \mu$ or $X$, and $r = 2$).

Parameters are often either moments or functions of moments. When this is the case, one technique is to estimate the parameter(s) in question by substituting sample moments for the corresponding population moments and solving the resulting equations. This is the "method of moments." It is so straightforward that any difficulty you may have in understanding it may arise because you expect a more difficult concept. For example, the population slope for standardized variables in a regression line may be simply estimated from the sample value of $r$ since the population value is the desired slope. The previous edition of this book assumed that samples were large enough to allow sampling error to be ignored. This essentially implies the method of moments.

Unfortunately, statistical research has often revealed flaws in the method of moments. Bowen and Huang (1990) provide an excellent illustration. Previously, Kenny and La Voie (1985) had used the method of moments to estimate a particular correlation useful in analyzing data obtained from randomly formed groups of subjects (the precise nature of this correlation need not be of concern). Population values are appropriately bounded by ±1. However, Bowen and Huang (1990) showed that estimates could easily fall out of bounds by large margins and developed a maximum likelihood algorithm to overcome this difficulty.

### Equal Weighting (the "It Don't Make No Nevermind Principle")

One very legitimate approach to estimating a series of parameters of the same type, such as regression weights or factor score weights (see Chapter 12) is to let all parameters equal one another. When the variables all have approximately equal variance, such as test items, it does not matter whether they are in raw or standardized form. However, if they differ considerably in scale, as might be the case for perfectly arbitrary reasons, the variables must first be standardized to prevent those with the largest variance from spuriously dominating the prediction. For example, if raw SAT scores ($\sigma = 100$) were simply added to high school grade point averages ($\sigma \approx .2$) to predict college grades, the greater variance of the SAT scores would determine the result and make grade point averages essentially irrelevant.

Equal weighting is especially appropriate for small samples where estimates usually produce large sampling error. There is no sampling error associated with equal weights since the parameters are not estimated but defined in advance. However, equal weighting introduces a second form of error because (probably) unequal population parameters are treated as equal. The relative magnitudes of the two sources of error determine the better strategy.

Kaiser (1970; Dawes, 1971; Dawes & Corrigan, 1974; Wainer, 1976) noted that equal weights are often just as effective in making predictions in a new sample as are optimal weights (least squares in his example). He used the term "it don't make no nevermind" to describe the outcome. Evidence for this point goes at least as far back as Wilks (1938). In some cases, though, equal weights sometimes impair ones' ability to predict. Perloff and Persons (1988; also see Paunonen & Gardner, 1991) provide relevant illustrations.

Evaluating the difference between equal and optimal weights is very easy to do on a computer. Correlate the equally weighted sum with the optimally weighted sum and, in a regression problem, the criterion, preferably in a new sample. The use of a new sample illustrates cross validation to minimize the role played by chance in determining optimum weights.

Using equal rather than optimal weights assumes that your research interest is in accuracy of prediction rather than in the weights themselves. This is particularly likely to be the case in applied problems. Many situations, however, dictate interest in the weights themselves, perhaps as measures of the relative importance of the various predictors. Obviously, equal weights do not address the issue.

### Properties of Estimators

Now that several approaches to define the best or optimal way to estimate a parameter have been mentioned, it is useful to note the four most desirable properties of an estimate: (1) It should be unbiased, (2) it should be efficient, (3) it should be consistent, and (4) it should be sufficient. Properties 1 and 2, bias and efficiency, are generally regarded as more important than properties 3 and 4, consistency and sufficiency.

**1** *Bias.* The estimate is unbiased if its expected value or average of all possible estimates is the same as the population parameter, i.e., if it tends neither to be too high nor too low.

**2** *Efficiency.* The estimate is efficient if values obtained from randomly different samples are similar (have small variance).

**3** *Consistency.* The estimate is consistent if it tends to fall closer and closer to the population parameter as sample size increases.

**4** *Sufficiency.* The estimate is sufficient if it utilizes all relevant sample information in estimating the parameter.

The mean-square error in an estimate combines the notions of bias and efficiency. Efficiency is the variance of estimates about the mean estimate (mean value of $\hat{\Theta}$), whereas mean-square error is the variance about the parameter ($\Theta$) The mean-square error and the efficiency will be equal if the estimator is unbiased. An estimator is sometimes both unbiased and most efficient. It is called a minimum variance unbiased estimator in that case.

It is not always possible to obtain sufficient estimators, but if they exist in a given situation, maximum likelihood estimators will be sufficient. Maximum likelihood estimators are also the most efficient and consistent in large samples. On the other hand, the lack of bias in ordinary least squares is a decided advantage in small samples (less than 10 observations per predictor). Not all estimation methods allow their properties to be deduced, the method of moments being a case in point, but computer simulations may be used. Maximum likelihood estimators are sometimes biased in small samples. Dividing the sample sum of squares by N does tend to underestimate $\sigma$ slightly, as illustrated in estimating the population standard deviation, but a great many statisticians feel that maximum likelihood's slight bias is offset by its other advantages, particularly its greater efficiency, in most situations.

Freedom from bias was once regarded as more important than efficiency. Opinions have changed, especially when the estimator is consistent so that the bias disappears in large samples. In contrast, ordinary least-squares estimators are unbiased but may be inefficient. We have noted how considerable efficiency is lost when one uses ordinary least squares with a heteroscedastic criterion (Draper & Smith, 1981). Maximum likelihood estimates have become increasingly popular because of the extremely wide variety of problems they may be applied to and the above statistical advantages. Even though they are complex, they actually simplify solutions to otherwise difficult problems, as Bowen and Huang (1990) illustrated. Although most procedures we will discuss use ordinary least squares and will probably continue to do so, maximum likelihood methods have been used with increasing frequency. At the same time, we have noted how maximum likelihood estimates may be biased in small samples. They are therefore not "magical" despite their many advantages. Bad data gathered from small samples used to estimate large numbers of parameters lead to bad estimates!

Virtually any maximum likelihood application provides standard errors of the estimates. They are useful in three major ways: (1) Dividing the parameter estimate by its standard error provides a *t* test to see if it is reasonable that the parameter is a value of interest (e.g., 0.), (2) the relative magnitudes of the standard errors indicate which are the least stable, and (3) the correlations among the estimates indicate interdependencies among the estimates. Winkler and Hays (1975) and Bush (1963) provide further information about maximum likelihood estimation.

## SUMMARY

The distinction between discrete (categorical) and continuous quantities is very important in psychometric theory. In particular, test items tend to be inherently categorical, whereas scale scores produced by aggregating items are continuous. However, our definitions of categorical and discrete differ somewhat from a mathematical definition. Mathematics defines a quantity as continuous if it is possible to obtain a value that is intermediate between any two other values, and discrete otherwise. All empirically defined quantities are discrete by this definition. Consequently, we will (somewhat arbitrarily) define a variable as continuous if it can assume more than 11 values, and discrete if it cannot.

Quantities are useful in science to the extent that they vary even if they are binary (dichotomous, so that they can assume only two values, such as answers on many tests, which are therefore also categorical) rather than continuous. The variance and its square root, the standard deviation measure this concept. Variables are transformed for various reasons, e.g., standardization. Adding a constant to each score does not affect the variance or standard deviation, but multiplying by a constant, $b$, increases the variance by $b^2$ and the standard deviation by $b$.

Studies of individual differences are usually concerned with variation among people, whereas experiments are usually concerned with variation in group means. In particular, nearly all studies are concerned with the correlations among two or more variables. The most widely used measure of correlation is the Pearson product-moment correlation ($r$) which describes the linear relation between two variables. Although there are many computational formulas, $r$ may be most simply defined as the average cross product of two sets of standard ($z$) scores. The "moment" part of the definition comes from the fact that the deviations used in obtaining $z$ scores are the first moments about the mean where a moment is the average difference between observations and a constant (the mean in this case) raised to a power (the first). Similarly, the covariance, which plays an important role in psychometric theory, is the average cross product of unstandardized deviation scores.

Many sources describe the phi coefficient, the point-biserial correlation, and Spearman's rank-order correlation, which are only computational short-cuts for hand calculation of $r$ in special cases. However, biserial and tetrachoric $r$ use binary data to estimate what $r$ would be if the data were continuous and normally distributed. They generalize to polyserial and polychoric $r$ which may be applied to categorical data in general. Although there are differences of opinion, we recommend that these estimates generally be avoided. Moreover, one should also avoid artificially categorizing variables save possibly to simplify data presentation.

Using $r$ involves three main assumptions. The relation between the variables should at least be monotonic and preferably linear; error affecting each variable should be of the same magnitude across levels of the other (homoscedastic), and error should be normally distributed. Normality is less important to description than inference, but skewness can cause $r$ to underestimate the magnitude of relationships. Two major factors that can limit $r$ are range restriction and differences in distribution shape, although the latter primarily occurs with categorical variables. In general, $r$ is directly related to true variance (variance predictable from the linear relation between the two variance) and inversely related to error variance (residual variance not predictable). Error variance tends to remain relatively constant as total (observed) variance increases, but true variance generally tends to increase, and so $r$ tends to increase as total variance increases. Similarly, the correlation between two categorical variables is limited by the similarity of their distributions which in turn reflects the similarities in proportions of people who pass on each of the two variables.

The correlation ratio, eta ($\eta$), measures correlation magnitude without assuming linearity. Eta is the square root of the ratio of true variance (variance predictable from any relation between the two variables) to total variance. It is also the square root of 1 minus the ratio of error variance to total variance.

Although they are distinct concepts, correlation and prediction are related by the role that $r$ plays in one form of prediction, linear regression—$r$ defines the slope of the line of best fit in predicting one standardized observable variable from another standardized observable variable. The $r^2$ defines the coefficient of determination or proportion of criterion variance accounted for by its relation to the predictor, and $r$ is the standard deviation of predicted scores ($z_{Y}' = rz_X$, assuming $z_Y$ is the criterion and $z_X$ is the predictor) in standardized form. In contrast, $1 - r^2$ is the coefficient of nondetermination or proportion of unaccounted criterion variance, and its square root is the standard error of estimate or standard deviation of residual scores ($z_{Y \cdot X} = z_Y - rz_X$). Regression and correlation thus illustrate the partitioning of variance important throughout statistics. Table 4-2 is crucial in defining the relations among predictor scores, criterion scores, predicted scores, and residual scores. Structural equations are a more general approach to prediction in which observed variables are functions of latent or unobservable variables.

Obtaining a correlation or the slope of a line of best fit are examples of statistical estimation where a decision rule provides estimators. A specific estimator is an estimate; e.g., a sample mean is an estimate of a population mean. Estimates should be close to the parameters of interest, and a loss function describes the disparity. Alternative loss functions are used in ordinary least-squares (historically the most popular), generalized least-squares, maximum likelihood, and Bayesian estimation. The method of moments is a widely used approach which people often use without realizing it (but one often posing hazards). When one estimates several parameters of the same form, another approach is to use equal weighting (assume their values are equal).

Many times, maximum likelihood and generalized least-squares estimation involve specifying parameters of a model as free (to be estimated from the data), constrained (defined in terms of another parameter), or fixed (set equal to a predefined variable). Constraining or fixing a parameter constrains a model by restricting the possible values parameter estimates may assume. If the estimated parameters of model A are defined as free and the corresponding estimates of model B are constrained or fixed, model B is a nested form (special case) of model A. The fit of each model and, more importantly, their difference in fit may be tested by a likelihood ratio chi-square, commonly symbolized as $G^2$. If the difference in $G^2$ is small, the constraint is appropriate to the situation; if it is large, the constraint is inappropriate.

In general, four properties are desirable in an estimator: (1) freedom from bias (the estimate should not be systematically too high or too low), (2) efficiency (estimates from different samples should be similar in magnitude), (3) consistency (any bias should disappear as sample size increases), and (4) sufficiency (the estimate should use all relevant information). Unfortunately, estimation strategies rarely possess all four properties. Least-squares estimates are generally unbiased but inefficient; maximum likelihood estimators are often biased but efficient. Recent statistical trends have emphasized the acceptability of the small amount of bias in maximum likelihood estimation given its greater efficiency and ability to test hierarchical models.

## SUGGESTED ADDITIONAL READINGS

Cohen, J., & Cohen, P. (1983). *Applied multivariate analysis/linear regression* (2d ed.). Hillsdale, NJ: Erlbaum Associates.

Edwards, A. L. (1985). *Multiple regression and the analysis of variance and covariance* (2d ed.) New York: Freeman.

Guilford, J. P., & Fruchter, B. (1978). *Fundamental statistics in psychology and education* (6th ed.). New York: McGraw-Hill.

Kenny, D. A. (1979). *Correlation and causality.* New York: Wiley.

Wherry, R. J. (1985). *Contributions to correlational analysis.* Orlando, FL: Academic Press.

## CHAPTER 5

# LINEAR COMBINATIONS, PARTIAL CORRELATION, MULTIPLE CORRELATION, AND MULTIPLE REGRESSION

## CHAPTER OVERVIEW

Linear combinations are weighted sums of variables that form the heart of psychometric theory. For example, the conventional practice of scoring tests by adding up the number of correct responses defines the total score as an equally weighted linear combination of item responses. This chapter begins with a consideration of their properties. In particular, the variance of the sum of an equally weighted linear combination is shown to be equal to the sum of the elements in the variance-covariance matrix defined by the variances and covariances of the elements of the linear combination. Simple extensions of this conclusion are then applied to obtain the variance of a weighted linear combination and of standardized variables. As part of the discussion, we will note how properties of items determine the shape of total score distributions. We will show how the common view that "a good test produces a normal distribution of scores" is false.

"Partial correlations" are correlations between two variables in which the effects of a third variable are removed. Similarly, "semipartial correlations" are correlations between two variables in which the effects of a third variable are removed from one, but not both, of the two. Both are integral to "multivariate analysis," which deals with the relations among several variables.

Multiple correlation and multiple regression occupy most of the chapter. "Multiple correlation" ($R$) deals with the correlation between an optimally weighted linear combination of predictors and a criterion, and "multiple regression" deals with defining the optimal weightings themselves. The optimal weights for standardized variables are called beta ($\beta$) weights, and the optimal weights for raw variables are called b weights. Both are usually estimated through the method of least squares. They describe the expected change in the criterion per unit change in a predictor, holding constant all other predictors. We will consider the factors that determine the magnitude of $R$. Perhaps contrary to expectation, $R$ seldom increases appreciably once two or three major predictors are included. One frequently overlooked point is that there is an upward bias in sample values of $R$; $R$ will spuriously increase with the number of predictors. Ways to incorporate categorical predictors are considered. Predictor importance is an extremely important topic as there are several definitions which vary considerably in meaning. For example, the variable having the largest validity or correlation with the criterion may not have the largest $\beta$ weight. Validity defines what the predictor has in common with the criterion ignoring other predictors, whereas a $\beta$ weight defines what the predictor has in common with the criterion controlling other predictors. A third definition is incremental validity of a predictor over a subset of predictors (covariates).

Although some regression problems concern only $\beta$ weights estimated with a fixed set of predictors, it is more common to select variables from a larger set. One important distinction is whether the situation involves (1) actuarially oriented prediction, which is characteristic of predictive validation, is data-driven, and places relatively little emphasis upon the processes underlying prediction, or (2) hypothesis testing, which is basic to construct validation, is theory-driven, and is concerned with details of these processes. Stepwise inclusion of variables selects predictors on the basis of sample data. It easily leads to spurious results and is *not* recommended, especially for hypothesis testing. In contrast, hierarchical inclusion of variables in a predefined order is an important strategy, especially for hypothesis testing. This approach stresses what new predictors add to previous knowledge. In addition, some situations suggest alternatives to $\beta$ weights, such as equal weighting. The concept of "it don't make no nevermind" states that the precise weightings of predictors are often unimportant to actuarially oriented prediction because different weightings often produce highly correlated linear combinations.

Finally, we briefly discuss certain related topics: (1) the analysis of covariance, which is a special case of hierarchical inclusion useful in reducing experimental error, (2) use of multiple regression to fit nonlinear functions, (3) canonical correlation, which concerns optimal relations between groups of predictor variables and groups of criterion variables, and (4) residual analysis which looks for systematic differences between observed and predicted values.

## VARIANCES OF LINEAR COMBINATIONS

Score distributions are often obtained by summing scores on individual variables (items). The simplest case of this linear model provides total scores as equally weighted linear combinations of item responses. Ordinary "number-correct" scores on classroom tests or sums of item responses on Likert-type items are outcomes of this model. Regression equations are weighted linear combinations in which the weights reflect what individual predictors have in common with the criterion, holding constant all other predictors.

There are some very important relations between the characteristics of linear combinations and the individual measures upon which they are based. These relations allow more complex methods of multivariate analysis to be easily developed. Because the results of most multivariate analyses are the same regardless of whether one starts with raw scores or deviation scores, it will be more convenient to work with deviation scores. Equation 5-1a is an equally weighted (also called unweighted, perhaps misleadingly, since there are weights, albeit equal ones) linear combination ($y$, the lowercase denoting that it is a deviation score $= Y - \overline{Y}$) of three individual variables, $x_1$, $x_2$, and $x_3$. The latter are likewise deviation scores, e.g., $x_1 = X_1 - \overline{X}_1$. Equation 5-1b is a weighted linear combination where $b_1$, $b_2$, and $b_3$ are weighting constants applied to the individual measures. In contrast, Eq. 5-1c is not a linear combination because it contains cross-product terms such as $x_1x_2$, and a variable raised to a power ($x_1^2$). However, if we define $x_4 = x_1x_2$, $x_5 = x_1x_3$, $x_6 = x_2x_3$, and $x_7 = x_1^2$, Eq. 5-1d *is* a linear combination, a most important "trick." This section will limit discussion to equations of the form of Eq. 5-1a, and later sections will consider those of the form of Eqs. 5-1b and 5-1d. We will not consider nonlinear combinations like Eq. 5-1c directly.

$$y = x_1 + x_2 + x_3 \tag{5-1a}$$
$$y = b_1x_1 + b_2x_2 + b_3x_3 \tag{5-1b}$$
$$y = x_1 + x_2 + x_3 + x_1x_2 + x_1x_3 + x_2x_3 + x_1^2 \tag{5-1c}$$
$$y = x_1 + x_2 + x_3 + x_4 + x_5 + x_6 + x_7 \tag{5-1d}$$

In Eq. 5-1a, each person's score on $y$ is obtained by summing the score on the three $x$ measures. The properties of $y$ would not be affected if some of the $x$ variables were subtracted rather than added. The mean of $y$ is zero because the means of the individual variables are zero (they are deviation scores), and the mean of a sum equals the sum of the individual means. This is also true of Eq. 5-1b but not of Eqs. 5-1c and 5-1d, unless the cross product and power terms are themselves transformed. The fact that $x_1$ and $x_2$ have means of zero does not imply that $x_1x_2$ or $x_1^2$ has means of zero. Indeed, a mean of numbers raised to an even-numbered power cannot have a mean of zero unless the numbers themselves are all zero.

Many mathematical properties of linear combinations can be deduced by substituting the linear combination in the equations for individual distributions. Thus, the variance of $y$ in linear combination 5-1a is obtained as follows:

$$\sigma_y^2 = \frac{\Sigma y^2}{N}$$
$$= \frac{\Sigma(x_1 + x_2 + x_3)^2}{N}$$
$$= \frac{1}{N}\,(x_1^2 + x_2^2 + x_3^2 + 2x_1x_2 + 2x_1x_3 + 2x_2x_3)$$
$$= \sigma_1^2 + \sigma_2^2 + \sigma_3^2 + 2(\sigma_{12} + \sigma_{13} + \sigma_{23}) \tag{5-2}$$

The variance of any sum of variables ($\sigma_y^2$) is generally obtainable from the individual variances of $x_i$ and $x_j$ ($\sigma_i^2$ and $\sigma_j^2$) and their covariance ($\sigma_{ij}$) as follows (note the change in notation—$x$ and $y$, without subscripts, sufficed in the previous chapter when we had only two variables to consider):

$$\sigma_y^2 = \Sigma\sigma_i^2 + 2\Sigma\sigma_{ij}\ \ i \neq j \tag{5-3a}$$

or, using Eq. 4-10:

$$\sigma_y^2 = \Sigma\sigma_i^2 + 2r_{ij}\Sigma\sigma_i\sigma_j\ \ i \neq j \tag{5-3b}$$

The variance of a sum ($y$) thus equals (1) the sum of the individual variances plus (2) twice the sum of all possible covariances among variables (see Eq. 2-3).

There is a very useful method for depicting the variance of a linear combination that greatly facilitates subsequent discussion. Numerical examples will be presented later. First, place the terms along the top and side of a table, as follows:

|       | $x_1$ | $x_2$ | $x_3$ |
|-------|-------|-------|-------|
| $x_1$ |       |       |       |
| $x_2$ |       |       |       |
| $x_3$ |       |       |       |

Next, multiply corresponding elements, as follows:

|       | $x_1$     | $x_2$     | $x_3$     |
|-------|-----------|-----------|-----------|
| $x_1$ | $x_1^2$   | $x_1 x_2$ | $x_1 x_3$ |
| $x_2$ | $x_1 x_2$ | $x_2^2$   | $x_2 x_3$ |
| $x_3$ | $x_1 x_3$ | $x_2 x_3$ | $x_3^2$   |

Next, sum over the number of people in the study ($N$), and, finally, divide each term by $N$. This produces variances in the main (or major) diagonal positions (the positions that run from the top left to bottom right of the table, which will be simply denoted "diagonal" hereafter). There are three diagonal entries in the present case—$\sigma_1^2$, $\sigma_2^2$, and $\sigma_3^2$. The remaining off-diagonal positions (six in this case) contain covariances, e.g., $\sigma_{12}$. We will treat the variances as covariances of variables with themselves in the discussion below. This produces the following table:

|       | $x_1$         | $x_2$         | $x_3$         |
|-------|---------------|---------------|---------------|
| $x_1$ | $\sigma_1^2$  | $\sigma_{12}$ | $\sigma_{13}$ |
| $x_2$ | $\sigma_{12}$ | $\sigma_2^2$  | $\sigma_{23}$ |
| $x_3$ | $\sigma_{13}$ | $\sigma_{23}$ | $\sigma_3^2$  |

(It is conventional to let the first subscript denote the row and the second subscript denote the column, as in Table 2-1. However, had we followed this convention, the point where $\sigma_{12} = \sigma_{21}$ would have been obscured.) This table contains all necessary data required to use Eq. 5-2 and compute the variance of $y$ from its $k$ individual members. The sum of the elements in the table is therefore the variance of $y$. Any rectangular table of variables such as the one above is called a "matrix." The matrix above is specifically called a "covariance matrix" or a "variance-covariance matrix." We will use the former term for simplicity and symbolize it as **C** (the use of boldface to denote matrices is standard notation). The covariance matrix of raw scores is identical to the covariance matrix of the corresponding deviation scores. Subscripts will later be used to distinguish different covariance matrices in particular problems. The symbol $\overline{C}$ will denote the sum of all the elements in the covariance matrix **C**. This use of a bar over **C** to indicate summing is unusual but convenient. It is more compact than the formal expression in summation notation, $\Sigma\sigma_{ij}$. Consequently, $\overline{C}$ is the variance of a sum of variables.

## Variance of a Weighted Sum

Linear combinations are often weighted, as in Eq. 5-1b. The weights ($b_i$) may be determined on some prior basis to give greater importance to certain variables. This might reflect a theory that says that one variable is twice as important as another. The weights may also be determined after the data are gathered by least-squares or another estimation method, as in multiple regression.

The variance of a weighted sum is obtained by an extension of the previous matrix approach used with an unweighted sum. The only difference is that weights for the variables are placed on the top and side of the covariance matrix, as follows:

|          | $b_1x_1$ | $b_2x_2$ | $b_3x_3$ |
|----------|----------|----------|----------|
| $b_1x_1$ |          |          |          |
| $b_2x_2$ |          |          |          |
| $b_3x_3$ |          |          |          |

As before, corresponding elements are multiplied, summed over the $N$ observations, and divided by $N$. Each element in the resulting matrix is a covariance multiplied by the product of the two weights for the two variables, an extension of Eq. 4-4. The resulting matrix is

|          | $b_1x_1$ | $b_2x_2$ | $b_3x_3$ |
|----------|----------|----------|----------|
| $b_1x_1$ | $b_1^2\sigma_1^2$ | $b_1b_2\sigma_{12}$ | $b_1b_3\sigma_{13}$ |
| $b_2x_2$ | $b_1b_2\sigma_{12}$ | $b_2^2\sigma_2^2$ | $b_2b_3\sigma_{23}$ |
| $b_3x_3$ | $b_1b_3\sigma_{13}$ | $b_2b_3\sigma_{23}$ | $b_3^2\sigma_3^2$ |

The variance of a weighted sum equals the sum of the elements in the weighted co-variance matrix ($\Sigma b_i b_j \sigma_{ij}$ in summation notation), as shown above. The variances of both weighted and unweighted sums equal $\overline{C}$. We state whether or not weights are involved when there is likelihood of confusion.

## Variance of a Sum of Standard Scores

The simplest case is when the individual variables have been standardized, as in the following linear combination:

$$y = z_1 + z_2 + z_3$$

The matrix arrangement for calculating the variance of a sum makes the result readily apparent. There are no weights, and so there are no $b$ terms. The variance of any set of standard scores is 1; consequently 1s will appear in the diagonal spaces. Since the covariance of any two sets of standard scores is $r$ (see Chapter. 4), $r$'s appear in the off-diagonal spaces. The result is a correlation matrix, illustrated as follows:

|       | $z_1$    | $z_2$    | $z_3$    |
|-------|----------|----------|----------|
| $z_1$ | 1.00     | $r_{12}$ | $r_{13}$ |
| $z_2$ | $r_{12}$ | 1.00     | $r_{23}$ |
| $z_3$ | $r_{13}$ | $r_{23}$ | 1.00     |

Correlation matrices will be symbolized as **R**. The variance of the sum of $k$ sets of standard scores equals the sum of all the elements in the correlation matrix of these sets of scores. The sum will be symbolized as $\overline{R}$. If these standardized variables are weighted before they are summed, products of the weights will appear in the correlation matrix just as was shown for a covariance matrix and $\overline{R}$ will equal $\Sigma b_i b_j r_{ij}$. The diagonal elements will always be positive because $b_i b_j$ will reduce to a positive number ($b_i^2$). However, off-diagonal values of $r$ might be either positive or negative depending upon whether (1) the direction of correlation is positive or negative and (2) the respective weights, $b_i$ and $b_j$, have the same or a different sign.

## Variance of Sums of Dichotomous Distributions

One of the most important cases in psychometric theory involves the variance of a sum of $k$ dichotomous variables, as in the total score variance for $k$ dichotomous items. The matrix representation of the variance of total test scores for a three-item test where each item is scored 1 or 0 is

|       | $x_1$       | $x_2$         | $x_3$         |
|-------|-------------|---------------|---------------|
| $x_1$ | $p_1 q_1$   | $\sigma_{12}$ | $\sigma_{13}$ |
| $x_2$ | $\sigma_{12}$ | $p_2 q_2$   | $\sigma_{23}$ |
| $x_3$ | $\sigma_{13}$ | $\sigma_{23}$ | $p_3 q_3$   |

The off-diagonal elements are again covariances, and the diagonal elements are variances (recall from Eq. 4-3 that the variance of a dichotomous variable is $pq$.) As the covariance of two variables is $r$ ($\Phi$ in the present case) times the product of their standard deviations, the covariance between any two items, such as 1 and 2, is

$$\sigma_{12} = r_{12}\sqrt{(p_1q_1)(p_2q_2)} \qquad (5\text{-}4)$$

Since $pq$ grows smaller as $p$ departs from .5 in either direction, the term under the radical will be largest when both $p$ values are near .5 and will decrease when either $p$ value is removed from .5. Similarly, the diagonal elements will be largest when the $p$ value for that item is near .5. These considerations are very important to future discussions of the variance of score distributions and test reliability. The variance of the sum of $k$ dichotomous items again equals the sum of the elements in the covariance matrix for these items, $\overline{C}$ we use a different symbol, $\overline{R}$ to discuss a correlation matrix.) With dichotomous items, $\overline{C}$ equals the sum of $pq$ values plus the sum of all off-diagonal covariances.

## Numerical Examples

Assume that the following is a variance-covariance matrix for variables $x_1$, $x_2$, and $x_3$.

|       | $x_1$ | $x_2$ | $x_3$ |
|-------|-------|-------|-------|
| $x_1$ | 50    | 20    | 30    |
| $x_2$ | 20    | 30    | 15    |
| $x_3$ | 30    | 15    | 40    |

The variance of the equally weighted sum of $x_1$, $x_2$, and $x_3$ is simply the sum of the nine elements in the matrix: $50 + 20 + 30 + \cdots + 40$ or 250.

Now, assume that $x_1$, $x_2$, and $x_3$ are given respective weights of 3, 2, and 1. This gives rise to the following matrix:

|        | $3x_1$ | $2x_2$ | $1x_3$ |
|--------|--------|--------|--------|
| $3x_1$ | $3^2 \cdot 50 = 450$ | $3 \cdot 2 \cdot 20 = 120$ | $3 \cdot 1 \cdot 30 = 90$ |
| $2x_2$ | $2 \cdot 3 \cdot 20 = 120$ | $2^2 \cdot 30 = 120$ | $2 \cdot 1 \cdot 15 = 30$ |
| $1x_3$ | $1 \cdot 3 \cdot 30 = 90$ | $1 \cdot 2 \cdot 15 = 30$ | $1^2 \cdot 40 = 40$ |

The variance of this unequally weighted linear combination is $450 + 120 + \cdots + 40$ or 1090.

For a third example, we will use Eq. 4-9 to convert the original variance-covariance matrix into a correlation matrix. This involves dividing each off-diagonal term (covariance) by the square root of the product of the on-diagonal terms (variances) that appear in the same row and in the same column. The diagonals of this correlation matrix are all 1s.

|  | $x_1$ | $x_2$ | $x_3$ |
|---|---|---|---|
| $x_1$ | $\dfrac{50}{\sqrt{50 \cdot 50}} = 1.00$ | $\dfrac{20}{\sqrt{50 \cdot 30}} = .52$ | $\dfrac{30}{\sqrt{50 \cdot 40}} = .67$ |
| $x_2$ | $\dfrac{20}{\sqrt{50 \cdot 30}} = .52$ | $\dfrac{30}{\sqrt{30 \cdot 30}} = 1.00$ | $\dfrac{15}{\sqrt{30 \cdot 40}} = .43$ |
| $x_3$ | $\dfrac{30}{\sqrt{50 \cdot 40}} = .67$ | $\dfrac{15}{\sqrt{30 \cdot 40}} = .43$ | $\dfrac{20}{\sqrt{20 \cdot 20}} = 1.00$ |

The variance of $z_1 + z_2 + z_3$, $x_1$ to $x_3$ expressed as $z$ scores, is obtained by adding the terms in this matrix: $1.00 + .52 + .67 + \cdots + 1.00 = 6.24$.

## CHARACTERISTICS OF SCORE DISTRIBUTIONS

The above principles plus some others that will be discussed in this section permit numerous deductions about the mean, variance, and shape of distributions of test scores to be developed. The principles will be developed with respect to test scores obtained by summing dichotomous items, but these principles also hold for multicategory items.

Let $Y = X_1 + X_2 + \cdots + X_k$ be an equally weighted linear combination (ordinary sum) of item responses (Note the use of $Y$ instead of $y$ since the item scores are not in deviation form). The mean $(\overline{Y})$ is by definition:

$$\overline{Y} = \frac{\Sigma X}{N}$$

Also by definition:

$$\overline{Y} = \frac{\Sigma(X_1 + X_2 + \cdots + X_k)}{N}$$
$$= \frac{\Sigma X_1}{N} + \frac{\Sigma X_2}{N} + \cdots + \frac{\Sigma X_k}{N}$$
$$= \overline{X}_1 + \overline{X}_2 + \cdots + \overline{X}_k \qquad (5\text{-}5)$$

The sum of scores on any item is simply the number of persons who passed the item. The mean score on the item ($p$ value) equals this sum divided by the number of persons ($N$). In other words, $p$ is the mean of an item scored as 1 or 0. The mean total score on a test comprised of such items ($\overline{Y}$) is therefore

$$\overline{Y} = p_1 + p_2 + \cdots + p_k \qquad (5\text{-}6a)$$
$$= \Sigma p_i \qquad (5\text{-}6b)$$

The mean thus equals the sum of the $p$ values. This holds for any type of dichotomous item (an item that is scored 1 or 0, e.g., an attitudinal item scored as agree or disagree, not just a pass-fail item).

## Variances

Since the variance of a sum equals the sum of the variances plus twice the sum of the covariances (Eq. 5-3a), the variance of any set of test scores depends on only these two factors. If the sum of the covariances is zero, the variance of total scores will equal the sum of the item variances. Since this section assumes the items are scored only as 1 or 0, the variance of test scores will equal the sum of $pq$ values. The sum of covariances will be zero if all correlations among items are zero *or* if negative correlations offset positive correlations.

Moreover, if the $k$ items are uncorrelated and all items have the same $p$ value, the sum of $pq$ reduces to $k(pq)$. In this special case, the total test scores forms a binomial distribution, illustrated in Fig. 5-1. This shows the expected number of heads ($p = .5$) obtained when $k = 10$ pennies are tossed 1024 times. The variance, $k(pq)$, will be $10(.5)(.5)$ or 2.5. This tie-in with the binomial distribution permits the development of many very useful principles about score distributions. Each coin in the example is analogous to a dichotomous test item: A head represents passing (a score of 1), and a tail represents failing (a score of 0). A toss of 10 coins represents the performance of one person on a 10-item test, and the number of heads is the person's score.

The foregoing discussion suggests several principles. First, the variance of score distributions tends to decrease as the item $p$ values get further from .5. This is so even

**FIGURE 5-1**    The expected distribution of heads and tails for 10 coins tossed 1024 times.

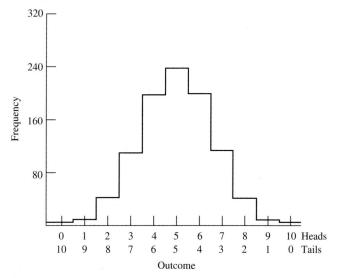

if the average $p$ value is .5, but the individual $p$ values vary widely about that point. Second, the average correlation (and thus covariance) among items and the total score variance are intimately related. High positive interitem correlations produce a large variance in test scores, and low correlations produce a small variance in test scores. Because high test reliability depends upon positive average item intercorrelations, a highly reliable test has a larger variance than a less reliable test (see Chapter 6). A binomial distribution is the limiting case of total unreliability, but this baseline is important to consider.

## Distribution Shape

The shape of the test-score distribution is determined by (1) the $p$ values, (2) the covariances among items, and (3) the number of items. As the number of items increases, the distribution becomes progressively smoother. The binomial distribution in Fig. 5-1 and, for that matter, in any 10-item test is a series of discrete steps rather than a smooth curve. The binomial distribution approaches the smooth normal distribution as the number of coins (items) is increased. Of course, this smooth appearance depends upon maintaining the same horizontal scale on the graph. If the horizontal axis were made longer as the number of coins or items was increased, the stair-step appearance would remain. However, since horizontal axes are not "stretched" in that way, the increase in number of coins or test items leads to an appearance of smoothing.

Real test scores based upon item sums are rarely normally distributed, even if the number of items is large, because items on a real test are positively correlated and not uncorrelated (independent). Items in a coin toss are expected to be uncorrelated: The outcome for one coin (heads versus tails) is independent of (uncorrelated with) the outcome for the other coins. Items on psychological measures must *not* be uncorrelated, however. Uncorrelated items have nothing in common; there is no central "theme" or factor, to their content, and they therefore measure different things. It is not sensible to name the total score (i.e., assume that it measures any trait) or even to add scores in the first place. Our use of items is not limited to pencil-and-paper tests. The principle applies equally to the number of items recalled in a memory study or to individual bar presses in a Skinner box. Most measures are comprised of items that are aggregated in some way. Seldom is only one response used to measure a trait.

Positive item intercorrelations also flatten the distribution of test scores, as may be seen in Fig. 5-2. The circles represent the distribution of simulated scores based upon the sum of 20 unrelated items (a totally unreliable test), and the squares represent the distribution of scores based upon 20 items whose average correlation was .10 (a low to somewhat reliable test by the standards discussed in Chapters 6 through 9). All items had a .5 probability of being answered correctly, and there were 1000 subjects. Note how the tails of the distribution for the moderately reliable test scores stretch out more widely in each direction relative to the height at the mean as compared to the distribution for the totally unreliable test scores. This also illustrates how a normal distribution of scores may be obtained by using a totally unreliable measure. Keep in mind, though, that the raw scores on the reliable measure may be normalized for convenience. Our concern is with the raw scores.

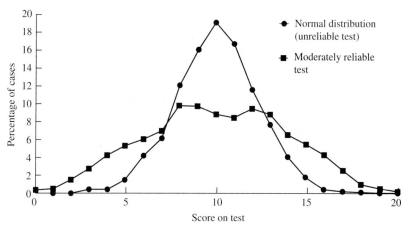

**FIGURE 5-2**   A normal distribution produced by random data (a totally unreliable test) and the flatter distribution of a moderately reliable test.

The amount of flattening depends upon the average item intercorrelations and the number of items, the two determinants of test reliability (see Chapters 6 through 9). Very high average item intercorrelations can produce a bimodal distribution, but this is very rarely seen. The limiting case is perfect interitem correlations where passing one item means passing all items and failing one item means failing all items. Total test scores fall at only two points—zero and perfect scores. Despite the difference in the two distribution shapes, most actual distributions obtained by summing items are sufficiently similar to the normal distribution because item correlations are typically low to allow use of the useful statistical properties of a normal distribution.

Whether a distribution is symmetric or skewed (lopsided) mainly depends on the average $p$ value and the number of items. The effects of $p$ can be illustrated with a 10-item test in which all $p$ values are .1 (only 10 percent of the subjects pass each item). The mean ($kp$) is 1.0. There is only one score possible below the mean (0), but there are nine possible scores above the mean (2 to 10 inclusive). Figure 5-3 presents a typical distribution for this case. Average $p$ values that deviate from .5 cause the distribution to be skewed, especially with small numbers of items. Average $p$ values below .5 tend to produce distributions that are positively skewed (skewed to the right), and the opposite, negative skew occurs for average $p$ values above .5 (skewed to the left). The nearer $p$ values are to .5, the more symmetrical the distribution tends to be.

Figure 5-4 contains representative distributions. One can tell if the average $p$ value is far removed from .5 simply by inspecting the shape of a score distribution. For example, a distribution with a pronounced positive skew implies the average item was difficult for that sample, and vice versa for a negative skew.

Another important principle is that the skewness tends to decrease as the number of items is increased, holding the average $p$ value constant. We previously showed that items on a 10-item test with average $p$ values of .1 will produce a distribution of total scores with a marked positive skew. However, a 100-item test with the same average $p$

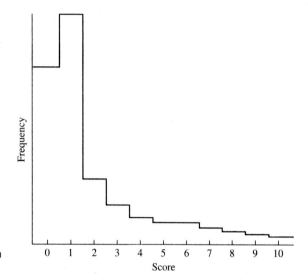

**FIGURE 5-3** A skewed distribution of test scores produced when each item has a $p$ value of .1.

value will be much less skewed. The limiting case of an infinitely long test will provide a symmetric distribution because there is ample room on such tests for scores to spread above and below the mean, regardless of the item $p$ values.

This process may be visualized through the analogy with coin tosses. Assume that 10 biased coins are used with the probability of each head being .2 and the probability of each tail being .8. The average number of heads over many tosses of the 10 coins will therefore be 2. This distribution will have a positive skew; the extreme of the distribution will stretch out over higher numbers of heads. Now increase the number of coins tossed on each trial. This will decrease the skewness. The distribution will be normal in the hypothetical limiting case when an infinite number of such biased coins is tossed per trial. A more elaborate proof of this principle follows from the central limit theorem in mathematical statistics.

The relative symmetry of the distribution is a function of the number of test items (or number of coins). It is not related to the number of people taking a test (or trials on which the coins are tossed).

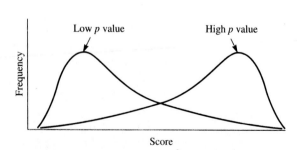

**FIGURE 5-4** Skewed scores distributions by a high average $p$ value and a low average $p$ value.

## COVARIANCE OF LINEAR COMBINATIONS

The previous section presented some useful principles regarding the characteristics of score distributions by "looking inside" the variance of a linear combination. This section considers some principles concerning the covariance between linear combinations of variables. The principles will be illustrated with two linear combinations, each having three variables, but these principles hold regardless of the number of variables in each combination. Numerical illustrations appear at the end of this section. The two linear combinations, again based upon deviation scores, are

$$y = x_1 + x_2 + x_3$$
$$w = x_4 + x_5 + x_6$$

The $x$'s could be six dichotomous items, continuous total scores, or a combination. The previous section demonstrated that the variance of $y$ equals the sum of the elements in its resulting covariance matrix, symbolized $\overline{C}_y$. Similarly, the variance of $w$ is symbolized $\overline{C}_w$. The covariance of the two linear combinations is obtained as follows:

$$\sigma_{wy} = \frac{\Sigma wy}{N}$$

$$= \frac{1}{N}\Sigma(x_1 + x_2 + x_3)(x_4 + x_5 + x_6)$$

$$\sigma_{wy} = \sigma_{14} + \sigma_{15} + \sigma_{16} + \sigma_{24} + \sigma_{25} + \sigma_{26} + \sigma_{34} + \sigma_{35} + \sigma_{36}$$

$$\sigma_{wy} = \Sigma\sigma_{ij} \tag{5-7}$$

Subscript $i$ goes from 1 to 3 ($y$), and subscript $j$ goes from 4 to 6 ($w$). The covariance of $y$ and $w$ equals the sum of all covariances between members of the two linear combinations. Note that neither individual variances nor covariances of members within each of the two linear combinations are involved. This covariance may be displayed in matrix form, just as the variance of a linear combination was displayed. The matrix representation is accomplished by placing the variables in one linear combination at the top of the matrix and the variables in the other linear combination on the side:

|   |       | $w$   |       |       |
|---|-------|-------|-------|-------|
|   |       | $x_4$ | $x_5$ | $x_6$ |
|   | $x_1$ |       |       |       |
| $y$ | $x_2$ |     |       |       |
|   | $x_3$ |       |       |       |

Corresponding terms are multiplied, summed over people, and divided by the number of people. The resulting matrix contains all covariances between the two sets of variables, as follows:

|       | $x_4$       | $x_5$       | $x_6$       |
|-------|-------------|-------------|-------------|
| $x_1$ | $\sigma_{14}$ | $\sigma_{15}$ | $\sigma_{16}$ |
| $x_2$ | $\sigma_{24}$ | $\sigma_{25}$ | $\sigma_{26}$ |
| $x_3$ | $\sigma_{34}$ | $\sigma_{35}$ | $\sigma_{36}$ |

The sum of the elements in the above matrix is the covariance of $w$ and $y$. It will be useful to speak of such a matrix as a matrix of "between" covariances to distinguish it from the matrix of "within" covariances involved in the variance of an individual linear combination. A between matrix will be symbolized as $\mathbf{C}_{wy}$ with different sets of double subscripts used as necessary to indicate the two linear combinations. The covariance of two linear combinations is then $\overline{C}_{wy} = \Sigma\sigma_{ij}$.

If weights were applied to the terms in each linear combination before they were summed, the weights would appear at the top and on the side of the matrix and multiplied as follows:

| | $b_4x_4$ | $b_5x_5$ | $b_6x_6$ |
|---|---|---|---|
| $b_1x_1$ | $b_1b_4\sigma_{14}$ | $b_1b_5\sigma_{15}$ | $b_1b_6\sigma_{16}$ |
| $b_2x_2$ | $b_2b_4\sigma_{24}$ | $b_2b_5\sigma_{25}$ | $b_2b_6\sigma_{26}$ |
| $b_3x_3$ | $b_3b_4\sigma_{34}$ | $b_3b_5\sigma_{36}$ | $b_3b_6\sigma_{36}$ |

The sum $(\overline{C}_{wy})$ then equals $\Sigma b_i b_j \sigma_{ij}$ instead of simply $\Sigma\sigma_{ij}$ for the equally weighted case. It is helpful to the understand linear combinations by looking at the "total" matrix of all possible variances and covariances. Table 5-1 contains this matrix for two linear combinations based upon three variables each. Lines drawn in the table show elements respectively concerned with (1) the variance of $y$, (2) the variance of $w$, and (3) the covariance of $y$ and $w$ (note that there are two of the latter; these are transposes of each other and are equivalent). Matrices 1 and 2 are within matrices, and matrix 3 is the between matrix.

The variances of the two linear combinations and the covariance between them can be obtained by summing the elements in the appropriate sections of this *partitioned* matrix. The following is the partitioning in a more concise form.

| | $y$ | $w$ |
|---|---|---|
| $y$ | $\mathbf{C}_y$ | $\mathbf{C}_{wy}$ |
| $w$ | $\mathbf{C}_{wy}$ | $\mathbf{C}_w$ |

If all variables were standardized, corresponding sections of the correlation matrix would be used in computation.

TABLE 5-1    TOTAL COVARIANCE MATRIX FOR TWO LINEAR
COMBINATIONS $y$ AND $w$

| | $y$ set | | | $w$ set | | |
|---|---|---|---|---|---|---|
| $y$ set | $\sigma_1^2$ | $\sigma_{12}$ | $\sigma_{13}$ | $\sigma_{14}$ | $\sigma_{15}$ | $\sigma_{16}$ |
| | $\sigma_{21}$ | $\sigma_2^2$ | $\sigma_{23}$ | $\sigma_{24}$ | $\sigma_{25}$ | $\sigma_{26}$ |
| | $\sigma_{31}$ | $\sigma_{32}$ | $\sigma_3^2$ | $\sigma_{34}$ | $\sigma_{35}$ | $\sigma_{36}$ |
| $w$ set | $\sigma_{41}$ | $\sigma_{42}$ | $\sigma_{43}$ | $\sigma_4^2$ | $\sigma_{45}$ | $\sigma_{46}$ |
| | $\sigma_{51}$ | $\sigma_{52}$ | $\sigma_{53}$ | $\sigma_{54}$ | $\sigma_5^2$ | $\sigma_{56}$ |
| | $\sigma_{61}$ | $\sigma_{62}$ | $\sigma_{63}$ | $\sigma_{64}$ | $\sigma_{65}$ | $\sigma_6^2$ |

## Correlation of Linear Combinations

The correlation between the two linear combinations $w$ and $y$ can be obtained using Eq. 4-9 as follows:

$$r_{wy} = \frac{\sigma_{wy}}{\sigma_w \sigma_y} \tag{5-8a}$$

This means that the correlation between two linear combinations of variables can be written as

$$r_{wy} = \frac{\overline{C}_{wy}}{\sqrt{\overline{C}_w} \sqrt{\overline{C}_y}} \tag{5-8b}$$

The numerator is the covariance of $w$ and $y$, the sum of the between terms $(\overline{C}_{wy})$. The denominator is the product of the standard deviations of $w$ and $y$, the sums of the within terms, $\overline{C}_w$ and $\overline{C}_y$. We strongly emphasize that there is no limit to the number of variables that can appear in $C_w$ or $C_y$, and $w$ and $y$ need not have the same number of variables in their respective linear combinations. Even if one linear combination had only two variables and the other had 400, all equations concerning variances, covariances, and correlations among linear combinations in this chapter would still be valid.

If all variables are standardized, Eq. 5-8a reduces to

$$r_{wy} = \frac{\overline{R}_{wy}}{\sqrt{\overline{R}_w} \sqrt{\overline{R}_y}} \tag{5-8c}$$

In the case of Eq. 5-8c, the elements in Table 5-1 contain $z$ scores on the top and side, 1s in the diagonal spaces, and correlations in the off-diagonal spaces. Thus, the sum of all the elements within a correlation matrix is the variance of the sum of a set of standard scores. Likewise, the sum of the elements in a between correlation matrix is the covariance of two sets of summed standard scores. If variables were weighted, the elements of the covariance or correlation matrix would also be appropriately weighted.

The correlation between a linear combination of variables with a single variable (i.e., one that is not a linear combination of other variables) is an important special case. The elements in the resulting variance-covariance matrix are schematized as follows:

|   |       |  $y$       | $x_1$ | $x_2$ | $x_3$ | $x_4$ |
|---|-------|------------|-------|-------|-------|-------|
|   | $y$   | $\sigma_y^2$ |       |       | $\overline{C}_{wy}$ |       |
| $w$ | $x_1$ |            |       |       |       |       |
|   | $x_2$ |            |       |       |       |       |
|   | $x_3$ | $\overline{C}_{wy}$ |   |       | $\overline{C}_w$ |   |
|   | $x_4$ |            |       |       |       |       |

In the above case, $\overline{C}_y$ reduces to $\sigma_y^2$ since the linear combination is but one variable. The sum of between covariances $(\overline{C}_{wy})$ equals the sum of all the elements in the first row or column of the matrix, excluding the diagonal term for $y$ $(\sigma_y^2)$. The correlation is

$$r_{wy} = \frac{\overline{C}_{wy}}{\sigma_y \sqrt{\overline{C}_w}} \tag{5-9a}$$

If all variables are $z$ scores, Eq. 5-9a reduces to

$$r_{wy} = \frac{\overline{R}_{wy}}{\sqrt{\overline{R}_w}} \tag{5-9b}$$

In that case, $\sigma_y^2$ falls out of the denominator of Eq. 5-9a since it is 1.0.

We have stressed that these equations hold equally well when the elements in linear combinations are dichotomous items. The diagonals of the total covariance matrix contain $pq$ values. The off-diagonal elements consist of phi ($\phi$) coefficients multiplied by the square root of the product of the two respective $pq$ values. Equations 5-9 thus also provide the correlation between the total scores on two tests composed of dichotomous items.

A variant on this procedure important in factor analysis (Chapters 11 through 13) is to correlate a given variable with a linear combination that includes that variable, e.g., to correlate $x_1$ with the sum of $x_1 + x_2 + x_3$. The procedure is really no different except that variable $x_1$ is entered twice—once as an individual variable and once as part of the linear combination. In an important special case, Eqs. 5-9 may be used to correlate a test item and the sum of scores on all test items, the item-total correlation which was introduce in Chapter 2 and which plays an important role in the next several chapters.

The principles developed so far in this chapter are the basis of multivariate crrelational analysis. Once they are thoroughly understood, it is relatively easy to understand such extensions as multiple correlation, factor analysis, and discriminant analysis. Reread the material if you do not understand the principles. Once you are comfortable with them, what lies ahead in this book will be greatly simplified.

**Numerical Example**

The following is a matrix of covariances for variables $y = x_1 + x_2 + x_3$ and $w = x_4 + x_5 + x_6$.

|   |       | $y$     |       |       | $w$   |       |       |
|---|-------|---------|-------|-------|-------|-------|-------|
|   |       | $x_1$   | $x_2$ | $x_3$ | $x_4$ | $x_5$ | $x_6$ |
|   | $x_1$ | 25.00   | 5.00  | 4.50  | −2.00 | −8.00 | −9.63 |
| $y$ | $x_2$ | 5.00  | 6.25  | 1.50  | −1.50 | −3.60 | −5.50 |
|   | $x_3$ | 4.50    | 1.50  | 9.00  | −1.50 | −3.60 | −5.78 |
|   | $x_4$ | −2.00   | −1.50 | −1.50 | 4.00  | 3.20  | −3.30 |
| $w$ | $x_5$ | −8.00 | −3.60 | −3.60 | 3.20  | 16.00 | 11.00 |
|   | $x_6$ | −9.63   | −5.50 | −5.78 | −3.30 | 11.00 | 35.00 |

The sum of the variances and covariances for $y$ ($C_y$, is $25.00 + 5.00 + \cdots + 9.00$ or $62.25$. Likewise, the sum of the variances and covariances for $w$ ($\overline{C_w}$) is $4.00 + 3.20 + \cdots + 35.00$ or $76.80$. The sum of the between terms ($\overline{C_{wy}}$) is $(-2.00) + (-1.50) + \cdots + (-5.78)$ or $-41.11$. Consequently, $r_{wy} = -41.11/\sqrt{(62.25)(76.80)}$ or $-.59$. The principles involved in using standardized scores instead of raw scores (i.e., converting the variance-covariance matrix to a correlation matrix) and in using unequal rather than equal (unit) weights are the same as previously illustrated.

## PARTIAL CORRELATION

The discussion of constructs in Chapter 3 stressed how science seeks to find a relatively small set of variables which explain a larger set of variables. This occurs when some combination of the smaller set correlates highly with each member of the larger set. For example, some have suggested that as few as 5 to 8 (factors) dimensions are sufficient to explain variation in personality [e.g., McCrae and Costa, (1985, 1987) and Dingman and Inouye (1986)]. Cattell (1946) and, more recently, Mershon and Gorsuch (1988) provide evidence for the need for 16. Even this latter figure is vastly less than the number of proposed personality traits as indexed through proposed scales. Reducing the number of "explainer" variables (constructs) is the essence of scientific parsimony.

One should demonstrate that a new variable actually adds something to existing constructs before that variable is added to the set of constructs. The concept of partialling is very important to this demonstration. Suppose a measure of anxiety correlates positively with the speed of solving simple arithmetic problems so that the investigators conclude that the measure is a useful explainer of speed in solving simple problems. Now suppose that other investigators find that both measures correlate positively with cognitive ability scores. Since IQ is known to be an important construct, it is mandatory to determine whether the new measure of anxiety adds to the prediction of problem solving. This can be accomplished by partialling IQ from the other two measures. If the partialled scores on the anxiety test still correlate with partialled scores on the problem solving measure, the anxiety measure will actually add to what the intelligence test explained. If not, there is no evidence to demonstrate that the anxiety test measures anything new.

A "partialed score" is simply the residual or error score when $r$ is used to estimate one variable from another (it might be useful to review the very important points contained in Table 4-2). The anxiety score, partialling the IQ score, is

$$z_{1-3} = z_1 - r_{13}z_3 \tag{5-10a}$$

where $z_1$ = standard score on an anxiety test
$\quad z_3$ = standard score on an intelligence test
$\quad r_{13}$ = PM correlation between the anxiety and intelligence test
$\quad z_{1-3}$ = partialled score on an anxiety test after variance explainable by IQ is
$\qquad$ removed

Similarly, the partialled score for the problem-solving test, holding IQ constant, is

$$z_{2-3} = z_2 - r_{23}z_3 \tag{5-10b}$$

where $z_2$ = a standard score in problem solving. Both Eqs. 5-10a and 5-10b are linear combinations. The symbols $z_{1-3}$ and $z_{2-3}$ are totally equivalent to the term $z_{Y \cdot X}$ used in the previous chapter. We have changed notation because there are more than two variables involved. As Table 4-2 indicated, these partialed scores are uncorrelated with the variable used for the estimation or covariate ($z_3$ in this case). Consequently any correlation between $z_{1-3}$ and $z_{2-3}$ is independent of the linear effects of the IQ measure. Such a correlation is called a partial correlation, symbolized as $r_{12.3}$. The equation is developed as follows. The correlation between any two variables, again using Eq. 4-9, is

$$r_{xy} = \frac{\sigma_{xy}}{\sigma_x \sigma_y}$$

The terms for partial correlation are

$$r_{12.3} = \frac{\sigma_{(1-3)(2-3)}}{\sigma_{(1-3)}\sigma_{(2-3)}} \tag{5-11}$$

The denominator is the product of the standard deviations of the two sets of partialled scores. Previously, Table 4-2 indicated that the variance of any set of partialled scores is 1 minus the squared correlation between the two variables. Consequently

$$r_{12.3} = \frac{\sigma_{(1-3)(2-3)}}{\sqrt{1 - r_{13}^2} \cdot \sqrt{1 - r_{23}^2}} \tag{5-12}$$

The covariance in the numerator equals the sum of cross products of the two sets of partialled scores divided by $N$, which can be expanded as follows:

$$\sigma_{(1-3)(2-3)} = \frac{1}{N} \Sigma(z_1 - r_{13}z_3)(z_2 - r_{23}z_3)$$

$$= \frac{1}{N} \Sigma(z_1 z_2 - r_{23}z_1 z_3 - r_{13}z_2 z_3 + r_{13}r_{23}z_3^2)$$

$$= r_{23} - r_{23}r_{13} - r_{13}r_{23} + r_{13}r_{23}$$

$$= r_{12} - r_{23}r_{13} \tag{5-13}$$

Reassembling the numerator and denominator gives Eq. 5-14 for the partial correlation:

$$r_{12.3} = \frac{r_{12} - r_{23}r_{13}}{\sqrt{1 - r_{13}^2}\sqrt{1 - r_{23}^2}} \tag{5-14}$$

It is important to remember that (1) the numerator in Eq. 5-14 is the covariance of two sets of scores from which $x_3$ has been partialled and (2) the denominator is the product of the standard deviations of the two sets of partialled scores.

Partial correlation is the expected correlation between two variables when a third variable is held constant, as if all subjects had the same intelligence test score in the above example. The expected zero-order (raw, unadjusted, or simple) correlation between anxiety and problem solving is the correlation obtained when intelligence is allowed to vary. However, if the relation between anxiety and problem solving varies with intelligence (is heteroscedastic), the partial correlation between anxiety and problem solving would depend upon which level of IQ was chosen. It would be an average across levels of IQ; IQ would be said to moderate the relation between anxiety and problem solving. The partial correlation might therefore underestimate the zero-order correlation obtained from subjects with a high IQ but overestimate the zero-order correlation for subjects with an average IQ (the important topic of moderation will be considered later in this chapter and elsewhere in this book). Because extreme heteroscedasticity is the exception rather than the rule, though, the partial correlation is usually a good estimate of the correlation found between two variables when a third variable is actually held constant. This provides very useful information in testing theories or in exploratory studies of correlations among variables.

A second important point is that the size of the partial correlation depends on the signs of the three correlations involved. If $r_{12}$ is positive, $r_{12.3}$ usually is smaller than $r_{12}$ when $r_{13}$ and $r_{23}$ have the same sign, regardless of whether the sign is positive or negative. It is usually larger than $r_{12}$ when $r_{13}$ and $r_{23}$ have different signs. The reverse is usually true in both instances when $r_{12}$ is negative. The word "usually" is essential in these three rules because there are instances in which the rules are incorrect. For example, let $r_{12} = .30$, $r_{13} = .10$, and $r_{23} = .80$. Here, $r_{12.3}$ is .37, which is larger than $r_{12}$, rather than smaller as would be expected from the first rule given above. If both $r_{13}$ and $r_{23}$ are zero, then $r_{12}$ and $r_{12.3}$ will be equal.

A third important point is that subjective ("eyeball") estimates of the amount of change expected from partialling a third variable are usually too large. Suppose that anxiety and problem solving correlate .60 and each correlates .40 with intelligence. One might think that partialling intelligence will markedly reduce the $r$ of .60. In fact, what occurs is as follows:

$$r_{12.3} = \frac{r_{12} - r_{13} \cdot r_{23}}{\sqrt{1 - r_{13}^2} \cdot \sqrt{1 - r_{23}^2}}$$

$$= \frac{.6 - (.4)(.4)}{\sqrt{1 - .16} \cdot \sqrt{1 - .16}}$$

$$= \frac{.6 - .16}{.84}$$

$$= .52$$

The $r_{12.3}$ is only .08 lower than $r_{12}$, which might not matter a great deal. It is very easy to be fooled about the size of a partial correlation before it is actually computed.

A fourth important point is that the covariate may itself be a linear combination of other variables. Thus, if $y$ is a linear combination of variables $x_1$ through $x_5$, there is nothing wrong with partialling $y$ from variables $x_6$ and $x_7$. This is basic to factor analysis, which consists essentially of successively partialling linear combinations of variables from the correlations among the variables.

Fifth, partialling eliminates only the linear effects of the covariate. If the covariate has a clearly nonmonotonic relation with either of the two remaining variables, that relation will *not* be adjusted as well. One simple way to handle this problem is to include successive powers of the covariate as additional covariates. That is, to fully remove the effects of $W$ from $X$ and $Y$, use $W$, $W^2$, $W^3$, ... $W^5$ (five powers are almost always sufficient; see Jensen, 1980). However, what has been said before about the minimal effects of slight nonlinearities applies. This strategy is needed only when there is a clear nonmonotonicity. Techniques for performing successive partialling will be considered shortly.

Similarly, partialling removes the effects of a construct only when the covariate accurately measures that construct. For example, if the IQ measure was unreliable or a poor measure of the general construct of intelligence, some effects of intelligence would remain in the relation between anxiety and problem solving.

This could be done with semipartial correlation (also called part correlation), which is very similar to partial correlation. The problem is to correlate $z_1$ with $z_{2-3}$, where problem solving is $x_1$, anxiety is $x_2$, and intelligence is $x_3$. These scores can be placed in the regular equation for $r$. Equation 5-15 results from expanding terms in a manner similar to partial correlation:

$$r_{1(2.3)} = \frac{r_{12} - r_{13}r_{23}}{\sqrt{1 - r_{23}^2}}$$

(5-15)

An additional term, the square root of $1 - r_{13}^2$, is in the denominator of the equation for a partial correlation (Eq. 5-14) but not for a semipartial correlation (Eq. 5-15). Since this cannot exceed 1, partial $r$ must always be larger than semipartial $r$ in absolute magnitude.

The partial correlation is reported far more often than the semipartial correlation. However, the semipartial correlation is important throughout multivariate analysis. Its square, called the uniqueness, describes the improvement in prediction when a new variable is added to a prediction equation.

### An Example of Partialling

We will now work through a problem to illustrate several points about partialling as well as a number of other points made in the previous chapter, particularly Table 4-2. We suggest that you make the calculations yourself both by hand and on a computer. The following are 10 observations on raw measures $X_1$, $X_2$, and $X_3$.

| Raw measure | | |
|---|---|---|
| $X_1$ | $X_2$ | $X_3$ |
| 7 | 9 | 7 |
| 12 | 6 | 15 |
| 15 | 8 | 13 |
| 10 | 8 | 9 |
| 19 | 9 | 12 |
| 13 | 8 | 12 |
| 10 | 6 | 13 |
| 12 | 8 | 11 |
| 15 | 10 | 9 |
| 14 | 9 | 10 |

You may readily verify that the respective means for $X_1$, $X_2$, and $X_3$ are 12.70, 8.10, and 11.10 and that their respective standard deviations are 3.34, 1.29, and 2.38 (using $N - 1$ in the denominator since this is what a computer package will probably use). Since a sample $z$ score $= (X - X)/s$, the first value of $z_1$ is $(7 - 12.70)/3.34$ or $-1.71$. These data provide the following series of $z$ scores:

| z scores | | |
|---|---|---|
| $z_1$ | $z_2$ | $z_3$ |
| −1.71 | .70 | −1.72 |
| −.21 | −1.63 | 1.64 |
| .69 | −.08 | .80 |
| −.81 | −.08 | −.88 |
| 1.89 | .70 | .38 |
| .09 | −.08 | .38 |
| −.81 | −1.63 | .80 |
| −.21 | −.08 | −.04 |
| .69 | 1.47 | −.88 |
| .39 | .70 | −.46 |

Use Eq. 4-6 to compute the correlations among these three variables. These should be as follows (within rounding error): $r_{12} = .344$, $r_{13} = .354$, and $r_{23} = -.730$. Next, compute the residuals, $z_{1-3}$ and $z_{2-3}$, partialling variable $x_3$ from variables $x_1$ and $x_2$, respectively, by means of Eq. 5-10. These are as follows:

| Residuals | |
|---|---|
| $z_{1-3}$ | $z_{2-3}$ |
| −1.10 | −.56 |
| −.79 | −.43 |
| .41 | .51 |
| −.50 | −.72 |
| 1.75 | .98 |
| −.04 | .20 |
| −1.09 | −1.05 |
| −.19 | −.11 |
| 1.00 | .83 |
| .55 | .36 |

Now, correlate these two residual terms. The $r$ will be approximately .94. This is $r_{12.3}$ and is the same value you obtain by using the much easier Eq. 5-14. Note that the partial correlation is much larger than the zero-order correlation in this highly artificial case because (1) $r_{12}$ (.34) is positive, (2) $r_{13}$ (.35) and $r_{23}$ (−.73) have opposite signs, and (3) $r_{23}$ is of large magnitude. Partialling removes a large effect that operates differentially on the two variables and whose presence therefore reduces $r_{12}$.

After completing this exercise, compute the semipartial correlation between $z_1$ and $z_{2-3}$ using both the above values and Eq. 5-15. You should obtain a value of .88 in both cases. Then do the same to obtain the semipartial correlation between $z_2$ and $z_{1-3}$ of .64. Finally, compute all means, standard deviations, and intercorrelations to verify Table 4-2. Include both the zero-order scores and $z$ scores to demonstrate that their correlations are 1.0. These data will be used again below.

### Higher-Order Partialling

After the effects of $x_3$ have been removed from variables $x_1$ and $x_2$, the effects of additional variables $x_4$, $x_5$, etc., may likewise be removed. That is, Eq. 5-14 may be applied to residuals and, for that matter, residuals of residuals, as may Eq. 5-15 for semipartial correlation. These covariates may be dichotomies such as gender. For example, one may wish to correlate scores on a reading achievement test with scores on a mathematics achievement test in grammar school children and correct for both age and gender. This is called higher-order partialling. The resulting correlations are designated $r_{12.34}$, $r_{12.345}$, etc. It does not matter in what order the variables are removed; $r_{12.34}$ is numerically equal to $r_{12.43}$. The concept of higher-order partialling is very important in multiple regression.

### Another Form of Partialling

Assume that you have obtained two measures, $x_1$ and $x_2$, from 10 members of each two groups ($A$ and $B$), such as males versus females, Democrats versus Republicans, etc. (The logic presented here can be simply extended to additional groups, and it is not necessary that the numbers in the two groups be equal.) The data are as follows:

| Group A | | Group B | |
|---|---|---|---|
| $x_1$ | $x_2$ | $x_1$ | $x_2$ |
| 18 | 11 | 10 | 23 |
| 19 | 14 | 16 | 24 |
| 32 | 15 | 19 | 27 |
| 37 | 22 | 21 | 24 |
| 24 | 12 | 20 | 29 |
| 34 | 13 | 14 | 21 |
| 28 | 11 | 14 | 24 |
| 31 | 19 | 16 | 27 |
| 25 | 8 | 19 | 21 |
| 30 | 14 | 20 | 25 |

Now, suppose you are interested in the relation between variables $x_1$ and $x_2$. If you were to compute the correlation over all 20 observations, thereby ignoring the group to which the observation belongs, you could readily verify the fact that $r = -.44$. This is known as a total correlation, as it is based upon the total set of scores, disregarding the group from which they were derived. It is very misleading. Look at group $A$. The relation $r_{12}$ is clearly positive (+.62), as it is in group $B$ ($r_{12} = +.38$). The source of this paradox is the negative correlation between the group means—group $A$'s mean on variable $x_1$ is larger than group $B$'s (27.8 versus 16.9), but the reverse is true for variable $x_2$ (13.9 versus 24.5). With only two groups, the correlation must be either $-1$ as here, or $+1$; it may take on intermediate values with more than two groups. Neglecting to take this correlation between group means into account has a strong but artifactual influence upon the total $r$.

An unconfounded measure, the pooled within-group correlation may be obtained by pooling (adding) the respective sums of squares ($\Sigma x^2$ values) and cross products ($\Sigma xy$ values) upon which $\sigma_{12}$, $\sigma_1^2$, and $\sigma_2^2$ are based in each group and dividing each by the total number of subjects. This correlation adjusts for group mean differences. It is a form of partialling since group mean differences are partialled out (it is identified as such in several statistical procedures). For example, the sum of cross products is 140.8 in group $A$ and 31.5 in group $B$, and so the pooled estimate is 172.3. After computing the two variances in a like manner, Eq. 4-8 may then be used to obtained the pooled within-group correlation of .55.

Another way to obtain this pooled within-group correlation is to define an additional variable denoting group membership. Thus, assign a 1 to all members of group $A$ and a 0 to all members of group $B$ (or the reverse, it doesn't matter, nor, for that matter do the numbers have to be 0 and 1, any two different numbers will do). Treat this as variable 3 in computing a partial correlation between variables 1 and 2. You will obtain the same value of .55.

The previous example illustrated "aggregation error"—what holds for each of several groups taken individually may not hold when the data are pooled across groups because differences among the groups form a third variable that may confound the outcome. When this effect is found when two or more samples are compared with regard to the incidence of some characteristic, the result is known as "Simpson's paradox" (Simpson, 1951). Bickel, Hammel, and O'Connell (1975) provide an important example involving adverse impact in faculty hiring, and Hintzman (1980) illustrates its relevance to memory data. Paik (1985) notes the relation between the phenomenon and correlational logic. Simpson's paradox will be discussed in two later contexts (Chapters 9 and 15).

Total, between-group, and within-group correlations play important roles in multivariate theory, especially discriminant analysis (see Chapter 14). An important thing to keep in mind is that the total correlation confounds group mean differences and covariation within groups. All combinations of positive, zero, and negative correlations between and within groups are possible, and the total correlation will be very misleading if there is a strong between-group correlation. The moral of the story is to be very careful about aggregating across categories.

## MULTIPLE CORRELATION AND MULTIPLE REGRESSION

Chapter 4 considered the related but distinct problems of linear correlation (describing the linear relation between pairs of variables) and linear regression (finding the line of best fit predicting a criterion from a predictor, usually by the method of least squares). The logic and method of least-squares regression are easily extended to estimating a criterion (dependent variable) from a linear combination of predictors (independent variables). Multiple correlation involves the magnitude of this relation. For the present, assume the criterion is continuous. Chapters 14 and 15 consider categorical criteria. It is not necessary to assume that the predictors are continuous; a later section will be devoted to the use of categorical predictors. Let the criterion be designated $z_y$ and the predictors be designated $z_1, z_2, ..., z_k$. Let any combination of the predictors used to estimate the criterion be designated $z_y'$ :

$$z_y' = \beta_1 z_1 + \beta_2 z_2 + \beta_3 z_3 \tag{5-16}$$

where $z_y'$ = estimate of $z_y$

$z_1, z_2, z_3$ = predictors

$\beta_1, \beta_2, \beta_3$ = weights for predictors

As noted in Chapter 4, $\beta$ is applied to a $z$ score, and $b$ is applied to a raw score. Both describe the expected change in the criterion per observed unit change in the predictor in their respective units, holding constant all other predictors. Unlike values of $r$, $\beta$ weights can exceed 1.0. The problem is to find a set of $\beta$ weights such that

$$\Sigma(z_y - z_y')^2 = \text{a minimum} \tag{5-17a}$$
$$\Sigma[z_y - (\beta_1 z_1 + \beta_2 z_2 + \beta_3 z_3)]^2 = \text{a minimum} \tag{5-17b}$$

After the last expression is squared and summed, calculus provides a solution for the $\beta$ weights by solving a set of simultaneous equations. The result is a unique set of $\beta$ weights for any problem in which the predictors are not linear combinations of each other. No solution is possible in this latter case, but commercial computer packages can detect the situation and attempt to delete the offending predictor(s). However, they may not choose the variable you wish deleted, and so you should look at the printout with extra care when relevant diagnostics appear.

### The Two-Predictor Case

Solving the equations necessary to obtain $\beta$ and the multiple correlation are very simple when there are only two predictors. This correlation is commonly symbolized $R_{y.12}$ for two predictors and $R_{y.1...k}$ in the general case, but we will use $R$ in most places for simplicity. (Be careful to distinguish italicized $R$, the symbol for the multiple correlation coefficient, from boldface $\mathbf{R}$, the symbol for a correlation matrix, and $\overline{R}$, the sum of the elements in $\mathbf{R}$.) Equations 5-18 and 5-19 are all that are needed:

$$\beta_1 = \frac{r_{y1} - r_{y2}r_{12}}{1 - r_{12}^2} \tag{5-18a}$$

$$\beta_2 = \frac{r_{y2} - r_{y1}r_{12}}{1 - r_{12}^2} \tag{5-18b}$$

$$R^2 = \frac{r_{y1}^2 + r_{y2}^2 - 2r_{y1}r_{y2}r_{12}}{1 - r_{12}^2} \tag{5-19}$$

The square root of $R^2$ then provides $R$. Note the similarity of Eqs. 5-18 to Eq. 5-15 for semipartial $r$; the difference is that a square root is taken in the denominator with semipartial $r$.

## Numerical Example

We will use the same data to illustrate the computation of $\beta$ and $R$ that we used to compute the partial correlation, using $x_1$ as the criterion and $x_2$ and $x_3$ as the predictors. Consequently, $x_1$ in the previous data corresponds to $y$ in Eqs. 5-18 and 5-19, $x_2$ corresponds to $x_1$, and $x_3$ corresponds to $x_2$. In the previous data, $r_{12} = .344$, $r_{13} = .354$, and $r_{23} = -.730$. The $\beta_2$ (the $\beta$ weight for variable $x_2$ in predicting $x_1$) = [.344 − (.354)(−.730)]/(1 − .730$^2$) or 1.290, $\beta_3$ = [.354 − (.344)(−.730)]/(1 − .730$^2$) or 1.295, and $R^2 = [.344^2 + .354^2 - 2(.354)(.344)(-.730)]/(1 - .730^2)$ or .902. The $R$ is therefore .95.

## The General Case

Computing $\beta$ weights is very simple on a computer but complex to do by hand when there are more than two predictors. Procedures for the general derivation of $\beta$ weights and $R$ are presented in books listed as Suggested Additional Readings. In particular, see Cohen and Cohen (1983), Draper and Smith (1981), Darlington (1990), or Pedhazur (1982) for extensive discussions of all aspects of multiple correlation and regression. The resulting $\beta$ weights can then be applied to the predictors to obtain $z_y'$, the least-squares estimates of $z_y$. In turn, one could correlate $z_y'$ with $z_y$ using the regular formula for $r$ (Eq. 4-9) to obtain $R$. Instead of correlating $z_y'$ with $z_y$, however, $R^2$ can be obtained more simply from the zero-order correlations and $\beta$ weights, regardless of the number of predictors, as follows:

$$R^2 = \beta_1 r_{y1} + \beta_2 r_{y2} + \cdots + \beta_k r_{yk} \tag{5-20}$$

The zero-order correlations between predictors and the criterion are commonly termed "validities" in the context of multiple correlation and regression. Standard output from commercial computer packages includes a significance test that the true value of $R$ is zero, the individual $\beta$ weights, their standard errors, and associated tests of significance from zero. The validities and correlations among predictors are often not standard output but may be (and should be) obtained along with other optional output to be discussed in later sections.

Equation 5-20 leads to the special case of Eq. 5-21 if the predictors are uncorrelated with one another:

$$R^2_{y.123} = r^2_{y1} + r^2_{y2} + r^2_{y3} \qquad (5\text{-}21)$$

Unfortunately, observable predictors are almost always intercorrelated, but methods of semipartial correlation can "untangle" these correlations to compute $R$. Equation 5-22 describes the untangling:

$$R^2_{y.123} = r^2_{y1} + r^2_{y(2.1)} + r^2_{y(3.12)} \qquad (5\text{-}22)$$

where $r_{y1}$ = zero-order correlation between $y$ and $x_1$ (validity of $x_1$)

$r_{y(2.1)}$ = semipartial correlation between $y$ and $x_2$, with $x_1$ partialled from $x_2$ but not $y$

$r_{y(3.12)}$ = semipartial correlation between $y$ and $x_3$, with both $x_1$ and $x_2$ partialled from $x_3$ but not $y$

It is irrelevant which variable is identified as $x_1$, $x_2$, etc.; the same value of $R$ is obtained if the first term on the right-hand side of the equation is $r^2_{y2}$ and the second term is $r^2_{y(1.2)}$. However, the ordering often reflects a theoretical hierarchy, as we will indicate later in this chapter. Although you will probably do all future problems on a computer, it is useful to explore Eq. 5-23. The first step is to square the first predictor's validity ($r_{y1}$). Next, obtain the semipartial correlation between the second predictor and the criterion, holding constant the first predictor. Enter its square as the second term in the equation. Third, obtain the semipartial correlation between the third predictor and $y$, holding constant the first two variables. Enter its square as the third term. This process can be carried out for any number of predictors. Successive terms in the equation are successively higher orders of squared semipartial correlations. The first term is the square of a simple correlation, the second term is the square of a first-order semipartial correlation, the third term is the square of a second-order semipartial correlation, and so on. Note that the $R^2$ in the above two-variable numerical example can be obtained within rounding error from the sum of (1) $r^2_{13} = .354^2 = .126$ and (2) $r^2_{1(2-3)} = .883^2 = .780$, using Eq. 5-10.

Semipartial correlations are used rather than partial correlations because the predictors must be partialled from one another but not from the criterion. Partial $r$ answers one hypothetical question: What would the correlation between two variables be if one or more other variables were held constant? This is hypothetically the same as assuming these other variables are actually constants, given homoscedasticity. The $R^2$ answers a different hypothetical question: What would the sum of the squared validities be if the predictors were independent of one another? However, this issue pertains to the predictors and not to the criterion. In $R$ (and therefore $R^2$), one wants to leave the criterion *intact* and not partial any variance attributable to the predictors. The problem is to determine how much an actual variable $Y$ correlates with a linear combination of predictors which have been orthogonalized (made to correlate zero with one another).

## Testing the Significance of R and Increments in R

Despite our emphasis upon statistical description rather than null hypothesis testing, we will illustrate how to test the significance of $R$ (actually, $R^2$). The test that $R = 0$ uses the $F$ statistic found in any statistics book (Eq. 5-23):

$$F = \frac{R^2/k}{(1 - R^2)/(N - k - 1)} \qquad (5\text{-}23)$$

where $k$ = number of predictors
$R^2$ = squared multiple correlation
$N$ = total number of subjects

The test has $k$ degrees of freedom in the numerator and $N - k - 1$ degrees of freedom in the denominator. If the obtained value is sufficiently large, it may be assumed that $R > 0$.

A closely related procedure, whose importance will be discussed later in this chapter, is to test the significance of the increment in $R$ from a base value obtained with $k_a$ predictors $(R_a)$ to a value of $R$ obtained with $k_b$ predictors that include the first $k_a$ $(R_b)$. We will also discuss why there is always a chance increment due to the bias inherent in the greater number of predictors, making $R_b > R_a$ (it is proper to refer to $R_a$ as a multiple correlation even when $k_a$ is 1). This increment is tested using Eq. 5-24:

$$F = \frac{(R_b^2 - R_a^2)/(k_b - k_a)}{(1 - R_b^2)/(N - k_b - 1)} \qquad (5\text{-}24)$$

where $k_a$ = number of predictors in the smaller set
$R_a^2$ = squared multiple correlation obtained from the smaller set of predictors
$k_b$ = number of predictors in the larger set (which *must* include all the predictors in the smaller set)
$R_b^2$ = squared multiple correlation obtained from the larger set of predictors
$N$ = total number of subjects

Again, consult a table of the $F$ distribution. The test has $k_b - k_a$ degrees of freedom in the numerator and $N - k_b - 1$ degrees of freedom in the denominator.

The following example, though simulated, came from the second author's experience. An executive was concerned about the effectiveness of a commercial multiscale personality test that was administered to store managers in a chain. The criterion was the judged effectiveness of the managers (assume that these are valid for purposes of the example). The executive was curious about the effectiveness of the profile as a whole. One scale was basically a short-form intelligence test. Call this predictor $x_1$ and assume that it correlates .35 with the criterion ratings (perceived effectiveness). Also assume that the $R$ between all 10 scales of the inventory (predictors) and this criterion is .45 and that there are 150 managers in the sample.

Equation 5-23 can be used to test the null hypothesis that the intelligence measure relates to job performance:

$$F = \frac{.35^2/1}{(1 - .35^2)/(150 - 1 - 1)}$$

$$= \frac{.1225}{.8775/148}$$

$$= 20.67$$

This value of $F$ is significant beyond the .01 level with 1 and 148 degrees of freedom. Equation 5-23 can also test the significance of the $R$ obtained from all 10 predictors in the personality profile:

$$F = \frac{.45^2/10}{(1 - .45^2)/(150 - 10 - 1)}$$

$$= \frac{.2025/10}{.7975/139}$$

$$= \frac{.02025}{.00574}$$

$$= 3.53$$

This is also significant beyond the .01 level, but with 10 and 139 degrees of freedom. Note that although $R$ is larger than when only one predictor was entered, the $F$ ratio is smaller. Equation 5-24 is used to evaluate the difference between the correlations obtained with 1 predictor and with all 10 predictors:

$$F = \frac{(.45^2 - .35^2)/(10 - 1)}{(1 - .45^2)/(150 - 10 - 1)}$$

$$= \frac{(.2025 - .1225)/9}{.7975/139}$$

$$= \frac{.0089}{.7975/139}$$

$$= \frac{.00889}{.00574}$$

$$= 1.55$$

This difference is *not* significant. The increase in $R$ from .35 with 1 predictor to .45 with 10 predictors reflects a bias due to the larger number of predictors which we discuss in the next section. We had every reason to use the intelligence scale (which probably could have been replaced by any of dozens) first, and so the result indicates how a little truth plus a lot of sampling error can lead up to a misleading conclusion about the test as a whole. This is an introduction to hierarchical model testing which we will discuss more fully later.

**Determinants of $R$**

The $R$ is determined by the following:

**1** The $R$ tends to be high when the predictors correlate highly with the criterion (have high validities). If all the predictors correlate zero with the criterion, $R$ must also be zero. Conversely, if some of the predictors have high correlations with the criterion, $R$ will also be high.

**2** The $R$ cannot be less than the highest validity. If, for example, one predictor correlates .50 with the criterion, $R$ cannot be less than .50, regardless of the other validities.

**3** The $R$ cannot be negative. The statistical procedures for deriving weights adjust their signs to make $R$ zero or positive. However, one can determine how individual variables relate to the criterion by looking at each of their validities.

**4** The $R$ is larger when the predictors have relatively *low* correlations among themselves. Each can then add something to the predictive power of others. If the correlations among predictors are high, they are highly redundant and so they will add little to the prediction. *When all correlations among predictors are zero, Eq. 5-21 shows that the $R^2$ equals the sum of the squared validities* $(\Sigma r_{iy}^2)$. Also, $\beta_i = r_{iy}$, where $i$ is a given predictor. These very important facts can be easily proved from the correlation of sums and will be used many times in discussing multivariate statistics. Thus, if two predictors correlate zero and each correlates .50 with the criterion, the $R^2$ is .50 = $.50^2$ + $.50^2$ and so $R$ = .71. On the other hand, if the two predictors correlate .50, $R$ decreases to .58 (see Eq. 5-19). Additional increases in the correlation between the predictors further reduce $R$. If the two predictors were perfectly correlated, $R$ would be .50.

**5** The relations among $R$, the predictors' validities, and their $\beta$ weights are often difficult to determine without performing the actual computation. This is particularly true when there is a mixture of positive and negative correlations. A suppressor relationship is an important special case. In a suppressor relationship, $\beta_i > r_{iy}$ for predictor $i$. Variable $x_i$ is also said to have a suppressor relationship when $r_{iy}$ and $\beta_i$ differ in sign but both are of substantial magnitude. In the following example, $R$ is higher (.69) than the zero-order correlation between $x_1$ and $y$ (.60). Tzelgov and Henik (1991) provide an extensive discussion of suppressor relationships with examples. The following illustrates how it may arise.

$$r_{1y} = .60$$
$$r_{2y} = .00$$
$$r_{12} = .50$$
$$\beta_1 = \frac{.6 - (.0)(.5)}{1 - .5^2} = .8$$
$$\beta_2 = \frac{.0 - (.5)(.6)}{1 - .5^2} = -.4$$
$$R^2 = (.8)(.6) + (-.4)(.0) = .48$$
$$R = .69$$

Despite the fact that $x_2$ is uncorrelated with $y$ and therefore has a validity of 0, its high correlation with $x_1$ ($r_{12} = .50$) supplies important information about variance in $x_1$ that is not correlated with variance in $y$. The squared correlation ($r^2{}_{12}$) describes this irrelevant variance. Consequently, when this component of variance is subtracted from $x_1$ (note that $\beta_2$ is negative), the predictive power of $x_1$ is increased. Actually, suppressor variables are rarely found in practice, but they illustrate the distinct surprises that sometimes come about when they do occur.

**6** The $R$ rarely increases dramatically as the number of predictors increases. Suppose 10 tests were investigated for their ability to predict college performance. A typical finding is that (a) one test correlates moderately with the criterion, (b) combining that test with another test of high validity increases $R$ above any of the zero-order correlations (validities), (c) adding a third test increases $R$ slightly, and (d) additional tests increase $R$ only slightly beyond that. Seldom are more than two or three tests needed in applied prediction problems, but there are counterexamples, e.g., the aforementioned study by Mershon and Gorsuch (1989). The $R$ usually does not continue to increase because the redundancy (high intercorrelations) among the predictors eventually catches up with the information obtainable from new predictors. Of course, it is always possible that a new, less redundant predictor will increase $R$. This search for important new constructs that add to prediction is at the core of psychology.

**7** The sample $R$ is systematically biased upward so that it tends to be larger than the population $R$. One major reason for the bias is that predictors are usually selected from a larger set, e.g., 3 tests may be selected from a set of 10. This selection takes enormous advantage of chance when it is based upon data and not theory. For example, if there are 10 predictors, 120 different sets of 3 predictors and 210 different sets of 4 predictors can be chosen from 10 initial predictors at random. Some predictors will correlate highly with the criterion because of sampling error rather than any inherent predictive ability and therefore correlate poorly in another sample. Chance also plays a role in determining the patterns of correlations among predictors.

Capitalization upon chance decreases with sample size and increases with the pool of possible predictors. For example, $R$ will be so spuriously high as to be worthless if 3 variables are selected from a group of 20 predictors in a sample of only 100. In contrast, the upward bias in $R$ will be negligible when 3 variables are selected from a group of 6 in a sample of 1000. See Green (1991) for a discussion of the issue of sample size in multiple regression.

It is not necessary to use least-squares regression weights in a prediction equation, and the next section will consider some alternative approaches. Weights defined in advance, such as equal weights, or added in a predetermined theoretical order and their associated values of $R$ are not subject to this spurious inflation, as are weights that are estimated from the data, e.g., $\beta$ weights. However, all are subject to the usual type I error (falsely concluding that a variable added to the equation improves prediction) and type II error (falsely concluding that the added variables do not improve prediction) present in any statistical inference.

Values of $R$ derived from $\beta$ weights are biased upward for a second reason even when predictors are not selected from a larger pool. Suppose three tests are used to predict a criterion. One is not taking advantage of chance in variable selection, since all predictors are used. However, chance still affects $R$ because we can know only the sample correlations and not the population correlations. This is true for *any* set of weights and the associated value of $R$ when variables are chosen on the basis of data. The $\beta$ weights extract all possible predictive power, but, in so doing, they capitalize on sampling error among correlations. A test that happens to have a large validity as a result of sampling error will have a large $\beta$ weight, and a test that happens to have a small validity will have a small $\beta$ weight.

Consequently, the $R$ obtained from a relatively small sample will tend to become smaller when reapplied to a larger sample. Large samples have less chance of producing unusually large correlations by chance because the parameter estimates are more stable. This tendency for $R$ to decrease as the sample grows larger is called "shrinkage". The following formula estimates the shrinkage in $R$ when it is reapplied to an infinitely large sample so that it is unbiased:

$$\hat{R}^2 = 1 - (1 - R^2)\frac{N-1}{N-k-1} \qquad (5\text{-}25)$$

where $\hat{R}$ unbiased estimate of the population multiple correlation
    $R$ = observed multiple correlation found in sample of size $N$
    $k$ = number of predictors

For example, suppose $R$ is .50 in a sample of $N = 100$ with $k = 8$ predictors. The unbiased estimate of the population $R$ ($\hat{R}$) is .44. Equation 5-25 indicates that the inflation in $R$ (bias) declines as the ratio of sample size to number of predictors increases. Bias is insignificant when the ratio is 100:1, but it is substantial when the ratio is 10:1. When there are as many predictors as people, $R$ will artifactually equal 1.0. This situation takes every opportunity of chance. It will hold even with random data because the equations producing an $R$ of 1.0 can *always* be solved when there are as many unknowns ($\beta$ weights) as subjects. Of course, this value of $R$ would not hold up if the weights were applied to a new sample. Lord and Novick (1968) developed this particular formula, modifying an earlier version by Wherry (1940).

As is true of most other problems in psychological measurement, nothing helps so much as a large sample. A sample of about 100 will provide a relatively unbiased estimate of $R$ when there are only 2 or 3 predictors, but a sample of 300 to 400 is needed when 9 or 10 predictors are used.

## Categorical Predictors

As noted in the section titled "Another Form of Partialling," categorical variables are now used quite commonly in multivariate analysis thanks to Cohen (1968). This use reflects the point made in Chapter 1 that a scale may be regarded as an interval scale when it contains only two points. This is the basis of the analysis of variance. If the variable takes on only two values, such as gender, one level may be coded 0 and the other coded 1. The choice will affect the sign of the resulting correlation with the criterion: If the group coded 1 has the higher mean, the correlation ($r_{pb}$, as discussed in Chapter 4) will be positive; otherwise it will be negative. The sign of the $\beta$ weight will be likewise determined. Otherwise, the choice of which variable is given which code makes no difference. A variable coded 0 or 1 is called a "dummy" or "indicator" variable. The independent variable's "scale" has interval properties, by definition, because the scale has only two points.

There are several ways to code a categorical variable that has more than two categories. These alternatives do not affect $R$, but one strategy may be more useful in a given setting than another because of differences in the way the resulting $\beta$ weights are interpretable. In all cases, $k$ categories will be used to form $k - 1$ individual predictor variables. For example, American voters may be classified as Democrats, Republicans, or Independents. One strategy is to define two dummy variables representing Democrats and Republicans, respectively. A Democrat is coded 1 on the first dummy variable and 0 on the second; a Republican is coded 0 on the first dummy variable and a 1 on the second, and an Independent is coded 0 on both variables. A third dummy variable for the Independent category is redundant because knowing that someone is neither a Democrat nor a Republican implies that he or she is an Independent. No one is coded 1 on both variables since the categories are mutually exclusive. The two dummy variables are therefore *negatively* correlated.

An alternative (among a literal infinity of others) is to code both Democrats and Republicans +1 and to code Independents −1 on one variable. This variable denotes whether the individual is or is not affiliated with a major political party. The second variable might be coded +1 for Democrats, −1 for Republicans, and 0 for Independents and represents whether a person is a Democratic or Republican given that he or she affiliated. This is called orthogonal coding because the correlation between the two resulting variables will be zero if there are equal numbers of people in the three categories.

A somewhat different issue arises when the categories form an ordinal scale, e.g., academic ranks (instructor, assistant professor, associate professor, and professor). The value of $R$ obtained from using three categorical predictors does not consider the relative magnitudes of the differences among the ranks, as it does not even assume the ranks are ordered. Coding the ranks as a single predictor (1 = instructor, 2 = assistant professor, 3 = associate professor, and 4 = professor) *does* assume they are equally spaced. The reduction in correlation using this single predictor as compared to using three categorical predictors is a measure of nonlinearity, as noted in the last chapter. If it is small, which it typically is when the criterion means for successive predictor values are monotonic, one predictor can replace several. Textbooks that discuss the details of multiple regression, such as Pedhazur (1982), present details on the use of categorical variables as predictors.

## Multicollinearity

A problem arises when the predictors are highly intercorrelated or multicollinear. This is not a practical problem when one or more predictors is an *exact* linear combination of the others since, as we have noted, no solution is possible without eliminating one or more or the chosen predictors. The more realistic problem is when one or more predictors is an *approximate* linear combination so that the solution proceeds to apparent completion.

Multicollinearity affects the stability of the regression weights in that slight changes in the data will produce substantial changes in the weights. However, it will not affect $R$ itself. This can be demonstrated by performing an orthogonal component analysis (see Chapter 11) on a set of multicollinear predictors. The resulting orthogonal components will not be multicollinear, by definition, but the values of $R$ produced by the original variables and their components will be identical. Among the many anomalies that can occur with unstable $\beta$ weights is that weight $\beta_i$ can be larger than weight $\beta_j$ but $\beta_i$ can be nonsignificant and $\beta_j$ significant. This is because the significance of a $\beta$ weight is tested by the ratio of its absolute value to its standard error ($t$) or this ratio squared ($F$), and $\beta_i$ can have a larger standard error than $\beta_j$. The high correlation between the two predictors in the numerical example given above ($-.729$) illustrates multicollinearity, but there is no magical value of the correlation to define multicollinearity exactly.

If your problem allows you to eliminate some predictors, try to locate the offenders. One statistic that is extremely useful is the tolerance of a predictor. This is 1.0 minus its squared multiple correlation with the other predictors (the criterion does not enter into this calculation). A variable with a very low tolerance is unlikely to add to prediction—its variance is largely shared with the other predictors, by definition. Unfortunately, no single predictor may have an unusually low tolerance relative to the others, yet multicollinearity may still be present. Another indicator of multicollinearity is when the determinant of the predictor correlation or variance-covariance matrix used in computing $R$ is small. Defining this quantity also goes beyond the scope of this book, but it is discussed in books listed as Suggested Additional Readings. Moreover, it may or may not be available, even as optional output (tolerances are available, though perhaps as optional output, in all the major packages). Some application (tests of theories, as we will discuss below) also dictate looking at all predictors. No procedure will be entirely satisfactory in this case, but the problem should be noted.

Other signs of an unstable solution are (1) a large standard error of the parameter estimates or its square, the variance, and (2) a large correlation among one or more parameter estimates. The latter are quite different from the correlations among the predictors but are readily obtainable. Large standard errors and correlations among estimates imply that alternative weightings are likely to produce similar results, meaning that the actual weights are not unique. Variables with large standard errors are also unlikely to be useful.

One way to handle a multicollinear set of predictors without eliminating any of them is a technique called ridge regression (Price, 1977; Darlington, 1968). It is a calculational device that goes beyond the scope of this text, and some (Morris, 1982; Rozeboom, 1979; Pagel & Lunneberg, 1985) are highly critical of it.

## Predictor Importance

It is extremely common to evaluate the relative importance of a set of predictors. Unfortunately, the concept is inherently ambiguous. A predictor that is most important by one criterion may not be by another. One definition of "importance" is the validity, defined earlier as the zero-order correlation between a predictor and a criterion. This (or its square) describes the information a predictor provides about the criterion, ignoring all other predictors. If you can use only one predictor, choose the one with the highest validity. The validity coefficient also remains unchanged as additional variables are entered or deleted.

Another definition of "importance" is the relation between a predictor and the criterion, holding constant all other predictors. This is indexed by the $\beta$ weights, but there are some statistical complications. One is that adding new predictors to the equation typically reduces the $\beta$ weights of all variables because the new variable typically has something in common with each of them, even if it is merely sampling error. When two predictors are highly correlated, *both* of their $\beta$ weights will be small because the effects of each will also be small when the other is controlled. Second, $\beta$ weights are much more sensitive to sampling error than are validities. Consequently, one should look at the standard errors of the $\beta$ weights as well as their absolute value. The "bottom line" is that each of a series of predictors may be highly valid, but none particularly important to independent prediction.

If the predictors have a common unit of measurement, the $b$ weights may be more useful than the $\beta$ weights. Range restriction (small predictor variance, perhaps due to sampling error) will reduce a $\beta$ weight. However, $\beta$ is divided by the predictor's standard deviation to produce $b$ (Eq. 4-21a), which partially offsets the range restriction. Using $b$ instead of $\beta$ is especially useful in comparing weights in different samples. The $b$ weights should not be used when the predictors are in different units since they are highly sensitive to these often arbitrary scale differences.

The "uniqueness" of a predictor is the difference in $R^2$ when (1) all variables are included in the model, called the saturated model, versus (2) the predictor in question is excluded from the model. This definition provides similar information to the $\beta$ weights and describes what the predictor adds to the other predictors. However, it is readily verified that the $t$ or $F$ statistic used to test the significance of a $\beta$ weight and a uniqueness are identical. The $\beta$ weights are readily available output from all computer programs; uniquenesses usually require effort to obtain. Although they are numerically different, they do not provide different information. The uniqueness is also numerically equal to the squared semipartial correlation between the added predictor and the criterion, controlling for the other predictors in the added predictor.

A third category of definitions is the improvement in prediction above that provided by one or more predictors known to be relevant to the criterion or incremental validity (Sechrest, 1963). One or more predictors serve as a covariate to provide a baseline for evaluating unknown predictor effects. For example, one might attempt to predict college grades from high school grades and a series of personality measures. Since high school grades are a known determinant of college grades, one would be much more interested in the increment the personality measures provide over high school grades than in their validities alone since the personality measures may be confounded with the same intellectual factors that are reflected in grades. The uniqueness–beta weight criterion is a special case in which the baseline is derived from all variables save the one in question.

The incremental validity criterion is intermediate to the zero-order correlation and uniqueness–beta weight criteria as far as defining predictor importance is concerned. Definitions based upon zero-order correlations do not take the redundancy of a given predictor into account at all. For example, $x_1$ and $x_2$ could contain all of the criterion-related variance, yet $x_3$ could still have the highest zero-order correlation. The $x_3$ could be important by itself yet useless in combination with $x_1$ and $x_2$. In addition, the increments to $R^2$ produced by an individual predictor depend upon its order of entry. Save for suppressor effects, the earlier it is entered, the larger its increment, so that its incremental validity lessens as variables with which it shares variance are entered ahead of it. In contrast, order of entry is immaterial to the values the β weights of a fixed set of predictors and the associated $R$.

On the other hand, the β-weight and uniqueness definitions are extremely stringent. A variable must measure something *novel* about the criterion in order to be important. Variable $x_3$ in the above example would have a β weight of zero, but it would still be valuable as it could be used to replace two other variables. Defining importance relative to the improvement in prediction does not require uniqueness with regard to *all* other predictors, only the covariate(s). It is therefore most useful in addressing the question of what a measure adds to what is already known in a given situation. Thus, if $x_1$ is the covariate, the incremental validity of $x_2$ corrects for $x_1$ but not $x_3$. Incremental validities are less affected by sampling error than β weights, though they are more affected than zero-order correlations.

There are other measures of predictor importance. Darlington (1968, 1990) provides an excellent discussion of these. Keep in mind that much of the "fury" about the best measure in prior discussions arose because different investigators conceived of importance differently. Decide first which meaning is most relevant to your study and act accordingly.

## SELECTION AND ALTERNATIVE WEIGHTINGS OF PREDICTORS

It is perhaps in the minority of cases that you will simply be concerned with the $R$ and β weights provided by a given set of predictors. One selects variables from a larger set (1) to find a parsimonious set of predictors that does a good job in estimating criterion scores or (2) hierarchically to test a theory about the relative importance of various measures

Consideration 1 implies that the researcher seeks a relatively small number of variables that will do an adequate job in predicting a criterion. Much applied effort is spent in obtaining the most predictive power with the smallest number of predictors. For example, 10 or more tests might be applied initially to predict success on a particular job ($Y$). If it is impractical to use more than 3 or 4 tests, the goal of the study is to find a small set of variables that has a higher value of $R$ with $Y$ than any other set of the same size. This approach is often called "actuarial prediction," as it implies that the investigator is uninterested in why the predictors achieve their goal. As noted in Chapter 3, this tends to be associated with the predictive validity paradigm, but even so, theoretical issues are often present, and so it is perhaps better to use the term "actuarially oriented prediction."

Consideration 2 implies an interest in the *processes* that determine a measure. It is inherent in construct validation. One example is whether a predictor is valid because of its direct effects or because of mediation. If predictor $x_1$ affects criterion $y$ directly, then it will maintain its relation when other possible variables (e.g., $x_2$) are controlled. Consequently, $r_{1y.2}$ and $\beta_1$ in an equation predicting $y$ from $x_1$ and $x_2$ will be sizable. However, if $x_2$ mediates the effect, these two quantities will be small even if $r_{1y}$ is large. For example, gender differences arise on many measures. However, many are interested in the extent to which these gender differences are biological outcomes versus due to such possible mediators as differential socialization. Path analysis (see Chapter 13) is one way to evaluate mediational effects. Whether or not a predictor's effects are direct or mediated by a third variable is less important to actuarially oriented prediction than to hypothesis testing. In contrast, a "moderator" is a variable which affects the correlation between two other variables. Thus, $r_{1y}$ may be large and positive under some conditions and small or even negative under others; e.g., a test may predict academic performance at one university and not at another. A later section of this chapter and Chapter 9 deal with evaluating moderator effects.

Predictor importance comes into play regardless of whether one's needs are purely in prediction or in evaluating processes. Vital to this issue is the distinction between variable selection that is data-driven versus guided by some form of prior theory. This distinction is very basic to multivariate analysis and will reappear in similar form in Chapters 11 through 13 when we consider the difference between exploratory (data driven) and confirmatory (theory driven) factor analysis. In the present case, nearly all psychometricians have a strong preference for using theory to guide variable selection when possible because of the tremendous role chance plays in data-driven procedures.

## Stepwise Inclusion of Predictors

Stepwise selection is a data-driven device for selecting variables which has its proponents (Darlington, 1968, 1990; Draper & Smith, 1981) and its critics (Cooley & Lohnes, 1971). We lean toward the latter position, especially and strongly when it comes to hypothesis testing.

In forward selection, the predictor with the highest zero-order correlation is entered first, followed by the variable that produces the largest increment in $R^2$ over the first variable, followed by the variable that produces the largest increment in $R^2$ over the first two, etc. The process ceases when no increment is significant. It would therefore stop at the first stage if no predictor correlated significantly with the criterion. Conversely, backward selection starts with all of the predictors, deleting in turn those whose presence is least missed (those producing the smallest decrease in $R^2$). An inferential criterion is again used to test the significance of the changes in $R^2$, the change being a decrement in this case. The two strategies can be combined by first adding predictors and then testing to see whether any previously added predictors have become redundant because of newer predictors, or vice versa.

The following common error illustrates why stepwise selection can be especially misleading in testing theories. Assume that $x_1$ and $x_2$ each relate to $y$, and that the stepwise solution results in the selection of $x_1$ but not $x_2$. It is *not* proper to conclude that $x_2$

is unimportant. What happened was that $x_1$ had a higher sample correlation than $x_2$, and that $R^2_{y.12}$ was not significantly greater than $r^2_{y1}$. This could easily happen because variables $x_1$ and $x_2$ were highly correlated *even if* there were no population difference between them or even if $r_{y2}$ was actually greater than $r_{y1}$ in the population. Limited sample size often contributes to this.

Another major reason to be conservative about using stepwise solutions is that existing algorithms offer little control for the role of chance in variable selection. This was noted at least as far back as Cohen (1968). Wilkinson (1979) made an important but largely ignored observation about predictor selection: Tests of significance for inclusion severely underestimate the role of chance because they do not correct for the multiple comparisons that are made. The significance level used to decide whether the first variable should be entered assumes that *one* particular variable has been chosen in advance, which is not the case, by definition.

For example, suppose there are 20 predictors and none are related to the criterion nor each other. The probability that a type I error will affect any given predictor is $\alpha$, by definition. Letting $\alpha = .05$, the probability of correctly concluding that the predictor is invalid is .95. Given that the predictors are independent, the probability that correct decisions will be made for all 20 predictors is $.95^{20}$ or .36. Conversely, the probability that at least type I error will arise is $1 - .36$ or .64, and so the odds are nearly 2 to 1 that a significant relation can be found even though the predictors are totally invalid. Setting $\alpha = .01$ still leaves a probability of .18 that at least one predictor will appear in the prediction equation. Despite the fact that over a decade has passed since Wilkinson's (1979) article, several major packages have failed to correct this error [see Hays (1988, Chap. 11) for a discussion of several methods for correcting for these multiple comparisons]. This spurious effect is very easy to demonstrate through computer simulation

There are perhaps defensible limited uses of stepwise selection, especially in actuarially oriented prediction, as when one is indifferent about which predictors are to be retained. The number of predictors should be relatively small to avoid the problem noted in the previous paragraph. It is also preferable to combine stepwise and hierarchical approaches, which we will discuss below, instead of using stepwise selection alone. Do *not* simply "dump" a large number of convenient variables into an analysis and interpret the results. Large samples are also an absolute necessity. If you wish to select from as many as 10 variables, employ 500 or more persons in the study. Whatever the sample size and amount of number of predictors selected, it is vital to examine the β weights, the $R$, and, especially, the variables selected in the initial investigation in a *new* sample. This is known as "cross validation." However, stepwise inclusion is inappropriate for model testing; that is what hierarchical inclusion is designed for (see below).

## All Possible Subsets Approaches

Another available approach is all possible subsets regression which provides $R$ estimates for all predictor combinations. This may be done with all $2^k$ models possible with $k$ predictors (each predictor may be included or not included, independently of all other predictors), or it may be limited to a specified number of predictors (in which case the term "some possible subsets" might be more apt even though the authors have not seen it used). An all (or some) possible subsets regression often illustrates (1) the slight effects of alternative models with the same number of predictors or (2) the consistent superiority of models containing certain predictors over others. It can also be generally informative as to the effects of swapping variables, (e.g., cheaper versus more costly ones) in and out of the equations. As long as one recognizes that the model producing the highest $R$ probably may have done so by chance and that the more successful predictors need to be cross-validated, these results can be quite informative. Keep in mind the gradual increase in $R$ expected from increasing the number of predictors (Eq. 5-25).

Even though all subsets regression is well within the capability of nearly every major statistical package, the downside to this approach is that the amount of information, to say nothing of paper, generated may be immense. For example, 10 predictors yield $2^{10}$ (1024) combinations of predictors. Whatever else is done, one should generally restrict the number of predictors searched.

### Hierarchical Inclusion of Variables

In a hierarchical process, variables are entered in an order determined by theory or other prior considerations (some authors term this "stepwise," but we limit this term to data-driven processes as considered above). It is especially appropriate if the theory is sufficiently well defined to define a complete hierarchy (order). The first variable or set of variables serve as a covariate for the second, the first and second serve as covariates for the third, etc. Hierarchical inclusion is incremental because its involves how much a given predictor(s) increments its predecessors. One controls for the effects of the preceding variables in testing the increment of a given variable. Hierarchical selection therefore is not concerned with what a predictor tells about the criterion but what it adds to what is already known based upon successive partialling. Equation 5-24 provides appropriate significance tests on the increments to $R^2$ precisely because order of variable entry has been specified in advance, in contrast to the procedure in stepwise inclusion.

Hierarchical selection or entry therefore involves incremental validity and successive partialling as discussed above. Further discussion is found in any textbook dealing with multiple regression, such as Pedhazur (1982, pp. 62–63). Decisions to retain or exclude variables can be based upon the magnitude of increment as well as on statistical significance.

To illustrate the use of hierarchical selection, consider the issue of evaluating the role of vocational interest in predicting college grades. By itself, a test of whether this measure predicts college grades is of limited value. A significant zero-order correlation could mean (1) there is some inherent role of vocational interest and therefore a direct relation between vocational interest and grades (2) better students have more of an academic interest than poorer students, and so the relation is mediated by academic ability; or (3) both. It is probably more informative to determine if vocational interest improves upon the prediction afforded by a known predictor of academic ability such as high school grades or possibly a combination of high school grades and SAT scores. This is a test of a direct effect, controlling for academic ability. High school grades, alone or in combination with SAT scores, may be sufficient as predictors. Note that it makes little sense to test the effects of adding the known measure (e.g., grades) to the unproven measure. The burden of proof is on the unproven measure. One important special case is to see whether an expensive predictor, such as expert judgment, improves prediction over the baseline provided by a inexpensive predictor such as past performance or some other actuarial basis. It is often not difficult to show that the expensive predictor relates to the criterion—the more important question is whether it is worth the cost (Dawes, 1971; Dawes & Corrigan, 1974; Goldberg, 1965, 1968a, 1968b).

If vocational interest measure predicts college grades because more able students have higher vocational interest scores and not because of any inherent relation between vocational interest and grades, its zero-order $r$ may be large but its increase in $R^2$ will be small. Natural hierarchies sometimes follow from theoretical considerations specific to the situation. Wickens and Olzak (1989) provide an example to be considered in Chapter 15. Perhaps the main point to consider is that simple effects are evaluated before more complex effects because of the principle of parsimony in science.

## Combining Strategies

Hierarchical strategies sometimes suffer from an ambiguity in the order of entering variables. For example, suppose there are seven variables, $x_1$ to $x_7$, you are considering for use in a regression equation. You know that $x_1$ should be entered first, as it has proven successful and is inexpensive to administer. However, you may have no rationale for some or all of the others. Even so, your one constraint reduces the number of possible orders from 7! (5040) to 6! (720). Further reflection before proceeding to look at the data may suggest others. For example, you may conclude that $x_2$ or $x_3$, but not $x_4$, $x_5$, $x_6$, or $x_7$, should come after $x_1$, and that $x_7$ really should come last. It is quite possible that this may leave you will a small enough set to explore individually.

Even though theoretical considerations usually limit the number of possible orders, the limitation may not be sufficient, and so stepwise selection under the relevant constraints may be defensible. The main idea is to avoid having a stepwise solution substitute for thought. You will not sacrifice anything of value by avoiding stepwise regression even though it is occasionally useful in deciding among variables when a theory is absent.

## Moderated Multiple Regression

Moderated multiple regression is a form of hierarchical entry designed to determine if the relation between two variables is influenced by a third or moderating variable. Moderating variables have come under extensive discussion in social psychology (Baron & Kenney, 1986; Bissonnette, Bernstein, Ickes, & Knowles, 1990a, 1990b; Paunonen & Jackson, 1985). The moderator may be either continuous or categorical. As noted in the previous discussion of partial correlation, partial correlations become misleading when the covariate is also a moderator.

The hierarchy of predictors is (1) the main predictor, denoted $x_1$; (2) the presumed moderator, denoted $x_2$; and (3) the joint effects of the two, defined as the cross products of their scores ($x_1 x_2 = x_3$). This cross product reflects the combined effects or interaction of the main predictor and moderator. It is an application of the principle illustrated when a nonlinear (cross-product) term in Eq. 5-1c was put in the linear form of Eq. 5-1d. For example, cognitive ability ($x_1$) might moderate the relationship between amount of study time ($x_2$) and grades ($y$), so that the order of entry would be cognitive ability, amount of study time, and their product. If cognitive ability were a dichotomy (which, hopefully it isn't save for this example), more able students would be coded 1, less able students would be coded 0, the cross products would be the study times for the more able students but scores of 0 for less able students.

Stage 1 uses amount of study time to predict grades. A significant correlation between it and the criterion (grades) at this stage ($r_{1y}$), using Eq. 5-23, would confirm the expected overall value of studying. Presumably, the sign of $r_{1y}$ would be positive because more study time would lead to higher grades.

Stage 2 involves using both the main predictor and the moderator. A large difference in $R^2_{y \cdot 12}$ between using the two predictors in conjunction versus the $r^2_{1y}$ for the main predictor alone indicates that more able students and less able students get different grades in general, holding study time constant. This test uses Eq. 5-24. The sign of the $\beta$ weight denotes whether the more cognitively able students performed better, as one would expect, or, improbably, worse. It is equivalent to stating that there is an intercept difference in the regression lines relating amount of study time to grades at different ability levels. Note that this test is quite different from one based upon a simple correlation between ability and grades ($r_{2y}$) which ignores amount of time spent studying. The effect of cognitive ability inferred from the moderator's $\beta$ weight at stage 2 controls for the relation between abilty and amount of time spent studying. The reason for adjusting for the overlap between amount of time spent studying and ability but not amount of time spent studying and grades (i.e., for using semipartial rather than partial correlation) was presented in introducing semipartial $r$ and is discussed further below.

Stage 3 involves the difference between the $R^2$ between the saturated model containing the main predictor, moderator, and cross-product term ($R^2_{y \cdot 123}$) and the $R^2$ obtained from the additive model using only the main predictor and moderator ($R^2_{y \cdot 12}$). This test also uses Eq. 5-24. Note that the more complex cross-product term is evaluated after its simpler components. Stage 3 is therefore a test of the uniqueness of the cross-product term. A significant difference in $R^2$ means that the slope of the regression line relating amount of time spent studying to grades varies with ability. This test is formally identical to testing an interaction in the ANOVA. The only difference is that the predictor, the moderator, or both may be (but need not be) continuous variables. This test is appropriate even when the $R^2_{y \cdot 12}$ from the additive model does not significantly differ from the $R^2_{y1}$ obtained from the main predictor alone or even when neither differs significantly from zero.

Figure 5-5 contains three of the outcomes possible with a dichotomous moderator. In Fig. 5-5a there is neither a slope nor an intercept difference between the two levels of the proposed moderator. As can be seen, this does *not* imply a lack of a grade difference between more and less able students—it merely indicates that the two groups

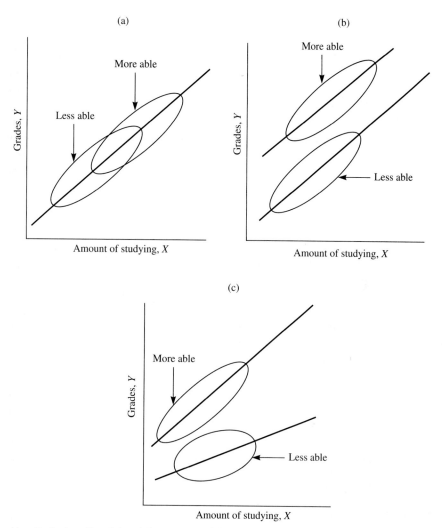

**FIGURE 5-5** Hypothetical scatter plots relating amount of time studied ($X$) to grades ($Y$) when (a) there is no difference between more and less able students in either slope or intercept, (b) there is an intercept difference favoring able students but no slope difference, and (c) there is both a slope and an intercept difference.

may be fit by a common regression line despite possible differences between them on both the predictor and on the criterion. Note that if we accept this as the final model, we attribute group differences in grades to the different amount of time spent studying and not ability per se.

Figure 5-5b presents perhaps a more likely possibility, an intercept difference favoring the more able students as well as an effect of amount of time spent studying. This says that even though they study the same amount of time, more able students will obtain better grades than less able students. However, the two effects are independent or additive—increasing the amount of time spent studying benefits both groups equally.

Figure 5-5c probably contains the most likely outcome, at least for a intellectually demanding curriculum. This illustrates both an intercept and a slope difference. The form of the relationship indicates that even though a more able student will get better grades than a less able student if they both study for an average amount of time, the more able student will benefit from additional study more than the less able student. This figure further illustrates heteroscedasticity. In one extreme case, the $r$ between amount of study and grades may be positive for more able students but zero for less able students. In an even more extreme case, $r$ may be positive in one group and negative in the other group, and so the overall regression line has a zero slope. Note that only the stage 3 result is relevant to moderation; when moderation occurs, statements about the main predictor (main effect) need to be qualified.

An alternative way to test the hypothesis that the relation between amount of time spent studying and grades is different for high and low cognitive ability subjects is to compare the magnitudes of $r$ between amount of time spent studying and grades in the two ability groups, using what the Fisher $Z'$ transformation (Hays, 1988). There are two major reasons for not doing this. First, Fisher's test requires that the proposed moderator be a dichotomy. A more serious problem is that it is generally more sensitive to both type I and type II errors arising from incidental differences in variability of the groups (Bissonnette, Bernstein, Ickes, & Knowles, 1990a, 1990b). Also note that moderated multiple regression and the $Z'$ test deal with slightly different issues—the former deals with regression, by definition, and the $Z'$ test deals with correlation.

Although we used amount of time spent studying as the predictor and cognitive ability as the moderator, we could have done the reverse. The result at stage 2 could well be different in this case since it tests the incremental effect of studying, controlling cognitive ability rather than the reverse. However, the result at stage 3 will be identical because both comparisons test the incremental effect of the cross product over the additive effects of cognitive ability and amount of time studying. The two questions therefore produce the same answer regarding moderation (interaction). Moderation is especially important to the highly controversial topic of test bias as it applies to groups defined on the basis of race or gender. This topic will be considered in Chapters 9 and 10. See Cronbach and related papers for a discussion of some recent methodological points.

## Variable Weighting

Once selected for inclusion in a linear combination, the next issue is how to weight the variables. The distinction between actuarially oriented prediction and model testing applies to weighting just as it does to variable selection. Indeed, variable selection is basically a special case of weighting in which omitted variables are given weights of zero. Optimal weighting, as defined through least squares $\beta$ weights or a similar estimation procedure, is but one of several possibilities for weighting the chosen variables. Optimal weightings are used in item response theory (Chapter 10), various forms of factor analysis such as principal components (Chapters 11 through 13), profile analysis, discriminant analysis and scaling (Chapter 14), and categorical modeling (Chapter 15), as well as in regression.

One problem with optimal weights is that they are highly subject to sampling error since the sampling error in a $\beta$ weight is a function of all the variables used in the analysis and not just the specific predictor and the criterion. Weights that are optimal in the original normative sample will not be optimal in a second sample because of (1) sampling error, which is a function of sample size, the number of variables, and their intercorrelation; and (2) systematic differences between the characteristics of the two samples. Regression weights may be robust across samples that have quite different means and variances, but this should not be taken for granted. Also, weights derived from a small, poorly constructed sample may generalize less well than equal weights—a bad pilot study may be worse than none at all. As a rule of thumb, but not a magical number, you should have 10 subjects per predictor in order to even hope for a stable prediction equation. The term "bouncing beta" describes the often large fluctuations in $\beta$ weights over samples due to sampling error.

Our entire discussion has been based upon the traditional approach to estimation, (ordinary) least squares. As noted in the previous chapter, generalized least squares and, especially, maximum likelihood are alternatives which are available in computer programs like LISREL. These methods are at least as demanding of large samples as ordinary least squares, but they have the advantage of allowing hypotheses about fixed and constrained parameters to be tested. For example, moderation may be tested by evaluating the difference in fit ($G^2$) between a model in which the regression weights are allowed to vary freely and a nested model in which they are constrained to equality among levels of the presumed moderator. Some models may make specific predictions about the values of regression weights which may be tested by allowing them to vary freely and then nesting a model in which the values are fixed appropriately. It seems probable that this approach will become increasingly popular relative to traditional approaches.

Equal weighting is an alternative to optimal weighting that appears in classical test theory (Chapter 6) and centroid and multiple group factor analysis (Chapters 11 and 13). The predictive properties of optimally weighted and equally weighted linear combinations are often nearly identical as long as the signs of the individual variables are chosen appropriately; i.e, variables which correlate negatively with the criterion are subtracted in the linear combination. For example, suppose optimal weights for Scholastic Aptitude Test (SAT) and grade point average (GPA) measures were obtained by multiple regression to predict academic performance in college. Now, suppose one were also to compute the equally weighted sum of SAT and GPA (in $z$ score or other form appropriate to eliminating the arbitrary scale differences). The $r$ between the two linear combinations might exceed .9 so that either combination, or, for that matter, *any* set of positive weights may predict the criterion as well as any other.

Kaiser (1970; also see Dawes, 1971; Dawes & Corrigan, 1974; Wainer, 1976) used the term "it don't make no nevermind" to describe this outcome. This is an important principle to keep in mind even though it should not stop you from using optimal weights if the data dictate or from looking at individual $\beta$ weights. You should routinely compare the results of optimal and equal weightings by correlating each linear combination with the criterion. If possible, cross validate the weights. High correlations among parameter estimates suggest that equal (or any other) weights will probably work as well as optimal weights, a corollary to the multicollinearity that may be present.

A compromise alternative is to use an empirical weighting that does not rely upon a formal definition of "optimal." For example, some advocate using validities (zero-order predictor-criterion correlations) instead of $\beta$ or $b$ weights when the normative base is small. Although there is little formal rationale for this procedure, it is a middle ground that allows more important variables to receive greater weight. In addition, it is not as sensitive to sampling error as optimal weighting since sampling error affects only the two involved variables. It may appear unpatriotic to use anything that is not optimal, but there is often good reason for not doing so. This book stresses the need for simple and direct approaches to problems. Optimal weighting is certainly not simple even though it may be necessary.

Actuarially oriented prediction usually does not require optimal weighting or any other specific choice, as its goals are pragmatic—to maximize the correlation between a linear combination of predictors and a criterion. In contrast, optimal weighting is necessary for some model testing. For example, if the hypothesis states that $x_1$'s effects are mediated by $x_2$, one tests the significance of $\beta_1$ in a model containing $x_1$ and $x_2$ as predictors, which requires optimal weights. However, the hypothesis may deal with whether $x_1$ relates more strongly to $y$ than $x_2$ does. This involves the relative magnitudes of $r_{1y}$ and $r_{2y}$ rather than optimal ($\beta$) weights. Some hypotheses, considered later in the chapters on factor analysis, can be tested with either optimal or equal weights.

Computing regression weights in a small sample for model-testing purposes is appropriate, assuming it addresses the issue at hand, as the lack of power handicaps all variables. One important distinction is between demonstrating the contribution of a predictor by showing that its $\beta$ weight is statistically different from zero and comparing the magnitudes of the $\beta$ weights associated with two variables. A demonstration normally requires a smaller sample size than a comparison because the standard error of a difference is usually larger than the standard error of a single variable even though both are functions of all variables. Sample size affects the confidence with which any conclusion can be reached, but it is especially risky to inspect relative magnitudes of predictors in small samples because of the instability of these weights.

Another possibility is to use some theory (which may simply be a hunch) that leads to unequal weights, rational weighting. Equal and rational weights are not affected by sampling error, by definition, since the weights are not estimated from the data. However, both may fail to incorporate relations that are present in the data and thus may not be the best choice. It is wise to compare the results of using unequal weights and using equal weights, just as it is wise to compare the results of using optimal weights and using equal weights. There is little reason to use rational weighting in prediction when the results correlate very highly with equal weighting; using equal weights helps sidestep unnecessary defense of the choice of weights.

## RELATED TOPICS

### The Analysis of Covariance

In the analysis of covariance (ANCOVA), a covariate is entered before treatment effects of more focal interest. The covariate is normally a continuous variable, and the treatment effects are normally categorical, but this is not necessary to the logic. This logic is nothing else than a hierarchical (incremental) approach to eliminate the effects of variables of lesser interest (we have noted that the ANOVA itself is a special case of multiple regression in which the predictors are categorical). The main, and most clearly appropriate, use of the ANCOVA is when the covariate and criterion are highly correlated but subjects have been assigned at random so that the covariate and treatment effects are uncorrelated. Putting the covariate in first may eliminate a source of variance that would have been part of the experimental error had it been ignored.

For example, suppose students are given a pretest on a topic, then assigned at random to different instructional groups, and then given a posttest on the topic. Pretest and posttest scores will probably be highly correlated because both tap individual differences in cognitive ability. In an ordinary ANOVA, cognitive ability forms part of experimental error and may be sufficiently great to eliminate differences due to instruction, especially in small groups. However, if the pretest scores are entered first, the part of individual differences assessed by the pretest become a systematic effect that is not part of the experimental error. The logic of this approach is sounder than simply using the simple difference score between the posttest and pretest since this simple difference does not use the correct correlation between the two in adjusting. In effect, simple difference scores overcorrect for the pretest, but the "it don't make no nevermind" (equal weighting) principle may also be applicable.

The ANCOVA is sometimes used to correct for preexisting group mean differences when the treatments must be administered to intact groups, e.g., classes that differ in ability. This is a somewhat questionable use, but one criterion for applicability is whether there is a causal relation between the treatment effect and the covariate. If there is, the covariance adjustment must be suspect. In either event, results of the ANCOVA should be interpreted with a caution to the reader.

### Nonlinear Relations

We have stressed that $r$ represents the relationship between two variables fairly well as long as this relationship is monotonic. This same principle holds in multiple $R$.

There is a second aspect of studying nonlinear relations. Trend analyses concern fitting different functions to data. These often form a polynomial series of the form $Y = b_1X + b_2X^2 + b_3X^3 + \cdots + b_kX^k$. One approach to fitting polynomials has much in common with moderated multiple regression. It was noted that the transformation of a variable from the nonlinear form of Eq. 5-1c to the linear form of Eq. 5-1d allowed the (relative) simplicity of linear methods to be used with nonlinear terms. The same principle may be used here. Let $X_1 = X$, $X_2 = X^2$, $X_3 = X^3$, etc., and test the significance of the increment in $R^2$ as each term is added in the sequence, starting with the simplest $(X_1)$. In this case, the successive terms are generally correlated, but there is a more elegant alternative approach using orthogonal polynomials that provides independent predictors (Winer, Brown, & Michels, 1991). Letting $X_1 = \log X$ or some other function allows nonpolynomial functions to be fit when appropriate.

## Residual Analysis

It is usually a simple matter to compute the residuals, $z_Y - z_y'$ (symbolized $z_{Y \cdot X}$ in the previous chapter where there was only one predictor). These residuals are not necessarily random. They are extremely important to applied prediction problems as a check on the completeness of the prediction (whether all systematic sources were accounted for) and the assumption of normally distributed error made in inference. Draper and Smith (1981) and Pedhazur (1982) are good sources for the mechanics.

Residual analyses are perhaps not performed often enough, but most major programs provide useful diagnostics on an optional basis. Some of the important things to look for are the following:

**1** *Outliers.* An outlier is an observation with a large residual. If the assumptions of the model are met, residuals will be normally distributed 5 percent of the observations will fall outside a $\pm 1.96$ standard error of estimate units, for example. However, outliers should be random observations. If they have some property in common, a relevant predictor has probably been omitted from the model. You may also detect coding errors by the inspection process.

**2** *Independence.* Magnitudes of residuals should be independent of predicted but not obtained scores (see Table 4-2). Lack of independence can arise from nonlinear predictor-criterion relations, among other factors.

**3** *Homoscedasticity.* The variance of residuals should be approximately equal across levels of the predictor. Homoscedasticity may be seen when residuals for different groups are compared. For example, the second author once served as an expert witness to examine faculty salaries. On average, females received less pay than males even after correcting for such variables as length of service. However, residuals for male faculty members were more variable than residuals for female faculty members, and so the lowest-paid faculty relative to relevant predictors were actually males.

Additional details may be obtained when the observations have a meaningful serial order. However, this is more likely to arise in areas like economics, where time series are common, than in psychology and related areas where most observations are randomly related to one another, e.g., individuals randomly sampled in some manner.

## Canonical Analysis

"Canonical analysis" is an extension of multiple correlation and regression in which an optimal weighting of predictors is related to an optimal weighting of criteria rather than a single criterion. The first canonical variables are the linear combinations of predictors and criteria producing the largest correlation (canonical correlation). These linear combinations are then partialled from the data. The search for new linear combinations and associated correlations is then repeated.

Redundancy analysis (Stewart & Love, 1968) is a closely related procedure (so closely related, in fact, that the two are often combined in the same computer procedures). This procedure is concerned with how much variance in the criterion is explained by an optimal combination of predictors, and vice versa. For example, a very high canonical correlation can arise when *one* predictor correlates highly with *one* criterion even if these individual variables are unrelated to all other variables. The canonical correlation might be misleading because very little of the total variance is explained by the relationship.Unfortunately, canonical analysis often tends to be used as a "multivariate fishing expedition." The interested reader is referred to the Suggested Additional Readings for a more detailed discussion.

## SUMMARY

The core of this chapter is the concept of a *linear combination* or sum of variables that may be equally or unequally weighted. A particularly useful "trick" is to take a nonlinear combination, such as one containing cross products of two variables or powers of individual variables, and make it a linear combination by redefining variables. One very fundamental relationship is that the variance of an equally weighted linear combination equals the sum of the individual variances plus two times the sum of the covariances. The resulting set of variances and covariances used in this computation, the variance-covariance matrix, is widely used in psychometric theory. Simple algorithms provide the variance of a weighted linear combination and linear combinations of standardized variables, in which case the variance-covariance matrix becomes a correlation matrix. Another important special case is when the individual variables are binary (dichotomous), such as items on many tests.

Characteristics of individual binary variables affect the distributions of the total scores (linear combination of item scores). In the limiting case of items that are totally uncorrelated (i.e., a totally unreliable test), this distribution will be normal. However, positive item correlations cause the distribution to flatten and, in the extreme and rare case of extremely high correlations, become bimodal. The item difficulties (probabilities of answering abilities' items correctly or $p$ values) also determine the shape of the distribution. Tests comprised of easy items will tend to be negatively skewed, and tests comprised of difficult items will tend to be positively skewed. Since these may be desirable outcomes, the commonly held belief that test scores should be normally distributed can be shown to be false. We next dealt with covariances and correlations between linear combinations, which are basic to multivariate analysis.

A partial correlation between two variables is the estimated correlation between them assuming one or more additional variables (covariates) are held constant. It is the correlation between the two sets of residual scores with respect to the covariates. A semipartial correlation is similar except that only one of the variables being correlated is adjusted. Partial and semipartial correlations are effective estimates only when the relation to the covariates is homoscedastic, (i.e., the correlation between the two variables is the same across levels of the covariate) and the covariate is valid and reliable. Some other key points are as follows: (1) the signs of the correlations among the variables being correlated are crucial in determining whether partialling increases or decreases the strength of relationship, (2) the effects of partialling are generally less than expected from examining the unpartialled (zero-order) correlation, (3) the covariate may be a linear combination of individual variables, and (4) partialling ordinarily removes only the linear effects of covariates. Removing the effects of more than one covariate is called higher-order partialling and is independent of the order in which the covariates are removed. A second form of partialling was discussed involving the concepts of within-group, between-group, and total correlations. These arise when two variables are correlated across different groups. It was noted how spurious effects can arise when variables are inappropriately aggregated across groups, i.e., total correlations are reported when the pooled within-group correlations are more appropriate. One special case of this artifact that appears with frequency data is called Simpson's paradox.

The multiple correlation ($R$) is the correlation between an optimal linear combination and a criterion, and multiple regression concerns the optimal weights that produce $R$. These weights are called beta ($\beta$) weights when applied to standardized scores, and $b$ weights when applied to raw scores. They describe the change in the criterion, holding constant other predictors per unit change in a predictor when the data are expressed as $z$ scores and raw scores, respectively. The weights are ordinarily complex to compute, but the case of two predictors is simple. Formulas were presented to test the significance of $R$ and of increments in $R$ as new predictors are added to old ones.

The $R$ (1) will be large when the zero-order correlations between predictors and the criterion (validities) are high, (2) cannot be lower than the highest validity, (3) can reflect unexpected results through *suppressor* relationships in which a $\beta$ weight exceeds the zero-order correlation or both are of substantial magnitude but of opposite sign, (4) illustrates a law of diminishing returns regarding the addition of predictors—rarely are more than two or three predictors needed for optimal prediction, and (5) is usually larger in a sample than in the population. The magnitude of this bias is directly related to the number of predictors and inversely related to the number of observations.

Predictors may be categorical. The general technique is to form $k - 1$ new variables from the original $k$ categories. In *dummy* coding, an observation is coded as 1 on a given variable if that observation belongs to a designated category (e.g., Democratic voters) and a 0 otherwise. In orthogonal coding, contrasts of interest are defined. For example, voters may be classified as 1 on one variable if they are either registered Democrats *or* registered Republicans and 0 if they are Independents. Democrats would be coded 1, Republicans −1 (or the reverse), and Independents 0 on the second contrast. The two contrasts therefore ask "Is the individual affiliated with a political party?" and "If so, which one?"

Highly intercorrelated predictors are *multicollinear*, which affects the stability of the $\beta$ weights (but not $R$)—alternative weights may predict as well as the optimal ones, and small changes in the data may produce large changes in the weights. One item of evidence for multicollinearity is a low tolerance (1.0 minus the multiple correlation of one predictor with the other predictors). Other (and related) signs of instability are when the predictors have large standard errors and when their estimates are highly correlated.

Many studies evaluate the importance of the various predictors. Unfortunately, the term has several meanings which address different questions. One definition is in terms of the relative magnitudes of the validities, which index what predictors share with the criterion, ignoring other predictors. In contrast, $\beta$ weights define what predictors share with the criterion, holding constant other predictors. Intermediate between these two definitions is the incremental validity or increase in $R^2$ produced by a given predictor plus a specified set of predictors over that produced by the specified set alone.

Variable selection depends upon the goal of the study (i.e., whether it is actuarially oriented and thus minimally concerned with how prediction occurs) versus hypothesis testing, as in construct validation. Two examples of hypotheses are "mediation," in which the effects of a predictor upon a criterion are produced indirectly by a third variable, and "moderation," in which the magnitude of correlation depends upon an additional variable. Regardless of the goals of the study, we recommend that stepwise variable inclusion be used with extreme caution if at all. This procedure involves selection on the basis of the sample data. It often leads to spurious estimates of significance and can easily be misinterpreted, as one variable can be included and another excluded, implying one is more unimportant on the basis of small, nonsignificant differences in correlation. A somewhat better procedure is all-subsets regression in which all possible combinations of predictors are examined. In order to use this effectively however, it is often necessary to minimize the number of combinations, i.e., use a "some possible subsets" approach, and be aware of the bias in sample values of $R$.

An even better approach is hierarchical inclusion in which the effects of variables are evaluated in a predetermined order based upon a theory. Moderated multiple regression is a particular form of hierarchical inclusion used to test moderator effects in which (1) the main predictor is entered at the first stage, (2) the presumed moderator is entered at the second stage, and (3) the cross product of the main predictor and presumed moderator are entered at the third stage. A significance difference in $R^2$ between the values obtained at stages 3 and 2 implies a moderation effect.

Variable weighting is closely related to variable selection, as a variable that is not selected may be regarded as having a weight of 0. Least-squares weighting is not the only viable approach, especially in actuarially oriented prediction. One alternative is equal weighting; the results of using optimal and equal weighting are almost indistinguishable. Generalized least-squares and maximum likelihood estimates may also be useful in testing certain specific hypotheses that can be stated in the form of differences in fit ($G^2$) between a nested and a more general model, e.g., models that constrain or fix parameters that are free in the more general model.

Some related topics include (1) the analysis of covariance in which the incremental effects of a predictor of interest are assessed, controlling for a variable of lesser interest (the covariate); (2) the analysis of trend and other nonlinear relationships; (3) canonical correlation, which is an extension of multiple correlation in which optimal linear combinations of predictors are correlated with optimal linear combinations of criteria, often unfortunately leading to "multivariate fishing expeditions," and (4) residual analysis. Residuals are the difference between observed and predicted scores. Large values (outliers) having some common property indicate a relevant predictor has been omitted. Other facets of the analysis may also provide useful information.

## SUGGESTED ADDITIONAL READINGS

Bernstein, I. H. (1988). *Applied multivariate analysis*. New York: Springer-Verlag.

Cohen. J., & Cohen, P. (1983). *Applied multiple regression correlation analysis for the behavioral sciences*. (2d ed.) Hillsdale, NJ: Erlbaum Associates.

Darlington, R. B. (1990). *Regression and linear models*. New York: McGraw-Hill.

Draper, N. R., & Smith, H. (1981). *Applied regression analysis* (2d ed.). New York: Wiley.

Pedhazur, E. J. (1982). *Multiple regression in behavioral research* (2d ed.). New York: Holt, Rinehart, & Winston.

Winer, B. J., Brown, D. R., & Michels, K. M. (1971). *Statistical principles in experimental design*. (3d ed.). New York: McGraw-Hill.

*Note*: Although packages such as SAS, SPSSX, SYSSTAT, and BMDP are broader in their scope, Gorsuch's *UniMult* program uniquely implements the principles described in this chapter.

# PART THREE

# CONSTRUCTION OF
# MULTI-ITEM MEASURES

Most measures are composites formed from aggregating individual items into a scale. Classical measurement theory aggregates items simply by summing item responses as in a "number correct" score on a classroom test. This part contains five chapters dealing with the process of aggregation. First, we consider the definition and role of measurement error both in individual and composite measures. This includes a discussion of one classical approach, sampling items from a domain (pool) of possible items. The succeeding chapter is concerned with actual assessment of test reliability. The third chapter employs these principles to discuss construction of the most common forms of tests. The fourth chapter deals with various special problems (guessing, speeded tests, adverse impact and test bias, halo effects in observations, response biases and response styles, and tests consisting of several scales). The final chapter presents modern developments, largely in the form of item response theory in which a scale score may be defined in terms of the pattern of responses. Scores on a test developed through such procedures need not bear a one-to-one relation to the number of correct respones.

## CHAPTER 6

# THE THEORY OF MEASUREMENT ERROR

**CHAPTER OVERVIEW**

Some error is involved in any measurement, whether it is the measurement of temperature, blood pressure, or intelligence. In order to assess its effects, we must know something about the processes that gave rise to the measure. Most of this chapter considers how random measurement error affects the internal consistency of linear combinations [e.g., scores on conventional, linearly scored tests (sums of correct responses)], which are the heart of classical test theory. Such scores may be contrasted with scores based upon patterns of item responses used in modern psychometric theory (Chapter 10).

There are several classical theories of measurement error. Several assume that the objects of measurement (e.g., people) have true scores on the attribute being measured but differ as to the definition of "true score." One definition is that the true score is the average score that would be obtained over repeated testings. Measurement error causes obtained scores to vary over the testings. The standard deviation of obtained scores over these generally hypothetical testings for a given individual defines the "standard error of measurement." Some, but not all of these models further assume that the measurement error is normally distributed about individual true scores and, moreover, is a constant for all objects of measurement.

A particularly useful model of a process that gives rise to true scores is called "domain sampling." Tests are constructed by selecting a specified number of measures at random from a homogeneous, infinitely large pool. This may be approximated by imagining that individuals are given successive sets of 10 problems, each of which consists of adding pairs of four-digit numbers. Under these conditions, the correlation of any given test score with the average of all test scores (the reliability index) can be shown to equal the square root of the correlation of any given test score with another given test score (the reliability coefficient). In turn, the reliability coefficient can be shown to estimate the ratio of variance in true scores to the variance in observed scores.

The "parallel test" model is one alternative to domain sampling. It assumes that two or more tests produce equal true scores but generate independent random measurement error. Although it defines rather than estimates the reliability coefficient, its major predictions are the same. The role of factorial complexity in measures of reliability is considered; a key point is that a test may measure more than one thing (factor) yet be highly reliable. In addition, we consider ways to estimate how precise a given reliability estimate is.

Some further deductions from the domain-sampling model are then presented. One deals with the expected change in reliability coefficient as the test length is increased. This is known as the Spearman-Brown prophecy formula. Cronbach's coefficient alpha ($\alpha$) is perhaps the most important outcome, as it provides actual estimates of reliability. The $\alpha$ is basically the ratio of the sum of the covariances among the components of the linear combination (items), which estimates true variance, to the sum of *all* elements in the variance-covariance matrix of measures, which equals the observed variance (see Eqs. 5-3). Other related deductions from the domain sampling model include the (1) estimation of true scores from obtained scores, (2) computation of the standard error of measurement from the reliability coefficient, and (3) attenuation. Attenuation deals with the fact that measurement error causes the observed correlation between two measures to be lower than it would be with more reliable measures, and formulas are given to estimate what the correlation would be in the absence of measurement error.

The next section of the chapter discusses models of reliability that lead to somewhat different predictions than those previously considered. The factorial domain-sampling model considers relations among groups of measures that do not necessarily measure the same thing and leads to generalizability theory, considered in Chapter 7. The binomial model is one of many that does *not* assume that measurement error is constant and normally distributed for all objects of measurement. In particular, measurement error associated with extreme true scores is estimated to be (1) smaller than the error associated with true scores nearer the mean and (2) skewed (positively for low scores and negatively for high scores).

In contrast to definitions of reliability based upon the internal consistency or covariances among components of a linear combination, "reliability" can also mean temporal stability. Temporal stability basically concerns the correlation between scores over repeated testings. It is important not to confuse the two types of definitions, as a measure can have high or internal consistency independently of high or low temporal stability. High internal consistency is *very* desirable, but temporal stability may or may not be: trait measures are intended to be reliable, but state measures are not.

## THE CONCEPT OF MEASUREMENT ERROR

It is common and appropriate to think of an obtained measure as deviating from a true value (the term will be given more precise meaning later in this chapter). Such measurement error can be a mixture of: (1) systematic and (2) random processes. When it is systematic, it can (1a) affect all observations equally and be a constant error or (1b) affect certain types of observations differently than others and be a bias. A miscalibrated thermometer that always reads three degrees too high illustrates a constant error in the physical sciences. If the thermometer were sensitive to some irrelevant attribute such as the color or the density of what was being measured, the error would be a bias. Finally, random error would be introduced if the person reading the thermometer were to transpose digits from time to time while recording observations.

There are obvious biases and random errors in the behavioral sciences, though the situation may be less obvious with constant errors. If clinician A were to judge the intelligence of each of a series of individuals five points higher than clinician B, they would be calibrated differently, but either or both could have a constant error since the true IQ is unknown. Indeed, the concept of a constant error could well be viewed as largely inapplicable to the behavioral sciences, to the extent that true values are rarely, if ever, known. However, a clinician, a rater, or an evaluative process may be sensitive to irrelevant attributes like race, gender, penmanship, etc., and thereby be biased. This would hold whether the person was prejudiced against a given group or "bent over backward to be fair." Likewise, unsystematic differences in ratings on repeated testing illustrate one form of random error when it can be assumed the person rated did not change.

This chapter is concerned with random errors. Random errors are important because they limit the degree of lawfulness in nature by complicating relationships. Suppose that perceived light intensity ($\Psi$) is a power function of physical intensity ($\Phi$) according to Stevens' law, with an exponent of .35 as in Eq. 2-2, so that $\Psi = \Phi^{.35}$. Random errors in measuring $\Phi$ or, more likely, $\Psi$ will cause the obtained curve to appear jagged and therefore more complex rather than smoother and simpler. These errors jumble nature's lawfulness in all of science. Systematic biases in psychological measures are also very important, and these will be discussed at several points in Chapters 7 through 10. Even if the concept of constant error was meaningful in the behavioral sciences, it affects all observations equally and therefore does not influence group comparisons, and so it need not be considered further. Indeed, it has no effect, by definition, unless a scale has a meaningful zero, i.e., is a ratio or absolute scale since it affects only the location of the scale mean (see Chapter 1).

Random errors influence measurements in the behavioral sciences in several ways. Scores on a particular classroom test are influenced by (1) the content sampled, e.g., luck in studying the right material, discussed below, (2) luck in guessing (Chapters 9 and 10), (3) state of alertness, and even (4) clerical errors, etc. Ratings of any form (e.g., evaluations of improvement in therapy) will reflect both random and systematic variation among judges and within a given judge over successive occasions. Specific sources of random error will be discussed later.

Random measurement errors are never completely eliminated; but one should seek to minimize them as much as possible and thus portray the ultimate lawfulness in nature. One definition of "reliability" is freedom from random error, i.e., how repeatable observations are (1) when different persons make the measurements, (2) with alternative instruments intended to measure the same thing, and (3) when incidental variation exists in the conditions of measurement. This definition implies homogeneity of content on multi-item tests and internal consistency or high correlations among components of the overall measure such as items on a conventionally scored test. For simplicity, we will assume that the constructs whose homogeneity is to be evaluated are static. A second, totally distinct definition is stability over time (occasions or waves), which will be considered briefly at the end of this chapter. It will also introduce the many problems involved in measuring change.

In other words, measurements must be stable whenever essentially the same results should be obtained. Science is concerned with repeatable phenomena, which implies the repeatability of its measurements. Random measurement errors impose limits on repeatability that will be explored from here to Chapter 10.

Measurement reliability is a classical issue in scientific generalization (see Chapter 1). Measurement is reliable to the extent that it leads to the same or similar results, regardless of opportunities for variations to occur. Reliable measures allow one to generalize from one particular use of the method to a wide variety of related circumstances. This link between the theory of reliability and scientific generalization will become even more apparent in discussing specific models of measurement error.

Of course, high reliability does not mean high *validity*. One could, for example, measure intelligence by having individuals throw stones as far as possible. Distances obtained by individuals on one occasion will correlate highly with distances obtained on another occasion. Being repeatable, the measures are highly reliable; but stone tossing is obviously not a valid measure of intelligence in the sense of Chapter 3; i.e., it will correlate with other measures of strength and not correlate with other measures of intelligence. Measurement error places limits on the validity of an instrument, but even its complete absence does not guarantee validity. Reliability is *necessary* but not *sufficient* to validity.

The theory of measurement error has been developed largely in the context of psychology and largely by psychologists. A perhaps common view is that measurement error is more of a problem in psychology than in the physical sciences, but this is only partially true. Measures in other areas of science often have as much, or more, random error than they do in psychology. Indeed, physiological blood pressure measurements are far less reliable than many psychological measures, and similar examples could be drawn from all of science. Even so, the development of the theory of measurement error by psychologists such as Spearman (1904) may partially reflect response to this common criticism. It may also reflect psychologists' healthy self-consciousness about measurement problems, or, perhaps, be simply an accident of history.

At the same time, the importance of measurement error may be overstated for at least two reasons. First, we will later show that measurement error does not harm most investigations as much as might be thought. Second, we will describe numerous equally important topics in psychological measurement throughout this book. Perhaps more has been written about measurement error than even more important topics like validity because the theory of measurement error lends itself so well to mathematical treatment. Nonetheless, the theory of measurement error *is* important to psychological measurement, and so this chapter and the next will be devoted to it.

The theory of measurement error to be presented is surely one of the most workable mathematical models in psychology. The theory can be derived with few assumptions about the nature of data, and the same formulas can be derived from different sets of assumptions. The theory is very robust in that it tends to hold even when particular assumptions are markedly violated. Although we will mention rather sophisticated, complex mathematical models of measurement error, you will hopefully be surprised how well the major conclusions from these more complex models agree with those derivable from a much simpler and more conventional theory to be emphasized.

## ONE FORM OF CLASSICAL TEST THEORY

Contrasting what is "classical" versus "modern" is always a bit risky, but we, like nearly all authors, will consider measures based upon linear combinations as classical. This implies the linear model of Chapter 2 that is used in scoring conventional tests as linear combinations of responses to individual items and may be contrasted with the emphasis upon scoring tests based upon the pattern of item responses discussed in Chapter 10 (response profiles). However, Thurstone's law of comparative judgment is also generally regarded as classical, if for no other reason than that it appeared more than 60 years ago, but it is not based upon linear combinations. Conversely, the Guttman (1950) scale is considered modern despite its long history because, as Chapter 2 noted, it is based upon response profiles rather than sums. This chapter is limited to scores obtained from the linear model. Furthermore, nearly all discussion involves equally weighted sums.

Figure 6-1*a* illustrates one classical theory of measurement error, which will be modified subsequently. This approach is but one of many that can be regarded as classical according to our definition in terms of using the linear model. Figure 6-1*b* is discussed later in the chapter in the section devoted to the binomial model, and its assumptions are different. Persons A, B, and C are each assumed to have true scores on an attribute that would be found with no errors of measurement. The true scores for the three individuals fall at progressively higher points along the continuum. Since the obtained score contains random error, it differs from the true score. If one could give many alternative test forms (e.g., words from a common pool used to provide different spelling tests), the *average* of the test scores would closely approximate the true score. For the present, we will assume that scores obtained from alternate forms are (1) distributed symmetrically above and below the true scores (i.e., are unbiased in the sense of Chapter 4), (2) normally distributed, (3) add in absolute value to the true score to provide the obtained score, and (4) have equal variance (are homoscedastic). These assumptions are not necessary to all classical approaches, although they are convenient for now. Further note the similarity to the discriminal dispersions of Thurstone scaling as in Fig. 2-4. This reflects the common statistical conception of how a constant (true score in this case) may vary because of the effects of a random (stochastic) process.

The more the obtained scores vary about the true score, the more measurement error there is. The "standard deviation" of each person's error distribution indexes the amount of error. If the standard deviation of errors were the same for all persons, which this most simple form of domain-sampling model assumes (but not alternatives such as the binomial form discussed below), one standard deviation could define the expected amount of error. This standard deviation of errors is called the "standard error of measurement" ($\sigma_{meas}$). It is common in the physical sciences to define the

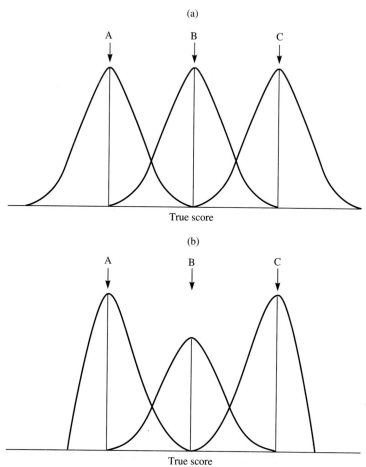

**FIGURE 6-1**  True scores and distributions of obtained scores for a person whose true score falls below the mean *(A)*, at the mean *(B)*, and above the mean *(C)* for the domain-sampling model *(a)* and the binomial model *(b)*.

reciprocal of $\sigma_{meas}$ as the precision or tolerance, but we will not follow this convention. The issues illustrated by Fig. 6-1 will be used to provide an extensive discussion of measurement error.

## THE DOMAIN-SAMPLING MODEL

We propose that the most useful model of measurement error considers any particular measure to be composed of responses to a random sample of items from a hypothetical domain of items. An example is a five-item test, on which each item requires the addition of pairs of four-digit numbers. Any given test could literally be generated by a program that randomly samples items from the $(10^4)(10^4)$ possibilities for any given item. Note that although this number is large, it is finite. The model assumes an infinite pool of possible items, but it works well as long as the pool of potential items is large.

Both individual difference measures and experimental measures can be thought of as arising from this process of domain sampling. The number of correct solutions to the above additional problems could either be used for ordinary grading or to compare instructional methods, for example. Many examples could be chosen to show how particular measures represent samples from a hypothetical domain of items. Many authors use the term "universe" or "population" of items instead of "domain" to refer to the hypothetical collection of items. We do not do so because of the possible confusion with the universe or population of persons or other objects of measurement.

One practical problem is that test items are usually *composed* rather than *sampled* from a well-defined domain. However, the model usually works well in practice because the variety of items composed for a test usually has effects similar to those of actual random sampling. The purpose of any particular measurement is to estimate the measurement that would be obtained if one could employ *all* the items in the domain, e.g., all possible four-digit addition problems.

We will denote the score that a subject would obtain *if* it were possible to test the whole domain as a true score. A sample of items (test) is reliable to the extent that the score it produces correlates highly with these true scores. One important part of our definition is that it that true scores are, in principle, obtainable by testing over the entire domain, even though that might be physically impossible. This process causes random error to "average out." One alternative to domain sampling is called "Platonic true score theory" (Sutcliffe, 1965) in which this true score is a given—the score is assumed rather than derived from the largely hypothetical process of repeated test administration. We do *not* intend this meaning even though Platonic true score and domain-sampling models make nearly identical predictions. Two alternative terms for true score are "domain score" and "universe score," but these do not communicate our intent of an error-free measure.

We will later expand the model to consider the possibility that the items in the domain vary in various ways, e.g., by the physical condition of the subject, the examiner's skill, the testing environment, etc. However, we will first simply consider the problem of testing a homogeneous group of subjects with a set of items in a homogeneous domain before complicating the model. We will later show that it is very simple to include additional factors that influence measurement error other than the sampling of items per se.

The domain-sampling model does not require that any specific number of items be sampled in order to define a particular measure. Each sample (test) can consist of a single item or many items. The model can also be developed without concern for the type of items employed or even their factorial composition. We will develop the domain-sampling model initially using standard ($z$) scores for individual variables. Measures are sums of standard scores on variables. We deliberately use the terms "variables" and "measures" in this section rather than "items" and "tests" to stress that the model is not limited to pencil-and-paper tests. Using $z$ scores rather than deviation ($x$) or raw ($X$) scores leads to results in terms of correlations ($r$) rather than variances

($\sigma_x^2$) and covariances ($\sigma_{xy}$). Of course, variables are usually not standardized before they are summed to obtain total scores; e.g., a score based upon dichotomous variables is usually the sum of a series of 0s and 1s. However, using $z$ scores has little effect on the deductions to be made and makes it much easier to understand the theory of reliability that follows from the model. Moreover, we will later switch from $z$ scores and correlations to raw scores, variances, and covariances to develop certain other statistics.

The model assumes an infinitely large correlation matrix containing all correlations among variables in the domain in which $r_{ij}$ denotes the correlation between variables $x_i$ and $x_j$. The average correlation in the matrix ($\bar{r}_{ij}$) indexes the extent to which a common core exists among the variables. It is *not* necessary that this core be a single factor in the sense of Chapters 11 through 13. The dispersion of correlations about this average indicates the extent to which variables vary in sharing this common core. If one assumes that all variables share equally in this core, the average correlations in each column of the hypothetical matrix would be the same and would equal the average correlation in the whole matrix ($\bar{r}_{ij}$). Keep in mind that we do not necessarily assume that *all* values of $r_{ij}$ are the same, but rather that the sum or average correlation for any *one* variable is the same as the sum or average for any *other* variable, which is much less restrictive.

If the above assumption holds, one may compute and not simply estimate the correlation of any particular variable with the sum of all variables in the domain, as follows. Since all variables are expressed as $z$ scores, the formula for the correlation of variable $x_1$ with the sum of scores on $k$ variables is

$$r_{1(1\ldots k)} = \frac{1/N \Sigma z_1(z_1 + z_2 + z_3 + \cdots + z_k)}{\sqrt{\Sigma z_1^2/N}\sqrt{1/N \Sigma(z_1 + z_2 + z_3 + \cdots + z_k)^2}} \tag{6-1}$$

Equation 6-1 is simply the expansion of the formula for the correlation of one variable with the sum of $k$ variables (Eq. 5-8c). This further illustrates how a single variable may be correlated with a linear combination that includes that variable. Variable $x_1$, a variable in the domain, is also part of the sum of variables $x_1$ through $x_k$. The numerator of Eq. 6-1 simplifies to

$$\frac{1}{N}-\Sigma z_1(z_1 + z_2 + z_3 + \cdots + z_k) = \frac{1}{N} - \Sigma(z_1^2 + z_1z_2 + z_1z_3 + \cdots + z_1z_k)$$

$$= \frac{1}{N}(\Sigma z_1^2 + \Sigma z_1z_2 + \Sigma z_1z_3 + \cdots + \Sigma z_1z_k)$$

$$= 1 + r_{12} + r_{13} + \cdots + r_{1k}$$

$$= 1 + (k-1)\bar{r}_{1j}$$

$$= 1 + (k-1)\bar{r}_{ij}$$

The expression in parentheses ($\Sigma z_1^2 + \Sigma z_1z_2 + \Sigma z_1z_3 + \ldots + \Sigma z_1z_k$) contains the product of sets of standard scores for variable $x_1$ with itself ($\Sigma z_1^2$) and all other variables (e.g., $\Sigma z_1 z_2$) in parentheses. The expression $1 + r_{12} + r_{13} + \ldots + r_{1k}$ results from dividing by the number of people ($N$). The elements in the sum are the correlation of variable $x_1$ with itself (1.0) and with each of the other variables, $r_{12}$, $r_{13}$, etc. This may be simplified to $1 + (k - 1)\bar{r}_{1j}$, where $\bar{r}_{1j}$ is the average correlation of variable $x_1$ with each of the other variables. The final result, $1 + (k - 1)\bar{r}_{ij}$, holds when this average correlation is the same as the average for *all* variables ($\bar{r}_{1j} = \bar{r}_{ij}$), the crucial assumption made above. Furthermore, the sum of the correlations of variable $x_1$ with the remaining $k - 1$ variables, *excluding* variable $x_1$ itself, is $(k - 1)\bar{r}_{ij}$.

The left-hand term of the denominator of Eq. 6-1 is the standard deviation of variable $x_1$ in $z$ score form and therefore 1.0, and so it "falls out" of the denominator. The right-hand term of the denominator is the standard deviation of the sum of the $k$ $z$ scores, *including* variable $x_1$. Chapter 5 showed this variance equals the sum of all terms in the intercorrelation matrix ($\mathbf{R}$) as an extension of Eqs. 5-3. There are $k^2$ elements in any intercorrelation matrix. Of these, $k$ are diagonal elements and $k^2 - k$ are off-diagonal elements. The sum of these diagonal elements equals $k$ since each of the $k$ diagonal elements in a correlation matrix is 1. Instead of adding the off-diagonal elements, one could obtain the same value by multiplying the average off-diagonal element ($\bar{r}_{ij}$) by $k^2 - k$. This makes no assumptions about the properties of $\mathbf{R}$, unlike the crucial assumption that $\bar{r}_{1j} = \bar{r}_{ij}$ made in the numerator. These considerations allow the denominator of Eq. 6-1 to be written as

$$\sqrt{k + (k^2 - k)\bar{r}_{ij}}$$

Reassembling numerator and denominator gives the following formula for the correlation of variable $x_1$ with the sum of the $k$ variables in the domain:

$$r_{1(1\ldots k)} = \frac{1 + (k - 1)\bar{r}_{ij}}{\sqrt{k + (k^2 - k)\bar{r}_{ij}}}$$

$$= \frac{1 + k\bar{r}_{ij} - \bar{r}_{ij}}{\sqrt{k + k^2\bar{r}_{ij} - k\bar{r}_{ij}}} \tag{6-2}$$

We next consider what happens when the potential pool of variables ($k$) approaches infinity so that $\bar{r}_{ij}$ is the average of an infinite number of correlations in a domain rather than a finite $k \times k$ matrix. The first step is to divide each term in the numerator and denominator by $k$:

$$r_{1(1\ldots k)} = \frac{1/k + \bar{r}_{ij} - \bar{r}_{ij}/k}{\sqrt{1/k + \bar{r}_{ij} - \bar{r}_{ij}/k}} \tag{6-3}$$

As $k$ approaches infinity, terms divided by $k$ approach zero. Since only two terms in Eq. 6-3 are not divided by $k$, the equation reduces to

$$r_{1(1...k)} = \frac{\bar{r}_{ij}}{\sqrt{\bar{r}_{ij}}} = \sqrt{\bar{r}_{ij}} \qquad k \rightarrow \infty \qquad\qquad (6\text{-}4)$$

The correlation of variable $x_1$ with the sum of an infinite number of variables in a domain therefore equals the square root of the average correlation among variables in the domain ($\bar{r}_{ij}$). The same holds for any other variable. This holds only when all variables have the same average correlation with other variables ($\bar{r}_{1j} = \bar{r}_{ij}$). If that is so, Eq. 6-4 can be written as

$$r_{1(1...k)} = \sqrt{\bar{r}_{1j}} \qquad k \rightarrow \infty \qquad\qquad (6\text{-}5)$$

By definition, the correlation of variable $x_1$ with the sum of the $k$ variables approaches the correlation of variable $x_1$ with true scores (the sum or average of scores on all possible variables) as $k$ approaches infinity, and so the following symbolic abbreviations will be useful:

$$r_{1(1...k)} = r_{1t} = \sqrt{\bar{r}_{1j}} \qquad k \rightarrow \infty \qquad\qquad (6\text{-}6)$$

The correlation $r_{1t}$ (the correlation between variable $x_1$ and true scores, i.e., the sum or average of all variables in the domain) equals the square root of the average correlation of variable $x_1$ with all other individual variables.

If you are troubled by the "ghostly" concept of infinity, think in terms of any big number. For example, a domain of 1000 possible variables would be indistinguishable from an infinity. Indeed, the results would be satisfactory with even 100 potential variables. The formulas derived so far, especially Eq. 6-6, are the foundations of the theory of measurement error, and many useful principles will be developed from them.

## Multi-item Measures

The previous section provided basic formulas for measurement error with respect to individual variables, which could be items or any other measures sampled from a hypothetical domain. Nearly all measures are composed of a number of items (we now return to this simpler term "items" even though what follows is also not limited to pencil-and-paper tests), but the model can be easily extended to multi-item measures. Think of dividing the infinitely large matrix of correlations among items into groups of $h$ items. The sum of scores in each group of items constitutes a test score which would range from 0 to $h$ if the items were dichotomously scored. If items were randomly sampled to form tests, correlations among different tests would tend to be the same. Such randomly sampled collections of items constitute "randomly parallel tests," and their means, standard deviations, and correlations with true scores would differ only by chance. Assuming that the average correlation of each test with the sum of all other tests is the same for all tests, one can proceed from Eq. 6-1 as before, but this time $z$ scores apply to whole tests rather than individual items. This leads to

$$\bar{r}_{1j} = \sqrt{\bar{r}_{ij}} \qquad\qquad (6\text{-}7a)$$

$$\bar{r}_{1j} = r_{1t}^2 \qquad\qquad (6\text{-}7b)$$

where $\bar{r}_{1j}$ = average correlation of test $x_1$ with all tests in domain
 $\phantom{where} r_{1t}$ = correlation between test $x_1$ and true scores in domain

This is *identical* to the result obtained with individual items, Eq. 6-6, and is presented as a separate equation merely to stress that it makes no difference whether the measure is a single item or the sum of several items. The crucial assumption of equal correlations among scoring units ($\bar{r}_{1j} = \bar{r}_{ij}$) is actually much more sensible with whole tests than with individual test items. Idiosyncracies of individual items (e.g., whether or not a particular addition item involves carrying) average out on whole tests, but may systematically affect correlations among individual items. Moreover, the $\bar{r}_{1j}$ between whole tests will be larger than the $\bar{r}_{1j}$ between individual items, so that values of $r_{1t}$ will also be higher for whole tests.

By convention, the correlation of one test, which can be a single item, with another test in the domain is called its "reliability coefficient," which will be symbolized as $r_{11}$ for variable $x_1$, $r_{ii}$ for variable $x_i$, and so on. The correlation between test $x_1$ and true scores ($r_{1t}$) is called its "reliability index." The reliability index is the square root of the reliability coefficient. The reliability coefficient cannot exceed the reliability index—the correlation between two fallible measures ($r_{12}$) cannot be higher than the correlation between a fallible measure and its true score ($r_{1t}$).

## Estimates of Reliability

The more tests that have been randomly sampled in a finite domain, the better the reliability estimates. For example, the square root of the average correlation between one 20-item spelling test and five other 20-item spelling tests ($\sqrt{\bar{r}_{ij}}$) should more closely approximate $r_{1t}$ than the square root of the correlation between the first test and one other test ($r_1 t$). However, reliability estimates are not obtained in practice by correlating a test with several other tests. Practical measures of reliability are usually based upon either (1) items within a single test or (2) between a test and one other test. We will later consider the efficiency of such estimates when only one correlation is used to estimate a hypothetical infinite number of correlations.

One may test the hypothetical square root relation between the reliability coefficient and reliability index empirically when it is meaningful to assume that $\bar{r}_{1j}$ equals $\bar{r}_{ij}$. Some measures are so readily obtainable that it is possible to retest the subject many times. For example, practice a sample of subjects at reaction time responses until their performance is stable to help satisfy the above assumption. Then run them for at least 100 trials to produce a domain of responses. Their reaction time on one trial is a one-item test. Correlate their results on one arbitrarily chosen trial (e.g., the tenth) with (1) their results on another arbitrarily chosen trial (e.g., the fifteenth) to estimate $r_{11}$ and (2) the average over all trials to estimate $r_{1t}$. These two correlations reflect the reliability of individual differences in a one-item test of reaction time and should closely approximate a square root relationship. The same may be done taking blocks of $k$ trials: Correlate one block with another block and then correlate either block with the overall average reaction time. Both correlations will be higher since this is now a $k$-item test, but the same square root relationship should hold.

## The Importance of the Reliability Coefficient

It will be helpful to restate several of the similar appearing terms that we have used. First, $r_{1t}$ or $r_{1(1...k)}$ is the correlation between a set of scores on a given test ($x_1$) and corresponding true scores, also known as the reliability index. It is exactly equal to the square root of $\bar{r}_{ij}$ or the average correlation between all pairs of tests in the domain, which may also be written as $r_{11}$. In turn, $\bar{r}_{ij}$ ($r_{11}$) may be estimated by $\bar{r}_{1j}$, the average correlation between test $x_1$ and the other tests in the domain, and $\bar{r}_{1j}$ may also be written as $r_{11}$, the reliability coefficient for test $x_1$. Many important principles can be developed about measurement error once a good estimate of $r_{11}$, and therefore of $r_{1t}$, is obtained. There are precise ways to estimate $r_{11}$, but we will delay discussion of how this is done and the precision of such estimates until later.

Although $r_{1t}$ is the correlation between an actual variable and a hypothetical variable rather than between two actual variables, it can be used in the same mathematical ways that any correlation can. Figure 6-2 is a scatter diagram of the relationship between a set of observed (fallible) scores on $x_1$ ($z_1$) and associated true scores ($z_t$). The reliability coefficient ($r_{11}$) used to generate these data was .81, and so the correlation between obtained and true scores (the reliability index or $r_{1t}$) is .9. The line of best fit (see Eq. 4-16) is

$$z'_t = r_{1t}z_1 = \sqrt{r_{11}}z_1$$

where $z'_t$ = estimated true $z$ score
  $z_1$ = observed $z$ score
  $r_{1t}$ = reliability index
  $r_{11}$ = reliability coefficient

The square of the reliability index ($r_{1t}^2$) equals the proportion of true-score variance explainable by a fallible measure, and vice versa. This is because the square of any correlation equals the variance in one variable explainable by variance in another variable (see Chapter 4, especially Eqs. 4-15b and 4-24b.) However, $r_{1t}^2$ is simply $r_{11}$, the reliability coefficient. Consequently, $r_{11}$ provides the proportion of true-score variance in the fallible measures (see Eq. 4-15b or 4-24c). This proportion takes on even more meaning when the fallible measure is expressed as a deviation score rather than a $z$ score since $r_{11}$ becomes expressible as

$$r_{11} = \frac{\sigma_t^2}{\sigma_1^2} \tag{6-9}$$

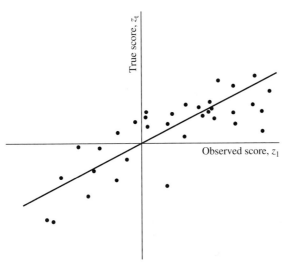

**FIGURE 6-2**    Regression line and scatter diagram between obtained scores and true scores for 20 hypothetical observations obtained when $r_{11} = .81$ ($r_{1t} = .9$).

where $\sigma_1^2$ = observed variance of variable $x_1$

$\sigma_t^2$ = variance of variable $x_1$ explainable by true scores

*reliability coefficient*

Equation 6-9 shows that $r_{11}$ equals the true-score variance in a measure divided by its actual (observed) variance. Viewing the reliability coefficient in this way facilitates the development of many principles about measurement error, but another model will be described before developing these principles.

## THE MODEL OF PARALLEL TESTS

We have already discussed a model for randomly parallel tests whose means, standard deviations, and correlations differ because of the sampling of items (content). We also stated that the best way to estimate the reliability is to correlate one test with a number of other tests from the same content domain. However, that is usually impractical; a test is usually correlated with only one other test, if that, to estimate its reliability. This could easily be inaccurate since one correlation estimates the average of many. Consequently one could rightly question whether the correlation between two tests meaningfully estimates the reliability of either.

If it is assumed that two tests actually are literally parallel and not just parallel in a statistical sense, $r_{11}$, and therefore $r_{1t}$, can be derived directly. Two tests are parallel if (1) they have the same standard deviation, (2) they correlate the same with a set of true scores, and (3) all of their variance that is not explainable by true scores is pure random error. It is sometimes useful to assume that the two tests have the same mean, but that assumption is not necessary here.

Several additional principles follow from assumption 3 that the variance in each test not explainable by true scores is pure random error. First, random errors balance one another, by definition, and so the mean of the error scores on each test is expected to be zero. Second, error scores on one test are uncorrelated with error scores on the other test, and, third, errors on both tests are uncorrelated with true scores, since pure random errors do not correlate with anything else except by chance. Of course, these three assumptions may not hold in a small sample, which is why we are primarily concerned with large samples.

The deviation scores on two parallel tests can be broken down as follows:

$$x_1 = t + e_1$$
$$x_2 = t + e_2$$

where $x_1$ = obtained deviation score on test $x_1$
  $x_2$ = obtained deviation score on test $x_2$
  $t$ = true score
  $e_1$ = error on test $x_1$
  $e_2$ = error on test $x_2$

Since only the fallible scores ($x_1$ and $x_2$) are observable, the only way to learn about the true and error scores ($t$, $e_1$, and $e_2$) is to correlate these fallible scores. If the correlations between each test and the true scores (which are assumed equal) were known, the result could be used in a regression equation to estimate scores on the two fallible variable, using the following steps.

These principles may be stated formally as follows:

$$\sigma_1 = \sigma_2$$
$$r_{1t} = r_{2t}$$
$$r_{te_1} = 0$$
$$r_{te_2} = 0$$
$$r_{e_1 e_2} = 0$$
$$\overline{X}_{e_1} = 0$$
$$\overline{X}_{e_2} = 0$$

Since error scores are uncorrelated with true scores:

$$\sigma_1^2 = \sigma_t^2 + \sigma_{e_1}^2 \tag{6-10}$$

and

$$\sigma_2^2 = \sigma_t^2 + \sigma_{e_2}^2 \tag{6-11}$$

The error-score variances must be equal because both the obtained score variances and the true-score variances of the two tests are equal.

Using Eq. 4-6 in conjunction with Eq. 4-9, the observed correlation between the two parallel tests is as follows:

$$r_{12} = \frac{\Sigma x_1 x_2 / N}{\sigma_1 \sigma_2}$$

Since $x_1$ and $x_2$ are the sum of true and error scores, and the two standard deviations in the denominator are equal,

$$r_{12} = \frac{\Sigma 33}{(t + e_1)(t + e_2)N}$$

$$= \frac{(\Sigma t^2 + \Sigma t e_1 + \Sigma t e_2 + \Sigma e_1 e_2)/N}{\sigma_1^2}$$

$$= \frac{\sigma_t^2 + \sigma_{te_1} + \sigma_{te_2} + \sigma_{e_1 e_2}}{\sigma_t^2}$$

The three covariances in the numerator ($\sigma_{te_1}$, $\sigma_{te_2}$, and $\sigma_{e_1 e_2}$) drop out because errors on the two parallel tests are assumed to be uncorrelated with true scores and with each other, leaving

$$r_{12} = \frac{\sigma_t^2}{\sigma_1^2} = r_{11} \qquad (6\text{-}12)$$

The correlation between two parallel tests equals the true-score variance in either test divided by the obtained variance of either test. This same ratio was derived from the domain-sampling model (Eq. 6-9). Since the ratio is the same for both tests, we will symbolize it as $r_{11}$ (or $r_{22}$ or $r_{xx}$) rather than $r_{12}$.

Various methods can be used to prove that the correlation of test $x_1$ with true scores equals the square root of the correlation between the two parallel forms. One method for showing this will prove especially useful later. An important consequence of the present assumptions is that the residual scores on the two tests (scores obtained by partialling the true scores from the two parallel tests) are uncorrelated because they are the error scores on the two tests and these errors are uncorrelated. Another way of saying this is that the partial correlation between the observed scores, adjusting for the true scores, is zero. Consequently, the numerator of this partial correlation must also be zero:

$$r_{11} - r_{1t} r_{2t} = 0$$

Since the model assumes that both tests correlate the same with true scores ($r_{1t} = r_{2t}$), $r_{11} = r_{1t}^2$ and $r_{1t} = \sqrt{r_{11}}$ (Eqs. 6-7). Correlating obtained scores with true scores leads to the development of many principles of measurement error, but we first need to consider relations between the two models thus far considered.

## PERSPECTIVES ON THE TWO MODELS

Two different-appearing models therefore reach the same conclusions about measurement error and in fact provide many other identical results. Actually, they are not different models—the parallel-test model is a special case of the more general domain-sampling model. If all sample tests in the domain have the same standard deviation and correlation with total scores in the domain (true scores) and the partial correlations among sample tests are zero when adjusted for true scores, the domain will consist of parallel rather than randomly parallel tests. The correlation between any two tests ($r_{ij}$) will then equal the average of all correlations among tests ($\bar{r}_{ij}$), and the square root of that correlation will be the correlation of any test with true scores ($r_{1t}$).

The three assumptions necessary for the parallel-test model require one to ignore the actual problem of estimating $r_{1t}$. According to the parallel-test model, the $r_{ij}$ between two tests in a domain defines rather than estimates the reliability. The domain-sampling model frankly acknowledges the problem of estimation.

Unfortunately, the parallel-test model is not a fruitful way to extend theories of measurement error. It is unclear what attribute the true scores have in common since true scores may be defined by only two tests. It is easier to think of a domain of possible test items and constructing an actual test by sampling these items, randomly or otherwise. If there were several supposedly parallel tests rather than two and their intercorrelations differed, what would the reliability be? One is in a quandary since the model explicitly assumes that all parallel tests have the same reliability. The domain-sampling model acknowledges this possibility: The estimated reliability of any one test is the average of its correlations with the other tests.

Although the parallel-test model makes three assumptions, only the least important of these (equality of variances) can be tested. Neither the assumption that (1) the two tests correlate equally with true scores or (2) errors on the two tests are uncorrelated (the partial correlation between observed scores, adjusting for true scores, is zero) can be directly tested. The parallel-test model has been popular because of its simplicity, but it ignores the issue of the precision of reliability estimation. Any result obtained from the parallel-test model specifying a characteristic of measurement error has a corresponding formula in the domain-sampling model estimating that characteristic. For example, the correlation between two tests specifies the reliability in the parallel-test model, but this correlation is considered only an estimate in the domain-sampling model. However, the domain-sampling model makes several deductions that have no counterpart in the parallel-test model. Specifically, issues related to the precision of reliability estimates obtained with different numbers of items and different distributions of correlations have no counterparts in the parallel-test model. This model can handle only questions about relations among numerous tests by postulating different parallel tests. Inevitably, this discussion relaxes the assumptions about parallelism; what starts as a parallel-test model evolves into a domain-sampling model.

The authors strongly favor the domain-sampling model as a theoretical framework for discussing and investigating reliability. Actually, the basic idea of randomly sampling items from a domain provides various models for measurement error, some of which will be discussed later in this chapter. We have thus far considered only the simplest case where the average correlation of each item with the others is the same for all items. This is not to say that the domain sampling model does not have problems being implemented in the real world. Our first example of a domain was to have students add four-digit numbers. However, we glossed over the fact that $1 + 1$ is just as much a member of that domain as is $9257 + 3481$. The difference in difficulty illustrates the idea of sampling error in the domain. One could introduce constraints to minimize the variation in difficulty for this specific problem (e.g., requiring four digits none of which is a zero), but this is not always possible. One perhaps never finds individual items that are alike as "peas in a pod," but summing items minimizes this problem.

We have noted that many problems, especially in personality research, also involve domain sampling only in the vaguest sense. A person may start with a plan to define a trait by sampling the assumed attributes of that trait. However, each item is quite clearly a distinct entity, so that thinking of randomly sampling is dubious. One uses the best set of items that can be obtained. The domain-sampling model's deductions may hold poorly, if at all, if this is the case. We will note below how the effects of doubling the number of items in a test derived under domain sampling are predictable in a straightforward fashion. However, the best items will usually be proposed first if this sampling process is not used. Lengthening the test may not achieve the desired end because it will involve including poorer items.

## Factorial Composition

It is *not* true that the domain-sampling and parallel-test models assume that all items measure only one factor. Both models would hold if items were divided between two (or more) factors, e.g., if the domain were divided between spelling and arithmetic items. Random samples of items from this two-factor domain would still tend to correlate the same with one another, and true scores would jointly reflect spelling and arithmetic ability. There would still be a square root relation between $r_{11}$ and $r_{1t}$, the key deduction from both models. Similarly, both models would hold if each item was a compound of a number of factors instead of having different items reflect different factors. For example, if each item simultaneously measured spelling and arithmetic ability, all item intercorrelations would be similar. The domain-sampling model concerns the extent to which one "anything" correlates with an infinite number of "anythings." This correlation (the reliability index, $r_{1t}$) is estimated or defined (according to the model chosen) by the square root of the average correlation of one or more anythings (the reliability coefficient, $r_{11}$, $r_{xx}$, etc.).

Factor composition, however, is important in two ways. First, correlations among real items are likely to vary more when different items measure different factors. This will later be shown to reduce the precision of the reliability estimates. Consequently, even though the domain-sampling model leads to unbiased reliability estimates in a factorially complex domain, such estimates might be unstable as a result of content-sampling error. The second important consideration is that investigators usually seek to investigate a unifactor domain to make the resulting measure interpretable. No one should care about studying the internal consistency of a polyglot domain of test materials. This book stresses that the purpose in developing a new measure is to define a *unitary* attribute. Even though the model holds for multifactor items, the results are more meaningful and estimates of reliability are more precise when items are dominated by a single factor. Unfortunately, high reliability does not imply that items measure only one factor.

## PRECISION OF RELIABILITY ESTIMATES

We have talked about the precision of reliability estimates from the domain-sampling model in a number of places. Such estimates are precise to the extent that different random samples of items correlate the same with true scores. If all items had exactly the same correlation with all other items in the domain, this correlation would completely specify the reliability. These items would therefore also have exactly the same correlation with true scores, i.e., the square root of any interitem correlation. There is random error in any actual sampling of items to the extent that these item intercorrelations vary. For example, if the correlations between $x_1$ and other items in the domain ranged only from .10 to .30, the average correlation of $x_1$ with a number of other items randomly selected from the domain would estimate the reliability of $x_1$ rather precisely. However, if the range was from $-.30$ to .60, the average correlation of $x_1$ with the other items would estimate the reliability poorly.

There is a double problem of sampling related to the precision of reliability estimates—the sampling of objects (usually people) and the sampling of items. We previously noted that it is very difficult to consider both sampling problems simultaneously. To do so would lead us into statistical complexities beyond the scope of this book. We also noted earlier that classical measurement theory is mainly a large-sample theory which assumes that a sufficient number of persons are studied to minimize sampling error from subjects. This is necessary not only to simplify measurement theory but also because measurement theory cannot usually tolerate the large doses of sampling error arising from a small number of subjects. Consequently, we will assume that a representative sample of 300 or more persons has been employed and focus on the primary concern of the theory of measurement error—sampling of items.

A domain of items is of interest only if the average correlation among items is positive. If the average correlation is zero or near zero, the items as a group have no common core, and it is useless to assume they measure a unitary attribute. Assuming that a core does exist, the next issue is the relative homogeneity of these correlations because it is most desirable that these correlations be relatively homogeneous.

Correlations always vary in magnitude. The particular statistical model we will use to evaluate the influence of this variation upon the precision of reliability estimates assumes that correlations are normally distributed about the average value and statistically independent of one another. Both assumptions must be somewhat slightly incorrect. If the average correlation is positive, the distribution of correlations must be negatively skewed and therefore nonnormal. Also, intercorrelations are not independent of one another, e.g., $r_{12}$ is not independent of $r_{13}$ because item $x_1$ is common to both. However, these assumptions are only slightly violated for typical test items, since their correlations usually range between .10 and .30. Conversely, be careful in applying them to correlations among multi-item tests because these correlations do often exceed .7.

We will explain below how test reliability is a direct function of the average correlation among items ($\bar{r}_{ij}$) for any given number of items. Longer tests are more reliable than shorter tests, but the test reliabilities are deducible from the $\bar{r}_{ij}$ in both cases. Because of this, the precision of any reliability estimate is a direct function of the precision of the estimates of $\bar{r}_{ij}$. Assuming such correlations are normally distributed, the approximate standard error in estimating $\bar{r}_{ij}$ is

$$\sigma_{\bar{r}_{ij}} = \frac{\sigma_{r_{ij}}}{\sqrt{\frac{1}{2}k(k-1)-1}} \tag{6-13}$$

where $\sigma_{\bar{r}_{ij}}$ = standard error in estimating $\bar{r}_{ij}$ from the whole domain
$\sigma_{r_{ij}}$ = standard deviation of the distribution of actual item intercorrelations
$k$ = number of test items

Equation 6-13 is merely an adaptation of the customary formula for the standard error of the mean, sampling items rather than people. In conventional applications, the standard error of average scores for people equals the standard deviation of scores divided by the number of persons. Each correlation in Eq. 6-13 is considered a score. The standard deviation of correlations within a test estimates the standard deviation of correlations in the whole domain. The denominator of Eq. 6-13 looks complicated at first glance, but it is only the square root of the number of possible correlations among $k$ items minus 1. The 1 is subtracted to obtain the proper degrees of freedom.

It is apparent from the formula that the error in estimating $r_{11}$ is directly related to the standard deviation of correlations among items and inversely related to the number of test items. This provides an important principle: Not only are longer tests more reliable than shorter tests (to be proven later), but their estimates of reliability are more also precise. The standard error in estimating $\bar{r}_{ij}$ from a 10-item test in which the average correlation among items is .20 and the standard deviation of correlations is .10 is

$$\sigma_{\bar{r}_{ij}} = \frac{.10}{\sqrt{(5)(9)-1}}$$

$$= \frac{.10}{\sqrt{44}}$$

$$= \frac{.10}{6.63}$$

$$= .015$$

One expects that 95 percent of normally distributed estimates lie in a ±2.0 standard error "band" above and below the estimated parameter, e.g., the mean. The analogous expectation here is that the average correlation among items will be similarly distributed over random samples of items. In the present case, the standard error for average correlations obtained from 10-item tests is only .015. One expects that 95 percent of the sample values will fall between .17 and .23. Lengthening the test to 40 items reduces the standard error to .0036!

This example illustrates that reliability estimates are rather precise even for tests as short as 10 items. Since most tests are longer than 10 items, sampling error due to item selection is vanishingly small, assuming the items have been sampled from a domain. This precision arises because the number of correlations among items increases roughly as the square of the number of items. This factor appears in the denominator of Eq. 6-13. For example, there are 780 possible correlations among 40 items. This provides the same precision for estimating the average correlation that would be obtained in sampling 780 people in order to estimate a mean. There is thus usually little error in estimating reliability due to random error in item selection.

Suppose that two tests assumed to come from the same domain correlate more poorly with one another than predicted from the average correlation among items within each test in a large sample. This would probably reflect systematic differences in item content when obtained from a large sample of subjects. We will discuss this point more fully later.

### Variances of Items

We have thus far assumed that all items are in $z$-score form, but items are rarely standardized before they are summed to produce test scores. One might wonder if differences in item variances disturb the principles that have been developed so far. For example, dichotomous items have different $p$ values and therefore different variances (Eq. 4-3). In fact, these differences do not complicate the domain-sampling model. The model could be developed from the item covariances as well as from item correlations and would produce the same principles. Also, differences in $p$ values of items usually have very little effect on the precision of reliability estimates, particularly on tests with 20 or more items (Cronbach & Azuma, 1962).

## FURTHER DEDUCTIONS FROM THE DOMAIN-SAMPLING MODEL

One may deduce other principles of measurement error from the domain-sampling model. These are useful both in the development of measurement theory and in handling everyday research problems.

### Test Length

We previously mentioned that the reliability of scores obtained from a domain sample increases with the number of items sampled ($k$). Thus, individual items may correlate poorly with true scores, but a 10-item test might correlate .50 with true scores, and a 100-item test might correlate above .90 with true scores. The rate of increase in reliability as a function of $k$ can be deduced using the following matrix, which depicts the correlations of items with true scores and one another:

|        | $t$      | $x_1$ | $x_2$ | $x_3$ | ... | $x_k$ |
|--------|----------|-------|-------|-------|-----|-------|
| $t$    | $r_{tt}$ |       |       | $r_{it}$ |  |       |
| $x_1$<br>$x_2$<br>$x_3$<br>...<br>$x_k$ | $r_{it}$ |  |  | $r_{ij}$ |  |  |

The first column and first row of the matrix contain correlations of true scores with all variables. All diagonal elements are correlations of items with themselves (1.0). The remainder of the matrix contains all possible correlations among items. The discussion in Chapter 5 about the correlation of sums allows the following:

$$r_{t(1...k)} = \frac{\Sigma r_{it}}{\sqrt{r_{tt}}\sqrt{k + 2\Sigma r_{ij}}} \tag{6-14}$$

Equation 6-14 is simply the correlation of the sum of $k$ variables with one variable $t$. The numerator is $k$ times the average correlation of items with true scores. The left side of the denominator is 1.0 and drops out of the equation. The right side of the denominator is the square root of the sum of intercorrelations among the $k$ items. There are, of course, $k$ diagonal elements. One can substitute 2 times the average correlation times the number of correlations for 2 times the sum of item intercorrelations, which allows Eq. 6-14 to be transformed to

$$r_{t(1...k)} = \frac{k\bar{r}_{it}}{\sqrt{k + k^2\bar{r}_{ij} - k\bar{r}_{ij}}} \tag{6-15}$$

The formula is theoretically correct, but since the numerator contains the average hypothetical correlation of items with true scores, it is of no practical use. However, square both sides of the equation ($r^2_{t(1...k)}$ will be symbolized as $r_{kk}$):

$$r_{kk} = \frac{k^2\bar{r}^2_{it}}{k + k^2\bar{r}_{ij} + k\bar{r}_{ij}} \tag{6-16}$$

Then, divide numerator and denominator by $k$:

$$r_{kk} = \frac{k\bar{r}^2_{it}}{1 + (k-1)\bar{r}_{ij}} \tag{6-17}$$

Since the correlation of any item with true scores may be estimated by the square root of the average correlation of that item with other items, $k\bar{r}_{ij}$ can replace $k\bar{r}^2_{it}$ in the numerator, producing

$$r_{kk} = \frac{k\bar{r}_{ij}}{1 + (k-1)\bar{r}_{ij}} \tag{6-18}$$

It is hard to overestimate the importance of Eq. 6-18 to the theory of measurement error. It is the general form of the Spearman-Brown prophecy formula, named after its originators. An example will illustrate use of the formula. Let the average correlation among items on a 20-item test be .25. Then

$$\begin{aligned} r_{kk} &= \frac{20(.25)}{1 + (19)(.25)} \\ &= \frac{5.00}{1 + 4.75} \\ &= \frac{5.00}{5.75} \\ &= .87 \end{aligned}$$

It was previously shown that $r_{kk}$ is the estimated square of the correlation of scores on a collection of items with true scores. Consequently the estimated correlation with true scores in the above example equals the square root of .87 or .93. In the equation, $r_{kk}$ is the reliability coefficient, which in this case is .87. This illustrates how a highly reliable total test score can be obtained from items that have an average intercorrelation of only .25 given a reasonable number of items, e.g., 20.

Although $r_{kk}$ was introduced to obtain the correlation of a collection of items with true scores, it equally well defines the expected correlation of one $k$-item test with other $k$-item tests in that domain. Thus, $r_{kk}$ also estimates the reliability of a test that is lengthened by a factor of $k$. The next chapter will show how this is used in actual research. Equation 6-18 holds regardless of the size of the units that are added. All one needs to know is the average correlation among the units. Thus the formula would hold if the $k$ units being combined were pairs of items, 10-item tests, or 1000-item tests. One comes to the same conclusion about the effects of lengthening a test with a particular number of items regardless of the number of items per test *if* the assumptions of the domain-sampling model hold. However, these assumptions often do *not* hold when, as we have noted, the measure begins with the best items. If subsequent items are not as good, the expected gain in lengthening the test may not be realized. Equation 6-18 assumes that each collection of items, regardless of size, represents a random sample from the domain, so that the tests are randomly parallel.

One of the most frequent previous uses of Eq. 6-18 was with "split-half reliability estimates." In this method, the items on a test are divided in half, and the two half-tests are correlated. The correlation describes the reliability coefficient for a test of "half length," and Spearman-Brown is used to infer the reliability of the whole test. However, computer methodology allows for a better approach, Cronbach's (1951) coefficient alpha, presented below. Nonetheless, it is useful to look at the special case of doubling a test's length:

$$r_{kk} = \frac{2r_{12}}{1 + r_{12}}$$    (6-19)

where $r_{12}$ = correlation between two half-tests

$r_{kk}$ = reliability of whole test

Thus, if the correlation between two halves of a test, such as the scores on the odd and even items, is .80, the reliability of the test as a whole is $(2)(.80)/(1 + .80) = 1.60/1.80 = .88$.

## The Reliability of an Item Sample and Coefficient Alpha

The logic of the previous section in determining the effect of test length on reliability can be extended to determine the reliability of any particular sample of measures. This reliability depends entirely on (1) the average correlation among items and (2) the number of items. These values, obtainable by any intercorrelation algorithm like SAS' PROC CORR, can be substituted in Eq. 6-18 to obtain a reliability estimate, but there is a much easier way to obtain the same result as $\bar{r}_{ij}$ can be used in the numerator instead of $r_{it}$. Equation 6-16 then is

$$r_{kk} = \frac{k^2 \bar{r}_{ij}}{k + k^2 \bar{r}_{ij} - k\bar{r}_{ij}}$$    (6-20)

If the average correlation in a set of test items is a good estimate of the hypothetical average correlation of all items in a domain ($\bar{r}_{ij}$), some very useful formulas can be deduced. Rather than introduce new terminology, a precise estimate of $\bar{r}_{ij}$ will be symbolized as the actual average correlation in the domain. Further note that the denominator in Eq. 6-20 equals the sum of the elements in the matrix of correlations among the $k$ variables, so that Eq. 6-20 can be rewritten as

$$r_{kk} = \frac{k^2 \bar{r}_{ij}}{\bar{R}}$$    (6-21)

The numerator equals the sum of all the elements in a matrix whose average element is $\bar{r}_{ij}$. This differs from the sum of elements in an actual item intercorrelation matrix ($\bar{R}$) in two important ways. First, the former matrix does not have variances on the diagonal (unities with $z$ scores). Consequently the sum of variances ($k$) must be subtracted from $\bar{R}$ to approximate the numerator. Second, it is only an approximation because the sum of elements with zeros in the diagonal equals $(k^2 - k)\bar{r}_{ij}$ rather than $k^2\bar{r}_{ij}$. In other words, the result needs to be inflated by the following ratio to obtain $k^2\bar{r}_{ij}$ after subtracting the sum of variances from $\bar{R}$:

$$\frac{k^2}{k^2 - k} = \frac{k}{k - 1}$$

This allows the reliability of a $k$-item test to be written as

$$r_{kk} = \frac{[k/(k-1)](\bar{R} - \Sigma\sigma_i^2)}{\bar{R}}$$

$$= \frac{k}{(k-1)} \left( \frac{\bar{R} - \Sigma\sigma_i^2}{\bar{R}} \right) \tag{6-22}$$

Since variables are expressed as $z$ scores, Eq. 6-22 reduces to

$$r_{kk} = \frac{k}{k-1} \frac{\bar{R} - k}{\bar{R}} \tag{6-23}$$

It has thus far been convenient to work with $z$ scores, but we will now work with the item covariances rather than with their correlations because the total score will most likely tbe based upon the sum of raw item responses and not their $z$ scores. This also means that we need not assume that all items have the same variance (same $p$ values for dichotomous items), a source of minor imprecision in estimating reliability. In that case Eq. 6-22 becomes

$$r_{kk} = \frac{k(\bar{C} - \Sigma\sigma_i^2)}{(k-1)\bar{C}} \tag{6-24}$$

Recall from Chapter 5 that $\bar{C}$ is the sum of the elements in a covariance matrix (**C**), in this case the square matrix of variances and covariances among items.

Equation 6-24 could actually be used to estimate the reliability of a $k$-item test from its item covariance matrix, but the discussion in Chapter 5 about the variance of sums suggests an even simpler approach. The sum of the elements in this covariance matrix is simply the variance in total scores, $\bar{C} = \sigma_y^2$. Thus, Eq. 6-24 may be rewritten as

$$r_{kk} = \frac{k}{k-1} \frac{\sigma_y^2 - \Sigma\sigma_i^2}{\sigma_y^2} \tag{6-25}$$

or

$$r_{kk} = \frac{k}{k-1} \left( 1 - \frac{\Sigma\sigma_i^2}{\sigma_y^2} \right) \tag{6-26}$$

Equation 6-26 is one of the most important deductions from the domain-sampling theory of measurement error, Cronbach's (1951) coefficient alpha ($\alpha$). This formula can also be derived from the parallel-test model, and very similar formulas can be derived from other mathematical models for measurement error. Coefficient $\alpha$ is also a special case of a broadly useful measure called the intraclass correlation (Hays, 1988; Winer, Brown, & Michels, 1991).

Although it may look very different, $\alpha$ is identical to Eq. 6-18 used in estimating the reliability of a $k$-item test when (1) the average item covariance rather than the average item intercorrelation is employed and (2) the average of the item variances ($pq$ values for dichotomous items) is substituted for 1 as the first part of the denominator in Eq. 6-18. All these considerations justify the vast importance of $\alpha$ in the theory of reliability. It represents the expected correlation of one test with an alternative form containing the same number of items. The square root of $\alpha$ is the estimated correlation of a test with errorless true scores. It is so pregnant with meaning that it should routinely be applied to all new tests.

When one investigates the reliability of a test composed of dichotomous items, $\alpha$ takes on the following special form

$$r_{kk} = \frac{k}{k-1}\left(1 - \frac{\Sigma pq}{\sigma_y^2}\right) \tag{6-27}$$

Equation 6-27 follows from Eq. 6-26 because $\Sigma pq$ equals $\Sigma \sigma_i^2$. This special case is called Kuder-Richardson formula 20 (KR-20) for historical reasons.

All that is needed for any test regardless of whether or not it is comprised of dichotomous items are (1) the individual item variances (values of $pq$ for dichotomous items, but this does not matter to a computer), which are summed to provide $\Sigma \sigma_i^2 (\Sigma pq$ for dichotomous items), (2) the variance in observed scores ($\sigma_y^2$); and (3) the number of test items ($k$). It is easy to compute, and there is no excuse for not computing it for *any* new measure.

Another way of looking at $\alpha$ further underscores its importance. We have stressed that the reliability coefficient is the estimated average correlation of a test with all possible tests of the same length obtained by domain sampling. Thus, $\alpha$ is the expected correlation of one test with another test of the same length purportedly measuring the same thing. It can also be viewed as the expected correlation between an actual test and a hypothetical alternative form even though that alternative form may never be constructed. If the actual test is called $x$ and the hypothetical test is called $y$, the covariance matrix of items on the two tests can be depicted as follows:

|   | $x$ | $y$ |
|---|---|---|
| $x$ | $\mathbf{C}_x$ | $\mathbf{C}_{xy}$ |
| $y$ | $\mathbf{C}_{xy}$ | $\mathbf{C}_y$ |

According to the domain-sampling model, the average diagonal term in $\mathbf{C}_x$ and $\mathbf{C}_y$ will be the same, and the average off-diagonal elements will also be also the same. It also is expected that the average elements in $\mathbf{C}_{xy}$ will equal the average off-diagonal element in $\mathbf{C}_x$ or $\mathbf{C}_y$. Thus, $\alpha$ can be derived from the correlation of sums (Chapter 5) as follows:

$$r_{xy} = \frac{\overline{C}_{xy}}{\sqrt{\overline{C}_y}\sqrt{\overline{C}_y}}$$

According to the model, $\bar{C}_x$ and $\bar{C}_y$ are approximately equal, and so the equation can be rewritten as

$$r_{xy} = \frac{\bar{C}_{xy}}{\bar{\bar{C}}_x}$$

The average coefficient in $\mathbf{C}_{xy}$ and thus their sum can also be derived from $\mathbf{C}_x$. One first subtracts the variances of diagonal items from $\mathbf{C}_x$ and then inflates the result by the previously developed factor $k(k-1)$ to produce $\alpha$.

## Numerical Example

The data in Table 6-1 may be used to illustrate the calculation of $\alpha$ for a three-item test ($k = 3$). You may readily verify that the sum of the elements in this variance-covariance matrix ($\bar{C} = \sigma_y^2$) is 47 and the sum of the diagonal elements ($\Sigma\sigma_i^2$) is 23. Consequently $\alpha = {}^3/_2(47 - 23)/47$ or .77. Although it may seem unrealistic to use a three-item test for any purpose other than an example, this could arise from using three raters to evaluate a series of individuals with respect to an attribute of interest. The result would describe the reliability of the composite (mean or average rating). The $\alpha$ measure is not limited to test items in the ordinary sense. The above result assumes that scores were not standardized. Note that the variance of $x_1$ is twice that of $x_2$, which will cause it to have heavier weighting in an equally weighted composite of raw scores. This can be avoided by standardizing the raw scores. However, it is much simpler to obtain a correlation matrix ($\mathbf{R}$) from the variance-covariance matrix ($\mathbf{C}$), using methods discussed in Chapter 5, and to apply Eq. 6-26 to $\mathbf{R}$. You may verify that $r_{12} = .71$, $r_{13} = .45$, and $r_{23} = .47$. The sum of all nine elements in $\mathbf{R}$ ($\bar{R}$) is 6.26, and the sum of the diagonal elements is $k$ or 3, and so $\alpha = {}^3/_2 (6.26 - 3)/6.26$ or .78. Standardization had essentially no effect. This may or may not hold true when $k$ is small but will tend to be the case for larger values of $k$. Also note that $\alpha$ is considerably greater than the average correlation among the three measures (.71 + .45 + .47)/3 or .53. This is in fact generally the case—the average correlation severely underestimates the reliability of a composite of three or more related measures. Related examples appear in Chapter 7.

TABLE 6-1    VARIANCES AND COVARIANCES AMONG THREE HYPOTHETICAL MEASURES

| | Measure | | |
| --- | --- | --- | --- |
| | $x_1$ | $x_2$ | $x_3$ |
| $x_1$ | 10 | 5 | 4 |
| $x_2$ | 5 | 5 | 3 |
| $x_3$ | 4 | 3 | 8 |

### Variance of True and Error Scores

Equation 6-12 provided the very basic definition of the reliability coefficient as

$$r_{11} = \frac{\sigma_t^2}{\sigma_x^2}$$

The reliability coefficient equals the estimated ratio of true-score variance to total (actual or observed) variance. Rearranging terms,

$$\sigma_t^2 = r_{11}\sigma_x^2 \tag{6-28a}$$

and

$$\sigma_t = \sqrt{r_{11}}\,\sigma_x \tag{6-28b}$$

True scores ($t$) are always, of course, hypothetical, so that they can only be estimated in practice. Unless observed deviation scores ($x$) are perfectly reliable, the variance of $t$ will always be less than the variance of $x$ by a factor of $r_{11}$. Since error scores are uncorrelated with true scores,

$$\sigma_x^2 = \sigma_t^2 + \sigma_e^2 \tag{6-29}$$

Because $\sigma_x^2$ and $\sigma_e^2$ are directly related, one might erroneously assume that reliable tests have smaller standard deviations than unreliable tests. Inspecting the formula for $\alpha$ (Eq. 6-26) shows that just the reverse is true. The larger the average item covariance, the more reliable the test. The reliability is zero when the sum of item covariances is zero. Note that the variance of a sum equals the sum of variances *plus* the sum of all covariances in the covariance matrix. The variance of a totally unreliable test equals the sum of variances only. Consequently the more reliable the test, the larger the variance of test scores. If, for example, two 20-item tests have the same average $pq$ value, the one with the larger variance is more reliable.

It is true that the error variance adds to whatever true (reliable) variance is present, but it also is true that the true variance adds to whatever error variance is present. The variance of scores of a completely unreliable measure equals the sum of the item variances. This is the lower limit on the variance of obtained scores. As the test becomes more reliable, the positive covariances cause the observed variance to increase. Whereas there is a severe limit on the size of the variance of errors, there is much less of a limit on the sum of covariance terms. For example, the item covariances on a moderately reliable 30-item test contribute at least three times as much to the variance of test scores as the item variances. Thus, reliable tests have larger observed variances relative to unreliable tests of the same length.

### Estimation of True Scores

The square root of $r_{11}$ is the estimated correlation of obtained scores with true scores ($r_{1t}$) and can be used to estimate true scores from obtained scores. Equation 4-21a provides the general form of the slope of the regression equation for estimating one deviation score from another deviation score (since these are deviation scores, Eq. 4-21b leads to an intercept of 0):

$$y' = \frac{\sigma_y}{\sigma_x} r_{xy} x$$

The problem is to estimate true deviation scores ($t'$) from obtained deviation scores ($x$). It was previously shown that the standard deviation of true scores ($\sigma_t$) equals $\sqrt{r_{xx}}\sigma_{x'}$, where $r_{xx}$ is the reliability of $x$. True deviation scores can be estimated as

$$t' = \frac{\sigma_t}{\sigma_x} r_{xt} x$$

$$= \frac{\sqrt{r_{xx}}\sigma_x r_{xt} x}{\sigma_x} \tag{6-30}$$

$$= \sqrt{r_{xx}} r_{xt} x$$

Since $r_{xt}$ equals the square root of $r_{xx}$,

$$t' = \sqrt{r_{xx}}\sqrt{r_{xx}} x$$
$$= r_{xx} x \tag{6-31}$$

True deviation scores ($t'$) are thus estimated as the product of the reliability coefficient and the obtained deviation scores.

Although Eq. 6-31 is the best least-squares estimate of true scores, the domain-sampling model does not assume that tests in the domain have linear regressions with true scores. Linearity of regression is not crucial to most of the principles that can be derived from the domain-sampling model (e.g., the effect of test length on reliability), but it is important to any relatively simple estimation of true scores. We presently assume (somewhat inaccurately) that the relationship between obtained scores and true scores is linear but will discuss this point more fully in Chapter 10.

As is true in any correlational analysis, obtained scores must be regressed to obtain a best least-squares estimate of true scores. This fact gives rise to an important principle: Obtained scores are biased estimates of true scores. Scores above the mean are biased upward, and scores below the mean are biased downward. The farther scores are in either direction from the mean obtained scores, the greater the absolute magnitude of bias. As a group, people with high obtained scores have a preponderance of positive measurement errors (good luck), and the opposite is true for people who have low obtained scores (bad luck).

This fact makes little difference in one sense because estimated true scores correlate perfectly with obtained scores. For this reason, there is usually little to be gained by estimating true scores, which we consider more fully in the next chapter, when constructs are static. In this case, the major importance of estimating true scores is to set confidence intervals for the effects of measurement error on obtained scores, which will be discussed in the next section.

The bias in obtained scores raises an important theoretical point, however. Suppose one actually had true scores which could then be used to estimate obtained scores. If both are in $z$-score form, the regression equation is

$$z'_x = r_{xt} z_t \qquad (6\text{-}32)$$

where $z'_x$ = estimate of an obtained standard score for $x$

$z_t$ = true score

$r_{xt}$ = correlation between true and obtained scores

Subtracting $z'_x$ from the actual values ($z_x$) provides the errors of estimation (residuals), which are errors due to unreliability. We have previously assumed that such errors of estimation are uncorrelated with the variable used for estimation (true scores), which is another way of saying that error scores and true scores are uncorrelated. However, errors of estimate are correlated with the variable being estimated (obtained scores):

$$r_{xe} = \sqrt{1 - r_{xt}^2} \qquad (6\text{-}33)$$
$$= \sqrt{1 - r_{xx}}$$

Thus if $x$ had a reliability of .64, obtained scores would correlate .60 with error scores. The correlation is positive: High obtained scores are biased upward, and low obtained scores are biased downward because errors correlate positively with obtained scores (see Table 4-2).

### The Standard Error of Measurement

One may compute the standard error in estimating obtained scores from true scores as in any regression problem. The standard error in estimating one variable in deviation-score form ($x$) from another variable in deviation or raw-score form ($y$) is

$$\alpha_{est} = \sigma_x \sqrt{1 - r_{xy}^2}$$

If $x$ is a set of obtained scores and $y = t$ is a set of true scores, Eq. 4-23b becomes

$$\sigma_{est} = \sigma_x \sqrt{1 - r_{xt}^2}$$
$$= \sigma_x \sqrt{1 - r_{xx}} \qquad (6\text{-}34)$$
$$= \sigma_{meas}$$

As noted in earlier in this chapter, the standard error in estimating obtained scores from true scores is called the standard error of measurement ($\sigma_{meas}$). This quantity is the expected standard deviation of scores for anyone taking a large number of randomly parallel tests. One can use it to set confidence intervals for obtained scores, but such confidence intervals are not symmetrical about the obtained score. Thus, it is *incorrect* to set the 95 percent confidence interval as equaling two standard errors of measurement below and two above the obtained score, although this is often done. The confidence interval *is* symmetric about the estimated true score ($t'$), as will be discussed more fully in the next chapter.

Using $\sigma_{meas}$ implicitly assumes that the distribution of errors has the same shape and size for people at different points on the continuum of true scores. The domain-sampling model does not make these assumptions, and they are not needed for the most important deductions from the model. They are required, however, to set confidence intervals for estimated true scores, but there are reasons to believe that both assumptions are usually incorrect. This matter will be discussed more fully subsequently.

## Attenuation

We said at the start of this chapter that measurement error is "bad" because it tends to obscure or attenuate the lawfulness in nature; correlations are lower than they would be in the absence of measurement error. The effect of measurement error upon observed correlations may be estimated. Similarly, one may also estimate how much higher the correlations between true scores would be than the correlation between fallible scores. One simple approach to developing the proper formulas is to assume that two tests from two different domains should have uncorrelated errors, and errors on either test should be uncorrelated with true scores on either test. The resulting correlation between fallible scores on the two tests can be "taken apart" as follows

$$r_{12} = \frac{\sigma_{12}}{\sigma_1 \sigma_2}$$

$$= \frac{(1/N)\Sigma(t_1 + e_1)(t_2 + e_2)}{\sigma_1 \sigma_2}$$

$$= \frac{(1/N)\Sigma(t_1 t_2 + t_1 e_2 + t_2 e_1 + e_1 e_2)}{\sigma_1 \sigma_2}$$

$$= \frac{(1/N)(\Sigma t_1 t_2 + \Sigma t_1 e_2 + \Sigma t_2 e_1 + \Sigma e_1 e_2)}{\sigma_1 \sigma_2}$$

Only the first term in the numerator is not zero, leading to

$$r_{12} = \frac{\sigma_{t_1 t_2}}{\sigma_1 \sigma_2} \tag{6-35}$$

The numerator shows that the covariance of obtained scores is equal to the covariance of true scores. If there were no measurement error, the covariance term in the numerator would remain the same, but the standard deviations in the denominator would shrink by the amount derived previously. Thus, if there were no error present, the correlation between the two sets of scores ($r'_{12}$) would be

$$\hat{r}_{12} = \frac{\sigma_{12}}{(\sqrt{r_{11}}\,\sigma_1)(\sqrt{r_{22}}\sigma_2)}$$

$$= \frac{\sigma_{12}/(\sigma_1\sigma_2)}{\sqrt{r_{11}}\sqrt{r_{22}}}$$

$$= \frac{r_{12}}{\sqrt{r_{11}}\sqrt{r_{22}}} \tag{6-36}$$

Equation 6-36 is known as the "correction" for attenuation, but it really only estimates how high the correlation would be if the two variables were made perfectly reliable rather than a true correction (these estimates can exceed 1.0!) In other words, Eq. 6-36 estimates the limiting value of the correlation between samples of items from two domains as the number of items from each domain increases. Equation 6-36 also applies to samples of items drawn from the same domain, but the result is trivial. The correlation between two such tests is expected to equal the product of the terms in the denominator, and so $r'_{12}$ equals 1.0.

One important principle that can be derived from Eq. 6-36 concerns the maximum correlation that any set of fallible scores can have with any other set of scores. If $r'_{12}$ were 1.0, $r_{12}$ would be limited only by the reliabilities of the two tests:

$$1.00 = \frac{r_{12}}{\sqrt{r_{11}}\sqrt{r_{22}}}$$

$$r_{12} = \sqrt{r_{11}}\sqrt{r_{22}} \tag{6-37}$$

The correlation between one test and another test may therefore be higher than its own reliability coefficient. In the limiting case, the correlation between the two tests would equal the square root of the reliability of the first test if the second test was perfectly reliable. The square root of the reliability is the correlation of a test with true scores or the "reliability index," the upper limit on the correlation between a sample of an item in one domain and a sample of items in another. The utility of the domain-sampling model would be open to serious question had any other conclusion been reached. The next chapter discusses various uses for formulas concerning attenuation.

## ALTERNATIVE MODELS

We have placed major emphasis in this chapter on the domain-sampling model because (1) it is relatively easy to understand, (2) it permits simple derivations of many important principles, and (3) deductions from the model have a high degree of internal consistency. Several different approaches led to the same formulas, and formulas serving quite different purposes were derived from one another. Other models compete with the domain-sampling model. For example, one of these is the parallel-test model. This was shown to be a special case of the domain-sampling model. Actually, this and other possible models we will now discuss are complementary to rather than competitive with the domain-sampling model. They supplement information provided by the domain-sampling model alone in the simple form in which it was presented.

## Factorial Domain-Sampling Model

The domain-sampling model we presented concerned a hypothetical infinite number of test items or other scoring units where all items measured the same attribute. No distinctions were made between possible subgroups of items within the domain, and the major problem for the development of statistical formulas for measurement error concerned the average correlation among items in the domain and the dispersion of correlations about that average. This is the simplest form of more complex domain-sampling models which classify the items in various ways within the overall domain in a very similar manner to the many ANOVA designs.

Each method of classifying the content within a domain is called a "factor" (but not in the sense of "factor analysis"), and there can be as many factors as there are types of measurement error to be investigated. For example, clinical psychologists might rate the improvement of patients in psychotherapy. The various psychologists might be one factor in the domain. A second factor might be the occasions over which ratings are obtained (e.g., weekly), and a third might be various measurement scales, perhaps evaluating behavior at home versus at work. This produces a three-factor design for structuring the content of the domain of measurements. Generalizability theory, discussed in the next chapter, deals with such factorial designs. It is particularly well suited to the common problem of estimating the interjudge reliability of three or more raters (when there are only two raters, the ordinary $r$ between them suffices).

## The Binomial Model

The binomial model (Lord & Novick, 1968) provides useful supplementary information to the domain-sampling model. This model assumes that errors have a binomial distribution about true scores. It can be illustrated in the special case where all items in a domain have $p$ values of .5. A person with an average true score would then have a probability of .5 of correctly answering any item selected at random from the domain. The expected score on any random sample of $k$ items is $k/2$, but this would be subject to binomial error over samples. Since errors are random, the scores obtained for two people on an item sample would be statistically independent. Consequently each person would produce a binomial distribution of obtained scores over tests. We mentioned previously that the shape and standard deviation of the binomial distribution depend on $p$ and the number of test items ($k$). The average person's distribution would be symmetric and approximate a normal distribution as $k$ increased.

A person with a high true score illustrates one key consequence of the model. That person would have a high probability of correctly answering any given item in the domain. Consequently the resulting distribution of obtained scores for different item samples ($\sigma_{meas}$) would be negatively skewed rather than symmetric and $\sigma_{meas}$ would be smaller than the average person's. The corresponding distribution for a person with a very low true score would be positively skewed, but $\sigma_{meas}$ would also be relatively small. The amount of skewness for persons at either extreme is inversely related to $k$ and would not be noticeable on long tests, e.g., 100 items.

The binomial model is a very sensible model for determining the shape and distribution of obtained scores, and so one should reconsider the simple model in Fig. 6-1$a$. Figure 6-1$b$ illustrates a more realistic outcome than assuming that the standard error of measurement is the same at all points on the true score continuum and the distribution of errors is normal. The figure indicates that the distribution of obtained scores tends to (1) have a smaller standard deviation and be positively skewed for a person like A who falls below the mean of the distribution, (2) have a larger standard deviation and be symmetric for a person like B who falls at the mean of the distribution, and (3) again have a smaller standard deviation but be negatively skewed for a person like C who falls above the mean of the distribution.

This means that the relationship between obtained scores and true scores is somewhat heteroscedastic since $\sigma_{meas}$ decreases toward the extremes of the distribution. The relationship between true and observed scores also tends to be slightly nonlinear. This and subsequent models predict an S-shaped (ogival) rather than a linear relation between true and observed scores. However, these potential modifications of the domain-sampling model are usually so slight as to have minor consequences for the results. Measurement error plays an important role in linear approaches to test scoring in Chapters 7 through 9. Its role in a different approach based upon the pattern of response, item response theory, will be considered in Chapter 10.

## RELIABILITY AS STABILITY OVER TIME

A second definition of "reliability" is stability over time. This is usually assessed by some form of correlation between scores on the same test, or, if memory for previous answers is likely to play a spurious role, parallel forms. One such measure is simply the correlation between observed scores, but this procedure may run into problems (Cronbach & Furby, 1970; Lord & Novick, 1968; for a partial defense of these measures, see Rogosa, Brandt, & Zimowski, 1982). This issue will be explored in the next section. Measures which have high temporal stability are called "trait measures," and measures which have low temporal stability are called "state measures" (Anastasi, in Wainer & Messick, 1983; Spielberger, Gorsuch, & Lushene, 1970), although the distinction is a continuum. Cognitive abilities tend to be traitlike, and mood is more statelike. In general, the longer the interval between testing, the lower the temporal stability.

Random error may attenuate measures obtained at two separate times, just as it may affect internal consistency (homogeneity). However, the two definitions are basically independent in that a test may have high temporal stability and high homogeneity, either, or neither. If a series of adults are asked to add the number of letters in the name given them at birth to their height and the "test" is repeated 2 years later, the correlation between the two measures should be 1.0 (high temporal stability), despite the zero correlation between the two items and consequent lack of internal consistency. Similarly, physiological measures like blood pressure and pulse rate are reasonably well correlated at any given time but tend to be unstable over time.

Measuring change in general is an extremely difficult problem. Collins and Horn (1991) have recently edited a volume that summarizes the many trends in this area. In general, it is important to consider several special cases because measures suitable in one situation may not be suitable in another. One such special case is "cumulative growth," in which true scores (if not observed scores) are expected to increase monotonically, as is true of the development of skills, versus situations in general, where there may be ups and downs in the true scores, such as mood. An even more special case is linear growth, in which the changes in true scores over time fall along a straight line versus situations in which this is not the case (certain nonlinear forms of growth, e.g., exponential growth, can be made linear by a transformation of variables).

The obvious minimum number of observation periods needed to study change, often called waves, is two. Some situations allow only this minimum, but many imply the need for more than two. At least three periods are needed to determine whether growth is linear, for example, and estimation of certain changes in scores is facilitated by having several waves. At a substantive level, gains found in a treatment group relative to a control group in an immediate posttest are often offset by subsequent recidivism in the treatment group. This assessment implies the need for a delayed posttest. Yet another consideration is whether the focus is on group changes (as in much research) or individual changes (as in individual classifications). In addition, some models for change can be handled from the perspective of domain sampling, perhaps requiring extensions in the form of multiple domains, as discussed more fully in the section titled "Generalizability Theory" in the next chapter; others, such as Collins and Cliff's (1990) approach to cumulative growth based upon an extension of Guttman scales (see Chapter 2), use item response theory. Statistical considerations that are specific to the situation, such as the degree of correlation among the measures and their reliability are also important.

## Difference Scores

A common denominator of any situation that involves change over time is the fact that one can compute an observed difference score. If we assume a two-wave study for simplicity, this may be denoted $d_i = x_{i2} - x_{i1} = (t_{i2} + e_{i2}) - (t_{i1} + e_{i1})$. The subscript $i$ denotes individual, $x_{i1}$ and $x_{i2}$ are the scores observed at the two time periods, $t_{i1}$ and $t_{i2}$ are the corresponding true scores, and $e_{i1}$ and $e_{i2}$ are the associated errors of measurement (assuming deviation scores only for simplicity of discussion). The use of simple difference scores is often criticized. We will shown in the next chapter that if $x_{i1}$ and $x_{i2}$ are highly correlated over subjects, as they are in many situations, especially when the time interval is short, $d_i$ will be highly *unreliable*. In addition, there will be a built-in correlation between $d_i$ and $x_{i1}$ of $1 - r_{12}$ if the scores are standardized, where $r_{12}$ is the correlation between $x_{i1}$ and $x_{i1}$. This correlation follows from the correlation of sums (see Chapter 5).

Rogosa et al. (1982), however, note that if it is reasonable to assume that the mean of the two sets of error scores is zero, the $d_i$ is an *unbiased* estimator of the true change $(t_{i2} - t_{i1})$. Moreover, the reliability and correlation with initial (baseline) tests are determinable. If there are wide individual differences in amount of true change, the difference score may have high reliability. In general, the stability of a measure such as $X$ can be low either because of wide variation in amount of change or because of low internal consistency, but these have very different implications. Rogosa et al. make an interesting side point by noting that most examinations of change concentrate upon the case in which amount of change is either negatively related or unrelated to change. This is often an artifact of standardizing $x_{i1}$ and $x_{i2}$ rather than letting their natural differences in variance contribute to the analysis. Real life contains many instances of a positive correlation in which the "rich become richer." Cogent arguments against standardization and in favor of letting variability differences remain date back at least to Thorndike (1966).

One commonly suggested alternative to simple difference scores are residual change scores based upon some form of partialling $x_{i1}$ from $x_{i2}$. The simplest form is the residual from the ordinary least-squares regression of the observed scores. Among its other problems is that it treats $x_{i1}$ as if it were error-free, i.e. as if it were $t_{i1}$. Further compounding this problem is that the error scores, $e_{i1}$ and $e_{i2}$ cannot be assumed independent over subjects. As noted in Chapter 4, generalized least-squares estimation is one approach to this problem, albeit beyond the scope of this book. Rogosa et al. discuss some other estimation procedures, but they too are complex. One intent is to improve the definition of change measures by taking more of the data into account than the individual differences.

Rogosa et al. note, and we agree, that the best measure of change is the difference in true scores, $t_{i2} - t_{i1}$. We will discuss the estimation of these scores individually in the next chapter. When it can be assumed that the errors are not highly correlated or if methods like generalized least-squares or structural equation modeling can be used to take this correlation into account, this may prove a useful approach. Before this is done, however, it is also useful to evaluate the reliability of the observed difference score since it is the simplest and most direct definition of change, despite its problems. Also, remember that standardizing the elements of a difference score may produce spurious results.

## One Other Consideration

Although Collins and Cliff's (1990) model for cumulative growth falls outside this chapter because of its use of the Guttman model, they make one extremely cogent point that is immediately relevant: Items that are useful in measuring static constructs may not be useful in measuring change (and, by implication, vice versa). For example, a general achievement item that deals with the ability to carry out addition problems would probably be failed by nearly all students early in grammar school and thus not discriminate within cohorts at this level. One would have good reason to exclude it from a test of early achievement. The same item may be too easy for more advanced students, and so one may also wish to exclude it in that group. However, items of this form can be extremely powerful predictors of change when the focus is upon that aspect of achievement. This argument applies to sentiments as well as judgments.

## SUMMARY

This chapter was concerned with measurement error that affects all observations randomly, as opposed to error that has a constant effect upon all observations or affects some but not all observations based upon some systematic characteristic (a bias). Conventional linear scoring was assumed so that the observed test score was a linear combination of item responses. Each object of measurement was assumed to have true scores on an attribute that could be found with no errors of measurement by repeated testing with alternative forms. It was initially assumed that scores obtained from alternative forms (1) were distributed symmetrically above and below the true scores (unbiased), (2) were normally distributed, (3) add to the true score to provide the obtained score, and (4) have equal variance (are homoscedastic). The standard deviation of obtained scores about a given true score produced by measurement error defines the standard error of measurement.

The notion of domain sampling was then introduced to study the internal consistency of measures. The idea is that there are an infinity of problems of a given type such as adding pairs of four-digit numbers. Constructing a test involves sampling items at random from this domain. The reliability index ($r_{it}$) is the correlation between a set of scores on a given test ($x_1$) and corresponding true scores. It is exactly equal to the square root of the average correlation between all pairs of tests in the domain ($\bar{r}_{ij}$, also written as $\bar{r}_{11}$). In turn, $\bar{r}_{ij}$ ($\bar{r}_{11}$) may be estimated by the average correlation between test $x_1$ and the other tests in the domain or reliability coefficient for test $x_1$ ($\bar{r}_{1j}$, also written as $r_{11}$). A key point is that the reliability coefficient equals the ratio of the variance of true scores to the variance of observed scores. Moreover, a high degree of internal consistency does not guarantee that a measure is unidimensional (measures only one thing).

The parallel-test model proceeds from somewhat different assumptions than the domain-sampling model. It assumes pairs of tests which (1) correlate equally with true scores, (2) possess independent (uncorrelated) error, and (3) have equal variance. In general, it *defines* the same relationships that domain-sampling models *estimate*, in particular the square root relationship between the reliability index and reliability coefficient. Consequently, major results are not limited to one particular model of reliability.

Reliabilities are usually estimated from a single test or, at most, the correlation of one test with an alternative form. Consequently, the precision of the reliability estimate needs be considered. This is inversely related to the standard deviations of item intercorrelations.

The domain-sampling model provides several important deductions:

**1** The Spearman-Brown prophecy formula estimates the expected increase in test reliability as a function of increased length.

**2** Even more important is Cronbach's coefficient alpha ($\alpha$) which estimates the reliability coefficient from the item intercorrelations.

**3** The reliability of a test increases as its total variance increases.

**4** The standard error of measurement for standardized variables is the square root of 1 minus the reliability coefficient.

**5** The distribution of obtained scores using the standard error of measurement is symmetric about the expected true score rather than the obtained score.

**6** Unreliability reduces or *attenuates* the observed correlation between measures, but it is simple to estimate what the correlation would be between perfectly reliable measures or, for that matter, measures of any given reliability.

We then considered some alternative models designed to broaden the applicability of the basic domain-sampling model. The factorial domain-sampling model handles items that are multidimensional, and the binomial model recognizes that the standard error of measurement for dichotomous items may be greater for individuals who score near the midpoint of a scale than individuals at the extremes. Finally, the chapter concluded with a second, completely distinct meaning of reliability: stability over time. Whereas internal consistency is always desirable, temporal stability may or may not be: Trait measures are designed to be temporally stable, but state measures are not. Moveover, measures of internal consistency such as $\alpha$ are independent of measures of temporal stability, which are normally based upon the correlation between repeated testings over time.

Measuring change is a very difficult problem. Models are now in the process of evolution to deal with such specific forms of change as cumulative growth (monotonic increases in performance) and, as a special case, linear growth. The simplest measure of change is the difference between two observed scores. This has been traditionally criticized because the reliability of differences between two positively correlated scores (as test-retest scores are likely to be) is low (see Chapter 7) and because there is an artifactual negative correlation between the observed change and the initial scores. However, the suggested alternatives, such as covarying the initial score from the second measure, also have problems. Consequently, observed differences need not be as fatally flawed as was once thought. Potentially better methods of measuring change can perhaps be derived by computing the change in estimated true scores. Estimation of true scores is considered in the next chapter. Two related points are that (1) one should not standardize the scores used to define change but let their natural units of variance contribute to the results and (2) items that may not be useful in measuring differences within a group because they are too easy or too difficult (or, in a more general sense, answered in a consistent direction) may be useful in measuring change.

## SUGGESTED ADDITIONAL READINGS

Lord, F. M., & Novick, M. R. (1968). *Statistical theories of mental test scores*. Reading, MA: Addison-Wesley.

Rogosa, D. R., Brandt, D., & Zimowski, M. (1982). A growth curve approach to the measurement of change. *Psychological Bulletin, 92*, 726–748.

*Note*: The vast majority of research into psychometric theory in the past 15 years has been oriented toward modern test (item response) theory, which we will discuss in Chapter 10. Further references will be provided at that point. Lord and Novick (1968) discuss both classical and modern approaches (of that time). Their book is still a widely cited classic, but it is very technical. Perhaps the single area in which classical test theory has been most expanded in recent years is generalizability theory, discussed in the next chapter. The references presented there typically are applicable to the issue of reliability in general.

## CHAPTER 7

# THE ASSESSMENT
# OF RELIABILITY

## CHAPTER OVERVIEW

Whereas the previous chapter presented the theory of reliability, this chapter will stress application of these principles. Some additional formulas will be developed to assess the effects of measurement error on research results and applied decisions. We previously said that measurements are reliable to the extent that they are repeatable and that any random influence which causes different measurements of the same variable to vary is a source of measurement error. The domain-sampling model was used as one approach to investigate such random sources of error. Each test is considered a random sample of items from a domain, and measurement error is present only to the extent that samples are limited in size. Thus, a long test with a positive average correlation among items is always a highly reliable test, the degree of reliability being estimated by Eq. 6-26.

This line of argument assumes that all measurement error arises from content sampling. But is content sampling the only factor that prevents measurements from being repeatable? We shall first look at some of the factors that reduce the repeatability of measurements and then see if they can be adequately handled by the domain-sampling model. In particular we will examine variation between two forms of a test as well as variation within a test. This forms part of the basis for the estimation of reliability in different circumstances, e.g., through alternative forms. Part of this discussion involves the long-range stability of measures.

Various practical uses of the reliability coefficient are considered as extensions of the material in Chapter 6. The correction for attenuation can be used to examine the correlation between two variables as the reliability of each is changed to a designated (higher or lower) level and not simply made perfect as was previously assumed. Confidence intervals about both obtained and true scores are explored. Finally, the effects of group dispersion (variability) are discussed—explicit in the definition of the reliability coefficient is the notion that its magnitude is directly related to the variance of obtained scores.

Information gained by evaluating a test's reliability can be used to make suitable modifications. The most obvious way to do this is to alter its length using the Spearman-Brown prophecy formula. Standards of acceptable reliability are presented. These depend upon what type of decision is to be made—tests used to contrast groups need not be as reliable as tests used to make decisions about individuals—but to a large extent, the issue is one of "How high is up?" Moreover, the importance of high reliability is also often exaggerated. Limited reliability is not the major reason limiting test validity, and, unfortunately, the search for reliable measures often causes people to replace relatively valid but somewhat unreliable measures with less valid measures.

Test construction proper largely consists of aggregating a series of extremely unreliable (and invalid) items into a reliable (and, at least sometimes, valid) scale. In contrast, scores from *whole* tests are often combined linearly into composite measures, e.g., differences between pre- and posttest scores used to measure change. The principles governing the formation and reliability of these composite measures are considered.

Chapter 6 illustrated how to obtain coefficient $\alpha$ from the variances and covariances among items. We also consider an approach developed by Hoyt (1941) that is based upon the analysis of variance. This is computationally very useful because computer programs for performing the ANOVA are more widely available than programs for computing $\alpha$ directly. However, the more important reason is that this approach leads to generalizability theory, which allows one to infer what are in effect reliabilities from domains that are not homogeneous. This topic occupies the remainder of the chapter.

## SOURCES OF ERROR

In practice, many factors prevent measurements from being exactly repeatable, the number and kinds of factors depending on the nature of the test and how the test is used. The following section describes some of these principal sources of measurement error. Stanley (1971) and Magnusson (1967) present very detailed lists.

### Variation within a Test

It is important to distinguish between measurement errors that (1) cause performance to vary from item to item within a test and (2) appear only when different forms of a test are used, either at the same or at different times. The domain-sampling model can handle case 1, but case 2 requires the model to be extended.

The major source of error within a test is item sampling. According to the domain-sampling model, each person has a particular probability of correctly answering each item, depending on the person's true score and the difficulty of the item. Someone whose ability is average for a given population and who answers items having $p$ values of .5 has a probability of .5 of correctly answering any item chosen at random from the domain. That person should correctly answer half the items on any test drawn from the domain. However, that expected proportion of .5 is accompanied by error.

The more items on the test, the smaller that error will be. The same logic applies to items that have no "correct" responses, i.e., sentiments. Each person has some probability of agreeing with each statement, which in turn leads to an expected number of agreements in an item sample. In turn, there is some variability in scores from test to test depending on the number of items per sample. This error due to item sampling is entirely predictable from the average correlation. Consequently, coefficient alpha ($\alpha$, Eq. 6-26) is the appropriate measure of reliability for any type of item.

Guessing, discussed more fully in Chapters 9 and 10, is a second source of measurement error, as an individual might pass one item and fail a second purely because of blind luck. Guessing causes performance to vary from item to item, lowering correlations between items and therefore overall test reliability. Many other factors produce variation among item scores within a test besides guessing, such as (1) subjects who intend to choose one answer but mark another by mistake, (2) clerical errors in hand-scored tests, (3) misreading a question because of confusing wording, (4) fatigue on long tests, and (5) random (but not systematic) grader errors on essay tests.

The domain-sampling model can handle all the errors that occur within a test. Consequently, the sampling process should be thought of as including the many situational factors such as guessing that influence responses (and therefore reliability) and not just content. How a person responds to any given item is then a function of situational factors as well as the chosen item. All such sources of error tend to lower the average correlation among items within the test, but the average correlation is still sufficient to estimate the reliability.

## Variation between Tests

The study of measurement error relating to variation between tests is performed most typically with alternative forms, which are intended to approximate randomly parallel tests. Chapter 6 noted that randomly parallel tests are random samples from a given domain of content and thus tend to have the same scores for any group of people. However, in many cases no actual sampling is done; rather, an individual constructs two tests which are intended to be similar in content. There is no guarantee that all the characteristics of randomly parallel tests are present, and so these are called alternative forms rather than randomly parallel forms. Having two such tests is widely useful, especially when a measure needs to be repeated. One way to construct such alternative forms is to combine the sets of items and randomly assign them to the two forms.

Scores derived from alternative forms administered after a time lapse will almost never correlate perfectly. The domain-sampling model can be used to predict this correlation. As was shown in the previous section, this prediction takes account of the many sources of error within each testing session as well as the sampling of content. There are, however, three major sources of error intervening between administrations of different tests that are not reflected in the average correlation of items within each test (Stanley, 1971). These sources of error cause the domain-sampling model to overestimate the actual correlation between forms.

The first is due to systematic differences in content of the two tests. We have stressed that items are usually composed rather than randomly sampled as assumed formally, especially outside the abilities domain. Differences in the way two tests are composed produce systematic differences not incorporated by the model. For example, different people might emphasize different kinds of words on spelling tests. This would make the correlation between the two tests less than predicted from the average correlation among the items within each test. The same is true of surveys constructed by different pollsters.

Systematic effects arising from subjectivity of scoring are a second potential cause of variation in scores on alternative forms. This is most easily seen when subjects are rated by different judges over occasions; the judges might have different standards. For example, one clinical psychologist might be behaviorally oriented, and a second psychoanalytically oriented. This would clearly lead them to look for different things in the behaviors of patients. This has nothing to do with differences in leniency. The two raters could have identical distributions of ratings yet differ in what they rated.

A third source of variation in test performance over occasions is an actual change in the subject in the attribute being measured, i.e., temporal instability. A person might feel much better on one occasion than on another, might study in the domain of content, or might change attitudes toward providing shelters for the homeless. Changes over time are especially important with mood-related measures and, to a lesser extent, other personality variables, but they are not necessarily trivial even with ability measures.

Systematic differences in test content, judgmental criteria, and temporal instability cannot adequately be handled by a model based solely on the random sampling of items. The model must also consider the random sampling of whole tests to handle these factors adequately. Consequently, tests should be thought of as randomly sampled over occasions, and correlations among tests may well be lower than predicted simply from the correlations among items within tests. In that case the average correlation among alternative forms administered on two or more occasions may estimate reliability more meaningfully than coefficient $\alpha$ obtained within tests. (Recall also from the end of the previous chapter that tests with a very low coefficient $\alpha$ may be temporally stable, so that alternative-form correlations may also be higher than within-test estimates of reliability.)

## ESTIMATION OF RELIABILITY

Because reliability is important to any measurement method, investigations of reliability should be made when new measures are developed. The following are some recommendations regarding how such investigations should be undertaken.

### Internal Consistency

Internal consistency describes estimates of reliability based on the average correlation among items within a test. This is partly a misnomer because coefficient $\alpha$ reflects both the number of items and their average correlation (which may be thought of as the internal consistency per se). Coefficient $\alpha$, including special cases like KR-20 for dichotomous items, should be applied to all new measurement methods even if other estimates of reliability are also necessary. However, the results of *any* internal consistency approach such as α or the split-half method (discussed later in this chapter) will be misleading on speed tests, as discussed in Chapter 9.

Coefficient α sets an upper limit for the reliability of tests constructed in terms of the domain-sampling model based upon observed correlations, a point we will return to later in this chapter. If α is very low, the test is either too short or the items have very little in common. In that case there is no point in obtaining other reliability estimates such as the correlation between alternative-forms because they will be even lower. If, for example, coefficient α for a 40-item test is only .30, the experimenter should reconsider the measurement problem, perhaps by choosing different types of items.

Even though coefficient α ignores certain potentially important sources of measurement error, it is surprising how little difference these sources of measurement error usually make. This is particularly true if the test instructions are easily understood and scoring is objective. Coefficient α based upon a sample of 300 or more subjects will usually be very similar to the alternative-forms correlation. The former might be .85 and the latter might be .80—it will rarely be as low as .60. Some exceptions will be discussed in the next section. Coefficient α usually provides a good estimate of reliability because sampling of content is usually the major source of measurement error for static constructs and also because it is sensitive to the "sampling" of situational factors as well as item content.

## Alternative Forms

It is also informative to obtain both coefficient α and alternative form correlations with most measures when possible. These alternative forms should ideally be parallel forms; but they often cannot be constructed in this way, especially with personality measures, for previously discussed reasons. The two forms should be administered about 2 weeks apart to allow variation in the traits to occur over time. If the correlation between alternative forms is markedly lower than coefficient α, say .20 or more, considerable measurement error is present from the three previously mentioned sources of error: systematic differences in content, subjectivity of scoring, and variation in the trait over time. Further investigation can determine the relative contributions of these factors. Also look for possible changes in level as well as correlation by evaluating possible mean differences over occasions.

The correlation obtained when the two forms are administered on the same day can be compared with the correlation obtained with a 2-week interval to investigate variation in scores over short periods of time. If the correlation between forms administered on the same day is much higher than the correlation obtained with a 2-week delay, variation in the trait over time is a major source of unreliability; i.e., the measure is statelike rather than traitlike in the sense of Chapter 6. This is not measurement error in the sense of a lack of internal consistency, since such changes are often both meaningful and desirable. For example, a mood measure should change over time because of normal mood swings. Regardless, trait variation over time will attenuate correlations with variables that are not measured at the same time. Conversely, if the correlations between alternative forms administered 2 weeks apart and on the same day are both low, people may be stable over time, but the two forms will differ in content. One form may be more reliable than the other, which will be reflected in a difference in their average correlation between items. This suggests that something went wrong in constructing one of the forms. It might be best to replace the less reliable form with a new form and correlate the new form with the more reliable form.

If the average correlation within the two test forms is substantial (e.g., .20) but the average cross correlation between items on the two forms is low (e.g., .10), the two forms probably reliably differ in content and thus measure somewhat different traits. This should lead the investigator to rethink the intended domain of content. Inspecting the content might reveal why the forms differ. This could lead either to emphasizing the content of one of the forms or to seeking items that bridge the gap in content. This circumstance will not arise if alternative forms are constructed by the previously mentioned method of randomly dividing a larger collection of items in half to form two randomly parallel tests.

It is somewhat more complicated to determine measurement error due to subjectivity of scoring. Assume that trait variation and content differences have both been ruled out as major sources of unreliability by the above methods. A separate set of comparisons are needed for each rater: If possible, have each score responses to alternative forms given (1) 2 weeks apart to one group of subjects and (2) on the same day to another group of subjects.

If correlations between raters are high for both groups, there is little unreliability from any source, including that due to subjectivity of scoring. If the correlation over the 2-week interval is substantially less than the correlation for tests taken on the same day, scoring is probably reliable but the trait is temporally unstable, which may be as desired. If both correlations are consistently low in various studies that use different raters, it is difficult to determine what went wrong since the rater is in essence part of the item.

Unreliability of scoring may indicate that the trait does not exist in any manner that is consistent over judges, or it may indicate that the raters are inconsistent, perhaps because of lack of training. Sometimes, judgmental unreliability can be overcome by using a more objective form of measurement. If the measurement problem is meaningful and one must employ subjective scoring methods, the rules for scoring should be improved. If this increases the reliability, unreliability of scoring contributed to the earlier measurement error. Sometimes a criterion exists to establish the accuracy of each rater. In other cases, one can only correlate each rater with the average rater. If one is clearly better than the others by either standard, have that individual train other raters.

If raters tend to agree with themselves when scoring the same subjects on alternative forms, one should ask whether or not there is measurement error because of differences among raters. This can be easily determined by correlating scores obtained from different raters on the same and alternative forms of the measure. Raters sometimes develop their own idiosyncratic methods of scoring and may not agree with one another even though each behaves consistently with his or her own rules. This works like other sources of measurement error to attenuate relations found between variables in research.

The need to investigate alternative forms of a measure depends very much on the type of measure. If the domain of content is easily specified, there is little subjectivity of scoring, and people tend to be stable over time, coefficient α provides an excellent estimate of reliability. This is true, for example, for most aptitude and achievement tests. Alternative forms are needed if the trait is suspected to vary considerably over relatively short periods of time, as is true for statelike measures such as moods and some attitudes.

Sometimes the experimenter must compose alternative forms to demonstrate that there is a definable domain of content. This occurs with some projective techniques, such as the Rorschach, where there is some question as to whether or not it is possible to construct an alternative form. If an alternative form cannot be constructed, the domain of content cannot be defined, and one cannot accurately communicate what is being measured, it is doubtful that anything of importance is being measured.

## Other Estimates of Reliability

Coefficient α and correlations between alternative forms (under the various conditions mentioned previously) are the basic estimates of reliability. There are other ways to estimate reliability which were once encountered in research reports, but most are not presently recommended for most measurement problems.

The split-half approach was once the dominant way to estimate reliability. In this method, test items are divided in half, usually by placing the even-numbered items in one group and the odd-numbered items in the other group. Scores on the two half-tests are then correlated. Equation 6-19 is then applied to the correlation between the half-tests to estimate the reliability of the whole test. This method was popular before computers became available because split-half correlations are easier to compute by hand than α (α can be shown to equal the average of all possible correlations obtainable by splitting the test in half different ways). The availability of computer programs makes this method generally obsolete, but it still has some applications (see Chapter 9). We have noted that any method based upon internal consistency is difficult to use with speed tests. In addition, split-half methods are likely to provide misleading estimates when items are ordered in terms of difficulty, as is often the case. Even if you do not have access to a program to compute coefficient α directly, it is very simple to obtain the required variance of the test as a whole and the sum of the item variances. An alternative approach, based upon the repeated measures, ANOVA (Hoyt's method), appears later in the chapter.

The retest method, in which the same people are retested by the same test after a period of time, is often used instead of the alternative-form method to determine reliability. However, the retest method often has serious problems, the most obvious being that memory for the first test usually influences the retest. Subjects tend to repeat their responses to the extent that they remember them. They also tend toward repeated work habits and similar guesses. All of these tendencies make the correlation between tests spuriously high.

Another difficulty with the retest method is that it does not fit very well into the domain-sampling model because it is only partly dependent on the interitem correlations.

In the model, the reliability of any fixed-length test is strictly a function of the average correlation among items. However, correlations between different items might be zero, but each item might correlate highly with itself over the two testings, even ignoring the role of memory. This is another way of saying that a measure that has no internal consistency may be quite stable over time.

Thus, a relatively high retest correlation can arise with low internal consistency. As we have stressed, a test should "hang together" in that the items should correlate highly with one another. Otherwise, it makes little sense to add scores over items and speak of the total score as measuring any attribute. The major information supplied by the retest method is negative: If the retest correlation is low, the alternative form correlation will be even lower. Logically, a measure which has low temporal stability will not be a good predictor of future behavior, by definition.

We recommend that the retest method generally not be used to estimate reliability, but there are some exceptions. Retests are sometimes relatively unaffected by a prior testing. Suppose, for example, an individual is required to rate the attractiveness of a large number of designs. It would be very difficult to remember individual ratings because of the sheer number of ratings and the nature of the stimuli, and so retest ratings would be relatively independent of the earlier test. Scores also tend to be more nearly independent as the time between testings increases.

## Long-Range Stability

We previously suggested a 2-week interval between administration of alternative forms. This is largely a matter of convenience to permit short-range fluctuations in abilities and personality characteristics to be manifest while minimizing subject attrition. It is often important to assess the stability of scores over longer periods of time— 6 months or more. If, for example, alternative forms given 6 months apart correlate less than those given 2 weeks apart, the difference reflects the dynamic nature of the trait. As mentioned previously, what is considered error and what is considered systematic depend on the way measurement tools are used, i.e., the scientific generalizations that are desired.

If a measure is to represent the relatively enduring status of a trait, it must remain stable over the period in which scores were employed for that purpose. The IQ is a good example of a relatively enduring characteristic of adults. It might change gradually over a period of years but not markedly within a year unless some unusual circumstance such as trauma intervenes. If a temporally unstable measure is used either to make practical decisions about people or in research, measurement error will reduce the validity of the decisions. The previous chapter introduced some of the psychometric issues related to measuring change. Collins and Horn (1991) present the views of many investigators who have been involved in this issue. Psychometricians have been accused of assuming that psychological traits remain largely stable throughout life and thus that very little can be done to improve people. It is in fact true that most past psychometric models assumed static traits for convenience. However, this property is not inherent in the concept of measurement error, and much current research is directed toward developing better models to describe change.

## USES OF THE RELIABILITY COEFFICIENT

The previous section showed that it is meaningful to think of a test as having a number of different reliability coefficients, depending on which sources of measurement error are considered. In particular, internal consistency needs to be separated from temporal stability. In practice, however, investigators tend to speak of a reliability coefficient for a test which summarizes the amount of measurement error expected from using the instrument in a given population and reflecting its internal consistency.

This striving for simplicity is understandable, but at least two types of reliability coefficients should be computed and reported for any test that will be employed widely. First, coefficient α (Eq. 6-26) should be reported for all forms of the test. Second, correlations should be reported among alternative forms. Alternative forms are not available for many tests employed in basic research in the behavioral sciences, but they are available for many commercially distributed instruments.

We previously said why correlations among alternative forms potentially reveal some sources of measurement error not detected by coefficient α even though the difference is usually small. The alternative forms should be administered at least 2 weeks apart in order to assess the measurement error due to temporal instability. Correlations between alternative forms administered on the same day contain important supplementary information about reliability when it is possible to obtain them.

Alternative forms should be independently scored by different persons if scoring is subjective. If, for example, five persons score the first form and five other persons score the second, coefficients can be obtained from the two sets of ratings. It is important to remember that coefficient α can be obtained from ratings as well as conventional test questions.

To the extent that different approaches to obtaining the reliability coefficient produce somewhat different results, the appropriate coefficient for gauging the stability of traits and in making statistical corrections depends upon the measurement method to be employed. If, for example, the measurement method requires raters, the reliability coefficient should take measurement error due to raters into account (see the section titled "Generalizability Theory" below for some specific procedures). The lowest reliability estimate obtained by a sensible approach is preferred in order to be on the conservative side when in doubt. One can then say that the reliability is no smaller than "so much," at the very least. Fortunately, most well-standardized tests usually provide similar reliability estimates, allowing these differences to be ignored.

The major use of reliability coefficients is to communicate the repeatability of the results. The reliability coefficient is one index of the effectiveness of an instrument, as at least some reliability is necessary for any type of validity. The reliability coefficient has several uses which are discussed in the following sections.

### Corrections for Attenuation

One of the most important uses of the reliability coefficient is to estimate the extent to which obtained correlations between variables are attenuated by measurement error. Previously, Eq. 6-36 was derived as the correction for attenuation:

$$r'_{12} = \frac{r_{12}}{\sqrt{r_{11}r_{22}}}$$

The $r'_{12}$ is the expected correlation between two perfectly reliable variables. If the correction is to be made for only one of the two variables, only that variable's reliability coefficient appears under the radical in the denominator.

There is some controversy about when the correction for attenuation should be applied. One could argue that it fools one into believing that a better correlation has been found than was actually obtained. Another justifiable criticism of many uses of the correction for attenuation is that it sometimes provides a very poor estimate of the correlation really obtained between variables when they are actually made more reliable. This can occur if the reliability estimate is poor; e.g., the sample is small. That poor estimates are often obtained is illustrated by the fact that corrected correlations sometimes are greater than 1.00! However, there are some appropriate uses of the correction for attenuation given good reliability estimates. One such use is in personality research to estimate the correlation between two traits from imperfect indicators of these traits. Determining the correlation between traits is typically essential in this area of research, but if the relevant measures are only modestly reliable, the observed correlation will underestimate the correlations among the traits.

Another important but often misleading use of the correction for attenuation is in applied predictive validity settings. If, as often happens, the criterion is unreliable, a correction on the criterion side may be misleading since you may or may not be able to improve its reliability. Sometimes improvement is possible, as by using multiple raters of performance instead of one. However, this is often not the case, as when an employee is known well by only one supervisor. A correction on the predictor side is justified only if one could actually improve its reliability, as by adding new items. By definition, a double correction is appropriate only when changes are actually contemplated in both the predictor and criterion.

Since perfect reliability is only a handy fiction, results from applying the foregoing formula for the correction for attenuation are always hypothetical. It is more important to estimate the increase in the correlation between two variables when the reliability is increased to a particular amount, which may be done using Eq. 7-1:

$$r'_{xy} = r_{xy} \frac{\sqrt{r'_{xx}r'_{yy}}}{\sqrt{r_{xx}r_{yy}}} \tag{7-1}$$

where $r'_{xy}$ = estimated correlation between variables $x$ and $y$ if their reliabilities are changed

$r'_{xx}$ = changed reliability for variable $x$

$r'_{yy}$ = changed reliability for variable $y$

$r_{xx}$ = obtained reliability for variable $x$

$r_{yy}$ = obtained reliability for variable $y$

Equation 7-1 can be illustrated where two tests correlate .30 and each test has a reliability of .60. If the reliability of each test is increased to .90, the expected correlation between the more reliable tests will be

$$r'_{xy} = .3 \; \frac{\sqrt{(.9)(.9)}}{\sqrt{(.6)(.6)}} = .45$$

Although $r_{xx} = r_{yy}$ and $r'_{xx} = r'_{yy}$ in the example, Eq. 7-1 works equally well if all four reliability coefficients differ from one another, if both reliabilities are lowered (as when one contemplates shortening a test), or if the reliability of one test is increased and the reliability of the other is decreased. It is particularly useful to employ Eq. 7-2 in conjunction with Eq. 6-18, the Spearman-Brown prophecy formula. For example, use the prophecy formula to estimate the effects of tripling a test's length upon its reliability and then use this new reliability to estimate the new validity.

If only one of the two reliabilities is to be changed, Eq. 7-1 simplifies to:

$$r'_{xy} = r_{xy} \; \frac{\sqrt{r'_{xx}}}{\sqrt{r_{xx}}} \qquad\qquad (7\text{-}2)$$

This version of the formula is useful in estimating how much a predictor's validity will change if its reliability is changed.

It should be evident from inspecting Eqs. 7-1 and 7-2 that corrected correlations are seldom dramatically different from the observed correlations. Thus, a dramatic increase in each test's reliability from .60 to .90 in the above example only increased their correlation from .30 to .45. This increase may well be important, but it is much less than intuition suggests. Furthermore, if only one variable's reliability was increased to .80, the original correlation of .30 would only increase to .35.

It is common to hear that some low correlations would probably have been much higher if the measures were more reliable. In one case, the average correlation was about .15, and the average reliability was about .60. Even if the average reliability of the tests were increased to .90, the average correlation could be less than .25. The investigator in this case was probably thinking about average correlations of .40 or .50, but these could not possibly occur. Two measures usually correlate poorly because they measure different things, not because they are plagued by measurement error.

## Confidence Intervals

The reliability coefficient may also be used to establish confidence intervals for obtained scores. Equation 6-34 showed that the standard error of measurement for variable $x$ is

$$\sigma_{\text{meas}} = \sigma_x \sqrt{1 - r_{xx}}$$

The standard error of measurement is the estimated standard deviation of obtained scores if any individual is given a large number of tests from a domain. The concept will be expanded upon later in this chapter to take different sources of error into account.

The $\sigma_{meas}$ is useful in establishing confidence intervals for scores to be expected on many alternative forms of a test. Chapter 6 noted, however, that one should establish such confidence intervals symmetrically about the person's true score and not the actual score. If, for example, an individual has an IQ of 130 on a particular test and the $\sigma_{meas}$ is 5, it is incorrect to say that the 95 percent confidence interval for that person extends from 120 to 140 ($130 - 2\sigma_{meas}$ to $130 + 2\sigma_{meas}$). Even though the practice in most applied testing has been to center confidence intervals about obtained scores, this is incorrect because obtained scores are biased, high scores tending to be biased upward and low scores downward (see Table 4-2 and Chapter 6). A related point is that this bias is due to unreliability affects averages of extreme groups: The means of extreme groups will always be less disparate on a retest than they were on the original measure because of regression toward the mean.

Before establishing confidence intervals, one must obtain estimates of unbiased scores. Unbiased scores are the average scores people would obtain if they were administered all possible tests with a constant number of items from a domain. These true scores are estimated as follows:

$$t' = r_{xx}x \qquad (7\text{-}3)$$

The individual in the previous example with an IQ of 130 has a deviation score $x$ of 30. If the reliability was .90, the estimated true score $t'$ would be 27 in deviation-score units. Adding back the mean IQ of 100 gives an estimated true score of 127 in IQ units. This approach allows one to establish confidence intervals for deviation scores or their raw-score equivalents. The correct procedure is to set the 95 percent confidence interval as extending from two standard errors of measurement below 127 to two standard errors above 127. If $\sigma_{meas}$ is 5, the interval then would extend from 117 to 137. If a person were administered a large number of alternative forms of the test, 95 percent of the obtained scores would be expected to fall in that interval; the average of the obtained scores would be 127 and not 130. A person with an IQ of 70 on that same test would have a 95 percent confidence interval extending from 63 to 83.

Equation 6-34 dealt with describing the probable range of observed scores for a fixed true score. Using the notation of Chapter 4, it would be appropriate to symbolize the standard error of measurement ($\sigma_{meas}$) as $\sigma_{x.t}$ because the intent is to predict scores on an observed variable ($x$) from a given true score ($t$). However, it is at least as possible that you may be interested in describing the probable range of true scores consistent with a given observed score. This requires Eq. 7-4 (Dudek, 1979), which provides the standard error of measurement in predicting true scores from observed scores:

$$\sigma_{t.x} = \sigma_x\sqrt{r_{xx}(1 - r_{xx})} \qquad (7\text{-}4)$$

The difference between Eq. 6-34 and 7-4 was noted as far back as Guilford (1936) who referred to the resulting quantities as the "standard error of a raw score" and the "standard error of a true score," respectively. Lord and Novick (1968) used the terms "standard error of measurement" and "standard error of estimation." Note that there is less error in estimating true scores from an observed score than the converse by a factor of the square root of $r_{xx}$ (i.e., $r_{xt}$), the reliability index. Regardless of which is used, the confidence interval should be centered around the estimated (regressed) observed score (Eq. 7-3).

Yet a third possibility discussed by Dudek (1979) is to estimate the probable range of scores on one form of a test ($y$) given a score on an alternative form ($x$). This involves estimating fallible scores from a given fallible score and leads to

$$\sigma_{y.x} = \sigma_y \sqrt{1 - r^2_{xx}} \qquad (7\text{-}5)$$

(It is assumed that $r_{yy} = r_{xx}$ since these are alternative forms).

Note that the results of using Eq. 7-5 will be numerically larger than the result of using Eq. 6-34 and therefore Eq. 7-4, but also keep in mind that different quantities are being estimated in the three cases. Lord and Novick (1968) term the result of Eq. 7-5 the "standard error of prediction."

One rarely estimates true scores in the applied assessment of static constructs except to center a confidence interval. The asymmetric confidence intervals relative to obtained scores are useful as a reminder that any obtained score is biased "outward" relative to the mean. In fact, estimated true scores correlate perfectly with obtained scores and have little practical utility in this context. It is easier to interpret the individual's obtained score. Most commercially distributed test manuals do an extremely poor job of reporting estimated true scores and confidence intervals for expected obtained scores on alternative forms. For example, intervals are often erroneously centered about obtained scores rather than estimated true scores. Often, the topic is not even discussed.

Unlike estimated true scores, confidence intervals are important to keep in mind when making decisions about individuals. It is perhaps sobering that obtained $z$ scores for an individual on a test whose value of $\alpha$ is .9, generally a more than acceptable value, will have an $\sigma_{meas}$ of approximately .3. This value is almost one-third the size of the distribution of scores in general and illustrates the fallibility of individual scores. This should not deter accepting the rank ordering of individuals, since this is the best bet of the true rank ordering.

There seldom is a need to estimate true scores *or* establish confidence intervals when comparing groups. The major concerns in such research are with how much the measurement error lowers correlations and how much it contributes to the error components in statistical treatments. However, the estimated true scores may be used to measure change over time, as noted in the last chapter. The main problem with using Eq. 7-3 to estimate true baseline and retest scores is that it does not take the possible correlation of errors into account. More complex methods of regression (e.g., generalized least squares) can overcome this problem. For a further discussion of the measurement of change, see Cronbach and Furby (1970), Nesselroade, Stigler, and Baltes (1980), Labouvie (1982), and Rogosa, Brandt, and Zimowski (1982). Donaldson (1983) discusses this problem in application to factor analysis.

## Effect of Dispersion on Reliability

The size of the reliability coefficient is directly related to the standard deviation of obtained scores for any sample of subjects since the reliability coefficient is a correlation coefficient. Equation 7-6 is a variant of Eq. 6-12 with slightly changed notation, reflecting the fact that total variance equals true score variance plus the variance of the errors of measurement:

$$r_{xx} = 1 - \frac{\sigma^2_{meas}}{\sigma^2_x} \tag{7-6}$$

The variance of the errors of measurement is approximately independent of the standard deviation of obtained scores. In other words, the standard error of measurement is considered to be a fixed characteristic of any measure, regardless of the sample of subjects under investigation. This is a relatively safe assumption unless one deals with persons at the extremes of the distribution, e.g., the upper and lower 10 percent of individuals. It should clear that the reliability coefficient will be larger in more variable samples.

For example, Bernstein and Garbin (1985) obtained scores on scale 2 of the Minnesota Multiphasic Personality Inventory, a depression measure. The scores were obtained from both job applicants and patients undergoing psychotherapy. The job applicants consistently "put their best foot forward" and did not admit to depressive symptoms. In contrast, some therapy patients had problems with depression, but others did not, and so that this group was quite varied. The respective standard deviations were 3.3 and 5.7. Consequently the coefficients α for the two groups were .31 and .63. At best, the former value only allows one to make statements about extreme scores (which is all it was used for). More detailed statements about level are possible in the therapy group.

Equation 7-6 estimates how much the reliability changes when the variance of obtained scores changes. If the error variance for one sample was 2.0 and the total variance was 8.0, the reliability would be .75. If a new sample had a total variance of 10.0, the error variance should remain at 2.0. Consequently, the reliability would be .80. After the standard error of measurement is found for one sample, it is thus easy to estimate what the reliability would be in another sample with a different standard deviation of scores. The accuracy of this estimate depends on the assumption of equal standard errors of measurement. This assumption is usually, but not necessarily, safe.

Even though the reliability varies with the dispersion of scores, this does not alter the meaning of the reliability coefficient in any particular sample of people. The reliability coefficient is the ratio of true-score variance to obtained-score variance. If that ratio is small, measurement error will attenuate correlations with other variables. If the total group of subjects in a study has a standard deviation of scores which is not much larger than the standard error of measurement, it is hopeless to investigate the variable in correlational studies. One situation where this is likely to happen is in studies of creativity. Subjects in these studies typically have an IQ of at least 120. The standard

*that's why one needs to establish reliability separately for every sample/study*

deviation of their IQs will not be much larger than the standard error of measurement, which severely limits correlation of IQ with the creativity measure.

In principle, this can be paradoxically welcome in experiments because it causes the observed variability of criterion scores to reflect measurement error rather than systematic individual differences in response to the treatment effects. This is most likely when subjects were homogeneous with respect to the dependent variable before the experiment was conducted. However, this is a very rare circumstance in practice. One usually finds substantial, reliable variance in individual differences relating to the dependent variable both before and after the experiment.

Keep in mind therefore that a reliability coefficient has numerical meaning only in reference to a specified population. The standard error of measurement (Eq. 6-34) should be relatively stable across populations which differ in variability because the resulting changes in the reliability coefficient and standard deviation are partially off-setting, at least in principle. Regardless, one can be misled (or misleading) by estimating coefficient $\alpha$ in one population and then assuming it will have the same value in a population whose variance is different.

## MAKING MEASURES RELIABLE

Of course, doing everything feasible to prevent measurement error from occurring is far better than assessing its effects after it has occurred. One reduces measurement error by (1) writing items clearly, (2) making test instructions easily understood, (3) adhering closely to the prescribed conditions for administering an instrument, (4) making subjective scoring rules as explicit as possible, and (5) training raters to do their jobs. Rules for scoring better individual intelligence tests are so explicit and clinicians usually so well trained that relatively little measurement error is present, even though clinicians can be a source of measurement error.

The ideal always is to remove subjectivity in scoring completely, which is generally impossible. For example, students of discrimination learning have long been interested in animals' "observing responses"—their tendency to look back and forth before responding. Conceivably, the number of such observing responses could be objectively recorded with a complex set of instruments, but if different raters, perhaps using videotapes, agree reasonably well in their scoring of observing responses, some subjectivity in scoring may be preferable to the expense and awkwardness of employing objective instruments, especially since they may tap the trait less well. Of course, there is a tradeoff with the additional goal of having measures that are unaffected by errors of human judgment.

### Test Length

A major way to make tests more reliable is to make them longer. For this and numerous other reasons in classical psychometrics, the maxim holds that a long test is a good test, other things being equal. This is true of both number of items in the usual sense and raters used in subjective scoring. If the reliability is known for a test with a given number of items, the Spearman-Brown prophecy formula can be used to estimate how much the reliability would increase if the number of items were increased by any factor $k$:

$$r_{kk} = \frac{kr_{11}}{1 + (k - 1)r_{11}} \qquad (6\text{-}18)$$

*[handwritten: can plug in α or alternate forms reliability estimate]*

If, for example, the reliability of a 20-item test is .70 and 40 items from the same domain are added to the test (making the final test three times as long as the original), the estimated reliability of the 60-item test will be

$$r_{kk} = \frac{(3)(.7)}{1 + (3 - 1)(.7)} = .88$$

The only assumption made in employing Eq. 6-18 is that the average correlation among the 20 items in the shorter test is the same as the average correlation among the 60 items in the augmented test. The assumption is violated if old items and new items differ systematically in content, as when they are drawn from different domains, or in reliability, as when the average correlation in the two sets differs. Either or both violations may occur when one selects the best items from the initial form. Under these conditions, the new reliability may be overestimated. Otherwise, Eq. 6-18 generally leads to fairly accurate predictions. This is particularly true when the shorter test contains at least 20 items. As noted in Eq. 6-13, the precision of the reliability estimate is directly related to the number of test items.

Equation 6-18 also can be used to estimate the effects of shortening a test on reliability. In this case $k$ equals the number of items on the shorter test divided by the number of items on the longer test, $r_{kk}$ is the estimated reliability of the shortened test, and $r_{11}$ is the reliability of the longer test. In the previous example, one could work backward from the reliability of .88 for the 60-item test and estimate the reliability of a 20-item test. By placing .88 as $r_{11}$ in Eq. 6-18 and making $k = \frac{1}{3}$, one recovers the original reliability of .70 for the 20-item test. Regardless of whether a test is lengthened or shortened, the precision of the estimate obtained from Eq. 6-18 depends mainly on the number of items on the shorter test. One would not expect a very precise reliability estimate using a 5-item test to estimate a 40-item test, or vice versa.

Equation 6-18 shows that reliability is a direct function of the number of test items and only this number for a given initial reliability. One might wonder how it could be accurate when there are other sources of measurement error in tests, e.g., temporal instability. As argued previously, the domain-sampling model considers many such sources of error. Coefficient $\alpha$ is sensitive to sources of measurement error that are present within the testing session as well as in the sampling of items. Alternative-form reliabilities can be made sensitive to all sources of error, including subjectivity of scoring and variations in abilities and personality characteristics over short periods of time.

If coefficient $\alpha$ is used in Eq. 6-18, the estimated reliability for a longer or shorter test takes the sources of error within the session and the sampling of content into account. If the alternative-forms correlation is used instead, the estimate also takes temporal instability and any other factors that may vary systematically between the two testings into account, e.g., the effects of using different raters in the two tests. This provides a good estimate of the alternative-form reliability for a longer or shorter test over the same period of time and with the same factors systematically varied.

Equation 6-18 also shows that the reliability necessarily approaches 1.0 as test length increases as long as the average correlation among items in a domain is positive. If the numerator and denominator of Eq. 6-18 are divided by $k$ and $k$ is allowed to approach infinity, $r_{kk}$ approaches 1.0. A positive average correlation means that the correlation between any two item samples ($r_{11}$) will also be positive. This might seem to be an easy way to obtain highly reliable tests, but the estimated number of required items may be prohibitively high when the average correlation is very small.

Equation 6-18 can also be modified to estimate the number of items required to obtain a particular reliability:

$$k = \frac{r_{kk}(1 - r_{11})}{r_{11}(1 - r_{kk})} \tag{7-7}$$

where $r_{kk}$ = desired reliability

$r_{11}$ = reliability of existing test

$k$ = number of times test would have to be lengthened to obtain a reliability of $r_{kk}$

The estimated lengthening of a 20-item test with a reliability of .50 required to obtain a reliability of .80 is

$$k = \frac{(.8)(1 - .5)}{(.5)(1 - .8)} = \frac{.4}{.1} = 4$$

Thus 80 items are required to achieve an estimated reliability of .80. A test of that length may be feasible, but see what happens when a 40-item test has a reliability of only .20 and a reliability of .80 is desired:

$$k = \frac{(.8)(1 - .2)}{(.2)(1 - .8)} = \frac{.64}{.04} = 16$$

A total of 640 items would be required to reach a reliability of .80. A 640-item test would almost always be impractical unless the items could be constructed very easily and administered very quickly. One can therefore see that if the average correlation among items in a domain is very low (e.g., only .05), the correlations between samples of items will be small and the number of items needed to achieve acceptable reliability will be prohibitively large.

## Standards of Reliability

A satisfactory level of reliability depends on how a measure is being used. In the early stages of predictive or construct validation research, time and energy can be saved using instruments that have only modest reliability, e.g., .70. If significant correlations are found, corrections for attenuation will estimate how much the correlations will increase when reliabilities of measures are increased. If these corrected values look promising, it will be worth the time and effort to increase the number of items and reduce measurement error in other ways. It can be argued that increasing reliabilities much beyond .80 in basic research is often wasteful of time and money. Measurement error attenuates correlations very little at that level. Strenuous and unnecessary efforts at standardization in addition to increasing the number of items might be required to obtain a reliability of, say, .90.

In contrast to the standards used to compare groups, a reliability of .80 may not be nearly high enough in making decisions about individuals. Group research is often concerned with the size of correlations and with mean differences among experimental treatments, for which a reliability of .80 is adequate. However, a great deal hinges on the exact test scores when decisions are made about individuals. If, for example, children with IQs below 70 are to be placed in special classes, it may make a great deal of difference whether a child has an IQ of 65 or 75 on a particular test. When selection standards are quite rigorous, decisions depend on very small score differences, and so it is difficult to accept any measurement error. We have noted that the standard error of measurement is almost one-third as large as the overall standard deviation of test scores even when the reliability is .90. If important decisions are made with respect to specific test scores, a reliability of .90 is the bare minimum, and a reliability of .95 should be considered the desirable standard. However, never switch to a less valid measure simply because it is more reliable.

## Limitations on the Reliability Coefficient's Utility

As noted in various points of this book, reliability estimates are usually based upon observed correlations and are thus affected by the similarities of the item distributions ($p$ values for dichotomously scored tests.) Assume, for example, that a test consists of a series of symptom descriptions. Most of the symptoms are rare, perhaps being endorsed 5 percent of the time, but one exceptional symptom occurs 50 percent of the time. Eliminating this exceptional item might actually improve coefficient $\alpha$. The same situation holds for abilities items (Loevinger, 1954). Should such items be eliminated?

From a strict domain-sampling framework, one would be strongly tempted to do so. After all, the domain-sampling model assumes equality of $p$ values within sampling error. However, suppose this disparity arose from the way the question was worded. It might be advantageous to include this item since it would help discriminate at the low end of the scale. The converse holds when an item has a disproportionately low $p$ value (see the section titled "Equidiscriminating Tests" in the next chapter).

One should be careful about thinking that an item is unrelated to a trait. Its low observed correlation may reflect statistical differences in its distribution relative to other items rather than differences in its content. Item selection based only upon the correlations between items and the total score can lead one to discard an item spuriously, especially if the process is stepwise like SPSS RELIABILITY. Such procedures do not take these statistical effects into account. The problem can be minimized considerably by looking at the item's distributional properties (e.g., its $p$ value) along with its correlation with total test score (discussed in more detail in the next chapter). If your sample is very large, biserial $r$, which attempts to control for the items's distributional properties, might be examined, but its large sampling error offsets its utility in samples of practical size. Finding useful items to construct a good scale is too difficult to allow these spurious influences to cause measures to be discarded prematurely.

Whereas heterogeneneities in item distributions may cause one to underestimate the worth of an item, a somewhat different problem may cause the sample estimate of $\alpha$ to be too high. As we have noted with regard to the multiple correlation (see Chapter 5), sampling error frequently causes statistics based upon sample correlations to be biased upward. In principle, $\alpha$ is a lower bound on the population reliability (the ratio of true variance to total variance). If it is based upon population correlations or covariances, it will equal the reliability when the items all relate linearly to the true scores and have equal variance (Lord & Novick, 1968, p. 88). However, a test with items that intercorrelate zero within the population, and therefore have zero population reliability, will probably produce a nonzero value of $\alpha$. Woodward and Bentler (1978) provide an estimate of the population lower bound for $\alpha$ that compensates for this bias.

$$\alpha_p = 1 - (1 - \alpha)F_\alpha \qquad (7\text{-}8)$$

where $\alpha$ = sample value of coefficient $\alpha$
$\quad F_\alpha$ = value obtained from a table of the $F$ distribution at a desired level of significance, e.g., .01 with $N - 1$ and $(N - 1)(k - 1)$ degrees of freedom
$\quad N$ = number of subjects
$\quad k$ = number of measures
$\quad \alpha_p$ = estimated true lower limit of the test's reliability

This correction will have minimal impact upon tests of at least moderate reliability and length if $\alpha$ is based upon 200 or more subjects.

## RELIABILITY OF LINEAR COMBINATIONS

So far, the discussion of reliability has been most concerned with the reliability of individual traits such as spelling ability, as manifested in the average correlation among items. Frequently, scale scores are linearly combined into composite measures, and it is usually desirable to evaluate the reliability of the composite. This is a separate issue from the reliability of the individual measures upon which it is based. One frequently used linear combination is the sum of the verbal and quantitative scores on the Graduate Record Examination. Simple linear combination based upon raw scores can be depicted as

$$Y = X_1 + X_2 + X_3 \qquad (5\text{-}1a)$$

(Capital letters are used since raw scores are typically combined).

Similar linear combinations are employed very frequently in basic research. One example might be to derive a measure of social participation ($Y$) as a linear combination of traits such as introversion-extroversion, social presence, and social anxiety ($X_1$, $X_2$, and $X_3$). The issue is to estimate the reliability of $Y$ from a knowledge of the reliabilities of the $X$ variables and their covariances.

One may be tempted to use Eq. 6-26 for coefficient $\alpha$ to estimate the reliability of $Y$. The result would be quite misleading unless the $X$ variables were all measures of the same trait, e.g., alternative forms of a test of spelling ability. The reliability of samples of items from the same domain depends entirely on the average correlation among the samples, but this is not true of samples of items from different domains.

Suppose that each test had a respectable reliability, but all three were mutually uncorrelated. Coefficient $\alpha$ would be zero, but it would be wrong to assume that the linear combination has a reliability of zero. The methods which will be developed extend the domain-sampling model to correlations among items from different domains of content and the reliability of linear combinations of these domains. The formulas to be developed for the reliability of linear combinations are analogous to those developed from the domain-sampling model and are really extensions of those for the one-domain case.

One proper approach to determining the reliability of a linear combination is to correlate alternative forms of the linear combinations. Thus alternative versions of $X_1$, $X_2$, and $X_3$, etc. (assuming they exist) could be administered on two different occasions. The correlation between total scores on the two occasions defines the reliability of the linear combination, assuming the traits are stable over the chosen time interval.

If alternative forms cannot be administered, the alternative-form reliability can be estimated as follows. The basic definition of the reliability of any variable is the ratio of true-score variance to total variance, e.g., Eq. 6-9. Thus the reliability of the linear combination is

$$r_{YY} = \frac{\sigma^2_{t_Y}}{\sigma^2_Y} \tag{7-9}$$

where $\sigma^2_{t_Y}$ = variance of true scores for linear combination

$\sigma^2_Y$ = variance of obtained scores for linear combination

In the example of a simple sum of three variables, the denominator was the variance of that sum, which equals $\bar{C}_Y$, the sum of all elements in the covariance matrix for the three variables. The numerator can be expressed as

$$\sigma^2_{t_Y} = \frac{1}{N}\Sigma(t_1 + t_2 + t_3)^2$$

By definition the true-score variance of $Y$ is the variance of the sum of the true scores for the $X$ variables, $t_1$, $t_2$, and $t_3$. Chapter 5 noted how the variance of a linear combination could be obtained by placing the variables in the sum on the sides of a square table, multiplying corresponding elements, and dividing each product by the number of people being studied ($N$). This results in a covariance matrix of true scores for the three variables. Each off-diagonal element is the covariance between two sets of true scores. Chapter 6 showed that the covariance of true scores for any two variables is identical to the covariance of obtained scores for these two variables. Thus the off-diagonal elements in the covariance matrix for true scores are identical to the off-diagonal elements in the covariance matrix for obtained scores.

The only difference between the two matrices is in the diagonal elements. Each diagonal element in the covariance matrix of obtained scores is a variance of obtained scores. Each diagonal element in the covariance matrix of true scores is the sum of the squares of true scores for that variable divided by $N$, i.e., the variance of true scores for that variable. Since the reliability of any variable in the linear combination equals the true-score variance divided by the obtained variance, the true-score variance equals the obtained score variance multiplied by the reliability. Thus the covariance matrix of true scores for the sum of three variables is

|       | $t_1$              | $t_2$              | $t_3$              |
|-------|--------------------|--------------------|--------------------|
| $t_1$ | $r_{11}\sigma_1^2$ | $\sigma_{12}$      | $\sigma_{13}$      |
| $t_2$ | $\sigma_{12}$      | $r_{22}\sigma_2^2$ | $\sigma_{23}$      |
| $t_3$ | $\sigma_{13}$      | $\sigma_{23}$      | $r_{33}\sigma_3^2$ |

Since the covariance matrix of true scores in the numerator of the equation differs from the covariance matrix in the denominator only in terms of diagonal elements, the former can be expressed in terms of the latter, as follows. To obtain the sum of the elements in the matrix of true scores, first subtract the sum of variances (the sum of diagonal elements) from the covariance matrix for obtained scores. Add to the remainder the sum of products of reliability coefficients and variances (the sum of diagonal elements in the covariance matrix for true scores). The reliability of the sum of variables will then be

$$r_{yy} = \frac{\bar{C}_Y - \Sigma\sigma_i^2 + \Sigma r_{ii}\sigma_i^2}{\bar{C}_Y} \tag{7-10}$$

$$= 1 - \frac{\Sigma\sigma_i^2 - \Sigma r_{ii}\sigma_i^2}{\bar{C}_Y} \tag{7-11}$$

Since $C$ is identical to $\sigma_Y^2$, Eq. 7-11 can be rewritten as

$$r_{YY} = 1 - \frac{\Sigma\sigma_i^2 - \Sigma r_{ii}\sigma_i^2}{\sigma_Y^2} \tag{7-12}$$

This version of the formula requires only the variance of the linear combination ($Y$), the variance of the individual variables in the linear combination, and estimates of each variable's reliability. For example, let (1) the variance of the sum of the three variables be 12, (2) the individual variances be 1, 2, and 3, respectively, and

(3) the individual reliabilities be 0.60, 0.70, and 0.80, respectively. The reliability of the sum is

$$r_{YY} = 1 - \frac{(1+2+3) - [(.6)(1) + (.7)(2) + (.8)(3)]}{12}$$

$$= 1 - \frac{(1+2+3) - (.6 + 1.4 + 2.4)}{12}$$

$$= 1 - \frac{6 - 4.4}{12}$$

$$= .87$$

If, as is often the case, variables were standardized before being summed, the co-variance of the sum of obtained scores would equal the sum of the elements in the correlation matrix for the variables being summed ($\bar{R}_Y$). The diagonal elements in the matrix would be 1s, and the off-diagonal elements would be correlations between variables in the sum. The covariance matrix for true scores would have off-diagonal elements equal to those in the correlation matrix for obtained scores, but the diagonal elements would be reliability coefficients rather than 1s. Equations 7-13 to 7-15 apply to the special case of standard scores:

$$r_{YY} = \frac{\bar{R}_Y - k + \Sigma r_{ii}}{\bar{R}_Y} \tag{7-13}$$

$$= 1 - \frac{k - \Sigma r_{ii}}{\bar{R}_Y} \tag{7-14}$$

$$= 1 - \frac{k - \Sigma r_{ii}}{\sigma_Y^2} \tag{7-15}$$

The $z$-score versions of the formula for the reliability of a sum can be illustrated when the three variables being summed each have reliabilities of .60 and each pair correlates .50. Then $k = 3$, and the sum of reliabilities equals 1.8. The variance of $y$ (lowercase is used because a linear combination of $z$ scores has a mean of .0 even though it rarely has a standard deviation of 1) equals $3 + (6)(.50) = 6$ (there being six off-diagonal elements in the correlation matrix), and so the result is

$$r_{YY} = 1 - \frac{3 - 1.8}{6} = .8$$

Going back to Eq. 7-15 one can see that in the special case where only two sets of standard scores are summed, the following special formula can be used:

$$r_{YY} = 1 - \frac{2 - r_{11} - r_{22}}{\sigma_Y^2} \tag{7-16}$$

The computations are as follows if each variable being summed has a reliability of .60 and their correlation is .50:

$$r_{YY} = 1 - \frac{2 - .6 - .6}{3} = .73$$

The variance of $y$ equals the sum of the elements in the two-variable correlation matrix, which equals 2.0 plus twice their correlation. This makes the denominator of the fraction on the right equal 3.0.

## Negative Elements

It has been thus far assumed that scores are being added, but the logic of Eq. 7-12 applies equally well when some variables are subtracted (have negative weights), as with the following linear combination:

$$Y = X_1 + X_2 - X_3$$

The fact that $X_3$ is subtracted does not affect the logic. There are still $k$ (three) variables, and the reliabilities of the three variables are not affected. The only term affected is the denominator $(\sigma_Y^2)$—the variance of the linear combination which is obtainable by the methods of Chapter 5. Furthermore, Eq. 7-15 could be applied if the three variables were standardized.

If variable $X_3$ correlates positively with the other two variables, placing a minus sign before it in the linear combination reverses the signs of the correlations of $X_3$ with the other two variables. It would also reduce $\sigma_Y^2$ compared to what it would have been had it been added rather than subtracted. Conversely, if $X_3$ correlated negatively with $X_1$ and $X_2$, the minus sign in the linear combination would increase $\sigma_Y^2$ over what it would have been had it been added. The larger the variance of the linear combination, the greater the reliability. Consequently, the pattern of positive and negative signs in the linear combination directly affects the reliability of the combination.

## Weighted Sums

The above method can be extended to weighted sums. The following is a weighted sum of standardized variables:

$$y = b_1 z_1 + b_2 z_2 + b_3 z_3$$

The variance of $y$ equals the sum of all elements in the weighted correlation matrix. As noted in Chapter 5, the diagonal elements contain squared weights, and each off-diagonal element contains the correlation between two variables multiplied by the products of the weights of the two variables. The sum of elements in this matrix that provides the variance of the observed weighted sums is divided into the sum of elements in the matrix that provides the variance of the true weighted sums. The off-diagonal elements are the same in the two matrices, but the diagonal elements in the latter are squared weights multiplied by reliability coefficients. Equation 7-15 can then be modified to obtain the following formula for the reliability of a weighted sum of standardized variables:

$$r_{yy} = 1 - \frac{\Sigma b_i^2 - \Sigma b_i^2 r_{ii}}{\sigma_y^2} \qquad (7\text{-}17)$$

where $b_i$ = weight for variable $z_i$

$r_{ii}$ = reliability of variable $z_i$

To apply Eq. 7-17, one first obtains the variance of the sum of weighted standard scores ($y$), which is the denominator of the right-hand term in the equation. The sum of squared weights is obtained for the numerator. The square of each weight is multiplied by the corresponding reliability, these products are summed, and the sum is subtracted from the sum of squared weights. The remaining algebra is simple.

When variables are expressed as deviation scores rather than as standard scores, Eq. 7-17 can be modified as follows to obtain the reliability of the weighted sum:

$$r_{yy} = 1 - \frac{\Sigma b_i^2 \sigma_i^2 - \Sigma b_i^2 \sigma_i^2 r_{ii}}{\sigma_Y^2} \qquad (7\text{-}18)$$

Equations 7-17 and 7-18 apply equally well when some of the weighted variables have minus signs in the linear combination.

## Principles Concerning the Reliability of Linear Combinations

Linear combinations of variables are frequently encountered in practice. We have already shown that a regression equation is a weighted linear combination of variables, weighted to correlate as highly as possible with a criterion variable. Chapters 11 through 13 will show that factors are also linear combinations of variables. Most other methods of multivariate analysis [e.g., discriminant analysis (Chapter 14)], involve linear combinations. Consequently the reliability of a linear combination of variables is an omnipresent issue in psychological measurement.

Although we previously said that the reliability of a sum cannot be estimated by coefficient $\alpha$ (Eq. 6-26), a close look at the basic formula for the reliability of a linear combination (Eq. 7-12) will show that the two formulas are very similar. The former contains a multiplier in which the number of test items is divided by the number of test items minus 1, but otherwise the two equations look much alike.

The main difference is that the sum of reliabilities multiplied by variances is subtracted from the sum of the variances in the numerator of the ratio to determine the reliability of a linear combination. Thus the reliabilities of the variables tend to increase the reliability of a linear combination over that predicted from coefficient $\alpha$. As mentioned previously, the similarity of these two equations is no accident: The formula for the reliability of a linear combination is an extension of the basic domain-sampling model to a multiple domain-sampling model. This is further evidence of the importance and extreme generality of the domain-sampling principle model.

Coefficient $\alpha$ is necessarily zero when all items are uncorrelated. A look at the standard-score version of the reliability of a sum of variables (Eq. 7-12) will show what happens when the correlations among variables are all zero. In that case $R = k$, the number of variables, reducing Eq. 7-12 to

$$r_y = \frac{\Sigma r_{ii}}{k} \qquad (7\text{-}19)$$

Equation 7-19 leads to the important deduction that the reliability of the sum is the average reliability of the variables when the variables are independent of one another. Thus if three standardized and uncorrelated variables had reliabilities of .60, .70, and .80, the reliability of their sum would equal .70. This would hold even if some of the variables were negatively weighted. Obviously, Eq. 7-20 also applies when the average correlation between measures is zero.

Another look at Eq. 7-15 shows what happens when the average correlation is not zero. The average correlation may be negative, which would occur if one computed the weighted difference between two variables. There is, however, a severe limit to the possible average negative correlation obtainable among the variables of a linear combination—two variables that each correlate negatively with a third probably correlate positively with each other.

One can readily determine this limit. Since the sum of all elements in a correlation matrix (including the diagonal elements) is the variance of their sum in standardized form and since a variance cannot be negative, a negative sum of off-diagonal correlations cannot be greater than the sum of diagonal values ($k$). By expressing the denominator of the ratio in Eq. 7-13 as $k$ plus the sum of off-diagonal correlations, one can see that the reliability approaches zero as the sum of off-diagonal correlations approaches minus the sum of reliabilities.

The higher the average correlation (assuming it is positive, as it usually is), the higher the reliability of the linear combination. To understand this rule, distinguish between correlations among variables before and after they are placed in linear combinations. This distinction is important because the correlation between two variables placed in a linear combination reverses sign if they are given different signs in the linear combination. In the simplest case, if two variables are positively correlated, the correlation will be negative for their difference, i.e., in the correlation matrix corresponding to the variance of the combination.

So far all the discussion of the reliability of linear combinations has concerned correlations after linear combinations are formed. To prevent confusion in that regard, all formulas were developed so that sums or averages of correlations did not explicitly appear. Instead, the correlations among variables in the linear combination were "hidden" in the variance of the linear combination. Of course, one would add or subtract variables depending on their signs in the combination when actually computing the variance of a linear combination. When that is done, the correct value is obtained for the variance of $y$. The remaining terms in the computing formulas are reliabilities when variables are standardized or both reliabilities and variances when they are deviation scores. Since reliabilities and variances are always positive, regardless of the signs variables are given, there is no way to become confused about the proper use of the formulas.

There is, however, considerable value in looking at correlations among variables *before* they are placed in linear combinations to show how much reliability may be expected from a particular linear combination. Here is an extreme case. If two variables correlate .60 and each has a reliability of .60, the reliability of their difference will be zero from Eq. 7-16. Obviously such a linear combination is worthless. Less extreme cases occur frequently in practice. If the two reliabilities are each .80 and the correlation between the two variables is .60, the reliability of the difference between the two variables will be only .50. In both cases the same reliability would have resulted if the correlations had been negative and the sums of the two variables computed.

Since the reliability of a sum increases with the size of the average correlation among variables, any set of signs in a linear combination that maximizes the positive sum of correlations will maximize the reliability. The problem is illustrated in the following correlation matrix for six variables:

|       | $x_1$ | $x_2$ | $x_3$ | $x_4$ | $x_5$ | $x_6$ |
|-------|-------|-------|-------|-------|-------|-------|
| $x_1$ | 1.0   | +     | +     | −     | −     | −     |
| $x_2$ | +     | 1.0   | +     | −     | −     | −     |
| $x_3$ | +     | +     | 1.0   | −     | −     | −     |
| $x_4$ | −     | −     | −     | 1.0   | +     | +     |
| $x_5$ | −     | −     | −     | +     | 1.0   | +     |
| $x_6$ | −     | −     | −     | +     | +     | 1.0   |

The matrix contains correlations among variables before they are placed in a linear combination. Variables $x_1$, $x_2$, and $x_3$ form a set whose members all correlate positively, and the same is true for variables $x_4$, $x_5$, and $x_6$. All correlations between members of the two sets are negative. If all variables were given positive signs, there would be more negative correlations than positive correlations. Consequently the sum of correlations might be near zero or even negative.

In this case, one could obtain the maximum reliability for any possible linear combination by giving negative signs to all three variables in either set (but not both). If one chose to give negative signs to variables $x_4$, $x_5$, and $x_6$, all correlations among the three would remain positive and would not change in size. They would remain positive because all three variables would still have the *same* sign. The important difference would be that the signs of all correlations between the two sets of variables, and therefore all correlations in the matrix, would become positive. This would maximize the variance of the linear combination and the reliability of the linear combination.

The problem is seldom as neat as this example suggests, however. An inspection of correlations among variables before they are placed in a linear combination often indicates that a planned linear combination of variables is not very reliable and that a different linear combination might be much more reliable. Of course, maximizing reliability is seldom the most important goal either in basic research or in applied work. For example, if a research hypothesis concerns how much better people do on the sum of three measures than they do on the sum of three other measures, there is no choice but to give positive signs to the first three variables and negative signs to the other three variables. Inspecting the correlations among the variables might show, however, that such a linear combination has a very low reliability, and so the study might be doomed before it is started.

## AN ANALYSIS OF VARIANCE APPROACH TO RELIABILITY

Any method which allows one to estimate true variance can be used to obtain a reliability coefficient. This includes methods for estimating error variance since the true variance can be obtained from the observed variance by subtraction. The reliability coefficient then follows as the ratio of true variance to total variance, Eq. 6-9.

Hoyt (1941) showed how the analysis of variance can be used to this end. This approach serves as the basis for generalizability theory (Cronbach, Gleser, & Rajaratnam, 1963; Cronbach, Gleser, Nanda, & Rajaratnam, 1972; Rajaratnam, Cronbach, & Gleser, 1963; Gleser, Cronbach, & Rajaratnam, 1965; for other antecedents see, Lindquist, 1953, and Medley & Mitzel, 1963, and for recent treatments see Brennan, 1983; Shavelson & Webb, 1991), considered in the next section.

### Some Basic Concepts

Although the ANOVA is usually taught in basic statistics as a means of testing group differences by means of the $F$ statistic, the emphasis here is upon estimating the magnitude of different sources of variance, and so we will consider some basic concepts. Standard sources such as Hays (1988) and Winer, Brown, and Michels (1991) treat the topic in depth.

The ANOVA, as noted in Chapter 5, is a special case of multiple regression. Categorical predictors (see Chapter 5) that reflect one or more treatments, which may be experimental manipulations or classificatory variables, are used. In the simple ANOVA, individual subjects fall in one, and only one, of several treatment groups which are considered different levels of a single factor (called a "facet" in generalizability theory). It is immaterial here whether the levels of the factor are fixed (the levels are specifically chosen because they are of interest to the researcher) or chosen at random, but it does matter in more complex designs. There is no intent to make statements about possible levels of a fixed factor that are not included for study. For example, an experiment may evaluate the effects of several different drugs. Other theoretically relevant drugs may exist, but the experiment is not applicable to them. In contrast, one seeks to generalize the results obtained from a random factor to levels that could have been included in the study but were not. The individuals chosen in an experiment are normally a random factor because one seeks to apply any conclusions beyond those actually studied.

We will let the first subscript for each score identify the individual within the group, and the second subscript denote the group, so that $X_{ij}$ is the $i$th individual within the $j$th group. In this case, there is no relation between the $i$th individual in one group and the $i$th individual in any other group. Because of this independence, individuals are said to be "nested" within groups. In the next design to be considered, individuals, in contrast, are crossed with another variable in that the $i$th individual is the same for the various levels of $j$. In some applications called "matched" or "blocked" designs, not considered here, the individual is not the same but is related in some way, e.g., in terms of comparable ability. The linear combination assumed to define $X_{ij}$ is the sum of (1) a constant or universal effect that applies equally to all individuals, (2) a treatment effect specific to the group to which the individual belongs, and (3) random error unique to each observation.

**1** The constant represents the population mean of all individuals. Its value ($\mu$) reflects how the stimuli are scaled and is usually not of interest. It is estimated from the sample grand mean of observations ($X_{..}$) (in this commonly used dot notation, the dots denote the variables over which averaging is performed, in this case both individuals and groups).

**2** The treatment effect for a given treatment level is the deviation between the population mean for the group to which the observation belongs ($\mu_j$) and $\mu$. It is estimated from the deviation between the sample group mean ($X_{.j}$) and $X_{..}$. This is usually of greatest interest because the null hypothesis in most inferential studies is that $\mu_j - \mu = 0$ for all groups, i.e., there are no group mean differences.

**3** The random error, denoted $e_{ij}$, reflects variation among individuals within groups (differences among individuals for whom the treatment is the same). It is assumed to be normally distributed when $F$ statistics are obtained in conventional applications of the ANOVA, but this is *not* necessary in generalizability theory when it is simply used descriptively. It is estimated as the deviation of $X_{ij}$ from the sum of the sample constant and treatment effects or, equivalently, as a deviation from $X_{.j}$.

Subtracting $X_{..}$ (the estimator of $\mu$) from each observation produces deviation scores. Squaring each deviation score, summing the squared scores over all observations to produce a sum of squares, and dividing by 1 less than the number of observations, the degrees of freedom for this effect, estimates the variance of all scores known as the total mean square ($MS_{total}$). This may be shown to be equal to (1) the variance of sample group means about the sample grand mean or mean square between groups ($MS_{between}$), and (2) the variance of individual scores about their sample group mean pooled over groups or mean square within groups ($MS_{within}$). These mean squares are simply special cases of the total, between-group, and within-group variance-covariance matrices discussed in Chapter 5. Calculations relevant to the ANOVA models used in psychometrics will be described in the following section.

We are presently interested in estimating variation in population treatment effects ($\sigma_t^2$) which cannot be observed directly. The $MS_{between}$ describes variation in sample treatment effects, but this value is also influenced by random error ($\sigma_e^2$) as well as $\sigma_t^2$, and so it is a biased estimator; it will undoubtedly exceed zero even when the population means are all the same. However, $MS_{within}$ can be shown to be an unbiased estimator of $\sigma_e^2$. The expected mean square (EMS) corresponding to any observed mean square describes the population sources of variance that are assumed to underlie it.

The major point is that one can obtain a least-squares estimate of $\sigma_t^2$ given $MS_{between}$ and $MS_{within}$. In particular, if there are exactly $n$ subjects in each group (the equal–$n$ case), $MS_{between} = n\sigma_t^2 + \sigma_e^2$ and $MS_{within} = \sigma_e^2$. As a result, $\sigma_t^2 = (MS_{between} - MS_{within}/n$. It is possible for estimates of $\sigma_t^2$ to be negative even though $\sigma_t^2$, a variance, itself must be positive, a shortcoming of the method of moments used in this estimation (see Chapter 4); treat $\sigma_t^2$ as zero if this is the case. We stress that we are *not* presently interested in the otherwise important fact that $F = MS_{between}/MS_{within}$. The present issue is one of estimating population sources of variance from sample data.

## Application to the Study of Reliability

More complicated ANOVA models are usually necessary for psychometric applications because the same individual typically responds to each item or may be judged by each of several judges ("treatment" in the previous section now corresponds to "item" or "judge"), and so individuals are crossed with items or judges. Responses to test items and/or judges' ratings form a basic data matrix (Fig. 2-1) with individuals (subjects, examinees, ratees) represented along rows and items or judges represented along columns. We will assume that the data are judges' ratings to make discussion comparable to that in the next section, but they could just as well be test items. The entries may be 1 or 0 (correct versus incorrect, pass versus fail, etc.), or they may fall along a multicategory continuum. One other reason for phrasing discussion in terms of judges' ratings is that it is easy to remember that $i$ denotes individuals and $j$ denotes judges. A third reason is to illustrate that ratings may be subject to the same analyses as item responses on an ordinary test.

These data form a repeated measures or treatment by subjects ANOVA design. Whereas the simple ANOVA contains only three effects (total, between-groups, and within-groups), the present design contains four: (1) total, as before, (2) variation among individuals, (3) variation among judges, and (4) residual variation due to the interaction of judges and individuals. This interaction reflects the fact that score $X_{ij}$ may not be exactly predictable from characteristics of the individual and judge alone and is error. It denotes that an individual rated relatively highly by one judge may be rated relatively poorly by another. In accord with the general principle that reliable tests produce a large variation in individuals' total test scores, we are most interested in maximizing variation among individuals (2) because this term directly reflects this desired variation. The somewhat complex role played by variation among judges, which also appears as variation in the difficulty of test items, will be considered in this chapter and the next.

Associated with each mean square is a sum of squares and degrees of freedom. The degrees of freedom for the total, individual, judge, and residual effects are the total number of observations minus 1, the total number of individuals minus 1, the total number of judges minus 1, and the product of the number of judges and the number of individuals minus 1, respectively. Each mean square is defined by the ratio of the corresponding sum of square to its degrees of freedom. Table 7-1 describes the partitioning process in terms of the observed scores ($X_{ij}$), the mean for each individual across judges ($X_{i.}$), the mean for each judge across individuals ($X_{.j}$), and the grand mean over judges and individuals ($X_{..}$). Computational formulas appear below.

TABLE 7-1   SOURCES OF VARIANCE, SUMS OF SQUARES, DEGREES OF FREEDOM, AND EXPECTED MEAN SQUARES IN A REPEATED MEASURES ANALYSIS OF VARIANCE DESIGN

| Source | Sum of squares | Degrees of freedom | Expected mean square |
|---|---|---|---|
| Individuals, ($i$) | $j\Sigma(X_{ij} - X_{i.})^2$ | $i - 1$ | $j\sigma^2_{ind} + \sigma^2_{residual}$ |
| Judges, ($j$) | $i\Sigma(X_{ij} - X_{.j})^2$ | $j - 1$ | $i\sigma^2_{judges} + \sigma^2_{residual}$ |
| Residual | $\Sigma(X_{ij} - X_{i.} - X_{.j} - X_{..})^2$ | $(i-1)(j-1)$ | $\sigma^2_{residual}$ |
| Total | $\Sigma(X_{ij} - X_{..})^2$ | $ij - 1$ | |

*Note:* $X_{ij}$ is the score for the $i$th individual made by the $j$th judge. $X_{i.}$ is that individual's mean, $X_{.j}$ is that judge's mean, and $X_{..}$ is the mean of all observations. The observed mean squares, not presented here, are simply the corresponding sums of squares divided by the degrees of freedom.

The reliability coefficient may be computed from these data using

$$r_{11} = \frac{MS_{ind} - MS_{residual}}{MS_{ind}} \tag{7-20}$$

In effect, the numerator of Eq. 7-20 estimates the product of the number of judges and true variance among individuals, and the denominator estimates the product of the number of judges and the observed variance among individuals. The terms for the number of judges cancel, leaving the expression as the ratio of true variance to total variance. This is the basic definition of any reliability coefficient.

The hypothetical results of having three judges rate eight people as pass versus fail are contained in Table 7-2.

The resulting variance-covariance matrix appears in Table 7-3. The sum of the elements of this matrix is 1.68, and the sum of the diagonal entries (variances) is .77. Using Eq. 6-26 for coefficient $\alpha$ with $k = 3$ measures (judges) results in

$$r_{11} = \frac{3}{2} \frac{(1.68 - .77)}{1.68}$$
$$= .81$$

TABLE 7-2   HYPOTHETICAL RATINGS OF EIGHT INDIVIDUALS BY THREE JUDGES

| Individual | Judge | | | Individual Total |
|---|---|---|---|---|
| | 1 | 2 | 3 | |
| 1 | 1 | 1 | 1 | 3 |
| 2 | 1 | 1 | 1 | 3 |
| 3 | 0 | 0 | 0 | 0 |
| 4 | 0 | 1 | 0 | 1 |
| 5 | 0 | 0 | 0 | 0 |
| 6 | 0 | 1 | 1 | 2 |
| 7 | 0 | 0 | 0 | 0 |
| 8 | 0 | 1 | 1 | 2 |
| Judge total | 2 | 5 | 4 | 11 |

TABLE 7-3   VARIANCE-COVARIANCE MATRIX AMONG
JUDGES' RATINGS DERIVED FROM TABLE 7-2

|  |  | Item | | |
| --- | --- | --- | --- | --- |
|  |  | $X_1$ | $X_2$ | $X_3$ |
| Item | $X_1$ | .21 | .11 | .14 |
|  | $X_2$ | .11 | .27 | .21 |
|  | $X_3$ | .14 | .21 | .28 |

In contrast, the computations needed for Hoyt's approach are as follows.

**1** *Total sum of squares.* Although the conceptual formula is given in Table 7-1, the computational formula is $\Sigma X_{ij}^2 - (\Sigma X_{ij})^2/N$. The expression $(\Sigma X_{ij})^2/N$ is known as the correction term. Square each observation, add the squares, and subtract the correction term. Thus, $1^2 + 1^2 + 0^2 + \cdots + 1^2 - 11^2/24$. Since $1^2 = 1$ and $0^2 = 0$, the present computation is simply $11 - 11^2/24$ or 5.96.

**2** *Sum of squares for individuals.* The computational formula is $(\Sigma X_{i.}^2)/j - (\Sigma X_{ij})^2/N$. Obtain the sum of squared sums for individuals, divide by the number of judges, and subtract the correction term. Thus, $(3^2 + 3^2 + 0^2 + \cdots + 2^2)/3 - 11^2/24$ or 3.96.

**3** *Sum of squares for judges.* The computational formula is $(\Sigma X_{.j}^2)/i - (\Sigma X_{ij})^2/N$. Obtain the sum of the squared sums for judges, divide by the number of individuals, and subtract the correction term. Thus, $2^2 + 5^2 + 4^2 - 11^2/24$ or .58.

**4** *Residual (error) sum of squares.* The residual sum of squares is the total sum of squares minus the sums of squares for individuals and judges: $5.96 - 3.96 - .58 = 1.42$.

**5** There are 7 *df* $(i - 1)$ for individuals, 2 *df* $(j - 1)$ for judges, and 14 *df* $[(i - 1)(j - 1)]$ for the residual. The 23 total degrees of freedom ($ij - 1$ or sum of the individual, judge, and residual degrees of freedom) is not needed.

**6** Divide each sum of squares by its associated degrees of freedom: (a) $MS_{ind} = 3.96/7 = .57$. (b) $MS_{residual} = 1.41/14 = .10$. (c) $MS_{judges}$ is not needed here but will be employed in a subsequent example and $= .58/2 = .29$). Hoyt's method therefore yields

$$r_{11} = \frac{.57 - .10}{.57}$$
$$= .82$$

The two estimates of $r_{11}$ would agree precisely if the results were carried to a greater degree of precision. You may be able to compute coefficient $\alpha$ directly (as in SPSS RELIABILITY, which is based upon Hoyt's approach) or fairly simply from the readily obtained item and total-score variances using a procedure like SAS PROC MEANS (choosing the option to obtain variances) and not need to use Hoyt's method. However, you may have conducted an ANOVA for other reasons and may find Eq. 7-20 easier. Either may be called coefficient $\alpha$ despite the difference in computational procedure, and the result links reliability theory and the familiar ANOVA.

## GENERALIZABILITY THEORY

### Basic Concepts

Generalizability theory is an extension of classical measurement theory in which different measures of the same individual may vary because what is measured differs as well as because of random error of measurement. It is an extension of domain-sampling theory to situations in which sampling proceeds factorially from more than one domain. Logically, it is closely related to issues in experimental design (Winer, Brown, & Michels, 1991), and so it might not appear relevant to clinicians and others doing field research. However, one of its major uses is when one or more judges (raters) evaluate a series of individuals with respect to multiple attributes, and so it is most useful in field studies. Two judges may disagree with each other because their judgments contain random measurement error in the sense previously described. However, they may also differ because they respond to different attributes.

For example, suppose two judges each rate a series of adolescents for aggressiveness. One judge may be more concerned with verbal aggression than the other, perhaps because of the unclear instructions they were given. The more they differ in what they consider "aggression," the less well they will agree and, in a more general sense, the more poorly both their ratings generalize to other possible judges. Although this causes their ratings to differ, it is *not* classical unreliability because it is nonrandom. In addition, specific judges are considered random samples from a universe or population of judges. An individual's trait score is the sum of an infinitely large number of judgments. Generalizability theory is essentially domain sampling in which one considers issues such as how well the ratings of a particular judge generalize to the domain of judges in general. One is usually not interested in a particular judge per se but rather in that judge as a representative of other potential judges.

To illustrate the difference between a classical analysis of a single judge's behavior (which is appropriate in certain contexts, but not here) and generalizability theory, consider Eq. 7-21 as a model for that judge's behavior:

$$x_{ij} = t_{ij} + e_{ij} \tag{7-21}$$

where $x_{ij}$ = observed rating of individual $i$ by judge $j$ as a deviation score
$t_{ij}$ = judge's systematic (true) component
$e_{ij}$ = judge's measurement error

The ratio of true variance (variance in $t_{ij}$ over individuals for a given judge) to the total variance (variance in $x_{ij}$ over individuals for a single judge) defines the extent to which that judge's ratings are influenced by random error and is a reliability coefficient ($r_{11}$) in the sense of sampling error as previously defined by Eq. 6-9. This reliability coefficient is directly related to the variance of $t_{ij}$ and inversely related to the variability of $e_{ij}$.

However, the reliability coefficient tells nothing about how that particular judge's ratings relate to other judge's ratings, which is at the heart of generalizability theory. A particular judge might be perfectly reliable yet differ systematically from the other judges, e.g., by rating an irrelevant attribute, such as the appearance of the individuals rather than their behavior. In order to consider differences among judges, assume that more than one judge evaluates the individual. Even when two judges evaluate the same attributes, one may be consistently more lenient or stringent than the other. Consider any given individual. The extent to which $t_{ij}$ varies across judges describes variation in how they conceptualize the trait. As noted above, variation in $t_{ij}$ over judges is not the same measurement error arising from simple domain sampling since it may also reflect systematic factors.

A generalizability coefficient or generic reliability coefficient (Lord & Novick, 1968) is a form of intraclass correlation (Hays, 1988, pp. 485–486) and is symbolized $\rho^2$. It describes how well the average judgments from a sample of one or more judges correlate with the average judgments from a population or universe of potential judges. A $\rho^2$ value, like an $r_{11}$ value, is defined as the ratio of true variance among individuals (symbolized $\sigma^2_{\text{ind}}$) to the sum of true variance plus random error variance ($\sigma^2_{\text{error}}$), which is in the spirit of the classical concept of reliability. However, what constitutes error variance depends upon how the ratings are structured in the sense of whether they reflect a single rating or a composite and whether the same or different raters rate the various individuals. It may or may not equal the $\text{MS}_{\text{residual}}$ as defined in Hoyt's method. Symbolically, $\rho^2$ may be expressed as

$$\rho^2 = \frac{\sigma^2_{\text{ind}}}{\sigma^2_{\text{ind}} + \sigma^2_{\text{error}}} \tag{7-22}$$

### Generalizability Studies and Decision Studies

Assume that judgments of aggressiveness are obtained from a study comparing the relative effectiveness of two or more forms of treatment. This type of study is known as a "decision ($D$) study" for the obvious reason that it is intended to make a decision, e.g., about the best form of treatment. Several considerations enter into designing a $D$ study properly. These include how many judges will evaluate each individual and whether or not a given judge will rate all individuals or not. Choice of strategy will be influenced by the extent to which $e_{ij}$ and $t_{ij}$ vary. One rarely has this knowledge at the beginning stages of inquiry, and it is wise to conduct a preliminary study to estimate these quantities. A study directed toward these issues or, more broadly, the degree to which an observed sample of measures generalizes to a population or universe, is called a "generalizability ($G$) study." Although a $G$ study is often a precursor of a $D$ study, it may be of interest in its own right.

Unfortunately, it is typical that no $G$ study is employed before conducting a $D$ study, and the judgmental strategy is made intuitively or upon the availability of judges. In other cases, generalizability data are obtained in parallel with the decision data. For example, one judge might evaluate all individuals, and a second judge may evaluate a subset of the individuals in conjunction with the primary judge as a check. Individuals seen by both judges contribute generalizability data. However, in both cases, the generalizability data cannot be used to select an optimal design for the main

(D) study. Clearly, the availability of a previous $G$ study, perhaps conducted by someone else, is important to an optimal outcome.

## A Single Facet Design

Hoyt's method is the simplest example of generalizability theory. It may be applied directly to what is called a single-facet $G$ study. We will apply the data from Tables 7-2
and 7-3 to perform a hypothetical evaluation of adolescent aggressiveness. A real
study would employ many more subjects, of course. Even though the eventual $D$ study
may use a single judge or have different judges evaluate different individuals, the most
useful $G$ study crosses judges with individuals—each judge evaluates each individual.
The minimum requirements for the study are two judges who each evaluate two individuals, but the stability of the resulting estimates improves as the square root of the
sample size. It is difficult to state the precise numbers of individuals and judges needed for the $D$ study without the $G$ study. Both the individuals and judges should be representative of those to be employed later: One should not conduct a $G$ study with highly trained judges if the $D$ study will use inexperienced judges, for example.

## Theoretical Considerations

The analysis is an extension of Eq. 7-21. One assumes that the systematic component
of a rating $(t_{ij})$ is the sum of three components: (1) a universal effect $(\mu)$ describing the
mean rating of all individuals by all judges in the domain, (2) the deviation of a particular individual's mean rating $(\mu_i)$ from $\mu$ $(\mu_i - \mu)$, and (3) the deviation of a particular
judge's mean rating $(\mu_j)$ from $\mu$ $(\mu_j - \mu)$. When $e_{ij}$ (which reflects both classical measurement error plus systematic disagreement among judges) is also considered, the
model simply states that a particular rating may be high because that individual is high
on that trait, because the judge tends to give high ratings, or because of error:

$$x_{ij} = \mu + x_{ij} = (\mu_i - \mu) + (\mu_j - \mu) + e_{ij} \tag{7-23}$$

Subtracting the scaling factor $(\mu)$ from both sides of the equation and expressing
the resulting term on the left-hand side, $X_{ij} - \mu$, as $x_{ij}$ provides

$$x_{ij} = (\mu_i - \mu) + (\mu_j - \mu) + e_{ij} \tag{7-24}$$

Recall that the corresponding sample sums of squares were 3.96, .58, and 1.42; the
degrees of freedom were 7, 2, and 14, and so the mean squares were .57, .29, and .10,
for individuals, judges, and error, respectively. As in the cases described above, appropriate computations can estimate three population variances from the sample mean
squares using the expectations provided in Table 7-1.

1  Residual error variance (variance in $e_{ij}$) $(\sigma^2_{\text{residual}})$
2  The variance of individuals over judges $(\sigma^2_i)$
3  The variance of judges over individuals $(\sigma^2_j)$

These population variance estimates are obtained as follows: The $\sigma^2_{residual}$ represents the error associated with a single average judge and is given simply by

$$\sigma^2_{residual} = MS_{residual} \tag{7-25}$$

However, the present case involves the sum (or average) of $j$ independent judges. Equation 7-26 describes the mean square for the composite error ($\sigma^2_{error}$) using the central limit theorem:

$$\sigma^2_{error} = \frac{\sigma^2_{residual}}{j} \tag{7-26}$$

Equation 7-27 estimates $\sigma^2_{ind}$:

$$\sigma^2_{ind} = \frac{MS_{ind} - MS_{residual}}{j} \tag{7-27}$$

Equation 7-28 estimates $\sigma^2_{judges}$:

$$\sigma^2_{judges} = \frac{MS_{judges} - MS_{residual}}{j} \tag{7-28}$$

Applying Eqs. 7-26 to 7-28 to the data yields

$$\sigma^2_{residual} = .10$$

$$\sigma^2_{error} = \frac{.10}{3} = .03$$

$$\sigma^2_{ind} = \frac{.57 - .10}{3} = .16$$

$$\sigma^2_{judges} = \frac{.29 - .10}{8} = .02$$

The conceptual form of the generalizability coefficient for these data is

$$\rho^2 = \frac{\sigma^2_{ind}}{\sigma^2_{ind} + \sigma^2_{residual}/j} \tag{7-29}$$

Substituting the corresponding mean squares leads to

$$\rho^2 = \frac{(MS_{ind} - MS_{residual})/j}{(MS_{ind} - MS_{residual})/j + MS_{residual}/j} \tag{7-30}$$

This simplifies in turn to a computational form:

$$\frac{MS_{ind} - MS_{residual}}{MS_{ind}} \tag{7-31}$$

Equation 7-31 is Hoyt's formula for the reliability, .82 in the present case, as it should be because "judges" play the same functional role as "items" (Lord & Novick's (1968) analysis is phrased in terms of "items".)

The standard error of measurement, which is the square root of the $\sigma^2_{error} = \sqrt{\sigma^2_{residual}/j} = \sqrt{.10/3} = .18$, may also be extracted from these data. A two-sided 95 percent confidence interval can be determined as ±1.96 times this standard error, and a 99 percent confidence interval can be determined as ±2.58 times this standard error. This assumes that the composite is expressed as the average of the three ratings. If the sum is used, multiply the resulting value by $j$.

The hypothetical data involve dichotomies, and so the concepts of standard error and confidence interval are strained. However, if these were ratings along a continuum, the confidence interval could be used to make absolute judgments about a score relative to a criterion or other reference point. For example, if the observed score is 3 ± .8 and the criterion for passing is a score of 2 or higher, the individual's score will be significantly higher than the cutoff. Likewise, the standard error of the difference between two scores can be estimated as $\sqrt{2}$ times the standard error of measurement. A confidence interval about this value can be used to determine whether two scores differ significantly from one another.

### Applying the Results of a Single-Facet G Study to a D Study

The power of the G study comes into play in choosing from some of the designs one might employ in a D study based upon preliminary data. Four possible designs are as follows:

**1** One judge may rate every individual.
**2** Multiple judges (not necessarily the same number as in the G study) may rate every individual.
**3** Raters and individuals may be paired so that each judge rates one and only one individual.
**4** Multiple judges may rate each individual, but each judge rates only one individual.

In each case, the appropriate generalizability coefficient follows from the general definition, Eq. 7-22. The individual component ($\sigma^2_{ind}$) does not change, but the error ($\sigma^2_{error}$) depends upon the design. For example, Eq. 7-32 describes the computation of $\rho^2$ conceptually if only one judge is selected at random from the domain of judges (option 1),

$$\rho^2 = \frac{\sigma^2_{ind}}{\sigma^2_{ind} + \sigma^2_{residual}} \qquad \text{(because } \sigma^2_{error} = \sigma^2_{residual}) \tag{7-32}$$

Substituting the mean squares used as estimators,

$$\rho^2 = \frac{(MS_{ind} - MS_{residual})/j}{(MS_{ind} - MS_{residual})/j + MS_{residual}} \tag{7-33}$$

This reduces to the computational form

$$\rho^2 = \frac{MS_{ind} - MS_{residual}}{MS_{ind} + (j - 1)MS_{residual}} \tag{7-34}$$

In the present case,

$$\rho^2 = \frac{.16}{.16 + .10} \qquad \text{(from Eq. 7-32)}$$

$$= \frac{.57 - .10}{.57 + (2)(.10)} \qquad \text{(from Eq. 7-34)}$$

$$= .61$$

Using a single judge instead of the average of three has the obvious effect of reducing the generalizability of the ratings. The standard error of measurement increases to $\sigma_{residual} = .32$.

Suppose you were planning to employ a particular judge in the $D$ study that you had used in the $G$ study, and further suppose that you used at least three judges in the original $G$ study. Equation 7-34 may underestimate or overestimate this judge's generalizability coefficient, depending upon whether he or she is better or poorer than the average judge. One index of a judge's "goodness" is that judge's correlation with the average rating. In the present case, the correlations for the three judges are .77, .87, and .92. Item-total correlations based upon a small number of variables (three in the present case) build in a substantial correlation between each of these variables and the total, but they do so for each variable so that the relative magnitudes are meaningful.

Recognizing that these correlations are based upon an unrealistically small number of observations (eight), the data suggest that the first rater is the most idiosyncratic and that the third rater is the least idiosyncratic. One may criticize the criterion of correlating a judge's ratings with the consensus (whether derived from a sample or from the population) as rewarding mediocrity, but unless there is a better yardstick, such as a physical definition of what is to be measured, this definition is most in keeping with the spirit of the model.

Equation 7-35 (Lord & Novick, 1968, p. 210, Eq. 9.8.4) may be used to estimate the generalizability coefficient for a specified judge. It assumes that at least three judges were used in the $G$ study, including the one designated.

$$\rho^2 = \frac{(j - 1)(\Sigma \sigma_{1i})^2}{2j\sigma_1^2 \Sigma \sigma_{ij}} \tag{7-35}$$

where $j$ = number of judges

$(\Sigma\sigma_{1i})^2$ = square of the sum of the covariances between the designated judge (judge 1)
and each of the other judges (judges $i$)

$\sigma_1^2$ = variance of the designated judges ratings

$\Sigma\sigma_{ij}$ = sum of the covariances between all pairs of judges other than pairs that include the designated judge (judges $i$ and $j$).

Recall from Chapter 4 that the covariance between two variables equals the product of their respective standard deviations and their correlation ($\sigma_{ij} = \sigma_i\sigma_j r_{ij}$).

When there are only three judges, where judge 1 is the designated judge and judges 2 and 3 are the two remaining, the formula simplifies to

$$\rho^2 = \frac{(\sigma_{12} + \sigma_{13})^2}{4\sigma_1^2\sigma_{23}} \tag{7-36}$$

Since Table 7-2 already contains the relevant data, one may estimate the generalizability expected from designating the first judge:

$$\rho^2 = \frac{(.11 + .14)^2}{(4)(.21)(.21)}$$
$$= .35$$

Likewise, the generalizability coefficient for the second rater is

$$\rho^2 = \frac{(.11 + .21)^2}{(4)(.27)(.14)}$$
$$= .68$$

And the generalizability coefficient for the third rater is

$$\rho = \frac{(.14 + .21)^2}{(4)(.29)(.11)}$$
$$= .96$$

Notice that in this atypical, but possible, example the third rater individually is more reliable than the sum of all three.

Now, assume that we are free to average the ratings of $k$ judges in the $D$ study, where $k$ may be a larger or smaller number than the $j$ used in the $G$ study (design 2). Again using the central limit theorem, $\sigma_{error}^2 = \sigma_{residual}^2/k$. Equation 7-37 describes the appropriate process:

$$\rho^2 = \frac{\sigma_{ind}^2}{\sigma_{ind}^2 + \sigma_{residual}^2/k} \qquad \text{(because } \sigma_{error}^2 = \sigma_{residual}^2/k) \tag{7-37}$$

Again substituting the mean squares used as estimators,

$$\rho^2 = \frac{(MS_{ind} - MS_{residual})/j}{(MS_{ind} - MS_{residual})/j + MS_{residual}/k} \tag{7-38}$$

which reduces to the computational form

$$\rho^2 = \frac{MS_{ind} - MS_{residual}}{MS_{ind} + (j - k)MS_{residual}/k} \tag{7-39}$$

Consequently, if two judges are chosen at random from the domain ($k = 2$), the estimated generalizability coefficient is

$$\rho^2 = \frac{.57 - .10}{.57 + (3 - 2)(.10/2)}$$
$$= .76$$

The estimated generalizability coefficient using four judges is

$$\rho^2 = \frac{.57 - .10}{.57 + (3 - 4)(.10/4)}$$
$$= .84$$

In this example, the differences in the generalizability expected using more than two judges is so small that it will not affect any validities in a noticeable manner. Indeed, you would be better off using a single judge who is known to be reliable. Your planning of the D study should consider its personnel costs.

The standard error of the mean rating is the square root of $\sigma^2_{residual}/k$. These are .22, .18, and .16 for two, three, and four judges, respectively. If the score is to be expressed as a sum of the $k$ judges, multiply these results by $k$.

Another approach to using $G$ data to estimate $\rho^2$ under either design 1 or design 2 is to apply the Spearman-Brown prophecy formula, Eq. 6-18, to the value of $\rho^2$ obtained in the $G$ study where $k/j$ is the factor by which the length of the test is altered. For example, if three judges were used in the $G$ study and you are planning to use six in the $D$ study, then simply determine the effect of making the test twice as long.

Design 3 assumes that a different judge rates each and every individual. For example, assume that a male and a female interact for a period of time and that each rates the other's sociability. The study provides two generalizability coefficients (men rating women and women rating men), but only one needs to be considered here. Variation among judges now becomes part of the error since judges are nested within individuals. A particular judge's tendency to give high or low ratings is canceled out in a crossed design because it applies equally to all individuals. However, part of the variation in an individual's rating is now determined by the "luck of the draw" in getting a high or a low rater. Ratings will vary more widely over individuals than in a crossed design because of the judges' idiosyncracies.

The design becomes a simple ANOVA. The total sum of squares now contains only two sources: (1) the individual effect, as before, and (2) the variation within each individual among judges pooled over individuals or the residual effect. The underlying sources of variation differ radically from the crossed design. The expected mean square for individuals equals $j\sigma^2_{ind} + \sigma^2_{judges} + \sigma^2_{residual}$, and the expected mean square for the residual is $\sigma^2_{judges} + \sigma^2_{residual}$. The presence of $\sigma^2_{judges}$ in both terms is the basis for the greater error variance. Equation 7-40 describes the generalizability coefficient:

$$\rho^2 = \frac{\sigma^2_{ind}}{\sigma^2_{ind} + \sigma^2_{judges} + \sigma^2_{residual}} \tag{7-40}$$

Equation 7-41 is a computational formula:

$$\rho^2 = \frac{MS_{ind} - MS_{residual}}{MS_{ind} + (j)MS_{judges}/i + (ij - i - j)MS_{residual}/i} \tag{7-41}$$

In the present case, this produces

$$\rho^2 = \frac{.57 - .10}{.57 + (3)(.57/8 + (8 \cdot 3 - 8 - 3)(.10/8)}$$
$$= .55$$

This demonstrates how variation among judges in the error term affects generalizability substantially even though it may sometimes be unavoidable. The standard error of the mean judgments is the square root of $\sigma^2_{judges} + \sigma^2_{residual} = \sqrt{.02 + .10} = .35$. In this artificial example, the judges are rather homogeneous ($\sigma^2_{judges} = .02$), which is not generally true.

Finally, consider design 4 where $k$ judges rate each individual, but each judge rates only one individual. Perhaps members of each of a series of committees rate their chair's effectiveness where no one serves on more than one committee. Because each individual (chair) is judged by several individuals, the generalizability coefficients will generally be higher than under design 3, just as they will generally be higher under design 2 than under design 1. Equation 7-42 describes the generalizability coefficient:

$$\rho^2 = \frac{\sigma^2_{ind}}{\sigma^2_{ind} + (\sigma^2_{judges} + \sigma^2_{residual})/k} \tag{7-42}$$

so that

$$\sigma^2_{error} = \frac{\sigma^2_{judges} + \sigma^2_{residual}}{k}$$

The formula defined in terms of mean squares is

$$\rho^2 = \frac{MS_{ind} - MS_{residual}}{MS_{ind} + j \cdot MS_{judges}/i \cdot k\ (i \cdot j - i \cdot k - j) \cdot MS_{residual}/(i \cdot k)} \tag{7-43}$$

Note that the $\sigma^2_{error}$ in Eq. 7-40 for design 3, $\sigma^2_{judges} + \sigma^2_{residual}$, is replaced by $(\sigma^2_{judges} + \sigma^2_{residual})/k$, which will be smaller. This is why one expects greater generalizability under design 4 than under design 3. Nonetheless, with $k = 2$ judges in the present case, the estimated generalizability is

$$\rho^2 = \frac{.57 - .10}{.57 + (3)(.57/8) + (8 \cdot 3 - 8 - 3)(.10/(8 \cdot 2))}$$
$$= .71$$

With $k = 3$ judges, the estimated generalizability is

$$\rho^2 = \frac{.57 - .10}{.57 + (3)(.57/8) + (8 \cdot 3) - 8 - 3)(.10/(8 \cdot 3))}$$
$$= .79$$

If adding judges has such a small effect, primary effort should be devoted to reducing variation among judges, as by devoting more effort to training. The standard errors for two, three, and four judges are, respectively, .24, .20, and .17, when scores are expressed as a mean. As above, multiply by $k$ if you express the score as a sum.

One can estimate generalizability coefficients for all four designs because the original $G$ study was conducted as a crossed design with multiple raters (design 2). As a result, variation among judges can be estimated separately from individual measurement error. Had design 1 been used, its data would have been useful only in a design-1 $D$ study because there is no way to estimate variation among judges. A design-3 $G$ study would have furnished data useful only in a design-3 or design-4 $D$ study, and a design-4 $G$ study would have furnished data useful only in a design-4 $D$ study. Variation among judges affects generalizability in a design-3 or a design-4 study, but it is completely confounded with measurement error.

In perhaps most cases, you can conduct a design-2 $G$ study by having a series of judges all rate a sample of individuals even if they cannot rate all the subjects in the $D$ study. This procedure is highly recommended because it allows you to explore all options. Of course, some problems inherently require different judges for each individual (design 3 or design 4).

It is common for judges to be assigned on the basis of scheduling convenience. One judge may be available at certain times, and another available at other times. This can be deadly if availability is confounded with a critical manipulation. For example, if one judge evaluates all the subjects in one treatment condition and another judge evaluates all the subjects in another condition, differences in the ratings of the two judges are completely confounded with treatment conditions. If there is a random relationship, there would be no confounding, but it is still difficult to infer the generalizability present in the study because it is neither a pure crossed or a pure nested design. One possibility is to present the generalizability coefficients one would estimate for the crossed and nested possibilities and note that the actual generalizability is at some intermediate point. To repeat, all of this is possible when a $G$ study has been conducted in advance.

## A Fixed-Facet Design

Judges in the above $G$ study were considered to be a random facet in the sense that they were initially considered to have been sampled at random. This meant that interest was directed toward their variability ($\sigma^2_{judges}$) rather than toward their individual properties as judges, save for analyses of individual judges.

Sometimes $G$ data are used as a basis for selecting judges in a subsequent $D$ study, creating a fixed facet. Suppose one is interested in a given individual as a potential judge. The facet of judges (actually "judge") is a fixed factor because the domain simply consists of this designated judge. The generalizability coefficient reduces to the ratio of this judge's true variance divided by his or her total variance, but this is an ordinary reliability coefficient ($r_{11}$), i.e., coefficient $\alpha$. The problem is how to estimate this quantity.

Each individual needs be judged more than once to infer the error in the judge's ratings. Assuming that the resulting correlation(s) are not inflated through memory of previous judgments and that the traits are temporally stable, coefficient $\alpha$ may be applied to the matrix of individuals by occasions of ratings (the result reduces to a test-retest correlation with only two occasions).

One may correlate the judgments with a physical criterion if one exists. For example, one may correlate a stockbroker's predictions about the future value of stocks with the value they actually obtain ("individuals" in this context are the different stocks). Likewise, one may correlate the judgments with the consensus of an expert panel. These examples, especially the first, are really validities rather than reliabilities, but they do address the general issue of how well the judge is performing.

## Higher-Order Designs

In a single-facet design, the total sum of squares reflects three sources—individuals, judges, and the residual. Now suppose that there are two facets, $A$ and $B$, e.g., aggressiveness in school and at play. These may be crossed in the universe in that all combinations of levels $A$ and $B$ may potentially be obtainable. For example, in principle, if $A$ were ratings made by a given judge when the individual was at play and $B$ were ratings made by the same judge when the individual was in the classroom, all combinations of levels could occur even if different samples of judges were used in actual research. In contrast, if the study was concerned with how teachers and peers rated the aggressiveness of individuals, the various levels of teacher and the various levels of peers would be inherently nested—teachers and peers would necessarily be distinct judges.

Seven sources of variation are present in a crossed design:

**1** Overall differences among individuals
**2** Differences among levels of $A$
**3** Differences among levels of $B$
**4** Differences among combinations of $A$ and $B$—the $A$-by-$B$ interaction
**5** Differences among individuals across levels of $A$—the $A$-by individual interaction
**6** Differences among individuals across levels of $B$—the $B$-by individual interaction
**7** The residual, which reflects differences among individuals across combinations of $A$ and $B$.

Whether or not each of these terms can be estimated and how to estimate them depends upon the specifics of the design—whether the sample facets are crossed or nested and whether a given facet is fixed or random. Analysis of variance considerations apply to these determinations. Rather than consider the specifics of the many possible cases, the reader is referred to the above sources on the topic of the analysis of variance and to Brennan (1983), Cronbach et al. (1972), and Shavelson and Webb (1991) for details.

Any given analysis may be highly complex and produce several different generalizability coefficients. Each one, though, can be used as a conventional reliability coefficient, e.g., to disattenuate correlations. In addition, results from a well-designed $G$ study can be used to dictate a wide range of $D$ studies, perhaps suggesting that some be avoided because of the lack of suitable generalizability. Most of the major developments concerning measurement over the last quarter-century have been in the domain of modern psychometrics, but generalizability theory illustrates an important extension based upon quite classical methods. Many studies use ratings, and it is essential to assess the ability of the raters through a procedure like generalizability theory (which, of course, is not limited to studies based upon ratings).

**SUMMARY**

Measurement error may emerge from several sources, but these fall into two main headings: (1) variation within a test produced by such factors as heterogeneity of item content and guessing and (2) variation between tests as produced by temporal instability. Alternative forms, in conjunction with a measure of internal consistency ($\alpha$) can be used to evaluate these influences. Conversely, $\alpha$ by itself may be inadequate. This is especially true for speeded tests. It is particularly useful to compare the results of administering alternative forms with a short time between them (e.g., at the same session) with alternative forms given with a longer time separation (e.g., 2 weeks). The basic outcomes are (1) $\alpha$ is substantial on both forms and the correlation between the two forms is high, implying a stable trait has been measured reliably, (2) $\alpha$ is substantial on both forms but the correlation between the two forms is low, implying the measure is more statelike; (3) $\alpha$ is low on both forms, implying the need to redefine the measures; and (4) $\alpha$ is high on one form but low on the other, implying the need to replace the latter form. There are additional considerations when raters provide the measures since one must assess the extent to which the raters are consistent with one another as well as over time.

Two other methods of estimating internal consistency were also considered. The split-half method, which involves correlating two separate sets of items on the test (usually odd versus even) is basically of historic interest and has an additional problem when items are ordered in terms of difficulty. The retest method involves giving the same test twice and suffers from the problem of subjects remembering their past responses and trying to respond consistently with these recollections. The section concluded with the issue of long-range stability: Many, but not all, traits are stable over time. Problems exist with regard to measuring dynamic traits.

We then considered some practical uses of the reliability coefficient. These include: (1) the estimated correction for attenuation, which deals with determining what the correlation between two variables would be as their reliabilities change; (2) confidence intervals; (3) estimation of true scores; and (4) the effects of changing the sample variance. Although neither confidence intervals nor true score estimation is necessary in most situations because obtained scores correlate perfectly with estimated true scores, it is important to recognize that any obtained score is only one in a probable range of scores whose size is inversely related to the test's reliability. In addition, three types of confidence intervals need to be distinguished: (1) the distribution of probable obtained scores for a given true score, (2) the distribution of probable true scores for a given obtained score, and (3) the distribution of probable obtained scores for a given obtained score on an alternative form.

The next topic was the practical matter of making measures more reliable. The most important concept is clarity, both as it applies to the logic of the measurement and the questions asked of those being tested. The Spearman-Brown prophecy formula is useful in estimating the effects of changing the test's length upon its reliability. Important cautions were noted about stressing any reliability estimate too much. One is that differences in item distribution may spuriously lower measures like $\alpha$ and suggest that items with deviant distributions do not belong as a part of the scale. In the next chapter we will show how deleting such items may be counterproductive. Conversely, sample estimates of $\alpha$ are biased upward. A correction that provides a better estimate of the lower limit of the population reliability (ratio of true variance to error variance) is introduced. However, this correction has a relatively small effect upon measures consisting of a large number of items and whose sample values of $\alpha$ are high and derived from a large sample.

Measures are often derived as composites of scale scores, i.e., as (perhaps weighted) linear combinations of whole tests. Some formulas and principles governing the reliabilities of these composites were discussed. In particular, assuming that the measures are not negatively correlated, the reliability of the composite will be higher than the individual reliabilities when the measures are added, but difference scores based upon positively correlated measures can be very unreliable.

There is a close linkage between the analysis of variance (ANOVA) and reliability coefficients. Consequently, some principles governing the ANOVA were presented. Unlike its most popular application, the determination of the $F$ statistic, the present emphasis is upon *estimating mean squares* from various sources. The variance in population means can be inferred from the difference between the mean square between groups (i.e., observed variance among means) and the mean square within groups. Extending this principle to an ANOVA design where all individuals answer a common series of items, (1) true variance is estimated from this difference in mean squares and (2) error variance is inferred from the mean square within groups. Consequently the ratio of the estimated true variance to the sum of the true variance and error variance is mathematically identical to $\alpha$.

This principle forms the basis of (and is a simple case of) generalizability theory. This theory allows one to evaluate both random sampling error that arises within a domain and systematic error that might arise because different judges evaluate different attributes. A generalizability study ($G$ study) evaluates the generalizabilities (effectively, reliabilities) obtainable under given measurement conditions. These results may then be used to choose the measurement conditions in a study whose purpose it is to apply these measures, a decision study ($D$ study). It is particularly useful to have several judges evaluate all individuals on all attributes being measured (a completely crossed set of measurement conditions or facets) in the $G$ study as opposed, for example, to having some judges evaluate certain individuals and other judges evaluate other individuals or to have some judges evaluate some attributes and other judges evaluate other attributes. The latter involves one or more nested facets. Using a completely crossed $G$ study allows one to estimate generalizability coefficients when the subsequent $D$ study (1) uses a single judge selected either at random or on a pilot rating performance, (2) uses multiple judges, each rating all individuals (as in the $G$ study), (3) raters and judges are paired (as when husbands and wives rate one another), or (4) groups of individuals are nested within particular judges. Generalizability theory is one of the most significant extensions of classical measurement theory and should be used more often, especially when data are in the form of ratings.

## SUGGESTED ADDITIONAL READINGS

Brennan, R. L. (1983). *Elements of generalizability theory*. Iowa City, IA: American College Testing Program.

Collins, L. M., & Horn, J. L. (1991). *Best methods for the analysis of change?* Washington, DC: American Psychological Association.

Cronbach, L. J., Gleser, G. C., Nanda, H., & Rajaratnam, N. (1972). *The dependability of behavioral measurements*. New York: Wiley.

Hays, W. L. (1988). *Statistics*. New York: Holt, Rinehart and Winston.

Magnusson, D. (1967). *Test theory*. Reading, MA: Addison-Wesley.

Shavelson, R. J., & Webb, N. M. (1991). *Generalizability theory: A primer*. Newbury Park, CA: Sage Publications.

Winer, B. J., Brown, D. R., and Michels, K. M. (1991). *Statistical principles in experimental design* (3d ed.). New York: McGraw-Hill.

*Note*: Brennan, Cronbach et al., and Shavelson and Webb provide expanded treatments of generalizability theory. Hays and Winer et al. are basic references on the ANOVA. Magnusson provides an excellent discussion of the various sources of measurement error. Collins and Horn's edited volume contains a broad survey of approaches to the issue of measuring change.

## CHAPTER 8

# CONSTRUCTION OF CONVENTIONAL TESTS

## CHAPTER OVERVIEW

This chapter considers the construction of general-purpose instruments, as opposed to those that are designed for specialized purposes. General-purpose instruments are intended to be employed very widely with diverse samples of subjects in either assessment or research. We assume that the intent is to maximize relevant individual differences among subjects. Ordinary classroom tests are included in this chapter even though they are usually applied to restricted samples because they employ the principles that are discussed. We will further assume that the measuring instrument is not highly speeded. Speeded tests will be discussed in Chapter 9. Except as noted, we will also generally assume that the underlying distribution of the trait to be measured is approximately normal even though an observed score distribution will not be truly normal (see Chapter 5, especially Fig. 5-2).

The measurement principles discussed in this book are not limited to pencil-and-paper measures. They therefore include psychophysiological indices of arousal, behavioral activity rates, and behavioral measures used to study memory, among others. The principles apply to measures of ability, achievement, personality, and attitudes; to both dichotomous and multicategory items; and to both judgments and sentiments. Some slight differences among different types of items will be noted, however.

Even though we stress constructing new measures, the principles are also applicable to selecting a preexisting measure. A good literature review will identify measures that are already available. Sources like the *Tenth Mental Measurements Yearbook* (Mitchell, 1989), which provides critical reviews of standardized tests, are invaluable. You may find a test which precisely fits your needs. It is more likely that you will find one that has fallen short, but you may be able to revise it successfully rather than start over from the beginning. For example, you may correct a poorly worded inventory. The total number of measures proposed in the literature (which is far larger than the published tests included in the *Yearbook*) has increased enormously since the last edition of this book. Unfortunately, this has not increased the number of good measures appreciably. Most measures are essentially unknown, because they have not been used enough to make a determination, rather than bad. Such unknown measures can often be profitably and simply modified for incorporation in your research. One could well argue that there are too many tests because not enough care has been given to determining what others with similar needs have attempted in earlier research. You should also become familiar with the various standards published by such groups as the American Psychological Association (1985, 1986a, 1986b, 1992).

Perhaps three-fourths of the time, simple, understandable, acceptable, and general methods exist to develop a measure based upon the linear model of classical psychometrics. Modern methods, involving use of response patterns as discussed in Chapter 10, may be equally suitable, but choice between various alternative methods will make little initial difference. This is particularly true when the measure is not designed for repeated testing. Since classical methods are much simpler, it is reasonable to consider whether someone who is unfamiliar with modern methods should spend time learning their details at the outset. This time could alternatively be spent broadening the scope of the validation research or increasing the sample size. A well-developed classical measure can usually be transformed to a measure based upon modern methods at a later date, and modern methods will not magically make an ill-conceived measure into a good measure.

Special methods of test construction are needed for about another 15 percent, such as speeded tests. Mixtures of various approaches are required or experts disagree about alternative approaches for the remainder of the cases, and these alternatives do make a real difference. Procedures relevant to this remaining one-fourth of the cases are discussed in Chapters 9 and 10.

Recall from Chapter 3 that tests may be evaluated by standards of content, construct, or predictive validity. The requirements for these three forms of validity are more similar than they are different, and most of what will be said about content validation, which is discussed first, applies to the two other situations. Predictive and construct validation, which reflect the needs of most research and clinical assessments, are especially similar in that both involve correlating the measure with a criterion.

Content validation begins with a domain of content that defines what is to be measured, including to whom the test is applicable, and a test plan that defines how it is to be measured. The resulting set of test items is then administered to a suitable group, usually after outside review. An item analysis defines each item's difficulty (e.g., what proportion of individuals answer it correctly) and discrimination (e.g., how highly it relates to the total test score). If the test is designed for repeated use in new samples, item selection provides a revised version of the test, which is readministered until a satisfactory version is obtained. Norms may be obtained in the process of obtaining a final version of the test. Although a content-validated test is not required to have any external correlates, such correlates are often useful. It is additionally important to assess possible bias, but that topic will be considered in the next chapter.

Construct validation begins with a hypothesis that implies a domain of content. It is important that the scale's content be homogeneous, but homogeneity is not easily assessed, as it is desirable that the methods used to infer the trait be heterogeneous. A scale's content must be unidimensional and unifactor. Unfortunately, decisions as to whether the content is homogeneous cannot be made solely on the basis of statistical criteria if the resulting scale is to have the desired degree of breadth. The simplest example of methodological heterogeneity is to key some sentiment items "true" (or "agree," etc.) and others "false." A multivariate approach, which often involves factor analysis, is necessary to understand items and constructs. However, there is an important difference between factoring whole tests and individual items; the factor analysis of individual items is fraught with problems. Rational and criterion-oriented (empirical) approaches to test construction, which were commonly used in the past, have been shown to be inadequate. Predictive validation really involves little that is new, but some differences between it and the other forms of validation are important.

The last major section of the chapter deals with common issues in testing. These are (1) how to reverse the direction of item keying; (2) unipolar versus bipolar attributes and items; (3) how to choose items to discriminate at a given point along the score continuum; (4) the closely related principle of equidiscriminating test construction, in which a slight amount of reliability is sacrificed in order to enhance overall discrimination; (5) weighting of items, and (6) the role of chance in item selection.

## CONSTRUCTION OF TESTS DESIGNED FOR CONTENT VALIDATION

Perhaps the most familiar testing situation is the classroom examination. Such tests are normally intended for one-time use. In contrast, other content-validated tests are designed for repeated use, such as tests used to license psychologists. The major difference between these two cases is that the tests designed for repeated use ordinarily require (1) greater potential legal scrutiny, (2) various nonpsychometric considerations like greater test security, and (3) several cycles of refinement before use. However, it is perhaps useful to ignore the first two differences by assuming that any test may be challenged and requires security. Moreover, even though it is obviously unwise to reuse a test in toto, sampling from an available item pool is an excellent way to construct classroom tests so they are often reused in similar form.

We will use a conventional definition of the term "achievement test" to denote measuring what a person has learned. As noted in Chapter 3, achievement tests are usually developed through content validation. That is a major difference between them and ability tests, which are usually construct-validated. Achievement tests may assess highly specialized knowledge, such as a classroom test on Shakespeare's *Macbeth*, or sample information more broadly, as in standardized tests given primary school students.

### The Domain of Content and Test Plan

Defining an appropriate domain of content or body of relevant material is essential to content validation (see Chapter 3). The domain includes both the material to be tested on and the population for whom the material is to be suitable. Population characteristics are extremely important, as items must be written to take the age, ability level (especially reading comprehension), and culture of those tested into account. The other major consideration is the test plan which dictates the format of the test. Having a domain of content and test plan available before the test is constructed is vastly more meaningful than attempting to determine content validity after construction. If potential users of the test agree in advance on the appropriateness of the content and test plan, arriving at an acceptable instrument is mainly a matter of technical skill and application.

Specifying the domain of content for an ordinary classroom examination can be as simple as stating which text chapters are to be covered. Sampling of assigned material need not be uniform (e.g., by constructing one question per page) nor parallel classroom emphasis, but it should reflect the more important material. Likewise, students need not be told explicitly what will be emphasized, but they should not be misled. People who are not skilled at making up tests often ask obscure questions in an attempt to create individual differences, but this is unnecessary. It is far more likely that questions will prove too difficult than too easy.

Defining the domain of content in tests designed for employment is often more difficult than it would seem. Most positions employing sufficient numbers to warrant standardized testing usually have a job description, but this may poorly reflect what the individual actually does on the job. A job analysis is used to make this determination. Ideally, one would actually observe employees, but it is more common to have them respond via questionnaire, which can lead to obvious distortions. Still, either procedure is better than making the determination in ignorance. For example, the average civilian, psychologists included, probably overestimates the frequency of armed confrontations police officers encounter and underestimates their need for interpersonal skills to mediate verbal disputes. In addition to the outline of content, the plan should describe (1) the types of items to be employed with examples, (2) the approximate number of items to be employed in each section and each subsection of the test, (3) how long the test will take to administer, (4) how it will be administered, (5) how it will be scored, and (6) the types of norms or other referencing that will be obtained.

The more widely a test is to be used and the greater its importance, the more thoroughly the completed plan needs be reviewed. The reviewers should be chosen broadly to include end users (e.g., personnel managers or teachers), subject-matter experts, psychometricians, and representatives of those who will be taking the test. The last-mentiond obviously can provide pilot data, but they also often provide valuable other commentary. Suggestions for changes are often made which require a revision of the test plan and a second review. Hopefully, the revised plan will receive general or near-general approval; the cycle is repeated if this is not the case.

## Test Items

Item formats include (1) short-answer (completion or "fill-in-the-blank"), (2) essay, (3) multiple-choice, (4) problem solving, and (5) other objective procedures such as matching or true-false. The nature of the material to be tested obviously plays an important role in the choice—students who need to be tested on spoken fluency in a foreign language cannot be properly evaluated by multiple-choice items. Such items are perfectly proper when one wishes to measure recognition of material, but circumstances often suggest measuring recall, which is better assessed by short-answer questions, and/or organizational ability, which implies the need for essay examinations or problems. All of these tests are adequate for measuring convergent thought about subject matter, but various forms of term papers (e.g., research proposals) are better suited to measure divergent thought and creativity. Legitimate philosophical differences exist among instructors as well, and the physical context of the class is important. An instructor who attempts to give an essay examination to a class of several hundred students without any assistants quickly learns the meaning of measurement error in grading. A given test may also combine formats, e.g., half short answer and half essay.

*If* an objective format directed toward measuring recognition is appropriate, there is every reason to employ conventional four or five alternative multiple-choice items over alternative formats such as matching. The test can be optically read, and computer programs are widely available to perform item analyses and obtain scores. Both multiple-choice and short-answer formats allow a broad sampling of the domain of content within reasonable time limits. Although essay examinations require subjects to use a broader range of skills (e.g., sentence construction), the feedback that is necessary to strengthen these skills is often not given. If you use more than one format, you may find it of interest to score the various formats separately, determine their reliabilities and correlate the scores. Scores on good multiple-choice items often correlate as highly with scores on essay items almost as highly as their respective reliabilities permit. High correlations between formats are especially likely when the class varies widely in academic ability. Moreover, scores on multiple-choice items usually are considerably more reliable. Alternative-form reliabilities are typically between .60 and .70 for essay examinations and between .75 and .90 for multiple-choice examinations. The broader the range of student abilities, the larger the expected reliability. At the same time, multiple-choice tests require the most time to construct in the absence of a good test bank, which makes short-answer formats especially attractive in classes of roughly 15 to 75. Essay formats are especially appropriate for smaller classes. Despite the applicability of the various formats to classroom testing and research, nearly all large-scale achievement tests employ multiple-choice items.

Of course, no test is better than the items of which it is composed. A good plan provides an intention to construct a good test, but unless items are skillfully written, the plan never materializes. Although there are some rules for writing good items (Berk, 1984, 1986; Flaugher, 1990; Thorndike, Cunningham, Thorndike, & Hagen, 1991), writing test items is an art that few people master. Nearly everything about item construction can be summed up by the word "clarity" as it applies to how well the item (1) is phrased, (2) relates to the domain, and (3) "points" the knowledgeable student toward what is demanded. For example, the question "What happened to art during the fifteenth century?" is so vague that respondents could legitimately take many different directions on an essay examination or select several different alternatives on a multiple-choice item.

At the same time you seek to be clear, try to avoid trivial questions. Askir dates, names, and simple facts is easy to do and can be unambiguous. These iter be made "picky" enough to calm neophyte test constructor's fears about making items too easy. However, these details are rarely very important; it is usually more important to determine how well students reason with the subject matter. Similarly, as easy as it is to make questions about statistics depend upon their memory for the correct formula, such rote memory is rarely, if ever, necessary in actual applications. Unfortunately, suitable items are often more difficult to construct than trivial ones.

The following principles, adapted from Thorndike et al. (1991), are useful for all forms of items. As obvious as some are, they are easily forgotten.

**1** Make the complexity of the items appropriate to the level of the students. This includes, but is not limited to, item wording. It also applies to numbers used in mathematical questions. Unless you are interested in skill at manipulating large numbers, small numbers, even single digits, are appropriate for most numerical problems.

**2** Define the task, including directions, as clearly as possible.

**3** Inform the students about grading standards, e.g., point assignments.

**4** Write the items as simply and in as straightforward a manner as possible.

**5** Know what mental processes you want the student to use and ask questions accordingly. Sometimes it is important to test factual knowledge (e.g., on licensing examinations), but in most academic situations, reasoning from facts is more important.

**6** Use novel material or organization to prevent students from merely reproducing lecture and text examples.

**7** Vary the complexity and difficulty of the items. This will improve your ability to discriminate at all knowledge levels for reasons considered later in the chapter. It is also a good idea to place some easier "ice breaker" items at the beginning to let students "settle in" to the examination, reduce their anxieties, and obtain practice at the specific type of item, if necessary.

**8** Make questions as independent as possible. In many mathematical problems, one miscalculation can make it nearly impossible for the student to demonstrate any knowledge they may possess. For example, it might be more useful to have students compute means, variances, and covariances in one problem and then compute a correlation with given variances and the covariance in another than to have them do both in one problem.

**9** Try to avoid negatively phrased items as much as possible. Use of a few is legitimate, such as multiple-choice questions that ask which alternative does not belong. Underscore the word "not" for clarity on such items.

**10** Never use double negatives.

For essay items:

**1** Start the question with words that clearly define the task, e.g. "Compare and contrast . . .".

**2** Phrase questions on controversial issues so that students are evaluated in terms of the evidence they present rather than the specific position they take.

**3** If all students are tested on the same material, have them answer the same questions and don't give choices. Although it is common to give students choices, they will then be compared against different standards.

For short-answer items:

**1** Omit only key words.
**2** Do not leave too many blanks.
**3** Put the blanks near the end of the question to make it more readable.
**4** Avoid specific determiners such as "all" and "none."
**5** Avoid ambiguous determiners such as "frequently" and "sometimes."
**6** Have each item express a single idea.

For multiple-choice items:

**1** Be sure that the stem (lead-in) clearly formulates the problem.

**2** Include as much of the item's content in the stem as possible. This avoids repeating material unnecessarily.

**3** Include only what is necessary in the stem.

**4** As in essay examinations, use novel material and examples to avoid having students reproduce the correct answer by rote.

**5** Be sure that distractors (incorrect alternatives) are plausible.

**6** Use "none of the above" or "all of the above" very sparingly, if at all. Multiple-choice items without these alternatives are comparative judgments of "which alternative is truest," a principle all teachers use when explaining the correct answer since incorrect alternatives may be *somewhat* true. Adding in either of the two options raises a second consideration: Are all (or any) of the alternatives "true enough to be true?" This problem is compounded when the correct answer is disproportionately "all (or none) of the above" because it then gives the uninformed student unnecessary information. Likewise, a student who is fairly sure that two alternatives are correct may choose "all of the above" without knowing whether additional alternatives are also correct.

**7** Make each alternative of approximately equal length and parallel grammatical construction.

**8** Randomize the location of the correct alternative.

**9** Make sure each alternative agrees grammatically with the stem, e.g., if the stem calls for the singular, make sure each alternative is phrased in the singular. Use "a(an)" to avoid giving cues about whether the correct alternative begins with a consonant or vowel.

**10** In general, try to eliminate any factor that makes the correct alternative stand out to an uninformed responder. The ideal is to make the alternatives look equally attractive to the uninformed.

**11** Try to formulate incorrect alternatives so that they detect common ways in which students may be misinformed. This often facilitates explaining to a student why a particular question was missed. For example, students in a course in abnormal psychology who are given a question describing the symptoms of a major depression should also be given the alternative of a bipolar disorder because they are often confused.

Test items should be reviewed after they have been constructed. Good multiple-choice questions are especially difficult to write. Instructors who don't have a teaching assistant will probably need to do their own reviewing, but several people should review a large-scale achievement test. These test construction experts should consider each item for its appropriateness, apparent difficulty, and clarity. Items surviving the review should then be reviewed by teachers and other potential users of the test.

## Test Length

The intended length of the test is another important consideration. This in turn reflects the time available and the desired reliability. The traditional 50-minute class obviously limits the number of items on a classroom examination, and the instructor's experience usually dictates the length appropriate to a given topic. Situational factors likewise enter into the time available for tests used for personnel selection. We have noted that unreliability somewhat attenuates correlations with other measures. Consequently a test may be too short, just it may be too long. It is difficult to estimate how many items should be used for a preliminary form unless one has had prior experience with similar tests. The correlations among the dichotomous items typically used on achievement tests tend to be lower than the correlations obtained with multicategory formats. This limits the reliability and requires the test to be longer in order to achieve the same degree of reliability. Finally, the more variable the target population, the smaller the number of items needed to achieve a given reliability.

Nothing is more informative than a good pilot study when a test is designed for repeated use. If one knows that items of a particular type tend to have high internal consistency (e.g., vocabulary items), the pilot version might only require twice as many items as eventually desired. Consequently, if 30 items have previously been shown to produce a coefficient α of .80 on a similar test and that reliability is acceptable, start with 60 initial items. If little is known about a given type of item or if it is known to be less internally consistent, be conservative and construct more items for the initial form, e.g., 100. As the Spearman-Brown prophecy formula indicates, adding items to increase reliability obeys a law of diminishing returns, and it is especially difficult to improve the reliability of a test that is already reliable substantially by adding more items.

An alternative strategy which is sometimes useful is to begin with a smaller number of items than is thought to be adequate, e.g., by constructing only 30 items when one suspects that 40 items will be eventually required to obtain a target coefficient α of .80. Apply these items to a relatively small sample of subjects, e.g., 100. If either the total collection of items (30) or the most homogeneous subset (e.g., the best 15 items) has a coefficient α of at least .60, it is probably worth constructing more items, gathering responses from a much larger group of subjects, and performing a more complete item analysis. The eventual labor of constructing the test in stages is greater than in doing everything in one large step, but the project can be abandoned without further loss of time and effort if the pilot results are very discouraging.

## Sample of Subjects

Items on tests designed for repeated use should be administered to a pilot sample. The pilot sample should be as similar to the eventual target population as possible in terms of range and level of ability. College students obviously provide only limited information about primary school children. However, the convenience of college student populations often makes them useful at preliminary stages. Tests that are poorly understood by college students will obviously be even more poorly understood by the less educated. The students may also provide feedback about various shortcomings in the procedures. The utility of college students is enhanced when the target population is difficult to locate. The intended final form must be run on the target population(s), as the need for a precisely representative sample is much greater in content validation than in predictive or construct validation.

The conditions of the pilot study should closely resemble the conditions of eventual use. If the test will require a severe time limit, use a time limit in the pilot study. Also, tests are often used with many different types of subjects. It may be difficult to ensure that the group of subjects used in test construction will be representative of all intended groups, but suitable efforts should be made. This applies especially to groups defined on the basis of ethnicity and gender. As in any pilot study, one cannot determine how many subjects should be used to obtain data for item analysis in advance without knowledge of results obtained in similar contexts. However, at least 200 normative subjects is a rule of thumb to provide sufficient stability to the analysis. Guadagnoli and Velicer (1988) have explored this "number of subjects" problem in detail.

## Item Analysis

Although content validity primarily rests on rational rather than empirical grounds, an item analysis is extremely useful if not essential. This furnishes a variety of statistical data regarding how subjects responded to each item and how each item relates to overall performance. We will first describe results for a given test, such as a classroom examination, and discuss how these results may be used for item selection in the next section. The utility of any item analysis is closely related to the stability of the estimates which in turn are closely related to sample size. However, much potential information can be gained from analyzing test results of even a small class. Suitable programs are widely available.

Any form of test can be subject to an item analysis, but multiple-choice tests provide the most detailed results. The most basic results are the proportions of response to each alternative. Since these are proportions and not correlations, they are quite likely to be meaningful in samples as small as 50 and are useful in three distinct ways. The third does not require multiple-choice formats.

**1** Be quite suspicious of any item if a distractor is chosen more often than the correct alternative. This suggests that either the instruction or the item itself is misleading.

**2** Distractors that are hardly ever chosen are too transparently incorrect and can be omitted or, preferably, replaced.

**3** The proportion choosing the correct alternative or item $p$ value is the classical index of item difficulty (a term that can also apply to sentiments, although "endorsement level" is more common). Items with extreme $p$ values should generally be excluded since they do not discriminate among individuals. An important exception is the use of a few simple ice-breaker items designed to reduce students' apprehension and to illustrate the remaining items. Chance is .0 on short-answer questions and $1/k$ on $k$-alternative multiple-choice tests. However, even if a class correctly answers a four-alternative item one-fourth of the time, they need not be guessing; they could be systematically distracted by a particular alternative. The next chapter considers guessing in more detail. The $p$ value contains all relevant information about item distributions for dichotomous items typically found on abilities and achievement tests. However, multicategory scoring is common on other tests, such as personality inventories designed for construct validation. In this case, the item mean is the extension of the $p$ value, and the standard deviation furnishes supplemental data about the extent to which responses were spread among categories.

Chapter 10 considers mastery learning, where individuals are intended to eventually respond correctly to most items, thus removing individual differences. A driver's test is a common example of a test designed for mastery learning. Not only would it be proper to ascertain whether applicants know the speed limit in a school zone, but it would be helpful if everyone got the question correct. Tests producing highly skewed distributions because the average score is very high or very low cannot correlate well with external criteria nor have much internal consistency, but this does not mean that they have not accomplished their intended purpose if that purpose is mastery learning of a domain of content.

Content-validated tests need not correlate with any other measure nor have very high internal consistency. Tests designed for mastery learning will have especially low internal consistency when the instruction has the desired effect. The demands of the situation may or may not dictate temporal stability, which is separate from both issues. If a content-validated measure is an achievement measure, which it usually is, its temporal stability will reflect the effects of any instructional manipulation. General achievement tests tend to be temporally stable because it is difficult to teach enough in a short period of time to alter scores appreciably. On the other hand, classroom tests are designed to be temporally unstable—if they were not, the educational intervention would be useless.

If the test begins with ice-breaker items, scores on these items might be psychometrically worthless because nearly everyone answers them correctly. However, it is often useful to score these items separately from the overall test to ensure that students have mastered the fundamentals of the test. Even though measures of psychopathology are usually developed by construct validation and for different purposes, similar logic is used to construct validity scales. For example, the $F$ scale of the MMPI consists of an extremely bizarre set of items that are infrequently endorsed even by severely impaired individuals. People who do endorse these items may be malingering or illiterate.

An item analysis must describe how each item relates to overall test performance and thereby provide discrimination indices, of which there are several. The best items on any test are the most discriminating. They probably are less ambiguous, they cannot be of extreme difficulty, and they tend to make individual differences on the final test more reliable. The simplest discrimination index is the ordinary PM item-total correlation ($r$) between each item and the total test score. If the item is scored dichotomously, it will be a point-biserial correlation ($r_{pb}$), but the computer program performing the analysis does not "know" or "care" that this is a special case. If the test is divided into sections, such as reading and science, the appropriate index is the correlation with the subtest score instead of the total test score.

One problem with this index of discrimination is that the item score is part of the total test score. This makes the correlation of an item with total scores higher than it would be if the item were correlated with the sum of the remaining items. Each item may correlate substantially with the total score on a test with 10 or fewer items even if it does not correlate with any of the other items, but the artifact is negligible on longer tests. This spurious source of item-total correlation, called "overlap," can be removed with the following formula:

$$r_{1(Y-1)} = \frac{r_{Y1}\sigma_Y - \sigma_1}{\sqrt{\sigma_1^2 + \sigma_Y^2 + 2\sigma_1\sigma_Y r_{Y1}}} \tag{8-1}$$

where $r_{Y1}$ = correlation of item $x_1$ with total scores ($Y$)

$\quad \sigma_Y$ = standard deviation of total scores ($Y$)

$\quad \sigma_1$ = standard deviation of item $x_1$

$r_{1(Y-1)}$ = correlation of item $x_1$ with sum of scores on all items ($Y$) exclusive of item $x_1$

For example, suppose a test has 80 items, item $x_1$ correlates .24 with total score, the $p$ value of this item is .5, and the variance of total scores is 191. In this case, $r_{1(Y-1)}$ is .22, which is only .02 less than the observed item-total correlation. The correction given in Eq. (8-1) is usually built into item analysis programs, and there is no reason not to use it even when its effects are slight.

Both the uncorrected and corrected item-total correlations ($r$) are biased in favor of items with $p$ values near .5. This bias causes tests to discriminate in the middle of the distribution rather than to be spread at all levels. We will later show why it is usually important to have a test discriminate at all levels by including relatively easy and difficult items. One possible way to overcome the effect of $p$ is to compute the biserial correlation ($r_{bis}$) between the item and total score. As discussed in Chapter 4, $r_{bis}$ assumes that the item score may be thought of as continuous, but unfortunately $r_{bis}$ has a very large sampling error which may offset any advantages it has in correcting for $p$. Moreover, the absolute magnitudes of $r_{bis}$ are misleadingly high since it makes more sense to think of the items as categorical rather than continuous.

Unfortunately, the sum of item scores ($Y$) is not really the criterion of interest. It changes as items are deleted in the selection process. Item response theory uses a complexly defined statistical estimate of trait magnitude, symbolized $\theta$ (see Chapters 2 and 10), and in effect correlates items with this estimate (though not in the sense of $r$). Another possibility is to correlate items with a set of "marker" items whose content is indisputably part of the domain rather than with the total test scores.

Three other possible discrimination indices are (1) the covariance between an item and total score, (2) the average correlation between a given item and all other items (the $\bar{r}_{1j}$ of Chapter 6), and (3) the proportion of people passing the item in the top half of the class minus the proportion of people passing the item in the bottom half of the class. Several variants of index 3 exist, e.g., the proportions passing in the top and bottom quarters. Measures like index 3 were popular as computational shortcuts before computer analyses were feasible. None of these three measures affords any particular advantage, and the rank orderings of items in terms of any one discrimination criterion tend to be highly similar to any other. Consequently, we suggest using the corrected item-total correlation, which we will assume in further discussion. If you use do not make the correction on a test with 10 or more items, no harm will result as the correction will have little effect.

Any item that fails to correlate with a relevant total score other than deliberately easy items should be carefully inspected. Such items may be valid, but that rarely is the case. It is more likely that the item is excessively difficult or easy, ambiguous, or has little to do with the domain. A cutoff of .3 is an arbitrary guide to defining a discriminating item. Most item-total correlations range from .0 to about .4. Negative values suggest bad wording, sampling error, or miskeying. The most discriminating items should describe meaningful aspects of the situation. One might question a classroom test where the most discriminating items are the color of the textbook cover, the correct spelling of the instructor's name, etc., even though these items probably do correlate positively with overall performance.

Item analysis programs may also include empirical estimates of trace lines (see Chapter 2), also referred to as correct response curves or item characteristic curves. Classical (linear model) estimates are obtained by computing the proportion of subjects passing the item at various levels of overall performance, as inferred from total test score. These proportions should increase across the various skill levels; i.e., the trace line should be monotonic as depicted in Fig. 2-7c. However, it need not have the mathematically well-defined form of Fig. 2-7a or 2-7b. The program may also provide the breakdown of chosen alternatives within the performance levels. Poorer and better students often choose different alternatives when incorrect, which in theory may provide diagnostically useful information. Unfortunately, these data are typically unstable. For example, if subjects are divided into quintiles on the basis of overall score, each subgroup in a class of 100 will have only 20 students.

Finally, the analysis should include coefficient α, which is obviously essential. Related statistics of somewhat lesser import may also be given, such as the value of α projected to a 100-item test or the average interitem correlation. Keep in mind, however, that item analysis of most achievement tests is secondary to content validity. Most of the effort to ensure validity takes place before any data gathering. This is somewhat, but not totally, different from construct and predictive validation. Thus, items are assumed to possess the desired content, so that the item analysis provides statistical information about the discriminatory capacity of the items in the target population when that is important, but ability to discriminate is not always essential to the test's use. The final decision to include or reject an item in either the initial or final version of a test is based primarily on human judgment, regardless of what the item analysis shows. Item analyses play a somewhat more important role in construct and predictive validation.

## Item Selection

If an item analysis is conducted on a preliminary form of a test, the next step is to select the "best" items to be used on the "final" version of the test (quotes are used because all tests need to be updated). This section is not directly necessary for classroom examinations and other tests that are intended to be used once. The primary criterion for including an item is the discrimination index, e.g., the corrected item-total $r$. Under all practical circumstances, items with high item-total $r$ values have more variance relating to what the items have in common and add more to the test's reliability than items with low $r$ values. How well this is done depends on the number of discriminating items ($r \geq .3$). The word "practical" was inserted in this guideline because Loevinger (1954) pointed out that if items are very highly correlated, subjects will basically divide into those who pass nearly all items and those who fail nearly all items even though their ability may be distributed along a continuum. This can happen for both judgments and sentiments when essentially the same question is asked. It will not happen if the item distributions are diverse.

A related consideration is that even though coefficient $\alpha$ is important to construct, content, and predictive validation (in that order), do *not* view maximizing it through item selection as an end in itself. As we will discuss later in the chapter, coefficient $\alpha$ will be maximized when the test items have maximally similar distributions ($p$ values for dichotomously scored items) and is therefore peaked (Lord, 1952a, 1952b), but that is not always the goal of test construction (Brogden, 1946; Loevinger, 1954). In fact, we will later show why it is desirable to mix easy and difficult items even if it sacrifices a slight amount of reliability (also see the section titled "Limitations on the Reliability Coefficient's Utility" in Chapter 7).

Thus, $p$ values may serve as a secondary criterion for item inclusion. We have noted that both the corrected and uncorrected item-total $r$ values are biased toward items with intermediate $p$ values. If $r$ were the only criterion, item difficulties might be concentrated in the .5 to .6 region. In turn, this would concentrate the ability of the test to discriminate in the middle of the attribute continuum. Having items of varied difficulties may cause a marginal sacrifice in coefficient $\alpha$. However, they will increase the test's ability to discriminate at all levels of the continuum as long as they correlate at least moderately with the total score. Quite often, the most discriminating items will have a spread of $p$ values. If so, fine.

If a sufficient number of items discriminate satisfactorily, item selection can proceed. If this number is limited and you cannot create an additional pool, you have no choice but to use the existing pool. Otherwise, repeat the preliminary testing with a new set of items and combine the new set with the initial set to construct the final form. Selection may proceed by investigating the reliability of successive item collections. First, rank the items in terms of their discrimination indices, e.g., item-total $r$ values. The basic strategy is to apply coefficient $\alpha$ to a set of items with the highest item-total correlations, replacing the least discriminating in this group with items having more desirable $p$ values if necessary. The size of this initial set can range from 5 to 30. More items are needed in this initial set when the average item-total correlation is low and the intended reliability is high. If this set produces the desired reliability, stop adding items. If not, add the next 5 or 10 items in the series, again making substitutions based upon the secondary $p$ value criterion, and recompute coefficient $\alpha$. Keep adding sets of 5 or 10 items until the desired reliability is reached.

In principle, it is possible to adopt a stepwise item selection procedure (see Chapter 6), such as SPSS' RELIABILITY. Both authors, as well as many other investigators, are opposed to the use of stepwise selection because of the extent to which it capitalizes upon chance. This is especially true when a theory can dictate selection. The arguments against a stepwise algorithm are weaker here because the suggested alternatives are also data-driven, and there is usually no theoretical reason to prefer one item over another. The key to successful item selection is readministration of the test in a new sample.

How many items need to be added depends on the item-total $r$ values and on the reliability of the first set of items. Adding very poorly discriminating items ($r < .05$) will add little if anything to coefficient $\alpha$. Conversely, sizable increments in the reliability can be achieved if there are numerous items which are at least moderately discriminating ($r > .20$). If the desired reliability is obtained, the item analysis is complete; if not, add more items. Much depends upon trial and error. If the reliability either fails to increase or decreases at any point, there is no use trying out larger numbers of items since you have already started with the best items.

One can plot coefficient $\alpha$ for tests of different lengths. Figure 8-1 shows a typical curve. Also shown is the expected increase in reliability from lengthening a five-item test when the five items have a reliability of .40 based upon the Spearman-Brown prophecy formula (Eq. 6-18). The obtained reliabilities are lower than predicted reliabilities because Eq. 6-18 assumes that the items added at each step have the same correlations with total scores as the original five items. The method of item analysis recommended here uses the most discriminating five items first so that later items correlate less with total scores. Consequently the obtained reliabilities will deviate progressively from the predicted reliabilities. Coefficient $\alpha$ may even *decline* as the least discriminating items are added.

Because selecting items takes advantage of chance, continue adding items until coefficient $\alpha$ is comfortably above the target reliability. For example, if a reliability of .80 is needed in the final test, it would be wise to keep selecting items until coefficient $\alpha$ reaches at least .85. If there is no predefined target reliability, stop adding items when the curve levels off, as it does in Fig. 8-1 past 50 items.

Assuming one can derive a set of items with the desired reliability, the next step is to plot the frequency distribution of total scores. Although there are legitimate exceptions (see Chapter 5, especially Fig. 5-2), the usual desired shape is symmetric and approximately normal because there is usually as much interest in low scores as in high scores. If the distribution is satisfactory, item selection is complete. If the distribution of scores is undesirably skewed, add easier or more difficult items as the case may be. Some applications, considered in the next chapter, work best with skewed distributions.

In principle, the standard error of the item-total $r$ may be used as a guide to the minimum acceptable discrimination index, but there is usually no need to be highly concerned about the statistical significance of item-total correlations, especially in large samples of people. Nearly all item-total correlations will be positive within

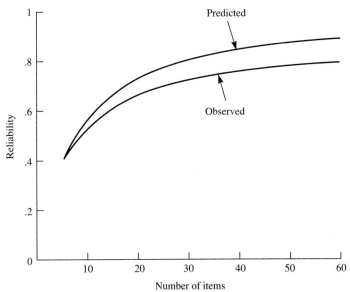

FIGURE 8-1    Predicted and obtained reliabilities of tests varying in length from 5 to 60 items when the reliability of the first 5 items is .40.

sampling error, and so one is being unduly conservative in rejecting items when their correlations with total scores are not statistically significant. If you do use inferential tests, it is appropriate to make them one-sided.

What should one do if this approach to test construction fails? The answer always involves going back and creating new items, perhaps oftotally different form, *or* abandoning the issue entirely. It will probably fail if the reliability of the first 30 dichotomous items is no more than .40. One probably has already used the best items, and so there probably will not be enough good items to improve the reliability. The measure may fail for three basic reasons.

**1** The items may be from a poorly defined domain where correlations among items are uniformly low. The reliability will grow slowly as the number of items increases, but the curve will not flatten out altogether. Achieving a reliable test will require a very large number of items if it is possible at all.

**2** The items may be factorially complex (multidimensional), so that clusters of items have relatively high correlations with one another but very low correlations with members of other clusters. This situation is very difficult to distinguish from an ill-defined domain. In both cases correlations with total scores are low and coefficient α tends to rise, but slowly, as more items are added. However, in this case, the range of interitem correlations will be relatively large. Unfortunately, "relatively large" depends upon the sample size and domain(s).

**3** Some items may have relatively high correlations with one another, but other items may have correlations near zero with all items. This implies that some good items can form the nucleus of a test, but the reliability cannot be increased by adding items. This condition can be detected by a sudden drop-off in the size of item-total $r$ values in the ranking, e.g., if the thirty-fifth item has an $r$ of .21 but the thirty-sixth item has an $r$ of only .09.

How can one recognize which of the three circumstances prevail, and what should be done after the circumstance is recognized? It is somewhat easy to distinguish the third circumstance from the other two by a marked falloff in item-total correlations at some point in the list of items. If that occurs, study the good items and try to determine the nature of their content. Try to construct more items of the same kind, administer them along with the original good items to a new group of subjects, and submit all items to another item analysis.

If the average item-total $r$ value is low, it is very difficult to tell whether this is because the domain is poorly defined or factorially complex. If the low value is caused by factorial complexity, it cannot be because of the presence of only two or three strong factors. Most investigators can probably guess that multiple factors are present and construct different tests to measure them. Moreover, item-total $r$ values will not necessarily be low, for reasons noted in Chapter 6—high reliability does not necessarily imply that the items measure only a single factor. All things held equal such as the number of items, items that measure only one factor will intercorrelate more highly on average than items that measure more than one and therefore generate a higher value of coefficient $\alpha$. However, the "all things" are not always "equal," and it is quite easy to find a set of items that measure multiple factors which produce a higher value of coefficient $\alpha$ than another set of items that measure a single factor but which contain more random error.

The bottom line is that you are most likely to find a small to modest number of items in the initial set that correlate well with total score, a fairly large number that do not correlate at all, and a sizable block in the middle. Even those items that are most discriminating do not correlate extremely well in an absolute sense. It is highly unlikely that you will find items which correlate more than .5 with total score. This means that 75 percent of the variance in even the best item is unrelated to total score. It illustrates the essential point that we stress throughout this book; test construction can be thought of as the process of making a reliable total score out of unreliable items. This can be done in a surprisingly high proportion of cases, but one should never lose sight of the inherent unreliability of individual items. We will be critical of approaches that take an alternative point of view at several points in this chapter and elsewhere.

## Norms

Establishing norms is one of the most important steps in standardizing large-scale achievement tests. Broadly speaking, "norms" are any statistical data that provide a frame of reference to interpret an individual's scores relative to scores of others since an absolute number correct has little meaning in isolation. If the test is designed to measure academic progress, norms might relate the score to those of a national cross section of representative students. Local norms, reflecting the region (perhaps city) or particular school are also useful.

Norms are less essential when a measure is intended for use in group research rather than individual decisions, but content-validated measures are usually intended for individual decision making. The main use of norms with measures of constructs and predictor tests is to indicate whether research results might have been different with different types of people, e.g., because of range restriction. Construction of norms for important achievement tests is almost as much work as construction of the tests themselves. (For some of the particulars, see Angoff, 1971.) Great care must be taken to ensure the adequacy of sampling and usually requires the testing of thousands of students. It is vital that the normative population represent different genders, races, and socioeconomic statuses well. Statistical analyses then produce the final norms. One usually obtains separate norms for different parts of the test and the various demographic groups.

Norms usually are expressed both as percentiles and as standard ($z$) scores to expedite communication. A "percentile" indicates the percentage of persons in the normative sample at or below a particular score. Thus if 80 percent of the students obtain a raw score of 122 or less, a person with a raw score of 122 is at the 80th percentile. Details for handling situations in which more than one individual obtains the same score are found in nearly all introductory and intermediate statistics textbooks, e.g., Hays (1988, pp. 183–185). The $z$ scores in turn are often transformed. Some commonly used transformations are the following.

**1** The deviation IQ, used in measurements of intelligence, in which $\mu = 100$ and $\sigma = 15$

**2** McCall $T$ scores, used in the MMPI and in educational statistics, in which $\mu = 50$ and $\sigma = 10$

**3** Scores on sections of the Scholastic Aptitude Test and Graduate Record Examination in which $\mu = 500$ and $\sigma = 100$

**4** Stanine (standard nine) scores, used in the military, in which $\mu = 5.5$ and $\sigma = 1$.

These scores are sometimes normalized (as in the revised MMPI), but sometimes they are not (as in the original MMPI) even though, strictly speaking, any of these transformations implies normalization. If the original distribution is approximately normal, the effects of normalization will be slight. Because a percentile rank denotes a person's standing directly, it is usually easier to interpret to a layperson than to a transformed standard score. However, it is extremely easy to translate back and forth between these measures, e.g., knowing someone has a $z$ score of +1 or a $T$ score of 60 denotes that they surpassed approximately 84 percent of the normative population. Also, transformed scores are either approximately linear with respect to raw scores (if the data are normalized) or exactly so (if they are not).

Classroom test norms are used to convert the numerical score on the test to whatever the institution uses for grading. Sometimes grades are "absolute," so that 90 to 100 is an A, 80 to 90 is a B, etc. This procedure is so standard in American primary and secondary education that it is difficult for those without a psychometric background to realize that it is an arbitrary outcome of the difficulties of the various measures comprising the average. It is much more meaningful to think of grades as reflecting judgments based upon the instructor's conception of the various categories, which are hopefully equitable in informing students of the quality of their performance.

Referencing a raw score to scores of others (e.g., as a percentile) is not the only way to make a score meaningful. A score may be criterion-referenced by describing its implications for relevant behaviors; e.g., a score of 50 on the admissions test means that the individual has a .75 probability of completing a given curriculum successfully. Alternatively, a score may be domain-referenced by relating it to the domain being measured, e.g., a score of 25 on a particular vocabulary test implies that the individual has a vocabulary of 150,000 words.

## The Role of External Correlates

We have stressed that measures designed through content validation basically need not correlate with any external criterion to be valid. Even though instructors hope that final examination scores correlate positively with whether or not students take additional courses in the area, they are not designed for that purpose, and it is no reflection on the test if there is no correlation or even if it is negative. Lack of positive correlation may, of course, be diagnostic of problems in the course, such as the extent to which the instructor motivates the students. The only meaningful issue is how content-related the items are, and that is better addressed by judgment than by statistics. As we have also noted, a content-validated test certainly might correlate with some relevant criterion, but spurious factors like range restriction might well attenuate this correlation if the test is used for selection, as is commonly the case.

A test need not have any construct or predictive validity to have content validity, but this does not mean that one should not correlate the test with other measures. Seeking external correlations is especially valuable when the test might be challenged on legal grounds. If a clerical position requires only high school-level reading skills, it is inappropriate to require college-level reading skills to take the test. Correlating test scores with reading comprehension scores furnishes much of the information relevant to this issue. Gender and ethnicity are frequent correlates of test scores, which often leads to legal challenges of tests used for employment. We consider the topic of bias in the next chapter, but for the present note that the best single line of defense is to have tests clearly content-referenced.

## CONSTRUCTION OF TESTS DESIGNED FOR CONSTRUCT VALIDATION

The domain of content for a content-validated achievement test can be rather arbitrary and heterogeneous, as it may be dictated by a source external to the investigator such as a job description. A classroom test may properly involve content sampled from a series of chapters chosen for scheduling convenience. In contrast, a test designed for construct validity cannot be developed without a theory that dictates the properties of that measure (see Chapter 3). This too must lead to a domain of content. We will stress the importance of making that measure homogeneous with regard to content.

We will further stress the many similarities between measuring personality traits and abilities. There are, of course, some differences between these situations. Personality tests are measures of typical performance, since most items ask what people usually do in a situation. Items used on such tests usually involve sentiments. In contrast, abilities tests are measures of optimum performance to determine what people can do at their best. Test items are usually judgments. However, we will focus on the more significant similarities, noting that historically personality measurement has borrowed more from abilities measurement than the reverse. Jackson (1971) provides a particularly thoughtful discussion of personality assessment.

This section will present something of a paradox: A good construct is homogeneous with respect to its content, but heterogeneous from the standpoint of the methods used to infer this content. Thus, a measure of numerical fluency should ask questions about the ability to manipulate numbers and be minimally sensitive to vocabulary. Likewise, a measure of depression should be minimally affected by anxiety. However, while seeking this homogeneity of *what* is measured, it is important that one define *how* it is measured broadly lest the same question be asked repeatedly. The resulting specific piece of behavior is unlikely to be able to address general issues of behavior. Knowing how to add 2 + 2 is an indicator of numerical fluency, and a sad mood is an indicator of depression, but there is more to both constructs.

### The Hypothesis and Domain of Content

Chapter 1 noted that some investigators are more formal than others in explicating a theory and that this diversity is healthy. However, it is important that an investigator at least be able to describe the properties of the attribute that is to be measured, regardless of whether this attribute is a personality trait or an ability. Recall that construct validation simultaneously tests the theory at the same time that it tests the measure, a difficult process of "bootstrapping." This book focuses upon the properties of the measure, but these include the ability to translate the deductions of the theory into meaningful correlates. In particular, the hypothesis should describe its domain of content, paralleling that required for content validation. The more properties the construct possesses, the more broadly it can be measured.

Any concept of numerical fluency thus implies questions that deal with simple operations upon numbers. Similarly, numerous investigators have been interested in measuring psychopathological traits like depression. The American Psychiatric Association's (1987) *Diagnostic and Statistical Manual*, (3d ed.) provides a listing of relevant symptoms for this and other conditions that can serve as starting point to define the domain. Questions, such as asking individuals whether they feel sad or appear sad to others, are therefore implicit. Independent behaviors that are observed in conjunction are particularly important. For example, there is nothing inherent in a sad mood that would cause an eating disturbance, but the fact that these constitute part of the clinical syndrome of depression allows both types of items to follow from the domain.

Once the domain has been defined, the creativity of the investigator is needed to formulate specific items that follow from the definition. Consequently, item pools should be regarded as samples of content, and they should be evaluated in terms of how well they sample the implied domain. In particular, earlier views of personality assessment (Meehl, 1945) stressed the importance of selecting items on the basis of their correlation with relevant criteria. We will criticize empirically oriented approaches to item selection later in this chapter although it is essential to validate scales.

Subtle items are often needed for personality measures, as lack of such items may allow individuals to fake results in the desired direction. However, as Jackson (1971) has noted, well-developed domains often define items whose responses would not be known by someone attempting to fake the item. The ability to generate such items is a benefit of a well-specified domain, particularly one that has been based upon prior research. The presence of eating and sleep disturbances in depression exemplifies less obvious features of the construct.

## Content Homogeneity

Chapter 3 contrasted the measurement (internal) and structural (external) properties of a test. The measurement properties include coefficient $\alpha$ reliability and temporal stability, which we have discussed, and homogeneity of content. A test's content is homogeneous when it has little measurement error (a high coefficient $\alpha$) and measures only one attribute. Homogeneity implies that the measures are mathematically unidimensional (i.e., that subjects vary along the scale measuring that trait in only one way) and unifactor in a sense to be specified in Chapters 11 through 13. Chapter 6 noted that a large value of coefficient $\alpha$ does not imply that measures are unidimensional. A measure of a construct may be heterogeneous either because it contains much random error or because its content is diverse.

The content of a construct *must* be homogeneous for its correlates to be interpretable unequivocally. If a test confounds several attributes, one cannot readily determine which or both are responsible for the correlation. The use of unnecessarily complex wording in measures designed to describe numerical fluency illustrates one form of this confounding in abilities measures. The California $F$ scale (Adorno, Frenkel-Brunskwik, Levinson, & Sanford, 1950) was once a widely used personality measure designed to assess fascist beliefs. Unfortunately, all of its items were keyed "yes," so that individual differences in the tendency to say yes were confounded with the trait in question. One of the dilemmas of construct validation is that the need for diverse correlates of a measure pushes investigators in one direction, and the need for homogeneity pulls them in another. Both are essential.

The heterogeneity of the content of these tests allows them to correlate with different measures for different reasons. A key point is that the confounding is not part of the definition of the construct. The term "numerical reasoning" implies nonverbal skills, and most conceptualizations of fascism do not include the simple tendency to say yes as part of the definition, though saying yes to authority figures could be. People who are high in the trait would differ from people low in the trait for different reasons, but these different reasons are inherent in the definition. This heterogeneity would be a legitimate part of the test if it were part of the domain of content implied by the construct. For example, some items on the MMPI's hysteria (Hy) scale describe symptom complaints and others describe naivete. If these can be regarded as components of the concept (which is a legitimate topic of debate), the confounding would be proper.

The homogeneity of a test's content is reflected in, but not completely defined by, the average correlation among items and in the pattern of those correlations. If the average correlation among items, and therefore the average item-total correlation, is low, the items are heterogeneous. This may be because of large amounts of random error or because a number of different factors are present in the items. The latter can produce clusters of relatively homogeneous items which might have either near-zero or negative correlations with one another. Despite the demands for breadth in a scale, it is necessary that (1) the average correlation with total scores be high and (2) the spread of correlations about this average be small.

Thissen, Steinberg, and Wainer (1991) outline three formal approaches to determining whether a set of items is unidimensional. These involve fitting the item responses to (1) a factor analytic model, as discussed in Chapters 11 through 13, (2) an item response theory (IRT) model as described in Chapter 10, and (3) a log-linear model as considered in Chapter 15. All three proceed from formal mathematical definitions that, while similar in an abstract sense, have somewhat different specific properties. However, measures designed to assess broad, useful traits may not fit any of these models, and the misfit may reflect desirable variation in method variance. Conversely, high average correlations, while important to content homogeneity, are not identical to it.

## Methodological Heterogeneity

Most attributes can be measured in several different ways. This implies methodological heterogeneity in the Campbell and Fiske (1959) sense of Chapter 3. Although the ability to add pairs of two-digit numbers quickly is germane to numerical fluency, defining numerical fluency solely in terms of such items would exclude fluency in the other fundamental operations of subtraction, multiplication, and division which are at least implicit in the domain. (There may be reasons to limit the definition to fluency in addition, but this should be made explicit in defining the domain of content.) The simplest example for sentiments is to have some items keyed "yes" (or "agree," etc.) and the remaining items keyed "no." Thus, some depression items would imply that "yes" denotes depression (symptom admission items) and other depression items would imply that "no" denotes depression (symptom denial items). These can often be constructed by suitable choice of wording, e.g., asking "I sleep as often as I usually do" instead of "My sleep has been disturbed recently." Being depressed is not identical to being "not undepressed." The former involves affirmation of symptoms, and the latter involves denial of positive mood states, which are not identical.

We will use the term "methodological heterogeneity" somewhat broadly to cover several different ways that measures purporting to reflect a given domain of content can be studied. These include, but are not limited to, systematic differences in (1) type of measure, e.g., self-description, observation; (2) situation, e.g., psychiatric evaluation, employee selection, etc.; (3) subject population, e.g., primary school students, college students, employees, retirees; and (4) item keying direction. Houts, Cook, and Shadish (1986) discuss their importance as part of what they term "critical multiplism," which deals with establishing a broad perspective on psychological research.

In general, failure to provide methodological heterogeneity leads to traits that are defined in extremely narrow terms and whose properties are confounded with the chosen method. Their narrowness will limit correlations with variables of interest to the general trait, and the confounding will cause them to correlate with variables that are not of interest. At the same time, it is not necessary that a measure apply to all possible methodological domains: A measure may require self-report and may be suitable only for use with adults, for example. Specifying the domain of methodology is as important as specifying the domain of content.

It is quite probable that addition items would correlate more highly with other addition items than with multiplication items on a test of numerical fluency and that symptom admission items would correlate more highly with other symptom admission items than with symptom denial items on a pathology measure. These are conditions which indicate that more than one factor is being measured, which in fact is the case. However, this multiplicity of factors may be an artifact of methodological heterogeneity, which is desirable, rather than content heterogeneity. If so, it would violate parsimony to attempt to use the measures separately. In particular, we support the rather traditional point of view that one should attempt to approximately balance the number of sentiment items keyed "yes" and "no" (agree versus disagree, etc.). Failure to do so confounds the measure of the trait with individual differences in willingness to say yes (acquiescence).

Methodological heterogeneity can therefore cause correlations among items to cluster, just as content heterogeneity can. If you have access to data obtained from a short scale on which items are keyed in different directions, say agree versus disagree, perform the following simple experiment. Correlate all items with each other. Then, compare the average correlation between items keyed in (1) the same direction versus (2) different directions. Your will probably find that the average correlation between items keyed in the same direction is larger than the average correlation between items keyed in different directions. This is evidence that "agree" and "disagree" items form different clusters or factors in the sense of Chapters 11 through 13. However, the factors represent differences in method rather than content. There are several examples of how item keying can produce clustering. These go at least as far back as Jackson and Messick (1962). The second author presents some recent examples that illustrate how the distinction between content and method variance is still often ignored (Bernstein & Eveland, 1982; Bernstein & Garbin, 1985; Bernstein, Teng, & Garbin, 1986). Deciding whether factors represent differences in method or content is not a statistical decision. It is a matter of defining the domain.

Correlations among clusters should first be corrected for attenuation since the observed scores are derived from very fallible parts of scales. The higher the correlation among clusters, the less possible it is for the clusters to relate differentially to external criteria, a point that follows directly from the logic of multiple regression (Chapter 5) and is implicit in Campbell and Fiske's (1959) work. There is no reason to separate groups of items whose average between-cluster correlation is high even if it is lower than the within-cluster correlation. Some recent methods of analysis easily provide statistically significant, but misleading, evidence that clusters are different. Two constructs are unparsimonious compared to one, and the two scales will be less reliable than the single composite scale. In addition, the regression weights in predicting a criterion will not differ from the equality implied by using a single scale. However, if the scales defined by different methods correlate very poorly with one another, say .7 or less, the construct needs reformulation.

We have used item keying as an example of method variance because it is very explicitly defined and easy to investigate. However, it is not the most important. The social desirability of response alternatives is perhaps the most important source of method variance for sentiments since it always accounts for much of the variance in response distributions over items concerned with sentiments, if not the most. Knowing the popularly chosen alternative for a given item will probably predict an individual's choice better than knowing the individual. In general, items should reflect a variety of situations. For example, measures of extraversion could ask whether the individual likes to go to parties with friends but should also include situations with strangers.

It is still somewhat a matter of debate how much individual differences with regard to such variables as social desirability are responsible for individual differences on substantive measures, but two possible artifacts should be kept in mind. One is that social desirability clearly varies over the context of testing—individuals seen in a psychotherapeutic setting find it more appropriate to endorse self-descriptive items about pathology than individuals seen in an employment setting. Indeed, it should not be very surprising that the second author noted that people seen in therapy for court-mandated child custody rulings portrayed themselves as "healthier" than people who voluntarily initiated therapy. Second, to the extent there are individual differences in tendency to respond on the basis of social desirability, tests may tend to correlate because they share social desirability variance. Chapter 9 considers additional incidental variables such as acquiescence.

This chapter is primarily concerned with scaling people rather than stimuli, but social desirability obviously plays a major role in both situations. Far more people claim they watch culturally approved events like the opera than actually do. The problem of eliminating social desirability in such areas as market research is actually more of a problem than it is in areas like personality assessment because the desirability is part of the stimulus. Chapter 9 illustrates the strategy of measuring the subject under conditions that provide differences in social desirability.

Although it is not employed in any single assessment device, the most obvious form of methodological heterogeneity is to combine self-report with behavioral observation or, alternatively, with a psychophysiological indicator. Raymond Cattell (1957, 1978; Cattell, Eber, & Tatsuoka, 1970) was one of the first to stress the importance of converging operations in personality measurement. The success with which this can be done depends upon the characteristics of the trait. As noted in Chapter 3, some traits, like depression, lend themselves to this particular form of multimethod converging operations since they tend to be reported by the individual and are apparent to external observers. Conversely, others, like anxiety, do not. Using different types of observers is another way to explore different methods. For example, peers and supervisors might rate individuals in a work setting, perhaps incorporating a generalizability analysis as discussed in Chapter 7.

## Relations among Measures and Constructs

Jackson (1971), among others, stresses the importance of a multivariate approach considering the relations of items to scales and scales to each other. Personality assessment, in particular, has long been afflicted by a multiplicity of construct names that are ill-differentiated from each other and most likely overlap in various ways. One must assess what is important *not* to incorporate into a scale as well as what is important. In a more general sense, numerical fluency needs to be considered at least in the context of verbal fluency, and depression needs to be considered in the concept of other pathologies.

An investigation of a given measure should include variables defined by methods other than that used by the proposed measure. For example, if the proposed measure(s) is(are) based upon self-report, as is perhaps most common, it is wise to include ability measures and measures based upon observation. Data derived solely from self-reports tend to be of limited value because a common method variance is imposed upon all measures, inflating the apparent structure.

Whereas many in the past took a narrow operationalist perspective ("Intelligence is what an IQ test measures"; also see Chapter 1), investigators now distinguish between a measure as an indicator of a construct and the construct itself. Methods of factor analysis, next considered, allow this to be implemented, but these methods also contain many hazards. However, when properly used, they allow data from several fallible measures to be combined into a more meaningful index. "Fallible" in this context means both imperfectly defining and unreliable in the classical psychometric sense. For example, researchers using demographic data often need to define a variable like the nation's economy at a given time. Measures like the unemployment rate, retail sales, and number of housing starts are all related to this concept, but no single measure can be regarded as definitive. Similar considerations hold for performance measures such as speed and accuracy of response. Linear combinations of indicators can provide the necessary breadth.

## The Role of Factor Analysis

Many investigators automatically think of using factor analysis whenever questions of structure arise. We will discuss specific strategies in Chapters 11 through 13. For now, we will stress an important conceptual difference between the factor analysis of whole tests (scale-level analysis), which we heartily encourage, and the factor analysis of individual items (item-level analyses), which we do not. There are defensible approaches to item-level multivariate analyses, but they are complex and typically unnecessary. Given that a domain has been well thought out, the same basic procedures used in the item analysis for content-validated tests generally suffice. Ordinary approaches to factoring items (i.e., those which may be appropriately applied to scale-level analyses) are almost guaranteed to produce spurious results. Such spurious results may lead to inappropriate criticism of sound scales or, what is basically the same thing, lead an investigator to falsely believe that the scale he or she has developed is inappropriately multidimensional when in fact it is not.

First, factor analytic results usually are clearest when correlations among measures vary considerably, especially when they fall in well-defined groups. For example, if some correlations are zero and others are .70, the measures will form strong factors. Two measures that each relate strongly to a factor will probably correlate substantially with each other and poorly with measures that relate strongly to other factors. Groups of measures will each then clearly define particular factors. This outcome is quite possible in scale-level factoring but is improbable in item-level factoring, simply because of the huge difference in reliability of whole tests versus individual items. The average correlation among items that are not simple variants of one another is less than .20 on most tests, and the variance of these correlations is small. Typically, two-thirds of the correlations among items are between .10 and .30. A larger range is just as likely to have arisen from sampling error than true population differences among correlations. This small variance of correlations makes it difficult to document different factors when they actually exist.

Correlations among multicategory items such as Likert scales and the variance of these correlations usually are higher than correlations among dichotomous items. Consequently, factor analyses of multicategory items have a slightly higher probability of not producing spurious outcomes, but correlations among multicategory items are still typically much lower than correlations among whole scales. Moreover, Bernstein and Teng (1989) found that multicategory items were actually more subject to artifact than dichotomous items with certain approaches to factoring.

Second, traditional exploratory approaches to factor analysis can encourage an unhealthy and unnecessary form of "shotgun empiricism" because they are not designed to test structures defined in advance. This is not true of factor analysis in general since confirmatory approaches can test theories of factor organization and exploratory approaches can be used properly. However, some investigators believe (though they may be loathe to admit it) that factor analyses and related methods automatically grind out the "true nature of things" in the absence of any theory. One can almost hear such individuals saying, "Give me a large enough collection of items to factor-analyze and a huge computer and I can completely determine the nature of human attributes." From a technical standpoint, modern computers allow such analyses to be conducted more easily, unfortunately.

The reader surely has heard about the evils of shotgun empiricism before. Progress in science must be guided by theories rather than by random efforts to relate things to one another. Good theories greatly reduce the amount of trial-and-error effort, and people who explore theories stand at the vanguard of each field of science. It is just as important to formulate theories regarding attributes to be measured as it is to develop methods of analysis. This point applies with great force when factor analysis is applied to a polyglot collection of items in the hope of obtaining important measures of human attributes.

A third problem is that conventions used in factor analysis evolved from the analysis of continuous variables and can be misleading when applied to item-level data which are inherently categorical (discrete). Conventional item-level factor analyses typically are plagued by two distinct problems, both of which lead, virtually without exception, one to conclude that a set of items are multidimensional when in fact they are unidimensional. Bernstein and Teng (1989) illustrate these problems and provide references to the long history of this problem (e.g., Ferguson, 1941; Carroll, 1945). The end result is that items with similar distributions will tend to correlate more highly with one another than with items with dissimilar distributions (see Chapter 4), assuming that there is any structure at all. Easy or commonly endorsed items will thus tend to form factors that are distinct from difficult or less commonly endorsed items even when they are simulated from a model that assumes they measure the same underlying variable and are unidimensional in the Guttman scale sense. Gorsuch (1983) provides a relevant illustration.

The results in short will bear more closely upon the univariate properties of items such as their direction of keying and response distributions rather than the multivariate structure. Not all journal reviewers are familiar with these artifacts even though they were noted over 50 years ago. Spurious arguments that scales are multidimensional are perhaps the most common artifact in the multivariate literature. Unfortunately, some of the newer methods of factor analysis are even more likely to provide spurious results than are older methods because they are more sensitive to all differences in correlation magnitude, including ones that arise spuriously from differences in the univariate structure of items.

## Item Analysis and Selection

The item analysis for tests designed for construct validation is very similar to the item analysis for tests designed for content validation. The item statistics ($p$ values for dichotomously scored items, mean and standard deviation for multicategory items) provide information about item difficulty for judgments and endorsement level for sentiments.

Whereas the corrected item-total correlation is the preferred discrimination index for content-validated tests, Jackson (1971; Neill & Jackson, 1970) suggests a variant for use in construction validation. The measure adjusts total score for irrelevant variables (his example involves social desirability) by using the difference between the squared item-total correlation and the squared correlation between the item and the irrelevant variable rather than the item-total correlation alone as the selection criterion. A variant is to look at the two correlations separately. One problem that may arise is that items that correlate highly with total score also correlate highly with the irrelevant variables. Jackson's procedure is not unlike the use of marker items in content validation since the intent is to improve upon the criterion with which the item is correlated over a fallible total score. Indeed, methods of item analysis largely differ in terms of what is defined as the criterion against which individual items are correlated.

In general, somewhat lower standards of reliability (coefficient $\alpha$) are tolerable for preliminary forms of construct-validated measures than for content-validated measures. This is not because of any difference in the two types of measures, but because a construct is more likely to be used to obtain correlations and less likely to be used for making decisions about individuals. We have stressed how the effects of measurement error, while not negligible, are usually not the major reason one fails to find correlations with external criteria. Ultimately, however, a construct-validated measure should have a high coefficient $\alpha$ given the need for content homogeneity and the likelihood that it will eventually be used for making decisions about individuals.

It is usually easier to modify a typical performance item used to measure sentiments than it is to modify a maximum performance item used in assessing abilities when its response distribution is undesirable. For example, suppose subjects are asked to agree or disagree with the question "I get headaches very frequently." The group sampled might provide an undesirably high proportion of "no" responses, limiting the item-total correlation. However, you have at least two options to improve the item's distributional characteristics; (1) use a multicategory format, e.g., a 5-point Likert scale—"very strongly agree" to "very strongly disagree"; and (2) change the modifier, perhaps dropping "very." It is usually difficult to make a judgment easier or harder without fundamentally changing its nature.

## The Inadequacy of Rational Approaches to Test Construction

The earliest (pre-1940) personality tests were constructed by a rational approach; items were included because they appeared to relate to what was being measured. People with no background in test construction often think in these terms. The MMPI evolved from the Bell Adjustment Inventory, which was developed in this way. For example, a depression item might have been included saying "I feel sad," and sad mood is a characteristic of depression. In a purely rational approach, no attempt is made to confirm that items correlate with the total score. Even though measures of reliability had long been used in measures of abilities (Kuder & Richardson, 1937), personality researchers paid less attention to the concept. One reason was that then, as now, many people who were interested in a measure did not consult with people knowledgeable about psychometric theory. Rational test construction is fundamentally inadequate (a better term than "incorrect" or "inappropriate") since it makes no attempt to confirm the hypothesis that gave rise to the item. Items on such scales may not correlate positively with total score or even correlate negatively. A depressive who is asked if he or she feels sad might well think, "The way I feel goes beyond being sad," and answer in the negative.

Earlier criticisms of rational approaches stressed that proposed items frequently were based upon incorrect assumptions and stressed the need to develop items that differentiated criterion groups, regardless of content. Meehl (1945) is probably the single most important reference for this empirical or criterion-oriented point of view. If more normals than depressives, or the reverse, stated that they ate lima beans, the question would be suitable on a depression scale. Content was irrelevant; indeed, the fact that an item bore no relation to the construct was viewed as a virtue. Empirical approaches led to many advances, the most important being the development of better methods of item analysis. Exploratory factor analysis became widely used because of its empirical orientation with, as we have suggested, mixed results. Empiricism played a strong early role in the abilities literature; J. McK. Cattell gave up his interest in measuring general ability using measures of sensory acuity because Wissler (1901; also see Cronbach, 1990) showed how heterogeneous these measures were.

The pendulum swung back from purely empirical approaches in the late 1960s, and Jackson (1971) documents this shift well. In retrospect, the problem with the original rational approach was *not* that most investigators generally lacked the ability to define relevant item content, although, of course, there are numerous instances in which this was true. The major problems were threefold: (1) the wording of individual questions was often flawed, (2) no methods of analysis were used to detect this, and (3) investigators paid insufficient attention to the similarity of their constructs to those of others (or, what leads to the same outcome, attempted to stress the unique aspects of theirs relative to others', thus ignoring the essential similarity). Anyone familiar with personality assessment is aware of how slight changes in wording can often make the difference between a suitable and an unsuitable item. In sum, our criticism of rationally developed tests is not based upon how items are constructed but the failure to evaluate the items after developing them.

### The Inadequacy of Empirical (Criterion-Oriented) Approaches to Test Construction

We have noted that the undeniable and appropriate success of the MMPI led investigators toward an empirical (criterion-oriented) approach. For those unfamiliar with its development, the principles are simple. First, a large pool of items was generated that was felt to be of use or had been used in clinical interviews in order to standardize these interviews. Clinical scales were constructed by choosing items to differentiate target groups, such as depressives or schizophrenics, from normals. Validity scales were also developed. Specifically, the defensiveness scale ($K$) corrects certain of the clinical scales for reluctance to admit to problems. In addition, 16 items were repeated to provide the familiar 566 total items on the test, and numerous supplementary scales were proposed. See Dahlstrom, Welsh, and Dahlstrom (1975a, 1975b) for further details on the original MMPI, and Hathaway and McKinley (1989) for information about its recent revision. We will limit our discussion to the individual scales even though practitioners typically base their decisions upon configurations of scale scores (profiles). This discussion is of general value because the issues are broadly applicable.

Even though the MMPI was ostensibly an example of an empirically derived test, we suggest that its best features actually illustrate the importance of defining domains of content. Its less successful applications were those that more strongly reflected purely empirical biases. First and foremost, the item pool was not generated randomly. It clearly reflected the experiences of the clinicians at making precisely the diagnostic decisions at which the MMPI has been most successful. Although much was (and is) unknown about the etiology and dynamics of major psychiatric disorders, the symptomatology has generally been known. Clinicians have long observed guilt (particularly of a religious nature), eating and sleeping disturbances, and behavioral retardation in addition to sad mood in depressives, for example. Moreover, depressives can be viewed as extreme points along a trait continuum. Similar considerations hold for the other diagnostic categories, such as schizophrenia, conversion disorders, and affective disorders. In general, the original item pool sampled these domains rather well.

Another feature of the MMPI is that its items also fall into categories defined by content, such as general health, occupational problems, and morale, somewhat independently of their role on clinical scales. In fact, the reuse of these content scales became an important development in the late 1960s (Wiggins, 1966, 1968, 1969, 1973). For our purposes, these scales provide methodological heterogeneity. For example, some depressives develop religiosity without showing sleep disturbances, whereas others do the reverse. Including both types of items increases the probability of correct diagnosis.

Proponents of empirical approaches to testing often have noted how difficult it is to determine which items fall on which scales. One problem with this argument is that an item analysis will reveal that many items on a given scale are invalid and that valid items were excluded because of sampling error, a major hazard in purely empirical methods. Even when an apparently relevant item correctly fails to appear on a scale, the failure may reflect details of wording. One could well argue that several items could be have been changed in the MMPI's recent revision. There was a legitimate issue of seeking optimal scales versus maintaining comparability of scales (which eventually dominated) that played a major role in this revision. Fortunately, lack of optimal item selection is mitigated by the forgiving nature of the linear model used in scoring. Whatever else one may say that is critical about the major clinical scales, few would claim they are too short. Of course, the difference between the actual scales and possible "optimal" ones is more important to making individual decisions than it is to group research.

MMPI scale items have long been classified as "subtle" and "obvious" based upon their relation to symptomatology (Wiener, 1948). Although one may debate the classification of individual items, it would be a major point in favor of empirical approaches if subtle items were to even approach obvious ones in their discriminative capacity. However, as Gynther and Burkhart (1983) note, this is clearly not the case. Subtle items were understandably sought after to help differentiate pathology from such response sets as "faking bad." The position taken here is that it is best to obtain separate measures for such purposes, which is, of course, precisely the role that the validity scales achieve.

Another point in favor of the empirical approach is the success of several of the supplementary scales that was not anticipated at the time the MMPI was originally developed. Ignoring issues of their construct validity, a few scales have gained apparent wide use, e.g., MacAndrew's (1965) alcoholism scale and Barron's (1953) ego strength scale. However, this number is an incredibly small fraction of those proposed, and both of these scales reflect rather traditional concerns of practitioners that may have been reflected in the item pool. One might argue that little would be lost if at least one of the clinical scales (masculinity-femininity, *Mf*) was deleted. In a great many of the ultimately unsuccessful attempts to derive supplemental scales, a true empirical approach was attempted but the items failed to replicate because the underlying traits (e.g., response to a particular drug or diagnostic subcategories) were ill-defined. Although we certainly recognize the legitimacy of debate on the issue, we conclude by noting that empirical methods did little to the MMPI that was not originally furnished by the (partially implicit) theories of those who generated the original item pool.

We have noted Raymond Cattell's early emphasis upon multiple methods to define constructs. The Sixteen Personality Factor (16-PF) Test was among the results of this

approach. However, we must be critical of one facet of his test development procedures. His stress upon methodological heterogeneity led him to seek items that correlate well with an appropriate criterion but poorly with each other. The logic follows
from the regression model (see Chapter 5), but the analogy to multiple regression is
strained. Multiple regression assumes that predictors are highly reliable. This logic can
apply to whole tests but clearly does not apply to individual items.

Moreover, it is difficult enough to find items outside the abilities domain which
correlate with total score without imposing the additional burden of having them correlate with an external criterion. Cattell's approach seeks items which are poorly correlated with total test score since they will be poorly correlated with the other items
that help determine the test score. However, items correlate with the criterion because they measure what the criterion measures. This makes it quite likely that items
that correlate with the criterion will correlate with each other. In other words, if we
were to take (1) the item-total correlation for each item, corrected or not, and (2) its
correlation with the criterion, we would find the two sets of numbers correlated over
items. Figure 8-2 illustrates this point. The desired items fall in the indicated upper-
left region of the figure. Because of the correlation between the two indices, the density of items in this region is relatively sparse. In this simulated example, the correlation was set at .5, and there are only three points in the somewhat arbitrarily chosen
selection zone.

We will also argue against this approach when constructing a predictor, but less ve-
hemently because of the greater importance of content homogeneity in measuring constructs.

FIGURE 8-2    Scatter plot of item correlations with a criterion and with total test scores.

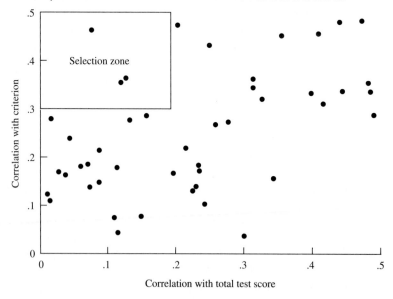

## Norms

A construct is somewhat less likely to require norms than a content-validated measure because of differences in their probable use. Nearly all measures derived from content validation are used for making decisions about individuals, where norms are important; many positions in industry, for example, involve ad hoc requirements that are of pragmatic rather than theoretical import. In contrast, constructs are often employed primarily in research and may never be used in individual classification or selection.

However, a well-developed measure that begins solely as a research tool may turn out to be of value in making individual decisions. At that point, norms may be required, but the considerations are no different from those involved in developing norms for content-validated measures. The same is true of measures derived under a predictive validity paradigm which, like content-validated measures, tend to be used for making decisions about individuals.

## Applying the Measure

Which populations a content-validated measure is to be used with is often implicit in its intended use. This dictates the level at which questions are worded. However, it is not uncommon to develop constructs or predictive measures without a clear idea of their limits of applicability, and most normative samples are chosen for convenience. However, the intended population should be incorporated in the definition of the domain. It is also desirable to evaluate the proposed measure in several populations which might also be targets of the measure. Although you will probably look at groups defined on the basis of gender and race in order to evaluate bias, the single most important starting point is generally reading level, assuming that the test requires the subjects to read, as in a self-descriptive inventory. Gorsuch, Henighan, and Barnard (1972) illustrate how a scale's properties may depend upon reading ability.

The authors strongly feel that good measures are hard to come by even if they work only in limited circumstances. A measure that has substantial validity in one population should not be dismissed for not working in others. It simply should not be used in that case. Failures to obtain desired correlations are quite common in the literature. Those who report a study might consider that such failures may represent real differences between populations in correlation magnitude (moderation, see Chapter 5) in reporting their results.

Our discussion applies in very similar form to behavioral observations and physiological measures. Reading skills (literacy) may not be an issue per se, but their socioeconomic correlates probably are, especially to ratings. Judges may naturally be able to make valid discriminations within their own group, but other groups may "all look alike" in their behavior. Moreover, it is not uncommon to find differences among lower socioeconomic groups defined on the basis of ethnicity even when these are much smaller or absent in the middle class (Pritchard & Rosenblatt, 1980a, 1980b; but also see Gynther, 1972; Gynther & Green, 1980). This problem is best addressed by appropriate training with feedback from those who are demonstrably skilled at making relevant discriminations.

## Some Examples of Constructs in the Abilities Area

Our previous discussion of the MMPI illustrated several points generally relevant to the measurement of sentiments. Turning briefly to examples involving the measurement of abilities, we have stressed that work in this area is more obviously relatable to the notion of domain sampling because abilities items, like adding four-digit numbers, often fall into well-defined classes. These classes in fact can be viewed as theories asserting that the particular skill common to the class is important. Much work has been based upon the rather traditional tasks derived from such sources as the Thurstones (T. G. Thurstone, 1941). Guilford (1967) proposed a model of intelligence that makes an explicit distinction between content and method. In fact, his model is based upon the tripartite classification of operations (what is to be done—evaluation, convergent production, divergent production, etc.), content (the material on which the operations are to be performed—figural, semantic, behavioral, etc.), and products (outcomes—units, classes, relations, etc.). For example, adding numbers involves convergent production as an operation (there is a single correct answer) upon symbolic content and the product is a unit (number). Unfortunately, the number of combinations of the three basic elements has proven rather large and unparsimonious to many investigators.

Several aspects of the abilities literature reflect this section's stress on having measures flow from at least some theory. In particular, the traditional (but incorrect) view that intelligence is a unitary phenomenon gave rise to the notion of "g" or general intelligence which in turn led to Spearman's (1904) development of factor analysis. At least two other theories follow from fairly conventional views of intelligence rather than highly elaborate models. Wechsler's extremely successful tests (see Mitchell, 1985) are organized around the distinction between verbal and performance skills. Similarly, the view that some cognitive abilities involve facts, but other, higher-level demands involve abstractions, led Horn and Cattell (1966; Horn, Donaldson, & Engstrom, 1981; Vernon, 1979) to contrast crystallized and fluid intelligence. Perhaps the example most familiar to college students is the distinction between verbal and quantitative ability on the SAT and GRE. In contrast, Earl Hunt, Robert Sternberg, and others whose roots are in cognitive psychology have developed highly elaborate information processing models of intelligence with attendant measures (e.g., Hunt, Pellegrino, Frick, Farr, & Alderson, 1988; Sternberg, 1977, 1988). One question for research is whether those measures that were originally developed for studying group differences, as produced by experimental manipulations, where individual differences are undesirable, will be as successful when adapted to the study of individual differences (see Cronbach, 1957).

## CONSTRUCTION OF TESTS DESIGNED FOR PREDICTIVE VALIDATION

A test designed solely to predict a criterion arguably need not require a well-defined domain of content. This could be taken to imply a purely empirical approach to item generation and selection. However, we hope to show that this is a poor strategy that is unlikely to yield a valid scale. Moreover, legal and ethical considerations also dictate considering bias in any measure, which we will do in the next two chapters.

Having a good idea of what determines the criterion is probably the single most important aspect of predictive validation. Sometimes an individual familiar with the task to be performed can furnish insights. Of course, these need not be correct. Chapter 5 presented an example of how all variation in outcome could be attributed to intelligence rather than a large set of individual attributes, and Chapter 3 illustrated other problems associated with practical criteria. Having someone tell you that virtues like intelligence, initiative, and mental stability are important is a starting point, but don't be surprised if these are unrelated or even negatively related to the outcome. You may or may not be able to do anything about the problem. If the situation allows you the luxury of repeated pilot work, consider the use of whole tests designed to measure possible attributes at the beginning, even if you are eventually going to use items sampled from these tests.

A typical situation that involves the development of a test for prediction is to anticipate improvement in a drug rehabilitation program. It is assumed that the often difficult problem of obtaining a suitable criterion measure (Chapter 3) has been resolved. The two essential ingredients in the development of a successful measure are (1) at least several hundred subjects to act as a normative pool for successive versions of the test and (2) a thorough literature review to suggest possible items or whole tests.

What is done is very similar to what is done either in content or construct validation. The major difference is that the focus is upon the single correlation between the scale and criterion (validity coefficient) rather than the suitability of the content, the scale's internal properties such as coefficient $\alpha$, or its relation to a diversity of criteria. Since most real-life criteria are somewhat heterogeneous factorially (i.e., are not "pure measures"), the difference between construct and predictive validation can be thought of as trading off some homogeneity of content, and therefore reliability, with ability to predict a specified criterion.

Requirement 1 can be relaxed somewhat if the goal is to test the utility of a preexisting measure. The primary considerations are the anticipated validity and the sampling error. A typical expected validity is .3 to .4, but it can be in the .5 to .6 range when the criterion is heavily determined by cognitive ability and there is wide variation in the relevant pool of individuals (Hunter & Hunter, 1984; Hunter & Schmidt, 1981; Schmidt, Hunter, & Pearlman, 1981). The sampling error in a single $r$ is $1/\sqrt{N-1}$, where $N$ is the sample size. Clearly, the smaller the anticipated validity, the larger the sample required. A sample of 50 is clearly the lowest tolerable limit on $N$ when the expected validity is .3 since $1/\sqrt{50-1} = .14$ and $(1.96)(.14)$ (the 95 percent confidence interval) $= .28$. Obviously, larger samples are really required. Moreover, if you are exploring the utility of several predictors, which is wise from the standpoint of economy, you need to take the resulting multiple comparisons into account.

In general, you will want to form a confidence interval around $r$. If this interval contains both the anticipated validity and zero, the experiment is inconclusive. Of course, having this confidence interval include zero denotes an inability to reject the null hypothesis, but a very low but nonzero validity (e.g., .1) also implies that the measure may not be useful. Higher standards should be imposed upon the validity for *developing* a measure than for testing a hypothesized measure because the development process capitalizes upon chance. The literature has no shortage of tests whose initial validity was simply due to chance. It is, of course, vital to cross-validate a test which has been developed through any form of empirically based item selection. The sample size required for cross validation is effectively the same as that needed for any other preexisting test. In addition, even though some outstanding tests have been very empirically driven and items designed for use in a predictor need not have any apparent relevance to the criterion, we stress the need for at least some theory. One cannot see all of the unsuccessful attempts to develop scales along a given line that have been unreported. Although there are many apparent successes in the literature, many of these are not replicable or hold only for limited populations.

### Item Analysis, Item Selection, and Norms

The principles of item analysis are similar to those used in developing other measures. Considerations of content homogeneity lead us to suggest using the total score or the score on marker variables rather than the criterion score to select items, but our reasons are not as compelling as they were for developing measures of constructs. However, correlations with a dichotomous criterion will be low, making it difficult to detect good items. There is less need to be concerned about item redundancy (correlations among items on the scale) unless it is so high as to suggest that the same item is being asked repeatedly. Even though internal consistency is relatively unimportant in predictive validation as compared to the development of construct measures, it is obviously not undesirable.

Norms are generally required for relevant populations. The principles required are the same as in developing a content-validated measure.

## PROBLEMS UNIQUE TO CERTAIN TESTING SITUATIONS

### Reversing the Direction of Keying

Items are often scored so that a high number (e.g., a 5) is in the keyed direction for some items (e.g., denotes shyness) but is in the nonkeyed direction for other items (e.g., denotes lack of shyness). "Flipping" item scores so that high scores on all items denote the presence of the trait is quite simple. To make a high item response ($X$) denote a low score on the key ($X'$) when there are $k$ categories, let $X' = k - X + 1$. Thus, a response of 2 on a 7-point scale becomes $7 - 2 + 1 = 6$ when the direction of scoring is reversed. This is applicable to dichotomously scored items where $k = 2$. Although methods of analysis can be used that do not require reversing the direction of keying, looking at the results is much easier if this is done early in the analysis. In particular, large negative correlations involving one or more items suggest a problem exists (which can be as simple as miskeying). This is more difficult to detect in the unreversed items.

### Unipolar versus Bipolar Attributes

Nearly all abilities and achievement attributes and many personality attributes are unipolar. The continuum extends in one direction from a zero point; it is difficult to think of "negative" intelligence. However, constructs such as liberal-conservative and introversion-extroversion are bipolar because they represent continuua with a neutral (zero) point and affirmative traits at the two poles. "Liberalism" does not denote the absence of "conservativism" any more than vice versa.

The distinction between absolute and comparative sentiments and judgments was made in Chapter 2. Asking people whether they like going to the movies is absolute, and asking whether they like going to the movies better than they like going to parties is comparative. Multicategory response scales can be used in both cases. Comparative items tend to relate exemplars of bipolar attribute poles and, as we have noted, are more sensitive than absolute items. A unipolar attribute usually implies absolute items, but a bipolar attribute can be assessed with either absolute or comparative items. Whether an attribute is assumed to be unipolar or bipolar is a function of the theory. The one key consideration is to be sure not to commit the logical fallacy of the "excluded middle" in which a person is both (e.g., liberal on some specific issues and conservative on others) because the attribute is multidimensional. If this is possible, replace the bipolar continuum with two separate continuua. The "neither" possibility is no problem since it is represented by the zero point(s).

Comparative items have an important use. Many scales are essentially checklists on which the score is a count of the number of absolute endorsements and the person's overall tendency to endorse items is a potential confounding factor. Suppose a measure of introversion-extroversion consists of a number of activities engaged in by introverts, such as reading books, and a number of other activities engaged in by extroverts, such as going to parties. The total score is the difference between the number of items endorsed in the two categories. However, this difference is a function of the willingness to endorse items—at the extreme, if no activities are endorsed, the difference must be zero. It may prove more useful to employ a forced choice comparing activities from each category. By not providing a neutral category, differences among numbers of endorsements are controlled. Be sure to choose alternatives within items that have approximately the same social desirability.

## Discrimination at a Point

Although most measurement problems involve discriminating over the entire continuum, the goal of construction is sometimes to most effectively discriminate persons from one another at a particular point in the distribution. Screening the top 10 percent of scholarship applicants for interview from the remaining 90 percent is one example. Mastery learning also involves selection at a point, but the intent is to discriminate the lowest scorers from the rest of the distribution. The MMPI is perhaps the best known test which was basically designed to discriminate at a point by detecting pathology. Although there are exceptions, most clinical scale items are infrequently endorsed symptoms. The distributions of raw scores on these scales thus tend to be positively skewed in the general population. This is a most appropriate strategy, although it is also responsible for the traditional difficulties of interpreting low scores.

Lord (1952a, 1952b) suggested that the most effective way to discriminate at a point is to control the $p$ values of items. He concluded that one should not choose items with $p$ values as extreme as the desired "split." Thus, to discriminate the upper 70 percent from the lower 30 percent, choose items with $p$ values closer on the .5

side of .7. Interesting as the point is, it is really secondary to the purpose of selecting valid items. The most discriminating item in the linear model for split is the one that correlates highest with that split. Thus, to discriminate at a point, select items as follows.

**1** Construct a test by previously described methods but have at least twice as many items in this test as eventually needed.

**2** Split subjects into the necessary divisions on the basis of total scores, e.g., the upper 70 percent from the lower 30 percent. Assign a 1 to subjects in the top group and a 0 to those in the bottom group.

**3** Compute the correlations between each dichotomous item and each dichotomized total test score ($r$). Note that these are phi coefficients ($\Phi$), unlike the correlations with total score, which are point-biserial correlations ($r_{pb}$).

**4** Rank the items from highest to lowest in terms of $r$. The items highest in $r$ are the most discriminating items at the particular point.

**5** The final test is obtained by selecting enough items high in $r$ to obtain the desired level of reliability.

Use the continuous scores rather than dichotomous scores in subsequent administrations of the test, of course.

This method of test construction can be improved by an iterative process. After selecting the first set of items on the basis of $r$, split subjects into the desired proportions on the revised test scores and recompute $r$ using the new split of high and low scores. The best items form a new test and repeat the procedure if required. However, iterations are seldom necessary. The items which initially had high values of $r$ will usually also have high values of $r$ after iteration.

Even though the items that individually have the highest values of $r$ with any split in terms of total scores will be the most discriminating items, there is no guarantee that the sum of scores on such items will be more discriminating than the sum of scores on some other set of items. The most discriminating set of $k$ items is the set that has the highest multiple correlation with dichotomized total scores. However, we do not recommend using the differential item weights produced by multiple regression because item unreliability violates the important assumption that the predictors (items) be reliable. The above method usually provides better discrimination at a point than any other feasible method. With or without iteration, it tends to select items that have $p$ values falling between .5 and the split. One therefore tends to select more items with $p$ values between .5 and .8 than between .5 and .2 in discriminating the upper 70 percent of people, and vice versa in discriminating the top 30 percent. The crucial consideration is the value of $r$ between dichotomous scores on the item and dichotomized total scores. One typically finds items with $p$ values near the split that have low values of $r$ and other items with $p$ values far removed from the split that have relatively high values of $r$, so $p$ by itself provides limited information. Similar considerations apply to multicategory items.

Tests should ordinarily *not* be constructed to discriminate at a particular point on the score continuum unless the situation specifically demands it. Such tests are useful for only a narrow range of purposes. Different points of discrimination may be important in different situations. A test constructed specifically to discriminate the top 80 percent of the people in one situation will probably be too easy when it has to discriminate the top 20 percent. In addition, the score at a particular percentile in one situation might correspond to a very different percentile in another situation. For example, if 70 percent of the people in one population exceed a raw score of 65, only 30 percent of the people in a less able population might exceed a score of 65. One usually wants to construct a general-purpose test that is discriminating at all levels of the attribute and hence can be used for different purposes in different situations. If, as is typically the case, a content-homogeneous test is desired, items should be selected in terms of their item-total correlations rather than their correlations with dichotomized scores. The refinement described in the next section will help ensure approximately equal reliability at different points on the continuum of scores on the eventual test.

## Equidiscriminating Tests

Items selected to discriminate most effectively at a particular point in the distribution tend to produce a test that is most reliable at that point. We have thus far been concerned with the *overall* reliability of a test in terms of coefficient $\alpha$ or, perhaps, the alternative forms correlation. This overall reliability is in effect an average of the reliabilities at different levels of the attribute. Instead of examining the overall reliability, consider the reliabilities at different levels of the attribute, as by computing coefficients $\alpha$ for subjects within each quintile (one-fifth of the distribution in terms of proportions of cases). Each of these five reliabilities will, of course, be lower than the overall reliability because the subjects within each quintile must vary less than subjects in general, but the error variance will be essentially the same (the standard error of measurement, Eq. 6-34, is more informative about the absolute level of measurement error in this case). However, we are most interested in the differences among these within-groups reliabilities and so $\alpha$ will suffice as a measure.

A test constructed to discriminate maximally at the 30th percentile by methods described previously would provide good reliability (discrimination) from the 20th to the 40th percentile but would provide poorer discrimination from the 60th to the 80th percentile. The rank order of individuals in the lower range would tend to change less than the rank order of those in the higher range on an alternative form constructed by the same standards. One can minimize these differences by constructing an equidiscriminating (EQD) test to equalize discrimination at different levels of the attribute. An EQD test is useful whenever (1) important practical decisions are made about people with regard to their particular test scores and (2) highly reliable distinctions are needed at all levels of the attribute. These circumstances tend to be the norm.

Observed item-total correlations, whether or not they are corrected for overlap, tend to favor the selection of items with $p$ values near .5, as we have noted. Consequently the test will tend to make its most reliable discriminations in the middle of the score range relative to either extreme. Similarly, the approximately normal nature of most score distributions causes most people to fall in the middle of the distribution. This bias toward selecting items of intermediate difficulty can be overcome somewhat by using $r_{bis}$, but this procedure requires very large samples. If one has the resources and can afford to use a relatively long test, a modification of the previously discussed method of developing general-purpose tests leads to the construction of an EQD test that has approximately the same reliability at all levels of the score continuum.

There are a number of approaches to constructing an EQD test; we recommend simply selecting items at multiple cutoff levels. For example, select one-third of the items to differentiate the top 25 percent of the people from the bottom 75 percent, another third to differentiate the top half of the people from the lower half, and a final third to discriminate the bottom 25 percent of the people from the top 75 percent. Each subgroup of items is obtained by the method discussed previously for maximizing discrimination at a particular point. However, select several subsets of items to discriminate at different levels of the score continuum to produce an EQD test.

Divisions are made where it is most important to make discriminations, and the number of divisions that are made depends on the resources available for constructing and employing the test. An EQD test requires from three to six divisions of the score continuum for which separate sets of items are selected. EQD tests are usually longer than conventional tests because they must discriminate well at all levels of the attribute. Since more room is required to select items than when items are selected purely in terms of item-total correlations: (1) the initial item pool must also be larger, (2) these items must vary greatly in their distributions, and (3) these items should correlate highly with total scores expressed as continuous numbers.

When all items are administered to a sample of subjects, the total sample is split at the desired percentile levels (e.g., 25, 50, and 75) and values of $r$ are computed between all items and dichotomized total scores in each case. Thus, first divide the total distribution of people at the 25th percentile, giving everyone above that point a score of 1 and everyone below a score of 0 and correlate each item with the dichotomized score. Rank the items in terms of $r$ and select items based upon the ranking. Repeat this process but divide subjects at the 50th percentile (median) and then at the 75th percentile. This produces two more rank orderings in terms of $r$.

After the three sets of item-dichotomy correlations are obtained, select an approximately equal number of items at each dichotomy to obtain the same average value of $r$ at each level. One might therefore wind up with 20 items at each of the three percentile levels whose average values of $r$ might, respectively, be .19, .21, and .18. Trial-and-error methods will probably be required to obtain such a result, as the $r$ obtained from dividing the distribution at the median will probably be higher than the $r$ obtained from dividing the distribution at the 25th or 75th percentile. Also, items that correlate well with one split are likely to correlate well with other splits, and items that correlate poorly with one split are likely to correlate poorly with others. One can, however, approximate the desired properties by shifting items from dichotomy to dichotomy. Because one should not attempt to construct an EQD test without reliable items, the final form should have at least a modestly high reliability. The fact that large numbers of items will be used also tends to produce a reliable result, but this final coefficient $\alpha$ must be computed.

Figure 8-3 describes the hypothetical results of an EQD test. Curve $a$ shows what might be found for a 40-item test constructed by selecting items only in terms of their item-total correlations. It illustrates that the reliability declines as one moves away

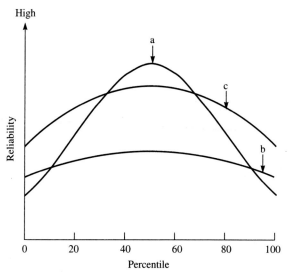

FIGURE 8-3    Hypothetical comparisons of (*a*) a 40-item homogeneous test, (*b*) a 40-item EQD test, and (*c*) a 100-item EQD test.

from the 50th percentile in either direction. In particular, the reliability falls off below the 25th percentile and above the 75th percentile.

Curve *b* shows the approximate results of a 40-item EQD test with eight items being selected specifically to discriminate at the 10th, 30th, 50th, 70th, and 90th percentiles. The function relating coefficient $\alpha$ to percentile is clearly flatter. This test tends to have a slightly lower overall reliability than a test using ordinary item selection procedures for the same number of items: The total area under curve *b* is smaller than the total area under curve *a*. However, an EQD test tends to be more reliable at the extremes.

Curve *c* estimates what might be obtained from a EQD test longer than that represented by curve *b*. The difference is that 20 rather than 8 items appear at each percentile level. This longer test should have higher overall reliability than *b*, substantially more reliability and better overall discrimination than *a*, except perhaps at the 50th percentile. Figure 8-3 also illustrates that the reliability of an EQD test tends to be somewhat higher near the 50th percentile than at either extreme even when maximum effort is given to equal discrimination. However, sufficiently long tests can provide excellent discrimination at the higher and lower levels of the percentile distribution using the EQD logic.

Dichotomies could be formed at 8 or 10 percentile levels rather than at 4 or 5, but this probably will have little effect upon the final test. One could improve the results at each stage by forming new distributions of total scores iteratively and recomputing *r* after items have been selected on the first go-around. Also, new items could be constructed and correlated with dichotomized scores at different levels of the existing test. A final refinement could be to adjust the average *r* value at each level. The ideal would be to obtain a collection of items whose average $r$ value with the dichotomy is the same at different splits. Thus if the test has 100 items with 20 at each of five splits, the ideal is for the average of the 100 values of $r$ at each split to be approximately the same since coefficient $\alpha$ is a function of these averages. One usually approximates this ideal by focusing on the average value of $r$ for the items selected specifically at each level. Since the values of $r$ for all items at each level have been obtained, it is simple to determine the degree of approximation to the ideal. If the average values of $r$ differ across percentile levels, add items of appropriate difficulty, if possible, to increase the average correlation where needed.

The concept of an EQD test was introduced in the first edition of this book (Nunnally, 1967) in passing as a largely hypothetical ideal rather than as a practicable solution to equating reliabilities across the score continuum. However, the need for instruments that have the properties of an EQD test has been spurred subsequently by recent advances (see Chapter 10), the growing realization that many otherwise reliable tests are not highly reliable on the extremes, and the availability of computers to perform the necessary statistical analyses. Although one may elaborate upon the general methods discussed here and there is room to develop some technical details, the overall logic for constructing an EQD test is simple. Employ correlational analysis to select subsets of items that are maximally discriminating at various points along the score continuum and then combine these items into one overall test.

It is seldom worth the trouble to develop an EQD test in basic research or classroom settings. The major requirement in basic research is to have sufficient overall reliability to evaluate different sources of individual differences. Limitations of time and available items typically preclude EQD construction in the classroom setting. However, at least an approximation of an EQD test should be constructed, resources permitting, where (1) people vary considerably with respect to the attribute in question, (2) it is important to make reliable distinctions at all points on the score continuum, and (3) test results are used to make important decisions. Even if one does not literally construct an EQD test, it is important not to make the maximization of an overall coefficient $\alpha$ an end in itself. Spreading item difficulties does sacrifice some overall reliability but improves discrimination and, quite possibly, validity (Loevinger, 1954).

## Weighting of Items

We have thus far assumed that all items are weighted equally in the linear composite. It is logically possible to weight items differentially—one could weight some items 3, others 2, and the remainder 1. We have not discussed this possibility because differential weights are almost always a total waste of time when a test has more than about 20 items—another reflection of Wainer's (1976) "it don't make no nevermind" principle. Various rules have been proposed for weighting items. Items could be weighted to maximize the correlation between total test scores and the criterion, e.g., by its regression weight or item-criterion correlation. We strongly recommended that this not be done since (1) it is generally unwise to construct tests in terms of item-criterion correlations and (2) the item-criterion (or item-anything correlation) usually contains considerable sampling error. In addition, the method cannot be used with content-validated tests, as there is no criterion to be weighted. A slightly more sensible approach is to weight items to maximize the total test score reliability by weighting each item in terms of its item-total correlation, but this makes little difference and is also unstable in most settings.

Weighting makes a difference when the weighted and unweighted scores on whole tests do not correlate highly *and* the weighted test is more reliable than the unweighted test. However, the evidence that differential weights seldom make a difference is overwhelming. Regardless of how differential weights are determined, the two sets of scores typically correlate in the high .90s as long as they are based upon at least 20 items. Differential weights may provide a slight benefit when (1) the number of items is relatively small (less than 20), (2) item-total correlations vary markedly, and (3) the sample consists of several hundred people. These conditions are seldom all present with dichotomous items. Some multicategory scales have considerably less than 20 items, and their item-total correlations vary more than those for tests composed of dichotomous items. Differentially weighting items might increase the reliability slightly, but this same increase in reliability might also result from adding two or three new items. In addition, the regression weights will have large standard errors and probably be poorer than equal weights in a new sample if the sample is relatively small and the number of items is large. In sum, total scores should nearly always be obtained by weighting items equally. If the reliability is undesirably low, increase the number and quality of items.

## Taking Advantage of Chance

All forms of item analysis tend to capitalize on sampling errors relating to the selection of people, so that the results will generally overestimate such quantities as coefficient $\alpha$. One takes advantage of chance *anytime* something is optimized from the data at hand—in multiple correlation, in selecting items in terms of item-total correlations, in selecting items for an EQD test, in seeking differential item weights, and in ridding a test of an unwanted factor. Since the opportunities to take advantage of chance are related positively to the number of variables and negatively to the number of persons, we suggest that there be at least twice as many subjects as items and that at least 200 subjects be used to construct a test designed for long-term use to minimize the role of chance. Items found to have a reliability of .84 might have an eventual reliability of .80, but the drop in reliability will seldom be more than that. If the exact level of reliability is crucial to item selection, strive for a reliability at least five points above the crucial level. The sample needed to construct an EQD test is even larger.

It is wise to investigate the extent to which item selection and related operations take advantage of chance by means of cross validation. Compute coefficient $\alpha$ and other appropriate statistics for a holdout group of at least 100 subjects after optimizing the test on the normative group.

## SUMMARY

This chapter considered tests designed for general use, including classroom tests. Such tests may be developed along principles of content, construct, or predictive validation. These are highly similar, but each has its own distinctive features. It is assumed that the tests are scored according to the linear model; i.e., the total score is the sum of responses to individual items.

Developing a test for content validation requires a domain of content, which defines the nature of the required subject matter and includes the population to which it will be administered, and a test plan. Defining the domain of content in industry may require a job analysis to determine what individuals with a given job actually do. The test plan includes the type of items to be used with examples, the approximate number of items, the length of administration, how it is to be administered, how it is to be scored, and the type of norms that will be required. Plans for major tests typically require consultation with various experts and revisions. Test items may be short-answer, essay, multiple-choice, problem-solving, or other objective formats such as true-false and matching. Choice of test item will reflect the needs of the situation. One consideration is whether recognition of the material is sufficient, in which case multiple-choice questions would be preferred; whether recall is essential, suggesting short-answer formats; or whether organizational ability is critical, in which case problem-solving or essay questions would be appropriate. Standard tips were provided to help phrase questions optimally, but the most essential point is clarity with respect to (1) phrasing, (2) the relation of the item to the content domain, and (3) pointing knowledgeable individuals in the appropriate direction.

The key to the development of any successful test is a good item analysis which provides information about how subjects responded to each item. For example, multiple-choice items for which distractors are chosen more often than the correct alternative are suspect, and distractors that are hardly ever or never chosen should be replaced. One major result of the analysis is the internal consistency reliability (coefficient $\alpha$). Data for each item include its response distribution and its discrimination. If an item is dichotomously scored, the information about its response distribution is completely contained in the probability of responding in the keyed direction ($p$ value). This is the item difficulty for judgments and the endorsement probability for sentiments. If an item allows several categories, the variance may also be of interest in addition to the mean. There are several measures of discrimination, but the item-total correlation, corrected for overlap, Eq. 8-1, is generally preferred. Some situations warrant the correlation of individual items with marker variables (a set of items known to relate to the domain) instead of the total score, though. Additional information is contained in the trace lines, which should be monotonic in the sense of Chapter 2. Item selection generally proceeds by choosing the items which are the most discriminating. Strategically, it is often useful to include some easy items at the beginning of the test as ice breakers. Hopefully, the item analysis provides a sufficient number of valid items.

The raw score is usually not informative by itself, and so it must be placed in context. Norms are statistical data that relate a person's score to the scores of others. The score may be expressed as a percentile, defining how many people in the target population fall at or below that score, or transformed in some other way. Some of these common transformations are $z$ scores ($\mu = 0$ and $\sigma = 1$), deviation IQ scores ($\mu = 100$ and $\sigma = 15$), McCall $T$ scores ($\mu = 50$ and $\sigma = 10$), SAT and GRE scores ($\mu = 500$ and $\sigma = 100$), and stanines ($\mu = 5.5$ and $\sigma = 1$). These usually imply that the raw scores are also normalized (transformed to the shape of a normal distribution), but normalization typically has little effect on tests comprised of several items because the obtained distribution of raw scores is typically a good approximation to a normal distribution. Norms are not the only way to make an obtained score meaningful. It may be criterion-referenced by estimating a criterion scores in some way, (e.g., the probability of success) or domain-referenced by relating it to the broader pool that is sampled. Some form of transformation is usually required when a measure is to be used for making individual decisions.

One also needs a domain of content in construct validation, but the domain is a function of the theory chosen by the investigator rather than imposed by such factors as course requirements or job demands. Personality constructs involve typical performance and are usually inferred from sentiments, whereas ability constructs involve maximum performance and are usually inferred from judgments. Nonetheless, other considerations are quite similar. Items should be homogeneous as to content and thus scale subjects unidimensionally and form one factor. The average item intercorrelation, and therefore coefficient $\alpha$, should be high. If a test contains more than one domain of content, its correlates cannot be interpreted unambiguously. However, items should be methodologically heterogeneous (diverse) in order to define a general construct. The simplest explicit example of methodological heterogeneity is to develop some sentiment items that are keyed "true" ("agree", etc.) and others that are keyed "false." Sampling over situations is another important way to achieve the needed diversity of method. Methodological heterogeneity can cause items to be multidimensional and consist of several factors, but this is a desirable outcome as long as the correlations among methods are high.

Constructs need to be studied in relation to other constructs, and items need to be studied in relation to irrelevant constructs as well as to the construct that they ostensibly relate to. This implies a multivariate approach to test development. Factor analysis is perhaps the most important of the multivariate tools. However, a distinction should be made between factor analyses of whole tests (scale-level analyses) and factor analyses of individual items (item-level analyses). Scale-level analyses are extremely important, but item level analyses are quite likely to lead one astray. First, a successful factor analysis requires that correlations vary widely, but correlations among items tend to be low and restricted in range by differences in item distributions. Moreover, traditional (but not more recent) methods tend to be exploratory and often lead to "shotgun empiricism." Ad hoc collections of items are factored with the intent of having the analysis provide meaningful scales rather than having a theory guide item generation and selection. Finally, although there are meaningful methods of factoring items, conventional methods of factoring were developed assuming that variables were continuous rather than categorical as items are. It is more important to employ careful methods of item analysis, particularly those which remove the effects of extraneous variables, such as direction of keying.

Students of human abilities have been concerned about validation for 100 years, but prior to 1940, students of personality measurement tended to accept an item as a legitimate measure of a construct if it rationally related to that construct. The development of the MMPI in the 1940s led to an empirical (criterion-oriented) approach in which items are selected because they correlate with a relevant criterion. We argue for the insufficiency of both approaches. Although items on rationally developed scales are usually (but far from universally) logically related to the construct, item analyses often reveal they are invalid because of problems in wording. Empirically developed scales often fail to replicate because they are highly sensitive to sampling error. Theory should provide a domain, and items should follow from that domain. This has been the dominant approach since the late 1960s. We note the role of implicit theory in the development of the MMPI, which was ostensibly derived by empirical procedures. In particular, the item pool probably reflected items that had been used successfully to define the traits associated with the pathological conditions that form its major clinical scales, and the validity scales serve to remove the effects of irrelevant variables. Because the scales are long, items falsely assigned to them have relatively little effect. However, where the MMPI was most truly empirical (e.g., in the formation of new scales designed to make discriminations that were not implicit in the original item pool), it has been least successful. The section concluded with several examples of how abilities measures reflect the importance of either a conventional theory (verbal versus performance ability, crystallized or fact-oriented versus fluid or abstract ability, and verbal versus quantitative ability) or one that is highly elaborated because it is based upon detailed research findings (the work of Robert Sternberg, Earl Hunt, and others, which incorporates developments in cognitive psychology). J. P. Guilford's work was an early recognition of the role of methodological heterogeneity.

Predictive validity requires the least discussion of the three forms of validation. The stress is on the test's relation with a suitable criterion, and so issues of theory are not likely to be as prominent. However, selection of a test for this purpose still needs some theory to determine what is important.

The final section of the chapter considered some special topics.

**1** One is how to reverse the direction of keying, as on tests where a given response category (e.g., "agree") is in the keyed direction for some items and in the nonkeyed direction for others.

**2** Unipolar attributes are those for which the opposite of having the trait is not having the trait (e.g., intelligence), and bipolar attributes are those for which the opposite is a trait in its own right (e.g., introversion-extraversion). Items may be comparative or absolute, as noted in Chapter 2. The greater sensitivity of comparative responses generally makes them preferable. One particular example involves having subjects make a choice between two activities reflecting either the poles of a single attribute or two different attributes instead of making absolute choices between the two separate sets.

**3** Some applications require discrimination at a point, e.g., separating the top 10 percent of a group from the bottom 90 percent without making discriminations within each of the separate groups. A simple way to do this is to obtain the values of $r$ between item scores and total scores dichotomized with respect to the two groups. Items with the largest values of $r$ are chosen instead of items that correlate most highly with the (continuous) total score.

**4** In an equidiscriminating test, item difficulties are deliberately varied to maintain the reliability of the test at all levels instead of maximizing the overall coefficient $\alpha$, which usually results in selecting items with $p$ values of approximately .5. This involves obtaining several values of $r$ for each item, respectively, dichotomizing the total score distribution at several levels along the continuum. Choose items with the largest values of $r$ within levels.

**5** If a test score is based upon 20 or more items, weighting items is generally unnecessary.

**6** Finally, the large role of chance in item selection was reiterated.

## SUGGESTED ADDITIONAL READINGS

If you have not had a basic course in tests and measurements that exposed you to the more common tests and items on these tests, read a standard reference in the area such as

Cronbach, L. J. (1990). *Essentials of psychological testing* (5th ed.). New York: Harper & Row.

There are now many reference works on available texts. Perhaps the most comprehensive is still the following:

Mitchell, J. V., Jr. (Ed.) (1989). *The Tenth Mental Measurement Yearbook*, Lincoln, NE: University of Nebraska Press.

A basic reference to construct validation of tests is

Jackson, D. N. (1971). The dynamics of structured personality tests: 1971, *Psychological Bulletin*, 78, 229–248.

The March 1986 issue of the *Journal of Personality* contains several papers devoted to important themes in personality research. In particular, Houts, Cook, and Shadish deal extensively with issues of methodological heterogeneity as an ingredient in their suggested research approach, which they term "multiplism." Briggs and Cheek and Judd, Jessor, and Donovan provide useful introductions to the role of factor analysis and structural analysis. However, neither makes the sharp distinction between item- and scale-level analysis that we feel is necessary.

## CHAPTER 9

# SPECIAL PROBLEMS IN CLASSICAL TEST THEORY

## CHAPTER OVERVIEW

Chapter 8 discussed principles for constructing general-purpose tests intended to have content, construct, or predictive validity. Although many auxiliary techniques are involved, instruments intended to have content validity are essentially constructed in terms of a rational appeal to the appropriateness of the item coverage; instruments intended to have construct validity are constructed to be homogeneous with respect to content but not to the methods of measurement, which is true, to a lesser extent, of instruments intended to have predictive validity. Such tests may be designed as general-purpose instruments for use with a variety of subjects and numerous purposes or simply as classroom examinations.

These tests are generally designed to produce large, reliable individual differences where they are employed and are the mainstay of research and applied work. However, there are special issues that also need to be considered: (1) speeded tests; (2) corrections for guessing; (3) the interrelated concepts of adverse impact, improper discrimination, test bias, and disparity; (4) halo effects; (5) response biases and response styles, which are measurement artifacts that are, respectively, situation-specific and generalizable; and (6) problems associated with multiscale tests. Some of these special issues apply only in situations that you may not encounter. For example, you may never need to construct a speeded test or have to deal with corrections for guessing or halo effects; other times additional analyses or slight modifications of previously discussed procedures may be required; and still other times major changes in test construction may be needed. Conversely, it is improbable that your work will be conducted exclusively on populations that are so homogeneous that bias is not an issue. In general, these issues will be examined from the standpoint of the classical linear model in which scores are simply sums of item responses, but we will again consider some of them from the perspective of item response theory in Chapter 10.

The main points of this chapter are as follows:

**1** There is a classical correction for guessing known as Abbott's formula. It assumes that subjects either know the correct answer or guess blindly. As such, it poorly describes what individuals actually do in taking a test. Guessing lowers test reliability somewhat because two individuals with the same underlying knowledge may get different scores because of differences in luck. However, the loss in reliability can be offset by adding a few items, if needed, and instructions not to guess potentially introduce individual differences in willingness to guess that are usually irrelevant to the test scores. Moreover, scores produced by Abbott's formula correlate perfectly with obtained scores when individuals attempt all items. We therefore strongly suggest that subjects simply be instructed to attempt all items.

**2** We have thus far been concerned with power rather than speed tests. A "power test" is one in which the presence of a time limit does not contribute to individual differences: The presence of a time limit per se, even one that makes some individuals uncomfortable, is not crucial. The main point in constructing a "speed test" is to choose a time limit that maximizes individual differences and therefore reliability. Unfortunately, the internal consistency method (coefficient $\alpha$) used to study reliability in power tests is inappropriate with speed tests, although test-retest methods are appropriate.

**3** A test has adverse impact if there is a disparity in outcomes between a reference group, commonly white males, and a focal group, commonly one of several legally protected groups such as females, Hispanics, and blacks. Adverse impact and related forms of disparity are legally important but do not imply bias, group differences in what the test measures, in and of themselves. Indeed, a failure to find group differences also implies bias, as when a scale fails to find a difference between the weights of adult men and women. Unfortunately, there are several definitions of bias which are often inconsistent when group differences exist. A basic ethical issue is whether it is more important to be fair to individuals or to groups. Approaches oriented toward individuals are based upon linear regression, often moderated multiple regression, and approaches oriented toward groups are based upon quotas. However, the modern methods of Chapter 10 have played an increasingly important role in the study of bias. "Reverse regression" is a paradoxical artifact of the regression model in which the same data may simultaneously appear to demonstrate that a focal group is both underpaid and underqualified. A different artifact, Simpson's paradox (Chapter 5), is shown to arise from improper aggregation. Methods of determining quotas, and the use of pooled versus separate group norms are also considered.

**4** Many investigators use behavioral ratings. A major problem with their use is that the rater may confound the specific attribute to be rated with other attributes, including an overall evaluation, producing a halo effect. Problems associated with traditional definitions of halo are considered, as are several causal models of halo.

**5** A "response bias" is a measurement artifact that emerges from a specific situation, whereas a "response style" is a characteristic of an individual that is consistent across situations. Sources of bias and ways to deal with it are considered. Perhaps the most widely discussed response style is social desirability. Although its role is clear in determining overall differences in response to items, its status as an individual difference variable is somewhat debatable. Moreover, it is important to separate the tendency to give a socially desired response with lack of self-knowledge. The section considers examples of other proposed response styles.

6 Chapter 8 noted the importance of taking a multivariate approach to the study of constructs. This naturally leads to the development of multiscale tests. Some of the problems in dealing with such tests are considered. One such problem is whether to repeat an item on more than one scale. This will artifactually produce a correlation between the scales since there will be a component in common even among subjects who answer randomly. However, an item may legitimately relate to two or more constructs because the constructs are inherently related.

## GUESSING

One of the distinctive features of objective format items is that subjects may respond correctly because of guessing rather than knowledge. Although our discussion of this topic will involve judgments, as in classroom examinations, the same issues can apply to sentiments even though the term "guessing" is strained. The fact that a response can be correct because of luck has led many to attempt to correct observed scores for guessing. There are two general classes of models. The first, which we will consider in greatest detail, is a blind guessing model: Guesses are assumed to produce random choice. Thus, each alternative on a four-alternative multiple-choice item has a .25 probability of being chosen. Blind guessing leads to Abbott's formula (Finney, 1947), which we will develop over the next few pages. In contrast, there are various sophisticated guessing models. For example, an individual might not know which answer is correct but can correctly rule out certain alternatives. Guessing has been examined extensively in experimental psychology, most explicitly in psychophysics where it has played a substantial role in the estimation of thresholds (see Chapter 2).

### The Blind Guessing Model and Abbott's Formula

The traditional model for guessing in a multiple-choice test assumes that a subject either (1) knows the correct response, and so the probability of a correct response is 1.0, or (2) guesses completely at random with equal preference for each alternative, and so the probability of a correct response is $1/K$, where $K$ is the number of alternatives. The blind guessing probability is therefore .5 on a true-false test, .25 on a four-alternative multiple-choice test, etc. This blind guessing assumption also appears in some item response theory models considered in Chapter 10. Lucky guesses are assumed not to occur in completion or other nonobjective formats.

The blind guessing model may be stated algebraically as

$$R = R_c + p(T - R_c) \tag{9-1}$$

where $R$ = observed number of correct (right) responses

$R_c$ = number of items a person knows, for which the probability of a correct response is 1.0

$p$ = probability of a lucky guess = $1/K$, where $K$ is the number of alternatives

$T$ = number of items attempted

Also let $N$ = total number of test items, $W$ = number of incorrect or wrong responses, and $U$ = number of items left blank (not guessed). Thus, $T = R + W$ and $N = T + U$. The only term that cannot be observed is $R_c$, which represents the number of correct responses the subject would obtain if he or she never guessed and left items blank when the correct answer was unknown. A useful but somewhat inaccurate analogy is that $R$ is the score a subject receives on a multiple-choice test and $R_c$ is the score a subject would receive on an equivalent short-answer test. We stress that this model assumes that guesses are totally random if the correct answer is not known; no alternative can be correctly eliminated, contrary to what anyone taking a test usually experiences. By definition, $R_c$ denotes the number of items a subject really knows and $T - R_c$ describes the opportunities to guess on the remaining items. The probability of a correct (lucky) guess is $p = 1/K$, and the probability of an incorrect response is $q = 1 - p = (K - 1)/K$. It is then simple to take Eq. 9-1 and solve for $R_c$:

$$R = R_c + pT - pR_c$$
$$= R_c - pR_c + pT$$
$$= R_c(1 - p) + pT$$
$$= qR_c + pT$$
$$qR_c = R - pT$$
$$R_c = \frac{R - pT}{q} \tag{9-2}$$

Since $p = 1/K$, $q = (K - 1)/K$, and $T = R + W$, Eq. 9-2 may be expressed as

$$R_c = \frac{R - (1/K)(R + W)}{(K - 1)/K}$$
$$= \frac{KR - R - W}{K - 1}$$
$$= \frac{(K - 1)R - W}{K - 1}$$
$$= R - \frac{W}{K - 1} \tag{9-3}$$

Equation 9-3 is one way to state Abbott's formula and is the final correction for guessing. The term "correction" is a misnomer because it only estimates the effects of guessing under unlikely assumptions. The model provides $R_c$ by subtracting a fraction, $1/(K - 1)$, of the number of the attempted but incorrect responses ($W$) from the actual number of correct responses ($R$). For example, assume (1) there are four alternatives per question, (2) the subject attempts 32 out of 40 items, and (3) the subject answers 20 of them correctly and 12 incorrectly. Thus,

$$R_c = 20 - \frac{12}{4-1}$$

$$= 16$$

The estimate is that the subject really knew the answers to 16 items and made 4 lucky guesses.

### Effects of Guessing on Test Parameters

The effects of blind guessing on the psychometric properties of score distributions are easily determined. First, guessing causes the estimated mean score to be larger than it would have been had the subjects left the items blank. The expected increase is $R - R_c$ and is directly related to the number of attempted but incorrect responses ($W$). In other words, $W$ reflects differences in the amount of guessing. If all subjects attempt all items, the expected gain from guessing is inversely related to $R_c$ (knowledge). People who know the least must guess the most, and they consequently stand to gain the most from guessing. Figure 9-1 shows the expected relationship between $R$ and $R_c$ for a $k = 4$ alternative, 40-item test. People who actually know every correct answer all obtain scores of 40, and people who actually know none of the answers obtain an average score of 10 by pure guessing. Note that $R_c$ and $W$ are linearly related with a slope of 1 because $K/(K-1)$ is a constant for a given test.

**FIGURE 9-1**    Expected scores when guessing is a factor ($R$) as a function of scores when guessing is not a factor ($R_c$). The figure assumes that $R$ is based on a 40-item multiple-choice test with four alternatives for each item and that each subject attempts all items.

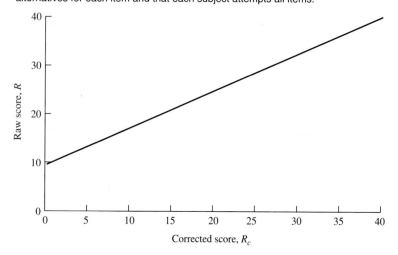

Regardless of the overall effects of guessing, there are individual differences in the amounts and results of guessing. Individuals with the same $R$ and $W$ will have different types of luck in guessing. One may answer every question correctly by guessing, and another may fail to answer any correctly, although both outcomes are improbable. The model for blind guessing assumes that the probabilities of correctly guessing on different items are independent, so that the expected variance in success of guessing, $R - R_c$, follows from the binomial theorem:

$$\sigma^2_{e_Y} = Npq \tag{9-4}$$

where $N$ = number of guesses = $T - R_c$
   $p$ = probability of a correct guess = $1/K$
   $q$ = probability of an incorrect guess = $(K - 1)/K$
   $\sigma^2_{e_Y}$ = expected variance of $R - R_c$ for people who guess on $N$ items

Again assume that there are $T = 40$ items, there are $K = 4$ alternatives, $R_c$ ranges from 0 to 40, and each person responds to each item. The model states that people who do not know any correct answers ($R_c = 0$) always guess, and so $N$ is 40, $p$ is .25, and $q$ is .75. The expected variance of their scores is $(40)(.25)(.75)$ or 7.5, and the expected standard deviation is $\sqrt{7.50}$ or 2.74. Conversely, individuals who know all the correct answers never guess ($N = 0$), and so $R = R_c = 40$ and the variance of both actual scores ($R$) and corrected scores ($R_c$) is zero. Since $p$ and $q$ are constants for a given test, the variance due to guessing ($\sigma^2_{e_Y}$) is an increasing linear function of the number of guessed items ($N$) and a decreasing linear function of the number of known items ($R_c$). Figure 9-2 illustrates the latter, which holds only if subjects attempt all items, as in most classroom multiple-choice tests and research. Situations in which subjects are urged not to guess when they are unsure of the correct answer will be discussed later.

The variance of errors due to guessing adds to the measurement error from previously considered sources. Figure 9-2 illustrates that the measurement error (unreliability) due to guessing decreases with actual ability. Guessing not only increases the scores of low-ability subjects more than those of high-ability subjects but also makes their scores less reliable. Since Eq. 9-4 involves the number of guessed items ($N$), it is only of theoretical interest. Estimates of the variance of scores contributed by guessing can be obtained by estimating $N$ since $p$ and $q$ are known. By definition, $N$ equals the total number of attempted items ($T$) minus the score that would be obtained in the absence of guessing ($R_c$):

$$N = T - R_c$$

Using Eq. 9-3,

$$N = T - \left( R - \frac{W}{K - 1} \right)$$

$$= T - R + \frac{W}{K - 1}$$

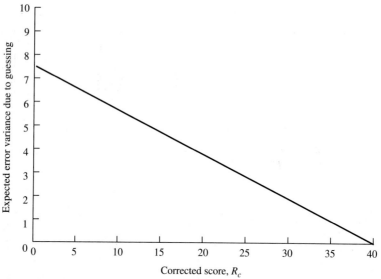

**FIGURE 9-2** Expected variance of errors because of guessing as a function of $R_c$. The figure assumes that there are four alternatives for each item on the multiple-choice test and that each subject attempts all the items.

Since $T - R$ equals the number of attempted but incorrect responses, we may rewrite this equation as

$$N = W + \frac{W}{K - 1} \tag{9-5}$$

Equation 9-5 therefore estimates the number of items on which the individual guesses blindly ($N$). Multiplying by $pq$ estimates $\sigma_{e_g}^2$, the amount of measurement error due to guessing for people with the same number of attempted but incorrect responses ($W$):

$$\sigma_{e_g}^2 = pq\left(W + \frac{W}{K - 1}\right) \tag{9-6}$$

Suppose, for example, $W = 8$ for many people, they all have the same $R_c$, and $K = 5$ alternatives per item:

$$\sigma_{e_g}^2 = (.2)(.8)(8 + 8/4)$$
$$= (.16)(10)$$
$$= 1.60$$

Thus, guessing causes the scores to have a variance of 1.6 points even though subjects all know the same amount.

### The Accuracy of the Correction for Blind Guessing

We have noted that the basic assumptions of blind guessing usually do not hold; subjects usually can eliminate at least one distractor. This means that the probability of a correct guess is greater than $1/K$. For example, if $K = 5$, but one distractor can always be eliminated, the number of attempted but incorrect responses ($W$) should be multiplied by $\frac{1}{4}$ rather than $\frac{1}{5}$ in Eq. 9-3. Since $W$ is actually multiplied by $\frac{1}{5}$, the actual effect of guessing is usually underestimated (Price, 1964). However, if some distractors are unusually plausible, Eq. 9-3 will overestimate the effects of guessing; even if subjects strenuously attempt not to guess, they may make many $W$ responses. One may argue that it is poor practice to include highly plausible distractors and that good methods of test construction tend to weed them out. Rather than employ such highly plausible distractors, it is better to compose distractors that all sound plausible to a student who knows very little about the topic. However, this is easier said than done. As most tests have few highly plausible distractors but provide ample opportunities for narrowing alternatives, the practical result is that the blind guessing model, Eq. 9-3, underestimates the amount of guessing and overestimates the number of items subjects know.

### Sophisticated Guessing Models

Signal detection theory, which was briefly introduced in Chapter 2 and is also discussed in Chapter 15, provides an illustration of how models developed in psychophysics can be applied to psychometric theory, in this case, to consider guessing (Green & Swets, 1967; Egan, 1975; Macmillan & Creelman, 1990; Nelson, 1986; Swets, 1986a, 1986b; Swets, Tanner, & Birdsall, 1961; Tanner & Swets, 1954). The basic (and reasonable) approach is to assume that each alternative possesses a "strength" or "truthfulness" and that the subject chooses the "strongest" (most truthful-appearing) alternative.

Formal models specify the mathematical properties of the strengths of the correct alternative and distractors. The model most relevant to a multiple-choice test is called the $K$-alternative forced-choice task. It is designed to handle tasks such as the ability to localize a briefly presented visual stimulus in one of $K$ spatial locations. The assumptions are that the effects of each stimulus vary randomly about a mean value on an interval scale of strength. The mean values of the incorrect alternatives are set at 0 with a standard deviation of 1, and the mean value of the correct alternative is set at a higher value, traditionally designated $d'$, with a standard deviation of 1. The specific values obtained for each alternative reflect random sampling. The subject is correct on a given trial when the values sampled for all $K - 1$ incorrect alternatives are less than the value sampled for the correct alternative; if one of the incorrect values exceeds the value sampled for the correct alternative, the subject will be incorrect. The chances of an incorrect response diminish as $d'$ increases, and so the better the subject, the larger his or her $d'$ parameter.

This particular formalization is clearly more suited to psychophysical applications where trials are much more likely to differ only by chance than in actual multiple-choice tests where (1) items vary in difficulty and (2) some distractors within items are more likely to be chosen than others. However, two particular deductions will usually hold even when the rather strict assumptions are relaxed.

**1** Allowing subjects a second guess when they are incorrect will show that they are not guessing blindly. The blind guessing model states that subjects must again guess blindly, this time among $K - 1$ (rather than $K$) alternatives. Sophisticated guessing models predict a higher probability of a correct second guess, which is almost universally the case (see the above references).

**2** The number of correct responses obtained when subjects respond to every trial is a sufficient estimator of $d'$; i.e., it uses all relevant information so that it is perfectly proper to instruct subjects to guess on every trial.

### Practical Considerations

Should one use a correction for blind guessing? Two reasons are commonly given for instructing subjects not to guess. First, guessing introduces a small amount of unreliability into test scores—reducing coefficient $\alpha$ by about .04 (Guilford, 1954; Lord, 1963; Price, 1964). Although it may be important in rare settings, this unreliability may nearly always be offset by making the test a few items longer. Second, some suggest that guessing fosters poor attitudes in students, as they are taught not to guess blindly in daily schoolwork but to investigate facts and "think out" unsolved problems. We consider it doubtful that multiple-choice tests warp many students' minds.

Instructing subjects not to guess poses at least two problems.

**1** It is difficult to frame such instructions clearly. The student is told that it does not pay to guess when in doubt, but this is rarely true. Students (and often teachers) do not understand the magnitude of the correction so that the penalty primarily stands as a vague and unnecessary threat.

**2** The effects of the instructions vary over students and create an irrelevant source of individual differences. A very conscientious student might lower her or his score appreciably by taking the instructions not to guess too seriously. There are degrees of guessing from blind to nearly complete knowledge, so that the meaning of "guessing" is ambiguous. Individual differences in guessing reflect personal idiosyncrasies more than intelligence or knowledge of the particular subject matter (Price, 1964). Consequently, individual differences in guessing will complicate the factor composition compared to that obtained when students attempt all items.

We therefore suggest that subjects be instructed to attempt every item. If subjects do attempt every item, there is no need to correct for guessing since there will be a perfect negative correlation between $W$ and $R$ and, more importantly, a perfect positive correlation between corrected ($R_c$) and obtained ($R$) scores. This strategy also follows from at least some sophisticated guessing models.

### Using the Model to Estimate Test Parameters

Even though we suggest that the blind guessing correction not be employed in test scoring, it does have utility in predicting the effects of guessing on test reliability and other important psychometric properties of score distributions.

First, it is often useful to distinguish between the possible and the effective score range. The possible range equals the number of test items plus 1. Of course, unless a test is given to as vast a sample as the SAT is, this range is unlikely to be filled, and guessing limits this range further. Assuming subjects attempt all items, the expected lower bound of the effective range is the expected number of items obtainable by pure chance ($Np$). This would be 10 on a 40-item, four-alternative test. Rarely, some scores may fall below 10 because of the variance in errors due to guessing ($\sigma_{e_\gamma}^2$).

The variance of scores below chance should be entirely totally unreliable, as it is due to random differences in guessing. This is commonly the case, but there are exceptions. Cliff (1958) found scores below the chance level on one form of a test correlated significantly with scores below chance level on an alternative form. This can arise when certain distractors successfully mislead very low-ability individuals. Below-chance performance also occurs when subjects deliberately try to do poorly (Theodor & Mandelcord, 1973).

### Multiple-Choice versus Short-Answer Tests

Multiple-choice tests and short-answer tests based upon the same material have been compared to study the effects of guessing. A short-answer test (which is assumed to be free of the effects of blind guessing) should be more reliable than a multiple-choice test by an explicit amount (see Nunnally, 1967, p. 584.), but Plumlee (1952) found that the difference in reliability was less than predicted. The short-answer test was not as reliable as predicted or, conversely, the multiple-choice test was more reliable than predicted. The actual difference was between one-half and two-thirds that predicted.

In actuality (see Chapter 8), multiple-choice items test recognition and short-answer items test recall. Recognition is usually easier than recall. The blind guessing model is not actually intended to estimate relations between a multiple-choice test and a corresponding short-answer test. It is intended to estimate relations between an actual multiple-choice test with a finite number of alternatives per item and a hypothetical multiple-choice test with an infinite number of alternatives per item. A short-answer test is not the same as a test with an infinite number of alternatives. Short-answer tests contain measurement error that is not present in multiple-choice tests. Good multiple-choice items "aim" knowledgeable students toward the correct answer. Items that are quite clear when presented in multiple-choice form are sometimes ambiguous when presented in short-answer form. Consider, for example, the item "An important product of Bolivia is _____" in which the multiple-choice alternatives are (1) coal, (2) tin (the correct answer), (3) diamonds, and (4) lead. If the same students were asked the item in short-answer form, the word "product" might be unclear, as it could refer to farming, manufacturing, mining, or other industries. Confusion produces measurement error in short-answer tests that partially offsets the effects of guessing on multiple-choice tests. It is one reason why the difference in reliability between the two formats is not as great as predicted.

Detailed evaluation of this difference in formats really requires a hypothetical test with an infinite number of alternatives. However, one may estimate the extent to which the blind guessing model predicts differences in reliability as a function of the numbers of alternatives, e.g., the relative reliability of a five- versus a four-alternative test obtained by randomly removing one distractor from each item. Numerous studies of this kind suggest that reliability increases as a function of the number of alternative responses, but by less than predicted by the blind guessing model (Nunnally, 1967, Chapter 15) and alternative models (Lord, 1976). There is generally a substantial increase from two alternatives (e.g., true-false) to three alternatives, a worthwhile increase from three to four alternatives, a small increase from four to five alternatives, and negligible increases beyond that point. Ebel's (1969) findings for simulated 100-item tests are typical. His reliabilities were .74, .83, .86, .87, and .88 for two through five alternatives, but the precise results also depended upon such factors as the average interitem correlations.

Data such as Ebel's involve the overall reliability. There is a larger gain in reliability for low-scoring individuals with an increased number of alternatives. Figure 9-2 showed that unreliability due to guessing declines rapidly as ability increases. Using more than four alternatives per item therefore reduces unreliability at the lower end of the trait continuum. If it were crucial to discriminate among low-ability individuals, seven or eight alternatives per item might be needed. In sum, it almost always pays to have more than two response alternatives, and seven or eight alternatives may be called for in rare instances. However, four or five alternatives nearly always suffice, the strategy followed on nearly all commercially distributed multiple-choice tests. The baseline provided by random guessing changes little per alternative beyond four—it decreases only from .25 to .20 as a fifth alternative is added, for example. Increase test reliability by adding more items rather than by adding more alternatives to each item.

## SPEED TESTS

Chapter 8 was concerned with power tests, i.e., tests on which individual differences are not due to the effects of a time limit. Although a given test may have a time limit to expedite test administration, it may be considered a power test if this time limit is sufficiently generous so that it does not affect the variance of test scores. In other words, a given test may be considered a power test to the extent that the correlation between scores obtained with the time limit and (probably) hypothetical scores obtained in the absence of any time constraints approaches 1.0 *even if* the two means are different. In a speed test, these individual differences emerge precisely because a highly restrictive time limit is imposed. A pure speed test consists of items that would be of trivial difficulty if subjects were given unlimited time. Consequently $p$ values would exceed .95 if the items were administered with no time limit. Simple addition problems given to literate adults $(23 + 12 = ?)$ are one example. The only way to obtain a reliable dispersion of scores with these items is to employ a highly restrictive time limit that prevents individuals from answering all the questions.

Simply imposing a time limit does not make a measure a speed test. Time limits are often imposed for practical reasons, e.g., classroom tests are typically limited to the available class time. Unless the time limit is severely restrictive, it will not influence the underlying traits measured by the tests. If scores obtained with and (usually hypothetically) without time limits are very highly correlated, the timed test can be considered a power test.

Unless the underlying trait obviously involves speed, it is generally ill-advised to employ a speed test in place of a power test. Much practical experience and a considerable amount of experimentation (e.g., Miller & Weiss, 1976) indicate that restrictive time limits cause test scores to be influenced by unwanted variance caused by incidental testing-taking habits unrelated to the underlying trait. Some general abilities, however, are intimately related to speed, such as numerical fluency and perceptual speed, as are various clerical aptitudes. Rules that apply to the construction of power tests generally do not apply to the construction of speed tests, and so special principles are needed.

### The Internal Structure of Speed Tests

The theory of reliability and the construction of power tests rely heavily upon the sizes and patterns of correlations among items (see Chapters 6 and 7). However, these correlations among items are artifacts of time limits and of the ordering of items within a test in speed tests. Consequently one cannot construct a speed test based on item intercorrelations. The average correlation among items on a speed test is directly related to the amount of time allotted for taking the test. The $p$ values of all items will be close to 1.0 if subjects are given unlimited time, which will range-restrict the correlations to zero. Conversely, these $p$ values will all be close to zero if subjects are given little time to take the test, which will also range-restrict the correlations. The average $p$ value between these two extreme time limits ranges from 0 to 1.0. If the limits produce average $p$ values near .5, the average correlation might be substantial.

The time limit affects the pattern of correlations among items and therefore the pattern of item-total correlations as well as the average correlation. Assume that the time limit produces an average $p$ value of .5 and that the test is made reliable by methods to be discussed. The item-total correlations will be artifacts of the ordering of items within a speed test. The $p$ values will decline from nearly 1.0 at the beginning of the test to nearly .0 at the end of the test. Both these early and late items must correlate poorly with the other items and therefore with total scores. In contrast, items near the middle of the test will correlate substantially with one another and with total test scores. Since the ordering of items on a speed test is arbitrary, these item-total correlations will also be arbitrary. It therefore makes no sense to select items on this basis. This is why a different form of item selection must be used for speed tests than for power tests. This section will consider the principles needed.

### The Item Pool

As in all test construction, the first step in constructing a speed test is to develop an item pool based upon a domain of content. Once a suitable domain is defined, the task is usually rather easy because the items are typically so simple that they can be composed by the dozens. Whereas it was possible to give some rules of thumb about the size of a power test's item pool, the size required for a speed test is very difficult to determine ahead of time. This is because the reliability of speed tests is not as highly related to the number of items as is the case with power tests. For example, a 50-item speed test using addition items might be more reliable than a 200-item test requiring subjects to say whether pairs of letter groupings are the same or different. The reliability of different types of speed tests is usually more closely related to the testing time required to obtain the most reliable distribution of scores than to the number of items. Thus, if the ideal testing times for two different speed tests are both 15 minutes, the tests will tend to have similar reliabilities even if the numbers of items differ. The number of items in the pool should depend on intuitive judgments about how rapidly they can be answered by the average person. If this pool is later found to be too small, it is usually easy to construct new items.

Assume, for example, that addition items are to be used with unselected adults. Previous experience might indicate that the average adult can correctly solve 2 such problems per minute and that about 80 such items will produce the desired reliability. The experimenter constructs 80 such items and experiments to determine the ideal time limit. At 2 problems per minute, this ideal time limit is approximately 40 minutes, but this should be determined empirically. Consequently, administer the items to five different randomly sampled groups with respective time limits of 30, 35, 40, 45, and 50 minutes. Quite often it is feasible to administer the test to a single group and score their results after each of a series of time limits. Although a more sophisticated measure will be discussed later, one simple approach is to select the time limit that produces the largest standard deviation of scores, interpolating as necessary. The reliabilities of a speed test under different time limits are highly related to the resulting standard deviations of scores. Hypothetical results from the above study are shown in Fig. 9-3. The standard deviation (and thus the reliability) will be highest at some intermediate point and taper off on either side of that point, in this case at 45 minutes.

**FIGURE 9-3**    Standard deviations of scores on a speed test as a function of different time limits.

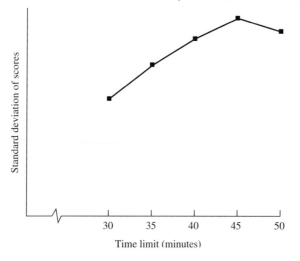

## Measurement of Reliability

It is *not* correct to measure the reliability of a speed test in terms of internal consistency (coefficient $\alpha$). The most appropriate measure of reliability is to correlate alternative forms. Thus, construct two 80-item tests of numerical computation in the previous example, rather than only one, and then use the correlation between the two sets of scores to estimate the reliability. A time-saving approximation to the alternative-form reliability is to use the split-half method (Chapter 7) on a single form of the test. Administer halves of the items with time limits of half that employed for the whole test. Use the Spearman-Brown prophesy formula, Eq. 6-18, on the correlation between the two halves since this correlation comes from half-tests. As a further check on the temporal stability of the attribute, administer the half-tests about 2 weeks apart instead of consecutively. The corrected correlation between halves will be a meaningful estimate of the reliability as long as performance within a testing session is not markedly influenced by fatigue.

The artifactual correlations among items are not the only reason that coefficient $\alpha$ poorly describes the reliability of speed tests. Chapter 6 noted that reliability is closely related to the standard deviation of total scores, which in turn is highly related to the average correlation among items within the test. Internal consistency measures (coefficient $\alpha$) cannot be legitimately employed with speed tests because they predict the alternative-form reliability only when one can assume that the average correlation among items within a test is the same as the average correlation between items on alternative forms. The average correlation between items on alternative forms of a speed test tends to be smaller than the average correlation between items within each test, so that internal consistency overestimates the alternative-form reliability of speed tests.

## Factor Composition

As mentioned previously, the patterns of correlations among items on a speed test are determined almost entirely by the time limit and the ordering of items within the test. Items near the middle of the test correlate more highly with other items than do items near either end of the test because they have larger variances. Some people will pass these items and others will not. In contrast, nearly everyone will pass early items and fail later items. In general, items will correlate more highly with items near their own ordinal position on the test than they do with items further removed in the ordering because of the similarities of their distributions (see Chapter 4). For example, the fourteenth item will probably correlate more highly with the thirteenth and fifteenth items than it will with the tenth and twentieth items. Items therefore tend to break up into different factors because of their proximity to one another, and items near the middle of the test will have the highest loadings on a general factor for reasons to be discussed in Chapter 11. This may be interesting mathematically, but it tells one nothing about factors of ability or personality. The proper way to learn about the factors present in speed tests is to apply the analysis to a set of whole tests (scale-level analyses) because these artifacts will not be present. As noted in the previous chapter, distributions of continuous scores on whole tests are usually sufficiently similar so that artifacts reflecting differences in distribution shape are not major considerations.

## Variables Relating to Speed

Speed instructions request subjects to work quickly. For example, word association usually stresses responding with the first word that comes to mind. Speed instructions usually do not force subjects to perform at any set speed, item per item, or to stop responding after any particular amount of time. Indeed, subjects are often not actually timed. Speed instructions therefore serve only to encourage rapid responses. They do not ensure rapid responses, prevent individual differences in rate of response, or necessarily lead to individual differences in rate of response.

Another variable relating to speed is preferred rate of response, which concerns how rapidly subjects like to respond. Preferred rate can be purely measured only when (1) responses are very easy (i.e., not mentally difficult or physically exhausting) and (2) the experimenter does not provide incentives for responding either quickly or slowly. Very few tasks meet these standards. Subjects might be told to tap a stylus at their preferred rate while that rate is recorded. If a word association test is given without speed instructions, a subject's total time is related to the preferred rate. However, individual differences in the ability to form associations would be a confounding factor. Preferred rate is the motivational component of the effects of speed on test scores. It concerns how rapidly the subject tries to work in a particular setting. Obviously, the purpose of speed instructions is to alter the preferred rate.

It is not clear whether preferred rate is a general personality trait or is largely specific to the task at hand, or how preferred rate interacts with speed instructions. The average person usually responds more quickly with speed instructions than without speed instructions, but this does not mean that changes in individual differences occur. A correlation of 1.0 between scores in the two situations, corrected for attenuation, means that speed instructions influence average rate of responding but not individual differences in preferred rate. Conversely, a zero correlation means that speed instructions erase individual differences in preferred rate. We know little about preferred rate because it is very difficult to investigate it independently of other variables. The apparent preferred rate is usually a mixture of how quickly subjects would like to respond and how quickly they can respond. A person of limited numerical ability may take considerable time to complete the problems even though that individual makes every effort to work quickly. Another person of superior ability may feel no pressure to work quickly but may complete the test quickly.

It is useful to distinguish between time-limit accuracy and response-time scores. Time-limit accuracy scores hold constant the amount of time needed to complete a set of problems for all subjects; the score for each subject consists of the number of problems correctly solved. Most classroom examinations are scored in this way, and time-limit accuracy scores are generally well suited to group testing. Response-time scores require each subject to work until one or more problems is solved; the score consists of the amount of time used. These tests usually require individual administration.

A final distinction is between paced and time-limit measures. Paced measures involve a time limit for each item or block of items. For example, subjects might be given 1 minute to solve each of 20 arithmetic problems. Pacing is seldom used in group testing because it is difficult to administer, but it is widely used when subjects are run individually. Time limits require subjects to complete as many problems as possible in the allotted time. There are often problems adjusting for a speed-accuracy tradeoff, as some individuals of the same skill may work rapidly and produce many errors, whereas others work slower but more accurately.

## Statistical Effects of Time Limits

Restrictive time limits obviously affect group mean scores but can have varied effects upon the reliability and validity once the time limit maximizing the variance is taken into account. A mean near the center of the usable score range (e.g., half of the number of items on a dichotomously scored short-answer test) tends to favor high reliability, but the relationship holds only loosely. The effect of the time limits on the distribution shape is important because it affects the reliability at different score (ability) levels. In particular, a highly restrictive time limit will produce a positively skewed distribution and provide more reliable discriminations among high-ability people than among low-ability people. A less restrictive time limit that produces a negatively skewed distribution will have the converse affect. These differences hold regardless of the variance and therefore the overall reliability. The overall reliability is related to the distribution shape only indirectly through the relation between shape and standard deviation.

These considerations do not specify how a restrictive time limit affects validity. One approach is to determine how a time limit affects the factor composition. Unfortunately, the factor composition of a pure power test is often unknown. However, the attenuation-corrected correlation, Eq. 6-36, between scores obtained with and without a time limit directly measures the extent that they measure the same thing. The square of this correlation defines the shared common variance (SCV) of the two measures. We will use this term specifically to describe the effects of speeding, although any attenuation-corrected correlation may be squared, of course. The SCV describes the effects of restrictive time limits on changes in the factor composition, and thus the validity, of different test materials. Alternative forms of a test can be constructed and administered to the same subjects on different days under different time limits, and the alternative forms reliabilities obtained to provide the desired data.

For example, suppose the reliability of scores under one time limit is .8, the reliability under a shorter time limit is .6, and the correlation between the two sets of scores is .7. The attenuation-corrected correlation is $.7/\sqrt{(.8)(.6)}$ or, approximately, 1.0, and so the SCV is also approximately 1.0. Thus, the scores obtained under more restrictive time limits have the same factor composition as the scores obtained under more generous time limits, but the former are more reliable. One must be careful to counterbalance testing sessions to control for practice effects. Investigate each alternative form in each time-limit condition in order to make this determination. Because of the labor involved in performing these kinds of studies, very few have been done. Morrison (1960) provides a thorough example.

## One-Trial Measures of the Effects of Time Limits

Computation of the SCV requires correlations among alternative forms administered under different time limits. Consequently all subjects must be administered several alternative forms. Proposals have been made for examining changes in factor structure due to varying time limits through item statistics rather than through alternative-forms correlations. Gulliksen (1950) and Morrison (1960) discuss these in detail.

One such approach is based upon the relative occurrence of errors of omission (items not attempted) and errors of commission (items attempted but answered incorrectly). A pure speed test could be defined as one in which all errors are omissions because the subject did not reach the item, rather than commissions because the subject answered the item incorrectly. The converse is true on a pure power test, and both types of error are found on a test that mixes speed and power. The simplest index of speeding based upon this distinction is the variance of errors of omission over subjects divided by the variance in the total number of errors (omissions plus commissions). More complex but related indices take the correlation between the two types of errors into account. A measure can be considered a speed test to the extent that the index approaches 1.0, and a power test to the extent that it approaches zero.

Indices of this form are appealing because they require neither construction nor administration of alternative forms. However, they are not recommended and have rightly fallen into disrepute. One unreasonable assumption they make is that errors of omission reflect speeding. In fact, the number of unattempted items is largely determined by the test instructions, penalties for guessing, and the overall atmosphere of test administration, regardless of any time limit. The experimenter can make the number of unattempted items large even with a very generous time limit simply by warning subjects not to guess when unsure. Conversely, one can produce many errors of commission on a test with a highly restrictive time limit and easy items by urging all subjects to answer all items in the allotted time even if they must guess wildly.

One-trial indices would still fail to provide important information even if their basic assumptions were sounder because these indices do not provide any information about the factor composition of scores. Investigations of factor composition necessarily are based on correlations of alternative forms or the same test administered to the same subjects under different time limits using methods described above.

### Correction for Guessing in Speed Tests

In principle, the blind guessing model has limited applicability to pure speed tests because there should be few errors of commission to correct for. The burden of preventing appreciable numbers of commission errors on pure speed tests rests on the effectiveness of instructions not to guess. However, low-ability subjects should ignore these instructions if there is no penalty. For example, assume that the problems require subjects to choose from a small number of alternatives, e.g., classify the sum of two numbers as odd or even. Low-ability subjects will probably benefit by hurriedly marking every item or even responding randomly unless there is some penalty for guessing. One cannot handle this problem by having all subjects attempt all items because that defeats the very purpose of designing the test so that the average subject can attempt only about half of the items. Consequently, if many commission errors arise, it more defensible to make the correction for guessing, Eq. 9-3, on speed tests than on power tests despite the flaws of the correction.

Errors of commission can also be minimized by using items that discourage guessing, such as short-answer or multiple-choice items with a large number of alternatives. Unfortunately, this introduces variances due to differences in reading fluency, which may be quite separate from the goals of the test. In general, guessing tends to be more of a problem on speed tests than on power tests if it is difficult to minimize the number of commission errors. The reliability and factor composition of the scores will depend greatly on the test instructions and on individual differences in test-taking strategies.

## Timed-Power Tests

A "timed-power test" is a measure designed to assess power but administered with a time limit, normally imposed for administrative purposes, e.g., classroom availability. The basic issue is how much of a time limit can be imposed without adversely influencing the distribution of obtained scores, i.e., causing the SCV between the actual test and one administered with unlimited time to be appreciably less than 1.0. Essentially, the issue is how much the testing time can be reduced from a limit subjects find "comfortable," defined somewhat arbitrarily as the time required for 90 percent of the subjects to report having ample time to complete the test. Although most of the evidence is circumstantial rather than direct, most of it indicates that the comfortable time can be decreased appreciably without seriously affecting any of the psychometric properties of tests save perhaps the mean.

For example, a vocabulary test is almost always given under power conditions even though time is required for the subject to look over each item and select the most appropriate answer. The intention is to measure knowledge of words rather than rapidity of response. In fact, additional time beyond the amount required to read and respond to the items does not materially change scores: If an individual does not know the meaning of the word "amalgamate," two additional minutes of staring at the word will not help select the correct alternative response. Consequently, time limits can often be imposed without affecting the psychometric properties of the test.

Obviously, there is a lower limit to the testing time at which point the reliability becomes adversely affected. For example, allowing 1 minute for a 40-item vocabulary test would yield a small standard deviation of scores and consequently low reliability. However, it requires an extremely limited amount of time to eliminate individual differences in this way. Some studies have found that doubling the usual time limit has little effect, and other studies have shown that halving the usual time limit does not even alter mean performance. When the mean was affected, the reliabilities usually dropped minimally. Even when the reliability was affected, the factor composition was minimally influenced. Restrictive time limits that change the reliability typically affect the factors underlying the reliable variance equally, so that the SCV remains high. Most of the important literature on this topic is now relatively old, e.g., Kendall (1964), Lord (1956), and Morrison (1960). Modern test theorists have generally focused on other issues, e.g., adaptive testing (Wainer, 1990).

Guilford (1954, pp. 366–370) and Morrison (1960) provide a relevant exception to the minimal effects of a time limit in which items become progressively more difficult. A very restrictive time limit causes individuals to respond to items that are easier than the items in general. The SCV for scores under timed and untimed conditions can be low because the easier items may measure different factors than the items in general, even when their content appears to be the same. For example, easy items on many quantitative tests tend to measure numerical skills, but difficult items tend to measure reasoning. Although this illustrates how restrictive time limits affect the factor composition of scores, it does not mean that speed per se introduces new ability factors. It means that restrictive time limits force the subject to take a somewhat different test than he or she would with a more generous time limit. The SCV would be high if items were randomly ordered in difficulty, allowing subjects to take the same kind of test under different time limits. Similar considerations hold for different types of items of the same difficulty.

If the mean score with a comfortable time limit is nearer the center of the effective range than either extreme, a good working rule is that the comfortable time can be cut on a power test by at least one-third without materially changing the standard deviation, reliability, or factor composition. This rule works because most subjects can perform effectively when asked to work faster than their preferred rate. They may be annoyed by having to work faster and frequently claim that the restrictive time limits hurt their performance, but that is not actually the case. Mildly restrictive time limits allow more efficient use of testing time. For example, one may employ more multiple-choice achievement items to sample content more widely. At the same time, there is a public relations facet to making individuals at least somewhat comfortable that should not be ignored. If an unavoidable time limit will make many individuals uncomfortable, the fact should be announced well ahead of time. If there is reason to believe that the time limit has influenced the mean on a classroom examination and grading is tied into absolute performance levels, an appropriate allowance should be made.

## Speed-Difficulty Tests

A speed-difficulty test is a measure in which items are easy but not extremely so, i.e., the $p$ values are in the .8 to .9 range without a time limit, but a restrictive time limit is used. It is much more difficult to determine the effects of speed on performance in this case than in the more traditional speed test where the $p$ values would all be close to 1.0 in the absence of a speed limit. Although the comfortable time on timed power tests can generally be cut by one-third without inducing important changes in psychometric properties, it is not safe to make this statement about speed-difficulty tests.

Whereas considerable research has been done to compare pure speed tests with pure power and timed power tests, very little has been done to compare speed-difficulty tests with either. Logically, one expects speed-difficulty tests to combine the pure speed and power factors, but this hypothesis is mainly untested. If it is correct, the mixture of factors in the speed-difficulty test may vary with different time limits. Perhaps the easiest way to avoid the ambiguity of speed-difficulty tests is to avoid their use. They are neither pure speed tests nor power tests, and so it is difficult to develop an adequate psychometric theory for them. They are often chosen for practical reasons to measure power rather than speed abilities. Numerous reasoning tests are of this kind, such as letter series and number series. The average item is relatively easy, and so the difficulty is increased by employing highly restrictive time limits. The items are used because it is very time-consuming to compose and administer large numbers of more difficult reasoning items within a comfortable time limit. These tests often fail to measure what is desired.

## Factors Measured by Speed and Power Tests

Spearman (1927) argued that the factors measured by power tests were the same as those measured by speed tests, however, his conjecture has not received wide support. Speed and power tests have generally been found to measure different factors. For example, speed tests involving the production of simple words tend to measure verbal fluency, but power tests involving the understanding of more difficult words tend to measure verbal comprehension. Similarly, simple perceptual judgments measure perceptual speed, but more difficult judgments measure spatial visualization. Speed and power tests using the same types of mental operations typically correlate positively but with a low SCV. Although the specific findings depend upon the type of material tested, and it is difficult to make explicit comparisons, performing simple problems quickly usually is quite different from performing difficult problems at a high level. The Galton-Spearman tradition has stressed the comparability of speed and accuracy measures of general intelligence (as is manifest in our language—someone who is smart is said to be "quick"). In contrast, the Binet tradition stresses problem-solving ability.

## Implications

Whether or not one wants to employ pure speed or power tests depends on the context. Most content-validated measures, such as standardized achievement tests, involve power rather than speed. Consequently, it is usually undesirable to use speed tests for such measures unless speed is an inherent part of the task, as is true of some clerical skills. Timed power tests are also somewhat undesirable with content-validated measures for previously discussed reasons. As noted, time limits may lower mean scores, which are often tied into grading standards.

Changes in the mean per se are generally less important to measures designed for predictive or construct validation. Speed may be more predictive than power in one instance and less predictive in another. Speed per se may be the topic of investigation. Having a theory guide the choice is highly desirable, if not mandatory, in the case of constructs. If power tests are appropriate, consider administering them at somewhat less than the comfortable time if testing time is at a premium. The bulk of the data indicate that this does not affect the critical psychometric properties. Finally, avoid speed-difficulty tests in developing constructs since their confounding of the two processes virtually guarantees lack of requisite content homogeneity.

## ADVERSE IMPACT, IMPROPER DISCRIMINATION, TEST BIAS, AND DISPARITY

Psychological tests are easily misused, and these misuses can have important legal ramifications for anyone who makes decisions about individuals. This section will be most concerned with misuses that affect groups of people sharing a common attribute such as gender or ethnicity, with particular, but not exclusive, emphasis placed upon legal implications. Females, Asian Americans, African Americans, Native Americans, Hispanic Americans, and Americans of Pacific Island ancestry are legally protected groups under Title VII of the 1964 Civil Rights Act. Although most of the discussion will use examples drawn from the workplace, parallel issues can arise over diagnoses and treatment and affect clinical, counseling, and school psychologists. The point is not discrimination per se but improper discrimination. To "discriminate" means to treat differently, and any evaluation must eventually treat people differently.

There are two basic arguments (called "theories" by lawyers, but not in the scientific sense) that are raised in employment discrimination.

**1** "Systematic discrimination" means that an individual or company deliberately seeks to exclude members of a protected group in initial hiring, promotion, or retention. It is the older of the two legal bases for illegal discrimination. Statistical evidence may play a role, but specific instances of intentional discrimination are usually more important. Statements like "We don't think a woman (black, Hispanic, etc.) can do the job" would bear most directly upon this argument, but the basis need not be this overt. Good faith is a basic defense. Some better known cases based upon this approach are *International Brotherhood of Teamsters v. United States* (1977), *Bazemore v. Friday* (1986), and *Rendon v. AT & T* (1989).

**2** "Disparate (adverse) impact" involves a procedure that appears neutral but which serves to exclude protected groups disproportionately, i.e., raises unnecessary barriers. Frequently, the plaintiff (complainant) alleges test bias—the test measures different things in different groups. *Griggs v. Duke Power* (1971) was an early disparate impact case. The suit was initiated by black employees who claimed that the employer's testing and educational requirements discriminated by race, serving to keep them at lower job levels. The original trial court found for the defendant in 1968 on the basis of a systematic discrimination argument; this decision was reversed by the U.S. Supreme Court. More recently, *Watson v. Ft. Worth Bank & Trust* (1990) established that disparate impact applied to selection by interview and not necessarily formal psychometric evaluation. Good faith is irrelevant to the defense; it must show that the practice yielding the disparity is a business necessity, which often involves validational research.

This section will be more concerned with disparate impact and, in particular, with test bias more than with systematic discrimination. Plaintiffs using the 1964 Act obviously wanted the broadest definition of improper discrimination to allow the use of psychometric and other statistical evidence. Recent decisions, such as *Wards Cove Packing Co. v. Atonio* (1990) made disparate impact cases more difficult to pursue. The Psychological Corporation (1978) summarized the early legal decisions. Bias has also been studied extensively at the level of individual items. Most of this work on item-level bias arises from item response theory, where it is known as differential item functioning rather than classical psychometrics. It will therefore be considered in the next chapter, and we will consider only bias in whole tests.

The *Guidelines* of the *Equal Opportunity Employment Commission* (1978, 1979) have legal status. They are also of interest to psychologists because they borrow heavily from material that had previously been adopted by the American Educational Research Association, American Psychological Association, National Council on Measurement in Education, and American Personnel and Guidance Association (for current standards, see American Educational Research Association et al., 1985; American Psychological Association, 1985, 1986a, 1986b, 1992; American Personnel and Guidance Association, 1978). The *Guidelines* define disparate impact in terms of the difference in success rate between individuals in the reference group and the focal group ("focal" has replaced "minority" among psychometricians because numerically large groups such as females have also obviously been victims of illegal discrimination). Prima facie (apparent but not conclusive) evidence for discrimination exists when the disparity is 20 percent or greater, the "four-fifths rule," although the figure is a rule of thumb. However, disparity is not conclusive evidence of bias in either the legal or psychometric sense.

Just as bias (in the everyday sense of the word) has had a long and virulent history, other factors may prevent focal (or reference) group members from being selected. Chapter 3 noted the criterion problem which reflects the difficulty people have in agreeing on what "best" means. Even if there is consensus about the criterion, finding a valid predictor is a second obvious problem. Third, temporal instability due to such factors as luck may arise—a potentially successful individual may be selected but become ill. Classical unreliability, while usually not the major problem, regresses individuals with the highest true scores toward the mean. All are probably at least as important as bias in preventing the best person from being selected, at least when standardized measures are used.

## Definitions of Bias

Defining bias is not a simple task and, as we shall see, plausible alternative definitions are often contradictory. Perhaps the most basic question asks to whom we should be fair—the individual or the group to which the individual belongs (Hunter & Schmidt, 1976)? Courts demand fairness to both, but the interests may be in opposition. Assume, for example, that 100 people are be hired for a given position where the criterion for success is unequivocal and a perfectly valid predictor exists. Perhaps nobody from a particular focal group is included in that number. Many argue that no focal group member should be selected. At the same time, others argue that it would be unfair to the focal group if this were done because of prior injustices and the need for diversity among those selected, e.g., hiring black police officers. The most recent legal trends, specifically the 1991 Civil Rights Act, have been in the direction of individual rather than group rights, but many proponents of group representation obviously exist.

To a large extent, this dilemma involves ethics. Psychometricians have no particular role to play in an ethical choice. Nonetheless, it is possible to analyze various positions that have been adopted. Hunter and Schmidt (1976) describe a person who opts for picking the best person and would use any valid predictor to this end (including race, sex, or ethnicity, perhaps giving credit on the predictor to focal group members to increase their scores if it improves overall validity) as an unqualified individualist, and a person who seeks the best individual but feels ethically bound to avoid race, sex, or ethnicity directly as a qualified individualist. Both may be contrasted with supporters of quotas, who are concerned with fairness at the group level. The several ways to form quotas will be noted below. Jensen (1980) has criticized the distinction between unqualified and qualified individualists, contrasting both with supporters of quotas.

## Disparity and Bias

Perhaps the most familiar lay definition of bias is that *any* group difference constitutes bias in and of itself. Judge Robert Peckham illustrated this definition when he banned the use of intelligence tests for the assessment of blacks that came before his court on the grounds that their lower scores arose from test bias (Landers, 1986). However, this position ignores the point that group differences may well reflect unbiased and valid measurement operations. Indeed, the weights provided by an ordinary scale would be suspect if there were no mean difference between randomly selected groups of adult males and females. If weight were job-related, the disparity would be defensible, and so disparate impact is therefore not sufficient to establish bias in any meaningful sense. Moreover, disparity is not necessary since test means may be the same in focal and reference groups, but individual scores may relate differentially to a criterion. This is known as "differential validity." Bias might affect the variability of a measure rather than the mean, as when the range of scores is attenuated in a focal population relative to a reference population. The second author observed this effect in unpublished data situations where supervisors were less likely to give females higher performance ratings than males. In order to avoid being seen as biased, the supervisors also gave females fewer low scores. This same process can also obviously affect reference group members.

## Test Bias, Regression, and the Cleary Rule

Although several statistical measures of test bias have been proposed (see Darlington, 1971; Hunter & Schmidt, 1976), the most important one is due to Anne Cleary (1968). The Cleary rule states that a test developed for use in construct or predictive validation is fair if it has the same regression equation in the focal and reference group, and biased if it does not (content validation will be considered separately). This rule can be applied to an individual test or to a composite score of several measures. It relates to the disparity in the consequences of using a test rather than in the predictor itself—a test is unbiased in a given group if its errors of prediction sum to zero. Courts have given heavy weight to this rule. If (1) reference and focal groups distributions on the predictor were identical, (2) they were matched on all relevant "third variables," and (3) the criterion could be assumed unbiased, the problem would reduce to whether or not there were group mean differences on the criterion. We will assume, often falsely, that the criterion is unbiased. However, reference groups commonly have higher mean scores on both predictor and criterion because of third variables such as prior experience, which is why statistical adjustments such as regression are necessary.

The Cleary rule implies that any criterion difference is (1) proportionate to the predictor difference and (2) independent of the level of the predictor. Issue 1 deals with whether or not there is an intercept difference between the focal and reference group regression lines, and issue 2 deals with whether or not there is a slope difference. An intercept difference implies that performance on the criterion systematically differs between members of the two groups at a given level of the predictor. However, it is immaterial whether there is or is not an intercept difference given a slope difference, which implies differential validity. Figure 9-4 portrays hypothetical outcomes reflecting (1) a fair test according to the Cleary common regression line rule, (2) intercept bias, and (3) slope bias. This is the same as Fig. 5-5 except for context.

An intercept difference implies bias because a reference subject and a focal subject

FIGURE 9-4    Relation between a predictor (*X*) and a criterion (*Y*) for a test which produces (*a*) neither an intercept nor a slope difference between focal and reference groups and is therefore fair in the regression sense, (*b*) an intercept but no slope difference, suggesting unfairness to the focal group, and (*c*) a slope difference, suggesting a different form of unfairness to the focal group. Note that in all three cases there is a disparity between reference and focal groups on both predictor and criterion.

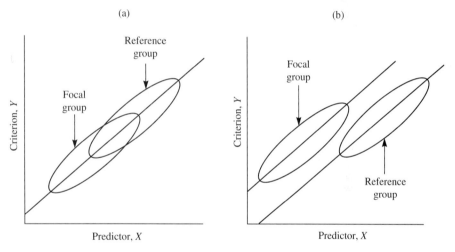

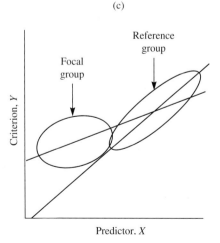

with the same score on the predictor will not have the same expected criterion performance. If the focal group's regression line fell *above* the reference group's regression line, there would be general agreement that the predictor is biased because the performance of focal group members would be systematically underestimated. If the focal group's regression line fell *below* the reference group's regression line, the same logic would lead individualists to argue that the test is biased against the reference group. However, proponents of quotas might not agree (see Thorndike, 1971) because they stress the social value of selecting focal group members and remediating prior injustices. By definition, bias would be a constant, independent of predictor score. A slope difference means that one group's criterion performance is predicted less well than the other's (differential validity). The extreme is single-group validity in which the slope for one group is zero. The common expectation is that the focal group's slope will be flatter since the predictor, having been developed upon the reference group, will be less predictive in the focal group.

Moderated multiple regression (Chapter 5, particular Fig. 5-5) is the most standard way to investigate possible slope and intercept differences. Denote the predictor $X$, the criterion as $Y$, and focal versus reference group membership (the possible moderator) $M$. Finally, let $I$ denote the cross product of $X$ and $M$ ($X$ itself for focal group members and 0 for reference group members when $M$ is coded 1 versus 0). As in any moderated multiple regression problem, first compute the correlation between predictor and criterion ($r_{XY}$), ignoring $M$ and $I$, to describe the predictor's overall validity. Next, add $M$ as a predictor and compute the multiple correlation predicting $Y$ from $X$ and $M$ ($R_{Y \cdot XM}$), ignoring $I$. Finally, add $I$ to $X$ and $M$ to the model and compute the multiple correlation with all terms (saturated model, $R_{Y \cdot XMI}$). A significant difference between $R^2_{Y \cdot XMI}$ and $R^2_{Y \cdot XM}$ or, equivalently, a significant $\beta$ weight for $I$ implies a slope bias. Jensen (1980) suggests an additional consideration—the standard errors for the two groups should be the same. If there is no evidence for slope bias, a significant difference between $R^2_{Y \cdot XM}$ and $R^2_{Y \cdot X}$ or a significant $\beta$ weight for $M$ in the saturated model implies an intercept bias. The empirical literature on bias assessed through the Cleary rule is complex. Houston and Novick (1987) reported black-white differences and Dunbar and Novick (1985) reported male-female differences. Jensen (1980) and Hunter and Schmidt (e.g., Hunter, Schmidt, & Rauschenberger, 1984) are good sources for the many possible artifacts leading to apparent bias. Conversely, one may fail to find bias because criterion measures themselves are biased. In addition, more evidence for bias is found when interviews, peer ratings, or supervisory ratings are used as predictors (Hunter, Schmidt, & Hunter, 1979). A test with a slope bias may favor low-scoring members of one group and high-scoring members of the other group.

## Applying Linear Regression to Salary Disputes

Linear regression is commonly used by courts to adjudicate salary disputes (the term "Cleary rule" is more typically applied to psychometric tests rather than processes used to determine salary even though the principles are the same). For purposes of discussion, we will assume that salary reflects qualifications which in turn may consist of easily measured but relevant variables like length of service plus a more vaguely defined merit component. Because salary is a continuous measure, the ordinary least-squares multiple regression methods of Chapter 5 may be employed. Regression can also be applied to categorical variables such as being hired versus not hired, promoted versus not promoted, assigned to one of several types of positions, and retained versus fired, but discriminant analysis or categorical modeling may be more appropriate than linear regression (see Chapters 14 and 15).

Class action lawsuits (those initiated on behalf of a group, legally protected or not, in contrast to those on behalf of a specific individual or individuals) involving salary and related group differences usually begin with the plaintiff describing a disparity favoring the reference group. The defense usually responds by stating that the reference group is more qualified than the focal group. Focal groups are often less qualified (e.g., may have less experience), perhaps because of previous injustices for which the various civil rights laws have not required redress. The plaintiff may also state that the disparity is increasing over time, but this can arise simply because raises are usually proportional to base salary—if there was a mean disparity between focal and reference groups of $1000 in 1 year and everyone was given a 5 percent raise, the disparity would also increase by 5 percent to $1050.

The disparity may be explained in terms of easily objectified measures like seniority. Unless the plaintiff can show that the focal group has more merit in a manner the company recognizes in some other way (e.g., in a different department or branch office), this may prove a satisfactory defense. Members within each of the two groups may be totally homogeneous as to qualifications (e.g., all reference group members were hired in 1985 and all focal group members were hired in 1990). In this case, seniority and group membership would be perfectly confounded, a problem inherent in any correlational problem. The issue might hinge on whether the disparity in salary due to experience is proportional to the disparity in comparable jobs.

Quite often the disparity cannot be simply explained, and even those companies that might have been fair may lack well-developed measures of merit. Actual application of the Cleary rule is thus often complicated. Consequently, if there were no mean difference in seniority, a disparity in mean salary could either reflect (1) true, appropriate, but perhaps implicit differences in merit or (2) illegal discrimination. The defense would then attempt to explicate merit by trying to emulate statistically the processes that previously may have been implicit, e.g., by attempting to show that the groups differed in some measure of productivity. These additional data would then be combined with seniority to redefine overall qualifications, returning the problem to the use of linear regression.

Regression-based methods of explaining disparities simply seek to determine what the disparity would be if there were no difference in qualifications, and the outcome may indicate no salary disparity, an intercept difference (which we have focused upon), or a slope difference (obtainable, as usual, from the product of qualifications and group membership). Attention centers upon disparities that adversely impact focal group members. One problem in evaluating predictors of measures like salary relative to tests is that the employees form a fixed population, and so the use of inferential tests is questionable (even though it is commonly done). An investigation of a test usually has no such imposed size limit.

## Reverse Regression

Birnbaum (1979b; also see Birnbaum, 1979a, 1981) performed an interesting twist on classical regression with data showing that a focal group was underpaid relative to a reference group, adjusting for qualifications. He then reversed the roles of predictor and criterion to predict qualifications from salary. Although one might logically expect the result to show that the focal members were overqualified for their salaries, precisely the reverse was noted—members of the focal group were simultaneously underpaid and underqualified! This paradox arises from the peculiarities of the regression model—what is considered error and is therefore minimized by least squares or other algorithms differs in the two cases: The regression line predicting $Y$ from $X$ is different from the regression line predicting $X$ from $Y$.

This reveals a problem with multiple regression. Although it is more natural to predict salary from qualifications than the converse, the term "qualifications" is often rather fuzzy and therefore somewhat unreliable. Salary disputes usually center on a discretionary (merit) component. The unreliability of merit violates a major assumption of the regression model, and so a structural model (see Chapter 4) may be more appropriate (McLaughlin, 1980; also see Birnbaum, 1981). The details of this approach are beyond the scope of this book.

## Residual Analysis

Discovering relevant "third variables" that account for disparities arising from a fair process is a combination of knowing the context in which the investigation is conducted, insight, and sometimes luck. One possible way to discover third variables is to conduct a residual analysis which analyzes what is left over after accounting for the variables employed in the regression analysis (see Chapter 5). The second author analyzed faculty salaries in response to a class action law suit filed by a former faculty member. One model employed a composite measure of qualifications that took academic rank, seniority, college of appointment (e.g., business, liberal arts, etc.), and group (focal versus reference) into account. The raw-score regression ($b$) weight for group describes the mean disparity in dollars and was relatively large in the model.

The next step was to determine the residual difference between actual and predicted salary for individual faculty members. This indicated a key variable had been neglected. Several reference group members but relatively few focal group members previously had been administrators. The policy was to pay faculty higher salaries as an inducement to take on these duties but not to lower their salaries when they left the position. A new model was constructed that included whether or not the individual had been a former administrator as a predictor. This model reduced the mean disparity considerably.

Plotting the residuals separately for the two groups revealed an additional point. The reference group residuals were much more variable than the focal group's. After adjustment both the lowest-paid and highest-paid faculty were in the reference group, even though the focal group earned less on average than the reference group. This illustrates the relevance of Jensen's (1980) concern about equal standard errors. Much of the difference in variability came from extremely senior outliers at the low end of the scale. The actual effects of seniority upon salary were not linear but "compressed" in that younger faculty got larger raises per additional year of service than older faculty.

## Simpson's Paradox Revisited

Simpson's paradox (Chapter 5), illustrating one form of aggregation error, is extremely important in the study of illegal discrimination (Bickel, Hammel, & O'Connell, 1975). For example, assume that a company accepts applicants for clerical positions which require 2 years of college and executive positions which require an M.B.A. Many more people thus apply for clerical positions than executive positions, but a lower proportion are actually hired. Further assume (1) that the selection processes for the positions are fair, (2) focal group applicants are less likely to be eligible for executive positions, and (3) the company doing the hiring is not responsible for this disparity. Table 9-1 illustrates the following.

**1** There were more focal group applicants than reference group applicants for clerical positions (1000 versus 500).

**2** A greater percentage of focal group applicants were hired for clerical positions than reference group applicants (100/1000 or 10 percent versus 25/500 or 5 percent).

**3** There were fewer focal group applicants than reference group applicants for executive positions (10 versus 100).

**4** A greater percentage of focal group applicants were hired for executive positions than reference group applicants (10/10 or 100 percent versus 60/100 or 60 percent).

**5** However, Only 11 percent of the focal group members were hired overall (110/1010) versus 14 percent of the reference group members (85/600).

Despite being hired at higher rates within each level, a lower rate of focal group members were hired overall, which is Simpson's paradox. Simpson's paradox would also be illustrated if the data represented those retained or promoted. Although the paradox pertains to aggregated percentages, the same principles could also be illustrated with regard to salary or any other continuous variable.

The heart of this paradox is that differences in a third variable, the distribution of applicants at the two levels, is confounded with focal group membership per se. Over 99 percent (1000/1010) of the focal group applied for clerical positions, but only 83 percent (500/600) of the reference group applied for clerical positions. Only 125 (100

**TABLE 9-1**   NUMBERS AND PERCENTAGES OF FOCAL AND REFERENCE APPICANTS AND HIREES FOR CLERICAL AND EXECUTIVE POSITIONS (HYPOTHETICAL DATA)

| Position | Focal applicants, $N$ | Reference applicants, $N$ | Focal hirees, $N$ (%) | Reference hirees, $N$ (%) |
|---|---|---|---|---|
| Clerical | 1000 | 500 | 100  (10) | 25  (5) |
| Executive | 10 | 100 | 10 (100) | 60 (60) |
| Overall | 1010 | 600 | 110  (11) | 85 (14) |

+ 25) of all 1500 (1000 + 500) clerical applicants were selected (8 percent), but 70 (10 + 60) of all 110 (10 + 100) executive applicants were hired (64 percent). There need not even be more focal group applicants at the clerical level and fewer at the executive level; all that is required is (1) a relative disparity in focal group applicants and (2) higher selection percentages at positions for which there are fewer applicants. Aggregating produces unweighted percentages that do not take these two factors into account. Though the data are fictitious, the example is quite relevant because the disparities in eligibility are all very real.

### Bias in Content-Validated Measures

Measures used for personnel selection are often based upon content validation. In principle, they need not be correlated with any criterion, and so the Cleary rule less obviously applies. In *U.S. v. State of South Carolina* (1977), the courts supported a measure of teaching effectiveness for which it was argued that no satisfactory criterion existed (as a rule, construct-validated measures that are not based upon extremely well-accepted theories have fared poorest and tests that are most clearly job-related have fared best). The primary issue is how well the test samples the content of the job. This is especially true of tests used for promotion or retention rather than initial hiring. Initial hiring decisions often use a cognitive ability (intelligence) measure for which the Cleary rule is applicable, but this may range-restrict the role of cognitive ability in promotion and retention. The latter decisions are based upon job performance, for which there may not be any standardized measure, and sample sizes are usually small. The following points are especially relevant.

1 Content on tests used for initial selection should not unfairly discriminate against focal group members. In particular, do not test for easily learned skills such as job vocabulary, as focal applicants may have poorer differential access to the jargon (*Dobbins v. International Brotherhood of Electrical Workers, Local 212*, 1968). This was clearly used as a discriminatory device in the past, allowing relatives of reference group employees unfair advantage. If people are trained in the jargon and it is important to communication, it may be appropriately used as a criterion for promotion and retention.

2 If possible, select the behaviors to be sampled through a careful job analysis that describes what people actually do on the job (see Chapter 8). In *U.S. v. City of St. Louis* (1978) the selection and promotion practices of the defendant were supported because of the thoroughness of their job analysis.

3 Test for invariance in the factor structure if the test(s) provide a profile of scores. A difference in the factor structure for reference and focal groups provides some evidence for bias even though equivalence (invariance) does not guarantee fairness. Factor invariance, which is also relevant to construct and predictive validity, is discussed in Chapter 13 and in more detail in technical sources such as Gorsuch (1983) and Harman (1976).

4 Knowledge of the correlates of the test is useful. Showing that a test correlates with other appropriate measures of performance on that job is an asset, especially con-

sidering the range restriction that may be present. Conversely, showing that a test correlates highly with irrelevant attributes is a liability. For example, a test designed to evaluate management performance might primarily reflect low-level clerical abilities.

## Barriers and Cutoffs

We have noted that the basis of the four-fifths rule is the desire to avoid placing unnecessary barriers in the path of members of a protected group. A disparity may arise in a test that is unbiased in the Cleary sense when an unnecessarily high cutoff is used, which, to a first approximation, occurred in *Commonwealth of Pennsylvania v. Flaherty* (1975). For example, a job might require the lifting of 50-pound weights, which need not create a huge gender disparity. However, requiring applicants for this job to lift a 200-pound weight may create a much larger gender disparity and lead to illegal discrimination if it cannot shown to be job-related.

Figure 9-5 illustrates the source of this particular problem. Assume that the measure (1) is sufficiently normal to have a reasonable "tail," (2) is valid in an appropriate sense, (3) is unbiased in the Cleary sense, and (4) produces slightly higher means in the reference group compared to the focal group. First, set the selection criterion at the median of the reference group. The disparity in rates of those passing will be of small, perhaps trivial magnitude, e.g., 48 percent of the focal group versus 50 percent of the reference group. However, if the criterion is high, the relative disparity in those passing can be extreme. For example, if it is set two standard deviations above the reference group's mean, roughly 2.5 percent of the reference group will pass, but practical-

**FIGURE 9-5**   Even though distributions of scores for the focal and reference groups may overlap considerably, the slight mean disparity favoring the reference group translates into a large disparity in relative numbers of individuals selected when the selection cutoff is quite extreme.

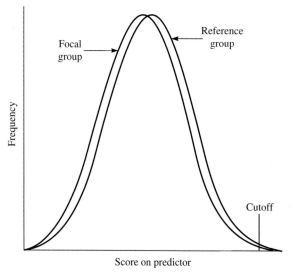

ly no focal group members will pass. As a result, only reference group members will be selected. The absolute disparity in the rates of those passing or failing will be small, but attention will naturally be drawn to the composition of those passing. A parallel situation arises when the criterion is set very low. Although nearly everybody in both groups passes, these who fail will nearly all be focal group members.

The crucial consideration is how much of the attribute is required. It is obviously unfair to the focal group to require that someone fall at the extreme of a dimension when only an average level is required. However, it is just as unfair to those doing the selecting to cite small mean differences in a general population as evidence for a barrier when the position demands very high scores on the attribute.

## Selection Fairness and Quotas

The above discussion is most applicable to a single test and dominated academic concern about bias until about 1970. It is still basic to the legal system. However, much subsequent work was devoted to what is called "selection fairness," which considers the overall social consequences of selection procedures. Discussion of this topic was stimulated by Cole (1973), Darlington (1971), McNemar (1975), and Thorndike (1971); see Cole and Moss (1989) for more recent developments. In particular, McNemar (1975) effectively defined "fairness" as the maximum predicted potential on the criterion. Unfortunately, what is considered fair depends very much on one's perspective, an issue that was foreshadowed by the distinction between individualists and proponents of quotas (and perhaps between qualified and unqualified individualists). Institutions, especially employers, are prone to be individualists, as are reference group members; members of focal groups likewise tend to be proponents of some form of quota (but, in both cases, not universally). We begin by noting five general definitions of fairness.

1 Pure regression, i.e., choosing people with the highest score
2 Compensated regression, i.e., using a common regression line but adjusting for some unfairness
3 Quotas using nonpsychometrically determined selection, e.g., random
4 Quotas using psychometrically determined selection, usually selecting the highest-scoring individuals within groups
5 Methods based upon the utility of decisions.

**Pure Regression** Although the term "best qualified" is commonly used to describe the individuals chosen under a pure regression model, it misses the point that the test is a predictor and usually a highly fallible one. The properties of this model have already been considered; in general it would be considered fair only if (1) selection was unbiased in the Cleary sense, (2) it met Jensen's (1980) requirement of equal standard errors of measurement, and (3) there was no need to diversify a population beyond that provided by the ordering of people on the predictor. If these conditions were met, the test would select people having the highest expected criterion performance.

**Compensated Regression**    Darlington (1971) suggested adding a constant to focal group scores as a form of bonus paralleling the veteran's bonus on civil service tests. People with the highest scores following the correction would then be selected. A major question, of course, is how much of a bonus is needed. If the test has a intercept bias, the correction could be the magnitude of the bias, but that would be a remedy, not a bonus, notwithstanding the rarity of pure intercept biases. In practice the value of his suggested correction was based upon the social value of focal group representation rather than simple compensation for bias.

A different approach has been suggested to provide equal marginal utility (equal risk), i.e., ensure that the last person selected in the focal and reference groups will have the same probability of success or expected performance on a continuous measure. Equal risk is violated when the group standard errors are unequal, even though the test may be fair in the Cleary sense. Unequal standard errors can arise from nonadditivity or when one of the groups is range-restricted. For example, requiring a college degree may be appropriate to a position, but it will result in a more highly selected group of blacks than whites. It can also cause an apparent slope bias. Further assuming that residuals are approximately normally distributed, the following procedure may be applied to select individuals whose probability of failure is less than some criterion amount ($\alpha$), which can be adjusted to select a desired proportion of individuals. This method can be used when there is a slope bias. However, it does not guarantee any form of diverse representation. Indeed, it really offers more benefit to an institution (e.g., an employer) by providing a better selection of employees when its conditions for use arise. At the extreme, no focal group member may exceed cutoff.

$$z = \frac{(Y_c - Y')}{s_{Y.X}} \tag{9-7a}$$

$$= \frac{Y_c - (bX + a)}{s_{Y.X}} \tag{9-7b}$$

where $X$ = predictor score

$\quad Y'$ = predicted criterion score

$\quad b$ = regression line slope relating predictor to criterion

$\quad a$ = regression line slope

$\quad s_{Y.X}$ = standard error of estimate

$\quad Y_c$ = cutoff on criterion

The probability of failure ($\alpha$) is the area under the normal curve below $Y_c$. For example, if $\alpha = .16$ (an 84 percent chance of success is desired) and scores have been standardized, the predicted criterion score is one standard deviation above the criterion mean ($Y_c = 1$). Let $r_{XY} = .30$ for a given group. Consequently $s_{Y.X} = \sqrt{1 - .30^2} = \sqrt{.91} = .95$. In order to achieve this predicted score, the obtained score on the predictor must be $1/.95 = 1.05$. Whether this is an advantage to a focal group member or not depends upon whether $\alpha$ is high or low and whether there are slope or intercept differences. If the group standard errors are equal and the test is fair in the Cleary sense, it will provide the same results as the pure regression model.

**Quotas Using Nonpsychometrically Determined Selection** Quotas in which choice is not made psychometrically may involve random choice or election by a suitable constituency. This category represents many laypersons' view of a population-based quota; e.g., if 10 percent of the population belongs to a focal group, 10 percent of these individuals should be selected. One relatively uncontroversial use is selection of individuals for inclusion in a research study, e.g., randomly selecting groups of males and females to study gender differences. Another example is the allotment of individuals by race and gender as delegates to political conventions. This form of quota is dictated when there is no valid predictor and the need for diverse representation is paramount. Random selection according to a quota is also reasonable when a content-validated test has provided a very large pool of qualified individuals and there is only marginal benefit from very high scores or the skills can be easily taught.

Unfortunately, the controversy over specific quotas hardly needs documentation. Groups defined by gender and ancestry are certainly not the only ones possible even in the relatively narrow legal sense, e.g., handicapped individuals have similar legal rights. Situations may demand representation of different religious groups. Those leading alternative lifestyles have also sought representation. Moreover, protected groups are not necessarily underrepresented—at this writing many programs in clinical psychology have been concerned that not enough males apply and that Asian Americans are well represented in many academic endeavors. Quotas that start as a guarantee of representation can also unfairly limit representation.

Multiple quotas (e.g., selection by gender, race, and ethnicity) raise an interesting problem. The question has been raised whether someone who is female, black, and Hispanic counts toward all three quotas. If the individual does, people who fulfill fewer quotas may have even more difficulty being selected than if no quota were imposed. Male black non-Hispanics may be disadvantaged by being counted only toward one quota, and a female black Hispanic may reflect different values than females in general, blacks in general, or Hispanics in general. However, if the individual counts toward only one quota, more positions could be required than there are positions to be filled. For example, if 50 percent must be allotted to females, 25 percent to blacks, 20 percent to Hispanics, and 10 percent to Asians, 105 percent of the positions would be accounted for. Population quotas must be based upon joint attributes, e.g., the percentage of individuals who are female *and* black *and* Hispanic rather than these marginal figures. Unfortunately, it may be difficult to locate individuals having the joint attributes because these percentages may be quite small even when there are as few as three attributes. This issue arises, less controversially as a rule, in marketing studies.

**Quotas Using Psychometrically Determined Selection** Assuming that the predictor and criterion can be satisfactorily represented as dichotomies, one possibility is simply to select individuals in accord with general quotas, e.g., population quotas. This is like random selection, but people are selected within groups on the basis of a valid, but perhaps biased, predictor. Three additional models can be understood with reference to an outcome matrix (see Table 9-2) which would be formed for each group (only the marginal data are needed for the third of these). For example, true positive is the number of individuals in a given group who exceed cutoff (pass) on both predictor

**TABLE 9-2**    AN OUTCOME MATRIX

|  | Pass predictor | Fail predictor | Sum |
|---|---|---|---|
| Pass criterion | True positives ($A$) | False negatives ($B$) | Actual positives ($A + B$) |
| Fail criterion | False positives ($C$) | True negatives ($D$) | Actual negatives ($C + D$) |
| Sum | Predicted positives ($A + C$) | Predicted negatives ($B + D$) | |

*Note:* $A$, $B$, $C$, and $D$ are cell frequencies associated with the four possible results of passing or failing a predictor and passing or failing a criterion, where passing is defined as exceeding a cutoff. Actual positive, actual negative, predicted positive, and predicted negative outcomes are marginal frequencies.

and criterion. Three other concepts derivable from the matrix used in traditional personnel selection are (1) the selection ratio or proportion of individuals to be selected, defined as the total number who pass over the total number of individuals, $(A + B)/(A + B + C + D)$; (2) the success ratio of those who are chosen (true positive over total positive $= A/(A + B)$; and (3) the base rate or ratio of those who succeed relative to the total, $(A + D)/(A + B + C + D)$.

The three models are based upon concepts (but, unfortunately, different concepts) of fairness. They can be used to rectify intercept or slope bias or to accommodate the need for additional cultural diversity in a test that is fair by Cleary's standards.

**1** The "equal-probability model" chooses predictor cutoffs in each group to equate the ratios of true positive to predicted positive—the success rate or $A/(A + B)$. It means that the probability of success will be the same in all groups; if half of the reference group succeeds under its cutoff, half of the focal group will also succeed under its (presumably different) cutoff. Linn (1973) suggested, but did not endorse, this model, and it may not be possible to obtain suitable cutoffs (Jensen, 1980).

**2** The "conditional-probability model" chooses cutoffs in each group to equate the ratios of true positive to actual positive, $A/(A + C)$. This allows all individuals who can succeed on the criterion to have the same selection probability, regardless of whether they are in the focal or the reference group (Cole, 1973).

**3** The "constant-ratio model" (Thorndike, 1971) chooses predictor cutoffs in each group to equate the ratios of predicted positive to actual positive, $(A + B)/(A + C)$. This means that if the reference group is 10 times the size of the focal group among those who succeed at the task, the proportions of those selected must also be in a 10:1 ratio. As noted above, the actual cells of the matrix ($A$, $B$, $C$, and $D$) are not needed; all one needs to do is select cutoffs that equate the selection ratios to the success ratios. Randomly generated quotas are a special case in which a predictor has no validity.

The equal-probability and conditional-probability models will usually provide better expected short-term performance than the constant-ratio model; the constant-ratio model will provide better short-term performance than selection from population quotas within groups, which in turn will provide better short-term performance than random selection when the focal group's predicted performance is well below that of the reference group. Conversely, the first two models are also less likely to satisfy focal group members. Since focal group members would have the same representation when selection is made by a predictor as randomly, there is little reason for preferring the latter. Proponents of quotas often argue about long-term benefits which are basically unknown. In all cases, focal group members who are selected may have lower scores than reference group members who are rejected. In contrast, a model using a single regression line (pure regression or the modification needed to accommodate unequal standard errors) picks those people with the highest expected criterion scores. If the test is fair according to the Cleary rule, it means that being fair to the individual means being unfair to the group, and vice versa. Moreover, criteria for selection to accept individuals fairly according to these rules will not necessarily reject individuals fairly according to the same rules (Peterson & Novick, 1976). Selecting individuals who eventually fail has an obvious cost to both employee and employer.

**Methods Based upon the Utility of Decisions**   Darlington's additive correction considered the utilities or costs and benefits of the various outcomes. A much more complex approach presented by Sawyer, Cole, and Cole (1976) considers this issue in more detail. The basic concept is standard in decision theory. The utility associated with the decision to accept an individual equals the benefit (reward) associated with successful performance times the probability that the individual will succeed plus the cost (penalty) associated with unsuccessful performance times the probability that the individual will fail. The two probabilities are conditional true and false positive probabilities. Conversely, the utility associated with the decision to reject an applicant equals the savings associated with not hiring the individual times the probability that the individual will fail plus the cost associated with not hiring a successful individual times the probability that the individual will succeed. These latter probabilities are the true and false negative probabilities. Because the costs and benefits are usually even more difficult to agree upon (especially when viewed from the different eyes of the institution and applicant) than quotas, we will not consider this model in detail. However, there may be situations where outcomes can be agreed upon.

It is important to note that Section 106 of the 1991 Civil Rights Act amends the 1964 Act by making it "an unlawful employment selection practice for [anyone making hiring decisions] . . . to adjust the scores of, use different cutoff scores for, or otherwise alter the results of, employment related tests on the basis of race, color, religion, sex, or national origin." Pending further legal decisions and legislation, this appears to rule out anything but a pure regression model in employment, though it may not affect college admissions. The act also reversed aspects of *Wards Cove Packing Co. v. Atonio* (1990) in which the Supreme Court ruled that if multiple potential practices can have disparate impact, the plaintiff had to show that a particular practice led to this impact. Equally important, the Court required the plaintiff to show that a business practice was not job-related. The Act returned the burden to the defendant once disparate impact is shown (where it had generally been felt to lie before the Court decision).

Many individuals have suggested that some focal groups do more poorly on abilities items because they have had less exposure to the content. Appropriate methods for evaluating the issue of bias involving particular items are considered in the next chapter.

### Pooled versus Separate Group Norms

It is common to form separate norms when focal and reference groups differ on a measure. For example, several MMPI scales are normed separately by gender and age. Whether or not it is appropriate to use separate norms depends upon the form of the question being asked. For example, younger individuals tend to endorse more items that denote impulsivity than older individuals. Some circumstances dictate asking how impulsive a person is for someone of that age, and others dictate ignoring age. Impulsivity would not be a matter of concern in a young person seen for therapy if the level was high for people in general but normal for that age. There would be a reasonable expectation that the individual would "outgrow" the condition. However, one would not wish to hire him or her for a position where impulsivity was undesirable, such as a police officer. To the extent that both types of questions may be asked, both separate and pooled norms are needed. Choice of norm is thus situation specific, and interpretations should be made accordingly.

## HALO EFFECTS

A "halo effect" is a rater's tendency to perceive an individual who is high (or low) in one area as high (or low) in other areas as well (Wells, 1907; Thorndike, 1920). It reflects "a failure to discriminate among conceptually distinct and potentially independent aspects of a ratee's behavior" (Saal, Downey, & Lahey, 1980, p. 450) and is a form of method variance-induced reduction in the divergent validity of ratings (see Chapter 3.) Many desirable traits have at least a small positive correlation (*true* halo), but a halo effect enhances these correlations (observed halo). Bernardin and Beatty (1984) have, however, noted negative halo effects, as when one underestimates the intelligence of someone who is physically attractive.

The traditional view of halo does not necessarily assume that the attributes under evaluation (true scores in the sense of classical psychometrics) are uncorrelated. Our discussion will therefore include situations in which the relation between the evaluations (observed scores) is either too high (traditional positive halo) or too low (negative halo). In addition, we use the term "relation" rather than "correlation" because halo effects are not always assessed in terms of correlations, although this is commonly the case. Halo effects are historically assumed to impair accuracy of judgment, so that the magnitude of a halo effect and judgmental accuracy are negatively related over judges or situations to the extent that accuracy can be defined. Cooper (1981) reported a paradoxical positive correlation between measures of halo and judgmental accuracy, but Fisicaro (1988) noted some problems with this conclusion.

In order to assess halo effects, one must obtain objective measures of the relevant attributes, e.g., the true correlations among the attributes. This has led various investigators to have subjects judge two or more physically defined attributes, e.g., Garner (1974), Santee and Egeth (1980), and Pomerantz and Pristach (1989), among many others. These experiments, considered further in Chapter 15, typically employ uncorrelated attributes—subjects might judge the height and width of rectangles that vary independently of one another. A classical finding is that misperceptions of height and width are related. Unfortunately, most studies require judgments that have no objective physical correlates. For example, a teaching effectiveness survey may have students rate how "clear" and "interesting" an instructor is. It is common to average expert ratings to define true scores, but this does not define true scores as unequivocally as do physical measures.

If possible, mask dimensions to eliminate halo. Imagine a marketing task involving judging the voice quality and visual appearance of television news reporters. Making both judgments while looking at a videotape with sound clearly allows halo effects to emerge. However, one could separately have the ratees (1) listen to an audio tape without video to judge voice quality and (2) look at a videotape without sound to evaluate visual appearance.

## Traditional Measures of Halo

Fisicaro (1988) describes two traditional classes of halo measures. Both attempt to estimate halo error ($H_E$) from an observed halo ($H_O$) and a true halo ($H_T$). Borman (1977) used the standard deviations of each judge's ratings (either in raw or standardized form) across dimensions for a given ratee and averaged these over ratees to yield $H_O$. The $H_T$ is the corresponding average standard deviation of the true scores. One possible measure of $H_E$ is simply the average difference between $H_O$ and $H_T$ over ratees. Since a positive difference for one ratee may cancel a negative difference for another ratee, the absolute halo error is based upon the absolute value of the average signed difference (Cooper, 1981), whereas the cumulative halo error is based upon the average absolute difference.

The second class of measures uses the correlation between dimensions over ratees for a given judge (Borman, 1979). Although the average of the resulting $(k^2 - k)/2$ such correlations for the $k$ dimensions may be used to define $H_O$, the Fisher $Z'$ transformation is preferable (see Chapter 5). This transformation corrects for the nonlinearity in the scale defining $r$. Equation 9-8 provides this transformation (also see Hays, 1988, pp. 590–592):

$$Z' = -\ln \frac{1}{2}\left(\frac{1+r}{1-r}\right) \tag{9-8}$$

The ln is the natural log function, and $r$ is the PM correlation. The average of the values of $Z'$ can then be transformed back to a value of $r$. This inverse transformation is given by

$$r = \frac{e^{2z'} - 1}{e^{2z'} + 1} \tag{9-9}$$

where, as usual, $e = 2.7182$. . . . Tables are widely available.

A value of $H_T$ can be obtained in like manner from the average dimensional intercorrelation between true scores and halo error computed as some form of difference (signed or unsigned) between $H_O$ and $H_T$. Unfortunately, Fisicaro and Lance (1990) have noted problems associated with any form of difference between observed and true halo which we will now consider. The problem is that any form of difference between $H_O$ and $H_T$ ignores measurement error. Suppose that there is actually a correlation of .5 between two attributes over ratees. A rater perceives a much higher correlation, say .8, but the actual ratings are attenuated back to .5 because of judgmental error. This falsely suggests no halo error; $H_O - H_T$ underestimates true halo.

Making the rater's judgments more reliable by obtaining multiple ratings of some or all the ratees on each of the dimensions is one way to overcome this problem. The observed correlation can be corrected for attenuation using Eq. 6-36. Fisicaro and Lance (1990) appropriately term the correlation between true and observed scores "correlation accuracy." However, it is basically the same as a reliability index of classical psychometrics (see Chapter 6) save that it is influenced by systematic as well as random factors. In fact, it is the square root of a generalizability coefficient in the sense of Chapter 7. Designate the true and observed scores for one dimension as $A$ and $a$, and the true and observed scores for a second dimension as $B$ and $b$. The correlation between observed scores (ratings) $(r_{ab})$ in the absence of halo error is $r_{Aa}r_{Bb}r_{AB}$. In other words, it is the true-score correlation weighted by the product of the two correlation accuracies. To obtain an appropriate measure of halo, subtract $r_{Aa}r_{Bb}r_{AB}$ and not simply the correlation between true scores $(r_{AB})$ from the correlation between observed scores $(r_{ab})$.

## Recent Developments in the Study of Halo

Fisicaro and Lance (1990) have developed three structural models (see Chapter 4) of halo.

**1** The "general-impression model" follows from the ordinary usage of the term "halo" but more specifically from King, Hunter, and Schmidt's (1980) definition as "the tendency of a rater to allow overall impressions of an individual to influence the judgment of that person's performance along several quasi-independent dimensions of job performance" (p. 507). A general impression $(G)$ affects observed scores but not true scores. The $G$ may be a composite of all attributes being rated or a separate attribute. For example, viewers separately judging auditory and visual characteristics of reporters may respond to their composite "pleasantness." Conversely, $G$ may also be a separate attribute—students may judge the "clarity" and "effectiveness" of their instructor in terms of how easy the instructor grades.

**2** The "salient dimension model" was anticipated by Robbins (1989; also see Anastasi, 1988; Blum & Naylor, 1968) who defined it as the "tendency for an evaluator to let the assessment of an individual on one trait influence . . . evaluation of that person on other traits" (p. 444). There is no composite or external variable $G$. One or more dimensions to be rated stand out, being easier to judge, and determine judgments on more subtle dimensions. For example, physical attractiveness has long been known to be a salient dimension (Walster, Aronson, & Abrams, 1966) and quite probably influences judgments of other dimensions such as honesty. Perceptually visual information frequently "captures" auditory information (Colavita, 1974), which is the basis of ventriloquism.

**3** The "inadequate discrimination model" refers to a "rater's failure to discriminate among conceptually distinct and potentially independent aspects of a (ratee's) behavior" (Saal, Downey, & Lahey, 1980, p. 415; cf. DeCotiis, 1977; Murphy & Reynolds, 1988). This involves mutual but perhaps unequal influences of one dimension upon another. As an example, viewers judging TV reporters may judge their voice partially in terms of their appearance, and vice versa. The general-impression model sometimes reduces to proportional contributions of each dimension upon the other, e.g., responding completely to *G* is the same as having each of two dimensions influence their own and other judgments equally. Likewise, the salient dimension model is a special case of inadequate discrimination where one of the influences is zero. The interpretation of halo error depends upon the applicable model and may become quite complex to estimate and require numerous simplifying assumptions when there are more than two dimensions. The simplest case is when a salient dimension influences one other dimension. In this case, the halo error equals the slope of the regression line in predicting the less salient dimension from the more salient dimension.

It is probably best to say that any of these models may fit in a given situation, but studies using ratings of multiple attributes must consider the problem of halo.

## RESPONSE BIASES AND RESPONSE STYLES

We define a "response bias" as a measurement artifact which emerges from the context of a particular situation that affects one or more people. Biases may systematically lead to one response over another, or they may produce randomness through confusion or carelessness. Systematic and random biases will be considered separately. A response style is a measurement artifact that is consistent across situations so that it qualifies as a personality variable. It is thus similar to a trait except that it is a "nuisance" variable that is incidental to the issues of interest. It may also be systematic (some people systematically prefer to choose socially desirable responses more than other people do) or random (some people are more careless than others). Both biases and styles are artifacts because what they are is at least partially independent of what one seeks to measure.

To understand the similarities and differences between the two, consider an ordinary political poll. Response biases and response styles could both cause someone who prefers one candidate or is indifferent to declare a preference for the other candidate. Political polls are notoriously influenced by the characteristics of the pollster. People are more likely to say that they plan to vote for candidate A if pollsters say they work for that candidate than if pollsters remains unidentified or say that they are associated with candidate B. Pollsters working for a given political candidate will disguise the fact if they want an honest result, or identify themselves if they wish to make the candidate look good when releasing the poll to the public.

The following hypothetical experiment can be used to evaluate the magnitude of bias associated with a pollster's identification. Assume that people are called twice during a political campaign, once by someone identified with candidate A and once under neutral identification. The result might be that 58 percent prefer candidate A when the pollster is identified with that candidate, but only 50 percent prefer candidate A when the pollster is unidentified. The order of calling needs to be counterbalanced over ratees to allow bias to be separated from shifts in the electorate over the course of the campaign. Identification changed the ratee's bias, but do not necessarily assume that the lack of identification and a consequent 50-50 split in the potential voters meant that this condition was unbiased. Either or both conditions might be biased relative to the actual election for any of a number of reasons. One candidate might belong to a racial minority, and the respondents might not wish to be considered bigots for choosing the opponent. The relative bias is at issue, not the absolute bias in a given condition of measurement. Measuring either relative or absolute bias is a thorny problem which requires the theoretical discussion of Chapter 15 (see Macmillan & Creelman, 1990).

Now, imagine that the same people are called twice more at some later date and asked whether they prefer brand X or brand Y cola. Paralleling the first situation, one market researcher is identified as working for brand X, and the other researcher is unidentified. There is no reason to assume that the change in bias due to the market researcher's identification is necessarily the 8 percent change observed in the political polling, but for simplicity assume it is also 8 percent. The issue of response style deals with the extent of overlap between the 8 percent of the people who responded differently to the political pollsters and the 8 percent who responded differently to the two market researchers, i.e., cross-situational consistency. In other words, if subjects are coded 0 (gave the same response) versus 1 (gave different responses) in each situation, how high is the correlation between the two measures?

Any of a number of words might be used to describe the tendency to respond in terms of the interviewer's identification, such as "compliance," but the term must characterize subjects in at least two situations at least to some extent. Consequently, biases might be present in both situations without there being any evidence for a consistent style if the changes are idiosyncratic, i.e., if the two groups of respondents are unrelated. Furthermore, even if a response style is consistent, it may not correlate with any other variable of interest. In that case, it would basically be a nuisance.

It is extremely simple to create biases; indeed, they are often unintended by-products of a flaw in the design of a study. Response styles were a popular research topic some years back but now have mostly faded from the literature. Consequently our discussion of them will be brief.

## Sources of Bias

The problems of controlling response biases depend upon whether one is primarily interested in studying people or scaling stimuli. Questions which everybody answers in the same way obviously cannot cast light upon how people differ, regardless of whether the content of the item makes it too easy or too difficult on an abilities test or the wording leads everyone in a common direction on any type of test. There are many advantages to asking questions (or, more generally, presenting stimuli) in such a way as to obtain a rectangular distribution of responses (equal response category usage), e.g., to have 20 percent of the sample choose each of five Likert-type alternatives.

These questions have the best opportunity of revealing individual differences. This does not deny the necessity of concentrating on questions that the overwhelming proportion of individuals answer in one way, as when one is measuring attributes of people that are relatively rare such as extreme psychopathology. One would probably not be successful in identifying extremely psychotic individuals by asking questions on which the general population is itself divided nearly equally.

The issue in scaling stimuli generally involves obtaining the most accurate measure of disparity among alternatives, e.g., of determining the probability that a candidate will be selected, which is probably not .5. The political poll example above illustrates the obvious importance of eliminating any biases that would cause the results to differ from the actual election when level is important. However, bias is less of a problem when interest centers on the correlation among measures, as in most research that scales people rather than level. Many points in this section are neglected even though they actually fairly obvious.

**1** *Avoid implying that one response is preferred over another.* Communicating a desired outcome creates what is known as a demand characteristic. This may either involve suggesting what the experimenter would like, so that making the preferred response will be doing the experimenter a favor, *or* that people who behave in one way are in some sense superior to others. Although the latter (e.g., telling people that psychotics tend to favor response A over response B) will generally create stronger biases, both are undesirable. Many subjects say they "tried to mess the experiment up" and do what was not desired, but most misleading results arise from attempts to cooperate. Instead of assuming that an experiment was free of demand characteristics, interview the subjects after the experiment about their perceptions. If subjects felt they were supposed to act in a certain way and it was physically possible for them to act in other ways, demand characteristics were probably operative even if they were unrelated or even opposed to the experimenter's intent. A colleague of the second author who was a priest but was also working toward a doctorate in experimental psychology unintentionally obtained demand characteristics in a word-naming task. He normally ran subjects in ordinary clothing but wore his clerical collar when he did not have time to change after celebrating mass. As you might well expect, the subjects gave a much higher percentage of religious words than usual.

**2** *Make all responses of equal effort.* This principal is violated in many subliminal perception experiments. A word is flashed at a rate that is ostensibly too rapid to permit conscious identification, and the intent is to show that the word influences behavior in more indirect ways. In order to show that the word is truly subliminal, some experimenters run an additional condition in which they flash the word and then ask subjects to write down what they saw as completely as possible. However, they also tell the subjects to simply draw a line across the page or make a similar response if they felt they saw nothing. Quite obviously, it takes more effort to write about what the subjects thought they saw than to simply respond in the negative. There is no incentive to respond completely and often a considerable disincentive. The subjects probably have little confidence about what they have seen, even though their judgments may be correct. They may feel their perceptions are incorrect or even silly. Bernstein and Eriksen (1965) surveyed several studies in which such biases were apparent. For example, Klein, Spence, Holt, and Gourevitch (1958) showed drawings of genitalia briefly to schizophrenic subjects in an attempt to modify their perception of a subsequent clearly visible stimulus. Quite obviously, subjects had nothing to gain if correct, but their medication might be strengthened for "hallucinating" if they were incorrect.

**3** *Pay attention to details of wording*, especially on questions used to scale people that have a binary response format. Keep the wording as simple as possible. Avoid "always" or "never" as much as possible, for example. The problem is less likely to be major with multicategory responses such as Likert scales since these either directly or indirectly supply alternative modifiers as part of the response scale, e.g., a question like "I feel unsure of myself (a) never, (b) rarely, (c) moderately often, (d) very often (e) always" (also see Chapter 8.)

**4** *Design the experiment to use tasks that are less subject to bias*. In particular, absolute judgments and sentiments tend to be more prone to bias than comparative judgments for reasons discussed in Chapter 2: "Do you like A?" brings up the question of how much liking is needed to answer in the affirmative: "Do you like A better than B?" is a more symmetric question.

**5** *Use converging operations* (Garner, Hake, & Eriksen, 1956). Garner et al. (1956) provide the following example based upon the then-popular "dirty word" studies (McGinnies, 1949). In this type of study, subjects are asked to identify briefly presented ordinary words and socially taboo words. The critical finding is that the ordinary words are usually identified better than the taboo words, raising the interesting theoretical question of how one knows a word is taboo unless it is identified in the first place. A problem is that subjects are generally less willing to *say* taboo words in the context of an experiment. Garner et al.'s (1956) approach is to have one group of subjects respond in an ordinary manner and have a second group respond by saying taboo words when they see ordinary words, and vice versa. The operations converge because neither condition alone is sufficient to separate the question of whether the difference is due to seeing or saying, but they jointly separate these two explanations by having the difficulties with each offset one another.

**6** *Provide clear instructions*. If one wants subjects to say yes and no with approximately equal frequency, don't keep this from them. Forced distributions, such as Q sorts (Stephenson, 1953; Kerlinger, 1986), are one way to minimize bias in category usage. Test administration includes not only the specific instructions but the atmosphere created by the administrator and can have both intended and unintended effects on bias responses. The second author was once approached by a student who was completing a dissertation concerned with modifying the attitudes and self-perceptions of parents of disabled children by different interventions. Various measures were given during a pretest, the intervention was introduced, and the measures were readministered during a posttest. The data were gathered during single sessions, but the parents were assigned randomly to the various groups. The results were that there were large group differences on the pretest, which is obviously inconsistent with the random assignment that had apparently taken place. What happened was that different test administrators were used in the various conditions, and their demeanors were sufficiently different to evoke different responses from the subjects.

**7** *Independently assess bias.* The MMPI contains several validity scales which measure carelessness, evasiveness, the tendency to present a positive image of one's self ("faking good"), and the tendency to present a negative image of one's self ("faking bad").

### Changes in Test Scores as Personality Changes

Not all changes in the distribution of test scores produced by the context of testing reflect changes in bias. For example, the second author has obtained MMPIs (1) screening individuals for positions where maladjustment is a potential danger to the general public, such as in police officers or security guards at a nuclear power plant and (2) for psychological and psychiatric evaluations. The MMPIs obtained in the second context are much more likely to suggest pathology. Personality test results should not be thought of as measuring properties of individuals that are invariant across situations since nontest behaviors exhibit similar changes. Part of the difference between the two situations may reflect a true difference in incidence of pathology. Although some individuals who apply for positions as police officers may be disturbed, it is reasonable to assume that the incidence is higher among those who are seeking professional help. However, part of this disparity also reflects the context of testing. A person being interviewed for a job may present a more positive view of himself or herself than when being interviewed for self-referred clinical evaluation.

This difference between the conditions is not simply a bias, as it describes legitimate differences in how people behave in different settings. Changes in response to formal test items mirror other changes in behavior. The problem in thinking of this as a change in bias is that one is forced to think of behavior as a rigid, fixed set of traits that are independent of the situation in which they occur. Indeed, it would be a sign of pathology for one to behave in the same manner at home and at work. Behavior is usually most strongly determined by the context in which it occurs and only secondarily by consistent individual differences. Moreover, there are trait-by-situation interactions: person A may exhibit more of a trait than person B in one situation, but person B may exhibit more of the trait in another situation (West, 1983).

### Carelessness and Confusion

Carelessness and confusion may both be outgrowths of the testing situation and therefore sources of bias—situations vary in the extent to which subjects are careful. They may also be styles—some people are more careful and/or less confused than others. The two are considered jointly because both introduce randomness into test responses. The tradeoff between speed and accuracy under a time limit is a form of carelessness or carefulness even though it is somewhat separable since some subjects are both rapid and careful. Since the effects of individual differences in motivation, fatigue, and physical health relate to carelessness and confusion, the comments in this section have some relevance for the former three variables also. Testing also may reveal illiteracy, which is perhaps the ultimate confusion about written material. Many different types of psychological measures illustrate the effects of carelessness and confusion. The original version of the MMPI contained 16 repeated questions, and it was common to see several pairs of these items answered inconsistently. Subjects may mark both ends of a series of rating scales. Pattern responding is common where the subject progressively marks the next higher step on each scale, marks all scales in the neutral category, or alternately marks the extreme ends of scales. Psychopathological subjects are especially likely to be careless and/or confused.

Research comparing the means of groups varying in carefulness or confusion (e.g., children versus adults, or normals versus psychiatrically impaired individuals) is most strongly affected. Such group differences in carelessness and confusion can artifactually inflate content differences of all types. The possibility of obtaining statistically significant group differences because of group differences in amount of carelessness or confusion is an ever-present danger in research. The danger is easiest to see when the groups are defined by a classificatory variable, but it can also arise as a by-product of experimental manipulations.

Carelessness and confusion are quite similar to blind guessing as discussed above, but the effects of all three differ from systematic measurement error. Although purely random error cannot produce true below-chance performance on abilities tests, this is not true of systematic attempts to respond incorrectly (Theodor & Mandelcord, 1973). The classical theory of measurement error (Chapter 6) deals with error that leads to a symmetric distribution of obtained (fallible) scores about subjects' true scores. Errors due to carelessness and confusion, however, not only lower the precision of obtained scores but also bias obtained scores toward the chance level on an abilities test and toward the middle of the measurement scale on a test of personality or sentiments. If all members of a group are equally careless or confused, the obtained rank order of scores will be the rank order of true scores within measurement error, but subjects with extreme scores will regress more toward the chance level (on abilities tests) or the midpoint (on personality tests) than subjects with true scores nearer chance or nearer the midpoint. The mean of the distribution of scores will shift toward the chance level or the midpoint, and the variability will be reduced. Carelessness and confusion produce unreliability but not systematic invalidity.

If, however, there are individual differences in amount of carelessness or confusion, systematic sources of invalidity can arise. For example, if opponents of an issue are more careless than proponents, the opponents' mean obtained scores will be closer to chance (on abilities tests) or midscale (on personality tests and surveys) than those of proponents. For example, the respective mean values might be 8 and 14 on a 20-item binary scale where the midpoint is 10, even though the true scores for both groups are equally far from the midpoint, e.g., 5 and 15. A person who scores at the apparent neutral point of 10 will therefore most likely be someone who actually is slightly opposed to the issue. The effects of individual differences in amount of carelessness or confusion are complexly interwoven with the type of item, the scoring key, and any possible correlation of carelessness or confusion with the trait in question. Regardless of the specific effects, individual differences in carelessness and confusion not only add to measurement error but also reduce validity.

Carelessness and confusion will obviously cause a person's true level of skill or ability to be underestimated because the score will be regressed toward chance. The effects on certain personality measures, such as the MMPI's maladjustment scales, are more interesting. As noted in Chapter 8's discussion of discriminating at a point,

MMPI items have a relatively low probability (typically around .3) of being answered in the keyed direction, but for good reason. Random responding produces $p$ values of .5. In other words, carelessness and confusion increase the chances of considering an individual maladjusted on the MMPI. Since careless and/or confused people are probably also more maladjusted, this outcome is not undesirable. Not all outcomes are that fortuitous, of course, and much training in the use of the MMPI properly is concerned with separating maladjustment due to carelessness and confusion from that resulting from intentional choice of item responses.

Individual differences in carelessness and/or confusion attenuate correlations with external measures compared to "cleaner" data because of the resulting increase in measurement error. However, systematic differences in carelessness or confusion may either increase or decrease correlations among measures, depending on the correlation between amount of carelessness and confusion with the traits in question. The usual result is a decrease because of the overall effects of randomness, but correlations may increase in magnitude when the correlation between carelessness or confusion and each of the traits is large and consistent.

If carelessness or confusion is likely to be a major problem, it may be advisable to measure these traits independently by interspersing a series of abilities items that are extremely easy or personality items that are unlikely to be answered in the unusual direction, like scale $F$ on the MMPI. To take an extreme case, college students who add $2 + 2$ incorrectly but can correctly solve a calculus problem are probably careless or confused. A more formal measure is the performance difference between easy and difficult items. Another strategy is the MMPI's use of repeated or near-repeated personality items and counting the number answered consistently. However, these measures provide only circumstantial evidence because they assume that responses are perfectly uniform when people are not careless or confused. Since the correlations among items are usually small, one should expect many inconsistencies in responses from item to item. It is far better to minimize carelessness or confusion ahead of time rather than evaluate it after the fact. One can do this by experimenting with the instructions to ensure that they are understandable, keeping the wording of items simple, and cross checking the results from different measuring instruments. If the measurement error due to carelessness or confusion is large, no sensible correction procedure can be applied. Attempting to do so would be like attempting to unscramble an egg.

When the tendency to guess and carelessness or confusion vary across subjects and relate to other variables, they take on the status of a response style. Guessing does not appear to be strongly related to any variable of interest. Obviously, carelessness and, especially, confusion are of some import as a manifestation of psychiatric impairment. Indeed, confusion is as valid a component of impairment as it is a response style. The tendency to avoid endorsing socially desirable statements also relates to pathology, although one might simply reflect the tendency to define maladjustment in part as nonconformity.

## The Role of Social Desirability

Social desirability in general refers to the tendency to choose items that reflect societally approved behaviors. We have noted that this is a particular problem in scaling stimuli: It is easy to overestimate the frequency with which adults actually go to the opera and underestimate the frequency with which they watch TV cartoons on Saturday mornings based upon their self-reports. This section is, however, concerned with the effect of the social desirability of responses upon scaling people. Although responses clearly vary in social desirability, it does not follow that this is a source of individual differences, the essential issue.

Although it had long been suspected that choosing socially desirable alternatives on items tended to dominate self-report inventories, Edwards (1953, 1970; 1990) was the first to document this well. His first major study involved 152 subjects who rated the social desirability of 140 self-report items on a 9-point scale. The mean rating of each item over subjects defined its social desirability. Edwards then obtained yes-no self-reports on these 140 items from a second group of subjects. He found a correlation of .87 over items between social desirability ratings and the endorsement probabilities of each item. Subjects thus tended to describe themselves in a socially desirable manner, but these data alone did not indicate that this tendency was a reliable individual differences variable (as noted earlier, behavior is most strongly determined by the situation, in this case item content). However, Edwards (1957) reported that a 39-item social desirability scale he developed from MMPI items correlated very highly with the principal dimension of variation in the overall MMPI and, indeed, suggested its use as a short form of the MMPI (Edwards & Walker, 1961). This finding is consistent with social desirability being an individual differences variable. Because he felt that individual differences in social desirability were irrelevant to personality traits, he stressed eliminating or controlling social desirability in personality measures. This spurred an enormous amount of research from 1955 to 1965. It became *de rigueur* to correlate proposed scales with social desirability measures (these specific measures will be considered shortly). Aspersion was cast upon those scales that correlated highly.

Block (1965; also see Block, 1990) and Rorer (1965) then offered major critiques. In particular, Block noted that Edwards' original social desirability scale actually consisted of a large number of substantive items describing anxiety. In other words, it measured a form of pathology as strongly as it did individual differences in social desirability. Block then developed an alternative scale of maladjustment that was neutral with respect to social desirability and showed that this scale was a valid predictor of maladjustment. These critiques led research away from emphasis upon social desirability (though it continued to be common practice to correlate scales with measures of social desirability). Walsh (1990) has suggested a somewhat different view: The results became so complex that the topic died of its own weight. Nonetheless, interest in social desirability has recently reawakened (Block, 1990; Edwards, 1990; Hogan & Nicholson, 1988; McCrae & Costa, 1983).

Four possibilities are that social desirability differences are

**1** Situation-specific (biases)
**2** Generalizable across situations as the by-product of conscious strategies (styles)
**3** Generalizable across situations as unconscious manifestations of a broader personality trait
**4** Not worth considering.

Specifically, the first two, if not three, of these positions imply that personality scales should be corrected for social desirability. Paulhus (1984, 1985) is particularly concerned with separating positions 2 and 3, but psychology has a long but unsuccessful history of separating the conscious from the unconscious. It is possible for a given measure to confound 1, 2, and 3 since they are not mutually exclusive.

The view that social desirability is situation-specific is implicit in the ordinary use of the MMPI's $K$ correction. Scale $K$ was empirically derived by Meehl and Hathaway (1946) to provide items that minimize classification errors (patients classified as normal on the basis of their scale scores, and vice versa). A fraction of the score on this scale is added to clinical scales to improve prediction, which makes the scores of defensive individuals more pathological (higher). A complete review of the validity of this procedure is beyond the scope of this book [see Dahlstrom, Welsh, & Dahlstrom (1975a, 1975b) for older studies and Graham (1990) for a recent discussion], but it is safe to say that there is at least some evidence that it is effective to this end. We have used the term "ordinary use" to denote that scale $K$ is considered separately from the substantive or clinical scales. In that sense, it is assumed to reflect the immediate situation so that a person's score could change as the situation changes. However, a moderate as opposed to a low or high level of $K$ is also assumed to be a positive indicator of adjustment, which is more closely related to position 3.

Viewing social desirability as a conscious process implies faking and is implicitly reflected in the standard use of MMPI scales $L$ and $F$. Scale $L$ consists of 15 highly approved behaviors such as not cursing and reading the editorial pages every day. People with high scores are assumed to be faking good by attempting to appear better adjusted than they really are (even though its full name is the "lie scale," few would literally view it in this manner, though). In contrast, scale $F$ consists of bizarre behaviors that are rarely endorsed even by psychopathological individuals. People with high scores are assumed to be "faking bad" by attempting to appear more poorly adjusted than they are, i.e., malingering. Unlike scale $K$, these scales are not used to adjust clinical scales, although the whole profile may be considered suspect or even unusable when these scales are extremely elevated. Edwards (1953, 1957) is often viewed as a proponent of the view that choosing socially desirable responses reflects conscious faking (Block, 1990; Hogan & Nicholson, 1988), but he vigorously denied this in his 1990 article.

Edwards' (1990) statement is consistent with position 3, and Walsh (1990) conceives of the ability to endorse socially desirable items as a major component of mental health. We have already noted Block's (1965, 1990) points in support of ignoring social desirability as an issue. More recently, McCrae and Costa (1984) argued that if social desirability is an irrelevant contaminant, controlling for it should increase validity. In fact, validities either decreased slightly or remained essentially unchanged following two separate types of corrections. Note that there is no contradiction between Edwards' (1953, 1957) findings that substantive and social desirability measures are highly correlated and McCrae and Costa's failure to find large changes in the validity of substantive measures when they are corrected for social desirability. Chapter 5 noted that zero-order and partial correlations do not differ as much as one would expect.

Edwards (1990) contrasted three types of social desirability scales. His original definition of a social desirability scale was one on which all items are keyed in the socially desirable dimension and the keyed response is also the modal response. His MMPI scale is of this form (ignoring its relation to anxiety). The second type of scale is illustrated by the Marlowe-Crowne Social Desirability Scale (Crowne & Marlowe, 1960), which has been the most popular such scale, and MMPI scale $L$ (McCrae & Costa, 1984, used these two scales). Both contain items for which the socially desired response is not modal. His third type of scale is obtained by finding items that change when subjects are given standard instructions versus instructions to fake good or give a good impression. Wiggins (1959) constructed a scale of this form. Scale $K$ of the MMPI reflects a somewhat similar approach since it too is empirically developed. Although the first two types of scales tend to correlate highly with each other, neither correlates highly with Wiggins' scale. Consequently, Edwards criticized McCrae and Costa (1984) for failing to incorporate Wiggins' scale, but he presented no data of his own to show that partialling out Wiggins' scale would improve validity.

Social desirability is certainly a major factor in self-description among normal individuals, but it does not explain all systematic variance. The major components of the tendency to choose socially desirable responses probably are the subjects' (1) actual adjustment, (2) self-knowledge (which includes memory for one's behavior; see Schwarz, 1990), and (3) frankness. Only component 3, frankness, can be clearly classified either as faking or as a response style in self-inventories. No one would classify actual adjustment or self-knowledge as a response style because the concept of response style would become so global as to lose all meaning. It is best to think of self-knowledge as an inherent limit upon what can be learned about a self-inventory. Evidence about the role in self-descriptions due to differences in frankness necessarily is indirect.

Subjects can indeed make themselves appear better adjusted on self-report inventories like the MMPI when they are instructed to fake good, i.e., not be frank. The data on the MMPI $K$ correction implies that its use does no harm at worst and probably is beneficial even though it is seldom employed for its original goal of providing psychiatric diagnosis. There is some risk in comparing the scores of two people who were tested under conditions that differed in amount of frankness. The rank ordering of people does change under different test instructions, types of items, and situational variables. This indicates that variation in frankness accounts for some substantive variance. However, these changes typically are not large. Consequently the correlations between scores obtained under the different conditions will be high. In sum, frankness probably accounts for some but not large amounts of individual differences in self-report inventories, and the tendency to choose socially desirable responses is probably one component of positive adjustment.

## Other Proposed Stylistic Variables

As above noted, there has been little interest in other stylistic variables following Rorer's (1965) critique, but they are briefly listed for completeness. They may also arise as biases.

**1** Yea-saying, also known as the "agreement tendency" and "acquiescence," is the tendency to choose "agree" or "true" as a response category. Nay-saying is the reverse.

This topic emerged from research conducted using the California $F$ scale (Adorno, Frenkel-Brunswik, Levinson, & Sanford, 1950), not to be confused with scale $F$ on the MMPI. The scale was unfortunately constructed so that all items were keyed in the "agree" direction, and the unfortunate consequences were discussed in Chapter 8. A scale consisting of items balanced in the direction of keying eliminates any potential problem in this area, as does improving the clarity of the item, since the style, to the extent that it exists, would presumably be most manifest with ambiguous items.

**2** The "extreme response tendency" refers to habitual choice of the extreme versus the middle categories on multicategory items, such as Likert formats. Subjects do vary in this tendency. For example, Price and Eriksen (1966) found paranoid schizophrenics used rating scale extremes more than nonparanoid schizophrenics or controls.

## MULTISCALE TESTS

Tests containing more than one scale (e.g., the MMPI) illustrate the adage that "The whole is different from the sum of its parts"; the relations among the scales form an important part of the data being studied. This is true whether the different scales presumably assess different content or whether some measure test-taking attitudes, such as the MMPI validation scales. This typically involves questions of factor analysis (Chapters 11 through 13).

A major consideration added in considering the relation among scales is that their correlation (corrected for attenuation) should be sufficiently low to indicate that the measures are actually distinct. "How low is low?" depends very much upon the context. At the one extreme, correlations that are very much greater than .6 make it difficult for the two scales to improve upon prediction of a criterion. In this case, the issue is not theoretical, nor is it necessarily whether the two predictors do better than one. What is at issue is whether an optimally weighted combination of the two tests leads to better prediction than simply combining the two tests into one instrument, which effectively weights the two tests simply in terms of their reliabilities. Having only one long instrument clearly makes for parsimony. One may additionally wish to raise the separate question of whether the two tests do better than one in reducing testing time.

At the other end, tests designed for occupational placement not only may correlate very highly but should correlate highly if the job requirements are very similar. As long as the tests are not completely redundant, there may be sufficient reason to use separate tests, although it may be possible to use one test and different cutoffs. Likewise, the point of some theoretical investigations is to show that two constructs are separable, and so any attenuation-corrected correlation below 1.0 may be of interest. Most situations are intermediate between these two extremes.

### Item Overlap

If two scales share items in common, as on the MMPI, they will have a built-in correlation even if answers are generated randomly. This obviously poses problems for the analysis which were brought most tellingly to light by Shure and Rogers (1965; also see Guilford, 1952). Before their paper, there had been many factorings of the

MMPI. A consistent finding was that one group of scales formed what was interpretable as a "neurotic" factor and a second group of scales formed a "psychotic" factor. Some used this as a model for psychopathology in general rather than the structure of the MMPI.

Shure and Rogers (1965) estimated the correlations among scales due entirely to item overlap using a method known as common-elements correlations (Dahlstrom & Welsh, 1960, p. 83) and then computed a second set of correlations among scales by deleting all overlapping items. These truncated scales (Welsh, 1956) are still sometimes used. The main finding was that factors derived from item overlap (common elements) were very similar to those obtained in prior studies; those based upon truncated scales were very dissimilar. The implication is that the MMPI's factor structure reflects the overlap of items rather than the content of the responses. Subsequent studies that have factored MMPI without correcting for overlap have been criticized by anyone familiar with Shure and Rogers results. Overlapping items also induce correlated error in the scales since responses are common to both.

Unfortunately, this places one in a dilemma. The item overlap is not totally an artifact of test construction, as it reflects real similarities among the traits in question. For example, people diagnosed as schizophrenic and people diagnosed as paranoid will answer certain questions alike but differently from the general population and other psychiatric groups. Even though not all schizophrenics are paranoid and not all people with paranoid symptoms are schizophrenic, the two traits are related. Although both scales were constructed from several studies, so that one cannot ascertain how many individuals diagnosed as paranoid schizophrenics were in both the paranoid and the schizophrenic groups, it is reasonable to assume that items common to both scales would still arise if such people were not allowed to appear in both groups (paranoid schizophrenics, being a large group within psychiatric hospitals, obviously cannot be totally excluded from the study). By analogy, individuals who are (1) culturally French and (2) culturally French-Canadian, among other groups, will endorse the item "My native language is French," and individuals who are culturally English will not even though one cannot be both French and French-Canadian at the same time.

If one grants that the item overlap is appropriate to the overlap of the concepts, since the concepts are related, it also follows that the reduction in correlations among scales obtained by eliminating overlapping items is artifactual because it describes correlations among scales that no one would use. Its effects are particularly troublesome when the eliminated items are among the more discriminating, as unpublished data by the second author suggest is in fact the case. Equally as unfortunate is that the resulting scales may be weakened when item overlap is eliminated or independence forced using the methods considered in Chapter 8. Consequently, item overlap can be described as "not indefensible," and correlations obtained with item overlap are at least as appropriate measures as correlations obtained with truncated scales. These interscale correlations may then be used to test the invariance of the MMPI's factor structure. However, this still does not mean that the original use of the factoring to determine dimensions of pathology is appropriate. These dimensions might have some meaning if the MMPI items were a random sample of relevant items. However, they are not. They are a fixed pool of items considered appropriate by clinicians.

## SUMMARY

Six major topics were considered in the context of classical test theory: (1) speeded tests, (2) corrections for guessing, (3) adverse impact, improper discrimination, test bias, and disparity, (4) halo effects, (5) response biases and response styles, and (6) problems associated with multiscale tests.

The traditional blind guessing model, which applies to multiple-choice tests, assumes that individuals either (1) know the correct answer or (2) choose alternatives randomly and with equal frequency. It leads to Abbott's formula, which estimates what an individual's score would be if he or she left unknown items blank. Guessing (1) increases the mean scores, (2) is inversely related to what an individual knows, and (3) is a source of individual differences and therefore unreliability because of differences in luck. However, partial knowledge causes guessing effects to be underestimated when Abbott's formula is used, but highly plausible distractors cause them to be underestimated. Alternative models, based upon signal detection theory, have two important consequences: (1) Subjects do *not* guess randomly—second guesses are more likely to be correct than the blind guessing model suggests; and (2) the number of correct responses is sufficient to estimate the key (knowledge) parameter of the model. Unfortunately, specific models for signal detection appropriate to the psychophysical applications where they were developed are difficult to use with ordinary tests. Further discussion noted that the small gain in reliability that may be achieved by a correction for blind guessing may be offset by making the test a little longer. Instructions designed to minimize guessing are difficult to make clear, and their effects may vary over subjects. However, the blind guessing model is useful in considering certain aspects of testing such as the difference between multiple-choice and short-answer tests. In general, we concluded by suggesting that there is little reason to use more than four or five alternatives per item, that test takers should be encouraged to answer all items, and that no correction for guessing should be used.

A test is a power test to the extent that scores obtained with a time limit (usually imposed for administrative convenience) correlate highly with scores obtained without a time limit, even though the means may be affected. Conversely, a pure speed test consists of items that would be of trivial difficulty were it not for the time limit. The internal structure of speed tests is quite difficult to infer, as correlations among items are arbitrarily determined by their proximity to one another. A primary consideration is the choice of a suitable time limit. The goal is to choose a limit that maximizes the variance among observed scores. One should *not* attempt to describe the reliability of a speed test in terms of coefficient $\alpha$. A more appropriate measure is the alternative-forms reliability. This may be accomplished in a single form by dividing the time limit in half, correlating the two halves, and applying the Spearman-Brown prophecy formula to the result.

Preferred rate of response describes how rapidly subjects prefer to work, a motivational concept. However, its practical measurement is obscured by the effects of such variables as instructions. Two useful distinctions are (1) time-limit accuracy, or number of problems correctly solved (which is especially suitable for group-administered tests) versus response time, or the average time per solution (which is better suited for individually administered tests) and (2) paced tests (in which a score is obtained for each item or block of items) versus time-limit tests in which the score is obtained at the end of the test as a whole. Paced tests are much more difficult to administer to large groups. In all cases, a problem is that subjects may trade-off accuracy for speed.

Because of the statistical artifacts in speeded tests, it is especially unwise to attempt to infer their factor structure at the item level (it is, however, perfectly appropriate to use the factor analysis of whole tests). However, the shared common variance (SCV) or squared correlation between the actual test and a test without a time limit, correcting for attenuation, is a useful way to determine whether a speeded test measures the same thing as its unspeeded counterpart. One-trial measures of the effects of speeding, based upon the relative incidence of errors of omission (characteristic of speeded tests) versus commission (characteristic of unspeeded tests) are discussed but not recommended because the relative incidence of the two types of errors are also strongly influenced by the instructions. A timed power test consists of items that are not of trivial difficulty but are administered with a restrictive time limit. An important point to keep in mind is that the time limit can be reduced considerably without affecting key psychometric properties even though individuals may find the test somewhat uncomfortable (and the discomfort should be avoided if possible). An exception arises when the items are ordered in terms of difficulty or some other important property; when the time available for the test is reduced, individuals take a somewhat different form of the test under the restrictive time limit. In contrast, a speed-difficulty test consists of items that have correct response probabilities in the .8 to .9 range. Such tests muddy the distinction between speed and power; as such they are not recommended. In general, speed and power measure somewhat different attributes of performance.

Although it is vital to make decisions as fairly as possible, the courts have been especially concerned about the employment rights of protected minorities such as females, blacks, and Hispanics. In general, there are two types of legal arguments raised about discrimination. Systematic discrimination implies intent to discriminate against and usually involves specific acts; good faith is a defense. In contrast, disparate (adverse) impact involves procedures that appear neutral on the surface but result in undue barriers to employment. Issues of test bias (differences in what the tests measure for different groups) are likely to be important. Good faith is *not* a defense though business necessity, often as manifested in a validational study, is. The *Guidelines* of the *Equal Opportunities Employment Commission* are significant both psychometrically and legally. They define a 20 percent disparity in rate of selection between the reference (dominant) group and the focal (protected) group as suggestive, but not conclusive, of illegal discrimination. This is called the four-fifths rule. We also noted that the criterion problem, lack of validity, temporal instability, and, to a lesser extent, unreliability are other major factors keeping the best person from being hired. Definitions of test bias raise the issue of to whom to be fair, the individual or the group to which the individual belongs, as their interests are often in conflict. The most common definition of fairness to individualists is identity of the regression lines in the reference and focal groups, a criterion that courts recognize widely. When applied to test bias, it is known as the Cleary rule. People stressing the importance of the group often argue for some form of quota.

The Cleary rule and other situations such as alleged salary discrimination often involve moderated multiple regression, as discussed in Chapter 5. Evidence for discrimination can arise either through a difference in intercept (a constant difference between groups) or slope (differential validity when applied to tests). In salary discrimination cases, an anomaly often arises from the unreliability of the predictors of salary when reverse regression is used (predicting qualifications from salary rather than the more usual converse); a focal group may appear to be underqualified at the same time that it is underpaid. Structural models are often used to eliminate this anomaly. Residual analysis is often useful in detecting neglected predictors and the source of unequal standard errors in the groups, a frequent source of apparent misfit of a regression equation. In addition, Simpson's paradox (Chapter 5) is shown to be relevant to categorical decisions such as hiring: The focal group may be hired in at least as high proportions as the reference group within levels but may have a lower overall rate of hiring because of improper aggregation and the effects of a difference in rate of application for the various positions.

Many tests used for personnel selection are content-validated and are appropriate if properly developed: Construct-validated measures based upon theories that are not widely accepted have been challenged most successfully and clearly job-related tests have been most easily defended. It is important that content-validated tests (1) not be based upon easily acquired vocabulary when the reference group has poorer access to that jargon, (2) be derived from a careful job analysis, (3) exhibit invariance of factor structure if they provide several measures, and (4) have appropriate correlates even though they are not necessary for content validity in the strict sense. Any form of test should not raise inappropriate barriers. A test that provides a small mean difference may lead to large disparities when a cutoff is located at a more extreme point; its appropriateness depends upon the application.

Selection fairness has dominated most work places since 1970. Some possible approaches are the following.

**1** Pure regression—select the person with the highest score on the predictor.

**2** Compensate for a constant (intercept) difference or to provide the social utility of additional focal group members as in the veteran's preference. Another form of compensation may be used when groups have unequal standard errors.

**3** Nonpsychometric quota selection (e.g., random or by vote) according to population quotas (problems are noted when several different types of quotas need to be filled).

**4** Psychometric quota selection which entails selection by a (possibly biased) predictor within groups according to quotas. The quotas may be defined (a) by the population, (b) to equate expected success rates, (c) to give all people who can succeed an equal chance of selection, or (d) by prior success rates.

**5** Maximize the utility of decisions.

It is important to note that the 1991 Civil Rights Act has basically made it illegal to use any form of job selection other than pure regression with an employment test. The final portion of this section dealt with conditions under which pooled versus separate test norms are more appropriate.

Halo effects are historically defined as failures to discriminate among conceptually separate dimensions. The dimensions may in fact be correlated (true halo). If the perceived correlation is larger than the true halo, there is said to be a positive observed halo, and if the correlation is lower, there is said to be a negative observed halo. Although it is desirable to define true halo in terms of physical measures, it is most often defined in terms of the average of a series of expert ratings. Traditional measures of halo unfortunately neglect the role of measurement error in judgment and thereby underestimate the magnitude of halo. Better measures correct the correlation between observed and true scores for unreliability (Fisicaro & Lance, 1990). Three models of halo have been suggested.

**1** The general-impression model in which judges react to their overall view of the person being rated (which can be either a composite of all dimensions or a separate dimension of its own) instead of the designated dimension.

**2** The salient dimension model in which judges react to one dimension that stands out the most.

**3** The inadequate discrimination model in which judges fail to differentiate the dimensions in question.

Response biases are sources of measurement error that are specific to a given situation, and response styles are analogous sources of error that generalize across conditions, thus serving as personality variables. Both may be systematic or random, as in careless and confused responding. Biases are basically nuisances. Some commonly suggested strategies for reducing their influence are (1) avoid suggesting one response is preferable, either overtly or tacitly, (2) make all responses of equal effort, (3) pay close attention to the wording of items, (4) use tasks that minimize bias (e.g., comparative rather than absolute judgments and sentiments), (5) apply converging operations, (6) make instructions clear, and (7) independently assess bias. Carelessness and confusion act somewhat like blind guessing in that they regress abilities measures toward chance and personality measures toward the mean of the measurement scale. However, systematic error may produce complex effects, including below-chance responding. Biases may also affect group comparisons if one group is more affected than another.

Although response styles were once a great topic of interest, they are currently of no more than secondary interest. Historically, the one of greatest interest was social desirability, since choice of response on self-report inventories is most strongly determined by the social desirability of the response. Moreover, preference for the socially desired response is a function of (1) level of adjustment, (2) knowledge of one's self, and (3) frankness. Other styles, such as yea- and nay-saying, were briefly noted.

Finally, we considered some of the issues that arise when a test has multiple scales. This provides a structure that can be analyzed. One major consideration is how high the scale intercorrelations are. Scales that are effectively redundant should be replaced by a single scale. Another important question is item overlap: Should the same question appear on more than one scale? The traditional view is that this is most undesirable since it will induce a correlation between scale scores even when subjects respond at random. However, one should not miss the additional point that often the same or similar items are dictated when the concepts measured are similar. For example, one would certainly ask if someone's native language was French in order to determine if that individual was culturally French, but the same item would also be highly discriminating if the issue was whether the person was culturally French-Canadian.

## SUGGESTED ADDITIONAL READINGS

Connolly, W. B., Jr., & Petersen, D. W. (1983). *Use of Statistics in Equal Employment Opportunity Litigation*. New York: Law Journal Seminars Press.

Fisicaro, S. A., & Lance, C. E. (1990). Implications of three causal models for the measurement of halo error. *Applied Psychological Measurement, 14*, 419–429.

Guion, R. M., & Gibson, W. M. (1988). Personnel selection and placement. In M. R. Rosenzweig & L. W. Porter (Eds.). *Annual Review of Psychology, 39*, 349–374.

Linn, R. L. (1989). *Educational measurement*. New York: ACE/Macmillan.

The Psychological Corporation. (1978). *Summaries of Court Decisions on Employment Testing*. New York: Psychological Corporation.

Reynolds, C. R. & Brown, R. T. (1984). *Perspectives on Bias in Mental Testing*. New York: Plenum Press.

## CHAPTER 10

# RECENT DEVELOPMENTS
# IN TEST THEORY

## CHAPTER OVERVIEW

We will now consider modern psychometrics, which consists largely of item response theory (IRT), notwithstanding the importance of generalizability theory (see Chapter 7). Any serious student of psychometrics will need to know the fundamentals of IRT even though classical procedures will suffice in most applications. Classical test scoring estimates the level of an attribute (ability, personality trait, etc.) as the sum, perhaps weighted, of responses to individual items (i.e., as a linear combination), whereas IRT, in contrast, generally uses the response pattern. Even though we will attempt to keep the discussion as simple as possible, some difficult mathematics is unfortunately necessary. The Suggested Additional Readings list several excellent references. Hambleton and Swaminathan (1985) and Hambleton, Swaminathan, and Rogers (1991) are particularly good (the former is the current standard), as is Hulin, Drasgow, and Parsons (1983).

Nearly all IRT research involves abilities, where the attribute of interest is some form of skill, symbolized $\theta$. We will assume a skill measure unless otherwise noted. However, $\theta$ can denote a personality trait or attitude without loss of generality even though this has not thus far been extremely common. In general, IRT uses information from item trace lines (see Chapter 2) assumed to be ogives (usually logistic functions) that relate $\theta$ to the probability of a given response (see Chapter 2). The location (threshold) of the trace line defines its difficulty, and the slope defines its ability to discriminate. Perhaps the most important concept in IRT is conditional (local) independence. Once an adjustment is made for $\theta$, responses to one item are independent of responses to any other item, and so $\theta$ contains all systematic information about responding.

The simplest IRT model is the one-parameter (Rasch) model in which the items are assumed to vary only with respect to their difficulty. The items are therefore assumed to be equally discriminating, and questions cannot be answered correctly by guessing. The classical measure of performance (sum of correct responses) is sufficient to estimate $\theta$. Inferential tests relevant to this and more complex models can be performed using the maximum likelihood test chi-square statistic ($G^2$) and the hierarchical strategy introduced in Chapter 4.

The next simplest or two-parameter model allows items to vary in both discrimination and difficulty but with the probability of a correct guess still assumed zero, whereas in a three-parameter model items can vary with respect to discrimination, difficulty, and the probability of being guessed correctly. A phenomenon called "Lord's paradox" arises in these models: A relatively nondiscriminating item may be easier than a more discriminating item for low-ability subjects but more difficult for high-ability subjects. The item information describes the ability of a given item to discriminate at a given level of $\theta$, and the test information or sum of the item information measures does so for the test as a whole. The relative efficiency of two tests is the ratio of their test informations.

Large samples are generally needed to estimate the parameters of any but the one- and, perhaps, two-parameter models, but developments in numerical estimation may change this situation. Two of the more interesting but, at present, largely impractical models are the Bock nominal model, which allows one to study how the choice of each alternative on a multiple-choice item changes with $\theta$, and the Samejima model designed for use with ordered response categories like Likert scales. Mokken (1971; Mokken & Lewis, 1982) has developed a nonparametric IRT. The section ends with a discussion of IRT's application to nonstandard testing situations and a brief introduction to the scoring algorithms.

The next major topic is differential item functioning (DIF), a term that has replaced "item bias" because of its relative neutrality. DIF occurs when item parameters differ across groups; e.g., an item is easier or more discriminating in one group than in another. A real example and a simulated example are presented. We then consider some alternative approaches to assessing DIF, including those based upon classical assumptions. The final part of the section considers the meaning of "content bias." The third major section considers the use of IRT in tailored tests in which different items are chosen for various individuals based upon their estimated ability. In computerized adaptive testing (CAT) a computer is used to present a tailored test. We then comment upon IRT in general. The final section considers achievement tests for mastery learning, which seek to have all subjects reach a given proficiency. IRT is one way to implement a mastery test, but it is not the only way.

## ITEM RESPONSE THEORY

IRT relies heavily on the concept of a trace line (item-characteristic curve), introduced in Chapter. 2. Recall that the trace line related an attribute to the probability of a designated response, such as a correct response on an abilities test. Trace lines are typically assumed to be ogives, which may be cumulative normal distributions, but they are more frequently logistic functions (Eq. 2-6) for mathematical convenience. We will not consider models with cumulative normal trace lines further. In general, a cumulative normal model exists for any logistic model, and the two have nearly identical properties. Other functions, most specifically exponentials, appear in special applications considered below. Once the parameters of the trace lines are estimated, the probability of any given response pattern is a function of the level of the attribute ($\theta$). One major goal of IRT is to estimate these parameters, including the standard errors. Another major goal is to choose the best value of $\theta$ for a given pattern. "Best" is often, but not universally, defined as a maximum likelihood estimate (see Chapter 4). Proponents of IRT note several reasons for its importance (some reasons for caution will be noted in a later section). Four that are particularly important are:

**1** An IRT can compare tests comprised of different items explicitly. Consequently IRT allows comparisons between different occasions for the same subject where memory for previous responses is a problem, even if the two tests have no items in common. This is termed "test-free measurement" and is important to tailored testing and computerized adaptive testing, discussed later.

**2** Subjects with the same classical score (number correct) may be shown to differ in $\theta$, depending upon the assumptions made by the IRT model.

**3** The classical estimate of attribute level (skill) or number correct on an abilities test is not linearly related to $\theta$ (Lord, 1980, pp. 49–51). Consequently a number correct scale is not an interval scale in the sense of Chapter 1. The usual relation is that number correct is an ogival function $\theta$.

**4** Classical estimates of difficulty and discrimination such as the probability of a correct response, $p$ value, and the item-total correlation ($r_{it}$) are not independent of one another, as they are dependent upon the subjects' abilities. Thus, an item whose $p$ value is .5 in a general population will have a lower value among the less able, but classical psychometrics cannot predict the magnitude of decrease. In principle, corresponding IRT estimates do not suffer from these problems.

IRT models generally assume conditional (local) independence, which states that $\theta$ contains all the systematic information about the subject's performance [Stout (1990) presents an alternative position]. This means that answers to individual items will be randomly related once $\theta$ has been partialled out. However, alternative IRT models vary as to (1) the number of different attributes or dimensions assumed to underlie the items; (2) item formats (binary as in short-answer and true-false tests, ordinal as on Likert scales, or nominal as in multiple-choice tests); and (3) number of item parameters. The latter depends in turn upon whether one assumes items vary in their ability to discriminate among individuals and whether or not the question can be answered correctly by pure guessing.

Different values of $\theta$ may fall along a continuum (latent trait theory) or form discrete and perhaps nominal categories (latent class theory). Haertel (1990) connects the two types of models, but not all psychometricians consider latent class theories IRT models for reasons that are beyond the scope of this text. One pragmatic reason for linking the two is that the same algorithm can usually estimate both latent trait and latent class parameters. Another is that latent class theory allows conditional independence to be readily illustrated. Most current research involves latent trait theories. We will assume for most of this discussion that a single trait underlies the item responses so that the items are unidimensional, but Bock and Lieberman (1970; also see Bock & Aitken, 1981) introduced multidimensional IRT models. quite a bit of work is currently being done with multidimensional IRT models. The Guttman scale, discussed in Chapter 2, was the first IRT, although its deterministic assumptions usually limit its utility.

Before getting too deeply into IRT concepts, it is essential to recognize that very large normative bases are required to implement all but the simplest and therefore sometimes unrealistic models using current estimation algorithms. Sometimes, however, the data allow simplifying assumptions (e.g., that certain parameters are equal), and the impact of these assumptions may be further minimized by constructing very short and highly homogeneous scales. IRT's emphasis upon very short scales is a significant departure from classical test theory. We will discuss later how this homogeneity may be counterproductive. As noted in Chapter 8, items should follow from a homogeneous domain of content, but it is important for a scale to possess methodological heterogeneity, such as keying personality items in both directions or sampling over situations.

The required normative base increases very rapidly with the number of parameters that need to be estimated, but so does the realism of the model, a familiar problem. Unfortunately, the average investigator is unlikely to have access to samples of sufficient size to use the more complex models. Many empirical investigations employing these more complex IRT models use data from the Scholastic Aptitude Test and like sources selected for their size. More efficient numerical estimation, may change this, but for now do not plan on using any of the complex models to be discussed below unless you are using an extremely short scale in a fairly large (200 to 500 subjects) sample.

## Conditional Independence

We have noted that conditional (local) independence means that item responses are independent once $\theta$ is held constant. It further implies that the joint probability of answering two or more questions correctly is the product of the individual probabilities. For example, if someone has a .5 probability of answering each of two individual items correctly, the probability that the individual will answer both items correctly is $.5^2$ or .25. Conditional independence is also assumed to hold for answers to the same item in a homogeneous subpopulation or group of individuals with the same value of $\theta$. This does *not* mean that item responses are independent over all individuals, for they will obviously be highly related to an extent determined by their internal consistency. However, this unconditional dependence is assumed to result entirely from the effects of $\theta$.

In order to appreciate the concept of conditional independence, consider a hypothetical two-item political survey asking 1000 potential voters whether they plan to vote for the Democratic or Republican candidate for (1) governor and (2) senator.

There are only two candidates in each race, and prospective voters must choose between them ("none of the above" is not permitted). The results are as follows:

| Gubernatorial | Senatorial candidate | | |
| --- | --- | --- | --- |
| candidate | Democratic | Republican | Total |
| Democratic | 460 | 180 | 640 |
| Republican | 80 | 280 | 360 |
| Total | 540 | 460 | 1000 |

Choice of the gubernatorial candidate obviously is related to choice of the senatorial candidate. If the two were independent, the number of individuals favoring the Democratic candidate in both races would be $(1000)(640/1000)(540/1000) = (640)(540/1000)$ or 345.6 instead of 460, and so forth for the remaining three options. Now assume that there are two homogeneous latent classes of voters, which will simply be labeled A and B. These *may* correspond to Democrats and Republicans, making the term "latent" questionable. However, they might also be groups differing on a dominant political issue, regardless of party affiliation. The type-A voters' preferences are as follows:

| Gubernatorial | Senatorial candidate | | |
| --- | --- | --- | --- |
| candidate | Democratic | Republican | Total |
| Democratic | 450 | 90 | 540 |
| Republican | 50 | 10 | 60 |
| Total | 500 | 100 | 600 |

Similarly, the type-B voters' preferences are as follows:

| Gubernatorial | Senatorial candidate | | |
| --- | --- | --- | --- |
| candidate | Democratic | Republican | Total |
| Democratic | 10 | 90 | 100 |
| Republican | 30 | 270 | 300 |
| Total | 40 | 360 | 400 |

Voting preferences for the two candidates *are* independent within each of the two classes even though they are not for voters as a whole. For example, the number of people preferring the Democratic candidate in both races among type-A voters is as expected: $450 = (540)(500/600)$, etc. In a like manner, the preference for the Democratic candidate for governor among type-A voters is 9:1 regardless of their candidate for senator. Note that type-A voters do not vote consistently one way and type-B voters do not vote consistently the other way, but choices are unrelated within groups.

Conditional independence means that the latent class (in this case) or trait information partials out all association. If we know peoples' choices for senator, we know something about their class membership, but once we know that class, the two choices become independent. Note the relation of these data to Simpson's paradox (see Chapters 5 and 9).

## One-Parameter Models

The simplest logistic latent trait IRT model assumes that items are equally discriminating but perhaps unequally difficult, and so it is called a one-parameter logistic (1PL) model. Each item is defined by a difficulty or location parameter that reflects the ogive's intercept, symbolized $b$. The Rasch (1960) model originally described a one-parameter model that used a particular form of estimation, but it is now synonymous with a 1PL model. Simpler equivalence or parallel models assume the items are also equally difficult, as in domain sampling, and employ one value of $b$ for the entire set of items but have no additional properties of interest to IRT. The Guttman scale in Chapter 2 is also a special case in which the items are perfectly discriminating. This means that their slopes are infinite—the ascending portion (slope) of the trace line is vertical as in Fig. 2-7a.

A 1PL model assumes that subjects who are low in the attribute have little chance of guessing the correct answer and that subjects who are high in the attribute are nearly certain to choose the correct answer. Consequently these models are more applicable to short-answer items rather than multiple-choice items scored as correct versus incorrect. Equations 10-1a and 10-1b equivalently describe the 1PL model in terms of the relation between the $p$ value for a given value of $\theta$, $p(\theta)$, and $\theta$ itself.

$$p(\theta) = \frac{e^{d(\theta - b)}}{1 + e^{d(\theta - b)}} \tag{10-1a}$$

$$= 1 - \frac{1}{1 + e^{-d(\theta - b)}} \tag{10-1b}$$

As before, $e = 2.18728. \ldots$ . The symbol $d$ is a scaling factor. Its usual value is 1.7, making the results comparable ($\pm.01$) to a cumulative normal distribution, or 1, so that it drops out of the model. Be careful when you read results from a computer program so that you will not assume the wrong scaling. Even within a given program, different options may provide different scalings.

The term "threshold" is borrowed from psychophysics (see Chapter 2). This parallel will be exploited in a subsequent discussion about tailored testing. The term gets its meaning because an individual with a given $\theta$ has a threshold (.5) probability of correct response when $b = \theta$, regardless of scaling, since $e^0/(1 + e^0) = 1/(1 + 1) = .5$. The probability of an incorrect response [$q(\theta)$] may also be defined by means of equations that parallel Eq. (10-1a) or (10-1b), but $q(\theta)$ is more simply calculated as $1 - p(\theta)$ by flipping the trace line at .5 on the ordinate. The $\theta$ and $b$ parameters are measurable on the *same* interval scale. The higher the subject is in $\theta$, the easier any item is for that subject, but the higher the value of $b$, the more difficult that item is. The $\theta$ and $b$ are defined relative to one another rather than absolutely because they are measured on an interval scale whose mean and standard deviation are arbitrary. If there is only a single group, $\theta$ is usually standardized, and so $\mu = 0$ and $\sigma = 1$. If the value of $b$ for a given item is positive, that item is relatively difficult for that group, and if the value is negative, that item is relatively easy. However, one may linearly transform the scale (see Chapter 1), which changes $\theta$ and $b$ by the same amount, maintaining their relation. In stricter notation, $\theta$ would require a different subscript for each subject and $b$ would require a different subscript for each item.

Table 10-1 contains parameter estimates from six items on a test given to 180 students in a class in abnormal psychology taught by the first author at the University of Texas at Arlington during the fall of 1989. The material covered the first seven chapters of Davison and Neale's (1986) *Abnormal Psychology* (4th ed.) and consisted of 56 four-alternative multiple-choice items involving such topics as the history of the field, assessment methods, and scientific methods. The average score was 34.0 items correct with a standard deviation of 7.5 items. Coefficient $\alpha$ was .82. The test as a whole and the student sample were typical of courses in abnormal psychology. The chosen six items had the highest item-total PM correlations ($r_{it}$), the classical discrimination index. The $p$ values were in the .5 range for the test as a whole. The table includes the 1PL estimates along with two additional models considered later. For simplicity, we will ignore the important point that these are multiple-choice items that have been dichotomized into correct versus incorrect rather than short-answer items. In fact, their probabilities of being answered correctly should start around .25 because of guessing and not around .0. Figure 10-1 contains the resulting six trace lines, using a $d$ of 1.

Although the rank ordering need not be exact, larger $p$ values are usually associated with smaller $b$ values since both index item difficulty. For example, item 32 had the highest $p$ value of the six items (.63) and the smallest value of $b$ (-.66). Conversely, item 5 had the lowest $p$ value (.48) and the largest value of $b$ (.08). Note that estimat-

TABLE 10-1    CORRECT ALTERNATIVES, CLASSICAL ITEM DIFFICULTIES ($p$), CLASSICAL DISCRIMINATIONS ($r_{it}$), AND IRT PARAMETER ESTIMATES FOR SIX CLASSROOM TEST ITEMS

| | | | | IRT model | | | | | |
|---|---|---|---|---|---|---|---|---|---|
| | | | | 1PL | 2PL | | 3PL | | |
| Item number | Correct answer | $p$ | $r_{it}$ | $b$ | $a$ | $b$ | $a$ | $b$ | $c$ |
| 5 | C | .48 | .35 | .08 | .66 | .11 | .51 | .99 | .23 |
| 7 | D | .58 | .25 | -.38 | .47 | -.71 | 4.28 | 1.16 | .50 |
| 20 | B | .59 | .36 | -.44 | 1.34 | -.37 | 2.41 | .42 | .35 |
| 22 | D | .52 | .38 | -.11 | 1.10 | -.11 | 12.87 | .55 | .36 |
| 32 | A | .63 | .41 | -.66 | 1.90 | -.47 | 1.55 | -.37 | .03 |
| 38 | D | .54 | .42 | -.22 | 1.13 | -.21 | 1.04 | .41 | .25 |

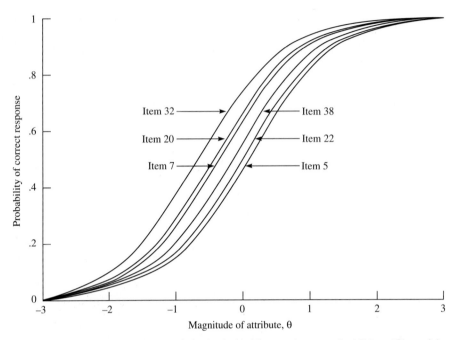

**FIGURE 10-1**    Trace lines for correct responses to six items derived from a classroom test fit to a 1PL model.

ing *b* for any item requires information from *all* items in the model (six in the present case), whereas estimating a *p* value uses information from that item alone.

Assume someone answers the first three items correctly but misses the last three items. Figure 10-2 contains the trace lines associated with this pattern of correct and incorrect answers. It was derived from Fig. 10-1 by flipping the three trace lines associated with items 22, 32, and 38 to define the probabilities of incorrect responses. According to Eqs. 10-1, the probabilities that these six events will each occur in an average subject ($\theta = 0$) are .47, .66, .68, $1 - .55 = .45$, $1 - .75 = .25$, and $1 - .59 = .41$. Given the assumptions of conditional independence, the probability of obtaining this pattern (+++−−−) is the product of these six individual probabilities or .009. Because of the small magnitudes of joint event probabilities, it is common to report the natural logarithm instead (−4.71).

If the subject was relatively unskilled ($\theta = -1$), the six probabilities would be .14, .26, .27, .82, .64, and .79 for a joint probability of .004 (ln = −5.50). On the other hand, if the subject was relatively skilled ($\theta = +1$), the six probabilities would be .83, .91, .92, .13, .06, and .11, and the joint probability would be .006 (ln = −7.46). It is therefore likelier that a person who is near $\theta = 0$ would obtain this particular pattern than a person who is very high or very low. Specifically, a person with $\theta$ of approximately −.3 would have the largest probability of obtaining this pattern (.011, ln = −4.49), and so −.3 is the maximum likelihood estimate to one decimal place for an individual who obtains this pattern. This person is slightly below average, which is

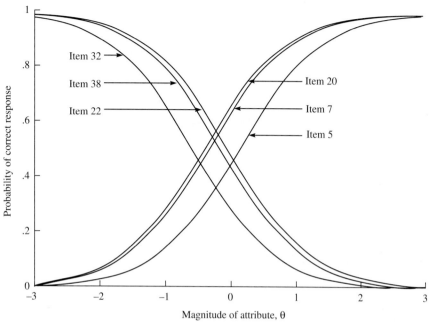

**FIGURE 10-2**    Trace lines for six items from a classroom test fit to a 1PL model. The first three were answered correctly, and the last three were answered incorrectly.

consistent with the fact that the individual's score of 50 percent (three of six items) is slightly below the six-item average score of 55.6 percent.

Figure 10-3 represents the likelihood (probability of the joint outcome) as a function of $\theta$. It is not difficult for you to obtain these values for yourself on a computer. Simply (1) choose a $\theta$, e.g., $-1$, (2) apply the values of $b$ from the 1PL model in Table 10-2 (.08, $-.38$, ..., $-.22$) to Eq. 10-1 to obtain six values of $p(\theta)$; (3) subtract $p(\theta)$ from 1 to obtain $q(\theta)$ for the last three items (if you wish to look at other response patterns, flip different items); (4) multiply the six probabilities together to obtain the likelihood; and (5) repeat the process for additional values of $\theta$ in the loop. The maximum value or mode at approximately $\theta = -.3$ is the maximum likelihood estimate. Because the mode is typically less stable than other measures of central tendency, the mean of the likelihood function provides an alternative, expected a posteriori estimate (Bock & Aitken, 1981; Bock & Mislevy, 1982). The maximum likelihood estimate can also be called the "maximum a posteriori" or "biggest after the fact."

This example began with a given set of trace lines. In practice, neither the trace line parameters (values of $b$) nor the abilities (values of $\theta$) are known. There are several different ways to estimate the two sets of parameters whose details are quite complex. Some estimate the two sets of parameters jointly; others alternate between solving for one and then using these tentative estimates to estimate the other.

The estimates of $b$ are usually of most interest, whereas the estimates of $\theta$ are usually only of interest in practical scaling problems. The standard errors of estimate of

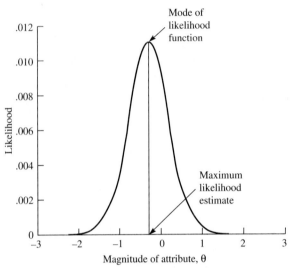

**FIGURE 10-3**   Likelihoods associated with the response pattern in Fig. 10-2 as a function of θ. Because of this particular function's symmetry, the mode is the same as the mean or expected a posteriori estimate, but this is not always the case.

the parameters are as important as the parameter estimates themselves. These errors are .08 for the common estimate of the slope (1.0) and range from .20 to .22 for the estimates of the location. By assuming that these statistics have a normal distribution (which has nothing to do with assuming that the trace line itself is logistic), one may test for differences between particular pairs of items and test individual items against particular parameter values to develop a model with fewer parameters. For example, the locations of items 5 and 38 do not differ from 0 nor from each other. In general, standard errors increase as the number of independent parameters estimated increases if these parameters differ slightly or not at all. On the other hand, the standard errors will also increase if two parameters that are really quite different are treated as equal. The standard errors also decrease with sample size.

Because items are assumed equally discriminating in a 1PL model, certain relations hold that are not true of IRT in general. The most important is that subjects who obtain the same number correct will have the same estimated value of θ. Consequently, if it is reasonable to assume the items are equally discriminating, all subjects who got three items correct would have an estimated θ of −.3. Number correct is a sufficient estimator of θ in the sense of Chapter 4 because the pattern data furnish no additional information about θ. Moreover, the relation between number correct and the estimate of θ will be monotonic. However, the number-correct scale is not the latent trait (θ) scale. For one thing, the number-correct scale ranges from 0 to the total number of items, whereas θ can take on any value. Consequently number correct is neither the maximum likelihood estimator nor the expected a posteriori estimator of θ.

Additional results of interest include the observed and expected frequencies for each pattern and the standardized difference between the two. Table 10-2 illustrates

TABLE 10-2    IRT STATISTICS ASSOCIATED WITH RESPONSE PATTERNS AS INFERRED
FROM A 1PL MODEL (SELECTED OUTPUT)

| | Frequency | | | Standard |
| Pattern | Observed | Expected | $\theta$ | error |
|---|---|---|---|---|
| – – – – – – | 5.0 | 8.3 | −1.51 | .71 |
| – – – – – + | 3.0 | 2.9 | −1.03 | .68 |
| – – – – + – | 2.0 | 4.5 | −1.03 | .68 |
| – – – – + + | 3.0 | 2.5 | −.59 | .65 |
| – – – + + + | 3.0 | 1.9 | −.17 | .65 |
| – – + – – + | 2.0 | 2.0 | −.59 | .65 |
| + – + + + + | 7.0 | 4.7 | .72 | .69 |
| + + + + – – | 2.0 | 1.8 | .27 | .67 |
| + + + + – + | 1.0 | 3.6 | .72 | .69 |
| + + + + + + | 22.0 | 18.3 | 1.23 | .73 |

Note: + denotes that the item was responded to correctly, and – denotes that it was
responded to incorrectly.

these results for 10 selected patterns that reflect a range of possible results. A – in a
pattern denotes incorrect, and a + denotes correct. By default, the program we employed (MULTILOG, Thissen, 1988) uses expected a posteriori estimates of $\theta$, which
we present, rather than the maximum likelihood estimates. Note that the second and
third pattern both contain one correct response and have the same estimated $\theta$ (−1.03).
Similarly, the fourth and sixth patterns both contain two correct responses and have
the same estimated $\theta$ (−.59), and the seventh and ninth patterns both contain five correct responses and have the same estimated $\theta$ (.72).

The quantity −2 times the natural logarithm of the likelihood provides an overall
test of the model. It equals $2 \Sigma o \ln(o/e)$, where $o$ and $e$ are the observed and estimated
(expected) frequencies of each pattern, and is a likelihood ratio chi-square test statistic
($G^2$) for the model as a whole in large samples (65.1 in the present case; see Eq. 4-22).
"Large" means at least 10 expected cases per pattern, which is not true in the present
case. As noted in Chapter 4, $G^2$ can also be used to test differences between a more
general and a nested model, even in relatively small samples. The difference between
two $G^2$ values is itself a $G^2$ statistic that is more robust with respect to sample size
than either of its constituents (Agresti & Yang, 1986). This difference $G^2$ indicates
whether the constraint(s) in the nesting degraded the model. For example, all six intercepts can be constrained (nested) to be equal (−.29). This caused $G^2$ to increase to
77.4, a difference of 12.3. The difference has 5 $df$ since the original model estimated
six values of $b$ but the nested model estimates only one. It is significant ($p < .05$),
which suggests that the items are not equally difficult, and so one can reject parallelism even though the differences are not large (the critical value of $G^2$ is 11.1). Thus,
tests of the overall model are sometimes possible, but tests of specific constraints are
more usually possible and in fact at least as important. Suitable programs, like MUL-
TILOG, allow considerable flexibility in specifying models. For example, it is possible

to estimate item 5's difficulty separately from that of the remaining items which in turn might be constrained to equality. Further tests of this form will be illustrated.

## Two-Parameter Models

Two-parameter logistic (2PL) models generalize 1PL models by allowing items to vary in their ability to discriminate, as well as in their difficulty. Like their 1PL counterparts, they assume that subjects low in $\theta$ are almost certain to miss the item and those high in $\theta$ are almost certain to answer the item correctly. Both models ignore guessing. The $a$ values are the discrimination indices with subscripts denoting the item in question inserted as needed. They define the slopes of the trace lines, i.e., how rapidly they rises with $\theta$. A 2PL model assumes Eqs. 10-2a and 10-2b, which are equivalent:

$$p(\theta) = \frac{e^{da(\theta-b)}}{1 + e^{da(\theta-b)}} \tag{10-2a}$$

$$= 1 - \frac{1}{e^{-da(\theta-b)}} \tag{10-2b}$$

The only difference between Eqs. 10-2 and 10-1 is addition of the slope parameter ($a$). As in the 1PL model, the probability of an incorrect response is 1 minus the probability of a correct response. Table 10-1 contains the 2PL estimates for the classroom examination, and Fig. 10-4 contains the resulting trace lines. Note the similarity between the classical discrimination index, $r_{it}$ and $a$; item 7 is least discriminating by both criteria, and item 32 has the second highest $r_{it}$ and largest $a$ (note that $r_{it}$ is based upon all 56 items, whereas $a$ is based upon the 6 chosen items only). The two indices also differ because $a$ and $b$ do not suffer from the inherent interrelation that $p$ and $r_{it}$ do. Table 10-1 also indicates that the values of $b$ obtained here and in the 1PL model are very similar for items 5, 20, 22, and 38 but differ somewhat for item 32 and considerably for item 7.

As noted above, increasing the number of estimated parameters from 7 (6 values of $b$ and a common value of $a$) in the 1PL case to 12 here (6 values of $b$ and 6 values of $a$) may make the parameter estimates less stable if the discriminations are not very different. This is why large populations are needed for more complex models. The standard errors ranged from .21 to .41 for $a$ and from .14 to .51 for $b$. All six of the $a$ estimates and two of the $b$ estimates are much larger than in the 1PL case, whereas four estimates of $b$ are slightly smaller. Moreover, the $G^2$ is decreased only to 54.7. Consequently the resulting difference $G^2$ is only 10.4 (65.1 − 54.7) which is nonsignificant with 5 $df$ (12 − 7 estimated parameters). This suggests accepting the equal discrimination inherent in a 1PL model if this was a real problem rather than an exercise. Recall that the items were chosen as the most discriminating to begin with and were thus not a random sampling of items, and the sample of 180 is at best moderate. However, $G^2$ is close to significance and probably would become so in a slightly larger sample.

A comparison of Figs. 10-1 and 10-4 reveals some important differences between the 1PL (including a Guttman scale) model versus the 2PL and more complex models.

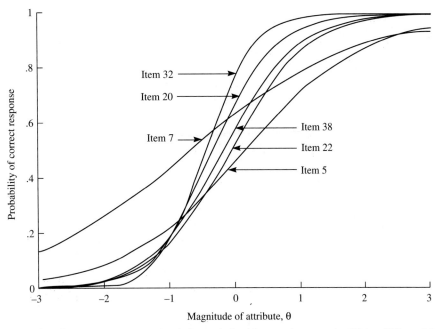

**FIGURE 10-4**    Trace lines for correct responses to six items derived from a classroom test fit to a 2PL model.

The rank order of item difficulties (values along the ordinate) in a 1PL model is the same, regardless of $\theta$; the trace lines are parallel in the sense of never crossing. However, the rank order of item difficulties depends upon the point chosen along the abscissa ($\theta$) in the 2PL case. Specifically, item 7 is easier for low-ability students than item 32 but more difficult for high-ability students because it is less discriminating. This differential effect of item discrimination on low- and high-ability subjects is called Lord's paradox (Lord, 1980). It can also be shown that the rank order of subjects is independent of the item difficulties of the items in a 1PL model but not in more complex models.

Despite the general need for complex estimation algorithms, the 2PL difficulties and discriminations may be estimated simply. First, use Eq. 10-3 to estimate $a$ from the item-total biserial correlation ($r_{bis}$), which itself is obtainable from the point-biserial correlation ($r_{it}$) using Eq. 4-26):

$$a = \frac{r_{bis}}{\sqrt{1 - r_{bis}^2}} \tag{10-3}$$

The difficulties are defined by

$$b = \frac{\Phi^{-1}(p)}{r_b} \tag{10-4}$$

The symbol $\Phi^{-1}(p)$ denotes the value of $z$ derived from the normal-curve cumulative probability of $p$. For example, item 5's point-biserial correlation with the total score on all 56 items ($r_{it} = .35$) may be multiplied by $\sqrt{pq}$ (Eq. 4-28) to obtain a biserial correlation of .44. This in turn leads to an estimate of $a = .44/\sqrt{1 - .44^2} = .49$. The estimate in Table 10-1 (.66) uses $d = 1$ rather than 1.7 in scaling. Multiplying .49 by 1.7 to convert it to the same metric yields .83. The comparison is biased because $r_{it}$ uses all 56 items and not simply the 6 chosen for example. Using Eq. 10-4, $\Phi^{-1}(p) = -.01$ for $p = .48$. Consequently $b = -(-.01)/.44 = .02$. Using an average value for $a$ in Eq. 10-4 estimates the $b$ parameters of a 1PL model.

Whereas $\theta$ varies monotonically with the unweighted sum of correct responses in the 1PL model, it varies monotonically with a weighted sum of correct responses in the 2PL model. The weighting factor is $a$. As in the 1PL model, the scale on which this weighted sum is defined is not the scale for $\theta$, and so a weighted sum is neither a maximum likelihood nor an expected a posteriori estimator. However, a weighted sum does contain all relevant information (is sufficient in the sense of Chapter 4). A person who answers a given number of more discriminating items will have a higher estimated value of $\theta$ than a person who answers the same number of less discriminating items. For example, the estimated $\theta$ is $-.71$ for a person who answers only question 32 and $-1.0$ for a person who answers only question 38 correctly because item number 32 is more discriminating ($a = 1.90$) than item number 38 ($a = 1.13$). Table 10-2 shows that both have the same estimated $\theta$ ($-1.03$) in a 1PL model.

## Three-Parameter Models

Three-parameter logistic (3PL) models incorporate a guessing parameter ($c$) which allows the ogive to begin above 0. This parameter represents the false positive rate—the probability that someone with a minimal score on the attribute correctly answers the item. It is particularly suitable for multiple-choice and true-false items. Without reading the item, a person would have a probability of $1/K$ of answering a $K$-alternative item correctly (see Chapter 9 for a further consideration of guessing). However, $c$ does not necessarily equal $1/K$, as a particularly attractive distractor may be chosen disproportionately. Equation 10-5 defines the 3PL model:

$$p(\theta) = c + \frac{(1 - c)e^{da(\theta - b)}}{1 + e^{da(\theta - b)}} \tag{10-5}$$

As above, the probability of an incorrect response is 1 minus the probability of a correct response.

Table 10-1 lists the $a$, $b$, and $c$ parameters for the classroom test example, and Fig. 10-5 shows the resulting trace lines. This model was much more difficult to fit than either of its predecessors and, more critically, produced much larger standard errors. Techniques can be used with all models to reduce these problems, which are beyond the scope of this book. They include imposing prior probabilities on the $c$ values (Lord, 1980). In particular, it would be reasonable to fix $c$ at .25 since the items all

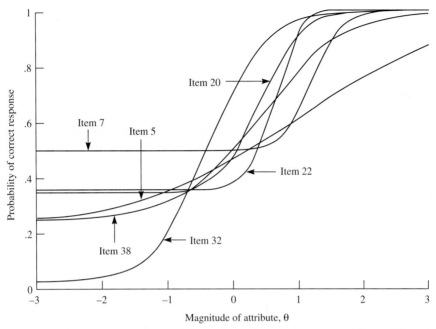

**FIGURE 10-5**    Trace lines for correct responses to six items derived from a classroom test fit to a 3PL model.

have four alternatives. This reduces it to a 2PL trace line in which the left asymptote is above 0.

Item 22 rises very steeply from a left asymptote of $c = .36$, but item 5 rises slowly from a slightly lower asymptote. Item 32 had an unusually low left asymptote, and item 7 had an unusually high asymptote. Regardless, the difference in fit of this model over a 2PL model is slight—the overall $G^2$ is 46.5, producing a nonsignificant difference of $G^2 = 8.2$ relative to the 2PL model ($df = 6$ since 18 parameters are estimated here versus 12). Indeed, the difference in $G^2$ between this model and the 1PL model is also nonsignificant ($G^2 = 18.6$ on 11 $df$).

Unlike the 1PL and 2PL models, it is not possible to make sufficient use of a subject's data by computing a sum (weighted or unweighted) of item responses. The concepts of test information and item information are necessary to estimate $\theta$.

### Item and Test Information

Any 1PL, 2PL, or 3PL trace line consists of three segments that may be approximated by straight lines. For example, the 3PL trace line for item 7 in Fig. 10-5 is flat [$p(\theta) \approx .5$] below $\theta = +.50$, rises steeply from $\theta = +.50$ to $\theta = +1.20$, and becomes flat again past $\theta = +1.20$. The slope of the trace line, symbolized $p'(\theta)$, is obtained from the tangent to the curve. It describes how $p$ changes as $\theta$ changes and is small, large, and then small again. The steeper the slope, the more information an item provides at that region of $\theta$. Item 7 in the 3PL is too difficult for moderate- to low-ability subjects ($\theta < +.5$) who are unlikely to answer the item correctly except by guessing; differences among them in response to the item will be largely due to chance. It will be too easy for high-ability subjects ($\theta > +1.2$) who are unlikely to miss it except through careless- ness. However, the item will be discriminating for subjects near the middle ($.5 \geq \theta \geq 1.2$). The same will hold for other items except that the values of $\theta$ will differ. In gen- eral, easy items discriminate best among low-$\theta$ subjects, and difficult items discrimi- nate best among high-$\theta$ subjects. The most useful items have difficulties ($b$) that are similar to the subject's $\theta$.

Technically, the item information function [$I(\theta)$] is the expected value of the accel- eration of the trace line. The acceleration describes the change in slope as $\theta$ changes. Equation 10-6 is an approximation that defines the item variance as the square of the slope divided by the item variance at that point. The item variance follows from ordi- nary binomial considerations.

$$I(\theta) = \frac{[p(\theta)']^2}{p(\theta)q(\theta)}$$

(10-6)

where $[p(\theta)']^2$ = squared trace line slope at a given value of $\theta$
$\qquad p(\theta)$ = probability of a correct response at that value of $\theta$
$\qquad q(\theta)$ = probability of an incorrect response at that value of $\theta$
$\qquad\quad = 1 - p(\theta)$

If you have been introduced to calculus, you may recognize the slope and accelera- tion as the first and second derivatives of the trace line, but calculus itself is not need- ed to understand any of these concepts. Maximum information arises in 1PL and 2PL models (which do not involve guessing) when $p(\theta)$ is .5 (when $b = \theta$).

The test information function [$T(\theta)$] is simply the sum of the individual item infor- mation functions:

$$T(\theta) = \Sigma I(\theta)$$

(10-7)

The additivity of the item informations is another consequence of the assumption of conditional independence, as it implies that each item's contribution is independent of that of the other items. The complex process of estimating $\theta$ in a 3PL model involves weighting responses by the corresponding item information. This in turn involves stressing different items for different individuals. By definition, it involves finding a value of $\theta$ that maximizes the joint probability of the pattern or some closely related quantity, using Eq. 10-5 to define each probability. More difficult items provide more information about high-ability subjects, and easier items provide more information about low-ability subjects. A subject who misses relatively few items and is therefore able will have a higher estimated $\theta$ if the missed items are easy than if they are diffi- cult. Precisely the converse is true of a subject who misses many items. Looking at the overall test information function indicates where the test discriminates best and most poorly so that items can be added or subtracted as needed.

The relative efficiency of test $y$ with respect to test $x$ is the ratio of their respective information functions:

$$RI(y, x) = \frac{T(y)}{T(x)} \tag{10-8}$$

Test $y$ may be a shortened form of test $x$, and so interest may center on what is lost and, of equal importance, where along the $\theta$ continuum it is lost in shortening $x$. Alternatively, the two tests may not have any items in common and interest may be directed toward determining how well they work at different $\theta$ levels; test $x$ may be more discriminating for better students, and test $y$ may be more discriminating for weaker students. The key point is that IRT stresses maximizing the test information function over the range of abilities that are of interest instead of maximizing reliability, as in classical psychometrics. Chapter 8 noted that maximizing coefficient $\alpha$ requires peaking the difficulties of the items on the test even though this effect of peaking is slight. This has led certain investigators to select out items of relatively high and low difficulty in an attempt to maximize reliability at the expense of other considerations. IRT suggests distributing item difficulties to discriminate across the full range of abilities, which we strongly agree with as in equidiscriminating test (see Chapter 8).

## The Bock Nominal Model

The 1PL, 2PL, and 3PL models have been the most widely used, in that order. Bock (1972) proposed a model for the analysis of nominal responses such as individual alternatives on a multiple-choice test. Equation 10-9 defines this model:

$$p(x = k/\theta) = \frac{e^{a_k\theta + c_k}}{\Sigma e^{a_i\theta + c_i}} \tag{10-9}$$

The expression $p(x = k/\theta)$ denotes the probability that a person of ability $\theta$ chooses response alternative $k$. The model assumes that there is a tendency to choose $k$ that is independent of $\theta$ ($c_k$), but this tendency changes at a rate of $a_k$ relative to $\theta$. The tendency to choose the correct answer should increase rapidly with $\theta$ and be reflected in a large positive value of $a_k$. The $a_k$ may also be positive for an incorrect alternative, providing it is smaller than the $a_k$ for the correct alternative, but the tendency to choose an incorrect alternative should generally decrease with $\theta$ ($a_k < 0$) or remain constant ($a_k = 0$). The symbols in the denominator, $a_i$ and $c_i$, denote the analogous tendencies associated with the various alternatives, including $k$. The model resembles Luce's (1959a) choice theory (Chapter 2), as it defines the probability of choosing a given alternative $k$ as the ratio of its value derived from an exponential function to the sum of a series of like values for all alternatives. Thus, although the absolute tendency to choose alternative $k$, $a_k\theta + c_k$, is a linear function of $\theta$, the observed probability, $p(x = k/\theta)$, is a function of this tendency relative to the other alternatives. Consequently $p(x = k/\theta)$ may vary in a complex manner with $\theta$.

TABLE 10-3    FREQUENCY DISTRIBUTION OF CHOICE OF
RESPONSE ALTERNATIVES WITHIN QUINTILES

| | Alternative | | | |
|---|---|---|---|---|
| Quintile | A | B | C | D |
| 1 (lowest) | 9 | 9 | 8 | 10 |
| 2 | 11 | 9 | 14 | 7 |
| 3 | 6 | 4 | 19 | 4 |
| 4 | 7 | 3 | 20 | 2 |
| 5 (highest) | 8 | 2 | 26 | 0 |

Item 5 asked about the history of psychopathology in the Dark Ages and will illustrate the model. Table 10-3 contains the frequencies with which subjects in each of five quintiles based upon total score chose alternative A (previously normal behavior came to be viewed as abnormal because of religious disapproval), B (discovering the secrets about the cause of mental disorders was an inevitable result of scientific inquiry), C (economics and religion had a strong effect on the degree to which science is valued, the correct answer), and D (one needs to distinguish demonic possession from mental disorder in the study of psychopathology). The total frequencies in each quintile are not exactly equal because of sampling error—two students omitted the question; our sample size was also extremely small.

The table indicates that the observed distribution of response choices for the lowest quintile was very nearly uniform. These students may have guessed blindly with equal preference for all four alternatives. A slight tendency for the correct response to dominate appears in the second quintile. This becomes stronger in each successive quintile, as it should. As a result, the other alternatives become less frequently chosen. However, the rate at which this occurs is different for the various alternatives. Alternative A is chosen with nearly the same relative frequency in all quintiles. The rate of decline is greatest for alternative D; none of the students in the top quintile chose it.

The $a_k$ estimates for the four alternatives were .38, −.30, .51, and −.60, and the $c_k$ estimates were .52, −.64, 1.38, and −1.27. Correct alternative C had the largest value of $a_k$ because it became dominant as $\theta$ increased. Note that the absolute tendency to choose A also increased with $\theta$, though not as rapidly as for C, but B and D showed the more common tendency to decrease with $\theta$. The differences among $c_k$ reflect differences in category choice among average subjects ($\theta = 0$) which, to a first approximation, describe students in the third quintile. Figure 10-6 shows the resulting trace lines.

Samejima (1979) extended Bock's basic model, and in turn Thissen and Steinberg (1984) further modified Samejima's. The modifications allow for blind guessing (see Chapter 9) and "don't know" responses.

## The Samejima Model for Graded (Ordinal) Responses

Samejima (1969, 1974) has developed and/or extended several IRT models. One of particular interest uses graded responses such as Likert-type scales. We will assume

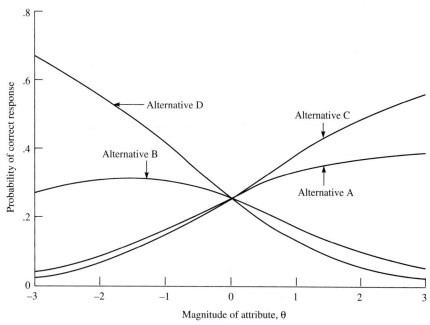

**FIGURE 10-6**    Trace lines for four alternatives from a classroom test fit to a nominal model. Alternative C is correct.

that higher-numbered categories are associated with larger values of $\theta$. A model of this form is applicable to personality and attitudinal data. Like all IRT models, it provides one trace line per response alternative, which is easy to miss when there are only two alternatives per response since they produce two trace lines that are flipped versions of each other. The Samejima model provides one monotonically decreasing trace line associated with the lowest category, nonmonotonic trace lines with successively higher peaks for intermediate categories, and a monotonically increasing trace line for the highest category. It is simplest to begin with a three category scale where 1 = disagree, 2 = neutral, and 3 = agree. Assume that 25 percent of the responses to a particular item are 1, 40 percent are 2, and the remaining 35 percent are 3.

Samejima's "trick" was to pool categories and obtain a series of dichotomies. For example, combining 2 and 3 responses produces a "do not disagree" category containing 75 percent of the cases (40 percent + 35 percent). It may be contrasted with the "disagree" category containing the remaining 25 percent. A trace line may be obtained for the "do not disagree" responses in which $p(x > 1)$ describes the probability of what serves in effect as a correct response, and $b_1$ describes the difficulty parameter. Next, pool the 1 and 2 categories to form a "do not agree" category. This contains 65 percent (25 percent + 40 percent) of the cases, and the contrasting "agree" category contains the remaining 35 percent. A second trace line defines "agree" (again, correct) responses, $p(x > 2)$, and has difficulty parameter $b_2$. Everyone who answered 2 is high (positive) in the first case and low (negative) in the second, but no one was low in the first case and high in the second. Consequently the probability of a high response must be lower in the second case (35 percent) than in the first (75 percent), and so $b_2$ must be numerically more positive than $b_1$. The slopes of the resulting trace lines are constrained to equality.

The results are preliminary trace lines describing probabilities of being in a given category *or* in a higher category. The instructions require that $p(x > 0) = 1$, as the person must choose a response of 1 or greater, and $p(x > 3) = 0$, as category 3 is the largest allowed. Final trace lines describing the probability of choosing each of the categories are obtained by subtraction. In general, $p(x = c)$, the probability that the response chosen falls in category $c$ is $p(x > c - 1) - p(x > c)$ (this meaning of $c$ has no relation to its use in a 3PL model). Thus, the probability that a person chooses category 1 (disagrees), $p(x = 1)$, is $p(x > 0) - p(x > 1)$ or $1.0 - p(x > 1)$. The probability that a person chooses category 2 (is neutral), $p(x = 2)$, is $p(x > 1) - p(x > 2)$. Finally, the probability that a person chooses category 3, $p(x = 3) = p(x > 2) - p(x > 3)$ or simply $p(x > 2)$ since $p(x > 3) = 0$.

Cheek and Buss' (1981) nine-item shyness scale will be used for illustration. Although the original form used 4-point Likert scales (1 = very much unlike me, 2 = somewhat unlike me, 3 = somewhat like me, and 4 = very much like me), the data were gathered on a 5-point scale by adding a neutral category. The scale was completed by 726 students enrolled in several sections of an introductory psychology course. Item 7 states "I feel inhibited in social situations." The distributions of responses to the five categories were 19.4 percent, 32.2 percent, 31.7 percent, 11.7 percent, and 5.0 percent, and the $r_{it}$ was .75, making it the most highly discriminating of the nine items. Figure 10-7 shows the preliminary trace lines, $p(x > c)$. The ordinate is spelled out more fully as "probability response > category." Each slope is constrained to equality, but the slopes may vary among items. The present slope is 2.57, the steepest of the nine items, which is consistent with its large $r_{it}$. There are only four curves, 1 less than

**FIGURE 10-7**    Preliminary trace lines using shyness data (Cheek & Buss, 1981) fit to the Samejima graded response model.

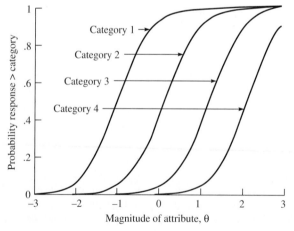

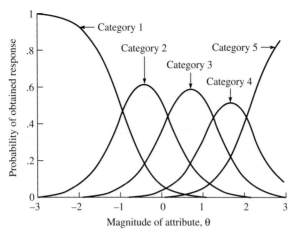

**FIGURE 10-8**    Final trace lines using shyness data (Cheek & Buss, 1981) fit to the Samejima graded response model.

the number of categories, because the curves describe relations between pairs of adjacent categories. If there are $k$ categories (four in the present case), there will be $k - 1$ (three) such pairs. The thresholds are at $-1.06$, $.06$, $1.12$, and $2.01$. The fact that the first threshold ($-1.06$) is closer in absolute value to zero, the distribution mean, than the last threshold ($2.01$) reflects the greater probability of a 1 response (19.4 percent) than a 4 response (5.0 percent).

Figure 10-8 shows the final trace lines that describe $p(x = c)$, where the ordinate is spelled out as the "probability of obtained response." There are five curves, one per category.

Similar sets of trace lines can be obtained for the remaining items. Their shapes will be similar, but they will be shifted and/or differ in spread as a function of the item distributions. For example, when more individuals choose category 1, the trace line for that category is displaced toward the right because more high-$\theta$ people choose that category. The remaining curves will have less spread because proportionally fewer people choose those categories.

## A Nonparametric Approach

A basic step in developing an IRT model is to postulate the specific shape of the trace line which, as we have seen, is most commonly the logistic ogive. Following general practice in statistics, such approaches may be called parametric. Mokken and Lewis (1982; also see Mokken, 1971) employ a nonparametric approach in that trace lines are only assumed to possess two ordinal properties. One is that these trace lines are monotonically increasing. As noted in Chapter 2, this is common to a great many approaches, including classical test theory. The second assumption is that the item difficulties maintain their same rank order regardless of ability level ($\theta$). This simply means that the trace lines *do not cross*. Following standard practice in IRT, Mokken and Lewis define difficulty as the item threshold, i.e., the magnitude of θ required for the probability of a correct response to equal .5. Items fulfilling these two conditions are called doubly monotonic. The trace lines of a 1PL model are doubly monotonic, but this is not the case with 2PL and 3PL models, as we have noted—only in the 1PL do the trace lines not cross. A person dominates an item when the probability that he or she will answer that item correctly direction is at least .5. It is sufficient to estimate θ by the number of items that the person dominates. Estimation uses an iterative routine. Mokken and Lewis (1982) provide an example drawn from the personality domain.

Mokken scales are closely related to Likert scales, but they do not assume that individual items perfectly "cut" the population in terms of θ based upon correct versus incorrect responses (and vice versa). We have considered that assumption to be a major reason why Likert scales are unrealistic. Mokken scales are also closely related to another trend in statistics associated with Clyde Coombs (e.g., Coombs & Kao, 1960). Coombs (and others, see Chapter 14) have stressed that ordinal relations in the data are usually sufficient to infer interval properties.

This nonparametric approach is extremely valuable in terms of helping describe such critical properties as dimensionality, which Mokken and Lewis (1982) define as the ability of each of a set of items to rank-order people in the same way. However, we would make the mildly critical point that assuming logistic traces is not empirically strong. Historically, parametric models in all areas of statistics (e.g., the ANOVA) have been fairly robust with respect to minor deviations from normality or, in this case, logistic form. A 1PL model is probably far more likely to misfit because one or more items are actually nonmonotone or differ in discrimination than because it has a nonlogistic monotone form. One very positive feature of the 1PL model is that a simple count of correct responses is sufficient to estimate ability; Mokken's approach to estimating ability is far more cumbersome for, it appears, little reward. Both 1PL and Mokken scales allow test-free measurement, and so the latter has no advantage in that sense.

## Other IRT Models

A number of different models exist, but nearly all are special cases of the models considered above, most specifically Bock's nominal model and Samejima's graded response model. Thissen and Steinberg (1986) provided a classification of models then available, but the number is steadily increasing. We have already noted that the 1PL model is a special case of the 2PL model obtained when the discrimination parameters ($a$) are constrained to equality, and the 2PL model is a special case of the 3PL model in which there is no opportunity to answer correctly by guessing ($c = 0$). Perhaps the most important development is multidimensional IRT in which an item may be a linear combination of several trace lines (Bock & Aitken, 1981; Bock & Lieberman, 1970). As we have noted at many points in this section, this highly attractive extension requires enormous numbers of subjects to implement. Four other types of models are those designed for (1) rating scales (Andrich, 1978, 1982, 1985; Rost, 1988; Wright & Masters, 1982), (2) partial credit (Masters, 1982; Glas & Verhelst; 1989), (3) continuous ratings (Mueller, 1987), and (4) nonmonotone deterministic items, as in Fig. 2-10 (Formann, 1988).

## Applications to Nonstandard Testing Conditions

A major point to consider is that the attribute levels of two different people (or the same person on different occasions) may be estimated just as well if they answer no items in common (or some but not all) as if they respond to the same set of items, the principle of test-free measurement. For any given set of items, either the maximum likelihood or expected a posteriori outcome for a given pattern estimates $\theta$, and these values may be compared with values of $\theta$ determined from other properly scaled items in the domain.

## Scoring Algorithms

Estimating relevant parameters (e.g., $a$, $b$, and $\theta$) is usually very complex. Although Eqs. 10-3 and 10-4 are useful approximation methods, especially as a check on computer-generated results, extensive use of IRT requires an appropriate computer program. Because of the idiosyncracies in many programs, relative lack of users, and, on occasion, bugs, IRT programs are more difficult to use than general-purpose programs like SPSS-X and SAS. The first author has contacted various program authors who were all quite happy to discuss problems, but there is no guarantee on this matter.

Some of the major differences among algorithms are:

**1** *Models analyzed.* BILOG (Mislevy & Bock, 1986) is designed for binary response models, but programs such as MULTILOG analyze both binary and multi-category data.

**2** *Restrictive assumptions.* MULTILOG assumes that $\theta$ is normally distributed within groups. This allows Bayesian considerations (e.g., prior probabilities) to be incorporated, but it is not necessary to IRT in general.

**3** *Computer suitability.* Older programs like LOGIST (Wood, Wingersky, & Lord, 1976) were written for and are available only for mainframes. Virtually any newer program is also designed for use on personal computers.

**4** *Cost.* IRT programs are generally expensive because they do not have a wide audience. However, LOGIST is available through the Educational Testing Service at a bargain price.

**5** *Form of numerical estimation.* Older programs like LOGIST use joint maximum likelihood estimation, but newer programs like MULTILOG use marginal maximum likelihood (Bock & Aitken, 1981; also see Orchard & Woodbury, 1972; Dempster, Laird, & Rubin, 1977) or conditional maximum likelihood (Wainer, Morgan, & Gustafsson, 1980) estimation. The latter two methods are generally preferable, as they are more efficient (yield smaller errors of estimate in a given sample) and provide explicit inferential ($G^2$) tests. Most algorithms are called full-information methods because the computations use response patterns; in contrast, limited-information methods (Mislevy, 1986) employ item means, variances, and covariances. Despite the somewhat negative term "limited information," these methods are not necessarily inferior. Maximum likelihood approaches have dominated, but generalized least squares is possible, as is ordinary least squares when inferential tests are not needed (Muthén, 1988). Computational details are beyond the scope of this book.

One usually obtains joint estimates of the abilities ($\theta$) and the item parameters ($a$, $b$, and $c$) from the *same* sample. However, it is generally preferable to develop the test and calibrate items on normative samples and then estimate $\theta$ separately in the target population to avoid capitalizing upon chance. This is no different from classical psychometrics where item pretesting and cross validation are highly desirable.

## DIFFERENTIAL ITEM FUNCTIONING (ITEM BIAS)

Differential item functioning exists when two or more groups differ in their trace lines, i.e., when parameters differ among groups. Thus, it is present if an item is relatively more difficult, discriminating, or easily guessed for one group than for the other. DIF is an item-by-group interaction in the analysis of variance sense. It may be evaluated by means of IRT, by classical assumptions, and by methods that are different from both, although most developments reflect the IRT tradition.

In particular, DIF implies that IRT's essential concept of conditional independence does not hold. Pattern information will not be random at a given level of $\theta$, as it will relate to group membership in a manner dependent upon the form of DIF. Thissen, Steinberg, and Wainer (1992) provide a detailed comparison of these approaches. Using the notation of the previous chapter, we will be concerned with item parameter differences between a reference group and a focal group. If two groups can be assumed equal in ability, classical methods can be used to detect certain forms of DIF very simply. For example, a difference in $p$ values obtained from the same item in different groups of equivalent ability does imply DIF. However, equality of $p$ values does not imply absence of DIF, since the item may not discriminate equally within the two groups. The problem becomes more difficult if the groups are not assumed equal in ability.

Some have used the term "item bias" in place of DIF. This is improper because if two items show DIF, one usually cannot determine where the bias lies unless one knows what the parameter differences should be, e.g., by having a suitable criterion or reason to believe that the groups are equal in ability. For example, suppose that item A is equally difficult for a focal and a reference group, but item B is more difficult for the focal group. If the two groups can be assumed to have the same ability, item B will be biased rather than item A. However, suppose the focal group is less able than the reference group. Item A might fail to assess that difference, but item B properly does. A third possibility is that neither difference in difficulty is proportional to the group differences in ability, so that both are biased. Similar considerations hold for differences in discrimination or guessing.

Even when a suitable criterion allows group differences in the attribute to be assessed, determination of where the bias lies may be difficult because individual items usually relate poorly to the criterion as compared to composite scales. Similarly, a test that mixes items with and without DIF may appear not to exhibit bias at the total-score level because of the low correlations between most predictors and criteria. Moreover, the word "bias" has pejorative connotations which are not always suitable. Suppose one group of subjects is taught by one method and a second group is taught by an alternative method. Items may and should be easier for the group taught by the more effective method. The term "bias" seems less appropriate than the term "DIF" here because the differences are due to a manipulation and not an inherent subject variable.

Unless one has evidence to the contrary, ethical and scientific considerations such as the law of parsimony dictate, assuming that there are no group differences in the attribute being measured. Similarly, one should choose items whose parameters are most similar across groups, whether these parameters are defined classically or through IRT. This is especially true when the groups differ in gender or ethnicity. However, differences in the distribution of the attribute (usually of unknown magnitude) clearly must exist in some situations, e.g., normal and pathological subjects certainly differ in level of pathology. Problems involving DIF are therefore often concerned with whether observed differences in either classical statistics (e.g., total scores, $p$, and $r_{it}$) or IRT-derived statistics (e.g., $\theta$, $a$ and $b$) are of appropriate magnitude. We will first consider DIF from an IRT perspective and further assume that the measure is valid (see Steinberg, Thissen, & Walner, 1990). The basic logic in determining validity from the IRT perspective is generally the same as it is from a classical perspective.

## A Substantive Example

Thissen, Steinberg, and Gerrard (1986) used IRT to evaluate possible DIF by gender in Mosher's (1966, 1968) Forced Choice Sex Guilt Inventory. They compared the fit of one model whose parameters were constrained to equality between groups, thus ignoring gender, with a second in which these parameters could differ between groups, thus controlling for gender (alternative tests will be considered later in the chapter). The difference in fit of the two models was substantial, implying that DIF was present. Males had higher thresholds ($b$) and were therefore less likely to report feeling guilty about prostitution or adultery but were more likely to report feeling guilty about homosexuality. Statements about gender differences in sexual guilt are therefore confounded with whether the items deal with prostitution and adultery or homosexuality. However, one cannot say whether prostitution and adultery items were biased, homosexuality items were biased, or both were biased relative to the remaining items. There were no gender differences in item discrimination ($a$) even though these values did vary, requiring a 2PL model.

An overall gender difference affecting all sexual behaviors does not imply DIF (see Chapter 3 and, especially, Chapter 9). For example, females may be more tolerant of homosexual behavior than males because they are more liberal than males. If overall differences in sexual guilt were the only determinant of the gender difference among particular items, there would be no DIF since the gender difference would disappear when $\theta$ (level of sexual guilt) was controlled. However, females cannot be more liberal toward some items and conservative toward others in the same domain. The critical finding is the lack of conditional independence—items differed in $b$ holding $\theta$ constant. The "crossover" exhibited by prostitution and adultery versus homosexuality items is interesting but not necessary for DIF since *any* group difference in $b$ (or $a$) suffices to establish this effect.

## A Simulated Example

The following computer simulation conducted by the second author illustrates DIF. Assume two populations. One group is average; $\theta$ is normally distributed with a mean of .0 and a standard deviation of 1. The second group is skilled; $\theta$ is normally distributed with a mean of .5 and a standard deviation of 1. Subjects ($n = 500$ per group) responded to five items in a manner consistent with a 1PL model, Eq. 10-1. The respective item difficulties ($b$) were −1, −.5, 0, +.5, and +1.5. For example, a given subject's skill ($\theta$) might be 0 in either group, though there are more average subjects near this value than skilled subjects. This value of $\theta$ then determined each $p$ value (e.g., .84 for item 1) regardless of group membership, and the specific response was determined by a random process. These are data without DIF because the same item parameters describe both groups even though, on average, one is more skilled (has a higher mean value of $\theta$). Figure 10-9a shows the obtained probabilities of a correct response ($p$) for each item. The average and skilled groups correctly answered 2.31 and 2.90 items, respectively.

Even when data do not have DIF, one should *not* expect the differences between the groups in $p$ to be the same for all items because $p$ and $\theta$ are not linearly related. However, if the items fit a 1PL model so that they differ only in the discrimination ($b$) parameters, differences in the normal deviates ($z$) corresponding to these $p$ values will be equal within sampling error. This is the basis of the delta plot method of detecting DIF, as described below. If the items fit a 2PL model and thus also vary in slope ($a$), the largest difference will be found with the most discriminating item. The obtained group differences in $z$ for each item are all approximately .35. For example, the $p$ values were .76 and .85 for item 1 in the average and skilled groups, respectively. The corresponding values of $z$ were .71 and 1.04 for a difference of .33.

A data set with DIF was then created. The data for items 1 to 4 were the same as above for both groups, as were the data for item 5 in the average group. However, item 5's difficulty was reduced to .0 for the skilled group, making it considerably more probable that they would answer the item correctly. Their resulting increase in $p$ to .62 appears in Figure 10-9b. The skilled group's average for the five items consequently increased to 3.32. The DIF is analogous to what was referred to as intercept bias in Chapters 3 and 9 because item 5's difficulty was manipulated. Items could have differed in discrimination and produce a slope bias, but they did not in this case.

## Differential Alternative Functioning

A particular form of DIF may arise on multiple-choice tests when an incorrect alternative (distractor) is disproportionately more attractive to one group than to another at a given attribute ($\theta$) level. For example, suppose a test of cognitive ability included the question "Which word is misspelled?" (a) technicolor, (b) trivial, (c) acedemic, and (d) modem." White males may have more exposure to computer-related concepts than others and be less likely to choose distractor d, which would make them miss the correct alternative, c. Bock's nominal model provides the most detailed analysis. The principles underlying the evaluation of differential alternative functioning are basically the same as those involved in overall DIF. This is difficult to evaluate in small samples where Bock's model lacks power.

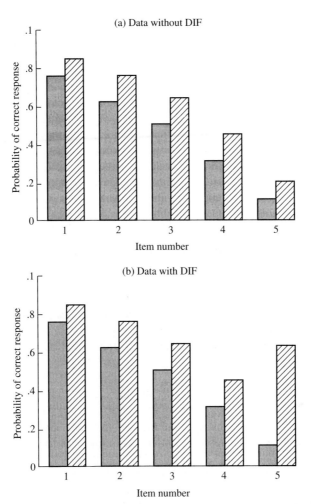

**FIGURE 10-9**    Correct response probabilities $p$ for five items in an average group (mean $\theta = 0$) and in a skilled group (mean $\theta = 1$). ($a$) Data without DIF and ($b$) data with DIF (simulated data).

## IRT Approaches to Assessing DIF

As in any area of statistics, there are issues of both description and inference to be considered. Rudner (1977) defined DIF as the area difference between the focal and reference groups' trace lines, symbolized $A$. Although an exact solution requires integral calculus, Eq. 10-10 provides a satisfactory approximation:

$$A = .005\Sigma\left(p\frac{F}{\theta} - p\frac{R}{\theta}\right)^2 \tag{10-10}$$

where $p(F/\theta) =$ focal group's trace line
$p(R/\theta) =$ the reference group's trace line

The limits of summation are from −4 to +4. An alternative is to sum the simple difference instead of the squared difference. This provides a signed measure, but its practical value is limited when the trace lines cross, i.e., when one group is superior at low levels of θ but the other group is superior at high levels. Linn, Levine, Hastings, and Wardrop (1981) developed a more complex weighted difference (cf. Levine, 1981; Levine, Wardrop, & Linn, 1982; Linn, Levine, Hastings, & Wardrop, 1981). For more recent technical discussion, see Raju (1988) and Rosenbaum (1987). Measures based upon group differences in the trace lines have the advantage of not exaggerating the differences that may arise if one simply looks at the item parameters. Recall from the earlier classroom test example that the 3PL trace lines looked very different from their 1PL and 2PL counterparts yet made very similar predictions. If a 1PL model fits reasonably well, the ordinary difference in difficulties (*b* values) describes the magnitude of DIF.

Perhaps the simplest IRT inferential test for DIF is based upon the difference between corresponding focal and reference group parameter estimates when the two groups are fit separately (Lord, 1977, 1980). For example, let $b_F$ and $b_R$ denote the discrimination estimates for a particular item in the focal and reference groups and $\sigma_{e_1}$ and $\sigma_{e_R}$ denote their associated standard errors. Equation 10-11 describes a test of the difference. Technically, this is a *t* test since the estimated difference is divided by the estimated standard error of that difference, but because the error degrees of freedom is usually quite large, the statistic is approximately distributed as *z* when $b_F = b_R$.

$$z = \frac{b_F - b_R}{\sqrt{\sigma_{e_F}^2 + \sigma_{e_R}^2}} \tag{10-11}$$

Slope and guessing differences may be tested analogously by substituting corresponding pairs of *a* or *c* values and their associated standard errors. Unfortunately, this approach provides no overall test of differences between the lines: It operates on an item-by-item, and, in more complex models, parameter-by-parameter basis. Performing this test for each item and parameter leads to the usual statistical problems of making multiple comparisons—the more comparisons you make, the more likely you will find evidence for DIF because of a type I error. Lord (1977, 1980) developed an omnibus test that uses a measure of multivariate distance between sets of trace lines, but this extension will not be considered here because it is difficult to implement.

Thissen, Steinberg, and Gerrard's (1986) above example used Thissen, Steinberg, and Wainer's (1988) likelihood ratio approach based upon the difference $G^2$ between a model in which corresponding parameter estimates are constrained to group equality versus one in which they are free to vary. In general, first choose the appropriate model by ignoring groups; i.e., decide among a 1PL, a 2PL, or perhaps another model. The chosen model (e.g., a 1PL) provides one $G^2$ value and a set of parameter estimates. Next, fit the same model to each group separately to obtain individual $G^2$ values and sets of parameter estimates for each group. The difference $G^2$ is the first $G^2$ value minus the sum of the latter $G^2$ values. Muthén and Lehman (1985) used this approach with limited information, generalized least-squares estimation. Thissen et al. (1988) suggest selecting items with known properties as anchors and constraining them to equality between groups. Differences among the remaining or studied items are then evaluated to obtain a somewhat more powerful test.

We fit the data in Fig. 10-9 without DIF to a 1PL model in which the $b$ parameters for all five items were constrained to equality between the two groups versus a model in which the $b$ parameters of items 1 to 4 were constrained to equality but the $b$ parameter for item 5 was allowed to vary. The difference $G^2$ was a nonsignificant .9, with 1 $df$ for the data without DIF. The separate estimates of $b$ for item 5 were 1.76 and 1.65 for the average and skilled groups, respectively. The respective standard errors were .14 and .11. The .11 difference in $b$ is therefore small compared to the standard errors (Eq. 10-11 provides a nonsignificant value of $z = .67$). In contrast, the difference $G^2$ value for the data with DIF was a highly significant 95.6, and the separate estimates of $b$ were 1.82 and .06, with standard errors of .14 and .06. Lord's $z$ statistic was a highly significant 11.55.

### Alternative IRT Approaches

Thissen et al. (1991) note that DIF may be evaluated using log-linear analysis (Tjur, 1982; Cressie & Holland, 1983; Thissen, Steinberg, & Mooney, 1989), a form of categorical modeling (Bishop, Fienberg, & Holland, 1975; Wickens, 1989) which is described in Chapter 15, or by certain forms of item factor analysis (Mislevy, 1986; Muthén, 1988), discussed in Chapter 13. These approaches are within the broadly defined IRT tradition. Unfortunately, categorical modeling requires items to have equal discrimination (i.e., to fit a 1PL model) and is therefore of limited applicability.

### Classical Approaches to Assessing DIF

Although we have stressed IRT approaches to the study of DIF, classical psychometricians have also examined this issue. Indeed, there are many similarities between IRT and classical approaches. Both recognize the importance of looking at performance conditional upon the estimated magnitude of the attribute rather than unconditional data (some classical approaches use unconditional data). The major difference is that IRT conditionalizes on the hypothetical entity $\theta$, whereas classical approaches conditionalize upon the observed (total) score or, sometimes, an external criterion (Angoff, 1982). One problem with matching on the basis of observed scores is that their fallibility may induce artifact. Moreover, the elegant likelihood ratio-based model testing possible with IRT is not possible with classical approaches, although some inferential techniques are available which we will present later.

The problem with describing DIF through classical methods is greatly simplified if it can be assumed that items are equally discriminating. We will show how differences in ability to discriminate (in effect, item reliabilities) may mimic DIF (Hunter & Schmidt, 1976). This is really no different from IRT because spurious evidence for DIF can arise from testing the wrong model, e.g, a 1PL with items that require a 2PL. Equal discrimination is not necessary in IRT since 2PL models can be contrasted with constrained and free parameters as well as 1PL models. However, life is much simpler when a 1PL fits the separate group data since there are fewer parameters to worry about, and the individual tests will have more power in a population of fixed size. Moreover, although the assumption of equal discrimination appears to be strong, careful item selection often allows this assumption to be met satisfactorily. To be specific, we previously noted that the $z$-score differences between the $p$ values for each item in Fig. 10-9 were each approximately .35 save for item 5 in the data with DIF. That difference (1.55) was disproportionately large. We know it reflects DIF because we know the data were generated to be equally discriminating, but the problem is that it can arise in other data from differences in discrimination.

For example, suppose item 5 was nondiscriminating ($r_{it} = 0$) but did not have DIF. The proportion of subjects in both groups passing that item would equal the item's $p$ value. The disparity would be zero even if the groups differed on the underlying attribute. On the other hand, if the item discriminated perfectly, the disparity would equal the mean true score disparity, which would be larger than any disparity observed with more typical, fallible items. Conversely, a nondiscriminating item with DIF could produce the same disparity between groups as a discriminating item without DIF if the magnitude of DIF matched the disparity in the attribute. The difference would be that the item with DIF would be answered correctly by random subsamples of subjects in each group rather than those higher in the attribute. Moreover, the item could combine DIF and validity so that it produced a disparity of "appropriate" size and was discriminating, though less so than other items.

Delta plots are one way to evaluate DIF. Convert the $z$-transformed $p$ values for each item to delta values by the relationship $\Delta = 4z + 13$ and plot the $\Delta$ values for the two groups against one another (Angoff & Ford, 1973), though the $z$ scores themselves obviously tell the same story as $\Delta$ since the two quantities are linearly related. Note that this method uses unconditional data. Figure 10-10$a$ and 10-10$b$ shows the respective delta plots for the data without and with DIF. A regression analysis (or, preferably, a structural analysis as introduced in Chapter 4 since neither group's data is error-free) can provide more detailed results. The distance from the line of best fit to each item may be used to describe the amount and direction of DIF. A delta plot *does* assume equal item discrimination.

It is better to see whether $p$ values (or item means for multicategory items) are the same within observed (total) score levels for focal and reference groups, as this does not require equal discrimination. Table 10-4 lists the frequencies with which subjects in the average and skilled groups passed each item at each total-score level in the two data sets. (These are the same for the average group in both cases, and so their data are presented only once.) Note that the percentages of average and skilled individuals passing each item in the data without DIF are approximately equal ($\pm 10$ percent) for each item at a given total-score level. Any disparity due simply to sampling error decreases proportionately as sample size increases. Using total score to partial out the level of the attribute largely eliminated the overall disparities in the $p$ values. Average subjects obviously answered fewer questions correctly, but there is no difference between groups at any given total-score level; i.e., there is conditional independence.

Now consider the data with DIF. There is a large disparity between groups for item 5 at total score levels of 1 to 4. The total score did not partial out the disparity for this item. No disparity is possible at 0 items correct because all these subjects had to have

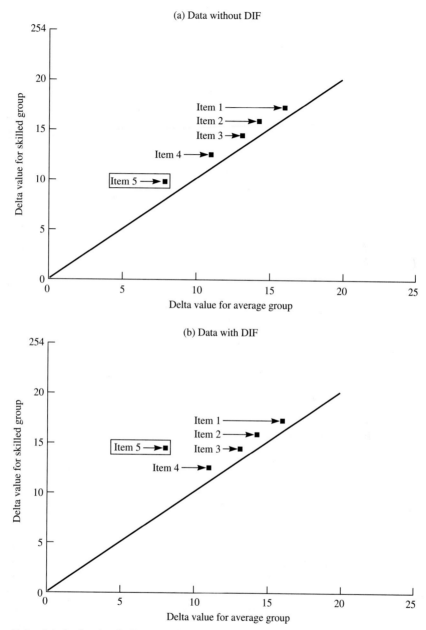

**FIGURE 10-10**    Delta plots for the data in Fig. 10-9. (*a*) Data without DIF and (*b*) data with DIF.

**TABLE 10-4**    OVERALL FREQUENCIES (*f*) AND PERCENTAGES OF INDIVIDUALS PASSING EACH ITEM AS A FUNCTIONOF TOTAL SCORE (SIMULATED DATA)

| Group | Total score | Item | | | | | |
|---|---|---|---|---|---|---|---|
| | | *f* | 1 | 2 | 3 | 4 | 5 |
| Average | 1 | 113 | 66 | 17 | 12 | 4 | 1 |
| Skilled, without DIF | 1 | 64 | 56 | 19 | 16 | 6 | 3 |
| Skilled, with DIF | 1 | 49 | 47 | 24 | 8 | 0 | 20 |
| Average | 2 | 103 | 82 | 67 | 33 | 16 | 3 |
| Skilled, without DIF | 2 | 121 | 88 | 63 | 25 | 20 | 3 |
| Skilled, with DIF | 2 | 72 | 83 | 33 | 28 | 19 | 36 |
| Average | 3 | 121 | 93 | 93 | 80 | 29 | 5 |
| Skilled, without DIF | 3 | 117 | 97 | 96 | 79 | 22 | 7 |
| Skilled, with DIF | 3 | 101 | 87 | 87 | 48 | 27 | 51 |
| Average | 4 | 82 | 98 | 100 | 98 | 88 | 17 |
| Skilled, without DIF | 4 | 130 | 98 | 100 | 98 | 85 | 18 |
| Skilled, with DIF | 4 | 117 | 98 | 99 | 92 | 38 | 72 |

*Note:* There were 52 in the average group, 30 in the skilled group without DIF, and 22 in the skilled subjects with DIF whose total score was 0 therefore missed all five items. Conversely, 29 in the average group, 66 in the skilled group without DIF, and 139 in the skilled group with DIF had a total score of 5 and therefore answered all five items correctly.

missed the item, and no disparity is possible at 5 items correct because all subjects had to have gotten the item correct, by definition.

Note that item 4 is apparently biased against the skilled group at a total score level of 4 since only 38 percent of these subjects answered the item correctly versus 88 percent of the average subjects. This illustrates one problem with using total score, which includes the response to item 4. Item 4 is the most difficult item for the skilled subjects, though not for the average subjects. Consequently, most skilled subjects with a score of 4 missed this particular item. This problem would be minimized somewhat by eliminating a given item from the total against which it is conditionalized, as in computing item-total correlations. It will not be eliminated, however, since DIF affects the rank orderings of the *p* values. Consequently, even when one can detect DIF, it is not simple to locate the offending item.

Jensen (1980) suggested dividing subjects randomly into "pseudogroups" independently of whether they are in the focal or reference group. Evidence for DIF in the pseudogroups simply reflects sampling error. Such data could then be compared to that obtained from real groups. Jensen's procedure belongs to a growing class of techniques for estimating measurement error in the absence of well-defined statistical theory by random sampling from a data base. Efron's bootstrap (Efron & Gong, 1983) procedure and Edgington's (1969; also see Noreen, 1989) randomization procedure are similar procedures.

Both Scheuneman (1979) and Camilli (1979) have proposed $\chi^2$ tests for data of the form of Table 10-4. Let $f_i$ denote the frequency with which a member of group $i$ passes a given item at a given total score level (e.g., 1 = average and 2 = skilled) or the reverse, $n_i$ denote the number in that group, and $p_i$ denote the probability of responding correctly $= f_i/n_i$. Now let $p$ denote the overall proportion of people passing the item at that total-score interval. This is the total number of people passing that item divided by the total number of people at that level, i.e., $(f_1 + f_2)/(n_1 + n_2)$ (a second subscript denoting the score level is implicit in all cases). Equation 10-12 defines Scheuneman's statistic:

$$\chi^2 = \sum \left[ \frac{(f_i - pn_i)^2}{pn_i} \right]$$  (10-12)

where summation proceeds over both score levels and groups.

Likewise, Eq. 10-13 defines Camilli's statistic:

$$\chi^2 = \sum \left[ \frac{n_1 n_2 (p_1 - p_2)^2}{(n_1 + n_2) p (1 - p)} \right]$$  (10-13)

Summation proceeds over categories but not groups since this is reflected by the expression $(p_1 - p_2)^2$. Omit total scores of 0 from the summation in Scheuneman's statistic and omit both 0 and perfect scores from Camilli's statistic since their presence would cause the denominator to be undefined. One problem is that scores on long tests need to be grouped to avoid small cell frequencies. This makes the outcomes somewhat ambiguous because the results depend upon how one forms the categories (Ironson, 1982).

Both measures are based upon group differences in $p$ at each observed score level. Scheuneman's statistic uses the squared difference between each $p$ and their mean, whereas Camilli's squares the difference between the two $p$ values. They are closely related algebraically but not identical. The most crucial difference is that Scheuneman's formula divides by a mean, whereas Camilli's divides by a variance. Scheuneman (1979) originally suggested that the inferential decisions be based upon $k - 1$ degrees of freedom, where $k$ is the number of categories, but Baker (1981) and others challenged the inferential standing of the measure. Camilli's statistic is tested with $k$ degrees of freedom and has a sounder inferential basis.

Scheuneman's statistic will be illustrated using the data with DIF for item 1. Table 10-4 indicates that 113 average subjects and 49 skilled subjects achieved a total score of 1. Of these, 75 average and 23 skilled subjects passed the items, and so $p_i = .66$ and .47 and $p = (75 + 23)/(113 + 49) = .60$. The result of Eq. 10-12 at this level is $[75 - (.605)(113)]^2/(.605)(113) + [23 - (.605)(49)] = .65 + 1.49 = 2.14$. The comparable sums for the remaining totals are .01, .24, and .00. Consequently $\chi^2$ is a nonsignificant 2.39 with 3 $df$.

Camilli's statistic is $[n_1 n_2 (p_1 - p_2)^2/[(n_1 + n_2) p (1 - p)] = [(113)(49)(.66 - .47)2]/[(113 + 49)(.6)(4)] = 5.40$ at a total score of 1. The results for the other observed scores are .09, 2.52, and .13 for a total $\chi^2$ of 8.14, which is nonsigificant with 4 $df$.

Table 10–5 lists the values of both statistics in both data sets. The data without DIF are correctly identified as such in all cases. Both indices are very large for the item containing DIF (5), but they are also modestly large for the other items. This further illustrates the problem of specifying which item has DIF when it affects the classical observed score.

**TABLE 10-5**   VALUES OF SCHEUNEMAN'S $\chi^2$ AND CAMILLI'S $\chi^2$ FOR FIVE HYPOTHETICAL ITEMS WITHOUT AND WITH DIF

| Item | Items without DIF | | Items with DIF | |
| --- | --- | --- | --- | --- |
| | Scheuneman | Camilli | Scheuneman | Camilli |
| 1 | .99 | 4.93 | 2.39 | 8.14 |
| 2 | .24 | 1.45 | 10.27* | 23.10** |
| 3 | 1.49 | 2.29 | 10.05* | 29.60** |
| 4 | 2.42 | 3.32 | 22.17** | 50.82** |
| 5 | 1.64 | 1.69 | 122.30** | 173.87** |

One variant on the above is to employ the sign of each discrepancy. A given component of the $\chi^2$ will be positive if $p_1$ is greater than $p_2$ and negative if $p_1$ is less than $p_2$. The result, however, will clearly not have a $\chi^2$ distribution. Several studies have compared the various classical and IRT indices, such as Ironson and Subkoviak (1979). In general, these indices do not correlate highly with one another. However, most item parameter differences are small. Consequently lack of correlation may be simply due to range restriction. To the extent that this is true, it is difficult to specify DIF in real applications. These do not exhaust the many approaches to DIF. Two that space does not permit us to consider are Holland and Thayer's (1988) use of the Mantel-Haenszel procedure, a form of chi-square, and Dorans and Kulick's (1986) standardization procedure.

## Content Bias

As noted in the previous chapter, standardized tests are often criticized for being biased because reference group members have had more exposure to the content than focal group members. Jensen (1980) is a basic reference to the data we will consider. We have delayed discussion of that point until we could survey empirical methods. Three issues need to be distinguished.

The first of these is that some items are biased and others are not, which implies acceptance of the concept of standardized testing with suitable items. The above procedures can be used to address hypotheses on the subject. The common finding is that items presumed to have the most differential exposure typically do *not* produce the greatest focal group deficit; these deficits are far more likely to arise on more abstract "culturally fair" items. Perhaps the major factor is the phenomenal role played by the mass media in exposing a diversity of individuals to common elements—vastly more people can recognize a Mercedes than are ever likely to own one. Obviously, one could choose vocabulary and other items for which there is differential exposure, e.g., perhaps by asking the general population to define the critical point on an $F$ distribution for $\alpha = .05$ with 3 and 40 *df*. It is probably true that more whites have gotten far enough in statistics to answer that question than members of other groups. However, the proportions will likely be so small in all groups that the item will never meet inclusion criteria in a well designed ability test (it would, of course, be quite suitable for a statistics achievement test, which is another story). The major point, though, is that procedures which allow this to be tested, which include the test construction criteria cited in earlier chapters, overwhelmingly tend to falsify the proposition.

There is a contrasting position which deals with disparities due to the overall testing process. Assume that the reference group consists of English speakers and the focal group consists of native French speakers. If the test content is predominantly verbal, the items on a test written in English might well appear to be fair in the sense of not showing DIF—items that are relatively easy for English speakers might also be relatively easy for French speakers even though the English speakers would consistently do better. The superiority of the English speakers could, of course, be reversed by using a test written in French, but this test could also be fair in the sense that differences in item difficulties between groups are relatively consistent.

It is doubtful that many people would be silly enough now to conduct such a study, but some data purportedly demonstrating the "inferiority" of immigrant groups in the early part of this century contained this blatant artifact (the "genetic" differences proposed to account for this were truly miraculous since they disappeared as soon as the immigrants' offspring had the chance to learn English). It is difficult to imagine anyone with the skill to conduct a research study who is ignorant of differences in language per se. However, certain overall differences certainly can and do exist with regard to such factors as test sophistication even within a language group, particularly as regards practice with multiple-choice tests and, perhaps ironically, the material found on a culturally fair test. These differences may also affect employment and educational criteria used in predictive validity. This empirical question goes well beyond the scope of this book, but it is important to keep in mind the wisdom of the term "differential item functioning" as opposed to "bias." The relative neutrality of the concept of DIF allows one to recognize that group differences may arise from artifact yet be consistent. In other words, a test may be fair by statistical criteria yet reflect artifactual overall differences.

The third issue relates back to the definition of fairness in terms of group equality (see Chapter 9), but this time the issue involves individual items rather than whole scores. It deals with attempts to mandate the "Golden rule," named after the Golden Rule Insurance Company. This company sued the State of Illinois over the examination they required to sell insurance because black applicants tended to do badly. The suit was settled in 1984 when the Educational Testing Service (ETS), who developed the test, agreed to changes that would increase the black pass rate. This basically involved choosing items that showed the least racial disparity. ETS later called the settlement "an error in judgment" (see Haney & Reidy, 1987, for a discussion), and the American Psychological Association's Committee on Psychological Tests and Assessments (1988) condemned the item selection procedure. One major effect of the settlement is for the test and tests constructed under the Golden rule to employ relatively easy items. It is quite likely that items which are content-valid and perhaps even highly important to the field would be eliminated. Similarly, it seems quite likely that the procedure might eliminate the most highly discriminating items.

## TAILORED TESTS AND COMPUTERIZED ADAPTIVE TESTING

We previously mentioned giving individuals a test where subjects receive different items. This is unlike conventional testing where all subjects receive all items. When this is done according to some plan, the result is known as a "tailored" or "adaptive" test. If, in addition, testing is under computer control, the tailored test is called a computerized adaptive test (CAT). A CAT can be administered on even the least expensive personal computers now available, but such accessories as light pens and a hard disk are useful—the more rapidly the computer responds, the easier it is to sustain the test taker's motivation. The limited exposure and consequent fear that people once had of computers is disappearing, though probably not equally in all groups. Multiple-choice items can be used, but they introduce the complication of guessing. Short-answer items avoid this problem, using text processors to handle incidental problems like typographical errors. From a technological standpoint, CAT is quite feasible at (relatively) little expense in testing small groups, and so it is not as esoteric as it seemed a decade ago. Tailored testing may be approached from a classical perspective, but nearly all recent developments have come from the IRT perspective. Wainer (1990) provides a comprehensive collection of recent papers on the topic. Hulin et al. (1983) provide an excellent summary, but much of the material they cite consists of technical reports that are difficult to access. Developing a tailored test is a highly complex procedure requiring the expertise of a specialist, but it is not difficult to present the information needed to make the nonspecialist an effective "consumer."

Conventional tests employ many items that generate little information, especially for subjects at the extremes of the attribute. Very able students are asked too many easy, time-wasting questions. Even worse, low ability students are asked too many difficult questions that may enhance any lack of self-confidence they may have. Tailored tests, in general, attempt to maximize the number of informative questions. That is, ignoring guessing for the moment, the selected items are intended to have $p$ values that are near .5 for the test taker so that they are at the most appropriate difficulty level. Tailored tests can be thought of as extending the concept of equidiscriminating testing considered in Chapter 8 in a very significant way. Abler students are asked relatively difficult items, and less able students are asked easier items. In principle, even though an individual is asked fewer questions than under conventional test administration, estimates should be at least as stable under tailored testing, if not more so.

Tailored testing is itself not new. If you have ever administered an individual intelligence test, you are familiar with the use of vocabulary items to get an approximate idea of the subject's intelligence. This information is then used to select the difficulty level of items on the remainder of the test. It would be obviously too time-consuming to ask the subject every question on the full test, e.g., to ask a normal adolescent questions that the average four-year old could answer. This use of a short test to determine items to be selected from a longer test is common to many forms of tailored testing.

Tailored testing is often but not necessarily a two-stage process. The first stage is a brief routing test, equivalent to the vocabulary test, that is used to direct a measurement test, equivalent to the rest of the individual intelligence test. However, tailored testing is possible without a routing test.

### Tailored Testing and Psychophysical Thresholds

Chapter 2 introduced the important concept of a threshold in psychophysics and its applicability to psychometrics. In psychophysics, the basic idea is to find a stimulus energy that is reported as being sensed half the time, e.g., to find a sound pressure level that is reported as being heard 50 percent of the time. Figure 2-2a portrayed the results as an ogival psychometric function relating the magnitude of the stimulus to the probability of responding that it was sensed. We noted at a later point in that chapter that the psychometric function and the trace line portray the same basic data. The point at which the psychometric function crosses the 50 percent point on the ordinate is the threshold, which is the difficulty (threshold) parameter ($b$) of IRT. Likewise, the slope of the psychometric function is the discrimination parameter ($a$). The major difference noted was that the abscissa in psychophysics was observable ($\Phi$, which was weight), whereas the abscissa in IRT is hypothetical ($\theta$).

In that example, the threshold was close to 200 grams, the magnitude of the standard, which it need not always be. The important point is that the subject hardly ever said that the 185-gram weight was heavier than the standard or that the 215-gram weight was lighter than the standard. The slope of the psychometric function is flat at these points because these points are uninformative about the threshold. These two points contribute one-third of the total number of trials and therefore one-third of the time required to obtain the threshold. Although we could have simply excluded these points from the experiment for this particular subject, we could not know this in advance. Had the subject's threshold been located somewhere else, these points might have been informative.

Considerable time can be saved using some form of the staircase method. Imagine selecting a magnitude ($X_1$) for comparison at some point along the continuum. Although it does not matter a great deal where $X_1$ is relative to the threshold, some time will be saved if the two are near one another. The subject responds as above, e.g., by pressing keys corresponding to the responses "yes" and "no" if the process is controlled by a computer. The basic algorithm is quite simple.

**1** If the subject responds yes, decrease the stimulus magnitude by amount $k$.
**2** If the subject responds no, increase the stimulus magnitude by $k$.

Assume that $X_1$ is below the subject's threshold. This leads to a sequence of "no" responses and corresponding increments in the magnitude of the stimulus. However, once the threshold is crossed, the subject responds yes and a downward sequence begins which is probably shorter than the first sequence. As soon as the stimulus falls below threshold, a third sequence of ascending magnitude begins. If allowed to continue indefinitely, ascending and descending sequences will alternate. However, the process need not continue indefinitely. A stopping rule, such as "stop at the fifth oscillation," can be adopted. Also, the magnitude of the change ($k$) can be decreased along the line to allow for a more precise determination; e.g., each time the subject reverses, $k$ can be reduced by some fraction such as 20 percent. The name "staircase" describes a "walk" up and down stairs of unknown height, in effect, and the process is used to determine the location of the middle "step." Data of this form can be used to construct a psychometric function that is just like that in Figure 2-2a. The major difference is that each trial involves a comparison stimulus that is generally closer to the threshold than a trial in the method of constant stimuli. Because each staircase trial is more informative, being nearer the threshold, fewer trials will be needed to estimate the psychometric function than in the method of constant stimuli.

### Applying the Staircase Principle to Psychometrics

In psychophysics, it is quite easy to select stimulus magnitudes in both the conventional method of constant stimuli and the tailored staircase method. quite literally, the "turn of a dial" provides a desired stimulus of repeatable magnitude. Unfortunately, this cannot be accomplished exactly with ordinary test items. The CAT process normally begins with a normed conventional test. Norming provides a pool of items of known threshold and discrimination. The more discriminating the items, the more efficient tailored testing will be compared to conventional methods. In short, the developer cannot simply take a piece of equipment off of a shelf and dial to select items; items must be developed with even more care than in an ordinary test, although some methods are more demanding than others.

### Flexilevel Tests

Lord's (1971, 1980) flexilevel test illustrates a simple way to accomplish tailored testing without using a computer. The test requires an odd number of items, say 81, that are arranged in order of difficulty for the population as a whole. Item 1 is the easiest, item 81 is the hardest, and item 41 is of median difficulty. Subjects begin at the median item and score their own responses. They proceed forward to a more difficult item if they are correct and backward to an easier item if they are incorrect, i.e., to items 42 and 40, respectively. If they get the first item correct and thereby proceed to item 42, they (1) attempt item 43 if they were correct a second time or (2) proceed back to item 40 if they were incorrect. Conversely, if they get the first item incorrect and thereby proceed to item 40, they (1) next attempt item 42, the item they would have attempted if they had gotten the first item correct, if the response to item 40 was correct or (2) proceed down to item 39 if incorrect. The process continues until half the number of items on the test have been attempted. The score for a subject who answers the last item correctly is the item's serial position in the test, and the score for a subject who answers the last item incorrectly is the serial position of the last correctly answered item plus .5. (In the unlikely event that the items formed a Guttman scale, the test could be stopped when an incorrect response followed a correct response, or vice versa.)

One problem with this method is that subjects may not follow the directions correctly. However, computer administration can overcome this problem. Another problem is that the method is less efficient than other tailored testing methods since the items asked in later stages are not necessarily near threshold. The method is relatively robust and requires relatively little normative data since it does not employ complex IRT estimation. All one basically needs is to trust the stability of the rank orderings of the item's $p$ values.

## More Complex Forms of Tailored Testing

The forms of tailored testing that are most similar to the staircase method of psychophysics are known as branching methods and normally require a computer.

**1** In "up-and-down branching," each change in difficulty (increase following a correct response or decrease following an incorrect response) is of constant magnitude ($k$). Assuming an IRT metric with $k = .2$, the first item would have a difficulty level near the group average ($b = 0$ and so $p = .5$). The second item would have a $b$ of $+.2$ if the first item was answered correctly, and the third item would have a $b$ of $+.4$ if the first two items were answered correctly. However, if the subject missed the first item, the item second item would have a $b$ of $-.2$, etc.

**2** In "H-L branching," the increases and decreases are of different but fixed magnitudes, and so items might become .2 units easier following an incorrect response but only .1 unit more difficult following a correct response.

**3** In "shrinking-step (Robbins-Monro) branching," changes in difficulty become progressively smaller. For example, items might be presented with steps of .4 until the first reversal (error following a string of correct responses or the converse), at which point the step size would decrease to .2. For example, a subject who gets the first four items correct but misses the fifth will have been presented with items of difficulty $b = 0, .4, .8, 1.2$, and 1.

Shrinking-step branching theoretically provides the best ability estimates but is the most difficult to implement (Lord, 1970).

Choosing the first item presents a problem since there is no information about $\theta$ at this point. The usual assumption is that the subject is of average ability ($\theta = 0$). However, tailored testing would not work very well if the eventual outcome was heavily dependent upon this initial estimate. Computer simulations (Lord, 1977) suggest that the final estimate of $\theta$ is relatively independent of the starting item. In addition, alternative methods need not lead to radically different item selections in a pool of fixed size since the same item is often chosen by different methods. After the first item, there are three common methods of determining working estimates of $\theta$ on successive trials.

**1** The simplest approach is to choose the item whose $b$ is nearest the working estimate of $\theta$. This may select items that are too difficult if guessing plays a major role, but Birnbaum (1968) developed a correction for guessing (also see Hulin et al., 1983; Lord, 1980).

**2** Maximum information item selection chooses the item that has the most expected information using Eq. 10-6 and the estimated $\theta$.

**3** Bayesian methods (Chapter 4) incorporate what is known about the population distribution of $\theta$ by choosing items with the largest product of (a) item information and (b) the prior probability of $\theta$ in the population. This prior probability is simply a weighting factor which is omitted in the maximum information method. Bayesian methods attempt to produce the maximum reduction in uncertainty about $\theta$ (Owen, 1975; Jensema 1974, 1977).

After the subject has responded, the new estimate of $\theta$ is used to choose the next item.

In addition to the rules governing item selection and branching, stopping rules are also obviously needed. One issue is the number of items. Simulated data presented in Hulin et al. (1983) suggest that the standard error decreases approximately linearly with the number of items. The simplest rule for deciding when to stop is to present a constant number of items. However, this produces wide differences among subjects in the stability of their $\theta$ estimates. An alternative is to compute the standard error (or, equivalently, its reciprocal, the test information) and stop testing when a criterion is reached. In all these methods, the computer records the items passed and failed and can estimate $\theta$ as described earlier in the chapter even though no two subjects may respond to the same items. This application most clearly illustrates the utility of IRT.

## Perspectives on Tailored Tests

Tailored testing is moving out of its highly experimental phase because computer technology is getting cheaper and IRT is becoming easier to use. Some (Urry, 1977; Lord, 1980; Wainer, 1990) suggest that it will replace conventional testing. Nonetheless, it still exists largely as potentiality. There are several major reasons why the death of conventional testing is not imminent.

**1** Tailored testing may not be justifiable or even possible in many areas. Development demands require material that is relatively stable over time and large normative samples. Much testing is in the classroom where textbooks in large-enrollment courses are now revised every 4 years and lectures are hopefully updated even more frequently. Given the diverse ways in which most courses are taught, it is difficult to pool data across instructors, let alone institutions. The problems are more severe in advanced classes since normative groups are much smaller.

**2** Legal challenges are quite likely to arise in employment and, to a less likely extent, education. People fired or not hired may well claim discrimination because they were asked different questions than successful individuals. Although using different questions makes perfectly good psychometric sense, it is difficult to explain IRT's logic or, equally important, to show that the data have met its assumptions to a judge or jury. They may not be convinced that the complainants probably would not have answered the more difficult items correctly because they could not answer simpler ones.

**3** The cost of tailored testing is still appreciable compared to that for traditional testing. A class of 200 individuals is not unusually large. Obviously, no one would expect 200 computers to be provided, but whatever the number involved, the cost would exceed that for traditional reproduction and scoring.

**4** Since students can be tested conventionally in one setting, the time factor is also not significant.

**5** Classical testing, while inefficient, does not require the extensive norming tailored tests do.

**6** Classical testing is also robust. A long traditional test is not affected by even several poor items.

**7** Even though the number of individuals who do not have even minimal computer literacy is diminishing, it is still far from zero and is likely to remain so given the decreases in funding of education. Many individuals with limited computer experience in general have extensive experience with playing games on computers, but the relation of this experience to educational testing is unclear.

At the same time, tailored testing can be quite feasible in countless circumstances. For example, large numbers of people may apply for jobs involving the same skills or cognitive abilities in large companies. It may be quite feasible to use a small number of computers, which may even serve other roles. The time saved can be used to broaden testing or to allow more people to be tested in greater depth.

## COMMENTARY ON IRT

One must consider both IRT's present state of implementation and its large possibility for improvement, especially in the efficiency of numerical estimation, to make a proper evaluation. These improvements will allow more sophisticated models to be applied to data bases obtainable by the average investigator.

**1** There are certainly many who are skeptical about various features of IRT and many others who ignore it. An increasing number of individuals are "friends" in the sense of being supportive and are often contributors to the growing literature in such sources as *Psychometrika* and *Applied Psychological Measurement*. However, there are very few sophisticated "enemies" in Békèsy's (1960) sense—individuals with sufficient motivation and an ability to detect problems that a friend would overlook.

**2** Too many users of IRT (or other) programs like MULTILOG probably treat them as "black boxes" and accept their output on faith. However, they must know the details of the solution and the meanings of the various options to prevent "garbage in–garbage out" analyses. In contrast, output from a classical psychometric analysis is relatively easy to understand.

**3** The step between the theory of estimation, especially that applicable to hypothetical large samples, and the reality of actual data is not trivial. Actual use of IRT may strain its assumptions, though not necessarily fatally.

**4** One of IRT's strongest points is its emphasis upon choosing items with a spread of difficulties in order to discriminate across levels of $\theta$. As noted previously, Lord (1952b) pointed out how a peaked test maximizes reliability. This led many, especially those who were unaware of the small magnitudes of difference, to seek to maximize coefficient $\alpha$ by choosing items of similar difficulty. Existing tests were often criticized unfairly and/or new tests were often made too hard for less able students and too easy for able ones. IRT stresses maximizing the test information, a different criterion which encourages spreading item difficulties.

**5** IRT's greatest potential lies in nonstandard testing situations like tailored testing or when repeated testings of the same individual are needed. However, this does not mean that classical methods, such as the construction of parallel forms, are inapplicable. Indeed, more data, perhaps in the form of computer simulations, are needed to delineate circumstances where IRT estimates might be unstable.

**6**  IRT's utility is much more limited if the goal is to scale individuals with a common set of items in a single testing like ordinary classroom examinations. Despite the curvilinear relation between $\theta$ and ordinary total score, their ordinary PM correlation will be extremely high and both will correlate to about the same degree with criteria.

**7**  Although there are theoretical advantages to $a$ and $b$ as measures of discrimination and difficulty instead of their classical counterparts, $r_{it}$ and $p$, the practical advantages are much less. An instructor who finds that a given question was answered by 60 percent of the class knows that $p$ would be higher in a more able class and lower in a less able class. The question of "how much" is rare. Moreover, the instructor is probably most interested in comparing items within a class to see which points were made effectively and which were not, and $p$ is satisfactory to this end.

**8**  IRT has considerable to offer in evaluating differential item functioning (DIF), a topic of both social and academic concern.

**9**  Potential users of IRT need to be aware of which assumptions are likely to work broadly and which may not. Despite the theoretical importance of such developments as nonparametric models (Mokken, 1971; Mokken & Lewis, 1982), there is little reason to worry about logistic, cumulative normal, or other possible trace line shapes because real data are likely to be so noisy as to preclude convincing empirical selection. This detail can probably be safely left to mathematical convenience. Indeed, it seems possible to construct a workable model with three-segment linear trace lines, though this possibility has not been pursued [see Stevens, Morgan, & Volkmann (1941), however, for a related situation where linear functions fit at least as well as ogives].

**10**  On the other hand, existing IRT models assume trace lines have right asymptotes of 1 so that subjects at high levels of $\theta$ never make false negative responses. Clearly, they do, even if through carelessness, which Lord (1980) clearly recognized. Consequently, all estimates of $\theta$ are probably multidimensional because of variations in carefulness. Likewise, only three-parameter models allow the left asymptote to begin above 0 and thus allow false positives among the low-$\theta$ subjects. Unfortunately, we have seen how difficult estimation is in a three-parameter model. It would probably be next to impossible in a four-parameter model with samples of realistic size.

**11**  The demands for large normative bases in more sophisticated models limit most users to models that offer the least relative to classical psychometrics. Recall that number correct is a sufficient estimator of $\theta$ in a one-parameter model if all people answer all items. This is also true in a practical sense of two-parameter models since weighted and unweighted sums usually correlate very highly.

**12**  IRT strongly favors short tests of extremely high homogeneity, in contrast to classical psychometrics. Consider the development of a symptom-oriented scale of a condition like depression. The scale will probably include items on sleep disturbances, sudden enhancement of religious tendencies, etc. An IRT analysis might indicate that these form separate scales. Unfortunately, the user may not be interested in assessing attributes defined that narrowly. Chapter 8 considered the important role of methodological heterogeneity.

**13**  Bock and Lieberman (1970; cf. Bock & Aitken, 1981) introduced multidimensional IRT models which are implemented in Mislevy and Bock's (1986) BILOG and

Muthén's LISCOMP (1988) programs. It is not clear how practicable it is to test multidimensional models in normal-sized samples because of the added number of parameters. Moreover, it is also not clear how informative the results would be. Consider a scale fit initially to a one-parameter, one-dimensional model. A two-parameter, one-dimensional model or a one-parameter, two-dimensional model with the same number of parameters might fit better. What could be concluded about dimensionality if both improvements were similar in magnitude?

**14** Like many procedures that have recently become popular, IRT model testing stresses statistical inference. Sophisticated users will recognize the limited utility of adding parameters based upon a marginally significant reduction in $G^2$ in a large sample. However, not all users are that sophisticated. Descriptive measures are important to put significance tests in proper context (Bentler & Bonnett, 1980).

**15** IRT can offer much to experimental psychology, particular perception and memory, by affording a better metric for what are commonly termed strength models. For example, students of memory since Ebbinghaus [see Crowder (1976) for a discussion of his work] have been aware that words at the beginning and end of a list are easier to learn than words in the middle, the serial-position effect. Some argue that items at extreme positions have "stronger memory traces," although there are alternative explanations. Many have attempted to quantify this relationship in terms of $p$. Such models should take into account the nonlinear nature of the scale. IRT could well be used to scale stimuli in terms of $\theta$ rather than $p$.

## ACHIEVEMENT TESTS FOR MASTERY LEARNING

Mastery learning appears in two distinct but related contexts in psychometrics (Lord, 1980, chapter 11).

**1** Deciding whether a person is a "master" or a "nonmaster," e.g., should be retained or not retained on a job based upon test scores. This is a traditional problem of binary classification which has been discussed most extensively in psychophysics. The issue involves determining one's ability to discriminate between pairs (usually) of stimuli that differ in a subtle manner (see Chapter 15).

**2** Training all or most people to an acceptable level of performance. According to one view, one would then not discriminate once the material had been mastered, e.g., law school graduates are attorneys once they pass the bar examination, no matter how many times they take it. An alternative view is to use trials to criterion rather than score on a one-shot testing as a basis for subsequent classification.

The former view was generally popular as a philosophy of education in the 1970s. Many stressed skill acquisition rather than evaluation. Part of the movement has become mainstream in the interim or was accepted even before that time. Recent demands for educational accountability have renewed interest in measuring competency in basic skills in the public schools. At the same time, there is probably more emphasis on evaluation (grades) now as opposed to then because of admission to professional schools, etc. Although a test designed for mastery can employ IRT principles, work has come from both classical and modern sources.

Mastery learning has been most extensively stressed in education (e.g., reading and mathematics), but it applies to all types of training programs (e.g., psychotherapy outcome). Quite apart from social philosophy, trials to criterion has a long history in laboratory research on learning and memory. Although mastery learning is traditional in one sense, it is also a recent development and thus a part of this chapter even if it is "recent" in a somewhat different sense than IRT. The main points of this section apply to both classically developed and IRT-based tests.

## Nature of Mastery Learning

A common corollary of using mastery learning to train people to an acceptable level of performance is the idea of giving individuals additional training and practice until a specified level of mastery learning is reached if their performance is unsatisfactory. The term "mastery learning" thus becomes somewhat of a misnomer in that the usual goal is to produce a satisfactory performance rather than true mastery (outstanding performance). A problem that is incidental to our discussion but important in practice is the strong tendency to change the definition of "mastery" rather than the individual when the educational process is costly.

Mastery learning—what it means, how it should be applied, which subject matters are suitable, if any, practicability of the goals, and problems of measuring results—is still controversial. Cronbach (1990) is a good source on these philosophical issues and the related topic of criterion referencing or tying mastery to the ability to perform specific behaviors. Our purpose is therefore limited to psychometric rather than philosophic issues. These measurement issues can be illustrated with simple arithmetic skills which might involve a grade school child's understanding of long division, including "carrying," use of decimals, and backward multiplication to check division. These are subgoals in an overall mastery of arithmetic at that level. The teacher intends for all students to demonstrate these skills, and students continue to receive practice until they all clearly showed a mastery of the concepts. Tests, including alternative forms, are easily developed for these simple skills.

## Test Construction

Mastery learning is basically a problem in achievement testing which is usually content-validated (see Chapters 3 and 8). That is, the test is constructed by rational appeal to the appropriateness of the content rather than experimentation or statistical results as in predictive or construct validation.

It may seem puzzling that there will be no test score variance in the ideal situation where all people master the material to the point of getting perfect scores and little variance in any real situation where people eventually perform at a high level. Consequently, the measure will not correlate with alternative forms or external criteria, and internal-consistency measures like coefficient $\alpha$ will approach zero. One should not be puzzled—tests constructed in terms of content validity need not be internally consistent or predictive. Moreover, this situation almost never occurs because (1) mastery learning is applicable to only certain types of subject matters, (2) abler students will outperform less able students even after mastery learning to provide at least some variance unless there is an artificial ceiling on test performance, and (3) mastery learning is frequently defined in a partly normative sense rather than purely in terms of instructional goals regarding particular skills. Furthermore, trials to criterion can have predictive validity, as quick learners on one task are typically quick learners on related tasks.

For these reasons, one may obtain large, reliable individual differences in mastery learning tests even with the best instructional efforts. There is nothing wrong with attempting mastery learning in any situation, and the appropriateness of the instruments is minimally dependent on empirical evidence and statistical results. At the same time, there is also nothing wrong with examining the variance actually obtained from achievement tests for that purpose to study internal-consistency reliability and predictive validity as incidental properties of the measure.

### Definition of "Mastery"

Mastery is not defined unequivocally in most situations, as any instructor who has had to defend a grading system to a student can attest. Mastery is typically defined in at least partly normative terms. This is most obviously true for nearly all types of speeded abilities. For example, the success of most athletes depends upon their foot speed, but many slow runners have a compensating skill and many fast runners do nothing else well. Foot speed is only probabilistically related to success. In the classroom situation, there is an irreducible component that must be left to the discretion of the instructor or, at the least, of a group of instructors.

A colleague told the first author about one form of mastery learning in a course in introductory psychology. The colleague gave three hour-long tests plus a final examination during the semester. All tests used four-alternative multiple-choice items. Mastery was defined as 80 percent correct based upon prior experience with the material. Consequently, any student who reached this level was given at least a C grade in the course. Higher grade levels were given B's and A's depending upon the instructor's judgment. Students falling below the 80 percent criterion were allowed additional study and could be retested up to five times per examination with alternative forms. The instructor reported that most students improved upon retestings to reach the mastery criterion, so that nearly all students received at least a C in the course. This situation is typical of mastery learning—the standards depend partly on the judgment of the instructor's definition of acceptable levels of performance and partly on normative data from previous uses of general-purpose tests. We neither approve nor disapprove of the above grading practice, but we will make some suggestions about appropriate methods of test construction when mastery learning depends partly on normative standards.

**1** The original normative information may come from well-standardized general-purpose achievement tests developed by experts or less formal classroom tests constructed by one instructor. However, these tests must possess good content validity.

**2** Auxiliary information (see Chapter 8) from the item analysis (the $p$ and $r_{it}$ values for each item) may also be helpful in helping improve discrimination at the point defining mastery, e.g., 80 percent correct.

**3** If item-total correlations are not available, the test can be slanted toward the difficulty level that is most discriminating at the mastery level.

The basic idea is that the test should be highly peaked because one is interested only in discriminating at the mastery point.

## Practical Problems

Whereas the logic for measuring mastery learning is reasonably clear, there are definite practical problems in carrying out that logic because mastery learning inherently requires much more performance assessment than conventional "one-shot" testing. This was obviously the case above where the instructor allowed students to be retested up to 20 times (five forms on four testing occasions), which entails a great deal of effort. Because of course revisions, the tests had to be updated continually. The sheer difficulties of scheduling, grading, and providing feedback to students required additional effort. Students may be happier when their grades run higher, as they often do in such courses, but it is often difficult to document that they have learned more.

One must assess performance levels continually in order to properly monitor instruction in testing for mastery learning of simple elementary school skills. This might require many brief tests to ensure that most students have mastered each subgoal of the overall unit of instruction. For the foregoing reasons, careful assessment obviously requires (1) considerable effort on the part of teachers to measure progress adequately, (2) "canned" testing materials for use by teachers, and/or (3) tailored testing such as CAT, discussed above.

## SUMMARY

Item response theory (IRT) employs the concept of a trace line as introduced in Chapter 2 which relates ability ($\theta$) to the probability of a designated response. Estimating $\theta$ in turn commonly requires the subject's pattern of responses rather than simply the number answered in the keyed direction. Four arguments made by proponents of IRT for its importance are the following.

**1** It provides test-free measurement: People or the same person on different occasions can be meaningfully compared even though they answer different items.

**2** Under fairly plausible assumptions, individuals who get the same number of answers correct can be shown to differ in underlying skill ($\theta$).

**3** Again under fairly plausible assumptions, number correct and $\theta$ are not linearly related.

**4** IRT provides better estimates of item difficulty and discrimination than the classical measures, proportion correct ($p$), and item-total product-moment correlation ($r_{it}$). The IRT measures are statistically independent; the classical measures have built-in dependencies.

Conditional (local) independence is a basic assumption for IRT models. It states that responses to the various items become independent once $\theta$ is controlled even though they should be highly related if θ is ignored. Most IRT current models assume that the trace line is a logistic ogive (alternative models assuming the normal ogive make the same fundamental predictions but are more mathematically cumbersome). Following standard practice, the location of this function, also called the threshold or intercept, is symbolized *b*, and the slope is denoted *a*. The *b* and *a* parameters, respectively, describe the difficulty and discrimination of the item. The simplest IRT model is associated with Rasch (1960) and assumes that items vary in difficulty but have the same ability to discriminate, and so the *b* terms vary across items but there is a single *a* term. This is called the one-parameter logistic (1PL) model. The trace lines therefore have the same slope but (possibly) different locations. Two special cases are the parallel (equivalence) model in which the items are also equally difficult and the Guttman scale on which the items are infinitely discriminating ($a = \infty$).

Estimating the parameters of an IRT model such as the 1PL is usually complex and iterative (open form). Each pattern of correct and incorrect responses provides a series of trace lines. At any point along the ability (θ) axis, the joint probability of the pattern can be obtained as the product of the individual probabilities, a consequence of conditional independence. This joint probability is the probability of the pattern for a given θ. The maximum value (mode) of the function relating this joint probability to θ is the maximum likelihood estimate and a common best estimate. An alternative is the average value or expected a posteriori estimate. The parameter estimates (*b* and perhaps θ) are basic outcomes, as are the standard errors of estimate. The overall fit of the model may be tested by means of a maximum likelihood chi-square ($G^2$) in very large samples. Hierarchical testing of nested models is also important (see Chapter 4) and applicable to smaller samples as well as larger ones. Assuming a 1PL model is appropriate, one may compare a model in which values of *b* are all allowed to vary versus a model in which some or all are constrained to equality or, perhaps less likely, are assigned specified values. In particular, comparing a general 1PL model with one in which the *b* values are constrained to equality tests for parallelism. The difference in $G^2$ (difference $G^2$) tests the significance of the reduction in fit produced by the constraint(s). If it is large, the constraint is unreasonable; if it is small, the constraint is reasonable. The 1PL has several important properties. The rank ordering of item difficulties is the same for all values of θ because the trace lines are parallel. The converse is also true; the rank ordering of abilities is the same regardless of the item difficulties. Although the scale for number correct differs from the scale for θ, number correct is a sufficient estimator of ability; the two measures bear a one-to-one relationship; subjects with the same number correct will obtain the same estimated θ.

In a two-parameter logistic (2PL) model, item discriminations (*a*) may vary as well as the difficulties. Lord's paradox arises in 2PL and more complex models—because the trace lines cross, a relatively discriminating item may be more difficult than a less discriminating item for someone of low ability but easier for someone of high ability. Both 1PL and 2PL models allow fairly simple parameter estimation. In a 2PL model, two subjects with the same number correct may achieve different values of θ as the estimated ability is related to both the number of items answered correctly and their difficulty. However, a weighted linear combination of correct answers using the biserial item-total correlation as the weight is sufficient to estimate ability. Hierarchical testing is also applicable to the 2PL and more complex models, as one can fit a 2PL and then constrain all values of $a$ to equality. If the difference in $G^2$ is small, a 1PL can be adopted.

A three-parameter logistic (3PL) model incorporates guessing, as would account for performance on multiple-choice tests. The role of each item in estimating $\theta$ depends upon its item information which is a function of the acceleration or rate of change in the slope of the trace line. The greater the item information, the larger the role played by the item for that subject. Assuming conditional independence, the test information is the sum of the item informations. The relative efficiency of one test relative to another is the ratio of their test information functions. Because three parameters are needed per item, a 3PL is difficult to apply to any but extremely large samples without constraints, such as fixing the guessing parameters at $1/K$, where $K$ is the number of alternatives.

Additional models were then discussed. Examples were presented of Bock's nominal model and Samejima's model for graded (ordinal) responses. Bock's model allows one to study changes in individual response alternatives on a multiple-choice test as a function of ability, and Samejima's allows one to study analogous changes for each response category on a Likert scale. Unfortunately, both are rarely used because of they require very large data bases. In contrast to preceding models that all assumed a particular (usually logistic) shape for the trace line, Mokken (1971; Mokken & Lewis, 1982) present a nonparametric approach. Items are said to be doubly monotonic when they are (1) all monotonically increasing and (2) do not cross. Data that fit a 1PL, including Guttman scales, fulfill Mokken's criterion, but the converse is not necessary. Ability can be estimated as the number of items the subject dominates by having at least a .5 probability of answering correctly. Other models were cited to illustrate the range of situations to which IRT has been applied. The application to nonstandard testing situations where subjects do not necessarily answer a common pool of items was discussed. The section ended with a consideration of some of the various differences among IRT algorithms.

The next topic considered was differential item functioning (DIF), which occurs when trace lines differ among groups. Items may be more difficult, discriminating, or more likely to be guessed by chance, holding $\theta$ constant. It is an item-by-group interaction in the ANOVA sense. DIF is preferable to item bias as a term since one does not necessarily know which items are responsible for the difference when DIF arises, and DIF may be present when the term "bias" is in applicable. Two examples were presented. One is based upon real data (Thissen, Steinberg, & Gerrard, 1986), and the other is simulated.

Differential alternative functioning is an extension of DIF and refers to group differences in choice of response alternatives on a multiple-choice test, again holding $\theta$ constant. Some variants on IRT approaches to DIF were discussed. One common procedure is to compute the difference in trace line area. One highly recommended inferential test is to compare the $G^2$ values for a model in which the item parameters vary freely among groups versus being constrained to equality. Procedures based upon classical approaches are then noted. These generally involve comparing the correct response probabilities among groups conditional upon ability defined in terms of obtained scores rather than inferred ability ($\theta$). A delta plot is another method in which $p$ values are converted to $z$ scores which in turn are transformed to $\Delta = 4z + 13$ for historic reasons. The resulting values for the various items obtained from the focal and reference groups are then plotted against one another. Deviations from linearity imply DIF. In general, it is more difficult to detect group differences in discrimination than differences in ability. Two $\chi^2$ tests developed by Scheuneman (1979) and Camilli (1979) were then presented. The section ended with a consideration of the popular term "content bias." We stress that one should look for group differences empirically and not simply assume them by inspecting content: Many empirical studies have shown that focal groups often do relatively better on presumed biased items than on fair items.

Tailored tests present different items to different individuals. One particular form of tailored test is the computerized adaptive test (CAT) in which a computer algorithm chooses items based upon the subjects previous responses. Conventional tests ask too many easy questions of high-ability subjects and, worse, difficult questions of low-ability subjects, which may affect their self-confidence adversely. A tailored test often begins with a routing test to provide a preliminary estimate of $\theta$. This then directs the actual measurement test. The idea is the analog of a psychophysical threshold in the sense of locating items with a 50 percent chance of being answered correctly. One particularly useful approach to finding the threshold is the staircase method: When the subject perceives the stimulus in a psychophysical situation (responds correctly to a test item), the next stimulus (item) is made more intense (difficult) and, conversely, when the subject fails to perceive the stimulus (responds incorrectly). Finally, stopping rules, perhaps based upon a constant number of items or a criterial standard error of $\theta$, terminate the process.

The simplest way to estimate a threshold for test items is Lord's flexilevel test, which uses an odd number of items that are ranked in order of increasing difficulty. Subjects begin with the median item and move forward to a more difficult item when correct and backward to an easier item when incorrect. Subjects answer half the number of items on the test. The score is the serial position of the last item attempted for someone who answers it correctly and the serial position of the last item correctly answered plus .5 for someone who misses the last item. More complex forms of tailored testing use branching methods. The change in difficulty (an increase or decrease depending upon the correctness of the response) may be (1) a constant (up-and-down branching), (2) greater in one direction than another (H-L branching), or (3) of progressively smaller magnitude (shrinking-step or Robbins-Munro branching). Tentative estimates of $\theta$ are achieved in several ways. The simplest chooses an item whose difficulty is nearest the working estimate; alternative methods choose the item that has the largest item information at that point (maximum information item selection) or the product of the item information and prior probability (Bayesian selection).

It has been suggested that tailored testing may replace conventional testing. However, there are several reasons why this is not likely to be the case. The greater developmental costs, the need for constant revision of test material, and possible legal challenges are but a few reasons. Traditional testing's much greater simplicity cannot be ignored, especially among subjects with limited computer experience.

We then put IRT in a broader perspective. The large number of advances have clearly been felt, but the enthusiasm of its proponents needs to be tempered by the need for more critical evaluation of such factors as the greater simplicity of the classical test model and its sufficiency in the vast majority of applications. Sample sizes required for some of the more complex and most interesting IRT models are beyond the availability of most potential users. More efficient algorithms, requiring fewer subjects, may change this. One of IRT's strongest points (which also applies to classical testing) is its emphasis upon choosing items with a range of difficulties rather than maximizing internal consistency reliability. IRT clearly can be used to address issues such as DIF better than classical methods. However, one should be cautious about the tendency of IRT-based tests to be too short and overly narrow with regard to sampling methods. Some proponents of IRT have also exaggerated the role of statistical inference as opposed to description. We suggest that someone who is not well versed in psychometric theory begin by constructing a test classically. A test that is good by classical standards will probably fit a suitable IRT model, and all the IRT in the world will not save a bad test.

The final section of the chapter dealt with achievement tests for mastery learning. Lord (1980) has noted two meanings of the term: (1) deciding whether someone who has met a criterion for mastery or not and (2) training people to reach a suitable level of proficiency. Recent trends in education, most specifically the need for accountability, have reawakened interest in mastery learning. One main issue is what constitutes mastery. In practice, it often means satisfactory rather than outstanding performance (true mastery). Recent trends have stressed criterion referencing—defining mastery in terms of the ability to perform specific behaviors. Specific test construction usually involves content validation. Moreover, tests producing uniformly high levels of performance might range-restrict individual differences and thus reduce internal consistency. In practice, this is not likely to be the case since the test is unlikely to eliminate all individual differences. The test is likely to require a normative definition of mastery. Careful selection of content is especially important. Item analysis is useful in selecting items of proper difficulty. A test designed for mastery learning should be peaked at the desired level of proficiency. Practical problems must be handled. Specifically, suitable items need to be generated, either as alternative forms or, perhaps, as an item pool for CAT, and performance standards need to be monitored.

## SUGGESTED ADDITIONAL READINGS

Hambleton, R. K., & van der Linden (1982). Advances in item response theory, *Applied Psychological Measurement, 6* (special issue).

Hambleton, R. K., & Swaminathan, H. (1985). *Item Response Theory*. Boston: Kluwer-Nijoff.

Hambleton, R. K., Swaminathan, H., & Rogers, L. (1991). *Fundamentals of Item Response Theory*. Newbury Park, CA: Sage Publications.

Hulin, C. L., Drasgow, F., & Parsons, C. K. (1983). *Item Response Theory*. Homewood, IL: Dow Jones-Irvin.

Linn, R. L. (1989) *Educational Measurement* (3d ed.). New York: ACE/Macmillan.

Thissen, D., & Steinberg, L. (1988). Data analysis using item response theory. *Psychological Bulletin, 104,* 385–395.

Thissen, D., Steinberg, L., & Gerrard, M. (1986). Beyond group-mean differences: The concept of item bias. *Psychological Bulletin, 99,* 118–128.

Wainer, H. (1990). *Computerized Adaptive Testing: A Primer.* Hillsdale, NJ: Erlbaum Associates.

Weiss, D. J., & Bock, R. D. (1983). *New Horizons in Testing: Latent Trait Theory and Computerized Adaptive Testing.* New York: Academic Press.

Wainer, H., & Braun, H. I. (1988) *Test Validity.* Hillsdale, NJ: Erlbaum Associates.

*Note:* The two books by Hambleton and Swaminathan are particularly recommended introductions. The two articles by Thissen are of especial interest to students of personality testing.

# PART FOUR

# FOUR

# FACTOR ANALYSIS

Much of psychometric theory is concerned with properties of linear combinations—the general linear model. Factor analysis is one application of this general linear model, as is multiple regression. Because of its importance and complexity, three chapters are devoted to it. The first chapter describes the factor analytic model in general in both algebraic and geometric terms. The chapter also considers how one may reduce most of the information contained in a large series of measures to a smaller number of variables (variance condensation). The next chapter concerns additional aspects of this process of exploring the structure of relations among a series of variables. The final chapter in this part deals with how one may test hypotheses about the organization of factors, which is known as confirmatory factor analysis.

## CHAPTER 11

# FACTOR ANALYSIS I: THE GENERAL MODEL AND VARIANCE CONDENSATION

**CHAPTER OVERVIEW**

Regardless of whether a set of items has been developed into a scale by classical or modern procedures, the ultimate worth of that scale or any other measure is defined by its relations to other variables, as noted in Chapter 3. Factor analysis describes a broad category of approaches to determining the structure of relations among measures. Among other applications, it may be used to determine

**1** Groupings or clusterings of variables
**2** Which variables belong to which group and how strongly they belong
**3** How many dimensions are needed to explain the relations among the variables
**4** A frame of reference (coordinate axes) to describe the relations among the variables more conveniently
**5** Scores of individuals on such groupings (considered in the next chapter).

In all cases, the variables are defined as combinations of entities known as factors. However, combinations appear in three contexts: (1) as what Bollen and Lennox (1991) call "effect indicators," where observable variables are regarded as outcomes of an underlying latent variable; (2) as components, where variables are simply transformed to other variables for convenience; and (3) as what Bollen and Lennox (1991) call "causal indicators," where the latent variable is regarded as the outcome of the observables. Common factor analysis is an example of the use of effect indicators. Also, some applications are exploratory in that the factors are defined to meet such mathematical objectives as maximizing the variance accounted for, but others are confirmatory in that the factors describe proposed substantive properties. Factor analysis is not one simple, statistical method that can quickly be described and exemplified with a few equations. Consequently three chapters are devoted to it. One key assumption we will make in this chapter and the next is that the variables are continuous. In particular, we will limit discussion to scale-level factoring until Chapter 13, at which point we will consider item-level factoring (factoring of categorical variables).

We first consider factor analysis as a general method of inquiry in an attempt to minimize some of the misuses that have occurred in the past. The key to a successful factor analysis is careful choice of variables and, to a somewhat lesser extent, subjects to ensure that all variables of interest correlate highly with other variables. One important strategy is to include marker variables whose properties are known. If each variable correlates highly with at least one other variable or if there are a large enough number of variables, most of the technical differences among methods of factoring, such as the difference between common factor analysis and component analysis, disappear because the various methods will produce very similar results.

This section introduces factor analysis as a general method of decomposing the variance of a measure into one or more common factors reflecting what variables share plus additional unique factors which normally describe variance in a measure that cannot be shared with other variables. Variables are expressed as weighted linear combinations of factors where the weightings are termed pattern elements. The component model is a special case of the general model that ignores unique factors. Although factor analysis is defined in terms of individual measures, computations are actually performed upon measures of relationship, which are usually, but not necessarily, correlations, and we compare the results of using different forms of relationships. The key concept of the correlation between a variable and a factor (structure element) and the important distinction between uncorrelated (orthogonal) versus correlated (oblique) factors are presented. We then show how factor analysis may be viewed both algebraically and geometrically. The unique variance is then broken down into two parts—measurement error (unreliability) and specific variance which is systematic but not shared with other variables in the analysis. This leads to a distinction between other types of factors, such as a general factor which relates to all variables and a group factor which relates to some, but not all, variables.

Exploratory factor analysis usually involves two stages. The first or direct solution condenses the variance shared among the variables and typically defines the number of factors. As initial factors are typically difficult to interpret, a second stage of rotation then makes the final result more interpretable. This chapter is limited to variance condensation (direct solutions, which are nearly always uncorrelated) in exploratory analyses.

Three approaches to condensation are discussed: (1) defining a factor's content in advance, e.g., as the sum of the variables in the analysis (centroid analysis); (2) maximizing a property of the sample data, e.g., by accounting for the most possible variance (principal component and principal axis analysis); and (3) estimating population parameters, e.g., choosing the most probable outcome given the data (maximum likelihood analysis). Additional ways to condense data are also discussed briefly.

We then present several rules for determining the number of factors to be retained for rotation from an initial solution. Part of the discussion is intended to show that one rule, the number of principal components whose eigenvalues exceed 1.0, may be very misleading even though it is the most popular default rule in computer packages.

Finally, we consider causal indicators. Many of the features required of causal indicators are less applicable, or different requirements arise in developing causal indicators.

## USES OF FACTOR ANALYSIS

### Factors as Groupings of Variables

Despite the diversity of what may be called factor analysis, there is one unifying principle to be kept in mind: factors (called composites, constructs, dimensions, indices, or axes depending upon the context) reflect combinations of observable variables (also called measures, tests, indicators, or simply observables). If everything to be known about anxiety could be summarized by a single observable measure ($X_1$), there would be no need to have the two classes of terms; the need for factor analysis arises because no single physical measure suffices.

Linear combinations are used in three different ways in the literature. Bollen and Lennox (1991) contrast two of these, but the third has at least equal significance.

**1** "Effect indicators" are linear combinations in which the observables are the results (effects, outcomes) of the factor. The observables are dependent variables, and the factor is an independent variable as in the discussion of regression theory in Chapter 5 (Bollen and Lennox do not imply a temporal relation in the sense of cause preceding the effect). As in any regression model, the factor, as an independent variable, is assumed to be error-free, but the observables contain error. A subject who does well on a test that is a good measure of the factor of verbal fluency does so as a consequence of being verbally fluent or because of luck; doing well on the test does not cause the individual to become verbally fluent. The factor is also broader in meaning than any of its fallible observables in that it is not completely defined by them individually or in combination.

**2** "Components" are simply linear combinations of observables and therefore observables in their own right. If $X_1$ and $X_2$ are two measures, their sum, $X_3 = X_1 + X_2$, and difference, $X_4 = X_1 - X_2$, are one possible pair of components (there are an infinity of others and they need not equal the number of variables). Although the equations describe $X_1$ and $X_2$ as dependent variables, they can be rewritten so that the two observables become dependent variables with no loss of meaning, e.g., $X_1 = 1/2(X_3 + X_4)$. Neither pair of variables contains any meaning that the other does not; knowing one pair implies knowing the other through a simple transformation, and if only one term in a given pair is unknown, the other pair is indeterminate. The transformation is largely made for convenience. For example, the sum and difference scores based upon a pretest and a posttest may be more useful in describing overall performance and learning. Bollen and Lennox (1991) do not discuss the component model.

**3** "Causal indicators" are linear combinations in which the factor depends upon the observables. The factor thus becomes the criterion in a regression analysis sense. Bollen and Lennox (1991) use socioeconomic status as an example. People have high socioeconomic status because they are wealthy and/or well-educated; they do not become wealthy or well-educated because they are of high socioeconomic status. Although their model identifies error solely with the factor, the fact that the observables (predictors in this case) can be observables implies that they may also contain error.

Most conceptions of factors in psychological research imply the first or second meaning, and so all but the last section of this chapter will be concerned with effect indicators. Moreover, we will see that viewing observables as effects of factors or as components leads to similar numeric outcomes in most well-designed studies.

## Exploratory and Confirmatory Analysis

To illustrate another way in which factor analyses differ, suppose that Prof. Adamik believes that a series of measures all involve some form of reasoning ability but does not propose any more precise organization. This investigator is concerned with discovering factors by exploration. On the other hand, assume that Prof. Brown proposes two major types of anxiety: (1) anxiety over possible physical harm and (2) anxiety over social embarrassment. Each proposed type of anxiety is measured by three tests which have distinct content but are assumed to share a common core. The hypothesis proposes two anxiety-related factors which factor analysis can confirm or disconfirm. If the average correlation of tests within each of the two sets was high both in an absolute sense and relative to the average correlation of tests between the two sets, the hypothesis would be supported even if the correlation between sets was not zero. Prof. Brown may use factor analysis to confirm or disconfirm the hypotheses about anxiety, and the specific methods should be somewhat different from Prof. Adamik's.

Prof. Adamik raised more of an open question about the number and kinds of factors derivable from a collection of variables, which leads to exploratory factor analysis. In contrast, Prof. Brown illustrated how a factor analysis may begin from a hypothesis stated before the data are gathered. A proper evaluation would involve confirmatory factor analysis. However, this distinction is a continuum rather than a sharp dichotomy. Some hypotheses are even more well developed than Prof. Brown's. For example, the hypothesis might involve parallelism—each test within the two sets is proposed to measure the respective attribute equally and contain the same proportion of error. Most investigations are somewhat more confirmatory than Prof. Adamik's and more exploratory than Prof. Brown's. Investigators usually have hunches, perhaps implicitly, about at least some of the underlying factors, but these may not be completely firm. Moreover, the results of any study may force initial hypotheses to be modified; e.g., one of the anxiety measures might be found to measure both proposed types of anxiety. However, the extremes of this continuum of confirmatory versus exploratory analysis are important to keep in mind. Totally exploratory analyses, in which there is no theoretical rationale for even having selected the variables, should be undertaken with extreme caution, if at all. Second, most factoring methods are clearly applicable to one or the other need, but not to both.

From another point of view, an exploratory analysis defines factors in the purely mathematical terms of best fit, typically "most variance accounted for," and eventually leads to factors which the investigator then interprets. It tends to be stepwise (data-driven) rather than direct (theory-driven). The analysis first condenses the variables into a relatively small number of initial (original) factors based upon the chosen statistical criterion. These initial factors are usually difficult to interpret; the goal is to explain the most variance (or related property) with the smallest number of factors. For example, five factors might explain 80 percent of the variance among 20 tests. This suggests that these factors described the relations among the initial 20 variables well. After condensation, the factors are usually transformed by rotation. A rotated factor is simply a linear combination of the initial factors. The rotated factors will explain exactly the same total variance as the initial factors even though the variables will relate to the rotated factors differently than they relate to the initial factors. Rotated factors divide up the variance more usefully.

In contrast, factors are defined directly in a confirmatory analysis. The intent is to have the factors incorporate the properties that have been hypothesized and then determine how well these fit the data. The properties that are tested include, but are not limited to, the number of factors and their contents of each factor—which variables belong to which factors. For example, six measures of introversion might be hypothesized to be explained by one factor. The hypothesis thus proposes one factor to which all measures belong. Using criteria to be described, this might or might not explain the data well.

The past 20 years have seen impressive developments in confirmatory factor analysis, even though some useful procedures are rather old. Testing reasonably explicit hypotheses offers many obvious advantages, but many previous investigators were unwilling to formulate hypotheses, did not trust their hypotheses, had so many variables that they could not anticipate their end result, or felt factor analysis could "magically" organize their data for them without their having to think, which it cannot. They often started with a large collection of "interesting" measures and let the results say what factors were present. Even worse, many studies were conducted simply because the data were there. Contemporary factor analysis is much more strongly confirmatory. Both authors view this as a generally healthy trend because it forces investigators to think about the organization of their data ahead of time and allows them to incorporate the very reasons they selected the variables. Of course, not every contribution to a rapidly developing area turns out to be useful, and more than a little of the contemporary confirmatory factor analysis literature is bogged down in details of using computer packages rather than interesting substantive findings. The remainder of this chapter will be concerned with condensing variance in exploratory factor analysis, which includes deciding how many factors to retain for rotation.

### Factor Analysis and Scientific Generalization

In general, relating variables to underlying groupings, testing for groupings, or discovering groupings can involve anything from a broad, essentially atheoretical, data-driven search to testing a highly developed theory. Different forms of factor analysis are well suited to these diverse needs. Articles about factor analysis appear in such sources as *Psychological Bulletin*, *Multivariate Behavioral Research*, *Applied Psychological Measurement*, and *Educational and Psychological Measurement* with great regularity. Any book on quantitative methods will contain at least one chapter on factor analysis (see Suggested Additional Readings). We recommend Gorsuch (1983) and Harman (1976). The former explains relevant principles well; the latter excels at outlining computations.

Although they are usually wedded in practice, one must distinguish between factor analysis as a set of concepts and factor analysis as a set of abstract mathematical procedures. Various theories of human ability and personality characteristics relate to factor analytic concepts without explicitly employing the associated mathematical techniques. For example, many aptitude test batteries have been constructed to measure a number of underlying factors, but the tests themselves were not formally developed from factor analysis.

Prof. Adamik verges closely toward the misapplication of applying factor analysis without any rationale, but the element of theory inherent in limiting the study to ability measures is an important consideration. Obviously, other procedures, such as stepwise multiple regression (which rivals if not surpasses factor analysis as the most misused multivariate procedure) can be criticized in similar ways. However, it should become clear why factor analysis is so often misused. The conceptual and mathematical models are both carefully thought out and interwoven in better factor analysis investigations. How to do this will be discussed at numerous points.

Because of the well-developed, elegant, highly complex methods of factor analysis that already exist, some have stressed the mathematics of factor analysis at the expense of empirical research. This can lead to the "tail wagging the dog." The experimenter should ask, "How much will this help my research program?" in judging the utility of any approach such as factor analysis. Many mathematical issues in the literature on factor analysis (or other areas) concern both vital and inconsequential topics from an empirical perspective. It is all to easy to subvert an important empirical problem by unnecessarily complex mathematics. Sometimes, very complex mathematical methods are required for the scientific problem at hand. However, most situations allow much simpler, direct, and practicable approaches.

We hope to show in the pages ahead that the basic ideas and principles underlying factor analysis are easy to understand. When particular problems are encountered that require specialized mathematical methods, the reader will have to do what nearly all psychometricians have done—go to the detailed accounts listed in the Suggested Additional Readings or to other referenced sources.

Factor analysis is a natural outgrowth of all topics that have been discussed so far in this book, specifically (1) the basic logic of measuring individual variables (test construction), (2) the statistical characteristics of individual variables, (3) the reliability and validity of individual variables, and (4) the relations among variables as manifest in the correlation of sums, multiple correlation and regression, and other multivariate measures of relationship. For example, both multiple correlation and factor analysis relate a linear combination of variables to a criterion. The difference is that in multiple regression the predictors and criterion are distinct entities, but in factor analysis the predictors (factors) are at least partially defined by the criteria (variables).

Factor analysis is a basic tool for explicating constructs—Chapter 3 noted that a major aspect of this explication is to determine the extent hypothesized measures of a construct measure the same thing versus break up into clusters of variables that measure different things. Another aspect is to study the statistical structure of a set of variables that measure a given construct *and* sets of other variables that presumably measure different constructs. Chapter 3 also illustrated experiments to determine whether presumed measures of a construct meet theoretical expectations. Although factor analysis is usually concerned with individual differences, it has also been used to study processes common to a group of people (Watson & Tellegen, 1985).

Applied psychometric research usually stresses groupings of measures rather than individual measures. For example, subtests used in achievement test batteries for the primary grades are commonly named reading comprehension, mathematical skills, language usage, etc. These names imply that the individual differences generalize beyond the chosen subtests. Thus, if it is proper to name a particular subtest "reading comprehension," that subtest should correlate substantially with other measures given the same or similar names. It should thus possess "convergent validity" in Campbell and Fiske's (1959) terminology and also relate strongly to a factor in an actual factor analysis. This discussion should make it clear that factor analytic concepts and methods are intimately related to scientific generalization. Hypotheses about factors concern the extent to which results go beyond specific variables given the same name. Such hypotheses require confirmation even if the initial hypotheses are rather vague, and so the specific analyses are exploratory. It is vital to ascertain the extent to which groups of variables go together empirically so that they can be given the same name.

We have thus far stressed the use of factor analysis to identify groups of variables and thereby define various constructs. However, such analyses of internal structure are only a prelude to more extensive investigations of the external correlates of these constructs, which may also involve a factor analytic design. Factor analysis is useful only to the extent that it aids in the development of principles of human behavior, and the best methods of analysis aid most in the search.

## Variable and Subject Selection

We cannot emphasize the importance of the selected variables enough. Factor analysis never has and never will succeed in finding a magical structure of any generality in an ill-defined set of variables. The following criteria for defining variables used in an analysis were adapted from Gorsuch (1988).

**1** The more variables in the set that a given variable correlates with and the higher the general level of correlation, the better. In general, the higher the level of intercorrelation, the easier it is to determine patterning of correlations, which is the general goal of factor analysis.

**2** Variables should be reliable. Chapters 6 and 7 considered the problem of attenuation due to unreliability. Attenuation affects measures of relationship like $r$, which we will show are basic to factor solutions. However, we have also seen that simple unreliability does not have the extreme effects upon measures like $r$ as much as many feel it does. Consequently, this point is subsidiary to point 1.

**3** The analysis should contain variables with known properties called marker variables. Quite often an investigator may be confronted with a largely unknown set of variables. In order to make sense out of these variables, include others which have been thoroughly studied. This will make the knowledge gained by the analysis cumulative with respect to prior analyses.

**4** Large sample sizes should be used to ensure that groupings are not simply effects of sampling error.

Gorsuch (1988) also properly notes the interaction between the nature of the variables chosen and factor analytic procedures appropriate to that situation. This particularly applies to rotation, considered in the next chapter.

The more observations there are relative to the number of variables, the better. We will downplay inferential testing because most major aspects of the data turn out to be significant; e.g., it is rare that all the correlations in a matrix can be assumed to be zero. Inferential criteria used to define factors tend to provide too many rather than too few. However, one should take advantage of the increasing availability of statistical tests for cases that may turn out to be exceptional. Statistical significance is necessary, but it is not sufficient.

The composition of the sample is also important. Suppose a series of measures that have previously been found to reflect equal amounts of verbal and quantitative abilities in a general population are administered to a sample that is range-restricted on one of these dimensions. Someone who is inexperienced in factor analysis may easily conclude that the tests measure different factors in this second population, which is probably not the case. Similarly, if the sample is more-or-less homogeneous, correlation magnitudes will be affected. Arbitrary use of criteria to define the number of factors, especially computer defaults, can easily lead one astray. In fact, studies which apply a previously studied set of variables to a new population are really not exploratory, and the investigator should consider the methods described in Chapter 13.

## BASIC CONCEPTS

It is very important to understand the meanings of some key terms and watch carefully how such terms are used in the literature. A slight change in terminology may make a very large difference in meaning. There are also some inconsistencies, especially in notation. Editors of the more empirically oriented journals often permit authors to employ terms loosely if not incorrectly. Some of the most important issues are as follows (others of somewhat lesser importance will be described later). We hope that succeeding generations of behavioral scientists do a much better job than the present one has in discussing the theory and results of factor analysis and in using its rich vocabulary.

Begin by assuming a data matrix of the form described in Fig. 2-1. Following convention, we will define this by a boldface $\mathbf{X}$. The rows of $\mathbf{X}$ describe different subjects, and the columns describe different variables. Again following convention that the row subscript precedes the column subscript, $X_{ij}$ describes a particular score on the $i$th subject and $j$th variable (measure), and so $X_{21}$ is the score of subject 2 on measure $X_1$. In general, $X$ with two subscripts denotes an observation on a particular subject, and $X$ with a single subscript denotes a variable ($X_1$). "Subject" can refer to any class of objects on which measurements are made, and so it may denote insects, vegetables, countries, rocks, or rivers as well as humans. Likewise, "variable" can refer to any quantifiable attribute, as has been the case throughout this textbook, so that it might be a standardized test, performance on a memory task, an autonomic response, etc. It is very important that there be a score for each subject on each measure and that the data matrix be much "taller" than it is "wide" (have more subjects than measures), but there are exceptions to both these points. The section on holes in the matrix in Chapter 2 applies to factor analysis, and the end of Chapter 12 will consider some alternative factor analytic designs where there may be more measures than people.

In addition, assume that (1) the number of observations is large relative to the number of variables and (2) no variable entered into the model is a linear function of the other variables. In particular, do not include the sum or average or a series of measures along with the individual measures. Both introduce spurious dependencies into the results, but methods for handling situation 1 will be considered in the next chapter. These basically involve reversing the roles of subjects and variables in the analysis.

## The General Factor Model

Earlier in this chapter, we contrasted three types of linear combinations. What Bollen and Lennox (1991) called effect indicators, because the observed variables are effects of the factors, are historically called common factors. Because a factor is viewed as broader in meaning than any specific variable, common factor analysis separates the variance that each variable can contribute to factors, called common variance, from the variance that is unique in itself. Unique variance is not, however, simply measurement error, as we will note in a later section of this chapter. In contrast, components are simply linear combinations of observables and therefore observables in their own right. All variance is considered systematic in a component model. An alternative way of saying this is that component models estimate the unique variance to be .0 for every variable.

Both models estimate the observed variable ($X_j$) as a weighted combination of factors ($F_p$). For example, Prof. Adamik's tests might be representable as a combination of a reasoning factor ($F_I$) and a verbal fluency factor ($F_{II}$). Some of this investigator's tests might be primarily a measure of $F_I$; others might be primarily a measure of $F_{II}$; still others might be nearly equal combinations of both, and the remainder may be unrelated to the two factors. The variance of each variable is analyzed into portions attributable to each factor.

Perhaps ironically, certain common factor algorithms produce unstable solutions when variables have little unique variance because they are highly intercorrelated, but high intercorrelations are highly desirable in component analysis. Proponents of common factor and component approaches disagree with one another strongly. However, as we hope to show, the two approaches will lead to very similar substantive outcomes when either (1) the number of variables is large or (2) each variable correlates highly with at least some of the remaining variables. The latter is an explicit goal (and the former perhaps an implicit goal) of any well-designed factor analytic study. Moreover, although some investigators limit the term "factor" to common factors as they do not consider component analysis to be factor analysis, we find it far more useful to think of component analysis as a special case of the more general factor analytic model in which error is ignored.

The weightings are called pattern (b) elements, which may be viewed as regression weights in the sense of Chapter 4, but not necessarily in the least-squares sense. The combinations will be assumed linear, even though nonlinear forms of factor analysis have been proposed (see McDonald, 1986). However, we will allow nonlinear transformations of variables to be made before they are entered into the analysis, as by defining a variable as the product or power of others (see Eq. 5-1d).

Equations 11-1 describe the general model:

$$X_j = b_{j\mathrm{I}}F_\mathrm{I} + b_{j\mathrm{II}}F_\mathrm{II} + b_{j\mathrm{III}}F_\mathrm{III} + \cdots + b_{ju}F_u \qquad (11\text{-}1a)$$
$$= \Sigma b_{jp}F_p \qquad (11\text{-}1b)$$

The subscript $i$ will index any subject (which we ignore for now), the subscripts $j$ and $k$ will index any two different variables, and the subscripts $p$ and $q$ will index any two different factors. However, as in Eq. 11-1a, we will denote particular common factors, such as the first in a series and the unique factor $u$. Keep in mind that each variable has its own unique factor in common factor analysis; more precise notation would describe the unique factors as $F_{u_1}, F_{u_2}, F_{u_3}, \ldots$, and their pattern elements as $b_{u_1}, b_{u_2}, b_{u_3}, \ldots$. It is extremely useful to think in terms of matrices (arrays). Just as $\mathbf{X}$ denotes the entire set of observations, we will denote the entire set of common factor pattern elements as $\mathbf{B}$, the entire set of unique factor pattern elements as $\mathbf{B}_u$, and the entire set of factors as $\mathbf{F}$. Formal matrix theory is not necessary for these chapters, but it provides an extremely compact way to describe Eqs. 11-1. The Suggested Additional Readings lists matrix-oriented mathematical presentations.

Factor analytic models are usually not designed to fit the data exactly, and so the equal sign in Eq. 11-1 is a misnomer in practice. The usual intent is to provide a good approximation. Each variable is predictable from the factors to a certain extent whether these factors are common factors or components, and the squared multiple correlation in predicting a given variable from the factors defines the communality of that variable, denoted $h^2$. Conversely, the estimated unique variance in a common factor model may contain some common factor variance that has not been included in the model if some factors have not been extracted. There are several possible measures of fit that have been used to describe the results of a particular model. Historically, the most popular, but not necessarily the best, is the proportion of variance accounted for, which is simply the average communality. One limitation it has is that the communality of each variable and therefore the proportion of variance accounted for generally increases as the number of factors increases for the same reason that all multiple correlations are biased with respect to number of predictors. This is true even when the additional factors are meaningless. There are several other measures of fit which we will consider later.

In contrast to the $h^2$ values reflecting the proportions of variance in the variables that are explained by the factors, it is also possible to compute multiple correlations that reflect the proportions of variance in the factors that are explained by the variables. These will always be 1.0 for components (even though the $h^2$ values for variables will generally be less than 1.0) because components are nothing other than linear combinations of the variables. Conversely, they will be less than 1.0 for common factors because they are broader than the variables that define them. Factors with low multiple correlations require additional variables for their definition. The same principles that applied to multiple correlation in Chapter 5 apply here—adding a variable that is highly correlated with other variables in a grouping does not add appreciably to the factor definition.

Also, do not think of factors as fixed entities; they may be rotated to form new factors, a process that will be discussed in the next chapter. For example, if $F_p$ and $F_q$ are pairs of factors, $F'_p$ can be defined as $.71F_p + .71F_q$, and $F'_q$ can be defined as $.71F_p - .71F_q$, among an infinity of other possible rotations. Although the weights for the new factors will also be changed so that **B** becomes transformed into **B'**, the new factors, $F'_p$ and $F'_q$, are just as proper to use in the model and are just as much factors as the original ones, $F_p$ and $F_q$. Rotation does not affect the individual $h^2$ values and overall indices of fit such as the proportion of variance accounted for.

## The Unit of Measurement

Factor analysis may be applied to data that have been standardized so that each variable has a mean of zero and a standard deviation of 1 over subjects, and so $X_j = z_j$. It is also commonly applied to deviation scores, where $X_j = x_j$, as well as raw scores. Historically, factor analysis has most commonly used standardized scores, but certain problems, such as comparing the factor structures of different groups, require alternative procedures. These alternative ways of defining the basic data have the following general effects:

**1** Standardizing the measures totally eliminates the effects of differences in the unit of measurement. It is common to denote the matrix of scores as **Z** in this case. This chapter and the next will assume that variables have been standardized.

**2** Expressing the measures as deviation scores eliminates effects of differences in the location of the variables (means) from the analysis but allows differences in variance to play a role. Certain inferential tests assume that these variance differences remain, i.e., the data being analyzed are raw or deviation scores. There is no standard symbol to denote the data matrix as a whole in this case.

**3** Expressing the measures as raw scores allows difference in both location and variance to affect the results.

**4** A logical possibility, which has not been used to our knowledge, is to divide raw scores by their standard deviation and thereby analyze X/s. This eliminates differences in variance but allows differences in location to remain.

## Estimating Correlations

This chapter will assume that the data have been standardized ($\mathbf{X} = \mathbf{Z}$) and so, following standard notation, the scores for variables $X_j$ and $X_k$ may be denoted $z_j$ and $z_k$, and the pattern weights are beta ($\beta$) weights. If we take pairs of scores, obtain their product, add the products over the $N$ subjects, and divide by $N$, the result, $\Sigma z_j z_k / N$, is the ordinary PM correlation of Eq. 4-6 (factor analysis has also been applied to the PM estimates discussed in Chapter 4, e.g., biserial and tetrachoric $r$, which we will discuss in Chapter 13). The right side of Eqs. 11-1 becomes a series of terms of the form $\Sigma b_{jp} b_{kq} F_p F_q / N = b_{jp} b_{kq} \Sigma F_p F_q / N$, which describe factor correlations. The set of all possible correlations among factors forms another matrix which we will symbolize as $\Phi$. Factors may be chosen so that all possible factor correlations are zero, which is known as an orthogonal (uncorrelated) solution. Transforming a set of correlated variables into a set of uncorrelated factors illustrates a second common goal of factor analysis. If one or more pairs of factors are correlated, the solution is known as oblique (correlated). Initial solutions obtained in exploratory analyses are nearly always orthogonal, but rotated factors and factors obtained in confirmatory analyses may or may not be, at the user's discretion. Historically, unique factors were assumed to be orthogonal with respect to one another and the common factors. This assumption is still made in most situations. However, more recent formulations allow the unique factors to be correlated with one another but still orthogonal with respect to common factors. The need for correlated error arises in special circumstances, as when one group of variables is obtained under one set of conditions and another group is obtained under a different set of conditions.

Equations 11-2 hold for the special case of orthogonal factors:

$$r_{jk} \approx \beta_{jI} \beta_{kI} + \beta_{jII} \beta_{kII} + \beta_{jIII} \beta_{kIII} + \ldots \qquad (11\text{-}2a)$$
$$\approx \Sigma \beta_{jp} \beta_{kp} \qquad (11\text{-}2b)$$

Summation in Eq. 11-2b proceeds over the $F$ factors. The relation is exact when there are as many factors as variables, and so = replaces $\approx$, but the result is not that important for reasons given earlier. It is useful to denote the matrix of estimated correlations as $\hat{\mathbf{R}}$ to distinguish it from the matrix of actual correlations $\mathbf{R}$. Various measures of disparity between $\hat{\mathbf{R}}$ and $\mathbf{R}$ serve as loss functions in the sense of Chapter 4 in describing how well a particular model fits the data. These serve the same general role in describing fit as the proportion of variance accounted for, but are increasingly replacing this latter measure because they have superior mathematical properties. For example, one loss function provides maximum likelihood estimates of the factors. One popular loss function is the square root of the average squared discrepancy between $\hat{\mathbf{R}}$ and $\mathbf{R}$, discounting the diagonal elements, or root-mean-square (RMS) error.

Analogous results can be obtained even if the raw data are not standardized. If deviation scores ($x_j$) are used in the analysis, covariances are estimated instead of correlations, and so the resulting matrices become $\mathbf{C}$ and $\hat{\mathbf{C}}$ (which are relatively standard symbols). Likewise, if raw scores are used in the analysis, mean sums of products are estimated, and the resulting matrices become $\mathbf{SP}$ and $\hat{\mathbf{SP}}$, which is less standard notation. Computations are performed upon correlations (covariances, mean sums of products) rather than $z$ scores (deviation scores, raw scores). The diagonal elements of $\mathbf{R}$ will contain communality estimates. These are 1.0 in a component analysis but are less than 1.0 in a common factor analysis. Communality estimates (elements of the form $r_{jj}$ in $\mathbf{R}$) are not the same as communalities ($h^2$ values). Alternative ways to define communality estimates are considered in the next chapter.

### Structure Elements

A factor can be correlated with an individual variable using the methods of Chapter 5. The factor structure consists of the PM correlations between each of the $F$ factors and each of the $V$ individual variables, and the individual correlations are called structure elements. The symbol **S** will denote the complete matrix of structure elements. Its columns, which describe the correlations between each variable and a given factor, will likewise be denoted $s_I$, $s_{II}$, $s_{III}$, etc. It is perfectly logical to symbolize individual structure elements as $s$ followed by appropriate subscripts to denote the factor and variable, but we will use the symbol $r$ to remind the reader that it is a correlation. For example, the correlation between variable $X_1$ and factor I is denoted $r_{1I}$. Thus, $s_I$ contains the correlations between each variable and factor I, $r_{1I}$, $r_{2I}$, ..., $r_{kI}$, and so on for the remaining factors. In particular, $r_{1I}$ is the correlation between $X_1$ and the average of all variables in a centroid solution. Depending on the nature of the variables and the method of factor analysis employed, some of the correlations might be high and others low; some might be positive and others negative.

As Chapter 5 noted, the beta weight for a predictor equals its correlation with the criterion (validity) when the predictors are uncorrelated. Consequently, the structure elements in an orthogonal solution are identical to the pattern elements: $\mathbf{S} = \mathbf{B}$, but this will not hold in an oblique solution. Thus, variables defined by orthogonal factors may be described as linear combinations in which the weights are the structure elements. Likewise, correlations may be estimated by the products of corresponding structure elements. These two very important results are stated algebraically as

$$z_j \approx \Sigma r_{jp} F_p \tag{11-3}$$

$$\hat{r}_{jk} \approx \Sigma r_{jp} r_{kp} \tag{11-4}$$

where $z_j$ = standardized score on variable $j$
$r_{jp}$, $r_k$ = structure elements for variables $j$ and $k$
$F_p$ = $p$th value of a series of orthogonal factors
$\hat{r}_{jk}$ = estimated correlation between variables $j$ and $k$

### Successive versus Simultaneous Factoring

Most problems require several factors to explain the data. The number of factors to be obtained is suggested by the first set of structure elements. If all variables have a high correlation with the first factor, this may be the only factor needed. If these correlations are near zero, there may not be any factors in the data. If they are moderately high (e.g., around .60), several factors may be needed. The end of the chapter presents common rules for determining the number of factors.

One way to obtain a series of factors, which is the way exploratory factors are normally obtained, is to define the first factor (I) and partial it from the data (see Chapter 5). The steps needed use the formula for a partial correlation (Eq. 5-14). The only difference is that the covariate is a linear combination rather than an individual variable. By definition, factor I will not only be linearly independent of the individual variables in the analysis ($X_1$, $X_2$, ...) but will also be independent of any linear combinations of these variables, i.e., additional factors. One result of this partialling is that it is possible to obtain a residual covariance matrix. Each element of this matrix ($c_{jk.I}$) may be obtained using

$$c_{jk.I} = r_{jk} - r_{jI}r_{kI} \tag{11-5}$$

where $c_{jk.I}$ = residual covariance between variables $X_j$ and $X_k$ after adjusting for factor I
$\quad r_{jk}$ = correlation between variables $X_j$ and $X_k$
$\quad r_{jI}$, $r_{kI}$ = structure elements for variables $X_j$ and $X_k$ (which numerically equal the pattern elements)

This residual covariance matrix $\mathbf{C}_I$ may be transformed into a residual correlation matrix, which we denote as $\mathbf{R}_I$. However, computations are usually performed on $\mathbf{C}_I$ rather than $\mathbf{R}_I$ because the correlations in the latter present an inflated picture of the residual variance. Nonetheless, Eq. 11-16 is useful in describing the relation between elements of the two matrices. Each element ($r_{jk.I}$) is defined by

$$r_{jk.I} = \frac{c_{jk.I}}{\sqrt{c_{jj.I}c_{kk.I}}} \tag{11-6}$$

Factor II can be defined by any linear combination of (partialled) variables in $X_I$, although some linear combinations are more useful than others, as was true of factor I. This process may be repeated until all $F$ factors have been extracted, and the successive residual covariance matrices may be denoted $\mathbf{C}_{II}$, $\mathbf{C}_{III}$,.... The absolute values of the elements of the successive matrices will shrink toward zero as more of the variance is explained (the RMS error may also be defined as the square root of the average squared residual value). Specifically, all terms must be zero in the last residual matrix in which $F = V$. The average value of the diagonal element of a given residual matrix ($\Sigma c_{jj.I}/V$, $\Sigma c_{jj.II}/V$, $\Sigma c_{jj.III}/V$, etc.) describes the proportion of variance left to explain (by definition it is 1.0 for $\mathbf{R}$ in a component solution because all diagonal elements are unity). The final result will be that the original matrix of correlations ($\mathbf{R}$) can be expressed as the sum of an estimated correlation matrix ($\hat{\mathbf{R}}$) plus the residual covariances that represent error in the model plus unique variance.

This method of successive extraction is the basis for obtaining the uncorrelated (orthogonal) factors of exploratory factor analysis. More than one factor can be extracted in a given step, but the factors extracted at that step will usually be correlated. This process of extracting simultaneous factors, which may be orthogonal or oblique, is characteristic of confirmatory approaches.

## Geometric and Algebraic Interpretations

There are some very useful analogies among geometry, algebra, and factor analysis. A vector can be thought of (1) as a line segment having both direction (orientation) and length (magnitude) in geometry and (2) as a set of numbers, such as test scores, in algebra.

Assume two line segments (vectors) are made to touch at a point so that they form an angle. If they are oriented in the same general direction, their angle will be small.

The cosine of this angle will be close to 1. This cosine can be obtained directly from trigonometry books, most hand calculators, and most computer languages. The more different the vectors are, the larger the angle (up to 90°) and the smaller the cosine. If two vectors are separated by 45°, the cosine of their angle is .71. Two unrelated vectors form right (90°) angles; their cosine will be 0. The cosine of the angle between the two vectors viewed geometrically is totally equivalent to their correlation if they are defined algebraically as two sets of numbers.

Components can be expressed as vectors sharing a common origin which are of length 1 (unit length). Each vector can be thought of as a "correlation yardstick" with the numbers 0, .1, .2, ..., .9, 1 along it. The correlation between any two variables may be obtained by extending a perpendicular line from either vector to the tip of the other. In Fig. 11-1, variable $X_2$ correlates .70 with variable $X_1$, and variable $X_3$ correlates .30 with $X_1$, as can be seen by lowering perpendiculars from $X_2$ to $X_1$ and from $X_3$ to $X_1$. In this figure, $X_2$ and $X_3$ are separated by an angle of 24°. The cosine of this angle (which can be measured with a protractor) is .91, and so their correlation is also .91. If the separation was 0°, their cosine, and consequently their correlation, would be 1. Conversely, if they met at right angles, their cosine and correlation would be 0, and they would be orthogonal.

Angles between 90° and 180° have negative cosines, and so negative correlations are represented by angles between 90° and 180°. For example, an angle of 180° has a cosine of −1, and an angle of 135° (45° beyond a right angle) has a cosine of −.71. Figure 11-2 illustrates a correlation of −.50. Each vector can be thought of as extending in both directions from the origin, so that it has both a positive and a negative direction. The negative direction is illustrated by the dashed line to the left of the origin at the end of variable $X_1$. Usually, only one end of the vector is illustrated, but vectors are understood to have a unit length on both sides of the origin. This permits the depiction of positive and negative correlations.

**FIGURE 11-1**    Geometric representation of the correlations among three variables.

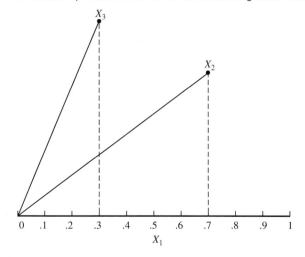

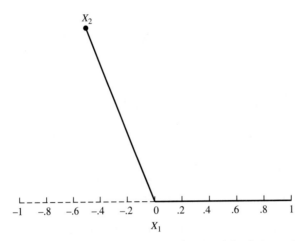

$X_2$

$X_1$

**FIGURE 11-2**  Geometric representation of a negative correlation between two variables.

By extension, a matrix can be regarded as a set of vectors as well as an array of numbers. Any correlation matrix, such as Table 11-1, can be thought of as a matrix of cosines among a set of vectors, where each vector represents one of the variables. The geometric configuration of these variables is shown in Fig. 11-3. Such configurations have an arbitrary frame of reference. That is, as long as the cosines among angles are left the same, the whole configuration can be rotated about the origin without changing the problem. Whereas $X_1$ appears below and to the right of the origin, $X_3$ could appear in this location by rotating all variables to the right through equal angles. The vector for $X_2$ would then slope downward to the left. It is important only that the configuration correctly show the relationships among the vectors.

The correlation matrix in Table 11-1 is an idealization of what is found in practice. It is unusual in that all the cosines (correlations) can be represented in two dimensions (a 2-space). This many correlations usually require more than three dimensions, making it necessary to represent the correlations in a hyperspace or a space of more than three dimensions. The fact that we cannot physically represent spaces of more than three dimensions does not hinder the use of geometric conceptions.

The use of unit-length vectors in physical space to portray correlation matrices as corresponding matrices of cosines is part of a more general geometric analogy. The re-

**TABLE 11-1**  A CORRELATION MATRIX (**R**) FOR FOUR VARIABLES (SIMULATED DATA)

|        | $X_1$  | $X_2$  | $X_3$  | $X_4$  |
|--------|--------|--------|--------|--------|
| $X_1$  | 1.00   | .73    | −.04   | −.67   |
| $X_2$  | .73    | 1.00   | .66    | .05    |
| $X_3$  | −.04   | .66    | 1.00   | .78    |
| $X_4$  | −.67   | .05    | .78    | 1.00   |

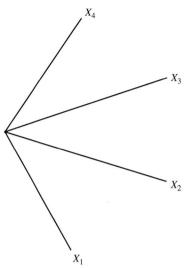

**FIGURE 11-3**    Geometric representation of the correlations in Table 11-4.

lationship between any two variables may be expressed as the cosine of the angle between their vectors multiplied by the lengths of the two vectors, known as the vector product. Variables in a common factor model may assume lengths that are both different from each other and less than unity because only part of a measure's variance is included in the analysis. The length of a common factor is the square root of its variance accounted for. In general, the lengths ($h_1$ and $h_2$) are the square roots of the corresponding diagonal elements of **R** and may be viewed as standard deviations. These diagonal elements, $h_1^2$ and $h_2^2$, are the squared lengths of the corresponding vectors and are variances. The relation between the two variables (vector product) is $h_1\cos_{12}h_2$ in this general case. It is in actuality a covariance (see Eq. 4-10, but note that the order of terms in that equation is equivalent to $\cos_{12}h_1h_2$). For example, if $h_1$ is .8 and $h_2$ is .9, then a correlation of .5 corresponds to a vector product (covariance) of .69 since $(.8)(.69)(.9) \approx .5$. The diagonal elements are 1 in a real correlation matrix such as Table 11-1 and in component analysis, so that $h_1$ and $h_2$ are also unity. Consequently, they need not appear in the vector product, and the covariance reduces to the earlier noted cosine of the angle between vectors, i.e., correlation.

Regardless of whether the vectors are all of unit length (component analysis) or of different lengths less than 1 (common factor analysis) and therefore regardless of what is placed in the diagonals of **R**, **R** can be depicted in terms of vectors in space. The discussion of multidimensional scaling in Chapter 14 will show how factor analysis can be applied to any system of vectors as depicted in Fig. 11-3. This is true regardless of variations in lengths of the vectors and whether the relationship $h_i\cos_{ij}h_j$ is based upon correlation coefficients or other measures of relationship. This geometric model is perfectly general, although we will also note some of its limitations. The component model depiction of **R** (unities in the diagonal) as cosines among unit-length vectors is a highly useful special case.

Factors are often spoken of as dimensions, and factoring is spoken of as dimensionalizing a space of variables, one of the initially stated goals of factor analysis. Imagine, for example, that the vectors for 20 variables all lie in a three-dimensional space. Factor analysis can be thought of as inserting a framework of three new vectors (factors) that explain the correlations (cosines) among the variables. Because all 20 vectors lie in a 3-space, the variables are redundant in the sense that they all can be "explained" by three factors.

In the present example, Fig. 11-4 contains the same variable vectors as Fig. 11-3, but two orthogonal factors have been inserted to serve as the two dimensions of the plane. Their role in providing a frame of reference to these data will be expanded upon in this chapter and the next. Similarly, the next chapter will show how rotating these two factors in the plane will preserve all relations among the vectors. Recall the hypothetical nature of these data; all vectors have unit length in the 2-space, and so two factors perfectly explain the data. If more than two factors are required, the vectors would not have unit length because they would also project into other dimensions.

The following are some useful principles regarding relations between factoring and hyperspace geometry.

**1** If a set of variables can be represented in an $F$-dimensional space, any linear combination of these variables is also a vector in that $F$-dimensional space, e.g., as in the above example where 20 variables fall in three dimensions. This is true regardless of the coefficients in the linear combination. Some of these coefficients can be zero, and some can be negative. In other words, a factor is a vector in the same space as the variables themselves, and factoring thus puts new vectors into the space. The important point is that these new vectors cannot "get out of" the space formed by the variables themselves.

**FIGURE 11-4**     Plot of centroid factors obtained from Table 11-4.

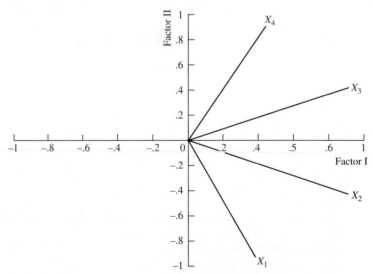

**2** If any set of variables lies in an $F$-dimensional space, any $F$ independent linear combinations of these variables constitutes a basis for the space. The term "independent" means that no vector can be expressed as a linear combination of the other vectors. In other words, no variable has a perfect multiple correlation with any other variable.

**3** It is easiest to visualize a basis when all factors are uncorrelated with one another. The factors (vectors) will all be at right angles to one another, and we are more used to dealing with right-angle coordinate systems than oblique systems. Moreover, if the factors lie in three dimensions, any three uncorrelated (orthogonal) factors will explain all the correlations among the variables.

**4** The number of factors (dimensions) required to represent a correlation matrix defines the rank of that matrix. Consequently, the goal of common factor analysis is sometimes described as finding the minimum rank of a matrix of correlations by a suitable choice of diagonal elements (communality estimates).

**5** The structure element relating a variable to a factor may be represented by the cosine of the angle between the vector for the variable and the vector for the factor. If the variables lie in an $F$-dimensional space, any $F$ orthogonal factors will explain the vectors for all variables. In that case the sum of the squared elements in each row of the structure matrix ($\mathbf{S}$) will equal 1, and the sum of cross products in any two rows of $\mathbf{S}$ will equal the correlation between the two variables (see Eq. 11-5). Thus a row of structure elements can be thought of as a set of cosines between a variable and a number of factors, and a column of structure elements can be thought of as a set of cosines between a factor and a number of variables.

**6** Because the number of factors usually does not explain correlations perfectly, the space of variables usually has more dimensions than there are factors. The factors then form a semibasis (approximate basis) of the space of variables rather than a true basis. Suppose, for example, that 10 variables require 10 dimensions, but only 5 factors are used. Some variables might lie almost entirely in the semibasis produced by the 5 factors, but others might lie mainly outside that space. The sum of squared structure elements for any variable ($h^2$) measures the extent to which that variable lies in the space defined by the factors and is the squared length of a vector in that space of factors. If, for example, the $h^2$ for a variable is .64, the length of the variable in the semibasis (factors) is .8.

As useful as these geometric interpretations are, they may be carried too far. First, there is nothing necessarily geometric about factoring. Factor analysis can be developed and used without ever discussing cosines of angles, dimensions, and the like. The geometric model is a useful isomorphism which may help one understand factoring, but it should be invoked only when it is useful. Chapter 14 and, especially, Chapter 15 will consider some limitations upon geometric approaches to measurement. Second, discussing the rank and the basis for a space can easily mislead one into assuming that these are frequently obtained. In fact, the rank of the correlation matrix in component analysis almost always equals the number of variables because each variable has some unique variance which cannot be explained by other variables. However, these concepts do play an important role in some applications.

The rank of the correlation matrix will probably equal the number of variables even when a small number of factors explains the variables in the population because sampling error usually prevents a perfect fit in the sample correlation matrix. However, investigators rarely try to explain the correlations among variables completely. They are usually more interested in prominent factors with moderate or large structure elements. A variable which correlates highly with a factor is called a "salient" for that factor. A value of .3 is a minimum value for a salient; a criterion of .5 or higher usually is better. In the language of hyperspace geometry, factor analysis is usually employed to establish a semibasis rather than a basis for a space of variables. From a statistical point of view, a good factoring method therefore explains as much variance ($h^2$) of the variables in the smallest space possible. Empirically, a good semibasis is one that (1) is easily interpreted and/or (2) relates most clearly to psychological theories.

## Components of Variance

If a factor model fit perfectly, it would partition the total variance of any variable (1.0 in standard score form) into the three terms of Eq. 11-7.

$$\sigma_x^2 = \text{variance due to measurement error} + \text{specific variance}$$
$$+ \text{common variance} \qquad (11\text{-}7)$$

The measurement error of variable $X_i$ is simply the squared standard error of measurement ($\sigma_{\text{meas}}^2$) from reliability theory and equals $1 - r_{ii}$, where $r_{ii}$ may be defined as coefficient $\alpha$. Thus, if the reliability of variable $X_1$ is .80, its measurement error variance is .20, and the systematic variance (the sum of common variance and specific variance) is .80. Specific variance is nonrandom but cannot be explained by relationships with other variables in the model. Common variance reflects covariation with factors. Although factor analysts differ as to how this is measured, one possible definition is $h^2$. Any measure therefore has some random variance due to unreliability, some variance that is repeatable but specific to the test itself (in the context of the model), and some variance that it shares with other tests.

Most actual analyses make no effort to separate specific variance from error variance. Consequently, these are lumped together and called unique variance ($u^2$). Equation 11-5 reduces to Eq. 11-8:

$$\sigma_x^2 = h^2 + u^2 \qquad (11\text{-}8)$$

A standardized variable's unique variance is $1 - h^2$.

Factor analysis is frequently described as partitioning variables into common and unique variance. Component analysis attempts to explain common variance with linear combinations of the variables; unique variance becomes in effect the residual not explained by obtained factors. We have previously mentioned that most studies allow some unanalyzed common variance to remain in the residual variance. Unfortunately, there is no foolproof way to distinguish common variance from unique variance. Component analysis also allows some unique variance of each variable to be included in the factors, confounding the two sources of variance and inflating structure elements

(Snook & Gorsuch, 1989; but also see Velicer & Jackson, 1990). Common factor analysis attempts to separate common variance from unique variance, but there are several methods for so doing that lead to distinct results in studies where the average communality is low.

Even though $u^2$ is usually not broken down into specific and error variance, a good argument can be made for doing so. If good measures of reliability are available and one is confident about the number of common factors underlying the data, this can be done by placing reliability coefficients rather than unities in the diagonals of **R** and using one of the methods of condensation to be discussed. Failure to make at least a conceptual definition between measurement error and specific variance leads to a common error in drawing conclusions from a factor analysis. Even if a test contains a series of scales which may be described by a single common factor, the various scales need not be redundant. They might be if all their unique variance is measurement error, but this is unlikely. It is quite possible that variance which is specific to a given scale on the test relative to other scales may be predictive of external criteria. For example, one of the scales on a maladjustment inventory might denote somatic complaints, and another scale might denote anxiety. The scale as a whole might be described by a common dissatisfaction factor. However, the somatic complaint scale might have incremental validity in predicting the outcome of, say, pain management. Indeed, whether the scale measures one or multiple factors is largely irrelevant to this outcome. Seeing how much of a difference exists between the reliability, as indexed by coefficient $\alpha$, and the variable's $h^2$, as inferred by using these reliabilities as communality estimates, is one way to make this determination.

In keeping with the principle we espouse that conclusions should not depend heavily on any one method of factoring, reestimate the specific variances using other communality estimates. In particular, put (1) unities (principal component analysis) and (2) squared multiple correlations in the diagonal. Both are standard options in every major computer package. The reliabilities will be smaller than 1.0 but larger than the squared multiple correlations (whose role is explained more thoroughly in the next chapter). Consequently, if the estimates are highly similar under all three procedures, you can feel more confident about the result, assuming your hypothesis about the number of common factors is correct and the reliability estimates are reasonable.

## Types of Factors

The distinction between common and unique factors is a very fundamental, mathematical one. Other important distinctions reflect the number and signs of the salients, which are admittedly somewhat vaguely defined as to magnitude.

**1** A "general factor" is one on which all measures are salients.

**2** A "group factor" is one on which some but not all variables are salients.

**3** General and group factors are collectively called common factors, even in a component analysis, because what they measure is common to more than one variable.

**4** If all salients on a common factor have the same sign, the factor is said to be unipolar.

**5** Conversely, if some salients are positive and others are negative, the factor is said to be bipolar. Polarity may be an artifact of how the variables are scored. For example, if one abilities measure is scored as number correct and a second is scored as errors, they will tend to correlate negatively. In this case, reverse (reflect) the direction of scoring of one of the variables (e.g., the error measure) because readers tend to associate better performance with higher numbers. On the other hand, affirmative outcomes may relate to each pole, particularly in the personality domain, e.g, introversion-extroversion. Introverts actively engage in certain behaviors, and extroverts actively engage in other behaviors. Finally, we will also see that bipolarity is an artifact of initial factor extraction, another major reason for rotation.

**6** A factor with only one salient is called a "singlet factor." For example, the masculinity-femininity (Mf) scale on the MMPI often appears as a singlet because it tends to correlate poorly with the other major scales. Singlet factors are similar to the unique factors of common factor analysis. However, singlet factors reflect an empirical outcome rather than a mathematical constraint.

**7** For completeness, a null factor has no salients.

The goal of finding groupings can be translated into a search for group factors. However, because abilities measures tend to intercorrelate positively, a general factor may also be present. A general factor is often also appropriate, e.g., many believe that there is a meaningful component that underlies all abilities measures. However, one does not know the limits of a general factor, i.e., what doesn't belong to the factor. Differences in methods of rotation will cause a general factor to have a more or less prominent role. Many historic differences in interpretation of data reflect this methodological difference. Bipolar factors are typically difficult to interpret since the factor is defined by the difference between what positively weighted variables have in common and what negatively weighted variables have in common. Many forms of rotation are designed to produce only group factors and eliminate bipolar factors which are artifactual. Finally, singlet and null factors are undesirable outcomes. They indicate that too many factors have been extracted or that a variable has been included which is unrelated to the others in the analysis.

## CONDENSING VARIANCE IN EXPLORATORY FACTOR ANALYSIS

Different methods for deriving exploratory factors may be defined in terms of the ways that weights are used to obtain linear combinations. There are three general approaches to this process. Each has a counterpart in confirmatory factor analysis that will be discussed in Chapter 13.

**1** In a rational approach, factors are defined before analyzing the data. Centroids are the simplest example in which a factor (usually a component) is the equally weighted sum of the variables.

**2** One may seek to optimize some property of the sample data. The most important example is principal component factor analysis. The symbol PrC will be used to denote a principal component. The abbreviation PC is traditionally more common, but most people now associate the latter with "personal computer." Each PrC maximizes the amount of variance that can possibly be explained, among many other useful properties.

**TABLE 11-2**    A CORRELATION MATRIX (**R**) FOR SIX VARIABLES (SIMULATED DATA)

|        | $X_1$ | $X_2$ | $X_3$ | $X_4$ | $X_5$ | $X_6$ |
|--------|-------|-------|-------|-------|-------|-------|
| $X_1$  | 1.00  | .75   | .83   | .32   | .28   | .36   |
| $X_2$  | .75   | 1.00  | .70   | .25   | .31   | .32   |
| $X_3$  | .83   | .70   | 1.00  | .39   | .25   | .33   |
| $X_4$  | .32   | .25   | .39   | 1.00  | .79   | .82   |
| $X_5$  | .28   | .31   | .25   | .79   | 1.00  | .76   |
| $X_6$  | .36   | .32   | .33   | .82   | .76   | 1.00  |

**3** One may use sample data to predict the results in a population. The most popular such approach is maximum likelihood (ML) exploratory factor analysis. It differs from methods like PrC in stressing statistical inference rather than assuming an indefinitely large sample.

Each of these three general exploratory approaches will be discussed in major sections of this chapter, and their confirmatory counterparts will likewise appear in major sections of Chapter 13. The essential point common to all three is that all seek to explain as much about the variables as possible with the fewest factors and thereby best condense variance. Table 11-2 is a matrix of correlations (**R**) generated by the hypothetical Prof. Brown to test the earlier stated hypothesis about the variables forming two groups of factors that measure separable aspects of anxiety. The measures presumed to form the first group (possible anxiety over harm measures) are $X_1$, $X_2$, and $X_3$, and the measures presumed to form the second group (possible anxiety over social embarrassment measures) are $X_4$, $X_5$, and $X_6$. Even though we suggest that the investigator's hypothesis be tested with a confirmatory approach, as in Chapter 13, these data will be used throughout the next two chapters to illustrate exploratory factor analysis, which is the way many investigators would test the hypothesis.

### The Role of the Correlation Matrix

As we have noted, factoring usually begins by computing a correlation matrix (**R**) even though basic equations such as Eq. 11-1 define factors in terms of observations. The **R** should be looked at in four different ways.

**1** Look to see if the data even warrant factoring. Factoring is not worthwhile unless there is a substantial number of large correlations even though determining how many large correlations there are or how large is large is somewhat arbitrary. There are statistical tests for sphericity (Bartlett, 1954) in which all correlations are zero. These test the null hypothesis that there are no factors in the data versus the alternative that there is at least one. Sphericity is far too liberal a criterion. It does not require many subjects and/or variables to reject the sphericity hypothesis even when all correlations are trivially low. (See the section titled "How To Fool Yourself with Factor Analysis" toward the end of Chapter 12.) You will rarely, if ever, obtain a spherical correlation matrix with real data because it requires almost random selection of variables with nearly total unreliability. This does not make the resulting **R** worth factoring. Six of the 15 correlations in the table are at least .7, which suggests that there is enough common variance to examine.

    **2** Look for groupings in the data. These will probably eventually form factors. In the present case, the correlations among variables $X_1$, $X_2$, and $X_3$ are all high, as are the correlations among $X_4$, $X_5$, and $X_6$.

    **3** Look at the signs and sizes within groupings. For example, if all signs are positive, as is true in the example, the variables all probably have something in common and may be given positive weights in the factor. The variables may still have something in common if some variables correlate negatively with other variables, but these variables might be given negative weights. The size of the correlations defines how strongly the factor (grouping) is defined.

    **4** Look at the correlation between groupings to help decide about the type of rotation you will use. If these are all very low, say .3 or less, you will be able to benefit from the simplicity of an orthogonal solution, as we will demonstrate. If these are higher, the strategy is more open to debate, as you will have to make an eventual choice between an orthogonal or an oblique rotation.

    One additional, but less important, thing to note about a correlation matrix is whether the column sums are all positive. If this is the case, as is true in Table 11-2, the matrix is said to have positive manifold. This will usually be true of abilities measures, but not necessarily of personality measures. When this occurs, most exploratory factoring methods will cause the first factor to be a general factor, and all later factors to be bipolar. Moreover, half of the weights that were positive on one of the later factors will be positive, and half negative on another of the later factors, and the same will be true of the weights that were negative. These are examples of bipolar factors, which were previously shown to be difficult to interpret in many situations. They may also be artifacts of the method of factoring.

## Properties of a Factor Solution

The data of Table 11-2 were factored by several methods, and the results appear in Table 11-3 [a similar demonstration appears in Jackson & Chan (1980)]. Chapters 12 and 13 will make further use of these data. We will use the three columns representing the centroid solution as an example of initial condensation.

    **1** Since initial solutions are nearly always orthogonal, the data in the first two columns of the first six rows can be regarded as either pattern elements (regression weights) or structure elements (correlations). They are often referred to as "loadings," but we will avoid this term because it becomes ambiguous in an oblique solution. Variable $X_1$ can be estimated as .77 times factor I plus .53 times factor II, Eq. 11-1; variable $X_1$ also correlates .77 and .53 with factors I and II, Eq. 11-3.

    **2** The $h^2$ value in an orthogonal solution equals the sum of squared structure (or pattern) elements: $.88 = .77^2 + .53^2$. Recall that it may be interpreted as the squared multiple correlation in predicting the variable from the factors.

    **3** The first two columns of the last row contain the factor variance or proportion of variance accounted for by each factor. These are obtained by averaging the squared structure (or pattern) elements over the number of variables, e.g., $.58 = (.77^2 + .73^2 + ...$

**TABLE 11-3** CENTROID, PRINCIPAL COMPONENTS, PRINCIPAL AXIS, AND MAXIMUM LIKELIHOOD STRUCTURE ELEMENTS OBTAINED FROM THE CORRELATIONS IN TABLE 11-2.

| Variable | Centroid | | | Principal component method | | | Principal axis method | | | Maximum likelihood | | |
|---|---|---|---|---|---|---|---|---|---|---|---|---|
| | I | II | $h^2$ | I | II | $h^2$ | I | II | $h^2$ | I | II | $h^2$ |
| $X_1$ | .77 | .53 | .88 | .77 | .54 | .88 | .77 | .55 | .89 | .81 | .49 | .89 |
| $X_2$ | .73 | .51 | .79 | .72 | .52 | .79 | .66 | .44 | .63 | .69 | .40 | .63 |
| $X_3$ | .77 | .51 | .85 | .76 | .52 | .85 | .74 | .49 | .78 | .77 | .42 | .77 |
| $X_4$ | .78 | −.52 | .88 | .79 | −.51 | .88 | .78 | −.49 | .85 | .75 | −.55 | .86 |
| $X_5$ | .74 | −.54 | .84 | .74 | −.54 | .84 | .71 | −.48 | .73 | .67 | −.53 | .73 |
| $X_6$ | .78 | −.49 | .86 | .79 | −.48 | .86 | .77 | −.45 | .79 | .74 | −.49 | .79 |
| Prop. var. | .58 | .27 | .85 | .58 | .27 | .85 | .55 | .23 | .78 | .54 | .23 | .78 |

*Note:* The proportion of variance accounted for by each factor (Prop. Var.) is the average of the squared structure elements. The total variance accounted for is the sum of the individual values and is given in the column labeled $h^2$.

$.78^2)/6$. Some computer programs (e.g., SAS) provide the sum rather than the average. Adding over factors in an orthogonal solution provides the proportion of variance explained by the model as a whole, $.58 + .27 = .85$ in this case. This figure also equals the average of the $h^2$ values. Explaining 85 percent of the variance among six variables with only two factors often implies a good fit of the model, but other considerations also apply.

    **4** Equation 11-2 or 11-4 may be used to estimate correlations. For example, $\hat{r}_{12} = (.77)(.73) + (.53)(.51) = .83$. It is slightly larger than $r_{12}$ (.75), which is characteristic of component solutions, as we will see.

    **5** As noted above, the positive manifold in the original correlation matrix causes factor I to be a general factor and factor II a bipolar factor.

    **6** Although rotation is needed to make the factors more interpretable, the variables proposed to form the physical harm group ($X_1$, $X_2$, and $X_3$) have a similar structure ($r_{jI} \approx +.75$ and $r_{jII} \approx +.50$), whereas the variables proposed to form the social embarrassment group ($X_4$, $X_5$, and $X_6$) also have a similar structure ($r_{jI} \approx +.75$ and $r_{jII} \approx -.50$). This is highly consistent with Prof. Brown's hypothesis.

Although the data in Table 11-3 provide the most important results, they do not provide the only results. The most important additional result is the matrix of residual correlations. If these are not both small and without apparent pattern, additional factors may be present in the data. This does not necessarily mean that the solution is wrong but rather that it is incomplete. Moreover, residual correlations in a component solution are larger in absolute value than residual correlations in a common factor solution with the same number of factors. In the present case, some of these correlations were quite large (>.50). Be careful to distinguish between this matrix of correlations (which SAS refers to as "partial correlations controlling factors," which they are) and the matrix of residual covariances (which SAS unfortunately terms "residual correlations"). The latter consists of differences between correlations which are not correlations themselves. The covariances will be quite small whether or not there is any pattern left to the data, as they can be only as large as 1.0 when a correlation matrix is factored.

## CENTROID CONDENSATION

We have noted that each variable is weighted equally in the centroid method, so that the factor is the equally weighted sum (or average, since they have the same properties in this case) of the variables. The first centroid is therefore the sum of all variables; the second centroid factor is the equally weighted sum of the variables after the overall (observed) average has been partialled, etc. This equal weighting can be applied to raw or deviation scores, in which case variables with greater variance will play a larger role in the sum, or it may be applied to standardized scores, making the raw score units irrelevant. As in any solution, structure weights define the magnitudes of correlations of variables with the factor, and so in this case they are correlations of individual variables with the average (or sum, since they have equivalent properties) of all variables.

The centroid method is basically obsolete because other methods to be discussed have somewhat superior properties. It is not implemented on any major computer package. However, it is useful to describe it briefly because it does have some advantages, especially for the student who is just beginning to explore the details of factor analysis.

**1** It is the easiest method to visualize because it defines a factor as an equally weighted sum of variables.

**2** It is very easy to calculate the solution by hand or with a spreadsheet, as it is one of the few methods that is noniterative. Instructors differ on the value of hand calculation, but both authors learned much about the process of factoring by calculating centroid factors on a small matrix. The appropriate steps may be found in Harman (1976). In particular, the first set of structure elements equals the sum of a given variable's correlations with all other variables (the sum in a given column or row of **R**) divided by the square root of the sum of all the entries in **R**.

**3** Because the factors are not estimated from sample data but defined in advance as equally weighted sums, centroids should be more robust in small samples than factors derived from estimated optimal weights.

**4** The centroid method maximizes the sum of the absolute values of the structure elements for each factor. It is therefore not devoid of useful mathematical properties.

**5** The logic of the centroid method follows directly from the straightforward logic of the correlation of sums (see Chapter 5).

**6** Geometrically, the variable vectors balance in all directions about the centroid. The two factors in Fig. 11-4 are actually centroids. Centroid factor I goes from left to right and can be seen to fall precisely in the middle of the variable vectors. The correlations of each variable with centroid factor I (the structure) are the vertical projections from the tips of the respective variable vectors to the factor axis in any method.

**7** The item-total correlations (*not* corrected for overlap) in an item analysis are structure elements on the first raw-score centroid (see Chapters 6 through 8). The idea of correlating a variable with the sum also appears in generalizability theory (Chapter 7).

## PRINCIPAL COMPONENT AND PRINCIPAL AXIS CONDENSATION

The PrC method was cited as the major example of an approach to condensation that optimizes a property of the sample data. Specifically, it maximizes the sum of squared structure elements so that each PrC explains more variance than any other type of component. Common factor approaches known as principal axes include several variants upon PrC factoring, differing only in the elements placed on the diagonals of **R**. Nearly all the options found in a typical computer package involve some form of one of these two methods, and the maximum likelihood method, considered in the next main section, uses many of the same basic computations.

### Principal Components

PrC analysis involves what is known by the rather foreboding name of "eigenanalysis," the solution to the characteristic equation of a matrix. The matrix in this case is **R** with unities in the diagonals. The mathematical rationale for the PrC method and various computational approaches are discussed in works listed in the Suggested Additional Readings. Although the concepts underlying PrC analysis have been long known, Hotelling (1933) first specified both the rationale and a practicable computational approach. The computations use one of several similar iterative algorithms which are generally easy to program but laborious to do by hand.

If you have been exposed to the multiplication of matrices (this paragraph may easily be skimmed if you have not), the steps to obtaining PrCs are quite simple. Multiply *any* arbitrary vector of $v$ elements into **R**. The result is a new vector. Normalize it (make it of unit length by dividing each element by the square root of the length). Multiply this normalized vector into **R**. The process of repeatedly taking the output vector ($\mathbf{v}_o$), normalizing it, and using it as the input vector ($\mathbf{v}_i$) on the next step will converge in that $\mathbf{v}_o$ will equal $\mathbf{v}_i$ times a length parameter ($\lambda$). At this point either $\mathbf{v}_o$ or $\mathbf{v}_i$ is the first eigenvector. Technically, it does not matter which because only the relative and not the absolute magnitudes of the elements are important. These relative values will be the same for the two vectors, even though computer programs usually output the normalized eigenvector. The $\lambda$ is the first eigenvalue. Multiplying the normalized eigenvector by the square root of $\lambda$ produces the first PrC. This first PrC can be partialled from **R** just as the first centroid factor can to produce a residual matrix. The iterative process can then repeated to provide up to $V$ eigenvectors, eigenvalues, and their associated PrCs.

We will denote the successive eigenvectors as $\mathbf{v}_I$, $\mathbf{v}_{II}$, .... Likewise, the associated eigenvalues will be denoted as $\lambda_I$, $\lambda_{II}$, ..., and the PrCs as $PrC_I$, $PrC_{II}$, .... All three sets of results are commonly provided by major computer packages, but the eigenvectors are largely unnecessary since the data they provide about the relative contribution of the variables is provided in the PrCs. The eigenvalues define the proportion of variance accounted for by each PrC. $PrC_I$ explains the most variance in **R** and therefore **X**; $PrC_{II}$ explains the most remaining variance, and so on.

## Mathematical Properties of Principal Components

Table 11-3 compares these PrCs with their centroid counterparts. These particular results are extremely similar—carried further, the total variances they account for are .8507 and .8506, respectively. A given number of PrCs must account for more variance than that number of centroids, by definition, and the difference can be much larger when factors are not so apparent.

The PrC method is the ideal way to condense variance in many respects. Some interesting and useful mathematical properties of PrC factoring are as follows:

**1** Each factor maximizes the variance explainable from the observed (unity diagonal) correlation matrix (**R**). This has several important implications: (a) The sum of squared structure elements on that factor is as large as possible. (b) The sum of squared structure elements in the residual matrix (RMS error) is as small as possible. In other words, (c) the sum of squared partial correlations obtained from the first residual matrix is at a minimum, and (d) the first PrC explains more of the actual standard score variance in the data matrix **X** than any other linear combination. Each PrC factor thus explains the most variance possible in a sample of subjects.

**2** Any $F$ principal components ($F \leq V$) explains as much or more total variance than any $F$ components obtained by any other method. This fortunate circumstance does not necessarily follow from the first statement above because a method could derive the most variance possible in an individual factor of **R** but not be best for any set of factors. In fact, the PrC method does maximize the variance explained for any number of factors.

**3** Each eigenvalue defines the total variance explained by that PrC, i.e., its sum of squared structure elements. Dividing each eigenvalue by $V$ provides the variance explained by each factor and, since eigenvectors are orthogonal, the sum over the $F$ factors defines the total variance explained.

**4** All component eigenvalues are either zero or positive (within rounding error) because eigenvalues are interpretable as variances.

**5** The number of positive (nonzero) eigenvalues represents the number of PrC factors needed to explain all the variance in a correlation matrix. For example, if only five eigenvalues are greater than zero in a $20 \times 20$ correlation matrix, then (a) five factors provide a complete geometric basis; (b) all residual correlations, including the diagonal elements, will be zero after extracting the fifth factor; and (c) all scores in **X** will be zero after five factors are partialled. Normally, all component eigenvalues are positive. Consequently as many components will be needed as there are variables to reduce the residual matrix totally to zero and thus totally explain the original **X** and **R** matrices. However, since the usual goal is approximation, some eigenvalues may be so small that the associated factors can be ignored.

**6** The sum of the eigenvalues equals the sum of the diagonal elements in **R**, called the trace. The sum of eigenvalues in a PrC analysis equals the number of variables ($V$). Since Table 11-3 is based upon six variables, the trace is 6.

**7** The PrCs are mutually orthogonal (uncorrelated) in two distinct senses. (a) The sum of the cross products of any two sets of structure elements, such as $s_I$ and $s_{II}$, will equal zero, which you may verify with the data in Table 11-3. This is known as geometric orthogonality. (b) the factors themselves are also uncorrelated, known as statistical orthogonality. Other initial and rotated factors may be statistically or geometrically orthogonal, but only PrCs are both. Although the two properties are useful, statistical orthogonality is more important than geometric orthogonality, and the two concepts must be kept distinct.

**8** The product of all eigenvalues in **R** equals its determinant, an important quantity used in the solution of systems of equations and, specifically, in factor analysis as a multivariate measure of variance. Because the number of factors required to explain a matrix of correlations exactly (i.e., the matrix rank) equals the number of positive eigenvalues, at least one root will be zero if there are more variables than factors. The product of the roots, and therefore the determinant, will be zero in this case, but, as we have noted, this is unlikely in a component solution.

**9** The eigenvalues, eigenvectors, and other by-products of PrC analysis have useful inferential properties. Harris (1985, pp. 260–264) provides a particularly good discussion; also see Morrison (1976). For example, one may test that the population eigenvalue corresponding to a given sample estimate is 1 or greater (the reason this test is useful is given below.) Although inferential testing has not been common in PrC, Bartlett's (1950, 1951) test for the significance of a residual correlation matrix is widely used in multivariate analysis. Rippe (1953) developed tests of factor significance (see Gorsuch, 1983; Harman, 1976). However, if you require much inferential testing, you may find the maximum likelihood method, discussed below, to be of greater value.

Note that despite these advantages, the results of the PrC solution, including the residual correlations, are indistinguishable from the centroid solution, which will generally be the case when each variable correlates highly with at least one other variable.

Since the correlations among variables is so important, it is useful to look at two extreme cases in some detail. In one, every variable in the population is perfectly correlated with every other variable so each element in **R** is 1.0. In this case, there will be only one eigenvalue that exceeds 1.0, and its value must be the number of variables ($V$) since that must be the total of all component eigenvalues. Such a matrix contains but one factor. In the other case, **R** is spherical, and so all off-diagonal values equal 0. The sum of all eigenvalues in the population **R** matrix will still be $V$, but this time each of $V$ eigenvalues will have a value of 1.0. However, any sample matrix it produces will not be exactly spherical. The first few eigenvalues will be slightly greater than 1.0, but since the trace of the sample **R** is still $V$, the last few eigenvalues must be less than 1.0 (Cliff, 1988; Gorsuch, 1983; Horn, 1965). Consequently early sample eigenvalues are biased upward and later sample values are biased downward.

We simulated some data to illustrate these points as well as the effect of sample size. Three population data matrices containing six variables were constructed. The first was spherical and thus contained no factors. The second contained correlations of .5 among all variables and therefore represented a single factor. The third contained two groups in which correlations were .5, but correlations between variables in different groups were .0. This therefore represents a two-factor solution. Samples of 50, which is far too small, and 1000, which is probably much larger than a typical investigator would use, were generated. Figure 11-5 shows the results in a series of what are known as scree plots (Cattell, 1966b) that represent the magnitude of each eigenvalue as a function of its serial position. The small-sample data are in Fig. 11-5*a*, and the large-sample data are in Fig. 11-5*b*.

The first thing to note that the spherical (no factor) data are far from flat lines at 1.0. The first eigenvalue ($\lambda_1$) is considerably above this point, and the last eigenvalue ($\lambda_6$) is considerably below it, especially in the small sample. This clearly illustrates the bias in the sample eigenvalues. Also note that the one-factor data contain one large eigenvalue and the two-factor data contain two large eigenvalues, but they appear more

**FIGURE 11-5**   Scree plot for six measures representing no factors (diamond), one factor (square), and two factors (circle). *(a)* Data simulated on a small sample (*N* = 50). *(b)* Data simulated on a large sample (*N* = 1000).

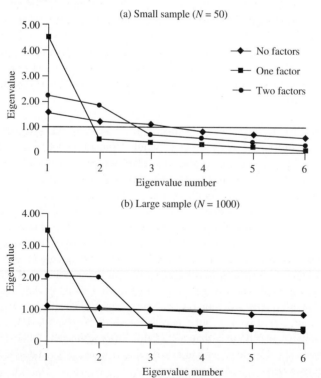

prominent in the smaller sample because the effects of the structure in the data are enhanced by the greater sampling error. These issues play an important role in the issue of deciding how many factors to retain, which we consider at the end of this chapter.

### Principal Axis Solutions

If numbers less than 1.0 are placed in the diagonal positions of **R** and the resulting matrix subject to an eigenanalysis, the result in generically known as a principal axis solution. Differences among the more common methods of determining these communality estimates will be considered in the next chapter. For now, it is sufficient to note that one popular method is to attempt to equate these estimates with the actual communalities by iterating the solution. Values of $h^2$ obtained from a given step become the values placed in the diagonal positions for the next step, and the matrix is refactored repeatedly until the output and input values converge. Unfortunately, this need not occur.

In a common factor solution, the successive eigenvectors still maximize the available sample variance and will reflect the related properties discussed under the heading "Principal Components." The sum of these common factor eigenvalues will equal the sum of the diagonal elements (trace of **R**), but this sum will be less than the number of variables ($V$). Extracting $V$ common factors will therefore lead to some meaningless ones that have large, negative eigenvalues. Common factor eigenvalues can still be thought of as variances accounted for. The only difference is that they are estimates of that limited portion of the total variance which is systematic—the common variance.

Because the variance to be explained is less in a common factor solution than in a component solution, the structure and pattern elements will usually be smaller. Table 11-3 illustrates this expected outcome quite clearly. One way to think of the difference is that the component elements are biased upward because they capitalize upon the error in the measures (Snook & Gorsuch, 1989). As a result, a common factor solution containing the same number of factors as a component solution will (1) estimate correlations better (note that in this case $\hat{r}_{12} = (.77)(.66) + (.55)(.44) = .75 = r_{12}$ to two decimal places), (2) produce smaller residual correlations (in absolute value) and, as a consequence, (3) produce a smaller RMS error. The common factor residual correlations were all less than .24 in the common factor solutions, which is a much more desirable outcome than either of the above component solutions. Keep in mind, however, that the common factor model estimates $V$ with more parameters (the communality estimates) than a component model, and so the gain in fit is not without a price. In addition, the multiple correlations describing factors in terms of variables will be less than 1.0, unlike a component solution (both were .91 here). This is why we will need to summarize the differences between the two basic models in the next chapter.

## MAXIMUM LIKELIHOOD AND RELATED FORMS OF CONDENSATION

We have mentioned that the linear combinations of variables in factor analysis may be defined to optimize some aspect of the expected relation between a sample and a population. This approach is epitomized by maximum likelihood (ML), generalized least-squares (GLS), and, to a lesser extent, unweighted least-squares (ULS) factoring. These methods are all based upon the common factor model. Our discussion will focus upon the ML method, as it its the most popular. Although all these algorithms are extremely complex, their logic is fairly simple. One usually begins by assuming that the individual measures are normally distributed, and so the sample covariance matrix will have a multivariate normal distribution (Wishart, 1928) whose properties may be used inferentially. Because of the importance of inferential testing, we distinguish between $\mathbf{R}_s$, the sample correlation matrix, and $\mathbf{R}_p$, the population correlation matrix. This parallels the distinction between $s$ and $\sigma$ in univariate statistics. The $\mathbf{R}_s$ is a maximum likelihood estimate of $\mathbf{R}_p$ if sampling is random, but (1) $\mathbf{R}_s$ is only one of many possible outcomes that could have arisen had different subjects been sampled and (2) although we are most interested in making statements about $\mathbf{R}_p$, it is unknown.

Assume that $F$ factors have been proposed to account for the interrelationship among $V$ measures. For the present, we assume that the factors are orthogonal so that a $V \times F$ pattern ($\mathbf{B}$) matrix would completely describe $\mathbf{R}_p$ if it were known. Some values, of course, are not permissible—elements in $\mathbf{B}$ cannot exceed 1 in absolute value because $\mathbf{B} = \mathbf{S}$, which consists of correlations. Moreover, some sets of pattern elements are equivalent to other sets of pattern elements even though the corresponding values are different because they are rotations of one another and therefore produce the same estimate of $\mathbf{R}_p$. Ignoring these complications, Eq. 11-2 or 11-4 can be used to estimate the correlations among the variables from the proposed pattern. We will use the symbol $\hat{\mathbf{R}}_p$ to denote this matrix of estimated correlations to emphasize that it is used to estimate $\mathbf{R}_p$ from a given set of pattern elements.

The better the $V \times F$ matrix of pattern elements has been chosen, the closer $\hat{\mathbf{R}}_p$ will be to $\mathbf{R}_p$. Indeed, the goal of all inferential approaches may be stated in terms of estimating unknowns (structure elements in this case) in the best way. Given that observations are in fact drawn from a multivariate normal population, it is possible to estimate how likely (probable) any discrepancy between $\hat{\mathbf{R}}_p$ and $\mathbf{R}_s$ is. ML factoring simply chooses the most probable set of pattern elements. Conventional ML factoring maximizes the correlation between factors and variables and is most traceable to Jöreskog and Lawley (1968). Rao (1955) developed a somewhat different form of ML factoring. If you employ ML factoring, be careful which version you use since they are not the same.

As example of the application of ML principles to factor analysis, assume the correlations among three variables ($\mathbf{R}_s$) are all .49. The investigator correctly assumes that one factor underlies the data. It is much more probable that the three unknown parameters (pattern elements) are .7, .7, and .7 than that they are .9, .4, and −.6. You may use Eq. 11-2 or 11-4 to verify that the first set of three values produces estimated correlations ($\hat{\mathbf{R}}_p$) of .49 which exactly reproduces $\mathbf{R}_s$. In contrast, the three correlations predicted from the second set of estimates are .36 [(.9)(.4)], −.54 [(.9)(−.6)], and −.24 [(.4)(−.6)], all of which are quite different from what was observed. The first set of weights will be the ML pattern, in fact, because of the exact fit; the second set is considerably less likely.

The fit is usually not exact, and so one needs an ML loss function to determine the best fit (least loss). Although this function requires a knowledge of matrix theory to define it exactly, it is basically a summary measure of the dissimilarity between the data ($\mathbf{R}_s$) and the best-fitting solution ($\hat{\mathbf{R}}_p$) and serves a role similar to that of the RMS error. Various iterative algorithms have been developed to minimize this loss function. Two chi-square test statistics may also be derived from the loss function to infer the significance of (1) the deviation of $\mathbf{R}$ from sphericity and (2) the residual variance. Descriptive measures of goodness of fit are also available based upon the relative magnitude of the loss function. The standard errors are, as always, important to consider since they may suggest simpler ways to define the factor and, if they are large, a poor solution. Unfortunately, the ML solution may fail to converge (Jackson & Chan, 1980), unlike PrCs. A second disadvantage is that they are sometimes biased. However, they are more efficient in the sense of Chapter 4 than alternatives.

## Usefulness of ML Factoring

The ML approach represents the inferential tradition in psychometrics and factor analysis in particular. This is in contrast to the descriptive (psychometric) approach that was dominant until the late 1960s as represented by PrCs. Despite this early dominance of the descriptive tradition, the foundations of ML factor analysis have a long history (Wishart, 1928; Lawley, 1940, 1941; Lawley & Maxwell, 1963) that predates the more recent innovations of Karl Jöreskog and his associates (Jöreskog, 1962, 1966, 1969a, 1969b, 1971, 1978; Jöreskog & Lawley, 1968; Jöreskog & Sörbom, 1989). ML's relatively long gestation period was not due to lack of interest in application. Applied researchers had long expressed interest in hypothesis testing (although, perhaps oddly, the inferential tests in PrC, which have long been known, were and are seldom used). The key has been the availability of computers which make the algorithms practicable.

Unfortunately, the user interested in ML as a "litmus test" for the number of factors will likely be disappointed. ML is quite sensitive to trivial sources of variance. Samples of 100 to 200, which are not extremely large in routine research, are quite sufficient to make the residual variance significant and may cause users to accept more factors than are practical. At the same time, simulated data that conform perfectly to the model's assumptions will generally reveal the mathematical adequacy of ML's foundations. The algorithms are also insensitive to *minor* violations of such assumptions as normality (e.g., Fuller & Hemmerle, 1966), as long as the distributions are continuous (Bernstein & Teng, 1989). However, this overdependence upon significance tests is not inherent in the method. Most major figures in the development of ML methods e.g., Bentler and Bonnett (1980) and Jöreskog and Sörbom (1989), have long issued cautions against rigid use of hypothesis testing, but their warnings have gone largely unheeded. It is important to determine whether a small but significant source of variance that causes a model to be rejected is important, unimportant, or spurious.

To take a common example, suppose one tests a set of measures in order to see if a one-factor model fits the data. Because of the number of measures, the set has to be broken down and administered on consecutive days. Unfortunately, tests administered on the same day will tend to form separate factors because individuals who are especially motivated on the first day will do slightly better on tests administered on that day compared to the second day, and vice versa. This could well cause one to reject the notion of unidimensionality even if it contributes only a small amount of variance. Its effects could be considered real but trivial. However, some applications make very specific hypotheses about the number of factors and thus dictate stricter use of hypothesis testing.

Two points limit the practical advantages of ML over PrC. First, PrC estimates are maximum likelihood estimates if all variance is systematic (unity diagonals). This assumption is certainly false in any given study, and so ML estimates will normally be less than 1 and thus differ from PrC estimates, but the difference may be small. ML can be employed with reliability coefficients or other prespecified communality estimates as fixed parameters. However, users most commonly treat the diagonals as free parameters in the sense of Chapters 4 and 10.

Second, all forms of estimation become nearly identical as the communalities increase (see Table 11-3). Since the PrC method is more straightforward and guaranteed to provide a solution, the ML method seldom has any advantage purely as an approach to condensation when nearly all the total variance is explainable. In other words, even though PrC falsely assumes that all variance is systematic, it tends to be either (1) convenient when the factor structure is well defined or (2) inappropriate because the variables intercorrelate so poorly and/or are so unreliable that *no* method of exploratory factor analysis will be fruitful. Moreover, ML solutions can be unstable when variables correlate highly. This is not true of PrC. In sum, proponents of ML favor it because of its inferential properties and its apparent advantages as an estimation device. We feel its advantages in exploration are more apparent than real. It may be useful to show that a factor does not account for a significant portion of variance, as when an investigator proposes that a set of measures are unidimensional and the residual after extracting this first factor is nonsignificant. However, this support of the null hypothesis is often unlikely because ML inferential tests are so powerful. The real power of ML is in confirmatory applications.

In the present case, the ML and principal axis results were nearly identical, which is not uncommon.

## Variants on ML Factoring

The major difference among ML, GLS, and ULS are in the loss function that they minimize. In particular, ULS minimizes the RMS error between $\mathbf{R}_s$ and $\hat{\mathbf{R}}_p$. We have noted that the PrC method does this when there are unities in the diagonal, so that it is a special case of ULS, but ULS also provides solutions in which these values are less than 1 (common factor analysis). ULS is more suitable than ML or GLS for highly nonnormal data. GLS minimizes a weighted sum of residuals. It gives more weight to those variables correlating most highly with the other variables in the analysis (having the largest squared multiple correlation) than to other variables. Browne (1984, 1987) has noted that ML's chi-square estimates are more likely to be inflated when the distribution is flatter than normal (platykurtic) and, perhaps, skewed. The result is a kind of tradeoff between efficient parameter estimation and accurate estimation of chi-square.

## OTHER METHODS OF CONDENSATION

In addition to the methods of condensation that have been discussed, numerous others are available. Most are now only of historical importance. Some are simply computational shortcuts that are now unnecessary with computers. Others are forms of principal axes that differ in terms of their communality estimates. Differences among these common factor models are generally slight and will disappear as the average correlation and number of variables increase. Any method that defines a factor is a potential approach to factor analysis, including, in principle, random definition. However, initial solutions are useful to the extent that they condense variance efficiently, and so one's needs can easily be met with the methods we have presented. Since you may encounter the names of some of these methods, we will describe them briefly.

**1** The square root method (also known as the solid staircase and diagonal method) defines a factor as an individual variable called the pivot. Each variable is therefore represented by its unique variance relative to its predecessors. Thus, factor I is the first pivot variable, and $s_I$ is the vector of correlations between each variable with this pivot. Factor II is the second pivot partialling out the first pivot, and $s_{II}$ contains the correlations between the variables and this second pivot, partialling out the first pivot, etc.

**2** Image analysis (Guttman, 1953) is a hybrid of component and common factor analysis which operates upon scores predicted from the remaining variables in the analysis instead of observed scores. Prediction produces an image-score matrix which can then be factored by PrC or any other approach. Image analysis is like a component solution in that factors are actual linear combinations (of scores in the image score matrix), but it is like common factor analysis in that it attempts to limit analysis to common variance. Its major drawbacks are that (1) structure elements are covariances of the image variables with linear combinations of the image variables, which are more difficult to interpret than variables or factors correlations; (2) it explains the variance common to a particular set of variables, whereas common factor theorists conceptualize common variance in broader terms; and (3) computer simulations suggest that it may not reproduce data as well as other methods.

**3** Minimum residual factor analysis (minres, Harman & Jones, 1966; also see Comrey, 1973) basically circumvents communality estimation by operating entirely on the off-diagonal elements of **R**. The resulting $h^2$ values provide the proper communalities, by definition. The major difference between the two is that Comrey derives one factor at a time, whereas Harman and Jones simultaneously extract a specified number of factors. The criterion for determining sets of structure elements is the obverse of the PrC analysis. PrC maximizes the variance explained; minres minimizes the RMS error, and so it is effectively an ULS solution.

**4** Alpha analysis (Kaiser & Caffrey, 1965; also see Bentler, 1968) maximizes the coefficient $\alpha$ reliability of the factors. It has some of the flavor of the ML method because it seeks to generalize from a sample to a population. However, ML estimation is concerned with generalizing to a population of subjects, whereas alpha analysis is concerned with generalizing to a population of measures. An alpha factor produces the highest correlation with the universe of possible variables and is therefore the best parallel form. Unfortunately, these properties are lost following rotation, as they apply to only the initial solution.

These and other approaches to condensation are presented in works listed in the Suggested Additional Readings. Gorsuch (1983) provides easily understood descriptions of many different factoring methods, and Harman (1976) provides step-by-step algorithms. Also see Thurstone (1947).

## DETERMINING THE NUMBER OF FACTORS

A rule must be used to determine the number of factors to be retained in exploratory factor analysis. This rule is largely independent of the method used to condense variance. Several rules have been proposed, of which the following are the most common, but none is a litmus test.

**1** The Kaiser-Guttman (Guttman, 1954; Kaiser, 1960, 1970) rule retains PrCs with eigenvalues of 1.0 or greater. This is probably the most widely used rule because computer packages commonly employ it as a default even in common factor solutions. The rule simply requires that a component account for at least as much variance as an individual variable. Unfortunately, the rule applies to the unknown population values rather then the observed sample values, and, as was shown in Fig. 11-5, earlier eigenvalues are biased upward. Moreover, the more variables there are, the less variance a factor needs to account for to reach criterion: A factor with an eigenvalue of 1.0 accounts for 10 percent of the variance when there are 10 variables but only 5 percent of the variance when there are 20 variables. Kaiser (1960) presented another rationale: A component will have negative reliability if its associated eigenvalue is less than 1. However, Cliff (1988; also see Gorsuch, 1973, 1983) has called this rationale into question, and it is *not* recommended, despite its wide use, because it tends to suggest too many factors.

**2** Figure 11-5 is a scree plot of successive eigenvalues against their ordinal position. "Scree" denotes the rubble at the bottom of a cliff, which geologists disregard in measuring the cliff's height. Cattell (1966b) used the term analogically to determine the number of factors by noting that the problem in factor analysis is to separate important early factors from the rubble of random error. The plot is therefore used to locate a transition point in the function. Whereas the Kaiser-Guttman rule employs absolute values of the eigenvalues, the scree rule uses relative changes in these values. The scree plot typically suggests fewer factors than the Kaiser-Guttman rule when the average level of correlation is low and/or the number of variables is large. Moreover, these excluded factors are typically unimportant. One should look at the scree plot even if some other criterion is used to determine the number of factors. The main disadvantage of the criterion is its subjectivity. See Gorsuch (1983) for further information.

**3** Horn (1969), Humphreys and Ilgen (1969), and Montanelli and Humphreys (1976) suggest factoring randomly generated data using the same number of subjects as variables as in the real study. The simplest form of their approach is to compare the two resulting scree plots. The earlier eigenvalues for the real variables should be larger than their random counterparts, but the later values should be smaller. The crossover point indicates where the random factors begin. Figure 11-5 illustrates this logic.

**4** It was once common to base factoring upon the proportion of variance accounted for, and computer packages still make this an option. There is no magic number, such as 90 percent, since this value depends heavily upon the average correlation, which in turn depends upon many considerations. Consequently, this rule is basically inapplicable as a device to determine the number of factors, although the data may be relevant on other grounds, e,g., comparing across studies.

**5** There are two broad classes of inferential ($\chi^2$ or $G^2$) tests usable in ML, GLS, and, in weaker form, PrC factoring. One can test for sphericity by testing for the equality of the eigenvalues either in **R** itself (Bartlett, 1954) or in the residual matrices following factor extraction (Bartlett, 1950, 1951). Testing **R** concerns whether there are any factors to be extracted; testing residual matrices tests whether those already extracted are sufficient. In general, these tests often lead to the acceptance of trivial factors (Gorsuch, 1973). As we have noted, statistical significance is necessary but not sufficient to warrant retaining a factor.

**6** One can use the above data to test the significance of extracted factors. For example, assume that the residual $G^2$ following extraction of one factor is 50 and the residual $G^2$ following extraction of a second factor declines to 20. The difference between the two is also a $G^2$ variable with degrees of freedom equal to the difference in degrees of freedom between the original tests. It tests the specific contribution of the added factor in explaining the variables. The comments made about residual testing also apply here.

**7** We have already noted that a common factor eigenvalue must be nonnegative because it is interpretable as a variance. However, this too is a necessary but not sufficient reason to retain a factor.

**8** Various means of testing the residual (partial) correlations and/or covariances have recently gained prominence. Specifically, Velicer (1976; Zwick & Velicer, 1982, 1986) proposed extracting factors to minimize an index based upon the average squared residual correlation (minimum average partial or MAP). The intent is to provide at least two salients per component, i.e., to define group factors whose importance we will consider below. It seeks to have a factor most heavily reflect the covariances (off-diagonal elements) rather than the variances (diagonal elements) of **R**. Velicer has shown that this method correctly infers the correct number of simulated factors very well, and the criterion is incorporated in Gorsuch's UniMult program. Although future research may reveal shortcomings, it appears to be a very sensible criterion.

**9** Any results should make theoretical sense. Quite apart from the above criteria, you have extracted too many factors for the data when fewer than two variables are salients on the rotated factors. Factors of interest describe things that variables have in common. By definition, there must be at least two defining variables for the concept of common to apply. The next chapter considers simple structure, which is a way to define this more explicitly.

## Consequences of Choosing a Given Number of Factors

Exploratory factor analysis is precisely that, a means to explore data for future research. The utility of the analysis depends upon the number of factors retained for rotation. Many users of factor analysis slavishly adhere to the defaults of their computer packages. This often arises because they are not aware of the details of factor analysis. Any method can produce misleading results if used in too rigid a fashion, and always following the defaults of a computer package is one obvious way to be rigid. We strongly urge looking at several alternative factorings, particularly exploring different numbers of factors.

Unfortunately, there is no completely safe way to err in choosing the correct number of factors. Extracting too many factors dilutes the structure of the rotated factors, reduces the number of salients, and thereby makes the resulting factors more difficult to interpret. Adding a component always increases the variance explained, but it lowers the average structure loading. On the other hand, you may miss subtle, but potentially important, facets of the data if you retain too few factors.

The structure of a given PrC is not affected by adding more PrCs, but a rotated factor's structure can change dramatically (a given principal axis structure may change slightly depending upon the method of communality estimation). Moreover, two sets of results that differ only by chance can appear quite different. For example, suppose two investigators conduct identical studies, but their respective values of $\lambda_4$ are 1.001 and .999. They will, respectively, retain three and four factors if they follow the Kaiser-Guttman rule slavishly, but the essential identity of their results can be demonstrated quite simply using methods discussed in Chapter 13.

## CAUSAL INDICATORS

As noted earlier in the chapter, Bollen and Lennox (1991) define a causal indicator as a combination that is the outcome of its indicators, such as socioeconomic status. Another example common to academics is to define merit in terms of scholarly productivity, teaching, and service to the university. Assume that suitable measures of these three terms exist. It can be seen that the considerations applying to a causal indicator are quite different than those that apply to common factors ("effect indicators" in Bollen and Lennox's terminology) and, in usual application, components. Among the differences Bollen and Lennox cite between causal and effect indicators, two stand out.

**1** Causal indicators need *not* be internally consistent. Because, in fact, measures of the three aspects of academic merit are not well defined, there has been much debate about the correlation between scholarship and teaching. From the present standpoint, this is irrelevant. Holding the other two measures constant, someone who has a highly scholarly publication record is more meritorious than someone who is less productive. The same holds for teaching. It is indeed possible for two aspects of a causal indicator to be negatively correlated yet both be appropriate. Negative correlations can arise because individuals have to choose between activities that define the construct.

**2** Breadth of definition is extremely important to causal indicators. It is again easy for many to relate to the idea that equating academic merit with scholarly productivity or, even more narrowly, number of publications, is too narrow by virtually any criterion save those applicable to the definition of common factors. If the same variables defining a causal indicator such as academic merit were effect indicators, they would be considered multidimensional and thus would not belong to the same factor. The need for a causal indicator, like any other composite measure, arises when a single observable fails to capture the meaning of a concept. But the failure in the case of causal indicators is a lack of something systematically measured by the other variables. However, the failure present with effect indicators arises because the observable describes something beyond the construct such as random error or another factor. If academic merit was equated with the sum of the above three indicators, it would become, in effect a component rather than a causal indicator. Strictly speaking, one would have no way to incorporate events that were not provided for in the definition.

We strongly agree with Bollen and Lennox's (1991) conclusion that investigators should be careful in defining the measurement model appropriate to their problem. They also note a problem associated with evaluating causal indicators. The criteria for good effect indicators can be established in terms of the fit of a factor model. Bollen and Lennox suggest that causal indicators be judged by their external correlates. However, causal indicators are often ends in themselves, as in salary and promotion decisions, where the idea of a correlate may or may not be clearly applicable. In such cases, one must rely upon a well-defined domain of content to justify the combination.

## SUMMARY

Factor analysis is a broad set of procedures designed to accomplish a variety of ends. This chapter considered finding (1) groupings or clusterings of variables, (2) which variables belong to which group and how strongly they belong, (3) how many dimensions are needed to explain the relations among the variables, and (4) a frame of reference (coordinate axes) for describing the relations among the variables more conveniently (Chapter 12 considers the additional goal of determining scores of individuals on such groupings).

What have been called factors are derived from combinations of variables, but combinations play different roles in different applications. In some cases, observable variables are viewed as effects of a broader, underlying variable, and so the underlying variable is only partially defined as a combination. In other cases, observable variables are simply transformed because the transformed variables are more useful than the original ones, but the transformed variables collectively have no properties that are not implicit in the original ones. As in the first case, an underlying variable may also be conceived of as broader in meaning than the observables that are combined to define it, but the underlying variable is viewed as the outcome of the observables. Most of this chapter was concerned with the first two of these meanings. Thus, factors may be viewed either as abstractions that have meaning beyond the specific variables that define them, or simply as linear combinations of observables and therefore observables in their own right. This is the traditional distinction between common factor and component analysis. Although some authors include only the term "factors" under the first of these headings, we also show that the second is a special case of the first. One consideration is that practical differences between the two tend to disappear as variables become more highly correlated.

It is most important that factor analysis not be used as a basis for blind inquiry. Successful analyses require variables that intercorrelate highly, are reliable, and are defined on large samples. Marker variables (i.e., variables with known properties) are very useful. In general, considerable care should be given to the choice of variables and subjects.

The distinction between exploratory and confirmatory factor analysis is very important. Exploratory factors are defined to achieve a mathematical objective, such as maximizing the variance accounted for. Exploratory factor analysis consists of two stages. In the first, variance is condensed, but the resulting factors are difficult to interpret. The second stage rotates these factors to make them more meaningful. In confirmatory analysis, factors are defined to achieve substantive criteria (e.g., because a theory states that particular variables are related to that factor), and the issue is how well they fit the data.

The general model relates a data matrix to factors, and variables are expressed as weighted linear combinations of the factors. Common factors relate to several variables, whereas unique factors relate to individual variables. Unique variance is treated as 0 in the component model but is an integral part of the common factor model. The weightings are provided by pattern elements. The communality ($h^2$) of a variable is defined as the squared multiple correlation between it and the set of factors. The average of these $h^2$ values is one measure of how well the model fits, the proportion of variance accounted for. Conversely, one may obtain multiple correlations predicting factors from variables, which describe how well defined the factors are. These multiple correlations are 1.0 by definition in a component solution. Factors are not fixed entities, as they may be rotated to make them more meaningful, but the process of rotation does not affect the individual $h^2$ values nor the overall fit.

The data matrix that is analyzed may consist of raw scores, deviation scores, or $z$ scores, among other possibilities. Choice of data determines what properties of the data affect the outcome. The most common choice is to factor $z$ scores, which eliminates differences among variables in their location and variability. Factoring raw scores allows both to contribute to the outcome, and factoring deviation scores allows differences in variability but not location to affect the outcome. The actual operations are performed upon measures of relationship which, in the case of $z$ scores, are PM correlations. If raw or deviation scores are used, the corresponding measures are mean sums of products and covariances, respectively. The diagonals of the correlation matrix contain what are called communality estimates. These are unities in a component solution and numbers less than unity in a common factor solution, but alternative forms of common factor analysis suggest the use of different communality estimates.

Factors may be chosen so that they are orthogonal (uncorrelated) or oblique (correlated) with respect to one another. If they are orthogonal, the observed correlations between pairs of variables may be estimated as the sum of the cross products of their corresponding pattern elements over vectors. The better the fit of the model, the better these correlations are estimated. Discrepancies between observed and estimated correlations provide a loss function that serves as a measure of fit in several formal models. Structure elements are correlations between variables and factors. In an orthogonal solution, these are numerically equal to the pattern elements, and so they may be used to estimate correlations.

Factors may be extracted successively by partialling each successive one from the data and repeating the process with new factors. This will always provide orthogonal factors. Alternatively, two or more factors may be obtained in a single step by simultaneous factoring. Simultaneous factors may be orthogonal or oblique. Exploratory factors are nearly always extracted successively; confirmatory factors may be extracted either way, but simultaneous factoring is more common.

Factor analysis may be considered from either an algebraic or a geometric perspective. Variables are algebraically vectors because they are sets of numbers, and they are geometrically vectors because they may also be expressed geometrically as directed line segments. Collectively, they form a matrix since a matrix may be defined as a set of vectors. The cosine of the angle separating pairs of vectors is equivalent to their correlation expressed algebraically. Components have a total length of 1.0, and common factors have a length that equals the square root of their variance accounted for in the common factor space they generate. Any set of $F$ vectors forms a basis of the space defined by $F$ factors as long as they are independent; i.e., none can be expressed as linear combinations of the rest. However, they are most easily visualized as dimensions when they are orthogonal because we are most used to dealing with right-angle coordinate systems. In practice, less than a complete basis (i.e., a semibasis) is obtained if it provides a sufficiently good approximation. In addition, one need not think of factoring in geometric terms if it is not useful in a given situation.

The complete common factor model analyzes observed variance into three parts: error variance, specific variance, and common variance. Error variance is unreliability (measurement error), specific variance is systematic variance that is not shared with other variables in the model, and common variance is shared variance. The unique variance equals the error and specific variance. Although it is somewhat difficult to separate error and specific variance, one measure may be obtained by factoring the data using reliabilities as communality estimates. The difference between the resulting coefficients $\alpha$ and $h^2$ values estimates the specific variance, and $1 - \alpha$ estimates the error variance. Even though a set of measures is unifactor, this does not mean that they are redundant because their specific variances may have incremental validity over the common factor(s).

A salient on a factor is a variable that is highly correlated with that factor. Somewhat arbitrarily, a value of .5 is considered high. Different types of factors are denoted by the number of salients and their signs. All variables are salients on a general factor, which makes them difficult to interpret because one does not know what does not belong to the factor. A group factor is one on which some, but not all variables are salients. They are much easier to interpret because they are defined by the common properties of the salients. General and group factors are considered common factors, though not necessarily in the common factor sense. They may be bipolar if some salients correlate positively and other negatively, or unipolar if all correlations are in the same direction. Bipolar factors may be appropriate outcomes of the relations in the data, as when some variables are associated with one pole of the factor and others are associated with the other pole. However, they very commonly emerge as artifacts of either scoring or the method of factoring. Two unimportant type of factors are singlets, which are defined by only one salient, and null factors, which are defined by none. In neither case is it possible to define a unifying property of the factor; their presence suggests refactoring with fewer factors or deleting variables.

There are three main ways to condense data. One is to define the content rationally. For example, in centroid factor analysis, the factor is the average of the variables. Another is to optimize a property of the sample data. This is illustrated by principal component analysis (a component approach) and principal axis analysis (a generic name given to several common factor approaches that differ as to communality estimation). The third major way is to attempt to estimate population factors from sample data. This is illustrated by maximum likelihood analysis. The correlation matrix plays a vital role in understanding the results. One should look (1) at the absolute magnitudes of the correlations to decide whether factoring is appropriate, (2) for groupings of variables in the data, (3) at the signs and sizes of the correlations within groupings, and (4) at the size of the correlation between groupings. If the latter are uniformly very low, say, less than .3, subsequent rotation should be orthogonal for simplicity. If not, the choice of orthogonal or oblique rotation is less clear. The correlation matrix is said to have positive manifold when the sum of each variable's correlation with the other variables is positive.

Centroid condensation is basically obsolete, but it is included here because it appears in other contexts and has some properties of interest. It (1) is easily visualized, (2) is highly suitable to hand calculation, perhaps being a useful way to understand the nature of factor analysis, (3) is robust, (4) maximizes the absolute values of structure and pattern elements, (5) follows from the correlation of sums, (6) provides the balance points of the variables, and (7) appears in item analysis and similar sources, e.g., as uncorrected item-total correlations.

Principal components are obtained from what are called the eigenvectors and eigenvalues of the correlation matrix. Its main properties are that (1) it maximizes the variance explained for individual factor loadings in terms of squared factor loadings; (2) it does the same for the collection of factors; (3) the individual eigenvalues equal the variances accounted for; (4) the eigenvalues are always 0 or greater and never negative; (5) the number of nonzero eigenvalues equals the basis (dimensionality) of the correlation matrix; (6) the sum of the eigenvalues equals the matrix trace (sum of communality estimates) which, in this component case, is also the number of variables); (7) PrCs are both geometrically orthogonal (the sum of the pattern elements for pairs of factors over variables equals zero) and statistically orthogonal (statistically independent); (8) the product of the eigenvalues equals the determinant of the correlation matrix, a measure of multidimensional variance that has other useful properties; and (9) various inferential tests are available. In principal axis analysis, similar properties hold. However, the matrix trace will no longer equal the number of variables, although it will continue to equal the sum of the communality estimates, and large negative eigenvalues are possible. In general, common factor solutions differ numerically from component solutions in that common factor pattern loadings tend to be smaller in absolute value and a given number of common factors will typically reproduce correlations better than a given number of components. However, this is gained at the expense of estimating additional parameters.

Maximum likelihood factors have properties similar to those of principal axis solutions, but they attempt to estimate population parameters and provide more detailed inferential (chi-square) tests of significance. They differ from generalized least squares and unweighted least squares in terms of the loss function they minimize. Generalized least squares may be more suitable in populations whose distributions are flatter than a normal distribution and perhaps skewed. Other methods of variable condensation were considered, but these are basically variations upon the method of principal axes or obsolete for various reasons.

The next issue concerned how to determine the number of factors. Perhaps the most popular rule was devised by Kaiser and Guttman, which is to select the same number of factors (either components or common factors) as the number of principal components whose eigenvalues exceed 1.0. However, the amount of variance a given factor that meets this criterion explains depends upon the number of variables in the analysis. In addition, the earlier sample eigenvalues have a positive bias, and the later ones have a negative bias. There are other problems associated with this rule. Cattell's (1966b) scree criterion involves plotting the values of the successive eigenvalues and separates the early from the late values based on dividing the function into two segments. A variation upon this principle is to generate a random correlation matrix with the same number of variables and sample size and use the point at which the scree plot for the real data falls below the scree plot for the random data as the criterion number of factors. Inferential tests upon (1) the residual variance and (2) the significance of extracted factors are still other possibilities. It has become increasingly popular to infer the number of factors from the data in the residual correlation matrix, specifically the minimum average partial. However, the major criterion is that the resulting factors should be meaningful after rotation. Unfortunately, extracting too many or too few factors can cause problems of this type.

The final section considered the situation in which observable variables are viewed as causes of a composite measure, as when income and education are used to define socioeconomic status. The considerations are different than the usual application of common factor analysis in which the converse is assumed. In this case, internal consistency is of minimal importance because two variables that might even be negatively related can both serve as meaningful indicators of a construct. A second major way in which this situation differs from common factor analysis is that the observable indicators need to be sampled broadly to capture the meaning of the construct. Evaluating the appropriateness of the observables is much more of a problem than it is in common factor analysis. If relevant correlates of the construct are available, it is important to consider the resulting validities. However, causal indicators are also used in evaluations where there may be no obvious criterion. In these cases, one must rely upon careful specification of the construct's domain of content.

## SUGGESTED ADDITIONAL READINGS

Bernstein, I. H. (1988). *Applied multivariate analysis*. New York: Springer-Verlag.

Gorsuch, R. L. (1983). *Factor analysis*. Hillsdale, NJ: Erlbaum Associates.

Guadagnoli, E., & Velicer, W. F. (1988). Relation of sample size to the stability of component patterns, *Psychological Bulletin, 103,* 265–275.

Hammer, A. G. (1971). *Elementary matrix algebra for psychologists and social scientists*. Rush-cutters Bay, Australia: Pergamon Press.

Harman, H. H. (1976). *Modern factor analysis* (3d ed., rev.). Chicago: University of Chicago Press.

Harris, R. J. (1985). *A primer of multivariate analysis*. Orlando, FL: Academic Press.

Hohn, F. E. (1973). *Elementary matrix algebra* (3d ed.). New York: Macmillan.

Huberty, C. J., & Barton, R. M. (1990). Review of applied multivariate statistics text books. *Applied Psychological Measurement, 14,* 95–101.

Searle, S. R. (1982). *Matrix algebra useful for statistics*. New York: Wiley.

*Note*: Gorsuch and Harman are standard textbooks on factor analysis. If you plan to work extensively with factor analysis or any other multivariate procedure, you should become familiar with multivariate analysis and matrix algebra. Huberty and Barton (1990) have surveyed the several books on multivariate analysis that were published around 1988. Hammer, Hohn, and Searle are all books on matrix algebra written for social scientists. Finally, Guadagnoli and Velicer attempt to answer the difficult question "How many subjects do I need?" empirically.

## CHAPTER 12

# EXPLORATORY FACTOR ANALYSIS II: ROTATION AND OTHER TOPICS

## CHAPTER OVERVIEW

This chapter begins by considering the process of rotation or transforming initial factors. Rotations place the variables nearer the factors designed to explain them, concentrate the variance of variables upon fewer factors, and, usually, provide factors that are more nearly equal in importance than the original factors. The problem is first considered from a geometric perspective, using the equivalence of the correlation coefficient to the cosine of an angle. Rotation is simplest with two orthogonal factors. We then consider several orthogonal factors, followed by oblique factors. Oblique rotations often allow factors to fall closer to groups of variables than orthogonal rotations, but they are more complicated; e.g., the pattern and structure become different. Investigators must decide whether the better factor definition is worth the added complexity. We then describe Thurstone's criterion for rotation, simple structure. This led him to the use of reference vectors, which are axes orthogonal to all factors save one. The topic is discussed because users of factor analysis will encounter it, even though the concept is largely obsolete. Rotations are now also usually analytic. We discuss three examples of analytic rotations, quartimax and varimax, which are orthogonal, and promax, which is oblique.

Factor analysis usually concerns variables and factors, but some applications concern individual scores and factor scores. The basic factor analytic model is easily extended to this situation. The goal is to define factor weights that provide these scores. This may be done explicitly in a component solution, but common factor scores can only be estimated, and this estimation is not unique, an outcome known as factor score indeterminacy. Although this may sometimes cause problems, it is not a reason to reject common factor analysis because (1) exact component weights are subject to sampling error and (2) scores on composite variables are usually estimated from salient variables and not explicit weight matrices.

A factor analysis provides a large number of matrices, vectors, and scalars, which we summarize. Despite the large number, virtually everything one needs to know can be derived from the structure matrix (**S**), the pattern matrix (**B**), and the factor correlation matrix ($\Phi$). This reduces to knowing **S** or **B** in an orthogonal solution, as they will be equal and all the correlations in $\Phi$ will be zero.

The next section concerns the common factor model. We suggest that the common factor model is conceptually superior to the component model, as it reflects many users' implicit view that constructs are broader than the measures that define them. Alternatively, the component model is superior in practice because a solution is guaranteed; even the most widely used common factor algorithms may fail to provide a solution.

Communality estimation involves what entries to place in the diagonals of **R**. The larger the numbers placed in these positions, the more variance there is to be explained and, as a result, the more factors that are needed. However, making the numbers too small will produce anomalies such as Heywood cases, in which the factors explain more than 100 percent of a variable's variance. A factorable matrix has the important mathematical property of being proportional to the product of another matrix and its transpose (the second matrix turned sideways). Such matrices are called Gramian. A Gramian matrix actually can be expressed as the product of an infinity of matrices and their associated transposes. For example, **R** can be derived from a matrix of $z$ scores (**Z**), but it can also be derived from structure matrices (**S**) of initial and rotated solutions. The number of factors needed to explain a matrix is the rank of that matrix; communality estimation can be viewed as a way to minimize the rank of **R**.

There are several suggested methods for deriving communality estimates. We first consider unities (component analysis). Spearman's (1904) hypothesis that all tests of mental ability share one and only one common factor ($g$) provides explicit communality estimates as the square of each variable's correlation with $g$. Other commonly used procedures are (1) statistical inferences about rank, (2) iterating the solution until the communality estimates equal the communalities' ($h^2$) values, (3) the squared multiple correlations between each variable and the remaining ones, (4) the internal-consistency reliability (coefficient $\alpha$), and (5) direct estimation, as in maximum likelihood. The last named has become especially popular.

We then compare the component and common factor solutions. Next, we note some difficulties with defining common variance. The general topic continues with an empirical discussion of the effects of the communality estimates as a function of the number of variables and their average correlation. This supports our suggestion that a component model be used to guarantee a solution unless the number of variables is small and the average correlation low.

We have thus far assumed a large number of subjects relative to variables and correlations computed among variables. However, in other situations the reverse is true or occasions replace either subjects or variables as a mode in the analysis. The most common alternative is a $Q$ design in which the roles of subjects and variables are reversed.

This raises the question of whether or not to standardize variables to the same mean and standard deviation. This should not be done if the variables are measurable on the same scale (commensurate) so that differences among variable distributions are meaningful, but should be done if these differences are arbitrary. Newer three-mode factor analytic models are discussed that allow subjects, variables, and a mode like occasions to be included in the same analysis.

The same method of variable condensation need not be used to extract all factors. Ad-lib factoring involves using different procedures to extract different factors. Most commonly, some of the factors are individual variables (pivots, as in the square root method discussed briefly in Chapter 11). Maintaining the orthogonality of these factors with respect to others allows their effects to be partialled.

Just as a factor may be viewed as an abstraction of variables, so may a higher-order factor be viewed as an abstraction of lower-order factors. Examples of this approach include such common tests as the Wechsler scales. We then discuss the many ways that a factor analysis can be misleading. A short postscript concludes the discussion of exploratory factor analysis.

## FACTOR ROTATION

With some rare exceptions (see Bernstein, 1988, for an example), initial factors are usually rotated to make the factor solution more interpretable. As this section will show, proper rotation will

**1** Strengthen the relation between variables and factors in that the factors will better represent variables that belong to it and not represent variables that do not belong to it. Numerically, this means that pattern and/or structure elements will tend to be either very high (close to 1.0) or very low. Geometrically, this means that the vector representing a particular factor will fall closer to groups of vectors that represent particular clusters of variables.

**2** Concentrate the variance shared by two variables that correlate highly on a single factor rather than on several factors. In particular, if the variables correlate positively, the structure elements on the factor they share will have the same sign as their correlation. This pair of variables will tend to have the same sign on some factors and different signs on other factors in the initial solution.

**3** Rotation will tend to level the variances of factors, i.e., make them more nearly equal in magnitude. The most common methods of condensation produce factors that account for progressively less variance and therefore are progressively less important. For example, Table 11-3 indicated that the first PrC accounted for over twice the variance of the second (.58 versus .27). Rotating can produce two factors that each account for nearly equal amounts of variance even though they do not change the total variance accounted for from .85. This process of leveling often makes the numbers of salients on each rotated factor more nearly equal in number. However, most solutions will still tend to contain a few major factors that account for most of the variance and a series of factors of lesser importance.

## Geometric Analogy

The rotation of factors makes the analogy between factoring and hyperspace geome-try most useful. Figure 11-4 illustrated the placements of two centroid vectors (fac-tors) in a 2-space of four variables. There is nothing to prevent one from rotating these two-factor vectors about the origin where the vectors touch. In an orthogonal (uncorrelated) rotation, the initial factors (say, I and II), which are almost always or-thogonal, are each rotated by the same amount to produce rotated factors I′ and II′ (primes will be used to identify rotated factors; although it usually matters which ini-tial factor is identified as I, II, ..., since they are usually extracted to account for pro-gressively less variance, it is arbitrary which rotated factor is labeled I′, II′, etc.). In an oblique (correlated or nonorthogonal) solution, each factor is rotated by a differ-ent amount. The term "oblique" is used because the rotated factors form angles that differ from 90°.

Figure 12-1 illustrates the process of rotation geometrically using the two principal axes from the six-variable problem in Table 11-2. Figure 12-1a contains the initial so-lutions. Note that the two axes are each rather separated from the two groups of vari-ables; indeed, each axis falls roughly midway between the two groupings. Principal axis I thus relates to both groups to an approximately equal extent, as does principal axis II. Figure 12-1b contains two orthogonal factors, I′ and II′, produced by rotating each of the principal axes by 45°. Each of these rotated factors (axes) falls much closer to the groupings than the original factors. Because they are at right angles, they form a new Cartesian (right-angle) coordinate system that can be used in place of the original one. Figure 12-1c contains an oblique rotation in which the two original factors are ro-tated by different amounts. These fall still closer to the groupings, but it is more com-plicated because the coordinate system is not Cartesian. It can be used as a coordinate system, but with more difficulty. However, the two oblique factors each fall closer to the relevant groupings. The outcomes in Fig. 12b and 12c each have advantages and disadvantages that we will discuss later in this section. This geometry would be the same had the initial factors been obtained through the PrC, ML, or any other method; indeed, the ML results look virtually identical to the one presented.

The structure elements for the six variables can be read from the rotated factors just as they were from the unrotated factors by projecting the variables perpendicularly onto each factor (see Fig. 11-1 or 11-2). Each variable's structure element on a rotated factor is the point where the perpendicular line meets the rotated factor. Equations 12-1 provide the appropriate solution when two orthogonal factors are each rotated by $\theta°$, producing a new pair of orthogonal factors.

$$r_{jI'} = (\cos \theta)(r_{jI}) + (\sin \theta)(r_{jII}) \tag{12-1a}$$

$$r_{jII'} = (-\sin \theta)(r_{jI}) + (\cos \theta)(r_{jII}) \tag{12-1b}$$

where $r_{jI'}$, $r_{jII'}$ = structure elements for variable $j$ on rotated factors I′ and II′
$r_{jI}$, $r_{jII}$ = structure elements for variable $j$ on original factors I and II

Note that factors I′ and II′ are each affected by both initial factors. The signs of all the structure elements for a given factor may be reversed, a process known as reflection.

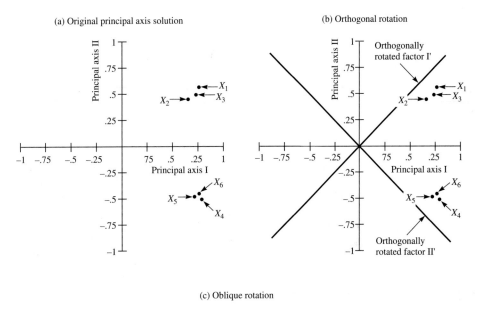

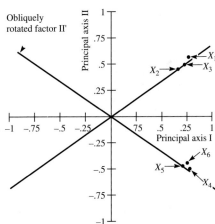

**FIGURE 12-1**    *(a)* Principal axis structure for the data Table 11-2, *(b)* 45° orthogonal rotation, and *(c)* an oblique (promax) rotation.

This is equivalent to rotating that factor by 180°. In addition, Eqs. 12-1 apply to the pattern elements as they are numerically equal to the structure elements.

Table 12-1 lists the orthogonally rotated factor structure derived from the principal axis solution in the previous chapter (Table 11-3). The values may be seen by looking at Fig. 12-1b and turning the page 45°. If you choose to work through the arithmetic yourself, $\sin 45° = \cos 45° = .71$. Two important properties of the unrotated structure matrix also apply to an orthogonal rotated structure matrix:

**1** Each variable's $h^2$ ($\Sigma r_{jp}^2$ over factors), which describes the proportion of its variance explained by the factors, is still the sum of the squared structure elements in its row. In fact, the $h^2$ does not change with any rotation, orthogonal or oblique. Consequently the initial and rotated factors explain exactly the same amount of variance. For example, $h^2$ for variable $X_1$ was originally $.77^2 + .55^2 = .89$. The $h^2$ following the rotation is $.93^2 + .16^2 = .89$.

**2**   The sum of products of squared structure elements ($\Sigma r_{jp} r_{kp}$ over factors) in any two rows of the initial and orthogonally (but not obliquely) rotated structure matrices are the same. Initial and rotated factors explain the same variance, even when the rotation is oblique. This figure is the estimated correlation between the two variables by Eqs. 11-2 or 11-4. For example, $r_{12}$ was previously shown to be $(.77)(.66) + (.55)(.44) = .75$. It is now $(.93)(.78) + (.16)(.16) = .75$. In other words, the two solutions are mathematically "just as good," but the rotated solution typically is more meaningful psychologically because the new factors fall closer to groups of variables and therefore represent them better. Thus, the investigator has every right to rotate if the rotated factors are more easily interpreted than the initial factors, as is usually so.

In summary, the first step in any exploratory factor analysis is to determine the starting points for rotation by condensing the common variance, and the second (rotation) step divides this common variance in a more easily interpreted form. In addition to placing the factors nearer variables, it tends to level the variances explained by each factor. Preferably, the number of salients on each factor will be equated along with the factor variances. In the example (1) initial factor I accounted for over twice the variance as initial factor II (.55 versus .23), but the rotated factors account for equal proportions (.39 each), (2) the rotated structure elements are much less equivocal than the original elements since the rotated elements are either much higher or much lower in absolute value, and (3) each factor has three salient and three nonsalient variables. Mathematically, rotation produces a new, more useful, coordinate system.

## Visual Rotation

The rotation angle of 45° was chosen visually. This is rarely done in application but is useful in understanding the process. First, graph the structure elements. One way to

**TABLE 12-1**   STRUCTURE ELEMENTS FOR THE CORRELATIONS IN TABLE 11-2 FOLLOWING A 45° ROTATION OF THE PRINCIPAL AXES

| Variable | I′ | II′ | $h^2$ |
|---|---|---|---|
| $X_1$ | .93 | .16 | .89 |
| $X_2$ | .78 | .16 | .63 |
| $X_3$ | .86 | .18 | .78 |
| $X_4$ | .20 | .90 | .85 |
| $X_5$ | .16 | .84 | .73 |
| $X_6$ | .23 | .86 | .79 |
| Prop. var. | .39 | .39 | .78 |

*Note:* Prop. var. is the proportion of variance accounted for by each factor. Factor II′ was reflected because all of its original signs were negative.

choose the angle is to place a transparent grid over the graph. Place the zero point of the grid over the zero point of the graph and place the abscissa of the grid along the vector for factor I. This makes the ordinate of the grid fall along the vector for factor II. The key step is to rotate the grid about the zero point until the points representing the variables fall as close as possible to the new (rotated) factors. Determine the angle with a protractor and apply Eqs. 11-1 or, if precision is not needed, read the structure elements for the resulting rotated factors, I' and II', from the grid.

Visual rotation is basically limited to examining two factors at a time. Thus one might start off by rotating I and II to obtain factors I' and II'. Next, rotate factors I' and III to produce factors I'' and III'. Factors II' and III' are then rotated to obtain factors II'' and III'', etc. The more factors there are, the more numerous the pairs of factors. This graphical method may take considerable time when several factors are rotated. Suppose, for example, that five factors are compared two at a time in all possible pairs in the first round of rotations. This requires 10 graphical comparisons, rotations, and computations of rotated structure elements. The full matrix of rotated factors usually does not fully achieve the goals stated above the first time. One usually goes through this process repeatedly, perhaps for as many as 10 to 20 such cycles. Analytic methods of rotation, which are used in practice, will be discussed later, as visual rotation is obviously too time-consuming to do by hand.

### Further Mathematics of Rotation

Although Eqs. 12-1 underlie all orthogonal rotations, the process becomes complicated when there are more than two initial factors, as is usually true in practice. If the original factors are orthogonal, as assumed thus far, the rotations may be expressed as linear combinations of the form

$$r_{jp'} = a_\text{I} r_{i\text{I}} + a_\text{II} r_{i\text{II}} + a_\text{III} r_{i\text{III}} + \ldots + a_F r_{iF} \tag{12-2a}$$

$$r_{jq'} = b_\text{I} r_{i\text{I}} + b_\text{II} r_{i\text{II}} + b_\text{III} r_{i\text{III}} + \ldots + b_F r_{iF} \tag{12-2b}$$

where $r_{jp'}$, $r_{jq'}$ = structure elements for variable $j$ on rotated factors $p'$ and $q'$
$a_\text{I}$, $a_\text{II}$, $a_\text{III}$, . . ., $a_F$ = rotation weights for factor $p'$ on initial factors I, II, III, . . ., F
$b_\text{I}$, $b_\text{II}$, $b_\text{III}$, . . ., $b_F$ = rotation weights for factor $q'$ on initial factors I, II, III, . . ., F
$r_{j\text{I}}$, $r_{j\text{II}}$, $r_{j\text{III}}$, . . ., $r_{jF}$ = structure elements for variable $j$ on initial factors I, II, III, . . ., F

These equations will have three major properties:

**1** The sum of the squared weights for rotation over the initial factors ($\Sigma a_p^2$ and $\Sigma b_p^2$, where $p = $ I, II, III, ..., F) must equal 1.0 for the rotated factors to maintain their original length. This was true both for the rotation in Eqs. 12-1 where $(.71)^2 + (.71)^2 = 1$ and, in a more general sense, $\sin^2 \theta + \cos^2 \theta = 1$. It will also be true for Eqs. 12-2.

**2** The sum of cross products ($\Sigma a_p b_p$) will equal zero. In Eq. 1, $(\cos \theta)(-\sin \theta) + (\cos \theta)(\sin \theta) = 0$.

**3** The rotation weights (values of $a_p$ and $b_p$) can be interpreted as correlations relating the original factors to the rotated factors, so that you can see where the rotated factors come from. If, for example, the weight for rotated factor II on initial factor I is

.95 and a method such as principal components or principal axes was used, the rotated factor will be very similar to the first principal component or principal axis. Since they are correlations, they can also be regarded as cosines of angles of rotation.

These three relations hold regardless of how many initial factors are employed in the rotation. We will denote the matrix of weights used in rotation as $\mathbf{T}$, since it is used to transform factors.

## Oblique Rotations

The rotated factors need not maintain right angles. Oblique factors place factor vectors through clusters of variables to maximize the correlations between variables and factor. The factors are thus conceptually independent but correlated. For example, height and weight are separate dimensions of size even though the two are correlated. Likewise, verbal and mathematical ability are distinct but correlated intellectual factors. Indeed, orthogonality is the exception rather than the rule.

In an oblique rotation, the sum of the cross products of the weights in $\mathbf{T}$ ($\Sigma a_p b_p$) will no longer be zero even though the two other properties will hold: $\Sigma a_p^2$ and $\Sigma b_p^2$ will equal 1, and the magnitudes of the weights are the correlations between the initial and rotated factors (cosines of angles of rotation). Whereas orthogonal rotations rotate each original factor by the same amount, oblique rotations rotate each original factor by different amounts. When an oblique rotation is employed, the correlations among the factors become an important part of the results, giving rise to a factor correlation matrix, defined as $\Phi$ in Chapter 11. The results of the oblique rotation portrayed in Fig. 12-1*c* appear numerically in Table 12-2. These results were derived from a particular analytic procedure known as promax, defined below. The correlation between the factors is .38, which means that the angle separating the two factors is 67°. Letting $\phi$ denote a particular factor correlation, the desired angle is the arc or inverse cosine of $\phi$, often symbolized $\cos^{-1}\phi$.

As can be seen, an oblique rotation generally allows factors to be placed closer to groups of variables since the groups are usually not independent. Oblique factors thus

**TABLE 12-2**   PATTERN ELEMENTS, STRUCTURE ELEMENTS, AND $h^2$ VALUES FOR TWO OBLIQUELY ROTATED PRINCIPAL AXES DERIVED FROM TABLE 11-2

| Variable | Pattern | | | Structure | | |
|---|---|---|---|---|---|---|
| | I′ | II′ | | I′ | II′ | $h^2$ |
| $X_1$ | .95 | −.01 | | .94 | .35 | .89 |
| $X_2$ | .79 | .02 | | .79 | .32 | .63 |
| $X_3$ | .87 | .02 | | .88 | .36 | .78 |
| $X_4$ | .01 | .92 | | .36 | .92 | .85 |
| $X_5$ | −.02 | .86 | | .31 | .86 | .73 |
| $X_6$ | .04 | .87 | | .38 | .89 | .79 |
| Prop. Var. | | | | .44 | .46 | .78 |

*Note:* Prop. var. is the proportion of variance accounted for by each factor. The factor correlation is .38, which corresponds to an angle of 67°. The actual solution was generated by means of a promax rotation, discussed later in text.

generally represent the salient variables better than orthogonal factors. However, several complications arise when factors are correlated.

**1** One no longer has the many simplifications possible with an orthogonal coordinate system. Chapter 14 will consider the relative ease with which distances between points in a right-angle (Cartesian) framework can be obtained when needed, for example.

**2** In an orthogonal solution, all relevant properties were contained in the structure matrix (**S**), as that matrix was numerically equal to the pattern matrix (**B**). The factor correlation matrix (**Φ**) played no role because all factor correlations were zero, by definition. All three become important in an oblique solution, although any one can be derived from the other two. Moreover, the more highly correlated the factors become, the more different **S** and **B** become. Figure 12-2 illustrates this geometrically. It specifically shows how changing the factor correlation does not affect the structure weight but

**FIGURE 12-2**    The relation between a structure element (correlation between a variable and a factor) and a pattern element (regression weight predicting a variable from a factor). *(a)* A more oblique rotation. *(b)* A less oblique rotation.

(a) More highly correlated factors

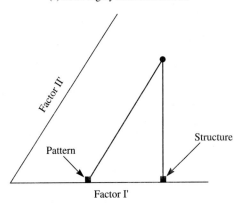

(b) Less highly correlated factors

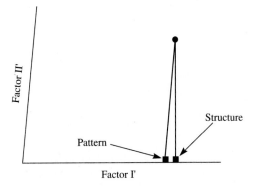

does affect the pattern weight. Figures 11-1 and 11-2 showed how a correlation can be depicted by drawing a perpendicular from one variable to another, in this case, a factor. A pattern element is obtained by drawing a line from the variable to the factor of interest, parallel to all other factors. The difference is illustrated in Fig. 12-2. In particular, note that variables which are not salients in Table 11-2 (e.g., variable $X_1$ on factor II) correlate about .3 with these factors, which is not trivial, even though their pattern elements are essentially zero. The difference becomes more extreme as the factor correlation increases, which may be seen by comparing Figs. 12-2a and 12-2b. Further note that the factor correlation affects only the pattern, not the structure.

**3** The $h^2$ for any given variable is no longer the sum of the squared structure (or pattern) elements. Instead, it becomes the sum of the product of the structure and pattern weight. Equations 12-3, which are formally identical to the computation of $R^2$ in Eq. 5-20, define $h^2$ as the sum of products of beta weights and correlations. These equations also apply to an orthogonal solution but are unnecessarily complex in that situation.

$$h^2 = r_{j1}b_{j1} + r_{j\text{II}}b_{j\text{II}} + r_{j\text{III}}b_{j\text{III}} + ... + r_{jF}b_{jF} \tag{12-3a}$$
$$= \Sigma r_{jp}b_{jp} \tag{12-3b}$$

In particular, $h^2$ for variable $X_1$ is $(.95)(.94) - (.01)(35) = .89$. This is the same as in the orthogonal rotation and original principal axis solution since rotations do not affect the overall fit of the model.

**4** Equations 11-2 and 11-4 describe an estimated correlation in terms of the sum of squared structure elements. However, this is no longer the case; estimation requires Eqs. 12-4:

$$\hat{r}_{jk} = r_{j1}b_{k1} + r_{j\text{II}}b_{k\text{II}} + r_{j\text{III}}b_{k\text{III}} + ... + r_{jF}b_{kF} \tag{12-4a}$$
$$= b_{j1}r_{k1} + b_{j\text{II}}r_{k\text{II}} + b_{j\text{III}}r_{k\text{III}} + ... + b_{jF}r_{kF} \tag{12-4b}$$
$$= \Sigma r_{jp}b_{xp} \tag{12-4c}$$
$$r_{jqi} = b_i r_{i\text{II}} + b_{\text{II}}r_{i\text{II}} + b_{\text{III}}r_{i\text{III}} + . . . + b_F r_{iF} \tag{12-4d}$$

For example, $\hat{r}_{13}$ (.84) may be expressed either as $(.95)(.88) - (.01)(.36)$ or as $(.87)(.94) + (.02)(.35)$.

**5** The variance accounted for by each factor remains the average squared structure element over variables. However, the total variance accounted for is no longer the sum of the individual variances accounted for because they will account for overlapping variance. Table 11-2 illustrates that the sum of the two factor variances (.44 and .46) exceeds the total variance accounted for (.78). However, it is still obtainable as the average $h^2$ value, as these do not change.

None of these differences provides such severe complications as to suggest that one avoid oblique rotations, but it is vital that one understand the difference between the pattern elements of **B** and the structure elements of **S** fully. Pattern elements are always regression weights and may be standardized into beta weights. As a result, they describe the change in a variable per unit change in an factor, holding all other factors constant. This describes the direct (intrinsic) relationship between the factor and the variable. Moreover, they are not correlations, as they can exceed 1.0 when factors are highly correlated. In contrast, structure elements reflect the relation between a variable and a factor, ignoring other factors. This describes the total relationship between the two, which is the product of their direct relationship and the indirect relationship produced by correlations among factors. It is also a correlation, and so its limits are ±1.0.

For example, suppose variable $X_j$ has a strong direct relationship to factor $p$, no direct relationship to factor $q$, but factors $p$ and $q$ are themselves highly related. Pattern element $b_{jq}$ will be small, but structure element $r_{jq}$ can be quite large. We have previously noted that a person of high verbal ability does better than a person of low verbal ability on a test that is mathematical even if their mathematical abilities are equal because of the positive correlation between verbal and mathematical ability. In addition, suppressor relationships can arise where the two have different signs. No interpretation of the data is complete without considering both items of information, and it is a major error to confuse pattern and structure by neglecting the role that factor correlations play in interpretation.

Factor analysts have debated the relative merits of orthogonal versus oblique rotation with almost as much vigor as much as they have debated the relative merits of components and the common factor issue. It is difficult to conclude that one position is "right" and the other "wrong" when they each have advantages and disadvantages. Orthogonal rotations offer the advantage of simplicity at the expense of poorer factor definition; oblique rotations offer the converse. Three rules of thumb may prove useful.

**1** Use orthogonal rotations until you feel confident about the distinction between pattern and structure. A common error made by those who are unclear about the distinction is to conclude that a good fit has been achieved when all the pattern elements are very high or very low in absolute magnitude. The next chapter will illustrate how this may be accomplished with variables that are randomly related. It is also essential that the structure matrix separate the variables and that the factor correlations not be extremely large.

**2** If the factor correlations in an oblique rotation are all very low, use an orthogonal rotation and gain the benefit of its simplicity. Experts differ on "How low is low?" Perhaps all would agree that there is no point to an oblique rotation if all factor correlations are less than .2 in absolute magnitude; we are inclined to suggest .3 as a criterion.

**3** If a factor correlation is very high in an exploratory problem, consider replacing the two factors with one. This will reduce the dimensionality of your solution by 1, often with little reduction in fit. Again, experts differ on "How high is high?," but a correlation of .5 should make you consider the option, and .7 would be a very strong reason. This consideration does not apply to confirmatory solutions. A common factor correlation of .9 in some settings may not be too high when it involves showing that two groups of variables are separable.

Because there are good things to say about both orthogonal rotations and oblique rotations and because both are mathematically legitimate, use boils down to a matter of taste. Most rotations in the early years of factor analysis were orthogonal. From about 1940 until recently, there was a swing toward the use of oblique rotations, but both are commonly seen now. Perhaps the single most popular current method of rotation used in computer programs (varimax) provides orthogonal rotations, but any general-purpose program also provides an oblique option such as promax.

The authors have a mild preference for orthogonal solutions in exploratory analysis because (1) they are so much simpler mathematically than oblique rotations, (2) there have been numerous demonstrations that the two approaches lead to essentially the same conclusions about the number and kinds of factors inherent in a particular matrix of correlations, and (3) it is easier to be fooled by an oblique than by an orthogonal rotation, as will be discussed more fully subsequently. In particular, Prof. Brown's hypothesis about two kinds of anxiety, stated early in Chapter 11, would be supported by any of the approaches considered—the initial solution, an orthogonal rotation, or an oblique rotation. Our preference for orthogonal rotations is "mild," because we will later show how estimating orthogonal factor scores performs the equivalent of additional rotations, causing these scores to be correlated even if the factors themselves are orthogonal. Oblique solutions are also the rule in confirmatory analyses. We can therefore understand why some prefer oblique rotations to place factor axes through dominant clusters of variables. Remember that any criterion for best rotation is psychological rather than mathematical since the initial factors or any other rotation is just as good mathematically, e.g., explains the same amount of variance.

If every solution was as clear as the example we have considered, there would be no argument about the criterion for rotation: Rotation is clearest when each variable correlates with one and only one factor. Unfortunately, this is not always possible. This rule need not require the same number of pure variables on all factors, only that each factor have some pure variables.

## Simple and "Simpler" Structures

Attempts to define an ideal rotation led to Thurstone's (1935, 1947; also see Gorsuch, 1983, pp. 178–179; Yates, 1987) concept of simple structure. Despite its name, simple structure describes the rotated pattern matrix (**B**). The general goal is to maximize the number of small pattern weights for a given number of factors. The two main properties of simple structure are the following.

**1** Each variable should have at least one very small pattern weight over factors.
**2** Each factor should have several variables with very small pattern weights.
Three other properties pertain to each possible *pair* of factors:
**3** Several variables should have one large and one small pattern weight.
**4** Most variables should have small pattern weights on both factors if there are more than four factors.
**5** Very few variables should have large pattern weights on both factors.

These criteria normally require oblique rotations, but they can be applied to orthogonal rotations. The overall objective is to provide clear group factors; a general factor is inconsistent with property 2. and, usually, properties 3 to 5. Not everyone agrees that general factors are undesirable, and so the concept of simple structure is somewhat controversial. Specifically, the tradition that began with Spearman (1904) and, somewhat later, Holzinger and Swineford (1937), prefers a general factor. Many applied problems also suggest a general factor (Gorsuch, 1966).

Cattell (1952) attempted to quantify simple structure in terms of what he called the "hyperplane count." This is the number of essentially zero pattern weights (typically defined as <.1 in absolute value) in the solution. Holding the total variance explained constant, the higher the hyperplane count, the better the approximation to simple structure. For example, both the principal axis and orthogonal rotations for Prof. Brown's hypothetical data have hyperplane counts of zero, but the promax rotation has a hyperplane count of 6 since $X_4$ to $X_6$ have small pattern elements on factor I' and $X_1$ to $X_3$ have small pattern elements on factor II'. Hoffmann (1979) proposed an alternative index based upon the number of salients in the solution. This is not really contrary to the concept of a hyperplane count, as both indices seek to minimize the number of intermediate-sized pattern elements.

It is usually possible to achieve some of the five goals of simple structure but difficult to achieve all of them. Different methods of analytic rotation considered later focus on different goals of simple structure. Consequently it is perhaps better to talk about simpler structure than about simple structure. A rotated structure matrix usually is simpler to interpret than an initial structure matrix, and some rotations are simpler to interpret than others. Generally, one seeks to rotate so that there are some relatively pure variables for each factor, as illustrated in Tables 12-1 and 12-2. Variables $X_1$ to $X_3$ correlate much more highly with factor I than with factor II, and vice versa for variables $X_4$ through $X_6$. This can be accomplished either graphically or, more commonly, with an analytic computer algorithm. Either orthogonal solutions (Fig. 12-1b) or oblique solutions (Fig. 12-1c) may be used, although Thurstone stressed oblique rotations. Moreover, the goal of a simpler structure, unlike Thurstone's, does not rule out a general factor.

## Reference Vectors

Thurstone (1935, 1947) and his colleagues developed a system of oblique rotation in their search for methods for defining simple structure. Yates (1987) describes this process, pointing out that Thurstone's goal was to best dimensionalize the space produced by the variables rather than to find groupings or clusters of variables. Nonetheless, factor analysis can and has been used as a fruitful approach to the identification of clusters.

Instead of placing oblique vectors through clusters of variables, they placed what are termed reference vectors 90° from each of the clusters save one. Figure 12-3 shows both the reference vectors and the promax rotated factors, and Table 12-3 lists the numeric results. In fact, the rotated factors are identical to their appearance in Fig. 12-1c. The principal axes have been deleted for clarity but would be depicted as vertical and horizontal vectors. Whereas the correlation between the rotated factors is +.38, corresponding, as was noted, to an angle of 67°, the correlation between the reference vectors is −.38, corresponding to an angle of 113°. Rotated factors and reference axes bear

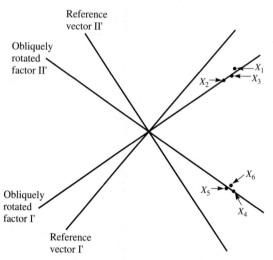

**FIGURE 12-3**   Reference structure corresponding to the promax rotation in Fig. 12-1c.

a complementary relationship to one another, but the relation is more complex with more than two factors. Rotation is rarely done by hand, and the specific need for reference vectors disappeared when Jennrich and Sampson (1966) developed a method for rotating to a simple structure directly from the initial factors, and so the concept is somewhat obsolete. However, reference vectors are reported in a variety of analytic rotations, making users curious what the term means, and reference vectors have some interesting properties.

When reference vectors are placed orthogonally to a cluster, the members of the cluster have near-zero correlations with that vector. Thus, variables $X_4$, $X_5$, and $X_6$ in Fig. 12-3 have correlations of nearly zero with reference vector I', and variables $X_1$, $X_2$, and $X_3$ have correlations of nearly zero with reference vector II'. The correlations of variables with the reference vectors (the reference vector structure) can be calculated by measuring the projected length of variables onto these vectors, as with any other structure. These correlations have two relevant properties:

**TABLE 12-3**   STRUCTURE ELEMENTS FOR THE OBLIQUE
REFERENCE VECTORS DEPICTED IN FIG. 12-3

|  | Reference vector | |
| --- | --- | --- |
| Variable | I' | II' |
| $X_1$ | .88 | −.01 |
| $X_2$ | .73 | .02 |
| $X_3$ | .81 | .02 |
| $X_4$ | .01 | .85 |
| $X_5$ | −.02 | .80 |
| $X_6$ | .04 | .80 |

**1** They are proportional to the pattern elements associated with the rotated factors that actually go through the clusters. In the present case, the constants of proportion that relate the pattern elements to the reference vector structure elements are approximately 1.08 within rounding error for both factors. For example, these terms are .95 and .88 for $X_1$ on factor I', whereas they are .86 and .80 for $X_5$ on factor II'. The ratios, .95/.88 and .86/.80, are approximately 1.08, but they depend upon the factor correlation.

**2** They represent the correlation between variables and the rotated factors, partialling out all other factors.

Consequently, reference vectors are an alternative to the pattern elements as an index of the direct effects of a factor upon a variable. Unfortunately, reference vectors cause more confusion than they facilitate the search for simple structure. They can be particularly troublesome to individuals who are not experienced in the use of factor analysis. If it is not easy to keep initial and rotated factors conceptually separate, a third set of axes emerges as a further complication. When there are three rather than two factors, one does not simply back off a factor vector 90° from a cluster—one backs off a plane 90° from a cluster; when there are more than three factors, one backs off a hyperplane. Reference vectors and rotated factors are sometimes confused in reporting results. A second difficulty is that clusters of variables are usually oblique, but positively correlated, e.g., abilities tend to correlate positively with one another. The reference vectors correlate negatively in this case, as we have seen. It is thus difficult to determine what they mean.

We suggest that any reference vector output simply be ignored and not reported further. Concentrate upon the rotated factors. The best way to accomplish an oblique rotation is to place the factors through clusters. This seldom provides a simple-appearing structure, but it does represent the actual relations among variables.

## ANALYTIC ROTATIONS

An analytic criterion is one that is stated mathematically rather than verbally or subjectively. Perhaps the single most popular is varimax, which we consider shortly. Numerous criteria have been formulated, usually based on some facet of Thurstone's conception of simple structure. Most are prefixed or suffixed by *max* or *min* because they either maximize something good about the rotation or minimize something bad. The "something good" commonly translates into an optimal angle of rotation. All require extremely complex computations and therefore, effectively, a computer program. Gorsuch (1983) provides an excellent discussion of the major existing methods. Kaiser (1970), Kaiser and Rice (1974), and Harman (1976) provide more mathematical details. There are far too many methods, variations on methods, and combinations of methods to discuss even the majority of analytic approaches. Consequently we will present some details of three methods: (1) quartimax, (2) varimax, and (3) promax. Quartimax and varimax are orthogonal, but promax is oblique. Others will be noted in passing.

## Quartimax

Although several investigators were working on essentially the same approach, Neuhaus and Wrigley (1954) are generally credited with developing the first analytic rotation method, quartimax. The quartimax method uses a fundamental consequence of simple structure: The variance of elements in each row of the structure matrix should be as large as possible. If factors can be rotated so that a variable correlates highly with one factor and poorly with others, the resulting variance of these correlations will be relatively large; that variable will be a relatively pure measure of the factor. Conversely, the variance of these correlations will be relatively small when a variable correlates moderately with several factors; it will be difficult to determine what property of the variable relates to each factor. Thus, maximizing the sum of variances in rows of the structure matrix relates variables more closely to factors. Since the variance of any row is affected by the sign of the structure elements as well as their size, the maximization criterion is applied to the squared elements rather than to the elements themselves. A variance is based upon squared observations, which become squares of squares in this case (hence the prefix *quarti*), and the algorithm maximizes the resulting fourth powers (hence the suffix *max*).

The quartimax method is useful when one wishes to stress a general factor (see Chapter 11) with which all variables correlate. However, initial factor I usually provides a better definition of a general factor, and quartimax it not suitable when a general factor is undesirable. Another problem is that the criterion is satisfied when all variables correlate highly with the same factor, which is then a general factor, by definition. Simpler structure is designed to locate clusters of variables; any method that tends to create too large a general factor (e.g., the first PrC) will not reflect clusters. The quartimax method has largely given way to varimax as an analytic orthogonal solution which locates clusters more successfully.

## Varimax

Kaiser's (1958) varimax approached the problem of orthogonal analytic rotation by maximizing the sum of variances of squared structure elements in the columns of the structure matrix rather than the rows, as in quartimax. This tends to produce some high correlations and some low correlations in each column of the matrix, which is an important aspect of simple structure.

Before computing the variance of squared structure elements in each column, the squared elements in each row of the structure matrix are divided by the sum of squares to normalize the variables. This makes them equally important in determining the rotated solution. The proper term for varimax is therefore "normalized varimax." There is an unnormalized version, but it is hardly ever used, and so "varimax" by itself implies the normalized version. There is also a rotation method known as equamax (Saunders, 1962) that is a compromise between quartimax and varimax. It makes factors more nearly equal in importance.

Varimax is the definitive orthogonal solution save that one should not argue against the existence of a general factor based upon a varimax structure alone. Varimax was designed to eliminate general factors (Gorsuch, 1966). In general it captures the meaning of simple structure within the confines of an orthogonal framework very well. The question is therefore not which orthogonal rotation to choose, but whether to use varimax or an oblique rotation. Moreover, if the varimax solution is extremely poor, it is often because no simple, clear factor solution is obtainable. This is the frequent outcome of throwing a polyglot collection of poorly constructed tests together or using too small a sample of subjects.

## Promax

Achieving an acceptable oblique, analytic solution has proven far more difficult than achieving an acceptable orthogonal solution. Many different methods have been proposed, none of which clearly dominates the field [see Harman (1976) and, especially, the excellent summary table on pp. 203–204 of Gorsuch, (1983)]. In general, some tend to produce factors that are too highly correlated, and others produce factors that are too nearly orthogonal. Some methods obtain a weighted combination of the two approaches and let the user choose an "obliqueness" parameter. Still others accept a poorer fitting solution in order to produce lower factor correlations.

The goal of promax (Hendrickson & White, 1964) is similar to that of varimax in that it seeks to maximize the spread (variance) of pattern elements on a factor. Promax starts with an orthogonal structure (e.g., a varimax rotation) and then determines an ideal pattern having greater spread than this orthogonal structure. This is accomplished by raising the elements of the orthogonal pattern matrix to a power. One ambiguity of the procedure is that the user sets this power, which is commonly 4.

To illustrate the principle of forming an ideal pattern by raising elements to a power, consider two variables which have pattern elements of .6 and .3. This ratio is 2:1. Raising both variables to the fourth power changes the individual values to .1296 and .0081 and the ratio to 16:1 ($2^4$:1). The ratio is the more crucial consideration since the process ultimately rescales the rotated factors to unit length. Rescaling preserves these ratios and also makes the absolute differences larger than they were in the orthogonal solution.

The next step is to rotate from the orthogonal solution to the ideal solution. The process involves a method of rotation known as Procrustes that is discussed more fully as a confirmatory procedure in the next chapter. It makes the actual obliquely rotated factors as close to the ideal factors as possible in a least-squares sense. Promax is widely implemented in computer packages. As noted, the structure in Fig. 12-1$c$ and Table 11-2 is a promax solution.

## ESTIMATION OF FACTOR SCORES

Estimating factor scores concerns how one assigns a score to an individual on a composite measure given scores on individual measures. As such, it is a general issue that goes beyond adoption of formal factor analysis, as it deals with the measurement of constructs. The problem may be described by restating the basic equation for the factor model, Eqs. 11-1, so that it applies to individuals by inserting the subject index $i$. This index applies to individual measures, and so $X_j$ becomes $X_{ij}$. However, it also applies to factors, which now become factor scores; $F_p$ becomes $F_{ip}$. It does *not* apply to the pattern weights. These are the same for each individual: A given factor is assumed to explain a given variable in proportion to the magnitude of its pattern weight, regardless of the individual involved.

$$X_{ij} = b_{j\mathrm{I}}F_{i\mathrm{I}} + b_{j\mathrm{II}}F_{i\mathrm{II}} + b_{j\mathrm{III}}F_{i\mathrm{III}} + \cdots + b_{ju}F_{iu} \qquad (12\text{-}5a)$$
$$= \Sigma b_{jp}F_{ip} \qquad (12\text{-}5b)$$

We will denote the complete set of factor scores as $\mathbf{X}_f$. Columns of $\mathbf{X}_f$ will contain $z$ scores, and so the mean values of $F_{i\mathrm{I}}$, $F_{i\mathrm{II}}$, $F_{i\mathrm{III}}$, ..., $F_{i\mathrm{F}}$, will be 0, and their standard deviations will be 1.0. The problem is to determine $\mathbf{X}_f$ given observed scores ($\mathbf{X}$) and pattern weights ($\mathbf{B}$).

Suppose factors are regarded as actual linear combinations of variables, as in an initial or rotated component solution (including image analysis). Factor scores can be calculated in that sample regardless of how many factors are extracted and how many variables there are. Specifically, Eq. 12-6 will provide a score on factor $p$:

$$F_{ip} = w_{1p}X_{i1} + w_{2p}X_{i2} + w_{3p}X_{i3} + \ldots + w_{vp}X_{iv} \qquad (12\text{-}6a)$$
$$= \Sigma w_{jp}X_{ij} \qquad (12\text{-}6b)$$

The complete set of values of $w_{ip}$ forms the factor-score weight matrix, denoted $\mathbf{W}$. The matrix is also called a scoring matrix, and its individual values are often called scoring coefficients. It is available at least as optional output from computer programs. Even though it has the same dimensions as $\mathbf{B}$ ($V$ rows and $F$ columns), it is distinct, though related through one of several complex transformations. This transformation is given in works on factor analysis or multivariate analysis listed in the Suggested Additional Readings for the previous chapter. However, it is often simple to describe. For example, factor score weights for a centroid solution are equal, though not necessarily 1.0, in order to maintain standardization, and principal component factor score weights are the pattern weights divided by their associated eigenvalues ($w_{jp} = b_{jp}/\lambda p$).

The following will hold in a component solution.

**1** If the solution is orthogonal, the correlation between any two columns of $\mathbf{X}_f$ will be exactly .0. If the solution is oblique, the correlation between any pair of columns will equal the factor correlation ($\phi$).

**2** Observed scores in $\mathbf{X}$, say $X_1$, will equal the sum of the factor scores in $\mathbf{X}_f$ weighted by the pattern elements ($\mathbf{B}$) if the components explain all the variance ($F = V$). Otherwise, they are least-squares approximations.

**3** The correlations obtained by weighting the factor scores to estimate the variables will exactly equal the correlation estimated by the various equations we have given that apply to factors, e.g., Eq. 12-2 for orthogonal factors or Eq. 12-4 in the general case.

**4** The multiple correlations obtained in "predicting" each of the $F$ factors from the $V$ variables will all be 1.0 since the factors are exact linear combinations of the variables.

**5** The elements of **W** are unique in that no other set of weights will have all these properties.

**6** Consequently, the elements of $\mathbf{X}_f$ are also unique.

These results follow because components, being exact linear combinations of the variables, have no properties other than those inherent in the collection of variables that define them. Keep in mind that the original scores (**X**) will be approximated only if a full-component model is used ($F = V$), which is normally not the case.

These properties do not apply to common factors because, as was noted early in Chapter 11, common factors have meaning beyond the particular variables that define them. However, that meaning is specific variance, whose content is not clearly defined, plus random measurement error. This causes the multiple correlations between the variables, as predictors, and the factors, as criteria, to be less than 1.0. In turn, it is possible to construct different **W** matrices, and therefore different $\mathbf{X}_f$ matrices, that will estimate **X** and **R** equally well. None will do so perfectly, but this is also generally true in component analysis. Furthermore, even though the factor solution may be orthogonal, the resulting factor scores may be correlated. In a more general sense, factor score correlations will not equal factor correlations. In a still more general sense, properties of factor scores will differ from properties of factors. Also, columns of $\mathbf{X}_f$ in a common factor solution are usually scaled so that their standard deviation is the multiple correlation between the variables and that factor rather than unity for mathematical convenience; their means are still 0, as in most component solutions.

The presence of multiple **W** and $\mathbf{X}_f$ matrices (actually an infinity) in a common factor analysis is called factor score indeterminacy. It is due to the fact that the common factor portion of an observed score, but not the unique portion, is determinate. McDonald and Mulaik (1979) provide a particularly good discussion even though the topic appears in all textbooks on factor analysis. Note that factor score indeterminacy is present even when there is only one factor in the solution. It therefore has nothing to do with the indeterminacy of factors that is present because any given solution can be rotated to another, equally acceptable solution.

How serious a problem is factor score indeterminacy? Schönemann (see Schönemann & Wang, 1972), a long-time critic of common factor analysis, considers it very important, but those who fall more in the common factor tradition feel it is less serious, e.g., McDonald and Mulaik (1979). It will be one of the points we will consider when we provide an overall discussion of component and common factor analysis later in this chapter. For now, we will consider it in the more practical context of how to best obtain composite scores. As we have stressed, the importance of exactly reproducing the original scores and correlations is very limited. Factor analysis is really not concerned with exactness, only good approximation. An exact result, even in the original sample, is usually not at issue because it would be rare to retain the necessary $V$ possible factors. Even if one did, sampling error will cause a **W** matrix obtained from one random sample to differ from the **W** matrix obtained from another random sample. Factor score weights are extremely subject to sampling error because each variable's weight on a given factor is affected by the relationships among all variables and their sampling error. The utility of any result lies in how similar it is to another obtained under similar conditions (efficiency, see Chapter 4) and the (unknown) population values (bias). In the sense that any sample estimate, such as **W**, is intended to generalize, it must be regarded as an estimate, not as an exact result.

As Gorsuch (1983), Harman (1976), and other texts note, good factor-score estimates have the following three properties.

**1** Factor scores should correlate as highly as possible with the factor they represent in the sense that the multiple correlation between the variables and the factor should be high. A measure of verbal ability should correlate as highly with true verbal ability as possible. This is called validity.

**2** Factor scores should not correlate with other factor scores beyond that implied by the correlation among the corresponding factors. It is most simply understood with orthogonal factors: Orthogonal factors should produce uncorrelated factor scores. Accordingly, this property is called orthogonality even though it is not descriptive when the underlying factors are oblique since the factor scores should then be correlated.

**3** Factor scores should not correlate with other factors beyond that implied by the correlation among the corresponding factors. It is also most easily understood in an orthogonal solution—factor scores should not correlate with factors that are orthogonal to the one in question. This is called univocality. For example, if verbal and mathematical ability factors have a correlation of .4, estimates of verbal ability should correlate .4 with estimates of mathematical ability.

There are many algorithms for estimating common factor scores. In general, a given algorithm will optimize one, but not all three objectives. The most common is multiple regression and is so identified in standard computer packages. By definition, it maximizes the correlation of the factors with the factor scores (objective 1). As with many of the issues we have discussed, clear solutions produced by well-defined factors will lead to highly similar results regardless of the method, including component analysis, where determination of factor scores is "exact" in the limited, sample-specific sense. We suggest you explore this issue in more detail by obtaining component and common factor scores from a computer package and exploring their respective properties. Many programs provide alternative algorithms to estimate common factor scores. Standard references, such Gorsuch (1983) and Harman (1976) discuss how to obtain correlations among factors, among factor scores, and between factors and factor scores.

Even though you may use the exact weights of a component solution or the formal estimates of a common factor solution, most applications involve an approximation. Approximations are commonly derived by adding scores of the salients that best define a factor, usually as the equally weighted sum or average (which have equivalent properties). Approximation is like an additional rotation (Gorsuch, 1983). One essentially places a factor axis among salient variables. If the estimation is an unweighted sum, it produces a rotation to the group centroid of the salients. We suggest you choose salients by looking at **W**, rather than **S** or **B**, since factors are being estimated, not variables. The elements in **W** are generally much smaller than the elements in **S** or **B** because of the way the different matrices are scaled.

Compute the correlations among these approximated scores and between these scores and the original variables (oblique multiple group factor analysis, discussed in the next chapter, can accomplish this quite conveniently), based upon both a component and a common factor solution. You may find that the correlations among the approximated scores differ widely from the correlations among the factors. In particular, approximations derived from an orthogonal solution may be very highly correlated. If this is so, the approximation is not very good, and you should use a different approximation. It is a very common error to treat such scores as orthogonal. At the same time, approximations, even equally weighted ones, usually do a good job of defining factor scores if the solution is well-defined.

### Practical Considerations in Obtaining Factor Scores

Determining factor scores is crucial to explicating constructs. For example, suppose two factors do a good job of accounting for the correlations among 20 supposed anxiety measures. The next step would be to relate these factor scores to experimental manipulations and other subject variables. Without continuing investigations of this kind, a factor analysis does little to advance science.

Because one of the better uses of factor analysis is to reduce a larger collection of variables to a smaller set of "potent explainers" (salients), you will probably find that you do not need to use all the measures. For example, three of five verbal abilities measures may suffice to define a construct reliably. It is seldom necessary to use more than three or four variables to approximate factor scores. Additional variables seldom improve the definition of the factor (see Chapter 5), so do not waste time gathering redundant information. As we have noted throughout this book, the weightings used for the composite are typically not critical and equal weighting will probably suffice, though there is nothing wrong with formal estimation (**W** itself, when available).

Conversely, it is usually poor practice to define a construct simply in terms of one variable, just as a singlet factor is usually not very useful. Most variables do not correlate highly with a group factor. Even when a structure element is .70, the variable shares only 49 percent of its variance with the factor. The rest is measurement error, specific variance, and common variance related to other factors. These extraneous sources of variance will contribute heavily to the factor score estimate. At a bare minimum, two variables should be used to estimate a factor. The multiple correlation between the two or more variables and the factor and the factor's reliability will likely be considerably higher than any of their individual correlations. Combining variables averages out their irrelevant variance, at least in part, even when they are weighted equally.

As in formal estimation, look at the multiple correlation of the variables with the factor if a common factor model is employed. Regardless of how statistically significant the factor is by ML or other criteria, a low multiple correlation (say, less than .70) implies that it is not sufficiently well-defined for continuing investigations. Mere statistical significance of a factor is not nearly as important as clear definition from a relatively small subset of the variables. Below this rule-of-thumb value, the factor has more error variance than valid variance. The variables would not represent the factor, and it would be of dubious value to perform extensive further investigation. When the $R$ between the variables and the factor is employed as a criterion, factors may be rejected that appear highly significant inferentially. Of course, even if a factor fails to meet the requirement of a high multiple correlation, it might be reinvestigated with new variables in a new factor analysis. However, it should only be reported when good factor score estimates are available.


## RELATIONS AMONG THE VARIOUS MATRICES

We have introduced a variety of matrices, vectors, and scalars (individual values), which it is useful to summarize. We begin with nine matrices.

**1** The data matrix **X** contains the data with the $N$ subjects as rows and the $V$ variables (measures, tests, observables, etc.) as columns. We have thus far assumed that the scores in each column of **X** have been standardized to a mean of .0 and a standard deviation of 1.0, and so it may also be called **Z**. Some designs require raw or deviation scores, however, especially when one is concerned with making detailed comparisons among groups. Although it is arbitrary in one sense whether subjects appear in rows and variables appear in columns, or vice versa, the mathematics of ordinary factor analysis requires that the matrix be much taller than wide. The end of this chapter considers alternative designs.

**2** The correlation matrix **R** is derived from **Z** and therefore **X**. It contains the correlations among the variables over subjects. If the columns of **X** are not standardized, the matrix will contain covariances or other measures of the relations among variables, and another symbol, such as **C**, would be more proper. Both the rows and columns of **R** correspond to the $V$ measures. The various residual matrices (**R**$_I$, **R**$_{II}$, etc.) are special cases of **R** rather than separate matrices.

**3** The factor structure matrix (**S**) contains correlations between the $V$ variables as rows and the $F$ factors as columns. This may refer to an initial or rotated solution. The reference structure is a special type of factor structure, namely, correlations between variables and factors, partialling out other factors.

**4** The factor pattern matrix **B** contains the regression weights used to predict the $V$ variables as rows from the $F$ factors as columns. The **S** and **B** matrices jointly produce $h^2$ values and predicted correlations. Furthermore, **S** = **B** if the solution is orthogonal.

**5** The factor correlation matrix ($\Phi$) contains the correlations among factors; both rows and columns correspond to the $F$ factors. It will be symmetric since it is a correlation matrix, e.g., the element in the first row and second column will equal the element in the second row and first column because both represent the correlation between factors I and II.

**6** The factor-weight matrix (**W**) contains weights used to determine the $F$ factors as columns from the $V$ variables as rows.

**7** The factor-score matrix (**X**$_f$) contains the scores for the $N$ subjects (rows) on the $F$ factors (columns). If an orthogonal solution is used and scores are obtained from components by exact methods or from certain common factor estimation procedures, scores in the various columns will be uncorrelated in the original sample. However, this will generally not be the case in a new sample.

**8** The transformation matrix ($\mathbf{T}$) contains sines and cosines of the angles of rotation. Both rows and columns correspond to the $F$ factors, but $\mathbf{T}$ is not symmetric.

**9** The *uniqueness* matrix ($\mathbf{U}$) employed in common factor analysis is closely related to the vector of $h^2$ values (see next item). It usually consists of zeros off the diagonal and values of $1 - h^2$ along the diagonal, but the off-diagonal entries may differ from zero in certain more complex models that attempt to estimate correlated error. It has $V$ rows and $V$ columns.

Three vectors are important:

**10** The vector of $h^2$ values contains the variances accounted for in the $V$ individual variables by the $F$ factors. In an orthogonal solution, these values equal the sum of squared elements in each row of $\mathbf{S}$ or $\mathbf{B}$. In general, they are the sum of the cross products of structure and pattern elements over factors. Their complements ($1-h^2$) appear in the diagonal spaces of residual matrices, e.g., the diagonal elements of $\mathbf{C}_1$ contain the complements of the $h^2$ values associated with a one-factor solution.

**11** The vector of factor variances (no symbol has been given) contains the variance accounted for by each factor. These may be expressed either as sums by adding the squared elements in $\mathbf{S}$ separately for each factor (columns) or as proportions by dividing the sums by the number of variables. These relations hold regardless of whether the solution is orthogonal or oblique. The column sums of squared initial structure elements also equal the corresponding eigenvalues in PrC or principal axis solutions.

**12** The squared multiple correlations ($R^2$ values) using variables to predict individual factors can be used to define the reliability of each factor. Factors are linear combinations of observed variables in a component solution, and so the resulting $R^2$ values will always be 1. They will be less than 1 in a common factor solution. Note that $h^2$ values use factors to predict variables, but $R^2$ values use variables to predict factors.

Two individual values (scalars) are important in describing the fit of the model.

**13** The proportion of variance accounted for is (1) the average $h^2$ value in any solutions or (2) the sum of the proportions of variances accounted for by each factor in an orthogonal solution. This is the traditional measure of fit.

**14** The square root of the average squared residual correlation (root-mean-square or RMS error) describes the loss function associated with an unweighted least-squares solution. Related loss functions appear in maximum likelihood and generalized least squares analyses. Loss functions have become increasingly important because of the inferential basis of many newer algorithms. The loss functions determine statistics such as chi-square.

Standard errors of pattern loadings are available from some programs using ML and related estimation algorithms, but this is unfortunately usually not the case.

As we have mentioned, relations among factors need not be the same as relations among factor scores, e.g., orthogonal factors can produce correlated factor scores. A good argument can be made for using separate symbols to define these matrices involving factor scores, but we will not do so for brevity. These parallel $\mathbf{S}$, $\mathbf{B}$, and $\Phi$. In addition, particular methods of condensation and rotation may provide other data, such as the number of iteration cycles required in estimation.

Fortunately, not all these matrices are important to the results of the analysis. Some, like $\mathbf{W}$ and $\mathbf{X}_f$ are important only when one obtains factor scores, which may or may not be the case. Actually, $\mathbf{X}$ and $\mathbf{R}$ are, respectively, obtained before the analysis, and so we need not be concerned with them at this point. The $\mathbf{T}$ matrix describes the rotation process, but it is not important in explaining relations among variables and between variables and factors.

Consequently, $\mathbf{S}$, $\mathbf{B}$, and $\Phi$ are the major matrices to consider. They produce the various other important quantities and directly index the relations among variables and factors. Moreover, only two of these three matrices contain independent information—matrix operations (discussed in standard references on multivariate analysis) provide the third once any two are given. Remember that $\mathbf{S}$ contains correlations between variables and factors and $\mathbf{B}$ contains regression weights to predict variables from factors. When standardized, these regression weights have the properties of beta ($\beta$) weights as discussed in Chapter 5.

## THE COMMON FACTOR MODEL

We have stressed that there has been impassioned, if not acrimonious, debate about the relative merits of the component versus the common factor model. The issue is largely one of considering composites as completely defined by the variables that define them and ignoring unique variance (i.e., making the composite an actual linear combination) versus allowing them to have additional meaning and attempting to separate common from unique variance (i.e., making the composite a hypothetical linear combination). The Suggested Additional Readings for this chapter will refer you to several position papers. We will summarize the main points of the debate in this section, starting with three that we consider paramount.

**1** In principle, the common factor model generally makes more sense: (a) It does not require much experience with tests to know that they are not perfectly reliable, (b) there are many ways to illustrate specific variance, such as the systematic differences between self-report and observational measures of personality traits, and (c) combining variables into a composite describes a broader trait rather than defining it exactly. Indeed, if one assumes traits, abilities, and the like have generality, one assumes a common factor model because the construct is present without having to apply the defining measures. Shakespeare was never given a formal intelligence test, but it is safe to conclude that his verbal ability was high. These features are all present in the common factor model but ignored in the component model. The latter model can lead to the rather counterproductive view that a construct is nothing other than its defining measures, so that it would cease to exist if one of its defining measures became unavailable. Moreover, all variables are given equal weight in a component solution performed upon a correlation matrix, but a common factor analysis of these same data properly gives more emphasis to variables that have the highest correlations with the other variables in the analysis. At the same time, common factor analysis is not devoid of conceptual problems, which we will discuss later in this section.

**2** In practice, the component model is the more reliable: (a) We will shortly review the several measures of common variance, which then determine unique variance by subtraction—their diversity suggests some ambiguity in the concept and (b) you will always be able to obtain a component solution but not necessarily a common factor solution. If you talk to any given proponent of common factor analysis, that individual will tell you why a particular measure of common variance is correct, but different individuals will not agree on which measure. Even more frustrating is when a solution fails to converge or provides any of the anomalies peculiar to common factor analysis that we will consider below. This is especially true when the design involves parallel analyses in different samples and results are obtainable in some, but not all, for no apparent reason. This is *not* necessarily caused by poorly chosen variables. Indeed, some methods of common factor analysis, including the more recently popular ones like maximum likelihood, become unstable because the common variance of one or more variables approaches 1.0. Some of the other possible anomalies are the following. (a) An $h^2$ value exceeds 1.0, called a Heywood (1931) case; (b) an estimated correlation ($\hat{r}_{ij}$) exceeds 1.0 in absolute value; and (c) any multiple or partial correlations among variables exceed 1 in absolute value. Actually, these illegitimate outcomes are unlikely when the $h^2$ values are below about .8, but they cannot occur in component analysis. Most common factor algorithms prevent these anomalies from occurring without causing the analysis to terminate abnormally, but the procedures are often ad hoc.

**3** If an exploratory study is well designed and the sample is large enough to minimize the spurious contributions of sampling error, the conclusions one reaches about groupings and their general relations will be the same in both cases. Many have questioned the value of factor analysis precisely because of the wide range of outcomes that have been reported in analyzing a given set of data by different methods, including, but not limited to, component versus common factor analysis. However, this diversity is usually an artifact of the variables chosen, not the general factor analytic model.

We therefore suggest that an exploratory study generally use a component solution, assuming the principles of good factor analytic design have been followed, in order to expedite a solution (we will shortly note an exception). However, a confirmatory study should generally employ a common factor model, as enough background research should have been done to eliminate many of the problems that can arise. However, this still is no guarantee that a solution can be obtained.

## The Problem of Communality Estimation

A common factor analysis requires a way to provide communality estimates, diagonal entries in **R**. In general, the larger these numbers are, the more trivial and/or spurious factors will appear. But the smaller they are, the greater the likelihood of an anomalous outcome, e.g., a Heywood case. The issue of communality estimation began with Spearman (1904). His general factor hypothesis, considered in more detail in the next chapter, was that all measures of intelligence reflect a single, error-free construct or general factor ($g$). In other words, $g$ is a true score. The hypothesis is a fascinating example of how a specific substantive theory gave rise to a mathematical model of the broadest possible application. It was sufficiently explicit to allow communality estimation designed to separate common and unique variance. The logic applies to any set of measures that are assumed to reflect only one common factor and is easily extended to the multifactor case.

## Factorable Matrices

It is tempting to ask why one cannot simply use any values in the diagonals and not worry about communality estimation. The answer in part is that these numbers represent the proportion of systematic variance assumed by the model, and so they are highly meaningful parameters, but there is another important consideration. Factor analysis can further be shown to require a symmetric matrix, none of whose eigenvalues are negative. Such matrices are called Gramian. This involves the "analysis" part of factor analysis. The total variance is decomposed into additive parts, but (1) eigenvalues define variances and (2) variances must not be negative. Further matrix theory states the following.

**1** A Gramian matrix is always proportional to the product of a second matrix with its transpose, which is the matrix turned on its side. The constant of proportionality is usually $1/N$. You do not need to know how to perform matrix multiplication, but **R** is always Gramian if unities are in the diagonal, because it is proportional to the product of **Z** and the transpose of **Z**.

**2** Any Gramian matrix will also be the product of an infinite number of other matrices multiplied by their transposes. Thus, **R** can be expressed as the product of any number of **B** or **S** matrices derived either from initial solutions or rotations as long as the solution is orthogonal (if it is oblique, the equation becomes slightly complicated). This follows from expressing Eq. 11-2 or 11-4 as a matrix multiplication.

**3** Even though **R**, with unities in the diagonal, will be Gramian by definition, so will other matrices. For example, the covariance matrix (**C**) with variances in the diagonal is also Gramian since it is derived from the product of a matrix of deviation scores with its transpose. We discussed these options in the previous chapter—the point is that mean sum-of-products or covariance matrices are just as factorable as correlation matrices.

**4** A matrix such as **R** may remain Gramian even though smaller numbers are used in the diagonals. However, such anomalous outcomes as Heywood cases arise when the communality estimates are too small. One approach to factor analysis is to choose numbers that will make the rank as small as possible while maintaining Gramian properties.

## Matrix Rank

We defined the rank of a correlation matrix in Chapter 11 as the number of factors required to explain all the correlations exactly. We further noted that the rank equals the number of linear combinations required to serve as a basis for a space when correlations are considered as cosines among vectors. Thurstone (1947) was the first to conceptualize the problem of factor analysis in terms of matrix rank. He saw that Spearman's g produced a correlation matrix of rank 1. Because most correlation matrices contain more than one factor, the rank of **R** determines the number of common factors needed. Thus, if five common factors could entirely explain **R** so that the coefficients in the fifth residual matrix were all zeros, the rank of the **R** in the diagonals would be 5. However, **R** must contain communality estimates and not unities for this to occur.

Unities in the diagonal cause the matrix to be of full rank—requiring as many factors as there are variables.

Although the concept of rank is mathematically important and provides a useful way to think about common factor analysis, there are numerous difficulties in putting this concept to actual use. First, sampling error will cause the rank of **R** to exceed $F$ even though $F$ factors underlie the population data. Second, if one were to force entries into the diagonal spaces to achieve fit, solving the necessary equations would require an inordinately large number of factors (Harman, 1976). Even when one places various restrictions on the nature of **R**, the rank required to find exact diagonal elements is frequently more than half the number of variables. Thus, finding communality estimates to fit a sample **R** matrix might require 10 or more factors to explain the correlations among only 20 variables.

Because of both sampling error and the very large number of factors required to fit any rank exactly, determining the number of factors required in a particular problem obviously involves finding a good rather than a perfect fit to the data. When unities are placed in the diagonals of **R** and some method of condensation is applied, such as PrC, the rank nearly always equals the number of variables, even though many of the factors explain trivial amounts of variance. This is also usually true when communalities estimates are placed in the diagonals. However, residual coefficients usually become very small after only a small number of common factors are extracted.

The concept of exact rank is mainly useful in pointing out the need for efficient methods of estimating the number of common factors required in particular problems, but the idea of approximate rank is more fruitful since it recognizes how sampling error may cause a fit to be inexact. The basic idea is to make the communality estimates large enough to maintain the Gramian properties of the matrix but small enough for the matrix not to be of full rank.

## Unities as Communality Estimates

Most exploratory analyses begin with a preliminary component analysis; i.e., the diagonal entries of **R** are 1s. Even though this section is concerned with common factor solutions, there are at least three good reasons for using unities as communality estimates, i.e., a component solution.

**1** The actual correlation of any variable with itself is 1, and so the diagonal elements of any real correlation matrix are unities.

**2** The formulas for the correlation of sums, Eqs. 5-9, require that structure elements be computed with unities placed in the diagonals of **R**. If anything other than unities is placed in these spaces, one is not correlating an actual variable with a linear combination of actual variables.

**3** As we have noted, the process guarantees a solution. The matrix will always be Gramian, and any of the rules of the previous chapter may be used to define the number of factors to be retained for rotation.

However, the general goal of common factor analysis to separate common and unique variance is not clearly achieved when unities are placed in diagonals of the correlation matrix. The two sources become somewhat mixed because each variable's uniqueness contributes to determining the various factors. Furthermore, the fact that one is not correlating variables with actual linear combinations is not necessarily a fault in common factor analysis.

### Communalities Derived from Hypotheses

Spearman's (1904) general factor hypothesis implies that if a single factor ($g$), accounts for all the correlations in $\mathbf{R}$, the structure matrix ($\mathbf{S}$) will, by definition, consist of a single column. Products of these structure elements will equal the correlations (and not merely the estimates) by Eq. 11-4 (or Eq. 11-2, since $\mathbf{S} = \mathbf{B}$ in a unifactor solution). Thus, $r_{12}$ will equal $r_{1I}r_{2I}$. However, this same logic leads to the expectation that the successive diagonal elements of $\mathbf{R}$, $r_{11}$, $r_{22}$, ..., will equal $r_{1I}^2$, $r_{2I}^2$, ..., rather than 1. In other words, the communality estimate for any variable is simply its squared structure element in $\mathbf{S}$. A variable would have to correlate perfectly with $g$ for its diagonal term to be 1, which is contrary to the assumption that the observed measures are fallible.

If $\mathbf{R}$ can be explained by one general factor but unities (or any number greater than the squared structure elements) are placed in the diagonals, more than one factor will be needed to explain the data, as the elements in the first residual matrix will clearly differ from zero. In fact, as many factors will be required as there are variables with unities in the diagonal. There will be a general factor, and the remaining factors will tend to explain rather small percentages of variance. However, if the squared elements in $\mathbf{S}$ are placed in the diagonals, a single factor *can* explain the data. Conversely, if numbers less than the squared structure elements are placed in the diagonal, anomalies such as Heywood cases will arise. As we have noted, most computer programs take some corrective steps, but some general-purpose matrix algebra will illustrate the outcome.

You can illustrate these results yourself very simply as follows.

**1** Make up a column of $V$ numbers to represent $\mathbf{S}$ (by convention, vectors are represented as columns of numbers, and so it is good practice to conform to this convention). These can be any numbers between +1 and −1, as they are correlations. They can be chosen at random, for example. Although it is not necessary, most should clearly differ from 0.

**2** Determine element $r_{ij}$ of $\mathbf{R}$, including the diagonal elements, as the product of elements $i$ and $j$ in $\mathbf{S}$.

**3** Factor the data using any major computer package. All major programs let you enter a correlation matrix as input instead of raw data, but the procedures vary from program to program. Make sure that the program will use the diagonal values you have specified as the communality estimates; i.e., do not allow the program to iterate. Specify the number of factors as $V$. This program will probably perform an eigenanalysis upon $\mathbf{R}$.

**4** Your result should be that the first factor consists of the initial values in $\mathbf{S}$. The associated eigenvalue ($\lambda_1$) will be the sum of squared values in $\mathbf{S}$, and the pattern will be the values of $S$ (since $S = B$). All the remaining eigenvalues will be 0, although you will probably see numbers reported for the patterns on the remaining factors. Other properties will follow the discussion of principal axis analysis provided in Chapter 11.

**5** Now repeat step 4, using values of 1.0 in the diagonals. This time, all the $V$ eigenvalues will exceed 0. You also will not reproduce $S$ with a single factor.

**6** Repeat the analysis a third time using values less than the squared structure elements. This is primarily an exercise in seeing how the program handles anomalous input, and so the results may vary from program to program.

Artificial matrices are often constructed to test the effectiveness of a particular method of common factor analysis, and the above is a simple way to become familiar with the process. More than one factor may be used, e.g., $S$ may contain $F$ columns rather than one. The values placed off the diagonals of $R$ are the sums of cross products of pairs of rows (Eqs. 11-2 or 11-4), and the values placed in the diagonals are the sums of squares across columns (factors). The equations of the previous chapter show that the result will contain exactly $F$ ($<V$) eigenvalues greater than zero. The pattern will not reproduce $S$, as it will be a rotation of it (more precisely, the values you enter will be a rotation of the principal axes). The fact that such clear-cut results can be obtained from common factor analysis based upon artificial data has motivated some psychometricians to search for such common factors in real data. However, we caution against too quick an allegiance to the common factor model since sampling error will preclude a perfect fit with real correlations. Keep in mind that we knew what to put in the diagonals in the demonstrations because we made up the data so that it would not contain sampling error.

## Statistical Criteria of Rank

We noted at the end of the previous chapter that there are statistical tests available to determine the number of significant factors. These test for rank as well, by definition. However, although these statistical tests are entirely appropriate, they usually suggest far too many trivial factors. Even when considerable previous experience indicates that no more than four or five factors explain a particular collection of tests such as those shown in Table 11-12, significance tests typically suggest a rank twice as large. Although these inferential tests are elegant, they do not solve the substantive and psychometric problems of obtaining a parsimonious solution. On the other hand, one certainly should not place any faith in a factor that was not statistically significant by this lenient standard.

## Iteration

Thurstone fully explored alternative ways to estimate communalities. He realized that any method of condensation, e.g., eigenanalysis, can provide the structure once these diagonal entries are known. If, for example, the exact rank is 4, all coefficients in the fourth residual matrix will be zero and the sum of squared structure elements for any variable ($h^2$) will equal that variable's communality estimate ($r_{ii}$) regardless of the method chosen to condense data. Unfortunately, this is a bootstrap operation since the communality estimates must be known before undertaking the condensation. They usually are not known but must be estimated.

Thurstone suggested an iterative method of estimating communalities. In its present form, initial communality estimates are placed in the diagonals. These estimates may be any number in principle (e.g., unities), but squared multiple correlations (SMCs) between each variable and the remaining variables in the matrix are most common for mathematical convenience (the general role of SMCs is discussed below). The process then proceeds through the following steps.

**1** The data are factored by any method of condensation, but an eigenanalysis (principal axis solutions) is most common.

**2** Communalities ($h^2$ values) are computed for each variable and compared with the initial values placed in the diagonal spaces (communality estimates).

**3** The communalities and communality estimates are compared. If they are similar (e.g., if the average squared difference over all variables is less than .01), the analysis is completed.

**4** If the overall difference between the communalities and the communality estimates exceeds the criterion, as it usually does on the first cycle, the $h^2$ values for each variable become the new communality estimates in the diagonals of **R**, and the next cycle begins at step 1.

This was the method we used to produce the principal axis solution in the previous chapter. It is necessary to know the number of factors to be extracted in advance. This is usually determined from a preliminary analysis using the Kaiser-Guttman rule by default. However, any of the criteria discussed in Chapter 11, such as Velicer's (1976) minimum average partial, can actually be used to define the number of factors because all major programs allow the default to be overridden, as we recommend.

There are major difficulties with iterative methods despite their popularity.

**1** First and foremost, there is no guarantee that the solution will converge, and it often does not (Gorsuch, 1973) because such anomalies as Heywood cases emerge. Failure to converge is not necessarily the sign of a model that fits poorly; it may occur in one data set and not in another that differs only by sampling error, as we have noted. Although it makes intuitive sense to have the final communality estimates match the communalities, the details of the mathematical justification are poor.

**2** The solution is not unique because the user usually defines the number of factors, and therefore the rank, before iteration. One can iteratively seek communalities for varying numbers of factors for the same data, but there is no assurance that any chosen number is correct. The only thing known is that the rank of the common factor **R** matrix (the matrix with communality estimates in the diagonals) must be less than the rank of the component **R** matrix (the matrix with unities in the diagonals). No iterative method exists for estimating both the number of factors and communality estimates simultaneously.

**3** Different initial communality estimates may converge to different communalities and structure elements. Indeed, the solution may converge to obviously wrong values. However, this problem is rarer than the other two.

## Squared Multiple Correlations

The squared multiple correlations between each variable in turn and the remaining variables are a common, noniterative form of communality estimation. The SMC for variable $X_1$ in a group of 20 variables is the $R^2$ between it and variables $X_2$ through $X_{20}$. These SMCs are extremely easy to obtain from **R** (see any standard text on multivariate analysis for the critical operation, known as matrix inversion). Guttman (1956) proved that the SMC is a lower bound for the communality. If the rank of a matrix is less than the number of variables, $h^2$ for any variable will be at least as large as the SMC for that variable.

The SMCs have the advantages of being (1) unique, (2) readily obtainable, and (3) definitive of at least one type of common variance.

There are four major difficulties with using SMCs as estimates of communalities, even though they obviously determine one type of common variance—the variance that a particular variable has in common with the other specific variables in **R**.

**1** The SMC does not relate clearly to the concept of common variance. Common variance is generally viewed as the variance a particular variable has in common with a set of common factors, not how much it has in common with the particular variables used in that study. A variable which is uncorrelated with the other variables in the study will have an SMC of zero, even though it may correlate very highly with variables not in the study.

**2** Computer simulations indicate that SMCs do not reproduce the actual communalities ($h^2$ values) generated from a known structure. They reproduce neither the initial structure elements nor the rank of the correlation matrix.

**3** There are some purely statistical problems in employing SMCs as communality estimates: They tend to increase spuriously with the number of variables in the analysis for reasons indicated in Chapter 5; each variable added to the analysis tends to increase the SMCs of variables already present even if it is unrelated in the population. Although people who employ the common factor model realize that communalities are different for different collections of variables, it is disturbing to find that they systematically increase when variables are added. Of course, the amount of increase is more noticeable when the original set of variables is small rather than large. The SMCs also increase because the new variables actually do have something in common with those already under consideration, but this still points to the same problem that they describe the specific variables in the study rather than some more general concept.

**4** SMCs tend to lead to Heywood cases with somewhat greater frequency than other methods because the estimates they produce tend to be smaller. We have noted that the smaller the diagonal values, the more likely Heywood cases are to emerge. If a Heywood case emerges using SMCs, the choice of a replacement value becomes especially unclear.

One practical problem is that most algorithms used to obtain the SMCs will not work when one or more of these values approaches 1.0. In that case, 1.0 is a perfectly proper value to use, but you may not be able to determine the other values in any simple manner. In general, SMCs are too *low* as communality estimates. Despite these problems, there is probably somewhat more of a reason to use SMCs as communality estimates than to iterate if one feels a common factor model is in order.

### Reliability Coefficients

One additional possibility is to use the internal-consistency (coefficient $\alpha$) reliabilities (Mulaik, 1966) if they are available. Whereas SMCs describe a lower limit on the communality, reliabilities provide an upper limit since they represent what the communalities would be if there were no specific variance, i.e., if all nonerror variance in a variable were common variance and if all unique error was unreliability. They possess the advantages of being unique, ready obtainable, and meaningful that the SMCs possess. Moreover, reliabilities are less likely to produce Heywood cases than SMCs because they will be larger. However, the assumption they make that all unique variance is unreliability can be very unrealistic.

### Direct Estimation

Communality estimates emerge directly in ML and other approaches derived from numerical analysis (generalized least squares, unweighted least squares, and minres; see Chapter 11). This is certainly a sensible approach since the communality estimates are just as much estimable unknowns as the pattern elements, but it succeeds only when the overall solution converges. This fails to happen often enough so that it is worth noting as a practical problem.

### Some Major Differences between Component and Common Factor Solutions

It is useful to subject an **R** matrix which provides clearly defined clusters of variables to component and various common factor analyses using a standard package like SAS, SPSS-X, or UniMult. Explore the various options for communality estimation. Results will tend to be ordered from the component model to SMCs. This has been done in part with the data in Table 11-2, and you might wish to repeat this with your own data (real or simulated). We have already noted some of the differences, and so this section is a partial summary. Obtain both orthogonal and alternative oblique rotations. Also obtain solutions with different number of factors. When you compare a component and a common factor solution, be sure it is based upon the same number of factors.

You should be able to verify the following points which are considered in the somewhat technical dispute between Velicer and Jackson (1990), who lean toward the component position, and Snook and Gorsuch (1989), Bentler and Kano (1990), and Widaman (1990), who support a common factor view. At the same time, part of your exploration will simply verify the mathematics of factoring.

**1** Component eigenvalues will exceed common factor eigenvalues because part of the unique variance excluded from common factor solutions remains in the component solution. Consequently a PrC solution will explain more total variance than a principal axis (common factor) solution for the same number of factors, but part of this is spurious. You can also verify that the sum of the component eigenvalues equals the number of variables, although the sum of the eigenvalues will equal the sum of the diagonal entries in both cases. If you extract too many factors, some common factor eigenvalues may also have large negative values.

**2** Structure elements obtained from the component solution will be higher than structure elements obtained from the common factor solution. The magnitude of difference is inversely related to the number of variables and directly related to the average correlation. This difference is another consequence of the fact that the unique variance in a common factor solution contributes to the component structure. This bias in the component factor structure is a mildly undesirable property of component solutions, but most exploratory analysis is concerned with the relative rather than the absolute magnitudes of these correlations. Users of a component model should, of course, be aware that the bias exists

**3** The residuals, or obtained correlations minus those predicted from the model, Eq. 11-6, will be smaller in absolute magnitude in the common factor solution for a given number of factors. A given number of common factors will fit the data better than a component solution. Consequently summary measures like the root-mean-square error will indicate better fit. Although this appears to give a clear advantage to the common factor model, this model needs to estimate more parameters (the communality estimates in the diagonals) to gain this improved fit, and there is disagreement on how to do this meaningfully.

**4** The absolute magnitude of the residuals will always decrease in a component solution with increasing numbers of factors, as will the root-mean-square error. This is not necessarily true of all common factor solutions: Increases in the magnitude of the residuals with increasing numbers of common factors imply that too many factors have been extracted. Whether or not this can happen depends upon the specific method of communality estimation.

**5** A component solution tends to overestimate the actual magnitudes of correlations because of the bias present, and so the average magnitude of the residuals will usually be negative when **R** has positive manifold. Common factor solutions will likely be less biased, and so the mean value will be closer to zero. An actual calculation will likely be unnecessary since the difference will be apparent simply by inspecting the signs of the residuals.

**6** The oblique rotation produced by the component solution will likely be more nearly orthogonal than the oblique rotation produced by the common factor solution. This is because the unique error that is part of the component structure will attenuate correlations.

**7** The initial structure derived from PrC or any noniterative principal axis method such as SMCs or reliabilities does not change as factors are added. This is because the diagonal entries in **R** do not change. However, the structure does change when iterative methods are used for communality estimation because the effects of iteration depend upon the number of factors extracted.

**8** The content, and therefore interpretation, of rotated factors changes substantially as the number of factors extracted changes relative to the number of variables, regardless of whether a component or a common factor solution is obtained.

**9** If you include a variable which is basically uncorrelated with any of the other variables (a randomly generated variable will do nicely), that variable will tend to produce its own singlet component but should not correlate with any common factor. This should not be a major practical problem because its lack of correlation with other variables will be visible in **R**, and so it can and should be excluded from the analysis.

**10** You will get a component solution without anything notable happening, but either you may not get a common factor solution, as by lack of convergence in some methods, or the solution may involve some ad hoc process like using the largest correlation of a given variable with the other variables.

**11** Most critically, the major conclusions you reach about factor content will probably be the same with both the component and the common factor solution if your groupings are well-defined.

## Some Conceptual Problems with the Common Factor Model

The mathematics of common factor analysis has evolved impressively to deal with a vital issue, the separation of "signal" from "noise." We have stressed that it makes more overall sense to think in terms of a common factor model (but probably to do a component analysis in exploring data). However, we do wish to express some concerns about common factor analysis at the conceptual level. Although the concept of common variance (and therefore unique variance) can be well defined mathematically, it is actually somewhat unclear in a substantive sense.

**1** One meaning of "common variance" is what a set of actual linear combinations in **X** explains. This implies a component model.

**2** Another meaning is what a variable has in common with other variables in a particular matrix. If this is what is intended, image analysis, a particular form of component analysis, can provide the definition. It is doubtful that the concept is often thought of this narrowly since a variable's communality is then not a property of itself; it is a property of the other variables chosen for analysis.

**3** A third meaning is a variable's reliable variance. If this is intended, internal-consistency reliabilities (coefficients $\alpha$) can be used as communality estimates to define the term. However, many common factor theorists criticize the use of the reliability coefficient as being too high since it neglects specific variance.

**4** A fourth meaning is what a variable shares with a domain of variables. This perhaps comes closest to a conceptual definition, but the word "domain" is ill-defined as compared to its prior use in the development of reliability theory. We found it useful to postulate the concept of a domain as a way of generating items in reliability theory. The concept could often be defined very explicitly, such as by randomly choosing pairs of four-digit numbers. Some applications required more of a stretch of the imagination (e.g., depression items) because the rules needed to generate them were less clear. However, none of these applications remotely resembled the vagueness in defining a domain of variables. Indeed, the domain can consist of variable that have yet to be developed. Even though it is reasonable to think in these terms, as when one is considering developing a new measure of anxiety, common variance thus possesses surplus meaning in the truest sense. Most researchers probably lack a well-defined idea of which variables are to be included and which are to be excluded in a particular domain, one necessary feature. Many investigations (especially the ones we suggest researchers avoid) lack any well-defined concept of domain. Indeed, the idea of a single domain becomes especially nebulous when the user believes there are two or more independent clusters of variables in the data.

**5** Common variance can be defined simply as parameter estimates, such as the $h^2$ provided by an ML algorithm. However, this verges upon the very weakness of component analysis—the narrow operational conception of the term. In practice, this definition becomes tied to the specific variables in the analysis since it is defined only by these variables. This raises the objections noted in point 2.

Numerous elegant models have been proposed to derive common factors, but none solve the conceptual issue of defining a domain. Impressive as recent developments in numerical estimation have been, maximum likelihood estimates of communalities do not resolve the issue of what communality means. We have indicated that communality estimates and the resulting communalities increase as the number of variables in the study increases. Indeed, common factor and component solutions become indistinguishable when more than about 20 variables are used. This is important pragmatically, and it further suggests that the only reason that any real measure does not have a communality of 1 is that too few variables, especially marker variables, were included in the analysis.

### Effects of Number of Variables and Average Correlation upon the Factor Structure

Table 12-4 shows the average centroid structure elements obtained with different numbers of variables and average correlation magnitudes, except for the last row (conclusions to be noted depend little on the method of condensation). This last row, marked $20_z$, shows the average centroid structure elements obtained using zeros in the diagonals.

**TABLE 12-4**   AVERAGE FIRST CENTROID STRUCTURE ELEMENTS AS A FUNCTION OF NUMBER OF VARIABLES AND AVERAGE CORRELATION AMONG VARIABLES (COMPONENT SOLUTION).

| | Average correlations among variables | | | |
|---|---|---|---|---|
| Number of variables | .00 | .20 | .40 | .60 |
| 5 | .45 | .60 | .72 | .82 |
| 10 | .32 | .53 | .68 | .80 |
| 15 | .26 | .50 | .66 | .79 |
| 20 | .22 | .49 | .66 | .79 |
| 25 | .20 | .48 | .65 | .78 |
| $20_z$ | .00 | .40 | .62 | .76 |

*Note:* The last row shows the results for 20 variables with zeros placed in the diagonals.

The first column corresponds to an average correlation of zero among variables. Because the diagonals are unities, the first centroid structure elements are not zero, but the size of such spurious correlations declines rapidly as the number of variables increases. If zeros are put in the diagonals, the average centroid structure element must then be zero, as indicated in the last row of the table. Although it is silly to factor a spherical matrix, $\mathbf{R}$ matrices with average correlations of .20 are often factored, especially by those with little background in the area. One can see that the diagonal unities make an important contribution to the first factor when there are only five variables, but this effect diminishes past 10 variables.

When the average correlation reaches .40, the diagonal unities play a minimal role even with a small number of variables. At 20 variables, the diagonal unities also play a trivial role. The last row indicates that structure elements derived with zeros and with ones in the diagonal are not very different, so that it really does not matter what you put in the diagonals when you have as many as 20 variables and decent correlations. Many other examples could be composed, and the results from many actual studies could be cited to show that the only problems in employing unities in the diagonals arise from low correlations *and* small numbers of variables. However, with even as few as 10 variables and at least modest correlations, one typically finds the same factor solution regardless of what goes in the diagonal spaces. The average correlation, assuming any care in the choice of variables, typically ranges between .4 and .8—not between 0 and 1. Therefore, the range of outcomes is fairly limited.

## FACTOR ANALYTIC DESIGNS

A factor analysis starts with a data ($\mathbf{X}$) matrix, which was illustrated in Table 11-1. Thus far, columns of $\mathbf{X}$ have been different variables and rows have been scores of subjects on those variables. Scores were standardized by columns so that each variable had a mean of 0 and a standard deviation of 1.0. Consequently $\mathbf{X} = \mathbf{Z}$. Correlations were obtained among variables (columns) over subjects (rows). The number of subjects was very large compared to the number of variables, and so subjects may be called the "long" dimension and variables the "short" dimension. This is the most common factor analytic design, called an $R$ design (Cattell, 1952; Gorsuch, 1983).

Looking more closely at this design, subjects are almost always selected, at least in principle, to form a random factor in the ANOVA sense. This allows the investigator to generalize results from the sample of subjects to the larger population. Indeed, inferential tests in $R$ design are meaningful because the correlations are computed over a random factor. In contrast, variables are ordinarily selected for specific reasons and are therefore a fixed factor. Moreover, scores for different subjects on the same variable are commensurate (measurable on the same scale, in this case an interval scale in the sense of Chapter 1); if subject 1 got a higher score on an ability test than subject 2, subject 1 would be assumed to be higher in that ability. The same would hold if covariances and mean sums of products were used instead of correlations to describe relations among measures. The purpose of these alternative measures is to allow differences in variable means and standard deviations to affect the outcome, as discussed in the previous chapter.

## Alternative Designs

Table 12-5 presents a series of alternative factor analytic designs, defined in terms of different long and short dimensions, and the symbols Cattell (1952) gave these designs.

The next most common alternative is used in only a small number of studies compared to $R$ design. It involves reversing or transposing the roles of subjects and variables and is called a $Q$ design. Consequently the rows of **X** contain variables, the columns contain subjects, and there are many more variables than subjects. The analysis looks for groupings of subjects rather than variables. Whereas variables produce factors and subjects produce factor scores in an $R$ design, the converse is true in a $Q$ design. Bernstein, Lin, and McClellan (1983) had Taiwanese and American subjects judge a relatively large number of college yearbook pictures for attractiveness. They were interested in whether the judgments of the two ethnic groups would tend to form clusters, which they did. This meant that two Taiwanese or two American subjects' judgments of attractiveness were generally more similar than those of a Taiwanese and an American.

An important issue in any design where correlations are obtained among subjects, such as a $Q$ design, is how to standardize variables. In ordinary ($R$ design) factor analysis, the average factor score for a given subject is generally not standardized, but the average for each variable is. If $Q$ data were analyzed in a parallel manner, subjects would be standardized but variables would not be. However, some applications of the $Q$ technique require variables to be standardized, but others do not. The key is whether the variables are commensurate. For example, when Bernstein et al. (1983) presented pictures to be judged, some evoked higher mean ratings over subjects than others, but this is a legitimate outcome since some people are simply more attractive than others. It is as proper to include these mean differences in the analysis as it is to include mean differences in ability among subjects in an $R$ design.

On the other hand, suppose that a different $Q$ study employed a series of variables that were each scored on measures whose scalings were arbitrarily related. For example, one variable might be a standardized intelligence test ($\mu = 100$ and $\sigma = 15$ over subjects), a second variable might be a reading comprehension measure scaled as a $T$ score ($\mu = 50$ and $\sigma = 10$), and a third measure might be a SAT score ($\mu = 500$ and $\Sigma = 100$), etc. This lack of commensurability due to arbitrary differences in scale has a profound but spurious effect on the correlations among subjects. The appropriate strategy

**TABLE 12-5**    ALTERNATIVE FACTOR ANALYTIC DESIGNS

| Name | Long dimension | Short dimension |
| --- | --- | --- |
| R | Subjects | Variables |
| Q | Variables | Subjects |
| P | Occasions | Variables |
| O | Variables | Occasions |
| T | Subjects | Occasions |
| X | Occasions | Subjects |

is to standardize each measure. Paralleling the $R$ design, this may be done so that subject means and standard deviations differ (single standardization). It may also be done so that both subject and variable means are standardized (double standardization). In the latter case, the data are subject-by-measure interactions in the ANOVA sense. Measures scaled so that each subject's mean is 0 are also called ipsitized, but this does not necessarily imply that the individual measures have been standardized nor that each subject's standard deviation is 1.0. The means and variances of variables are treated as equal in single and double standardization since there is no basis for treating them differently. For example, consider the data in Table 12-6 which represent the population means and standard deviations plus scores of two subjects on five measures in their original form, following single and double standardization.

The correlation between the first two sets of scores (obtained scores) is essentially 1.0 ($r = .99$). However, this is an artifact of the wide difference in scale among the five measures. Indeed, a correlation of this magnitude would probably be obtained if each pair of measures in a given row were sampled randomly using the population parameters: Scores for $X_1$ and $X_4$ will generally be low and scores for $X_3$ and $X_6$ will generally be high, with scores on $X_2$ and $X_5$ in the middle, regardless of the structure of the data. Ipsitizing the two columns by subtracting the two subject means (249 and 195) from each measure would not affect $r$.

Standardizing the scores in each row provides the next pair of columns. There is a substantial negative correlation between these two columns ($r = -.85$). The reason is that subject 1 has relatively high scores on the first three measures but relatively low scores on the last three measures. The converse is true of subject 2. The term "relatively" applies to each subject's mean over all measures (.86 and $-.60$, respectively). Doubly standardizing, as in the last pair of columns, causes each subject's mean and standard deviation to become 0 and 1.0 over the five measures. If the first three and last three measures described verbal and mathematical ability, subject 1 would be described as being above average in overall ability, but more verbal than quantitative, and subject 2 would be described as below average in overall ability, but more quantitative than verbal.

TABLE 12-6   ORIGINAL SCORES, SINGLY STANDARDIZED SCORES, AND DOUBLY STANDARDIZED SCORES FOR TWO SUBJECTS ON FIVE MEASURES

| Measure | Scale | | Original subject | | Singly standardized subject | | Doubly standardized subject | |
|---|---|---|---|---|---|---|---|---|
| | $\mu$ | $\sigma$ | 1 | 2 | 1 | 2 | 1 | 2 |
| $X_1$ | 50 | 10 | 65 | 40 | 1.50 | −1.00 | 1.31 | −1.45 |
| $X_2$ | 100 | 15 | 120 | 90 | 1.33 | −.67 | .97 | −.24 |
| $X_3$ | 500 | 100 | 600 | 425 | 1.00 | −.75 | .28 | −.54 |
| $X_4$ | 50 | 10 | 55 | 44 | .50 | −.60 | −.74 | .00 |
| $X_5$ | 100 | 15 | 105 | 95 | .33 | −.33 | −1.08 | .97 |
| $X_6$ | 500 | 100 | 550 | 475 | .50 | −.25 | −.74 | 1.27 |

The correlation between the singly and doubly standardized values over variables will always be the same because the correlation adjusts for the column mean and standard deviations in the same way that doubly standardizing does. The question, however, is whether this correlation captures what we want of the similarity between the two subjects. We certainly want these two subjects in the example to be different, and a correlation of $-.85$ certainly implies a difference. However, suppose subject 3 had the same overall mean as subject 1 but the same pattern as subject 2. That subject's five scores would correlate perfectly with subject 2's, despite their difference in overall ability, and so subject 3 would also correlate $-.85$ with subject 1. This is probably not an intended outcome. We could prevent it from happening by using a measure other than the correlation, most specifically the mean sum of products of the singly standardized scores since that would incorporate mean differences. This is a major part of profile analysis, considered in Chapter 14.

There have been numerous attempts to show that nothing can be obtained from a $Q$ design that could not be obtained from an $R$ design. Given certain assumptions, the results obtained from a $Q$ design can be transformed to the results expected in an $R$ study, and vice versa (Burt, 1941). This is not likely to be useful for several reasons. First, these assumptions are stringent and rarely hold in actual studies. Second, the number of factors and best rotational choice for a $R$ study need not be the best for a $Q$ study even when these assumptions do hold. Third, and most importantly, $R$ and $Q$ designs have very different implications for psychological theory.

If one is interested in grouping variables, an $R$ design should be used, but if one is interested in grouping persons, a $Q$ design should be used. Most theories concern clusters of variables, where an $R$ design is most valuable. It is relatively simply to think of a factor as an idealized variable, e.g., anxiety. It is also relatively easy to think of this ideal variable as being closer to some indicators than to others based upon the factor structure. In contrast, a $Q$ design concerns clusters of people, and each factor is a prototypical "person" defined by his or her pattern of responses. Factors are such things as idealized personality types, and the correlations among actual people specify to what extent they are mixtures of the various types. Such constructs are somewhat more difficult to conceptualize than constructs of an $R$ design. This is one reason why an $R$ design is used much more frequently than a $Q$ design. There is a more pragmatic reason—it is easier and cheaper to get small amounts of time from large numbers of subjects (especially in subject pools) than to get large amounts of time from small numbers of subjects. These points are not intended to be critical of the $Q$ design which both authors have used. Indeed, Chapter 14 contains an example of a form of $Q$ analysis developed by the first author, called "raw score factor analysis."

An interesting approach is to obtain repeated measures on the same variable on different occasions with a single subject. For example, the subject's weight, diastolic blood pressure, systolic blood pressure, pulse rate, and other variables might be measured daily for a period of time. This is known as a $P$ design if the number of occasions is large compared to the number of measures, so that correlations are obtained among measures over occasions. Its transpose, correlating a small number of occasions over a large number of measures, is called an $O$ design. Occasions replace subjects as a dimension of the analysis in both cases. However, there is no way to generalize the results directly since neither occasions nor measures are random effects. One possibility is to conduct parallel analyses on different individuals and show that their pattern of results is the same. Nunnally (1955) used an $O$ design with a woman who repeatedly rated her self-concept from 16 different points of view, e.g., "the way you really are" and "the way your parents view you." These were intercorrelated, resulting in a $16 \times 16$ **R** matrix. A factor analysis found three "selves," whose changes were investigated over the course of psychotherapy. In this case, the subject herself was the topic of interest. There was minimum interest in generalizing to other individuals, though the results hopefully generalized to the woman's future behavior.

Two other designs employ only a single measure, such as "How are you feeling," for different subjects over occasions. Occasions replace measures in $Q$ and $R$ designs. In a $T$ design, the number of occasions is small compared to the number of subjects, and occasions are intercorrelated over subjects. In an $X$ design, the converse is true. It is somewhat improbable that factor analysis would address the typical issues of interest. Since occasions is an ordinal variable, an investigator would probably be interested in functional relationships (e.g., does the mean for the single measure increase or decrease over time) rather than correlations between the measures at different times. An ANOVA with trend tests would probably be more valuable.

## Three-Mode Factor Analysis

Subjects, variables, and occasions are termed data modes. In traditional factor analysis, only two modes (e.g., variables and subjects) are studied at a time, and the third (e.g., occasions) is limited to a single value. For example, an $R$ design, the most popular design, employs subjects and measures (variables) obtained on one occasion, and the data are contained in a two-way matrix. In a three-mode problem, each mode is represented at more than one level. For example, one might obtain MMPI profiles containing several measures (scale scores) from several subjects before and after psychotherapy (two occasions). The same data structure would arise if each of several words or other concepts were rated on each of several attributes by a group of subjects. This structure forms a three-mode "data solid." Tucker (1963, 1964, 1966) has extended conventional factor analysis to the three-mode situation. Bentler and Lee (1978, 1979) have provided an inferential foundation for the approach. Jones and Iacobucci (1989) supply an illustration using 78 subjects (college students), 15 concepts (names of politicians, such as Jimmy Carter and Ronald Reagan) and 27 rating scales.

The analysis forms three correlation matrices by aggregating over the two other modes. Thus, subjects are correlated over both concepts and rating scales, concepts are correlated over both subjects and rating scales, and rating scales are correlated over both subjects and concepts. Each of these three matrices is then factored by any suitable method such as PrC, producing three factor structures (subjects, concepts, and rating scales). Each individual analysis is based on the product of two other modes rather than a single mode; e.g., concepts are intercorrelated over a combination of 27 rating scales and 78 subjects for a total of $(27)(78) = 2106$ "observations" and not simply 27 rating scales or 78 subjects. With the exception of the way an observation is defined, the three individual analyses are no different from any other factor analysis. At the same time, the fact that observations always combine two modes does raise methodological questions since correlations over one mode holding another constant may be quite different from the converse correlations. Furthermore, neither the 15 concepts nor the 27 rating scales are independent of one another in the sense that the 78 subjects are. Jones and Iacobucci discuss these methodological issues.

The novel aspect of the analysis is a special type of factor pattern called a core matrix which interrelates factors from the three modes. Columns of the core matrix are factors derived from one mode (e.g., subjects), and rows are factors derived from a second mode (e.g., ratings) separately for each level of the third mode (e.g., concepts). The core matrix can reflect whatever organization of the three modes is of greatest interest.

## AD-LIB FACTORING

It is not necessary to employ the same method of factoring to obtain successive factors. Subsequent factors need not be a PrC just because factor I may have been. An ad-lib approach to factoring is especially useful in dissecting the common variance among variables when there are hypotheses to guide the analysis, but these are not sufficiently well developed to suggest a confirmatory approach. However, the most useful function of ad-lib factoring is to partial one or more variables from a larger set of variables. The partialled variables can be a composite (linear combination) or, perhaps more frequently, individual variables. Adjusting a set of cognitive abilities for overall intelligence as defined by the first PrC would illustrate the first use; adjusting these measures for gender and/or ethnicity would illustrate the second.

Nunnally and Hodges (1965) provide an application of ad-lib factoring to the study of individual differences in word association. Each variable described the tendency to give a particular type of associate. Three scales had previously been studied; the question of interest was the structure of five new scales, controlling for the three old ones. The authors used the square root method [discussed briefly in Chapter 11 and more fully in Gorsuch (1983) and Harman (1976)] with the three old scales applied successively as pivots. This meant that the first three factors thus simply consisted of these scales in turn. Because succeeding factors are orthogonal to earlier factors, and vice versa, all factors starting with the fourth are independent of these three variables *and* any linear combination of them (see Chapter 5, if nonlinear effects may be present). Although their subsequent analysis employed a confirmatory procedure to test a proposed structure, it could have simply been an exploratory analysis, such as PrC.

If you rotate from an ad-lib solution, be sure that the factors being controlled are omitted from the rotation process or else the rotated factors will no longer be independent of the corresponding variables. For example, Nunnally and Hodges had to exclude the first three from the rotation. Many computer programs make it easy to remove one or more PrCs from a correlation matrix since they allow the user to store residual covariance matrices. Thus, one may remove the first PrC by analyzing **R** after specifying the extraction of one factor. Convert the stored residual covariance to a correlation matrix by the methods of Chapter 11 and then factor the resultant by any method desired. It is often even easier to remove individual variables since this option may be provided directly by the program. However, the more popular programs make it difficult to limit rotation to selected factors.

Ad-lib factoring to remove irrelevant variables allows a more direct test of the explanatory power of hypotheses about the nature of psychological constructs and a potentially more thorough exploration of new groupings of variables. It is easy to let good ideas get lost in the mechanics of a ready-made, rigid approach to factoring. This is especially true when one slavishly follows the other defaults of computer packages. Some of this rigidity reflect programmers who "know what's right for you" but much more reflects the lack of willingness of users to explore options fully.


## HIGHER-ORDER FACTORS

Correlated factors produce factor correlations which in turn may themselves be factored, providing higher-order factors. This may be viewed as providing successive levels of increasing abstraction to the factors. Factors obtained at the first stage are called first-order factors and may be closely tied to specific variables. For example, suppose that 40 variables are factored and the results rotated obliquely to produce 10 factors. The $10 \times 10$ factor correlation matrix ($\Phi$) can itself be factored by any method and the results rotated as desired to produce more abstract second-order factors. Assume that four factors are obtained. Since there are more than two second-order factors, the correlations among the second-order factors could also be analyzed to obtain still more abstract third-order factors, etc. Gorsuch (1983) describes how to link the original variables to the higher-order factors and thereby provide the structure of all variables on higher-order factors. Normally, a common factor model is employed, and rotations obviously have to be oblique.

Higher-order factors are appealing to the many psychologists who favor hierarchically organized theories. Higher-order factors are basic to Cattell's (1966a) Sixteen Personality Factor (16PF) Test. Gorsuch (1983), a student of Cattell's, suggests its applicability to the thorny problem of factoring categorical data as in item-level factoring considered in the next chapter. He further provides an illustration of how higher-order factors reduce the likelihood of being misled by other artifactual factors (Gorsuch, 1983, p. 294).

Two cautions should be noted.

**1** It may be more difficult to understand higher-order factoring than conventional factoring. The average student has difficulty understanding first-order factors without having to deal with higher-order factors. This is less of a problem at the highest order of factors than at intermediate levels where misinterpretations can easily emerge.

**2** The information in a multilevel factor hierarchy can be often be communicated more simply with only two levels and sometimes only one level. A second-order factor often tends to be a general factor in which structure elements reflect the overall tendency of variables to correlate among themselves. Much the same information is obtainable from the initial PrC or principal axis structure elements. There is nothing wrong with describing an initial general factor even if that factor is subsequently rotated in conjunction with other factors.

On a more positive note, second-order factors have often proven useful in summarizing the results of large analyses that produced many factors. For example, the various Wechsler intelligence scales (e.g., Wechsler, 1989) consist of several individual tests which are used to estimate verbal and performance IQ measures which in turn produce an overall IQ measure. Even though the scales were not formally developed through factor analysis, it is quite reasonable to think of verbal and performance IQ as first-order factors and overall IQ as a second-order factor. The presence of the second-order factor makes it explicit that the first-order factors are related but separable aspects of intelligence.

## HOW TO FOOL YOURSELF WITH FACTOR ANALYSIS

Here are some cautions about using factor analysis.

**1** The easiest way to fool yourself with factor analysis is to ignore the correlations that underlie the analysis. Variables that define a factor may have negligible correlations with one another. The fact that two such variables can correlate with a "common" factor merely reflects the successive partialling of factors. For example, suppose that $X_1$ and $X_2$ each correlate $+.50$ with factor I, $X_1$ correlates $+.50$ with factor II, and $X_2$ correlates $-.50$ with factor II. A careless investigator might define factor I in terms of what $X_1$ and $X_2$ have in common and define factor II as a contrast between $X_1$ and $X_2$. However, Eq. 11-2 or 11-4 shows that $X_1$ and $X_2$ are uncorrelated in the plane defined by the two factors. If factors I and II account for much of the overall variance, the overall correlation between $X_1$ and $X_2$ would be nearly zero. Mathematically there is nothing wrong with this outcome, but it is easily misinterpreted and not likely to be useful unless the two factors each contain several other salients which correlate with $X_1$ and $X_2$.

**2** A second common error is to overinterpret the meaning of "small" to include moderate but salient structure elements, e.g., those between .30 and .60. This is especially true in component analyses conducted with a small number of variables because of the mathematics inherent in any method of condensation and the bias present in component approaches. Condensations make the squared or absolute structure elements on successive factors as large as possible. These structure elements may look substantial even if the absolute value of the average correlation in **R** is rather low. As an extreme example, suppose that there are only four variables which have correlations of precisely zero with each other. Each variable will have a structure element on factor I of approximately .5. As advised above, always inspect **R** to ensure that salient variables correlate substantially with one another.

**3** The meaning of orthogonal factors is often misinterpreted. Although the factors themselves are uncorrelated, factor score estimates are generally correlated, and these correlations need be determined separately.

**4** Confusion often arises between an experimental dependency and the substance of what is being measured. This can occur in a number of ways. Perhaps the most common dependency arises because items appear on more than one scale of a test, as in the MMPI (see Chapter 9). Item overlap forces correlations among the scales and thus enhances any inherent factor overlap. Another way to obtain experimental dependency is to include one or more combinations of the individual variables in the analysis along with these individual variables. This error arises when sums or differences of variables are included along with the variables themselves. This should simply be avoided. There is no reason to include these combinations along with the original variables. Certain forms of factor analysis, such as ML or those using SMCs as communality estimates will terminate abnormally, but partial item overlap of items will not cause this to happen. Minimize any form of experimental dependency among variables; the intent of factor analysis is to investigate the "natural" structure of variables rather than one forced through experimental dependence.

**5** Subject selection provides another possible source of artifact. Factors can arise from differences in age, sex, education, etc., if subjects are relatively heterogeneous with respect to these variables. Whether one wants samples that are homogeneous or heterogeneous with respect to these variables depends on the population to which the results are to be generalized. For example, if the factors are to reflect individual differences among children at a particular age level, the sample should be relatively homogeneous with respect to age. If this is not possible, some form of ad lib factoring is one possibility. An alternative is to form separate covariance matrices for each group (e.g., age levels, genders, or ethnicities), pool (add) the separate matrices, and compute the correlation from this pooled matrix. Standard references on multivariate analysis describe the pooling process. Certain computer packages designed for other purposes (e.g., SAS PROC DISCRIM) can be used to this end. On the other hand, if the factors are to reflect developmental trends, children should vary in age.

**6** Factor analysis allows one to take great advantage of chance and thus spuriously demonstrate almost anything in a small enough sample. The authors have seen some horrible examples in which the number of subjects was no more than the number of variables, in which case handsome factors are built in. Unfortunately, any of the methods described in this book can be misused to provide such spurious, nonreplicable results.

**7** Yet another common error is to rotate so as to obscure the actual groupings of variables more than they are elucidated. This is particularly likely if one interprets the factor pattern ($\beta$ weights describing variables in terms of factors) and ignores the factor structure (variable-factor correlations) and factor correlations of highly correlated factors.

**8** It is also easy to confuse a linear correlation with the concept of correlation in general. The relation between some variables may be highly curvilinear, perhaps U- and/or inverted U-shaped, in which case the PM correlation will seriously underestimate the strength of relationship (relations that are monotonic but not linear are unlikely to cause major problems). For example, in life-span developmental research, very young children and the elderly may be more like one another than either are like those in the middle for some variables, e.g., strength. Chapter 5 noted how one may include powers of variables that you have good reason to suspect are curvilinearly related to other variables, e.g., $age^2$, $age^3$, ... (four or five powers are usually sufficient). Look at scatter plots, which are usually easy to obtain, and also look at correlations between these powered variables: If $age^5$ correlates poorly with other variables, but lower powers have at least moderate correlations, delete $age^5$ but keep the lower powers. These powered variables may be partialled by ad-lib factoring if they are nuisance variables, or they may be kept in the analysis if they are of interest.

**9** A ninth (but not the last possible) way is to analyze categorical measures such as items as if they were continuous. This is probably the most common error found in articles published in better journals because item-level factoring seems so natural, the appropriate data are easy to gather from "captive sources" like classes, and the problem has largely been ignored in the more empirical sources (despite being in the literature for a long time, cf. Ferguson, 1941). Most item-level factorings produce too many factors and, in particular, nearly always suggest multidimensionality even in a unidimensional scale. This topic will be considered at length in the next chapter.

## AN OUTLOOK ON EXPLORATORY FACTOR ANALYSIS

Both authors strongly feel that a proper and flexible outlook on factoring is more important than an extremely detailed technical understanding as long as one grasps the major concepts. Factor analysis is like any other multivariate or psychometric procedure. *None* are "royal roads to truth," as some apparently feel, or simply bases for shotgun empiricism, as others claim. Since it is usually necessary to combine scores from several variables to obtain valid measures of constructs, some method is required to determine the legitimacy of particular combinations. The patterns of correlations among variables is vital to determining this legitimacy. It is also important to determine whether members of an assumed cluster of variables actually do correlate higher with one another than they do with variables outside that clusters if one is to make valid scientific generalizations by naming the assumed cluster. Factor analysis is nothing more than a set of tools for examining clusters of correlations and providing a frame of reference in the space defined by a set of measures, and it is indispensable for that purpose.

### Practical Considerations in Factor Analysis

We conclude our discussion of exploratory factor analysis with these final practical considerations.

**1** Consider whether the theory is well developed enough to profit from a confirmatory approach, as discussed in the next chapter, since you probably have some theory that guided you to select the variables in the first place. Exploratory factor analysis can be used to test theories and, if the theory consists simply of defining relatively independent clusters, an orthogonal solution will probably find them if they are there. However, a confirmatory approach will probably help guide you through the succeeding steps of theory development better.

**2** Don't worry extensively about the choice of a component or common factor model to analyze the data, despite the attention we have given this distinction. One draws almost identical inferences from either approach in *most* analyses. Unless the numbers placed in the diagonal spaces are so low as to provide ridiculous outcomes (a Heywood case and/or large negative eigenvalues), the diagonals of **R** do not have that great an impact on the number and content of exploratory factors, especially if you keep inflation of the component factor structure in mind. It is safe to say that the diagonal entries are of minor concern when there are 20 or more variables in the analysis, as long as any care at all has been given to the selection of variables. Consequently, if there are 20 or more variables in the exploratory factor analysis, we strongly recommend a component solution, i.e., unity diagonals. Although 20 variables is not a magic number, one is surely safe pursuing the recommended course at this point. Put in other terms, the false assumption that the variables are error-free made in component analysis becomes a "convenient fiction" at this point.

**3** Problems may arise when only a small number of variables is studied, say less than 10, and the average correlation is low. The choice of diagonal entries in that case can have a substantial influence on the resulting factor structure. If an exploratory factor analysis is conducted with less than 20 variables, unclear groupings of variables, and no marker variables, some form of communality estimation may be warranted if the sample size is sufficient to minimize the role of sampling error. A common factor solution might prove more fruitful than a component analysis, especially when the number of variables is less than 12. If a component solution is used, keep the inflation of structure elements in mind. At the same time, this might be a good time not to use factor analysis.

**4** Orthogonal rotations usually lead one to essentially the same major groupings as oblique rotations. If you employ an orthogonal rotation, there is every reason to choose varimax. A varimax solution will usually do as well as any oblique rotation while providing the simplification of orthogonality. One can avoid dealing with separate pattern, structure, and factor correlation matrices if one is willing to sacrifice some proximity of the factors to the variables. However, it is easy enough to examine a promax or other oblique solution as long as you consider the misleading effects of high factor correlations. The nice thing about the ready availability of personal computers is that you can verify these points yourself very quickly by trying out a variety of options.

**5** If groupings are well-defined, different factoring methods generally lead to the same conclusions. Each factor should have some variables which correlate with it nearly exclusively (most variables correlating highly with that factor should not correlate more than .3 with any other factor), and at least four tests, including marker variables whose inclusion we stress, should correlate above .5. Unless a factor is at least that strong, it is best to ignore it. Factor solutions that lack such clear-cut groupings can change in different approaches, so that differences between component and common factor analysis and methods of rotation may make a difference. Solutions that are highly method-dependent are poor solutions and might best be left unreported. Consider how you selected the variables to make the next study better. We cannot repeat enough how factor analysis should not be used to find "magic" in an arbitrarily selected set of variables.

## SUMMARY

Factors are usually rotated to make solutions more interpretable, which typically has three effects: (1) strengthening relations between variables and factors, (2) concentrating variance shared by two variables onto a single factor, and (3) making the factor variances more nearly equal. Orthogonally rotated factors remain at right angles because each initial factor is rotated by the same amount, but obliquely rotated factors involve rotating each initial factor by a different amount. The rotated factors are not at right angles.

Rotations are linear transformations which do not affect the $h^2$ values, estimated correlations, or overall fit. Orthogonal rotation weights have three major properties: (1) The sum of the squared weights for any one factor equals 1 since the factor maintains its length, (2) the sum of cross products for pairs of factors equals zero, and (3) the weights represent cosines of angles between original and rotated factors and therefore their correlations. The total variance accounted for remains the sum of the variances accounted for by the individual factors, as with the initial (orthogonal) factors, and the pattern ($S$) matrix contains all relevant information.

Oblique rotations allow factors to be placed nearer groups of variables. Properties 1 and 3 of an orthogonal solution hold, but not property 2, and factor correlations become an important part of the outcome. In general, the oblique rotations are more complicated because (1) one no longer has the benefit of a right-angle coordinate system and (2) the structure matrix ($S$), the pattern matrix ($B$), and the factor correlation matrix ($\Phi$) all contribute important information, though any one can be derived from the other two. Pattern elements represent the intersection of a line from the variable to the factor parallel to other factors, whereas structure elements represent lines drawn perpendicularly to the factor (see Chapter 11). The equations for $h^2$ and the estimated correlations become complicated because both $S$ and $B$ are needed, as in multiple regression with correlated predictors. The total variance accounted for is still the average $h^2$ value, but no longer the sum of the individual variances accounted for, because of overlapping factor variance. We suggest that you use orthogonal rotations until the distinction between pattern and structure is clear; it is easier to be misled by an oblique solution than an orthogonal solution. Moreover, if an oblique rotation leads to very low factor correlations, replace it with an orthogonal solution to gain the advantage of its simplicity and, if two factors are highly correlated, try replacing them with a single factor.

Thurstone's concept of simple structure is designed to best dimensionalize a space. The goal is to maximize the number of small pattern weights. Cattell's (1966a) hyperplane count attempts to quantify this concept, but Hoffmann (1979) proposed an alternative definition based upon the number of large pattern elements. Because simple structure is not always achievable, the goal of rotation is better stated as providing a simpler structure with some relatively pure variables for each factor. In addition, simple structure means avoiding a general factor.

Reference vectors are vectors which are at right angles to all but one factor. They are largely obsolete since better methods have become available, but they are commonly described in computer printouts and have two interesting properties: (1) They are proportional to the pattern weights and (2) they represent the correlation between variables and a factor, controlling for all other factors. Nonetheless, we suggest you ignore reference vector data since they add to the other difficulties normally present in reporting factor analytic results.

Rotation is now generally analytic, rather than visual. The first analytic rotation was quartimax, an orthogonal process which maximizes the average variance of squared structure elements over factors (squaring is used to eliminate signs). However, if all variables have their largest correlation with the same factor, quartimax will produce a general factor, contrary to the goals of simple structure. Varimax maximizes the average variance of squared structure elements within factors and much more nearly meets the goal of simple structure and has become the standard orthogonal rotation by far. There are many analytic oblique rotations, but none dominates use. One that is fairly popular is promax, which rotates obliquely to a target matrix and increases the disparity between large and small elements.

The next major section dealt with the determination of composite scores for individuals, factor scores, by extending the basic factor model to apply to individual observations rather than variables in general. The goal is to obtain a factor weight ($\mathbf{W}$) matrix defining factors in terms of variables. This matrix may be defined exactly in a component solution, and so the scores will fulfill the results of the model. Specifically, (1) orthogonal factors will produce uncorrelated factor scores, and the correlation between factor scores produced by oblique factors will equal the factor correlation, (2) observed scores will equal the weighted sum of the factor scores if there are as many components as variables, (3) correlations produced by weighting factor scores will equal correlations estimated from the factors ($\mathbf{S}$ and/or $\mathbf{B}$), (4) the multiple correlations of the variables in predicting the factors will be 1.0, and (5) the $\mathbf{W}$ matrix will be unique, as will (6) the matrix of the factor scores it produces ($\mathbf{X}_f$).

These relations do not hold in a common factor solution because of the unique variance—an infinity of $\mathbf{W}$ matrices can be obtained to estimate the factor scores, an outcome known as factor-score indeterminacy. The properties of the different solutions will vary somewhat. Good factor-score estimation has three goals—factor scores should (1) correlate maximally with the factors they represent (be valid), (2) not correlate with other factors beyond that implied by the factor correlation (be orthogonal), and (3) not correlate with other factor scores beyond that implied by the factor correlation (be univocal). No single estimation procedure can accomplish these three goals, unfortunately, though the most common, multiple regression, usually is sufficient. However, factor-score indeterminacy is not as major a problem for the common factor model as it appears. For one thing, the unique properties of the component solution hold only in the original sample. Most applications actually involve approximations, typically derived from the equally weighted sum of salient variables. One should examine the properties of such approximations since they may be highly correlated even though the factors they represent are orthogonal. In practice, three or four salient variables are usually sufficient to define a factor score, but one should avoid limiting the definition to one variable.

The next section interrelated the major matrices, vectors, and scalars thus far discussed: $\mathbf{X}$ (raw score = $\mathbf{Z}$ when standardized by columns), $\mathbf{R}$ (correlation or some other measure of relationship), $\mathbf{S}$ (factor structure), $\mathbf{B}$ (factor pattern), $\Phi$ (factor correlation), $\mathbf{W}$ (factor weight), $\mathbf{X}_f$ (factor score), $\mathbf{T}$ (transformation from initial to rotated factors), and $\mathbf{U}$ (uniqueness). The major vector output consists of the $h^2$ values, the factor variances, and the multiple correlations predicting factors from variables. The scalars are the proportion of variance accounted for in the model as a whole and the root-mean-square error or some equivalent loss function. The $\mathbf{S}$ matrix contains all needed information in an orthogonal solution, but **S**, **B**, and $\Phi$ are needed in an oblique solution (though one of the three is redundant). Moreover, relations among factors need not be the same as relations among factor scores, and so additional matrices may be defined for factor scores to describe their properties.

We suggest that the common factor model makes more conceptual sense than the component model. We normally think of a construct as standing apart from its defining variables, and an individual may be viewed as having a score on a construct even in the absence of these defining measures. However, common factor analysis may lead to various anomalies in practice. Consequently we suggest that exploratory factor analysis use a component approach in order to guarantee a solution.

Factor analysis requires decisions about what to place in the diagonals of **R**, the problem of communality estimation. If these entries are too large, trivial and/or spurious factors will emerge, but if the entries are too small, the solution may be anomalous. A matrix must be Gramian in order to be factored, meaning that can be expressed as the product of a second matrix and the transpose of that second matrix (the matrix turned on its side). If a matrix is Gramian, it can be expressed as the product of an infinite number of different matrices and their transposes. Moreover, as was noted in Chapter 11, the matrix need not contain correlations, but if a correlation matrix is Gramian, its corresponding covariance matrix and sum-of-products matrix will be also. Using numbers less than 1 can allow the matrix to retain its Gramian properties but be of smaller rank and thus require fewer factors to explain it.

We reviewed several procedures for estimating communalities, including unities (component solution), which are not devoid of meaning. The major ways to estimate common factor communalities are (1) to have the hypotheses define the communality estimates, (2) to employ statistical criteria based upon rank, (3) to iterate communality estimates until they converge to the communalities, (4) to use squared multiple correlations, which generally provide the lowest estimates, (5) to use reliabilities, which provide the highest estimates, and (6) to use direct estimation, e.g., maximum likelihood.

Next we compared the empirical properties of component and common factor solutions. Some of the major differences are the following. (1) Component eigenvalues are larger than common factor eigenvalues; (2) component structure elements are also larger than common factor structure elements; (3) component residual correlations are larger than common factor eigenvalues for a given number of factors; (4) absolute values of component residual correlations always decrease with the number of factors, but this is not necessarily true of common factors; (5) component solutions provide biased estimates of the obtained correlations; (6) an oblique rotation derived from a component solution will tend to be more nearly orthogonal than an oblique rotation derived from a common factor solution because unique variance in the component correlation attenuates the factor correlation; (7) the initial structure in a PrC or noniterative principal axis method does not change as factors are added, but it does change when iterative methods are used; (8) changing the number of factors can have a dramatic impact upon rotated factors in both a component and a common factor solution; (9) a variable that is uncorrelated with other variables in the analysis will tend to provide its own singlet component, but will be eliminated from a common factor solution; and (10) you may or may not be able to obtain a common factor solution and/or the common factor solution may involve an ad hoc process to resolve an anomaly, but the major conclusions you reach will be the same in both cases.

Even though we argue for the conceptual superiority of the common factor model, it is not without problems, as several meanings of common variance are possible: (1) the *actual* variance accounted for by linear combinations, but this is effectively a component solution; (2) the variance shared with variables in the set being analyzed, which is estimated by image analysis, a form of component analysis; (3) the reliable variance, which in principle ignores specific variance; (4) the variance shared with a domain of variables, but the concept of domain is vague; and (5) a parameter estimate, which may be empty.

In order to alleviate some of the concerns about communality estimation, we provided data on the estimated magnitude of structure elements as a function of the number of variables and their average correlation. In practice, communality estimates are important only when the number of variables is small *and* their average correlation is low. Both problems can be prevented by a suitable design.

We have thus far considered the most typical design in which correlations are obtained among variables and the number of subjects is large compared to the number of variables, called an *R* design. Subjects are usually chosen at random, but variables are not. Variables, but not subjects, are standardized. Subjects are assumed to be measurable on the same scale (commensurate). The next most popular design, called a *Q* design, reverses the roles of subjects and variables. One must decide whether to standardize scores of subjects. This depends upon whether mean and standard deviation differences among subjects are meaningful. Although it has been argued that *R* and *Q* designs should yield the same outcomes, they are usually intended for different purposes. In still other designs, occasions replace variables or subjects, but these alternative designs usually raise questions that are not factor analytic in nature. Some newer factor analytic models involve three-mode analysis in which variables, subjects, and occasions can be jointly studied.

The same method of condensation need not be used to extract all factors. It is particularly useful to combine factors derived from single variables (pivots in the sense of the square root method defined in Chapter 11) with principal components or principal axes and then rotate orthogonally to these pivots. This ad-lib factoring adjusts for (covaries) the pivots, which might be incidental to the main purpose of the study.

Just as factors may be viewed as abstractions of variables, so may higher-order factors (factors derived from other factors rather than from variables) be viewed as abstractions of lower-order factors. Even though they were not developed formally by factor analysis, the Wechsler scales illustrate this approach.

The chapter concluded with a series of ways to fool yourself with the results of a factor analysis, as by ignoring high factor correlations in an oblique solution, and a short postscript on exploratory factoring containing five practical considerations: (1) use a confirmatory method if it is suitable, (2) don't worry extensively about the component versus common factor issue, (3) avoid studies with small numbers of variables that intercorrelate poorly, (4) orthogonal and oblique rotations will probably lead to the same conclusions, and (5) major groupings will probably be identified regardless of method.

## SUGGESTED ADDITIONAL READINGS

Gorsuch, R. L. (1990). Common factor analysis versus component analysis: Some well and little known facts, *Multivariate Behavioral Research*, *25*, 33–39.

Gorsuch, R. L. (1988). Exploratory factor analysis. In J. R. Nesselroade & R. B. Cattell (Eds.), *Handbook of Multivariate Experimental Psychology*, pp. 231–258. New York: Plenum.

Snook, S. C., & Gorsuch, R. L. (1989). Component analysis versus common factor analysis: A Monte Carlo study, *Psychological Bulletin, 106*, 148–154.

Velicer, W. F., & Jackson, D. N. (1990). Component analysis vs. common factor analysis: Some issues in selecting an appropriate procedure, *Multivariate Behavioral Research*, *25*, 1–28.

Widaman, K. F. (1990). Bias in pattern loadings represented by common factor analysis and component analysis, *Multivariate Behavioral Research*, *25*, 89–95.

*Note*: The sources listed in the previous chapters also deal with the topics considered in this chapter. In addition, the above are some of the relatively less technical works on matters that are under debate.

## CHAPTER 13

# CONFIRMATORY
# FACTOR ANALYSIS

## CHAPTER OVERVIEW

We have thus far let one of several mathematical definitions of "best" dictate the organization of linear combinations and then interpreted the content of the resulting factors. We will now essentially reverse the procedure by beginning with some form of theory that at least partially dictates the content of the factors and see how well that theory fits the data. These theories fall into several classes.

At the least theoretical end, one may wish to compare the factor organization of alternative data sets provided by different subjects, sets of variables, or solutions based upon the same variables. There may be actually little or no theory behind the organization in this case. Prof. Smith may have conducted an exploratory factor analysis of a series of problem solving measures in adolescents, and Prof. Martinez may have studied these same variables in adults. You might be interested in the similarity of the two solutions. Similarly, you may wish to compare a set of maximum likelihood (ML) factors with a set of principal components (PrCs). Still another application is to evaluate factor score estimates. Chapter 12 noted that the properties of components parallel their factor scores in the original sample: Orthogonal components produce uncorrelated factor scores. This is not necessarily true of common factors and their estimated scores nor of any factor scores obtained in a new sample.

The next step up in terms of theory testing, though not necessarily in terms of the complexity of the analysis, concerns hypothesized groupings of variables. In Chapter 11, we described a hypothetical personality researcher who had proposed that anxiety over physical harm was separable from anxiety over social embarrassment. That investigator administered two sets of four tests each that were assumed to measure two respective types of anxiety. A key aspect of the hypothesis is that it makes no statement about how the tests are weighted. The investigator might prefer that they all be equally reliable and relate equally to the factor or outside criterion, but the theory does not require this. All the theory states is that the variables go together in the sense of measuring a construct in common. It is therefore a *weak* theory (Bernstein, 1988) or, within the tradition of structural equation modeling we will consider in this chapter (Jöreskog, 1974), congeneric. An important special case is when a single factor is assumed to underlie all variables, i.e., Spearman's (1904) general factor hypothesis introduced in the previous chapter.

As a theory becomes more highly developed, statements become more precise. One might propose that (1) the two constructs are orthogonal, (2) the two constructs are redundant, (3) tests within groups have equal pattern elements (true variance) and so they are tau-equivalent, and (4) given that they are tau-equivalent, they also have equal error variance so that they are parallel. All these involve hypotheses about measurement.

Another possibility is the testing of causal hypotheses. For example, one investigator may hypothesize that anxiety over bodily harm is directly related to perceived danger, but another investigator may argue that the relationship is mediated by one's perceived competence in handling the danger. Assuming that perceived danger, perceived competence, and anxiety about bodily harm are all measurable, the first hypothesis states that a perceived danger and anxiety about bodily harm will still be correlated after controlling perceived competence; the second hypothesis states that the correlation will disappear following this control. Both measurement and causal hypotheses are examples of strong theories (Bernstein, 1988).

Two broad sets of approaches will be considered. One follows directly from the correlations of sums and the resulting geometry (see Chapter 5). This gives rise to multiple group analysis and related procedures. It is quite suitable for comparing alternative factor solutions and testing weak theories. Also following in this tradition is the use of forced rotations, which includes Procrustes. Although the phrase "methods based upon properties of linear combinations" is value-free and descriptive, we will use the less cumbersome term "classical." Classical methods are more difficult to apply to the testing of strong theories but may be used in some cases.

In contrast, ML, GLS, and ULS estimation may be used to handle all three situations through the analysis of covariance structures (ACS). Although the term LISREL (*li*near *s*tructural *rel*ations, Jöreskog & Sörbom, 1989) is a very common synonym for ACS, it is ambiguous because it also describes a particular computer program. This particular program in turn has competitors which may be used to this same general end, such as Bentler's (1989) EQS. The notation we will use arbitrarily follows LISREL rather than EQS, but we will use the term "ACS" to refer to the abstract model. References to LISREL imply the specific computer program we used to evaluate examples. We will not evaluate the advantages and disadvantages of alternative computer programs save one, Muthén's (1988) LISCOMP, because its extension to ACS is basic to a major topic in this chapter, the analysis of categorical variables such as scales.

Because of the relative simplicity of Spearman's general factor solution and the related problem of defining the structure of a single factor, we will begin by reviewing its logic.

## SPEARMAN'S GENERAL FACTOR SOLUTION

Charles Spearman (1904) was the originator of factor analysis, and even recent theorists have been strongly influenced by his ideas. Although he later modified his position (Spearman, 1927), his early theory was that one general factor ($g$) underlies all mental abilities. This $g$ factor was thought of as the mental yardstick of intelligence—the only one needed to explain the common ground among all individual differences in abilities. Thus, arithmetic, spelling, and judgments of illusions were thought to share in $g$. Spearman additionally theorized that each source of individual differences (each test) possessed a unique factor. Unique factors for different tests were assumed to be uncorrelated. Consequently $g$ accounts for all correlations among tests. The theory is sometimes called Spearman's two-factor theory because each test is assumed to consist of a general factor and a unique factor. As a mathematical model, it is not limited to abilities measures; e.g., it can be used to evaluate a series of anxiety measures if it is proposed that each of the tests has only anxiety in common.

Spearman used the following line of reasoning. If $g$ completely accounts for correlations among tests, these correlations can be accounted for by the correlations of each test with $g$. For example, say that there are five measures, $X_1$ to $X_5$, whose intercorrelations are $r_{12}$, $r_{13}$, etc. The correlations of each with $g$ are $r_{1g}$, $r_{2g}$, etc. According to the logic of PM correlational analysis, the partial correlation between two observables, holding $g$ constant, would be zero if $g$ can explain the correlation between them. Consequently, if $g$ explains the common variance among the five variables, all partial correlations among these five variables holding $g$ constant (e.g., $r_{12.g}$) will be zero. It can further be shown that the correlation between any two variables equals the product of their correlations with $g$. For example, consider the following variation upon Eq. 5-14, partialling $g$ from the correlation between $X_1$ and $X_2$:

$$r_{12.g} = \frac{r_{12} - r_{1g}r_{2g}}{\sqrt{1 - r_{1g}^2}\ \sqrt{1 - r_{2g}^2}} \tag{13-1}$$

The only way for $r_{12.g}$ to be zero is for the numerator to be zero, and the only way for the numerator to be zero is for the correlation between the two tests ($r_{12}$) to equal the product of their correlations with $g$ ($r_{1g}r_{2g}$). Thus, the correlations in any matrix explainable by $g$ equal the products of their correlations with $g$.

We will symbolize the correlations of $X_1$ to $X_5$ with $g$ (structure elements) as $a$, $b$, $c$, $d$, and $e$ rather than as $r_{1g}$, $r_{2g}$, etc., to simplify notation. Then, $r_{12} = ab$, $r_{13} = ac$, $r_{23} = bc$, etc. Assuming the correlations can be explained by $g$, the full correlation matrix (**R**) equals the products of the correlations with $g$, as shown in Table 13-1. We will employ Spearman's method for calculating the diagonal elements, which was discussed in the previous chapter, as part of the solution.

Matrices that can be explained by $g$ have some interesting characteristics. One characteristic of Table 13-1 is that the elements in any column are proportional to those in any other columns, exclusive of diagonal elements. For example, the elements in columns 1 and 2 provide

**TABLE 13-1**    CORRELATIONS AMONG FIVE TESTS EXPRESSED
AS CORRELATIONS WITH A GENERAL FACTOR

|       |       | Test  |       |       |       |
|-------|-------|-------|-------|-------|-------|
| Test  | $X_1$ | $X_2$ | $X_3$ | $X_4$ | $X_5$ |
| $X_1$ |       | $ab$  | $ac$  | $ad$  | $ae$  |
| $X_2$ | $ab$  |       | $bc$  | $bd$  | $be$  |
| $X_3$ | $ac$  | $bc$  |       | $cd$  | $ce$  |
| $X_4$ | $ad$  | $bd$  | $cd$  |       | $de$  |
| $X_5$ | $ae$  | $be$  | $ce$  | $de$  |       |

$$\frac{r_{13}}{r_{23}} = \frac{r_{14}}{r_{24}} = \frac{r_{15}}{r_{25}} \tag{13-2}$$

This can be seen by substituting the products of the correlations with $g$ for the correlation between the measures:

$$\frac{r_{13}}{r_{23}} = \frac{ac}{bc} = \frac{a}{b}$$

$$\frac{r_{14}}{r_{24}} = \frac{ad}{bd} = \frac{a}{b} \tag{13-3}$$

$$\frac{r_{15}}{r_{25}} = \frac{ae}{be} = \frac{a}{b}$$

The elements in any two columns are therefore proportional to the correlations of the two variables with $g$, ignoring pairs of elements where either is a diagonal element. This holds for any two rows of **R** as well as for any two columns.

The first tests of $g$ were made by examining the proportionality of columns in **R** using tetrads. A tetrad consists of two elements from any column (e.g., $r_{14}$ and $r_{24}$) and the corresponding two elements from any other column (e.g. $r_{15}$ and $r_{25}$). If Eq. 13-2 holds so that the two pairs are proportional, products of the form $r_{14}r_{25} - r_{15}r_{24}$ will equal zero, a condition known as the vanishing tetrad. All tetrads will vanish in the population **R** matrix if the methods of Chapter 12 are used to obtain communality estimates. If you are familiar with the concept of a determinant, you will also recognize that vanishing tetrads imply that all $2 \times 2$ determinants (which are the values of the tetrad differences, e.g., $r_{14}r_{25} - r_{15}r_{24}$) will be zero. This also implies that the matrix is of rank 1, providing the correlations are not all zero. Harman (1976) discusses how such tetrads were investigated and how Spearman's model was later expanded to include possible factors beyond $g$. However, there are now better ways to test the hypothesis that a single factor explains **R** than examining tetrads. Nonetheless, we will present Spearman's method as the easiest form of factor analysis to calculate by hand for the benefit of those who wish to learn by direct calculation.

Assuming **R** fits the model exactly, the structure can be computed directly. Equation 13-4a provides the squared correlation of $X_1$ with $g$ ($a^2$):

$$\frac{r_{12}r_{23}}{r_{23}} = \frac{(ab)(ac)}{bc} = \frac{a^2bc}{bc} = a^2 = r_{1g}^2 \qquad (13\text{-}4a)$$

Equation 13-4b provides the same result:

$$\frac{r_{14}r_{15}}{r_{45}} = \frac{(ad)(ae)}{de} = \frac{a^2de}{de} = a^2 = r_{1g}^2 \qquad (13\text{-}4b)$$

In a matrix of five variables, there are six different equations that can be used to infer the correlation of any variable with $g$ since there are six ways the four remaining variables can be combined in pairs. All give the same result in the population. This will not occur in practice because of sampling error, and so the different equations will provide slightly different estimated correlations with $g$. A pooled estimate of the squared correlation between $X_1$ and $g$ ($a^2$) can be obtained by (1) adding the numerators of all equations, (2) adding the denominators, and (3) dividing as in Eq. 13-5. Spearman and Holzinger (1924, 1925) also studied the sampling distribution of these estimates.

$$a^2 = \frac{r_{12}r_{13} + r_{12}r_{14} + r_{12}r_{15} + r_{13}r_{14} + r_{13}r_{15} + r_{14}r_{15}}{r_{23} + r_{24} + r_{25} + r_{34} + r_{35} + r_{45}} \qquad (13\text{-}5)$$

The numerator is the sum of paired products of correlations between $X_1$ and each of the other variables, and the denominator is the sum of all correlations *not* involving $X_1$. Parallel expressions estimate the correlations of $X_2$ to $X_6$ with $g$.

Equation 13-6 is a simpler way to obtain these estimates:

$$r_{ig}^2 = \frac{L^2 - Q}{2(M - L)} \qquad (13\text{-}6)$$

where $r_{ig}^2$ = squared correlation of variable $X_i$ with $g$
$L$ = sum of correlations in column $i$, excluding the diagonal element
$Q$ = sum of squared correlations in column $i$
$M$ = sum of all correlations below diagonal of matrix

As noted in Chapter 12, Spearman's special case solves the problem of communality estimation that plagued later factor analysis. It is a tribute to his intellect that he recognized that the problem existed. The results are similar to the structure of the first centroid but differ because correlations with the centroid factor involve diagonal terms.

Table 13-2 illustrates application of Spearman's result to simulated data. Imagine that a Prof. Hatfield has developed five measures of aggression, $X_1$ to $X_5$. The tests are

TABLE 13-2   COMPUTATIONAL PROCEDURES FOR DETERMINING CORRELATIONS WITH A GENERAL FACTOR

| | $X_1$ | $X_2$ | $X_3$ | $X_4$ | $X_5$ |
|---|---|---|---|---|---|
| | | | **Correlations** | | |
| $X_1$ | | .72 | .62 | .51 | .47 |
| $X_2$ | .72 | | .56 | .49 | .46 |
| $X_3$ | .62 | .56 | | .42 | .38 |
| $X_4$ | .51 | .49 | .42 | | .29 |
| $X_5$ | .47 | .46 | .38 | .29 | |
| Column sums ($L$) | 2.32 | 2.23 | 1.97 | 1.70 | 1.60 |
| Column sums of squares ($Q$) | 1.38 | 1.29 | 1.01 | .75 | .66 |
| | | | | | $M = 4.91$ |
| $r_{ig}^2$ | .77 | .69 | .49 | .33 | .29 |
| $r_{ig}$ | .88 | .83 | .70 | .58 | .54 |

| | $X_1$ | $X_2$ | $X_3$ | $X_4$ | $X_5$ |
|---|---|---|---|---|---|
| | | | **Residual coefficients** | | |
| $X_1$ | | −.01 | .00 | .01 | .00 |
| $X_2$ | −.01 | | −.02 | .01 | .02 |
| $X_3$ | .00 | −.02 | | .01 | .00 |
| $X_4$ | .01 | .01 | .01 | | −.02 |
| $X_5$ | .00 | .02 | .00 | −.02 | |

all in standard score ($\mu = 0$, $\sigma = 1$) and are all defined by a single factor ($g$). The population correlations between $X_1$ to $X_5$ and $g$ are .9, .8, .7, .6, and .5, respectively, because the tests are of decreasing reliability. The raw data look like the following:

```
1.30     .77    1.30    2.20     1.14
-.22    -.51     .74    -.87     -.77
-.21   -1.27     .18   -1.00    -1.28
-.91   -1.91    -.73    1.18     -.86
 .07    -.27    -.15     .23     -.05
```

After estimating the correlations with $g$, a matrix of their cross products may be obtained and subtracted from the **R** to produce a residual covariance matrix. Examining the size and patterning of these values can lead to a decision about the general factor hypothesis. Our calculations maintained the full precision of the raw data but were rounded to two decimal places for presentation (yours may differ through rounding error). As can be seen, the residuals are all of trivial magnitude (less than ±.02 in all cases). Moreover, the five structure estimates (.88, .83, .70, .58, and .54) are very close to the parameters generating the data (.9, .8, .7, .6, and .5).

A more modern approach is to obtain a single exploratory ML factor and test the residual for significance, using the likelihood ratio chi-square ($G^2$) distribution. Other tests, discussed below, are more complex but lead to basically the same outcome. Our ML results were that the $G^2$ value testing the null hypothesis that there were no common factors in the data was 949.64, which is significant well beyond the .001 level with 10 $df$. This confirms the presence of at least one factor. The $G^2$ value associated with the residual was only 2.31, which is not significant with 5 $df$. This indicates that the single factor was sufficient to explain the correlations. The structure estimates were nearly identical to those obtained from Spearman's procedure (.88, .82, .70, .58, and .54). Recall that even when the data conform as closely to the model as the present data do, the ML procedure is not guaranteed to converge, however. Similar results were obtained from other common factor solutions and, for reasons discussed in Chapter 12, the structure of the first PrC was slightly larger in magnitude.

Although Spearman laid the foundation for factor analysis, numerous contrary findings made his hypothesized $g$ untenable as a substantive explanation of how cognitive abilities relate. It became quite obvious that a single factor could not explain the correlation matrices obtained from larger sets of more diverse measures, such as verbal skills, spatial skills, perceptual skills, numerical skills, etc. Additional factors were obviously needed. This required both an augmentation of theory and the development of mathematical procedures that went beyond testing for only a general factor. Various efforts were made to extend Spearman's factoring method to the multifactor case. Most of these basically consisted of inferring factors from clusters of partial correlations in the residual matrix produced by removing $g$. One widely used method of this form was Holzinger and Swineford's (1937) bifactor method cited in the previous chapter. However, two major changes took place in extending Spearman's original to the multifactor case.

First, factoring gradually switched from confirmatory to exploratory analysis because groupings of residual correlations were inferred from their sizes rather than specified before the analysis. Second, the mathematics of obtaining correlations with $g$ did not provide an adequate basis for developing a general logic for exploratory factor analysis. The efforts to obtain additional factors consisted largely of trial-and-error techniques requiring numerous assumptions about patterns of correlations in the matrix. These methods had no solid mathematical basis as the centroid, PrC, and ML methods do.

This change in emphasis from confirmatory to exploratory analysis took place around 1930. The resulting forms of exploratory analysis (e.g., PrC plus varimax) have been greatly refined and applied widely. However, a variety of psychological theories and prior data have provided more definite hypotheses about factor structures in the last 20 years. Consequently testing hypothesis with factor analysis has returned to vogue, and there is great interest in confirmatory factor analysis. Spearman's old, elegant model for $g$ is still a perfectly good procedure for testing the hypothesis that a particular collection of variables is dominated by only one common factor. When its results are radically different from ML, the data probably deviate so radically from a single factor structure that the correlations with $g$ are of no interest.

## COMPARING FACTORS IN DIFFERENT ANALYSES

An important research problem is to determine how similar sets of factors are in different analyses, as in the example given at the beginning of the chapter concerning the two investigators who studied a series of abilities measures in populations of different ages. Science cannot progress on the particular; its most valuable discoveries are general. A single exploratory (or, for that matter, confirmatory) analysis has limited value. Results contribute to our knowledge when they are replicable under different conditions. Groups differing in age, gender, and ethnicity, are the most obvious, but not the only, ways to generalize. It is also useful to explore differences across populations. One might find that there is greater variability in a verbal ability factor among members of group A than group B or that two uncorrelated factors in group A are highly correlated in group B. However, such differences are meaningful only when there is some degree of factorial similarity to provide a basis for comparison.

In investigating such issues, it is essential to remember that factors can be viewed as linear combinations of variables—actual linear combinations in component analysis and hypothetical (estimated) linear combinations in common factor analysis. Similarly, factor scores are linear combinations of observed scores—again, actual in the case of component factors and hypothetical in the case of common factors. Both must be sharply distinguished from structure elements (correlations between variables and factors).

Gorsuch (1983) discusses three situations where one might compare factors and/or factor scores:

**1** One set of variables, such as a set of cognitive abilities measures, has been given to the same subjects (same variables–same subjects). The goal might be (a) to compare alternative factor solutions, (b) to evaluate the properties of factor score estimates, or (c) to compare exact or estimated factor weights with approximations based upon salient variables.

**2** One set of variables is given to two different groups (same variables–different subjects). The goal is to test for factor invariance.

**3** Two or more distinct sets of variables are given to a single group of subjects (different variables–same subjects). The goal is to relate factors obtained from one set of variables to factors obtained from other sets of variables.

There is a vital functional difference between the same variables–same subjects case (1) and the different variables—same subjects case (3), but you cannot tell which is which simply from looking at the variables. The choice depends upon the goals of the analysis. A case-1 factor may contain salients from different sets, but case 3 provides separate factors for each set of variables.

## Classical Approaches to Testing Factor Invariance

Assume that an investigator has obtained either a series of measures from the same subjects on two occasions (case 1) or the same measures from two different groups of subjects (case 2) and wishes to compare the resulting factor structures.

Investigators commonly determine the similarity of the two sets of results based upon corresponding structure elements (factor-variable correlations) or, even worse, pattern elements (beta weights predicting variables from factors) or factor-score weights (beta weights predicting factors from variables.) We cannot suggest strongly enough that this *not* be done, especially when the variables underlying these factors are highly correlated, as they should be. The "it don't make no nevermind" principle

(Kaiser, 1970; Wainer, 1976) we have stressed is that two sets of weights that appear highly different may generate linear combinations that are highly correlated when the underlying variables are highly correlated.

Conversely, it is possible to rotate two orthogonal factors so that their structure (and therefore pattern) elements become highly similar; e.g., $X_1$ correlates .4 with both factors and $X_2$ correlates .3 with both factors. This is because statistical and geometric orthogonality are distinct concepts (see Chapter 11); orthogonal factors can produce structure elements that are correlated. Only PrC and principal axis analyses produce uncorrelated factors with uncorrelated factor structure elements, and rotation destroys this property. Do not base comparisons upon the similarity of structure (or pattern or factor-score) elements because these elements are *not* the factors.

One classical approach is to correlate the scores produced by the two factors, which is also the correlation between the factors in a component solution. When the same measures are obtained from all subjects, it does not even matter whether the two factors are based upon the same or different variables, i.e., whether case 1 or case 3 holds. Factors I and II are each defined by a set of factor weights. These weights were symbolized in terms of a single matrix (**W**) in Chapters 11 and 12 but are better viewed as two distinct vectors here, symbolized $\mathbf{w}_x$ and $\mathbf{w}_y$ (the use of lowercase boldface to denote vectors is conventional). One may correlate the two sets of factor scores by applying $\mathbf{w}_x$ and $\mathbf{w}_y$ to the data matrix **X**, and the procedure generalizes to scores on multiple factors. However, it is much simpler to apply the vectors to **R** instead of **X**. An alternative and somewhat popular procedure, which dates back to Burt (1948), is the coefficient of congruence. This is a formal measure of the similarity of two sets of pattern elements. It provides a simplified measure of the correlation between components, but it can lead to anomalous results in other settings. Consequently we do not recommend it for the reasons we do not recommend any comparison based upon factor patterns (for details, see Gorsuch, 1983; Harman, 1976).

We will illustrate how these calculations follow directly from the methods of Chapter 5. Recall the mythical Prof. Hatfield's five aggression measures. Equally mythical Prof. McCoy administers these ($X_1$ to $X_5$) to 500 people institutionalized for acts of violence and finds that these measures correlate .9, .8, .7, .8, and .8 with Prof. McCoy's factor I because $X_4$ and $X_5$ are more reliable than they were in the original study. These correlations appear in Table 13-3.

TABLE 13-3  COMPUTING THE CORRELATION PRODUCED BY TWO SETS OF FACTOR WEIGHTS

| Variable Weight | | Correlation Matrix | | | | |
| --- | --- | --- | --- | --- | --- | --- |
| | | $X_1$ | $X_2$ | $X_3$ | $X_4$ | $X_5$ |
| $X_1$ | .29 | 1.00 | .75 | .62 | .75 | .74 |
| $X_2$ | .28 | .75 | 1.00 | .58 | .67 | .66 |
| $X_3$ | .26 | .62 | .58 | 1.00 | .61 | .55 |
| $X_4$ | .23 | .75 | .67 | .61 | 1.00 | .66 |
| $X_5$ | .21 | .74 | .66 | .55 | .66 | 1.00 |
| Accumulative sum | | .99 | .94 | .86 | .93 | .90 |

Prof. Hatfield's factor weights ($\mathbf{w}_x$) were .29, .28, .26, .23, and 21, whereas Prof. McCoy's factor weights ($\mathbf{w}_y$) were .25, .24, .21, .24, and .23. Note that McCoy's $X_4$ and $X_5$ have larger weights than Hatfield's because McCoy's were more reliable. These trends also appear in Prof. McCoy's factor structure, which is not presented. We will illustrate the calculation using Prof. McCoy's correlation matrix.

**1** The variances produced by $\mathbf{w}_x$ and $\mathbf{w}_y$ and their covariance are needed, as in any correlation. These quantities in turn require what we will term intermediate vectors. The weights $\mathbf{w}_x$ appear in the first data column of Table 13-3. Accumulatively cross-multiply these by the correlations in the first column of the correlation matrix: $(.29)(1.00) + (.28)(.75) + (.26)(.62) + (.23)(.75) + (.21)(.74) = .99$. This is the first element of the intermediate vector (the process illustrates matrix multiplication).

**2** Repeat this for the remaining columns in the correlation matrix. This produces the values .94, .86, .93, and .90, as shown at the bottom of the table, that constitute the remainder of the intermediate vector.

**3** Accumulatively multiply the corresponding terms in $\mathbf{w}_y$ and the intermediate vector to obtain the covariance of the two linear combinations: $(.29)(.99) + (.28)(.94) + (.26)(.86) + (.23)(.93) + (.21)(.90) = 1.095$.

**4** Accumulatively multiply the intermediate vector by $\mathbf{w}_x$ instead of $\mathbf{w}_y$ to obtain the variance produced by $\mathbf{w}_x$. The result is 1.201.

**5** Place the values of $\mathbf{w}_y$ instead of $\mathbf{w}_x$ in the first column and accumulatively multiply the resulting intermediate vector by $\mathbf{w}_x$ to obtain the variance produced by $\mathbf{w}_y$. The result is 1.0. This will always be the case when component weights are applied to their corresponding matrix.

**6** The correlation, as always, is the covariance divided by the square root of the product of the variances: or $1.095/\sqrt{(1.201)(1)}$ or 1.0 within rounding error. Had you used the structure weights (variable-factor correlations), the variance would equal the variance accounted for by the factor. However, the covariance would be affected in a parallel manner, leaving the correlation unaffected. When structure elements other than those produced by PrC are used, the correlation will differ from the proper value obtained using factor weights.

The correlation between the two sets of weights can be determined in a like manner for Prof. Hatfield's correlation matrix, and either set of weights can be compared to equal weights (1, 1, 1, 1, 1). In fact, all of these correlations are .999 or larger. When the results for both matrices are as similar as they are here, report this fact and one arbitrarily chosen set of results. Otherwise, report both sets of results and explore the reason for the difference; e.g., see if one group may have been range-restricted.

The fact that the correlations between Prof. Hatfield and Prof. McCoy's factors are all so high means that their properties are practically identical. Clearly, it is very strained to say that two factors are different when their factor scores correlate above .95, as is often true. We strongly recommend the present method for most problems (an exception will be noted) because it is sensitive to both the structure elements and the correlations among the observed variables and not just to the structure elements themselves. This point may appear obvious given the similarity in magnitude of correlation and factor weights, but the results of an ACS analysis, presented below, will be of interest.

## Some Practical Aspects of Comparing Factor Structures

**1** Some lack of invariance in a component solution may reflect unreliability. Equation 7-12 can be used to estimate the reliability of the factors, and Eq. 6-36 can then be used to correct the correlation between factors for attenuation. The result approximates the correlation between common factors, which are theoretically error-free.

**2** Lack of factor invariance across groups could imply that group differences moderate the correlations among groups, or it could simply arise from sampling error. Bernstein, Garbin, and McClellan (1983; also see Jensen, 1980) formed pseudogroups to evaluate this issue. Assume you have obtained correlation matrices from samples of 500 males and 500 females. Compute two additional correlation matrices. Obtain one by selecting half the males and half the females at random, and obtain the other from the remaining cases (e.g., the even sequence numbers, assuming these are random). These two matrices define the pseudogroups, and correlations between corresponding factors obtained from them can differ only through sampling error. They provide a baseline for evaluating the correlation between factors obtained from the male and female correlation matrices.

**3** Imagine comparing a set of cognitive abilities measures in groups of engineering and liberal arts students at a fairly selective university in order to compare the resulting factor structures. If the engineering subjects are uniformly high in numerical ability, they will be range-restricted on relevant measures, but they may vary more widely in verbal ability. As a consequence, verbal skills might dominate their major dimension of variation (PrC I). Just the reverse may be true of the liberal arts students. The comparison may profit by using the initial rather than rotated factors. Comparing rotated factors confounds differences in the overall structure with differences in rotation (e.g., the angle of rotation might be 30° in one group and 40° in the other) which would be superimposed on any difference in the composition of the PrCs.

**4** Comparing pairs of weights in each group can become cumbersome when there are several groups (e.g., whites, blacks, Hispanics, and Asians) since there will be two correlation matrices to compare for every pair of groups. Moreover, the correlation matrices used to compare whites and blacks will both be different from the correlation matrices used to compare Hispanics and Asians. Standard references on multivariate analysis (see Chapter 11) describe how to obtain the pooled within-group covariance matrix, which may then be used to obtain a composite correlation matrix. For applications, see Kaiser, Hunka, and Bianchini (1971) and Bernstein, Teng, Garbin, and Grannemann (1987). However, examine the separate matrices for systematic differences in variance and/or covariance. Appropriate procedures may be found in the multivariate texts listed in Chapter 11.

**5** Comparing the two professors' factors was greatly simplified because the properties of component factor scores are identical to the properties of their corresponding factors. In common factor analysis, this is not generally the case. Consequently circumstances may arise in which one wishes to compare two common factors, a factor with factor-score estimates derived either from that or another factor, or two sets of factor-score estimates. Gorsuch (1983) deals with this issue in detail. The basic idea is to use the structure matrix ($\mathbf{S}$) to investigate properties of factors, and the factor weight matrix ($\mathbf{W}$) to investigate properties of factor-score estimates.

**6** Case 3, discussed above, involves two sets of variables that are administered to the same subjects, say, 10 demographic and 15 attitudinal measures, which are intended to yield separate sets of factors. Factor the $10 \times 10$ matrix of demographic correlations separately from the $15 \times 15$ matrix of attitudinal measures. Then obtain the $25 \times 25$ matrix containing all possible correlations both within and between sets. Assume the first variables in the matrix are the demographic ones. Augment the demographic weights on its factor(s) by adding 15 zeros at the end of each. Then, augment the attitudinal weights on its factor(s) by adding 10 zeros at the beginning of each. The procedure used to evaluate the similarities of the two professors' factors can also be used to compare these two groups of factor-score weights.

## Comparing Overall Solutions

The above discussion was directed toward comparing pairs of factors and/or factor scores. A rather different problem involves the overall similarity of two solutions. Consider two investigations, each of which employs the same variables, case 2 above. Each investigation provides a two-factor solution. Denote the two factors obtained from one study as $I_x$ and $II_x$, and the two factors obtained from the second study as $I_y$ and $II_y$. Using the above principles, you discover that the correlation between $I_x$ and $I_y$ is only .7, and that the same is true of $II_x$ and $II_y$. What does the fact that the two pairs of factors have only 50 percent overlap say about the overall solutions?

The answer is that you don't know. It is possible that a simple rotation may transform $I_x$ and $II_x$ into $I_y$ and $II_y$, but it is also possible that this is not so. That is, all four factors may lie in the same plane [i.e., be coplanar (in general, share a common hyperplane that is a subspace of the overall solution)] or they may not, depending upon other possible relations (e.g., between $I_x$ and $II_y$). Following the above logic, the extent to which $I_y$ falls in the plane defined by $I_x$ and $II_x$ may be defined by its multiple correlation with the latter factors. The extent to which $I_x$ and $II_x$ are related to $I_y$ and $II_y$ may be inferred from a canonical correlation analysis involving the two groups of factors. (Standard textbooks on multivariate analysis discuss canonical correlation analysis.)

Cliff (1966; also see Meredith, 1964) developed a system of forced rotation to make two sets of factors as similar as possible. His procedure is one of a larger class of such procedures including Procrustes, discussed later as a confirmatory procedure. Although the details of the method involve a very complex eigenanalysis, the solution is readily programmed. Basically, $I_x$ and $II_x$ are rotated to form $I'_x$ and $II'_x$. Simultaneously, $I_y$ and $II_y$ are rotated to form $I'_y$ and $II'_y$. The angles of rotation make the sum of the squared distance between $I'_x$ and $I'_y$ and between $II'_x$ and $II'_y$ as small as possible. The relevant computations are described in Gorsuch (1983) and Harman (1976). Cliff's method is orthogonal in that both $I_x$ and $II_x$ are each rotated by the same amount and $I_y$ and $II_y$ are also rotated by the same amount (but probably a different amount than $I_x$ and $II_x$). However, oblique methods, which allow all four factors to be rotated by different amounts, are also available.

## ACS Approaches

Approaches based upon the ACS compare the fit of two solutions. In one, parameters are estimated separately for each group, and in the other, they are constrained to equality. This is fundamentally the same logic used in Chapter 10 with item response theory to test for differential item functioning and comes from the same roots in numerical estimation. The parameters involved in comparing the correlational structure are the pattern weights, the factor correlations (in a multifactor solution), and the uniquenesses (the reason that ACS stresses pattern elements over structure elements will be given later in this chapter). Unlike classical methods which can be used with both component and common factor solutions, ACS effectively makes sense only as a common factor solution.

Parameters that can vary freely among groups must provide better overall fit than fixed or constrained parameters, by definition, but the inferential question is whether this fit is significantly better (i.e., whether the $G^2$ values for the two models differ by more than chance), and the descriptive question is how much better the fit is. Comparing groups often requires that one analyze either the covariance matrix (the values of $\Sigma x^2/N$ and $\Sigma xy/N$) or the mean sum-of-products matrix (the values of $\Sigma X^2/N$ and $\Sigma XY/N$, also called the moment matrix) rather than $\mathbf{R}$. Strictly speaking, the $G^2$ test used to evaluate models should always be based upon the covariance matrix or the mean-sum-of-products matrix rather than the $\mathbf{R}$ matrix, though it often does not differ appreciably when $\mathbf{R}$ is used. The mean-sum-of-products matrix is needed when mean differences are under investigation. For example, it allows one to test whether groups that have been given a set of abilities measures differ in overall ability. There has been much recent discussion about when to use these other matrices and when to use $\mathbf{R}$ (Cudeck, 1989). Computer programs provide standardized output as an option to place the parameters in the same metric that $\mathbf{R}$ would produce, as well as standard errors.

We will provide a detailed example later. For the moment, we note that Prof. Hatfield's and Prof. McCoy's solutions were significantly different by ACS criteria, despite the .999+ correlation between the corresponding components. Is it a mistake to conclude that the two solutions are different? Earlier we suggested that one not look at differences in pattern weights as implying a difference in factor structure, yet that is precisely what is done here. We suggest it *is* a mistake to conclude differences exist if one's primary interest is in the properties of the composites they generate. However, it is just as proper to ask questions about properties of individual tests in relation to the structure, and ACS is certainly correct in noting between-group differences caused the very nature of the simulation. However, to ignore the trivial effects of these differences upon the composite is a failure "to see the forest for the trees."

## TESTING WEAK THEORIES (THEORIES CONCERNING GROUPINGS OF VARIABLES)

Weak theories concern how variables group, e.g., that $X_1$, $X_2$, and $X_3$ define one factor, $X_4$, $X_5$, and $X_6$ define a second factor, etc. The correlations among factors is also of interest in determining how separable the factors are, but the factors are not assumed independent. Moreover, the investigator is not concerned with whether the proposed factors completely explain the relations among variables. For example, measures from two separate factors may share method variance in the sense of Chater. 5. This would not be counter to the weak theory as long as it is minor compared to the differences among the proposed types of tests. In other words, the proposed groupings need not be exhaustive. The example involving hypothetical Prof. Brown's research on two forms of anxiety used in Chapters 11 and 12 will be used here.

The two main classical approaches are the multiple group method, which usually defines factors as the equally weighted sum of variables presumably comprising each cluster, and Procrustes (forced rotation). The classical approach treats weights as equal if there is no basis for treating them as different (both methods can be used to test proposed unequal weightings, but that is an issue of strong theory). In contrast, ACS numerically estimates optimal linear combinations. Although we will argue in favor of the multiple group method over Procrustes, Procrustes is available in at least one major computer package (SAS), but the multiple group method is not. However, it is simple to write a multiple group program in a matrix-oriented language like SAS PROC IML. Bernstein (1988) provides a program written in a precursor form of PROC IML which SAS can translate into usable form.

## Multiple Group Confirmatory Analysis

The multiple group method was developed nearly simultaneously by Thurstone (1945) and Holzinger (1944). It is also called the group centroid method because it is only a variation of the centroid method discussed in Chapter 11. Centroid analysis places a factor among *all* the variables in the analysis. Multiple group analysis places factors through proposed groupings. The factors are usually correlated, and so a third name is the oblique multiple group method, but it is also possible to extract orthogonal factors. The mathematics is extremely simple, following directly from the correlation of sums (Chapter 5). The analysis may be applied to correlations (standardized variables), covariances (deviation scores), or mean sums of products (raw scores), but we will use correlations. We will use a component model, but a common factor model may also be employed.

The basic results are as follows.

**1** The factor structure (**S**): the correlations between each of the variables and the centroids

**2** The factor correlations ($\Phi$): the correlation s among the centroids

**3** The pattern (**B**): the regression weights predicting variables from the centroids.

As in any factor analysis, other quantities of interest like the $h^2$ values may be derived from these three matrices.

In the present case, Prof. Brown's proposed bodily harm factor, factor I, is defined simply as $X_1 + X_2 + X_3$, and the social anxiety factor, factor II, is likewise defined as $X_4 + X_5 + X_6$. Factor I is the centroid (average) of variables $X_1$, $X_2$, and $X_3$, and factor II is the centroid of variables $X_4$, $X_5$, and $X_6$ (as with rotated factors, which factor is denoted I and which is denoted II is arbitrary).

The concept of a hypothesis matrix is basic to confirmatory factor analysis even though it does not appear explicitly in the calculations that we will present. A hypothesis matrix has one column per factor and one row per variable. The process of specification in weak multiple group analysis defines which variables are associated with which factors. A +1 or a −1 includes the variable in a given row with the centroid (group) represented by the column, and a 0 excludes it. The sign reflects the relation between that variable and the others in the group.

In the present case, the hypothesis matrix is

$$
\begin{array}{cc}
1 & 0 \\
1 & 0 \\
1 & 0 \\
0 & 1 \\
0 & 1 \\
0 & 1
\end{array}
$$

In contrast, the overall centroid would be represented as

$$
\begin{array}{c}
1 \\
1 \\
1 \\
1 \\
1 \\
1
\end{array}
$$

If, for reasons to be made clearer later, factor I is to be defined as the sum of variables $X_1$, $X_3$, and $X_5$, and factor II as the sum of variables $X_2$, $X_4$, and $X_6$, the hypothesis matrix would be

$$
\begin{array}{cc}
1 & 0 \\
0 & 1 \\
1 & 0 \\
0 & 1 \\
1 & 0 \\
0 & 1
\end{array}
$$

It is easier to apply the formula for the correlation of sums to a correlation matrix ($\mathbf{R}$), covariance matrix, or mean-sum-of-products matrix than to a data matrix ($\mathbf{X}$). The analysis relies heavily upon the general formula for the correlation of equally weighted sums of standard scores, Eq. 5-8c, which can be written in the form of

$$
r_{\text{I,II}} = \frac{\bar{R}_{\text{I,II}}}{\sqrt{\bar{R}_\text{I}}\,\sqrt{\bar{R}_\text{II}}} \tag{13-7}
$$

where $r_{I,II}$ = correlation between linear combinations I and II

$\bar{R}_{I,II}$ = sum of all elements in the cross-correlation matrix between the two linear combinations

$\bar{R}_I, \bar{R}_{II}$ = sum of elements within the respective correlation matrices

If either linear combination is an individual variable rather than a sum of several variables, the corresponding term ($\bar{R}_I$ or $\bar{R}_{II}$) equals 1 and the numerator ($\bar{R}_{I,II}$) equals the sum of correlations between the individual variable and the members of the linear combination.

Table 13-4 contains a worked-out example of the multiple group method testing Prof. Brown's hypothesis. The correlation matrix is partitioned so that the top left contains the correlations within factor I ($X_1 + X_2 + X_3$), the bottom right contains the correlations within factor II ($X_4 + X_5 + X_6$), and the bottom left (or top right) contain the correlations between the two sets. These values of $\bar{R}_I$, $\bar{R}_{II}$, and $\bar{R}_{I,II}$ are $1.00 + .75 + .83 + \cdots$ or 7.56, $1.00 + .79 + .82 + \cdots$ or 7.74, and $.32 + .25 + .39 + \cdots$ or 2.81. Consequently, assuming an oblique solution, the factor correlation $\phi_{I,II}$ is $2.81/\sqrt{(7.56)(7.74)}$ or .37.

The correlation of any variable with group centroid I (the sum of $X_1$, $X_2$, and $X_3$) is obtained from Eq. 13-7 as follows. Since these structure elements equal the correlations of individual variables with the sum of $X_1$ to $X_3$, only one term appears in the denominator, $\sqrt{\bar{R}_I} = 2.75$. The numerator is the sum of correlations of each variable

**TABLE 13-4**   COMPUTATIONAL PROCEDURES FOR OBTAINING MULTIPLE GROUP FACTORS

| | Correlation Matrix | | | | | |
|---|---|---|---|---|---|---|
| | $X_1$ | $X_2$ | $X_3$ | $X_4$ | $X_5$ | $X_6$ |
| $X_1$ | 1.00 | .75 | .83 | .32 | .28 | .36 |
| $X_2$ | .75 | 1.00 | .70 | .25 | .31 | .32 |
| $X_3$ | .83 | .70 | 1.00 | .39 | .25 | .33 |
| $X_4$ | .32 | .25 | .39 | 1.00 | .79 | .82 |
| $X_5$ | .28 | .31 | .25 | .79 | 1.00 | .76 |
| $X_6$ | .36 | .32 | .33 | .82 | .76 | 1.00 |

$$\bar{R}_I = 7.56 \qquad \sqrt{\bar{R}_I} = 2.75$$
$$\bar{R}_{II} = 7.74 \qquad \sqrt{\bar{R}_{II}} = 2.78$$
$$\bar{R}_{I,II} = 2.81$$

| | Sum of correlations with groups | | Structure | |
|---|---|---|---|---|
| | I | II | I | II |
| $X_1$ | 2.58 | .96 | .94 | .35 |
| $X_2$ | 2.45 | .88 | .89 | .32 |
| $X_3$ | 2.53 | .97 | .92 | .35 |
| $X_4$ | .96 | 2.61 | .35 | .94 |
| $X_5$ | .84 | 2.55 | .31 | .92 |
| $X_6$ | 1.01 | 2.58 | .37 | .93 |

with $X_1$ to $X_3$. For example, the sum of the correlations of $X_1$ with $X_1$, $X_2$, and $X_3$ variables is 2.58 (1.00 + .75 + .83), and so the structure element for $X_1$ on factor I is 2.58/2.75 or .94. The remaining five structure elements for factor I are defined analogously. Unfortunately, computing the pattern elements is cumbersome and not particularly instructive to do by hand. It is the matrix product of **S** and what is known as the inverse of $\Phi$ (see p. 616 for the definition of an inverse). We will present these pattern elements later when we compare the various procedures for performing a confirmatory analysis.

In an oblique solution, the structure for factor II is obtained in the same general way that the structure for factor I was obtained. The difference is that one divides sums of correlations with $X_4$ to $X_6$ by $\sqrt{\overline{R_{II}}}$ rather than dividing sums of correlations with $X_1$ to $X_3$ by $\sqrt{\overline{R_I}}$. This illustrates simultaneous extraction of factors as discussed in Chapter 11, in contrast to the successive extraction that characterizes exploratory factoring. However, we could have made factor II orthogonal to factor I, using successive extraction. Factor II would be obtained from a residual matrix following extraction of factor I ($\mathbf{R_I}$) rather than from **R** itself. A third option is to extract factor II first, generate a residual matrix, and then extract factor I. The orthogonal group centroid structure may also be obtained by transforming the oblique factors, as described in Harman (1976) and other standard references on factor analysis.

Table 13-4 shows the structure, which is almost identical to the promax solution in Table 12-2. For example, $r_{II}$ is .94 in both cases. The difference in obliqueness is trivial, cos $(\phi) = .37$ here versus .38 previously. Both rotated factors go through clusters of variables. There is, however, a very important difference in how the two sets of results are obtained: Factors were defined mathematically in the exploratory solution but were hypothesized in advance in the group centroid solution. We therefore solved for these multiple group factors directly. The two approaches need not provide similar results, particularly when the number of variables is large (more than 20) and numerous factors are extracted. Note that the structure matrix in Table 13-4 does not look especially simple. The variables that define factor I have correlations of about .3 with factor II, and vice versa. The reasons are the same as noted in the discussion of oblique rotations in Chapter 12. However, the structure elements for the three variables that define each factor are all much higher ($\approx$.9) than the structure elements of the three variables excluded from the factor ($\approx$.3), and so the nature of each factor is clear.

The multiple group method can be used to test for any number of hypothesized factors. If a single common factor ($g$) is hypothesized to underlie a group of variables, the first group centroid contains all the variables. In other words, one simply extracts the first centroid factor, as illustrated by the second hypothesis matrix above. The method can be easily extended to more than two groups of variables. Oblique factors can be determined directly from the correlation matrix by sectioning off the variables that constitute the various groups. Formulas for the correlation of sums are applied to each of these sections. After all factors are extracted from **R**, they can be mutually orthogonalized by the transformation mentioned above. These orthogonal structure elements can be used to obtain a final matrix of residuals. Consequently, one can compute a residual matrix after extracting four factors without computing earlier residual matrices. All variables need not to be assigned to a group factor. There are often firm hypotheses about the factorial composition of some variables, but other variables may be included on a more exploratory basis. The correlation of sums can be used to compute their structure elements without affecting the structure elements for the original variables.

It is important to be able to disconfirm a hypothesized set of groupings. Both authors have worked quite extensively on this problem (for applications, see Bernstein, 1988; Bernstein & Teng, 1989; Bernstein, Teng, & Garbin, 1986; Bissonnette & Bernstein, 1990). Several statistics are useful toward this end besides the structure elements themselves and the overall fit of the model (proposed groupings) in terms of the proportion of variance accounted for or the root-mean-square error. In order to put the overall fit in perspective, it is useful to determine the fit of a like number of PrCs (two in the present case) since that imposes a mathematical upper limit on the fit.

It is also useful to determine the fit of a like number of pseudofactors. These involve assigning variables to groups as arbitrarily and as independently of the proposed organization as possible. That was why we formed a hypothesis matrix with $X_1$, $X_3$, and $X_5$ assigned to one factor and $X_2$, $X_4$, and $X_6$ assigned to the other. These groupings are examples of pseudofactors. Pseudofactors may be formed in a variety of ways in more complicated models. One set of proposed pseudofactors may be used to test that proposed factors I, II, and III are all separable from one another, and another set may be used to test that factors II and III are separable from each other given that factor I is separable from both of them. For technical reasons, pseudofactors are guaranteed only to provide solutions in a component analysis. Bernstein (1988) describes the details of the process of forming pseudofactors.

Other useful data may be provided by the (1) average off-diagonal correlation within each group of variables that define a factor, (2) the residual correlation matrix obtained after all factors have been extracted, (3) the correlations between the proposed factors and the PrCs or principal axes, and (4) the factor correlations.

These data are used as follows:

**1** A variable assigned to a group might not correlate highly with the centroid for that group, which means that the variable does not have much in common with the other variables. This is unlikely to happen when the groups contain only a small number of variables because each variable is prominently represented in the centroid—at least a modest correlation is built in because the factor is partially defined in terms of that variable. As the number of variables defining the factor increases, the spurious effect of variable-factor overlap diminishes. When six or fewer variables define each centroid, however, the structure elements will be inflated.

**2** The average off-diagonal correlation is a less biased measure of the extent to which variables group, especially when only a few variables define the factors. Table 13-4 indicates that these average correlation are .76 and .79 for factors I and II, respectively. Both of these averages are lower than the structure elements, even though they are large.

**3** Another possible way to handle the potentially misleading effect produced by the overlap of items on factors is to place communality estimates in the diagonal spaces of the correlation matrix and perform a common factor analysis. However, this has a very strong tendency to produce spurious outcomes such as Heywood (1931) cases.

**4** Very strong disconfirming evidence can arise when a variable has a higher correlation with a factor to which it is not assigned than its own factor. While unlikely, for the reasons given above, it does happen.

**5** It is preferable that residual correlations be small and not systematic. However, this is relative, especially to the information provided by pseudofactors. The RMS residual may be large in proportion to the average absolute correlation in the original matrix because the groupings are in fact ill-chosen and so explain the common variance poorly. However, the theory may be incomplete in the sense of having failed to account for additional and possibly meaningful relations that exist above and beyond those postulated. One source of additional systematic variance is that due to method (see Chapter 3). For example, some of the Prof. Brown's anxiety measures may be based upon self-report, and others may be based upon observation. Secondary groupings may form on this and similar bases even though the original theory is not wrong. Examining residuals provides room for further discoveries as multiple group factoring may be used as part of an ad lib strategy, as discussed in Chapter 12.

**6** The model should *not* be evaluated simply by looking at the absolute level of fit. When variables are highly intercorrelated, the absolute fit will be good regardless of how variables are assigned to groups by the "it don't make no nevermind" principle (Kaiser, 1970; Wainer, 1976), as long as they are given proper signs within groups. The more relevant comparison is to the fit of a like number of PrCs. Any grouping will explain *some* variance; the extent to which they fall in the hyperspace generated by a like number of PrCs describes their appropriateness. Were they to explain as much variance as the PrCs after correcting for chance, they would be rotations of these earlier, most important dimensions, which would be strong support for the model. Note that part of the disparity between the two reflects sampling error—a PrC solution capitalizes on chance because it selects optimum weights for that sample; a multiple group solution, using prior weights, does not. Bernstein, Teng, and Garbin (1986) show how to cross-validate the PrCs to estimate how much of the disparity arises from capitalization on chance.

**7** Likewise, the fit must be appreciably better than the arbitrary assignment of variables to factors (pseudofactors) for the factors to have divergent validity.

**8** Factor correlations provide additional data about possible redundancies; e.g., if factors I and II correlate .8, they probably can be replaced by a single factor (but this is highly context-dependent, as noted in Chapter 12). Redundancy may also exist when all factors intercorrelate modestly but no single factor correlation is extremely high.

**9** Sometimes the fit of a given number of pseudofactors is very similar to the fit of a like number of PrCs. This implies that *no* model will fit better than an arbitrary assignment. It is another sign of redundant factors.

**10** If the proposed factors correlate poorly with the first few PrCs, they probably represent trivial sources of variation.

Do *not* directly compare the fit of one set of proposed groupings to another if the number of groupings (factors) is not the same. The proportion of variance accounted for is an average squared multiple correlation, which is biased upward with the number of predictors (factors in this case) as noted in Chapter 5. The RMS error is likewise affected. Compare each model to its appropriate pseudofactor baseline instead. You may be unable to decide between one solution that is more parsimonious (contains fewer factors) but less complete (explains less variance) than another.

We will evaluate the solution presented in Table 13-4 after considering alternative approaches. The authors are "sold" on the general usefulness of the multiple group method for testing weak theories. It may be fully confirmatory, as when the proposed organization is fully defined in advance, or it may be partially exploratory, as when variables are included that have not been assigned to any group.

## Procrustes Confirmatory Analysis

Another approach to confirmatory factor analysis is through forced rotation. The rotation is a least-squares approximation to a hypothesized factor structure that typically starts with PrCs or principal axes. However, any method of component or common factor condensation can be employed. The rotation may be either orthogonal or oblique (the more common procedure). Some versions allow the user to stipulate the sizes of factor correlations in oblique solutions, or this can be left up to the method of forced rotation. We have also noted that Procrustes is part of a broad family of forced rotations, including promax rotations and Cliff's (1966) approach to comparing two obtained factor solutions. Cramer (1974) provides a useful discussion of the various forms of Procrustes. The name "Procrustes" comes from the innkeeper in Greek mythology who had a bed that would fit anyone. If the visitor was too short for the bed, Procrustes stretched the visitor on a rack. If a visitor was too tall to fit the bed, Procrustes trimmed the length of the visitor's legs to fit the bed.

Procrustes uses a hypothesis matrix that generally looks identical to its multiple group counterpart, including the use of equal weighting, but it has a different meaning. Multiple group analysis specifies factors in terms of variables, but Procrustes specifies variables in terms of factors. Consequently multiple group analysis fits factor weights, but Procrustes fits pattern weights. Which is preferable is a matter of debate. Strategically, weak theories describe the composition of factors rather than variables; e.g., tests $X_1$, $X_2$, and $X_3$ may be proposed to measure a particular trait. The multiple group method embodies these hypotheses more directly than Procrustes. Conversely, the formal factor analytic model, Eqs. 11-1, defines variables in terms of factors.

One major objection to Procrustes is that the methods are "too flexible" in that *any* hypothesis matrix may be fit by a suitable cutting and stretching of the original factors so that Procrustes methods take advantage of chance. Many parameters (the pattern elements and factor correlations) float free, and so it is difficult for the process *not* to resemble the hypothesis matrix. For example, Horn and his associates (e.g., Horn & Knapp, 1973) obtained good simple structures from what we term pseudofactors. Indeed, since the Procrustean rotation takes place in the space defined by the number of factors, it will explain as much variance and have the same RMS error as a like number of PrCs, regardless of whether the groupings are appropriate or not. However, there will be other evidence of misspecification; e.g., the factor correlation will be extremely high and neither the pattern nor the structure may resemble the incorrectly hypothesized groupings particularly well. The problem described by Horn arises when one evaluates a solution in an absolute sense rather than in the context of alternative solutions.

Procrustes methods are no longer widely employed for confirmatory factor analysis because of the popularity of ACS. Even though Horn's critique may not be totally appropriate, we see no clear advantage to Procrustes in evaluating proposed groupings of variables. If it is used, the same criteria that were applied to the multiple group method can be used, save that results relating to the proportion of variance accounted for will be meaningless since they will not differ among PrC (or principal axes), proposed, and pseudofactor solutions.

## ACS Confirmatory Analysis

We have noted that ML, GLS, and ULS estimation are even more useful and popular as confirmatory methods than as exploratory methods and that they can be used to compare factor structures. ACS describes confirmatory approaches based upon such numerical estimation that compares three models differing as to the restrictions placed upon their parameters: the elements of the pattern matrix ($\mathbf{B}$), the factor correlation matrix ($\Phi$), and the uniqueness matrix ($\mathbf{U}$). As we have noted in Chapters 4 and 10, the estimation algorithms are extremely complex. Some applications have thus far been implemented only with GLS since its mathematics is often simpler, and it converges upon the ML estimates in very large samples (unfortunately, "how large" is difficult to state). Unless one or more variable deviates markedly from normality, there seem to be few advantages to ULS for continuous variables. Our examples employ ML estimation.

The three basic models are the following.

**1** An unconstrained (saturated) model is one in which all parameters are allowed to vary freely. It is a best-case scenario. However, an infinity of such models can be obtained by rotation. The model thus explains nothing because it is not identified; i.e., it has no unique solution. Whether or not a model is identified is a difficult and complex topic that is beyond the scope of this book. A necessary but not sufficient condition is that the number of estimated parameters be smaller than the number of known values, e.g., sample correlations. Unconstrained models exhaust the degrees of freedom available for model testing; however, it is important to keep in mind that the model will not fit perfectly.

**2** A substantive model is one in which parameters are fixed at specified values or constrained to equality with one another, as in the above comparisons of factor structures. Specifically, a weak model treats a pattern element as a free parameter if a variable is proposed to relate to that factor and fixes it at zero if a variable is not proposed to relate to that factor. This is the equivalent of specifying values at 1 and 0 in the multiple group and Procrustes methods. Factor correlations and uniquenesses are also free parameters.

**3** A null model is one in which there is no structure because the matrix being analyzed (e.g., $\mathbf{R}$) is spherical. The $\mathbf{B}$ matrix contains only zeros, and so all factor correlations are also zero, by default. It is a worst-case scenario. There are some controversies over null model selection (Tanaka, 1987).

The basic inferential property of a model is its $G^2$, i.e., the sample size times the value of the fitting function. We will denote the $G^2$ values associated with the unrestricted (saturated), substantive (weak in this case), and null models as $G_u^2$, $G_s^2$, and $G_n^2$ and their associated degrees of freedom as $df_u$, $df_s$, and $df_n$. The $G_u^2$ and $df_u$ are both 0 since the unrestricted model fits perfectly but exhausts all the degrees of freedom, by definition. A substantive (constrained) model cannot fit as well as an unconstrained model because no estimate of a free parameter is ever zero nor are any pair of estimates ever exactly equal because of sampling error. However, if the difference in fit between the models is slight, parsimony dictates accepting the substantive model because it contains fewer free parameters. Similar considerations hold in comparing the substantive model to the null model, which contains the fewest free parameters (none). These three basic models are depicted in Table 13-5 where an $F$ denotes a free parameter and an 0 denotes a parameter fixed at zero. Fixed parameters may assume values other than zero in other applications, but the same logic holds.

When we consider the testing of strong theories, we will consider alternative substantive (constrained) models, particularly those that form a hierarchy of progressive constraints. As in hierarchical multiple regression (Chapter 5), the process controls for (partials, in effect) variables previously considered. ACS bears kinship to both the multiple group and Procrustes approaches. It is similar to multiple group analysis in that one obtains a solution directly from **R** or related matrices rather than condensing and rotating separately, but it is similar to Procrustes in defining variables in terms of factors.

Chance can play a major role in model testing when an investigator refits models until an acceptable solution is reached, a not-uncommon situation. One way this can occur is for the investigator to add or eliminate variables on factors after looking at the effects of a given factor definition. We also cannot stress too much that sample sizes must be much larger than in multiple group analysis because more parameters

**TABLE 13-5**  ALTERNATIVE SPECIFICATIONS OF MODELS WITH SIX VARIABLES AND TWO FACTORS

| Variable | Unconstrained model factor | | Weak model factor | | Null model factor | |
|---|---|---|---|---|---|---|
| | I | II | I | II | I | II |
| $X_1$ | F | F | F | 0 | 0 | 0 |
| $X_2$ | F | F | F | 0 | 0 | 0 |
| $X_3$ | F | F | F | 0 | 0 | 0 |
| $X_4$ | F | F | 0 | F | 0 | 0 |
| $X_5$ | F | F | 0 | F | 0 | 0 |
| $X_6$ | F | F | 0 | F | 0 | 0 |

*Note*: *F* denotes a free parameter, and 0 denotes a parameter fixed at zero. The uniquenesses and factor correlation are not shown but are free parameters in the unconstrained and weak models. The uniquenesses are fixed at 1, and the factor correlation is fixed at 0 in the null model.

are estimated. Multiple group analysis takes very little advantage of chance because factor weights are defined as unities in advance of the analysis. These weights are sample-optimized in ACS, and so they capitalize upon chance, by definition. If your sample is small, consider multiple group analysis, which we suggest should be done anyway for the weak theory problems under present discussion. Even though ACS offers more powerful inferential tests than the multiple group method, we have stressed that these inferential tests are a mixed blessing. To our knowledge, there are no suitable inferential tests for use with Procrustes.

Tests of Prof. Brown's particular hypothesis about the two kinds of anxiety (variables $X_1$ to $X_3$ and $X_4$ to $X_6$) involve two common factors and six variables. There are 19 possible parameters: 12 pattern weights (6 variables by 2 factors), 1 factor correlation, and 6 uniquenesses (measurement errors, making the usual assumption that only the diagonals of **U** differ from zero). The model would be constructed somewhat differently if covariances or mean sums of products were used, which probably would be the case in practice, but the principles would be the same. There are only $(6)(5/2) = 15$ sample correlations in **R**, but the 6 diagonal values are also treated as observations. This provides 21 "known" values, even though the diagonals must be 1.0. This is one reason why it is technically incorrect to test a model inferentially using **R** rather than a covariance or mean-sum-of-products matrix, where the diagonal elements are meaningful observations. However, many strong applications of ACS involve difference $G^2$ values between substantive models in which this spurious effect is eliminated by subtraction. The constrained (weak) model estimates 13 parameters (6 pattern elements, 1 factor correlation, and 6 uniquenesses), and so 8 (21–13) are available for model testing.

There has been great recent emphasis upon developing descriptive measures. Unfortunately, there is much less agreement about the proper descriptive measure than there is about the proper inferential test. Our discussion follows recent reviews by Bentler (1990) and McDonald and Marsh (1990). Also see Bollen (1990) and Mulaik, James, Van Alstine, Bennett, Lind, and Stilwell (1989). We have stressed the importance of description because it is counterproductive to reject a model based solely upon a significant $G^2$ in a very large sample. Because error in the model reflects the unique variance, this problem tends to become more severe as the communality of the variables increases. Conversely, the fitting function times the sample size may not have a $G^2$ distribution in a small sample. Another assumption, multivariate normality, may not hold, but the evidence suggests ACS is relatively robust as long as the data are continuous.

Bentler and Bonnett (1980) introduced the distinction between measures of comparative fit and incremental fit. Comparative fit is concerned with testing a given model such as the weak model under consideration. Incremental fit is concerned with testing differences between two nested models, e.g., between the weak model and stronger assertions to be discussed. To simplify the discussion, we will assume that models being compared are based upon the same numbers of subjects. This might not be the case, as in comparing the fit of a given model in two populations. Most, but not all, descriptive measures are intended to be coefficients that fall between 0 (no fit) and

1 (perfect fit) in the population. Some are also guaranteed to fall between 0 and 1 in the sample, but others are not. In addition, some attempt to correct for the number of degrees of freedom in a model and therefore overcome a bias toward better fit in a model with more free parameters; others do not. Although there is a strong tendency to view coefficients in excess of .9 as indicative of good fit, it is difficult, if not impossible, to state a criterion value with any assurance.

We will present four broad classes of descriptive indices. Each class has variants that differ in order to achieve some statistical goal, e.g., to correct for the number of degrees of freedom. The current literature seems sufficiently complex for us to avoid endorsing any one, but all are justifiable.

**1** The first class consists of measures that act like squared multiple correlations ($R^2$ values), at least in some cases, by comparing the variance explained by the model to a total variance. Jöreskog and Sörbom's (1989) goodness-of-fit index (GFI) compares the similarity of the observed (sample) and estimated (model) correlation, covariance, or mean-sum-of-product matrices. Unfortunately, it is difficult to describe without matrix notation. See the above source (the LISREL reference manual) and other sources on the analysis of covariance structures such as Long (1983a, 1983b) and Byrne (1990) for further information. Unfortunately, it has an upward bias like the multiple correlation, so that the fit apparently improves as the number of free parameters increases. It is thus poorly suited to comparing alternative models with different degrees of freedom. Jöreskog and Sörbom's (1989) adjusted goodness-of-fit index (AGFI) attempts to correct for the degrees of freedom and is perhaps the most popular descriptive index currently used.

**2** A second class is based upon the differences between the substantive and worst (null) models. These are based upon an index proposed originally for exploratory ML analysis by Tucker and Lewis (1972) which compares this difference to the difference between the best (unrestricted) and worst models. In perhaps the simplest version, Bentler and Bonnett's (1980) normed-fit index (NFI), distances are defined in terms of $G^2$ values:

$$\text{NFI} = 1 - \frac{G_n^2}{G_s^2} \qquad (13\text{-}8)$$

An incremental version of the NFI is obtainable by placing the difference in $G^2$ between two substantive model values in the numerator of Eq. 13-8. The nonnormed-fit index (NNFI) introduces a correction for the number of degrees of freedom. The expected value of $G^2$ in the absence of any misspecification is degrees of freedom itself. The difference, $G^2$ minus degrees of freedom is an estimate of the degree of misspecification for a given number of free parameters beyond that expected by chance. Consequently the NNFI replaces values of $G^2$ with $G^2$ minus degrees of freedom. More recently, Bentler (1990) introduced a family of estimates of this form, two of which are termed the comparative-fit index (CFI) and the fit index (FI). Bollen (1989) also proposed a coefficient of this general form.

**3** The third class is based upon differences between a best and a substantive model. Akaike's (1974, 1987) information criterion (AIC) is commonly defined as

$$\text{AIC} = G_s^2 + 2p \qquad (13\text{-}9)$$

The symbol $p$ denotes the number of parameters estimated by the model, e.g. 13 for the present weak model. The AIC is the Pythagorean distance (see Chapter 14) between the two sets of parameters. The AIC's two components denote the respective contributions of sampling error and the number of free parameters to any misfit. McDonald and Marsh (1990) note that it becomes increasingly biased toward models with more free parameters as sample size increases.

**4** The loss (fitting) function itself may be used. For example, the root-mean-square residual has been previously defined as the square root of the average squared discrepancy between the predicted and obtained correlations or covariances and is the ULS loss function. Unlike the previous classes of measures, a small RMS denotes a good fit. It is perhaps the most strongly biased class of measures in favor of models with more free parameters. The ML and GLS fitting functions and related terms such as the model $G^2$ have similar properties. Consequently, it is least recommended.

### A Comparison of the Three Approaches

We will now apply the three methods to the data in Table 11-2 to test the proposition that there are two (correlated) factors among the six variables. We have assumed a sample size of 500, which is reasonable and not extremely large. The component eigenvalues of **R** were 3.49, 1.61, .37, .22, .19, and .11. Any criterion for selecting factors would suggest at least two; most would suggest exactly two, but the residual $G^2$ associated with the ML residual was 109.09 with 4 $df$ ($p < .0001$). Although this implies the need for additional factors, we will consider this issue later since even a residual $G^2$ of this large magnitude may reflect trivial sources of variation. Table 13-6 contains details of the solutions: the structure, pattern, $h^2$ values, variances accounted for by each factor individually and as a total, and factor correlation. A component solution was used for the multiple group solution and Procrustes, and a common factor solution was used for ACS. Consequently, some of the differences among the results reflect general differences between components and common factors.

The multiple group solution contains the same structure elements as in Table 13-4. The pattern elements are consistent with the proposed organization, but, as we have noted, this can be deceiving. The important findings are the following.

**1** About .85 of the total variance is explained by this grouping, which is the same (to three decimal places) as that explained by the PrCs.

**2** All $h^2$ values are similar to this .85 figure, meaning that variables were equally explained by the model.

**3** The factor correlation (.37) is not so high as to suggest redundancy.

**4** Less important, but not trivial, is that the two factors explain approximately the same amount of variance (.48 and .49) because the two groupings are fairly parallel.

**TABLET 13-6** FACTOR SOLUTIONS FOR MULTIPLE GROUP, PROCRUSTES, AND ACS SOLUTIONS: "CORRECT" GROUPINGS

| Variable | Pattern | | Structure | | $h^2$ |
|---|---|---|---|---|---|
| | I | II | I | II | |
| Multiple group solution: | | | | | |
| $X_1$ | .94 | .00 | .94 | .35 | .88 |
| $X_2$ | .90 | −.01 | .89 | .32 | .79 |
| $X_3$ | .92 | .01 | .92 | .35 | .85 |
| $X_4$ | .01 | .94 | .35 | .94 | .88 |
| $X_5$ | −.04 | .93 | .31 | .92 | .84 |
| $X_6$ | .03 | .92 | .37 | .93 | .86 |
| Prop. var. | | | .48 | .49 | .85 |
| Procrustes component solution | | | | | |
| $X_1$ | .94 | .00 | .94 | .35 | .88 |
| $X_2$ | .90 | −.01 | .89 | .32 | .79 |
| $X_3$ | .92 | .01 | .92 | .35 | .85 |
| $X_4$ | .01 | .94 | .35 | .94 | .88 |
| $X_5$ | −.04 | .93 | .31 | .92 | .84 |
| $X_6$ | .03 | .92 | .37 | .93 | .86 |
| Prop. var. | | | .48 | .49 | .85 |
| ACS solution: | | | | | |
| $X_1$ | .94 | .00 | .94 | .37 | .88 |
| $X_2$ | .80 | .00 | .80 | .32 | .64 |
| $X_3$ | .89 | .00 | .89 | .35 | .78 |
| $X_4$ | .00 | .92 | .37 | .92 | .85 |
| $X_5$ | .00 | .85 | .34 | .85 | .73 |
| $X_6$ | .00 | .89 | .36 | .89 | .79 |
| Prop. var. | | | .45 | .46 | .78 |

Note: The groupings are correct in that $X_1$ to $X_3$ are assigned to factor I and $X_4$ to $X_6$ are assigned to factor II. The three factor correlations are .37, .37, and .40. The ACS $G^2$ value was 117.36 based upon $n = 500$ subjects ($p < .0001$ with 8 $df$); the ACS goodness-of-fit index was .93, and the ACS-adjusted goodness-of-fit index was .82.

The Procrustes solution is nearly identical to the multiple group solution. However, the fact that it accounts for as much variance as the first two PrCs is an artifact of the method rather than a result of interest. The ACS results are similar to both once its common factor nature is considered (see Chapter 12). Its distinctive feature is that the fixed pattern elements for $X_4$ to $X_6$ on factor I and for $X_1$ to $X_3$ on factor II are *exactly* zero (ACS programs generally do not provide the structure matrix, and so these were obtained by hand; the LISREL program we employed also referred to the $h^2$ values as "squared multiple correlations"). Note in addition that the $G^2$ value was significant, as was true of the exploratory ML solution, implying a rejection of the model given this sample size, although the goodness-of-fit statistics provided by ACS were fairly good (GFI = .93 and AGFI = .82). Finally, all of the solutions were similar to their promax counterparts.

Before considering why the misfit occurred, it is instructive to look at obviously incorrect groupings, and so $X_1$, $X_3$, and $X_5$ were assigned to pseudofactor I, and $X_2$, $X_4$, and $X_6$ were assigned to pseudofactor II. These data are presented in Table 13-7.

The effect of this misspecification appears at several places in the multiple group solution:

**1** The pattern does not resemble the pseudofactors. Indeed, the pattern actually resembles the correct grouping more than it does the pseudofactor groupings.

**2** The structure does not differentiate the two factors well—all elements are at least .59 in magnitude.

TABLE 13-7   FACTOR SOLUTIONS FOR MULTIPLE GROUP, PROCRUSTES, AND ACS SOLUTIONS: "PSEUDOFACTOR" GROUPINGS

| Variable | Pattern | | Structure | | $h^2$ |
|---|---|---|---|---|---|
| | I | II | I | II | |
| Multiple group solution: | | | | | |
| $X_1$ | 1.20 | −.39 | .88 | .60 | .83 |
| $X_2$ | .61 | .15 | .74 | .65 | .55 |
| $X_3$ | 1.17 | −.37 | .87 | .59 | .80 |
| $X_4$ | −.24 | 1.05 | .63 | .86 | .76 |
| $X_5$ | .02 | .76 | .64 | .77 | .60 |
| $X_6$ | −.37 | 1.20 | .61 | .89 | .84 |
| Prop. var. | | | .54 | .54 | .73 |
| Procrustees solution: | | | | | |
| $X_1$ | 1.21 | .62 | .81 | −.14 | .88 |
| $X_2$ | 1.13 | .58 | .77 | −.15 | .79 |
| $X_3$ | 1.18 | .63 | .78 | −.13 | .85 |
| $X_4$ | .62 | 1.20 | −.15 | .81 | .88 |
| $X_5$ | .55 | 1.16 | −.19 | .81 | .84 |
| $X_6$ | .64 | 1.19 | −.12 | .78 | .76 |
| Prop. var. | | | .32 | .33 | .85 |
| ACS | | | | | |
| $X_1$ | .91 | .00 | .91 | .44 | .83 |
| $X_2$ | .00 | .36 | .17 | .36 | .13 |
| $X_3$ | .90 | .00 | .90 | .43 | .82 |
| $X_4$ | .00 | .89 | .43 | .89 | .78 |
| $X_5$ | .33 | .00 | .33 | .16 | .11 |
| $X_6$ | .00 | .92 | .44 | .92 | .84 |
| Prop. var. | | | .36 | .36 | .59 |

*Note*: The groupings are pseudofactors in that $X_1$, $X_3$, and $X_5$ are assigned to factor I and $X_2$, $X_4$, and $X_6$ are assigned to factor II. The factor correlations are .82, −.64, and .48. The ACS $G^2$ value was 976.65 based upon an assumed $n = 500$ subjects ($p < .0001$ with 8 $df$); the ACS goodness-of-fit index was .69, and the ACS-adjusted goodness-of-fit index was .19.

**3** The factor correlation is extremely high (.82), unlike that found with the correct groupings.

**4** The individual $h^2$ values, and therefore the proportion of variance accounted for, are smaller than in the "correct" solution—.73 versus .85 for the model as a whole. Note, however, that this model, which is as wrong as possible without using incorrect signs, still accounts for nearly three-fourths of the total variance, an illustration of the "it don't make no nevermind" principle that we have frequently cited.

Procrustes also fails to provide a structure that resembles the pseudofactors or that is simple in any sense, and the factor correlation is very high (−.64). As noted, it is an artifact of the method that this solution still accounts for .85 of the total variance. This deceptively good fit is the basis of Horn's critique.

ACS shows the effects of misspecification somewhat differently.

**1** Four of the six free pattern elements are of appropriately large magnitude, but the other two are extremely small. The two that are large on each factor are the two that correlate highly with each other, and their $h^2$ values are also much higher than that of the third variable assigned to the group.

**2** As in the other two approaches, the factor correlation is higher than in the correct solution, but in this case, the difference is not especially large (.48 versus .40).

**3** The $G^2$ is much higher than in the correct solution, and the GFI and, especially, the AGFI, are much lower.

As noted in Chapter 12, common factor solutions are not always obtainable. This is likely to be true whenever you attempt to fit pseudofactors because an extremely high factor correlation may cause the program to terminate without providing estimates.

These data were not constructed with a particular disparity in mind, and so we explored the reasons for the significant ACS $G^2$ value in the correct grouping by changing the specifications, just as an investigator would in a real problem. One strategy is to free the parameters that were fixed at zero. This might significantly improve the fit if, for example, one of Prof. Brown's ostensive social embarrassment items also reflected anxiety over physical harm, or vice versa. However, this did not help the situation. The largest pattern element that had previously been fixed at 0 was only .17, and the difference $G^2$ was not significant. Adding a third factor defined by $X_2$, $X_3$, and $X_4$ *did* improve the fit, even though the residual $G^2$ of 14.23 was still significant with 3 *df* (keep in mind that these additional tests are no longer truly confirmatory, and so one should not accept the alpha levels as true). This factor had no pattern element larger than .35, and so it was trivial. It might reflect such effects as method variance in a real problem. Had the sample been smaller, of course, even the original model would have fit, but one should never sacrifice power in order to gain an acceptable fit. We conclude by accepting the proposed groupings, especially because a weak model contains the potential for unspecified sources of variance.

In sum, the disparity between the correct and pseudofactor solutions makes it clear that, contrary to what you may have heard, you *cannot* prove anything with factor analysis. You have to know what to look for, and each of the three methods found the misspecification quite easily in this extreme case; ACS also provided evidence to reject a good but not perfect model. Both authors suggest that the correct groupings are at least a good first approximation to the data and would never criticize someone for accepting this as a solution, the ACS $G^2$ statistic notwithstanding. Although ACS and exploratory ML (which are effectively identical in testing the hypothesis that all variables load on one general factor) are certainly appropriate, neither should preempt use of Procrustes and, especially, the multiple group method, especially in small samples. The advantages of ACS are more apparent with strong theories.

## FACTORING CATEGORICAL VARIABLES (ITEM LEVEL FACTORING)

Thus far we have assumed that variables are continuous in the sense of Chapter 4. This includes scores on multi-item scales with 11 or more dichotomous items per scale (somewhat fewer multicategory items are needed to qualify). At this scale level, ordinary PM correlations index similarity of content (i.e., what is measured), even though extremely disparate distributions and, especially, floor and ceiling effects can have spurious effects. A "floor effect" is a value that observations cannot fall below, such as zero errors on a learning task, and a "ceiling effect" is a value that observations cannot exceed, such as a perfect score. If values of the observed variable fall at the floor or ceiling, the distribution is said to be censored. In some cases, the variable is not observed, in which case the distribution is said to be truncated. Distributions of continuous variables need not be normally distributed and will not be when they are scores on multi-item tests. However, as long as floor or ceiling effects are not strong influences upon the data, analyses that assume normality are not likely to produce misleading results.

The same cannot be said about analyses using categorical data, e.g., item-level factoring. The problems we will discuss are generally greater with dichotomous items than with multicategory items, such as Likert scales, but this is not always true (see Bernstein & Teng, 1989, for an example). The problem is that the resulting PM correlations are affected by the similarity of their distributions as well as the similarity of their content. Moreover, categorizing affects the factor structure even when the variables (items) have identical distributions (e.g., a series of equally difficult true-false items) because the correlations are lower than they would be if the data were continuous.

Consider a series of eight continuous measures. These measures are parallel in that each correlates .5 with a single factor ($g$). Consequently their measurement errors are $\sqrt{1 - .5^2}$, and the population correlation between any two will be .25 (see Eqs. 11-2 or 11-4). The measures are also standardized to a mean of 0 and a standard deviation of 1. A series of 1000 observations of this form was generated to produce what we will call latent measures. In turn, these latent measures were categorized in the following four different ways.

**1** All eight observed measures were a 0 if their latent counterparts were less than zero and a 1 if they were more than zero. These measures could denote incorrect and correct on abilities tests or no and yes sentiments. The results simulate a set of items of average difficulty ($p = .5$) to form the dichotomous-same data set.

**2** The first four observed measures were a 0 if their latent counterparts were less than −1, and 1 if they were greater than −1. The last four observed measures 5 to 8 were considered a 0 if their latent counterparts were less than +1, and a 1 if they were greater than +1. These mimic four easy items ($p = .84$) followed by four difficult items ($p = .16$) to form the dichotomous-different data set.

**3** All eight variables were a 0 if their latent counterparts fell below $-.44$, a 1 if they fell between -.44 and +.44, and a 2 if they fell above +.44. The three response categories have equal population frequencies and form the trichotomous-same data set.

**4** Finally, the first four measures were a 0 if their latent counterparts fell below +1, a 1 if they fell between +1 and +1.5, and a 2 if they fell above +1.5. The three responses have expected response proportions of .84, .09, and .07. Conversely, the last four measures were a 0 if their latent counterparts fell below $-1.5$, a 1 if they fell between -1.5 and $-1$, and a 2 if they fell above $-1$. These produce converse proportions to form the trichotomous-different data set.

The factor analytic tradition provides at least seven logical approaches to inferring the dimensionality of the data. Two other approaches may be used that are not directly derived from classical factor analysis (both are formally equivalent to factor analysis). One is to fit the data to an IRT model (Chapter 10), which may require very large samples. It is important to note the formal equivalence of IRT and classical factor analysis as models. The other is to use categorical modeling (Chapter 15), which is not well suited to items that vary in difficulty. The factor analytic approaches are as follows.

**1** Simply pretend that you are factoring continuous data and use a classical approach. This is what nearly all inexperienced individuals do. We will show why it will almost certainly suggest that unidimensional data are multidimensional.

**2** Pretend that you are factoring continuous data and use ACS, an approach that has become increasingly popular. We will show how ACS's greater inferential power is unfortunately even more likely to produce spurious results.

**3** Use a classical method but take the categorical nature of the data into account using simple methods to be described.

**4** Use classical methods, but factor polychoric (tetrachoric correlations for dichotomous items) estimates of PM correlations (see Chapter 4).

**5** Use ACS to factor PM correlations but take the categorical nature of the data into account.

**6** Use ACS to factor polychoric correlations. The newest version of ACS (version 7.1) has a preprocessor called PRELIS that computes these estimates, but there are other ways to obtain these quantities (e.g., Martinson & Hamdan, 1975, as modified by Beardwood, 1977).

**7** Use an extension of ACS, Muthén's (1988) LISCOMP, specifically designed to evaluate categorical data.

We do not consider approach 1 or 2 to be viable. Approach 3 is satisfactory for most applications, but the others can also be viable as long as one realizes the effects of categorization. One major problem with real data is that investigators tend to think that the results reflect the effects of item content. Thus, if the data suggest two factors, investigators look at what items in the first set have in common, assign a label, and then do the same with the items in the second set. This is a stimulating and enjoyable enterprise, especially if you have constructed the items. However, you *must* keep in mind that the structure may simply reflect statistical properties of the items. It is a bit embarrassing to have someone point out to you, especially in print, that your ego anxieties, id anxieties, and superego anxieties subscales can more parsimoniously be viewed as highly common anxieties, moderately common anxieties, and uncommon anxieties subscales. It is especially poor practice to develop a set of items and construct subscales based upon an exploratory factor analysis since that analysis will reflect item distribution differences in large part.

The coefficient $\alpha$ reliability of the latent data set is .74, which is reasonable for a relatively short test; the reliabilities of the categorized data sets vary from .52 to .61. This illustrates one effect of categorization. The latent data clearly illustrate that the data reflect a single factor. Each expected correlation is .25, and the observed correlations ranged from .22 to .30. This range of correlations can be shown to reflect sampling error. Because the expected correlation between each variable and factor I (g) is .5, the expected $h^2$, which is also the expected proportion of variance accounted, is $.5^2$ or .25. The expected value of the first eigenvalue is (8)(.25) or 2 since there are eight measures. However, the earlier sample values, including the first (2.81), are biased upward and the later sample values are biased downward for reasons noted in Chapter 11. Figure 13-1 shows the scree with $\lambda_2$ to $\lambda_8$ sloping gradually downward (the trichotomized data are omitted for clarity).

The categorization inherent in item responses induces two quite distinct effects. One that is always present is the loss of information which polychoric and polyserial correlations attempt to regain. Consequently the correlations observed in the dichotomized-same data set are clearly lower, ranging from .14 to .22, and the correlations observed in

**FIGURE 13-1** Scree plots of eigenvalues for (1) eight latent continuous measures, (2) eight measures dichotomized at $z = 0$, (3) four measures dichotomized at $z = -1$ and four measures dichotomized at $z = +1$, and (4) eight measures trichotomized at $z = -0.44$ and $z = +0.44$.

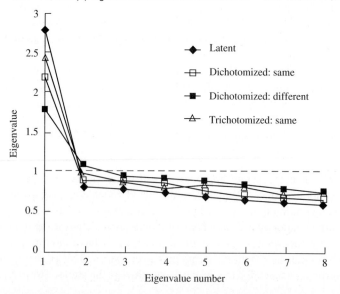

the trichotomized-same data set ranged from .17 to .25. The difference between the two categorized data sets illustrates how dividing data into two approximately equal categories loses more information than dividing data into three approximately equal categories. This loss of information affects $\lambda_1$ directly; the corresponding values are 2.16 and 2.43 instead of the previously noted value of 2.81. Conversely, $\lambda_2$ to $\lambda_8$ are larger for the categorized data because the sum of all eigenvalues must be 8. In neither case did the second eigenvalue exceed the criterion value of 1. However, this is solely a function of the small number of items; simulations using larger numbers of items will easily produce values of $\lambda_2$ in excess of 1. The existence of these difficulty factors (perhaps a bad name considering that they are found in all areas) has been long known (Carroll, 1945; Ferguson, 1941) and ignored just as long, unfortunately.

The second statistical effect of categorization arises from the fact that item distributions usually are heterogeneous. Although our examples were exaggerated for didactic reasons, we have observed them in real data (e.g., Bernstein et al., 1986). This causes items to cluster on the basis of the similarities of their distributions. For example, four of the six correlations among the pairs of easy dichotomized-different items exceeded .15, but no correlation between an easy and a difficult item was this high. Similar trends held for trichotomized-different items. In both cases, the clustering caused two eigenvalues to exceed 1.0. The resulting two factors were defined by items with similar item distributions, e.g., the easy items in the dichotomized-different condition formed one factor, and the difficult items formed a second factor after varimax rotation.

If one were to replicate this study, and the item distribution differences were also to replicate, the spurious multidimensional factor structure would also replicate. Hence, replicability is not in itself evidence that categorical data require multiple dimensions. It might simply suggest the similarities of the distributions in the two studies. Conversely, if the item distributions were to change (e.g., because of differences in skill), the factor structure would also change. In both cases, a multivariate procedure (factor analysis) is being used to explore a univariate issue—item distribution differences.

We have previously mentioned a third consideration of a less statistical nature that can arise in personality tests when items are keyed in different directions; factors tend to arise based upon item keying because endorsing a trait is not equivalent to denying its absence. In a sense this is true (content-related) factor variance, but it is method and not trait variance in the Campbell and Fiske (1959) sense. Gorsuch (1983) suggests some additional approaches to item-level factoring. These include forming groups of items and higher-order factoring. In particular, he suggests that difficulty factors tend to form a common higher-order factor. Gorsuch (1984) provides an example.

## ACS and Related Approaches with PM Measures

It does not matter whether one uses an exploratory ML solution with a single factor specified or a confirmatory ACS solution with pattern elements allowed to vary freely to test for unidimensionality. The $G^2$ and degrees of freedom will be the same within rounding error.

The residual $G^2$ for the latent data was quite small and not significant (21.47), correctly identifying the data as unifactor. Paradoxically, the $G^2$ value obtained from the dichotomous-same data was even smaller, 14.72, which apparently also correctly identifies the data as being unifactor. However, recall that this test statistic is based upon the difference in fit between the substantive model and a best-fitting model. In the present case, this best-fitting model fit poorly because of the low correlation magnitudes, and so the difference between models was small. The remaining three residual $G^2$ values were all highly similar (31.83, 31.55, and 31.29). The first two barely reached significance ($p < .05$), and the third just missed it. All comparisons were based upon 20 $df$ [(8)(7/2) = 28 known correlations minus 8 estimated pattern elements]. We also attempted GLS solutions. These were nearly identical to the ML results for the latent data. However, estimation failed in several cases with the categorized data. This could also have happened with ML, but it did not.

Consider a set of items designed to measure how frequently you perform a number of activities, such as going to the movies, sporting events, etc. The stems for each question are (a) at least once a week, (b) at least once a month, (c) at least once a year, and (d) hardly ever (less than once a year). Now, consider the specific item "going to the movies." You saw (or, what is really at interest, *thought* you saw) 14 movies. However, you aren't allowed to report this number directly; you must choose one of the four alternatives. This number in your head (14) is the latent variable that underlies your choice of a response from (a) to (d). This item really translates to the following form. Let $X$ denote the number of times you thought you went to the movies:

1  If $X \geq 52$, then answer (a).
2  If $52 > X \geq 12$, then answer (b).
3  If $12 > X \geq 1$, then answer (c).
4  If $1 < X$, then answer (d).

The numbers 4, 12, and 52 on this scale are thresholds in the IRT sense that convert the latent variable to an observable variable. They do so quite explicitly in this case, but the cutoffs are less explicit in most applications, as when the stems are "frequently" and "seldom." The model infers these latent variables from the observables; an item with $k$ categories requires $k - 1$ thresholds. In the present case, the true cutoffs are (1) at 0 in the dichotomized-same data, (2) at $-1$ for items 1 to 4, and at $+1$ for items 5 to 8 in the dichotomized-different data, (3) at $-.44$ and $+.44$ in the trichotomized-same data, and (4) at 1 and 1.5 for items 1 to 4 and at $-1.5$ and $-1$ for items 5 to 8 in the dichotomized-different data. The eight latent variables each correlate .5 with the one common factor that underlies them all.

The proportion of 1 responses to items 1 and 2 observed in the dichotomized-same data were .47 and .52. These observed cutoffs correspond to thresholds of .06 and $-.05$ which are obtained by taking the $z$ score corresponding to the proportion and changing its sign—the higher the proportion, the lower the threshold. The values could be used to determine polychoric correlations which might then be factored (method 6 above). However, LISCOMP tests models that estimate these values along with other parameters (e.g., the pattern weights), and so they need not be the same as the observed values. In the present case, the observed thresholds and those estimated with LISCOMP fit equally well. Their corresponding RMS error values for the dichotomized-same data were .0440 and .0433.

LISCOMP uses a GLS algorithm for categorical data because there are some technical problems presently associated with developing ML algorithms. In principle, there seems to be no reason why an ML algorithm will not eventually be obtained. We found it difficult to obtain GLS estimates with dichotomous data and high item intercorrelations, though it was less likely to be a problem with three or more categories. Perhaps these problems will abate when ML estimation becomes possible. LISCOMP can be used to place further restrictions on parameters, e.g., the user can specify that all thresholds are to be equated to one another. This logic is the same as in ACS. In addition to modeling categorical variables, it can also be used to analyze censored and truncated distributions.

LISCOMP has considerable potential as an analytic tool, but the current version of the program as of this writing (version 1.1) shares problems with other ACS programs providing solutions reliably. This is especially true with dichotomous data and high interitem correlations. We reiterate our suggestion that the average user stick to classical methods for analyzing item-level data but be aware of the artifacts that may suggest multidimensionality.

## Multiscale Analyses

Suppose, for example, that you have proposed that the first four dichotomously scored items on an eight-item test form scale A and that the second four dichotomously scored items form scale B. One can use multiple group analysis with the following hypothesis matrix:

$$
\begin{matrix}
1 & 0 \\
1 & 0 \\
1 & 0 \\
1 & 0 \\
0 & 1 \\
0 & 1 \\
0 & 1 \\
0 & 1 \\
\end{matrix}
$$

In the continuous-variable case, the fit of the resulting model would be compared to the fit of the first two PrCs and to a pseudofactor model, perhaps of the form

$$
\begin{matrix}
1 & 0 \\
0 & 1 \\
1 & 0 \\
0 & 1 \\
1 & 0 \\
0 & 1 \\
1 & 0 \\
0 & 1 \\
\end{matrix}
$$

This will not suffice with categorical data since the fit may reflect similarities of item distributions. That is, if items 1 to 4 are endorsed more often than items 5 to 8 for some reason, the two groups of items will tend to form separate factors even though all eight measures may reflect unidimensional latent data. A more suitable baseline is achieved by ranking the items in terms of their $p$ values. Assign the four items with the highest $p$ values to one factor, and the four items with the lowest $p$ values to the second factor. Call this a mean model in distinction to the pseudofactor and substantive models discussed above. If the rank ordering of items is 1, 5, 2, 3, 8, 4, 7, 6 (it doesn't matter whether the ranking is from high to low or the converse), the hypothesis matrix will be

$$
\begin{array}{cc}
1 & 0 \\
1 & 0 \\
1 & 0 \\
0 & 1 \\
1 & 0 \\
0 & 1 \\
0 & 1 \\
0 & 1
\end{array}
$$

This model provides a better baseline for dichotomous data. If the proposed matrix and the mean model are the same, or very similar (as is the case here), one cannot clearly determine whether it is the content of the items or their statistical distributions that are causing items to cluster, assuming both models fit better than pseudofactors. The analysis has gone as far as it can go without constructing additional items; e.g., if the factor I items are easier as a group than the factor II items, attempt to construct some difficult factor I items and some easy factor II items. The mean model suffices as a baseline with dichotomous data because the item's $p$ value completely summarizes the distributional properties. Multicategory items require additional tests. Construct two other models, called the variance and skewness models, by ranking items on the basis of these two additional item statistics. Generally, these are not independent of one another: Items with means near the end of the scale tend to have smaller variances than items with means near the middle of the scale because of range restriction (censoring), items with a small mean tend to be positively skewed, and items with a large mean tend to be negatively skewed.

   The above analysis, which forms correlations from variables that are scored as 1 versus 0, standardizes each item. Gorsuch (1983) notes that if the reciprocal of the items' standard deviations are used in place of 1s, the results are totally equivalent to an ordinary item analysis. Structure coefficients are item-total correlations (not corrected for overlap), and factor correlations are correlations between scales.

## TESTING STRONG THEORIES

We have been concerned with whether or not proposed groupings of variables exist (weak theories), which we suggest are tested more at least as easily through multiple group analysis as ACS. We now turn our attention to strong theories, where ACS is uniquely applicable.

Spearman's $g$ illustrates the simplest category of strong theories. It is not enough to demonstrate that a series of measures are dominated by a single factor; one must show that this single factor is the *only* factor, unless perhaps additional factors are defined by method variance. If the mythical Prof. Brown had intended measures $X_1$, $X_2$, and $X_3$ to measure only anxiety about physical harm and measures $X_4$, $X_5$ and $X_6$ to measure only anxiety about social embarrassment (allowing, in both cases, for random measurement error), the theory would be strong and, as we have seen, incorrect.

Strong theories exploit the effects of being able to fix and/or constrain parameter estimates. The ways that this can be done are limitless. However, certain strong tests are especially likely and are good ways to illustrate the properties of ACS. In general, they assume that groups of variables measure the same thing that we would describe as conforming to a weak theory but that the ACS tradition refers to as *congeneric* ("measuring the same thing," Jöreskog, 1974). These tests may be combined with each other and with tests that compare different groups.

**1** *Orthogonality.* The factor correlation was left as a free parameter in testing Prof. Brown's model because the model did not say that the two classes of measures were independent of one another. Had that been proposed, the factor correlation would have been fixed at .0. Assuming that nothing else was changed in the specification, the difference in $G^2$ between the two would illustrate the effects of nesting and would explicitly test orthogonality given that the pattern had been correctly specified. Note that the overall $G^2$ might be large because the pattern had been incorrectly specified, but the difference $G^2$ specifically tests for orthogonality.

**2** *Redundancy.* Conversely, suppose one or more factor correlations were very high. You might suspect that two or more factors can be replaced by one. Simply fix the appropriate factor correlations at 1.0 to see how much the fit is degraded. This also illustrates that fixed parameters need not always be 0.

**3** *Tau-equivalence.* Suppose a series of measures can be assumed congeneric. It is quite possible that the variances of the raw scores (or deviation scores, since they will be equal) vary because the measures differ in true and unique variance and are therefore unequally reliable. One might wish to test for equality of true variance. This may be accomplished by comparing the fit of a model in which pattern elements and uniquenesses are both free with a model in which pattern elements are constrained to equality but uniquenesses remain free. The difference $G^2$ in this case specifically tests for equality of pattern. This test requires that one analyze either the covariance matrix or the mean-sum-of-products matrix.

**4** *Parallelism.* Parallelism implies that the measures have equal pattern elements and equal uniquenesses, i.e., that they are tau-equivalent and equally reliable. The test involves constraining the pattern elements to one another and the uniquenesses to one another. It may be evaluated as a difference $G^2$ relative to the more general model in which both sets of parameters are free or relative to the tau-equivalent model. Note that tests which meet the criterion for parallelism need not differ only in measurement error; they can differ in the nature of their specific variance as long as the magnitudes are the same. Parallelism also requires that one analyze either the covariance matrix or the mean sum-of-products matrix.

## Introduction to the Full ACS Model

In order to appreciate the complexity of the ACS model and its range of applicability, assume that an investigator has obtained three indicators (the term used in ACS to denote what we have called variables) of each of the following four constructs (factors, in more traditional language).

**1** Psychopathology: two MMPI scales and a clinical rating
**2** Intelligence: verbal ability, quantitative ability, and social intelligence measure as found on a number of personality inventories
**3** Job performance: a peer evaluation, a supervisory evaluation, and a self-evaluation
**4** Job satisfaction: a peer evaluation, a supervisory evaluation, and a self-evaluation.

Although the issue will not be pursued, the six measures in constructs 3 and 4 may be further analyzed in ACS using a multitrait-multimethod approach as discussed in Chapter 3; see Browne (1984) and Cole and Maxwell (1985).

Assume that data from a large number of individuals have been gathered. The data form a $12 \times 12$ correlation or covariance matrix which may be used to investigate the following hypotheses.

**I** The three indicators of psychopathology define a construct.
**II** The three indicators of intelligence define a second construct.
**III** The three indicators of job performance define a third construct.
**IV** The three indicators of job satisfaction define a fourth construct.
**V** Psychopathology impairs job performance.
**VI** Intelligence facilitates job performance.
**VII** Job performance facilitates job satisfaction.

Hypotheses I to IV are weak. In ACS terminology, they involve the measurement portion of the full model, and the principles are the same as previously considered. However, hypotheses V to VII are of quite a different form. They involve relations among constructs which are similar in many ways to higher-order factoring. These proposed relations are causal in nature and involve the structural portion of ACS.

ACS further distinguishes between two types of constructs and indicators, exogenous and endogenous. Exogenous indicators and constructs are assumed to be determined by sources outside the model. In this model, psychopathology and intelligence are assumed exogenous. The causes of each (genetics, early family history, stress, etc.) are not at issue in the particular study. By definition, an exogenous construct is never assumed to be caused by any other construct. In contrast, endogenous indicators and their associated constructs may potentially be influenced (caused) by other constructs in the model (both exogenous and endogenous). Job performance and job satisfaction are hypothesized to be endogenous. The full ACS model thus has three distinct aspects:

**1** A measurement model that relates exogenous constructs to indicators
**2** A measurement model that relates endogenous constructs to indicators
**3** A structural model that relates exogenous and/or endogenous constructs to endogenous constructs.

However, a given study need not use more than one or two of these aspects.

We have stressed the importance of structure elements over pattern elements because of the difficulties that frequently affect people inexperienced with oblique rotations. ACS does precisely the converse because it allows effect strengths in both the measurement and structural portions of the model to be described in the same way. Unfortunately, most ACS programs do not even report structure elements, which we feel is a mistake.

## ACS Notation

In order to get a better idea of the structural model and learn about the complex notation used in LISREL (alternative programs use different, but just as complex, notation), consider Fig. 13-2.

Figure 13-2 is a path diagram of the proposed organization of the data. We will discuss the meaning of "path" in more detail shortly, but it is simply the direct effect of one variable upon another. Variables in squares are observables, with $X$ denoting exogenous indicators and $Y$ denoting endogenous indicators. Subscripts distinguish

**FIGURE 13-2** A path diagram interrelating three proposed measures of psychopathology and three proposed measures of intelligence as exogenous indicators, and three proposed measures of job performance and three proposed measures of job satisfaction as endogenous indicators.

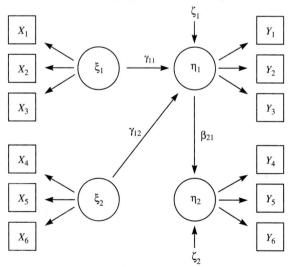

between both constructs and indicators. Hence, $X_1$ to $X_3$ are the three psychopathology indicators, $X_4$ to $X_6$ are the three intellectual indicators, $Y_1$ to $Y_3$ are the three job performance indicators, and $Y_4$ to $Y_6$ are the three job satisfaction indicators. Terms in circles are constructs (factors). Greek lowercase xi ($\xi$) denotes exogenous constructs, and Greek lowercase eta ($\eta$) denotes endogenous constructs. Consequently $\xi_1$ denotes psychopathology, $\xi_2$ denotes intelligence, $\eta_1$ denotes job performance, and $\eta_2$ denotes job satisfaction. Arrows imply relations between constructs and between indicators and constructs.

Gamma ($\gamma$) denotes a causal relation (path) between an exogenous construct and an endogenous construct, and beta ($\beta$) denotes a path between two endogenous constructs. The first subscript denotes the proposed effect, and the second subscript denotes the proposed cause. Thus, the arrow drawn from $\xi_2$ to $\eta_1$ describes the hypothesis that intelligence is causally related to job performance (being smart causes better job performance), $\gamma_{12}$. Likewise, the arrow drawn from $\eta_1$ to $\eta_2$, which is identified as $\beta_{21}$, describes the hypothesis that job performance ($\eta_1$) causes job satisfaction ($\eta_2$). In this proposed model, intelligence is assumed unrelated to job satisfaction, and so there is no path identified as $\gamma_{22}$.

Figure 13-2 is good for depicting the overall proposed model without excessive "clutter," but it ignores several important details. Figure 13-3 contains these missing elements in the exogenous portion of the model, and Figure 13-4 contains parallel elements in the endogenous portion of the model. The uniqueness of endogenous variable $i$ is symbolized as $\varepsilon_i$, and the correlation between endogenous constructs $j$ and $k$ is symbolized by $\psi_{jk}$. It is often useful to refer to an aggregate of exogenous or endogenous variable elements, e.g., all of the exogenous path coefficients. Following more general statistical practice, the resulting matrix or vector is described by boldface. Consequently the set of $\lambda_x$ values is denoted $\boldsymbol{\lambda}_x$.

**FIGURE 13-3**   Details of the exogenous portion of the full model depicted in Fig. 13-2.

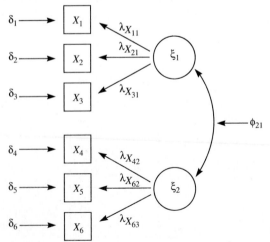

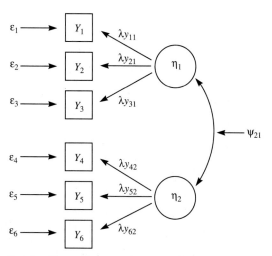

**FIGURE 13-4**   Details of the endogenous portion of the full model depicted in Fig. 13-2.

It is sometimes necessary to distinguish between the true (parameter) value and the estimate notationally. As in other areas of statistics, a circumflex (hat) is used to describe an estimate. Consequently $\hat{\beta}_{21}$ is the estimated strength of the effect of job performance upon job satisfaction whose true value is $\beta_{21}$. A particularly important application of this principle applies when we algebraically combine all the parameter estimates used in a particular model. The result is an estimate of the correlation, covariance, or sum-of-products matrix being analyzed and is denoted $\hat{\Sigma}$. As in the measurement model described previously, the analysis makes $\hat{\Sigma}$ as close as possible to the sample $\Sigma$ matrix, which is assumed to be the best estimate of the unknown population $\Sigma$ matrix. We will assume that these are ML estimates, but they may also be GLS or ULS estimates, and a variety of strategies are possible. Table 13-8 summarizes the various symbols (one further symbol will be mentioned below simply for completeness that plays an extremely minor role in the model).

## Assumptions

The full ACS model may be described in terms of equations that describe the exogenous measurement model, the endogenous measurement model, and the structural model. These are given by Eqs. 13-10a to 13-10c, respectively. They merely state formally what has already been presented in this general section and, in the case of the two measurement models, what has been considered starting in Chapter 11.

$$x = \lambda_x \eta + \varepsilon \qquad (13\text{-}10a)$$

$$y = \lambda_y \xi + \delta \qquad (13\text{-}10b)$$

$$\eta = B\eta + \Gamma\xi + \zeta \qquad (13\text{-}10c)$$

**TABLE 13-8    ACS NOTATION**

| Variable | Type | Matrix Element Name | Name | Role |
|---|---|---|---|---|
| Indicator | Ex | **X** | $x$ | Observables |
| Construct | Ex | $\Phi^*$ | $\xi$ | Factors and factor interrelations |
| Pattern | Ex | $\Lambda_x$ | $\lambda_x$ | Regressions of exogenous indicator on construct |
| Uniqueness | Ex | $\Theta_\delta^*$ | $\delta$ | Errors in measurement model |
| Indicator | En | **Y** | $y$ | Observables |
| Construct | En | $\Upsilon$ | $\eta$ | Factors and factor interrelations |
| Pattern | En | $\Lambda_y$ | $\lambda_y$ | Regressions of endogenous indicator on construct |
| Uniqueness | En | $\Theta_\varepsilon^*$ | $\varepsilon$ | Errors in measurement model |
| Path | Ex→En | $\Gamma$ | $\gamma$ | Causal effect of exogenous variables |
| Path | En→En | B | $\beta$ | Causal effects of endogenous variables |
| Error | Ex→En | | $\zeta$ | Errors in structural model |
| Overall model | | $\Sigma$ | | Observed data relations, e.g., covariances |
| Overall model | | $\hat{\Sigma}$ | | Estimated data relations, e.g., covariances |

*Note*: Ex, Exogenous; En, endogenous. Matrices contain regression weights unless denoted by an asterisk (*), in which case they contain covariances (correlations when standardized).

Equations 13-10a and 13-10b provide a standard factor analytic definition of observed scores as the product of a factor score and regression weight plus measurement error as presented in Eqs. 11-1. Equation 13-10c may appear unusual because a matrix ($\eta$) appears on both sides of the equality and is therefore defined in terms of itself. In fact, the $\eta$ on the right describes a different quantity (set of path coefficients) than the one on the left. This equation merely says that a given path coefficient is a function of other path coefficients ($\eta$ and $\xi$) plus measurement error ($\zeta$).

Jöreskog and Sörbom's (1989) statement of ACS make the following major assumptions.

**1** Errors of measurement ($\delta$ and $\varepsilon$) are assumed to be uncorrelated with constructs ($\eta$ and $\xi$), but they may be correlated among themselves. Ordinarily, all measurement error is assumed independent, but this need not be the case in ACS. Errors of measurement may be correlated because certain variables are measured on the same day and other variables are measured on different days. Some programs estimate a matrix of covariances between exogenous errors ($\delta$) and endogenous errors ($\varepsilon$), symbolized $\Theta$, but there is little use for this in most applications.

**2** Errors of measurement are also assumed to be uncorrelated with structural measurement error ($\zeta$).

**3** An endogenous variable cannot "cause itself," so that the diagonal terms of **B** are zero (a more technical restriction on this matrix that goes beyond this text is described in the ACS manual).

## Properties of Path Coefficients

We will now consider the properties of the two matrices of path coefficients, $\Gamma$ and $\mathbf{B}$, in more detail. At a purely descriptive level, $\gamma_{12}$ merely describes the change in the first endogenous construct, $\eta_1$ (job performance in the example), produced by a unit change in the second exogenous construct, $\xi_2$ (intelligence), holding constant all other constructs, both exogenous and endogenous (psychopathology and job satisfaction in the example). Likewise, $\beta_{21}$ describes the analogous effect upon $\eta_2$ (job satisfaction) produced by $\eta_1$ (job performance). Save for the fact that these terms are all constructs, their properties are really no different from the properties of regression weights considered in Chapter 5 and pattern elements as discussed in chapters on factor analysis. As we have stressed, pattern elements index the direct effect of one variable upon another by holding constant all other variables. Consequently two constructs, just like two observables, may be correlated, yet the regression weight (pattern element) relating one to the other may be zero.

Assume for a moment that the model depicted in Fig. 13-2 is correct. It says that there is no path connecting $\xi_1$ and $\eta_2$; i.e., psychopathology per se does not cause higher or lower job satisfaction. There may well be a high correlation between the two—the more psychopathological individuals may be the more dissatisfied. However, one could attribute this to other constructs; e.g., more psychopathological individuals might perform their jobs more poorly and those who do their job more poorly on the job might be more dissatisfied. Holding constant (partialling) job performance would eliminate the correlation between psychopathology and job satisfaction. In other words, the relation between psychopathology and job satisfaction is mediated by job performance. The model may be wrong. There may be a relationship between psychopathology and job satisfaction, holding both intelligence and job performance constant, e.g., more disturbed individuals may in fact be more dissatisfied with their job. This model, with its added path, is depicted in Fig. 13-5.

## A Note on Inferring Causality from Correlational Data

If one simply sticks to this essentially mathematical interpretation of path coefficients, there is little to argue with and much to find beneficial about these mathematical deductions. However, most users impute a stronger meaning to these terms, namely, causation, and many raised in the tradition that "correlation is not causation" are bothered by inferring causation from measures which were not manipulated experimentally. We share this skepticism to a large extent. For example, suppose the amount of rainfall and the proportion of people carrying umbrellas are highly correlated. One possible interpretation is (1) that rain causes people to carry umbrellas. Two other possibilities are (2) carrying umbrellas causes rainfall, and (3) a third variable, such as the weather forecast—people may carry umbrellas because the forecast causes them to expect rain. Alternative 2 is obviously implausible, as it requires the effect to precede the cause in time, but alternative 3 is obviously quite viable and perhaps testable by giving subjects incorrect weather reports. It is difficult not to

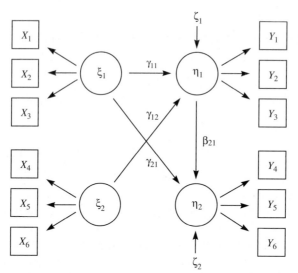

**FIGURE 13-5**    A modification of the model proposed in Fig. 13-2 in which it is further assumed that psychopathology affects job satisfaction.

think of a situation in which third (or fourth, etc.) variables do not operate. Including more variables in the network, on the one hand, allows control over these third variables, but, on the other, makes it more difficult to focus upon key variables. As one goes through all the assumptions made in a typical analysis, it is difficult not to consider alternative ways to formulate the model. The exogenous-endogenous distinction suffers from this same basic problem of equivocality. By considering a variable such as psychopathology or intelligence as exogenous, it is removed, by fiat, from the influence of other variables.

One can attempt to address the issue by treating the variables as endogenous so that they may be the object as well as the subject of causal linkages. ACS does not require any exogenous variables, but it does require at least one endogenous variable. However, the more such paths allowed in the model, the greater the chance that the model will not be identified in the sense previously described of providing a unique solution (the reader is referred to works listed in Suggested Additional Readings for the technical aspects of identification). Merely being flexible about allowing relations does *not* necessarily solve the problem. Consequently assumptions made to rule out possible paths are a necessary and important part of the analysis.

At the same time that we are critical of the strong use of causality in ACS and path analysis in general, we do not wish to lose sight of some real benefits. Questions of whether the relation between two variables disappears once other variables are controlled are interesting and important. ACS is a powerful tool allowing these issues to be addressed while simultaneously addressing questions of how multiple indicators of constructs define these constructs.

## Model Specification in ACS

There is a total of eight matrices in a full ACS model:

**1** The exogenous pattern ($\Lambda_x$)
**2** The covariances among the exogenous constructs ($\Phi$)
**3** The exogenous uniquenesses ($\Theta_\delta$)
**4** The endogenous pattern ($\Lambda_y$)
**5** The covariances among the endogenous constructs ($\psi$)
**6** The endogenous uniquenesses ($\Theta_\varepsilon$)
**7** The path coefficients from exogenous variables to endogenous constructs ($\Gamma$)
**8** The path coefficients among endogenous constructs (**B**).

As we have noted, every element in each matrix must be specified as a fixed parameter, a free parameter, or a constrained parameter. In addition to introducing constraints consistent with the substantive demands of the model, other constraints are necessary to impose a unit of measurement. Many pitfalls might produce an unidentified model.

For example, the exogenous factor pattern $\Lambda_x$ could be constructed in the following form, where the six rows are the six exogenous indicators and the two columns are the two exogenous constructs (psychopathology and intelligence). The symbols Fr and 0, respectively, denote free parameters and parameters fixed at zero:

$$
\begin{array}{cc}
\text{Fr} & 0 \\
\text{Fr} & 0 \\
\text{Fr} & 0 \\
0 & \text{Fr} \\
0 & \text{Fr} \\
0 & \text{Fr}
\end{array}
$$

One of several possible ways to provide the unit necessary for the first construct (psychopathology) is to fix the element in the first column and row at 1.0.

The matrix of variances and covariances among exogenous constructs ($\Phi$) will have two rows and two columns since there are two constructs. All four elements will be free parameters. Since it is more likely that $\Sigma$ will be analyzed as a covariance matrix or a sum-of-products matrix than a correlation matrix, the diagonals are not necessarily 1.0, but ACS can provide standardized output, and so you can also evaluate $\Phi$ as a correlation matrix. Proper specification of $\Lambda_x$ will also ensure that the factor variances are defined. Although there are four elements in $\Phi$, only three estimates are needed because of its symmetry; only those variables below the diagonal are considered in a symmetric matrix. Consequently $\Phi$ takes the following form.

$$
\begin{array}{cc}
\text{Fr} & \\
\text{Fr} & \text{Fr}
\end{array}
$$

The exogenous uniqueness (error variance) matrix ($\Theta_\delta$) has six columns and six rows corresponding to the six endogenous variables. Because the error terms are considered uncorrelated, the terms off the diagonal are fixed at zero, leaving only the diagonal terms to be estimated. Consequently, $\Theta_\delta$ takes on the following form.

$$
\begin{matrix}
\text{Fr} & & & & & \\
0 & \text{Fr} & & & & \\
0 & 0 & \text{Fr} & & & \\
0 & 0 & 0 & \text{Fr} & & \\
0 & 0 & 0 & 0 & \text{Fr} & \\
0 & 0 & 0 & 0 & 0 & \text{Fr}
\end{matrix}
$$

There is generally no logical connection between the dimensions of the three corresponding endogenous matrices, but they have the same form as the exogenous matrices in this problem.

The matrix of path coefficients relating exogenous constructs (columns) to endogenous variables (rows) or $\Gamma$ will have two rows and two columns in this case, though it will generally not be square and therefore not symmetric. According to the model proposed in Fig. 13-2, both exogenous constructs are assumed to affect the first endogenous construct (job performance), and so the elements in the first row will both be free parameters. Likewise, neither exogenous construct is assumed to affect the second endogenous construct, and so the elements in the second row are fixed at zero:

$$
\begin{matrix}
\text{Fr} & \text{Fr} \\
0 & 0
\end{matrix}
$$

On the other hand, the model proposed in Fig. 13-5 implies a path between psychopathology and job satisfaction, and so the matrix appears as:

$$
\begin{matrix}
\text{Fr} & \text{Fr} \\
\text{Fr} & 0
\end{matrix}
$$

Finally, the path coefficient relating the endogenous variables to each other (**B**) is square since both the rows and columns are endogenous variables, but it is usually not symmetric. Since the only specification postulated is an effect of job performance ($\eta_1$) on job satisfaction ($\eta_2$) and since causes appear in columns and effects in rows, the matrix is:

$$
\begin{matrix}
\text{Fr} & 0 \\
0 & 0
\end{matrix}
$$

The 12 observables provide 12 variances and $(12)(11/2) = 66$ covariances, for a total of 78 distinct elements in $\Sigma$. The exogenous measurement model requires 15 parameters, the endogenous measurement model requires 15 parameters, and the structural model requires 3 parameters, leaving 55 $df$ to test the model. Each ACS program has its own syntax for implementing these constraints which we will not discuss here. A given specification can often be achieved several different ways; e.g., you can fix an entire matrix and then free selected elements, or vice versa. The output normally tells you how each variable has been interpreted. One of the first things you should do is to check to see if the model has been specified as intended. You may find that this has not been done even if you are highly experienced. Fortunately, computer programs describe the specification with reasonable clarity.

## Recursive and Nonrecursive Models

One thing that we did not do in either version of the model was to allow causal effects to operate in both directions. That is, we assumed that job satisfaction did not affect job performance when we assumed that job performance affected job satisfaction. In a more general sense, no path through the structural model crossed itself. A "recursive model" is one in which no possible path crosses itself, and a "nonrecursive model" is one with a crossing, as would arise from reciprocal causation.

It was extremely difficult to test a nonrecursive model before ACS. Among the many things that ACS did in unifying correlational analysis was to make analysis of a nonrecursive path model as easy as analysis of a recursive path model since the only difference between the two types of models is in the specification of the structural model. In a recursive model, a free or constrained parameter in the $i$th row and $j$th column must be associated with a parameter fixed at 0 in the $j$th row and $i$th column, whereas this need not be the case in a nonrecursive model. In general, the rows and columns in **B** can be rearranged to form a triangular pattern of zeros in a recursive model. Although it is possible to have an identified nonrecursive model, lack of recursion often leads to lack of identifiability. Although nonrecursive models often have appeal for their flexibility, they have very distinct pitfalls.

## Cross-lagged Correlation

Cross-lagged correlation has been suggested as an approach to inferring causation (Duncan, 1969; Kenny, 1975). It may be implemented as a strong theory in ACS. In its simplest (two-wave) case, two variables are each studied at two points in time. For example, assume that each of a large number of clinical supervisors has an associated trainee. Each supervisor rates the proficiency of each trainee, and each trainee rates the quality of supervision of each supervisor. Both ratings are made on two occasions, e.g., at 6 months and at the end of a year. Designate the two supervisory ratings as $X_1$ and $X_2$, and the two trainee ratings as $Y_1$ and $Y_2$.

Correlating over pairs yields six correlations (or covariances): $r_{x_1y_1}$ and $r_{x_2y_2}$ (correlations between two variables measured at the same time), $r_{x_1x_2}$ (correlations between the same variable measured at different times), and $r_{x_1y_2}$ and $r_{x_2y_1}$ (correlations between different variables measured at different times). The last-named cross-lagged correlations are of greatest interest. Although the analysis has several features, the key is the relative magnitude of $r_{x_1y_2}$ and $r_{x_2y_1}$. In essence, if $r_{x_1y_2}$ is greater than $r_{x_2y_1}$, then $X$ causes $Y$. Conversely, if $r_{x_1y_2}$ is greater than $r_{x_1y_2}$, then $Y$ causes $X$. Finally, if both correlations are of similar magnitude, the relations between the two could be attributed to a third variable.

Claims appeared in the literature that cross-lagged methods could put correlational research on a par with experimental research as far as inferring causality was concerned, e.g., Crano and Mellon (1978). The wide applicability of cross-lagged methods from 1970 to 1985 and the general interest in inferring causality from correlation make it important that we briefly define the technique. However, everyone considering this method should read Rogosa's (1980) profound critique. His penetrating mathematical analysis of the difference between the two correlations reveals its dependence upon the magnitudes of the other four correlations. He notes, and provides plausible examples, of how both unequal cross-lagged correlations could arise in the absence of causal effects, equal causal effects, or causal effects that are actually in the direction opposite those apparent in the correlations.

## Applying ACS

Once a model has been properly specified, ACS then estimates the desired parameters and provides the diagnostic information discussed above and considered further in works listed in the Suggested Additional Readings. Since the additional concepts are either regression weights or covariances, there literally is nothing in this complete ACS model that was not considered in the more restricted confirmatory factor analytic setting. One should consider not only the summary $G^2$ but descriptive measures of fit and the statistics available for individual parameters. Free parameters that yield numerically small estimates might be fixed at zero. Fixed parameters whose derivatives are large might be freed, e.g., one might consider the specific relaxation implied by Fig. 13-5 relative to Fig. 13-2. These possible parameter relaxations should be thought of in advance as possible alternative models based upon substantive considerations.

Keep in mind that the overall fit of an ACS model is a joint function of all parameters even if they are not of equal interest. In the present application, the path coefficients ($\Gamma$ and $\mathbf{B}$) are clearly of most concern, followed by the pattern elements ($\Lambda_x$ and $\Lambda_y$). The uniqueness of ($\Theta_\delta$ and $\Theta_\varepsilon$) are often of least importance. Note that 12 of the 33 parameters estimated, over one-third, were uniquenesses in the example used in this section. This is not atypical and is a far cry from component analysis where these terms were disregarded. If one's interest is in weak theories, the "tail clearly wags the dog." Recall that at its core, ACS is basically a numerical estimation program. However, those within the common factor tradition, including Thurstone, see factor analysis as the separation of common variance from error and view the emphasis placed upon the uniquenesses as most proper.

## Reapplying ACS

It is rare that one simply fits a model and stops. Hopefully, the investigator has formulated several alternative hypotheses, as we have done in Fig. 13-5, to make meaningful modifications. However, most modifications are data-driven by unexpected findings. ACS's diagnostic information allows parameters to be added by freeing previously fixed or constrained parameters or deleted by fixing previously free parameters.

As in nearly all multivariate applications, the standard errors of estimates and the correlations among estimates are extremely important. Large standard errors relative to other parameters and a high correlation between two estimates imply that the estimation process is unstable. The derivatives of the fitting function with respect to fixed parameters describe the expected change in the function with a slight change in the parameter. A large value implies that the value chosen for the parameter is not correct. For example, if a variable actually belonged to a factor to which it was assigned a zero value, its' derivative would be large. Freeing the parameter to take on a more optimal value would improve the fit. But be careful that freeing the parameter does not cause the model to become unidentified. Conversely, if a parameter estimate is close to zero, little fit will be lost by fixing the parameter at zero. Likewise, if a factor correlation is close to 1, try fixing it at 1 to eliminate the factor. In both cases, use the ratio of the parameter's value to its standard error of estimate, which is a $t$ ratio.

ACS provides a variety of other information useful for respecification. Once this is done, the result is no longer strictly confirmatory, no matter how plausible the outcome is. The most recent versions of ACS can automatically respecify a model for you. Logically, this is not very different from using stepwise multiple regression in that it gets the program to do your thinking for you. Moreover, exert care in trying to explain a small but significant decrease in the residual $G^2$ in a large sample if that parameter greatly complicates your theoretical interpretation. Finally, keep in mind that the alpha levels are no longer true once you start respecifying on the basis of the data. It is always useful to replicate the model on a new sample.

### Classical Approaches to Strong Theories

Strong theories differ in "strength." For example, suppose that you wish to construct parallel forms of a test. Form A has a mean of, say, 10.3, a standard deviation of 4.1, and a coefficient $\alpha$ reliability of .84. Form B has a mean of 10.4, a standard deviation of 4.0, and a coefficient alpha reliability of .83. The correlation between forms is .80, so that it becomes $.80/\sqrt{(.84)(.83)}$ or .96 when corrected for attenuation. Do these slight disparities from parallelism make a difference, even if significant? In most situations, probably not. If you ran a pre-post design, randomly administering one form on the pretest and the other on the posttest, the effect of any disparity would be neutralized. On the other hand, if you had hoped to use either form as part of a college admissions process, you would not wish to use a common criterion though separate cutoffs would be defensible.

Classical methods are quite useful if you only need to approximate the conditions of a strong model such as parallelism. For example, multiple group analysis makes misspecifications more manifest than ACS since it does not force pattern weights to zero. The tendency of multiple group factors to point out a more correct solution is especially valuable in theory modification. Regression methods may then be used on the equally weighted sums that represent the constructs to infer path strengths. You have fewer decisions to make about parameters than you do in ACS. A multiple group model will never fit a sample as well as an ACS model because you have not optimized it for that sample, but it may be more robust across samples. However, ACS $G^2$ tests are much more systematic than classical methods and are more appropriate if needed to test models in a strict sense. The point of the above paragraph was not to decry ACS. It was to note that you should be skeptical about any method of data analysis as a "royal road" to truth. The more your substantive conclusions remain the same across different methods of analysis, the less you have to worry about them being artifacts of any particular method. Perhaps theories will someday be so highly developed in all areas and investigators will always gather large amounts of data. At that time (which certainly is the present in certain areas), ACS will be mandatory. However, this is clearly not now the case universally. Cliff (1983b) describes some useful cautions.

## SUMMARY

In contrast to previous chapters, where exploratory factors were defined to meet mathematical criteria such as accounting for the most variance, this chapter concerned confirmatory factors defined to meet substantive (theoretical) objectives. The goal of confirmatory factor analysis is to see how well proposed factors explain the data. There are two general traditions. Classical approaches stress the algebra of linear combinations and place relatively little emphasis upon statistical inference. A newer approach is based upon ML and related techniques of numerical estimation used to infer population parameters from sample data. It stresses statistical inference, although many descriptive measures have also been proposed. This tradition is perhaps most commonly called LISREL, but we use the designation analysis of covariance structures (ACS) to avoid confusion with LISREL as a specific computer program.

Factor analysis began with Spearman's (1904) hypothesis that measures of intelligence consist of a common factor ($g$) plus a unique error. If $g$ accounts for all the common variance, partialling it out should reduce all correlations to 0 within sampling error. All tetrads (correlations in paired rows and columns) will vanish. The difference in cross products of the tetrad values is also the second-order determinant. A matrix that contains correlations which are not all zero but whose tetrads vanish is of rank 1. Even though ML and related methods can provide explicit tests on the sufficiency of $g$ and the original theory is substantively incorrect, Spearman's logic is important since it is simple to apply and relates to unifactor hypotheses in general.

It is important to be able to compare factor structures so that results may be related across studies and establish generality. Three general situations have been distinguished: (1) the same variables may be given to the same subjects, as when one compares alternative factor solutions or factors to factor scores, (2) the same variables may be given to different subjects to look for factor invariance, and (3) different variables may be given to the same subjects to relate two or more classes of factors. One should *not* simply look at the pattern, structure, or factor weights to infer similarity, since these could generate highly similar factors or factor scores when the underlying variables are highly correlated. Correlating factor scores is sounder.

Some practical considerations in making comparisons classically are (1) lack of correlation between sets of factors may reflect unreliability; (2) conversely, it could represent true group differences that moderate relationships; (3) correlating rotated factors among groups confounds differences in correlational structure with differences in rotation angles—correlating unrotated solutions eliminates the latter artifact; (4) use the pooled within-groups covariance matrix for multiple comparisons if the individual matrices are similar; (5) equations comparing factors involve the structure matrix, whereas equations comparing factor scores involve the factor weight matrix. Relevant procedures were then discussed. We also discussed how to compare overall structures, as opposed to individual factors, using forced rotations.

ACS compares factors across groups by evaluating the difference between a model in which relevant parameters are constrained to equality across groups versus being allowed to vary freely. These parameters may come from the factor pattern, the factor correlation matrix, or the uniqueness matrix when a correlation ($\mathbf{R}$) matrix is analyzed. However, problems typically require analyzing the covariance or mean-sum-of-products matrices. The former allows groups to be compared as to variability on the factor, and the latter allows groups to be compared on both variability and location. Factors which are highly correlated may still each be significant, so proper interpretation is very important.

Weak theories propose groupings of variables but do not assert that groupings are independent or exhaustive. Three approaches were presented. All three require the proposed groupings to be specified by a hypothesis matrix. In multiple group analysis, factors are defined as sums of variables, and the properties of these sums define the solution. For example, the correlation between sums from two groupings defines their factor correlation, and the correlation of individual variables with groups defines the factor structure. In Procrustes, variables are defined terms of factors. A set of original factors are rotated to best fit the proposed organization in a least z squares sense. Unlike the multiple group method, the rotation always takes places within the hyperspace defined by the appropriate number of factors, and so the solution artifactually explains as much variance as a like number of original factors, whether or not the grouping is appropriate. ACS tests a weak theory by evaluating a model in which pattern weights for variables assigned to a factor are treated as free parameters and pattern weights for variables not assigned to a factor are fixed at zero. The factor correlation(s) and uniquenesses are additional free parameters. We then described the importance of arbitrarily chosen groupings (pseudofactors).

Next, we discussed evaluating the results. A variable that correlates poorly with its assigned grouping in multiple group analysis is probably misspecified, but the correlation is inflated because the variable belongs to the group with which it is correlated. Looking at the average off-diagonal correlation or performing a common factor analysis may reduce the bias somewhat. Even stronger evidence for misspecification is when a variable correlates more highly with another grouping than the one to which it is assigned. Looking at residuals may suggest further relations even though a weak theory does not require them to be nonsystematic. Do *not* give much credence to the absolute level of fit (e.g., proportion of variance accounted for), which may be high even with a major misspecification when variables are highly correlated, but the fit *must* clearly exceed that provided by pseudofactors. The factor correlation should not be extremely high. If the pseudofactors fit nearly as well as PrCs, too many factors have probably been proposed. Finally, the proposed factors should correlate highly with the early PrCs in order to represent major sources of variation.

ACS compares three models. The unconstrained (saturated) model uses all the data to obtain a best fit. It explains nothing and is not unique. The substantive model describes the proposed groupings, and the null model assumes there is no structure (no common variance). Inferential tests are based upon the respective values of $G^2$ which is the sample size times the value of the appropriate fitting function, e.g., ML. The substantive model must be identified, meaning that its solution is unique. In general, a substantive model's fit may be comparative, assessing the model itself, or incremental, assessing the model in relation to another nested model in the hierarchy. However, weak model testing is comparative. One should not dismiss a model because of significant $G^2$ in a very large sample, and various descriptive measures have been proposed. We discussed four classes of measures: (1) those that are like squared multiple correlations, which estimate the proportion of total variance accounted for by the proposed model, (2) those that compare the fit of the proposed model to the null model, (3) those that compare the fit of the proposed model to the saturated model, and (4) those based upon the fitting function. A major problem is to avoid a bias in favor of models with more free parameters; the fitting function is especially subject to this artifact. Two examples, one involving a correct grouping and the other involving an incorrect grouping were compared. The ACS solution suggested a misfit in that the residual $G^2$ was significant, but this reflected a trivial source of variance.

Many erroneously feel that item-level (discrete, categorical) data can be factored in the same way as scale-level (continuous) data. However, even though correlations usually describe the similarity of content of continuous measures, they do not for discrete data. Categorization attenuates correlations and thus diffuses the factor variance. Even though the underlying data may be unifactor, the analysis may suggest additional, spurious factors. In addition, categorical measures tend to group on the basis of the similarities of their distributions. A third source of artifact is that items with the same keying will tend to correlate more highly than items with opposite keying because of shared method variance.

Several ways to deal with categorical data were considered. One is to factor polychoric estimates rather than correlations themselves, but this has problems as well as advantages. Muthén's (1988) more recent LISCOMP was considered. It exploits the equivalence of factor analysis and item response theory. Observable responses are linked to underlying continuous variables which in turn are linked to factors. Response probabilities are assumed to reflect thresholds along the underlying continua. Unfortunately, some problems were noted in reliably obtaining estimates, especially with dichotomous data and high underlying correlations. Another approach involves the similarity of obtained factors to those defined on the basis of univariate item statistics, e.g., $p$ values.

We then considered testing strong theories using ACS. The simplest strong theory is that proposed groupings are exhaustive, as in Spearman's $g$. The test simply involves looking at the residual $G^2$. More specific examples include testing (1) that groupings are independent by fixing their factor correlation at 0, (2) that groupings are redundant by fixing their factor correlation at 1.0, (3) for equality of true variances (tau-equivalence) by constraining the pattern weights to equality, and (4) for parallelism by constraining the pattern weights to equality and the uniquenesses to equality.

The full ACS model relates two groups of factors (constructs) and their associated variables (indicators). Endogenous terms are assumed to originate outside the model, whereas endogenous variables are caused, at least in part, by exogenous variables and other endogenous variables. Indicators are related to their constructs through a measurement model, the confirmatory factor analytic model thus far discussed. The remaining relationships arise from the structural model that defines paths among constructs. Path coefficients describe the direct relationship between constructs which are, by definition, pattern elements. The resulting model contains a series of eight matrices whose elements must be specified as fixed, constrained, or free. These are the (1) exogenous pattern, (2) covariances among the exogenous constructs, (3) exogenous uniquenesses, (4) endogenous pattern, (5) covariances among endogenous constructs, (6) endogenous uniquenesses, (7) path coefficients from exogenous constructs to endogenous constructs, and (8) path coefficients among endogenous constructs. The considerations involved in specification were discussed.

Perhaps the majority of models are recursive in that paths do not cross and there is no reciprocal causation (if A causes B, then B does not cause A). However, ACS allows nonrecursive models to be evaluated just like recursive ones, although it is often somewhat more difficult to ensure identification. Cross-lagged correlation is another topic related to causation. In its simplest case, it involves obtaining two measures at two different points in time. Inferences about causation are made based upon the pattern of correlations. However, a cogent critique by Rogosa (1980) should give users of this procedure cause to seek alternatives.

Several things need be considered in evaluating an ACS model. Free parameters which provide small numeric estimates might be fixed at zero, estimates that are very similar might be constrained, and fixed parameters that suggest an instability might be freed. It is rare that the first ACS model tested is ideal. It is preferable that an investigator has a series of alternative models in mind that lead to a theory-based modification. Look at the standard errors. Moreover, once the model is respecified in the original sample, the original alpha levels are no longer true; one will tend to capitalize upon chance. Consequently replication in a new sample is strongly suggested. We conclude by noting how certain classical approaches may be useful when the goal is simply to approximate such conditions as parallelism.

## SUGGESTED ADDITIONAL READINGS

Anderson, J. C., & Gerbing, D. W. (1988). Structural equation modeling in practice: A review and recommended two-step approach. *Psychological Bulletin, 103,* 411–423.

Bentler, P. (1990). Comparative fit indexes in structural models. *Psychological Bulletin, 107,* 238–246.

Breckler, S. J. (1990). Application of covariance structure modeling in psychology: Cause for concern? *Psychological Bulletin, 107,* 260–273.

Byrne, B. M. (1990). *A primer of LISREL.* New York: Springer-Verlag.

Cudeck, R. (1989). Analysis of correlation matrices using covariance structure models. *Psychological Bulletin, 105,* 317–327.

McDonald, R. P. (1990). Choosing a multivariate model: Noncentrality and goodness of fit. *Psychological Bulletin, 107,* 247–255.

*Note*: The Suggested Additional Readings for Chapters 11 and 12 also list works that discuss classical approaches to confirmatory factor analysis. Those given here are selections from the increasingly large ACS literature. The April 1990 issue of *Multivariate Behavioral Research* contains several papers dealing with model respecification in ACS.

# PART FIVE

# ADDITIONAL STATISTICAL MODELS, CONCEPTS, AND ISSUES

Several additional models are useful in psychometric theory, and this final part consists of two chapters devoted to them. The first of these chapters concerns ways to group profiles. This may arise when one's interest is in finding latent groups, as in cluster analysis, profile analysis, and multidimensional scaling. In contrast, it may involve ways to best discriminate among existing groups, as in discriminant analysis. In most cases, measures of interest are based upon the similarity of one observation to another; however, measures of dominance (preference) may also be analyzed. Part of this material involves a further consideration of the geometric model presented in the chapters on factor analysis. The last chapter involves ways to analyze categorical data such as ethnicity or religion. This discussion also illustrates some alternative, nongeometric models.

## CHAPTER 14

# PROFILE ANALYSIS, DISCRIMINANT ANALYSIS, AND MULTIDIMENSIONAL SCALING

## CHAPTER OVERVIEW

Although factor analysis is probably the most common way to study similarities among measures, it is only one of a number of possible methods. This chapter will consider the four most popular alternative ways to study similarity. First, *cluster analysis* began as an alternative to factor analysis. Second, like factor analysis, profile analysis and discriminant analysis are usually concerned with scaling people, although they can be applied to scaling stimulus objects as well. Finally, multidimensional scaling is usually concerned with scaling stimuli, but it also has some special uses in scaling people. It is particularly useful when data fail to fit the unidimensional scaling models discussed in Chapter 2.

Like factor analysis, cluster analysis, profile analysis, and discriminant analysis begin with a rectangular data matrix ($\mathbf{X}$). Variables define the columns of $\mathbf{X}$, and people define the rows. Just as one major purpose of most exploratory factor analysis is to discover clusters of variables, the same is true of classical cluster analysis. Each cluster consists of variables that tend to measure the same thing and something different from other clusters. In contrast, profile analysis and discriminant analysis are concerned with relations among people, as in $Q$-design factor analysis. We will show that similar mathematical procedures underlie conventional factor analysis, profile analysis, and discriminant analysis. The same is true to a large extent of multidimensional scaling. Currently, these methods are largely exploratory in the sense of Chapters 11 and 12, rather than confirmatory in the sense of Chapter 13.

Most of this chapter concerns data that are like correlations in the sense of describing similarity, referred to in many sources as proximity measures, e.g., Davison (1983). Dominance relations, as exemplified by preferences, are a very different form of data. Methods appropriate to the study of dominance relations will be considered in the last main section of this chapter.

Do not confuse similarity and dominance judgments even though both may be used to scale stimuli and the resulting scales may in fact be quite similar. They require quite different methods of analysis. For one thing, there is no counterpart in the study of dominance that matches the power of the PM correlation as seen in factor analysis and other multivariate procedures. Second, similarity relations are symmetric: If stimulus a is highly similar to stimulus b, then stimulus b is highly similar to stimulus a. The correlation between stimuli a and b ($r_{ab}$) is the same as the correlation between stimuli b and a ($r_{ba}$). On the other hand, dominance relations are asymmetric: If you prefer stimulus a to stimulus b, you cannot prefer stimulus b to stimulus a.

## CLUSTER ANALYSIS

The original purpose of cluster analysis (Tryon & Bailey, 1970; Lorr, 1983) was very similar to a common goal of factor analysis. As the name implies, cluster analysis consists of methods of classifying variables into groups, or clusters. A "cluster" is defined as it was in Chapter 11—variables that have high correlations with one another compared to their correlations with other variables. However, cluster analysis employs different methods for exploring groupings. Chapter 15 will introduce a somewhat different approach to clustering, Schvaneveldt's (1990) Pathfinder model.

One traditional approach is as follows. Reflect (reverse the direction of) variables as in centroid factor analysis to maximize the sum of positive correlations in the matrix if their sum of correlations with the remaining variables is negative. Next, find the highest correlation in the matrix. The two involved variables form the nucleus of the first cluster. Then look for variables that correlate highly with these and include them in the cluster. The nucleus for the second cluster is formed by finding two variables that have a high correlation with each other but a low correlation with members of the first cluster. Include variables that correlate highly with the two variables serving as the nucleus of the second cluster in this second cluster. Proceed in this same way to obtain additional clusters.

If clusters were quite clear, cluster analysis would be a more direct way of identifying groups of variables than factor analysis. Unfortunately, this is seldom the case for several reasons. When there are but a few variables, the patterns of relationship are often visible by simply inspecting the correlation matrix ($\mathbf{R}$), as was true of the six-variable problem used in Chapters 11 through 13. However, it is easy to get lost in a large matrix. Also, groupings may be apparent in the residual matrices following factor extractions that were not originally discernible in $\mathbf{R}$. McQuitty (e.g., McQuitty & Koch, 1976) has developed a number of clustering routines for large matrices. Unfortunately, these methods involve numerous subjective decisions about the number of clusters and their composition.

If you think of factor analysis as a form of cluster analysis (which has considerable merit), we recommend multiple group factor analysis to determine how well predefined clusters hang together. ACS is a second possibility. If clusters are not predefined, multiple group analysis can still be used. Include the variables having the highest correlations with one another in the first group centroid. Obtain a residual matrix and form a second factor using those variables which have the highest residual correlations with one another, etc. Whether one uses trial-and-error methods of cluster analysis or formal factor analysis, factors can be thought of as clusters. We have stressed how subsequent work with factors almost always involves sums of three or four salient variables at most.

In recent years, cluster analysis has come to describe grouping people on the basis of the similarity of their profiles (score vectors). This is the problem of profile analysis to which we now turn.

## PROBLEMS IN PROFILE ANALYSIS

"Profile analysis" is a generic term for all methods concerned with grouping people, and what we speak of here as profile analysis is frequently called cluster analysis. However, there are some key differences between clustering people in profile analysis and clustering variables in conventional factor analysis. One important class of profile analysis problems involves groups that are known in advance of the analysis. The purpose is to use the data to best distinguish groups from one another. For example, one might collect MMPI scale scores from groups of psychiatric patients and try to use the MMPI profiles to distinguish among these groups. Discriminant analysis can be used to address this problem. In discriminant analysis, one simultaneously tests hypotheses regarding the differentiation of these groups using these profiles and forms maximally discriminating linear combinations of those measures.

The other major class of problems in profile analysis occurs when groupings of people are not stated in advance of the analysis. In this case, the purpose of the analysis is to cluster individuals in terms of their profiles and thereby discover meaningful latent groupings. Discriminant analysis thus determines the extent to which previously defined groups hang together, and the clustering of profiles attempts to discover latent groups of people that hang together. Typically, relatively few people fall into pure clusters; most people combine the traits that define the clusters.

### Characteristics of Score Profiles

The term "profile" comes from the practice in applied testing of plotting scores on a battery of tests as a profile. Figure 14-1 contains examples of profiles for subjects 1, 2, and 3 on six variables. They have been separately standardized over people, as discussed in Chapter 12.

A profile contains three items of information: level, dispersion, and shape. The level is typically defined by the person's mean score over the variables in the profile, i.e., by simply averaging that person's scores. Subect 1's level is clearly higher than subject 2's, and subject 2's is higher than subject 3's. However, the mean denotes little unless all variables are pointed in the same direction and concern the same domain of behavior, i.e., have large positive intercorrelations. Levels describing poorly related measures are essentially meaningless. This does not mean that one should not incorporate unrelated or negatively related measures in a profile; it only means that their level

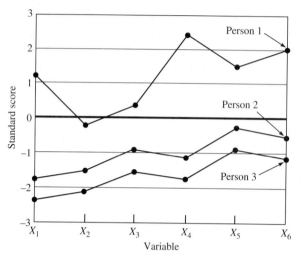

**FIGURE 14-1** Score profiles for two people on six variables.

will not be meaningful. Moreover, even if the variables all relate to the same domain of behavior, the level is difficult to interpret if variables are pointed in different directions; e.g., some scores denote maladjustment and others denote adjustment.

As the word implies, the dispersion (also called the scatter) defines how widely scores in a profile diverge from the average (level). One way to describe the dispersion of a person's profile is as the standard deviation of scores. Subject 1's dispersion is larger than that of subjects 2 and 3, whose dispersions in turn are identical. Whereas levels may be compared directly, assuming the individual measures are positively correlated so that the process is meaningful, dispersions are much more difficult to compare because they depend upon the correlations among variables in the profile. The more highly correlated the measures are, the smaller the dispersions will be. A particular person's dispersion is therefore meaningful only relative to the dispersions of other people. One way to facilitate comparing dispersions is to obtain the distribution of dispersions over people and convert them to percentiles, although this is seldom done.

The last remaining information in the profile, the shape, concerns where the "ups and downs" in the profile occur. Even though two people may have the same level and dispersion, their high and low points might be quite different. The shape obtained from a profile of abilities measures indicates an individual's particular talents. The shape is definable from the rank order of scores for each person. Thus, subject 1's rank ordering from high to low in Fig. 14-1 is $X_4$, $X_6$, $X_5$, $X_1$, $X_3$, and $X_2$. In contrast, the rank orderings of subjects 2 and 3 are $X_5$, $X_6$, $X_3$, $X_4$, $X_2$, and $X_1$. Their shapes are identical even though their levels are different.

Level, shape, and dispersion are interdependent over people. The dispersion must be relatively small because of range restriction when the level is either very high or very low so that there is generally a moderate curvilinear correlation between dispersion and level. If a person's dispersion is small, the ordering of variables (shape) represents only tiny differences in performance and may simply reflect measurement error (see Chapter 7). Consequently one should not interpret a profile's shape unless the dispersion is relatively large. The physical appearance of a particular profile also depends on the order of listing the variables. This ordering is usually arbitrary, and so the physical appearance of the profile can typically be changed arbitrarily without affecting level, dispersion, or shape. In some cases such as trials on a learning curve, variables are naturally ordered.

The profiles shown in Fig. 14-1 could have depicted the average scores for groups of people rather than individuals. The term "profile analysis" is frequently used to refer to the statistical description of differences among group profiles, which includes inferential tests on the significance of the group differences (these methods are discussed extensively in works concerned with multivariate analysis listed in the Suggested Additional Readings). However, significance testing should not be confused with the more major problem of describing the clustering of profiles and discriminant analysis which is considered here.

## CLUSTERING OF PROFILES

Although there has been considerable controversy over how to cluster profiles (see Lorr, 1983), there are some straightforward methods for handling the problem. Assume that each of $N$ people has been measured on $V$ variables. There are marked differences in the levels of the individual profiles, but differences in shape are especially interesting. The study concerns individual differences in the patterns of these responses to determine whether people fall into meaningfully defined clusters. Nunnally (1962) placed the problem of clustering profiles in the general perspective of multivariate analysis and demonstrated that all major clustering problems could be handled by the same powerful factor analytic methods more traditionally employed to study correlations among variables.

### Measures of Profile Similarity

The first step in clustering is to define profile similarity. If profile level and dispersion are unimportant, one suitable measure is the PM coefficient over profile elements, as in $Q$ design factor analysis (see Chapter 12). The measurements for each person are standardized by subtracting the individual's level (mean) from each of the individual measures and dividing by the dispersion of the profile. The correlation between two people is the average cross product of these standardized scores, Eq. 4-6, but, as in $Q$-design factor analysis, the average is computed over profile elements ($V$) rather than people ($N$, see Chapter 12).

If the profile level, profile dispersion, or both are important aspects of similarity, as they often are, the PM correlation is *not* a proper measure of the similarity of two profiles. The computations equate all profiles for level and dispersion; each profile level becomes 0, and each profile's dispersion (standard deviation) becomes 1. The PM coefficient is sensitive only to similarities in shape and not in level or dispersion. Two examples that indicate how this could produce misleading results are (1) the profiles of

subjects 2 and 3 in Fig. 14-1 correlate perfectly, which hides their obvious level difference, and (2) two people could have the same shape and level on their profiles, also
producing a PM correlation of 1, but they could differ in dispersion.

The two primary standards for choosing a measure of profile similarity are that (1)
it should include all relevant information and (2) it should lend itself to formal mathematical analysis. The first is largely a matter of situational demands, but a given measure may place severe limits on the methods of analysis that can legitimately be employed. If level, dispersion, and shape are all important, the similarity measure should
obviously consider all three types of information. Later, however, we argue that it is
sometimes better to ignore one or more of the three sources of information. Numerous
measures have been proposed for various purposes (Cronbach & Gleser, 1953; Helmstadter, 1957; Muldoon & Ray, 1958; Tryon & Bailey, 1970).

One possible measure that considers level, dispersion, and shape is the sum of the
absolute differences in scores. This is zero for two identical profiles and grows larger
as profiles differ in level, dispersion, or shape. Although it makes sense descriptively,
it suffers from the same fault as many other proposed measures of profile similarity: It
does not lend itself to mathematical analysis because it is difficult to work with absolute differences.

## Distance Measure

One very appealing measure of profile similarity is the distance measure ($D$) (Osgood
& Suci, 1952; Cronbach & Gleser, 1953). $D$ is the generalized Pythagorean distance
between two points in Euclidian space. We will define the properties of a Euclidian
space later in the chapter; for now, just think of it as the space around us which one ordinarily studies in geometry. With two people and two variables, $D$ is the length of the
hypotenuse of a right triangle, as illustrated in Fig. 14-2. The square of the distance
between the points for subjects 1 and 2 is obtained as follows:

$$D_{ab}^2 = (X_{a1} - X_{b1})^2 + (X_{a2} - X_{b2})^2 \qquad (14\text{-}1)$$

The square root of the above expression is the distance ($D$) between the two points. If
the number of variables ($V$) exceeds two, the squared distance is

$$D_{ab}^2 = (X_{a1} - X_{b1})^2 + (X_{a2} - X_{b2})^2 + \cdots + (X_{ak} - X_{bk})^2 \qquad (14\text{-}2a)$$
$$= \Sigma(X_{aj} - X_{bj})^2 \qquad (14\text{-}2b)$$

The distance $D$ between the two points corresponding to the profiles for two people
equals the square root of the sum of squared differences on the profile variables, regardless of the number of variables. The number of terms involved ($V$) describes the
number of dimensions in the space. When $V = 1$; (i.e., the space is unidimensional),
$D = (X_a - X_b)$.

All scores for a person on the $V$ variables define a point in a $V$-space of variables.
Each variable is plotted at right angles to the others. [More complex methods that do
not assume that the variables are orthogonal exist (cf. Bernstein, 1988, Chapter 9), but

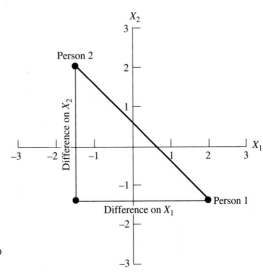

**FIGURE 14-2**    Distance between two people on two variables.

this issue will be considered below.] This point summarizes all the information about the person's profile. Although it is not physically possible to represent such points for more than three variables (dimensions) at a time, the logic of measuring distance with $D$ still holds.

$D$ is intuitively appealing because it considers profile level, dispersion, and shape. Also, it lends itself to powerful methods of analysis. For these reasons, the authors generally recommend, as others have, that profile analysis be based upon $D$. Many algorithms begin by computing $D$ between all possible pairs of individuals to form an $N \times N$ symmetric distance matrix (Lorr, 1983; Osgood, Suci, & Tannenbaum, 1957; Sawrey, Keller, & Conger, 1960; Tryon & Bailey, 1970). People with small $D$s have similar profiles, and people with relatively large $D$s have dissimilar profiles. However, we will shortly discuss a transformation of $D$ that is at least as useful.

### Hierarchical and Overlapping Clustering

There are several ways to define the best clustering of $G$ groups based upon a set of $N$ individual profiles. One is to maximize the variance of profiles between groups relative to the pooled within-group differences. Specifically, the two most similar profiles, in terms of $D$ or a related measure, are grouped into a cluster.

In hierarchical clustering, one proceeds sequentially by grouping the two most similar profiles in this way and treating their average scale values on the original two profiles as a new single profile. Next, these two most similar profiles are grouped. This grouping may include the profile that was averaged at step 1 or two different profiles. The process proceeds until only a single profile remains. At each step, a measure of the homogeneity of clusters is obtained, such as the ratio of between- to within-group profile variation, which steadily decreases. Conversely, measures reflecting error (within-group variation) steadily increase as the number of clusters decreases. Both changes occur because the clusters steadily become more dissimilar. One way to decide upon the number of profiles to be retained is to look for an "elbow" in the curve relating the criterion measure to the number of clusters. A tree diagram can be used to plot the history of the clustering process.

Most forms of clustering limit a subject to one and only one cluster. An exception is overlapping clustering which allows a subject to belong to multiple clusters. Lorr (1983) discusses these and other clustering methods.

## RAW-SCORE FACTOR ANALYSIS

Most proposed methods of cluster analysis that analyze matrices of distance measures are based upon trial and error. Consequently they lack a general algebra, are indeterminate, and are messy to compute. This section considers one useful method for clustering, raw-score factor analysis (Nunnally, 1962). As the name implies, it is based upon scores that have *not* been standardized over subjects. It also illustrates (1) a $Q$ design, since the measures of relationship are applied among people over variables, and (2) that factor analysis need not always be applied to a correlation matrix. Imagine that there are profiles of six people (1 to 6) on 10 variables. Table 14-1 and Fig. 14-3 contain the distances ($D$) between all pairs of individuals. These hypothetical distances were chosen to fall exactly in a 2-space, which will never happen in actual research. There is nothing sacred about the way points in Fig. 14-3 fall on the page. They could be shifted to the right or left or rotated as long as their final positions maintain the same distances among the six points. Distances are ratio measures (see Chapter 1), and so they may be multiplied by a constant without disturbing the configuration. For example, if all the distances in Fig. 14-3 were multiplied by 2.5, the geometric configuration would be remain the same, but it would be spread out more on the page. However, one cannot *add* a constant to these distances without affecting the configuration of points. Adding a constant will probably change the number of dimensions required to contain the points.

Figure 14-3 and Table 14-1 indicate that there are two clusters, respectively, defined by subjects 1, 2, and 3 and subjects 4, 5, and 6. It is, of course, unlikely that an actual

**TABLE 14-1**   MATRIX OF D VALUES FOR POINTS SHOWN IN FIG. 14-3

| Person | Person | | | | | |
| --- | --- | --- | --- | --- | --- | --- |
| | 1 | 2 | 3 | 4 | 5 | 6 |
| 1 | .0 | 1.0 | 1.4 | 7.8 | 7.1 | 6.4 |
| 2 | 1.0 | .0 | 1.0 | 7.2 | 6.4 | 5.8 |
| 3 | 1.4 | 1.0 | .0 | 6.4 | 5.7 | 5.0 |
| 4 | 7.8 | 7.2 | 6.4 | .0 | 1.0 | 1.4 |
| 5 | 7.1 | 6.4 | 5.7 | 1.0 | .0 | 1.0 |
| 6 | 6.4 | 5.8 | 5.0 | 1.4 | 1.0 | .0 |

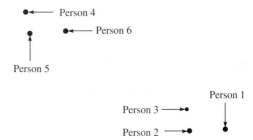

**FIGURE 14-3**    Interpoint distances for six people.

study would employ so few cases and provide such definite clusters; if this were to happen, refined methods of analysis would not be needed. A method of factor analysis that uses $D$ measures will be described which can recover these clusters. It can be used equally well with any number of people, regardless of how apparent the clusters are. The method was derived by Suci (Osgood, Suci, & Tannenbaum, 1957). Suci and the first author cooperatively explored his method of factoring $D$ and found it to be a special case of raw score factor analysis. Chapter 11 noted that values of $\Sigma X/Y$ can be factored just as $r$ can be factored. Since $N$ (which represents the number of profile elements and not people) is a constant, it can be ignored, so that factor analysis can be performed using sums of cross products ($\Sigma XY$) as the basis measure of similarity.

### An Example of Raw-Score Factor Analysis

We will provide a worked-out example of raw-score cross-product factoring because of its relative unfamiliarity. The first step is to obtain the sum of raw cross products over the profile variables as in the following example for subjects 1 and 2 for four variables, $X_1$ to $X_4$. These scores need *not* be standardized.

| Variable | Subject 1 | Subject 2 | Cross products |
|----------|-----------|-----------|----------------|
| $X_1$ | 1.5 | 1.0 | 1.5 |
| $X_2$ | .5 | 2.0 | 1.0 |
| $X_3$ | −2.0 | −1.0 | 2.0 |
| $X_4$ | 1.2 | −.5 | −.6 |

The sum of cross products for subjects 1 and 2 is 3.9 (1.5 + 1.0 + 2.0 − .6). The sums obtained for all pairs of subjects produce a symmetric matrix of raw cross products—the mathematics places no limits on the scoring units employed for each variable. We will later consider common units for all variables (e.g., standardizing all variables), as in Fig. 14-1.

Table 14-2 shows a hypothetical matrix of cross products which was constructed to be compatible with the $D$ values shown in Table 14-1 by working backward from the distances. In practice, the distances would be obtained by summing actual cross products. Note that large sums of cross products in Table 14-2 correspond to small $D$ values in Table 14-1, and vice versa. Each diagonal entry is simply the sum of an individ-

TABLE 14-2    RAW-SCORE CROSS PRODUCTS AND FACTOR SOLUTION
FOR POINTS SHOWN IN FIG. 14-3

|  | Person | | | | | |
| Person | 1 | 2 | 3 | 4 | 5 | 6 |
| --- | --- | --- | --- | --- | --- | --- |
| 1 | 36 | 30 | 30 | 6 | 6 | 12 |
| 2 | 30 | 25 | 25 | 5 | 5 | 10 |
| 3 | 30 | 25 | 26 | 11 | 10 | 15 |
| 4 | 6 | 5 | 11 | 37 | 31 | 32 |
| 5 | 6 | 5 | 10 | 31 | 26 | 27 |
| 6 | 12 | 10 | 15 | 32 | 27 | 29 |

ual's squared profile elements ($\Sigma X^2$). This parallels placing unities in the diagonal spaces of a correlation matrix in component analysis.

Any of the methods of factoring correlation coefficients can be applied to these cross products: PrC, principal axis, multiple group or ACS confirmatory analysis, etc. We will use a PrC analysis so that you can repeat the relatively simple computations. One problem you may confront if you attempt the analysis is that you must tell the program that you are analyzing covariances and not correlations. Actually you are not; the terms are values of $\Sigma XY$ rather than $\Sigma xy/N$. However, the program will then allow numbers larger than 1 to appear in the matrix. The program may standardize the structure to correlations, which is not what you want. Obtain the normalized eigenvectors and multiply each element by the square root of the associated eigenvalue. You can tell if the eigenvalues are on the proper scale by seeing that their sum equals the sum of the diagonal elements of the matrix. Equation 12-1, or, if you have several factors, Eqs. 12-2, may be used for rotation. The varimax rotation applied to standardized data is not the same as the varimax rotation that should be applied to the cross products because all vectors are not the same length, but it is usually satisfactory. The rotated structure clearly describes the clusters shown in Fig. 14-3 and Tables 14-1 and 14-2. Figure 14-4 shows a plot of the rotated structure; the interpoint distances are identical to those in Fig. 14-3.

## How Raw-Score Factor Analysis Works

Variables in profiles can be described by mutually orthogonal axes in Euclidian space unless they are extremely highly correlated. If they are, the original variables can be factored and rotated orthogonally to provide more meaningful composite measures, and the raw scores replaced by factor scores. Each profile can be plotted as a point in the space, and $D$ measures the distance of such points from one another. Raw-score factor analysis provides a basis (or semibasis) for the profile space; i.e., the factors provide a geometric frame of reference.

Because any sufficient basis preserves distances between points, the structure preserves the original $D$ value. This can be tested with the data in Table 14-2 by obtaining

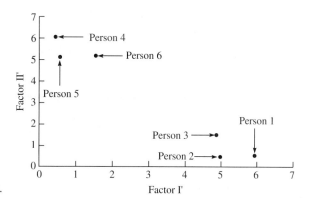

**FIGURE 14-4**    Rotated factor structure.

$D$ values from the rotated structure. For example, the $D$ between subjects 1 and 2 is almost exactly 1.0, which is what was given in Table 14-1. Similarly, all the $D$ values can be calculated from either the centroid or rotated structure matrix. If factoring is not complete, the factor matrix will serve to explain most of the distances. Thus information about clusters that can be obtained from a matrix of $D$ values also can be obtained from a matrix of cross products. Whereas it is complex to factor matrices of $D$ values directly, it is simple to factor cross-product matrices. Consequently, although it is useful to think of a profile as a point in Euclidian space, these points are better analyzed with the sums of cross products than with $D$.

There is a simple relationship between the two measures:

$$
\begin{aligned}
D_{ab}^2 &= \Sigma(X_{aj} - X_{bj})^2 \\
&= \Sigma(X_{aj}^2 + X_{bj}^2 - 2X_{aj}X_{bj}) \\
&= \Sigma X_{aj}^2 + \Sigma X_{bj}^2 - \Sigma 2X_{aj}X_{bj}
\end{aligned}
\tag{14-3}
$$

$$
\Sigma X_{aj}X_{bj} = \frac{\Sigma X_{aj}^2 + \Sigma X_{bj}^2 - D_{ab}^2}{2}
$$

Standardizing both profiles over the $V$ profile variables and dividing both sides of Eq. 14-3 by $V$ produces

$$
r_{ab} = 1 - \frac{D_{ab}^2}{2V}
\tag{14-4}
$$

Thus, when two profiles are standardized over profile variables (not people), the PM correlation between the two profiles is a monotonically decreasing function of $D^2$, and thus of $D$.

Raw score factor analysis is part of a more general model for factoring vector products, though we will discuss some limits upon the utility of geometric analogies in the next chapter. Chapter 11 developed this model by translating any correlation into

$h_i \cos_{ij} h_j$, where $h_i$ and $h_j$ equaled the lengths of the vectors depicting the two variables (square roots of diagonal elements) and $\cos_{ij}$ equaled the cosine of the angle between them. The more general method permits one to factor any matrix of elements of the form $h_i \cos_{ij} h_j$ that can be legitimately construed to lie in a Euclidian space. In raw score factor analysis, $h_1$ equals the square root of the sum of squared elements in subject 1's profile, $h^2$ equals the square root of the sum of squared elements in subject 2's profile, and $\cos_{12}$ equals the cosine between the two vectors (profiles). These lengths are not unity, as in component factoring of correlation matrices, or some fraction of unity, as in common factor analysis, but are determined by the actual sums of squared profile elements.

We will consider factoring in multidimensional scaling where there are no variables over which cross-product terms can be summed later in the chapter. The data are a symmetric matrix of similarity measures. If either the raw judgments or some modifications of them can be construed as vector products ($h_i \cos_{ij} h_j$), this matrix can be factored and rotated too.

## Transformations of Variables

Two types of transformations are important in profile analysis: transformations of individual variables, considered in this section, and transformations of profiles, considered in the next section. The most common variable transformation is standardization, i.e., making the mean of a variable 0 and its standard deviation 1. This is the simplest way to handle the problem that an observed variable's standard deviation (over people) often reflects arbitrarily chosen units of scaling. Thus, SAT scores have a standard deviation of 100, whereas their grade point averages might have a standard deviation of 1.5. These differences artifactually influence the profiles unless something like standardization is employed. In general, standardize all variables unless differences in their units are meaningful. If the differences are small, standardizing will not have much effect.

A second issue regarding the transformation of variables arises when observed variables are correlated over people, as they almost always are. Sometimes, as with human abilities measures, these correlations may be substantial. Some have argued that it makes no sense to employ $D$ or to perform cross-products analyses on these observed variables if they are correlated at all. Replacing the original variables with orthogonal components is a possible solution to this problem. However, there are two arguments in favor of analyzing the original variables even though they are correlated—one mathematical and one theoretical. The mathematical argument is that the use of $D$ and cross-products analysis is not restricted to uncorrelated variables. Correlated variables are commonly depicted algebraically and geometrically with orthogonal axes. The depiction is used to determine the degree of correlation. For example, scatter plots use orthogonal or uncorrelated coordinates in order to examine the relationship between two variables.

A more general example will help show why correlated variables can be depicted as orthogonal. Equation 14-4 showed that the correlation ($r$) between two profiles is a monotonically decreasing function of $D$. When $r$ is derived from two variables rather than two profiles, $D$ is the distance between two variables in a space of people rather than two people in a space of variables. In that instance, each person is represented by an axis which is orthogonal to the axes for all other people. The $r$ between any two variables can be obtained either as a function of $D$ or as the average product of standard scores. People are viewed as independent (orthogonal or uncorrelated) dimensions because their data are obtained independently. No one seriously questions the customary use of correlational analysis simply because it is usually depicted in a space of orthogonal people. Yet, some think it is not correct to use $D$ or the sum of cross products unless the variables are orthogonal. For the same reason, there is no strong mathematical argument for insisting upon variables being uncorrelated in order to compute the $D$ statistic or perform cross-products analysis over people.

Although there is no obvious mathematical necessity for having uncorrelated variables, substantial correlations among the variables do make it difficult to interpret the results. On the one hand, it is improbable that a well-conceived problem would involve clustering of profiles based upon unrelated variables. Variables in an overall theoretical system probably correlate at least modestly. The structure of these correlations determines the redundancy of the variables and thus the extent to which they differentially influence $D$ and any cross-products factors used to explain the distance space. For example, two highly correlated reasoning tests will make approximately the same contribution to $D$ and have essentially the same influence on raw-score cross products. If two people have similar scores on these tests, they will tend to have similar profiles, even though they may differ substantially in other respects. The potential problems caused by substantial correlations among profile variables relate to the generalizability of results that can be obtained from profile clustering.

Ideally, the variables included in a cluster analysis should be representative of some specified domain of variables, e.g., physiological variables relating to stress or tests representative of different factors of reasoning. The $D$ statistic indexes dissimilarity, which raises the knotty question of "Dissimilar with respect to what?" This question can be answered only if investigators can define the domain of variables and thus declare the traits over which results can be generalized. Two approaches will help ensure generalizability. The first is to sample the variables thought to be important in a specified domain, e.g., reasoning abilities. The study would include a little of everything thought to be important, have the broadest feasible coverage, and involve a relatively large number of measures. A complementary approach to selecting variables can be used if a more definite theory is available about the domain of variables. For example, if prior results suggest six major reasoning ability factors, tests that measure these specific traits should be included in the profiles.

If generality can be ensured either by sampling or structured selection of variables, the $D$ statistic and the cross-products analysis can be interpreted directly even if there are some substantial correlations among the variables. That is, it makes sense to say that two individuals are similar over a sufficient mapping of the variables from a domain, even if some of the variables correlate substantially. The chosen variables can be factored before performing cross-products analysis if the original variables are highly correlated, as noted earlier. One might find, for example, that four factors explain most of the common variance. Factor scores over people could be obtained on the four factors, the $D$ statistic could be computed using these factor scores, and cross products could then be factored over the profile elements. However, a factor analysis may raise more problems than it solves. First, one may end up with so few variables that there is not much room to perform cross-products factor analysis. Second, the specific variance of each variable will be excluded from $D$, so that one may throw away the most important part of the data.

One approach is to employ component analysis and extract as many factors as there are variables. This will represent the full variance of all variables on $D$ in an orthogonal space. The resulting cross-products analysis is mathematically proper, but the results might be difficult to interpret. However, this may be the wisest approach if it is difficult to define the domain of variables clearly and/or the variables are highly intercorrelated.

### Transformations of Profiles

Regardless of what transformations, if any, are made of the distributions of individual differences on variables, possible transformations of intraindividual distributions of profile scores also need to be considered. If it is meaningful to consider level, dispersion, and shape in clustering profiles, these should be permitted to vary when cross products are analyzed. If, however, one or more of these aspects are irrelevant, they should be eliminated before the analysis. For example, if level is unimportant, all profile means should be equated, typically to zero, using the methods of Chapter 12. Then form cross products among the resulting deviation scores about each person's level.

### DISCRIMINANT ANALYSIS

Discriminant analysis is employed to distinguish predefined groups from one another on the basis of their score profiles. Examples of groups are different types of psychiatric patients, vocational groups, and college seniors majoring in different fields. Mathematically, there is no limit to the types of variables that can be employed, but problems may arise in interpreting the results. These problems will be discussed later.

There are three related problems in discriminant analysis:

**1** Determining the statistical significance of differences in score profiles for two or more groups

**2** Maximizing the discrimination among groups by forming linear combinations among the variables

**3** Establishing classification rules to place new individuals into one of the groups.

The first of these is most important when sizes are small. Appropriate tests such as Wilks' lambda are discussed in all major textbooks on multivariate analysis (see the Suggested Additional Readings). Rejecting the null hypothesis allows one to infer that the group profiles differ. We have previously noted two reasons why statistical tests are not highly important in most research problems when sample sizes are at least moderate. First, the results of such tests are frequently difficult to interpret. For example, groups may not differ significantly on any of the original variables, but the overall difference between profiles may be significant. Such tests combine the information from the different variables into an overall significance test. It may be difficult to interpret a significant difference in overall profiles unless some, and preferably most, variables differ significantly. At best, such tests provide rather meager information about the significance of differences. At the same time, they are important in ruling out the null hypothesis when sample sizes are small, as they are in much laboratory research. This inferential aspect of discriminant analysis is known as the multivariate analysis of variance (MANOVA). Moreover, it *is* proper to aggregate a series of fallible measures into a more reliable composite, which discriminant analysis often does. An even more important reason is that merely knowing that the average profiles differ among groups does not tell one how to combine the information or classify new subjects.

The major problem in discriminant analysis is to maximize the discrimination among groups. Most of this section will consider issues related to that problem. The problem of classifying new individuals will be discussed later in the section.

### Geometric Interpretation of Discriminant Analysis

The geometric model previously given for profile analysis will help explain discriminant analysis. If there are $N$ people and $V$ variables, any person's profile can be represented as a point in $V$-dimensional space. Each axis of the space consists of one of the variables, and the axes are depicted as mutually orthogonal. In discriminant analysis, it is useful to think of a particular group as being concentrated in a region of the space. Discriminant analysis provides the most information when members of a given group cluster in a given region and different groups occupy different regions rather than being scattered throughout the space. The tighter the clustering of groups in the $V$ space and the less overlap there is among groups, the more useful the information.

Figure 14-5 illustrates a simplified example of a space for two groups (males and females) on two variables ($X_1$ and $X_2$), e.g., raw scores on two physiological stress in-

**FIGURE 14-5**  Scores of females (open circles) and males (open squares) on two hypothetical measures of physiological reaction to stress. The solid circle and solid square are the group centroids.

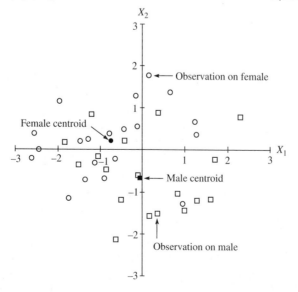

dicators. Each female is represented by an open circle, and each male is represented by an open square. It can be seen that the two groups tend to occupy different regions of the space: Males tend to be high on $X_1$ and low on $X_2$, and females tend to be low on $X_1$ and high on $X_2$. However, both groups overlap on each variable.

The solid circles and solid squares in Fig. 14-5 represent the centroids for males and females, respectively. Simply stated, a "centroid" is the average profile of a group. The average score for the group is obtained for each variable, and the resulting means are plotted as though they were scores for an individual. Points for individuals balance in all directions around a group centroid, just as variables balance around a centroid factor. If groups are well discriminated, centroids are far apart, and the members of each group hover near their centroid.

Instead of depicting each person as an individual point, it is more convenient to depict regions of scatter for the groups as a whole. This is done in Fig. 14-6 for the profile points depicted in Fig. 14-5. The amount of overlap between the contours of scatter indicates the extent to which the two variables fail to discriminate between the two groups. The individual scatter plots are circular because the two hypothetical measures are uncorrelated within each of the two groups. The two regions of scatter are of equal size and shape in the diagram, i.e., homoscedastic. This implies that the distinguishing characteristics of the groups are additive with respect to the underlying variables. This need not be the case in reality; the group scatter may be heteroscedastic, which greatly complicates the analysis and renders the figure of little value. Bernstein (1988) discusses this issue at length (also see Chapter 15).

FIGURE 14-6    Areas of scatter for males and females on two measures of physiological reaction to stress.

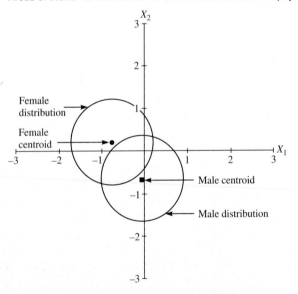

### Linear Discriminant Function

Some means of combining the information from the two variables to best discriminate members of the two groups is helpful in the problem depicted in Figs. 14-5 and 14-6. This could potentially be done with various functions of the variables, but a simple linear function has been used most often. Such a function is referred to as a linear discriminant function:

$$Y = b_1 X_1 + b_2 X_2$$

where $Y$ = scores on linear discriminant function
$X_1, X_2$ = raw scores on variables
$b_1, b_2$ = weights for variables

Weights $b_1$ and $b_2$ are applied to raw scores on variables $X_1$ and $X_2$ for each person in each group. This produces a new score for each person, called a discriminant score ($Y$, which we will use to symbolize both the linear relation and the individual scores; a more formal notation would use a subscript to denote scores, e.g., $Y_i$ for the $i$th subject) which combines the information from $X_1$ and $X_2$ to discriminate among groups.

Figure 14-6 illustrates how a linear function can discriminate between two groups. The weights define a line in the space ($Y$), and the discriminant scores of all individuals can be projected on that line as in Fig. 14-7. These discriminant scores on $Y$ can be "taken out" of the space for the variables and depicted separately as a frequency distribution (Fig. 14-8). The distributions of the discriminant scores overlap much less than the individual distributions of $X_1$ and $X_2$: $Y$ has condensed the discriminant information present in the two variables.

Obtaining the weights requires a rule for optimization, as is true whenever optimum weights are sought. Just as multiple regression weights are usually obtained by the least-squares principle of minimizing the sum of squared errors of prediction, linear discriminant weights maximize the following ratio.

$$\frac{\text{Variance between means on } Y}{\text{Variance within groups on } Y}$$

In fact, Fisher (1936) noted that this optimization rule maximizes the $F$ ratio of between-means variances to within-group variances, and so it is an extension of an ordinary one-way analysis of variance (ANOVA). The discriminant function provided by the weights produces a score for each person.

After proposing an optimization rule, Fisher used calculus to derive the linear discriminant functions' weights. This is especially simple with only two groups, regardless of the number of variables. The solution involves a special use of multiple regression analysis in which members of one group receive a score of 1 and members of the other group receive a score of 0 (since correlational analysis standardizes the group scores, any other two numbers, do as well, and it does not matter which group is given which score). The predictors are used to best estimate group membership.

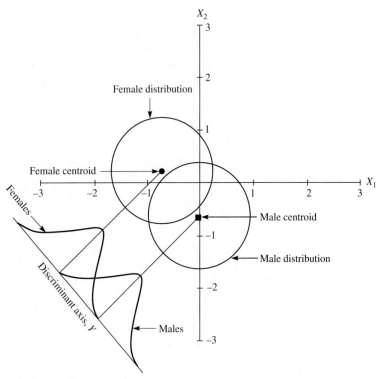

**FIGURE 14-7** Projection of scores onto a discriminant function $Y$.

**FIGURE 14-8** Distribution of scores on a discriminant function.

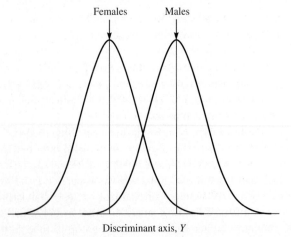

## Multiple Linear Discriminant Functions

Most research problems involve more than two groups. It is both possible and usually desirable to derive more than one discriminant function to provide a multiple discriminant analysis (MDA) when there are at least three groups and two predictors. The first discriminant function is that linear combination of the variables which maximizes the ratio of between-means variance to within-group variance. A second discriminant function is derived from the residual variances and covariances among variables in much the same way that a second principal component is obtained. It serves as the second-best explainer of variance. Additional discriminant functions are obtained analogously. There will be as many possible discriminant functions as the lesser of (1) the number of variables or (2) 1 less than the number of groups. The resulting family of linear discriminant functions is

$$Y_1 = a_1X_1 + a_2X_2 + \cdots + a_kX_k$$
$$Y_2 = b_1X_1 + b_2X_2 + \cdots + b_kX_k$$
$$Y_3 = c_1X_1 + c_2X_2 + \cdots + c_kX_k$$

$$\cdots\cdots\cdots\cdots$$

$$Y_h = h_1X_1 + h_2X_2 + \cdots + h_kX_k$$

(even though we have previously used the symbol $b$ to denote unstandardized regression weights, which the above are, it is simpler to use different letters and a single subscript here than to use double subscripts). The weights provide a discriminant score for each person on each discriminant function. Discriminant scores on any two functions (e.g., $Y_1$ and $Y_2$) are uncorrelated with one another (orthogonal) over all subjects. However, these discriminant scores are usually correlated within a particular group. Note that the numbers we are using for the various discriminant functions correspond notationally to the Roman numerals we previously used to define the various factors. The computational procedures underlying MDA are discussed in detail in works concerned with multivariate analysis cited in the Suggested Additional Readings. The mathematical procedures involve a special type of eigenanalysis based upon a matrix we will designate **A**, rather than a correlation matrix. The same measures must be applied to all subjects. There need not be the same number of individuals in each group.

Whereas subjects were not classified into a priori groups in the data matrix **X** depicted in Table 11-1, they are in discriminant analysis, as indicated in Table 14-3. The symbols $G_1$, $G_2$, . . . , $G_h$ denote the various groups. It is conceptually helpful to assume that each variable has been standardized over all subjects. Each measure will therefore sum to zero over groups, but the group averages need not be zero. Similarly, the average variance of a given measure weighted by group size will be 1, but it may be more or less in a given group (although this is the most common way to standardize data, it is not the only way, and different computer programs may standardize data differently). Only the general element ($z_{ij}$) is shown for each group on each measure.

We will symbolize the first discriminant function $Y_1$, again using the same symbol to denote the linear function and the scores it produces. The resulting scores maximize the proportion of variance explained. The set of $V$ weights forms a vector of weights,

**TABLE 14-3** DATA MATRIX PARTITIONED FOR DISCRIMINANT ANALYSIS

| | Measures (variables) | | | | |
|---|---|---|---|---|---|
| Person (objects) | $z_1$ | $z_2$ | $z_3$ | ... | $z_k$ |
| Group 1 | $z_{11}$ | $z_{12}$ | $z_{13}$ | ... | $z_{1k}$ |
| Group 2 | $z_{21}$ | $z_{22}$ | $z_{23}$ | ... | $z_{2k}$ |
| Group 3 | $z_{31}$ | $z_{32}$ | $z_{33}$ | ... | $z_{3k}$ |
| | | | ...... | | |
| Group h | $z_{h1}$ | $z_{h2}$ | $z_{h3}$ | ... | $z_{hk}$ |

and the first such vector $\mathbf{v}_1$ is mathematically equivalent to the first eigenvector of a PrC analysis. The calculation is extremely similar to the way trial vectors were accumulatively multiplied into correlation matrices in Chapter 11 to derive PrCs.

Again paralleling the ANOVA, applying $\mathbf{v}_1$ to the scores produces linear combinations that maximize the previously discussed ratio of the sums of squares between group means to the pooled sums of squares within groups. Whereas it is customary to compute sums of squares directly from lists of scores in the ANOVA, we have shown in Chapter 5 and elsewhere that variances of sums and weighted sums can be obtained from covariance matrices. The analysis employs the covariance matrix between group means, denoted $\mathbf{B}$, and the pooled covariance within groups, denoted $\mathbf{W}$. The $\mathbf{B}$ matrix uses sums of squares and cross products based upon group means, and the $\mathbf{W}$ matrix uses sums of squares and cross products obtained within each group and added over groups. One therefore seeks $\mathbf{v}_1$ to maximize the corresponding ratio of variances:

$$\frac{\mathbf{B}\mathbf{v}_1}{\mathbf{W}\mathbf{v}_1} = \text{a maximum}$$

The actual calculation involves an analogy to what may be done in ordinary scalar division—multiplying the numerator of a ratio by the inverse (reciprocal) of the denominator (computing $a/b$ as $ab^{-1}$). Here $\mathbf{B}$ is multiplied by the inverse of $\mathbf{W}$, symbolized in matrix algebra terminology as $\mathbf{W}^{-1}$. Unfortunately, $\mathbf{W}^{-1}$ does not bear a simple relationship to $\mathbf{W}$. It is *not* obtained by any simple process like taking the reciprocal of each element in $\mathbf{W}$. Rather, any inverse such as $\mathbf{W}^{-1}$ is a specially computed matrix which produces what is called an identity matrix when it is multiplied by the original matrix. An identity matrix is a symmetric matrix with unities on the diagonals and zeros off the diagonal. Thus, the inverse of a matrix is the analog of the inverse of any variable in ordinary algebra. Given $\mathbf{W}^{-1}$, the normalized vector of weights for $Y_1$ can be stated as

$$\mathbf{W}^{-1}\mathbf{B}\mathbf{v}_1 = \text{a maximum}$$
$$\mathbf{A}\mathbf{v}_1 = \text{a maximum}$$

In other words, $\mathbf{A}$ is the product of $\mathbf{W}^{-1}$ and $\mathbf{B}$, and the problem is of exactly the same form as PrC analysis ($\mathbf{A}$, unlike a correlation matrix, $\mathbf{R}$, is normally not symmetric, but this difference is only important computationally). One can derive $\mathbf{V}_1$ iteratively by applying essentially the same computational routine to $\mathbf{A}$ as was done to $\mathbf{R}$ in PrC analysis. The process produces the first eigenvalue ($\lambda_1$) and the first vector of discriminant weights ($\mathbf{v}_1$) based upon the first eigenvector. This eigenvalue describes the amount of total variance explained by $Y_1$. Each variable will have a weight in $\mathbf{v}_1$, although some weights may be near zero. Accumulatively multiplying these weights by the scores produces the discriminant axis ($Y_1$). Additional results include the mean and standard deviation of the discriminant scores for each group and a test of significance on whether the groups differ on $DF_1$.

Obtaining $Y_1$ allows computation of a residual matrix ($\mathbf{A}_1$). Performing the iterative process upon $\mathbf{A}_1$ produces a second normalized vector of weights ($\mathbf{v}_2$) and an associated discriminant function ($Y_2$). One can continue to derive discriminant functions until they (1) are not statistically significant, (2) explain only tiny portions of the original variance, even though this amount may be significant, or (3) are not of theoretical or practical importance. By definition, each discriminant function must explain less variance than any of its predecessors.

## Placement

Placement concerns the assignment of new individuals to a group when their membership is unknown. This might be an Air Force recruit who is to be assigned to a technical specialty or a student who is seeking career counseling. Placements are usually made by comparing the target person's profile with the average profiles for people known to belong to the various groups. One potential difficulty is that one must first know the group membership of a representative group of persons to make valid placement decisions. If these average group profiles are not different from one another, placement is hopeless—flipping coins would do as well. Placements may employ either the observed or discriminant scores. Cooley and Lohnes (1971) and Bernstein (1988) compare various suggested approaches and provide an overall discussion of the logic and methods of placement.

Assume that MDA has provided discriminant scores for all the people in the various groups and each group centroid. Most applications assume that these discriminant scores are normally distributed within each group. This allows one to compute contours of equal density about the centroid for each group. Since these are con*tours* about the group *cen*troid, they are often referred to as centours (Cooley & Lohnes, 1971). It is easiest to visualize such centours in the plane provided by two discriminant functions, but the logic applies to any number of discriminant functions. In this 2-space, the scatter of group members about the group centroid can be pictured as a series of ellipses reflecting various proportions of the group. These are in effect confidence intervals and are portrayed in Fig. 14-9.

As mentioned earlier, discriminant scores are usually correlated within a particular group even though they are uncorrelated over all groups. The higher this correlation, the more elliptical the centour, as is true of any scatter plot. These centours indicate the percentages of people farther in and farther out relative to the centroid.

The centour score for an individual estimates the percentage of persons in a group that are further from the centroid than that individual. For example, a centour score of 75 means that the individual is closer to the centroid than 75 percent of the members

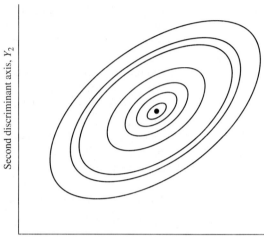

**FIGURE 14-9**   Centour ellipses around the centroid for one group on two discriminant functions.

Second discriminant axis, $Y_2$

First discriminant axis, $Y_1$

of the group, regardless of direction. Individuals are placed in the group for which their centour score is highest. An individual with respective centour scores of 75, 25, and 10 for three groups would be assigned to the first group.

Centour scores need not add up to 100 percent for any one subject and may vary among subjects. One person could have high centour scores for a number of groups, and another person could have very low centour scores for all groups. The extent to which centour scores successfully place a person is directly related to the variability of that person's centour scores. If these scores are highly similar to one another, classification will probably not be successful. If this is the case for most of the subjects, the variables used for placement have been ill-chosen.

### Evaluation of Discriminant Analysis

In spite of the differences in purpose of factor analysis and discriminant analysis, they are closely related mathematically. MDA is based on linear combinations of variables so that a discriminant function is also a factor. We have also noted that linear discriminant functions are obtained by PrC factoring of a special matrix describing discrimination among versus within groups. Discriminant functions, then, are special types of factors that discriminate among a priori groups of subjects even though it is highly unlikely that discriminant functions derived from a set of variables corresponded to their PrC factors. MDA is both conceptually and mathematically a powerful tool which has not been employed nearly as much as it should have been in the behavioral sciences, although Hake (e.g., Hake, Faust, McIntyre, & Murray, 1967; Rodwan & Hake, 1964) pioneered its application in experimental psychology. Still, the main use of MDA in basic research has been in the form of the MANOVA. Unfortunately, this is simply a way to obtain an overall (omnibus) test of the significance of group differences. This use ignores the much greater descriptive role of MDA in understanding the structure of the variables. A particularly useful question is whether the measures that discriminate among groups all relate to a single attribute (factor), in which case the group mean differences are said to be concentrated. For example, groups A, B, and C may have the same rank order on all measures. In contrast, some measures may order the groups as A, B, and C, but others may order them B, C, and A. In this case the group mean differences are said to be diffuse. No single attribute underlies group differences in a diffuse structure.

MDA was introduced into psychology through applied testing programs for personnel selection and placement. Early applications employed ability tests rather than noncognitive measures such as personality traits, interests, and values. These early applications were intended to provide an effective strategy to assign people to jobs or training programs. Unfortunately, these early applications were rather unsuccessful, and the close association of the methods with these specialized problems in personnel selection tended to hide the methodology from the broader field of psychology. MDA is potentially useful in many applied problems. However, some logical issues must be confronted.

**1** How should the groups be defined before the analysis. Some problems dictate this in an obvious, reliable manner (e.g., in comparing males and females or members of different professions), but group definition is less obvious in other cases. As one example, if MDA is applied in studying psychiatric classifications, some classifications are so unreliable as to preclude clear results. A practical issue in this case might be whether to treat people suffering from major depression and bipolar (manic-depressive) disorders as separate groups or to pool their data. Obtaining a random sample of subjects in the various groups is vital but often difficult.

**2** If abilities tests are used, a decision must be made whether to include (a) all subjects who were tested, (b) people who meet at least a minimum level of competence, or (c) only outstanding individuals.

**3** Discriminant analysis is needed with ability tests only when there is a curvilinear or no relationship between test scores and the desirability of placing an individual in a particular group. If this relation is linear, one could simply place the individual in the highest group for which his or her scores are minimally acceptable.

**4** Placement based upon centours provides a related problem. An individual who is far removed from the centroid in any direction would be declared not fit for the group. This could lead to anomalies like a person being too smart to be a nuclear physicist or too psychotic to be schizophrenic. However, this problem does not exist in all methods of classification and is discussed in Cooley and Lohnes (1971) and Bernstein (1988). Centours might be much more fruitfully applied to noncognitive attributes such as interests, personality traits, attitudes, and values. The assumption of "just the right amount" of such traits to determine group compatibility makes more sense than with abilities in these cases.

**5** It is often inappropriate to assume that people who currently are members of definable groups, especially occupations, should be in these groups. Actually, people frequently become members of occupational groups partly because of prior errors in classification, including racial and gender discrimination. Methods like MDA may actually serve to perpetuate rather than eliminate misclassifications.

MDA has proven more helpful in understanding the structure of group centroid differences than it has in classification because of the large amount of scatter about the group centroids (within-group variance) relative to distances among centroids. In other words, discriminant functions frequently do not explain a large amount of variance. There may be significant group differences, but the within-group variance may be so large that classification is difficult. Nonetheless, MDA may help understand why groups differ and thus guide future test development.

## PATTERN ANALYSIS

What has been spoken of as profile analysis is called pattern analysis by some. We find it useful to distinguish between the two based upon the data employed in each. We will use the term "profile analysis" when the variables are continuous, the term "pattern analysis" when the variables are discrete (categorical). Chapter 10 has already dealt with one highly sophisticated form of pattern analysis, item response theory.

A "pattern" is simply any complete set of responses to a collection of items, e.g., agree, agree, disagree to three attitudinal items. It may refer to the actual responses of a particular individual, the most popular responses in a group of people, or even a hypothetical set of responses. Even though two people obtain the same total test scores, they rarely make the same errors. As we saw in Chapter 10, some feel that analyzing patterns of response might offer better measures than those obtained from the linear model.

As in our prior discussion of continuous measures, problems relating to pattern analysis fall into the two categories of discovering latent groups and discriminating among existing groups.

## Discovering Latent Groups

Numerous trial-and-error methods have been proposed to cluster people on the basis of their response patterns (see Tryon & Bailey, 1970; Lorr, 1983). One proper approach, however, is to employ cross-products analysis, just as was used with continuous measures. The first step in the analysis is to compute an index of response agreement over items for each pair of individuals. If two individuals respond in the same way to an item, regardless of what that response is, that is counted as an agreement. The two types of responses on ability tests are correct and incorrect and are often agreement and disagreement on nonability tests.

If the responses are dichotomous, one index of agreement is the mean cross product of scores, treating one response category as +1 and the other as −1 (any other distinct pair of numbers will be mathematically equivalent). Thus if two people both pass or both fail an ability item, their item cross product is 1; but if one person passes the item and the other fails the item, their item cross product is −1. Similarly, if two people both agree or both disagree with a nonability item, their cross product is 1; but if they give different responses, their cross product is −1. Sums of such cross products over items are then divided by the number of items. Any of the methods of factor analysis previously considered can be used with these mean sums of cross products. An approach based upon factor analysis has certain advantages. Each person's structure element on the first initial factor is an index of his or her agreement with the consensus of all subjects. The factor structure denotes groupings of individuals, as is true of other factor analytic applications described in this chapter. However, the cautions about factoring categorical data discussed in Chapter 13 need to be kept in mind. In particular, differences among individuals in their tendency to choose the more probable alternative can account for a substantial portion of the discrepancy between two individuals.

### Discriminating among Existing Groups

Discriminant analysis can be applied to sets of dichotomous scores (patterns) in a manner analogous to the application of discriminant methods to continuous scores (profiles, see Maxwell, 1961). For example, one might diagnose psychiatric illness in patients on the basis of their symptom pattern, where a symptom is scored 1 when present and 0 when absent. Overall and Klett (1971) have also presented some interesting possibilities. However, the item response theory methods of Chapter 10 are uniquely suited to this issue. In particular, the same methods used to study differential item functioning can be used even though the interpretation is different. Most of the questions one would ask can be phrased in terms of group differences in difficulty or discrimination parameters.

### Evaluation of Pattern Analysis

In spite of its interesting possibilities, pattern analysis suffers from a crippling flaw: It takes individual items too seriously, a concern we also have about item response theory. As noted previously, individual items are usually heavily loaded with unique error: pure measurement error plus reliable variance specific to individual items. We have stressed that test items usually correlate poorly with one another; correlations above .30 are the exception. In other words, most of the variance in each item is trivial, and pattern analysis seeks to find important information in that trivia. It has not worked. Studies in which pattern analysis has been employed either failed to obtain clear results or, when they apparently did, the results did not hold up in subsequent samples (which explains the dearth of published results). Pattern analysis of test items is unfortunately ideal for taking advantage of chance because (1) each item has a large measurement error component; (2) there is usually a relatively large number of items, which gives more room to take advantage of chance; and (3) methods of analysis, such as MDA, capitalize on chance. Perhaps better results might be obtained by using data that are more reliable than ordinary test items, such as the presence or absence of well-defined symptoms. Some categorical measures, of course, are reliable.

## MULTIDIMENSIONAL SCALING

We will use the term "multidimensional scaling" (MDS) to focus on the scaling of stimuli rather than the scaling of people. As is implicit in the name, we assume that the stimuli may vary complexly among themselves in such psychological attributes as pleasantness, liberal versus conservative, etc. Although MDS employs the same mathematical models as factor analysis and discriminant analysis, it is normally used for a different purpose. However, it does overlap with the forms of factor analysis considered in this chapter. MDS can be used to study individual differences among people, but (1) studies of individual differences are adequately handled by the multivariate procedures discussed previously in this book and (2) the procedures which will be discussed are mainly important for scaling stimuli. MDS is an extension of the unidimensional scaling methods discussed in Chapter 2, which noted that unidimensional scaling methods should be applied only when there is good reason to believe that the data vary along one dimension. Good unidimensional scaling requires the experimenter to minimize extraneous differences among the stimuli to prevent them from influencing judgments or preferences. In unidimensional scaling, the investigator must know the psychological dimension on which responses are to be made in advance of the study.

Suppose, for example, one wishes to study perceived weight, which, under proper conditions could be viewed as a single dimension. The weights should all be the same shape, color, and, ideally, size. The most important facet of the study is the control obtained by instructions to subjects. Each subject must be carefully instructed to make judgments or preferences with regard to the dimension of interest and be warned about letting other variables influence the responses.

In MDS, subjects are usually not instructed to respond with respect to a particular dimension; rather, they are asked to respond only in terms of overall similarities and differences among the stimuli, e.g., to judge whether stimulus a is more similar to stimulus b or to stimulus c. MDS is used in two related types of studies. In one type, the investigator does not know what dimensions people typically use in responding to a class of stimuli, and the purpose of such investigations is to learn the dimensions. For example, subjects might judge the similarity of well-known political figures. These similarity judgments might require only one dimension (probably like versus dislike), or they might require several dimensions reflecting positions on various social issues such as abortion. The purpose of the study would be to learn about the "natural" dimensions that people employ in their judgments.

The second type of study in which MDS is employed concerns judgments rather than sentiments. Although the major physical dimensions that differentiate the stimuli might be known, it might not be clear how these dimensions affect the psychological processes underlying judgments. For example, suppose one obtains similarity judgments for a set of red chips that vary systematically along the physical dimensions of saturation (pureness) and reflectance (proportion of light reflected or physical intensity). The results might indicate that subjects actually employ only one subjective dimension even though there are two physical dimensions of variation: Saturation and intensity combine into a single dimension of "vividness." Alternatively, subjects might employ the two physical dimensions in their judgments, but one is much more influential than the other; e.g., they are more sensitive to variation in saturation than reflectance, or vice versa. Still another possibility is that more than two dimensions are needed to explain the data because of the way the physical dimensions interact.

MDS has become a very popular tool because (1) many behavioral scientists are sufficiently sophisticated in mathematics and statistics to understand the complex methods involved, (2) computers are now readily available to perform the analyses, and (3) the outcomes have proven useful to the behavioral sciences. The most comprehensive recent sources on the topic are listed in the Suggested Additional Readings. Davison (1983) is an excellent source.

## Spatial Conceptions of MDS

Spatial models are extremely important in MDS, even more so than in factor and profile analysis. The terms used to refer to the experiments and methods of analysis are spatial in nature, e.g., "dimension," "proximity," "origin," and "rotation." Indeed, one of its most prominent developers has noted (Shepard, in Shepard, Romney, & Nerlove, 1972) that one of MDS' most attractive features is that it allows one to summarize complex relations among numerous stimuli in terms of simple two-dimensional representations showing pairs of relations in three or four dimensions.

MDS essentially requires subjects' responses to be converted to a spatial representation, either directly or by the use of assumptions about the data. Perhaps more simply, it is quite natural to think of similar stimuli as falling "nearer" one another than more dissimilar stimuli. Indeed, the analogy is so compelling (even for many who are not mathematically oriented) that we often have to think twice to realize that it is only an analogy.

Euclidian space is by far the most frequently employed spatial geometric model for MDS. A Euclidian space is basically the geometry of flat surfaces in which the generalized Pythagorean theorem of Eq. 14-2 holds. This is the space that we observe in the world around us, and so it is also referred to as real space. Thus, while sitting in a room, one is literally in a Euclidian 3-space. All the geometric properties of the room could be computed from familiar theorems of geometry; e.g. the area of a wall equals its width times its height. One of the most important properties of a Euclidian space is the triangle (Cauchy-Schwarz) inequality which states that the distance from one point $a$ to a second point $b$ ($D_{ab}$) measured directly cannot be greater than the sum of their distances through a third point $c$ ($D_{ac} + D_{cb}$). It is called the triangle inequality because it implies that one side of a triangle cannot be longer than the sum of the other two sides. In particular, both Eq. 14-2 and the triangle inequality dictate that $D_{ab} = D_{ac} + D_{cb}$ in a one-dimensional space, e.g., the distance from First Street to Fourth Street along First Avenue is the sum of the distance from First Street to Third Street and the distance from Third Street to Fourth Street (in this one-dimensional case, several models produce the same distance). Finally, we will assume that distances are positive numbers and therefore not directed: $D_{ab} = D_{ba}$, although distances are considered directed (signed) in some applications so that $D_{ab} = -D_{ba}$.

Technically, distances between cities can differ from those based upon Eq. 14-2 since they are measured on the surface of a globe and not on a flat surface. Intercontinental distances between cities therefore follow a non-Euclidian distance model, but the error in measuring distances within a smaller area, say the United States or, better, within a given state, can be neglected. It is very useful to conceptualize MDS and other forms of multivariate analysis in terms of Euclidian spatial models because very powerful systems of mathematics can be adopted, e.g., those in factor analysis and discriminant analysis.

Various non-Euclidian models have been considered in MDS (see Coombs, 1980; Coombs, Dawes, & Tversky, 1970; Shepard, Romney, & Nerlove, 1972; Torgerson, 1958). Perhaps the simplest one is the city block model in which distances are measured in terms of how one gets from one corner of a city block (say First Street and First Avenue) to another (say Second Street and Second Avenue). One could walk one to First Street and Second Avenue (Second Street and First Avenue would work just as well), turn, and walk another block for a total of two blocks. The shortest distance in Euclidian space is to walk straight through the buildings from one corner to the opposing corner. This is 1.4+ blocks, $\sqrt{1^2 + 1^2}$, but it is has limited applicability since one ordinarily cannot walk through buildings as if they were an empty field. Euclidian and city block distance measures are part of a broader class of measures referred to as Minkowski $r$ metrics which are important in the next chapter. MDS also considers nonmetric spaces derived from rank orders rather than assumptions about distances. Theoretically at least, one should contrast classical methods, which assume that data are at least interval and perhaps, though not necessarily, Euclidian, with ordinal methods, which are used to infer a metric. Much of the output of these two classes of analyses will be similar, as it concerns the structure of the stimuli, but the logic of ordinal methods is far more complex. Most of our discussion will assume the Euclidian model since it is by far the simplest. We will discuss some more formal properties of distance in the next chapter and consider an approach to scaling that employs non-Euclidian distance measures at that point.

Once points are located in (mapped into) a Euclidian space, powerful methods of analysis can dimensionalize the space, place it in a coordinate system, and locate each stimulus with respect to the resulting coordinate axes. The logic is the same as that used with the $D$ measure and raw-score factor analysis. This logic grew out of a historic paper by Young and Householder (1938) and has been manifested subsequently in numerous mathematical methods for handling multivariate problems in factor analysis, clustering, MDA, and MDS. The primary experimental and analytic problem in MDS is therefore to obtain data that can be mapped into a Euclidian space.

## An Overview of Alternative Approaches to MDS

One situation-specific issue is whether to gather data from a large sample of people, as in market research, or to study a single individual in detail, as in a case study. This distinction between nomothetic and ideographic measurement has long been made in the psychology literature. It has some important methodological implications. For example, observations made by two different people are independent, whereas observations made at two different times by the same person are obviously not. This may raise a problem for inferential tests, but a well-designed ideographic study that minimizes the correlated error in subjects' responses (e.g., by providing breaks to keep them from developing a set to respond in the same way on a block of ratings) can mitigate the problem.

Two broad, interrelated issues involved in choosing an MDS model are (1) the empirical (psychophysical) aspect of data gathering and (2) the mathematical aspect that deals with the assumed properties of the data and the choice of the specific MDS model used to analyze these data. At the empirical level, Chapter 2 contrasted direct and indirect methods. Direct methods assume that subjects can provide data which can be analyzed as obtained; e.g., subjects can report intervals through magnitude estimation. This section considers two types of direct methods: similarity and attribute ratings. The method of paired comparison, also discussed in Chapter 2, is the simplest way to obtain similarity ratings. For example, the goal of the study might be to scale 10 well-known U.S. senators. They would be arranged in 45 [(10)(9/2)] pairs, and subjects would be asked to judge the similarity of the members of each pair, perhaps on a 10-point scale (subjects are *not* asked which senator they prefer, as that would generate the dominance data considered in the last major section of this chapter). Certain MDS programs require subjects to judge dissimilarity or difference rather than similarity, but this is not a major complication. Conversely, attribute ratings require subjects to judge each stimulus with respect to a series of attributes, e.g., to rate individual senators with regard to specific policy issues.

Chapter 2 also discussed indirect methods, which require that judgments of stimuli be confused and that different responses be made to the same stimulus over trials. They are predicated on the probabilistic nature of judgments: The more similar stimuli are, the more often they are confused. For example, subjects might be offered cola drinks a, b, c, . . ., and asked to identify a given sample by name. The results may be portrayed in a confusion matrix containing the joint frequencies of identifying actual cola $i$ as cola $j$. The basic idea is that if cola a is more similar to cola b than cola c, the probability of judging cola a as cola b will be higher than the probability of judging cola a as cola c. Indirect methods depend upon errors of judgment. The Fullerton-Cattell law, upon which these are based, states that one cannot directly compare two stimuli which are never confused with one another (although each may be compared to a third stimulus). The subjects never compare the colas directly. Not all indirect methods use confusion; some use correlations to index similarity, as will be described below. Whereas direct methods are most clearly suited to normal subjects judging stimuli that they are familiar with and are interested in judging, indirect methods have the advantage of being more usable with impaired populations or with animals.

The most important, but not the only, mathematical consideration is the level of measurement assumed to underlie the data. For example, one investigator might treat similarity ratings as ratio data and adopt a model that assumes that a similarity rating of 4 literally means twice the similarity of a rating of 2. Another investigator may decide that it is better to treat the measures as interval rather than ratio data. That investigator assumes that a rating of 4 is midway between a rating of 2 and 6 but not necessarily twice that of 2. Finally, a third investigator may simply consider the data as ordinal so that a 3 simply denotes greater similarity than a 2.

Most applications of MDS reduce the data to a symmetric $V \times V$ matrix of dissimilarities, where $V$ is the number of stimuli. Data from individual subjects are usually lost in the process of aggregation. An alternative is individual differences scaling (Carroll & Chang, 1970; Carroll, 1972) which compares subjects or groups of subjects. A family of methods, which include individual differences algorithms, that has dominated the MDS literature uses what is known as the alternating least-squares estimation algorithm (Takane, Young, & de Leeuw, 1977; Young, Takane, & Lewyckyj, 1978). It forms the basis of the ALSCAL program which will be discussed in a later section.

As we consider the various MDS methods or, for that matter, any other methods discussed in this book, keep in mind the adage that one "cannot make silk a purse out of a sow's ear." Applying complex methods to poorly gathered data, either in the sense of ill-conceived sets of variables or poorly controlled observations, is most unlikely to lead to meaningful discoveries. There are obvious advantages and disadvantages in employing strong psychophysical scaling methods and strong methods of MDS, where "strength" is defined in terms of the assumptions made. Unfortunately, the stronger the assumptions, the more likely it is that they will be inapplicable and produce spurious results. Nearly all methods have ways to test the validity of the assumptions, and these are important. MDS is capable of producing quite valuable results when properly applied, as are, of course, the methods considered elsewhere.

When subjects provide proximity information, as when they produce distances between stimuli directly, one may seek MDS methods that make strong mathematical assumptions. If subjects can actually produce good proximity information, much information would be lost using a method of MDS that does not utilize all this potential information. Even though there is less danger when using weaker psychophysical and/or MDS methods, the results are more limited. These strong methods allow a great deal of information to be obtained rather easily if one is willing to make a variety of assumptions about the data-gathering process and methods of analysis. However, there is a risk of producing spurious results because the assumptions are faulty. Conversely, the experimenter can require subjects to supply only weak psychophysical information, such as rank orderings, and apply methods of MDS that make few assumptions about the spatial representation of the stimuli. In so doing, the experimenter may lose potential information. He or she must know both the options and the situation to make an informed choice. It is usually reasonable to employ stronger methods with trained subjects who make decisions about familiar, distinctive, and salient stimuli. Similarly, it is quite risky to use these methods with groups like psychiatric patients when the stimuli are not interesting to the subjects and/or are not clearly differentiated.

### Psychophysical Methods Based upon Similarity

Most methods of MDS use some form of overall perceived similarity judgment rather than judgments of specific, predefined attributes. Several are adaptations of tasks originally discussed in Chapter 2. The first four of these generally involve some form of paired comparison.

**1** Direct magnitude estimation (Stevens, 1956, 1958) involves having the subject numerically estimate the perceived similarity or dissimilarity of stimulus pairs. Normally, one pair is chosen as a referent and given a desired scale value. If, for example, subjects are asked to judge the similarity of senators, they might be instructed to rate Senator Smith and Senator Hong as 10. If they feel that Senators Brown and Gomez are twice as dissimilar when compared to one another as Senators Smith and Hong are when compared to one another, the appropriate response will be 20. Although it is not necessary to treat the resulting data as ratio measurement, the assumption is more justified here than with any of the alternatives. A variant is to have subjects draw a line whose length equals the relative magnitude of the rating.

**2** Category ratings employ a format like the following.
How similar are Senators Smith and Hong? (circle one)

1    2    3    4    5    6    7    8    9
Very similar                      Very dissimilar

Variants upon this procedure include sorting the pairs into categories, e.g., placing cards with the names of the stimulus pairs into stacks corresponding to the categories. Categorization typically is nonlinear in the sense that the distance from category 1 to category 2 usually cannot be assumed to be the same as the distance from category 4 to category 5. Ratio measurement that is sometimes possible with magnitude estimation is therefore not appropriate to categorization.

**3** The principle is the same in ranking as it is in rating except that subjects rank order the pairs in terms of their similarity. Generally, rankings require more complex methods than ratings to form the proximity matrix.

**4** Forced categorization, in which there are designated numbers of stimuli to be placed in each category, is essentially a compromise between ranking and rating.

**5** It is a particularly useful procedure to have the subject make free sorts of the stimuli into categories based upon their apparent similarity. The subject is often given complete freedom to define "similarity," and often the number of categories. However, it is more typical for the experimenter to define an upper and lower limit to the number of categories. The data matrix reflects the number of times that subjects place members of a given pair of stimuli in the same category. This is perhaps the most popular method when the number of stimuli is too large to allow paired comparisons and one seeks only ordinal data.

**6** In the method of triads, subjects are shown all possible groups of three stimuli (e.g., Senators Smith, Hong, and Khoury) and asked to pick the most dissimilar of the three. These data produce the proportions of times that one stimulus is judged more similar to a second stimulus than to a third stimulus. Thus, $_aP_{bc}$ denotes the proportion of subjects that say stimulus a is more similar to stimulus b than to stimulus c. Although there are usually more triads, $V(V-1)(V-2)/6$, than there are pairs, $V(V-1)/2$, each triad is usually simpler to judge than each pair. It is also possible to obtain metric information directly from the subject when the number of triads is not great.

**7** Bisection is another method adapted from Stevens. In unidimensional scaling, the subject sees two stimuli, such as lights varying in luminance, and adjusts a third to appear halfway between them. In multidimensional scaling, the task is much more complex since it involves choosing a pair of stimuli whose distance is half that of two other pairs of stimuli. The experimenter shows subjects stimulus pair ab and stimulus pair cd. The subject chooses stimuli ef so that their distance is midway between the distances of ab and cd. This method has several drawbacks: it is likely to be confusing, it cannot be easily used in scaling a fixed set of stimuli, and it produces only an interval scale of distance. Ratio estimation methods are more understandable to subjects and produce ratio scales with less effort. Interval methods make more sense in unidimensional scaling. They are included for completeness since MDS methods predicated upon interval measurement exist and will be discussed below. Variants on bisection include trisection and interval estimation, where the subject rates the distance of one pair of stimuli relative to two other pairs. These variants have the same liabilities as bisection.

The distinction between the way bisection is used in unidimensional scaling and MDS points up an important general difference between the two. In unidimensional scaling, response proportions describe how often one stimulus is judged greater than another stimulus with respect to a specified attribute such as loudness. However, in MDS these proportions describe how often the distance (i.e., difference) between two stimuli is judged greater than the distance between two other stimuli. Unidimensional methods produce scales with respect to an attribute; MDS produces scales reflecting distances among stimuli. The attribute(s) that produce these distances are inferred later in the analysis.

The following is an illustrative interval scale of distances between three pairs of stimuli. Assume that it is an interval scale rather than a ratio scale, and so the zero point is irrelevant.

The distance between pairs ab and bc is much smaller than the distance between pairs bc and cd. Mathematical models transform proportions, which are not linearly related to distances and are therefore ordinal, to relative distances. These methods therefore provide an interval scaling of all possible distances between stimuli in a set from these (ordinal) proportions. The next step is to transform interval data to ratio data. The ends of the line are anchored only by "Smaller distances" and "Larger distances." However, the ratios of the three intervals depicted are meaningful (e.g., the interval bc-cd is several times larger than the interval ab-bc) and therefore provide a ratio scale.

There are several methodological problems with paired comparisons. For example, we have assumed $V(V-1)/2$ trials because stimuli are usually presented in only a single order. If subjects are asked "How similar is Senator Smith to Senator Hong?" they are normally not asked "How similar is Senator Hong to Senator Smith?" If in fact both pairs are presented, requiring $V(V-1)$ trials, it would not be surprising to find a difference over subjects because of space biases (also known as position or order effects). If so, the proximity matrix will not be symmetric when rows represent the first stimulus and columns represent the second stimulus (or the reverse). MDS methods normally require symmetric proximity matrices, and so the two numbers are typically averaged. This is not a problem if the position biases are small, but if they are large, subjects may not be taking the rating task as seriously as they should.

A subject's judgmental criteria typically vary over the list of pairs, so that if a given pair is repeated at different points on the list, the ratings may also vary. This may be random, or it may be systematic. Systematic error might arise if a given pair is rated as more similar when it follows a highly dissimilar pair (a contrast effect) or, conversely, when it follows a highly similar pair (an assimilation effect). Randomizing orders both by choosing which member of the pair goes first and by placing the pair unsystematically in the list is one way to overcome these problems. A more elegant solution is the Ross ordering [Ross (1934); Cohen & Davison (1973) provide a computer program], which balances order and time effects. A third possibility discussed by Davison (1983) is to use a rotating standard. In our senator rating example, Senator Smith would be compared to the remaining $V-1$ senators in turn. Next, Senator Hong would be compared to the remaining $V - 2$ senators in turn; Senator Herrera would be compared to the remaining $V - 3$ senators, etc. This tends to provide a clearer standard for each pair, especially early in the list, but we agree with Davison's preference for either Ross or random ordering. When $V$ is very large, so that it is impractical to have a subject rate all possible pairs, present randomly selected subsets, chosen with the constraint that each pair must appear equally often over subjects (MacCallum, 1979; Spence & Domoney, 1974) or use free sorting.

Perhaps the most important advice we can give is to view the task from the standpoint of the subject. Consider the effort required of them and how motivated they are likely to be. One general question that is very often asked is "How many observations?" Davison (1983) suggests that this equal $40F/(V - 1)$, where $F$ is the expected number of dimensions and $V$ is the number of stimuli. Of course, the number of dimensions is often at issue, so prepare for the worst case (the largest number of interpretable dimensions). It normally requires at least two and preferably three salients to define a given dimension, as in factor analysis. Consequently it is usually fruitless to attempt to interpret, say, a four-dimensional solution with fewer than 12 stimuli. It is probably better to assume that flaws are present in either the problem or the data-gathering process, redo the study, or consider a different problem.

Guilford's (1954) *Psychometric Methods* has long been regarded as the "bible" of rating scale methodology. Although too much can be made of issues like whether to have the scales vertical or horizontal, the issue of the number of ratings that have to be made is very important. Keep in mind that the number of stimulus pairs increases roughly as the square of $V$. Subjects will nearly always provide data (i.e., respond rather than stalk out of the experiment), but they may not provide meaningful data.

## Psychophysical Methods Based upon Attribute Ratings

Some experimenters have a specific set of attributes in mind to be judged. For example, the Senate may be considering a tax plan, foreign aid appropriations, support for the arts, etc., and the experimenter may wish to focus on these specific issues. Likewise, prior research may have defined attributes along which colas may vary (sweetness, sharpness, intensity of flavor). In each case, stimulus ratings provide data for which methods of profile analysis are applicable. The usual, but not the only, way to analyze these data is to compute distance ($D$) measures from the profiles. This $D$ matrix may then be transformed in various ways discussed below to permit an MDS analysis or to employ raw-score factor analysis. Attribute ratings are commonly gathered even though the main analysis uses similarity ratings.

## Indirect Methods

A proximity matrix may be formed in several ways using indirect methods, depending upon the problem at hand. These matrices usually require much larger numbers of observations than matrices obtained from direct methods to ensure the resulting data are stable. The particular method is usually dictated by the nature of the problem, and the following are perhaps the three most common forms of data.

**1** *Confusion matrices.* As previously noted, a confusion matrix describes the probability that the subject will chose category $j$ in response to stimulus $i$. We will assume that the stimuli appear in the columns of the matrix and that the responses appear in the rows. Consequently the matrix will be square and the diagonal entries (which typically play no role in MDS analysis) will represent the probability of a correct choice. The probabilities are often made conditional upon the stimulus and therefore add to 1 within columns. Element $X_{12}$ will therefore be the probability that response 2 was chosen given that stimulus 1 was presented. Students of perception deal with such matrices routinely. Confusion matrices need not be symmetric; i.e., the probability of choosing response $j$ to stimulus $i$ may be quite different from the probability of choosing response $i$ to stimulus $j$ because of response biases in choosing categories and other reasons. Although it is common to average the two values to provide the symmetry needed in most methods, this is inappropriate when the disparities are large. Later, we will present a distance measure derived by Shepard (1957, 1958, also see Luce, 1963) that does not require averaging.

**2** *Joint (co-occurrence) probability matrices.* Joint or co-occurrence matrices describe the probability that two events will both be present. For example, consider the following symptoms of depression: (1) sleep difficulties, (2) difficulty in concentrating, (3) religious preoccupation, and (4) retardation of behavior. A given patient may have none, some, or all of these symptoms. If a given patient has symptoms 1 and 2, a count is added to elements 11, 12, 21, and 22 of the matrix. Consequently the diagonal elements of this matrix contain the frequencies with which the individual symptoms occur, and the off-diagonal elements contain their joint frequencies. The frequencies are divided by the number of subjects to obtain joint probabilities. This matrix is inherently symmetric and uses much, but not all, of the data; e.g., it does not use the information about which triads of symptoms occur.

**3** *Transition matrices.* Transition matrices describe the probability that a subject will change preference from one stimulus to another. For example, matrix element $ij$ describes the probability that a person who originally chose cola brand $i$ changed to cola brand $j$. Although this method involves preferences, it is a similarity method because it assumes that a person changes preference to the most similar stimulus. Like a confusion matrix, this matrix can be quite asymmetric, and averaging element $ij$ and $ji$ may not always be appropriate. Also, if preferences are highly stable, the elements off the diagonal will be quite small compared to the elements on the diagonal, which describe consistent choices.

Having explored some of the alternative psychophysical methods, we will now turn to the mathematical procedures used to analyze the resulting data.

### Vector-Space Ratio Methods

The strongest assumption possible in MDS is that subjects directly produce a vector space containing $h_i \cos_{ij} h_j$ for all pairs of stimuli. This normally requires direct similarity ratings as obtained through magnitude estimation. Even so, many investigators may not choose to assume that the data have interval properties. Vector product MDS is one example of this general approach. Assume that subjects have judged the similarity of pairs of stimuli on a continuum running from 0 (total dissimilarity) through 1 (identity or zero dissimilarity). The first author had subjects scale adjectives describing emotions in order to derive a set of factored rating scales in an unpublished study. Nine adjectives were investigated, and three adjectives were hypothesized to define each of three underlying factors. The adjectives "happy," "contented," and "pleasant" (group A); "vigorous," "healthy," and "strong" (group B); and "loving," "romantic," and "warm" (group C).

Subjects rated the similarity of meaning for each of 36 [(9)(8/2)] pairs in terms of the proportion of stimulus contexts in which one word could be substituted for the other without altering the meaning of a sentence. Since all nine adjectives had positive connotations, the scale was unipolar rather than bipolar. The responses of 34 college students were used to form a symmetric matrix of proportions. The highest proportion (maximum similarity) was .80 ("happy" and "contented"), and the lowest proportion (maximum dissimilarity) was .30 ("pleasant" and "strong"). These data can be converted directly to vector products. Averaging the data over subjects describes the group proportions or, alternatively, the proportions produced by a modal individual. The square roots of each average, e.g., $.89 = \sqrt{.80}$ for "happy" and "contented" and $.55 = \sqrt{.30}$ for "pleasant" and "strong," define the vector product in a proportion square root (PS) analysis.

If one can assume that the underlying data are ratio-level measurements, these square roots meet all the requirements for a vector product space, and so they can be factored. Each vector (adjective in the example) was assumed to be of unit length, so unities were placed in the diagonals. Alternatively, a common factor model could have been employed using communality estimates. The number of important factors defines the dimensionality of the space, exactly as in factor analysis. The structure consists of the projections of the adjectives on the underlying factors. The squared structure elements define the proportion of variance in the adjective explained by the factor, and correlations among oblique factors describe how the dimensions relate.

The first step in this case was to employ confirmatory multiple group analysis. Three group centroids were simultaneously (obliquely) placed in groups A, B, and C, each defined by the three aforementioned adjectives. Whereas the results generally confirmed the hypotheses, there were some systematic departures. The group A and C centroids were highly correlated, and some of the words did not behave exactly as expected: "pleasant" and "warm" did not correlate as highly with their hypothesized factors as had been anticipated. They shared enough meaning to form a fourth factor of their own. The matrix of PS coefficients was also subjected to a PrC analysis. Four factors were extracted and rotated to a varimax criterion. The results of this analysis, shown in Table 14-4, were generally similar to the results of the multiple group analysis. Boxes have been drawn around the structure elements of the three variables that were intended to represent each of the three factors. These results show how the original hypotheses were largely confirmed, but an unexpected result was also obtained.

This pilot work suggested that the original hypotheses were generally along the right lines, indicated improved groupings of words, and provided a starting point for much more extensive investigations of emotion-related words. Most important for the

TABLE 14-4    VARIMAX ROTATED VECTOR PRODUCT PRC
FACTORS FOR EMOTION-RELATED WORDS

| Word | Factor | | | |
|---|---|---|---|---|
| | I | II | III | IV |
| Happy | .66 | .39 | .45 | .42 |
| Contented | .70 | .34 | .49 | .26 |
| Pleasant | .53 | .26 | .35 | .69 |
| Vigorous | .15 | .84 | .24 | .36 |
| Healthy | .55 | .74 | .20 | .15 |
| Strong | .22 | .87 | .33 | .10 |
| Loving | .45 | .29 | .75 | .31 |
| Romantic | .28 | .31 | .85 | .21 |
| Warm | .19 | .32 | .64 | .62 |

present discussion is that the study exemplifies vector product MDS using PS analysis. Factor analysis can be applied in a straightforward manner whenever such vector products are obtainable from the subjects' responses. Even if you employ a more elaborate commercial MDS program as discussed below, you should compare its results with a direct approach like this one to get a feel for the unity of the scaling.

PS analysis can be applied to bipolar rating scales ranging from complete agreement through complete disagreement, including a zero indifference point. Attach negative signs to disagreements; e.g., proportional disagreements of .25 and .64 become PS coefficients of $-.50$ and $-.80$.

Vector product MDS can be applied to a wide variety of classes of stimuli, particularly when individuals judge pairs of familiar stimuli. Of course, it runs the risk of requiring subjects to do more than they are capable of doing if they cannot produce a vector space directly. One necessary criterion is that a Euclidian space is appropriate. This assumption is violated in vector product MDS if there are any large negative eigenvalues, since that indicates that the matrix does not have the Gramian properties necessary for factoring. None of the nine possible eigenvalues shown in Table 14-4 were negative, but this problem may arise in other applications. More complex forms of MDS, such as ALSCAL, prevent this from occurring.

## Euclidian Distance Ratio Methods

Some approaches to psychophysical scaling provide distance estimates between stimuli directly, as in magnitude estimation, or indirectly, as when attribute ratings are converted to distances by means of the $D$ measure. In contrast, formal scaling models convert indirect measures to distances. Shepard (1957, 1958; also see Luce, 1963) has provided one widely used distance measure that can be applied to confusion and transition probability data. Let $p_{ii}$ and $p_{jj}$ represent the probabilities of correctly identifying stimuli i and j and $p_{ij}$ and $p_{ji}$ describe the respective probabilities of misclassifying stimulus i as j and vice versa. Equation 14-5 describes the inferred distance between i and j ($D_{ij}$) based upon these four probabilities:

$$D_{ij} = \sqrt{\frac{p_{ij}p_{ji}}{p_{ii}p_j}j} \qquad\qquad (14\text{-}5)$$

Luce's (1959a, 1963) choice theory, as described in Chapter 2, shows how the logarithm of a probability, as in a co-occurrence matrix, may be used to define distance. Thus, if two behaviors always occur together, so that the probability of event j is 1 given event i, the distance between them is ln 1 or 0 (natural logarithms typically define the metric). More use is made of this transformation in choice theory analysis of dominance relations.

Only ratios between distances are important in a Euclidian model because the dimensionality and configuration are not influenced when all distances are multiplied by a constant, as when one shifts from the English and American foot to the more nearly universal meter. Thus, all one needs to know are the distances up to a constant of proportionality. That is, it must be possible to say, for example, that the distance between points $a$ and $b$ is twice the distance between points $b$ and $c$. Since a ratio scale must have a rational origin, it must also be possible for two stimuli to have zero distance between them (be coincident). Chapter 1 noted that a ratio scale is invariant only over transformations of the type $bX$. Any ratio scale $X$ can be multiplied or divided by an arbitrary constant $a$, and the resulting scale $X'$ will also be a ratio scale. Thus, MDS distances are determined only up to a constant of proportionality.

Since ratio scales are not invariant under the more general class of linear transformations, $bX + a$, distances will not be preserved when a constant is added to all distances. Adding an arbitrary constant might change the shape of the triangle connecting three points or the number of dimensions required to represent half a dozen points. The space might become non-Euclidian; i.e., the generalized Pythagorean theorem of Eq. 14-2 may not hold. However, the changes produced by adding a constant may be exploited to transform interval measures into a ratio scale that produces Euclidian distances, as we will show in the next section.

As mentioned previously, a careful distinction must be made between ratio estimates of distances, as discussed here, and ratio estimates of scale values, as discussed in Chapter 2. The latter, for example, requires subjects to estimate the ratio of the brightness of one light to that of another. The analogous ratio estimation of distance requires the subjects to judge the ratio of differences in the brightness of lights $a$ and $b$ versus $b$ and $c$. MDS tasks concern judgments about the relative size of differences between the stimuli rather than about the absolute amount of an attribute possessed by stimuli. Unfortunately, knowing the distances of points (stimuli) from each other does not imply knowing the distance of each point from an origin. Knowing distances from an origin allows them to be converted directly to vector products which can then be factored. Assume that these distances are determined by some appropriate method so that the issue becomes one of applying MDS to these distances. Figure 14-10 shows hypothetical distances between six senators. The example is simplified because most studies scale considerably more than six stimuli and more than two dimensions would probably be required.

Lines could have been drawn in Fig. 14-10 between all pairs of stimuli to denote distances, but we did not do that to simplify the illustration. The question is how to dimensionalize these distances. If the points fit as neatly in a plane as illustrated, there would

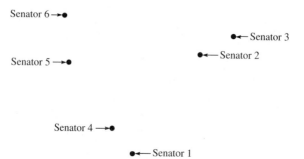

**FIGURE 14-10**    Space of distances of six senators.

be no problem. One could simply pencil in two dimensions with a ruler, but the exact placement would be a matter of choice, as is the rotation of factors in factor analysis. The dimensions could be scaled arbitrarily. For example, ¼ inch could equal a score of 1, so that ½ inch would equal a score of 2, etc. The senators' scores would allow the dimensions to be interpreted as liberal-conservative, isolationist-international activist, etc., and investigated in subsequent studies. However, methods must be developed to handle all cases since it unlikely that real stimuli can be represented exactly in a 2-space.

The distances in Fig. 14-10 provide no hint about an origin, and so none has been provided. There are a number of ways to place an origin in the space. One is to make one of the points the origin and represent all other points as vectors extending from it. This is not satisfactory because (1) there will be some error in establishing the point and (2) even if that were not the case, the results of subsequent analyses would depend very much on the point which was chosen. A better choice of origin is the centroid or average of the points. This is done in a 2-space of points by putting an arbitrary pair of orthogonal coordinates in the space and computing the average scores of all points on these coordinates. Figure 14-11 represents the points in Fig. 14-10 as vectors extending from this centroid.

**FIGURE 14-11**    Space of points for six senators with an origin at the centroid.

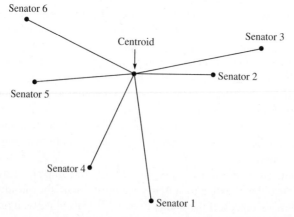

**TABLE 14-5**    THE FACTOR STRUCTURE OF SIX
SENATORS ON TWO ROTATED FACTORS

| Senator | Factor | |
|---|---|---|
| | I | II |
| 1 | .02 | −.31 |
| 2 | .26 | −.05 |
| 3 | .74 | .07 |
| 4 | −.16 | −.13 |
| 5 | −.37 | .03 |
| 6 | −.42 | .35 |

In the more usual case in which the points cannot be exactly represented in a 2-space, calculating the distance of each point from the centroid of the space is still straightforward. The matrix of distances of stimuli from one another contains all the necessary information, and simple formulas can be used to calculate the distance of each stimulus from the centroid of these differences (see Torgerson, 1958, Chap. 11). The resulting matrix of distances between stimuli can be converted to a factorable matrix of vector products. Table 14-5 and Fig. 14-12 show the results of a PrC factoring of the vectors shown in Fig. 14-11. The structure is expressed in the same units as those used to define the distances of points from one another and from the centroid of the space. Further information might suggest that the factors denote, respectively, liberalism-conservatism and whether the United States should be active or restrained in world affairs.

**FIGURE 14-12**    The structure elements for six senators on two centroid factors.

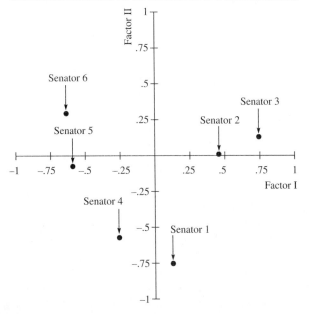

## Interval Methods

The limitations of psychophysical methods designed to directly produce interval data for MDS (e.g., bisection) were noted above. Logically, one could obtain data using ratio methods and treat the data as interval. This has as many problems as the use of interval psychophysical methods. If one mistrusts the ratio nature of such scales, the data should be analyzed as ordinal, and if one trusts the ratio nature, ratio methods of analysis are suitable. At the same time, the importance of obtaining a unit of measurement from ordinal data cannot be overestimated since much scaling is a two-step process which first transforms ordinal data into interval scale measures and then transforms the resulting measures into relative differences in distance. (Some models, such as Eq. 14-5, and methods of data collection accomplish both in a single step.) We will now consider the most common way to transform interval data to ratio data, the additive constant.

In the present case, the principle of the additive constant is to add or subtract a number from the measures to make them obey Euclidian (or other, such as the city block) assumptions in a minimum number of dimensions. The goal is to make the data obey such Euclidian theorems as the generalized Pythagorean theorem, Eq. 14-2, and the triangle inequality. For example, assume that three values on an interval scale are 5, 6, and 7. If we subtract a number larger than 5 (add a number less than −5) from any of them, at least one value will become negative and produce a negative distance. If we subtract 5 from each (add −5), which is permissible since they are measured on an interval scale, the resulting values (0, 1, and 2) will not qualify as distances along a ratio scale because they violate several Euclidian (as well as non-Euclidian) distance assumptions. Most obviously, the first two points will fall at the same place in space (be coincident) since there is zero distance between them. However, their distances to a third point will be different (1 versus 2).

However, if we subtract 2 (add −2) from each of the original measures, the resulting values will be 3, 4, and 5. Since $3^2 + 4^2 = 5^2$, the three points will form the vertices of a right triangle in 2-space. They will therefore qualify as distance measures. However, if we were to subtract 4 from each measure (add −4), the resulting measures would be 1, 2, and 3. These fall in a one-dimensional space as follows: $a$—$b$——$c$, where — represents 1 unit. Since a one-dimensional space is simpler than a two-dimensional space, 4 would be the best additive constant.

A suitable additive constant allows any three measures to be converted to distances in a two-dimensional space. In general, any $V$ measures can be described in a hyperspace of $V - 1$ dimensions. The problems posed by subtracting 5 arise whenever the constant makes the values too small. Conversely, any constant that is far removed from all the values in either the positive or negative direction will allow the resulting distances to fall in $V - 1$ dimensions. A large value is therefore "safe" for the same reason that putting unities in the diagonal of a correlation matrix (component factoring) is safe. However, too large a constant will enhance measurement error. The best additive constant allows the particular stimuli to be scaled in the smallest, most parsimonious space. MDS therefore seeks to make the constant large enough to provide Euclidian distances but small enough to minimize the dimensionality.

Although it is always possible to choose a constant that will allow $V$ measures to be scaled in $V - 1$ dimensions, no constant will generally allow a large set of measures to achieve a dimensionality of 1 or even $V - 2$. Measurement errors also usually prevent the data from falling in a space of less than $V - 1$ dimensions. However, a suitable constant can usually make the resulting values *close* to fulfilling the distance requirements of a space that is (1) Euclidian and (2) contains fewer than $V - 1$ dimensions using indices described below. Proponents of non-Euclidian models (e.g., the city block model) would drop the first requirement if they could achieve the second. For example, they would properly argue that the city block model is more parsimonious if a set of data would require two dimensions in a city block metric but five in a Euclidian metric.

There is no direct way to determine an additive constant that will produce a ratio scale in the fewest dimensions. Torgerson (1958) has described iterative methods for doing this that are widely used in MDS. One way to estimate the additive constant is as follows. More complex algorithms used in programs such as ALSCAL are slightly different but employ the same basic logic.

**1** Choose a trial value, typically the average of all interval measures (centroid).

**2** Use this constant to convert the interval measures to approximate distances.

**3** Determine the distance of each point from the centroid of the points by previously discussed methods.

**4** Convert the distances to vector products by methods which have been also discussed previously.

**5** Perform a PrC analysis upon the matrix of vector products.

**6** If the PrC analysis provides large, negative roots, the space is non-Euclidian, and so a larger additive constant must be chosen and the analysis repeated from step 2.

This iterative approach is employed until the smallest additive constant consistent with a Euclidian space is obtained. Because error in the data will prevent an exact fit to Euclidian requirements, the iterations cease when the fit is within some criterial value that depends upon such factors as the particular model being used. Torgerson (1958) and Messick and Abelson (1956) describe this process in detail. It is typically not difficult to achieve a good fit with a limited number of iterations. This is obviously well suited to computer algorithms. The final additive constant simultaneously provides the desired scaling. The number of factors defines the dimensionality of the space, and the factor structure indicates the amount of each attribute (dimension) possessed by each stimulus.

## Ordinal Methods and ALSCAL

We have seen that use of the additive constant allows interval measures to be transformed into ratio distances, but the key problem is to convert ordinal data, as might be obtained from free sorting or triad methods, to interval measures. Some procedure is therefore needed to obtain a unit of measurement. In a sense, this involves "bootstrapping" since the subject was not required to use an interval in making judgments, and so one is therefore not obvious in the data. It is a demand placed upon on the scaling model. In some cases, equations like Eq. 14-5 are applicable, but we will now consider a more general algorithm, ALSCAL (Young & Lewyckyj, 1980; also see Kruskal, 1964; Kruskal & Wish, 1978; Takane, Young, & de Leeuw, 1977, Young, Takane, & Lewyckyj, 1978). Material in this section is derived from Chapter 6 of Young and Lewyckyj (1980), although their discussion deals with a more complex MDS model.

ALSCAL may be thought of as both a specific computer program and a mathematical model. It actually combines and is therefore a "superset" of several other MDS and dominance scaling programs. Although we will focus on ordinary nonmetric MDS, we will illustrate some of its other options. In ALSCAL parlance the data are referred to as two-way, one-mode because the data input is in the form of a two-dimensional table of dissimilarities, but both dimensions of the table consist of the stimuli (objects) to be scaled. ALSCAL is an acronym for *a*lternating *l*east-*s*quares *scal*ing. This name is derived from the presence of two types of parameters that the program estimates, optimal scaling parameters and model parameters. The program alternates between tentative least-squares estimates of the two until they each converge to their respective values. The distinction between the two types of parameters may be better understood by considering four basic matrices: (1) the raw data (e.g., similarity ratings), which are in the form of a symmetric $V \times V$ matrix of dissimilarities (a program option can convert similarities into dissimilarities), where $V$ is the number of stimuli that are at least of ordinal level; (2) disparities, which are an optimal rescaling of the raw data and are contained in a second $V \times V$ matrix; (3) distances, in the form of a third $V \times V$ matrix but which are derived from model parameters (coordinate values, i.e., loadings) using Eq. 14-2; and (4) the model parameters themselves, which are in the form of a $V \times F$ matrix, where $F$ is the number of dimensions specified in the analysis.

ALSCAL's goal is to make the disparity and distance matrices as similar as possible. Two critical differences between these matrices are that (1) the disparity matrix is at least monotonically related to the data (depending upon whether ordinal, interval, or ratio models are chosen), whereas the distances are ratio-level functions of the model parameters; and (2) the disparity matrix is typically of full rank (all $V$ of its rows and columns are linearly independent); the distance matrix is of rank $F$ (has $F$ linearly independent columns or rows) since it is determined by the matrix of model parameters. The algorithm is called conditional least-squares estimation because scaling parameters are conditional upon model parameters, and vice versa.

An outline of the operation of ALSCAL is as follows, ignoring various normalizing operations.

**1** An additive constant transforms the raw data into approximate distances on a ratio scale. The approximate distances are made to obey the triangle inequality and be positive.

**2** A scalar product matrix is obtained from the data matrix. The values in this matrix are doubly centered in that the mean score for each subject is zero and the mean score for each variable is also zero. Ordinary factor analysis uses singly centered data in which variable means are zero but subject means are not. We described single and double standardizing in Chapter 12 when we were concerned with adjusting both means and standard deviations. Here we are concerned only with adjusting means.

**3** The principal components of the scalar matrix define the initial model parameters, and the number of components is determined by the number of dimensions selected by the user.

**4** Equation 14-2 is applied to the model parameters to provide the matrix of distances.

**5** Optimal scaling then produces the disparities and is the one novel ingredient of ALSCAL compared to what we have discussed. The disparities are rank-ordered and placed in a vector. Assume that observation $X_{13}$ consists of the two stimuli that are judged similar most often. Its value appears as the first element in this vector. The distances are placed in a second vector based upon this same ordering. Consequently the first element of this second vector is the distance between points 1 and 3 in the model. This need not be the smallest distance, and so the second set of distances need not be in rank order. When two or more values in the vector of distances are out of order, they are replaced with their mean. These values become the new disparities. Ultimately, the data and disparities will be at least ordinally related. Interval scaling further requires that the disparities and distances be linearly related, and ratio scaling further requires that they be related by a multiplicative constant.

**6** The disparities are normalized, and a measure of fit called SSTRESS (squared stress) presented in Kruskal (1964) is computed by means of Eq. 14-6. Alternative SSTRESS formulas are used for different types of matrices; we report the one known as formula 1:

$$\text{SSTRESS} = \sqrt{\frac{\Sigma(d^2 - \hat{d}^2)}{\Sigma d^4}} \tag{14-6}$$

SSTRESS describes misfit in terms of the difference between the squared distances ($d^2$) and the squared disparities ($\hat{d}^2$). Double subscripts describing the stimulus row and column have been omitted. The smaller this value, the better the fit.

**7** The iterative process minimizes SSTRESS. If SSTRESS is sufficiently small on the first cycle or if it changes by less than a criterial amount over iterations, the process ends. If it changes by more than the criterial amount, the disparity matrix is refactored, and so the program loops back to step 3.

**8** When SSTRESS has stabilized, the coordinate values are individually chosen to minimize the rate of change in SSTRESS with regard to a given coordinate. This is done for each coordinate and each point in turn and repeated until all coordinates stabilize.

The output may include some or all of the following results.

**1** *The iteration history of changes in SSTRESS.* In general, better data and a proper choice of transformation tend to produce more rapid convergence, but only in a general way. A failure to converge certainly is a sign that the data do not fit the chosen model and/or number of dimensions.

**2** *The STRESS* (again, formula 1; see Kruskal, 1964). STRESS is like Eq. 14-6 except that it uses $d$ and $\hat{d}$ instead of $\hat{d}^2$ and $\hat{d}^2$. It should also be as small as possible. If it is large, consider adding another dimension if there are enough stimuli to interpret the results (at least two and preferably three salient stimuli per dimension) or relaxing the constraints on the transformation; e.g., use ordinal instead of interval scaling. Remember that adding a dimension will usually improve fit simply because you have added more free parameters, although adding dimensions can actually make the fit worse (this is very strong evidence that the added dimension is not necessary when it happens). Relaxing the scaling constraints will also improve the fit on grounds that are partially spurious. If you both increase the number of parameters and reduce the scaling constraints, look for error messages telling you that you may be trying to estimate too many parameters with too little data (numbers of observation pairs).

**3** *The squared correlation between the disparities and the distances*, *RSQ*. This is the ratio of the variance accounted for by the model to the variance in the data. Similar considerations apply here as is the case with STRESS and SSTRESS, although larger values of RSQ imply a better fit. Since three indices describe the fit of the data to the proposed space, avoid being too optimistic by selecting the most favorable one.

**4** *The coordinate values.* These are scaled so that the mean of each dimension is zero. As a result, all dimensions must be bipolar, unlike in classical factor analysis. The average variance of coordinate values will be 1.0, but, like the principal components they are, the values on the first dimension will vary more than the values on the second dimension, etc.

**5** Optionally, *a graphical representation of these coordinates*, two dimensions at a time. This can generate a lot of paper when you are scaling stimuli in many dimensions.

**6** Optionally, a *plot of linear fit*. This describes the relation between the disparities and the distances. The amount of scatter in this plot describes overall lack of fit. These data underlie SSTRESS, STRESS, and, most directly, RSQ.

**7** Optionally (with ordinal transformations), *a plot of transformation*. This describes the relation between the disparities and the observations. For example, if it is necessary for MDS to compress the data (e.g., if $X$ is a ratio scale but the data are of the form $X^2$), the function will be concave downward. Conversely, if it is necessary for MDS to expand the data (e.g., if $X$ is a ratio scale but the data are of the form $\sqrt{X}$), the function will be concave upward. The precise form of the transformation used to obtain disparities from data is not mathematically important, but it is psychologically desirable that the transformation be at least somewhat meaningful.

**8** Optionally (with ordinal transformations), a plot of nonlinear fit. This describes the relation between the distances and the observations. This plot combines, and therefore confounds, the information in results 6 and 7.

Dimensions are interpreted by contrasting the properties of salient stimuli which fall at the poles of a given dimension. This is similar to the interpretation of exploratory factors. Interpretation may be facilitated by regressing the dimensional values for the stimuli upon individual attribute ratings or similar data. Since the dimensions are orthogonal, the beta weights are the correlations between the dimensions and the particular attribute and may be used as cosines to incorporate the attribute ratings along with the stimuli into the graphical depiction. A given dimension is therefore also describable by the attributes with which it correlates most highly.

## Some Empirical Properties of Alternative MDS Solutions

The second author conducted a simple computer simulation which you may wish to repeat in order to learn more about MDS. Define an arbitrary set of $V$ (say a dozen) points (stimuli) in a 2-space by choosing two random numbers for each. You could use a 1-space by choosing a single random number or a more complex space by choosing several random numbers, but a 1-space is restricted as to what it will demonstrate, and a larger space is unnecessarily complicated. Standardize these scores so that the two means are 0 and the two standard deviations are 1. These constitute true data. Next, obtain a matrix of $D^2$ values using Eq. 14-2 and take the square root of each resulting value to obtain (ratio) distances. Submit these distances to an MDS program like ALSCAL. First, choose the ratio option and two dimensions since these are correct for the data; then look at alternative solutions.

The correct solution should converge rapidly and fit well; the ALSCAL indicators SSTRESS and STRESS will be nearly zero, and RSQ will be nearly 1.0, as they should. Note, however, that the scale values generated by the program will not be the same as the true values for two reasons. One is that ALSCAL produces scale values that are principal components: Values on the first dimensions vary maximally, and values on the second dimension vary minimally since the data falls exactly in 2-space. The original data were not expressed as principal components. Cliff's algorithm, discussed in the previous chapter (1966, see Harman, 1976, pp. 347–352), can rotate the two sets of coordinates to maximum congruence and eliminate this artifactual difference. A matrix language like SAS' PROC IML allows Cliff's procedure to be employed directly, but the two solutions may be compared by simply plotting them on separate pieces of graph paper and rotating one manually until they appear to be as similar as possible. Even after this is done, the two solutions will not coincide. ALSCAL provides a mathematically acceptable solution, but it need not agree with the true data. This is *not* due to error in the scaled distances because there is none.

Next, add an arbitrarily chosen constant to each of the distances. This destroys their ratio properties but preserves the interval of measurement. The fit of the transformed data using the ratio option with the transformed data will be poorer than the fit of the true data with the ratio option. Now, use the interval option to find the additive constant. It should produce the same good fit in both data sets. The fit of the interval data under the ratio option may also be quite good in an absolute sense since the original data were error-free. Consequently, a good fit under the ratio option does not guarantee that the underlying data fulfill ratio assumptions.

Now, distort the interval measures to the ordinal level. One way to do this is to raise all the values to a power; e.g., square each number. Neither the ratio nor the interval option will provide as good a fit as the ordinal solution. Look at the transformation plot, if available. It should complement the distortion.

## MDS of Correlation Matrices

Since MDS may be applied to any similarity (proximity) matrix, it may be applied to a correlation matrix. It is therefore useful to consider its pros and cons relative to a PrC analysis of the same data. Davison (1985) summarizes the rather substantial literature. His presentation is quite well balanced in describing the pros and cons of each approach. His points are applicable to both the component and common factor approaches, since dimensionality is typically determined from a preliminary component solution, e.g., the number of eigenvalues ≥1. We will further assume that the component analysis is performed upon correlations rather than covariances or mean sums of products, which will not affect any conclusions.

Although both MDS and factor analysis involve eigenanalysis, the data being analyzed are not the same. Component analysis uses singly centered data that adjust variable means to equality (0). However, MDS uses doubly centered data that also adjust for subject differences. Consequently,

**1** MDS will provide a space of one less dimension than a factor analytic solution.

**2** The origin of the space will be shifted to the centroid of the points in metric MDS.

**3** The MDS solution will essentially be the same as the factor analytic solution, ignoring the first factor if the subject means are independent of the MDS scalar products *or*

**4** The MDS and overall factor solutions will be essentially the same if the average correlation between each variable and all other variables is nearly zero, as when each has a mixture of positive and negative correlations.

Some researchers have suggested that MDS is preferable to factor analysis because it reduces the dimensionality of the space—a nonmetric MDS solution often leads to a solution that has several and not just one fewer dimensions than a factor analysis. Although we have argued that science's goal of parsimony makes a reduction of dimensionality advantageous, it may be an artifact of the process of double centering and the parameters needed to transform the data. It may also eliminate important data. We have seen that the artifice of choosing a suitably large additive constant can make any set of data unidimensional.

Davison (1985) appropriately stresses the importance of the context in which the analysis is performed. The first factor in abilities testing is typically extremely important as it describes general intelligence. However, the first factor obtained from preferences is often trivial, as it represents differences among subjects in their overall bias toward high versus low ratings. Excluding it from the analysis (which can be done with ad-lib factoring as well as MDS) would be a useful simplification. In essence, the choice between whether or not to let a general factor remain in the solution is more important than the choice between factor analysis and MDS.

## Scaling of Individual Differences

The next step in complexity beyond evaluating the structure of a single proximity matrix is to compare two or more matrices. We have already touched upon this issue in showing how Cliff's (1966) matching procedure can be used to compare a set of true values with an MDS solution. Carroll and Chang's (1970; Carroll, 1972) individual differences scaling (INDSCAL) model is a particularly attractive way to compare MDS solutions. Although the term "individual" implies "person," the model is perhaps more useful in comparing groups, such as males versus females, rather than individuals because the results are of more general interest. It also provides a form of three-mode factor analysis (see Chapter 12). We are usually more interested in seeing how groups differ than in how John and Mary differ, although applied measurement often dictates the latter issue. The term "individual" will therefore denote both a group of people sharing a common attribute as well as a single person. The data are known as three-way, two modes because they can be viewed as a rectangular "solid" of similarity measures. Two of the dimensions (modes) are defined by the stimuli to be scaled, as in classical MDS, and the third dimension is individuals, and so there are three modes of data but only two types.

INDSCAL assumes that individuals share the same dimensions. Group differences in similarity reflect group differences in the relative weights given these dimensions. Mathematically, an extension of the generalized distance measure, Eq. 4-2, called the weighted (Euclidian) distance measure, is used:

$$D^2_{abi} = w_{1i}(X_{a1i} - X_{b1i})^2 + w_{2i}(X_{a2i} - X_{b21})^2 + \cdots + w_{ri}(X_{ari} - X_{bri})^2$$
$$= \Sigma w_{ji}(X_{aji} - X_{bji})^2 \qquad (14\text{-}7)$$

Extending the previous notation, $D^2_{abi}$ is the squared distance between stimuli a and b produced by individual i. The $X$ subscripts respectively denote the stimulus, dimension number, and individual, the key new concept is the weight applied to each dimension ($w_{ji}$), denoting the dimension and individual, respectively. Simply think of $w_{ji}$ as defining how much relative attention subject i pays to dimension j.

As in ordinary MDS, the solution provides overall measures of fit and coordinates for each stimulus pooled over individuals. Unlike an ordinary MDS solution, which can be rotated, an INDSCAL solution cannot be rotated without loss of its essential properties. The solution also describes the fit of each individual similarity matrix. The other key data are the $w_{ji}$ values which are scaled to equal the RSQ values for that individual. Consequently an individual who responds more randomly than average will have lower $w_{ji}$ values. The $w_{ji}$ values for different individuals can be used to provide an index of how similar the individuals are in terms of how they weight (pay attention to) the dimensions. One caution is that the $w_{ji}$ values are vector coordinates. The absolute similarity of $w_{ji}$ values is not important; the similarity of the orientation of these values is important. Other indices that may be provided describe how heavily a given individual weights a particular dimension relative to the average individual.

## An Example of the Use of MDS

We will describe a study by Garbin and Bernstein (1984) because it shows how the results of MDS based upon global similarities may be complemented by attribute ratings. Many other appropriate and interesting examples of MDS also appear in the literature. The stimuli scaled were 24 randomly generated three-dimensional "lumps." Subjects judged the shapes under visual conditions where they looked at but did not touch the stimuli and under haptic conditions where they made judgments purely by feel. Within each condition, they (1) sorted the forms into between four and nine groups and (2) rated each form on twelve 9-point bipolar scales using attributes like small versus large and narrow versus wide. The theoretical issue was the extent to which perceptual equivalence of the structures obtained in different sensory modalities exists and under what conditions it breaks down. A relevant example of lack of perceptual equivalence is when our tongue tells us that our tooth has a large cavity, but its appearance is visually small. Perceptual equivalence means that the visual and haptic sortings can be rotated into one another.

The structure of the attribute ratings was inferred from confirmatory (multiple group) factor analysis using three proposed factors (size, shape, and symmetry). These proposed factors accounted for 85 percent of the variance in the visual condition as compared to 86 percent by the first three principal components and 60 percent by pseudofactors (see Chapter 13). This indicates that the three proposed factors accounted for the major dimensions of variation. Similar results held in the haptic condition. Variables also correlated most highly with their assigned factors, and correlations between conditions for a given attribute typically were also high. However, the three proposed factors were at least moderately correlated in both conditions. For example, shape and symmetry correlated .61 and .64 in the visual and haptic conditions, respectively.

Classical MDS analyses on the overall data (ignoring conditions) indicated that the fit improved sizably in going from one to two dimensions but little gain thereafter. Consequently, two-dimensional solutions were retained for further investigation. As in factor analysis, the usual practice is to look for a "break" or "elbow" in the fit (scree) as the number of dimensions is increased, assuming that there are enough stimuli to interpret a higher-dimensional solution. The authors next used INDSCAL (which requires at least a two-dimensional solution) to compare the visual and haptic conditions. The results were that corresponding stimuli were generally located near one another in the visual and haptic solutions, but a few stimuli did change locations.

The third step was to correlate the attribute ratings and the MDS solution coordinates over stimuli. Dimension I was basically a size factor, and dimension II was basically a shape-symmetry factor in both conditions. In sum, the study noted substantial but not total equivalence between modalities. Garbin's (1988) subsequent work has attempted to specify these differences.

### Some Concluding Comments

This chapter has thus far extended the analysis of similarity relationships from the factor analysis of cross products of various forms (correlations, covariances, mean sums of products) in the previous chapters. Throughout this book, we have tried to avoid suggesting that a particular method of data analysis can be a "magic road to truth." Although certain forms of data analysis can clearly lead you astray, two proper methods should lead you to similar conclusions once you make allowances for their idiosyncrasies, such as MDS' elimination of a general factor.

Before discussing the analysis of dominance (preference) ratings, it is useful to briefly consider four points about MDS.

**1** The last edition of this book noted that there were few applications of MDS to substantive areas in psychology. This is no longer true. Whereas earlier applications tended simply to scale stimuli, it is now virtually mandatory for the authors to demonstrate additional properties of the solution, as by correlating scale values with some external criterion. Confirmatory MDS models (Bentler & Weeks, 1978; Heiser &

Meulman, 1983) have appeared, although they have not had the impact of confirmatory factor analytic models.

**2** Subsequent work has supported the utility of the trial-and-error methods present in alternating least-squares solutions, even though the previous edition expressed concern about these methods. Indeed, ALSCAL has to be ranked among the most profound statistical contributions in the recent literature since using similarity ratings in factor analysis may yield nonsensical (non-Gramian) results. However, we continue to advocate that investigators who use MDS also explore more direct factor analytic approaches, at least as a didactic tool.

**3** One criticism of both factor analysis and MDS applications to scaling stimuli is that both treat the stimuli as equally variable in the space assumed to underlie the scale. Indeed, the observations are treated as points having no variance. An alternative view is that some stimuli are better defined, and thus have less variance, than others. Consequently, stimuli should be viewed as occupying regions of lesser or greater size. This alternative point of view will be considered in the next chapter in the form of Ashby and Townsend's (1984; Ashby & Perrin, 1988) general recognition model.

**4** You may have a strong desire to scale the similarity of the U.S. presidents that may have arisen from your profound knowledge of U.S. history. You personally would not mind making the more than 800 paired comparisons involved in that method and devoting at least as much attention to the last as to the first comparison. However, don't assume that is also true of your subjects, especially when they are recruited from the usual introductory course subject pool. Consider the task from their standpoint. Ethically, they are free to leave the experiment at any time, but they are usually polite enough stay, especially when your judgments require what they perceive as the proper level of academic dryness. This does not mean that they are paying attention or responding on some meaningful basis; they will nearly always provide data, but it may not be meaningful. The key is *careful* pretesting of the target population.

## DOMINANCE (PREFERENCE) SCALING

We noted at the beginning of the chapter that proximities (similarities) are fundamentally different from dominance relations (preferences). One is the power of the correlation coefficient in analyzing at least some similarities. Unfortunately, there is no exact counterpart that can dimensionalize a space of dominance relations as conveniently as factor analysis or MDS, even though it is not based upon measures like the PM correlation. Specifically, one cannot take a $V \times V$ dominance matrix ($V$ denoting the number of stimuli) and perform operations that are exact counterparts of dimensionalizing a correlation matrix. This does not mean that psychometric theory is bereft of ways to analyze dominance data. Multidimensional extensions of Thurstone scaling (see Chapter 2) are one possibility, which unfortunately is far less well developed than factor analysis. We will shortly consider an approach called unfolding which uses a different form of data, usually rank orderings of stimuli either by different people or by a single person on different attributes.

If your goal is to perform the equivalent of a factor analysis with dominance-based data, you may wish to consider recasting the problem in terms of actual similarity judgments. A common strategy is to include an ideal stimulus among those to be compared. For example, a marketing study of automobiles might include a hypothetical "dream car." In principle, the degree to which the ideal stimulus is preferred to an actual stimulus, and therefore the extent to which an actual stimulus is preferred to another actual stimulus, is determinable by their similarities to the ideal stimulus.

The idea that dominance relations maybe multidimensional is not very different from the idea that similarity may be multidimensional. For example, a person may judge the designs and performance of automobiles a, b, and c. The conclusion may be that automobile c is most dissimilar in design and automobile b is most dissimilar in performance. The same person may also prefer the design of automobile c and the performance of automobile b. Unfortunately, there may be a substantial judgmental difference. Subjects readily grasp the idea of ranking stimuli in terms of preference; any indecision usually reflects inabilities to choose among certain stimuli. Indeed, they may ask "Similar in what respects?" when told to classify them on the basis of overall similarity. Moreover, there is a tendency toward unidimensionality of preferences that is not present with similarity. This simplifies getting a unidimensional preference scale as a (perhaps, linear) combination of physical attributes but complicates determining multiple dimensions of preference. In addition, not all dominance relations are preferences in the ordinary sense, and subjects may also have difficulty describing dominance relations other than preferences.

## The Unfolding Concept

Coombs' (1964, 1980) unfolding concept is currently the most highly developed approach to the study of preference. It uses ordinal dominance relations to obtain interval scales. The thrust of Coombs' general efforts, especially here, is to show how much data are inherent in a rank ordering (alternating least squares also reflects this broad tradition). Chapter 1 of this book played down the representational tradition of measurement which stresses formal adherence to axioms of measurement. We did so because of the number of counterproductive criticisms of the form, "You haven't shown that $X$ is an interval scale, so you have no business doing an ANOVA on your data." However, we also acknowledged the contributions of this tradition. Unfolding is a major example.

We will use rank orders of preferences among four candidates for political office as an example. Given enough subjects, all the $4! = (4)(3)(2)(1) = 24$ possible orderings will probably be obtained. This will be the case for at least two distinct reasons: (1) Raters respond on the basis of different dimensions (issues in this case) or combinations of dimensions—one person may care only about senior citizens' issues, and another person may care only about abortion; and (2) even when two people agree on the importance of a dimension, they may differ as to where along the dimension they fall and therefore where they prefer the candidate to fall. One person may favor more taxation to benefit social programs; a second may favor less taxation; and a third may fall in between the other two.

Assume for the moment that the potential voters agree upon the issue but vary as to where they stand on this issue. All differences in preference may be reduced to variations along a single dimension $(X)$ that exists in principle as an interval scale. We will focus, as Coombs did, upon the data inherent in the simple preference orders. Specifically, assume that candidates a, b, c, and d are located 7, 20, 31, and 47 units from an (arbitrary) origin on the underlying scale, where – denotes 1 unit.

Consider a person whose relatively extreme views fall at the origin. This subject is 7 units removed from a, 20 units from b, 31 units from c, and 47 units from d. If preference can be defined as the distance from an ideal point, that individual should prefer a to b, b to c, and c to d to produce a preference ordering of abcd. Furthermore, any voter who falls at or below 13 on this scale will have this same rank ordering, as indicated in the diagram. The ordering for people who fall between 14 and 19 is bacd since they fall closer to candidate b than candidate a. Using this same principle, it is possible to identify four other regions: (1) cabd from 20 to 27, (2) dabc from 28 to 33, (3) dcab from 34 to 39, and, finally (4) dcba above 40 (a and c are tied at 19, and a and d are tied at 27). Thus, whereas there are 24 ways to order four candidates in general, the underlying scale constrains these to 6. The alternating least-squares algorithm may be used here, as in MDS, to provide scale values.

What happens if someone provides a different rank ordering, such as adbc? Assuming the rating is systematic, the rater must be using a different attribute or dimension to rate the stimuli, and the stimuli must rank order differently along this second dimension. This provides the basis for a multidimensional analysis of preference.

## Multidimensional Unfolding and ALSCAL

The simplest form of multidimensional unfolding (MDU) uses what is called two-way, two-mode data which are judgments of a series of stimuli on one or more attributes—the term "two-way" denoting that the table is two-dimensional and the term "two-mode" denoting that the dimensions are different from one another. The data may reflect an individual subject or a group average. Conversely, "attributes" can also refer to different omnibus evaluations made by separate groups of subjects. Although we have concentrated upon unfolding as a technique to convert ordinal data to an interval scale, MDU may be used in ALSCAL and other programs with data that are already assumed to be interval or ratio. A joint Euclidian model is used to define distances. The model has the same form as Eq. 14-2, but it employs differences between a given stimulus and a given attribute over dimensions rather than differences between two stimuli. In addition to providing coordinates for the location of the stimuli in the $F$-dimensional space, the attributes are also located in this same space, which is why the term "joint" is used. A variant of this model provides individual difference scaling. The data are three-way, three-mode in that they are dominance judgments generated by a series of subjects on each of several attributes over stimuli. A weighted joint Euclidian model is used. It parallels Eq. 14-7 except that it involves differences between attributes and objects rather than between pairs of objects. These differences are weighted by a parameter that describes the relative attention paid to each attribute.

MDU has been used much less than MDS. Similar questions apply as have been raised above, but there is many fewer data that bear upon its practical use. Given the naturalness with which subjects make preference judgments, the technique certainly should be explored more fully.

## SUMMARY

This chapter was largely concerned with ways to study similarities, although the closing section dealt with the study of dominance relationships. There is a major difference between the two—similarity relationships are inherently symmetric, and dominance relationships are inherently asymmetric. Consequently, different methods of analysis are needed. In particular, the PM correlation is not applicable to the study of dominance relationships.

Cluster analysis describes a variety of procedures for obtaining groupings. The general idea is to form a nucleus of the two most similar objects (stimuli or people). Objects are added to this nucleus using a variety of techniques, including subjective ones. The term "profile analysis" is often used to describe cluster analysis of people. Profiles have three interdependent aspects: (1) level (how high or low the average element is), (2) dispersion (how much the highs and lows differ from each other), and (3) shape (which measures the highs and lows). Different measures of profile similarity incorporate or ignore these various aspects. One useful measure is the distance ($D$) measure, which is defined as the square root of the summed discrepancies between two people over the measures defining the profile. Most commonly, an individual profile is assigned to a single cluster, but clustering can be overlapping so that a given profile can be assigned to more than one cluster. Clustering can also be hierarchical in that higher-order clusters can be formed from lower-order clusters.

One advantage of using $D$ is that it can be converted to a sum-of-cross-products measure and subjected to raw-score factor analysis. This uses values of $\Sigma XY$, which are the sum of cross-products between two individuals over their profile elements. These data can be factored just as a correlation matrix is factored. The length of the vector describing each person is the square root of the sum of that individual's squared profile elements rather than 1.0, as in component analysis, or some fraction of 1.0, as in common factor analysis. Small values of $D$ between individuals correspond to large values of $\Sigma XY$, which will lead to the individuals having a similar factor structure.

Although it is possible to orthogonalize the profile elements, we suggested that this not be done unless they have extremely high correlations. The reason is that the original measures are usually chosen on some meaningful basis and the correlational structure is part of that basis. Furthermore, the methods described in Chapter 12 can be used to adjust for level when that is an irrelevant part of the analysis.

In contrast to other methods considered in the chapter which are concerned with the discovery of latent groupings, discriminant analysis is concerned with forming linear combinations of variables to best discriminate among existing groups. There are basically three separate issues: (1) determining whether multivariate group differences are significant, (2) combining predictors in an optimal manner, and (3) forming classification rules to place unknown individuals into groups. The first of these is most important with small samples and is the multivariate analysis of variance (MANOVA). Geometrically, the issue of combining predictors is one of placing an axis in a hyperspace. Individuals are points in the space. The better the grouping, the more tightly clustered groups are at different points in space. Specifically, the linear discriminant function is the axis (line) maximizing the variance between groups relative to the variance within groups. Discriminant scores are the linear combinations obtained from optimally weighting the predictors. When there are at least three groups and two predictors, it is possible to obtain multiple discriminant functions. The first function maximizes the discrimination possible in the observed scores. Additional functions maximize the discrimination possible in the residual data, partialling out earlier discriminant functions. The process is quite similar to successive (orthogonal) factoring. Mathematically, the problem of discriminant analysis involves an eigenanalysis of the product of two matrices. One is the covariance matrix between groups on the various predictors. The other is the inverse of the covariance matrix within groups, where an inverse is the matrix counterpart of a reciprocal. Placement may be accomplished in several ways. One is the use of centroid contours (centours) around a group, which are a form of confidence intervals about the multivariate average (centroid) of each group. A centour score for an individual is the percentage of individuals in a group that fall further from the centroid than that individual.

Multiple discriminant analysis is particularly well suited to exploring the structure of group differences. In particular, it can be used to decide whether these differences are concentrated or diffuse. In a concentrated structure, one factor underlies group differences, and so the groups tend to rank-order similarly on all measures. In a diffuse structure, more than one factor underlies these group differences, and so groups may rank-order in one way with respect to some variables and in a different way with respect to others. Early applications of multiple discriminant analysis in applied situations revealed several ambiguities and limitations: (1) It is not always clear how to define the groups, (2) it is not always clear who should be placed in the group, (3) it is not needed when there is a strong relationship between test scores and the desirability of group membership, (4) placements based upon centour scores may lead to anomalies such as an individual being too smart to be a nuclear physicist, and (5) not all people in a given group belong there, and so the analysis may serve to perpetuate past errors. Nonetheless, MDA is quite useful in understanding the structure of group differences.

Pattern analysis describes the study of categorical (discrete) measures. As with continuous measures, the problem may involve the discovery of latent groups of describing differences among existing groups. One approach to the discovery of latent groups is to classify responses between people as agreements versus disagreements, obtain a measure of relationship, and factor the result. Although this addresses the issue, the problems inherent in factoring categorical data discussed in Chapter 13 need be kept in mind. Even though discriminant analysis can be applied to categorical measures, a sounder approach is to use item response theory (Chapter 10). Specifically, the same methods used earlier to study differential item functioning can be used to study pattern differences, although the interpretation is different. An important caution in any pattern analysis is to keep the unreliability of such measures in mind.

Multidimensional scaling describes a class of procedures used to scale stimuli. It is an outgrowth of unidimensional scaling (Chapter 2), but responses concern relations among stimuli rather than stimuli themselves. The study may be concerned with discovering natural dimensions of similarity or how subjects combine known dimensions. Classical MDS assumes that the data are at least interval in character, but newer, ordinal methods produce distances from ordinal data. Several models of distance have been used, but the most popular is the Euclidian model for which the generalized Pythagorean distance theorem and triangle inequalities hold. The former states that the distance between two points is the square root of the distances along the individual dimensions; the latter states that the distance along two sides of any triangle is at least as great as the distance along the third side.

There are two components of an MDS study: (1) the empirical aspect of gathering the data, and (2) the mathematical aspect of deciding the properties of the data, specifically the level of measurement it represents. The latter also includes whether to incorporate individual differences into the analysis or not. One way to gather data is through extensions of the direct psychophysical tasks discussed in Chapter 2. One broad class of these methods provides measures of the overall similarity of the stimuli. These include (1) direct magnitude estimation, (2) category ratings, (3) rankings, (4) forced categorization, (5) free sortings, (6) the method of triads, and (7) bisection. Many of these are paired comparison methods. A second broad class of methods involve ratings of specified attributes. A third category uses indirect methods also discussed in Chapter 2. These include matrices derived from (1) confusions, (2) joint (co-) occurrences, and (3) transitions.

Vector-space approaches to MDS obtain ratio-level data directly from similarities, perhaps derived from magnitude estimations. A variant on this approach is vector product MDS in which the square root of similarity judgments is treated as a vector product, allowing factor analysis to be employed. Unfortunately, these methods do not guarantee a factorable (Gramian) matrix. An alternative Euclidian distance model provides distances from confusion data. One popular measure is the square root of the ratio of the product of the probabilities of incorrect classifications of stimulus pairs to the product of correct classifications.

One way to obtain ratio data from interval measures is to employ an additive constant which causes the measures to meet the Pythagorean distance and triangle assumptions. If the constant is large enough, the data will necessarily meet Euclidian assumptions but in the largest possible space. A smaller value will provide a space of fewer dimensions. There is an inherent similarity between this issue and the communality estimation problem in factor analysis. An iterative procedure is described to compute the additive constant.

The alternating least-squares algorithm (ALSCAL) has dominated approaches to MDS that convert ordinal data to ratio scales. The name is derived from the fact that the procedure alternates between estimating optimal scaling and model parameters. Disparities, which are functions of the data, and distances, which are functions of the model parameters, are made as similar as possible. The fit of the model is derived from the similarity of these two types of data. The procedure is described and followed by simulation that explores ALSCAL's properties.

It has been suggested that MDS be applied to correlation matrices. MDS will in fact provide a solution with one fewer dimension than a factor analytic solution, but that is in effect an artifact. Other relations between the two are that the origin of the MDS solution will be shifted to the group centroid and the MDS solution will be essentially the same as the MDS solution, ignoring the first factor, if the subject means are independent of the MDS scalar products. Conversely, the MDS and overall factor solutions will be essentially the same if the average correlation between each variable and all other variables is nearly zero, as when each has a mixture of positive and negative correlations. The difference between MDS and factor analysis is less important than the decision about whether to let a general factor remain in the data or not. This general factor is important to the study of abilities but not to the study of preferences.

Individual differences scaling was considered next. It employs a weighted Euclidian model. Individuals (which can be groups) are all assumed to respond to the same dimensions but may pay attention to these dimensions differentially. An example of its application was provided. The general discussion of MDS then concluded. One important point is that the all MDS models view stimuli as points in space. As such, they are assumed to be equally well-defined. Alternative models that treat less well-defined stimuli as being more spread out in space are considered in the next chapter.

We then considered methods based upon dominance measures. Despite the long history of Thurstone scaling, there are no methods for dimensionalizing a matrix of dominance measures that have the degree of acceptance that factor analysis and MDS do with similarity measures. One approach is to convert a dominance problem to a similarity problem by including a subject's ideal stimulus as an object to be scaled. Similarity models can then be applied to the data. The most important modern dominance scaling procedure is unfolding. The basic idea is that a preferential ordering reflects distances from the subject's ideal point to the various alternatives. Consequently, even though $V$ stimuli can be rank-ordered $V!$ ways, this number is severely constrained when the underlying mechanism is an unfolding. ALSCAL provides a multidimensional extension of the model using the joint Euclidian distance model in which distance is based upon the difference between a stimulus and an attribute over dimensions. This has been extended to the individual difference case where subjects may pay differential attention to the various dimensions.

## SUGGESTED ADDITIONAL READINGS

Davison, M. L. (1983). *Multidimensional scaling*. New York: Wiley.

Guilford, J. P. (1954). *Psychometric methods* (2d ed.). New York: McGraw-Hill.

Lanterman, E. D., Feger, H., & Coombs, C. W. (1980). *Similarity and choice*: *Papers in honour of Clyde Coombs*. Bern: Haber.

Lorr, M. (1983). *Cluster analysis for social scientists*. San Francisco: Josey-Bass.

Schiffman, S. S., Reynolds, M. C., & Young, F. W. (1981). *Introduction to multidimensional scaling*: *Theory, methods, and applications*. New York: Academic Press.

*Note*: Standard textbooks on multivariate analysis, as considered in Chapter 11, discuss many of the issues in this chapter, especially discriminant analysis. The Fall 1983 issue of *Applied Psychological Measurement* was devoted to multidimensional scaling and contains several interesting papers.

# THE ANALYSIS OF CATEGORICAL DATA, BINARY CLASSIFICATION, AND ALTERNATIVES TO GEOMETRIC REPRESENTATIONS

## CHAPTER OVERVIEW

The opening paragraph of this book defined "measurement" to include both scaling and classification. However, nearly all discussion has thus far been concerned with scaling. This is because most of our concern with discrete variables (in the sense of Chapter 4, not the mathematical sense) has been directed toward aggregating items into scales. This is certainly a proper and major focus since responses to "I get many headaches" or "The mean equals _____ divided by the number of observations" are properly viewed as too laden with error to be of much value on their own. Consequently they are aggregated, and most interest lies in the composite measure. This is not an inherent property of discrete variables. Even though there may be some ambiguity associated with classifying individuals by religion, ethnicity, etc., each of these variables may be of interest in its own right and enter into strong relations with other variables. This is particularly true of experimental manipulations which are inherently categorical.

Categorical modeling describes a rich variety of methods that can be used with discrete variables. Some of them are applicable to nominal measures in the sense of Chapter 1, others to ordinal measures, and still others relate one or more interval measures to discrete criteria. Even though the Pearson chi-square, Eq. 4-32, used to test model fit dates back very far (Pearson, 1900), methods paralleling the sophistication of those available for continuous variables, such as multiple regression, are very recent in origin. The authors' experience has been that students in psychology tend to get much less exposure to these methods than students in some other areas, such as sociology. Yet, we feel they are very useful in psychology, and so at least an introduction is necessary in a text such as this one. In particular, categorical modeling will be shown to offer a way of aggregating predictors that has advantages over multiple regression (Chapter 5) and discriminant analysis (Chapter 14) when the criterion is discrete. We will therefore compare the three methods later in the chapter.

The simplest problem in categorical modeling involves stimuli and responses that each occur at only two levels. In fact, categorical modeling can be applied to any of the following problems, regardless of the number of levels that are involved.

**1** Assume you have two or more nominal or ordinal variables and you wish to study relations (associations) among them. Further assume that there is no clear distinction between which are predictors (independent variables) and which are criteria (dependent variables). Various questions may be posed about the associations among these variables, e.g., whether there is a relation between ethnicity and income, correcting for differences in level of education.

**2** Now assume that some variables are clearly predictors and others are clearly criteria. One may wish to know which predictors relate to the criteria and their weightings, as in ordinary (continuous variable) multiple regression. For example, you may wish to see how well choice of different brands of a product relates to demographic variables.

**3** In one important special case of problem 2, logistic regression, one or more predictors is quantitative. This is no different from the former problem in a general sense, but variables like age need to be specified differently from variables like ethnicity in the analysis and there is a complication in analyzing the outcome.

**4** In yet other special cases of problem 2, one is interested both in the individual and combined (joint) properties of the various predictors and criteria. This situation is the categorical (discrete) analog of the analysis of variance (ANOVA) and the multivariate analysis of variance (MANOVA).

**5** You may wish to test specific properties of a two-dimensional matrix. For example, you may want to determine if the distributions of psychiatric diagnoses are the same among ethnic groups. The null hypothesis that the distributions are the same is called marginal homogeneity. Another question is whether a matrix is symmetrical within sampling error, as when classifications of two individuals are compared with each other.

The simple case of two stimuli with their associated responses involves binary classification. The theory of signal detection, introduced in Chapter 2, is an important way to study binary classification. The task discussed at that point was judging whether a particular stimulus event had occurred or not. It was noted that there is a problem in separating a subject's accuracy in making judgments from bias or differential use of the response categories reflecting judgmental criteria. Two important aspects of signal detection theory are (1) it was initially an outgrowth of Thurstone scaling and (2) later applications, particularly by Wickens and Olzak, (1989), showed how categorical modeling could be used to address fundamental issues, e.g., separating accuracy from bias.

Signal detection theory is also important because vector-based methods we have considered, such as factor analysis and MDS, define stimuli as points in space. By definition, mathematical points have no size, and so they differ only in location. Although we did not exploit the fact in Chapter 2 in order to simplify the later description of these vector-based methods, classical Thurstone scaling really considers stimuli as regions in a one-dimensional space defined by their discriminal dispersions. When we did consider stimuli as regions in the discussion of discriminant analysis, it was also simpler to consider the case in which the regions were of the same shape and size. Later in this chapter, we will consider alternative nongeometric models in which similarity is not defined in spatial terms and non-Euclidian models in which similarity is defined spatially but some alternative to the Pythagorean theorem, Eqs. 14-1 and 14-2, defines distance. In particular, we will discuss the following.

**1** *General recognition theory* (Ashby & Townsend, 1984), which extends signal detection theory and Thurstone scaling to dual judgment tasks. Stimuli are viewed as producing bivariate distributions which may or may not have the same size and shape and, as in the theory of signal detection, the forms of the decision criteria are important to consider. Ashby and Townsend also derive consequences of viewing stimuli as points in Euclidian space and show that these do not necessarily hold empirically. They propose that similarity be defined in terms of distributional overlap.

**2** *Tree representations*, as employed in Tversky and Hutchinson's (1986) nearest-neighbor analysis. Tree representations provide a very different way to define similarity and may be especially useful in scaling constructs, as opposed to physical objects.

**3** Non-Euclidian distance measures, as reflected in Schvaneveldt's (1990) Pathfinder model. This model provides one measurement foundation for neural networks used in connectionist approaches to cognition. It defines distance through a generalization of the Pythagorean theory, Minkowski $r$ metrics, introduced in Chapter 14.

## CATEGORICAL MODELING

Most forms of categorical modeling take advantage of the facts that

**1** The joint probability of two independent events, $p_i$ and $p_j$, is the product of their individual probabilities, $p_{ij} = p_i p_j$,

**2** The natural logarithm of this product (ln) equals the sum of the natural logs, $\ln(p_i p_j) = \ln p_i + \ln p_j$, and

**3** Natural logarithms have useful mathematical properties.

Crucial aspects of these methods hold using common (base 10) logs, but natural logs are more convenient. Point 2 allows for linear methods that parallel continuous variable statistics. Because these models deal with linear functions of logarithms of probabilities, they are called log linear. Much credit for the development of these methods is due to Leo Goodman (cf. Goodman, 1978). Two additional areas of statistical research contributed to our ability to address these issues. One is represented by the work of Bishop, Fienberg, and Holland (1975), and the other by the work of Grizzle, Starmer, and Koch (1969; Koch, Landis, Freeman, Freeman, & Lehnen, 1977). When these traditions originally emerged, a major issue was Bishop et al.'s use of maximum likelihood (ML) estimation versus Grizzle et al.'s use of generalized least-squares (GLS) estimation. However, the major difference from our perspective is the applicability of Goodman's (1978) work and Bishop et al.'s (1975) work when there is no clear distinction between independent and dependent variables and the applicability of Grizzle et al.'s (1969) and others' work when there is a clear distinction. The term "log linear" will apply to the Goodman-Bishop et al. approach, and the term "predictor-criterion model" will describe Grizzle et al.'s approach. Moreover, there are additional models which are not log linear in nature, but these will not be considered here (see the above references). Over the years, both ML and GLS estimation have been made available as options for categorical problems (as noted previously, GLS solutions are also often used as preliminary ML estimates, and the two converge upon one another in very large samples). One general algorithm can handle most categorical modeling problems. We will assume ML estimation, as it is by far the most common.

Several categorical modeling programs are widely available. We will make special reference to SAS' PROC CATMOD in discussion because of its flexibility. BMDP's BMDP4F and SPSSX's LOGLINEAR are also useful. None of these, especially PROC CATMOD, is easy to use, and we do not recommend reporting results based upon any one of these procedures until you have become extremely familiar with it. For one thing, parameters are defined differently than in the more widely used SAS regression and ANOVA procedures. Second, it must be invoked repeatedly (at least in the current releases of SAS) to obtain an important class of results from hierarchical models in the sense of Chapters 4, 10, and 13.

In this introductory section, we will assume that there are two variables and that each has two levels. The next major section will consider more-complex, higher-order designs that exploit the power of categorical modeling. To make the discussion tangible, suppose that one wishes to study the association between two dichotomous variables, e.g., male and female voters ($X$) are asked which of two candidates, A or B, they prefer ($Y$) to look for what has been called the gender gap. Although it is common to poll equal numbers of males and females, suppose interviewees are sampled from a list of eligible voters. Random sampling will yield a disparity in $X$ that is proportional to the district (population) disparity rather than equality. If the district contains a high proportion of the elderly, females may well outnumber males. Further assume that candidate A is generally preferred to candidate B. Consider two possible outcomes presented in Table 15-1. In one, gender and candidate preference are independent (the proportions of females and males preferring each candidate are the same),

**TABLE 15-1**    TWO POSSIBLE OUTCOMES REFLECTING THE RELATION BETWEEN VOTER GENDER AND CANDIDATE PREFERENCE

| Preferred candidate, Y | Outcome I voter gender, X | | | Outcome II voter gender, X | | |
|---|---|---|---|---|---|---|
| | Female | Male | Total | Female | Male | Total |
| A | 420 | 280 | 700 | 500 | 200 | 700 |
| B | 180 | 120 | 300 | 100 | 200 | 300 |
| Total | 600 | 400 | 1000 | 600 | 400 | 1000 |

*Note*: Outcome I reflects independence of voter gender and candidate preference, and outcome II reflects association (nonindependence).

and in the other they are associated (nonindependent). The outcomes were constructed so that the marginal frequencies in rows (700 and 300) and columns (600 and 400) are the same.

The magnitude of a possible gender gap may be described in several possible ways. In an inferential sense, the respective evidence for independence and association can be derived by using Eq. 4-32 to obtain the respective Pearson $\chi^2$ values of 0 and 126.98 (ns and $p < .001$ with 1 $df$). However, describing effect magnitudes is a problem when an association is present. You might note that 70 percent of females and 70 percent of males prefer candidate A to B under outcome I for a disparity of 0 percent, whereas 83 percent of females and 50 percent of males prefer candidate A to B under outcome II for a disparity of 33 percent. An alternative is to report the phi coefficients ($\Phi$) between gender and preference (Chapter 4), which are, respectively, 0.0 and 0.36. Unfortunately, both disparities and values of $\Phi$ are influenced by the marginal proportions. Different marginals, as in a district with more nearly equal proportions of genders, will provide a different disparity in proportion and value of $\Phi$ even when the underlying strength of association can be shown to remain the same in terms of a formal model. Log-linear models provide better ways to describe strength of association.

## Two-Way Independence

We have noted that independence (lack of association) implies that $p_{ij} = p_i p_j$ and that $\ln p_i p_j) = \ln p_i + \ln p_j$. It is useful to describe the latter in terms of frequencies, ($f_{ij}$), where $i$ and $j$ denote the outcomes of events 1 and 2. This frequency equals $Np_{ij}$. Consequently Eq. 15-1 describes independence.

$$\begin{aligned}
f_{ij} &= Np_{ij} \\
&= Np_i p_j \\
\ln(f_{ij}) &= \ln(Np_i p_j) \\
&= \ln N + \ln p_i + \ln p_j
\end{aligned} \tag{15-1}$$

Applying Eq. 15-1 and letting the first subscript denote the row (candidate) and the second subscript denote the column (voter gender),

$$\begin{aligned}
\ln f_{11} &= \ln 1000 + \ln(700/1000) + \ln(600/1000) \\
&= 6.91 - 0.36 - 0.51 \\
&= 6.04
\end{aligned}$$

The natural log of 420, the actual number of females preferring candidate A under outcome I (independence of gender and preference), is also 6.04. Likewise,

$$\begin{aligned}
\ln f_{12} &= \ln 1000 + \ln(700/1000) + \ln(400/1000) \\
&= 6.91 - 0.36 - 0.92 \\
&= 5.63
\end{aligned}$$

$$\ln f_{21} = \ln 1000 + \ln(300/1000) + \ln(600/1000)$$
$$= 6.91 - 1.20 - 0.51$$
$$= 5.20$$
$$\ln f_{22} = \ln 1000 + \ln(300/1000) + \ln(400/1000)$$
$$= 6.91 - 1.20 - 0.92$$
$$= 4.79$$

You may verify that these sums also equal the natural log of the observed frequencies for the three remaining cells, a direct consequence of the independence of row and column effects. Under these conditions, the disparity in log frequencies between the first and second rows is the same in each column and equals the marginal disparity in log frequencies: $\ln 420 - \ln 180 = \ln 280 - \ln 120 = \ln 700 \ln 300 = .85$. The same is true of the columns: $\ln 420 \ln 280 = \ln 180 - \ln 120 = \ln 600 - \ln 400 = 0.40$. These relations also hold if the frequencies are divided by $N$ to produce probabilities.

These are very similar to the relationships that hold in an ordinary (continuous-variable) $2 \times 2$ ANOVA with equal sample sizes when there is no interaction, i.e., when row and column effects are additive. Consult a source like Hays (1988) if you are unfamiliar with or rusty on the ANOVA. Equation 15-2 describes the resulting ANOVA model (a more complex statement of the ANOVA model is necessary to describe the individual observations and the associated variability within groups).

$$\bar{X}_{ij} = \mu + \beta_i + \beta_j \tag{15-2}$$

We will use the symbol $\beta$ to draw attention to certain similarities between regression effects and effects in categorical modeling; $\lambda$ is an alternative symbol in wide use. This equation states that each mean ($\bar{X}_{ij}$) equals the grand mean ($\mu$) plus a treatment effect associated with the row ($\beta_i$) plus a treatment effect associated with the column ($\beta_j$). A constraint normally introduced onto the various $\beta$ values is that $\Sigma\beta_i = \Sigma\beta_j = 0$. This can be accomplished for $\beta_i$ by expressing each row mean as a deviation from the grand mean and can be accomplished for $\beta_j$ by expressing each column mean as a deviation from the grand mean. Alternatively, each $\beta_j$ can be defined as plus and minus half the difference between the two column means. For example, if the means for the first row are 2 and 4 and the means for the second row are 6 and 8, the row means will be 3 and 7, the column means will be 4 and 6, and the grand mean will be 5. Consequently the $\beta_i$ values are $-2$ and $+2$ [either because $7 - 5 = 2$ and $3 - 5 = -2$ or because $\pm 1/2$ of $-2 - (+2) = \pm 2$], and the $\beta_j$ values are $-1$ and $+1$. The entry in the first row and column (2) therefore can be expressed as $5 - 2 - 1 = 2$.

In a like manner, the log-linear model can be written as

$$\ln f_{ij} = \mu + \beta_i + \beta_j \tag{15-3}$$

This time, $f_{ij}$ is the mean of the logs of the cell frequencies which in turn is the log of the geometric mean of the frequencies (the $K$th root of the product of the $K$ frequencies, where $K$ is the number of cells, four in the present case). This equals 5.41

for the sample data. In order to estimate the $\beta_i$ values, compute the mean of the two log frequencies in the first row, (ln 420 + ln 280)/2, minus the mean of the two log frequencies in the second row, (ln 180 + ln 120)/2 or 0.85. Because of the independence of rows and columns, this will also equal the disparity between the logs of the row sums, ln 700 − ln 300 and therefore the log of their ratio which we have noted to be 0.85.

This log ratio is called the logit or log-odds ratio (LOR) of the effect. It is called the latter because it equals the log of the odds favoring the first outcome over the second since ln(700/300) = ln 700 − ln 300. Plus and minus half this value (±0.42) provide the desired values of $\beta_i$. Likewise, the difference between the logs for the two columns sums is (ln 420 + ln 180)/2 − (ln 280 + ln 120)/2 or 0.20. This again equals the difference between the logs of the marginal frequencies and therefore the logit, so that the two desired values of $\beta_j$ are 0.20 and −0.20. In this model, therefore,

$$5.41 + 0.42 + 0.20 = 6.03 = \ln f_{11} \text{ (within rounding error)}$$
$$5.41 - 0.42 + 0.20 = 5.19 = \ln f_{21}$$
$$5.41 + 0.42 - 0.20 = 5.63 = \ln f_{12}$$
$$5.41 - 0.42 - 0.20 = 4.79 = \ln f_{11}$$

The grand mean thus provides one parameter estimate, the row effect provides a second (although there are two values of $\beta_i$, only one is free to vary since their sum must be zero), and the column effect provides a third. Equation 4-22 can be applied to the disparity between the observed and predicted values, providing a likelihood ratio chi-square, $G^2 = 2 \Sigma o \ln(o/e)$ to test the departure from independence for significance. It would be based upon 1 $df$—the number of entries in the table (4 in the present case) minus the number of estimated parameters (3 in the present case).

## Association (Nonindependence)

A large value of $G^2$ implies that a model based upon only the grand mean, row effect, and column effect fails (i.e., there is association of rows and columns), which may be illustrated using nonindependence outcome II. The log frequency of $f_{11}$ under outcome II is 6.21. The difference between observed and obtained log frequencies of 0.17 reflects the association between gender and preference. The remaining differences for $f_{12}$, $f_{21}$, and $f_{22}$, are −0.33, −0.58, and 0.51, respectively. These log disparities do not add to zero (as in the ANOVA), but the disparities themselves do. A more complex model that contains an additional parameter, Eq. 15-4, is needed.

$$\ln f_{ij} = \mu + \beta_i + \beta_j + \beta_{ij} \tag{15-4}$$

These data are like an ANOVA with unequal sample sizes. As before, one parameter of the model is the mean of the cell means (log geometric mean of the observations) or 5.36. Although we cannot use the log ratio of the marginal frequencies to estimate the row effect ($\beta_i$), we can use plus and minus half the difference between the averages of the two log cell frequencies over columns:

$$\frac{\ln 500 + \ln 200}{2} - \frac{\ln 100 + \ln 200}{2} = \frac{6.21 + 5.30}{2} - \frac{4.61 + 5.30}{2} \text{ or } \pm 0.40.$$

We can do the same for columns to obtain the two values of $\beta_j$, which are $\pm 0.06$. The final parameters are obtained from the two pairs of diagonal entries as

$$\frac{\ln f_{11} + \ln f_{22}}{2} - \frac{\ln f_{21} + \ln f_{12}}{2} = \frac{\ln 500 + \ln 200}{2} - \frac{\ln 100 + \ln 200}{2}$$

$$= \frac{6.21 + 5.30}{2} - \frac{4.61 + 5.30}{2}$$

These parameters are $\pm 0.40$, just like $\beta_i$ in this case, but this is purely a coincidence. The sign of a given term is positive if $\beta_i$ and $\beta_j$ have the same sign, which is true of $f_{11}$ and $f_{22}$ (their parameters are, respectively, both positive and both negative), and negative if they have different signs, which is true of $f_{12}$, and $f_{21}$. Consequently Eq. 15-4 provides the following four equations:

$$5.36 + 0.40 + 0.06 + 0.40 = 6.22 = \ln f_{11} \quad \text{(within rounding error)}$$
$$5.36 - 0.40 + 0.06 - 0.40 = 4.62 = \ln f_{21}$$
$$5.36 + 0.40 - 0.06 - 0.40 = 5.30 = \ln f_{12}$$
$$5.36 - 0.40 - 0.06 + 0.40 = 5.30 = \ln f_{22}$$

This saturated model reconstructs the logs of the original frequencies in terms of a row effect, a column effect, and an association term, which is like an interaction in the ANOVA. However, we have gained little since we have estimated four quantities to explain four known quantities. This exhausts the degrees of freedom and thus precludes the model from being tested. However, the model furnishes one useful item— the association parameter ($\beta_{ij}$) of 0.40 describes the gender gap, adjusting for the rows and column marginal totals. $\beta_{ij}$ reflects both association and random error but, as is generally true, the contribution of random error declines as the sample size increases.

Equation 15-3 can be used to test outcome II. Since the marginal frequencies are the same under both outcomes, the $\beta_i$ and $\beta_j$ estimates will be the same, $\pm 0.42$ and $\pm 0.20$, as is the average of the four log frequencies, 5.36. The differences (residuals, as in ordinary regression analysis) between observed and predicted values are 0.23 and $-0.97$ for the first row and 0.16 and 0.56 for the second row. The observed values, $o$ (500, 100, 200, and 200), and expected values, $e$ (400, 180, 280, and 120), provide a $G^2$ value of 126.54. This is very close to the value obtained from Eq. 4-32 for the Pearson $\chi^2$ (126.98). Equation 15-4 can be applied to outcome I; the estimate of $\beta_{ij}$ is zero.

## Alternative Models for the $2 \times 2$ Case

We have thus far considered two models. One defined the joint probabilities as the sum of the row and column effects, Eq. 15-3, and the other incorporated an additional associative parameter, Eq. 15-4. Equation 15-3 is a special case of Eq. 15-4 in which $\beta_{ij} = 0$ (i.e., a nested model in the sense previously described in Chapters 4, 10, and 13), and so Eq. 15-4 is therefore a generalization of Eq. 15-3 in which a parameter is added. Equations 15-5a, 15-5b, and 15-6 define some additional models:

$$\ln f_{ij} = \mu + \beta_i \qquad (15\text{-}5a)$$

$$\ln f_{ij} = \mu + \beta_j \qquad (15\text{-}5b)$$

$$\ln f_{ij} = \mu \qquad (15\text{-}6)$$

Equations 15-5a and 15-5b each contain only one effect—rows but not columns in Eq. 15-5a, and columns but not rows in Eq. 15-5b. Both have meaning—the two genders could be of unequal size but prefer the two candidates equally, i.e., there is no gender gap. Likewise, the genders could be of equal size, but each group could prefer one candidate over the other by the same margin. Both models have 2 *df*. Finally, if the population contained equal numbers of males and females, if there was equal candidate preference, and if there was no gender gap, Eq. 15-6 would hold. It has 1 *df* that reflects the overall sample size. It is called a homogeneity model because it defines all cell frequencies as equal. Comparable parameter estimates for Eqs. 15-5 are the same as in the independence model, Eq. 15-3. Specifically, $\beta_i$ is 0.42 in Eq. 15-5a and $\beta_j$ is 0.20 in Eq. 15-5b because the marginal totals are the same. In contrast, the parameters for the associative model, Eq. 15-4, are based upon cell rather than marginal frequencies, and so they differ in the two outcomes. Note that Eqs. 15-5 are generalizations of Eq. 15-6 and restrictions of Eqs. 15-3 and 15-4 but that they are not generalizations of one another. The parameter for the homogeneity model, Eq. 15-6, is simply $N$ divided by the number of cells (4 in the present case).

So far, the models we have considered do not exhaust all possibilities. Equations 15-7 illustrate two others:

$$\ln f_{ij} = \mu + \beta_i + \beta_{ij} \qquad (15\text{-}7a)$$

$$\ln f_{ij} = \mu + \beta_j + \beta_{ij} \qquad (15\text{-}7b)$$

Equation 15-7a describes an overall difference in candidate preference and a gender gap but assumes the number of males and females sampled are the same. This could be the outcome of a study which chose equal numbers of males and females by intent. However, that study would likely consider gender as an independent variable and candidate preference as a dependent variable. Consequently it would be tested with Grizzle et al. (predictor-criterion) models, considered below, rather than the Goodman-Bishop et al. log-linear models presently considered which make no such distinction. The log-linear model implies that no constraints were put on sampling by gender, so that the outcome reflects equal numbers of males and females in the population, perhaps an unlikely outcome. Equation 15-7b has similar properties: It states that overall candidate preference is split equally at 50-50, but that there is an overall difference in numbers of males and females and a gender gap. Perhaps 400 males and 350 females preferred candidate A and 100 females and 650 males preferred candidate B. It too is unlikely. Both models have 2 *df*.

One final model is

$$\ln f_{ij} = \mu + \beta_{ij} \qquad (15\text{-}8)$$

This states that there are equal numbers of males and females and equal preference for the two candidates, but that there is a gender gap. This is perhaps even less plausible than Eqs. 15-7. The preference for one candidate would have to be exactly as strong among males as the preference for the other candidate among females. This is the analog of what is called a complete crossover interaction in the continuous-variable case. This model also has 2 *df*.

Equations 15-3 through 15-6 are hierarchical, and Eqs. 15-7a through 15-8 are nonhierarchical. Any association term ($\beta_{ij}$ in the present case) in a hierarchical model must contain its lower-order constituents, $\beta_i$ and $\beta_j$. Lower-order terms may exist in either type without their association, as can be seen in Eq. 15-3. Early algorithms required the model tested to be hierarchical, but this is no longer the case.

There is at present considerable debate over the use of nonhierarchical models (Rindskopf, 1990; Wickens, 1989). The second author has never been impressed with one argument against them—that it is unlikely that an association could occur in the absence of a lower-order effect, e.g., that a gender gap could occur when there are exactly the same number of males and females. In fact, *any* null hypothesis is unlikely; if we had access to the population data, we probably would always find a difference. However, null hypothesis testing has been a useful heuristic. A better argument is that higher-order terms are best computed as deviations from lower-order terms and used only when simpler models fail.

Wickens (1989) and Bishop et al. (1975) both note that restricting discussion to hierarchical models has little practical effect because nonhierarchical models can usually be translated into hierarchical models by redefining variables. Suppose candidate A actively endorses issues supported by women and candidate B actively opposes these issues. We could define $X$ as gender, as before, but define $Y$ as whether or not voters select the candidate that is consistent with their gender. The $\beta_{ij}$ then measures relative candidate preference. Defining variables in this way causes testing differences in numbers of males and females without testing overall preference to be hierarchical and testing overall preference without testing differences in numbers of males and females to be nonhierarchical.

## Measures of Association in the 2 × 2 Design

The $\beta_{ij}$, its logit (twice the absolute value of $\beta_{ij}$), and the odds ratio itself (without taking logs) are equivalent ways to describe the strength of an association. Although the odds ratio has the advantage of not requiring users to think in terms of logs, it has the disadvantage of not being symmetric. Cross-product ratios range from 1 to $\infty$ when $p = .5$ but range only from 0 to 1 when $p \leq 1.5$. It is therefore difficult to compare cases in which $p$ is above .5 versus below .5. In contrast, $\beta_{ij}$ and the logit merely change sign. It is moderately desirable for measures to be bounded by $-1$ and $+1$ or by 0 and $+1$ (be co-efficients). We have already discussed $\Phi$, which is certainly popular despite its dependence upon the marginal totals. Yule (1900, 1912; see Bishop et al., 1975) proposed two coefficients. First let $\alpha$ be the odds ratio:

$$\alpha = \frac{p_{11}p_{22}}{p_{12}p_{21}} \qquad (15\text{-}9)$$

Note that Shepard's distance measure, Eq. 14-5, is the square root of the reciprocal of $\alpha$.
    Yule's (1900) measure of association ($Q$) is

$$Q = \frac{\alpha - 1}{\alpha + 1} \qquad (15\text{-}10a)$$

Yule's (1912) measure of colligation ($Y$) is

$$Y = \frac{\sqrt{\alpha} - 1}{\sqrt{\alpha} + 1} \qquad (15\text{-}10b)$$

These measures are most useful when levels of both variables have the same meaning. For example, we might interview male-female couples about their choice of candidates. One variable in the $2 \times 2$ table is the male's choice of candidate, and the other variable is the female's choice. The $Q$ measure equals the conditional probability that they will choose the same candidate minus the conditional probability that they will choose different candidates. It will be positive when there is a preponderance of agreements, negative when there is a preponderance of disagreements, and zero when the two are equal. Moreover, it cannot exceed 1 in absolute value. The $Y$ measure is generally similar, but it is designed to address the issue of what would be the case if the row and column marginal probabilities were equally split, e.g., if the proportions of males and the proportions of females favoring each candidate were both .5. However, both $Q$ and $Y$ are sensitive to differences in marginal totals (Swets, 1986a).
    One additional way to correct for differences in marginal frequency is to compute the tetrachoric correlation (see Chapter 4). However, the criticisms made of it at that point (e.g., its large sampling error) are still applicable. We suggest that the associative effect ($\beta_{ij}$) or the LOR be used to define strength of association, especially when there is also interest in the marginal probabilities, which can be defined as $\beta_i$ and $\beta_j$ or their corresponding logits. These measures allow marginal probabilities and associative effect to be expressed in the same metric and have the useful property of symmetry.

## More about $G^2$

We have already noted how Eq. 4-22 may be used to compare obtained and expected (predicted) frequencies to obtain $G^2$ values. These are residual values describing the model's lack of fit. Two other $G^2$ values may be obtained:

**1** A difference $G^2$ may be obtained between two models as in Chapter 10. The residual $G^2$ for Eq. 15-5a must be larger than the residual $G^2$ for Eq. 15-3. The difference $G^2$ between them has 1 $df$ and tests the significance of adding $\beta_j$ to the model.

**2** An effect $G^2$ is obtained by squaring the ratio of a given effect to its standard error (which is computed by a relatively complex algorithm described in such sources as the SAS manual). This tests the significance of its presence in the model, i.e., whether it can be assumed to differ from zero.

Although difference and effect $G^2$ values are often numerically similar, their interpretations are different. Both also depend upon what other variables have been included in the model.

We will illustrate the computation of these various terms using outcome II. Table 15-2 lists the observed proportions, the expected proportions for each of several models, and the residual $G^2$. We will use association notation to describe these models by placing quantities that are assumed to be associated in brackets. Thus, $[XY]$ denotes the saturated model of Eq. 15-4, $[X][Y]$ denotes the independence model of Eq. 15-3, and $[X]$ denotes the model of Eq. 15-5a in which only row effects are present. The symbol – denotes the homogeneity model of Eq. 15-6, and NH followed by the parameters denotes the nonhierarchical models of Eqs. 15-7a, 15-7b, and 15-8.

Application of Eq. 4-22 provides a residual $G^2$ of 2 {500 [ln(500/250)] + 200[ln(200/250)] + 200 [ln(20/250)] + 100 [ln(100/250)]} = 2(346.57 − 44.63 − 44.63 − 91.63) = 331.36 for the homogeneity model. The difference $G^2$ for X ($G_X^2$) equals the homogeneity residual $G^2$ (331.36) minus the $[X]$ residual $G^2$ (291.10) = 40.26, and the difference $G^2$ for Y ($G_Y^2$) equals the homogeneity residual $G^2$ (331.36) minus the $[Y]$ residual $G^2$ (166.81) = 164.45. The $G_Y^2$ is larger than the $G_X^2$, and the residual $G^2$ for Y is smaller than the residual $G^2$ for X because the disparity in Y proportions (0.7 versus 0.3) is greater than the disparity in X proportions (0.6 versus 0.4).

The model $[X]$ residual $G^2$ – the model $[X][Y]$ residual $G^2$ (291.10 − 126.54) produces the difference $G^2$ for Y correcting for X ($G_{X/Y}^2$) of 164.56. Likewise, the model $[Y]$ $G^2$ minus the model $[X][Y]$ $G^2$ (166.81 − 126.54) produces the X difference $G^2$ correcting for Y ($G_{X/Y}^2$) of 40.27. These are identical to their uncorrected counterparts $G_X^2$ and $G_Y^2$, but this need not be the case with more complex models. Finally, the independence $[X][Y]$ residual $G^2$ minus the associative $[XY]$ residual $G^2$ (126.54 − 0) pro-

TABLE 15-2   OBSERVED PROPORTIONS, EXPECTED PROPORTIONS, AND RESIDUAL $G^2$ FOR ALTERNATIVE MODELS

| Model parameters | $f_{11}$ | $f_{12}$ | $f_{21}$ | $f_{22}$ | $G^2$ |
|---|---|---|---|---|---|
| Homogeneity, $\mu$ | 0.25 | 0.25 | 0.25 | 0.25 | 331.36 |
| $[X]$, $\mu$, $\beta_i$ | 0.30 | 0.20 | 0.30 | 0.20 | 291.10 |
| $[Y]$, $\mu$, $\beta_j$ | 0.35 | 0.35 | 0.15 | 0.15 | 166.81 |
| $[X][Y]$, $\mu$, $\beta_i$ $\beta_j$ | 0.42 | 0.28 | 0.18 | 0.12 | 126.54 |
| $[XY]$, $\mu$, $\beta_i$, $\beta_j$, $\beta_{ij}$ | 0.50 | 0.20 | 0.10 | 0.20 | 0.0 |
| Observed | 0.50 | 0.20 | 0.10 | 0.20 | |

duces the association difference $G^2$ ($G^2_{XY}$) of 126.54. All effects are significant well be-yond the .01 level. Note that the initial $G^2 - G^2_Y - G^2_{Y/X} - G^2_{XY}$ (331.36 − 164.56 − 49.27 − 126.54) = 0, as does the initial $G^2 - G^2_X - G^2_{Y/X} - G^2_{XY}$. This additivity is like the additivity of sums of squares in the ANOVA. The effect $G^2$ values are generally similar to the difference $G^2$ values though numerically distinct; e.g., the effect $G^2$ for $X$ is 150.76 in $[X][Y]$ and in $[X]$.

Which $G^2$ should be used—difference or effect? In general, these address different questions. The difference $G^2$ defines the reduction in uncertainty or variance in the contingency table as a particular effect is considered. It defines the effect adjusting for effects previously included in the model but ignoring effects incorporated at a later stage. Its value is in demonstrating that effects like $X$, $Y$, or its association add to previous effects. Although the effect $G^2$ can be used to this same end by evaluating it at the time of entry, its primary value lies in describing the unique contribution of an effect in the model that is ultimately selected, adjusting for all other variables in that model.

If you are familiar with the notation SAS uses for its regression and ANOVA programs, there is an analogy between the difference $G^2$ and the type I (sequential or hierarchical) sums of squares and between the effect $G^2$ in the final model as the type II (simultaneous) sums of squares. Statistical theorists tend to emphasize selection of a particular model out of alternatives. These alternatives grow at a geometric rate with the number of variables. In contrast, most empirical investigations are more directed toward identifying particular contingencies.

## The Generalized Logit Variant

We have defined the logit of a particular event as $\ln[p/1 - p)] = \ln(p/q) = \ln p - \ln q$, where $p$ is the probability of a given event and $q$ is its complement when there are two events. By extension, the generalized logits of a series of probabilities that add to 1.0 are obtained by taking the log of the ratio of all but one to the remaining event or baseline. Any event may serve as the baseline, although the last event in the series is a common default choice. Recall that under outcome II, the four cell frequencies, $f_{11}, f_{21}, f_{12}$, and $f_{22}$, are 420, 180, 280, and 120. It does not matter whether we divide these by $N$ (1000) because $N$ will be eliminated in the process of forming the generalized logits. The generalized logits are therefore $\ln(420/120) = 1.25$, $\ln(180/120) = 0.41$, and $\ln(280/120)$ or 0.85. These are all positive because $f_{22}$, the baseline, is the smallest frequency. When it is not, some generalized logits may be negative. Note that the fourth possible logit, $\ln(120/120)$, is 0. This will always be the case, and so it may be ignored.

Several log-linear modeling programs use generalized logits instead of the original frequencies. The result reduces the number of observed quantities by 1 and eliminates the parameter $\mu$, which is not of interest, from the model. The various parameter estimates and $G^2$ values remain the same.

## Structural and Random Zeros

A random zero in a table states that an event could have occurred but did not. This may imply a sample was too small to obtain a relatively rare event. Many random zeros in a table indicate problems in the analysis, especially when they are found at the same level across a given variable. This problem may be handled by collapsing levels (relevant assumptions will be considered later in the chapter). In contrast, a structural zero arises from the intent of the study. Chapter 14 dealt with transition matrices where one dimension reflected a classification at one point in time and the second dimension reflected a later classification. If the analysis considers only those who change preference, the diagonal entries will be structural zeros; e.g., if a study involves change of academic majors, students are excluded if their major remains the same. Another common situation providing structural zeros is when individuals are given a list of stimuli, say political candidates or vegetables, and asked to name their top two choices. By definition, a given stimulus cannot be both a first and second choice, and so the diagonal positions of the matrix must contain zeros. Models with structural zeros are a bit more difficult to work with than ordinary models, but not extremely so (see Wickens, 1989).

## Multiple Levels on a Variable

Chapter 1 introduced the important point that any nominal variable at $K$ levels can be represented as $K - 1$ separate variables such as dummy codes, each with 1 $df$. Chapter 5 showed how this could be applied to ordinary (continuous variable) regression. Exactly this same principle applies to categorical modeling. Effect $G^2$ values, difference $G^2$ values, and residual $G^2$ values can be obtained for the separate variables. In addition, difference and residual (but not effect) $G^2$ values can be obtained for the effect as a whole. As in ordinary regression, there are an infinite number of ways to define the individual variables, but only a few are likely to be of practical interest. For example, schizophrenia, bipolar disorder, and major depression are three common psychiatric diagnoses. Assume that patients in all three groups are classified as having shown improvement or not in response to therapy. Response to therapy has 1 $df$, but diagnostic category and the association of diagnostic category with response to therapy each have 2 $df$. One way to define the diagnostic category effect is to compare two groups separately with a third (baseline) group. This is analogous to dummy coding in multiple regression and is a common default procedure. However, it may be more useful to divide the 2 $df$ into comparing (1) schizophrenics versus the two mood disorder groups and (2) the two mood disorder groups with each other, ignoring schizophrenics. The association with response to therapy may be defined analogously.

Individual comparisons may be nonsignificant, but the overall effect may be significant for two reasons:

**1** Two groups being compared against a baseline group may differ from one another but not from the baseline group.

**2** The $G^2$ needed for significance with $K$ degrees of freedom is not $K$ times that required with the 1 $df$ involved in comparing two groups; the overall effect is not additive with respect to its component individual effects.

One important issue is how to describe the overall effect magnitude. Chapter 9 of Wickens (1989; also see Wickens & Olzak, 1989) presents some alternative measures. One is the information transmitted or $0.72135/N$ times the difference $G^2$ associated with the set of variables. The general logic of this measure is discussed in Garner and Morton (1969). Unfortunately, it is not independent of $K$.

## Higher-Order Designs

More models become possible as variables are added, most of which require open-form (iterative) estimation. For example, a model may have three variables, three first-order associations of the form $\beta_{ij}$, and a second-order association of the form $\beta_{ijk}$. Models of this form may be used to explore Simpson's paradox (see Chapters 5 and 9) where there may be no association between $X$ and $Y$ at each level of a third variable ($Z$) but $X$ and $Y$ are associated when $Z$ is ignored. It is also possible for the direction of association to change when a third variable is controlled as opposed to ignored, as we will show. In general, a problem with three variables produces five types of models that we have previously considered:

**1**  A homogeneity model in which all cells have equal frequency in the population and there are no associations: –

**2**  Three one-way independence models in which two variables have equal frequency and there are no associations: $[X]$, $[Y]$, and $[Z]$

**3**  Three two-way independence models in which one variable has equal frequency and there are no associations: $[X][Y]$, $[X][Z]$, and $[Y][Z]$

**4**  A three-way independence model: $[X][Y][Z]$

**5**  A saturated model: $[XYZ]$.

In addition, there are three new types of models:

**6**  Three one-factor independence models in which two variables are associated, but both are independent of a third: $[XY][Z]$, $[XZ][Y]$, and $[YZ][X]$

**7**  Three conditional independence models in which one variable is associated with the two other, but the two are independent of each other: $[XY][XZ]$, $[XY][YZ]$, and $[XZ][YZ]$

**8**  A homogeneous association model in which all pairs of variables are related, but there is no three-way association: $[XY][XZ][YZ]$.

There are also several nonhierarchical models that we will ignore for simplicity. Because there are so many possible models, it is important that the order of variable entry be well formulated in advance, as effect magnitudes are order-dependent. One problem encountered is that this ordering may be arbitrary. As effects may be highly correlated, it is wise to look at alternative orderings. More specific models may be tested in special circumstances (see the section titled "More Specific Categorical Models" below).

We simulated a homogeneous association model in which all two-way (first-order) associations are present but there is no three-way association to saturate the model:

$$\ln f_{ijk} = 6 + \beta_i + \beta_j + \beta_k + \beta_{ij} + \beta_{ik} + \beta_{jk} \qquad (15\text{-}11)$$

The number 6 defines the sample size as the geometric mean of each group. Assume that the study concerns 5-year survival after treatment for cancer.

**1** One variable ($I$) is the year of treatment (1950 or 1990), and the associated values of $\beta_i$ are −0.2 and +0.2. Making the first value negative causes the overall rate to increase.

**2** A second variable ($J$) describes the overall outcomes, and the associated values of $\beta_j$ are +0.8 for success and −0.8 for failure, i.e., people generally survived.

**3** A third variable ($K$) reflects the type of cancer (A, B, or C); the three values of $\beta_k$ are +0.3, −0.2, and −0.1, and so there is a predominance of type A cancer.

**4** The parameters reflecting the association of year and outcome were $\beta_{11} = \beta_{22} = -0.1$ and $\beta_{12} = \beta_{21} = +0.1$, reflecting higher survival rates in 1990 than in 1950 due to medical advances.

**5** The parameters reflecting the association of year and type were $\beta_{ik} = -0.60$, +0.05, and +0.55 for the three types in 1950 and $\beta_{ik} = +0.60$, −0.05, and −0.55 for 1990. These represent the change in distribution of the three forms of cancer over time.

**6** Finally, the associations between outcome and type of cancer were $\beta_{jk} = -0.50$, −0.03, and +0.53, and so the associations for nonsurvival were $\beta_{jk} = +0.50$, +0.03, and −0.53. These mean that type A cancer is most life-threatening and type C cancer is least life-threatening.

The observed quantities generated by these parameters are given in Table 15-3. It will be useful if you verify the analysis. The proportion surviving is simply the number surviving over the total for that year and type, e.g., 298 people survived type A cancer in 1950, 200 did not, and 298/(298 + 200)= 0.60. The parameter estimates differed trivially from the actual parameters because of rounding error. Consistent with the lack of three-way association, the residual $G^2$ for the homogeneous association model was exactly 0 with 2 $df$. The residual $G^2$ values for the year by outcome, year by type, and outcome by type associations were 32.61, 1493.63, and 2216.36, respectively. All three terms are clearly significant, and so the simpler conditional independence models can properly be rejected. Note what has happened though. The survival rates for the individual forms of cancer all increased and the percentage change was greatest for the most difficult form of cancer to treat, type A. There is a positive association between year and probability of survival within types. However, in 1950, 2625 individuals (298 + 555 + 1772) survived and 496 (200 + 145 + 151) did not survive. Consequently the survival rate that year was 2625/(2625 + 496) or 0.84. The corre-

**TABLE 15-3** SIMULATED SURVIVAL FIGURES FOR THREE TYPES OF CANCER IN 1950 AND 1990

| | 1950 survival rate | | | 1990 survival rate | | |
|---|---|---|---|---|---|---|
| Type | Yes | No | p(surv) | Yes | No | p(surv) |
| A | 298 | 200 | .60 | 1808 | 812 | .69 |
| B | 555 | 145 | .79 | 915 | 160 | .85 |
| C | 1772 | 151 | .92 | 1074 | 61 | .95 |

*Note*: p(surv) is the probability of surviving or number surviving divided by the total for that type and year.

sponding figure in 1990 was 0.79, and so there is a decline in overall survival. This is an artifact of the changing distribution of type of cancer, i.e., Simpson's paradox. Log-linear modeling is a powerful way to investigate phenomena such as these which often give rise to the paradox.

## Predictor-Criterion Models

Models have thus far not distinguished between predictors and criteria, but one might well argue that it would be more natural to ask how candidate preference depends upon gender and how cancer survival depends upon year, type, and their associations in the above examples. These involve predictor-criterion models. Various methods exist to fit such models, including those that model the criterion response probabilities directly. This is especially useful for ordinal criteria such as whether a patient got worse, remained the same, or responded positively to therapy or interval criteria. We will model the generalized logits of the criteria for the voting example. When the criterion is a dichotomy, there is one response function (e.g., the relative preference for candidate A over candidate B) that is modeled as a function of the predictor(s).

Equations 15-12 describe four models that may be applied to the voting data in Tables 15-1 and 15-2:

$$\text{logit } Y = 0 \qquad\qquad (15\text{-}12\text{a})$$
$$\text{logit } Y = \beta_0 \qquad\qquad (15\text{-}12\text{b})$$
$$\text{logit } Y = \beta_i \qquad\qquad (15\text{-}12\text{c})$$
$$\text{logit } Y = \beta_0 + \beta_i \qquad\qquad (15\text{-}12\text{d})$$

**1** Equation 15-12a treats all four probabilities as homogeneous, so that the resulting three logits are all zero. It has 3 *df* because one of the four cells ($f_{22}$ in the present case) provides the baseline against which three observed logits are obtained. It states that the two outcomes are (a) equally probable (preferences are divided 50-50) and (b) unrelated to the predictor (gender).

**2** Equation 15-12b states that the two outcomes are not equally probable, and $\beta_0$ describes the log of their ratio. However, $\beta_0$ is independent of the predictor (gender) and is the intercept of a regression equation with a slope of zero. This intercept plays a role similar to that of $\mu$ in log-linear models, but it describes the natural log of the relative preference rather than the absolute frequency.

**3** Equation 15-12c states that the preference is related to the predictor, but the overall ratio of preference for candidate A over candidate B is 1, and so the log ratio is zero. Females prefer candidate A by a given amount, and males prefer candidate B by that same amount. The $\beta_i$ parameter is basically a slope parameter that relates the difference in candidate preference to gender.

**4** Equation 15-12d holds when the predictor (gender) is related to the criterion (candidate preference) and there is an overall candidate preference.

In more complex models, individual effects are designated $\beta_j$, $\beta_k$, . . .; two-way (first-order) associations among predictors are designated $\beta_{ij}$, $\beta_{ik}$, . . . .

The residual $G^2$ values for these four models under outcome II were 166.81, 126.54, 2.24, and 0. The last-mentioned arises by necessity because Eq. 15-12d is a saturated model. The intercept is fitted before the slope because the intercept is the simpler concept; the intercept depends only upon the criterion, but the slope is a joint function of the predictor and the criterion. Consequently, the difference $G^2$ for the intercept term is $166.81 - 126.54$ or 40.27, and the slope adjusting for the intercept is $126.54 - 0$ or 126.54, both of which are significant. The first of these $G^2$ values establishes an overall preference, but the point of greater interest is that the $G^2$ for the slope is identical to its value in the log-linear model. However, the slope effect in the saturated model (the gender gap, $\beta_i$) is 0.80 or twice what it was in the log-linear model. This is because predictor-criterion models describe ratios of outcomes, whereas log-linear models describe how individual outcomes differ from 0.5. In a dichotomy, $\ln(p/q)$ will be twice $\ln(p/0.5)$, and so it will also be twice $\ln(q/0.5)$, but the corresponding $G^2$ values will be identical since both $\log(p/0.5)$ and $\log(q/0.5)$ contribute to the $G^2$ value in a predictor-criterion model.

Predictor-criterion models have fewer terms than their log-linear counterparts because they use only those terms that relate to the criterion. This model ignores any overall disparity between males and females. If the ratio of females to males were to change but their relative preferences were to remain the same, $\beta_i$ (0.80) would not change.

## Multiple Response Categories in Predictor-Criterion Models

In order to consider what happens when there are more than two response categories, it is necessary to consider three major cases:

**1** Multiple nominal levels of a single attribute, e.g., political party affiliation, including independents

**2** Multiple quantitative levels of a single dimension, e.g., got worse, remained the same, or improved in therapy

**3** Combinations of two or more attributes; e.g., an subject might be asked whether faint tones were presented to the left ear, right ear, both ears, or neither. Garner and Morton (1969) and Wickens and Olzak (1989) have studied judgments of this form. We will briefly describe the kind of analysis Wickens and Olzak performed. A later section will consider Ashby and Townsend's contributions, e.g., Ashby and Townsend (1986).

In all cases, the multiple levels are analyzed by combining a hypothesis matrix (also called a design matrix) representing the desired response effects with a hypothesis matrix representing the stimulus effects into an overall effect matrix. The same options exist for multiple response levels as exist for multiple stimulus levels (see the section "Multiple Levels on a Variable"). If the dependent variable is a composite of two separate responses, as in the example of the tones presented to the two ears, one may model each separate response plus the association of the two responses, which denotes whether the two responses are the same or different. In particular, the four response categories may be arranged as tone in (1) both ears, (2) left ear alone, (3) right ear alone, and (4) neither ear. The contrast of (1) + (2) versus (3) + (4) represents responses to the left-ear stimulus; the contrast of (1) + (3) versus (2) + (4) represents responses to the right-ear stimulus; and the contrast of (1) + (4) versus (2) + (3) (association) represents whether the two responses were the same or different.

Logically, response and stimulus associations are no different, and so the four stimuli may be partitioned in the same way. The data matrix contains 16 cells (4 stimuli by 4 responses). In the present case, the experimenter defines the frequencies of each of the 4 stimulus combinations, usually as equal, but these quantities may vary freely in nonexperimental settings. There are 12 remaining degrees of freedom. Three effects, each with 1 $df$, represent the intercepts or marginal effects, which are biases in using the response categories. For example, the subject may tend to say the left-ear stimulus was presented more often than it really occurred or favor same rather than different response combinations. The remaining 9 $df$ represent combinations of three stimulus effects and three response effects.

The direct relations between the left-ear stimulus and its response and between the right-ear stimulus and its response will probably be the strongest contingencies in terms of both $\beta$ and $G^2$. Once these effects and two separate response biases (but not their association) are included in the model, any other effects represent judgmental nonindependence. For example, whether or not a stimulus is presented to the left-ear may affect the accuracy of judging the right-ear stimulus. A tendency to use the same or different response categories (an association between the two marginal biases) also denotes lack of independence.

## Some Important Assumptions

Wickens (1989) describes three assumptions critical to the use of both $\chi^2$ and $G^2$. These also apply to descriptive measures.

1 The observations must be operationally independent of one another.
2 The observations must have the same distribution.
3 There must be a large number of observations.

Operational independence means that classifying one variable has no built-in influence on classifying the other even though the results may be empirically related. For example, patients given therapy A versus therapy B may either improve or not improve. It is assumed that the same standards are used to classify improvement in the two therapy groups, preferably by a blind method. Of course, the goal of the study is to see if there is a difference in improvement between the groups. As obvious as the requirement of operational independence is, it is often violated in practice. Violations can arise in many ways. For example, if the political poll illustrated Table 15-1 were to be conducted by having unbiased interviewers call up people, each call could be viewed as independent of the other calls. However, if interviewer biases affected their interviewing strategy, subjects interviewed by one interviewer might have something in common that subjects interviewed by another interviewer might not (one possibility in this case would be to include interviewers as a variable). Likewise, if people were interviewed in a group so that their answers could be overheard, there might be a tendency toward conformity.

The independence rule is often interpreted as requiring the observations to come from different individuals. This would eliminate many applications in which individual subjects are observed on many trials. For example, traditional psychophysics uses a small number of subjects, each of whom makes many judgments. Clearly, one would not wish to run $N$ individuals for one trial each. However, a composite data matrix will contain two sources of variability—between and within subjects. One possibility is to estimate parameters from individual subjects, average the estimates, and add the $G^2$ values. Although there are often clear departures from independence in a subject's repeated observations (e.g., their tendency to want to balance out responses), parameters obtained from individual subjects do not contain any between-subject variation and do not seem to do statistical "harm." The composite $G^2$ will have $N$ degrees of freedom. This approach is more conservative than simply using the aggregate data. Moreover, the variability in the parameter estimates describes the consistency of the effect over subjects: It makes a great deal of difference in interpretation whether a mean value of $\beta_{ij}$ of 0.1, for example, represents individual values ranging from 0.05 to 0.15, which would denote very high stability, versus from −0.05 to +0.35, in which case the composite would be of lesser value. If the number of parameters ($K$) is small and $N$ is large, the $G^2$ test itself can be bypassed in favor of parametric tests on the parameter. For example, an ordinary single-group $t$ test can evaluate the null hypothesis that the mean $\beta_{ij}$ is zero. Simply divide the obtained mean by the standard error of the mean (the standard deviation of the estimates divided by $N$). Mixing between- and within-subject errors also relates to assumption 2 since the two sources are probably of different magnitudes. Individual estimation does not really solve this problem completely if there are latent groups. For example, if the data in Table 15-1 was derived from a mixture of people with more versus less traditional values, any effect might hold differentially in the two groups. This is basically the problem of specification as in ordinary multiple regression (see Chapter 5).

Estimating parameters from individual subjects in more complex designs may be difficult when the number of parameters is large compared to the number of observations per subject. The second author suggests forming "supersubjects" by randomly pooling subjects. For example, Bernstein, Bissonnette, and Welch (1990) used a complex design involving 32 parameters with 50 subjects based upon 80 responses per subject. They could not estimate each subject's parameters. Five supersubject groups of 10 subjects each were formed. The standard deviations of each set of parameters were multiplied by $\sqrt{10}$ to estimate their variability over individual subjects, using the central limit theorem in reverse. One possible extension is to form groups on the basis of some external characteristic of interest to study the relation between this characteristic and relevant parameters. The logic parallels that of forming pseudofactors.

Finally, assumption 3 deals with the point that Eqs. 4-22 and 4-32 hold only in large samples—$G^2 = 2 \Sigma o\ [\ln(o/e)]$ is asymptotically distributed as chi-square. It is extremely difficult to say how many total observations are needed. The traditional caveat is five expected observations per cell. Thus, if one variable is at three levels, another is at four, and observations are equally divided among levels of both variables, the rule would dictate a minimum of (3)(4)(5) or 60 observations. However, Wickens' (1989, p. 29) suggests that this is too strict. Size becomes more important when there is an sharp imbalance in marginal frequencies. The appropriate strategy is to pool categories when there are too many categories for the number of observations. Two important considerations are that (1) the combined categories should make sense and (2) pooling with respect to one variable be done independently of the other variables in the analysis. For example, if one variable is levels of agreement with regard to an attitudinal item, it might make sense to pool "agree" and "strongly agree," but whether these two categories or "disagree" and "strongly disagree" or both are pooled should not depend upon what this variable is being related to.

As in other applications, unreliability of the classifications can attenuate relationships. This is particularly important to consider in predictor-criterion models for the same reason that it is important in ordinary regression: The model attributes error to the criterion rather than to the predictors, which may in fact be incorrect. This does not mean that one can ignore the issue in log-linear models.

### Log-linear Modeling and Item Response Theory

The logistic distribution was introduced in Chapter 2, and we have previously noted that the one-parameter logistic (Rasch) model in Chapter 10 may be written as a log-linear model [see Thissen, Steinberg, & Wainer (1992) who provide additional references]. In particular, the log probability of the response profile (vector) is a linear function of the item difficulties.

Let $\mathbf{X}$ denote a profile of responses such as "correct, correct, correct, incorrect, correct" on a five-item abilities test. It replaces the previous term $f_{ij}$ that was used to describe a two-dimensional table because there are now as many subscripts (dimensions) as there are items. Equation 15-13 describes the relationship between the probability of achieving a given profile and the log-linear parameters of a single group. It is slightly simpler to model probabilities instead of frequencies.

$$\ln[p(\mathbf{X})] = \Sigma\beta_i X_i + \beta_0 \tag{15-13}$$

$p(\mathbf{X})$ = probability of obtaining a given response profile
 ln = natural logarithm function
 $\beta_i$ = difficulty of item $i$
 $X_i$ = response to the ith item (correct vs. incorrect)
 $\beta_0$ = overall group ability

The units of measurement may be defined when there is only one group by fixing $\beta_1$ and $\beta_0$ at 0. The remaining $\beta_i$ values become the difficulties of the remaining items relative to the first item.

Equation 15-14 allows the model to examine differential item functioning (DIF) in two groups by including association terms that reflect differences in item difficulty between groups.

$$\ln[p(\mathbf{X})] = \Sigma\beta_i X_i + \beta_g + \Sigma\beta_{gi}g_{xi} \tag{15-14}$$

The quantity $\beta_g$ represents the skill of one group relative to that of another and controls for group differences in overall ability. The $\beta_{gi}g_{xi}$ are group-by-item associations. If they are present, one or more items varies in relative difficulty across groups. If these $\beta_{gi}g_{xi}$ terms are zero, Eq. 15-15 holds:

$$\ln[p(\mathbf{X})] = \Sigma\beta_i X_i + \beta_g \qquad (15\text{-}15)$$

The difference in $G^2$ between Eqs. 15-15 and 15-14 tests for DIF. Keep in mind that this assumes that the items vary only in difficulty and not in discrimination and that there is no guessing. More complex IRT models are not log linear in nature. If your interest is in these complex models, consider a program specifically designed for IRT, such as MULTILOG (Thissen, 1988). However, the methods of Chapters 6 through 9 will often tend to produce items whose discriminations are essentially the same.

There are certain similarities between IRT and categorical modeling, but the differences are equally important. In particular, IRT is latent variable modeling, categorical modeling is not, in general. However, there is much positive transfer in learning the two because of their joint use of log-linear relationships.

## More Specific Categorical Models

There are several more specific models that appear in certain categorical modeling applications. One such model is quasi-independence, which means that two variables are unrelated in the presence of structural zeros (i.e., fit Eq. 15-3 rather than the more general Eq. 15-4) but would be related if structural zeros were real, nonzero observations. For example, first and second choices among events may be independent when people cannot select the same stimulus twice, but they may be highly related when they are given this option.

Several interesting models arise when the rows and columns of a two-dimensional table have the same levels, e.g., when people are asked whether or not they would consider buying each of two brands of automobiles. In this case, the levels of each dimension (brand) are yes versus no. The cells contain the joint frequencies of the two judgments, e.g., the number of people who would buy both brands. Another example is to ask two clinicians to diagnose a series of patients as schizophrenic or not. Yet another is to obtain a transition matrix of first and second preferences. The latter is complicated. The diagonals of the matrix will probably contain structural zeros since a given stimulus cannot be both a first and a second choice, but these diagonals are relatively unimportant to the analysis. The tone detection experiment provides another example. The present discussion generalizes to more than two dimensions (e.g., to three or more brands of cars) and more than two levels, but we will limit discussion to dichotomous classifications at two levels.

The strongest possible relationship is symmetry—the matrix remains the same within sampling error when rows and columns are reversed; e.g., two brands of automobiles are judged equivalently, two clinicians perform equivalently, etc. This model formally states that $p_{ij} = p_{ji}$ for all values of $i$ and $j$. Given symmetry, the best estimate of the expected values of $p_{ij}$ and $p_{ji}$ is their corresponding sample average. If each factor has $K$ levels, the complete table has $K^2$ entries. However, the $K$ diagonal values are unimportant to the model, and so there are $K(K - 1)$ observed quantities. Half of these are constrained to equal the other half. Consequently, there are $K(K - 1)/2$ constraints, leaving $K(K - 1)/2$ degrees of freedom to test the model.

Deviations from symmetry can result from either differential association or lack of marginal homogeneity. Differential association means that the effect of $i$ upon $j$ ($\beta_{ij}$) differs from the effect of $j$ upon $i$ ($\beta_{ji}$) independently of marginal (overall) preferences. For example, suppose people have to make a second choice of a vegetable from a menu after being told that their first choice is unavailable. Differential association means that people are more likely to choose corn after initially choosing string beans, or vice versa, controlling for overall preference. In contrast, marginal homogeneity implies that the marginal distributions are the same for rows and columns. Thus, two clinicians might use diagnostic categories with the same frequency, or the overall preference for two automobiles may be the same. Conversely, if one clinician is more likely to use a given diagnostic category than another or one automobile is more popular, the result will be marginal heterogeneity. Marginal homogeneity is rather unlikely in a transition matrix since something with a very high probability of being a first choice has a low chance of being a second choice. In the extreme, a stimulus that is always the first choice will never be the second choice. This model has $K - 1$ degrees of freedom. Data that do not fit a symmetry model because of marginal heterogeneity but do not have differential association fit a quasi-symmetry model which has $(K - 2)$ $(K - 1)/2$ degrees of freedom. Testing for quasi-symmetry is relatively difficult to describe. See Wickens (1989).

## Logistic Regression

Logistic regression relates levels of a quantitative predictor to a categorical response. It began as a way to obtain dose-response curves relating drug dosage to a target response such as symptom alleviation. Its only difference from previously considered predictor-criterion models is that numeric values of the predictor replace a series of contrasts. Consequently, the predictor employs 1 $df$ rather than $K - 1$ degrees of freedom. Both are therefore part of the more general class of linear models. This predictor may also be combined with other predictors (quantitative or nominal) in the overall analysis. For example, one can study the joint effects of varying drug dosage and the presence or absence of psychotherapy upon symptom remission. The term "logistic regression" describes the mathematical function fit to the relation between the continuous variables. This is the same logistic function introduced in Eq. 2-6 and discussed extensively in Chapter 10. It may be written as Eq. 15-16 in terms of the probability of $X$:

$$p(X) = \frac{e^{bX + a}}{1 + e^{bX + a}} \qquad (15\text{-}16)$$

As usual, $e = 2.71828+$. As in ordinary regression, $b$ is a slope parameter and $a$ is an intercept parameter. Indeed, some simple algebra will make this equation look just like a regression equation, $Y = bX + a$.

$$p(X)(1 + e^{bX+a}) = e^{bX+a}$$
$$p(X) + p(X)e^{bX+a} = e^{bX+a}$$
$$p(X) = e^{bX+a} - p(X)e^{bX+a}$$
$$= e^{bX+a}[1 - p(X)]$$
$$\frac{p(X)}{1 - p(X)} = e^{bX+a}$$

Since the natural logarithm (ln) is the inverse of the exponential transformation, $\ln e^X = e^{\ln(X)} = X$ and $\ln\{p(X)/[1 - p(X)]\} = \text{logit } X$, taking natural logarithms of both sides produces the desired outcome, Eq. 15-17.

$$\ln\left[\frac{p(X)}{1 - p(X)}\right] = \text{logit } X = bX + a \qquad (15\text{-}17)$$

In other words, the logit of $X$ is a linear function of $X$. Figure 15-1 relates $p(X)$ to logit $X$. Like many other functions used in curve fitting (e.g., the cumulative normal distribution), it is linear over much of its range except at the extremes of $p(X)$ where, unfortunately, the data are least likely to be stable.

The six points in the psychometric function in Fig. 2-2 may be fit as an example using a program like SAS PROC CATMOD. These paired values are (185, 0.08), (190, 0.15), (195, 0.28), (205, 0.80), (210, 0.85), and (215, 0.95). The resulting estimate is logit $X = 0.18X$ - 36.89. Various terms like the absolute threshold discussed in Chapter 2 may be derived from the parameter estimates.

**FIGURE 15-1**    Logit $X$ as a function of $p(x)$.

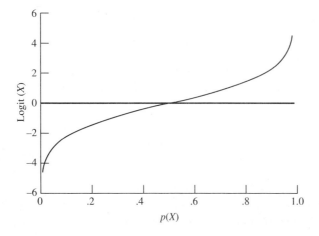

### Comparing Groups with Logistic Regression

Logistic regression is especially useful in comparing functions across groups. For example, assume the dosage of a drug ($X$) has been varied to determine its effectiveness, e.g., whether or not patients improve. Denote the probability of a target response such as improvement as $p$. Although one might study a single new drug when the outcome of conventional treatment is well known, it is more common to compare a drug with a control (placebo) medication or another drug. The possible results of comparing the two drugs form a hierarchy of models:

**1** Logit $X = 0$. The regression lines for both drugs are independent of dosage and $p = .5$. This model implies that (a) both drugs are ineffectual and (b) the baseline probability of the target response is .5.

**2** Logit $X = a$, where $a \neq 0$. The regression lines for both drugs are independent of dosage at a common $p \neq .5$. Both drugs are still ineffectual, but the target response has some probability other than .5.

**3** Logit $X = bX + a$. The regression lines for both drugs have identical nonzero slopes with dosages. This is unlikely when one of the drugs is a placebo, but it may arise from comparing two potentially active drugs.

**4** Logit $X = bX + a_g$. The intercepts ($a_g$) differ for the drugs, but their slopes are the same, and so the regression lines are parallel. The drugs differ in threshold for the criterion response, but changes in dosage are equally effective. This too is more likely when both drugs are potentially active.

**5** Logit $X = b_g X + a_g$. Both the drug slopes ($b_g$) and intercepts ($a_g$) are different; the drugs differ in effectiveness.

The outcomes are diagrammed in Fig. 15-2.

Within each model, special cases may exist of importance to specific applications. For example, given that the groups have a common slope and intercept (model 3), a test that $a = 0$ ($p = .5$) may be relevant. Second, if model 5 holds, perhaps only one of the two drugs is effective, the case of interest when the other drug is a placebo. Likewise, given different slopes (model 5), one may wish to test for equal intercepts and, perhaps, that this common value of $a$ is 0. Testing the five models and these additional cases uses principles derived from hierarchical evaluation of residual $G^2$ values previously discussed.

### An Illustrative Problem

This section involves a somewhat more complex example using real data obtained from 300 male and female adolescents of African-American or Hispanic ethnicity. They were weighed; their height was measured, and they were asked whether or not they considered themselves overweight as part of an overall study of adolescent health care. The data were obtained by Prof. Judith Keith at a series of publicly supported clinics located in Dallas, Texas. Although there are perhaps better ways to define degrees of over- or underweight, we used the simple ratio of weight (in kilograms) to height (in centimeters) along with gender and ethnicity to predict self-perception of

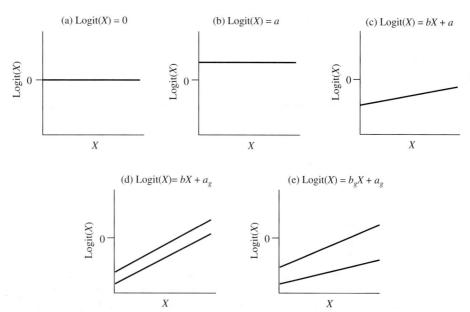

**FIGURE 15-2** Five logistic regression models: (*a*) logit $X = 0$ (homogeneity with $p(X) = .5$); (*b*) logit $X = a$ (homogeneity with $p(X) \neq .5$); (*c*) logit $X = bX + a$ (common slopes and intercepts); (*d*) logit $X = bX + a_g$ (common slope, separate intercepts); and (*e*) Logit $X = b_g X + a_g$ (separate slopes and intercepts).

obesity. These ratios ranged from 1.19 to 4.18. The sample was 62 percent African American versus 38 percent Hispanic and 23 percent male versus 77 percent female. Table 15-4 lists the residual $G^2$ values and the associated degrees of freedom arising from the successive models identified as A, B, . . ., I.

The design extracts an overall linear trend, gender differences, ethnicity differences, and all possible associations. Each residual $G^2$ value is subtracted from its predecessor to produce the difference $G^2$ values in Table 15-5. Thus, the difference in $G^2$ for a model in which $p$ is a free parameter (299.64) and the $G^2$ value obtained when $p$ is fixed at .5 (384.88) tests the hypothesis that half of the subjects consider themselves overweight and half consider themselves underweight, ignoring weight/height ratio, gender, and ethnicity. This $G^2$ (85.24) is highly significant with 1 *df*, and so this hypothesis may be rejected.

Model 1 ($p = .5$) is not of great interest since there is no reason to think that half the population considers themselves overweight. The associated value of $\beta$ (−1.32) denotes that 21 percent of the sample thought themselves overweight. However, this is simply the logit of the observed proportion in the null model. The slope effect (difference $G^2 = 7.57$) denotes that larger weight/height ratios are associated with higher probabilities of self-reported overweight, an expected outcome. The most interesting finding is the ethnicity effect: African Americans were more likely to consider themselves obese than Hispanics at a given weight/height ratio (difference $G^2 = 7.40$, all

TABLE 15-4 RESIDUAL $G^2$ VALUES REFLECTING PERCEPTIONS OF BEING OVERWEIGHT AS A FUNCTION OF WEIGHT/HEIGHT RATIO, RACE, AND GENDER

| Adjustment | $G^2$ | df |
|---|---|---|
| A. None | 384.88 | 272 |
| B. Intercept | 299.64 | 271 |
| C. Slope (W/H ratio) | 292.07 | 270 |
| D. Gender | 291.39 | 269 |
| E. Ethnicity | 283.68 | 268 |
| F. Gender by ethnicity | 283.20 | 267 |
| G. Slope by gender | 283.19 | 266 |
| H. Slope by ethnicity | 282.70 | 265 |
| I. Slope by gender by ethnicity | 282.68 | 264 |

Note: Adjustments described are cumulative; e.g., the slope adjustment also includes the intercept adjustment.

$p < .01$). It is also of interest to note that there was no effect of gender; adolescent males and females used the same criteria for obesity. The slope and ethnicity effects in the final model estimates were 0.97 and 0.86. The latter value of $\beta$ denotes a fairly large group difference: At any given weight/height ratio, African Americans were 2.36 times as likely to consider themselves obese as Hispanics.

## A Note on Residuals

Although a goal of categorical modeling is to find a nonsaturated model in which the residual is nonsignificant, many applications of logistic regression pose a hazard if one relies too heavily upon this criterion. The number of degrees of freedom available to test alternatives models depends upon the number of cells and not the number of observations. In previous categorical models, the number of cells was the product of the number of levels of each variable. Typically, the residual in a model with categorical

TABLE 15-5 DIFFERENCE $G^2$ VALUES CORRESPONDING TO THE ADJUSTMENTS OF TABLE 15.4

| Effect | How computed | $G^2$ |
|---|---|---|
| Intercept | A – B = (384.88 – 299.64) = | 85.24*** |
| Slope (W/H ratio) | B – C = (299.64 – 292.07) = | 7.57** |
| Gender (Gen.) | C – D = (292.07 – 291.38) = | 0.69 |
| Ethnicity (Eth.) | D – E = (291.39 – 283.68) = | 7.40** |
| Gen. by Eth. | E – F = (283.68 – 283.20) = | 0.48 |
| Slope by Gen. | F – G = (283.20 – 283.19) = | 0.01 |
| Slope by Eth. | G – H = (283.19 – 282.70) = | 0.49 |
| Slope by Gen. by Eth. | H – I = (282.70 – 282.68) = | 0.02 |

*$p < .05$.
**$p < .01$.
***$p < .001$.

predictors has relatively few degrees of freedom, perhaps six or less. This may be the case in logistic regression if the continuous variable achieves a relatively small number of levels, as when drug dosage is manipulated by the experimenter.

However, the number of distinct levels may be quite large when they occur naturally, as was the case in our perceived obesity example. The 300 subjects produced 278 distinct weight/height ratios, and the various residual terms at different stages had many (260+) degrees of freedom. This residual contains a mixture of random error and systematic effects, e.g., nonlinearity. Suitable procedures exist for examining many of these systematic components. However, the critical point is that a residual may be nonsignificant yet bury an important influence, and so a nonsignificant residual may be relatively meaningless when it is based upon many degrees of freedom.

### Predicting Categorical Criteria

We have now considered three ways to model a categorical criterion as a weighted linear combination of predictors: (1) ordinary regression (Chapter 5), (2) discriminant analysis (Chapter 14), and (3) categorical modeling. Keeping in mind that there are several variations upon each procedure, it is useful to compare and contrast them. We begin by assuming that the criterion is dichotomous. We will denote these levels as 1 and 0 and their associated probabilities as $p$ and $q$.

**1** Ordinary regression and discriminant analyses typically employ unweighted least-squares estimation, whereas categorical modeling usually uses maximum likelihood or generalized least squares. The similarities and differences among them were discussed in Chapter 4. It is also important to mention regression based upon minimum chi-square (see Marascuillo & Levin, 1983). This has been specifically suggested for regressing predictors upon a dichotomous criterion. It overcomes the problem that the error variance will not be constant for different values of the predictor, as ordinary least-squares regression assumes. The actual error variance will in fact be binomial, equaling $pq$, reaching a maximum at $p = q = .5$ and decreasing as $p$, and therefore $q$, become more extreme.

**2** Ordinary regression and categorical modeling are both concerned with prediction, but they predict different quantities. Regression is concerned with predicting values that correspond to group membership (0 versus 1), making a linear combination of the predictors $(z'_y)$, fall as close to the obtained outcomes $(z_y)$ as possible. Unfortunately, when these predicted values are negative or exceed +1, they are difficult to interpret. Different forms of categorical modeling allow different entities to be predicted, but it is most common to predict either the natural logarithm of the probability of target group membership or, equivalently, its logit. Consequently, the results are bound to meaningful values in all cases. Discriminant analysis, in contrast to both, is concerned with classification, i.e., making the groups as homogeneous as possible with respect to the linear combination. Specifically, the algorithm maximizes the ratio of between-group variation to within-group variation. However, membership probabilities can be inferred in several different ways from discriminant data, as discussed in most multivariate analysis texts (see the Suggested Additional Readings for Chapter 11).

Discriminant analysis programs also typically allow the user to incorporate Bayesian considerations (Chapter 4): (a) prior probabilities of group membership, (b) rewards for correct classification, and (c) penalties for misclassification.

**3** Even though ordinary regression and discriminant analyses employ different criteria to form linear combinations, their weightings will be equivalent. This does not mean identical, because regression produces a unique set of weights, and discriminant analysis does not. A given form of categorical modeling also produces a unique set of weights, but these will differ, in general, from ordinary regression and discriminant weights.

**4** The significance test for $R^2$ in ordinary regression is equivalent to the overall significance test in discriminant analysis but, again, both differ from the test used in categorical modeling.

**5** Because it is oriented toward classification, commercial discriminant analysis programs provide extensive output about its success. Categorical modeling programs like SAS PROC CATMOD also provide relevant information. However, programs for ordinary regression do not.

**6** Discriminant analysis provides explicit ways of assessing and dealing with heteroscedasticity. Both ordinary regression and categorical modeling ignore this issue. We will consider some of the substantive consequences in the next major section.

If there are more than two groups, ordinary regression is basically inappropriate. If the groups are defined nominally, the results will depend upon the order of the numbers arbitrarily given them. Even if they fall along a continuum, regression will capture the nature of the differences only when (1) differences are completely concentrated (in the sense of Chapter 14) along a single dimension and (2) the groups are equally spaced along this dimension. In addition, there are several overall significance tests suggested for use in discriminant analysis that may lead to different results, but hypothesis testing in categorical modeling is somewhat less equivocal. In general, discriminant analysis and categorical modeling are both suited to diffuse and concentrated structures. Standard multivariate texts also describe how indices of concentration can be obtained from the data.

In general, the choice breaks down to the use of discriminant analysis versus categorical modeling. Obtaining similar results from both adds to the confidence that one would have in either alone. You will probably find one or the other is more convenient for your particular applications, but some familiarity with both is highly recommended. For example, logistic regression is the most appropriate way to compare intercepts and slopes over groups when the criterion is categorical. To repeat, discriminant analysis deals more directly with classification, and categorical modeling deals more directly with estimating the probability of group membership. However, either can be used for the other goal with some effort.

## BINARY CLASSIFICATION

Chapter 2 introduced the very common problem of binary classification in which a stimulus assumes two levels and subjects attempt to associate each level with its own, correct category. One particular form of this problem is to judge the presence versus absence of some attribute. The original situation involved detecting a faint sensory event such as a tone, but it was later applied to various judgments, including those made by presumed experts, such as diagnosing a particular condition. A major issue is to separate sensitivity or ability to make a correct choice from or differential use of response categories by means of independent indices. Thus, suppose a subject makes the same discrimination under two conditions but is induced to report the attribute's presence when uncertain in one case but not in the other. The sensitivity index should not change, but the bias index should. The logic, known as the theory of signal detection (TSD), emerged from auditory psychophysics (Chapter 2), statistical decision theory (Chapter 4), and Thurstone scaling (see Chapter 2). Luce (1959a, 1963) developed an alternative model that is empirically indistinguishable from those based upon Thurstone's. Macmillan and Creelman (1991) present the most current treatment of this topic.

The need to separate response bias from sensitivity arises in a variety of applied problems. For example, a consultant may suggest individuals not be hired because of their potential "dishonesty." An error is to assess the consultant's proficiency by simply looking at the probability of correctly identifying an individual as dishonest. This makes no sense in isolation; it may be reduced to an absurdity if the consultant simply calls every job candidate dishonest. Every dishonest individual will be correctly identified, but every honest individual will be incorrectly called dishonest, and nobody will be hired. We now turn to a consideration of this general issue.

## Classical Signal Detection

Consider a yes-no task in which there are two possible events:

**1** A faint tone (signal) is embedded in noise on signal-plus-noise $(s + n)$ trials versus
**2** The signal is absent on noise $(n)$ trials.

The subject is asked to say yes on $s + n$ trials and no on $n$ trials. Table 15-6 describes the four possible outcomes. Note its similarity to Table 9-2. Identical logic applies to stimuli presented to other sensory modalities and to discriminations between two affirmative stimuli. It is also possible to apply the logic of TSD to other judgmental tasks. Two that are particular important are the following.

**1** Rating tasks in which the subject is allowed to express degrees of confidence about the judgment.
**2** Forced-choice tasks in which there are multiple observation intervals. The subject is asked to say which one contains the signal. For example, a visual stimulus could

**TABLE 15-6**  A 2 × 2 DECISION MATRIX FOR A YES-NO SIGNAL DETECTION TASK

| | Response | |
|---|---|---|
| Stimulus | Yes | No |
| Signal plus noise, $s + n$ | $f_{11}$ (hit) | $f_{12}$ (miss) |
| Noise, $n$ | $f_{21}$ (false alarm) | $f_{22}$ (correct rejection) |

*Note*: The hit rate is $f_{11}/(f_{11} + f_{12})$, and the false alarm rate is $f_{21}/(f_{21} + f_{22})$.

be presented either above or below fixation and the subject asked where. Response bi-ases usually play less of a role in forced-choice tasks than in yes-no tasks.

TSD stresses the hit rate and the false alarm rate, which are the conditional proba-bilities of saying yes on $s + n$ trials and on $n$ trials, respectively. The complementary miss rate and correct rejection rate of saying no are unnecessary because of their re-dundancy. Note the difference between TSD and categorical modeling, which uses cell and marginal probabilities rather than conditional probabilities. We will relate the two later in this section.

Many models have been developed to provide the desired sensitivity and bias para-meters in the yes-no task in Table 15-6 from the hit rate and the false alarm rate. Chap-ter 2 considered Case V of Thurstone scaling. Its three main assumptions were:

1  Stimuli varied along one dimension.
2  Their discriminal dispersions were assumed independent of one another.
3  Their discriminal dispersions were further assumed to be equal.

We will first show how this leads to one TSD model, the equal variance Gaussian. This is by far the simplest and most widely used model. We will then drop assumption 3 to obtain the unequal variance Gaussian model, which is also important. In the equal variance Gaussian model, noise is assumed to be normally distributed on an interval intensity (strength) axis, $X$ (many deductions require only that $X$ be ordinal). Let the mean of the noise ($n$) distribution be 0 on this scale and let its standard deviation be 1 to define one unit. Now assume that the signal increments the noise by a constant amount on each trial. Adding a constant to a random variable such as noise provides the signal plus noise ($s + n$) distribution and shifts the distribution by that constant. However, it does not affect its variability. It is standard practice to denote this incre-ment as $d'$. The two distributions reflect the subjects' varied sensory experience over trials in response to fixed stimuli.

In order to convert these into "yes" and "no" responses, the subject establishes a criterion at some point along $X$ as depicted in Fig. 15-3 (more specific forms of the model further predict the best location for this criterion based upon the probabilities of the two stimulus alternatives and the consequences of the responses). Call this location $X_c$. If a given observation ($X_i$) falls at or to the right of the criterion ($X_i \geq X_c$), the sub-ject says yes, and if it falls to the left of the criterion ($X_i < X_c$), the subject says no. The hit rate is simply the area under the $s + n$ distribution to the right of $X_c$, and the false alarm rate is simply the area under the $n$ distribution to the right of $X_c$. The miss rate is therefore the area under the $s + n$ distribution to the left of $X_c$, and the correct rejection rate is the area under the $n$ distribution to the left of $X_c$. In the present case, $d'$ is 1.0 and $X_c$ is at +.1. Because of the location of $X_c$, the subject's hit rate will be .82, and the false alarm rate will be .46. This is derivable from normal curve statistics—$X_c$ is 0.9 z-score units below the mean of the $s + n$ distribution and 0.1 unit above the mean of the $n$ distribution. If the two stimuli are equally probable, the subject will say yes (0.82 + 0.46)/2 = 64 percent of the time and no 36 percent of the time. Note that the subject says yes less often as the criterion moves to the right because less of each distribution falls to its right. Conversely, the subject will say yes more often as it moves to the left. You can verify these relationships yourself by working with the figure.

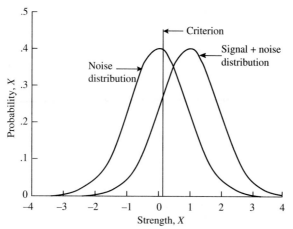

**FIGURE 15-3**   The location of a criterion ($X_c$) relative to a signal-plus-noise ($s + n$) and a noise ($n$) distribution in the equal variance Gaussian signal detection model.

A receiver operating characteristic (ROC) curve describes the hit rate as a function of the false alarm rate for different criteria produced by having the subject say yes more or less often under different conditions. ROC curves are often more informative when hit and false alarm rates are expressed as $z$ scores because the relationship between them becomes linear with a slope of $+1$ if there is equal variance. Because the slope is $+1$, the subject's sensitivity can be defined as $d' = z$(hit rate) $- z$(false alarm rate), regardless of where the criterion is located.

An equally important consequence is that the ratio of the ordinate of the $s + n$ distribution ($Y_{s+n}$) to the ordinate of the $n$ distribution ($Y_n$) increases monotonically as $X_c$ moves to the right. This ratio describes the likelihood of signal relative to noise. The ratio is called beta ($\beta$), but it is not a regression weight. In other words, $\beta$ and $X$ are monotonically related—the more conservative the criterion for saying yes (the further it is to the right), the more probable it is that yes will be correct. Moreover, $\beta$ is a standard measure of bias. Subjects, who need not even understand the concept of likelihood, can therefore choose according to the likelihood principle by responding in terms of $X$.

Figure 15-4 describes the equal variance ROC curve. Figure 15-4*a* employs probabilities, and Fig. 15-4*b* employs $z$ transformations. The diagonal line in Fig. 15-4*a* denotes chance performance (the hit rate equals the false alarm rate). The likelihood ratio at the criterion of 0.1 ($\beta$) is .27/.40 or .68. Large ratios imply that the criterion is to the right, where hit and false alarm rates will both be low.

It is often more reasonable to assume that both $s$ and $n$ vary over trials, especially when $s$ is not a single physical event but a member of a class of events. For example, recognition memory tasks involve exposing subjects to a list of words during a training period. During a subsequent test phase, subjects are given a second list containing a mixture of words presented during the training phase (old words) and new words which they attempt to classify. Signal detection approaches to this task assume that the familiarity of a word can be defined along a strength continuum and that training in-

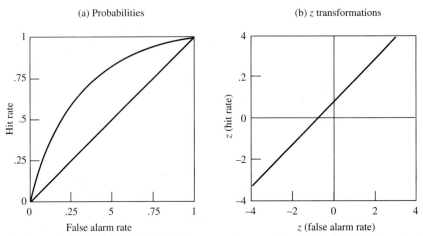

**FIGURE 15-4**   Receiver operating characteristic (ROC) curves for the equal variance Gaussian signal detection model: (*a*) probabilities and (*b*) *z* transformations.

crements the strengths of old words. This assumption is reasonable, and some form of signal detection seems warranted to separate sensitivity about the discrimination from a bias in saying "old" versus "new". However, it is less reasonable to assume that each old word's familiarity is incremented by exactly the same amount. To the extent that the increment varies over words, an equal variance model will not hold. In general, the equal variance model is quite unlikely to hold whenever the stimuli are heterogeneous; the $s + n$ distribution will be the more variable. One should check results, using methods discussed in works listed the Suggested Additional Readings, most specifically Macmillan and Creelman (1991), before using the $d'$ measure, which evaluates only the mean difference and ignores any variance difference. Assuming an equal variance model when there is a large disparity in variance may seriously confound sensitivity and bias.

Figure 15-5 illustrates the unequal variance Gaussian model when the variance of the signal-plus-noise distribution exceeds the variance of the noise distribution, and Fig. 15-6 shows the resulting ROC curves. The standard deviation of $s + n$ in these figures was made twice the standard deviation of $n$. This is unusually large but makes the results clearer. The important points are that (1) the ROC curve based upon probabilities dips below the chance diagonal and (2) the $z$-transformed ROC curve slopes downward. The slope in fact equals the ratio of the standard deviation of the $n$ distribution to the standard deviation of the $s + n$ distribution (0.5). This downward slope means that the particular value of $d'$ computed from the difference in $z$-transformed hit and false alarm rates varies with the criterion ($X_c$) generating it.

A related consequence is that strength ($X$) and signal likelihood will no longer be monotonically related, as they were under equal variance. Signal is more likely at both low and high values of $X$ (approximately $-2.0$ and $0.5$ in the present case) so that a subject who employs a single value of $X_c$ will be systematically in error. In order to make most effective use of the data, the subject must transform the data into some form of deviation from the point at which noise is most likely.

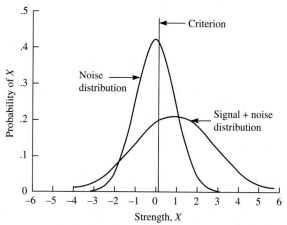

**FIGURE 15-5** The location of a criterion ($X_c$) relative to a signal-plus-noise ($s + n$) and a noise ($n$) distribution in the unequal variance Gaussian signal detection model.

## Categorical Modeling Approaches to the Equal Variance Gaussian Model

The effect magnitudes of a categorical model can be used to infer sensitivity and bias in the equal variance Gaussian case. This may be accomplished using either a log-linear or a predictor-criterion approach. We will illustrate the latter. The intercept parameter predicting yes versus no from signal plus noise versus noise measures bias, and the association parameter measures sensitivity. One consideration is whether the indices should be hierarchical or simultaneous. Thus, one could (1) estimate the intercept, ignoring the slope, and then estimate the slope adjusting for the intercept; or

**FIGURE 15-6** Receiver operating characteristic (ROC) curves for the unequal variance Gaussian signal detection model: (a) probabilities and (b) z transformations.

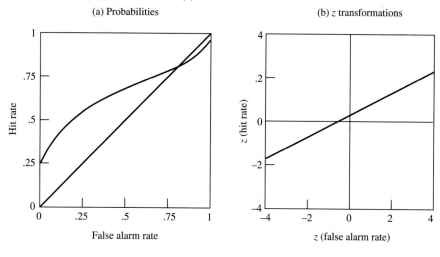

(2) estimate both parameters from the same model. Both are reasonable possibilities. Macmillan and Creelman (1990) discuss this problem in detail. The data must at least approximately conform to an equal variance model. The second author has conducted computer simulations indicating that the larger the $s + n$ variance is relative to the $n$ variance, the more the bias is underestimated and the sensitivity is overestimated. Categorical modeling is especially useful when there are additional variables in the study (for an example, see Bernstein et al., 1990).

## General Recognition Theory

Although we have not compared them explicitly, we have presented three general approaches to scaling stimuli and people.

**1** Stimuli are represented as points in a mathematical space that is usually, but not necessarily, Euclidian. As mathematical points, they occupy *no* space. This is a purely geometric and vector-based approach exemplified by factor analysis and MDS.

**2** Stimuli are represented as equal distributions. This was depicted multidimensionally in discriminant analysis (Fig. 14-6) and unidimensionally in the equal variance Gaussian model (Fig. 15-3). Stimuli are therefore inherently ambiguous, but equally so.

**3** Stimuli are represented as unequal distributions. This is depicted unidimensionally in Fig. 15-5, but the possibility of a multidimensional representation was raised in passing in the discussion of discriminant analysis in Chapter 14. Stimuli are assumed to vary with respect to the clarity of their definition. "Equal" and "unequal" apply simply to variance in the forms of TSD we have presented so far. However, the concept also applies to multidimensional differences in correlation magnitude.

Treating stimuli (or people) as points has an important simplicity, but the resulting constancy may be questioned, as it was in TSD and other models. The possibility of variation that is explicit in the two latter representations has clear appeal. However, geometric and equal distribution representations make relatively similar predictions compared to unequal distribution representations.

The consequences of treating distributions as unequal have been most explicitly considered as part of general recognition theory (Ashby, 1988, 1989; Ashby & Gott, 1988; Ashby & Maddox, 1990; Ashby & Perrin, 1988; Ashby & Townsend, 1986, also see Eriksen, 1960; Garner, 1974; Garner & Morton, 1969; Hake, Faust, McIntyre, & Murray, 1967; Olzak & Wickens, 1983; Wickens & Olzak, 1989). Information theory (Garner, 1962; Miller, 1956) and, especially, Thurstone scaling are important precursors. The topic concerns the ability of subjects to judge stimuli that vary along two or more dimensions, e.g., to simultaneously judge heights and widths of rectangles that vary in each dimension or to judge workers' competence independently of their physical attractiveness. These dimensions need not vary independently of one another, but this is ordinarily the case in experiments unless the experimenter wishes to study the effects of dimensional correlations (redundancy) upon judgments. We will use the term "dimension" in discussion, although many authors use the term "feature" or "attribute" when a property such as "wearing glasses" is presence or absence and so the "dimension" is dichotomous. We will assume for purposes of discussion that a subject is shown a series of rectangles that vary in height and width and is asked to judge each dimension, a task that is similar to Ashby and Townsend's. We will assume that the issue is one of accuracy of judgment, although reaction time is also a commonly used measure. The following are common ways to obtain these judgments. In all cases, the physical differences in height and width might or might not be equal, but they must be chosen to preclude perfect discrimination.

**1** In a complete rating task, the number of responses per dimension exceeds the number of stimulus levels per dimension, and so the subject might be asked to judge each dimension to the nearest fraction of an inch on separate rating scales even though only a few levels are employed.

**2** In a complete identification task, the number of stimulus levels and response levels per dimension are equal. The most important of such tasks is the simplest—stimuli and responses are both dichotomies. Thus, there might be four rectangles (short-narrow, short-wide, tall-narrow, and tall-wide).

**3** In a categorization task, the number of stimulus levels per dimension exceeds the number of responses per dimension, so that the subject might be asked to dichotomize or trichotomize stimuli that vary over several levels.

**4** In a filtering task, subjects judge one dimension and ignore the other, but both vary randomly as in the above tasks.

**5** In a condensation task, subjects respond to a combination of the two as alternative to these independent judgments. For example, they may be asked to place tall-narrow and short-wide rectangles in one pile and short-narrow and tall-wide rectangles in a second pile.

**6** In control task, subjects judge each dimension when the other is held constant.

Garner (cf. Garner, 1974) introduced an important distinction involving integral versus separable dimensions. Integral dimensions, such as hue (color) and lightness are perceived in an interdependent manner despite being varied independently. Condensation is relatively easy, but filtering is difficult. Conversely, separable dimensions like size and shape can be readily separated, and so filtering is easy, but condensation is difficult. Integrality and separability are not distinct classes—a given pair of dimensions generally falls along a continuum.

General recognition theory begins with the basic assumption of discriminal dispersions as made in Thurstone scaling and TSD. We will let $X$ and $Y$ denote the two physical dimensions (i.e., heights and widths) and $x$ and $y$ denote their internal (psychological) representations. Any given rectangle has a unique $X$ and $Y$ value (e.g., 3 inches by 4 inches), but the $x$ and $y$ values it evokes are random variables over trials. It is further assumed that random variation in $x$ and $y$ has a bivariate normal distribution, as discussed in the section titled "Discriminant Analysis" in Chapter 14 and in standard multivariate textbooks. The probability that a given stimulus (A) (e.g., the short-narrow rectangle) will fall at a given point in space is denoted $f_A(x, y)$, where $f$ is the bivariate normal distribution. Each stimulus distribution has an $x$ and a $y$ location (mean), a $x$ and a $y$ standard deviation, and a covariance or correlation. Figure 15-7 illustrates two of the possible forms the elliptical scatter may assume for a given stimu-

(a) $X$ and $Y$ are independent

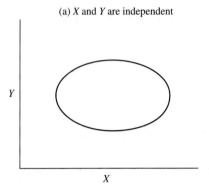

(b) $X$ and $Y$ are positively correlated

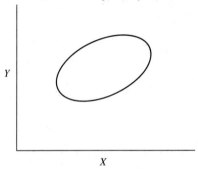

**FIGURE 15-7**   Elliptical scatter associated with bivariate normal error. (*a*) Independent error but greater error along the *x* dimension. (*b*) Positively correlated error.

lus. Although the axes are labeled $X$ and $Y$ because the units are physical, the scatter occurs psychologically in $x$ and $y$. Figure 15-7*a* illustrates independent error that is greater along the $X$ dimension than the $Y$ dimension. Figure 15-7*b* illustrates positively correlated error between $x$ and $y$ (negative correlated error is also possible though not shown). The amount and direction of error correlation, if any, is extremely important and defines the perceptual component of the theory.

By extension from signal detection theory, criteria are placed along the two dimensions to provide response categories and define regions of the 2-space. Consequently, there is a short-narrow region, a short-wide region, a tall-narrow region, and a tall-wide region. These may or may not have equal areas. The properties of these criteria and their associated regions constitute the decisional portion of the model.

Figure 15-8*a* is an important special case of the model. This outcome illustrates both perceptual and decisional independence:

**1** The major axis of the elliptical scatter in each stimulus is parallel to one of the axes defining the physical dimensions, and the minor axis is parallel to the second axis. Consequently there is no within-group correlation between perceived dimen-

(a) Perceptual independence

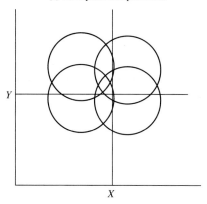

(b) Negative within-group correlations

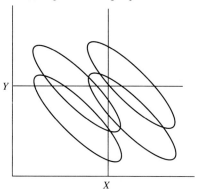

**FIGURE 15-8** (*a*) Contours of equal probability under complete independence. (*b*) Lack of perceptual independence (negatively correlated perceptual noise) with decisional independence.

sions. In this case, the major axis is oriented vertically, but it could just as well be oriented horizontally or the scatter plot could be circular. The main point is that there is no covariation in the random error—perceived variation in height is independent of perceived variation in width. Figure 15-8*b* illustrates a violation of perceptual independence due to the correlation between perceived height and perceived width.

**2** The stimuli therefore all have the same shape, i.e., are homoscedastic.

**3** The scatter plot centroids have a rectangular pattern. Ashby and Townsend term this rectangularity "dimensional independence." This outcome is a multidimensional extension of Thurstone's Case V. Both homoscedasticity and rectangularity are necessary because departures from decisional independence may arise from either heteroscedasticity or nonrectangularity even though the correlations may be the same for all combinations (Fig. 15-9 illustrates these two effects). Three consequences follow if there is both perceptual and decisional independence: (a) "perceptual separability" means the perceptual effect of one dimension is independent of the level of the other dimension (varying height has the same perceptual effect on both wide and narrow

(a) Differences in correlation magnitude

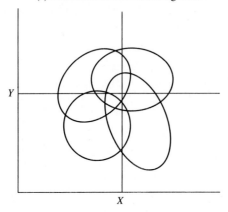

(b) Dimensional interdependence with
perceptual interdependence

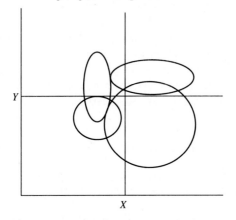

**FIGURE 15-9**    (*a*) Lack of perceptual separability—heteroscedasticity (differences in the variance-covariance matrices produced by the stimuli). (*b*) Lack of rectangularity due to dimensional interdependence with perceptual independence.

rectangles); (b) "sampling independence" means the two accuracies are independent of one another—accuracy in judging the dimensions jointly is the product of their separate accuracies (the probability of correctly identifying a tall-narrow rectangle is the product of the probabilities of identifying it as tall and as narrow), and (c) "marginal response invariance" means that the accuracy in judging one dimension is the same for different levels of the second dimension (the accuracy in judging tall rectangles is the same for wide and narrow rectangles). Outcomes b and c, but not outcome a, involve the subject's decision criteria.

    **4** The decision criteria for a given dimension are perpendicular to that dimension because of decisional separability. For example, assume that the locations of the tall and short stimulus means are at 1 and 0 along the subjective height dimension. The criterion need not be placed at 0.5 along this axis—the subject may have a response bias—but it must be at the same point for both wide and narrow stimuli. Figure 15-10 depicts lack of decisional separability when there is perceptual independence and perceptual separability.

Perceptual independence applies to individual stimulus combinations, and it is quite possible for one stimulus combination to possess independence and another to possess a dependency or correlation. In contrast, both perceptual separability and decisional separability are properties of the collection of stimulus combinations and their associated effects.

The analysis of a classification task begins with a test for marginal response invariance. If the probability of correctly judging one dimension depends upon the other (e.g., if the accuracy of height judgments depends upon width, and vice versa), one cannot generally determine whether this arises from a lack of perceptual separability (different sensory effects for a given dimension across levels of a second dimension), a lack of decisional separability (nonindependent decision criteria), or both. The lack of a general algorithm to test for perceptual and decisional separability when marginal response invariance fails is a limitation of the Ashby-Townsend model, since it frequently does fail, but it is not a fatal flaw. Ashby (1988) illustrates some considerations involved in deciding whether effects are perceptual or decisional in nature. We will consider log-linear modeling to that end below.

If marginal response invariance holds, one then tests for sampling independence. If it also holds (i.e., if the accuracy in judging a combined dimension equals the probabilities of the separate accuracies), there is perceptual independence (independent error). If it fails, there is perceptual and decisional separability but not perceptual independence. These do not exhaust the possible considerations. If the accuracies in making judgments of a given dimension do not depend upon whether the other dimension is also judged, based upon a comparison to a control task, the subject exhibits perfor-

**FIGURE 15-10**    Lack of decisional separability with perceptual separability.

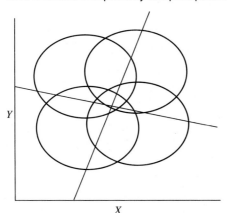

mance parity. Lack of parity often implies a limited capacity of the judgmental process and integrality of the dimensions.

## Application to Condensation Tasks

Decisional separability is a rational strategy when subjects make separate judgments of two dimensions or in filtering tasks. Lack of decisional separability is consequently of empirical interest. In contrast, optimal condensation demands decisional dependence. For example, a tennis player must possess both strength and control over his or her racquet to deliver an effective shot, among other attributes. Suppose players on a college tennis team are classified as successful versus unsuccessful in terms of their competitive ability as depicted in Fig. 15-11a. There will probably be a lack of perceptual independence in the sense of a positive within-group correlation. Because successful performance is positively related to both dimensions, there will

**FIGURE 15-11** (a) Distributions of successful and unsuccessful tennis players on the basis of racquet control and racquet strength. (b) Partitioning the classes by a discriminant function. Observations are predicted to be successful when the fall to they top and right. (c) A nonlinear optimal decision rule that is optimal when there is heteroscedasticity.

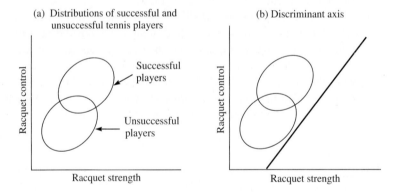

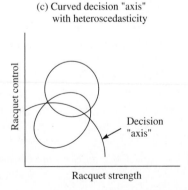

also be a positive between-group correlation; high scores on either dimension lead to success.

A key issue is how to partition the data into predicted successes and failures. Ashby and Maddox (1990) and Ashby and Gott (1988) have considered this general problem. If the within-group correlations are of the same magnitude, one may employ a discriminant function as discussed in Chapter 14 (see Hake, et al., 1967; Hake & Rodwan, 1966; Hake, Rodwan, & Weintraub, 1966; Rodwan & Hake, 1964). The discriminant function, by definition, maximizes between-group variation relative to within-group variation and reduces the situation to a univariate problem. The function may be used as a signal detection strength axis and partitioned to provide classification.

When the scatter plots are of different shapes, a different strategy is necessary. One optimal decision rule is to measure the probabilities that a given observation is a random deviation from each of the two groups and to assign the observation to the "nearer" (more probable) group (see Hake et al., 1967). Bayesian considerations (Chapter 4) may also be included. For example, if one population is larger than the other, one could require that the probability that the observation came from the smaller group exceed the probability that it came from the larger group. This may lead to a nonlinear decision rule, as in Fig. 15-11b. Needless to say, subjects could well have difficulty performing optimally under these conditions.

## MDS, Dissimilarity Judgments, and General Recognition Theory

Simplifying Ashby and Perrin's (1988) notation slightly, let the perceived dissimilarity of stimuli A and B be denoted as $d(A, B)$. As noted in the last chapter, MDS produces distance relations among stimuli by transforming a data matrix in various ways that depend upon the definition of distance (ordinary Euclidian, weighted Euclidian, cityblock, etc.) and the data's measurement level (ratio, interval, ordinal). Ashby and Perrin (1988) describe four deductions from the Euclidian model.

**1** The dissimilarities of perceived stimuli to themselves or self-dissimilarities are all equal; i.e., $d(A, A) = d(B, B) \, d(C, C) \ldots$ .

**2** The dissimilarity of two stimuli cannot be less than their self-dissimilarities, a condition known as minimality. Thus, $d(A, B) \geq d(A, A)$ and $d(A, B) \geq d(B, B)$.

**3** Dissimilarities are symmetric: $d(A, B) = d(B, A)$.

**4** The triangle inequality of Chapter 14 holds, so that $d(A, B) + d(B, C) \geq d(A, C)$.

Although these assumptions seem reasonable, they may be violated. Whether or not this is possible depends upon how the data are gathered. To save time, most paired comparison tasks do not compare stimuli to themselves and present different stimuli in only one order. Violations of deductions 1, 2, and 3 cannot be detected under these conditions. However, these violations may be detected if all possible pairs of stimuli are presented. If they occur, MDS is inappropriate.

Ashby and Perrin (1988) illustrate how various anomalies may arise when the distributions are unequal, i.e., when the variances or within-group correlations differ. For example, suppose a clinician rates the physical and verbal hostility of a series of patients on each of several days. Patient A varies in physical assaultiveness but rarely engages in verbal hostility, patient B is consistently not hostile, and patient C shows considerable variation in verbal hostility but little physical assaultiveness. Assume for simplicity that the two types of hostility are uncorrelated over days for each of the three patients. Figure 15-12 contains these scatter plots. Patients A and B overlap substantially because neither is verbally hostile, patients B and C overlap substantially because neither is physically hostile, but patients A and C overlap very little.

The distances drawn between the means of the three scatter plots in Fig. 15-12 obviously fit a Euclidian framework (which follows from the fact that they were drawn on a flat surface). However, the issue is whether one actually perceives the similarities and dissimilarities among patients as dictated by their physical proximity. They well might not be. Patients A and B may be perceived as similar because of their lack of verbal hostility, and patients B and C may be seen as similar because of their lack of physical hostility. However, patients A and C may appear highly dissimilar. Consequently the sum of the distances from A to B and from B to C may well be less than the distance measured directly from A to C, thus violating the triangle inequality. James (1890) pointed out this anomaly many years before any distance models were formalized, and Tversky and Gati (1982) examined its implications in depth.

Based upon this and related examples, Ashby and Perrin (1988) proposed a measure of similarity based upon distributional overlap. As noted above, the perceptual component of the theory states that variability in the perceived stimulus produces a distribution of effects in stimulus A, $f_A(x, y)$. For example, let A be the short-narrow stimulus. The decisional component of the theory states that a given response can be represented as an area in the space. Let the response in this case be the short-wide combination. The similarity of the short-narrow stimulus to the short-wide response is defined as that portion of the short-narrow stimulus distribution that falls in the short-wide response region, $f_A(x, y)$. This need not be the same as $f_B(y, x)$, so that their model can account for asymmetries in judgment. Their definition of similarity

**FIGURE 15-12**   Scatter plots for three patients observed over time with regard to verbal and physical hostility.

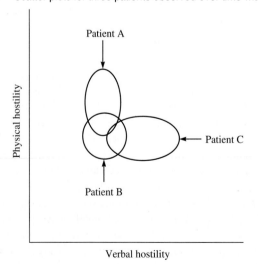

in terms of overlap is a multivariate extension of the way classical signal detection theory treated the problem of unequal variance. This approach also accounts for other violations of predictions made by Euclidian models, including the triangle inequality.

Does Ashby and Townsend's work mean that we should discard MDS, since nearly everything we have previously discussed defines similarity in terms of distance? Ashby and Perrin (1988) distinguish quite explicitly between MDS as a device for scaling stimuli and as a theory of perceived similarity. If one's intent is to describe the structure of stimuli, MDS would still be appropriate, but that is quite different from assuming that the subjects' perceptions follow a geometric process. Of course, if the perceived distributions of the stimuli are homoscedastic, a geometric or equal variance representation may be applicable.

## Implications for Measurement

Thus far, Ashby, Townsend, and their colleagues have generally relied upon preexisting Thurstonian algorithms [see Ashby (1988) and Ashby and Perrin (1988) for an relevant discussion]. However, both the analysis of covariance structures (ACS, see Chapter 13) and categorical modeling explicitly appear potentially quite useful and readily available as tools.

Consider a dual rating task in which it is reasonable to assume decisional separability and recall that decisional separability is necessary to evaluate lack of perceptual independence in detail. ACS can compare the resulting variance-covariance matrices as follows. A general model allows all five parameters of the covariance matrices (two means, two variances, and a covariance) obtained from each stimulus combination plus the measurement error to vary freely and therefore be estimated separately. If there are $K$ stimuli, the data furnish $K$ means, $K$ variances, and $K^2 - K$ covariances for a total of $K^2 + K$ terms, but $6K$ parameters need to be estimated, leaving $K^2 + K - 6K$ or $K^2 - 5K$ degrees of freedom. Obviously the design requires six or more stimuli. This model is too general to be of interest in itself; its importance lies in the following restrictions.

Perceptual separability (assuming decisional separability) implies homoscedasticity of the distributions for each stimulus. This is testable by constraining each of the variances, covariances, and unique error to equality over stimuli but letting the locations vary freely. This model estimates $2K$ (two means per stimulus) + 4 parameters. It is a nesting of the general model, and so the difference may be tested with $(K^2 + K - 2K - 4) - (K^2 + K - 6K) = 4K + 4$ $df$. If the difference is significant, individual stimuli may be examined to evaluate lack of separability further.

Assuming perceptual separability, perceptual independence may be evaluated by constraining each of the covariances to zero. This model estimates two means per stimulus and two variances and unique errors constrained to equality over stimuli for a total of $2K + 3$ parameters. It is nested within the separability model and has $(K^2 + K - 2K - 3) - (K^2 + K - 2K - 4) = 1$ $df$. It considers whether the common covariance term of the separability model can be considered to be zero.

We have already noted the problems associated with using ACS to analyze data that fall into a small number of categories, and so this procedure is not recommended in classification tasks, especially binary classification. Log-linear modeling offers a useful alternative approach. Again assume a binary classification task as discussed above where $X$ and $Y$ denote the two physical dimensions and $x$ and $y$ denote the associated responses (not, as above, their internal representations). The data matrix has 16 cells (4 stimuli and 4 responses), but the 4 stimuli are constrained by the presentation probabilities, leaving 12 $df$.

These may be analyzed by the methods described in the section titled "Multiple Response Categories in Predictor-Criterion Models." In particular,

**1** Lack of independence in using combinations of categories (marginal biases to use of the same or different response categories) indicates lack of decisional separability.

**2** Associations among $X$, $Y$, or their combination upon $x$ or $y$, adjusting for simpler effects, indicate a violation of marginal response invariance.

**3** Associations among $X$, $Y$, or their combination upon same versus different responses, adjusting for simpler effects, imply a correlation in the error terms that underlie errors, i.e., lack of perceptual independence.

Ashby (1988) and Wickens and Olzak (1989) discuss the implications of using a rating task.

## NONGEOMETRIC AND NON-EUCLIDIAN MODELS

A major point to be gleaned from the previous discussion is that proximity (similarity) measures based upon a purely geometric (spatial, point) representation of the stimuli can produce anomalous results when some stimuli are more ambiguous than others (i.e., have more perceptual variance) or the dimensions being judged are perceived as interdependent. The same arguments apply to scaling people and dominance relationships (preferences).

### Nearest Neighbors

Tversky and Hutchinson (1986) noted a problem associated with geometric (spatial) representations of proximity data. Assume that $K$ stimuli have been rated for similarity. They used judgments of relatedness among 20 common names of fruits plus the word "fruit" itself obtained by Mervis, Rips, Rosch, Shoben, and Smith (1975). The data produce a $21 \times 21$ matrix of means, where larger numbers denote greater relatedness on a 5-point scale. By definition, stimulus j is the nearest neighbor of stimulus i if stimulus j is closer (has a smaller distance) to stimulus i than any other stimulus is to stimulus i; e.g., the letter B is the nearest neighbor to the letter A in terms of its serial position in the Roman alphabet. Assuming that ratings are at least ordinally related to distances, the nearest neighbor of a given stimulus is the stimulus with the highest mean similarity rating. Excluding ties, a given stimulus can have only one nearest neighbor, but that nearest neighbor can also be the nearest neighbor of other stimuli. In particular, "fruit" was the nearest neighbor of every specific fruit save for "olive" and "lemon" whose nearest neighbors were, respectively, "date" and "orange."

Tversky and Hutchinson (1986) show how geometry constrains the number of points that may have the same nearest neighbor. Specifically, no stimulus can be the nearest neighbor of more than 2 points in a one-dimensional space. For example, if three stimuli are ordered X—Y—Z, Y is the nearest neighbor of X and Z. If stimulus W is added and also has Y as its nearest neighbor, W becomes the nearest neighbor of X or Z depending upon whether it falls to the left or right of Y. Likewise, no stimulus can be the nearest neighbor of more than 5 points in a two-dimensional space or of more than 11 points in a three-dimensional space. Even though Mervis et al.'s (1975) two-dimensional MDS representation appeared reasonable, it failed to reflect this aspect of the data.

Tversky and Hutchinson (1986) derived two statistics. Let $N_i$ equal the number of stimuli for which stimulus i is the nearest neighbor. Since the index runs from 0 to $N$ (the number of stimuli), there are $N + 1$ terms. Because each stimulus has only one nearest neighbor (ignoring ties), the sum of these terms is $N + 1$ and the mean is 1.

**1** The centrality ($C$) of the data set reflects the extent to which one or a few stimuli dominate the data. It is defined as $\Sigma N_i^2/(N + 1)$ which equals the sample variance plus 1. The $C$ will be at its maximum of $(N^2 + 1)/(N + 1)$ when one stimulus is the nearest neighbor of all other stimuli save itself, and it will be at its minimum value of 1 if each stimulus is the nearest neighbor of only one other stimulus.

**2** The reciprocity of a given relationship describes the extent to which that relationship is symmetric. Let $R_i$ denote the rank order of stimulus j's similarity to stimulus i, where stimulus j is the nearest neighbor of stimulus i. It will equal 1 if stimulus i is also the nearest neighbor of stimulus j (reciprocity), as when two people are each other's closest friend, and equal $N + 1$ when the relationship is totally asymmetric, as when person j prefers person i the most but person i despises person j. The overall reciprocity of the set ($R$) is simply the average of the individual $R_i$ values. A low value of $R$ implies high reciprocity, and vice versa. Its minimum value is 1, which occurs when each stimulus is the nearest neighbor of its own nearest neighbor. Its maximum value of $N_2 + 1/(N + 1)$ reflects total lack of reciprocity. It can be shown that $C \leq 2R - 1$.

Tversky and Hutchinson (1986) explored a number of data sets which were either perceptual, involving similarities among physical stimuli such as hues and letters of the alphabet, or conceptual, like the words in the Mervis et al. (1975) study. In general, geometric representations, and therefore MDS-type models, fit perceptual judgments fairly well but did not fit conceptual judgments. The obtained $R$ was considerably higher than the $R$ inferred from the MDS solution.

## Tree Representations

Tversky and Hutchinson (1986) discussed an alternative way to represent data, known as an additive tree, that may prove more useful for conceptual judgments than the geometric MDS approach. Additive trees are discussed more fully in Sattath and Tversky (1977; also see Tversky, Rinott, & Newman, 1983). Figure 15-13a illustrates a simple additive tree. The distance (dissimilarity) between two stimuli is proportional to the horizontal distances along the tree limbs (the vertical distances are immaterial); the lo-

(a) A simple tree representation

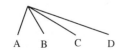

A    B     C     D

(b) A binary tree that
illustrates reciprocity

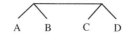

A    B     C    D

(c) A singular tree that illustrates
that one stimulus (A) is the
nearest neighbor of all others

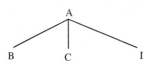

B     C       D

(d) A nested tree that illustrates
superior-subordinate relations

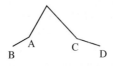

B    A   C  D

**FIGURE 15-13**    (*a*) A simple additive tree. (*b*) A binary tree reflecting complete reciprocity. (*c*) A singular tree (star or fan) that emerges when one stimulus is the nearest neighbor of all other stimuli. (*d*) A nested tree (brush) reflecting a hierarchy where each position is more closely related to its subordinates than to its superiors or peers.

cations of the stimuli are referred to as nodes. This representation, unlike the geometric one of MDS, can accept a very high degree of centrality (many items sharing the same nearest neighbor). Figure 15-13*b* indicates a special form known as a binary tree which arises from complete reciprocity. In the extreme case, both *C* and *R* are at their minimum values of 1. No individual is the nearest neighbor of more than one other individual, and the nearest neighbor relation is completely symmetric. Preference ratings among a series of contented couples would form this pattern. Figure 15-13*c* depicts what is variously referred to as a singular tree, a star, or a fan. Both *C* and *R* are high because a small number of stimuli tend to be foci for other stimuli, serving as their nearest neighbors. Students in classes who do not know each other well and who compare themselves to each other and their instructor might form such a relationship. Figure 15-13*d* depicts a nested tree or brush in which *C* is low but *R* is high. Only the longest branch is not a nearest neighbor, but each point is closer to a point on its shorter branch than on its longer branch. Tversky and Hutchinson (1986) exemplify this pattern with a military hierarchy—each level is closer to its subordinates than to its superiors.

Tversky examined several alternatives to geometric representation other than additive trees, including hybrids of geometric and other models. These include common and distinctive features (Tversky, 1977) and discrete clusters (Sattath & Tversky, 1977; also see Carroll, 1976; Johnson, 1967; Shepard & Arabie, 1979). The latter is a modification of more traditional forms of geometric clustering considered previously.

Tversky's work highlights some deficiencies in the geometric approach that has dominated psychometric theory and multivariate analysis, including this book. However, his findings also strengthen the applicability of geometric models like MDS to physically defined stimuli. It is perhaps unlikely that classical geometric methods will ever be totally replaced, but tree algorithms will likely offer added flexibility to measurement. We therefore stress the importance of this work as a caution to the blind use of MDS and related methods, especially with semantically defined sets, but not as any dictum to avoid their use. Further note that even though a tree representation is non-geometric, it does represent stimuli as points rather than as distributions as in general recognition theory.

### Network and Graph-Theoretic Approaches

In general, graph theory deals with the structure of a series of nodes (points) and their connections. Tree representations and clustering are thus both based upon graph theory [for this particular application of clustering, see Johnson, (1967)]. In the present context, nodes are stimuli and connections are the strength of their relationships. They might be used to depict the strengths of word associations to a cognitive psychologist or interactions in a small group of people to a social psychologist. Some relations are nondirected (symmetric) in that the connection from stimulus i to stimulus j is the same as the connection from j to i. Consequently the distance from i to j ($d_{ij}$) equals the distance from j to i ($d_{ji}$). Distances between cities are nondirected—the distance from Dallas to London equals the distance from London to Dallas. Other relations are directed (asymmetric), and so $d_{ij} \neq d_{ji}$. Liking someone may not be reciprocated. The term "graph" by itself implies nondirected distances, and the term "directed graph" or "digraph" implies directed distances. Trees, as discussed above, are a special type of graph or digraph in which each stimulus (node) is connected (linked) to every other stimulus but one cannot form a cycle or path through the graph back to the starting point.

Cartwright and Harary (1956) introduced graph theory into psychology. Its first major use was in "sociometry," the study of interaction patterns and affective relations in small groups. Figure 15-14 describes patterns of communication among eight committee members, A to H. For simplicity, we assume that "speaking to" is reciprocal, which it need not be, and so the figure is a graph rather than a digraph. Figure 15-4a shows a group polarized into two factions—A, B, C, and D communicate only among themselves (but A also does not speak to D) and E, F, G, and H communicate only among themselves. Polarization may arise for many reasons, e.g., political, ethnic, or gender. Figure 15-14 shows lack of polarization. Even though everybody does not speak to everybody else, patterns of communication are idiosyncratic.

Cognitive psychology has recently used graph-theoretic concepts to study hypothetical neural networks which have been proposed to explain a variety of phenomena. This approach is called connectionism or parallel distributed processing (Rummelhart, McClelland, & the PDP research group, 1988a, 1988b). Schvaneveldt's Pathfinder model (1990; Schvaneveldt, Durso, Goldsmith, Breen, Cooke, Tucker, & DeMaio, 1985; Schvaneveldt, Dearholt, & Durso, 1989; Schvaneveldt, Durso, & Dearholt, 1988; Schvaneveldt, Durso, & Mukherji, 1982) is a particularly good example of the application of graph theory. The model produces a tree representation (either as a graph or a digraph) of scaled distances called a Pathfinder net (pfnet) based upon dis-

(a) A group that is polarized into two factions

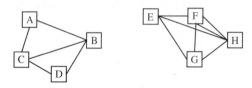

(b) A group that is not highly polarized

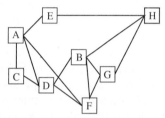

**FIGURE 15-14** (*a*) A graph reflecting a highly polarized group. (*b*) A graph for a nonpolarized group in which some people do not communicate with others.

tances as defined by their inverse, proximities. Stimuli i and j may be directly linked, linked through additional stimuli, or not linked at all. It uses Minkowski *r* metrics, introduced in Chapter 14, to account for proximities with a minimum of internode connections. Equation 15-18 defines the *r*-metric distance from i to j ($d_{ij}^r$) in terms of the distances from i to k ($d_{jk}^r$) and from j to k ($d_{jk}^r$):

$$d_{ij}^r = (d_{ik}^r + d_{jk}^r)^{1/r} \tag{15-18}$$

The parameter *r* may vary from 1 to infinity. For example, $r = 1$ produces the city-block metric used in the initial graph-theoretic research, and $r = 2$ produces the Euclidian metric which this book has stressed. Although Pathfinder can define distances in these more conventional manners, it is novel for its emphasis on the dominance metric in which $r = \infty$ and $d_{ij}$ equals the larger of $d_{ik}$ and $d_{jk}$. In general, the larger the value of *r*, the smaller the value of $d_{ij}$. Tversky and Gati (1982) also explored nonmetric situations where $r < 1$.

Nodes i and j of a pfnet are directly connected if and only if $d_{ij}^r$ is less than the sum of all indirect path lengths through other nodes, e.g., $d_{ik}^r + d_{jk}^r$. In other words, the triangle inequality of Chapter 14 must be satisfied for either all paths or, optionally, paths of a certain length. Pathfinder estimates these $d_{ik}^r$ values (path lengths or weights), which may be displayed graphically, and indexes the similarity of two networks. One particular reason to estimate similarity is to establish the stability of data by comparing networks obtained from split halves. Pathfinder presently has two important limitations:

**1** Measurement is deterministic. Pathfinder does not optimize the proximities to remove the effects of sampling error nor does it allow ordinal or interval transformations, as MDS does.

**2** Proximities are treated as unipolar, and so Pathfinder does not provide for negative (inhibitory) relations. Consequently, it cannot analyze a correlation matrix with negative correlations since these become infinite distances, just as zero correlations do, rather than strong negative relations.

We simulated three sets of proximities among 12 nodes ($X_1$ to $X_{12}$) to illustrate one of Pathfinder's uses, clustering, starting with data in which there was no sampling error. In the first- or single-cluster case, all pairwise proximities were 0.72. In the second or correlated cluster, case, the pairwise proximities were 0.72 among $X_1$ to $X_6$ and $X$ to $X_{12}$, but 0.46 among nodes in different sets, e.g., $X_2$ and $X_9$. Finally, in the uncorrelated cluster case, the pairwise proximities were also 0.72 among $X_1$ to $X_6$ and $X$ to $X_2$, but were 0.0 between variables in different sets. We used a dominance metric and required the triangle inequality to apply to all possible paths to minimize the number of connections. Pathfinder incorporates a threshold proximity below which distances are assumed infinite. This was set at 0.1. Distances were defined as 1 plus the threshold minus the proximities, another program option.

The single-cluster graph (pfnet) is presented in Fig. 15-15$a$ (we have omitted the symbol $X$ for simplicity). It linked every stimulus with every other stimulus at the same distance (0.38 unit). This was because all links are 0.38 ($1 + 0.1 - 0.72$), and so this value is perforce the largest distance between any links, and the largest distance determines the path length in a dominance metric.

Perhaps paradoxically, the correlated cluster graph in Fig. 15-15$b$, also linked every stimulus with every other stimulus with paths of the same length, 0.64 unit. The distances between links in the same cluster were 0.38 unit as above, but the distances between links in different clusters were 0.64 unit ($1 + 0.1 - 0.46$). Paths between any two stimuli, whether or not they are in the same cluster, contain links from different sets; e.g., the path from $X_1$ to $X_2$ includes a link from $X_1$ to $X_6$ and a link from $X_6$ to $X_2$. These between-cluster links establish the path length because they are larger than the within-cluster path lengths. Figure 15-15$a$ and 15-15$b$ were drawn to different scales. They are equivalent (i.e., their similarity is 1.0) because the paths are of the same length in each case but the lengths are different. Whether or not this equivalence of the two solutions is psychologically valid is an interesting question to examine.

Finally, the uncorrelated cluster solution provided the two disjoint graphs in Fig. 15-15$c$. Within each cluster, each node was linked to every other at a distance of 0.38 unit, but there were no paths linking nodes in the two clusters.

We then introduced sampling error into each of the three data sets to make them resemble real data. Proximities in the single-cluster solution varied from 0.65 to 0.73. Proximities in the correlated cluster case varied from 0.73 to 0.77 within clusters and from 0.44 to 0.54 between clusters, and proximities in the uncorrelated cluster case ranged from 0.72 to 0.76 within clusters and from −0.01 to 0.10 within clusters. These

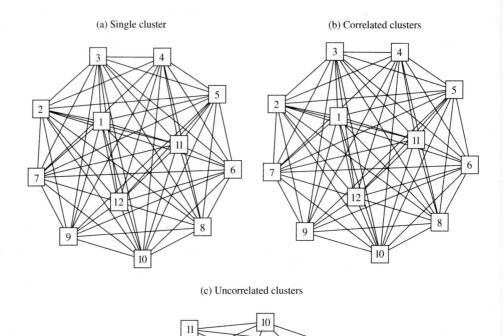

(a) Single cluster

(b) Correlated clusters

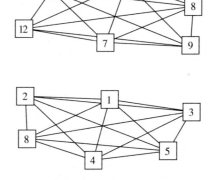

(c) Uncorrelated clusters

**FIGURE 15-15** Graphs (pfnets) for (*a*) single-cluster data, where all measures are equally similar to one another, (*b*) two correlated clusters, where variables within the same cluster are equally similar and variables in different clusters are less highly related, and (*c*) two uncorrelated clusters, where variables within the same cluster are equally correlated but the two clusters are unrelated. Even though the configurations (*a*) and (*b*) are equivalent, the path lengths are different.

results appear in the three graphs in Fig. 15-16. As can be seen, the underlying struc-ture is considerably less clear, save for the uncorrelated cluster case.

## Conclusions

Our goal is writing this chapter was to call attention to the potential usefulness of sev-eral procedures that have attracted somewhat less interest among psychometricians than those discussed in earlier chapters. Psychologists, especially those in experimental

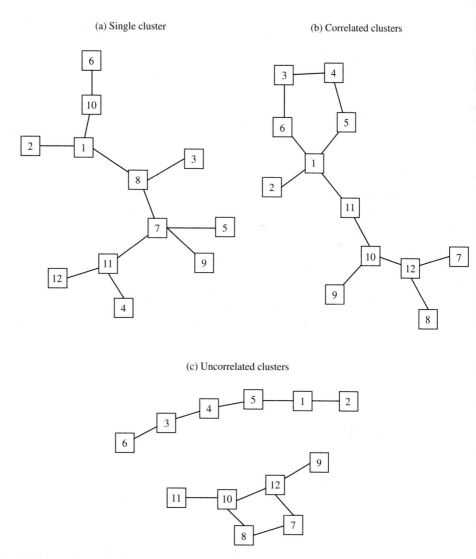

**FIGURE 15-16**   Solutions obtained from (*a*) single cluster data, (*b*) correlated cluster data, and (*c*) uncorrelated cluster data when sampling error is introduced.

areas, should find these methods especially useful. It is particularly important that categorical models directly address frequently studied substantive issues such as judgmental independence. Similarly, Ashby and Townsend's general recognition model flows from the signal detection theory and Thurstonian traditions and, in the process, introduces several relevant distinctions. Although tree and network models are also applicable to current problems, perhaps a bit more caution is advised before abandoning tried and true geometric models, especially factor analysis. One advantage of factor analysis is that the skilled user has a large literature available to know its limitations. Moreover, one key application of geometric models, its use with perceptual stimuli, has actually been strengthened. At the same time, anyone seriously interested in measurement needs to know alternative methods of representing data structures.

The issues raised in the last section of this chapter one further point. We strongly argued in the first chapter that formal approaches to measurement can be counterproductive. This is certainly true to the extent that one becomes bogged down in issues like "Is a score that sums across items truly defined on an interval scale?" We have steadfastly argued in defense of summing to get on with the business of applying the powerful methods of multivariate analysis and psychometric theory. However, once that is done, one can then proceed to the more positive features of the representational position as seen in the work of Tversky, Schvaneveldt, and others.

## SUMMARY

Categorical modeling has been applied to several traditional problems: (1) studying relations among categorical variables (log-linear modeling), (2) predicting categorical variables from other categorical variables (predictor-criterion modeling), (3) predicting a categorical variable from a quantitative variable (logistic regression), (4) partitioning sources of variance, as in the continuous-variable ANOVA and MANOVA, and (5) testing matrices for specific properties such as symmetry. The basic logic of most categorical modeling is (1) the probability that two independent events will jointly occur is the product of their individual (marginal) probabilities, (2) consequently the natural logarithm of this joint probability is the sum of the natural logarithms of the individual probabilities, and (3) natural (base $e$) logarithms are mathematically more convenient than common (base 10) logarithms. The logit or log-odds ratio of two events is the natural log of their ratio.

The log probabilities of individual events are related to regression ($\beta$) weights used to test for independence. If two individual events are binary, the model used to test for independence uses 3 $df$, leaving 1 $df$ to test for their association. If there is an association, an additional parameter needs be added to the model. The resulting saturated model cannot be tested, but the magnitude of the associative parameter can be estimated. Related models can test hypotheses that either or both the row or column probabilities are .5 using hierarchical principles discussed in Chapters 4, 10, and 13.

Strength of association may be defined by (1) the value of $\beta$ associated with an effect, (2) the effect logit or 2 times $\beta$, and (3) the odds ratio itself ($\alpha$) or square root of the reciprocal of Shepard's distance measure, Eq. 14-5. Yule derived two additional measures from $\alpha$: (4) the measure of association or conditional probability of agreement between two responses, and (5) the measure of colligation, which corrects the measure of association for marginal differences. Tetrachoric $r$ is another, less highly recommended possibility. Three inferential statistics are (1) the residual likelihood ratio chi-square ($G^2$) based upon the disparity between predicted and obtained model frequencies; (2) the difference $G^2$ between two nested models, which evaluates the significance of the constraint(s); and (3) the effect $G^2$, which tests whether or not a given parameter differs significantly from zero.

The generalized logit of an event is the log ratio of its probability relative to an baseline event, regardless of the number of possible events. Generalized logits can be modeled just like log probabilities and produce equivalent results.

There is an important distinction between structural and random zeros in a model. A structural zero is a constraint introduced to eliminate one or more cells (e.g., the diagonals), from a model. In contrast, random zeros are empirical outcomes. Many random zeros imply too small a sample and/or poorly chosen categories.

The information transmitted is a measure of effect strength of a multilevel variable. Difference and residual, but not effect, $G^2$ values test such effects inferentially. A multivariable analysis was then performed to evaluate data containing Simpson's paradox.

Predictor-criterion models designate variables as predictors or criteria, unlike log-linear models which do not. A predictor-criterion analysis can be conducted as a log-linear analysis, but not necessarily the converse. Comparable effects will produce the same $G^2$ value. A predictor-criterion model will have fewer terms because it includes only relations between predictors and criteria, not among predictors or criteria. Effects present in more complex designs depend upon whether variables are quantitative or not and whether one considers combinations of effects. These effects include (1) marginal biases (unequal outcomes), (2) direct predictor-criterion relations, and (3) higher-order effects.

Categorical modeling's three main assumptions are that (1) categories are operationally independent, and so there are no built-in relationships; (2) all observations have the same distribution; and (3) the number of observations is large. Repeated observations from subjects are a problem because the results confound variability between subjects and within subjects. If the ratio of observations per subject to estimated parameters is large, estimates can be obtained separately for each subject and pooled. If this ratio is small, consider randomly grouping subjects and estimating parameters from each group. The consistency of the parameter estimates should be evaluated in both cases. A traditional requirement is five expected subjects per cell, but this may be too conservative. Finally, classification should be reliable.

Item response models assuming equal discrimination (i.e., Rasch models) can be written as log-linear models, allowing tests of differential item functioning (Chapter 10). However, more complex item response models are *not* log linear. Moreover, item response theory is inherently latent variable modeling; categorical modeling is not.

Quasi-independence means that categories are unrelated in the presence of structural zeros even though they may be related when these observations are included in the model. Symmetry means that all $\beta_{ij} = \beta_{ji}$. It may not hold because of either differential association (inherent associative asymmetry) or marginal heterogeneity (differences in row and column distributions). A model that is asymmetric because of marginal heterogeneity is quasi-symmetric.

Logistic regression relates a quantitative predictor to a categorical criterion. Group differences in slope may be evaluated independently of differences in intercept, and vice versa. However, logistic regression usually provides more residual degrees of freedom than other categorical modeling problems, and so important sources of variance may be present in a nonsignificant residual.

Binary classification was introduced in the context of the theory of signal detection (TSD) in Chapter 2. In a yes-no task subjects judge the presence or absence of an attribute. The important data are the hit rate (conditional probability of saying yes when the attribute or signal is present) and the false alarm rate (conditional probability of saying yes when the signal is absent). The subject is assumed to locate a response criterion along a decision axis. The response is yes when the observation exceeds criterion, and no otherwise.

The most common TSD model is based upon Case V Thurstone scaling. This equal variance Gaussian model assumes that the variability (discriminal dispersions) in the absence of signal (the noise distribution, $n$) is the same as the variability in the presence of the signal (the signal-plus-noise distribution, $s + n$). The predicted receiver operating characteristic (ROC) curve, which relates $z$ transformations of the hit and false alarm rates over criteria, is linear with a slope of 1. The mean difference between standardized distributions ($d'$) describes sensitivity, and the ratio of the ordinate of the $s + n$ distribution to the $n$ distribution at the response criterion ($\beta$) describes bias. In addition, the likelihood ratio (the ratio of the probability of $s + n$ to the probability of $n$, conditional upon the observation) is a monotonically increasing function of $X$: The larger the magnitude of the observation, the more probable it is that signal is present.

If, however, signal is also variable, an unequal variance Gaussian model is more applicable. The $z$-transformed ROC curve is still linear, but its slope is the ratio of the standard deviation of the $n$ distribution to the standard deviation of the $s + n$ distribution. In addition, the likelihood ratio does not increase monotonically with $X$: Both large and small observations are more likely to contain signal than are intermediate-sized observations. Categorical modeling can be used for the equal variance but not the unequal variance model.

In contrast to geometric (vector-based) approaches, TSD and Thurstone scaling treat stimuli as regions of either equal or unequal size. General recognition theory (Ashby & Townsend, 1986) extends this conception to dual judgments. Several tasks are relevant to the issue, although only the first three actually involve dual judgments: (1) ratings—there are more response levels per dimension than stimulus levels; (2) identification— the two are equal; (3) categorization—there are more stimulus levels than response levels; (4) filtering—one dimension is responded to and the other is ignored; (5) condensation—subjects judge a combination of attributes; and (6) control— an irrelevant dimension is held constant. Results depend upon the dimensions being judged. Integral dimensions are relatively easy to condense but difficult to filter; separable dimensions are the converse.

Perceptual independence means that the sensory variation (discriminal dispersion) is uncorrelated between dimensions for each stimulus pair, and decisional independence means that the criteria used to classify dimensions are independent of each other. When both perceptual and decisional independence occur, (1) the stimulus centroids form a rectangular pattern; (2) the sensory variation about each centroid is of the same magnitude and shape; (3) perceptual separability holds for each stimulus—sensory variation in one dimension is independent of variation in the other; (4) the stimuli exhibit sampling independence—the accuracies dual judgments will be the product of the separate accuracies; and (5) the stimuli exhibit marginal response invariance—the accuracy of judging a dimension will be the same at all levels of the other dimension. Performance parity means that dual judgment accuracy is the same as accuracy obtained when separate judgments are made.

If marginal response independence fails under dual judgments, one cannot determine whether it is due to lack of perceptual or decisional independence. If both marginal response independence and sampling independence hold, there is perceptual independence. If marginal response independence holds but sampling independence does not, there is perceptual and decisional separability but not perceptual independence.

If psychological similarity depends upon proximities in Euclidian space, four properties should hold: (1) Stimuli must be equally dissimilar from themselves, (2) stimuli must be more dissimilar to all other stimuli than to themselves (minimality), (3) dissimilarity must be symmetric, and (4) the triangle inequality of Chapter 14 must hold. Ashby and Townsend show how all of these may fail. They propose that similarity be based upon distributional overlap. Their model is then related to the analysis of covariance structures and categorical modeling.

Tversky and Hutchinson (1986) note other problems with traditional geometric conceptions. They define the nearest neighbor of a stimulus as that stimulus that is most similar to it. Geometry constrains the properties of nearest neighbors. For example, only two stimuli can be the nearest neighbor of a given stimulus in a one-dimensional space. Judgments of the similarity of physical stimuli usually do not violate these geometric constraints seriously, but judgments of concepts usually do. Two properties of nearest-neighbor analysis are the extent to which similarity relations show: (1) centrality—one or a few stimuli tend to be nearest neighbors of most stimuli (foci), and (2) reciprocity—if stimulus A is the nearest neighbor of B, then B is the nearest neighbor of A. They propose a tree structure as an alternative to spatial representation; similarity is represented by distances along branches. Three types of tree structure are (1) binary—there is complete reciprocity and low centrality (no stimuli are focal), as in affective judgments of contented couples; (2) singular (star or fan)—a few stimuli are focal and reciprocity is high, as in a class where students do not know one another but know the instructor who in turn knows them; and (3) a nested tree (brush) in which centrality is low but reciprocity is high, as in a hierarchy.

Graph theory concerns nodes (points) and their connections (paths). If connections can be asymmetric, the graph is directed, and if connections are symmetric, the graph is nondirected. Schvaneveldt's (1990) Pathfinder model uses Minkowski $r$ metrics in which the path length from one node (stimulus) to another is the $r$th root of the sum of their path lengths through a third stimulus raised to the $r$th power. If $r = 1$, distances obey the city block metric of Chapter 14; if $r = 2$, distances obey the Euclidian metric; and if $r = \infty$, distances obey a dominance metric in which the length is simply the larger of the individual lengths. Although the present form of the model is limited in that it does not correct for measurement error nor handle inhibitory relationships, it appears to be a useful way to describe similarity.

## SUGGESTED ADDITIONAL READINGS

Ashby, F. G., & Perrin, N. A. (1988). Toward a unified theory of similarity and recognition. *Psychological Review*, *95*, 124–150.

Ashby, F. G., & Townsend, J. T. (1986). Varieties of perceptual independence. *Psychological Review*, *93*, 154–179.

Bisop, Y. M. M, Fienberg, S. E., & Holland, P. W. (1975). *Discrete multivariate analysis: Theory and practice*. Cambridge, MA: MIT Press.

Goodman, L. A. (1978). *Analyzing quantitative/categorical data: Log-linear models and latent structure analysis*. Lanham, MD: Abt.

Macmillan, N. A., & Creelman, C. D. (1991). *Detection theory: A user's guide*. Cambridge: Cambridge University Press.

Schvaneveldt, R. W. (1990). *Associative networks: Studies in knowledge organization*. Norwood, NJ: Ablex.

Wickens, T. D. (1989). *Multiway contingency tables analysis for the social sciences*, Hillsdale, NJ: Erlbaum Associates.

# REFERENCES

Adorno, T. W., Frenkel-Brunswik, E., Levinson, D., & Sanford, R. N. (1950). *The authoritarian personality*. New York: Harper.

Agresti, A., & Yang, M. (1986). An empirical investigation of some effects of sparseness in contingency tables. *Computational Statistics & Data Analysis, 5*, 9–21.

Akaike, H. (1974). A new look at the statistical model identification. *IEEE Transactions on Automatic Control, 19*, 716–723.

Akaike, H. (1987). Factor analysis and AIC. *Psychometrika, 52*, 317–332.

American Educational Research Association et al. (1985). *Standards for psychological and educational testing*. Washington, DC: American Psychological Association.

American Personnel and Guidance Association. (1978). Responsibilities of users of standardized tests. *Guidepost*, 5–8.

American Psychiatric Association (1987). *Diagnostic and statistical manual of mental disorders* (3d ed., rev.). Washington, DC: American Psychiatric Association.

American Psychological Association. (1985). *Standards for educational and psychological tests*. Washington, DC: American Psychological Association.

American Psychological Association (1986a). *Ethical principles of psychologists*. Washington, DC: American Psychological Association.

American Psychological Association (1986b). *Guidelines for computer-based tests and interpretation*. Washington, DC: American Psychological Association.

American Psychological Association (1992). Ethical principles of psychologists and code of conduct. *American Psychologist, 47*, 1597–1611.

Anastasi, A. (1986). Evolving concepts of test validity. *Annual Review of Psychology, 37*, 1–16.

Anastasi, A. (1988). *Psychological testing* (6th ed.). New York: Macmillan.

Anderson, J. C., & Gerbing, D. W. (1988). Structural equation modeling in practice: A review and recommended two-step approach. *Psychological Bulletin, 103*, 411–423.

Anderson, N. H. (1981). *Foundations of information integration theory*. New York: Academic Press.

Anderson, N. H. (1982). *Methods of information integration theory*. New York: Academic Press.

Andrich, D. (1978). A rating formulation for ordered response categories. *Psychometrika, 43*, 561–573.

Andrich, D. (1982). An extension of the Rasch model for ratings providing both location and dispersion parameters. *Psychometrika, 47*, 105–113.

Andrich, D. (1985). An elaboration of Guttman scaling with Rasch models for measurement. In N. B. Tuma (Ed.), *Sociological methodology*. San Francisco: Josey-Bass.

Angoff, W. H. (1971). Norms, scales, and equivalent scores. In R. L. Thorndike (Ed.), *Educational measurement* (2d ed.). Washington, DC: American Council on Education.

Angoff, W. H. (1982). Uses of difficulty and discrimination indices for detecting item bias. In R. A. Berk (Ed.), *Handbook of methods for detecting item bias*. Baltimore, MD: Johns Hopkins University Press.

Angoff, W. H., & Ford, S. F. (1973). Item-race interaction on a test of scholastic ability. *Journal of Educational Measurement, 10*, 95–106.

Ashby, F. G. (1988). Estimating the parameters of multidimensional signal detection theory from simultaneous ratings on separate stimulus components. *Perception and Psychophysics, 44*, 195–204.

Ashby, F. G. (1989). Stochastic general recognition theory. In D. Vickers and P. L. Smith (Ed.), *Human information processing: Measures, mechanisms, and models*. Amsterdam: Elsevier Science Publishers.

Ashby, F. G., & Gott, R. E. (1988). Decision rules in the perception and categorization of multidimensional stimuli. *Journal of Experimental Psychology: Learning, Memory, and Cognition, 14*, 33–53.

Ashby, F. G., & Maddox, W. T. (1990). Integrating information from separable dimensions. *Journal of Experimental Psychology: Human Perception and Performance, 16*, 698–612.

Ashby, F. G., & Perrin, N. A. (1988). Toward a unified theory of similarity and recognition. *Psychological Review, 95*, 124–130.

Ashby, F. G., & Townsend, J. T. (1986). Varieties of perceptual independence. *Psychological Review, 93*, 154–179.

Baker, F. B. (1981). A criticism of Scheueneman's item bias technique. *Journal of Educational Measurement, 18*, 97–108.

Baker, B. O., Hardyck, C. D., & Petrinovich, L. F. (1966). Weak measurement vs. strong statistics: An empirical critique of S. S. Stevens' proscriptions on statistics. *Educational and Psychological Measurement, 26*, 291–309.

Baron, R., & Kenney, D. (1986). The moderator-mediator variable distinction in social-psychological research. *Journal of Personality and Social Psychology, 51*, 1173–1182.

Barron, F. (1953). An ego-strength scale which predicts response to psychotherapy. *Journal of Consulting Psychology, 17*, 327–333.

Bartlett, M. S. (1950). Tests of significance in factor analysis. *British Journal of Psychology* (Statistical Section), *3*, 77–85.

Bartlett, M. S. (1951). A further note on tests of significance in factor analysis. *British Journal of Psychology* (Statistical Section), *4*, 1–2.

Bartlett, M. S. (1954). A further note on the multiplying factors for various $\chi^2$ approximations in factor analysis. *Journal of the Royal Statistical Society, 16*, 296–298.

*Bazemore v. Friday. (1986)*. 478 United States 385.

Beardwood, J. E. (1977). A remark on algorithm AS 87: Calculation of the polychoric estimate of correlation in contingency tables. *Applied Statistics, 26*, 121.

Békèsy, G. (1960). *Experiments in Hearing*. New York: McGraw-Hill.

Bentler, P. M. (1968). Alpha-maximized factor analysis (alphamax): Its relation to alpha and canonical factor analysis. *Psychometrika, 3*, 335–345.

Bentler, P. M. (1985). *Theory and implementation of EQS: A structural equations program*. Los Angeles, CA: BMDP Statistical Software.

Bentler, P. M. (1986). *LaGrange multiplier and Wald tests for EQS and EQS/PC*. Los Angeles: BMDP Statistical Software.

Bentler, P. M. (1989). *EQS structural equations program manual*. Los Angeles: GMDP Statistical Software.

Bentler, P. M. (1990). Comparative fit indexes in structural models. *Psychological Bulletin, 107*, 238–246.

Bentler, P. M., & Bonnett, D. G. (1980). Significance tests and goodness of fit tests in the analysis of covariance structures. *Psychological Bulletin, 88*, 508–606.

Bentler, P. M., & Kano, Y. (1990). On the equivalence of factors and components. *Multivariate Behavioral Research, 25*, 67–74.

Bentler, P. M., & Lee, S.-Y. (1978). Statistical aspects of a three-mode factor analysis model. *Psychometrika, 43*, 343–352.

Bentler, P. M., & Lee, S.-Y. (1979). A statistical development of three-mode factor analysis. *British Journal of Mathematical and Statistical Psychology, 32*, 87–104.

Bentler, P. M., & Weeks, D. G. (1978). Restricted multidimensional scaling models. *Journal of Mathematical Psychology, 17*, 138–151.

Berk, R. A. (1984). *A guide to criterion-referenced test construction*. Baltimore: Johns Hopkins University Press.

Berk, R. A. (1986). *Performance appraisal: Assessing human behavior at work*. Boston, MA: Kent.

Bernardin, H. J., & Beatty, R. W. (1980). *Performance appraisal: Assessing human behavior at work*. Boston: Kent.

Bernstein, I. H. (1988). *Applied multivariate analysis*. New York: Springer-Verlag.

Bernstein, I. H., Bissonnette, V., & Welch, K. (1990). Perceptual and response interdependencies in semantic priming. *Perception and Psychophysics, 48*, 525–534.

Bernstein, I. H., & Eriksen, C. W. (1965). Effects of "subliminal" prompting on paired-associate learning. *Journal of Experimental Research in Personality, 1*, 33–38.

Bernstein, I. H., & Eveland, D. (1982). State vs. trait anxiety: A case study in confirmatory factor analysis. *Personality and Individual Differences, 3*, 361–372.

Bernstein, I. H., & Garbin, C. P. (1985). A comparison of alternative proposed subscale structures for MMPI scale 2. *Multivariate Behavioral Research, 20*, 223–235.

Bernstein, I. H., Garbin, C. P., & McClellan, P. G. (1983). A confirmatory factoring of the California Psychological Inventory. *Educational and Psychological Measurement, 43*, 687–691.

Bernstein, I. H., Lin, T.-D., & McClellan, P. (1982). Cross- vs. within-racial judgments of attractiveness. *Perception and Psychophysics, 32*, 495–503.

Bernstein, I. H., & Teng, G. (1989). Factoring items and factoring scales are different: Spurious evidence for multidimensionality due to item categorization. *Psychological Bulletin, 105*, 467–477.

Bernstein, I. H., Teng, G., & Garbin, C. P. (1986). A confirmatory factoring of the self-consciousness scale. *Multivariate Behavioral Research, 21*, 459–475.

Bernstein, I. H., Teng, G., Garbin, C. P., & Grannemann B. (1987). Invariance in the MMPI's component structure. *Journal of Personality Assessment, 51*, 522–531.

Bickel, P. J., Hammel, E. A., & O'Connell, J. W. (1975). Sex bias in graduate admissions: Data from Berkeley. *Science, 187*, 398–404.

Binet, A., & Simon, T. (1905). Méthodes nouvelles pour le diagnostique du niveau intellectuel des anormaux. *Année Psychologie, 11*, 191–244.

Birnbaum, A. (1968). Some latent trait models and their use in inferring an examinee's ability. In F. M. Lord and M. R. Novick (Eds.), *Statistical theory of mental test scores.* Reading, MA: Addison Wesley.

Birnbaum, M. H. (1974). Reply to the devil's advocates: Don't confound model testing and measurement, *Psychological Bulletin, 81*, 854–859.

Birnbaum, M. H. (1979a). Is there sex bias in salaries of psychologists? *American Psychologist, 34*, 719–720 (Comment).

Birnbaum, M. H. (1979b). Procedures for the detection and correction of salary inequities. In P. R. Pezzullo & B. E. Brittingham (Eds.), *Salary equity.* Lexington, MA: Lexington Books.

Birnbaum, M. H. (1981). Reply to McLaughlin: Proper path models for theoretical partialing. *American Psychologist, 36*, 1193–1195 (Comment).

Bishop, Y. M. M., Fienberg, S. E., & Holland, P. W. (1975). *Discrete multivariate analysis: Theory and practice.* Cambridge, MA: MIT Press.

Bissonnette, V., & Bernstein, I. H. (1990). Artifacts can replicate: A reply to Piliavin and Charng, *Personality and Social Psychology Bulletin, 16*, 554–561.

Bissonnette, V., Ickes, W., Bernstein, I. H., & Knowles, E. (1990a). Item variances and median splits: Some discouraging and disquieting findings. *Journal of Personality, 58*, 595–601.

Bissonnette, V., Ickes, W., Bernstein, I. H., & Knowles, E. (1990b). Personality moderating variables: A warning about statistical artifact and a comparison of analytic techniques. *Journal of Personality, 58*, 567–587.

Block, J. (1965). *The challenge of response sets: Unconfounding meaning, acquiescence, and social desirability in the MMPI.* New York: Appleton-Century-Crofts.

Block, J. (1990). More remarks on social desirability. *American Psychologist, 45*, 1076–1077 (Comment).

Blum, M. L., & Naylor, J. C. (1968). *Industrial psychology.* New York: Harper & Row.

Bock, R. D. (1972). Estimating item parameters and latent ability when the responses are scored in two or more nominal categories. *Psychometrika, 37*, 29–51.

Bock, R. D., & Aitken, M. (1981). Marginal maximum likelihood estimation of item parameters. *Psychometrika, 46*, 443–459.

Bock, R. D., & Jones, L. V. (1968). *The measurement and prediction of judgment and choice.* San Francisco: Holden-Day.

Bock, R. D., & Lieberman, M. L. (1970). Fitting a response model for $n$ dichotomously scored items. *Psychometrika, 35*, 179–197.

Bock, R. D., & Mislevy, R. J. (1982). Adaptive EAP estimation of ability in a microcomputer environment. *Applied Psychological Measurement, 6*, 431–444.

Bollen, K. A. (1990). Overall fit in covariance structure models: Two types of sample effect sizes. *Psychological Bulletin, 107*, 256–259.

Bollen, K., & Lennox, R. (1991). Conventional wisdom on measurement: A structural equation perspective. *Psychological Bulletin, 110*, 305–314.

Boring, E. G. (1950). *A history of experimental psychology* (2d ed.), Englewood, NJ: Prentice-Hall.

Borman, W. C. (1977). Consistency of rating accuracy and rating errors in the judgment of human performance. *Organizational Behavior and Human Performance, 20*, 238–252.

Borman, W. C. (1979). Format and training effects on rating accuracy and rater error. *Journal of Applied Psychology, 64*, 410–421.

Bowen, J., & Huang, M.-H. (1990). A comparison of maximum likelihood with method of moment procedures for separating individual and group effects. *Journal of Personality and Social Psychology, 58*, 90–94.

Breckler, S. J. (1990). Application of covariance structure modeling in psychology: Cause for concern? *Psychological Bulletin, 107*, 260–273.

Brennan, R. L. (1983). *Elements of generalizability theory*. Iowa City, IA: American College Testing Program.

Bridgman, P. W. (1928). *The logic of modern physics*. New York: Macmillan.

Brogden, H. E. (1946). Variation in test validity with variation in the distribution of item difficulties, number of items, and degree of their interrelation. *Psychometrika, 10*, 1–20.

Browne, M. W. (1984). Asymptotic distribution-free methods for the analysis of covariance structures. *British Journal of Mathematical and Statistical Psychology, 37*, 62–83.

Browne, M. W. (1987). Robustness of statistical inference in factor analysis and related models. *Biometrika, 74*, 375–384.

Burt, C. W. (1941). *The factors of the mind: An introduction to factor analysis in psychology*. New York: Macmillan.

Burt, C. W. (1948). The factorial study of temperamental traits. *British Journal of Psychology* (Statistical Section), *1*, 178–203.

Bush, R. R. (1963). Estimation and evaluation. In R. D. Luce, R. R. Bush, & E. Galanter (Eds.), *Handbook of Mathematical Psychology* (Vol. 1). New York: Wiley.

Byrne, B. M. (1990). *A primer of LISREL*. NY: Springer-Verlag.

Camilli, G. (1979). A critique of the chi-square method for assessing item bias. Unpublished paper. Laboratory of Educational Research, University of Colorado.

Campbell, D. T., & Fiske, D. W. (1959). Convergent and discriminant validation by the multitrait-multimethod matrix. *Psychological Bulletin, 56*, 81–105.

Carroll, J. D. (1945). The effect of task difficulty and chance success on correlations between items or between tests. *Psychometrika, 10*, 1–20.

Carroll, J. D. (1957). Biquartmin criterion for rotation to oblique simple structure in factor analysis. *Science, 126*, 1114–1115.

Carroll, J. D. (1972). Individual differences and multidimensional scaling. In R. N. Shepard, A. K. Romney, & S. Nerlove (Eds.), *Multidimensional scaling: Theory and applications in behavioral sciences* (Vol. 1). New York: Academic Press.

Carroll, J. D. (1976). Spatial, nonspatial, and hybrid models for scaling. *Psychometrika, 41*, 439–463.

Carroll, J. D., & Chang, J. J. (1970). Analysis of individual differences in multidimensional scaling via an *N*-way generalization of "Eckart-Young" decomposition. *Psychometrika, 35*, 238–319.

Cartwright, D., & Harary, F. (1956). Structural balance: A generalization of Heider's theory. *Psychological Review, 63*, 277–293.

Cattell, R. B. (1946). *The description and measurement of personality*. New York: World Book Company.

Cattell, R. B. (1952). *Factor analysis*. New York: Harper & Row.

Cattell, R. B. (1966a). Higher order factor structures and reticular vs. hierarchical formulae for their interpretation. In C. Banks & P. L. Broadhurst (Eds.), *Studies in psychology*. London: University of London Press.

Cattell, R. B. (1966b). The scree test for the number of factors. *Multivariate Behavioral Research, 1*, 245–276.

Cattell, R. B. (1978). *The scientific use of factor analysis in behavioral and life sciences*. New York: Plenum Press.

Cattell, R. B., Eber, H. W., & Tatsuoka, M. M. (1970). *Handbook for the sixteen personality factor questionnaire (16PF)* Champaign, IL: Institute for Personality and Ability Testing.

Cheek, J. M., & Buss, A. H. (1981). Shyness and sociability. *Journal of Personality and Social Psychology, 41*, 330–339.

Cleary, T. A. (1968). Test bias: Prediction of grades of Negro and white students in integrated colleges. *Journal of Educational Measurement, 10*, 43–56.

Cliff, N. R. (1958). The predictive value of chance-level scores. *Educational and Psychological Measurement, 18*, 607–616.

Cliff, N. R. (1966). Orthogonal rotation to congruence. *Psychometrika, 31*, 33–42.

Cliff, N. R. (1983a). Evaluating Guttman scales: Some old and new thoughts. In H. Wainer, H. and S. Messick (Eds.), *Principles of modern psychological measurement: A festschrift for Frederic M. Lord*. Hillsdale, NJ: Erlbaum Associates.

Cliff, N. R. (1983b). Some cautions concerning the application of causal modeling methods. *Multivariate Behavioral Research, 18*, 115–126.

Cliff, N. R. (1988). The eigenvalues-greater-than-one rule and the reliability of components. *Psychological Bulletin, 103*, 276–279.

Cohen, H. S., & Davison, M. L. (1973). Jiffy scale: Fortran IV programs for generalized Ross-ordered paired comparisons. *Behavioral Science, 18*, 76.

Cohen, J. (1968). Multiple regression as a general data-analytic system. *Psychological Bulletin, 70*, 426–443.

Cohen, J. (1983). The cost of dichotomization. *Applied Psychological Measurement, 7*, 249–253.

Cohen, J. (1990). Things I have learned (so far). *American Psychologist, 12*, 1304–1312.

Cohen, J., & Cohen, P. (1983). *Applied multivariate analysis/linear regression* (2d ed.). Hillsdale, NJ: Erlbaum Associates.

Colavita, F. B. (1974). Human sensory dominance. *Perception and Psychophysics, 16*, 409–412.

Cole, D. A., & Maxwell, S. E. (1985). Multitrait-multimethod comparisons across populations: A confirmatory factor analytic approach. *Multivariate Behavioral Research, 20*, 389–417.

Cole, N. S. (1973). Bias in selection. *Journal of Educational Measurement, 10*, 237–255.

Collins, L. M., & Cliff, N. R. (1990). Using the longitudinal Guttman simplex as a basis for measuring growth. *Psychological Bulletin, 108*, 128–134.

Collins, L. M., & Horn, J. L. (1991). *Best methods for the analysis of change?* Washington, DC: American Psychological Association.

*Commonwealth of Pennsylvania v. Flaherty* 983 F.2D 1267 (3rd cir., 1975).

Comrey, A. L. (1973). *A first course in factor analysis*. New York: Academic Press.

Connolly, W. B., Jr., & Petersen, D. W. (1983). *Use of statistics in equal employment opportunity litigation*. New York: Law Journal Seminars Press.

Cooley, W. W., & Lohnes, P. R. (1971). *Multivariate data analysis*. New York: Wiley.

Coombs, C. H. (1964). *A theory of data*. New York: Wiley.

Coombs, C. H. (1980). *Similarity and choice: Papers in honour of Clyde Coombs*. Bern: H. Huber.

Coombs, C. H., Dawes, R. M., & Tversky, A. (1970). *Mathematical psychology: An elementary introduction*. Englewood Cliffs, NJ: Prentice-Hall.

Coombs, C. H., & Kao, R. C. (1960). On a connection between factor analysis and multidimensional unfolding. *Psychometrika, 6*, 267–272.

Cooper, W. H. (1981). Ubiquitous halo. *Psychological Bulletin, 90*, 218–244.

Coren, S., & Ward, L. M. (1989). *Sensation and perception* (3d ed.). Fort Worth, TX: Harcourt Brace Jovanovich.

Cramer, E. M. (1974). On Browne's solution for oblique procrustes rotation. *Psychometrika, 39*, 159–163.

Crano, W. D., & Mellon, P. M. (1978). Causal influences of teachers' expectations on children's academic performance: A cross-lagged panel analysis. *Journal of Educational Psychology, 70*, 39–49.

Cressie, N., & Holland, P. W. (1983). Characterizing the manifest probabilities of latent trait models. *Psychometrika, 48,* 129–141.

Cronbach. L. J. (1951). Coefficient alpha and the internal structure of tests. *Psychometrika, 6,* 297–334.

Cronbach, L. J. (1957). The two disciplines of scientific psychology. *American Psychologist, 12,* 671–684.

Cronbach, L. J. (1971). Test validation. In R. L. Thorndike (Ed.), *Educational measurement* (2d ed.). Washington, DC: American Council on Education.

Cronbach, L. J. (1990). *Essentials of psychological testing* (5th ed.). New York: Harper & Row.

Cronbach, L. J., & Azuma, H. (1962). Internal-consistency reliability formulas applied to randomly sampled single-factor tests: An empirical comparison. *Educational and Psychological Measurement, 22,* 645–666.

Cronbach, L. J., & Furby, L. (1970). How should we measure "change"—or should we? *Psychological Bulletin, 74,* 68–80.

Cronbach, L. J., & Gleser, G. C. (1953). Assessing similarity between profiles. *Psychological Bulletin, 50,* 456–473.

Cronbach, L. J., Gleser, G. C., Nanda, H., & Rajaratnam, N. S. (1972). *The dependability of behavioral measurements.* New York: Wiley.

Cronbach, L. J., Gleser, G. C., & Rajaratnam, N. (1963). Theory of generalizability: A liberalization of reliability theory. *British Journal of Mathematical and Statistical Psychology, 16,* 137–173.

Cronbach, L. J., & Meehl, P. E. (1955). Construct validity in psychological tests. *Psychological Bulletin, 52,* 281–302.

Crowder, R. G. (1976). *Principles of learning and memory,* Hillsdale, NJ: Erlbaum Associates.

Crowne, D. P., & Marlowe, D. (1960). A new scale of social desirability, independent of psychopathology. *Journal of Consulting Psychology, 24,* 349–354.

Cudeck, R. (1989). Analysis of correlation matrices using covariance structure models. *Psychological Bulletin, 105,* 317–327.

Dahlstrom, W. G., & Welsh, G. S. (1960). *An MMPI handbook: A guide to use in clinical practice and research.* Minneapolis, MN: University of Minnesota Press.

Dahlstrom, W. G., Welsh, G. S., & Dahlstrom, L. E. (1975a). *An MMPI handbook* Vol. I. Minneapolis: University of Minnesota Press.

Dahlstrom, W. G., Welsh, G. S., & Dahlstrom, L. E. (1975b). *An MMPI handbook.* Vol. II. Minneapolis: University of Minnesota Press.

Darlington, R. B. (1968). Multiple regression in psychological research and practice. *Psychological Bulletin, 69,* 161–182.

Darlington, R. B. (1971). Another look at culture fairness. *Journal of Educational Measurement, 8,* 71–82.

Darlington, R. B. (1990). *Regression and linear models.* New York: McGraw-Hill.

Davison, G. C., & Neale, J. M. (1986). *Abnormal Psychology* (4th ed.). New York: Wiley.

Davison, M. L. (1983). *Multidimensional scaling.* New York: Wiley.

Davison, M. L. (1985). Multidimensional scaling vs. components analysis of test intercorrelations. *Psychological Bulletin, 97,* 94–105.

Davison, M. L., & Sharma, A. R. (1988). Parametric statistics and levels of measurement. *Psychological Bulletin, 104,* 137–144.

Davison, M. L., & Sharma, A. R. (1990). Parametric statistics and levels of measurement: Factorial designs and multiple regression. *Psychological Bulletin, 107,* 394–400.

Dawes, R. M. (1971). A case study of graduate admissions: Application of three principles of human decision making. *American Psychologist, 26,* 180–188.

Dawes, R. M., & Corrigan, B. (1974). Linear models in decision making. *Psychological Bulletin, 81*, 95–106.

DeCotiis, T. A. (1977). An analysis of the external validity and applied relevance of three rating formats. *Organizational Behavior and Human Performance, 19*, 247–266.

Dempster, A. P., Laird, N. M., & Rubin, D. B. (1977). Maximum likelihood from incomplete data via the EM algorithm (with discussion). *Journal of the Royal Statistical Society*, Ser. B, *39*, 1–38.

Digman, J. M., & Inouye, J. (1986). Further specification of the five robust factors of personality. *Journal of Personality and Social Psychology, 50*, 116–121.

*Dobbins v. International Brotherhood of Electrical Workers, Local 212* (1968). 292 Federal Supplement 413 (Southern District of Ohio).

Donaldson, G. (1983). Confirmatory factor analysis models of information processing stages: An alternative to difference scores. *Psychological Bulletin, 94*, 143–151.

Dorans, N. J., & Kulick, E. M. (1986). Demonstrating the utility of the standardization approach to assessing unexpected differential item performance in the Scholastic Aptitude Test. *Journal of Educational Measurement, 23*, 355–368.

Draper, N. R., & Smith, H. (1981). *Applied regression analysis* (2d ed.). New York: Wiley.

Dudek, F. J. (1979). The continuing misinterpretation of the standard error of measurement. *Psychological Bulletin, 86*, 335–337.

Duncan, O. D. (1975). *Introduction to structural equation models.* New York: Academic Press.

Ebel, R. L. (1969). Expected reliability as a function of choices per item. *Educational and Psychological Measurement, 29*, 565–570.

Edgington, E. S. (1969). *Statistical inference: A distribution-free approach.* New York: McGraw-Hill.

Edwards, A. L. (1953). The relationship between the judged desirability of a trait and the probability that the trait will be endorsed. *Journal of Applied Psychology, 37*, 90–93.

Edwards, A. L. (1957). *Techniques of attitude scale construction.* New York: Appleton-Century-Crofts.

Edwards, A. L. (1970). *The measurement of personality traits by scales and inventories.* New York: Holt.

Edwards, A. L. (1985). *Multiple regression and the analysis of variance and covariance* (2d ed.). New York: Freeman.

Edwards, A. L. (1990). Construct validity and social desirability. *American Psychologist, 45*, 207–209 (Comment).

Edwards, A. L., & Walker, J. N. (1961). Social desirability and agreement response set. *Journal of Personality and Social Psychology, 62*, 180–183.

EEOC et al. (1978). Adoption by four agencies of Uniform Federal Guidelines on Employee Selection Procedures. *Federal Register, 43*, 38290–38315.

EEOC et al. (1979). Adoption of questions and answers . . . . *Federal Register, 44*, 11996–12009.

Efron, B., & Gong, G. (1983). A leisurely look at the bootstrap, the jackknife, and cross-validation. *American Statistician, 37*, 36–48.

Egan, J. P. (1975). *Signal detection theory and ROC analysis.* New York: Academic Press.

Engen, T. (1972a). Psychophysics I: Discrimination and detection. In J. W. Kling & L. A. Riggs (Eds.), *Woodworth & Schlossberg's Experimental Psychology* (3d ed.) (Vol. 1, Chap. 1). New York: Holt, Rinehart, and Winston.

Engen, T. (1972b). Psychophysics II: Scaling methods. In J. W. Kling & L. A. Riggs (Eds.), *Woodworth & Schlossberg's Experimental Psychology* (3d ed.) (Vol. 1, Chap. 2). New York: Holt, Rinehart, and Winston.

Eriksen, C. W. (1960). Discrimination and learning without awareness: A methodological survey and evaluation. *Psychological Review*, *67*, 279–300.

Fechner, G. T. (1860/1966). *Elements of Psychophysics*. New York: Holt, Rinehart, & Winston.

Ferguson, G. A. (1941). The factorial interpretation of test difficulty. *Psychometrika*, *6*, 323–329.

Finney, D. J. (1947). *Probit analysis*. Cambridge: Cambridge University Press.

Fisher, R. A. (1936). The use of multiple measurements in taxonomic problems. *Annals of Eugenics*, *7*, 179–188.

Fisicaro, S. A. (1988). A reexamination of the relation between halo error and accuracy. *Journal of Applied Psychology*, *73*, 239–244.

Fisicaro, S. A., & Lance, C. E. (1990). Implications of three causal models for the measurement of halo error. *Applied Psychological Measurement*, *14*, 419–429.

Flaugher, R. (1990). Item pools. In H. Wainer (Ed.), *Computerized adaptive testing: A primer*. Hillsdale, NJ: Erlbaum Associates.

Formann, A. K. (1988). Latent class models for nonmonotone dichotomous items. *Psychometrika*, *53*, 45–62.

Fuller, E. L., Jr., & Hemmerle, W. J. (1966). Robustness of the maximum likelihood estimation procedure in factor analysis. *Psychometrika*, *31*, 255–266.

Fullerton, G. S., & Cattell, J. M. (1892). *On the "perception of small differences,"* University of Pennsylvania Philosophy Series. Philadelphia: University of Pennsylvania.

Gaito, J. (1980). Measurement scales and statistics: Resurgence of an old misconception. *Psychological Bulletin*, *87*, 564–567.

Garbin, C. P. (1988). Visual-haptic perceptual nonequivalence for shape information and its impact upon cross-modal performance. *Journal of Experimental Psychology: Human Perception and Performance*, *14*, 547–553.

Garbin, C. P., & Bernstein, I. H. (1984). Visual and haptic perception of three-dimensional solid forms. *Perception and Psychophysics*, *36*, 104–110.

Garner, W. R. (1960). Rating scales, discriminability, and information transmission. *Psychological Review*, *67*, 343–352.

Garner, W. R. (1962). *Uncertainty and structure as psychological concepts*. New York: Wiley.

Garner, W. R. (1974). *The processing of information and structure*. Hillsdale, NJ: Erlbaum Associates.

Garner, W. R., Hake, H. W., & Eriksen, C. W. (1957). Operationalism and the concept of perception. *Psychological Review*, *63*, 317–329.

Garner, W. R., & Morton, J. (1969). Perceptual independence: Definitions, models, and experimental paradigms. *Psychological Bulletin*, *72*, 233–259.

Ghiselli, E. E. (1966). *The validity of occupational aptitude tests*. New York: Wiley.

Glas, C. A. W., & Verhelst, N. D. (1989). Extensions of the partial credit model. *Psychometrika*, *54*, 635–660.

Gleser, G. C., Cronbach, L. J., & Rajaratnam, N. S. (1965). Generalizability of scores influenced by multiple sources of variance. *Psychometrika*, *30*, 395–418.

Goldberg, L. R. (1965). Diagnosticians vs. diagnostic signs: The diagnosis of psychosis vs. neurosis from the MMPI. *Psychological Monographs*, *79*, 9 (Whole no. 602).

Goldberg, L. R. (1968a). The diagnosis of psychosis vs. neurosis from the MMPI. Paper presented at the Third Annual MMPI symposium. Minneapolis, MN.

Goldberg, L. R. (1968b). Simple models or simple processes. *American Psychologist*, *23*, 483–496.

Goldiamond, I. (1958). Unconscious indicators of perception: I. Subliminal perception, subception, unconscious perception. An analysis in terms of psychophysical methodology. *Psychological Bulletin*, *55*, 373–411.

Goodman, L. A. (1978). *Analyzing quantitative/categorical data: Log-linear models and latent structure analysis.* Lanham, MD: Abt.

Gorsuch, R. L. (1966). The general factor in the test anxiety questionnaire. *Psychological Reports, 19*, 308.

Gorsuch, R. L. (1973). Using Bartlett's significance test to determine the number of factors to extract. *Educational and Psychological Measurement, 33*, 361–364.

Gorsuch, R. L. (1983). *Factor analysis.* Hillsdale, NJ: Erlbaum Associates.

Gorsuch, R. L. (1984). Measurement: The boon and bane of investigating religion. *American Psychologist, 39*, 228–236.

Gorsuch, R. L. (1988). Exploratory factor analysis. In J. R. Nesselroade & R. B. Cattell (Eds.), *Handbook of Multivariate Experimental Psychology.* New York: Plenum.

Gorsuch, R. L. (1990). Common factor analysis versus component analysis: Some well and little known facts. *Multivariate Behavioral Research, 25*, 33–39.

Gorsuch, R. L., Henighan, R. P., & Barnard, C. (1972). Locus of control: An example of dangers in using children's scales with children. *Child Development, 43*, 579–590.

Graham, J. R. (1990). MMPI-2: Assessing personality and psychopathology. New York: Oxford University Press.

Green, S. (1991). How many subjects does it take to do a regression analysis? *Multivariate Behavioral Research, 26*, 499–510.

Green, D. M., & Swets, J. A. (1967). *Signal detection theory and psychophysics.* New York: Wiley.

Greenwald, A. G., Pratkanis, A. R., Leippe, M. R., & Baumgardner, M. H. (1986). Under what conditions does theory obstruct research progress. *Psychological Review, 93*, 216–229.

*Griggs v. Duke Power* (1971). 401 United States 424.

Grizzle, J. E., Starmer, C. F., & Koch, G. G. (1969). Analysis of categorical data by linear models. *Biometrics, 25*, 489–504.

Guadagnoli, E., & Velicer, W. F. (1988). Relation of sample size to the stability of component patterns. *Psychological Bulletin, 103*, 265–275.

Guilford, J. P. (1936). *Psychometric methods.* New York: McGraw-Hill.

Guilford, J. P. (1952). When not to factor analyze. *Psychological Bulletin, 49*, 26–37.

Guilford, J. P. (1954). *Psychometric methods* (2d ed.). New York: McGraw-Hill.

Guilford, J. P. (1967). *The nature of human intelligence.* New York: McGraw-Hill.

Guilford, J. P., & Fruchter, B. (1978). *Fundamental statistics in psychology and education* (6th ed.). New York: McGraw-Hill.

Guion, R. M. (1965). *Personnel testing.* New York: McGraw-Hill.

Guion, R. M., & Gibson, W. M. (1988). Personnel selection and placement. *Annual Review of Psychology, 39*, 349–374.

Gulliksen, H. (1950). *Theory of mental tests.* New York: Wiley.

Guttman, L. (1950). The basis for scalogram analysis. In S. A. Stouffer et al. (Eds.), *Measurement and Prediction.* Princeton, NJ: Princeton University Press.

Guttman, L. (1953). Image theory for the structure of quantitative variates. *Psychometrika, 18*, 277–296.

Guttman, L. (1954). Some necessary conditions for common factor analysis. *Psychometrika, 19*, 149–161.

Guttman, L. (1956). "Best possible" systematic estimates of communalities. *Psychometrika, 21*, 273–285.

Gynther, M. D. (1972). White norms and black MMPIs: A prescription for discrimination. *Psychological Bulletin, 78*, 386–402.

Gynther, M. D., & Burkhart, B. R. (1983). Are subtle MMPI items expendable? In J. R. Butcher & C. D. Spielberger (Eds.), *Advances in personality assessment* (Vol. 2). Hillsdale, NJ: Erlbaum Associates.

Gynther, M. D., & Green, S. B. (1980). Accuracy may make a difference, but does a difference make for accuracy? A response to Pritchard and Rosenblatt. *Journal of Consulting and Clinical Psychology, 48,* 268–272.

Haertel, E. H. (1990). Continuous and discrete latent structure models for item response data. *Psychometrika, 55,* 477–494.

Hake, H. W., Faust, G. W., McIntyre, J. S., & Murray, H. G. (1967). Relational perception and modes of perceiver operation. *Perception & Psychophysics, 2,* 469–478.

Hake, H. W., & Rodwan, A. S., (1966). Perception and recognition. In J. B. Sidowski (Ed.), *Experimental methods and instrumentation in psychology.* New York: McGraw-Hill.

Hake, H. W., Rodwan, A. S., & Weintraub, D. (1966). Noise reduction in perception. In K. R. Hammond (Ed.), *Egon Brunswik's psychology.* New York: Holt, Rinehart and Winston.

Hambleton, R. K. (1980). True score validity and standard setting methods. In R. A. Berk (Ed.), *Criterion referenced measurement: The state of the art.* Baltimore: Johns Hopkins University Press.

Hambleton, R. K., & Swaminathan, H. (1985). *Item response theory.* Boston: Kluwer-Nijoff.

Hambleton, R. K., Swaminathan, H., & Rogers, L. (1991). *Fundamentals of item response theory.* Newbury Park, CA: Sage.

Hambleton, R. K., & van der Linden, W. J. (1982). Advances in item response theory, *Applied Psychological Measurement, 6* (Special Issue).

Hammer, A. G. (1971). *Elementary matrix algebra for psychologists and social scientists.* Rushcutters Bay, Australia: Pergamon Press.

Hammond, K. R., Hamm, R. M., & Grassia, J. (1986). Generalizing over conditions by combining the multitrait-multimethod matrix and the representative design of experiments. *Psychological Bulletin, 100,* 257–269.

Harman, H. H. (1976). *Modern factor analysis* (3d ed., rev.). Chicago: University of Chicago Press.

Harman, H. H., & Jones, W. H. (1966). Factor analysis by minimizing residuals. *Psychometrika, 31,* 351–368.

Harris, R. J. (1985). *A primer of multivariate analysis.* Orlando, FL: Academic Press.

Hartline, H. K. (1940). The receptive field of optic nerve fibers. *American Journal of Physiology, 130,* 690–699.

Hathaway, S. R., & McKinley. J. C. (1989). *Minnesota Multiphasic Personality Inventory—2: Manual for administration and scoring.* Minneapolis, MN: University of Minnesota Press.

Hayduk, L. A. (1987). *Structural equation modeling with LISREL.* Baltimore: Johns Hopkins University Press.

Hays, W. L. (1988). *Statistics.* New York: Holt, Rinehart and Winston.

Hedges, L. V., & Olkin, I. (1985). *Statistical methods for metanalysis.* Orlando, FL: Academic Press.

Heiser, W. J., & Meulman, J. (1983). Constrained multidimensional scaling, including confirmation. *Applied Psychological Measurement, 7,* 381–404.

Helmstadter, G. C. (1957). An empirical comparison of methods for estimating profile similarity. *Educational and Psychological Measurement, 17,* 71–82.

Hendrickson, A. E., & White, P. O. (1964). Promax: A quick method for rotation to oblique simple structure. *British Journal of Statistical Psychology, 17,* 65–70.

Henryssen, S. (1971). Gathering, analyzing, and using data on test items. In R. L. Thorndike (Ed.), *Educational measurement* (2d ed.). Washington. DC: American Council on Education.

Heywood, H. B. (1931). On finite sequences of real numbers. *Proceedings of the Royal Society of London, 134*, 486–501.

Hills, J. R. (1971). Use of measurement in selection and placement. In R. L. Thorndike (Ed.), *Educational measurement* (2d ed.). Washington, DC: American Council on Education.

Hintzman, D. L. (1980). Simpson's paradox and the analysis of memory retrieval. *Psychological Review, 87*, 398–410.

Hoffmann, R. J. (1978). Complexity and simplicity as objective indices descriptive of factor solutions. *Multivariate Behavioral Research, 13*, 247–250.

Hogan, R., & Nicholson, R. A. (1989). The meaning of personality test scores. *American Psychologist, 43*, 621–626.

Hohn, F. E. (1973). *Elementary matrix algebra* (3d ed.). New York: Macmillan.

Holland, P. W., & Thayer, D. T. (1988). Differential item performance and the Mantel-Haenszel procedure. In H. Wainer & H. Braun (Eds.), *Test Validity*. Hillsdale, NJ: Erlbaum Associates.

Holzinger, K. J. (1944). A simple method of factor analysis. *Psychometrika, 9*, 257–262.

Holzinger, K. J., & Swineford, F. (1937). The bi-factor method. *Psychometrika, 2*, 41–54.

Horn, J. L. (1965). An empirical comparison of various methods for estimating common factor scores. *Educational and Psychological Measurements, 25*, 313–322.

Horn, J. L. (1969). On the internal consistency reliability of factors. *Multivariate Behavioral Research, 4*, 115–125.

Horn, J. L., & Cattell, R. B. (1966). Refinement and test of the theory of fluid and crystallized intelligence. *Journal of Educational Psychology, 57*, 253–276.

Horn, J. L., Donaldson, E., & Engstrom, R. (1981). Apprehension, memory and fluid intelligence decline in adulthood. *Research on Aging, 3*, 33–84.

Horn, J. L., & Knapp, J. R. (1973). On the subjective character of the empirical base of the structure-of-intellect model. *Psychological Bulletin, 80*, 33–43.

Horst, P. (1966). *Psychological measurement and prediction*. Belmont, CA: Wadsworth.

Hotelling, H. (1933). Analysis of a complex of statistical variables into principal components. *Journal of Educational Psychology, 24*, 417–441, 298–520.

Houston, W. M., & Novick, M. R. (1987). Race-based differential prediction in Air Force technical rating programs. *Journal of Educational Measurement, 24*, 309–320.

Houts, A. C., Cook, T. D., & Shadish W. R., Jr. (1986). The person-situation debate: A critical multiplist perspective. *Journal of Personality, 54*, 52–105.

Hoyt, C. J. (1941). Test reliability estimated by analysis of variance. *Psychometrika, 6*, 153–160.

Huberty, C. J., & Barton, R. M. (1990). Review of applied multivariate statistics text books. *Applied Psychological Measurement, 14*, 95–101.

Hulin, C. L., Drasgow, F., & Parsons, C. K. (1983). *Item response theory*. Homewood, IL: Dow Jones-Irwin.

Humphreys, L. G., & Fleishman, A. (1974). Pseudo-orthogonal and other analysis of variance designs including an individual difference variable. *Journal of Educational Psychology, 66*, 464–472.

Humphreys, L. G., & Ilgen, D. (1969). Note on a criterion for the number of common factors. *Educational and Psychological Measurement, 29*, 571–578.

Hunt, E. B., Pellegrino, J. W., Frick, R. W., Farr, S. A., & Alderson, A. (1988). The ability to reason about movement in the visual field. In E. A. Fleishman (Ed.), *Human performance and productivity*. Hillsdale, NJ: Erlbaum Associates.

Hunter, J. E., & Hunter, R. (1984). Validity and utility of alternative predictors of job performance. *Psychological Bulletin, 96,* 72–98.

Hunter, J. E., & Schmidt, F. L. (1976). Critical analysis of the statistical and ethical implications of various definitions of test bias. *Psychological Bulletin, 83,* 1053–1071.

Hunter, J. E., & Schmidt, F. L. (1981). Fitting people to jobs: The impact of personnel selection on national productivity. In E. A. Fleishman (Ed.), *Human performance and productivity.* Hillsdale, NJ: Erlbaum Associates.

Hunter, J. E., Schmidt, F. L., & Hunter, R. (1979). Differential validity of employment tests by race: A comprehensive review and analysis. *Psychological Bulletin, 86,* 721–735.

Hunter, J. E., Schmidt, F. L, & Jackson, G. B. (1982). *Metanalysis: Cumulating research findings across studies.* Beverly Hills, CA: Sage.

Hunter, J. E., Schmidt, F. L., & Rauschenberger, J. (1984). Methodological, statistical, and ethical issues in the study of test bias. In C. R. Reynolds & R. T. Brown (Eds.), *Perspectives on bias in mental testing.* New York: Plenum Press.

*International Brotherhood of Teamsters v. United States,* 431 United States 324 (1977).

Ironson, G. H. (1982). Use of chi-square and latent trait approaches for detecting item bias. In R. A. Berk (Ed.), *Handbook of methods for detecting item bias.* Baltimore: Johns Hopkins University Press.

Ironson, G. H., & Subkoviak (1979). A comparison of several methods for assessing item bias. *Journal of Educational Measurement, 16,* 209–225.

Isaac, P. D. (1970). Linear regression, structural relations, and measurement error. *Psychological Bulletin, 74,* 213–218.

Jackson, D. N. (1971). The dynamics of structured personality tests. *Psychological Review, 78,* 229–248.

Jackson, D. N., & Chan, D. W. (1980). Maximum-likelihood estimation in common factor analysis: A cautionary note. *Psychological Bulletin, 88,* 502–508.

Jackson, D. N., & Messick, S. J. (1962). Response styles and the assessment of psychopathology. In S. J. Messick and J. Ross (Eds.), *Measurement in personality and cognition.* New York: Wiley.

James, W. (1890). *The principles of psychology.* New York: Holt, Rinehart, and Winston.

Jennrich, R. I., & Sampson, P. J. (1966). Rotation for simple loadings. *Psychometrika, 31,* 313–323.

Jensema, C. J. (1974). The validity of Bayesian tailored testing. *Educational and Psychological Measurement, 34,* 757–766.

Jensema, C. J. (1977). Bayesian tailored testing and the influence of item bank characteristics. *Applied Psychological Measurement, 1,* 111–120.

Jensen, A. E. (1980). *Bias in mental testing.* London: Methuen.

Johnson, S. C. (1967). Hierarchical cluster schemes. *Psychometrika, 32,* 241–254.

Jones, L. A., & Iacobucci, D. (1989). The structure of affect and trait judgments of political figures. *Multivariate Behavioral Research, 24,* 257–276.

Jöreskog, K. G. (1962). On the statistical treatment of residuals in factor analysis. *Psychometrika, 27,* 335–354.

Jöreskog, K. G. (1966). Testing a simple structure hypothesis in factor analysis. *Psychometrika, 31,* 165–178.

Jöreskog, K. G. (1969a). A general approach to confirmatory maximum likelihood factor analysis. *Psychometrika, 34,* 183–202.

Jöreskog, K. G. (1969b). Efficient estimation in image factor analysis. *Psychometrika, 34,* 51–75.

Jöreskog, K. G. (1971). Statistical analysis of sets of congeneric tests. *Psychometrika, 36,* 109–133.

Jöreskog, K. G. (1974). Analyzing psychological data by structural analysis of covariance matrices. In R. C. Atkinson, D. H. Krantz, R. D. Luce, & P. Suppes (Eds.), *Contemporary developments in mathematical psychology* (Vol. II). San Francisco: Freeman.

Jöreskog, K. G. (1978). Structural analysis of covariance and correlation matrices. *Psychometrika, 43*, 443–477.

Jöreskog, K. G., & Lawley, D. N. (1968). New methods in maximum likelihood factor analysis. *British Journal of Mathematical and Statistical Psychology, 21*, 85–96.

Jöreskog, K. G., & Säorbom, D. (1989). *LISREL:* Analysis of linear structural relationships by the method of maximum likelihood (Version VII). Mooresville, IN: Scientific Software.

Kaiser, H. F. (1958). The varimax criterion for analytic rotation in factor analysis. *Psychometrika, 23*, 187–200.

Kaiser, H. F. (1960). The application of electronic computers to factor analysis. *Educational and Psychological Measurements, 20*, 141–151.

Kaiser, H. F. (1970). A second generation Little Jiffy. *Psychometrika, 35*, 401–417.

Kaiser, H. F., & Caffey, J. (1965). Alpha factor analysis. *Psychometrika, 30*, 1–14.

Kaiser, H. F., Hunka, S., & Bianchini, J. (1971). Relating factors between studies based upon different individuals. *Multivariate Behavioral Research, 6*, 409–422.

Kaiser, H. F., & Rice, J. (1974). Little Jiffy Mark IV. *Educational and Psychological Measurement, 34*, 111–117.

Kendall, L. M. (1964). The effects of varying time limits on test validity. *Educational and Psychological Measurement, 24*, 789–800.

Kendall, M. G. (1948). *Rank correlation methods.* London: Griffin.

Kendall, M. G., & Stuart, A. (1967). *The advanced theory of statistics* (Vol. 2) (2d ed.). New York: Hafner.

Kenny, D. A. (1975). Cross-lagged panel correlation: A test for spuriousness. *Psychological Bulletin, 82*, 887–903.

Kenny, D. A. (1979). *Correlation and causality.* New York: Wiley.

Kenny, D. A., & La Voie, L. (1985). Separating individual and group effects. *Journal of Personality and Social Psychology, 48*, 339–348.

Kerlinger, F. N. (1986). *Foundations of behavioral research* (3d ed.). New York: Holt, Rinehart, & Winston.

King, L. M., Hunter, J. E., & Schmidt, F. L. (1980). Halo in a multidimensional forced-choice performance evaluation scale. *Journal of Applied Psychology, 65*, 507–516.

Klein, G. S., Spence, D. P., Holt, R. R., & Gourevitch, S. (1958). Cognition without awareness: Subliminal influences upon conscious thought. *Journal of Abnormal and Social Psychology, 57*, 255–266.

Koch, G. G., Landis, J. R., Freeman, J. L., Freeman, D. H., & Lehnen, R. G. (1977). A general methodology for the analysis of experiments with repeated measurement of categorical data. *Biometrics, 33*, 133–158.

Krantz, D. H., Atkinson, R. C., Luce, R. D., & Suppes, P. (Eds.) (1974). *Contemporary developments in mathematical psychology.* (Vol. 2). San Francisco: Freeman.

Krathwohl, D. R., & Payne, D. (1971). Defining and assessing educational objectives. In R. L. Thorndike (Ed.), *Educational measurement* (2d ed.). Washington, DC: American Council on Education.

Kruskal, J. B. (1964). Nonmetric multidimensional scaling. *Psychometrika, 29*, 1–27; 115–129.

Kruskal, J. B., & Wish, M. (1978). *Multidimensional scaling.* Beverly Hills, CA: Sage.

Kuder, G. F., & Richardson, M. W. (1937). The theory of the estimation of test reliability. *Psychometrika, 2*, 151–160.

Kuffler, S. W. (1953). Discharge patterns and functional organization of mammalian retina. *Journal of Neurophysiology*, *16*, 37–68.

Labouvie, E. W. (1982). Measurement of individual differences in intraindividual change. *Psychological Bulletin*, *88*, 54–59.

Landers, S. (1986). Judge reiterates IQ test ban. *APA Monitor*, *17*, 18.

Lang, P. J. (1969). The mechanics of desensitization and the laboratory study of fear. In C. M. Franks (Ed.), *Behavior therapy: Appraisal and status*. New York: McGraw-Hill.

Lanterman, E.-D., Feger, H., & Coombs, C. W. (1980). *Similarity and choice: Papers in honour of Clyde Coombs*. Bern: Haber.

Lawley, D. N. (1940). The estimation of factor loadings by the method of maximum likelihood. *Proceedings of the Royal Society of Edinburgh*, *60*, 64–82.

Lawley, D. N. (1941). Further investigators into factor estimation. *Proceedings of the Royal Society of Edinburgh*, *61*, 176–185.

Lawley, D. N., & Maxwell, A. E. (1963). *Factor analysis as a statistical method*. London: Butterworth.

Levine, M. V. (1981). Weighted item bias statistics. Report 81-5. Urbana-Champaign: Department of Educational Psychology, University of Illinois.

Levine, M. V., Wardrop, J. L., & Linn R. I. (1982). Weighted mean squares item bias statistics. Paper presented at the annual meeting of the American Educational Research Association, New York.

Lindquist, E. F. (1953). *Design and analysis of experiments in psychology and education*. Boston: Houghton-Mifflin.

Linn, R. L. (1973). Fair test use in selection. *Review of Educational Research*, *43*, 343–357.

Linn, R. L. (1989). *Educational Measurement* (3d ed.). New York: ACE/Macmillan.

Linn, R. L., Levine, M. V., Hastings, C. N., & Wardrop, J. L. (1981). Item bias in a test of reading comprehension. *Applied Psychological Measurement*, *5*, 159–173.

Loehlin, J. (1987). *Latent variable models: An introduction to factor, path, and structural analysis*. Hillsdale, NJ: Erlbaum Associates.

Loevinger, J. (1954). The attenuation paradox in test theory. *Psychological Bulletin*, *51*, 493–504.

Loevinger, J. (1957). Objective tests as instruments of psychological theory. *Psychological Reports*. Monograph No. 9, *3*, 635–694.

Long, J. S. (1983a). *Confirmatory factor analysis*. Beverly Hills, CA: Sage.

Long, J. S. (1983b). *Covariance structure models*. Beverly Hills, CA: Sage.

Lord, F. M. (1952a). A theory of test scores. *Psychometric Monographs*, No. 7.

Lord, F. M. (1952b). The relationship of the reliability of multiple choice items to the distribution of item difficulties. *Psychometrika*, *18*, 181–194.

Lord, F. M. (1953). The relationship of test scores to trait underlying the test. *Educational and Psychological Measurement*, *17*, 510–521.

Lord, F. M. (1956). A study of speed factors in tests and academic grades. *Psychometrika*, *21*, 31–50.

Lord, F. M. (1963). Formula scoring and validity. *Educational and Psychological Measurement*, *23*, 663–672.

Lord, F. M. (1970). Some test theory for tailored testing. In W. H. Holtzman (Ed.), *Computer-assisted instruction, testing, and guidance*. New York: Harper & Row.

Lord, F. M. (1971). The self-scoring flexilevel test. *Journal of Educational Measurement*, *8*, 147–151.

Lord, F. M. (1974). Individualized testing and item characteristic curve theory. In D. H. Krantz, R. C. Atkinson, R. D. Luce, & P. Suppes (Eds.), *Contemporary developments in mathematical psychology* (Vol. 2). San Francisco: Freeman.

Lord, F. M. (1976). *Optimal number of choices per item—A comparison of four approaches*. Research Bulletin RB 76-4. Princeton, NJ: Educational Testing Service.

Lord, F. M. (1977). A study of item bias using item characteristic curve theory. In Y. H. Poortinga (Ed.), *Basic problems in cross-cultural research*. Amsterdam: Swets & Zeitlinger.

Lord, F. M. (1980). *Applications of item response theory to practical testing problems*. Hillsdale, NJ: Erlbaum Associates.

Lord, F. M., & Novick, M. R. (1968). *Statistical theories of mental test scores*. Reading, MA: Addison-Wesley.

Lorr, M. (1983). *Cluster analysis for social scientists*. San Francisco: Josey-Bass.

Luce, R. D. (1959a). *Individual choice behavior*. New York: Wiley.

Luce, R. D. (1959b). On the possible psychophysical laws. *Psychological Review, 66*, 81–95.

Luce, R. D. (1963). Detection and recognition. In R. D. Luce, R. R. Bush, & E. Galanter (Eds.), *Handbook of mathematical psychology* (Vol. 1). New York: Wiley.

Luce, R. D. (1977). Thurstone's discriminal process fifty years later. *Psychometrika, 42*, 461–490.

Luce, R. D. (1990). "On the possible psychophysical laws" revisited: Remarks on cross-modal matching. *Psychological Review, 97*, 66–77.

MacAndrew, C. (1965). The differentiation of male alcoholic outpatients from non-alcoholic psychiatric patients by means of the MMPI. *Quarterly Journal of Studies on Alcohol, 26*, 238–246.

MacCallum, R. (1986). Specification searches in covariance structure modeling. *Psychological Bulletin, 100*, 107–120.

Macmillan, N. A., & Creelman, C. D. (1990). Response bias: Characteristics of detection theory, threshold theory and "nonparametric" indices. *Psychological Bulletin, 107*, 401–413.

Macmillan, N. A., & Creelman, C. D. (1991). *Detection theory: A user's guide*. Cambridge: Cambridge University Press.

Magnusson, D. (1967). *Test theory*. Reading, MA: Addison-Wesley.

Marascuilo, L. A., & Levin, J. R. (1983). *Multivariate statistics in the social sciences: A researcher's guide*. Belmont, CA: Brooks-Cole.

Marks, L. E. (1974). On scales of sensation: Prolegomena to any future psychophysics that will be above to come forth as science. *Perception and Psychophysics, 16*, 358–376.

Martin, B. (1961). The assessment of anxiety by physiological behavioral measure. *Psychological Bulletin, 58*, 234–255.

Martinson, E. O., & Hamdan, M. A. (1975). Calculation of the polychoric estimate of correlation in contingency tables. *Applied Statistics, 24*, 272–278.

Masters, G. N. (1982). A Rasch model for partial credit scoring. *Psychometrika, 47*, 149–174.

Maxwell, A. E. (1961). Canonical variate analysis when the variables are dichotomous. *Educational and Psychological Measurements, 21*, 259–271.

McCrae, R. R., & Costa, P. T., Jr. (1983). Social desirability scales: More substance than style. *Journal of Consulting and Clinical Psychology, 51*, 881–888.

McCrae, R. R., & Costa, P. T., Jr. (1984). *Emerging lives, enduring dispositions: Personality in adulthood*. Boston, MA: Little, Brown.

McCrae, R. R., & Costa, P. T., Jr. (1985). Updating Norman's adequate taxonomy: Intelligence and personality dimensions in natural language and in questionnaires. *Journal of Personality and Social Psychology, 49*, 710–721.

McCrae, R. R., & Costa, P. T., Jr. (1987). Validation of the five factor model of personality across instruments and observers. *Journal of Personality and Social Psychology, 52*, 81–90.

McDonald, R. P. (1986). Describing the elephant: Structure and function in multivariate data. *Psychometrika, 51*, 513–534.

McDonald, R. P. (1990). Choosing a multivariate model: noncentrality and goodness of fit. *Psychological Bulletin, 107*, 247–255.

McDonald, R. P., & Marsh, H. W. (1990). Choosing a multivariate model: Noncentrality and goodness of fit. *Psychological Bulletin, 107*, 247–255.

McDonald, R. P., & Mulaik, S. A. (1979). Determinacy of common factors: A nontechnical review. *Psychological Bulletin, 86*, 297–306.

McGinnies, E. (1949). Emotionality and perceptual defense. *Psychological Review, 566*, 244–251.

McLaughlin, S. D. (1980). A theoretical partialing in survey research. *American Psychologist, 35*, 851.

McNemar, Q. (1975). On so-called test bias. *American Psychologist, 30*, 848–851.

McQuitty, L. L., & Koch, V. L. (1976). Highest column entry hierarchical clustering: A redevelopment and elaboration of elementary linkage analysis. *Educational and Psychological Measurement, 36*, 243–258.

Medley, D. M., & Mitzel, H. E. (1963). Measuring classroom behavior by systematic observation. In N. L. Gage (Ed.), *Handbook of research in teaching*. Chicago: Rand McNally.

Meehl, P. E. (1945). The dynamics of "structured" personality tests, *Journal of Clinical Psychology, 1*, 296–303.

Meehl, P. E., & Hathaway, S. R. (1946). The K factor as a suppressor variable in the MMPI. *Journal of Applied Psychology, 30*, 525–564.

Melzack, R. (1975). The McGill pain questionnaire: Major properties and scoring methods. *Pain, 1*, 277–299.

Meredith, W. (1964). Notes on factorial invariance. *Psychometrika, 29*, 177–185.

Mershon, B., & Gorsuch, R. L. (1988). Number of factors in the personality sphere: Does increase in factors increase predictability of real-life criteria? *Journal of Personality and Social Psychology, 55*, 675–680.

Mervis, C. B., Rips, L., Rosch, E., Shoben, E. J., & Smith, E. E. (1975). Relatedness of concepts. Unpublished manuscript. Ann Arbor, MI: University of Michigan.

Messick, S. J., & Abelson, R. P. (1956). The additive constant problem in multidimensional scaling. *Psychometrika, 21*, 367–376.

Michell, J. (1986). Measurement scales and statistics: A clash of paradigms, *Psychological Bulletin, 100*, 398–397.

Miller, G. A. (1956). The magical number seven, plus or minus two. *Psychological Review, 63*, 81–97.

Miller, T. W., & Weiss, D. J. (1976). *Effects of time limits on test taking behavior*. Research Report 76-2. Minneapolis: University of Minnesota.

Mislevy, R. J. (1986). Bayes model estimation in item response models. *Psychometrika, 51*, 177–195.

Mislevy, R. J., & Bock, R. D. (1986). *PC-Bilog: Item analysis and test scoring with binary logistic models*. Mooresville, IN: Scientific Software.

Mitchell, J. V., Jr. (Ed.) (1985). *The ninth mental measurement yearbook*, Lincoln: University of Nebraska Press.

Mitchell, J. V., Jr. (Ed.) (1989). *The tenth mental measurement yearbook*, Lincoln: University of Nebraska Press.

Mokken, R. J. (1971). *A theory and procedure of scale analysis with application in political research*. The Hague: Mouton.

Mokken, R. J., & Lewis, C. (1982). A nonparametric approach to the analysis of dichotomous item responses. *Applied Psychological Measurement, 6*, 417–430.

Montanelli, R. G., & Humphreys, L. G. (1976). Latent roots of random data correlation matrices with squared multiple correlations on the diagonal. A Monte Carlo study. *Psychometrika, 41*, 341–347.

Morris, J. D. (1982). Ridge regression and some alternative weighting techniques: A comment on Darlington. *Psychological Bulletin, 91*, 203–209.

Morrison, D. F. (1976). *Multivariate statistical methods* (2d ed.). New York: McGraw-Hill.

Morrison, E. J. (1960). On test variance and the dimensions of the measurement situation. *Educational and Psychological Measurement, 20*, 231–250.

Mosher, D. L. (1966). The development and multitrait-multimethod matrix analysis of three measures of three aspects of guilt. *Journal of Consulting and Clinical Psychology, 30*, 25–29.

Mosher, D. L. (1968). Measures of guilt in females by self-report inventories. *Journal of Consulting and Clinical Psychology, 32*, 690–695.

Mueller, H. A (1987). Rasch model for continuous ratings. *Psychometrika, 52*, 165–182.

Mulaik, S. A. (1966). Inferring the communality of a variable in a universe of variables. *Psychological Bulletin, 66*, 119–124.

Mulaik, S. A., James, L. R., Van Alstine, J., Bennett, N., Lind, S., & Stilwell, C. D. (1989). Evaluation of goodness-of-fit statistics for structural equation models. *Psychological Bulletin, 105*, 430–445.

Muldoon, J. F., & Ray, O. S. (1958). A comparison of pattern similarity as measured by six statistical techniques and eleven clinicians. *Educational and Psychological Measurement, 18*, 775–781.

Murphy, K. R., & Reynolds, D. H. (1988). Does true halo affect observed halo? *Journal of Applied Psychology, 73*, 235–238.

Muthén, B. (1988). *LISCOMP* program manual. Mooresville, IN: Scientific Software.

Muthén, B., & Lehman, J. (1985). Multiple group IRT modeling: Application to item bias analysis. *Journal of Educational Statistics, 10*, 133–142.

Nairn, A., & Nader, R. (1980). *The reign of ETS: The corporation that makes up minds*. New York: Nader.

Neill, J. A., & Jackson, D. N. (1970). An evaluation of item selection strategies in personality scale construction. *Educational and Psychological Measurement, 30*, 647–661.

Nelson, T. O. (1986). ROC curves and measures of discrimination accuracy: A reply to Swets. *Psychological Bulletin, 100*, 128–132.

Nesselroade, J. R., Stigler, S. M., & Baltes, P. B. (1980). Regression towards the mean and the study of change. *Psychological Bulletin, 88*, 622–637.

Neuhaus, J. O., & Wrigley, C. (1954). The quartimax method: An analytical approach to orthogonal simple structure. *British Journal of Statistical Psychology, 7*, 81–91.

Noreen, E. W. (1989). *Computer intensive methods for hypothesis testing: An introduction*. New York: Wiley.

Nunnally, J. C. (1955). An investigation of some propositions of self-conception: The case of Miss Sun. *Journal of Abnormal and Social Psychology, 50*, 87–92.

Nunnally, J. C. (1962). The analysis of profile data. *Psychological Bulletin, 59*, 311–319.

Nunnally, J. C. (1967). *Psychometric theory*. New York: McGraw-Hill.

Nunnally, J. C. (1972). *Educational measurement and evaluation* (2d ed.). New York: McGraw-Hill.

Nunnally, J. C., & Hodges, W. F. (1965). Some dimensions of individual differences in word association. *Journal of Verbal Learning and Verbal Behavior, 4*, 82–88.

Olzak, L. A., & Wickens, T. D. (1983). The interpretation of detection data through direct multivariate frequency analysis. *Psychological Bulletin, 93*, 574–585.

Orchard, T., & Woodbury, M. A. (1972). A missing information principle: Theory and applications. *Proceedings of the 6th Berkeley Symposium on Mathematical Statistics and Probability, 6*, 697–715.

Osgood, C. E., & Suci, G. J. (1952). A measure of relation determined by both mean differences and profile information. *Psychological Bulletin, 49*, 251–262.

Osgood, C. E., Suci, G. H., & Tannenbaum, P. H. (1957). *The measurement of meaning*. Urbana, IL: University of Illinois Press.

Overall, J. E., & Klett, C. J. (1972). *Applied multivariate analysis*. New York: McGraw-Hill.

Owen, R. J. (1975). A Bayesian sequential procedure for quantal response in the context of adaptive mental testing. *Journal of the American Statistical Association, 70*, 351–356.

Pagel, M. D., & Lunneborg, C. E. (1985). Empirical evaluation of ridge regression. *Psychological Bulletin, 97*, 342–355.

Paik, M. (1985). A graphic representation of a three-way contingency table: Simpson's paradox and correlation. *American Statistician, 39*, 53–54.

Parker, S., Casey, J., Ziriax, J. M., & Silberberg, A. (1988). Random monotone data fit simple algebraic models: Correlation is not confirmation. *Psychological Bulletin, 104*, 417–423.

Paulhus, D. L. (1984). Two-component model of socially desirable responding. *Journal of Personality and Social Psychology, 46*, 598–609.

Paulhus, D. L. (1985). Self-deception and impression management in test responses. In A. Angleiter & J. S. Wiggins (Eds.), *Personality assessment via questionnaire: Current issues in theory and measurement*. New York: Springer-Verlag.

Paunonen, S. V., & Gardner, R. C. (1991). Biases resulting from the use of aggregated variables in psychology. *Psychological Bulletin, 109*, 520–523.

Paunonen, S. V., & Jackson, D. N. (1985). Idiographic measurement strategies for personality and prediction: Some unredeemed promissory notes. *Psychological Review, 92*, 599–619.

Pearson, K. (1900). On the criterion that a given system of deviations from the probable in the case of a correlated system of variables is such that it could have reasonably be supposed to have arisen from random sampling. *The London, Edinburgh, and Dublin Philosophical Magazine and Journal of Science*, 5th Ser., *50*, 157–175, 2.

Pedhazur, E. J. (1982). *Multiple regression in behavioral research* (2d ed.). New York: Holt, Rinehart, and Winston.

Perloff, J. M., & Persons, J. B. (1988). Biases resulting from the use of indices: An application to attributional style and depression. *Psychological Bulletin, 103*, 95–104.

Peterson, N. S., & Novick, M. R. (1976). An evaluation of some models for culture-fail selection. *Journal of Educational Measurement, 13*, 3–20.

Plumlee, L. B. (1952). The effect of difficulty and chance success on item-test correlation. *Psychometrika, 17*, 69–86.

Pomerantz, J. R., & Pristach, E. A. (1989). Emergent features, attention and perceptual glue in visual form perception. *Journal of Experimental Psychology: Human Perception and Performance, 15*, 635–649.

Popper, K. R. (1959). *The logic of scientific discovery*. New York: Basic Books.

Prediger, D. J. (1989). Ability differences across occupations: More than *g*. *Journal of Vocational Behavior, 34*, 1–27.

Price, B. (1977). Ridge regression: Application to nonexperimental data. *Psychological Bulletin, 84*, 759–766.

Price, D. B. (1964). *A group approach to the analysis of individual differences in the randomness of guessing behavior on multiple-choice tests and the development of scoring methods to take such differences into account.* Research Bulletin No. 64-59. Princeton, NJ: Educational Testing Service.

Price, R. H., & Eriksen, C. W. (1966). Size constancy in schizophrenia: A reanalysis. *Journal of Abnormal Psychology, 71*, 155–160.

Pritchard, D. A., & Rosenblatt, A. (1980a). Racial bias in the MMPI: A methodological review. *Journal of Consulting and Clinical Psychology, 48*, 268–272.

Pritchard, D. A., & Rosenblatt, A. (1980b). Reply to Gynther and Green. *Journal of Consulting and Clinical Psychology, 48*, 273–274.

Psychological Corporation. (1978). *Summaries of court decisions on employment testing.* New York: Psychological Corporation.

Rajaratnam, N. S., Cronbach, L. J., & Gleser G. C. (1963). Generalizability of parallel stratified tests. *Psychometrika, 30*, 39–56.

Raju, N. S. (1988). The area between two item characteristic curves. *Psychometrika, 53*, 495–502.

Rao, C. R. (1955). Estimation and tests of significance in factor analysis. *Psychometrika, 20*, 92–111.

Rasch, G. (1960). *Probabilistic models for some intelligence and attainment tests.* Copenhagen: Denmarks Paedagogiske Institut.

*Rendon v. AT&T (1989).* 883 F.2D 388 (5th cir., 1989).

Reynolds, C. R., & Brown, R. T. (1984). *Perspectives on bias in mental testing.* New York: Plenum Press.

Rindskopf, D. (1990). Nonstandard log-linear models. *Psychological Bulletin, 108*, 150–162.

Rippe, D. D. (1953). Application of a large sampling criterion to some sampling problems in factor analysis. *Psychometrika, 18*, 191–205.

Robinson, D. N. (1981). *An intellectual history of psychology* (rev. ed.). New York: Macmillan.

Rodwan, A. S., & Hake, H. W. (1964). The discriminant function as a model for perception. *American Journal of Psychology, 77*, 380–392.

Rogosa, D. R. (1980). A critique of cross-lagged correlation. *Psychological Bulletin, 88*, 245–258.

Rogosa, D. R., Brandt, D., & Zimowski, M. (1982). A growth curve approach to the measurement of change. *Psychological Bulletin, 92*, 726–748.

Rorer, L. G. (1965). The great response-style myth. *Psychological Bulletin, 63*, 129–156.

Rosenbaum, P. R. (1987). Comparing two item characteristic curves. *Psychometrika, 52*, 217–234.

Ross, R. T. (1934). Optimum order for presentation of pairs in paired comparisons. *Journal of Educational Psychology, 25*, 375–382.

Rost, J. (1988). Rating scale analysis with latent class models. *Psychometrika, 53*, 327–348.

Rovinelli, R. J., & Hambleton, R. K. (1977). On the use of content specialists in the assessment of criterion-referenced test item validity. *Dutch Journal of Educational Research, 2*, 49–60.

Rozeboom, W. W. (1966). *Foundations of the theory of prediction.* Homewood, IL: Dorsey Press.

Rozeboom, W. W. (1979). Ridge regression: Bonanza or beguilement. *Psychological Bulletin, 86*, 242–249.

Rudner, L. M. (1977). An approach to biased item identification using latent trait measurement theory. Paper presented at the annual meeting of the American Educational Research Association, New York.

Rumelhart, D. E., McClelland, J. L. & the PDP Research Group. (1986). *Parallel distributed processing: Explorations in the microstructure of cognition* (Vol. 1). Cambridge, MA: Bradford.

Rumelhart, D. E., McClelland, J. L. & the PDP Research Group. (1986). *Parallel distributed processing: Explorations in the microstructure of cognition* (Vol. 2). Cambridge, MA: Bradford.

Saal, F. E., Downey, R. G., & Lahey, M. A. (1980). Rating the ratings: Assessing the psychometric quality of rating data. *Psychological Bulletin, 88,* 413–428.

Sackett, P. R., Zedeck, S., & Fogli, L. (1988). Relations between measures of typical and maximum job performance. *Journal of Applied Psychology, 73,* 482–486.

Samejima, F. (1969). *Estimation of latent ability using a response pattern of graded scores.* Psycho Metrika Monograph No. 17, 34 (4 pt 2).

Samejima, F. (1974). Normal ogive model on the continuous response level in the multidimensional latent space, *Psychometrika, 39,* 111–121.

Samejima, F. (1979). A new family of models for the multiple choice item. Research Report 79-4. Department of Psychology, University of Tennessee. Knoxville, Tn.

Santee, J. L., & Egeth, H. E. (1980). Independence versus interference in the perceptual processing of letters. *Perception and Psychophysics, 31,* 101–116.

Sattath, S., & Tversky, A. (1977). Additive similarity trees. *Psychometrika, 42,* 319–345.

Saunders, D. R. (1962). Trans-varimax. *Psychometrika, 26,* 395.

Sawrey, W. L., Keller, L., & Conger, J. J. (1960). An objective method of grouping profiles by distance functions and its relation to factor analysis. *Educational and Psychological Measurement, 20,* 651–673.

Sawyer, R. L, Cole, N. S., & Cole, J. W. L. (1976). Utilities and the issue of fairness in a decision theoretic model for selection. *Educational and Psychological Measurement, 13,* 59–76.

Scheuneman, J. (1979). A new method for assessing bias in test items. *Journal of Educational Measurement, 16,* 143–152.

Schiffman, S. S., Reynolds, M. C., & Young, F. W. (1981). *Introduction to multidimensional scaling: Theory, methods, and applications.* New York: Academic Press.

Schmidt, F. L., & Hunter, J. E. (1977). Development of a general solution to the problem of validity generalization. *Journal of Applied Psychology, 62,* 529–540.

Schmidt, F. L., Hunter, J. E., & Pearlman, K. (1981). Task differences and validity of aptitude tests in selection: A red herring. *Journal of Applied Psychology, 66,* 166–185.

Schmidt, F. L., Pearlman, K., Hunter, J. E., & Hirsh, H. R. (1985). Forty questions about validity generalization and metanalysis. (With commentary by P. R. Sackett, M. L. Tenopyr, N. Schmitt, & J. Kehoe.) *Personnel Psychology, 38,* 697–798.

Schoenberg, R. (1982). *MILS: A computer program to estimate the parameters of multiple indicator structure models.* Bethesda, MD: National Institutes of Health.

Schönemann, P. H., & Wang, M. M. (1972). Some new results in factor indeterminacy. *Psychometrika, 37,* 61–91.

Schvaneveldt, R. W. (Ed.) (1990). *Associative networks: Studies in knowledge organization.* Norwood, NJ: Ablex.

Schvaneveldt, R. W., Dearholt, D. W., & Durso, F. T. (1988). Graph theoretic foundations of Pathfinder networks. *Computers and Mathematics with Applications, 15,* 337–345.

Schvaneveldt, R. W., Durso, F. T., & Dearholt, D. W. (1989). Network structures in proximity data. In G. H. Bower (Ed.), *The psychology of learning and motivation: Advances in research and theory* (Vol. 24). New York: Academic Press.

Schvaneveldt, R. W., Durso, F. T., & Mukherji, B. R. (1982). Semantic distance effects in categorization tasks. *Journal of Experimental Psychology: Learning, Memory and Cognition, 8,* 1–15.

Schvaneveldt, R. W., Durso, F. T., Goldsmith, T. E., Breen, T. J., Cooke, N. M., Tucker, R. G., & DeMaio, J. C. (1985). Measuring the structure of expertise. *International Journal of Man-Machine Studies, 23,* 699–728.

Schwarz, N. (1990). Contributions of cognitive psychology to questionnaire construction. *Research methods in personality and social psychology, 11*, 98–119.

Sechrest, L. (1963). Incremental validity: A recommendation. *Educational and Psychological Measurement, 23*, 153–158.

Searle, S. R. (1982). *Matrix algebra useful for statistics.* New York: Wiley.

Shavelson, R. J., & Webb, N. M. (1991). *Generalizability theory: A primer.* Newbury Park, CA: Sage.

Shepard, R. N. (1957). Stimulus and response generalization: A stochastic model relating generalization to distance in a psychological space. *Psychometrika, 22*, 325–345.

Shepard, R. N. (1958). Stimulus and response generalization: Tests of a model relating generalization to distance in psychological space. *Journal of Experimental Psychology, 55*, 509–523.

Shepard, R. N., & Arabie, P. (1979). Additive clustering: Representation of similarities as combinations of discrete overlapping properties. *Psychological Review, 86*, 87–123.

Shepard, R. N., Romney, A. K., & Nerlove, S. B. (Eds.) (1972). *Multidimensional scaling* (Vol. 1). New York: Seminar Press.

Shure, G. H., & Rogers, M. S. (1965). Note of caution on the factor analysis of the MMPI. *Psychological Bulletin, 63*, 14–18.

Siegel, S., & Castellan, N. J., Jr. (1988). *Nonparametric statistics for the behavioral sciences* (2d ed.). New York: McGraw-Hill.

Simpson, E. H. (1951). The interpretation of interaction in contingency tables. *Journal of the Royal Statistical Society*, Ser. B., *13*, 238–241.

Snook, S. C., & Gorsuch, R. L. (1989). Component analysis versus common factor analysis: A Monte Carlo study. *Psychological Bulletin, 106,* 148–154.

Spearman, C. (1904). General intelligence: Objectively determined and measured. *American Journal of Psychology, 15*, 201–293.

Spearman, C. (1927). *The abilities of man.* New York: Macmillan.

Spearman, C., & Holzinger, K. J. (1924). The sampling error in the theory of two factors. *British Journal of Psychology, 15*, 201–293.

Spearman, C., & Holzinger, K. J. (1925). Note on the sampling error of tetrad differences. *British Journal of Psychology, 16*, 86–88.

Spence, I., & Domoney, D. W. (1974). Single subject incomplete designs for nonmetric multidimensional scaling. *Psychometrika, 39*, 469–490.

Spielberger, C. D., Gorsuch, R. L., & Lushene, R. D. (1970). *Test manual for the State-Trait Anxiety Inventory.* Palo Alto, CA: Consulting Psychologists Press.

Stanley, J. C. (1971). Reliability. In R. L. Thorndike (Ed.), *Educational measurement* (2d ed.). Washington, DC: American Council on Education.

Steinberg, L., Thissen, D., & Wainer, H. (1990). Validity. In H. Wainer (Ed.), *Computerized adaptive testing: A primer.* Hillsdale, NJ: Erlbaum Associates.

Stephenson, W. (1953). *The study of behavior.* Chicago: University of Chicago Press.

Sternberg, R. J. (1977). *Intelligence, information processing, and analogical reasoning.* Hillsdale, NJ: Erlbaum Associates.

Sternberg, R. J. (Ed.) (1988). *Advances in the psychology of human intelligence* (Vol. 4). Hillsdale, NJ: Erlbaum Associates.

Stevens, S. S. (1946). On the theory of scales of measurement. *Science, 103*, 677–680.

Stevens, S. S. (1951). Mathematics, Measurement, and Psychophysics. In S. S. Stevens (Ed.), *Handbook of Experimental Psychology.* New York: Wiley.

Stevens, S. S. (1956). The direct estimation of sensory magnitude—Loudness. *American Journal of Psychology, 69*, 1–25.

Stevens, S. S. (1958). Problems and methods of psychophysics. *Psychological Bulletin*, 55, 177–196.

Stevens, S. S. (1960). Ratio scales, partition scales, and confusion scales. In H. Gulliksen & S. Messick (Eds.), *Psychological scaling: Theory and Applications*. New York: Wiley.

Stevens, S. S. (1961). The psychophysics of sensory function. In W. A. Rosenblith (Ed.), *Sensory communication*. Cambridge, MA: MIT Press.

Stevens, S. S. (1975). *Psychophysics: Introduction to its perceptual, neural, and social prospects*. New York: Wiley.

Stevens, S. S., Morgan, C. T., & Volkmann, J. (1941). Theory of the quantum in the discrimination of loudness and pitch. *American Journal of Psychology*, 54, 315–335.

Stewart, D. K., & Love, W. A. (1968). A general correlation index. *Psychological Bulletin*, 70, 160–163.

Stine, W. W. (1989a). Interobserver relational agreement. *Psychological Bulletin*, 106, 341–347.

Stine, W. W. (1989b). Meaningful inference: The role of measurement in statistics. *Psychological Bulletin*, 105, 147–155.

Stout, W. F. (1990). A new item response theory modeling approach with applications to unidimensionality assessment and ability estimation. *Psychometrika*, 55, 293–326.

Suppes, P., & Zinnes, J. L. (1963). Basic measurement theory. In R. D. Luce, R. R. Bush, & E. Galanter (Eds.), *Handbook of mathematical psychology* (Vol. 1). New York: Wiley.

Sutcliffe, J. P. (1965). A probability model for errors of classification: II. Particular cases. *Psychometrika*, 30, 129–155.

Swets, J. A. (1986a). Indices of discrimination or diagnostic accuracy: Their ROCs and implied models. *Psychological Bulletin*, 99, 100–117.

Swets, J. A. (1986b). Form of empirical ROCs in discrimination and diagnostic tasks: Implications for theory and measurement of performance. *Psychological Bulletin*, 100, 181–198.

Swets, J. A., Tanner, W. P., Jr., & Birdsall, T. G. (1961). Decision processes in perception. *Psychological Review*, 68, 301–340.

Takane, Y., Young, F. W., & de Leeuw, J. (1977). Nonmetric individual differences multidimensional scaling: An alternating least squares method with optimal scaling features. *Psychometrika*, 42, 7–67.

Tanaka, J. S. (1987). "How big is big enough?": Sample size and goodness of fit in structural equation models with latent variables. *Child Development*, 58, 134–146.

Tanner, W. P., Jr., & Swets, J. A., (1954). A decision-making theory of visual detection. *Psychological Review*, 61, 401–409.

Theodor, L. H., & Mandelcord, M. S. (1973). Hysterical blindness: A case report and study using a modern psychophysical technique. *Journal of Abnormal Psychology*, 82, 552–553.

Thissen, D. (1988). *Multilog: Multiple categorical item analysis and test scoring using item response theory*. Mooresville, IN: Scientific Software.

Thissen, D., & Steinberg, L. (1984). A response model for multiple choice items. *Psychometrika*, 49, 501–519.

Thissen, D., & Steinberg, L. (1986). Taxonomy of item response models. *Psychometrika*, 51, 567–578.

Thissen, D., & Steinberg, L. (1988). Data analysis using item response theory. *Psychological Bulletin*, 104, 385–395.

Thissen, D., Steinberg, L., & Gerrard, M. (1986). Beyond group-mean differences: The concept of item bias. *Psychological Bulletin*, 99, 118–128.

Thissen, D., Steinberg, L., & Mooney, J. (1989). Trace lines for testlets: A use of multiple-categorical-response models. *Journal of Educational Measurement*, 26, 247–260.

Thissen, D., Steinberg, L., & Wainer, H. (1988). Use of item response theory in the study of group differences in trace lines. In H. Wainer & H. I. Braun (Eds.) *Test validity*. Hillsdale, NJ: Erlbaum Associates.

Thissen, D., Steinberg, L., & Wainer, H. (1992). Detection of differential item functioning using the parameters of item response models. In P. W. Holland & H. Wainer (Eds.), *Differential item functioning*. Hillsdale, NJ: Erlbaum Associates.

Thorndike, E. L. (1920). A constant error in psychological ratings. *Journal of Applied Psychology, 4*, 25–29.

Thorndike, R. L. (1966). Intellectual status and intellectual growth. *Journal of Educational Measurement, 57*, 121–127.

Thorndike, R. L. (1971). *Educational measurement* (2d ed.). Washington, DC: American Council on Education.

Thorndike, R. M., Cunningham, G. K., Thorndike, R. L., & Hagan, E. (1991). *Measurement and Evaluation in Psychology and Education* (5th ed.). New York: Macmillan.

Thurstone, L. L. (1927). A law of comparative judgment. *Psychological Review, 34*, 273–386.

Thurstone, L. L. (1935). *Vectors of the mind*. Chicago: University of Chicago Press.

Thurstone, L. L. (1945). A multiple group method of factoring the correlation matrix. *Psychometrika, 10*, 73–78.

Thurstone, L. L. (1947). *Multiple factor analysis*. Chicago: University of Chicago Press.

Thurstone, T. G. (1941). Primary mental abilities of children. *Educational and Psychological Measurement, 1*, 105–116.

Tjur, T. (1982). Connection between Rasch's item analysis model and a multiplicative Poisson model. *Scandinavian Journal of Statistics, 9*, 23–30.

Torgerson, W. S. (1958). *Theory and methods of scaling*. New York: Wiley.

Townsend, J. T., & Ashby, F. G. (1984). Measurement scales and statistics: The misconception misconceived. *Psychological Bulletin, 96*, 394–401.

Tryon, R. C., & Bailey, D. E. (1970). Cluster analysis. New York: McGraw-Hill.

Tucker, L. R. (1963). Implications of factor analysis of three-day matrices for measurement of change. In C. W. Harris (Ed.), *Problems in measuring change*. Madison: University of Wisconsin Press.

Tucker, L. R. (1964). The extension of factor analysis to three-dimensional matrices. In H. Gulliksen & N. Fredriksen (Eds.), *Contributions to mathematical psychology*. New York: Holt, Rinehart, & Winston.

Tucker, L. R. (1966). Some mathematical notes on three-mode factor analysis. *Psychometrika, 31*, 279–311.

Tucker, L. R., & Lewis, C. (1972). A reliability coefficient for maximum likelihood factor analysis. *Psychometrika, 38*, 1–10.

Tversky, A., & Gati, I. (1982). Similarity, separability, and the triangle inequality. *Psychological Review, 89*, 123–154.

Tversky, A., & Hutchinson, J. W. (1986). Nearest neighbor analysis of psychological spaces. *Psychological Review, 93*, 3–22.

Tversky, A., Rinott, Y., & Newman, C. M. (1983). Nearest neighbor analysis of point processes: Applications to multidimensional scaling. *Journal of Mathematical Psychology, 27*, 235–250.

Tzelgov, J., & Henik, A. (1991). Suppression situations in psychological research: Definitions, implications, and applications. *Psychological Bulletin, 109*, 524–536.

*U.S. v. City of St. Louis* (1978). 434 United States 1026.

*U.S. v. State of South Carolina* (1977). 410 Federal Supplement 948.

Urry, V. W. (1977). Tailored testing: A successful application of item response theory. *Journal of Educational Measurement, 14*, 181–186.

Velicer, W. F. (1976). The relation between factor score estimates, image scores, and principal component scores. *Educational and Psychological Measurement, 36*, 149–159.

Velicer, W. F., & Jackson, D. N. (1990). Component analysis vs. common factor analysis: Some issues in selecting and appropriate procedure. *Multivariate Behavioral Research, 25*, 1–28.

Vernon, P. E. (1979). *Intelligence: Heredity and environment.* San Francisco, CA: Freeman.

Wainer, H. (1976). Estimating coefficients in linear models: It don't make no nevermind. *Psychological Bulletin, 83*, 213–217.

Wainer, H. (1990). *Computerized adaptive testing: A primer.* Hillsdale, NJ: Erlbaum Associates.

Wainer, H., & Braun, H. I. (1988). *Test Validity.* Hillsdale, NJ: Erlbaum Associates.

Wainer, H., & Messick, S. J. (1983). *Principles of Modern Psychological Measurement.* Hillsdale, NJ: Erlbaum Associates.

Wainer, H., Morgan, A., & Gustafsson, J. E. (1980). A review of estimation procedures for the Rasch model with an eye toward longish tests. *Journal of Educational Statistics, 5*, 35–64.

Wald, A. (1950). *Statistical decision functions.* New York: Wiley.

Walsh, J. A. (1990). Comment on social desirability. *American Psychologist, 45*, 289–290 (Comment).

Walster, E., Aronson, V., & Abrams, D. (1966). Importance of physical attractiveness in dating behavior. *Journal of Personality and Social Psychology, 4*, 508–516.

Ward, L. M. (1974). Power functions for category judgments of duration and line length. *Perceptual and Motor Skills, 38*, 1182.

*Wards Cove Packing Co. v. Atonio* (1990). 490 United States 642.

Watson, D., & Tellegen, A. (1985). Toward a consensual structure of mood. *Psychological Bulletin, 98*, 219–235.

*Watson v. Ft. Worth Bank & Trust* (1990). 487 United States 977.

Wechsler, D. (1989). Manual for the Wechlser preschool and primary scale of intelligence—Revised. San Antonio, TX: Psychological Corporation.

Weiss, D. J., & Bock, R. D. (1983). *New horizons in testing: Latent trait theory and computerized adaptive testing.* New York: Academic Press.

Wells, F. L. (1907). A statistical study of literary merit. *Archives of Psychology, 1*(7).

Welsh, G. S. (1956). Factor dimensions *A* and *R*. In G. S. Welsh & W. G. Dahlstrom (Eds.), *Basic readings on the MMPI in psychology and medicine.* Minneapolis: University of Minnesota Press.

Wesman, A. G. (1971). Writing the test item. In R. L. Thorndike (Ed.), *Educational measurement* (2d ed.). Washington, DC: American Council on Education.

West, S. G. (1983). Personality and prediction: Nomothetic and idiographic approaches. *Journal of Personality, 51* (Special Issue), 275–604.

Wherry, R. J. (1940). The Wherry-Doolittle selection method. In A. Stead & P. Shartle (Eds.), *Occupational counseling techniques.* New York: American Books.

Wherry, R. J. (1985). *Contributions to correlational analysis.* Orlando, FL: Academic Press.

Wickens, T. D. (1989). *Multiway contingency tables analysis for the social sciences.* Hillsdale, NJ: Erlbaum Associates.

Wickens, T. D., & Olzak, L. A. (1989). The statistical analysis of concurrent detection ratings. *Perception & Psychophysics, 45*, 514–528.

Widaman, K. F. (1990). Bias in pattern loadings represented by common factor analysis and component analysis, *Multivariate Behavioral Research, 25*, 89–95.

Wiener, D. N. (1948). Subtle and obvious keys for the MMPI. *Journal of Consulting Psychology, 12*, 164–170.

Wiggins, J. S. (1959). Interrelationships among MMPI measures of dissimulation under standard and social desirability instructions. *Journal of Consulting Psychology, 23*, 419–427.

Wiggins, J. S. (1966). Substantive dimensions of self-report in the MMPI item pool. *Psychological Monographs, 80*, 22(whole no. 630).

Wiggins, J. S. (1968). Personality structure. *Annual Review of Psychology, 19*, 293–350.

Wiggins, J. S. (1969). Content dimensions in the MMPI. In J. N. Butcher (Ed.), *MMPI: Research development and clinical application*. New York: McGraw-Hill.

Wiggins, J. S. (1973). *Personality and prediction: Principles of personality assessment*. Reading, MA: Addison-Wesley.

Wilkinson, L. (1979). Response variable hypotheses in the multivariate analysis of variance. *Psychological Bulletin, 82*, 408–412.

Wilks, S. S. (1938). Weighting systems for linear functions of correlated variables when there is no dependent variable. *Psychometrika, 3*, 23–40.

Winer, B. J., Brown, D. R., and Michels, K. M. (1991). *Statistical principles in experimental design* (3d ed.). New York: McGraw-Hill.

Winkler, R. L., & Hays, W. L. (1975). *Statistics: Probability, inference, and decision* (2d ed.). New York: Holt, Rinehart, & Winston.

Wishart, J. (1928). The generalized product-moment distribution in samples from a normal multivariate population. *Biometrika, 20*, 32–52.

Wissler, C. (1901). *The correlation of mental and physical tests*. New York: Columbia University Press.

Wood, R. L., Wingersky, M. S., & Lord, F. M. (1976). *LOGIST—A computer program for estimating examinee ability and item characteristic curve parameters*. Princeton, NJ: Educational Testing Service.

Woodward, J. A., & Bentler, P. M. (1978). A statistical lower bound to population reliability. *Psychological Bulletin, 85*, 1323–1326.

Woodworth, R. S., & Schlossberg, H. (1954). *Experimental Psychology* (rev. ed.). New York: Holt.

Wright, D. D., & Masters, G. N. (1982). *Rating scale analysis: Rasch measurement*. Chicago: Mesa Press.

Yates, A. (1987). *Multivariate exploratory data analysis*. Albany: State University of New York Press.

Young, G., & Householder, A. S. (1938). Discussion of a set of points in terms of their mutual distances. *Psychometrika, 3*, 19–22.

Young, F. W., & Lewyckyj, R. (1980). *ALSCAL user's guide*. Chapel Hill, NC: Institute for Research in the Social Sciences, University of North Carolina.

Young, F. W., Takane, Y., & Lewyckyj, R. (1978). Three notes on ALSCAL. *Psychometrika, 43*, 433–435.

Yule, G. U. (1900). On the association of attributes in statistics: with illustrations from the material of the childhood society. *Philosophical Transactions of the Royal Society of London*, Ser. A, *194*, 257–319.

Yule, G. U. (1912). On the method of measuring association between two attributes. *Journal of the Royal Statistical Society, 75*, 579–642.

Zwick, W. R., & Velicer, W. F. (1982). Factors influencing four rules for determining the number of components to retain. *Multivariate Behavioral Research, 17*, 253–269.

Zwick, W. R., & Velicer, W. F. (1986). Comparison of five rules for determining the number of components to retain. *Psychological Bulletin, 99*, 432–442.

# AUTHOR INDEX

# SUBJECT INDEX